CLYMER®

BMW

K-SERIES • 1985-1997

The world's finest publisher of mechanical how-to manuals

PRIMEDIA
Business Magazines & Media

P.O. Box 12901, Overland Park, Kansas 66282-2901

Copyright ©2002 PRIMEDIA Business Magazines & Media Inc.

FIRST EDITION
First Printing January, 1990
Second Printing August, 1991

SECOND EDITION
First Printing January, 1996
Second Printing October, 1997
Third Printing April, 1999
Fourth Printing December, 2000

THIRD EDITION
Updated by Jay Bogart to include 1996-1997 K1100 models
First Printing September, 2002
Second Printing May, 2004

Printed in U.S.A.

CLYMER and colophon are registered trademarks of PRIMEDIA Business Magazines & Media Inc.

ISBN: 0-89287-831-2

Library of Congress: 2002111051

AUTHOR: Ed Scott.

TECHNICAL PHOTOGRAPHY: Ed Scott, with assistance by Curt Jordan, Jordan Engineering, Santa Ana, California.

TECHNICAL ILLUSTRATIONS: Mitzi McCarthy.

TOOLS AND EQUIPMENT: K & L Supply Co. at www.klsupply.com.

PRODUCTION: Elizabeth Couzens.

COVER: Mark Clifford Photography, Los Angeles, California.

Chapter One
General Information   1

Chapter Two
Troubleshooting   2

Chapter Three
Lubrication, Maintenance and Tune-up   3

Chapter Four
Engines   4

Chapter Five
Clutch   5

Chapter Six
Transmission and Gearshift Mechanisms   6

Chapter Seven
Fuel Injection System, Emission Controls and Exhaust System   7

Chapter Eight
Electrical System   8

Chapter Nine
Cooling System   9

Chapter Ten
Front Suspension and Steering   10

Chapter Eleven
Rear Suspension and Final Drive   11

Chapter Twelve
Brakes   12

Chapter Thirteen
Frame, Body and Frame Repainting   13

Chapter Fourteen
Supplement   14

Index   15

Wiring Diagrams   16

CLYMER®

Publisher Shawn Etheridge

EDITORIAL

Managing Editor
James Grooms

Associate Editor
Jason Beaver
Lee Buell

Technical Writers
Jay Bogart
Michael Morlan
George Parise
Mark Rolling
Ed Scott
Ron Wright

Editorial Production Manager
Dylan Goodwin

Senior Production Editor
Greg Araujo

Production Editors
Holly Messinger
Shara Pierceall
Darin Watson

Associate Production Editor
Susan Hartington
Julie Jantzer
Justin Marciniak

Technical Illustrators
Steve Amos
Errol McCarthy
Mitzi McCarthy
Bob Meyer
Mike Rose

MARKETING/SALES AND ADMINISTRATION

Advertising & Promotions Manager
Elda Starke

Advertising & Promotions Coordinators
Melissa Abbott
Wendy Stringfellow

Art Director
Chris Paxton

Sales Managers
Ted Metzger, Manuals
Dutch Sadler, Marine
Matt Tusken, Motorcycles

Business Manager
Ron Rogers

Customer Service Manager
Terri Cannon

Customer Service Supervisor
Ed McCarty

Customer Service Representatives
Shawna Davis
Courtney Hollars
Susan Kohlmeyer
April LeBlond
Jennifer Lassiter
Ernesto Suarez

Warehouse & Inventory Manager
Leah Hicks

PRIMEDIA
Business Magazines & Media
P.O. Box 12901, Overland Park, KS 66282-2901 • 800-262-1954 • 913-967-1719

The following books and guides are published by PRIMEDIA Business Directories & Books.

More information available at *primediabooks.com*

CONTENTS

QUICK REFERENCE DATA IX

CHAPTER ONE
GENERAL INFORMATION 1
Manual organization
Notes, cautions and warnings
Safety first
Service hints
Special tips
Torque specifications
Fasteners
Lubricants

Expendable supplies
Parts replacement
Serial numbers
Miscellaneous information labels
Basic hand tools
Test equipment
Mechanic's tips
Riding safety

CHAPTER TWO
TROUBLESHOOTING 22
Operating requirements
Emergency troubleshooting
Engine starting
Engine performance

Engine noises
Excessive vibration
Front suspension and steering
Brake problems

CHAPTER THREE
LUBRICATION, MAINTENANCE AND TUNE-UP 28
Routine safety checks
Service intervals
Bike cleaning
Tires and wheels

Battery
Periodic lubrication
Periodic maintenance
Tune-up

CHAPTER FOUR
ENGINES 83
Engine principles
Servicing engine in frame
Engine removal-installation
Crankshaft cover, cylinder head cover and
  timing chain cover
Camshafts, timing chain and chain
  tensioner assembly
Cylinder head
Valves and valve components

Oil/water pump
Intermediate housing
Starter clutch and gears
Oil pan, lower crankcase half and output shaft
Pistons and connecting rods
Crankshaft
Cylinder block
Break-in

CHAPTER FIVE
CLUTCH 172
Clutch
Clutch release mechanism

Clutch cable

CHAPTER SIX
TRANSMISSION AND GEARSHIFT MECHANISMS 187
Transmission and gearshift operation
Transmission housing

Transmission shafts and gearshift mechanism
Transmission shafts

CHAPTER SEVEN
FUEL INJECTION SYSTEM, EMISSION CONTROLS AND EXHAUST SYSTEM . . . 225
Fuel injection system description
Fuel injection system components
Depressurizing the fuel system
Fuel injection precautions
Troubleshooting
Fuel injectors and fuel supply pipe
Throttle housing and intake manifold
Pressure regulator
Air flow meter
Fuel injection control unit
Throttle valve switch
Fuel injection system adjustments
Air filter case

Throttle cable replacement
Choke cable replacement
Fuel pump
Fuel filler cap
Fuel tank
Fuel gauge sensor
Fuel level sender (models so equipped)
Gasoline/alcohol blend test
Crankcase breather system (U.S. only)
Evaporative emission control system (California
 models)
Exhaust system

CHAPTER EIGHT
ELECTRICAL SYSTEM 274
Charging system
Alternator
Voltage rectifier
Ignition systems
Ignition system troubleshooting
Hall transmitter unit
Ignition control unit
Ignition coils
Spark plug secondary wires
Starting system
Starter
Starter relay

Lighting system
Headlight
Taillight/brake light and license plate light
Turn signals
Switches
Electrical connectors
Instrument cluster
Relays
Horn
Fuses
Chassis wiring harness
Wiring diagrams

CHAPTER NINE
COOLING SYSTEM 342
Hoses and hose clamps
Cooling system check
Pressure check
Radiator
Cooling fan

Thermostat
Connector pipe
Coolant recovery tank
Hoses

CHAPTER TEN
FRONT SUSPENSION AND STEERING 354

Front wheel
Front hub
Wheel balance
Tire changing
Tire repairs

Handlebar
Steering head and stem
Steering head bearing race
Front fork

CHAPTER ELEVEN
REAR SUSPENSION AND FINAL DRIVE 392

Rear wheel
Shock absorber
Swing arm and drive shaft

Final drive unit
Pinion gear-to-ring gear adjustment
Taper roller bearing preload

CHAPTER TWELVE
BRAKES 423

Front brake pad replacement
Front master cylinder
Front caliper
Rear disc brake
Rear brake pad replacement
Rear master cylinder and reservoir
Rear caliper
Brake hose and line replacement (non-ABS models)
Brake disc (front and rear)

ABS brake system
Brake hose and line replacement (ABS equipped
    models)
Pressure modulator and mounting bracket
Trigger sensor
Bleeding the system
Rear drum brake (K75C models)
Rear brake pedal

CHAPTER THIRTEEN
FRAME, BODY AND FRAME REPAINTING. 485

Kickstand (sidestand)
Center stand
Footpegs
Safety bars
Locks
Handle
Fenders
License plate bracket

Seat
Rear cowl and storage tray
Body panels (K75 models)
Body panels (K100 models)
Luggage and rack
Optional equipment
Windshield cleaning (all models)
Frame

CHAPTER FOURTEEN
SUPPLEMENT

SUPPLEMENT.. 544

Engine starting and engine performance
Routine maintenance checks
Service intervals
Tires and wheels
Battery
Periodic lubrication
Periodic maintenance
Tune-up (K100RS [1991-1992], K1, K1100LT-ABS, K1100RSA)
Engine removal/installation (4-valve engines)
Crankshaft cover, cylinder head cover and timing chain cover
Camshafts, timing chain and chain tensioner assembly
Cylinder head
Valve and valve components (4-valve cylinder head)
Throttle housing and intake manifold
Air flow meter
Fuel injection control unit (Motronic)
Fuel injection system adjustments
Air filter case
Fuel pump
Exhaust system
Ignition system (K100RS [1991-1992], K1 and all K1100 models)
Ignition control unit (Motronic)
Ignition coils
Ignition output stage
Headlight
Turn signals (K1 models)
Radiator
Coolant recovery tank
Hoses
Front wheel (3-spoke type)
Front hub
Tire balancing (3-spoke type)
Handlebar
Steering damper (K1, K100RS)
Steering head and stem (K75, K75RT, K75S)
Front fork (K75, K75RT, K75S, 1992-on)
Front fork (K1, K100RS, K100LT)
Front fork (K1100LT, K1100RS)
Rear wheel
Swing arm and drive shaft (K1, K100RS [1991-1992], K1100LT and K1100RSA [1993-on])
Final drive unit (K1, K100RS [1991-1992], K1100LT and K1100RSA)
Pinion gear-to-ring gear adjustment
Tapered roller bearing preload
Front brake pad replacement (dual piston caliper)
Front master cylinder
Front caliper (dual piston caliper)
Rear master cylinder (K75 [1993-on], K100 [1990-1992], K1, K1100)
Brake hose and line replacement (non-ABS models)
Brake disc (K1, K100RS, K1100LT, K1100RSA)
ABS brake system
Pressure modulator and mounting bracket
Footpegs (K1)
Fenders
Seat
Rear cowl
Body panels (K75RT)
Body panels (K1 models)
Body panels (K1100LT)
Body panels (K1100RS)
Luggage and rack

INDEX.. 665

WIRING DIAGRAMS.. 668

QUICK REFERENCE DATA

TIRE INFLATION PRESSURE (COLD)*

Model	Rider only		Rider and passenger	
V-Rated Tires				
	psi	kPa	psi	kPa
K75, K75C				
No speed limit				
Front	29	200	33	230
Rear	26	250	42	290
K75RT				
No speed limit				
Front	32	220	36	250
Rear	36	250	42	290
K75S				
No speed limit				
Front	32.5	225	—	—
Rear	36	250	—	—
Up to 112 mph (180 kmh)				
Front	—	—	32.5	225
Rear	—	—	39	270
Over 112 mph (180 kmh)				
Front	—	—	39	270
Rear	—	—	42	290
K100 (all models 1985-1989)				
No speed limit				
Front	32.5	225	—	—
Rear	36	250	—	—
Up to 112 mph (180 kmh)				
Front	—	—	32.5	225
Rear	—	—	39	270
Over 112 mph (180 kmh)				
Front	—	—	39	270
Rear	—	—	42	290
VR-Rated Tires**				
K100 (all models 1985-1989)				
No speed limit				
Front	37	255	—	—
Rear	40.5	280	—	—
Up to 112 mph (180 kmh)				
Front	—	—	37	255
Rear	—	—	43.5	300
Over 112 mph (180 kmh)				
Front	—	—	43.5	300
Rear	—	—	46	320
K100 (all models 1990-on)				
K1100 (all models)				
Front	32	220	36	250
Rear	36	250	42	290

*Tire inflation pressure for factory equipped tires. Aftermarket tires may require different inflation pressure.
** BMW does not recommend installing VR-rated tires on the K75 models.

MAINTENANCE AND TUNE UP TORQUE SPECIFICATIONS

Item	N•m	ft.-lb.
Oil drain plug	20	15
Oil filter cover Allen bolts	10	7
Oil pan Allen bolts	10	7
Cylinder head cover bolts	10	7
Spark plug	20	15
Camshaft bearing cap nuts	9	7
Camshaft driven sprocket bolt	54	40

OIL QUANTITY AND RECOMMENDED TYPE

Item	Quantity	Recommended type
Engine oil		
Oil change	3.5 liter (3.7 qt.)	API SF or SG
Oil change and filter	3.75 liter (4.0 qt.)	
Transmission oil	0.85 liter (0.9 qt.)	Hypoid gear oil GL5
		SAE 90 above 5° C
		(41° F)
		SAE 80 below 5° C
		(41° F)
		SAE 80W 90 (optional)
Final drive unit oil		
Overhaul	0.25 liter (0.26 qt.)	Hypoid gear oil GL5
Oil change	0.23 liter (0.24 qt.)	SAE 90 above 5° C
		(41° F)
		SAE 80 below 5° C
		(41° F)
		SAE 80W 90 (optional)
Front fork oil		
K75 models (1986-1989)		Bel-Ray SAE5, Castrol Extra
Standard	320-330 cc	Light, Castrol DB Hydraulic
	(10.7-11 oz.)	Fluid, Castrol Shock Absorber
		Oil 1/318, Castrol LMH, Golden
Sport suspension	270-290 cc	Spectro Very Light, Mobil Aero
	(9.23-9.8 oz.)	HFA, Mobil DTE 11, Shell Aero
		HFA, Mobil DTE 11, Shell Aero
		Fluid 4, Shell 4001
K75 (all models 1990-on)	410 cc (13.8 oz.)	
K100	320-330 cc (10.7-11 oz.)	
K100RS, K100RS (ABS),		
K100RT, K100LT, K100LT		
(ABS) (1985-1989)		
Standard	350-360 cc (11.7-12 oz.)	
Sport suspension	270-290 cc (10.7-11 oz.)	
K100LT, K100RS (1990-on)	400 cc (13.5 oz.)	
K1	440-450 cc (14.8-15.2 oz.)	
K1100		
Left-hand leg	349-351 cc (11.7-11.8 oz.)	
Right-hand leg	399-401 cc (13.4-13.6 oz.)	

COOLANT CAPACITY AND MIXING RATIO

Capacity	
Engine and radiator	
K75	2.5 liters (2.6 qts.)
K100, K1, K1100	3.0 liters (3.2 qts.)
Recovery tank	0.4 liters (0.8 qt.)
Anti-freeze/water ratio	
Temperature down to -28° C (-18° F)	60% distilled water 40% BMW anti-freeze
Temperatures below -36° C (-31° F)	50% distilled water 50% BMW anti-freeze

TUNE UP SPECIFICATIONS

Valve clearance*
  Intake: 0.15-0.20 mm (0.006-0.008 in.)
  Exhaust: 0.25-0.30 mm (0.010-0.012 in.)
Spark plug type
  1985-1989 K100, all years K75
    Bosch X5DC or Champion A 85 YC
  1990-on K100, K1
    Bosch X5DC or Beru 12-5DU
  K1100
    Bosch XR5DC or Beru 12 R-5DU
Spark plug gap
  Recommended 0.6-0.7 mm (0.024-0.28 in.)
  Maximum gap limit 0.9 mm (0.036 in.)
Compression pressure (1985-1989)
  Good: more than 1012 kPa (145 psi)
  Normal: 848-1012 kPa (123-145 psi)
  Poor: less than 848 kPa (123 psi)
Compression pressure (1990-on)
  Good: more than 1000 kPa (145 psi)
  Normal: 850-1000 kPa (123-145 psi)
  Poor: less than 850 kPa (123 psi)
Idle speed 900-1,000 rpm

* Cylinder head maximum temperature: 35° C (95° F).

BULB REPLACEMENT

Item	Voltage/wattage	Number designation
Headlight	12 volt 60/55 watt	H4-halogen (Phillips)
Parking lamp	12 volt 4 watt	T 8/4
Taillight	12 volt 10 watt	R 19/10
Brakelight	12 volt 21 watt	R 25/1
Turn signals	12 volt 21 watt	P25-1
Instrument cluster		
Turn signal indicator	12 volt 4 watt	T8/4
All others	12 volt 3 watt	W 10/3

INTRODUCTION

This detailed, comprehensive manual covers the BMW K75, K100, K1 and K1100 Series bikes from 1985-1997. Chapter Fourteen contains all procedures and specifications unique to 1990 and later models.

The expert text gives complete information on maintenance, tune-up, repair and overhaul. Hundreds of photos and drawings guide you through every step. The book includes all you will need to know to keep your BMW running right. Throughout this book where differences occur among the models, they are clearly identified.

A shop manual is a reference. You want to be able to find information fast. As in all Clymer books, this one is designed with you in mind. All chapters are thumb tabbed. Important items are extensively indexed at the rear of the book. All procedures, tables. photos, etc., in this manual are for the reader who may be working on the bike for the first time or using this manual for the first time. All the most frequently used specifications and capacities are summarized in the *Quick Reference Data* pages at the front of the book.

Keep the book handy in your tool box. It will help you better understand how your bike runs, lower repair costs and generally improve your satisfaction with the bike.

CHAPTER ONE

GENERAL INFORMATION

MANUAL ORGANIZATION

All dimensions and capacities are expressed in English units familiar to U.S. mechanics as well as in metric units. Refer to **Table 1** for decimal and metric equivalents.

This chapter provides general information and discusses equipment and tools useful both for preventive maintenance and troubleshooting.

Chapter Two provides methods and suggestions for quick and accurate diagnosis and repair of problems. Troubleshooting procedures discuss typical symptoms and logical methods to pinpoint the trouble.

Chapter Three explains all periodic lubrication and routine maintenance necessary to keep the BMW running well. Chapter Three also includes recommended tune-up procedures, eliminating the need to constantly consult chapters on the various assemblies.

Subsequent chapters describe specific systems such as the engine, clutch, transmission, fuel injection, exhaust, suspension and brakes. Each chapter provides disassembly, repair and assembly procedures in simple step-by-step form.

If a repair is impractical for a home mechanic, it is so indicated. In some cases a complicated procedure is included so that you have the option of performing this procedure yourself or having it done by a professional mechanic. It is usually faster and less expensive to take such repairs to a BMW dealer or competent repair shop. Specifications concerning a particular system are included at the end of the appropriate chapter.

Some of the procedures in this manual require special tools. These special tools are shown either in actual use or alone. Well equipped mechanics may find they can substitute similar tools already on hand or can fabricate their own.

Tables 1-4 are at the end of this chapter.

NOTES, CAUTIONS AND WARNINGS

The terms NOTE, CAUTION and WARNING have specific meanings in this manual. A NOTE provides additional information to make a step or procedure easier or clearer. Disregarding a NOTE could cause inconvenience, but would not cause equipment damage or personal injury.

A CAUTION emphasizes areas where equipment damage could occur. Disregarding a CAUTION could cause permanent mechanical damage; however, personal injury is unlikely.

A WARNING emphasizes areas where personal injury or even death could result from negligence. Mechanical damage may also occur. WARNINGS *are to be taken seriously.* In some cases, serious injury or death has resulted from disregarding similar warnings.

Throughout this manual keep in mind 2 conventions. "Front" refers to the front of the bike. The front of any component, such as the engine, is the end which faces toward the front of the bike. The "left-" and "right-hand" sides refer to the position of the parts as viewed by a rider sitting on the seat facing forward. For example, the throttle control is on the right-hand side and the clutch lever is on the left-hand side. These rules are simple, but even experienced mechanics occasionally become disoriented.

SAFETY FIRST

Professional mechanics can work for years and never sustain a serious injury. If you observe a few rules of common sense and safety, you can enjoy many hours servicing your own machine. If you ignore these rules you can hurt yourself or damage the bike.

1. *Never* use gasoline as a cleaning solvent.
2. Never smoke or use a torch in the vicinity of flammable liquids such as cleaning solvent in open containers.
3. If welding or brazing is required on the machine, remove the fuel tank to a safe distance, at least 50 feet away.
4. Use the proper sized wrenches to avoid damage to nuts or bolts and injury to yourself.
5. When loosening a tight or stuck nut, think about what would happen if the wrench should slip. Be careful; protect yourself accordingly.
6. Keep your work area clean and uncluttered.
7. Wear safety goggles during all operations involving drilling, grinding or the use of a cold chisel.
8. Never use worn tools.
9. Keep a fire extinguisher handy and be sure it is rated for gasoline and electrical fires.

SERVICE HINTS

Most of the service procedures covered are straightforward and can be performed by anyone reasonably handy with tools. It is suggested, however, that you consider your own capabilities carefully before attempting any operation involving major disassembly of the engine.

Take your time and do the job right. Do not forget that a newly rebuilt engine must be broken in the same as a new one. Keep the rpm within the limits given in your BMW owner's manual when you get back on the road.

1. There are many items available that can be used on your hands before and after working on your bike. A little preparation prior to getting "all greased up" will help when cleaning up later. Before starting out, work Vaseline, soap or a product such as Invisible Glove (**Figure 1**) onto your forearms, into your hands and under your fingernails and cuticles. This will make cleanup a lot easier. For cleanup, use a waterless hand soap such as Sta-Lube and then finish up with powdered Boraxo and a fingernail brush (**Figure 2**).

> *CAUTION*
> *BMW has determined that the use of S100 Total Cycle Cleaner may damage, or even remove, the electrolyte-dip matte black from*

components on the bike. This includes both engine and frame components. If your bike is still under warranty, BMW will not cover any damage caused by using this cleaner.

2. Repairs go much faster and easier if the bike is clean before you begin work. There are special cleaners, such as Gunk or Bel-Ray Degreaser, for washing the engine and related parts. Just spray or brush on the cleaning solution, let it stand, then rinse it away with a garden hose. Clean all oily or greasy parts with cleaning solvent as you remove them.

> *WARNING*
> *Never use gasoline as a cleaning agent. It presents an extreme fire hazard. Be sure to work in a well-ventilated area when using cleaning solvent. Keep a fire extinguisher, rated for gasoline fires, handy in any case.*

3. Special tools are required for some repair procedures. These may be purchased from a BMW dealer or motorcycle shop, rented from a tool rental dealer or fabricated by a mechanic or machinist (often at a considerable savings).
4. Much of the labor charged for by mechanics is to remove and disassemble other parts to reach the defective unit. It is usually possible to perform the preliminary operations yourself and then take the defective unit to the dealer for repair.
5. Once you have decided to tackle the job yourself, read the entire section *completely* while looking at the actual parts before starting the job. Make sure you have identified the proper procedure. Study the illustrations and text until you have a good idea of what is involved in completing the job satisfactorily. If special tools or replacement parts are required, make arrangements to get them before you start. It is frustrating and time-consuming to get partly into a job and then be unable to complete it.

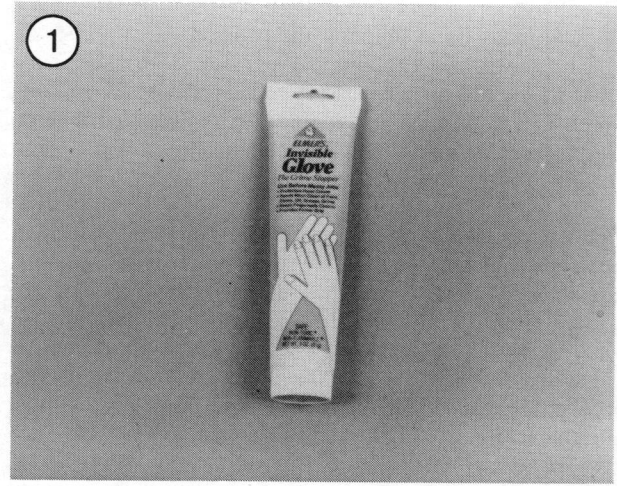

6. Simple wiring checks can be easily made at home, but knowledge of electronics is almost a necessity for performing tests with complicated electronic testing gear.

7. Whenever servicing the engine or transmission, or when removing a suspension component, the bike should be secured in a safe manner. If the bike is to be parked on the side stand or center stand, check the stand to make sure it is secure and not damaged. Block the front and rear wheels if they remain on the ground. A small hydraulic jack and a block of wood can be used to raise the chassis. If the transmission is not going to be worked on, shift the transmission into first gear if the front wheel is raised.

8. Disconnect the negative battery cable when working on or near the electrical, clutch, or starter systems and before disconnecting any electrical wires. On most batteries, the negative terminal will be marked with a minus (-) sign and the positive terminal with a plus (+) sign.

WARNING
Never disconnect the positive battery cable unless the negative cable has been

disconnected. Disconnecting the positive cable while the negative cable is still connected may cause a spark. This could ignite the hydrogen gas given off by the battery, causing an explosion.

9. During disassembly of parts, keep a few general cautions in mind. Force is rarely needed to get things apart. If parts are a tight fit, such as a bearing in a case, there is usually a tool designed to separate them. Never use a screwdriver to pry parts with machined surfaces such as crankcase halves. You will mar the surfaces and end up with leaks.

10. Make diagrams (or take a Polaroid picture) wherever similar-appearing parts are found. For instance, crankcase bolts are often not the same length. You may think you can remember where everything came from, but mistakes are costly. There is also the possibility you may be sidetracked and not return to work for days or even weeks, in which interval carefully laid out parts may have become disturbed.

11. Tag all similar internal parts for location and mark all mating parts for position (A, **Figure 3**). Record number and thickness of any shims as they are removed. Small parts such as bolts can be identified by placing them in plastic sandwich bags (B, **Figure 3**). Seal and label them with masking tape.

12. Place parts from a specific area of the engine (e.g. cylinder head, cylinder, clutch, shift mechanism, etc.) into plastic boxes (C, **Figure 3**) to keep them separated.

13. When disassembling transmission shaft assemblies, use an egg flat (the type that restaurants get their eggs in) (D, **Figure 3**) and set the parts from the shaft in one of the depressions in the same order in which is was removed.

14. Wiring should be tagged with masking tape and marked as each wire is removed. Again, do not rely on memory alone.

15. Protect finished surfaces from physical damage or corrosion. Keep gasoline and hydraulic brake fluid off plastic parts and painted and plated surfaces.

16. Frozen or very tight bolts and screws can often be loosened by soaking with penetrating oil, such as WD-40 or Liquid Wrench, then sharply striking the bolt head a few times with a hammer and punch (or screwdriver for screws). Avoid heat unless absolutely necessary, since it may melt, warp or remove the temper from many parts.

17. No parts, except those assembled with a press fit, require unusual force during assembly. If a part is hard to remove or install, find out why before proceeding.

18. Cover all openings after removing parts to keep dirt, small tools, etc., from falling in.

19. Wiring connections and brake components should be kept clean and free of grease and oil.

20. When assembling 2 parts, start all fasteners, then tighten evenly.

21. When assembling parts, be sure all shims and washers are installed exactly as they came out.

22. Whenever a rotating part butts against a stationary part, look for a shim or washer.

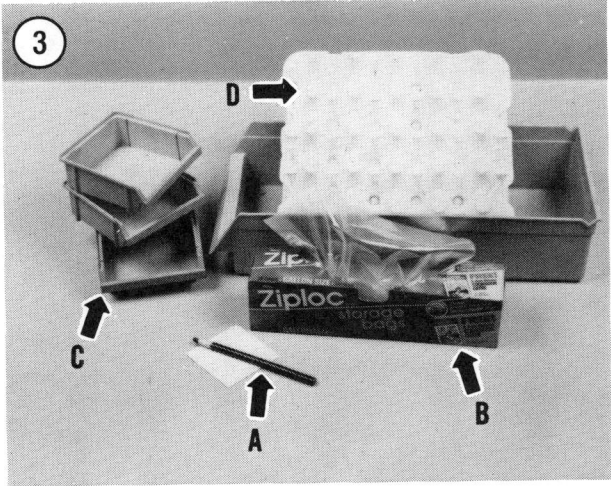

23. Use new gaskets if there is any doubt about the condition of the old ones. A thin coat of oil on gaskets may help them seal effectively.

24. Heavy grease can be used to hold small parts in place if they tend to fall out during assembly. However, keep grease and oil away from electrical and brake components.

25. High spots may be sanded off a piston with sandpaper, but fine emery cloth and oil will do a much more professional job.

26. Carbon can be removed from the head, the piston crowns and the exhaust ports with a dull screwdriver. Do *not* scratch machined surfaces. Wipe off the surface with a clean cloth when finished.

27. A baby bottle makes a good measuring device for adding oil to the front forks. Get one that is graduated in fluid ounces and cubic centimeters. After it has been used for this purpose, do *not* let a small child drink out of it as there will always be an oil residue in it.

28. Some operations require the use of a press. It would be wiser to have these performed by a shop equipped for such work, rather than trying to do the job yourself with makeshift equipment. Other procedures require precise measurements. Unless you have the skills and equipment required, it would be better to have a qualified repair shop make the measurements for you.

CAUTION
BMW has determined that the use of S100 Total Cycle Cleaner may damage, or even remove, the electrolyte-dip matte black from components on the bike. This includes both engine and frame components. If your bike is still under warranty, BMW will not cover any damage caused by using this cleaner.

29. When washing down the exterior of the bike, avoid the use of high-pressure water (some coin-operated car washes) and do not point any water spray directly at the following parts or areas:
  a. Final drive unit.
  b. Wheel hubs.
  c. Instrument cluster.
  d. Ignition switch and handlebar switches.
  e. Fuel injection assembly.
  f. Brake master cylinders.
  g. Muffler outlet.
  h. Under the seat and fuel tank.

NOTE
BMW offers a paint sealant (clear coat) to protect the painted surfaces from air pollution (e.g. acid rain and industrial fallout). The sealant, BMW part No. 88 882 000 001, is compatible with the existing paint used on BMW motorcycles.

SPECIAL TIPS

Because of the extreme demands placed on a bike, several points should be kept in mind when performing service and repair. The following items are general suggestions that may improve the overall life of the machine and help avoid costly failures.

1. Use a locking compound such as Loctite Threadlocker No. 242 (blue Loctite) on all bolts and nuts, even if they are secured with lockwashers. This type of Loctite does not harden completely and allows easy removal of the bolt or nut. A screw or bolt lost from an engine cover or bearing retainer could easily cause serious and expensive damage before its loss is noticed. Make sure the threads are clean and free of grease and oil. Clean with an aerosol electrical contact cleaner before applying the Loctite. When applying Loctite, use a small amount. If too much is used, it can work its way down the threads and stick parts together not meant to be stuck. Keep a tube of Loctite in your tool box. When used properly it is cheap insurance.

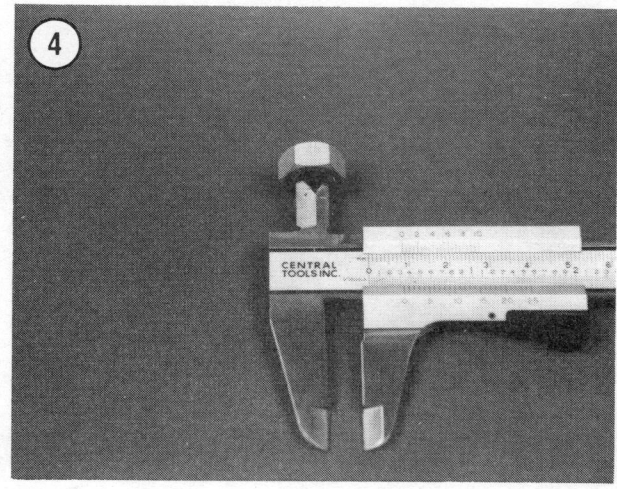

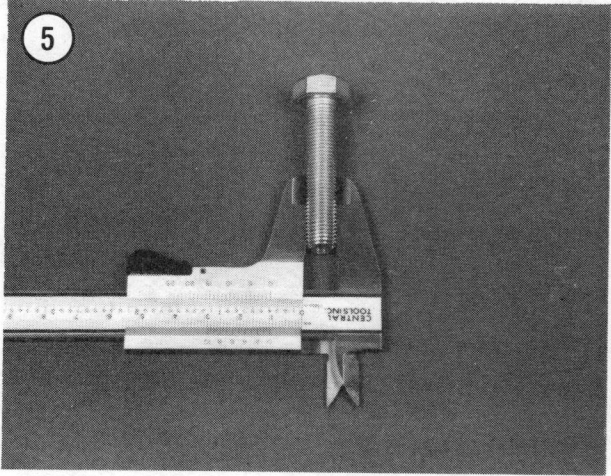

2. Use a hammer-driven impact tool to remove tight fasteners, particularly engine cover screws. These tools help to prevent the rounding off of bolt heads.

3. When replacing missing or broken fasteners (bolts, nuts and screws), especially on the engine or frame components, always use BMW replacement parts. They are specially hardened for each application. The wrong 50-cent bolt could easily cause serious and expensive damage, not to mention rider injury.

4. When installing gaskets in the engine, always use BMW replacement gaskets *without* sealer, unless designated. These gaskets are designed to swell when they come in contact with oil. Gasket sealer will prevent the gaskets from swelling as intended, which can result in oil leaks. These BMW gaskets are cut from material of the precise thickness needed. Installation of a too-thick or too-thin gasket in a critical area could cause engine damage.

TORQUE SPECIFICATIONS

Torque specifications throughout this manual are given in Newton meters (N·m) and foot-pounds (ft.-lb.). Newton meters have been adopted in place of meter kilograms (mkg) in accordance with the International Modernized Metric System. Tool manufacturers offer torque wrenches calibrated in both Newton meters and foot-pounds.

Existing torque wrenches calibrated in meter kilograms can be used by performing a simple conversion. All you have to do is move the decimal point one place to the right; for example, 3.5 mkg = 35 N·m. This conversion is accurate enough for mechanical work even though the exact mathematical conversion is 3.5 mkg = 34.3 N·m.

Refer to **Table 2** for standard torque specifications for various size screws, bolts and nuts that may not be listed

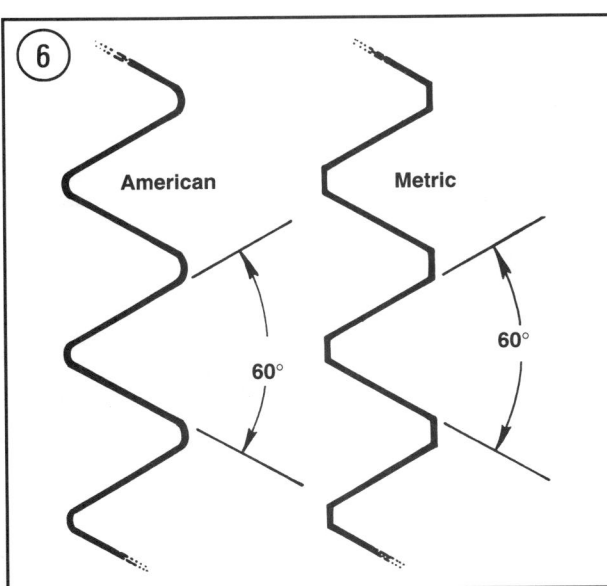

in the respective chapters. To use the table, first determine the size of the bolt or nut. Use a vernier caliper and measure the inside dimension of the threads of the nut (**Figure 4**) and across the threads for a bolt (**Figure 5**).

FASTENERS

The materials and designs of the various fasteners used on your BMW are not arrived at by chance or accident. Fastener design determines the type of tool required to work the fastener. Fastener material is carefully selected to decrease the possibility of physical failure.

Threads

Nuts, bolts and screws are manufactured in a wide range of thread patterns. To join a nut and bolt, the diameter of the bolt and the diameter of the hole in the nuts must be the same. It is just as important that the threads on both be properly matched.

The best way to tell if the threads on 2 fasteners are matched is to turn the nut on the bolt (or the bolt into the threaded hole in the piece of equipment), with your fingers only. Be sure both pieces are clean. If much force is required, check the thread condition on each fastener. If the thread condition is good but the fastener jams, the threads are not compatible. A thread pitch gauge can also be used to determine pitch. BMW motorcycles are manufactured with metric standard fasteners. The threads are cut differently than those of American fasteners (**Figure 6**).

Most threads are cut so that the fastener must be turned *clockwise* to tighten it. These are called right-hand threads. Some fasteners have left-hand threads; they must be turned *counterclockwise* to be tightened. Left-hand threads are used in locations where normal rotation of the equipment would tend to loosen a right-hand threaded fastener. When left-hand threads are used in this manual they are identified in the text.

ISO Metric Screw Threads

ISO (International Organization for Standardization) metric threads come in 3 standard thread sizes: course, fine and constant pitch. the ISO coarse pitch is used for most common fastener applications. The fine pitch thread is used on certain precision tools and instruments. The constant pitch thread is used mainly on machine parts and is used on all metric thread spark plugs.

ISO metric threads are specified by the capital letter M followed by the diameter in millimeters and the pitch (or the distance between each thread) in millimeters. For example, an M8-1.25 bolt is one that has a diameter of 8 millimeters with a distance of 1.25 millimeters between each thread. Use a vernier caliper and measure the inside diameter of the threads of the nut (**Figure 4**) and across the threads for a bolt (**Figure 5**).

Machine Screws

There are many different types of machine screws. **Figure 7** shows a number of screw heads requiring different types of turning tools. Heads are also designed to protrude above the metal (round or hex) or to be slightly recessed in the metal (flat). See **Figure 8**.

Bolts

Commonly called bolts, the technical name for these fasteners is cap screws. Metric bolts are described by the diameter and pitch (or the distance between each thread). For example, an M8-1.25 bolt is one that has a diameter of 8 millimeters and a distance of 1.25 millimeters between each thread. The measurement across two flats on the head of the bolt (**Figure 9**) indicates the proper wrench size to be used. Use a vernier caliper and measure across the threads (**Figure 10**) to determine the bolt diameter and to measure the length (**Figure 11**).

Nuts

Nuts are manufactured in a variety of type and sizes. Most are hexagonal (6-sided) and fit on bolts, screws and studs with the same diameter and pitch.

Figure 12 shows several types of nuts. The common nut is generally used with a lockwasher. Self-locking nuts have a nylon insert which prevents the nut from loosening; no lockwasher is required. Wing nuts are designed for fast removal by hand. Wing nuts are used for convenience in non-critical locations.

To indicate the size of a nut, manufacturers specify the diameter of the opening and the threads per inch. This is similar to bolt specifications, but without the length dimension. The measurement across 2 flats on the nut indicate the proper wrench size to be used (**Figure 13**).

Self-locking Fasteners

Several types of bolts, screw and nuts incorporate a system that develops an interference between the bolt, screw, nut or tapped hole threads. Interference is achieved in various ways: by distorting threads, coating threads with dry adhesive or nylon, distorting the top of an all-metal nut, using a nylon insert in the center or at the top of a nut, etc.

Self-locking fasteners offer greater holding strength and better vibration resistance. Some self-locking fasteners can be reused if in good condition. Others, like the nylon insert nut, form an initial locking condition when the nut is first installed; the nylon forms closely to the bolt thread pattern, thus reducing any tendency for the nut to loosen. When the

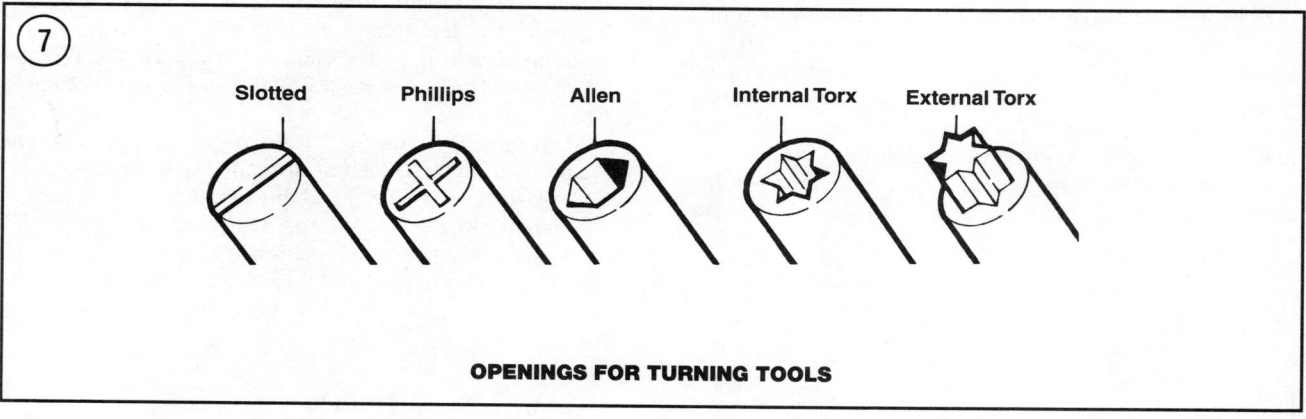

⑦ **OPENINGS FOR TURNING TOOLS**

Slotted　Phillips　Allen　Internal Torx　External Torx

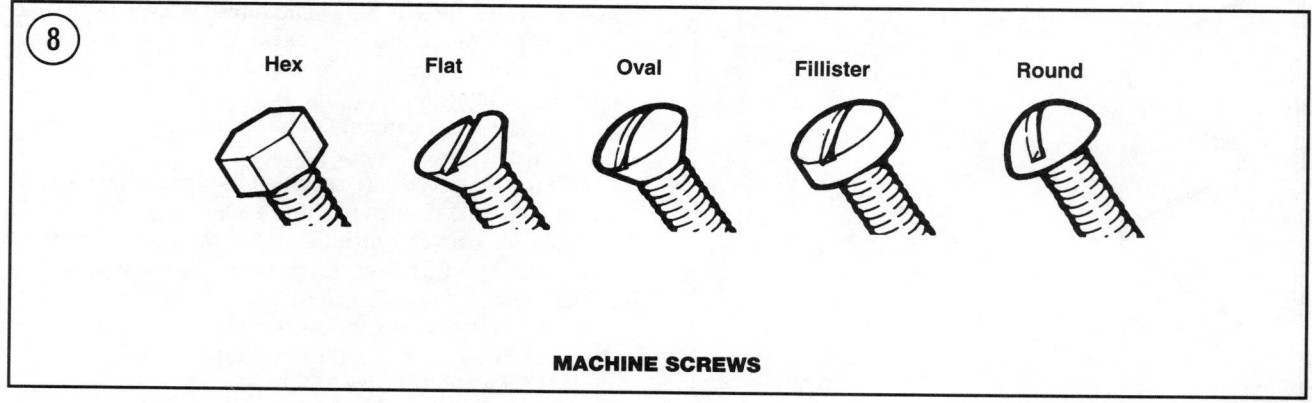

⑧ **MACHINE SCREWS**

Hex　Flat　Oval　Fillister　Round

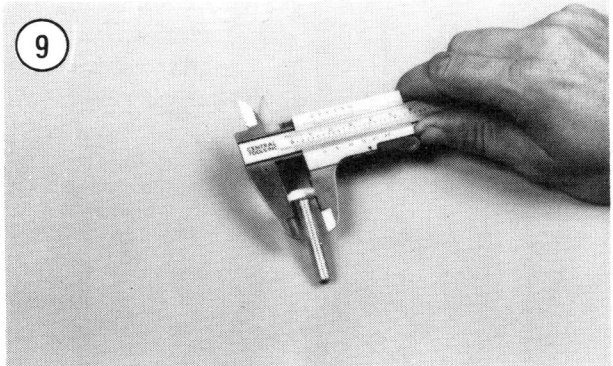

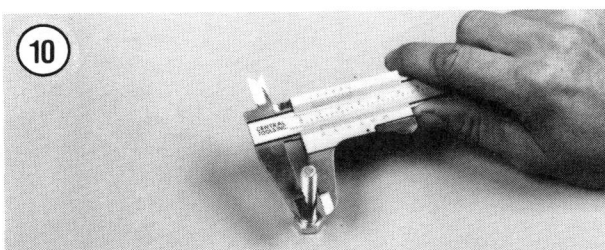

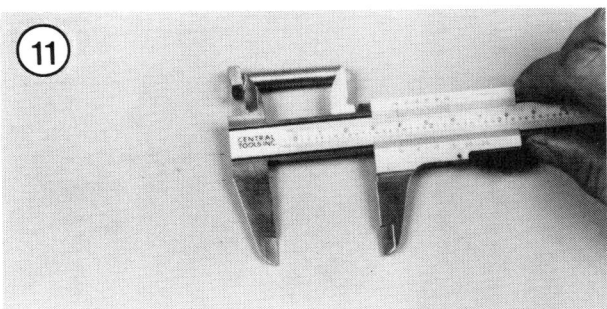

nut is removed, its locking efficiency is greatly reduced. For greatest safety it is recommended that you install new self-locking fasteners whenever they are removed.

Washers

There are 2 basic types of washers: flat washers and lockwashers. Flat washers are simple discs with a hole to fit a screw or bolt. Lockwashers are designed to prevent a fastener from working loose due to vibration, expansion and contraction. **Figure 14** shows several types of lockwashers. Washers are also used in the following functions:

    a. As spacers.
    b. To prevent galling or damage of the equipment by the fastener.
    c. To help distribute fastener load during torquing.
    d. As fluid seals (copper or laminated washers).

Note that flat washers are often used with a fastener to provide a smooth bearing surface. This allows the fastener to be turned easily with a tool.

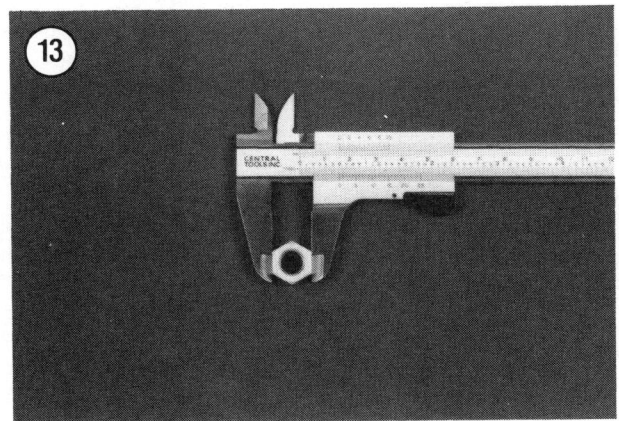

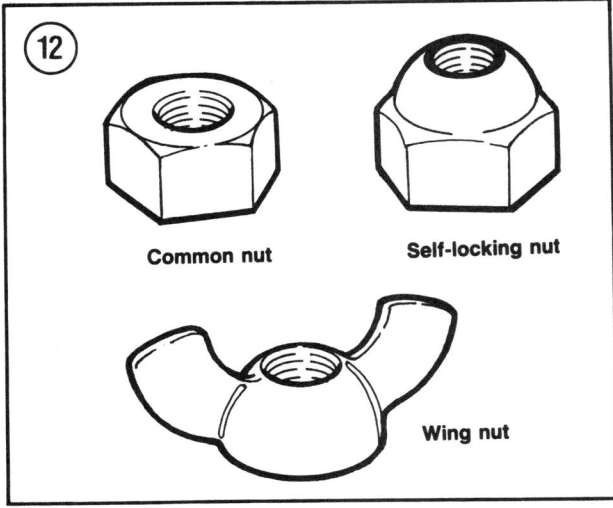

Common nut   Self-locking nut

Wing nut

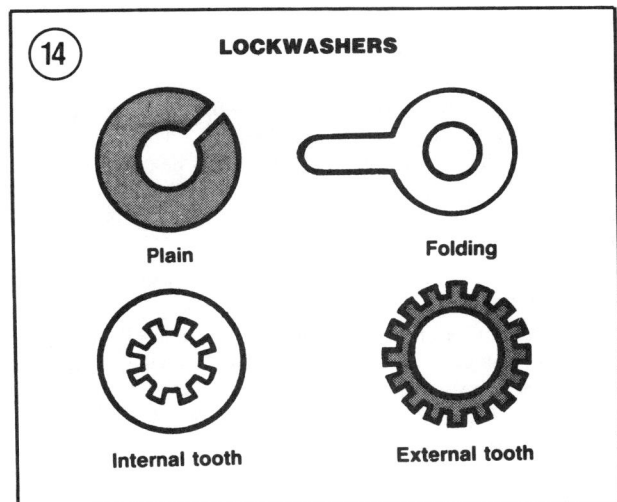

LOCKWASHERS

Plain   Folding

Internal tooth   External tooth

Cotter Pins

Cotter pins (**Figure 15**) are used to secure fasteners in a special location. The threaded stud or bolt must have a hole in it. Its nut or nut lock piece has castellations around its upper edge into which the cotter pin fits to keep it from loosening.

Once fully inserted, the ends of the cotter pin are bent around the outside of the nut to secure it. Cotter pins should not be reused as their ends may break which would allow the cotter pin to fall out and perhaps the fastener to unscrew itself.

Circlips

Circlips (or snap rings) can be internal or external design. They are used to retain items on shafts (external type) or within tubes (internal type). In some applications, circlips of varying thickness are used to control the end play of parts assemblies. These are often called selective circlips. Circlips should be replaced during installation, as removal weakens and deforms them.

Two basic types of circlips are available: machined and stamped circlips. Machined circlips (**Figure 16**) can be installed in either direction (shaft or housing) because both faces are machined, thus creating two sharp edges. Stamped circlips (**Figure 17**) are manufactured with one sharp edge and one rounded edge. When installing stamped circlips in a thrust situation (transmission shafts, fork tubes, etc.), the sharp edge must face away from the part producing the thrust. When installing circlips, observe the following:

  a. Compress or expand the circlip only enough to install or remove it.
  b. After the circlip is installed, make sure it is completely seated in its groove.

Transmission circlips become worn with use and increase side play. For this reason, always use new circlips whenever a transmission is to be reassembled.

LUBRICANTS

Periodic lubrication assures long life for any type of equipment. The *type* of lubricant used is just as important as the lubrication service itself, although in an emergency the wrong type of lubricant may be better than none at all. The following paragraphs describe the types of lubricants most often used on motorcycle equipment. Be sure to follow the motorcycle's manufacturer's recommendations for lubricant types.

If any unique lubricant is recommended by BMW it is specified in the service procedure.

Generally, all liquid lubricants are called "oil." They may be mineral-based (including petroleum bases), natural based (vegetable and animal bases), synthetic-based or emulsions (mixtures). "Grease" is an oil to which a thickening base has been added so that the end product is semi-solid. Grease is often classified by the type of thickener added; lithium soap is commonly used.

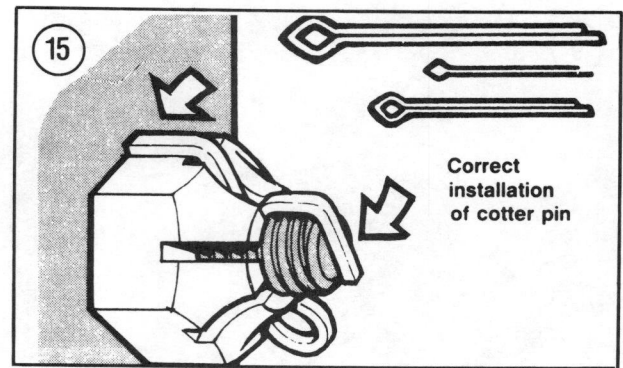

Correct installation of cotter pin

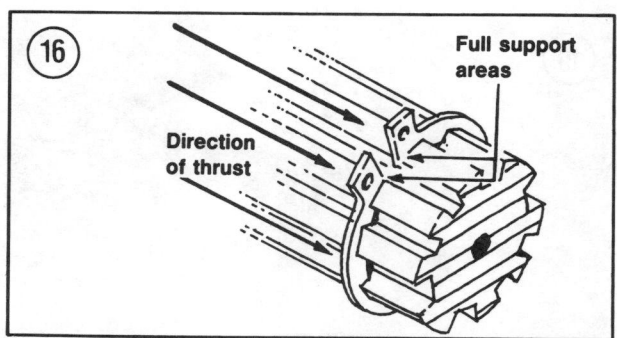

Full support areas

Direction of thrust

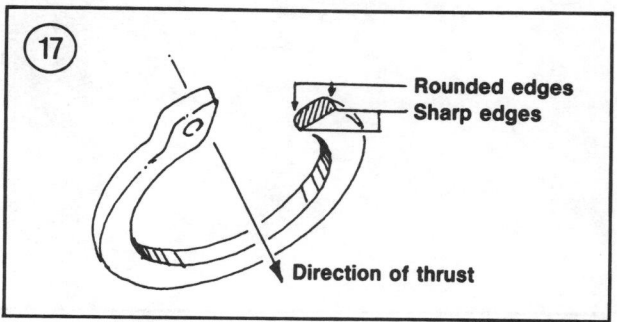

Rounded edges
Sharp edges

Direction of thrust

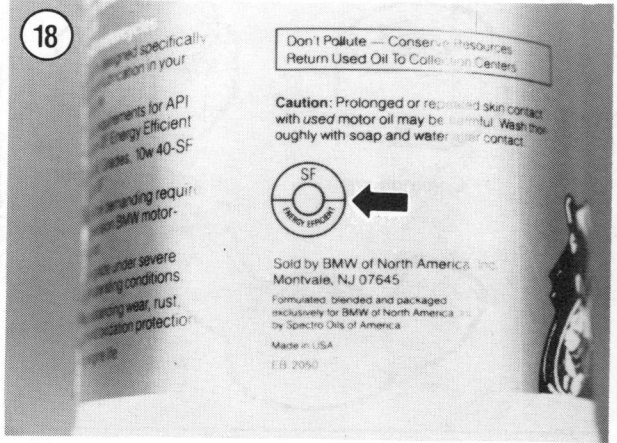

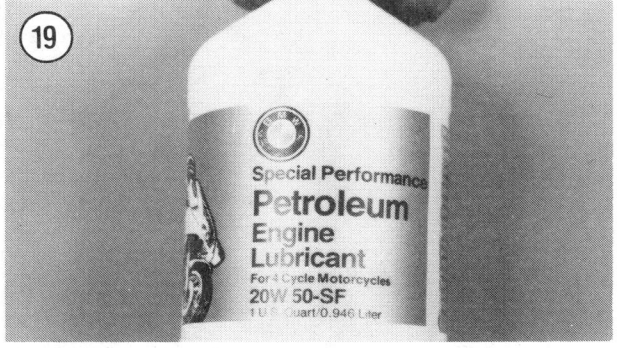

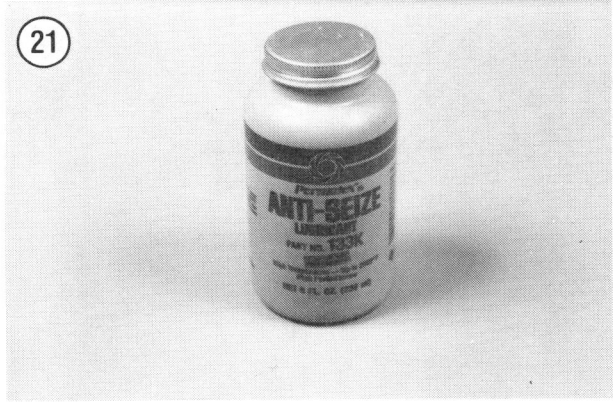

Engine Oil

Oil for motorcycle and automotive engines is classified by the American Petroleum Institute (API) and the Society of Automotive Engineers (SAE) in several categories. Oil containers display these ratings on the top of the can or on the bottle label (**Figure 18**). It is suggested that the oil (**Figure 19**) manufactured for and sold by BMW dealers be used in this engine. A substitute brand of oil may be used but first confer with a BMW dealer regarding which type is compatible.

API oil classification is indicated by letters; oils for gasoline engines are identified by an "S." The engines covered in this manual require SF or SG graded oil.

Viscosity is an indication of the oil's thickness. The SAE uses numbers to indicate viscosity; thin oils have low numbers while thick oils have high numbers. A "W" after the number indicates that the viscosity testing was done at low temperature to simulate cold-weather operation. Engine oils fall into the 5W-30 and 20W-50 range.

Multi-grade oils (for example 10W-40) maintain a consistent viscosity at low temperatures and at high temperatures. This allows the oil to perform efficiently across a wide range of engine operating conditions. The lower the number, the better the engine will start in cold climates. Higher numbers are usually recommended for engines running in hot weather conditions.

Grease

Greases are graded by the National Lubricating Grease Institute (NLGI). Greases are graded by number according to the consistency of the grease; these range from No. 000 to No. 6, with No. 6 being the most solid. A typical multipurpose grease is NLGI No. 2. For specific applications, equipment manufacturers may require grease with an additive such as molybdenum disulfide (MOS2).

BMW has recommended several extreme-pressure greases for the splines joining the clutch friction plate and transmission input shaft. Staburags NBU 30 PTM grease (**Figure 20**) was originally used, while BMW Lubricant #10 is the latest recommendation.

Also recommended for the swing arm pivot is Permatex Anti-Seize lubricant (**Figure 21**), or equivalent. This is necessary to prevent the pivot points from corroding and locking up.

EXPENDABLE SUPPLIES

Certain expendable supplies are required during maintenance and repair work. These include grease, oil, gasket cement, wiping rags and cleaning solvent. Ask your dealer for the special locking compounds, silicone lubricants and other products (**Figure 22**) which make vehicle maintenance simpler and easier. Cleaning solvent or kerosene is available at some service stations or hardware stores.

PARTS REPLACEMENT

BMW makes some minor changes during a model year. When you order parts from the BMW dealer or other parts distributor, always order by engine and frame number. Write the numbers down and carry them with you. Compare new parts to old before purchasing them. If they are not alike, have the parts manager explain the difference to you.

SERIAL NUMBERS

You must know the model serial number and vehicle identification number (VIN) for registration purposes and when ordering replacement parts.

The frame serial number is stamped on the right-hand side of the frame (**Figure 23**) just above the rear brake master cylinder reservoir. The vehicle identification number (VIN) is on the left-hand side of the frame (**Figure 24**). The engine serial number is located on a raised pad on the right-hand side of the cylinder block (**Figure 25**) to the rear of the oil level sight glass.

MISCELLANEOUS INFORMATION LABELS

Miscellaneous labels relating to tire inflation pressure, emission control, paint code numbers, etc. are located under the seat on the rear fender and storage compartment cover (**Figure 26**).

BASIC HAND TOOLS

A number of tools are required to maintain a bike in top riding condition. You may already have some of these tools for home or car repairs. There are also tools made especially for bike repairs; these you will have to purchase. In any case, a wide variety of quality tools will make bike repairs easier and more effective.

Top quality tools are essential; they are also more economical in the long run. If you are now starting to build your tool collection, stay away from the "advertised specials" featured at some parts houses, discount stores and chain drug stores. These are usually a poor grade tool that can be sold cheaply and that is exactly what they are—*cheap*. They are usually made of inferior material and are thick, heavy and clumsy. Their rough finish makes them difficult to clean and they usually don't last very long.

Quality tools are made of alloy steel and are heat treated for greater strength. They are lighter and better balanced than cheap ones. Their surface is smooth, making them a pleasure to work with and easy to clean. The initial cost of good quality tools may be more but it is cheaper in the

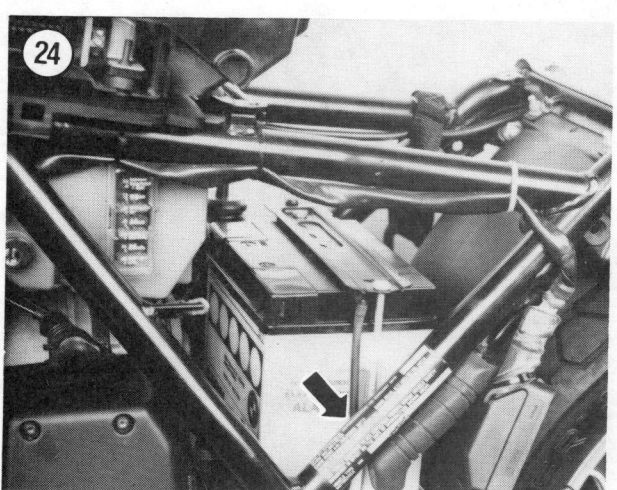

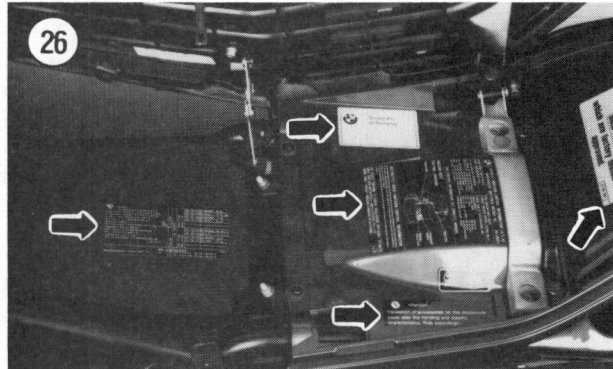

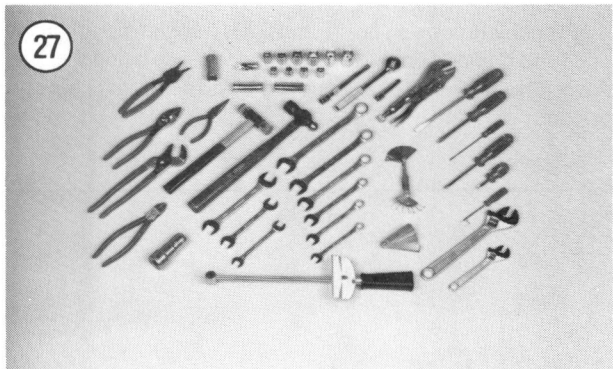

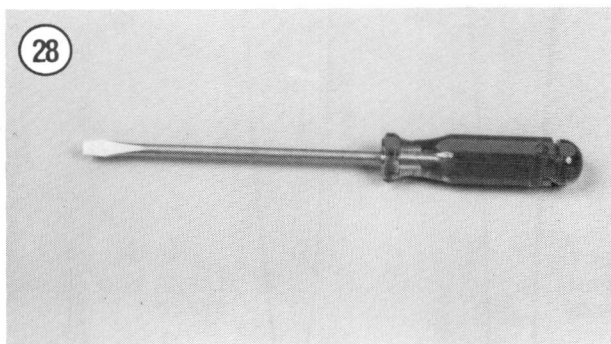

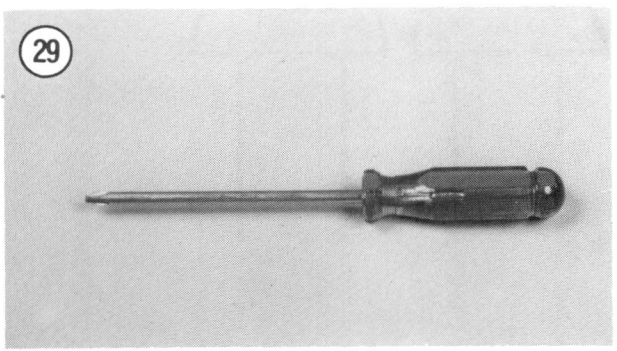

long run. Don't try to buy everything in all sizes in the beginning; do it a little at a time until you have the necessary tools.

Keep your tools clean and in a tool box. Keep them organized with the sockets and related drives together and the open end and box wrenches together, etc. After using a tool, wipe off dirt and grease with a clean cloth and place the tool in its correct place. Doing this will save a lot of time you would have spent trying to find a socket buried in a bunch of clutch parts. Also, be careful when lending tools—make sure they are returned promptly.

The following tools are required to perform virtually any repair job on a bike. Each tool is described and the recommended size given for starting a tool collection. **Table 3** includes the tools that should be on hand for simple home repairs and/or major overhaul as shown in **Figure 27**. Additional tools and some duplicates may be added as you become more familiar with the bike. Almost all motorcycles and bikes (with the exception of the U.S. built Harley and some English bikes) use metric size bolts and nuts. If you are starting your collection now, buy metric sizes.

Screwdrivers

The screwdriver is a very basic tool, but if used improperly it will do more damage than good. The slot on a screw has a definite dimension and shape. A screwdriver must be selected to conform with that shape. Use a small screwdriver for small screws and a large one for large screws or the screw head will be damaged.

Two basic types of screwdriver are required to repair the bike—common (flat blade) screwdrivers (**Figure 28**) and Phillips screwdrivers (**Figure 29**).

Screwdrivers are available in sets which often include an assortment of common and Phillips blades. If you buy them individually, buy at least the following:

    a. Common screwdriver—5/16 x 6 in. blade.
    b. Common screwdriver—3/8 x 12 in. blade.
    c. Phillips screwdriver—size 2 tip, 6 in. blade.

Use screwdrivers only for driving screws. Never use a screwdriver for prying or chiseling. Do not try to remove a Phillips or Allen head screw with a common screwdriver; you can damage the head so that the proper tool will be unable to remove it.

Keep screwdrivers in the proper condition and they will last longer and perform better. Always keep the tip of a common screwdriver in good condition. **Figure 30** shows how to grind the tip to the proper shape if it becomes damaged. Note the symmetrical sides of the tip.

Pliers

Pliers come in a wide range of types and sizes. Pliers are useful for cutting, bending and crimping. They should never be used to cut hardened objects or to turn bolts or nuts. **Figure 31** shows several pliers useful in bike repairs.

Each type of pliers has a specialized function. Slip-joint pliers are general purpose pliers and are used mainly for holding things and for bending. Vise Grips (**Figure 32**) are used to hold objects very tightly like a vise. But avoid using them unless absolutely necessary since their sharp jaws will permanently scar any objects which are held.

Needlenose pliers are used to hold or bend small objects. Channel lock pliers can be adjusted to hold various sizes of objects; the jaws remain parallel to grip around objects such as pipe or tubing. There are many more types of pliers. The ones described here are most suitable for bike repairs.

Box, Open-end and Combination Wrenches

Box-end, open-end and combination wrenches are available in sets or separately in a variety of sizes. On open and box end wrenches, the number stamped near the end refers to the distance between 2 parallel flats on the hex head bolt or nut. On combination wrenches, the number is stamped near the center.

Open-end wrenches are speedy and work best in areas with limited overhead access. Their wide flat jaws make them unstable for situations where the bolt or nut is sunken in a well or close to the edge of a casting. These wrenches grip only two flats of a fastener so if either the fastener head or the wrench jaws are worn, the wrench may slip off.

Box-end wrenches require clear overhead access to the fastener but can work well in situations where the fastener head is close to another part. They grip on all six corners of a fastener for a very secure grip. They are available in either 6-point or 12-point. The 6-point gives superior holding power and durability but requires a greater swinging radius. The 12-point works better in situations with limited swinging radius.

Combination wrenches (**Figure 33**) have open-end on one side and box-end on the other with both ends being the same size. These wrenches are favored by professionals because of their versatility.

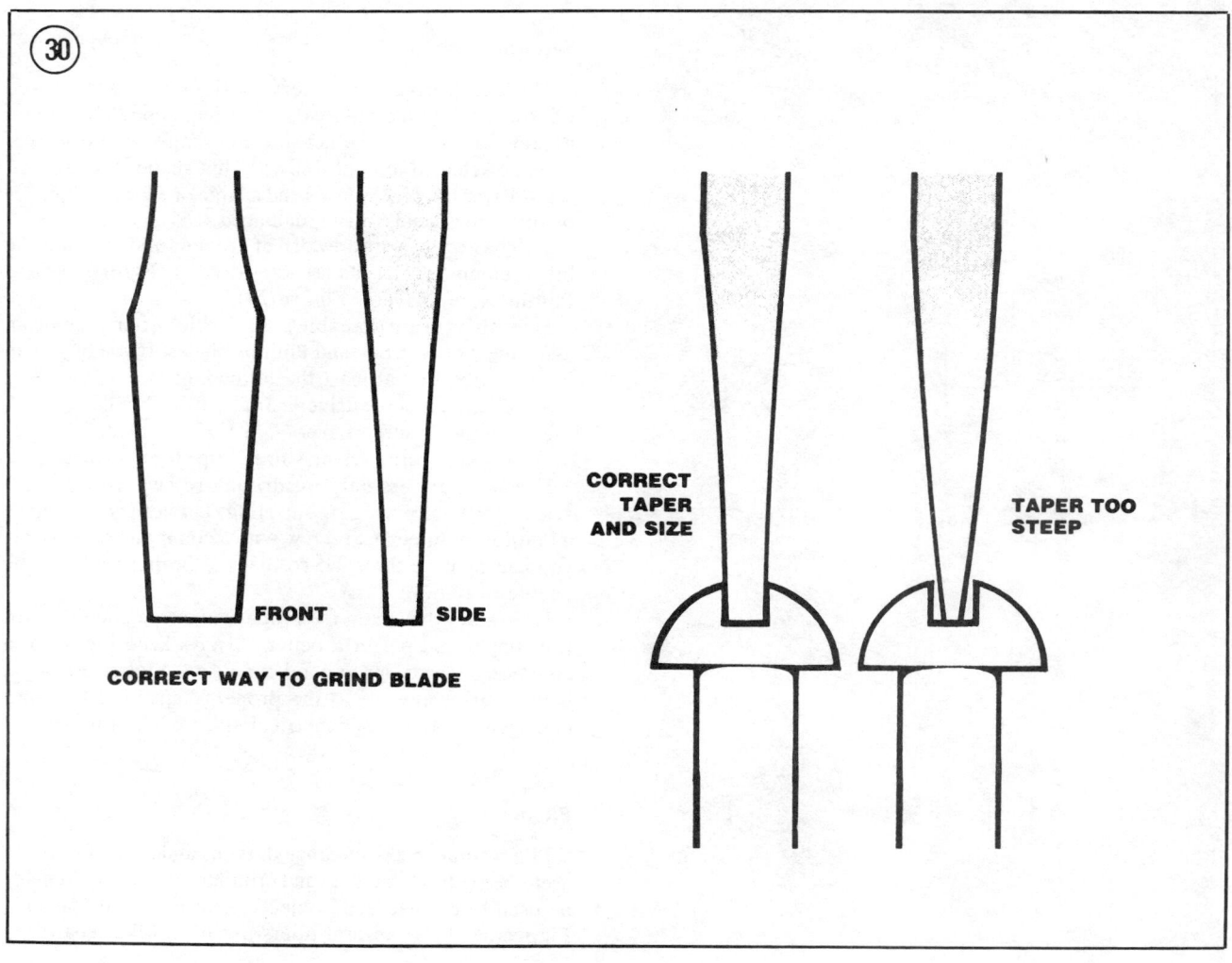

(30)

FRONT   SIDE

CORRECT WAY TO GRIND BLADE

CORRECT TAPER AND SIZE

TAPER TOO STEEP

Adjustable (Crescent) Wrenches

An adjustable wrench (sometimes called Crescent wrench) can be adjusted to fit nearly any nut or bolt head which has clear access around its entire perimeter. Adjustable wrenches (**Figure 34**) are best used as a backup wrench to keep a large nut or bolt from turning while the other end is being loosened or tightened with a proper wrench.

Adjustable wrenches have only two gripping surfaces which make them more subject to slipping off the fastener and damaging the part and possibly injuring your hand. The fact that one jaw is adjustable only aggravates this shortcoming.

These wrenches are directional; the solid jaw must be the one transmitting the force. If you use the adjustable jaw to transmit the force, it will loosen and possibly slip off.

Adjustable wrenches come in all sizes but something in the 6 to 8 in. range is recommended as an all-purpose wrench.

Socket Wrenches

This type is undoubtedly the fastest, safest and most convenient to use. See **Figure 35**. Sockets which attach to a ratchet handle are available with 6-point or 12-point openings and 1/4, 3/8, 1/2 and 3/4 inch drives. The drive size indicates the size of the square hole which mates with the ratchet handle.

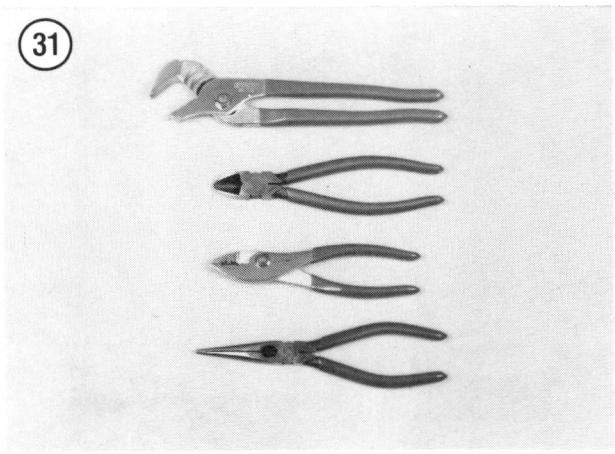

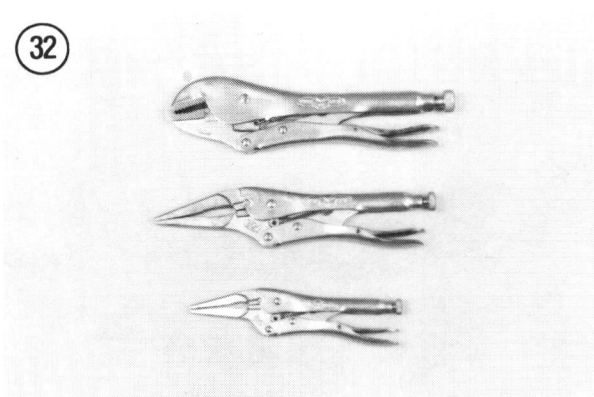

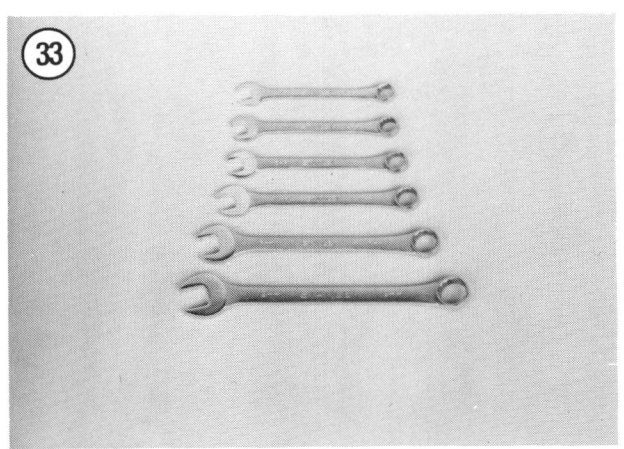

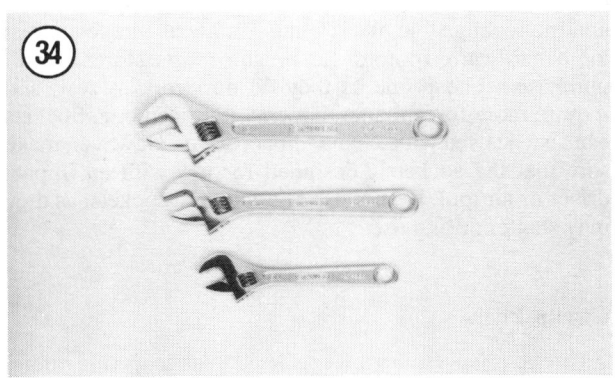

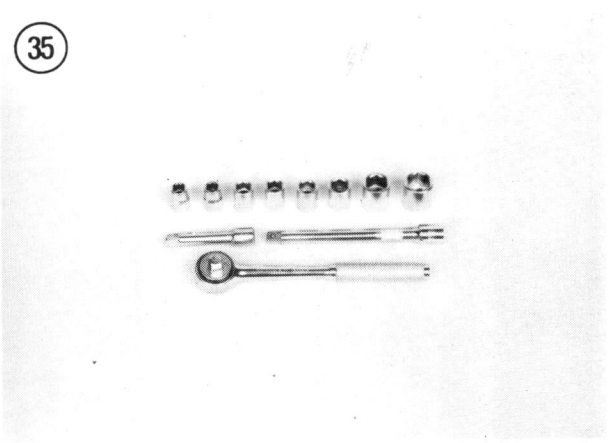

Allen Wrenches

Allen wrenches (**Figure 36**) are available in sets or separately in a variety of sizes. These sets come in SAE and metric size, so be sure to buy a metric set. Allen bolts are sometimes called socket bolts.

BMW uses Allen bolts for the major fasteners on both the engine and the frame components. Some times the bolts are difficult to reach and it is suggested that a variety of Allen wrenches be purchased (e.g. socket driven, T-handle and extension type) as shown in **Figure 37**.

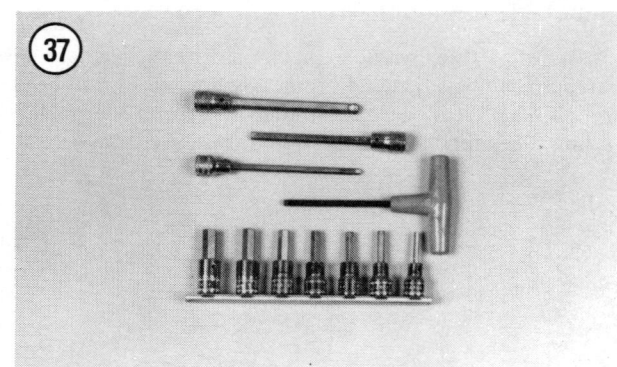

Torque Wrench

A torque wrench is used with a socket to measure how tightly a nut or bolt is installed. They come in a wide price range and with either 3/8 or 1/2 in. square drive (**Figure 38**). The drive size indicates the size of the square drive which mates with the socket. Purchase one that measures 0-280 N·m (0-200 ft.-lb.).

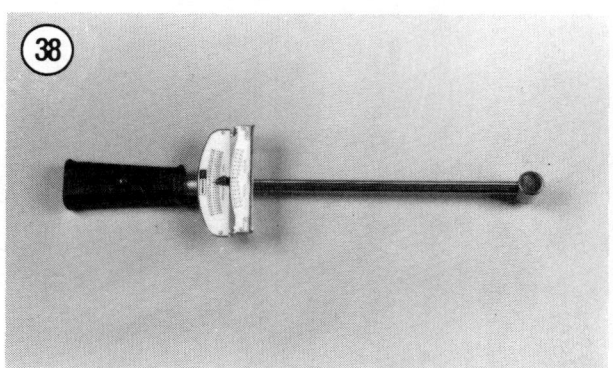

Impact Driver

This tool might have been designed with the bike in mind. This tool makes removal of fasteners easy and eliminates damage to bolts and screw slots. Impact drivers and interchangeable bits (Figure 39) are available at most large hardware, motorcycle or auto parts stores. Don't purchase a cheap one as they do not work as well and require more force than a moderately priced one. Sockets can also be used with a hand impact driver. However, make sure that the socket is designed for use with an impact driver or air tool. Do not use regular hand sockets, as they may shatter during use.

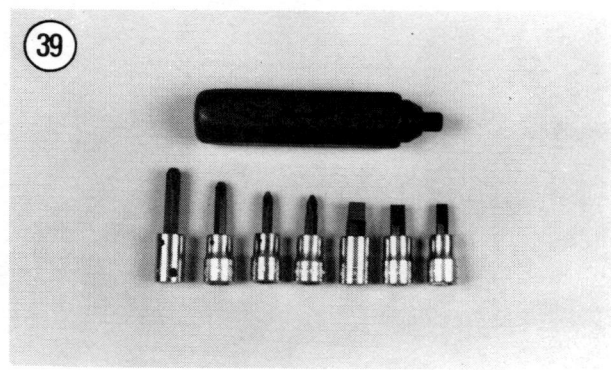

Circlip Pliers

Circlip pliers (sometimes referred to as snap-ring pliers) are necessary to remove the circlips used on the

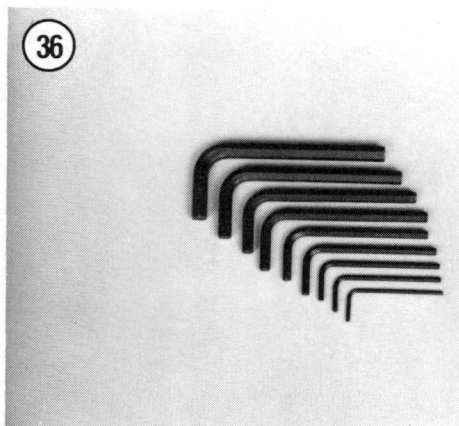

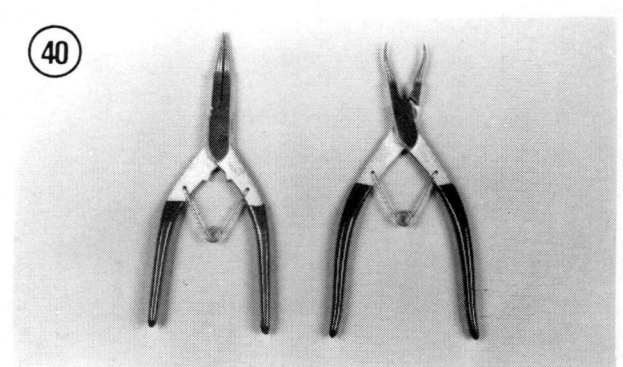

1

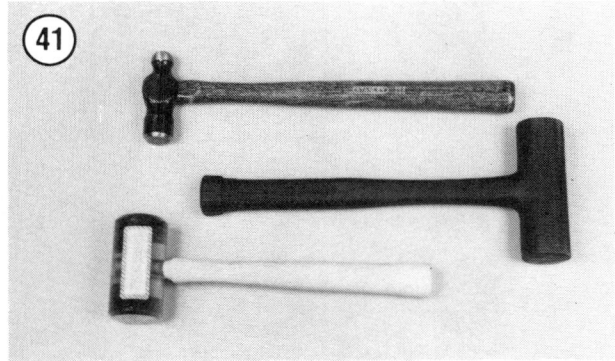

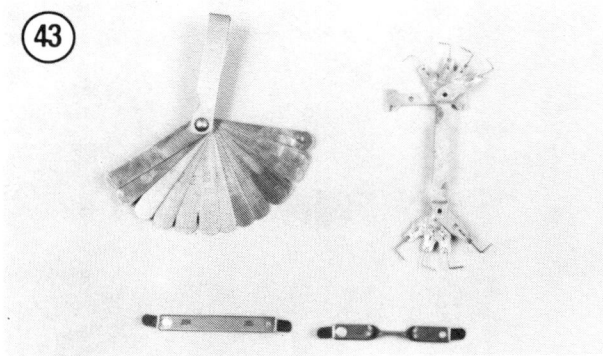

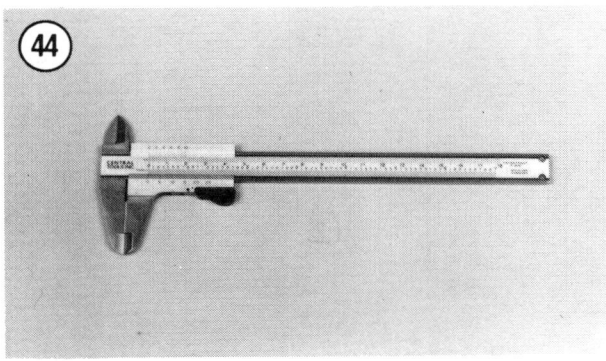

transmission shaft assemblies. See **Figure 40**. There are two kinds of circlip pliers. External pliers (spreading) are used to remove circlips that fit on the outside of a shaft. Internal pliers (squeezing) are used to remove circlips which fit inside a gear or housing.

WARNING
Because circlips can sometimes slip and "fly off" during removal and installation, always wear safety glasses.

Hammers

The correct hammer is necessary for bike repairs. Use only a hammer with a face (or head) of rubber or plastic or the soft-faced type that is filled with buck shot. See **Figure 41**. These are sometimes necessary in engine teardowns. *Never* use a metal-faced hammer on the bike as severe damage will result in most cases. You can always produce the same amount of force with a soft-faced hammer.

Spark Plug Gauge

This tool (**Figure 42**) has both flat and wire measuring gauges and is used to measure spark plug gap. This device is available at most auto or motorcycle supply stores.

Ignition Timing Device

A BMW special tool set-up is necessary to check and adjust the ignition timing. The BMW ignition tester (part No. 12 3 650) and the dial gauge adaptor (part No. 00 2 580) and a dial indicator are necessary for ignition timing. This ignition system does not use a strobe light for timing inspection.

Feeler Gauges

Feeler gauges come in assorted sets and types (**Figure 43**). Some are strictly flat, some are a combination of flat and wire. Others are used specifically for valve adjustment and are bent at a certain angle to make it easy to use them in the normally tight working areas of a cylinder head.

Vernier Caliper

This tool (**Figure 44**) is invaluable when it is necessary to measure the inside, outside and depth measurements with close precision. It can be used to measure the thickness of shims and thrust washers. The vernier caliper can be purchased from large hardware and motorcycle dealers or mail order houses.

Micrometers

The micrometer (**Figure 45**) is used for very exact measurements of close-tolerance components. It can be used to measaure the outside diameter of a piston and for crankshaft and camshaft bearing journal inspection measurements. These instruments are relatively expensive and you may choose to have these components measured by a BMW dealer or machine shop instead of purchasing a costly set.

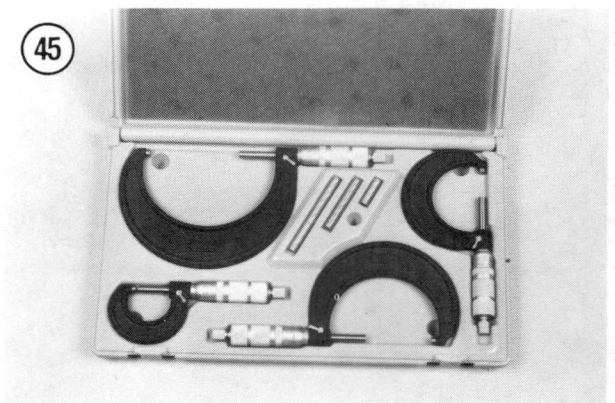

Tap and Die Set

A complete tap and die set (**Figure 46**) is a relatively expensive tool. But when you need a tap or die to clean up a damaged thread, there is really no substitute. Be sure to purchase one for *metric* threads if your are working on German or Japanese bikes. British and Italian bikes use a unique thread of their own and the Harley-Davidson uses American standard (SAE).

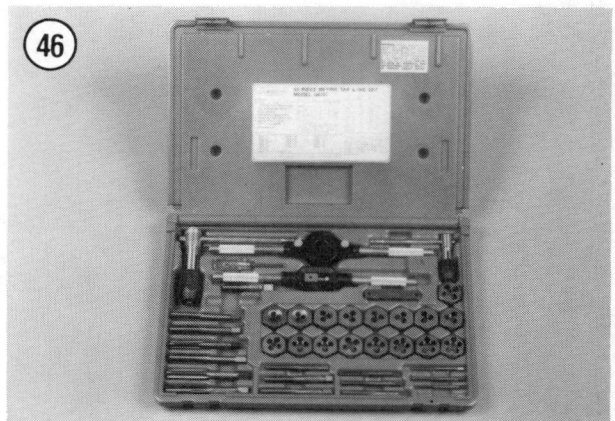

Tire Levers

When changing tires, use a good set of tire levers (**Figure 47**). Never use a screwdriver in place of a tire lever; refer to Chapter Ten for tire changing procedures using these tools. Before using the tire levers, check the working ends of the tool and remove any burrs. Don't use a tire lever for prying anything but tires.

Other Special Tools

A few other special tools may be required for major service. These are described in the appropriate chapters and are available either from BMW dealers or other manufacturers as indicated.

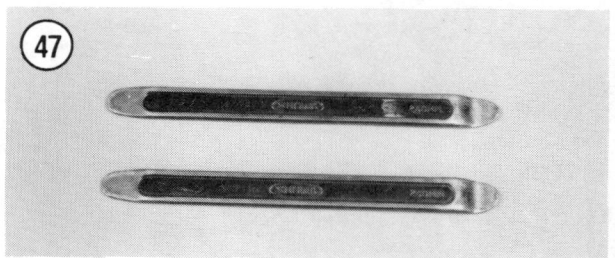

TEST EQUIPMENT

Multimeter or Volt-ohm Meter

> *CAUTION*
> *Due to the sensitivity of the computer-controlled fuel injection and ignition systems, the multimeter **must not** be used to test either of these systems. Refer to exact test procedures in the fuel and electrical chapters for types of test equipment which can or cannot be used.*

This instrument (**Figure 48**) is invaluable for electrical system troubleshooting and service. A few of its functions may be duplicated by homemade test equipment, but for the serious mechanic it is a must. Its uses are described in the applicable sections of the book.

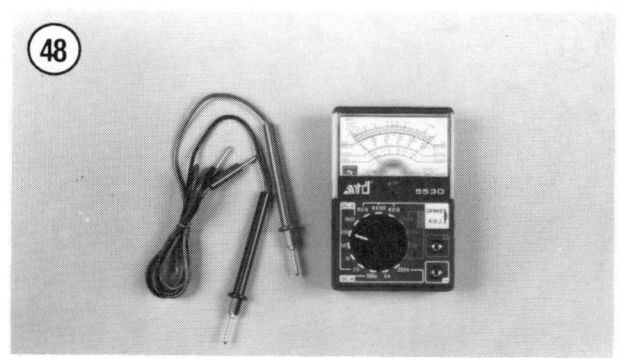

Portable Tachometer

A portable tachometer is necessary for tuning (**Figure 49**). Ignition timing and carburetor adjustments must be performed at the specified engine speed. The best instrument for this purpose is one with a low range of 0-1,000 or 0-2,000 rpm and a high range of 0-4,000 rpm. Extended range (0-6,000 or 0-8,000 rpm) instruments lack accuracy at lower speeds. The instrument should be capable of detecting changes of 25 rpm on the low range.

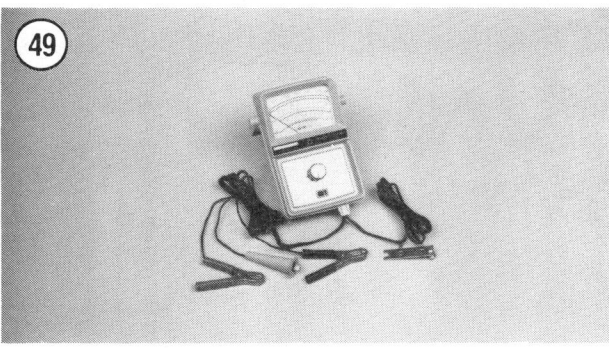

Compression Gauge

A compression gauge (**Figure 50**) measures the engine compression. The results, when properly interpreted, can indicate general ring and valve condition. They are available from motorcycle or auto supply stores and mail order outlets.

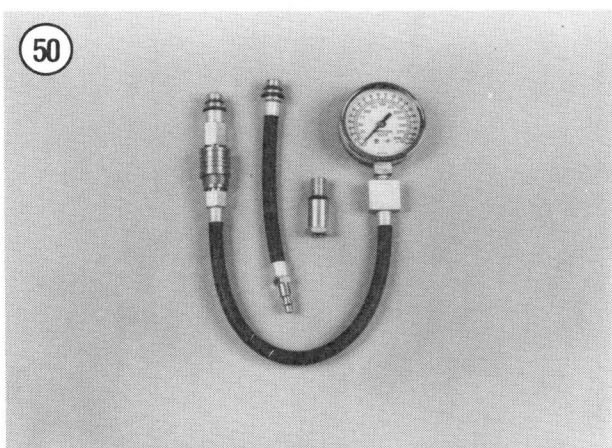

MECHANIC'S TIPS

Removing Frozen Nuts and Screws

When a fastener rusts and cannot be removed, several methods may be used to loosen it. First, apply penetrating oil such as Liquid Wrench or WD-40 (available at any hardware or auto supply store). Apply it liberally and let it penetrate for 10-15 minutes. Rap the fastener several times with a small hammer; do not hit it hard enough to cause damage. Reapply the penetrating oil if necessary.

For frozen screws, apply penetrating oil as described, then insert a screwdriver in the slot and rap the top of the screwdriver with a hammer. This loosens the rust so the screw can be removed in the normal way. If the screw head is too chewed up to use a screwdriver, grip the head with Vise Grip pliers and twist the screw out.

Remedying Stripped Threads

Occasionally, threads are stripped though carelessness or impact damage. Often the threads can be cleaned up by running a tap (for internal threads on nuts) or die (for external threads on bolts) through or over the threads. See **Figure 51**. Use a screw pitch gauge (**Figure 52**) to determine the exact thread pitch prior to using a tap or die for thread cleanup. To clean or repair spark plug threads, a spark plug tap (**Figure 53**) can be used.

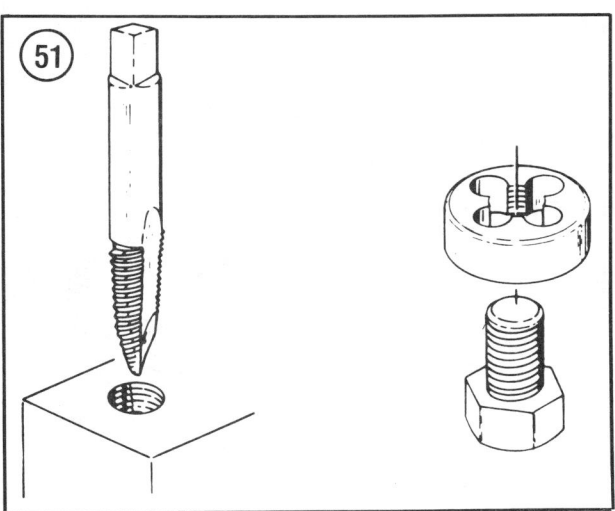

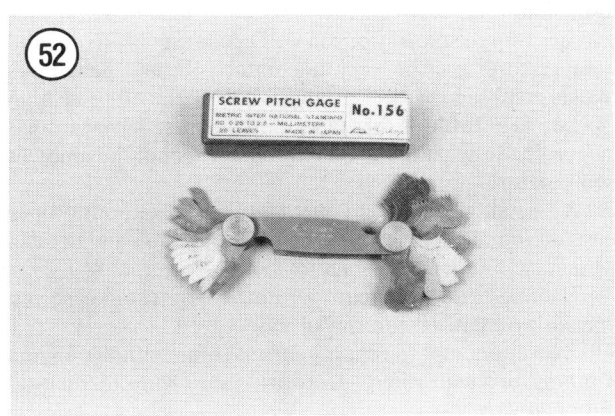

If the internal threads in a part are damaged beyond the use of a tap, the damaged threads can be replaced with a HeliCoil, or equivalent master thread repair pack (**Figure 54**). These kits have all the necessary items to repair a damaged internal thread.

Removing Broken Screws or Bolts

When the head breaks off a screw or bolt, several methods are available for removing the remaining portion.

If a large portion of the remainder projects out, try gripping it with Vise Grips. If the projecting portion is too small, file it to fit a wrench or cut a slot in it to fit a screwdriver. See **Figure 55**.

If the head breaks off flush, use a screw extractor. To do this, centerpunch the remaining portion of the screw or bolt. Drill a small hole in the screw and tap the extractor into the hole. Back the screw out with a wrench on the extractor. See **Figure 56**.

RIDING SAFETY

General Tips

1. Read your owner's manual and know your machine.
2. Check the throttle and brake controls before starting the engine.
3. Know how to make an emergency stop.
4. Never add fuel while anyone is smoking in the area or when the engine is running.
5. Never wear loose scarves, belts or boot laces that could catch on moving parts.
6. Always wear eye and head protection and protective clothing to protect your *entire* body. Today's riding apparel is very stylish and you will be ready for action as well as being well protected.
7. Riding in the winter months requires a good set of clothes to keep your body dry and warm, otherwise your entire trip may be miserable. If you dress properly, moisture will evaporate from your body. If you become too hot and if your clothes trap the moisture, you will become cold. Even mild temperatures can be very uncomfortable and dangerous when combined with a strong wind or traveling at high speed. See **Table 4** for wind chill factors. Always dress according to what the wind chill factor is, not the ambient temperature.
8. Never allow anyone to operate the bike without proper instruction. This is for their bodily protection and to keep your machine from damage or destruction.
9. Use the "buddy system" for long trips, just in case you have a problem or run out of gas.
10. Never attempt to repair your machine with the engine running except when necessary for certain tune-up procedures.

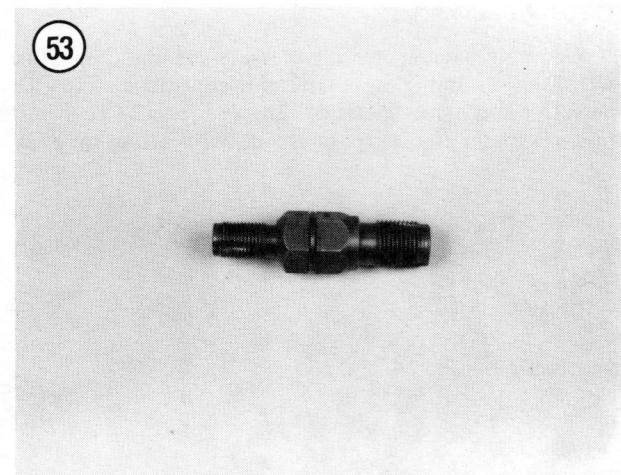

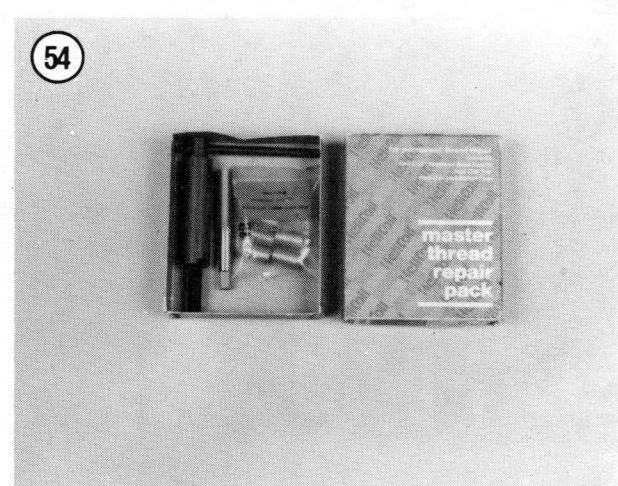

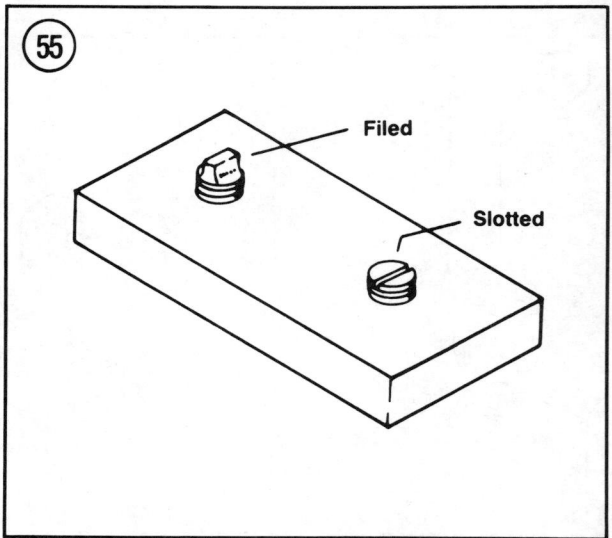

11. Check all of the machine components and hardware frequently, especially the wheels and the steering.

Operating Tips

1. Avoid dangerous terrain.
2. Keep the headlight, turn signal lights and taillight free of dirt.
3. Always steer with both hands.
4. Be aware of the terrain and avoid operating the bike at excessive speed.
5. Do not panic if the throttle sticks. Turn the engine stop switch to the OFF position.
6. Do not tailgate. Rear end collisions can cause injury and machine damage.
7. Do not mix alcoholic beverages or drugs with riding—*ride straight*.
8. Check your fuel supply regularly. Do not travel farther than your fuel supply will permit you to arrive at the next fuel stop.

1

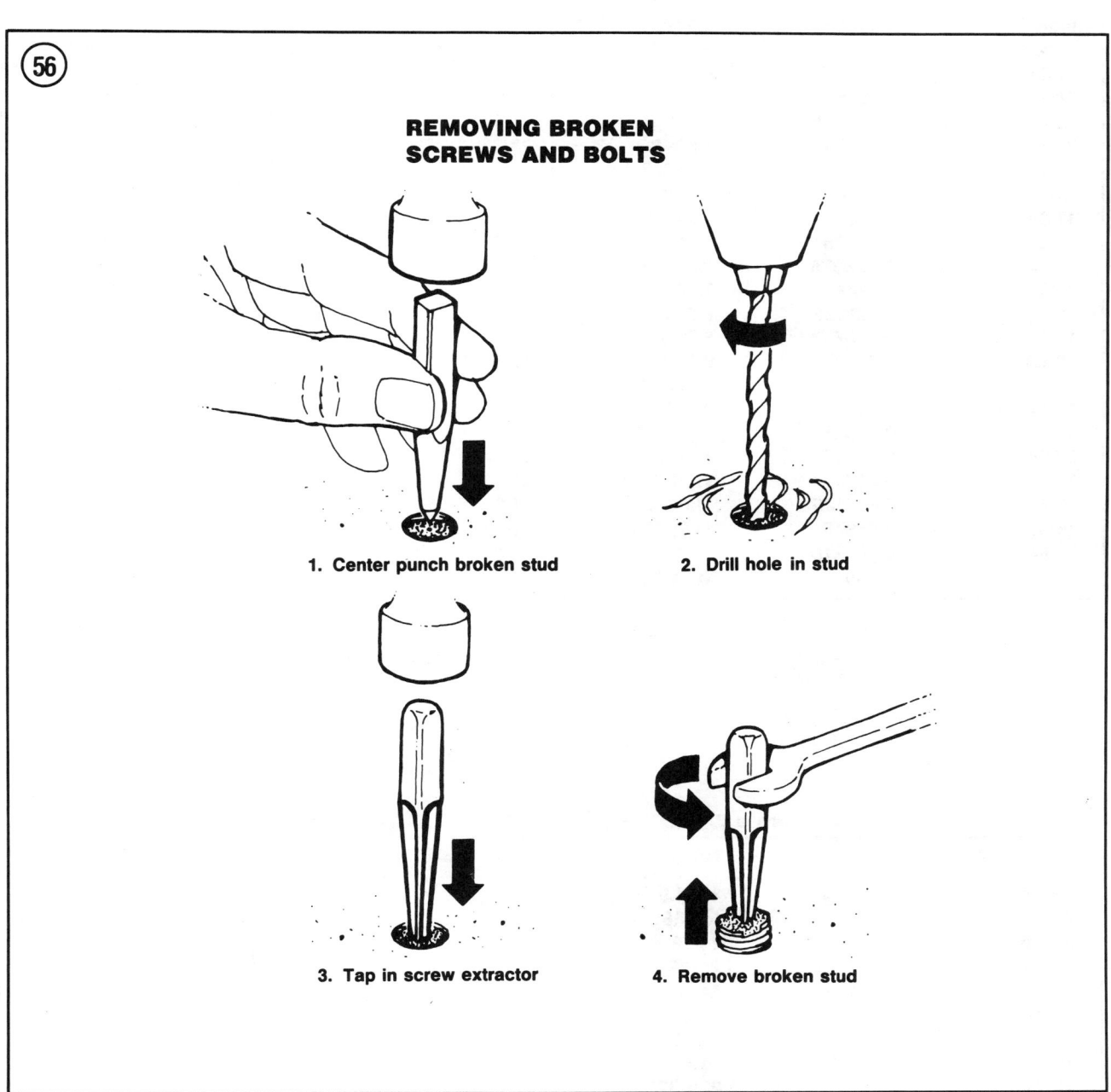

(56)

REMOVING BROKEN SCREWS AND BOLTS

1. Center punch broken stud

2. Drill hole in stud

3. Tap in screw extractor

4. Remove broken stud

Table 1 DECIMAL AND METRIC EQUIVALENTS

Fractions	Decimal in.	Metric mm	Fractions	Decimal in.	Metric mm
1/64	0.015625	0.39688	33/64	0.515625	13.09687
1/32	0.03125	0.79375	17/32	0.53125	13.49375
3/64	0.046875	1.19062	35/64	0.546875	13.89062
1/16	0.0625	1.58750	9/16	0.5625	14.28750
5/64	0.078125	1.98437	37/64	0.578125	14.68437
3/32	0.09375	2.38125	19/32	0.59375	15.08125
7/64	0.109375	2.77812	39/64	0.609375	15.47812
1/8	0.125	3.1750	5/8	0.625	15.87500
9/64	0.140625	3.57187	41/64	0.640625	16.27187
5/32	0.15625	3.96875	21/32	0.65625	16.66875
11/64	0.171875	4.36562	43/64	0.671875	17.06562
3/16	0.1875	4.76250	11/16	0.6875	17.46250
13/64	0.203125	5.15937	45/64	0.703125	17.85937
7/32	0.21875	5.55625	23/32	0.71875	18.25625
15/64	0.234375	5.95312	47/64	0.734375	18.65312
1/4	0.250	6.35000	3/4	0.750	19.05000
17/64	0.265625	6.74687	49/64	0.765625	19.44687
9/32	0.28125	7.14375	25/32	0.78125	19.84375
19/64	0.296875	7.54062	51/64	0.796875	20.24062
5/16	0.3125	7.93750	13/64	0.8125	20.63750
21/64	0.328125	8.33437	53/64	0.828125	21.03437
11/32	0.34375	8.73125	27/32	0.84375	21.43125
23/64	0.359375	9.121812	55/64	0.859375	21.82812
3/8	0.375	9.52500	7/8	0.875	22.22500
25/64	0.390625	9.92187	57/64	0.890625	22.62187
13/32	0.40625	10.31875	29/32	0.90625	23.01875
27/64	0.421875	10.71562	59/64	0.921875	23.41562
7/16	0.4375	11.11250	15/16	0.9375	23.81250
29/64	0.453125	11.50937	61/64	0.953125	24.20937
15/32	0.46875	11.90625	31/32	0.96875	24.60625
31/64	0.484375	12.30312	63/64	0.984375	25.00312
1/2	0.500	12.70000	1	1.00	25.40000

Table 2 GENERAL TORQUE SPECIFICATIONS

Thread diameter	N·m	ft.-lb.
5 mm	3.4-4.9	30-43 in.-lb.
6 mm	5.9-7.8	52-69 in.-lb.
8 mm	14-19	10.0-13.5
10 mm	25-39	19-25
12 mm	44-61	33-45
14 mm	73-98	54-72
16 mm	115-155	83-115
18 mm	165-225	125-165
20 mm	225-325	165-240

Table 3 WORKSHOP TOOLS

Tool	Size or specification
Screwdriver	
Common	1/8 × 4 in. blade
Common	5/16 × 8 in. blade
Common	3/8 × 12 in. blade
Phillips	Size 2 tip, 6 in. overall
Pliers	
Slip joint	6 in. overall
Vise-grips	10 in. overall
Needlenose	6 in. overall
Channelock	12 in. overall
Snap ring	Assorted
Wrenches	
Box-end set	Assorted
Open-end set	Assorted
Crescent	6 in. and 12 in. overall
Socket set	1/2 in. drive ratchet with assorted metric sockets
Socket drive extensions	1/2 in. drive, 2 in., 4 in. and 6 in.
Socket universal joint	1/2 in. drive
Allen	Socket driven (long and short), T-handle driven and 90°
Hammers	
Soft faced	—
Plastic faced	—
Metal faced	—
Other special tools	
Impact driver	1/2 in. drive with assorted bits
Torque wrench	1/2 in. drive
Flat feeler gauge	Metric set

Table 4 WIND CHILL FACTOR

Estimated Wind Speed in MPH	Actual Thermometer Reading (°F)											
	50	40	30	20	10	0	−10	−20	−30	−40	−50	−60
	Equivalent Temperature (°F)											
Calm	50	40	30	20	10	0	−10	−20	−30	−40	−50	−60
5	48	37	27	16	6	−5	−15	−26	−36	−47	−57	−68
10	40	28	16	4	−9	−21	−33	−46	−58	−70	−83	−95
15	36	22	9	−5	−18	−36	−45	−58	−72	−85	−99	−112
20	32	18	4	−10	−25	−39	−53	−67	−82	−96	−110	−124
25	30	16	0	−15	−29	−44	−59	−74	−88	−104	−118	−133
30	28	13	−2	−18	−33	−48	−63	−79	−94	−109	−125	−140
35	27	11	−4	−20	−35	−49	−67	−82	−98	−113	−129	−145
40	26	10	−6	−21	−37	−53	−69	−85	−100	−116	−132	−148

*

Little Danger (for properly clothed person)   **Increasing Danger**   **Great Danger**

*Danger from freezing of exposed flesh.

*Wind speeds greater than 40 mph have little additional effect.

CHAPTER TWO

TROUBLESHOOTING

Diagnosing mechanical problems is relatively simple if you use orderly procedures and keep a few basic principles in mind.

The troubleshooting procedures in this chapter analyze typical symptoms and show logical methods of isolating causes. These are not the only methods. There may be several ways to solve a problem, but only a systematic, methodical approach can guarantee success.

Never assume anything. Do not overlook the obvious. If you are riding along and the engine suddenly quits, check the easiest, most accessible problems first. Is there gasoline in the tank? Has a spark plug wire cap become loose? Check the ignition switch and key. Sometimes the weight of the key ring may turn the ignition off suddenly.

If nothing obvious turns up in a quick check, look a little further. Learning to recognize and describe symptoms will make repairs easier for you or a mechanic at the shop. Describe problems accurately and fully. Saying that "it won't run" isn't the same as saying "it quit at high speed and won't start" or that "it sat in my garage for 3 months and then wouldn't start."

Gather as many symptoms together as possible to aid in diagnosis. Note whether the engine lost power gradually or all at once. Remember that the more complicated a machine is, the easier it is to troubleshoot because symptoms point to specific problems.

After the symptoms are defined, areas which could cause the problems are tested and analyzed. Guessing at the cause of a problem may provide the solution, but it can easily lead to frustration, wasted time and a series of expensive, unnecessary parts replacements.

You do not need fancy equipment or complicated test gear to determine whether repairs can be attempted at home. A few simple checks could save a large repair bill and time lost while the bike sits in a dealer's service department. On the other hand, be realistic and don't attempt repairs beyond your abilities. Service departments tend to charge a lot for putting together a disassembled engine or transmission that may have been abused. Some dealers won't even take on such a job—so use common sense and don't get in over your head.

OPERATING REQUIREMENTS

An engine needs 3 basics to run properly: correct fuel/air mixture, compression and a spark at the correct time. If one or more are missing, the engine just won't run. The electrical system is the weakest link of the 3 basics. More problems result from electrical breakdowns than from any other source. Keep that in mind before you begin tampering with fuel injection adjustments and the like.

If the bike has been sitting for any length of time and refuses to start, check and clean the spark plugs and then look to the gasoline delivery system. This includes the fuel tank, fuel filter, fuel pump and the fuel line to the fuel injector fuel pipe. Gasoline deposits may have formed and gummed up the fuel injectors or filter. Gasoline tends to lose its potency after standing for long periods. Condensation may contaminate the fuel with water. Drain the old fuel and try starting with a fresh tankful.

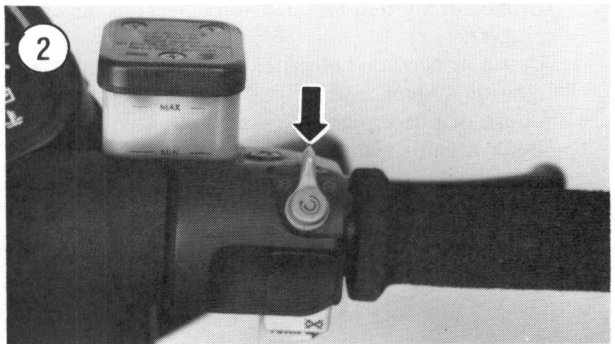

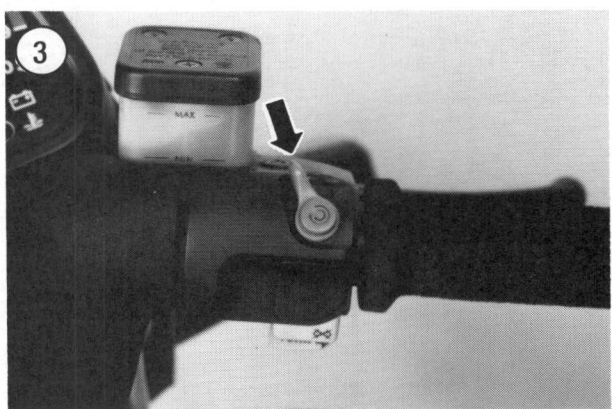

EMERGENCY TROUBLESHOOTING

When the bike is difficult to start or won't start at all, it does not help to wear down the battery with the starter. Check for obvious problems even before getting out your tools. Go down the following list step by step. Do each one; you may be embarrassed to find your engine stop switch is stuck in the OFF position, but that is better than wearing down the battery. If it still will not start, refer to the appropriate troubleshooting procedure which follows in this chapter.

WARNING
*Do **not** use an open flame to check in the tank.*
A serious explosion is certain to result.

1. Is there fuel in the tank? Open the filler cap (**Figure 1**) and rock the bike. Listen for fuel sloshing around.
2. Make sure the engine stop switch is in the ON position (**Figure 2**) and not in the OFF position (**Figure 3**).
3. Are the spark plug wire caps on tight? Remove the Allen screws (A, **Figure 4**) securing the spark plug cover (B, **Figure 4**) and remove the cover. Using a pair of pliers, push on and slightly rotate each spark plug cap to clean the electrical connection between each plug and its connector. Refer to **Figure 5** for K75 models or **Figure 6** for K100 models.

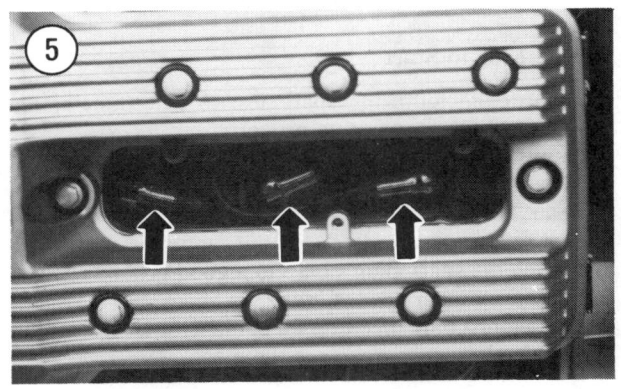

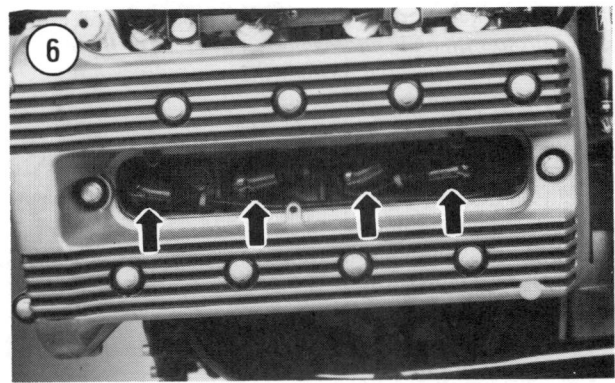

2

NOTE
In ambient temperatures below 0° C (32° F), disengage the clutch to make engine starting easier. By doing this the transmission input shaft will not turn during the cranking procedure.

4. Is the choke in the correct position? The choke lever should be in one of the following positions:
   a. Position 1 (at right angles to the handlebar hand grip) as shown in A, **Figure 7**: ambient temperature is below 10° C (50° F).
   b. Position 2 (mid-way point of lever) as shown in B, **Figure 7**: ambient temperature is above 10° C (50° F).
   c. Position 0 (in line with the handlebar hand grip) as shown in **Figure 8**: when the engine is at normal operating temperature.

ENGINE STARTING

An engine that refuses to start or is difficult to start is very frustrating. More often than not, the problem is very minor and can be found with a simple and logical troubleshooting approach.

The following items show a beginning point from which to isolate engine starting problems.

Engine Fails to Start

Perform the following spark test to determine if the ignition system is operating properly.
1. Remove one of the spark plugs from the cylinder head as described under *Spark Plug Removal/Cleaning* in Chapter Three.
2. Connect the spark plug wire and cap to the spark plug and touch the spark plug's base to a good ground such as the engine cylinder head (**Figure 9**). Make sure the spark plug is against bare metal, not a painted surface. Position the spark plug so you can see the electrodes.

WARNING
If it is necessary to hold the high voltage lead, do so with an insulated pair of pliers. The high voltage generated by the Hall transmitter unit could produce serious or fatal shocks.

3. Crank the engine over with the starter. A fat blue spark should be evident across the plug's electrodes.
4. If the spark is good, check for one or more of the following possible malfunctions:
   a. Obstructed fuel line(s).
   b. Low compression.
   c. Leaking head gasket.
   d. Choke not operating properly.

   e. Throttle not operating properly.
   f. Fuel injection control not functioning properly or not operating at all.
   g. Fuel pump not operating properly or not operating at all.
   h. Fuel pump relay not operating properly or not operating at all.
   i. Fuel system pressure regulator not operating properly or not operating at all.
5. If spark is not good, check for one or more of the following:
   a. Weak ignition coil(s).
   b. Weak or faulty ignition control unit.
   c. Broken or shorted high tension lead(s) to the spark plug(s).
   d. Loose or corroded electrical connectors within the ignition system.
   e. Loose or broken ignition coil ground wire(s).
   f. Weak or faulty Hall transmitter in the ignition system.

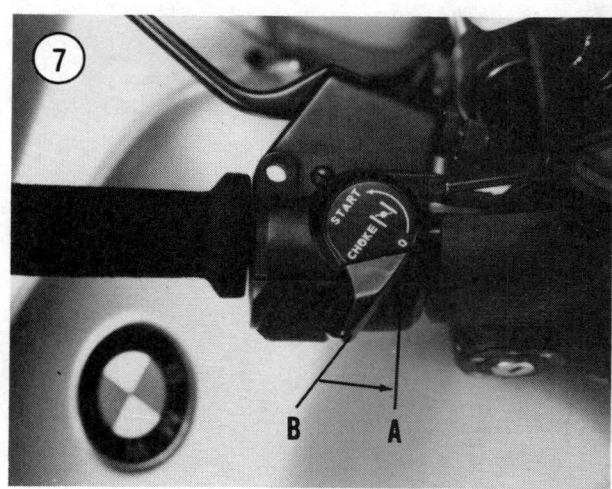

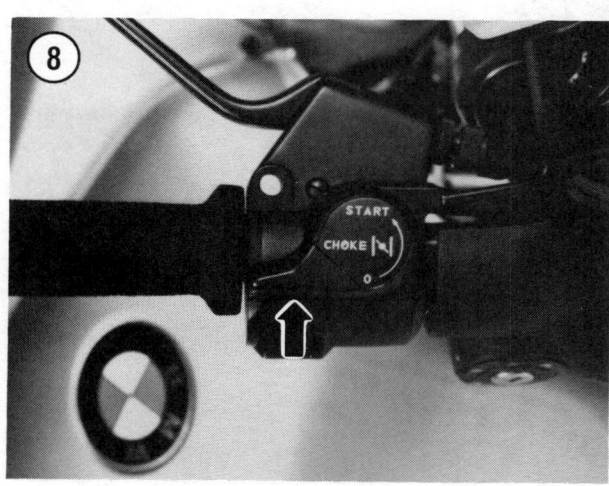

Engine is Difficult to Start

Check for one or more of the following possible malfunctions:
a. Fouled spark plug(s).
b. Improperly adjusted choke.
c. Contaminated fuel system.
d. Weak ignition coil(s).
e. Weak or faulty ignition control unit.
f. Weak or faulty fuel injection control unit.
g. Incorrect type ignition coil(s).
h. Poor compression.
i. Loose or corroded electrical connectors in the fuel injection system.

Engine Will Not Crank

Check for one or more of the following possible malfunctions:
a. Discharged battery.
b. Defective starter motor, starter relay or start switch.
c. Broken starter gears.
d. Seized piston(s).
e. Seized crankshaft bearings.
f. Broken connecting rod(s).
g. Locked-up transmission or clutch assembly.

ENGINE PERFORMANCE

In the following check list, it is assumed that the engine runs, but is not operating at peak performance. This will serve as a starting point from which to isolate a performance malfunction.

The possible causes for each malfunction are listed in a logical sequence and in order of probability.

Engine Will Not Start or is Hard to Start

a. Fuel tank empty.
b. Obstructed fuel line(s) or fuel filter.

c. Low compression.
d. Leaking head gasket.
e. Choke not operating properly or improperly adjusted.
f. Throttle not operating properly.
g. Fuel injection control not functioning properly or not operating at all.
h. Fuel pump or fuel injector(s) not operating properly or not operating at all.
i. Fuel pump relay not operating properly or not operating at all.
j. Fuel system pressure regulator not operating properly or not operating at all.
k. Loose or corroded electrical connectors in the fuel injection system.
l. Improper choke operation.
m. Fouled or improperly gapped spark plug(s).
n. Ignition timing incorrect (faulty component in system).
o. Broken or shorted ignition coil(s).
p. Improper valve timing.
q. Clogged air filter element.
r. Contaminated fuel.

Engine Will Not Idle or Idles Erratically

a. Fuel pump or fuel injector(s) not operating properly.
b. Fuel pump relay not operating properly.
c. Fuel system pressure regulator not operating properly.
d. Weak or faulty fuel injection control unit.
e. Obstructed fuel line.
f. Loose or corroded electrical connectors in the fuel injection system.
g. Fouled or improperly gapped spark plug(s).
h. Leaking head gasket or vacuum leak.
i. Weak or faulty ignition control unit.
j. Incorrect type ignition coil(s).
k. Ignition timing incorrect (faulty component in system).
l. Improper valve timing.
m. Poor compression.

Engine Misses at High Speed

a. Fouled or improperly gapped spark plug(s).
b. Improper ignition timing (faulty component in system).
c. Weak or faulty ignition control unit.
d. Broken or shorted high tension lead(s) to the spark plug(s).
e. Loose or corroded electrical connectors within the ignition system.
f. Loose or broken ignition coil ground wire(s).
g. Weak or faulty Hall transmitter in the ignition system.
h. Weak ignition coil(s).
i. Improper valve timing.
j. Obstructed fuel line.

**Engine Continues to
Run with Ignition Off**

   a. Excessive carbon build-up in engine.
   b. Vacuum leak in intake system.
   c. Contaminated fuel or incorrect octane rating.

Engine Overheating

   a. Coolant level low.
   b. Faulty water pump faulty or thermostat.
   c. Improper ignition timing (faulty component in system).
   d. Improper spark plug heat range.
   e. Engine oil level low.

Engine Misses at Idle

   a. Fouled or improperly gapped spark plug(s).
   b. Spark plug cap(s) faulty.
   c. Ignition cable(s) insulation deteriorated (shorting out).
   d. Dirty or clogged air filter element.
   e. Loose or corroded electrical connectors within the ignition system.
   f. Fuel pump or fuel injector(s) not operating properly.
   g. Fuel system pressure regulator not operating properly.
   h. Weak or faulty fuel injection control unit.
   i. Obstructed fuel line.
   j. Fouled or improperly gapped spark plug(s).
   k. Leaking head gasket or vacuum leak.
   l. Weak or faulty ignition control unit.
   m. Incorrect type ignition coil(s).
   n. Ignition timing incorrect (faulty component in system).
   o. Improper valve timing.
   p. Poor compression.

**Engine Backfires—
Explosions in Muffler**

   a. Fouled or improperly gapped spark plug(s).
   b. Spark plug cap(s) faulty.
   c. Ignition cable(s) insulation deteriorated (shorting out).
   d. Ignition timing incorrect (faulty component in system).
   e. Improper valve timing.
   f. Contaminated fuel.
   g. Burned or damaged intake and/or exhaust valves.
   h. Weak or broken intake and/or exhaust valve springs.

**Pre-ignition (Fuel Mixture
Ignites Before Spark Plug Fires)**

   a. Hot spot in combustion chamber (piece of carbon).
   b. Valve(s) stuck in guide.
   c. Overheating engine, coolant level low.

Engine Overheating

   a. Coolant level low.
   b. Faulty temperature gauge or temperature sensor.
   c. Thermostat stuck in the closed position.
   d. Passages blocked in radiator, hoses or water jackets in the cylinder block and cylinder head.
   e. Fan blades bent or missing.
   f. Faulty fan motor.
   g. Faulty water pump.
   h. Improper ignition timing (faulty component in system).
   i. Improper spark plug heat range.

Smoky Exhaust and Engine Runs Roughly

   a. Fuel injector(s) not operating properly.
   b. Fuel system pressure regulator not operating properly.
   c. Weak or faulty fuel injection control unit.
   d. Choke not operating correctly.
   e. Water or other contaminants in fuel.
   f. Clogged fuel line.
   g. Clogged air filter element.

**Engine Loses Power at
Normal Riding Speed and Lacks Power**

   a. Engine overheating.
   b. Improper ignition timing (faulty component in system).
   c. Incorrectly gapped spark plug(s).
   d. Spark plug wires and/or caps defective.
   e. Loose or corroded electrical connectors within the ignition system.
   f. Fuel pump or fuel injector(s) not operating properly.
   g. Fuel system pressure regulator not operating properly.
   h. Weak or faulty fuel injection control unit.
   i. Obstructed fuel line.
   j. Fouled or improperly gapped spark plug(s).
   k. Obstructed muffler.
   l. Dragging brake(s).

ENGINE NOISES

1. *Knocking or pinging during acceleration*—Caused by using a lower octane fuel than recommended. May also be caused by poor fuel. Pinging can also be caused by spark plugs of the wrong heat range. Refer to *Spark Plug Selection* in Chapter Three.

2. *Slapping or rattling noises at low speed or during acceleration*—May be caused by piston slap (excessive piston to cylinder wall clearance).

3. *Knocking or rapping while decelerating*—Usually caused by excessive rod bearing clearance.

4. *Persistent knocking and vibration*—Usually caused by excessive main bearing clearance.

5. *Rapid on-off squeal*—Compression leak around cylinder head gasket or spark plugs.

EXCESSIVE VIBRATION

Usually this is caused by loose engine mounting hardware. If not, it can be difficult to find without disassembling the engine.

FRONT SUSPENSION AND STEERING

Poor handling may be caused by improper tire pressure, a damaged or bent frame or front steering components, a worn front fork assembly, worn wheel bearings or dragging brakes.

BRAKE PROBLEMS

Sticking brake pads may be caused by a stuck piston in a caliper assembly or warped pad shim or disc. Sticking brake shoes may be caused by worn brake shoe return springs or an out-of-round drum.

2

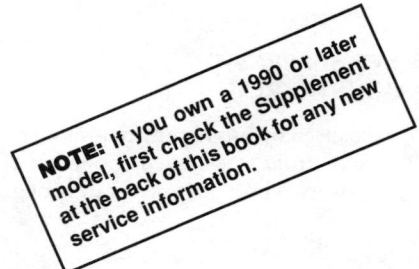

NOTE: If you own a 1990 or later model, first check the Supplement at the back of this book for any new service information.

CHAPTER THREE

LUBRICATION, MAINTENANCE AND TUNE-UP

A motorcycle, even in normal use, is subjected to tremendous heat, stress and vibration. When neglected, any bike becomes unreliable and actually dangerous to ride.

To gain the utmost in safety, performance and useful life from the BMW K-series motorcycle it is necessary to make periodic inspections and adjustments. Minor problems are often found during these inspections that are simple and inexpensive to correct at the time. If they are not found and corrected at this time they could lead to major and more expensive problems later on.

Regular cleaning of the bike is also very important. It makes routine maintenance a lot easier by not having to work your way through built-up road dirt to get to a component for adjustment or replacement. Routine cleaning also allows you to see a damaged component that can be repaired or replaced as soon as the damage occurs. If a damaged part is allowed to continue to deteriorate it may create an unsafe riding condition that could lead to a possible accident.

Start out by doing simple tune-up, lubrication and maintenance. Tackle more involved jobs as you become more acquainted with the bike.

The service procedures and intervals shown in **Table 1** are recommended by the BMW factory. **Tables 1-7** are located at the end of this chapter.

ROUTINE SAFETY CHECKS

The following safety checks should be performed prior to the first ride of the day.

General Inspection

1. Quickly inspect the engine for signs of oil, coolant or fuel leakage.

2. Check the tires for embedded stones. Pry them out with your ignition key.
3. Make sure all lights work.

> *NOTE*
> *At least check the brake light. It can burn out at any time. Motorists cannot stop as quickly as you and need all the warning you can give.*

4. Inspect all fuel lines and fittings for wetness. If the bike is equipped with a front fairing this is difficult, but it is still a good idea to check for fuel leakage.
5. Make sure the fuel tank is full of fresh gasoline.
6. Check the operation of the front and rear brakes. Add hydraulic fluid to the front master cylinder, and on models so equipped, the rear master cylinder if necessary.
7. Check the operation of the clutch. If necessary, adjust the clutch free-play as described in this chapter.
8. Check the throttle and the rear brake pedal. Make sure they operate properly with no binding.
9. Inspect the front and rear suspension. Make sure they have a good solid feel with no looseness.
10. Check tire pressure. Refer to **Table 2**.
11. Check the exhaust system for damage.
12. Check the tightness of all fasteners, especially engine mounting hardware.

Engine Oil Level

Refer to *Engine Oil Level Check* under *Periodic Lubrication* in this chapter.

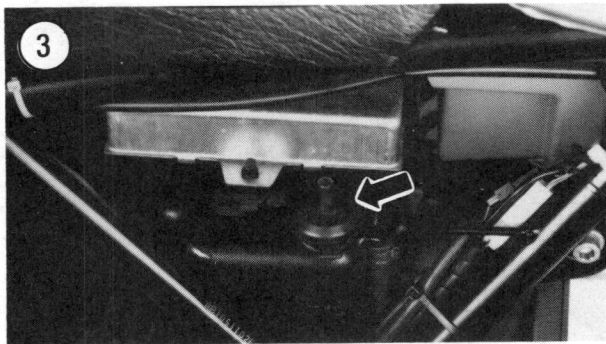

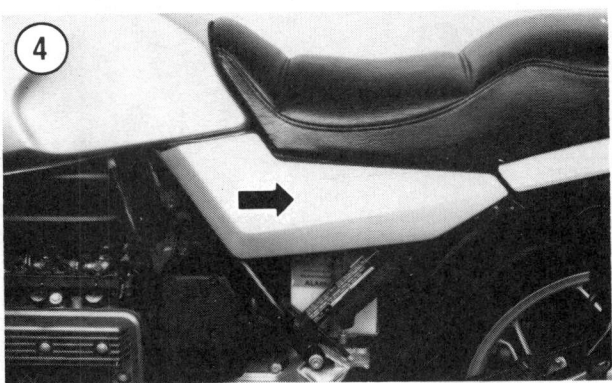

Coolant Level

Check the coolant level *when the engine is cold* since the coolant level in the reserve tank will vary depending on the engine operating temperature.

Always add coolant to the coolant reserve tank as this tank is never pressurized. The remainder of the cooling system is under an operating pressure and the coolant is very hot when the engine has been run.

If the coolant level is very low, it will be necessary to refill the cooling system through the coolant filler cap located under the fuel tank. If this is necessary, refer to *Coolant Change* under *Periodic Maintenance* in this chapter. If the coolant reserve tank requires repeated refilling, inspect the cooling system for the probable cause; correct the problem immediately.

1. Remove the frame right-hand side cover (**Figure 1**) and check the level in the coolant reserve tank.
2. The level should be at the MAX mark (**Figure 2**) on the transparent level-check tube on the front of the tank.
3. If necessary, remove the reserve tank fill cap (**Figure 3**) (not the coolant filler cap) and add coolant until the level is to the MAX mark. For the recommended coolant-to-purified water ratio, refer to *Coolant Change* under *Periodic Maintenance* in this chapter.

Tire Pressure

Tire pressure must be checked with the tires cold. Correct tire pressure, listed in **Table 2**, varies with the load you are carrying. Refer to *Tire Pressure* under *Tires and Wheels* in this chapter.

Battery

Remove the frame left-hand side cover (**Figure 4**) and check the battery electrolyte level. The level must be maintained at a distance 5-10 mm (0.20-0.40 in.) below the black upper section of the battery or on models so equipped, between the MAX and MIN markings (**Figure 5**).

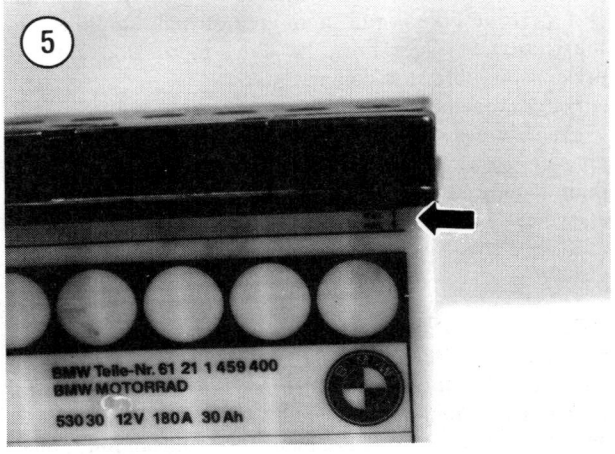

For complete details see *Battery Removal, Installation and Electrolyte Level Check* in this chapter.

Check the level more frequently in hot weather; electrolyte will evaporate rapidly as engine and ambient temperatures increase.

Evaporative Emission Control System

The evaporative emission control system consists of a sealed fuel filler cap, one hose and a pressure relief valve (**Figure 6**) between the fuel tank and the crankcase. Inspect the hose to make sure it is not kinked or bent and that it is securely connected to the fuel tank and the engine crankcase.

Refer to the vacuum hose routing label (**Figure 7**) located under the seat on the rear fender.

Lights and Horn

With the engine running, check the following.
1. Pull the front brake lever on and check that the brake light comes on.
2. Push the rear brake pedal down and check that the brake light comes on soon after you have begun depressing the pedal.
3. Turn the ignition switch ON. Press the headlight dimmer switch to the high, the low and flashing positions (A, **Figure 8**) and check to see that both headlight elements are working in the headlight.
4. Turn the turn signal switch to the left (B, **Figure 8**) and right (**Figure 9**) positions and check that all 4 turn signals are working.
5. Push the horn button (C, **Figure 8**) and make sure that the horn blows loudly.
6. If the horn or any of the lights failed to operate properly, refer to Chapter Eight.

SERVICE INTERVALS

The services and intervals shown in **Table 1** are recommended by the BMW factory. Strict adherence to these recommendations will ensure long service from the BMW. If the bike is run in an area of high humidity, the lubrication services must be done more frequently to prevent possible rust damage.

For convenience when maintaining your motorcycle, most of the services shown in these tables are described in this chapter. However, some procedures which require more than minor disassembly or adjustment are covered elsewhere in the appropriate chapter.

BIKE CLEANING

Regular cleaning of the bike is very important. It makes routine maintenance a lot easier by not having to work your way through built-up road dirt to get to a component for adjustment or replacement. It also makes the bike look like new even though it may have many thousands of miles on it.

If you ride in an area where there is a lot of rain or road salt residue in the winter, clean the bike off more often in order to maintain the painted, plated and polished surfaces in good condition. Keep a good coat of wax on the bike during the winter to prevent premature weathering of all finishes.

Washing the bike should be done in a gentle way to avoid damage to the painted and plated finishes and to components that are not designed to withstand high-pressure water. Try to avoid using the coin-operated car wash systems as the cleaning agents may be harmful to the plastic parts on the bike. Also the rinse cycle is usually fairly high pressure and will force water into areas that should be kept dry.

Use a mild detergent (mild liquid dish washing detergent) or a commercial car washing detergent available at most auto parts outlets. Be warned, these detergents will remove some of the wax that you have applied to the finish. Follow the manufacturer's instructions for the correct detergent-to-water mixture.

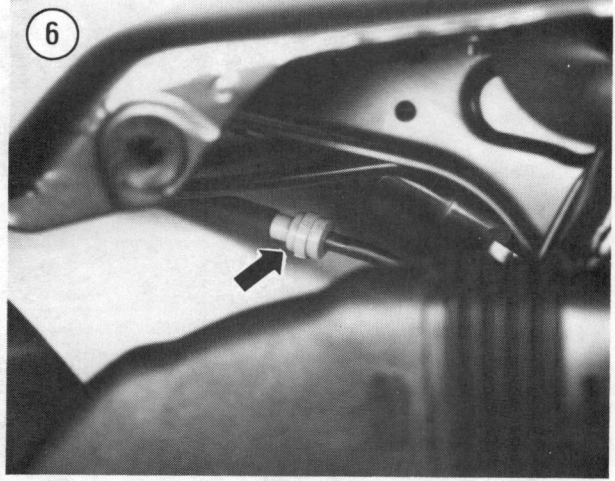

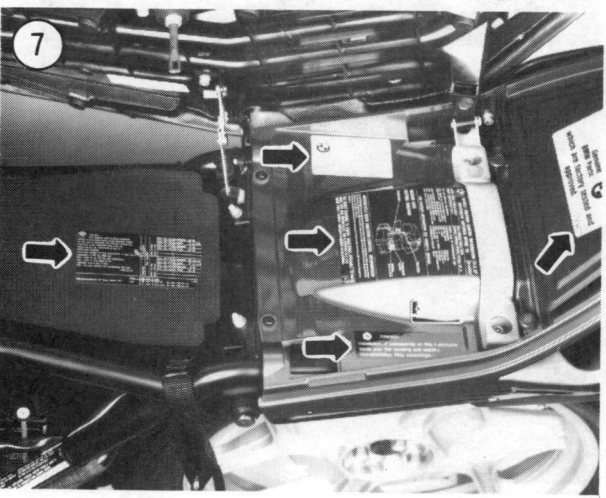

CAUTION
*BMW has determined that the use of **S100 Total Cycle Cleaner may damage**, or even remove, the electrolyte-dip matte black from components on the bike. This includes both engine and frame components. If your bike is still under warranty, BMW will not cover any damage caused by using this cleaner.*

If the lower end of the engine and frame are covered with oil, grease or road dirt, first remove this dirt with a commercial cleaner like Gunk Cycle Cleaner, or equivalent. Keep this cleaner off of the plastic components (fairing panels, engine spoiler, frame side covers, luggage cases, etc.) as it may damage the finish. Follow the manufacturer's instructions and rinse with *plenty of cold water*. Do not allow any of this cleaner residue to settle in any pockets as it will stain or destroy the finish of most painted parts.

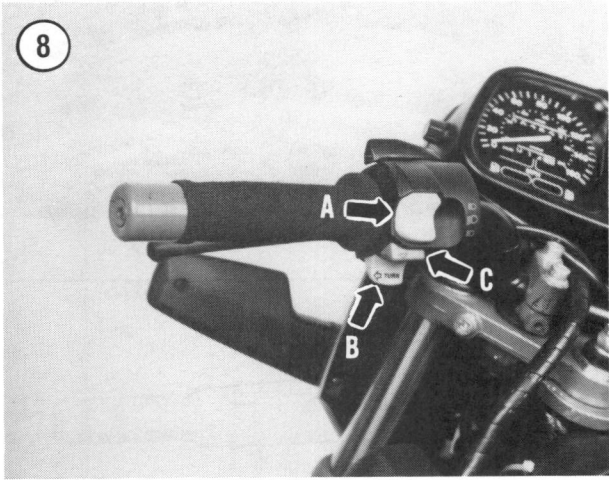

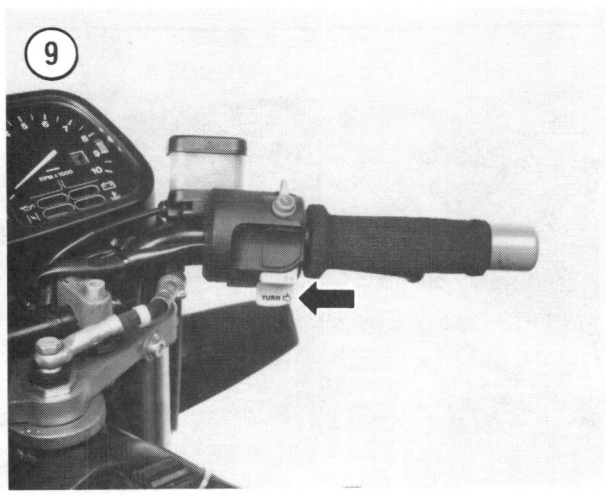

Use a commercial tar-stain remover to remove any severe road dirt and tar stains. Be sure to rinse all areas thoroughly with plenty of clean water to make sure all of the tar-stain remover is rinsed off of all surfaces.

Prior to washing the plastic and painted surfaces of the bike make sure the surfaces are cool. Do not wash a hot bike as you will probably end up with streaks since the soap suds will start to dry prior to being rinsed off.

CAUTION
Do not allow water (especially under pressure) to enter the air intake, brake assemblies, electrical switches and connectors, instrument cluster, wheel bearing areas, swing arm bearings, the breather tube on the final drive unit or any other moisture sensitive areas of the bike.

After all of the heavily soiled areas are cleaned off, use the previously described detergent, warm water and a soft natural sponge and carefully wash down the entire bike, including the wheels and tires. Don't use too much detergent as it will be difficult to thoroughly rinse off all of the soap suds. After all areas are washed, rinse off the soap suds with *low-pressure cold water*. Make sure all of the detergent residue is thoroughly rinsed off.

Take the bike off the center stand and lean it to both sides to allow all water to drain off the top of the cylinder block and other horizontal surfaces. If you have access to compressed air, *gently* blow excess water from areas where the water may have collected. Do not force the water into any of the sensitive areas mentioned in the previous CAUTION. Gently dry off the bike with a chamois, a clean soft turkish towel or an old plain T-shirt (no transfers or hand-painted designs).

Be careful cleaning the windshield as it can be easily scratched or damaged. Do not use a cleaner with an abrasive or a combination cleaner and wax. Never use gasoline or cleaning solvent. These products will either scratch or totally destroy the surface finish of the windshield.

Clean the windshield with a soft cloth or natural sponge and plenty of water. Dry thoroughly with a soft cloth or chamois—do not press hard.

WARNING
The brake components may have gotten wet. If they are damp or wet they will not be operating at their optimum effectiveness. Be prepared to take a longer distance to stop the bike right after washing the bike. Ride slowly and lightly apply the brakes to dry off the pads.

Start the bike and let it reach normal operating temperature. Take the bike out for a *slow and careful* ride around the block to blow off any residual water. Bring the bike back to the wash area and dry off any residual water streaks from the painted and plated surfaces.

Once the bike is thoroughly dry, get out the polish, wax and Armor All and give the bike a good polish and wax job to protect the painted, plated and polished finishes.

TIRES AND WHEELS

Tire Pressure

Tire pressure should be checked and adjusted to maintain the smoothness of the tire, good traction and handling and to get the maximum life out of the tire. A simple, accurate gauge (**Figure 10**) can be purchased for a few dollars and should be carried in your motorcycle tool kit. The appropriate tire pressures are shown in **Table 2**.

> *NOTE*
> *After checking and adjusting the air pressure, make sure to install the air valve cap (**Figure 11**). The cap prevents small pebbles and dirt from collecting in the valve stem; this could allow air leakage or result in incorrect tire pressure readings.*

Tire Inspection

The tires take a lot of punishment so inspect them periodically for excessive wear, cuts, abrasions, etc. (**Figure 12**). If you find a nail or other object in the tire, mark its location with a light crayon prior to removing it. This will help locate the hole for repair. Refer to Chapter Ten for tire changing and repair information.

Check local traffic regulations concerning minimum tread depth. Measure the tread depth of the tire tread using a tread

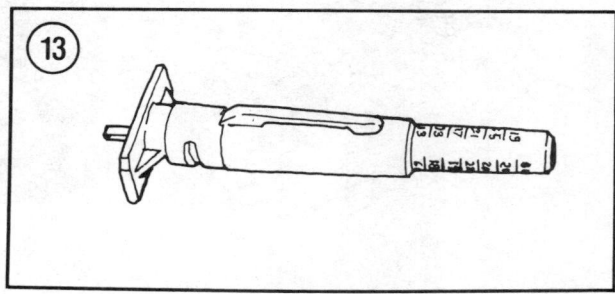

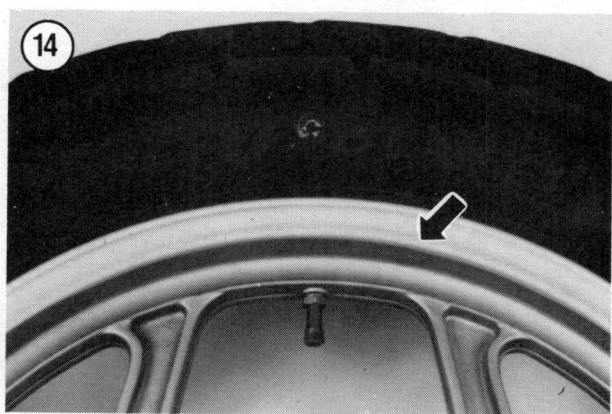

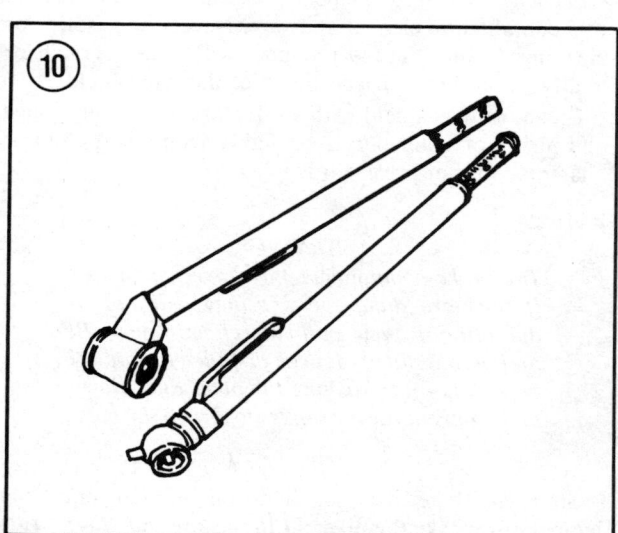

depth gauge (**Figure 13**) or small ruler. BMW recommends that original equipment tires be replaced when the tread depth has worn to 2.0 mm (0.08 in.) or less.

Rim Inspection

Frequently inspect the wheel rims (**Figure 14**). If a rim has been damaged it might have been knocked out of alignment. Improper wheel alignment can cause severe vibration and result in an unsafe riding condition. If the rim portion of an alloy wheel is damaged, the wheel must be replaced as it cannot be repaired.

BATTERY

Removal, Electrolyte Level Check and Installation

The battery is the heart of the electrical system. Check and service the battery at the interval indicated in **Table 1**. The majority of electrical system troubles can be attributed to neglect of this vital component.

1. Remove the seat as described under *Seat Removal/Installation* in Chapter Thirteen.
2. Remove the left-hand frame side cover (**Figure 4**).
3. Remove the storage tray cover (**Figure 15**).
4. Carefully pull out on the front edge and remove the protective cover (**Figure 16**) from the fuel injection control unit.
5. Insert a long screwdriver through the hole (A, **Figure 17**) in the storage compartment tray. Insert the screwdriver blade into the keeper on the electrical connector and move the handle toward the front of the bike (**Figure 18**).
6. Release the keeper, pull the electrical connector (**Figure 19**) toward the rear and disconnect it from the fuel injection control unit.

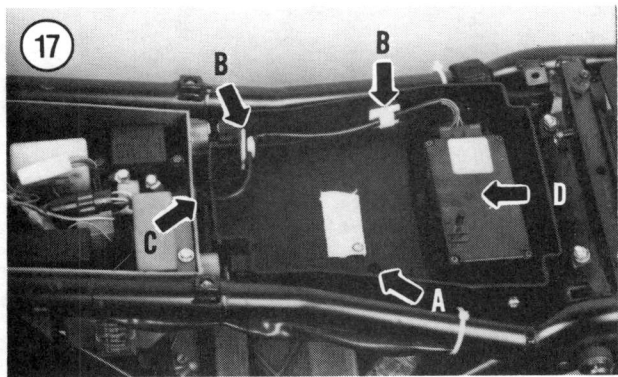

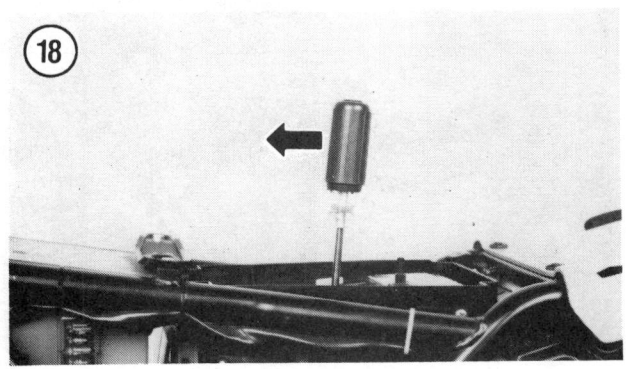

7. On models equipped with the BMW electronic alarm system, perform the following:

   a. Remove the screws (A, **Figure 20**) securing the alarm unit to the storage tray.

   b. Unhook the electrical wires from the clips (B, **Figure 17**) on the side of the storage tray.

   c. Pull the alarm wires out of the notch and grommet (C, **Figure 17**) at the front of the storage tray.

   d. Remove the alarm unit (D, **Figure 17**).

8. Pull the storage tray (along with the fuel injection unit) up and out of the frame (B, **Figure 20**) and remove it.

9. Flip up the protective covers and disconnect the battery leads (**Figure 21**). First disconnect the battery negative (-) lead then the positive (+) lead.

10. Remove the long bolts (A, **Figure 22**) securing the battery hold-down strap (B, **Figure 22**) and remove the strap.

11. Disconnect the breather tube and vent elbow (**Figure 23**) from the battery. Leave the breather tube routed through the frame.

12. Lay several thick layers of old newspapers on top of your workbench where you intend to place the battery. This will protect the work bench surface if there is electrolyte residue on the sides and bottom of the battery.

13. Carefully lift the battery upward and toward the rear then remove the battery from the frame.

14. Set the battery on the newspapers (**Figure 24**).

15. The electrolyte level should be maintained between the 2 marks on the battery case (**Figure 25**).

WARNING
Protect your eyes, skin and clothing. If electrolyte gets into your eyes, flush your eyes thoroughly with clean water and get prompt medical attention.

CAUTION
Be careful not to spill battery electrolyte on plastic, painted or plated surfaces. This liquid is highly corrosive and will damage the finish. If it is spilled, wash it off immediately with soapy water and thoroughly rinse with clean water.

16. Use a coin or wide-bladed screwdriver and remove the caps (**Figure 26**) from the battery cells.

17. Add distilled water to correct the level. *Never* add electrolyte (acid) to correct the level.

NOTE
If distilled water has been added, reinstall the battery caps and gently shake the battery for several minutes to mix the existing electrolyte with the new water.

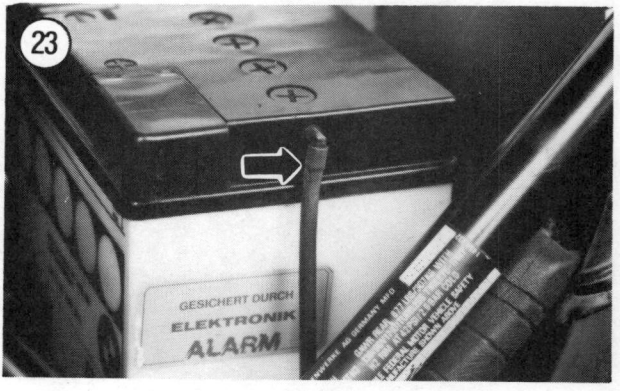

CAUTION
*If distilled water is going to be added to a battery (while the battery is installed in the bike) in freezing or near freezing weather, add it to the battery, dress warmly and then ride the bike for a **minimum of 30 minutes**. This will help mix the water into the electrolyte in the battery. Distilled water is lighter than electrolyte and will float on top of the electrolyte if it is not mixed in properly. If the water stays on the top, it may freeze and fracture the battery case.*

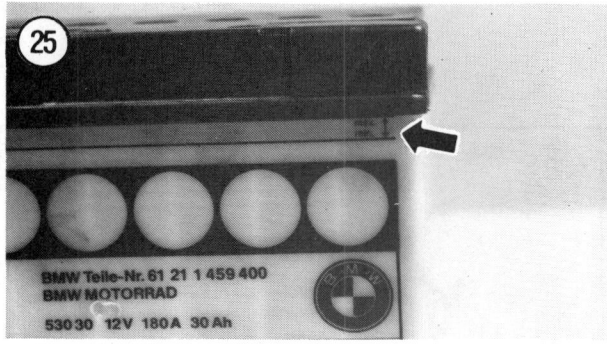

18. After the fluid level has been corrected and the battery allowed to stand for a few minutes, remove the battery caps and check the specific gravity of the electrolyte with a hydrometer. See *Battery Testing* in this chapter.

19. After the battery has been refilled, recharged or replaced, install it by reversing these removal steps, noting the following.

20. Clean the battery terminals (**Figure 27**), electrical cable connectors and surrounding case and reinstall the battery in the frame.

21. Coat the battery terminals with Vaseline or protective spray (**Figure 28**) to retard corrosion and decomposition of the terminals.

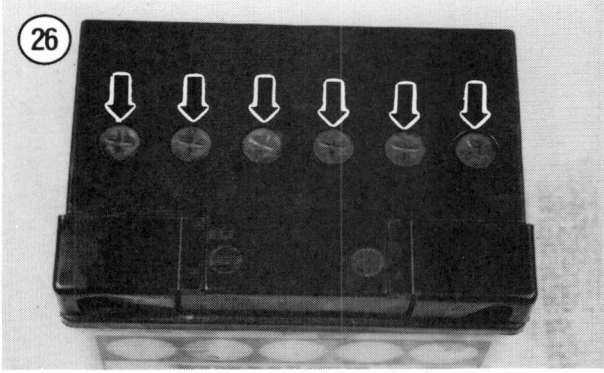

CAUTION
If the breather tube was removed from the frame, be sure to route it so that residue will not drain onto any part of the bike's frame. The tube must be free of bends or twists as any restrictions may pressurize the battery and damage it.

CAUTION
The battery must be installed in the frame correctly so that the battery cables will be attached to the correct terminals (positive to positive and negative to negative). The factory equipped battery cables will be difficult to attach if the battery is installed backwards with the terminals located at the rear.

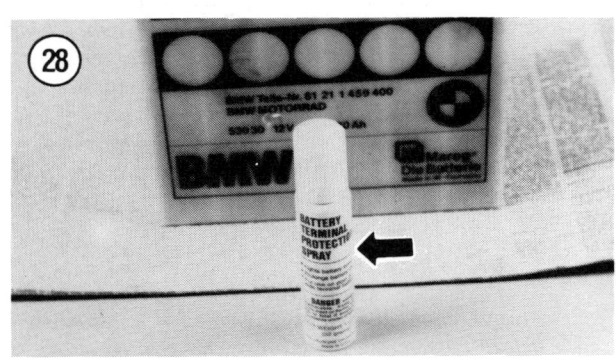

22. Position the battery so the battery cable terminals are toward the front (A, **Figure 29**) and the vent tube elbow receptacle (B, **Figure 29**) is on the left-hand side. Install the battery.

23. Do not overtighten the battery hold-down strap bolts as the strap may damage the battery case. Tighten the bolts so that the battery is held securely in place. This is especially true on the K75 models that are equipped with a smaller battery.

Testing

Hydrometer testing is the best way to check battery condition. Use a hydrometer with numbered graduations from 1.100 to 1.300 rather than one with just color-coded bands. To use the hydrometer, perform the following,

1. Use a coin or wide-bladed screwdriver and remove the caps (**Figure 26**) from each battery cell.

2. Squeeze the rubber ball, insert the tip into the cell and release the pressure on the ball.

3. Draw enough electrolyte to float the weighted float inside the hydrometer. Note the number in line with the surface of the electrolyte (**Figure 30**); this is the specific gravity for this cell.

4. Squeeze the rubber ball again and return the electrolyte to the cell from which it came. The specific gravity of the electrolyte in each battery cell is an excellent indication of that cell's condition. A fully charged cell will read from 1.260-1.280, while a cell in good condition reads from 1.230-1.250 and anything below 1.140 is discharged. Refer to **Figure 31**. If the cells test in the poor range, the battery requires recharging. The hydrometer is useful for checking the progress of the charging operation. **Table 3** shows approximate state of charge.

5. Install the caps onto each battery cell and tighten securely.

Charging

> *WARNING*
> *During the charging process, highly explosive hydrogen gas is released from the battery. The battery should be charged only in a well-ventilated area away from any open flames (including pilot lights on home gas appliances). Do not allow any smoking in the area. Never check the charge by arcing (connecting pliers or other metal objects) across the terminals; the resulting spark can ignite the hydrogen gas.*

> *CAUTION*
> *Always remove the battery from the bike's frame before connecting the battery charger. Never*

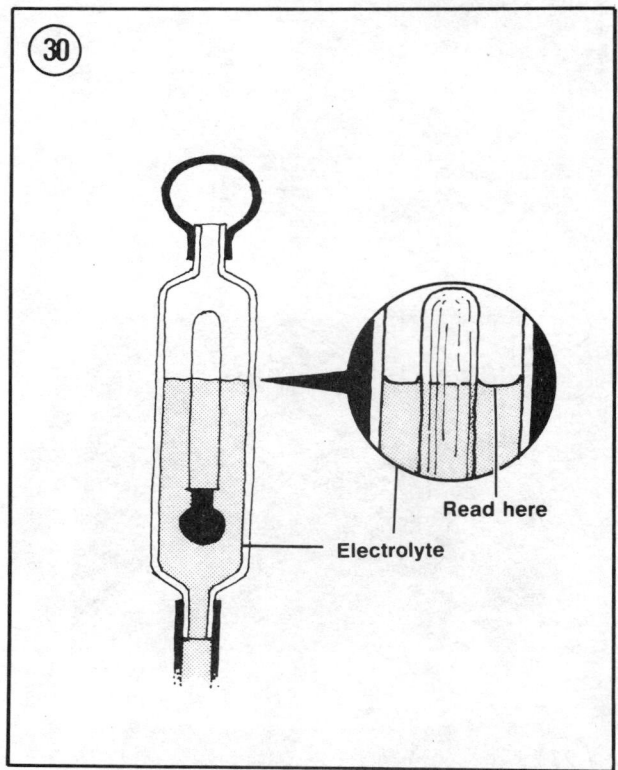

recharge a battery in the bike's frame; the corrosive mist that is emitted during the charging process will corrode all surrounding surfaces.

1. Connect the positive (+) charger lead to the positive (+) battery terminal and the negative (-) charger lead to the negative (-) battery terminal.

2. Use a coin or wide-bladed screwdriver and remove the caps (**Figure 26**) from each battery cell.

STATE OF CHARGE	
Specific Gravity	**State of Charge**
1.110-1.130	Discharged
1.140-1.160	Almost discharged
1.170-1.190	One-quarter charged
1.200-1.220	One-half charged
1.230-1.250	Three-quarters charged
1.260-1.280	Fully charged

(31)

3

(32)

3. Set the charger to 12 volts and switch the charger ON. If the output of the charger is variable, it is best to select a low setting—1 1/2 to 2 amps.

CAUTION
The electrolyte level must be maintained at the upper level (Figure 25) during the charging cycle; check and refill as necessary.

4. After the battery has been charged for about 8 hours, turn the charger OFF, disconnect the leads and check the specific gravity of each cell. It should be within the limits specified in **Table 3**. If it is, and remains stable for 1 hour, the battery is considered charged.
5. Install the caps onto each battery cell and tighten securely.
6. Clean the battery terminals (**Figure 27**), electrical cable connectors and surrounding case and reinstall the battery in the frame, reversing the removal steps. Coat the battery terminals with Vaseline or protective spray (**Figure 28**) to retard corrosion and decomposition of the terminals.

CAUTION
Route the breather tube so that is does not drain onto any part of the frame. The tube must be free of bends or twists as any restriction may pressurize the battery and damage it.

New Battery Installation

When replacing the old battery with a new one, be sure to charge it completely (specific gravity 1.260-1.280), as described in this chapter, before installing it in the bike. Failure to do so or using the battery with a low electrolyte level will permanently damage the new battery.

PERIODIC LUBRICATION

Oil

Oil is graded according to its viscosity, which is an indication of how thick it is. The Society of Automotive Engineers (SAE) system distinguishes oil viscosity by numbers. Thick oils have higher viscosity numbers than thin oils. For example, an SAE 5 oil is a thin oil while an SAE 90 oil is relatively thick.

Grease

A good quality grease (preferably waterproof) should be used (**Figure 32**). Water does not wash grease off parts as easily as it washes oil off. In addition, grease maintains its lubricating qualities better than oil on long and strenuous rides.

Engine Oil Level Check

Engine oil level is checked with the oil level inspection window, located at the right-hand side of the engine on the cylinder block.
1. Place the bike on the center stand and on level ground. A false reading will be given if the bike is tipped either to the right or left.

2. Start the engine and let it idle for 2-3 minutes.

3. Shut off the engine and let the oil settle for 1-2 minutes.

4. Look at the oil level inspection window. Refer to **Figure 33** or **Figure 34**. The oil level should be between the upper (maximum) and lower (minimum) marks.

CAUTION
Check the oil level inspection window (Figure 33) for tightness and leakage. If either is detected, pry out and replace the window assembly. If desired, apply rubberized locking compound to the sealing area on the new assembly, then seat into place. Crankcase pressure can eject a loose/leaking inspection window, causing loss of engine oil.

5. If the level is below the lower mark, perform the following:

   a. Unscrew the oil filler cap (**Figure 35**) located on the right-hand side of the engine crankcase cover.

   b. Insert a small funnel into the filler hole.

   c. Add the recommended weight engine oil indicated in **Figure 36** to correct the level. To raise the oil level from the lower to the upper mark it will take approximately 0.6 liters (1 pint) of oil for all models.

Engine Oil and Oil Filter Change

Change the engine oil and the oil filter at the same time as the factory-recommended oil change interval indicated in **Table 1**. This assumes that the motorcycle is operated in moderate climates. In extreme climates, oil should be changed every 30 days. The time interval is more important than the mileage interval because acids formed by combustion blowby will contaminate the oil even if the motorcycle is not run for several months. If the motorcycle is operated under dusty conditions, the oil will get dirty more quickly and should be changed more frequently than recommended.

Oil for motorcycle and automotive engines is classified by the American Petroleum Institute (API) and the Society of Automotive Engineers (SAE) in several categories. Oil containers display these classifications (**Figure 37**). It is suggested that the oil (**Figure 38**) manufactured for and sold by BMW dealers be used in this engine. A substitute brand of oil may be used but first confer with a BMW dealer regarding which type is compatible.

Use only a high-quality detergent motor oil with an API classification of SF or SG. Try to use the same brand of oil at each change. Refer to **Figure 36** for correct oil viscosity to use under anticipated ambient temperatures (not engine oil temperature).

NOTE
Never dispose of motor oil in the trash, on the ground, or down a storm drain. Many service stations accept used motor oil and waste haulers provide curbside used motor oil collection. Do not combine other fluids with motor oil to be recycled. To locate a recycler, contact the American Petroleum Institute (API) at www.recycleoil.org.

1. On models so equipped, remove the engine spoiler as described under *Engine Spoiler Removal/Installation* in Chapter Thirteen.

2. Start the engine and let it reach operating temperature; 15-20 minutes of stop-and-go riding is usually sufficient.

3. Turn the engine off and place the bike on level ground on the center stand.

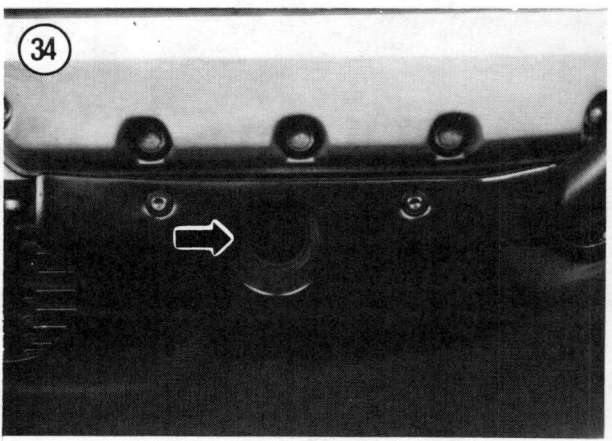

WARNING
During the next step, hot oil will spurt from the drain plug hole. Be ready to move your hand away quickly once the drain plug is removed so hot oil will not run on your hand and down your arm.

4. Place a drain pan under the oil pan and remove the drain plug with an 8 mm Allen wrench. Refer to **Figure 39** and **Figure 40**. Allow the oil to drain for at least 15-20 minutes.
5. Unscrew the oil filler cap (**Figure 35**) located on the right-hand side of the engine crankcase cover; this will speed up the flow of oil.

6. Remove and discard the sealing washer on the oil pan drain plug. Replace the sealing washer every time the drain plug is removed.

NOTE
The following steps are shown with the engine removed and turned upside down for clarity.

7. Install the oil drain plug and new sealing washer. Tighten the drain plug to the torque specification listed in **Table 4**.

3

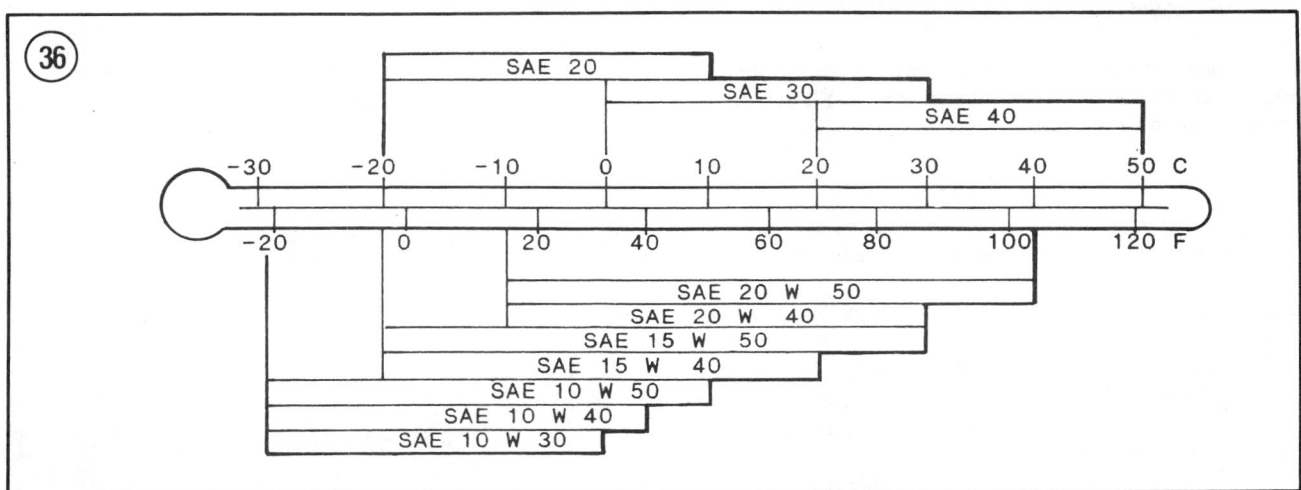

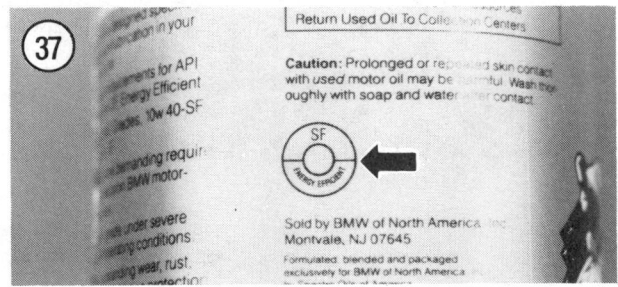

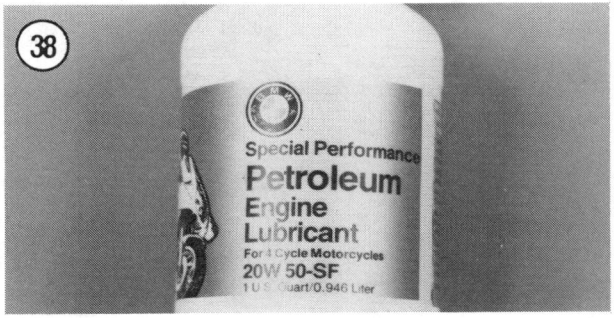

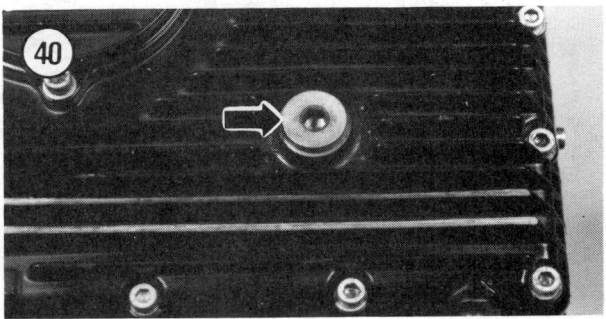

NOTE
Prior to removing the oil filter cover, thoroughly clean off all road dirt and oil around it. This prevents any dirt from entering the oil pan.

NOTE
Make sure the oil drain pan is still positioned correctly as some residual oil will run out after the oil filter cover is removed.

WARNING
The exterior of the oil filter cover is hot from engine heat—protect your hands from burning.

8. Using a 5 mm Allen wrench, remove the Allen bolts (A, **Figure 41**) securing the oil filter cover (B, **Figure 41**) to the oil pan and remove the cover (**Figure 42**).

WARNING
The exterior of the oil filter is hot from engine heat—protect your hands from burning.

9A. If you use the special oil filter wrench, perform the following:
  a. Using the BMW special oil filter wrench (part No. 11 4 650) (**Figure 43**) and socket wrench, unscrew the oil filter (**Figure 44**) from the crankcase.
  b. Remove the oil filter wrench from the filter and place the filter in a heavy plastic bag to contain any residual oil.
  c. Close off the end of the bag to prevent oil from draining out.
  d. Clean off the inner surface of the oil filter cover with a shop rag and cleaning solvent. Remove any oil sludge if necessary. Wipe it dry with a clean, lint-free cloth.

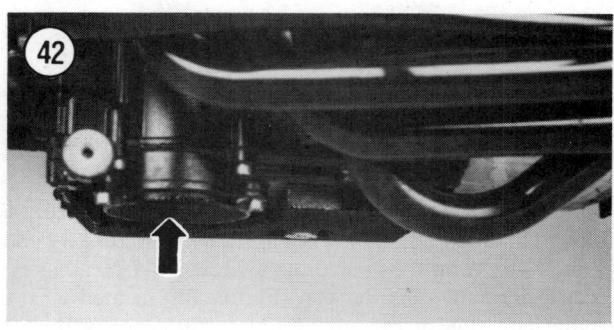

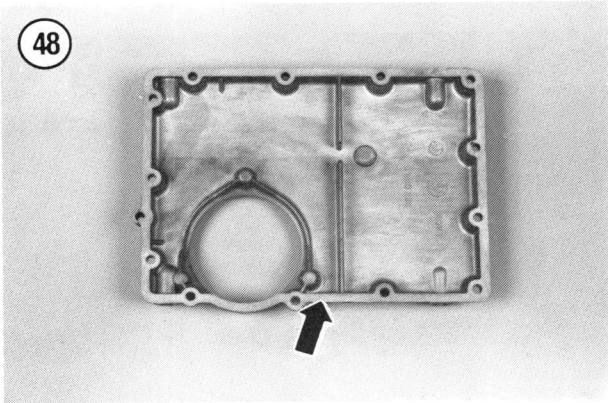

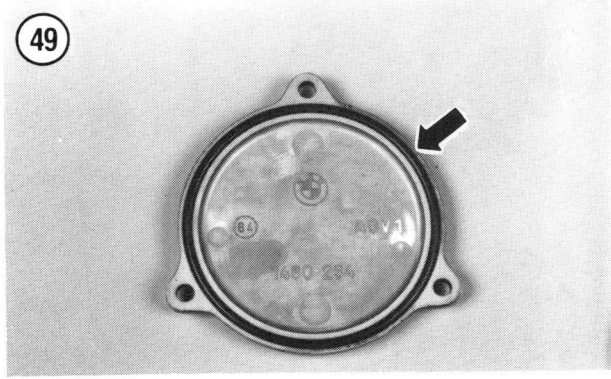

3

WARNING
The inner surface of the oil pan hole is sharp where the oil filter fits into it. Protect your hands and finger while installing the new oil filter.

   e. Screw on the new oil filter *by hand* until the rubber ring just touches the crankcase surface. At this point there will be a very slight resistance when turning the filter.

   f. Tighten the oil filter an additional 1/2 turn *by hand only* using the oil filter wrench *without* a socket wrench. If a socket wrench is used the filter will probably be overtightened, which will make filter removal difficult and may cause an oil leak.

NOTE
Prior to removing the oil pan, thoroughly clean off all road dirt and oil around the entire perimeter of the oil pan. This will prevent any dirt from entering the crankcase.

9B. If you do not have an oil filter wrench, perform the following:

   a. Remove the Allen bolts securing the oil pan (**Figure 45**) and remove the oil pan.

   b. Unscrew the oil filter (**Figure 46**) from the crankcase and place the filter in a heavy plastic bag to contain any residual oil. Close off the end of the bag to prevent oil from draining out.

   c. Apply a light coat of clean engine oil to the rubber seal on the new oil filter.

   d. Remove and clean the oil pump strainer as described in this chapter. Also clean the oil pan as described in this procedure.

   e. Screw on the new oil filter *by hand* until the rubber ring just touches the crankcase surface. At this point there will a very slight resistance when turning the filter.

   f. Tighten the oil filter an additional 1/2 turn *by hand only*. If a filter wrench is used the filter will probably be overtightened, which will make filter removal difficult an may cause an oil leak.

   g. Clean off all gasket residue from the mating surface of both the crankcase (**Figure 47**) and the oil pan (**Figure 48**). For a final clean up, use an aerosol electrical contact cleaner and wipe dry with a lint-free cloth.

   h. Apply a light coat of Three Bond No. 1216 to the sealing surface of the oil pan and install the oil pan.

   i. Tighten the Allen bolts, in a crisscross pattern, to the torque specification listed in **Table 4**.

10. Inspect the oil filter cover O-ring seal (**Figure 49**) for deterioration; replace if necessary.

11. Make sure the O-ring seal (**Figure 49**) is in place in the recess in the oil filter cover. Make sure it is correctly seated to prevent an oil leak.

12. Apply a light coat of clean engine oil to the O-ring seal on the oil filter cover and install the cover.

13. Install the Allen bolts securing the cover and tighten in a crisscross pattern to the torque specification listed in **Table 4**.

14. Insert a funnel into the oil fill hole and fill the engine with the correct viscosity and quantity of oil. Refer to **Table 5**.

15. Install the oil filler cap and tighten securely.

16. Remove the oil drain pan from under the engine and discard the oil properly.

17. Start the engine, let it run at idle speed and check for leaks.

18. Turn the engine off and check for correct oil level; adjust as necessary.

19. On models so equipped, install the engine spoiler as described under *Engine Spoiler Removal/Installation* in Chapter Thirteen.

Oil Pump Filter Screen and Oil Pan Cleaning

The oil filter screen and oil pan should be cleaned every time the oil pan is removed from the engine.

1. Drain the engine oil as described in this chapter.

NOTE
The following steps are shown with the engine removed and turned upside for clarity.

2. Remove the Allen bolts securing the oil pan (**Figure 45**) and remove the oil pan.

3. Remove the bolt (A, **Figure 50**) securing the oil pump strainer (B, **Figure 50**) and remove the strainer from the oil pump.

4. Remove the O-ring seal from the end of the pipe where it attaches to the oil pump. Always remove the O-ring whenever the assembly is removed.

5. Thoroughly clean the strainer with cleaning solvent and a medium soft brush. Be sure to clean out any built-up oil sludge on the screen.

6. Dry with compressed air. Make sure there is no solvent residue left in the strainer as it will contaminate the new oil.

7. Clean the oil pan with cleaning solvent and a brush. Clean off any built-up oil sludge with a scraper and cleaning solvent. Thoroughly dry with compressed air.

8. Inspect the oil pan and the cooling fins for damage. If any of the fins are damaged and broken off (**Figure 51**), check where they were attached to the oil pan. If just the fin(s) is broken off but the oil pan is not cracked or damaged, the oil pan can be reused. If any fractures are evident this may lead to an oil leak and the oil pan should be repaired or replaced.

9. Install a new O-ring seal onto the end of the pipe where it attaches to the oil pump. Apply a light coat of clean engine oil to the O-ring seal after it is installed.

10. Install the oil strainer into the oil pump and install the bolt. Tighten the bolt securely.

11. Clean off all gasket residue from the mating surface of both the crankcase (**Figure 47**) and the oil pan (**Figure 48**). For a final cleanup, use an aerosol electrical contact cleaner and wipe dry with a lint-free cloth.

12. Apply a light coat of Three Bond No. 1216 to the sealing surface of the oil pan and install the oil pan.

13. Tighten the Allen bolts, in a crisscross pattern, to the torque specification listed in **Table 4**.

14. Refill the engine with the correct viscosity and quantity of oil as described in this chapter.

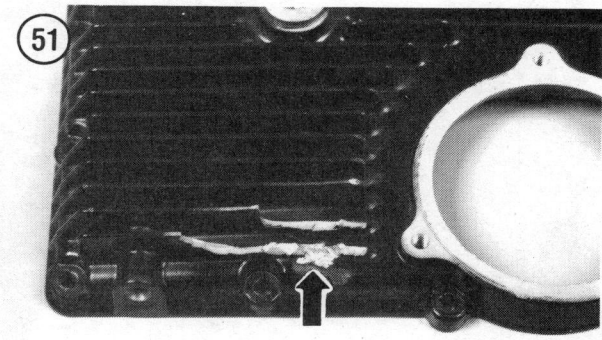

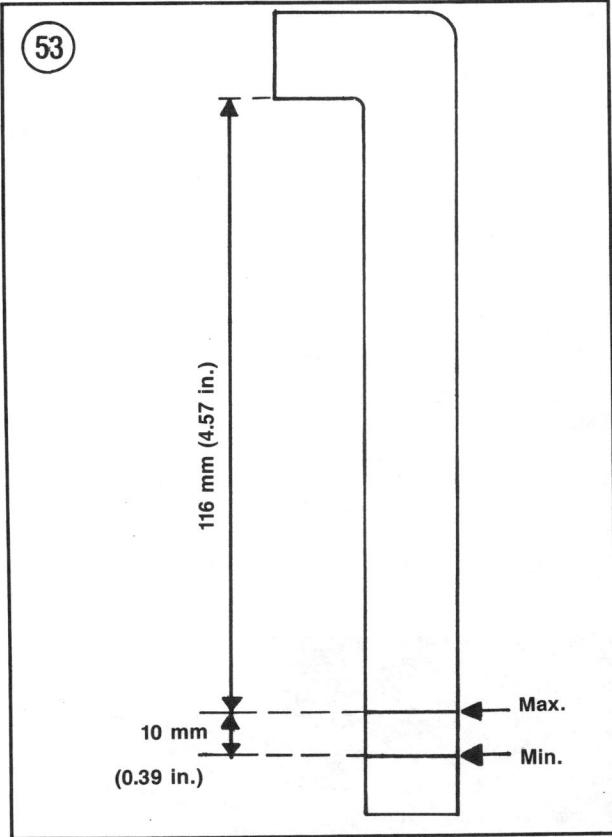

116 mm (4.57 in.)

10 mm

(0.39 in.)

Max.

Min.

3

Transmission Oil Level Check

Inspect the transmission oil level at the interval listed in **Table 1**. If the bike has been run, allow it to cool down (at least of 10 minutes), then check the transmission oil level. When checking the transmission oil level, do not allow any dirt or foreign matter to enter the case opening.
1. Place the bike on the center stand on level ground.
2. Wipe the area around the oil filler cap clean. Use an 8 mm Allen wench and unscrew the oil filler cap and sealing washer (**Figure 52**).

NOTE
If you have lost the shock absorber spring adjusting wrench, refer to **Figure 53** *and fabricate one out of metal or plastic using the dimensions furnished on the drawing.*

3. Use the shock absorber spring adjusting wrench or the fabricated tool to check the oil level. Wipe off the wrench or tool to keep dirt and foreign matter out of the transmission case.
4. Insert the wrench or fabricated tool into the opening in the transmission case and set it on the machined surface of the case opening (**Figure 54**).

NOTE
Add only enough oil to bring the oil level up to the MAX line. Do not overfill the case by adding too much oil. The oil level should **never** *be above the MAX line.*

5. Withdraw the tool and check the oil level on it. The oil level should be up to the MAX line on the tool. If necessary, add the recommended oil to bring the oil up to the correct level.
6. If the oil level is low, add the recommended type of oil listed in **Table 5**.
7. Inspect the sealing washer on the oil filler cap; replace if necessary.
8. Install the sealing washer (**Figure 55**) and the oil filler cap and tighten securely.
9. Wipe off any spilled oil from the transmission case.

Transmission Oil Change

Replace the transmission oil at the interval listed in **Table 1**.
To change the transmission oil you will need the following:
  a. Drain pan.
  b. Funnel.
  c. 8 mm Allen wrench (oil filler cap plug).
  d. 19 mm box wrench (drain plug).
  e. 1 liter (1 quart) of hypoid gear oil.

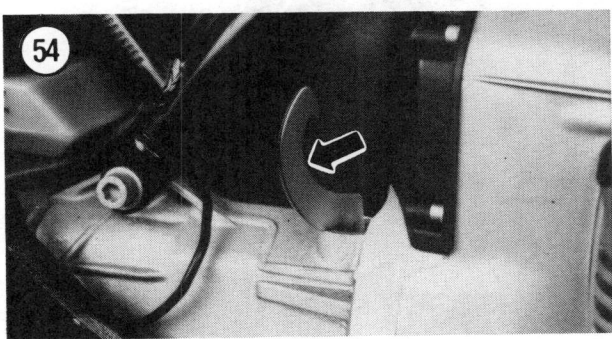

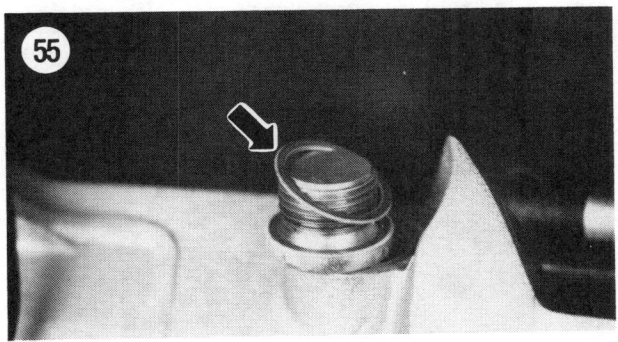

2. Ride the bike until the transmission oil reaches normal operating temperature. Usually 10-15 minutes of stop and go riding is sufficient. Shut the engine off.

3. Place the bike on the center stand on level ground.

NOTE
*Prior to removing the drain plug, loosen the oil filler cap. If you are unable to loosen the oil filler cap, do **not** remove the oil drain plug as you will end up with an empty transmission and no way to refill it. Take the bike to a dealer and have them loosen the oil filler cap for you.*

4. Wipe the area around the oil filler cap clean and unscrew the oil filler cap and sealing washer (**Figure 52**). This will speed up the flow of oil.

5. Place a drain pan under the drain plug.

WARNING
During the next step, hot oil will spurt from the drain plug hole. Be ready to move your hand away quickly once the drain plug is removed so hot oil will not run on your hand and down your arm.

6. Remove the drain plug (**Figure 56**) with a box wrench. Allow the oil to drain for at least 15-20 minutes.

7. Remove and discard the sealing washer on the transmission oil drain plug. Replace the sealing washer every time the drain plug is removed.

8. Install the drain plug and new sealing washer. Tighten the drain plug securely.

9. Insert a funnel into the oil fill hole and fill the transmission with the correct viscosity and quantity of oil. Refer to **Table 5**.

10. Install the oil filler cap and tighten securely.

11. Remove the oil drain pan from under the transmission and discard the oil as outlined under *Engine Oil and Filter Change* in this chapter.

12. Ride the bike until the transmission oil reaches normal operating temperature. Usually 10-15 minutes of stop and go riding is sufficient. Shut the engine off.

13. Check the transmission oil level as described in this chapter and readjust if necessary.

Clutch and Input Shaft Spline Lubrication

Lubricate the input shaft splines and clutch friction plate splines at the interval listed in **Table 1**.

This is a very complicated procedure since the transmission case assembly must be completely removed from the engine to accomplish it. If the clutch is operating satisfactorily and there is no erratic operation you *may* want to consider not performing this procedure. BMW has included this procedure for the K-series bikes because there was an inherent problem with the older Boxer models.

During clutch engagement and disengagement the clutch friction plate moves back and forth on the splines of the input shaft a slight amount. On the older Boxer models this caused an abnormal wear pattern on the input shaft splines that eventually required replacement of the input shaft. Get the advice of a BMW dealer regarding this procedure and whether it should be performed or not.

If you do *not* perform this procedure and there is a problem with the input shaft the BMW warranty may not cover any parts replacement costs.

Final Drive Oil Level Check

Inspect the final drive oil level at the interval listed in **Table 1**. If the bike has been run, allow it to cool down (at least 10 minutes), then check the final drive oil level. When checking the final drive oil level, do not allow any dirt or foreign matter to enter the case opening.

1. Place the bike on the center stand on level ground.

2. Wipe the area around the oil filler cap clean.

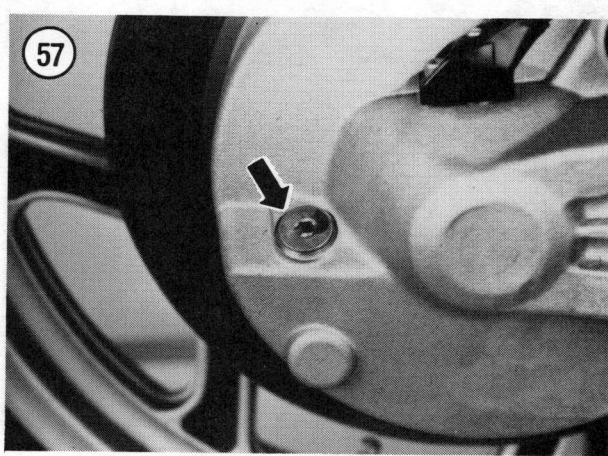

3. Use a 6 mm Allen wench and unscrew the oil filler cap and sealing washer (**Figure 57**).

4. Look down into the oil filler cap threaded hole in the final drive unit.

5. The oil level is correct if the oil is up to the lower edge of the filler cap hole (approximately 12 mm/0.48 in. from the top surface of the oil filler hole).

6. If the oil level is low, add the recommended type of oil listed in **Table 5**.

7. Inspect the sealing washer (**Figure 58**) on the oil filler cap; replace if necessary.

8. Install the sealing washer and the oil filler cap and tighten securely.

9. Wipe off any spilled oil from the final drive case.

Final Drive Oil Change

Replace the final drive oil at the interval listed in **Table 1**. To change the final drive oil you will need the following:

a. Drain pan.
b. Funnel.

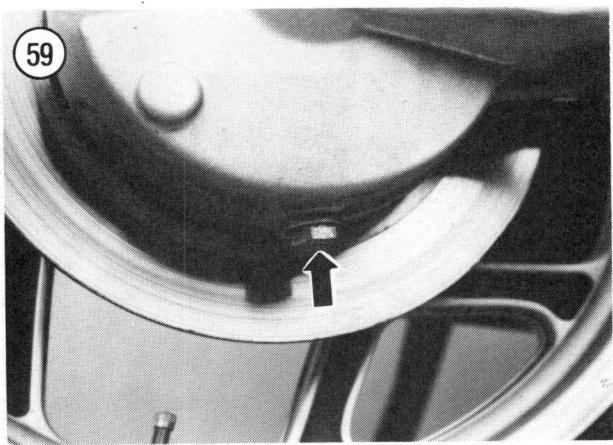

c. 6 mm Allen wrench (oil filler cap plug).
d. 19 mm box wrench (drain plug).
e. 0.26 liter (9 ounces) of hypoid gear oil.

1. Ride the bike until the final drive oil reaches normal operating temperature. Usually 10-15 minutes of stop and go riding is sufficient. Shut the engine off.

2. Place the bike on the center stand on level ground.

NOTE
*Prior to removing the drain plug, loosen the oil filler cap. If you are unable to loosen the oil filler cap, do **not** remove the oil drain plug as you will end up with an empty final drive unit and no way to refill it. Take the bike to a dealer and have them loosen the oil filler cap for you.*

3. Wipe the area around the oil filler cap clean and unscrew the oil filler cap and sealing washer (**Figure 57**). This will speed up the flow of oil.

4. Place a drain pan under the drain plug.

WARNING
During the next step, hot oil will spurt from the drain plug hole. Be ready to move your hand away quickly once the drain plug is removed so hot oil will not run on your hand and down your arm.

5. Remove the drain plug (**Figure 59**) with a 19 mm box wrench. Allow the oil to drain for at least 15-20 minutes.

6. Remove and discard the sealing washer on the final drive unit oil drain plug. Replace the sealing washer every time the drain plug is removed.

7. Install the drain plug and new sealing washer. Tighten the drain plug securely.

8. Insert a funnel into the oil fill hole and fill the transmission with the correct viscosity and quantity of oil. Refer to **Table 5**.

9. Install the oil filler cap and sealing washer and tighten securely.

10. Remove the oil drain pan from under the final drive unit and discard the oil as outlined under *Engine Oil and Filter Change* in this chapter.

11. Ride the bike until the transmission oil reaches normal operating temperature. Usually 10-15 minutes of stop and go riding is sufficient. Shut the engine off.

12. Check the final drive unit oil level as described in this chapter and readjust if necessary.

Front Fork Oil Change

It is a good practice to change the fork oil at the interval listed in **Table 1** or once a year. If it becomes contaminated with dirt or water, change it immediately.

1. Place the bike on the center stand.

2. Remove the plastic trim cap (**Figure 60**) from the top of each fork tube.
3. Place a drain pan under the right-hand and left-hand fork sliders.
4. Using a box wrench, remove the oil drain plug (**Figure 61**) from each fork slider.
5. On some models it may be necessary to partially remove the handlebar assembly to gain access to the fork spring retainer and oil filler plug. Refer to *Handlebar Removal/Installation* in Chapter Ten.

NOTE
Figure 62 is shown with the fork assembly removed for clarity. It is not necessary to remove the fork assembly to change the fork oil.

6. Using a 22 mm open-end wrench, hold onto the fork spring retainer to prevent it from turning. Refer to **Figure 63** and A, **Figure 62**.
7. Using an 8 mm wrench, remove the oil filler plug (B, **Figure 62**) from the fork spring retainer.
8. Repeat Step 5 and Step 6 for the other fork leg.
9. Allow the fork oil to drain for 10-15 minutes to allow the fork oil to drain out.
10. Inspect the sealing washer on the drain plug; replace if damaged in any way.
11. Install the sealing washer and drain plug in each fork leg and tighten securely.
12. Sit on the seat and apply the front brake. Lean on the handlebars and compress the front forks several times to expel any additional fork oil. Get off of the seat.
13. On models so equipped, remove the engine spoiler as described under *Engine Spoiler Removal/Installation* in Chapter Thirteen.
14. Lean the bike back on the center stand and place wood blocks under the oil pan to support the bike with the front wheel off the ground.
15. Insert a small funnel into the opening in the fork spring retainer.

NOTE
Use the recommended weight fork oil or the fork damping will be very stiff.

NOTE
To measure the correct amount of fluid, use a plastic baby bottle. These bottles have measurements in fluid ounces (oz.) and cubic centimeters (cc) on the side.

16. Fill the fork leg with the correct viscosity and quantity of fork oil. Refer to **Table 5**. Remove the small funnel.
17. Repeat Step 15 and Step 16 for the other fork leg.

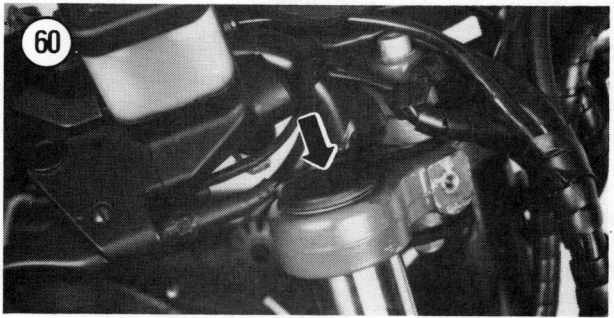

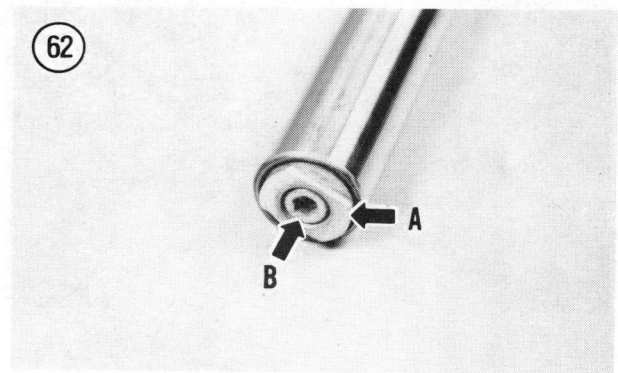

18. After the fork oil has been added to both fork legs, remove the wood blocks from under the oil pan.

19. Sit on the seat and apply the front brake. Lean on the handlebars and compress the front forks several times to expel any trapped air in the fork assemblies and to distribute the fork oil. Get off of the seat.

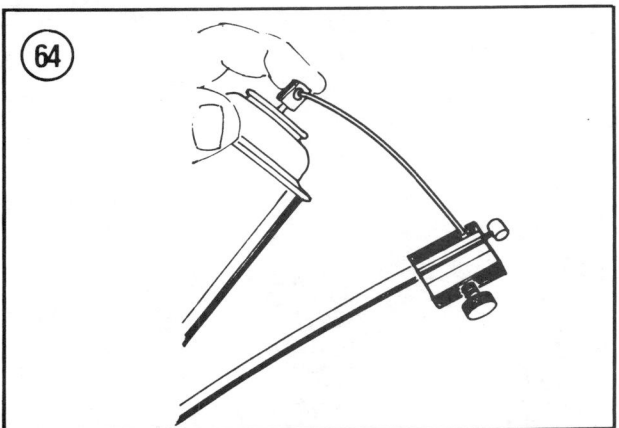

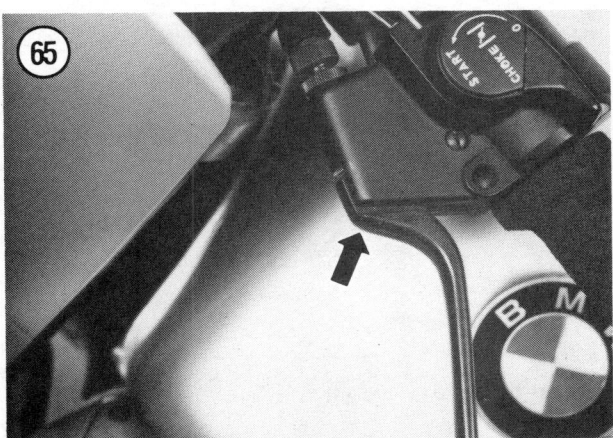

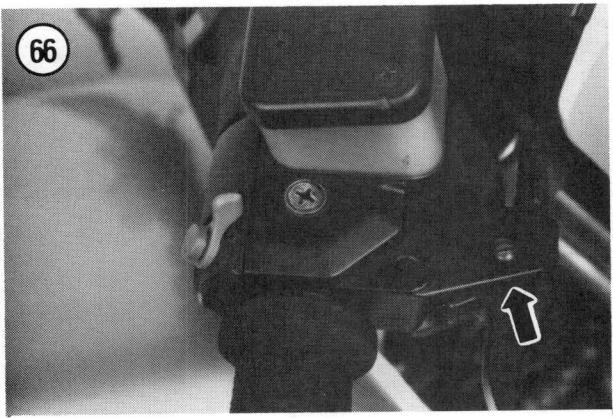

20. Inspect the sealing washer on the oil filter plug. Replace if damaged in any way.

21. Install the sealing washer and oil filter plug in each fork spring retainer and tighten securely.

22. Install the plastic trim cap.

23. Repeat Steps 19-21 for the other fork assembly.

24. On models so equipped, install the engine spoiler as described under *Engine Spoiler Removal/Installation* in Chapter Thirteen.

25. Road test the bike and check for leaks.

Control Cables

> *CAUTION*
> *Original equipment BMW cables have an internal liner and **do not** require lubrication. Lubricant oils may cause the liner to swell making cable operation erratic.*

Lubricate non-lined cables at the interval listed in **Table 1**. They should also be inspected at this time for fraying and the cable sheath checked for chafing.

Lubricate control cables with a cable lubricant and a cable lubricator available at most motorcycle dealers.

> *NOTE*
> *The main cause of cable breakage or cable stiffness is improper lubrication. Maintaining the cables as described in this section will assure long cable service life.*

1. Disconnect the cable from the clutch, the choke and the throttle grip assemblies. Refer to Chapter Five and Chapter Seven for cable removal procedures.

2. Attach a lubricator following the manufacturer's instructions (**Figure 64**).

> *NOTE*
> *Place a shop cloth at the end of the cable(s) to catch all excess lubricant that will flow out.*

3. Insert the nozzle of the lubricant can in the lubricator, press the button on the can and hold down until the lubricant begins to flow out of the other end of the cable.

> *NOTE*
> *If the lubricant does not flow out of the other end of the cable, check the entire length of the cable for fraying, bending or other damage.*

4. Remove the lubricator, reconnect the cable(s) and adjust the cables as described in this chapter.

Miscellaneous Lubrication Points

Lubricate the clutch lever (**Figure 65**), front brake lever (**Figure 66**), sidestand pivot point, center stand pivot point

(**Figure 67**) on each side and the footpeg pivot points (**Figure 68**). Use SAE 10W-40 engine oil.

If the sidestand and center stand pivot points will not respond to lubrication by the engine oil, remove the assemblies, clean and lubricate them as described in Chapter Thirteen.

PERIODIC MAINTENANCE

Disc Brake Fluid Level

The fluid level should be up between the MAX and MIN marks within the reservoir. Refer to **Figure 69** for the front brake and to **Figure 70** for the rear brake.

If the brake fluid level reaches the lower level mark, visible through the master cylinder's transparent reservoir, the fluid level must be corrected by adding fresh brake fluid.

Front master cylinder

1. Place the bike on level ground and position the handlebars so the front master cylinder reservoir *is level*.
2. Clean any dirt from the area around the top cover prior to removing the cover.
3. Remove the screws securing the top cover. Remove the top cover (**Figure 71**), spacer and the rubber diaphragm.
4. Add brake fluid until the level is to the MAX line on the master cylinder reservoir (**Figure 69**).

> *WARNING*
> *Use brake fluid from a sealed container and clearly marked DOT 4 only and specified for disc brakes. Others may vaporize and cause brake failure. Do not intermix different brands or types of brake fluid as they may not be compatible. Do not intermix a silicone based (DOT 5) brake fluid as it can cause brake component damage leading to brake system failure.*

> *CAUTION*
> *Be careful when handling brake fluid. Do not spill it on painted or plated surfaces or plastic parts as it will destroy the surface. Wash the area immediately with soapy water and thoroughly rinse it off.*

5. Reinstall the rubber diaphragm, spacer and the top cover. Tighten the screws securely.

Rear master cylinder

1. Place the bike on level ground so the rear master cylinder reservoir *is level*.
2. Clean any dirt from the area around the top cover prior to removing the cover.

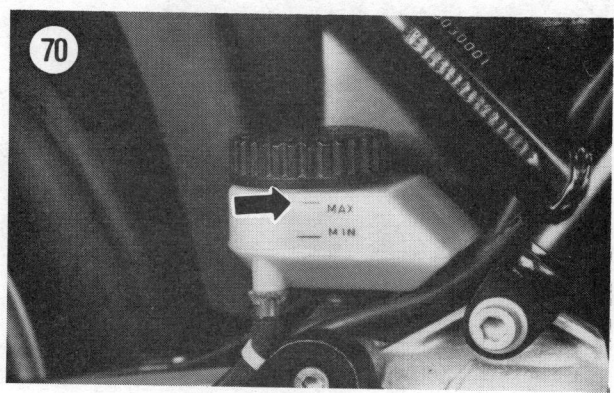

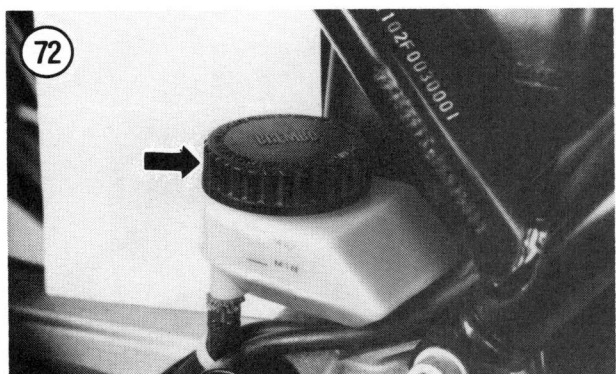

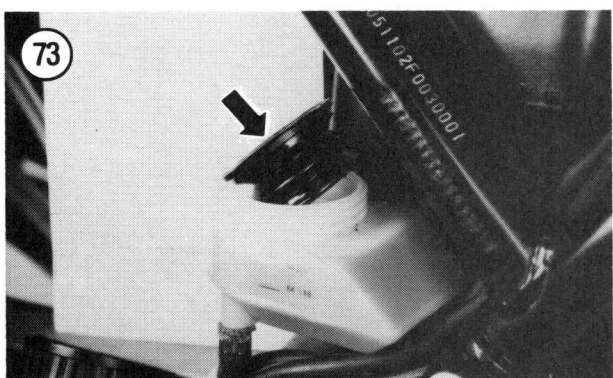

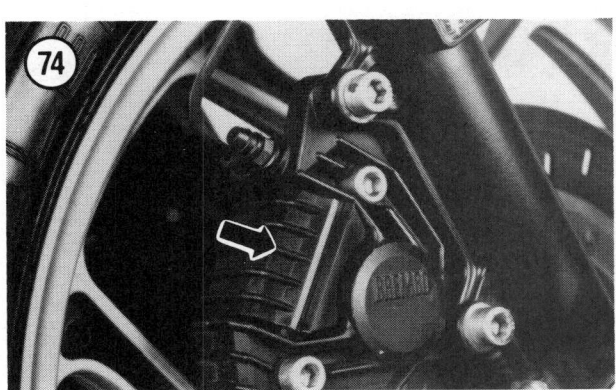

3. Unscrew and remove the top cover (**Figure 72**) and the rubber diaphragm (**Figure 73**).

4. Add brake fluid until the level is to the upper level line within the master cylinder reservoir (**Figure 70**).

> *WARNING*
> *Use brake fluid from a sealed container and clearly marked DOT 4 only and specified for disc brakes. Others may vaporize and cause brake failure. Do not intermix different brands or types of brake fluid as they may not be compatible. Do not intermix a silicone based (DOT 5) brake fluid as it can cause brake component damage leading to brake system failure.*

> *CAUTION*
> *Be careful when handling brake fluid. Do not spill it on painted or plated surfaces or plastic parts as it will destroy the surface. Wash the area immediately with soapy water and thoroughly rinse it off.*

5. Reinstall the rubber diaphragm and the top cover. Tighten the top cover securely.

Disc Brake Lines

Check the brake lines and hoses between the master cylinders and the brake calipers. If there is any leakage, tighten the connections and bleed the brakes as described under *Bleeding the System* in Chapter Twelve. If this does not stop the leak or if a brake line is obviously damaged, cracked or chafed, replace the brake line and bleed the system as described in Chapter Twelve.

Disc Brake Pad Wear

Inspect the brake pads for excessive or uneven wear.

1. Using a flat bladed screwdriver, carefully pry off the plastic cover on the caliper assembly. Refer to **Figure 74** for the front caliper or **Figure 75** for the rear caliper.

2. Look down into the caliper assembly and check the pad thickness.

3. Replace both pads if they are worn to the service limit dimension of 1.5 mm (1/16 in.) as described under *Brake Pad Replacement* in Chapter Twelve.

4. If the brake pads are okay, reinstall the plastic cover.

Disc Brake Fluid Change

Every time the reservoir cap is removed, a small amount of dirt and moisture enters the brake fluid. The same thing happens if a leak occurs or any part of the hydraulic system is loosened or disconnected. Dirt can clog the system and cause unnecessary wear. Water in the brake fluid vaporizes at high temperature, impairing the hydraulic action and reducing the brake's stopping ability.

NOTE
On models equipped with the ABS system, the brake fluid change must be performed by a BMW dealer as a power bleeder must be used.

To maintain peak performance, change the brake fluid as indicated in **Table 1**. To change brake fluid, follow the *Bleeding the System* procedure in Chapter Twelve. Continue adding new fluid to the master cylinders and bleeding out at the calipers until the fluid leaving the caliper is clean and free of contaminants.

WARNING
Use brake fluid from a sealed container and clearly marked DOT 4 only and specified for disc brakes. Others may vaporize and cause brake failure. Do not intermix different brands or types of brake fluid as they may not be compatible. Do not intermix a silicone based (DOT 5) brake fluid as it can cause brake component damage leading to brake system failure.

Rear Drum Brake Lining Wear Indicator

The rear brake is equipped with a brake lining wear indicator. This enables you to check the brake lining condition without removing the rear wheel and brake assembly for inspection purposes.

1. Have an assistant apply the rear brake fully.

2. Observe where the pointer on the brake camshaft (A, **Figure 76**) falls within the embossed wear range (B, **Figure 76**) on the final drive unit.

3. If the pointer falls within this range the brake lining thickness is within specification and the linings do not require any service.

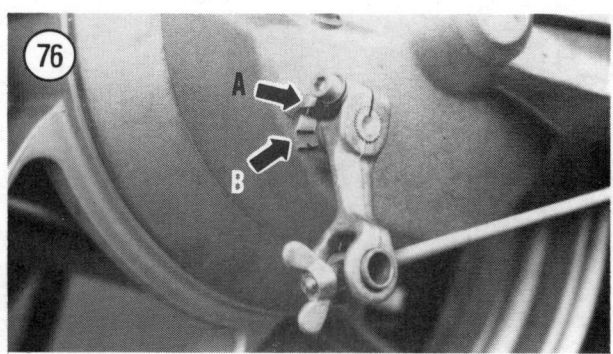
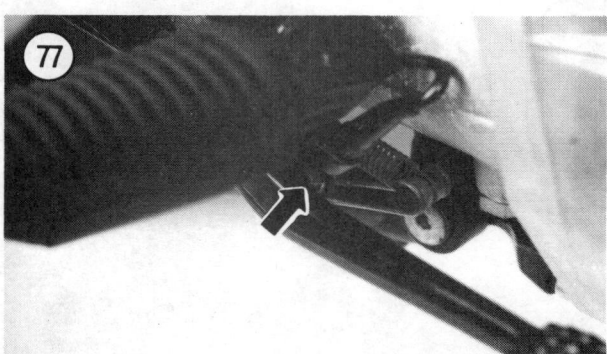
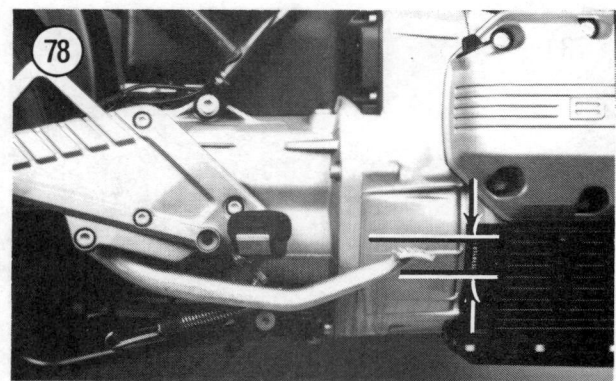
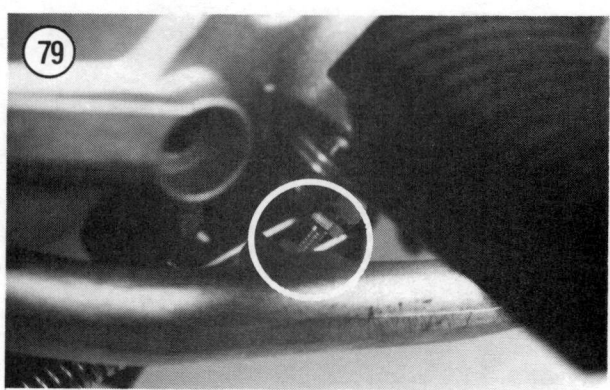

4. If the pointer falls outside of this range or to the lower line, the brake linings are worn to the point that they require replacement.

5. If necessary, replace the rear brake linings as described under *Rear Drum Brake* in Chapter Twelve.

Rear Disc Brake Pedal Height Adjustment

The rear brake pedal height should be adjusted at the interval listed in **Table 1**. The pedal height should be

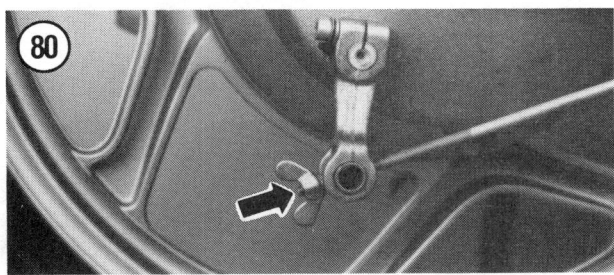

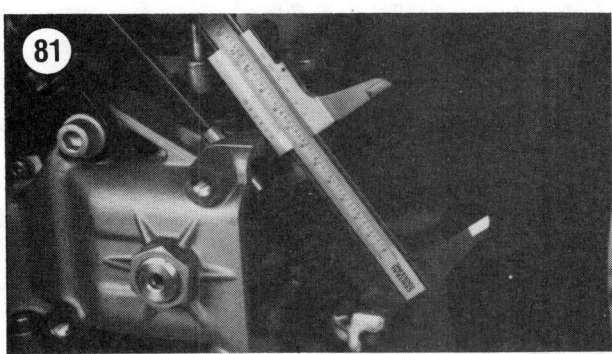

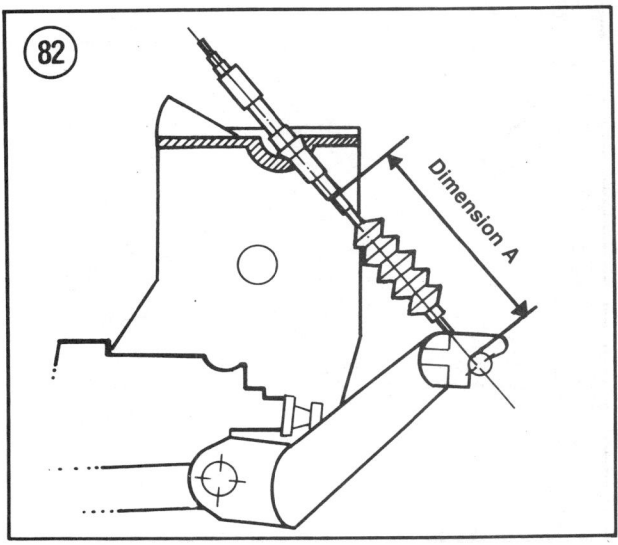

adjusted for individual rider preference. The top of the brake pedal should be positioned so it is close the rider's boot sole in the normal riding position.

To adjust the brake pedal height, perform the following:
  a. Loosen the locknut and turn the adjust bolt (**Figure 77**) in either direction until the desired height is achieved.
  b. Hold onto the adjust bolt and tighten the locknut securely.

Rear Drum Brake Pedal Height and Freeplay Adjustment

The rear brake pedal height and freeplay should be adjusted at the interval listed in **Table 1**. The pedal height will change with brake shoe wear. The pedal height should be adjusted for individual rider preference. The top of the brake pedal should be positioned so it is close to the rider's boot sole in the normal riding position.

The brake pedal freeplay should not exceed 20 mm (1.2 in.) as shown in **Figure 78**.

1. Place the bike on the center stand.
2. Make sure the brake pedal is in the at-rest position.
3. To adjust the brake pedal height, perform the following:
  a. Loosen the locknut and turn the adjust bolt (**Figure 79**) in either direction until the desired height is achieved.
  b. Hold onto the adjust bolt and tighten the locknut securely.
4. To adjust the freeplay, perform the following:
  a. Turn the rear wheel slowly and tighten the wing nut (**Figure 80**) on the end of the brake rod until the brake shoes just make contact with the brake drum. You will hear a slight grinding sound when contact is made—*stop*.
  b. At this point, loosen the wing nut 3-4 complete turns.
  c. Turn the rear wheel slowly. The brake shoes should *not* be contacting the brake drum at this time. If you can hear brake shoe contact, and there is brake pedal free play, the brake shoe return spring(s) may be stretched or broken.
     Refer to *Rear Brake Drum* in Chapter Twelve and correct the problem.

Clutch Adjustment

Adjust the clutch at the interval indicated in **Table 1**.
1. At the clutch lever on the transmission case, perform the following:
  a. Using a vernier caliper, measure the distance between the end of the clutch cable sheath and the clutch cable nipple (**Figure 81**).
  b. The correct distance (dimension "A") is 73-76 mm (2.9-2.96 in.) as shown in **Figure 82**.

2. To adjust, at the clutch hand lever, loosen the locknut (A, **Figure 83**) and turn the cable adjuster (B, **Figure 83**) in either direction until the correct amount of clutch cable is exposed.

3. Tighten the cable adjuster locknut (B, **Figure 83**) securely.

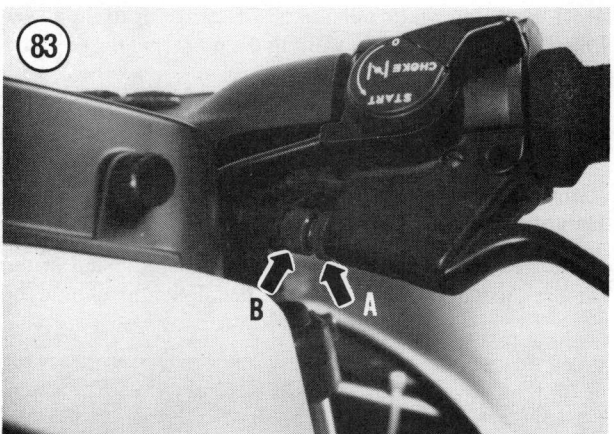

> *NOTE*
> *Figure 84 is shown with the engine and transmission assembly removed from the frame for clarity. It is not necessary to remove these components to perform this procedure.*

4. On the transmission case, perform the following:
    a. Loosen the locknut (A, **Figure 84**) and loosen the adjust bolt (B, **Figure 84**) 2-3 full turns.
    b. Turn the locknut all the way out until it is against the backside of the adjust bolt head. If the locknut is not positioned in this manner, the locknut could touch the transmission case prior to the adjust bolt touching the clutch pushrod. This would give a false reading and an incorrect clutch adjustment.
    c. Slowly turn the adjust bolt in by hand until it touches the clutch pushrod. When resistance is felt—*stop*.
    d. Hold onto the adjust bolt with a wrench and tighten the locknut with another wrench. Tighten the locknut securely.

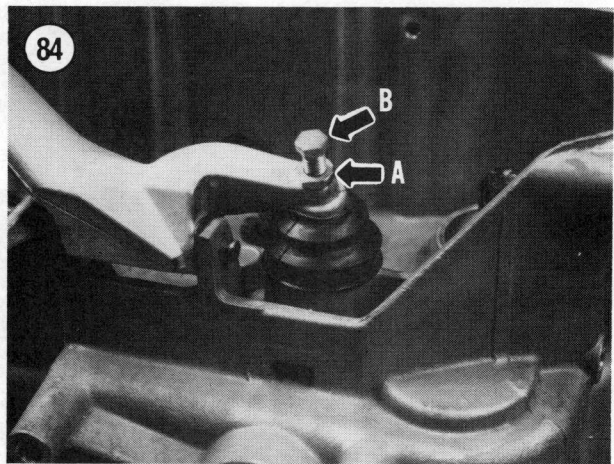

5. Adjust the handlebar clutch lever free play as follows:
    a. Loosen the locknut (A, **Figure 83**) and turn the cable adjuster (B, **Figure 83**) in either direction until the dimension A free play is achieved. Dimension A is the distance between the cable end of clutch hand lever and the lever housing (**Figure 85**). Dimension A is 1.5-2.5 mm (0.06-0.10 in.) on K75 models or 3.5-4.5 mm (0.135-0.175 in.) for K100 models.
    b. Tighten the cable adjuster locknut (A, **Figure 83**) securely.

6. After adjustment is complete, check that the locknut(s) is tight at the clutch actuating lever on the crankcase cover and at the hand lever.

7. Road test the bike to make sure the clutch fully disengages when the lever is pulled in; if it does not, the bike will creep in gear when stopped. Also make sure the clutch fully engages; if it does not, the clutch will slip, particularly when accelerating in high gear.

8. If the proper amount of adjustment cannot be achieved using this procedure, the cable has stretched to the point where it needs replacing. Refer to *Clutch Cable Replacement* in Chapter Five for complete procedure.

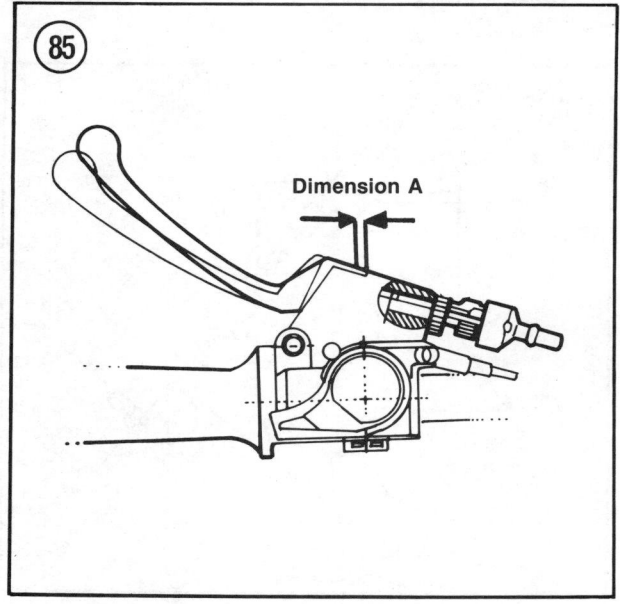

Camshaft Chain Tensioner Adjustment

There is *no* provision for cam chain tensioner adjustment on this engine. Camshaft chain tension is maintained automatically.

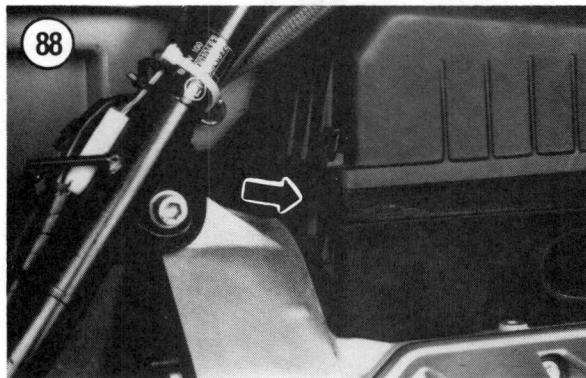

3

Air Filter Element

The air filter element should be removed and cleaned at the interval listed in **Table 1**. The air filter element should be replaced at the interval listed in **Table 1** or sooner if soiled, if severely clogged or broken in any area.

The air filter removes dust and abrasive particles from the air before the air enters the fuel injection system and the engine. Without the air filter, very fine particles could enter the engine and cause rapid wear of the piston rings, cylinders and bearings and might clog small passages in the fuel injectors and/or throttle housing. Never run the bike without the air filter element installed.

Proper air filter servicing can do more to ensure long service from your engine than almost any other single item.

Air Filter Element
Removal/Cleaning/Installation

1. Place the bike on the center stand.
2. On models so equipped, remove the radiator trim panel as described under *Radiator Trim Panel Removal/Installation* in Chapter Thirteen.
3. On models so equipped, remove the left-hand knee pads and lower panel on the right-hand side as described under *Front Fairing Removal/Installation* in Chapter Thirteen.
4. Remove the fuel tank as described in this chapter.
5. Remove the air guide as follows:
    a. Remove the bolts (A, **Figure 86**) securing the front section of the air guide to the radiator.
    b. Pull the lower section of the air guide channel (B, **Figure 86**) out of the air filter air box.
    c. Remove the air guide channel.
6. Unhook the front and rear spring clamps securing the upper case to the lower case. Refer to **Figure 87** and **Figure 88**.
7. Raise the upper case away from the lower case and withdraw the air filter element (**Figure 89**) out through the right-hand side.
8. Wipe out the interior of the air box with a shop rag dampened with cleaning solvent. Remove any foreign matter that may have passed through a broken element.
9. Gently tap the air filter element to loosen the dust.

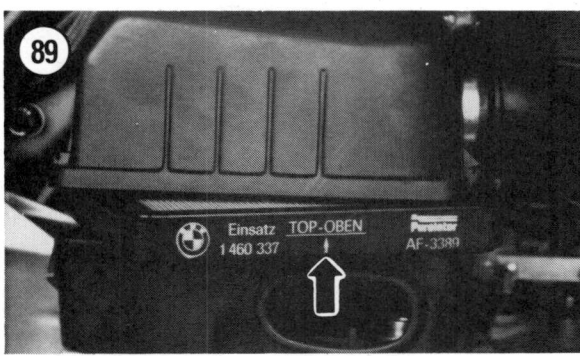

> *WARNING*
> *Never clean the air filter element in gasoline or low flash point cleaning solvent. If this type of cleaner is used, the residual solvent or vapors could cause a fire or explosion after the filter is reinstalled and the engine started. Do not clean the element in any type of solvent—only blow it out with compressed air.*

> *CAUTION*
> *In the next step, do not direct compressed air toward the bottom surface of the element. The*

normal air flow through the air filter element, when the engine is running, is from the bottom side up through the element and out through the top side. Therefore any dirt will be on the bottom surface of the element. If air pressure is directed to the bottom surface it will force the dirt and dust into the pores of the element, restricting air flow.

10. Apply compressed air toward the top side, or throttle housing side, of the element to remove all loosened dirt and dust from the element. This is reversing the normal air flow through the filter.

11. Inspect the element; if it is torn or damaged in any area it must be replaced. Do *not* run the bike with a damaged element as it may allow dirt to enter the engine.

12. Apply a light coat of multipurpose grease to the sealing edges of the air filter element. This will assure an air-tight fitting of the element to the air filter case.

13. Position the air filter element with the TOP-OBEN arrow (**Figure 89**) facing *up*.

14. Install the air filter into the lower case and press it down to make sure it seats correctly. Make sure the element is correctly seated in the air box so the sealing surface is tight up against the air box surfaces.

15. Install the upper case onto the lower case and make sure it is correctly seated all the way around the perimeter. Secure the upper case to the lower case with the spring clamps. Make sure the spring clamps have snapped over-center and are holding tightly.

16. Apply a light coat of rubber lube or Armor All to the lower section of the air guide channel where it fits into the gasket on the air filter lower case. This will make installation easier.

17. Install the air guide as follows:
   a. Install the lower section of the air guide channel (B, **Figure 86**) into the air filter air box.
   b. Move the air guide channel into position.
   c. Install the bolts (A, **Figure 86**) securing the front section of the air guide to the radiator. Tighten the bolts securely—but not too tight as the plastic mounting tabs may be damaged.

18. Install all body panels removed as described in Chapter Thirteen.

Fuel Filter

The cartridge type fuel filter is located within the fuel tank. There is also a fuel strainer attached to the inlet end of the fuel pump. This fuel strainer should be removed and cleaned when there is evidence of fuel blockage even after the cartridge fuel filter has been replaced. Fuel strainer service is covered under *Fuel Pump Removal/Installation* in Chapter Seven.

Replace the fuel filter at the interval listed in **Table 1**.

WARNING
Gasoline is very volatile and presents an extreme fire hazard. Be sure to work in a well-ventilated area away from any open flames (including pilot lights on household appliances). Do not allow anyone to smoke in the area and have a fire extinguisher rated for gasoline fires handy.

NOTE
If you have large hands this job will be very difficult. You must work down inside the filler cap opening in the fuel tank and disconnect the fuel hoses. If your hands are large, you may have to find someone with small hands to perform this procedure for you.

1. Remove the frame left-hand side cover.

2. Disconnect the battery negative lead as described under *Battery* in Chapter Three.

NOTE
The fuel filter can be removed with the fuel tank installed on the bike or removed. This procedure is shown with the fuel tank removed;

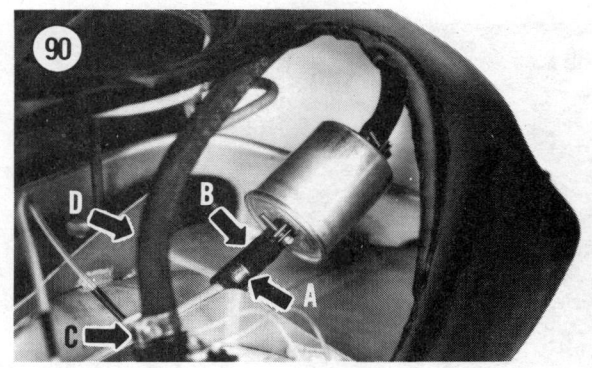

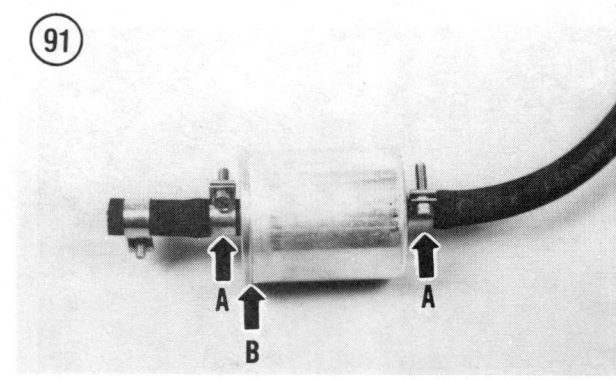

also, the left-hand side of the tank has been cut away for clarity.

3. Open the fuel tank filler cap.

4. Siphon off all fuel in the tank and store it in a suitable sealed metal container.

5. If compressed air is available, blow out the interior of the fuel tank to evacuate most of the fumes.

6. Protect the painted surface of the fuel tank with heavy cloths. Apply duct tape around the filler cap area.

7. Remove the fuel filler cap assembly as described under *Fuel Filler Cap Removal/Installation* in Chapter Seven.

8. Using a long flat-bladed screwdriver, loosen the clamping band (A, **Figure 90**) on the short length of hose running from the fuel filter to the fuel outlet line in the fuel tank. Loosen the band at the fuel line end of the hose. Slide the short fuel hose (B, **Figure 90**) off of the fuel line.

9. Using a long flat-bladed screwdriver, loosen the clamping band (C, **Figure 90**) securing the long length of hose to the top of the fuel pump. Loosen the band at the fuel pump end of the hose.

10. Disconnect the fuel hose (D, **Figure 90**) from the top of the fuel pump.

11. Withdraw the fuel filter and fuel hose from the fuel tank.

12. Loosen both hose clamps (A, **Figure 91**) and disconnect both lengths of fuel hose from the fuel filter.

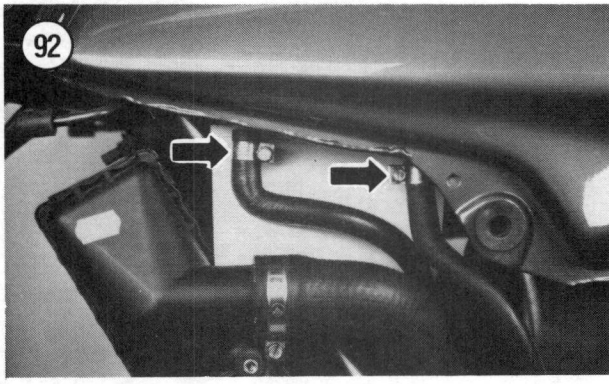

13. Inspect both fuel hoses for damage or deterioration; replace at this time if necessary.

NOTE
If you are unable to find the fuel flow directional arrow on the fuel filter, position the fuel filter with the caped end (B, Figure 91) on the end with the short piece of fuel hose.

14. Correctly position the new fuel filter so the fuel flow is correct. There is a directional arrow on the fuel filter case to indicate fuel flow direction through the filter.

15. Install both fuel hoses onto the new fuel filter and tighten the hose clamps securely.

16. Carefully install the fuel filter and fuel hose assembly into the fuel tank.

17. Look down into the fuel tank and make sure the fuel hoses are not bent or kinked. Straighten out if necessary.

18. Connect the short length of fuel hose (B, **Figure 90**) to the fuel outlet line in the fuel tank.

19. Using a long flat-bladed screwdriver, tighten the clamping band (A, **Figure 90**) on the short length of hose at the fuel line.

20. Connect the long length of fuel hose (D, **Figure 90**) to the fuel pump.

21. Using a long flat-bladed screwdriver, tighten the clamping band (C, **Figure 90**) on the long length of hose at the fuel pump.

22. Install the fuel filler cap assembly as described in Chapter Seven.

23. Refill the fuel tank and close the fuel filler cap.

24. Connect the battery negative lead as described under *Battery* in Chapter Three.

25. Install the frame left-hand side cover.

Fuel Hose Inspection

Inspect the fuel feed and fuel return hoses (**Figure 92**) from the fuel tank to their respective components. If either is cracked or starting to deteriorate it must be replaced. Also make sure the hose clamps are in place and holding securely.

WARNING
A damaged or deteriorated fuel line presents a very dangerous fire hazard to both the rider and the vehicle if fuel should spill onto a hot engine or exhaust pipe.

Cooling System Inspection

At the interval indicated in **Table 1**, the following items should be checked. If you do not have the test equipment, the tests can be done by a BMW dealer, automobile dealer, radiator shop or service station.

1. Have the coolant filler cap (**Figure 93**) pressure tested. The specified cap relief pressure is 110 kPa (16 psi). The

cap must be able to sustain this pressure for a minimum of 6 seconds. Replace the cap if it does not hold pressure or if the relief pressure is too high or too low.

> *CAUTION*
> *If test pressure exceeds the specifications the radiator may be damaged.*

2. Leave the coolant filler cap off and have the entire cooling system pressure tested (**Figure 94**). The entire cooling system should be pressurized up to, but not exceeding, 110 kPa (16 psi). The system must be able to sustain this pressure for 6 seconds. Replace or repair any components that fail this test.
3. Test the specific gravity of the coolant with an antifreeze tester (**Figure 95**) to ensure adequate temperature and corrosion protection. The system must have at least a 50/50 mixture of antifreeze and distilled water. Never let the mixture become less than 40% antifreeze or corrosion protection will be impaired. Never let the mixture exceed 50% antifreeze or cooling system damage will result.
4. Check all cooling system hoses for damage or deterioration. Replace any hose that is questionable. Make sure all hose clamps are tight.
5. On models so equipped, remove the radiator trim panel as described under *Radiator Trim Panel Removal/Installation* in Chapter Thirteen.
6. Carefully clean any road dirt, bugs, mud, etc. from the radiator core. Use a whisk broom, compressed air or low-pressure water. If the radiator has been hit by a small rock or other item, *carefully* straighten out the fins with a screwdriver.

> *NOTE*
> *If the radiator has been damaged across approximately 20% or more of the frontal area, the radiator should be recored or replaced as described under **Radiator Removal/Installation** in Chapter Nine.*

7. On models so equipped, install the radiator trim panel as described under *Radiator Trim Panel Removal/Installation* in Chapter Thirteen.

Coolant Change

The cooling system should be completely drained and refilled at the interval indicated in **Table 1**.

It is sometimes necessary to remove the radiator or drain the coolant from the system on order to perform a service procedure on some parts of the bike. If the coolant is still in good condition (not time to replace the coolant), the coolant can be reused if it is kept clean. Drain the coolant into a *clean* drain pan and pour it into a *clean* sealable

container like a plastic milk or bleach bottle. This coolant can then be reused if it is still clean.

> *WARNING*
> *Ethylene glycol is poisonous and may attract animals. Do not leave the coolant where it is accessible to pets or children.*

CAUTION
Use only a high quality ethylene glycol antifreeze specifically labeled for use with aluminum engines, preferably the BMW type mentioned in this procedure. Do not use an alcohol-based antifreeze.

In order to better protect aluminum engines, antifreeze manufacturers are using a high percentage of silicates while blending antifreeze. This chemical creates a silicate gel dropout which tends to create what is referred to as "Green Goo." This goo coats parts of the cooling system—especially the inner surfaces of the cooling tubes in the radiator—and the buildup increases when used with hard water. Also using a higher than recommended percentage of antifreeze-to-water will increase the development of "Green Goo."

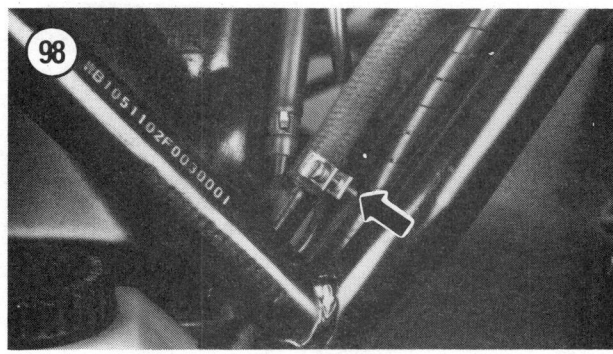

As the "Green Goo" builds up in the cooling system it actually creates an insulating coating, thus reducing the cooling system's effectiveness. This will lead to overheating problems resulting in expensive engine damage.

BMW has developed an antifreeze that eliminates this problem. It does not contain any phosphates or nitrites and will prevent the buildup of "Green Goo." This antifreeze is available from BMW dealers (part No. 81 22 9 407 638) in gallon containers. It is more expensive than the typical antifreeze, but is worth it because it eliminates this problem.

Always use a mixture of 40% antifreeze and 60% water. This percentage is the best overall cooling performance and offers a better cooling efficiency than a 50/50 ratio. This mixture affords protection down to -28 degrees C (-17 degrees F). If additional protection is needed change the percentage to 50/50 ratio. *Never* exceed this percentage of antifreeze.

In areas where freezing temperatures occur, add a higher percentage of antifreeze to protect the system to temperatures far below those likely to occur. **Table 6** lists the recommended amount of antifreeze for protection at various ambient temperatures.

The following procedure must be performed when the engine is cool. Never drain the coolant when it is hot as it will result in skin burns on your hands, arms and face.

CAUTION
Be careful not to spill antifreeze on painted surfaces as it will destroy the surface. Wash immediately with soapy water and rinse thoroughly with clean water.

1. Place the bike on the center stand.
2. On models so equipped, remove the engine spoiler as described under *Engine Spoiler Removal/Installation* in Chapter Thirteen.
3. Remove the fuel tank as described under *Fuel Tank Removal/Installation* in Chapter Seven.
4. Remove the coolant filler cap (**Figure 96**). This will speed up the draining process.
5. Place a drain pan under the water/oil pump at the front left-hand side of the engine.
6. Using a 5 mm Allen wrench, remove the drain plug (**Figure 97**) and allow the coolant to drain for 10-15 minutes.
7. Do not install the drain plug yet.
8. Take the bike off the center stand and tip the bike from side to side to drain any residual coolant from the cooling system. Place the bike back onto the center stand.
9. Install the drain plug on the water/oil pump and tighten securely.
10. Remove the coolant recovery tank as follows:
    a. Loosen the hose clamp (**Figure 98**) at the base of the coolant recovery tank.
    b. Pull the coolant recovery tank (**Figure 99**) up and out of the locating receptacles in the battery holder base.

c. Remove the hose from the base of the tank. Place your finger over the tank fitting as the coolant within the tank will drain out.

NOTE
On some models a black residue and paint flecks will come out while draining the coolant. On these models, the inside surface of the water pump cover was painted black and this paint has come off, has entered the cooling system and usually settles in the coolant recovery tank. Thoroughly rinse out the inside of the coolant recovery tank to remove this residue prior to installation.

d. Drain the coolant from the tank.
e. Install by reversing these removal steps, noting the following.
f. Make sure the locating tabs on the coolant recovery tank are properly indexed into the receptacles in the battery holder base.

11. Refill the cooling system. Use the recommended mixture of antifreeze and purified water. See **Table 6**.

12. Slowly add the coolant through the coolant cap filler neck, not the reserve tank. By adding the coolant slowly there will be less air trapped within the cooling system. Add coolant until the level reaches the base of the filler neck. Do not install the radiator cap at this time.

13. Add coolant to the reserve tank up to the MAX line (**Figure 100**).

14. Partially install the fuel tank to the point where the fuel lines are connected correctly but there is still access to the radiator filler cap. Refer to *Fuel Tank Removal/Installation* in Chapter Seven.

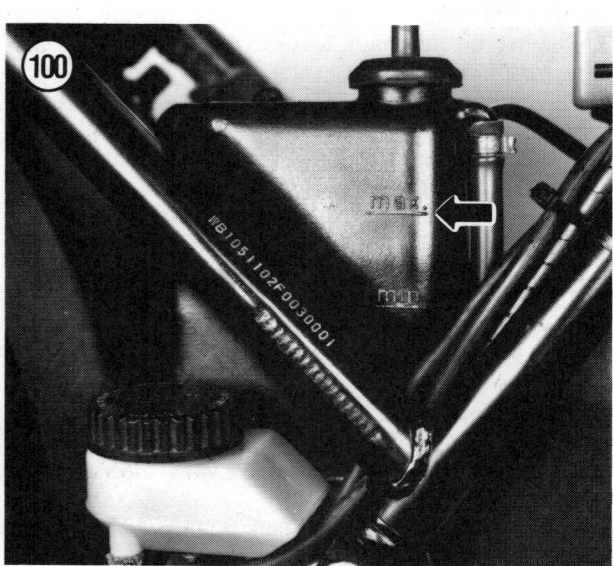

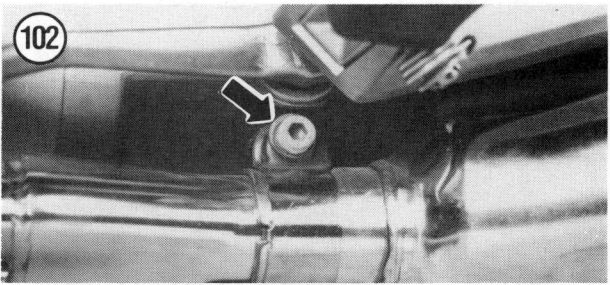

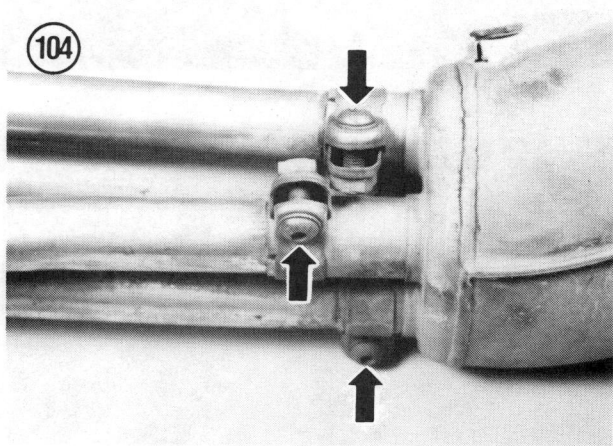

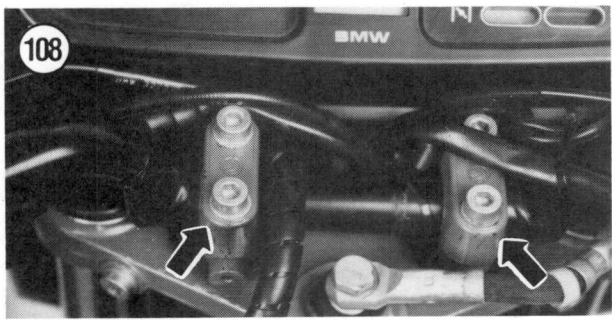

15. Start the engine and let it run at idle speed until the engine reaches normal operating temperature.

16. As the engine warms up and the coolant circulates the trapped air bubbles will work their way out of the system. When the thermostat opens, additional air bubbles will exit the radiator filler neck. Continue to add coolant until the coolant is free of bubbles.

17. Make sure there are no air bubbles in the coolant and that the coolant level stabilizes at the correct level. Add coolant as necessary.

18. Install the coolant filler cap.

19. Complete the fuel tank installation.

20. On models so equipped, install the engine spoiler as described *Engine Spoiler Removal/Installation* in Chapter Thirteen.

21. Test ride the bike and readjust the coolant level in the reserve tank if necessary.

22. Add coolant to the reserve tank to the correct level.

Exhaust System

Check for leakage at all fittings. Refer to **Figure 101** and **Figure 102** for K75 models or to **Figure 103** and **Figure 104** for K100 models. Tighten all bolts and nuts. Replace any gaskets if necessary. Refer to *Exhaust System* in Chapter Seven.

Wheel Bearings

The front wheel bearings should be inspected at the interval listed in **Table 1**. They should also be inspected and serviced, if necessary, every time the wheel is removed or whenever there is a likelihood of water contamination. The correct service procedure is covered in Chapter Ten.

The rear wheel is not equipped with any bearings. The rear suspension bearings are located within the final drive unit.

Front Suspension Check

1. Apply the front brake and pump the forks up and down as vigorously as possible. Check for smooth operation and check for any oil leaks.

2. Make sure the upper and lower fork bridge bolts are tight (**Figure 105**) on each side.

3. Remove the plastic trim cap (**Figure 106**) from the top of the fork leg. Make sure the fork top cap bolt (**Figure 107**) is held securely in place with the snap ring on each fork leg.

4. To remove the impact pad covering the handlebar upper holder bolts, perform Steps 1-5 of *Handlebar Removal* as described in Chapter Ten. Make sure all Allen bolts are tight securing the handlebar upper holders (**Figure 108**).

5. Make sure the front axle clamp bolts are tight. Refer to **Figure 109** and **Figure 110**.

6. Check the tightness of the front axle bolt (**Figure 111**).

7. Replace the steering head bearings at the interval listed in **Table 1**. The correct service procedure is covered in Chapter Ten.

> *CAUTION*
> *If any of the previously mentioned bolts and nuts are loose, refer to Chapter Ten for correct procedures and torque specifications.*

Rear Suspension Check

1. Place a wood block(s) under each side of the frame to support it securely with the rear wheel off the ground.

2. Push hard on the rear wheel (sideways) to check for side play in the rear swing arm bearings. Remove the wood block(s).

3. Check the tightness of the shock absorber upper and lower mounting bolt and nut (**Figure 112**).

> *NOTE*
> *In Step 4, the footpeg assemblies are removed for clarity.*

4. Make sure the swing arm pivot bolts and locknut are tight as follows:
   a. At the right-hand pivot point, check mounting bolts (A, **Figure 113**) and lockwashers securing the fixed pivot pin (B, **Figure 113**).
   b. At the left-hand pivot point, check the locknut (A, **Figure 114**) and the adjustable pivot pin (B, **Figure 114**) for tightness.

5. Make sure the rear wheel bolts are tight. Refer to **Figure 115** for disc brake models or **Figure 116** for drum brake models.

> *CAUTION*
> *If any of the previously mentioned bolts and nuts are loose, refer to Chapter Eleven for correct procedures and torque specifications.*

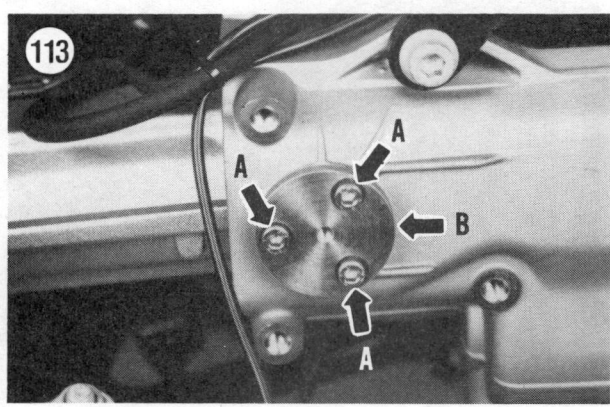

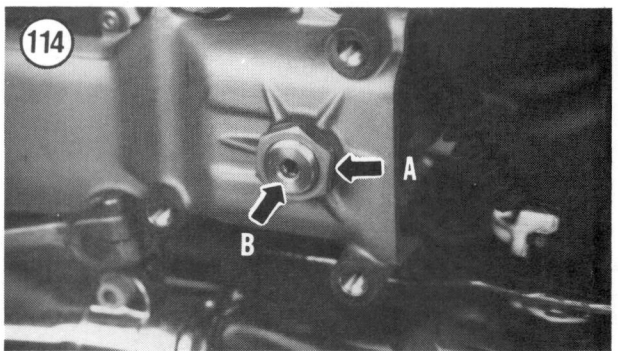

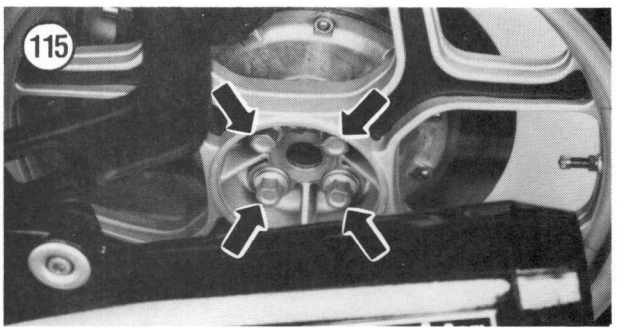

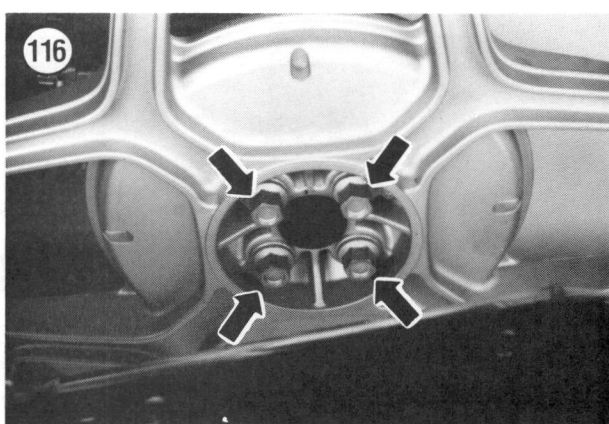

Nuts, Bolts and Other Fasteners

Constant vibration can loosen many of the fasteners on the motorcycle. Check the tightness of all fasteners, especially those on:
a. Engine mounting hardware.
b. Engine crankcase covers.
c. Handlebar and front forks.
d. Gearshift lever.
e. Brake pedal and lever.
f. Exhaust system.
g. Lighting equipment.
h. Body panels and luggage.

Steering Head Adjustment Check

Check the steering head bearings for looseness at the interval listed in **Table 1**.

Place a wood block(s) under each side of the frame to support it securely with the front wheel off the ground.

Hold onto the front fork tube and gently rock the fork assembly back and forth. If you feel looseness, refer to Chapter Ten.

Speedometer Sensor Cleaning

The electronic speedometer receives its impulses from a sensor located on top of the final drive unit. Within the final drive unit is a castellated ring that rotates with the rear wheel. As the castellations pass by it triggers the sensor which in turn sends the pulses to the electronic speedometer. At the interval listed in **Table 1**, remove and clean the speedometer sensor.

1. Remove the screw (A, **Figure 117**) securing the speedometer sensor.
2. Carefully remove the sensor (B, **Figure 117**) from the final drive unit. If necessary, use a screwdriver and gently pry the sensor up and out.
3. Inspect the O-ring seal (**Figure 118**) for damage; replace if necessary.
4. Clean off all dirt and grease from the end of the sensor that is down in the final drive unit.

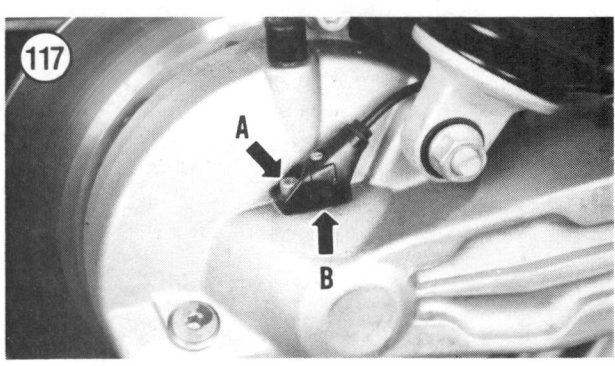

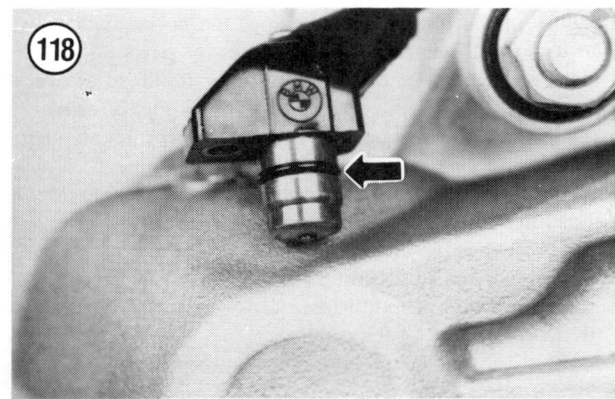

5. Make sure the O-ring seal is in place and install the speedometer sensor into the final drive unit.

6. Install the screw and tighten securely—do not overtighten as the plastic housing may fracture.

Crankcase Breather

NOTE
Figure 119 is shown with the air filter case removed for clarity.

Inspect the breather hose (**Figure 119**) from the cylinder block outlet to the air plenum chamber. If it is cracked or starting to deteriorate it must be replaced. Make sure the hose clamps are in place and holding securely.

Evaporative Emission Control System (Models So Equipped)

When the bike is stopped after a ride, the fuel and fuel vapor in the fuel tank expands due to engine heat (or ambient temperature). When the pressure within the fuel tank reaches 20 kPa (2.9 psi) the pressure relief valve (**Figure 120**) opens allowing the fuel vapor to enter the engine crankcase via a vent hose. It is stored in the crankcase until the engine is started.

When the engine is restarted, the vacuum in the air intake system pulls the fuel vapor from the crankcase and mixes it with the incoming fresh air, thus burning it in the engine.

There is no routine maintenance on the evaporation emission control system other than to inspect the hoses and the pressure relief valve whenever the fuel tank is removed. Make sure the hoses are not kinked or damaged.

Make sure all vapor hoses are correctly routed and attached. Inspect the hoses and replace any if necessary.

TUNE-UP

Perform a complete tune-up at the interval listed in **Table 1** for normal riding. More frequent tune-ups may be required if the bike is ridden in stop-and-go traffic. The purpose of the tune-up is to restore the performance lost due to normal wear and deterioration of parts.

The spark plugs should be routinely replaced at every other tune-up or if the electrodes show signs of erosion. In addition, this is a good time to clean the air filter element. Have the new parts on hand before you begin.

Because the different systems in an engine interact, the procedures should be done in the following order:

a. Adjust valve clearances.
b. Check ignition timing.
c. Run a compression test.
d. Replace the spark plugs.
e. Set the idle speed and synchronize the fuel injector throttles.

Table 7 summarizes tune-up specifications.

NOTE
It is a good idea to start the engine after each one of the tune-up procedures is completed and make sure it runs okay. If for some reason, the procedure was not done correctly or a faulty new part(s) was installed, you can then concentrate on that specific procedure and correct the problem. If you wait until all of the tune-up procedures are completed and then the

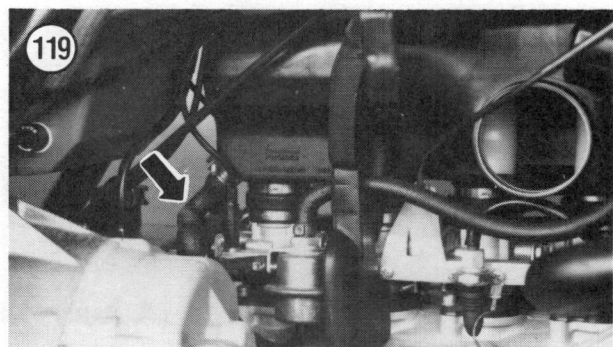

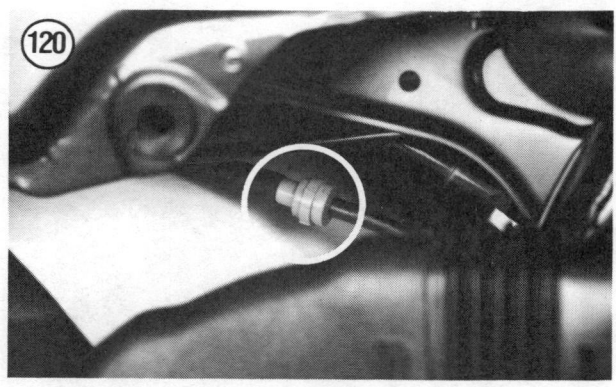

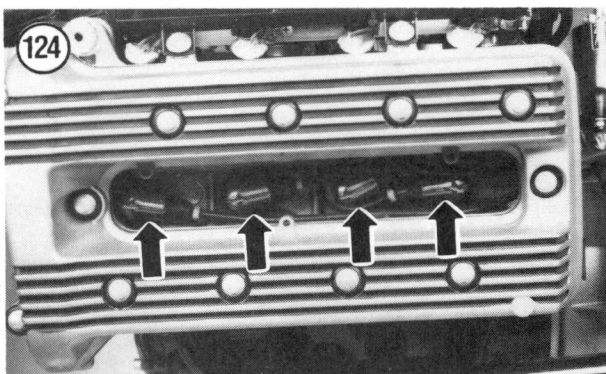

bike runs worse or does not start at all, then you have to narrow it down to which one of the procedures is causing the problem.

To perform a tune-up on your BMW, you will need the following tools and equipment:

  a. 5 mm Allen wrench.
  b. BMW spark plug wrench and wheel lug nut wrench (in factory tool kit) or 18 mm spark plug wrench.
  c. Socket wrench and assorted sockets.
  d. Flat feeler gauge.
  e. Compression gauge.
  f. Spark plug wire feeler gauge and gapper tool.
  g. Assorted BMW special tools for valve clearance that are described and listed in the valve clearance procedure.
  h. Manometer for synchronizing fuel injector throttles.

Valve Clearance Measurement

Measure the valve clearance at the interval listed in **Table 1**.

Valve clearance measurement must be performed with the engine cool, at room temperature. The maximum temperature the cylinder head can be is 35 degrees C/95 degrees F. If the temperature is greater than that specified the clearance measurement will not be correct. The correct valve clearances are listed in **Table 7**. The intake valves are located at the top of the cylinder head and the exhaust valves are located at the bottom.

> *NOTE*
> *Measure the valve clearance very accurately. This adjustment procedure is quite complicated and you will only want to perform it once. This is not like turning an adjustment screw on a rocker arm adjuster, where you can go back and forth easily until the clearance is correct. If you do not accurately measure the first time, chances are you will have to re-purchase the spacers and repeat the procedure until the clearance is correct. Once the clearance is correct, it will usually remain correct for many thousands of miles and will probably only have to be checked and not readjusted.*

1. Place the bike on the center stand.
2. Shift the transmission into 5th gear.
3. Remove the screws and lockwashers securing the spark plug cover panel and remove the panel. Refer to **Figure 121** for K75 models or **Figure 122** for K100 models.
4. Using a crisscross pattern, loosen the bolts securing the cylinder head cover. Refer to **Figure 123** for K75 models or **Figure 124** for K100 models. Remove the bolts, the cover and the rubber gaskets. Don't lose the spring (**Figure 125**) on one of the camshaft bearing caps.

3

CAUTION
CAUTION
Follow spark plug removal procedure in this chapter carefully to prevent engine damage.

5. Remove all spark plugs from the cylinder head as described in this chapter. This will make it easier to rotate the engine by hand during this procedure.

NOTE
There is no specific sequence to checking the valve clearance, but to avoid confusion, start at the front of the engine with the No. 1 cylinder and work toward the back checking the remaining cylinders in order.

NOTE
*To obtain the correct measurement, the camshaft lobe must be directly opposite the lifter surface (**Figure 126**).*

NOTE
The following steps are shown with the engine removed from the frame for clarity. It is not necessary to remove the engine to inspect and adjust the valves.

NOTE
The intake camshaft is located at the upper side of the cylinder (next to the fuel injectors) and the exhaust camshaft is located at the lower side of the cylinder head (next to the exhaust pipe).

6. Rotate the engine using the rear wheel until the front or No. 1 cylinder's intake camshaft lobe is directly opposite the lifter surface as shown in **Figure 126**.
7. With the engine in this position, check the clearance of the No. 1 cylinder's intake valve.

NOTE
*Measure the valve clearance with a flat **metric** feeler gauge. If adjustment is necessary, it will be easier to calculate valve lifter spacer selection in the following procedure.*

NOTE
Measure the clearance very accurately. The adjustment procedure is quite complicated and you will only want to perform it once. This is not like turning an adjustment screw on a rocker arm adjuster, where you can go back and forth easily until the clearance is correct.

If you do not accurately measure the first time, chances are you will have to re-purchase the spacers and repeat the procedure until the clearance is correct. Once the clearance is correct, it will probably maintain this clearance for many thousands of miles and will probably not have to be readjusted—only remeasured.

8. Check the clearance by inserting a flat *metric* feeler gauge between the camshaft and the top surface of the valve lifter spacer (**Figure 127**). When the clearance is correct, there will be a slight drag on the feeler gauge when it is inserted and withdrawn.
9. Measure the valve clearance for the intake valve on the No. 1 cylinder. Write down the clearance for the intake valve on a piece of paper noting the cylinder number and intake clearance number. This clearance dimension will be used during the adjustment procedure, if adjustment is necessary.
10. To correct the valve clearance, the spacer on top of the valve lifter must be replaced with one of a different thickness. These spacers are available from BMW dealers in 0.05 mm increments that range from 2.00 mm to 3.00 mm in thickness. The thickness is marked on the spacer face that contacts the valve lifter body, not the camshaft.
11. Rotate the engine using the rear wheel until the front or No. 1 cylinder's exhaust camshaft lobe is directly opposite the lifter surface as shown in **Figure 126**.

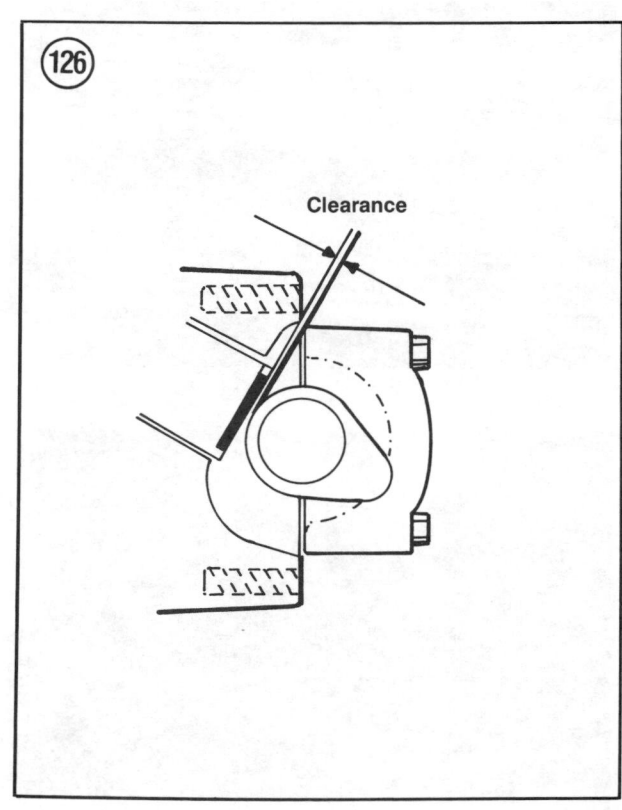
(126)
Clearance

12. With the engine in this position, check the clearance of the No. 1 cylinder's exhaust valve.

13. Repeat Steps 6-11 for the valves in the remaining cylinders. Record the clearance for both the intake and exhaust valves.

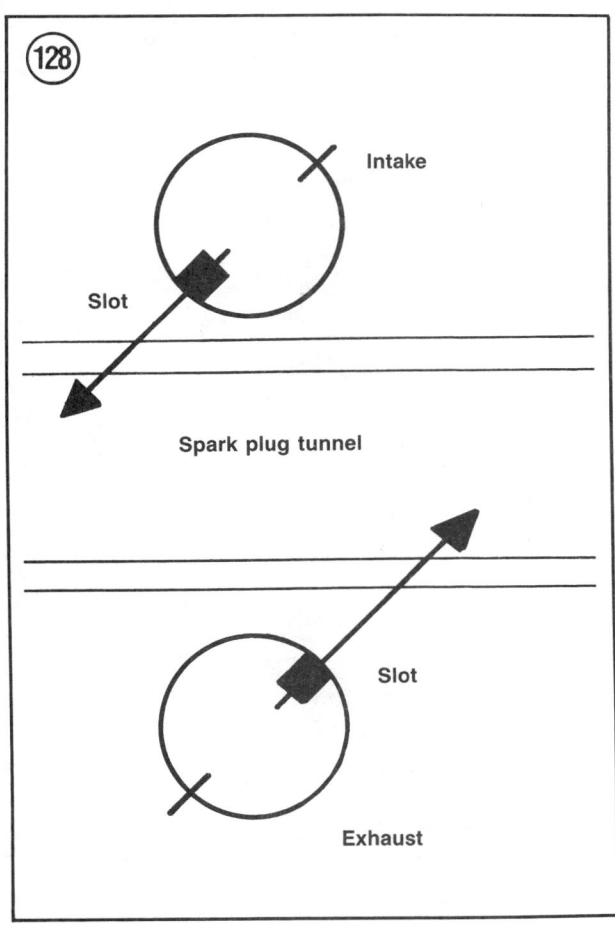

Intake

Slot

Spark plug tunnel

Slot

Exhaust

Valve Clearance Adjustment

CAUTION
*Do **not** try to perform this procedure with substitute tools as you will end up damaging some portion of the valve train. As is typical with all Clymer books, we try to suggest substitute tools whenever possible—this is **not** the procedure for substitute tools. Use only the BMW special tools.*

Special BMW tools are required for valve clearance adjustment. These special tools are available from BMW dealers and they are as follows:

    a. Decompressor lever: BMW part No. 11 1 720.
    b. Valve lifter holder: BMW part No. 11 1 722.

NOTE
The correct valve clearance is 0.15-0.20 mm for the intake valves and 0.25-0.30 mm for the exhaust valves. For the best performance, adjust the valve clearance to the smaller dimension.

There is no specific sequence for adjusting the valve clearance, but to avoid confusion, start at the front of the engine with the No. 1 cylinder and work toward the back. Determine which cylinder(s) require valve clearance adjustment. This procedure takes into account that at least one valve requires adjustment in each cylinder. If both valves in one of the cylinders are within specifications, skip that cylinder and proceed to the next cylinder.

The top of the valve lifter has a slot. This slot must be positioned as noted in order to gain access to the spacer for removal.

1. Rotate the rear wheel until the front or No. 1 cylinder is at top dead center (TDC) on its compression stroke. To determine TDC for the No. 1 cylinder, perform the following:

    a. Rotate the rear wheel (in normal forward rotation) until the intake camshaft has completely opened and then allowed the *intake valve* to close.

    b. Using a small flashlight, direct the light into the spark plug hole to observe the piston as it moves up in the cylinder.

    c. Continue to rotate the rear wheel until the No. 1 cylinder's piston reaches the top of its stroke. This will be TDC on the compression stroke.

2. Rotate the valve lifter(s) until the slot is positioned at a 45° angle as shown in **Figure 128**. This slot must be positioned as noted in order to gain access to the spacer for removal.

3. Install the decompressor lever (BMW special tool, part No. 11 1 720) next to the camshaft lobe (**Figure 129**) and onto the top of the spacer. Pivot the tool handle down (**Figure 130**) until it depresses the valve lifter and spacer. Hold the tool in this position.

4. On the other side of the camshaft lobe install the valve lifter holder (BMW special tool, part No, 11 1 722) between the camshaft and the valve lifter (**Figure 131**). The valve lifter holder must be positioned so that it touches the outer ledge of the valve lifter only. It cannot touch the spacer as the spacer is going to be removed later in this procedure.

CAUTION
Make sure the valve lifter holder is correctly positioned on the outer ledge of the valve lifter and camshaft. If the holder is not located properly, it may slip off of the shoulder when the decompressor lever is removed. If this happens the valve lifter may be gouged, causing a burr which will make free movement of the valve lifter impossible, thus leading to expensive parts replacement.

5. Make sure the valve lifter holder is seated correctly on the valve lifter outer ledge and remove the decompressor lever from the camshaft.

6. Use a magnetic tool and lift the spacer up and out of the valve lifter (**Figure 132**) or use an angled scribe (**Figure 133**) (or dental tool) and remove the spacer part of the way until it can be removed with a pair of tweezers.

NOTE
If working on a well run-in engine (high mileage), measure the spacer with a micrometer to make sure of the exact spacer thickness. If the spacer is worn to less than the indicated thickness marked on it, it will throw off calculations for a new spacer. Also measure the spacer in this manner if the spacer number is either worn off or is illegible as shown in **Figure 134.**

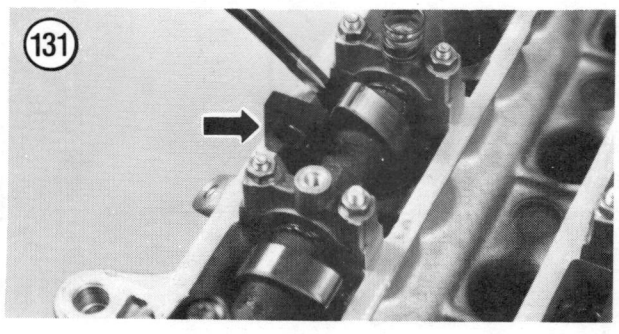

7. Turn the spacer over and note the thickness number (**Figure 135**).

8. For correct spacer selection proceed as follows:

NOTE
For calculations use the mid-point of the specified clearance. For example, if the intake valve clearance is 0.15-0.20 mm the mid-point is 0.18 mm; if the exhaust valve clearance is 0.25-0.30 mm the mid-point is 0.28 mm.

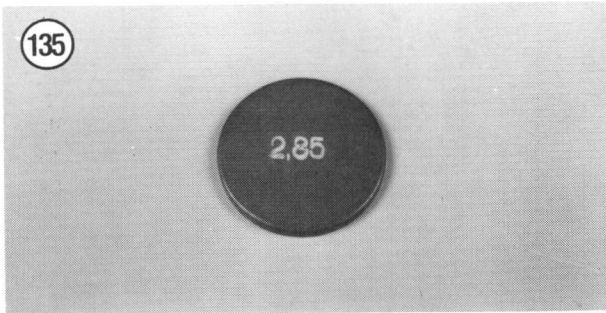

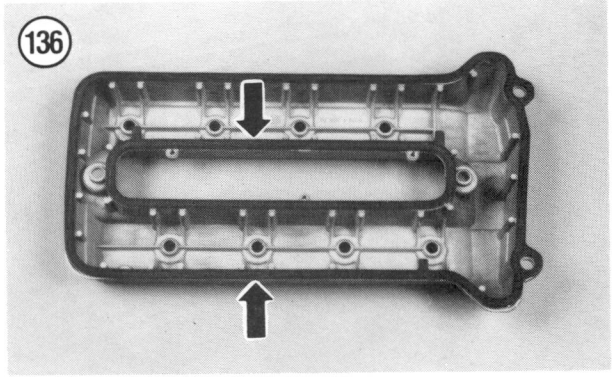

NOTE
*The following numbers are for **examples only**.*
*Use the numbers written down during the **Valve Clearance Measurement** procedure.*

3

Examples:	Intake	Exhaust
Actual measured clearance	0.50 mm	0.41 mm
Subtract specified clearance	– 0.18 mm	– 0.28 mm
Equals excess clearance	0.32 mm	0.13 mm
Existing spacer number	220	245
Add excess clearance	+ 32	+ 13
	252	258
Equals new spacer number (round off to the nearest spacer number)	250	260

9. Position the new spacer with the thickness number facing down and install the new spacer into the lifter. Make sure the spacer is correctly positioned within the recess in the valve lifter—it cannot be cocked or the lifter will be damaged. After the spacer is installed, rotate it around with a pair of tweezers or small screwdriver to make sure it is correctly seated.

10. Reinstall the BMW decompressor lever next to the camshaft lobe. Pivot the tool handle down until it is positioned correctly on the valve lifter and spacer. Hold the tool in this position.

11. Remove the BMW valve lifter holder from between the camshaft and the valve lifter.

12. Remove the BMW decompressor lever from the camshaft.

13. Repeat this procedure for all valve assemblies that are out of specification.

14. After all valve clearances have been adjusted, using the rear wheel, rotate the engine several complete revolutions to seat all new components.

15. Reinspect all valve clearances as described in this chapter. If any of the clearances are still not within specification, repeat this procedure until all clearances are correct.

16. Install all spark plugs into the cylinder head as described in this chapter.

17. Inspect the rubber gaskets (**Figure 136**) on the cylinder head cover; replace if necessary.

18. Install the cylinder head cover and tighten the bolts in a crisscross pattern to the torque specification listed in **Table 4**.

19. Install the spark plug cover panel and install the screws and lockwashers. Tighten the screws securely.

20. After the valves are adjusted correctly, synchronize the fuel injector throttle butterflies and adjust the idle speed as described in this chapter and Chapter Seven.
21. Start the bike and make sure it runs correctly.

Ignition Timing

Check the ignition timing at the interval indicated in **Table 1**.

Special BMW tools are required for checking ignition timing. These special tools are available from BMW dealers and they are as follows:

a. Ignition tester: BMW part No. 12 3 650.
b. Test lead: BMW part No. 12 3 651.
c. Dial gauge extension: BMW part No. 00 2 580.

> *WARNING*
> *The ignition system is electronic. The high voltage generated by the ignition signal generator and ignitor unit could produce serious or fatal shocks if any of the ignition components are touched while the engine is running. If it is necessary to hold any of the high voltage leads, do so with an insulated pair of pliers.*

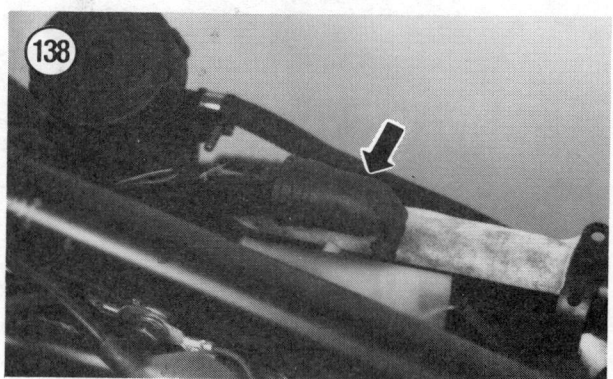
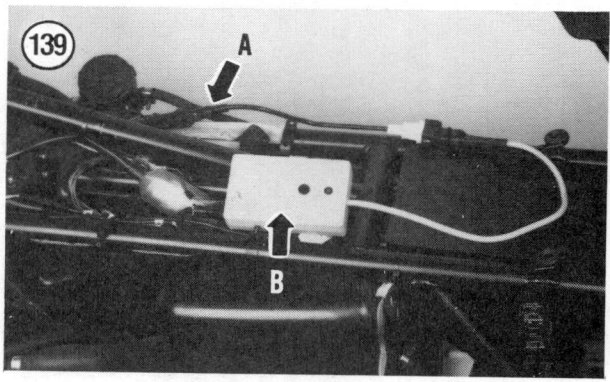
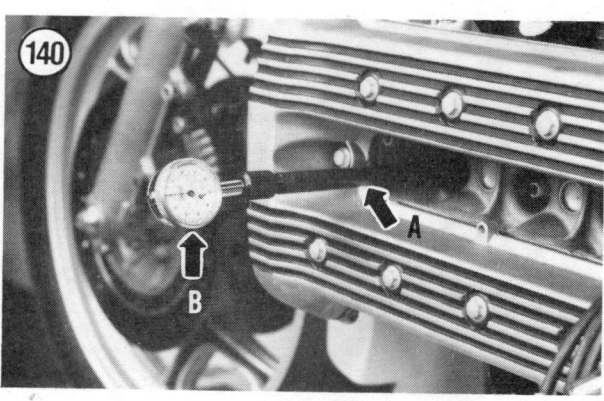

1. Remove the fuel tank as described under *Fuel Tank Removal/Installation* in Chapter Seven.
2. Remove the screws and lockwashers securing the spark plug cover panel and remove the panel. Refer to **Figure 121** for K75 models or **Figure 122** for K100 models.
3. On models so equipped, remove the engine spoiler as described under *Engine Spoiler Removal/Installation* in Chapter Thirteen.
4. Remove the bolts securing the Hall transmitter cover (**Figure 137**) and remove the cover and gasket.
5. Remove the spark plugs as described in this chapter. This will make it easier to rotate the engine during this procedure.
6. Pull back the rubber boot (**Figure 138**) and disconnect the Hall transmitter electrical connector located next to the upper right-hand frame rail.
7. Connect the BMW test lead (A, **Figure 139**) to the Hall transmitter electrical connector.
8. Connect the BMW ignition tester (B, **Figure 139**) to the test lead. The diode (small light) on the face of the ignition tester should now be ON.
9A. On K75 models, install the dial gauge extension into the No. 3 or rear cylinder. Attach a dial gauge to the extension.
9B. On K100 models, install the dial gauge extension (A, **Figure 140**) into the No. 1 or front cylinder. Attach a dial gauge (B, **Figure 140**) to the extension.

NOTE
Figure 141 is shown with the engine removed for clarity. This procedure can be performed with the engine in the frame.

10. Use an Allen socket and socket wrench on the Allen bolt on the end of the crankshaft (**Figure 141**). Rotate the engine *counterclockwise* until the piston (No. 3—K75 or No. 1—K100) reaches top dead center (TDC).

11. Zero the dial gauge (**Figure 142**) and lock it in this position.

12. Slightly rotate the engine in both directions to make sure the piston is at TDC. If necessary, zero the dial gauge again.

13. Again use an Allen socket and socket wrench on the Allen bolt on the end of the crankshaft. This time rotate the engine *clockwise*—against normal rotation—until the piston reaches firing position. This dimension is 0.24 mm (0.009 in.) before top dead center (BTDC).

14. With the engine at BTDC the diode (**Figure 143**) on the ignition tester should go OFF. If the diode goes OFF the ignition timing is *correct;* proceed to Step 20. If the diode is still ON the ignition timing is *wrong;* proceed to the next steps.

15. Remove the Allen socket and socket wrench.

16. Loosen the base plate Allen screws (A, **Figure 144**) and gradually rotate the base plate assembly (B, **Figure 144**) in either direction until the diode light goes OFF. When the diode light goes OFF the ignition timing is correct.

17. Once again gradually rotate the base plate assembly back and forth until the diode light again goes OFF—stop and tighten the base plate mounting screws securely.

18. Again use an Allen socket and socket wrench on the Allen bolt on the end of the crankshaft. This time rotate the engine *counterclockwise* until the piston goes beyond the firing position.

19. This time rotate the engine *clockwise*—against normal rotation—until the piston reaches firing position. This dimension is 0.24 mm (0.009 in.) before top dead center (BTDC). The diode light must go OFF. If the diode light goes OFF the ignition timing is now correct. If the diode light did not go off, repeat Steps 10-18 until the timing is correct.

20. Remove the Allen socket and socket wrench.

21. Disconnect the dial gauge and remove the extension from the engine.

22. Disconnect the BMW ignition tester and the test lead from the Hall transmitter electrical connector.

23. Connect the Hall transmitter electrical connector. Make sure the electrical connector is free of corrosion and is tight. Pull the rubber boot back over the connector.

24. Install the spark plugs as described in this chapter.

25. Install a new gasket (**Figure 145**) and install the cover. Install the cover bolts and tighten them securely.

26. On models so equipped, install the engine spoiler as described under *Engine Spoiler Removal/Installation* in Chapter Thirteen.

27. Install the spark plug cover panel, lockwashers and bolts. Tighten the bolts securely.

28. Install the fuel tank as described under *Fuel Tank Removal/Installation* in Chapter Seven.

Compression Test

Check the cylinder compression at the interval indicated in **Table 1**. Record the results and compare them to the results at the next interval. A running record will show trends in deterioration so that corrective action can be taken before complete failure.

The results, when properly interpreted, can indicate general cylinder, piston ring and valve condition.

1. Warm the engine to normal operating temperature, then shut it off.

2. Place the bike on the center stand.

3. Shift the transmission into NEUTRAL.

4. Remove the screws and lockwashers securing the spark plug cover panel and remove the panel. Refer to **Figure 121** for K75 models or **Figure 122** for K100 models.

5. Remove all spark plugs from the cylinder head as described in this chapter. This will make it easier to rotate the engine during this procedure.

6. Reconnect the spark plug leads to each spark plug.

> *CAUTION*
> *Each spark plug must be grounded to the cylinder head or cover to prevent damage to the ignition system.*

7. Position the spark plugs to that they are grounded on the top of the cylinder head cover.

8. Connect the compression tester to the No. 1 cylinder following the manufacturer's instructions.

9. Using the starter, crank the engine over 2-3 revolutions until there is no further rise in pressure.

10. Remove the tester and record the reading. When interpreting the results, actual readings are not as important as the difference between the readings. The recommended "Good," "Normal" and "Poor" cylinder compression pressures are listed in **Table 7**. If the reading(s) is less than that listed under *poor* in **Table 7** this would indicate broken rings, leaky or sticking valves, a blown head gasket or a combination of all.

If a low reading (10 % or more) is obtained in a cylinder(s) it indicates valve or ring trouble. To determine which, carefully lay the bike as far as possible on its right-hand side. Pour about a teaspoon of engine oil through the spark plug hole onto the top of the piston. Turn the engine over once to distribute the oil, then take another compression test and record the reading. If the compression increases significantly, the valves are good but the rings are defective. If the compression does not increase, the valves require servicing. A valve(s) could be hanging open or burned or a piece of carbon could be on a valve seat.

11. Remove the spark plugs from the spark plug leads.

12. Install the spark plugs as described in this chapter.

13. Start the bike and make sure it runs correctly.

Spark Plug Selection

Spark plugs are available in various heat ranges, hotter or colder than plugs originally installed at the factory.

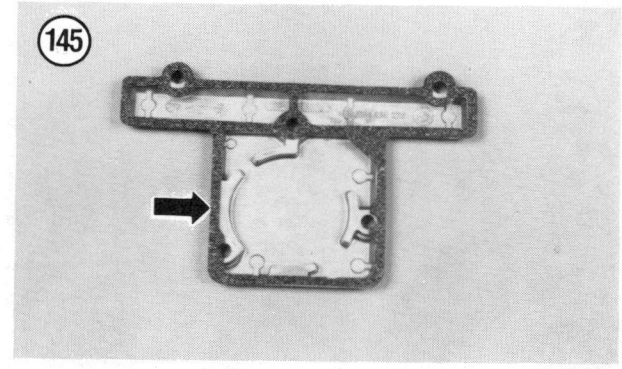

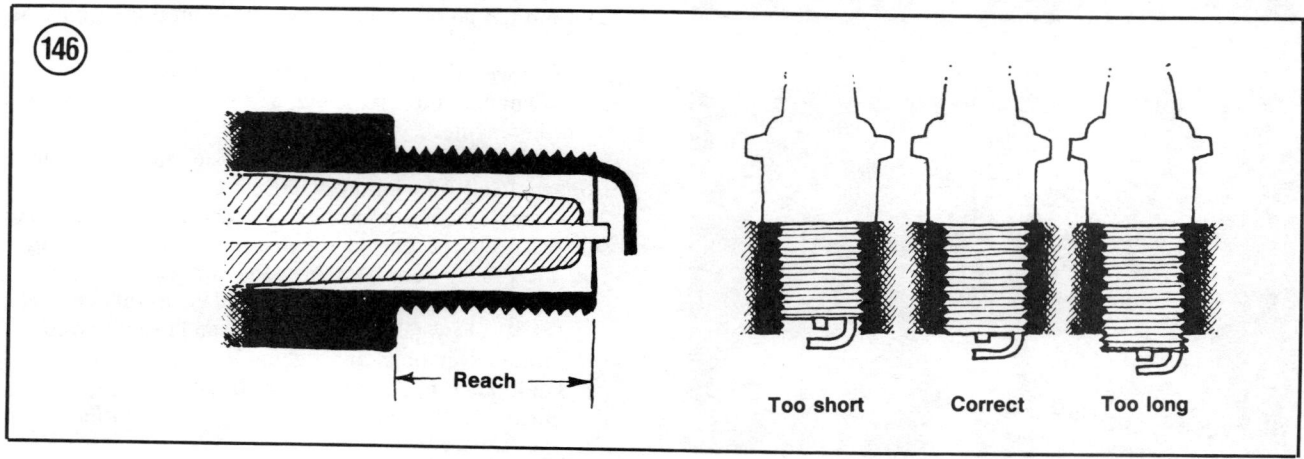

Reach

Too short   Correct   Too long

Select a plug of the heat range designed for the loads and temperature conditions under which the bike will be run. The use of incorrect heat ranges can cause a seized piston, scored cylinder wall or damaged piston crown.

In general, use a hot plug for low speeds, low engine loads and low temperatures. Use a cold plug for high speeds, high engine loads and high temperatures. The plug should operate hot enough to burn off unwanted deposits, but not so hot that it is damaged or causes preignition. A spark plug of the correct heat range will show a light tan color on the portion of the insulator within the cylinder after the plug has been in service.

The reach (length) of a spark plug (**Figure 146**) is also important. A longer than normal plug could interfere with

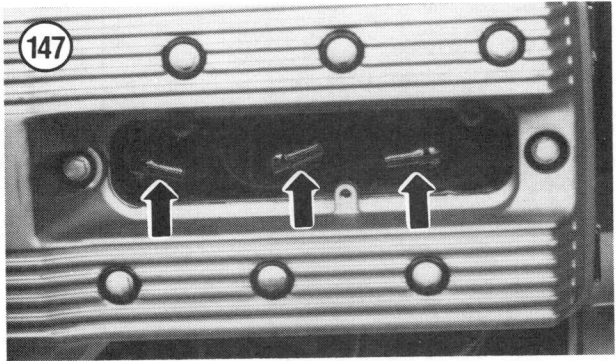

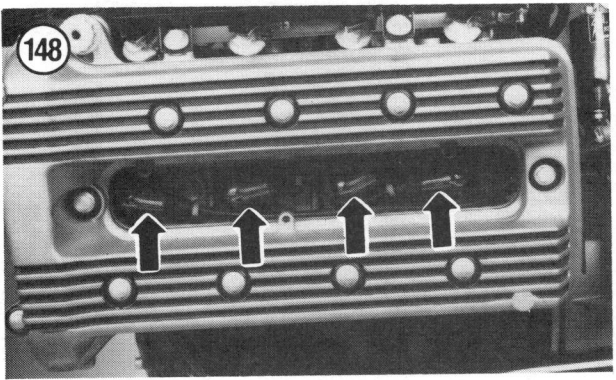

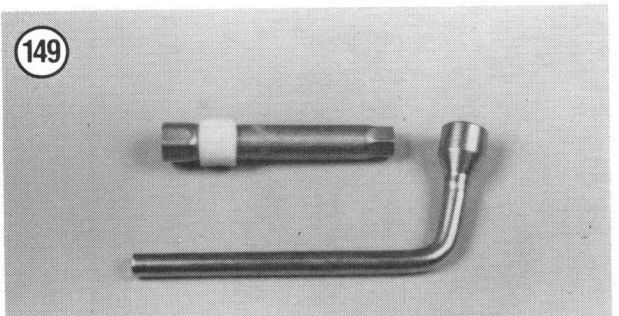

the valves and pistons, causing permanent and severe damage. The BMW factory recommends a single heat range for all conditions and it is listed in **Table 7**.

Spark Plug Removal/Inspection

CAUTION
Do not turn the engine over with the starter or try to run the engine with any of the spark plug leads disconnected. If this is done components within the ignition system will be damaged.

WARNING
Do not touch any of the spark plug leads or suppressors while the engine is running. The high voltage generated by this ignition system could lead to serious or fatal electrical shocks.

1. Place the bike on the center stand.
2. Remove the screws and lockwashers securing the spark plug cover panel and remove the panel. Refer to **Figure 121** for K75 models or **Figure 122** for K100 models.

CAUTION
Prior to removing the spark plug wires, note the routing of the wires within the cylinder head cavity. The wires must be rerouted in this manner to keep from being damaged.

3. Using a pair of slip joint pliers, pull on the metal suppressor cap on the spark plug wire and carefully remove the spark plug wire from each spark plug. Refer to **Figure 147** for K75 models or **Figure 148** for K100 models.

CAUTION
If any dirt falls into the cylinder when the plugs are removed, it could cause serious engine damage.

4. Use compressed air and blow away any dirt that may have accumulated in the cylinder head cavity around each spark plug well.

NOTE
Keep the spark plugs in the order from which they were removed (cylinder No. 1, No. 2, etc.). If one of the spark plugs shows signs of abnormal engine operation it is a good idea to know its cylinder number.

5. Remove the spark plug with the spark plug wrench and lug nut wrench (**Figure 149**) or a 18 mm spark plug wrench.

If using the BMW factory tools turn the spark plug wrench with the wheel lug nut wrench (**Figure 150**).

> *NOTE*
> *If plug is difficult to remove, apply penetrating oil around base of plug and let it soak in about 10-20 minutes.*

6. Inspect the spark plug carefully. Look for a broken center porcelain, excessively eroded electrodes and excessive carbon or oil fouling. Replace such a plug. If deposits are light, the plug may be cleaned in solvent with a wire brush or in a special spark plug sandblast cleaner.

7. Insert a wire feeler gauge between the center and the side electrode of the plug (**Figure 151**) and inspect the gap. The correct gap is listed in **Table 7**.

> *NOTE*
> *If the spark plug gap has opened to 0.9 mm (0.036 in.) it must be replaced. For optimum performance, replace all 3 or 4 spark plugs at the same time.*

8. If the gap is correct, you will feel a slight drag as you pull the wire through. If there is no drag or the gauge won't pass through, replace the spark plug as it *must not be gapped,* even with a spark plug gapping tool.

New Spark Plug Gapping and Installation

A new plug must be carefully gapped to ensure a reliable, consistent spark. You must use a special spark plug gapping tool with a round feeler gauge.

> *CAUTION*
> *BMW does **not** recommend regapping a used spark plug. They believe that the side electrode (ground) may be weakened and break off if it is adjusted after a spark plug has been in use.*
> ***Gap new spark plugs only.***

1. Remove the new plug from the box. If removed, install the small piece onto the spark plug (**Figure 152**). These are sometimes loose in the box and must be used.

2. Insert a round feeler gauge between the center and the side electrode of the plug (**Figure 151**). The correct gap is listed in **Table 7**.

3. If the gap is correct, you will feel a slight drag as you pull the wire through. If there is no drag or the gauge won't pass through, bend the side electrode *with the gapping tool* (**Figure 153**) to set the proper gap.

4. Put a *small* amount of oil or aluminum anti-seize compound (**Figure 154**) on the threads of the spark plug.

5. Screw the spark plug in by hand until it seats. Very little effort is required. If force is necessary, you have the plug cross-threaded; unscrew it and try again.

6A. If you are installing new spark plugs, tighten the spark plug an additional 1/2 turn after the gasket has made contact with the cylinder head. Then tighten to the torque specification listed in **Table 4**.

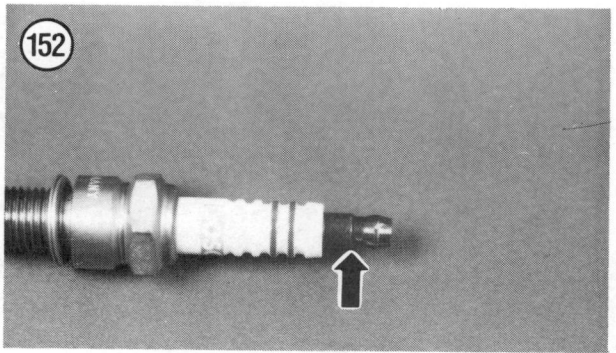

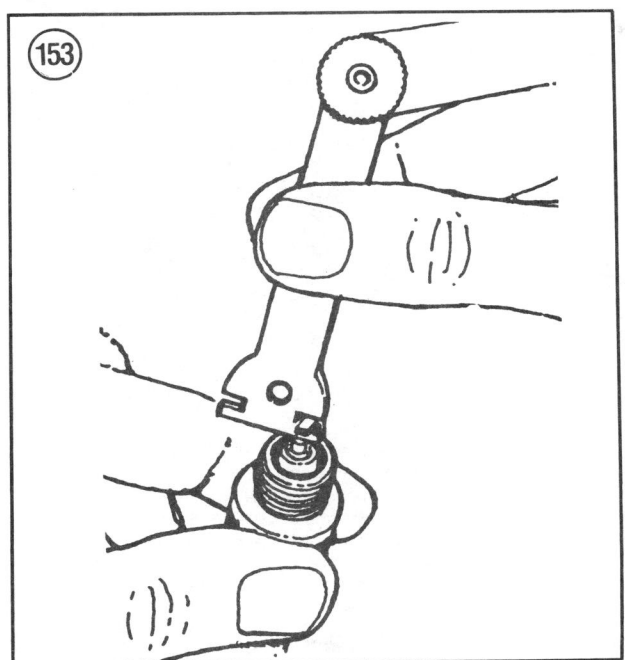

6B. If you are reinstalling old spark plugs and are reusing the old gaskets, tighten only an additional 1/4 turn after the gasket has made contact with the cylinder head.

CAUTION
*Do not overtighten. This will only squash the gasket and destroy its sealing ability. Overtightening may also lead to thread damage in the cylinder head which will require inserting a HeliCoil thread repair kit (**Figure 155**) or if damage is severe, a new cylinder head.*

7. Use a pair of slip joint pliers to install the spark plug wire and metal suppressor cap; make sure all wires are on tight.
8. Be sure to route the spark plug wires within the cylinder head cavity the same as they were, as noted during removal.
9. Install the spark plug cover panel and secure with the screws and lockwashers. Tighten the screws securely.
10. Start the bike and make sure it runs correctly.

Reading Spark Plugs

Much information about engine and spark plug performance can be determined by careful examination of the spark plugs. This information is more valid after performing the following steps.
1. Ride the bike about 6 miles (10 km) at moderate speeds to thoroughly warm up the engine.
2. Ride back to your work area where you can remove the spark plugs and examine them.
3. Turn the engine switch (**Figure 156**) to the OFF position, close the throttle and simultaneously pull in the clutch or shift to NEUTRAL; coast and brake to a stop.

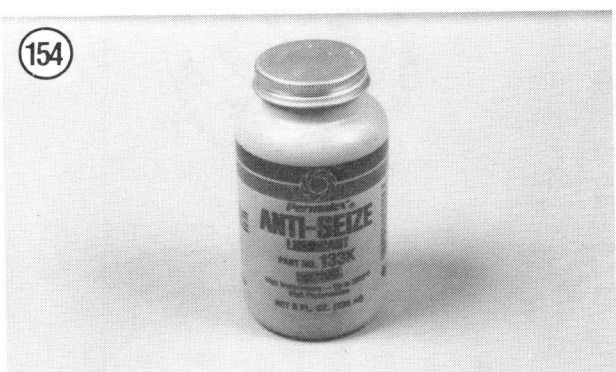

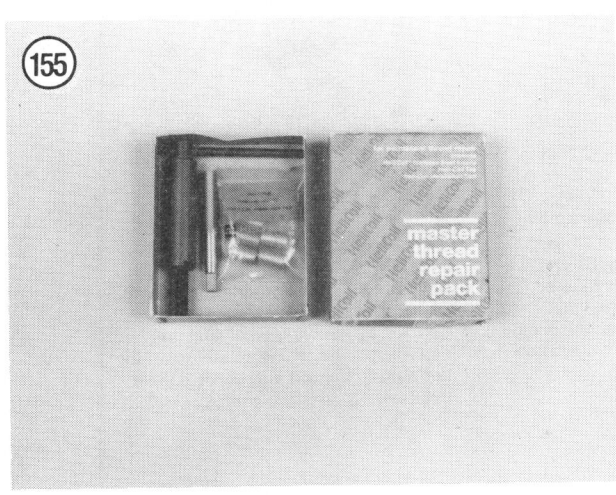

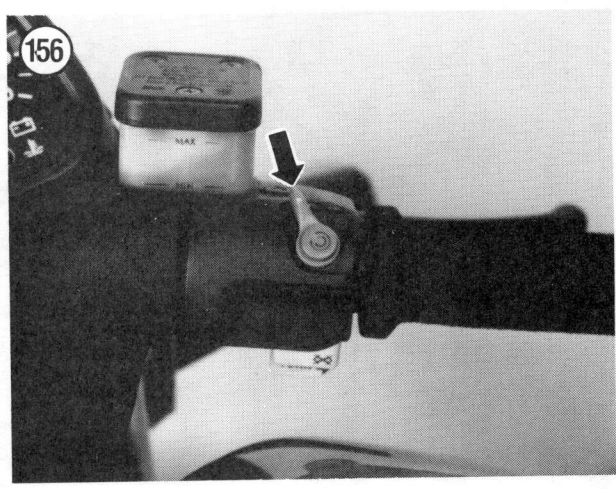

SPARK PLUG CONDITION

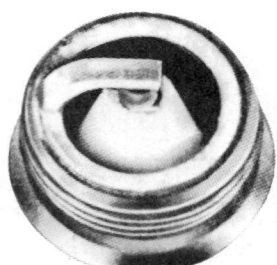

NORMAL

- Identified by light tan or gray deposits on the firing tip.
- Can be cleaned.

GAP BRIDGED

- Identified by deposit buildup closing gap between electrodes.
- Caused by oil or carbon fouling. If deposits are not excessive, the plug can be cleaned.

OIL FOULED

- Identified by wet black deposits on the insulator shell bore and electrodes.
- Caused by excessive oil entering combustion chamber through worn rings and pistons, excessive clearance between valve guides and stems, or worn or loose bearings. Can be cleaned. If engine is not repaired, use a hotter plug.

CARBON FOULED

- Identified by black, dry fluffy carbon deposits on insulator tips, exposed shell surfaces and electrodes.
- Caused by too cold a plug, weak ignition, dirty air cleaner, too rich a fuel mixture, or excessive idling. Can be cleaned.

LEAD FOULED

- Identified by dark gray, black, yellow, or tan deposits or a fused glazed coating on the insulator tip.
- Caused by highly leaded gasoline. Can be cleaned.

WORN

- Identified by severely eroded or worn electrodes.
- Caused by normal wear. Should be replaced.

FUSED SPOT DEPOSIT

- Identified by melted or spotty deposits resembling bubbles or blisters.
- Caused by sudden acceleration. Can be cleaned.

OVERHEATING

- Identified by a white or light gray insulator with small black or gray brown spots and with bluish-burnt appearance of electrodes.
- Caused by engine overheating, wrong type of fuel, loose spark plugs, too hot a plug, or incorrect ignition timing. Replace the plug.

PREIGNITION

- Identified by melted electrodes and possibly blistered insulator. Metallic deposits on insulator indicate engine damage.
- Caused by wrong type of fuel, incorrect ignition timing or advance, too hot a plug, burned valves, or engine overheating. Replace the plug.

4. Remove one spark plug at a time, as described in this chapter, and examine it. Compare it to the following and to **Figure 157**:

   a. If the plug has a light tan or gray colored deposit and no abnormal gap wear or electrode erosion is evident, the plug and the engine are running properly.

   b. If the plug is covered with soft, dry soot deposits, the fuel injection system is malfunctioning, probably with a too-rich mixture or a dirty or blocked air filter element. Also the spark plug heat range may be too cold.

   c. If the plug is brightly colored from overheating, the fuel injection system is malfunctioning, probably

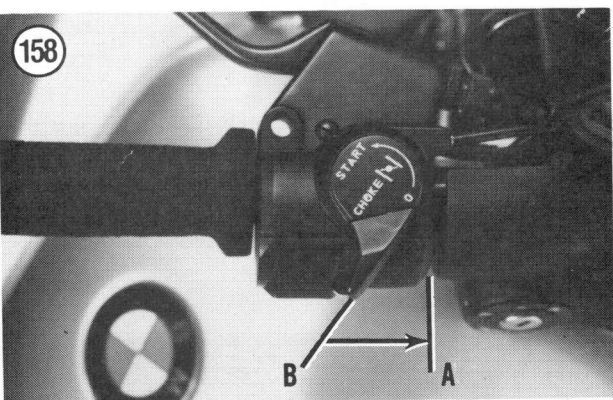

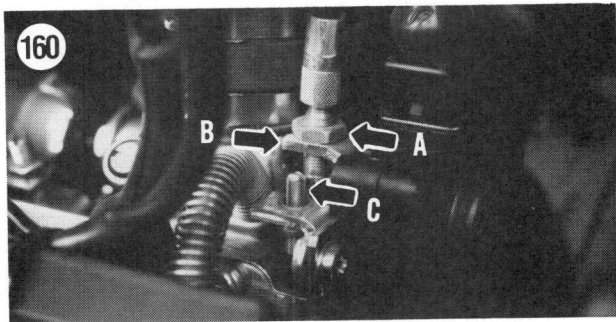

with a too-lean mixture. Also the ignition timing may be too far advanced or the spark plug heat range may be too high. There may also be deposits in the combustion chamber.

   d. If the plug exhibits a black insulator tip, a damp and oily film over the firing end and a carbon layer over the entire nose, it is oil fouled. Engine oil is passing by the valve guides or piston rings and fouling the plug. An oil fouled plug can be cleaned, but it is better to replace it.

5. If the existing spark plug is okay, reinstall it. If not, replace with a new one.

6. Repeat Step 4 and Step 5 for the remaining spark plugs. If any of the spark plugs are questionable, replace all 3 or 4 plugs as a set for maximum performance.

Fast Idle Adjustment For Cold Starting

NOTE
The choke lever and cable are used to increase engine idle speed during cold starting. It does not work like a choke mechanism used with carburetors.

Before making this adjustment, the air filter element must be clean and the engine must have adequate compression. See *Compression Test* in this chapter. Otherwise this procedure cannot be done properly.

1. On models equipped with a front fairing, remove the left-hand knee pad as described under *Front Fairing Removal/Installation* in Chapter Thirteen.

2. Move the choke lever to the all the way toward the front to the No. 1 position (A, **Figure 158**).

3. At the throttle linkage on the fuel injection throttle assembly, note the distance the idle stop screw (**Figure 159**) has moved up and away from its stop. The specified distance is as follows:

   a. K75 models: 1.5 mm (0.059 in.).

   b. K100 models: 1.0 mm (0.039 in.).

CAUTION
Do not try to adjust by turning the idle stop screw. This screw is not to be turned for this procedure. Adjustments are to be made at the choke cable adjuster at the end of the cable.

4. If the idle stop screw movement is not within specification, perform the following:

   a. At the end of the choke cable, loosen the choke cable adjuster locknut (A, **Figure 160**).

   b. Rotate the adjuster (B, **Figure 160**) in either direction until the correct dimension is obtained.

   c. Tighten the locknut securely (A, **Figure 160**).

5. Move the choke lever to the middle point or to the No. 2 position (B, **Figure 158**).

6. At the throttle linkage on the fuel injection throttle assembly, note the distance the idle stop screw (**Figure 159**) has moved up and away from its stop. The specified distance is as follows:

    a. K75 models: 3.0 mm (0.118 in.).

    b. K100 models: 2.5 mm (0.098 in.).

> *CAUTION*
> *Do not try to adjust by turning the idle stop screw. This screw is not to be turned for this procedure. Adjustments are to be made at the threaded stud adjuster next to the end of the choke cable.*

7. If the idle stop movement is not within specification, turn the threaded stud adjuster (C, **Figure 160**) in either direction until the correct dimension is obtained.

8. On models so equipped, install the left-hand knee pad as described under *Front Fairing Removal/Installation* in Chapter Thirteen.

Idle Speed Adjustment

Before making this adjustment, the air filter element must be clean and the engine must have adequate compression. See *Compression Test* in this chapter. Otherwise this procedure cannot be done properly.

1. Perform *Throttle Housing Butterfly Synchronization* as described in Chapter Seven.

2. Start the engine and let it reach normal operating temperature. Usually 10-15 minutes of stop-and-go riding is sufficient. Make sure the choke lever is moved all the way back toward the hand grip in the open position (**Figure 161**).

3. Turn the engine off and place the bike on the center stand.

4. On models so equipped, remove the left-hand knee pad as described under *Front Fairing Removal/Installation* in Chapter Thirteen.

5. Connect a portable tachometer following the manufacturer's instructions.

6. Start the engine and note the idle speed. The recommended idle speed is listed in **Table 7**.

7. Turn the idle adjust screw (**Figure 159**) in or out to adjust the idle speed to the correct speed.

8. Open and close the throttle a couple of times; check for variations in idle speed. Readjust if necessary.

> *WARNING*
> *With the engine running at idle speed, move the handlebar from side to side. If the idle speed increases during this movement, the throttle cable may need adjusting or it may be incorrectly routed through the frame. Correct this problem immediately. Do **not** ride the bike in this unsafe condition.*

9. Disconnect the portable tachometer.

10. After the idle speed is correctly adjusted, start the engine and let it idle. Slightly rotate the throttle grip. There should be a "click" coming from the idle switch as the throttle cable free play has been taken up. If there is no click, the idle adjust screw is turned in too far and must be backed out.

Table 1 MAINTENANCE SCHEDULE *

Perform these procedures at specific monthly intervals. This is especially true if the bike is not routinely ridden.

Every 3 months	•Check the battery electrolyte level. Refill if necessary.
Every 3 months or at least every 2,000 miles (1242 km).	•Change engine oil and filter if the bike is used at outside temperatures below 0° C (32° F)
Every 6 months	•Change engine oil and filter if the bike is used for short trips only. •Lubricate the clutch splines and input shaft splines if bike is used in high humidity areas. Perform this procedure if clutch operation is erratic.
Every 12 months	•Change engine oil and filter. •Change transmission oil. •Change final drive oil. •Change front fork oil. •Change brake fluid and bleed the brake system. •Lubricate the clutch splines and input shaft splines. Perform this procedure if clutch operation is erratic.
Every 2 years	•Drain and replace engine coolant.
Before each ride	•Inspect tire and rim condition. •Check tire inflation pressure. •Check fuel supply. Make sure there is enough fuel for the intended ride. •Check brake operation and for fluid leakage. •Check for fuel leakage. •Check coolant level and for coolant leakage. •Check the oil level in the engine, transmission and final drive unit. •Check for smooth clutch and throttle operation. •Check for smooth gearshift operation. •Check steering for smooth operation with no excessive play or restrictions. •Check headlight, taillight/brake light and turn signal operation. •Check horn operation.
Every 4,500 miles (7,240 km)	•Change engine oil and filter •Check battery electrolyte level •Make sure battery cables are clean and properly secured. •Check spark plug condition and gap. Do *not* regap. •Clean or replace air filter element if bike is ridden in dirty or dusty conditions.

(continued)

3

Table 1 MAINTENANCE SCHEDULE (continued)

Every 4500 miles (7,240 km) (cont.)	• Lubricate clutch cable nipples at each end. • Check all fuel line connections for wetness or damage. Tighten hose clamps if necessary. • Check the fuel tank vent and drain lines. • Check brake fluid level in master cylinder(s). • Check all brake lines and hoses for leakage or damage. • Check brake pads for wear. • Check brake discs for wear or damage. • Check brake rear brake drum and linings for wear. • Check and adjust clutch if necessary. • Lubricate control cables. • Lubricate center stand and sidestand pivot points. • Inspect tire tread depth and inflation pressure. • Check tightness of rear wheel mounting bolts. • Check tightness of muffler heat shield bolts. • Check tightness of sidestand pivot bolt. • Check for smooth clutch and throttle operation. • Check for smooth gearshift operation. • Check steering for smooth operation with no excessive play or restrictions. • Check and adjust engine idle speed. • Check all running and illumination lights. • Check horn operation.
Every 8,500 miles (13,680 km)	• Replace all spark plugs. • Check valve clearance. • Check ignition timing. • Run a compression test. • Replace air filter element. • Replace fuel filter if poor quality fuel has been used. • Replace transmission oil. • Replace final drive oil. • Replace front fork oil. • Check and adjust throttle free play. • Check and adjust brake pedal height. • Check coolant level and antifreeze percentage. • Clean speedometer inductive sensor in final drive unit. • Check and adjust steering head bearings. • Check and adjust swing arm bearing play. • Check wheel bearings. • Check tightness of front axle bolt and clamping bolts. • Check tightness of sidestand and center stand pivot bolts. • Check tightness of shock absorber mounting bolts

(continued)

Table 1 MAINTENANCE SCHEDULE (continued)

Every 8,500 miles (13,680 km) (cont.)	•Check tightness of engine mounting bolts and nuts •Check tightness of exhaust system fasteners.
Every 16,000 miles	•Replace the fuel filter (25,750 km)
Every 25,000 miles	•Replace the steering stem bearings (40,232 km)

* This BMW factory maintenance schedule should be considered as a guide to general maintenance and lubrication intervals. Harder than normal use and exposure to mud, water, sand, high humidity, etc. will naturally dictate more frequent attention to most maintenance items.

3

Table 2 TIRE INFLATION PRESSURE (COLD)*

	Rider only		Rider and passenger	
Model	psi	kPa	psi	kPa
K75, K75C				
No speed limit				
Front	29	200	33	230
Rear	36	250	42	290
K75S				
No speed limit				
Front	32.5	225	—	—
Rear	36	250	—	—
Up to 112 mph (180 kmh)				
Front	—	—	32.5	225
Rear	—	—	39	270
Over 112 mph (180 kmh)				
Front	—	—	39	270
Rear	—	—	42	290
K100 (all models)				
No speed limit				
Front	32.5	225	—	—
Rear	36	250	—	—
Up to 112 mph (180 kmh)				
Front	—	—	32.5	225
Rear	—	—	39	270
Over 112 mph (180 kmh)				
Front	—	—	39	270
Rear	—	—	42	290

(continued)

Table 2 TIRE INFLATION PRESSURE (COLD)* (continued)

Model	Rider only		Rider and Passenger	
	psi	kPa	psi	kPa
VR-Rated Tires**				
K100 (all models)				
No speed limit				
Front	37	255	—	—
Rear	40.5	280	—	—
Up to 112 mph (180 kmh)				
Front	—	—	37	255
Rear	—	—	43.5	300
Over 112 mph (180 kmh)				
Front	—	—	43.5	300
Rear	—	—	46	320

* Tire inflation pressure for factory equipped tires. Aftermarket tires may require different inflation pressure.
** BMW does not recommend installing VR-rated tires on the K75 models.

Table 3 STATE OF CHARGE

Specific Gravity	State of Charge
1.110-1.130	Discharged
1.140-1.160	Almost discharged
1.170-1.190	One-quarter charged
1.200-1.220	One-half charged
1.230-1.250	Three-quarters charged
1.260-1.280	Fully charged

Table 4 MAINTENANCE AND TUNE-UP TORQUE SPECIFICATIONS

Item	N•m	ft.-lb.
Oil drain plug	20	15
Oil filter cover Allen bolts	10	7
Oil pan Allen bolts	10	7
Cylinder head cover bolts	10	7
Spark plug	20	15

Table 5 OIL QUANTITY AND RECOMMENDED TYPE

Item	Quantity	Recommended type
Engine oil		
Oil change	3.5 liter (3.7 qt.)	API SF or SG
Oil change and filter	3.75 liter (4.0 qt.)	
Transmission oil	0.85 liter (0.9 qt.)	Hypoid gear oil GL5
		SAE 90 above 5° C
		(41° F)
		SAE 80 below 5° C
		(41° F)
		SAE 80W 90 (optional)
Final drive unit oil		
Overhaul	0.25 liter (0.26 qt.)	Hypoid gear oil GL5
Oil change	0.23 liter (0.24 qt.)	SAE 90 above 5° C
		(41° F)
		SAE 80 below 5° C
		(41° F)
		SAE 80W-90 (optional)
Front fork oil		
K75 models (1986-1989)		Bel-Ray SAE5, Castrol Extra
Standard	320-330 cc	Light, Castrol DB Hydraulic
	(10.7-11 oz.)	Fluid, Castrol Shock Absorber
		Oil 1/318, Castrol LMH, Golden
Sport suspension	270-290 cc	Spectro Very Light, Mobil Aero
	(9.23-9.8 oz.)	HFA, Mobil DTE 11, Shell Aero
		Fluid 4, Shell 4001
K100	320-330 cc (10.7-11 oz.)	
K100RS, K100RS (ABS),		
K100RT, K100LT, K100LT (ABS)		
Standard	350-360 cc (11.7-12 oz.)	
Sport suspension	270-290 cc (10.7-11 oz.)	

Table 6 COOLANT CAPACITY AND MIXING RATIO

Capacity	
Engine and radiator	
K75	2.5 liters (2.6 qts.)
K100 and K1100	3.0 liters (3.2 qts.)
Recovery tank	0.4 liters (0.8 qt.)
Anti-freeze/water ratio	
Temperature down to -28° C (-18° F)	60% distilled water
	40% BMW anti-freeze
Temperatures below -36° C (-31° F)	50% distilled water
	50% BMW anti-freeze
* BMW does not provide coolant ratio specifications for -29° to -35° C.	

Table 7 TUNE-UP SPECIFICATIONS

Valve clearance *
  Intake: 0.15-0.20 mm (0.006-0.008 in.)
  Exhaust: 0.25-0.30 mm (0.010-0.012 in.)
Spark plug type
  Bosch X5DC or Champion A 85 YC
Spark plug gap
  Recommended 0.6-0.7 mm (0.024-0.028 in.)
  Maximum gap limit 0.9 mm (0.036 in.)
Compression pressure
  Good: more than 1012 kPa (145 psi)
  Normal: 848-1012 kPa (123-145 psi)
  Poor: less than 848 kPa (123 psi)
Idle speed 900-1,000 rpm

* Cylinder head maximum temperature: 35° C (95° F).

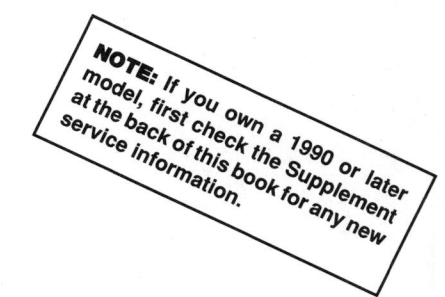
CHAPTER FOUR

4

ENGINES

The BMW K-Series bikes are equipped with a liquid-cooled, 4-stroke, 3 or 4 cylinder engine with double overhead camshafts. The camshafts are chain-driven from the drive sprocket on the front end of the crankshaft.

This chapter provides procedures for complete service and overhaul including information for removal, disassembly, inspection, service and reassembly of the engine. Although the clutch is located within the engine, it is covered in Chapter Five to simplify this material.

Service procedures for all models are virtually the same. The engine used in this chapter is a 4 cylinder from a K100 model. Where differences occur they are identified.

Before starting any work, re-read Chapter One of this book. You will do a better job with this information fresh in your mind.

Throughout the text there is frequent mention of the right-hand and left-hand side of the engine. This refers to the engine as it sits in the bike's frame, *not* as it sits on your workbench. "Right-" and "left-hand" refer to a rider sitting on the seat facing forward.

Refer to **Table 1** for complete specifications for the 3-cylinder 740 cc engine or to **Table 2** for the 4-cylinder 980 cc engine. Tables 1-5 are located at the end of this chapter.

ENGINE PRINCIPLES

Figure 1 explains how the engine works. This will be helpful when troubleshooting or repairing the engine.

SERVICING ENGINE IN FRAME

The following components can be serviced while the engine is mounted in the frame (the bike's frame is a great holding fixture for breaking loose stubborn bolts and nuts):
a. Fuel injection assembly.
b. Exhaust system.
c. Alternator and starter.
d. Camshafts and cylinder head.
e. Hall transmitter.

ENGINE REMOVAL/INSTALLATION

Engine removal and installation is the opposite of most current Japanese bikes. With the BMW, the frame is removed from the engine instead of removing the engine from the frame. The engine, clutch and transmission housing should remain as a complete unit, then be disassembled after the frame is removed. The clutch and transmission housing can be removed from the frame as an assembly leaving the engine in the frame. The engine *cannot* be removed leaving the clutch and transmission housing in the frame. This is due to the various frame mounting points and where they attach to these components.

> *WARNING*
> *Due to the size and weight of parts to be removed, this procedure requires at least 3 people.*

1. Remove the seat as described under *Seat Removal/Installation* in Chapter Thirteen.

① **4-STROKE OPERATING PRINCIPLES**

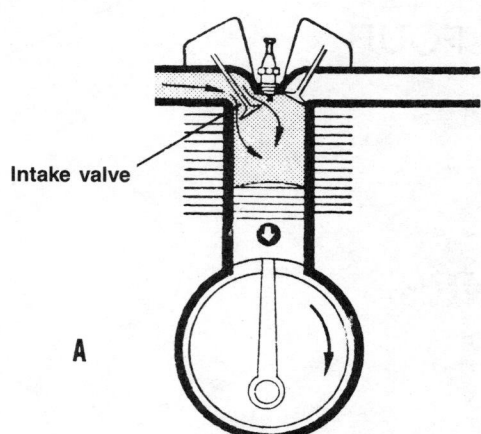

Intake valve

A

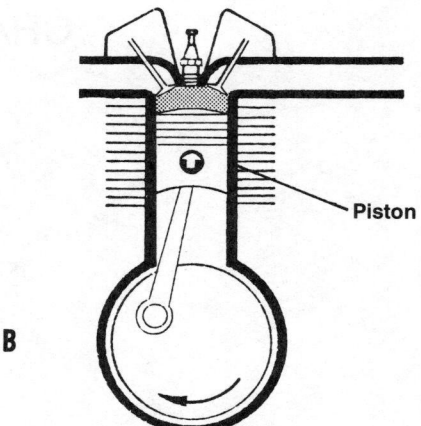

Piston

B

As the piston travels downward, the exhaust valve is closed and the intake valve opens, allowing the new fuel/air mixture to be drawn into the cylinder. When the piston reaches the bottom of its travel (bottom dead center or BDC), the intake valve closes and remains closed for the next revolution-and-a-half of the crankshaft.

While the crankshaft continues to rotate, the piston moves upward, compressing the fuel/air mixture.

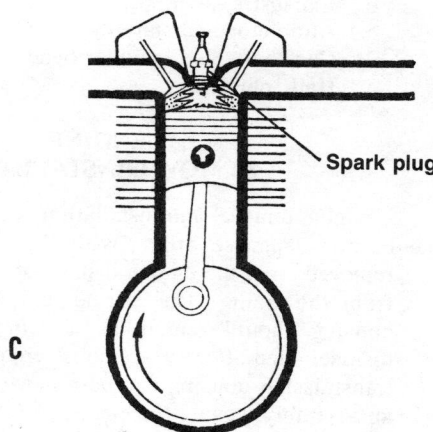

Spark plug

C

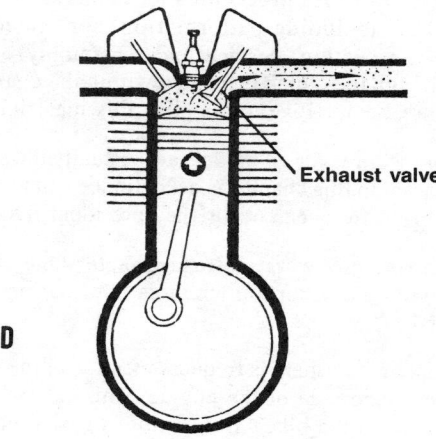

Exhaust valve

D

As the piston almost reaches the top of its travel, the spark plug fires, igniting the compressed fuel/air mixture. The piston continues to top dead center (TDC) and is pushed downward by the expanding gases.

When the piston almost reaches BDC, the exhaust valve opens and remains open until the piston is near TDC. The upward travel of the piston causes the exhaust gases to be pushed out of the cylinder. After the piston has reached TDC, the exhaust valve closes and the cycle starts all over again.

2. On models so equipped, remove the front fairing as described under *Front Fairing Removal/Installation* in Chapter Thirteen.

3. Remove the fuel tank as described under *Fuel Tank Removal/Installation* in Chapter Seven.

4. Remove the battery as described under *Battery* in Chapter Three.

5. Remove the exhaust system as described under *Exhaust System Removal/Installation* in Chapter Seven.

6. Remove the fuel injection control unit as described under *Fuel Injection Control Unit Removal/Installation* in Chapter Seven.

7. Drain the engine oil and remove the oil filter as described under *Engine Oil and Filter Change* in Chapter Three.

8. Drain the engine coolant as described under *Coolant Change* in Chapter Three.

9. Remove the radiator and coolant hoses as described under *Radiator Removal/Installation* in Chapter Nine.

10. Remove the rear cowl as described under *Rear Cowl Removal/Installation* in Chapter Thirteen.

11. Remove the rear fender as described under *Rear Fender Removal/Installation* in Chapter Thirteen.

12. Loosen the adjusting barrel at the clutch hand lever and disconnect the clutch cable from the hand lever.

13. Disconnect the clutch cable from the clutch release arm.

14. Disconnect the following electrical connectors:
   a. Alternator.
   b. Starter.
   c. Hall transmitter.
   d. Oil pressure indicator switch.
   e. Choke electrical switch.
   f. Ground strap.
   g. Oil pressure switch.
   h. Neutral indicator switch.

15. Disconnect the throttle cable from the throttle housing as described under *Throttle Cable Replacement* in Chapter Seven.

16. Disconnect the choke cable from the throttle housing as described under *Choke Cable Replacement* in Chapter Seven.

17. Remove the coolant recovery tank as described under *Coolant Recovery Tank Removal/Installation* in Chapter Nine.

18. Remove both footpeg assemblies as described under *Footpegs Removal/Installation* in Chapter Thirteen.

NOTE
If you are just removing the engine and are not planning to disassemble it, do not perform Step 19.

19. If the engine is going to be disassembled, remove the following parts while the engine is still in the frame. Removal is described in this chapter unless otherwise noted:
   a. Alternator and starter (Chapter Eight).
   b. Camshafts and cylinder head.
   c. Hall transmitter (Chapter Eight).

20. Take a final look all over the engine to make sure everything has been disconnected.

21. Place a suitable size jack, with a piece of wood to protect the oil pan, under the engine. Apply a small amount of jack pressure up on the engine, clutch and transmission housing assembly.

22. Remove the bolts and washers securing the center stand and sidestand assembly and remove the assembly.

CAUTION
Continually adjust jack pressure during engine removal and installation to prevent damage to the mounting bolt threads and hardware.

23. Refer to **Figure 2** and remove the following mounting bolts, nuts and washers:
   a. Right-hand front bolt and washer (**Figure 3**).
   b. Right-hand upper rear bolt and washer (A, **Figure 4**).
   c. Right-hand lower rear bolt and washer (B, **Figure 4**).
   d. Left-hand front bolt and washer (**Figure 5**).
   e. Left-hand rear bolt and washer (**Figure 6**).

WARNING
The following steps require the aid of at least 2 helpers to safely remove the front fork, front wheel and frame assembly from the engine assembly.

24. Have one of the assistants hold onto the engine assembly, then gradually raise the frame assembly up and off of the engine assembly. Move the frame away from the engine and place it where it will be stored.

25. A special BMW tool (part No. 46 5 620) is available to fit onto the rear frame down tubes and hold the frame assembly in its normal attitude just as though it was attached to the engine assembly. This tool is expensive and is unnecessary. With the front wheel on the ground, carefully rest the rear sections of the frame on wood blocks on the floor.

26. If necessary, remove the transmission housing from the engine as described under *Transmission Housing Removal/Installation* in Chapter Six.

27. If necessary, remove the clutch assembly from the engine as described under *Clutch Removal* in Chapter Five.

28. Install by reversing these removal steps, noting the following.

29. Tighten the engine-to-frame mounting bolts to the torque specifications in **Table 3**.

30. Fill the engine with the recommended type and quantity of oil; refer to Chapter Three.

31. Fill the engine with the recommended type and quantity of coolant; refer to Chapter Three.

32. Adjust the clutch as described under *Clutch Adjustment* in Chapter Three.

33. Start the engine and check for leaks.

4

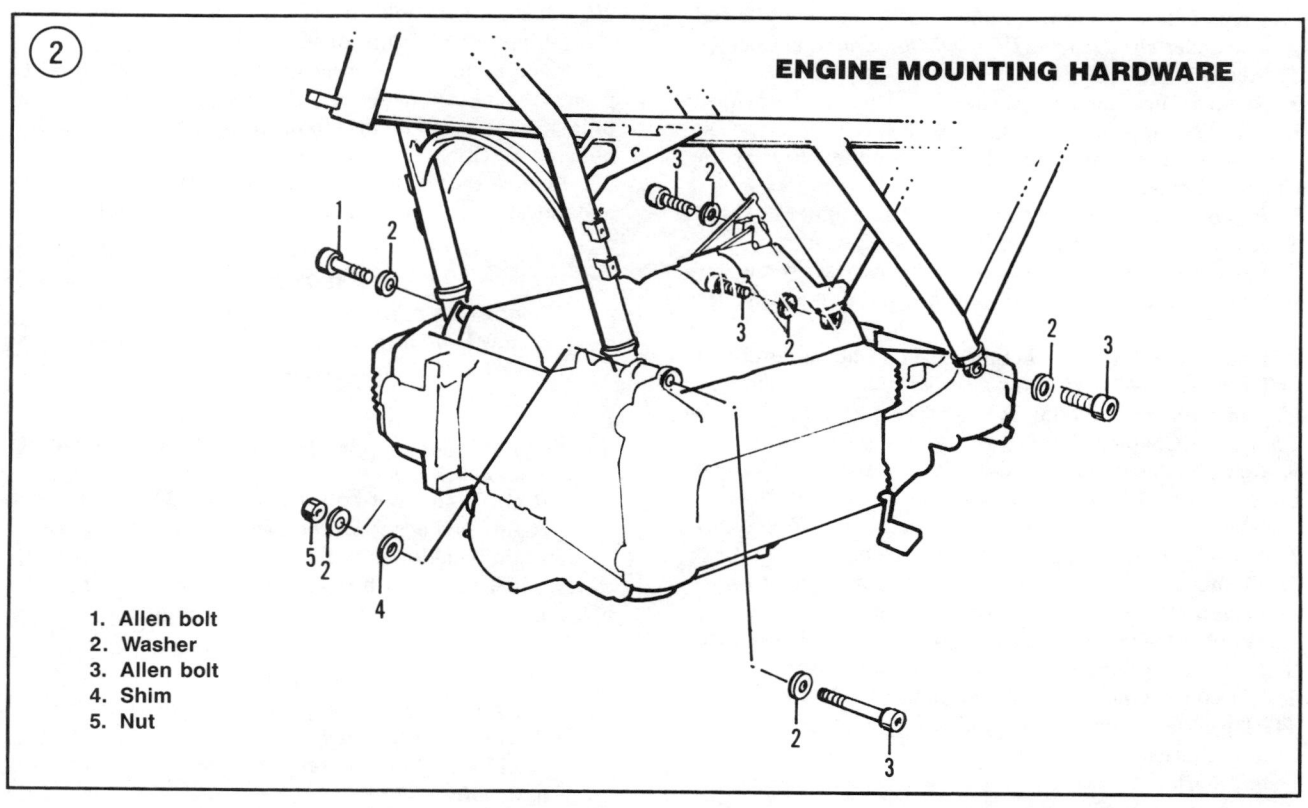

② ENGINE MOUNTING HARDWARE

1. Allen bolt
2. Washer
3. Allen bolt
4. Shim
5. Nut

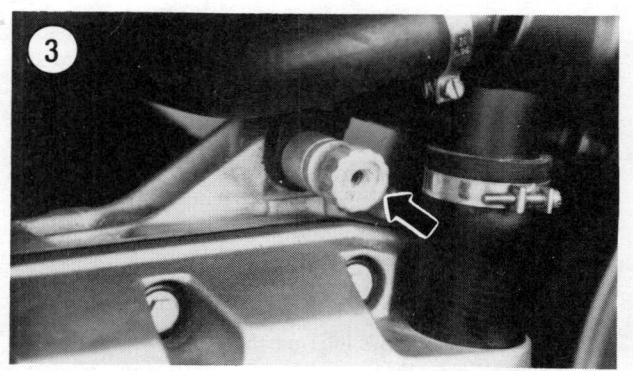

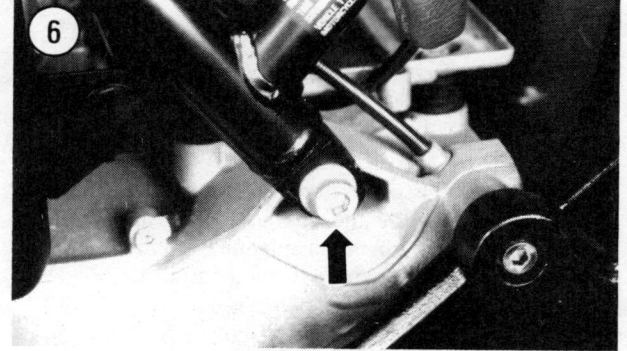

CRANKSHAFT COVER, CYLINDER HEAD COVER AND TIMING CHAIN COVER

Removal

> *NOTE*
> *This procedure is necessary for cylinder head removal.*

Refer to the following illustrations for this procedure:
a. **Figure 7**: Crankshaft cover.
b. **Figure 8**: Cylinder head cover.
c. **Figure 9**: Timing chain cover.
1. Place the bike on the center stand.
2. On models so equipped, remove the engine spoiler as described under *Engine Spoiler Removal/Installation* in Chapter Thirteen.
3. On models so equipped, remove the lower sections of the front fairing and/or the radiator trim panel as described in Chapter Thirteen.
4. Drain the engine oil and remove the oil filter as described under *Engine Oil and Filter Change* in Chapter Three.

5. Drain the engine coolant as described under *Coolant Change* in Chapter Three.
6. Loosen both clamps (**Figure 10**) on the front coolant hose that travels through the crankshaft cover. Move the clamps back off of the fittings and onto the hose.

> *NOTE*
> *The following steps are shown with the engine removed from the frame and the fuel injection assembly removed for clarity. It is not necessary to remove the engine to remove the crankcase cover, cylinder head cover and timing chain cover.*

7. Using a crisscross pattern, loosen then remove the bolts securing the crankshaft cover (**Figure 11**) and remove the cover and gasket. Don't lose the rubber grommets under the bolts.
8. Remove the Hall transmitter unit as described under *Hall Transmitter Unit Replacement* in Chapter Eight.
9. If the engine is still in the frame, disconnect and remove the spark plug secondary wires as described under *Spark Plug Secondary Wires Replacement* in Chapter Eight.

4

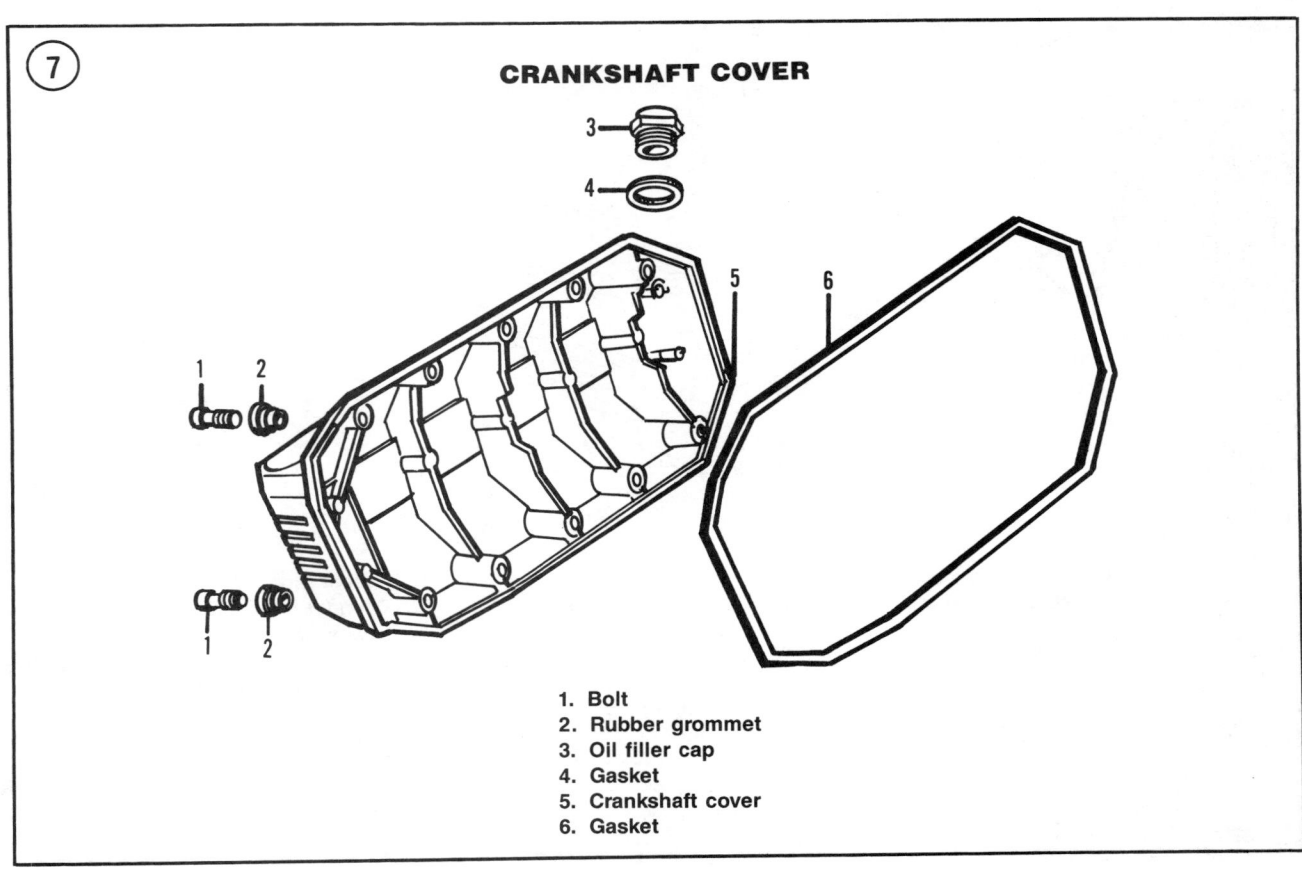

⑦ **CRANKSHAFT COVER**

1. Bolt
2. Rubber grommet
3. Oil filler cap
4. Gasket
5. Crankshaft cover
6. Gasket

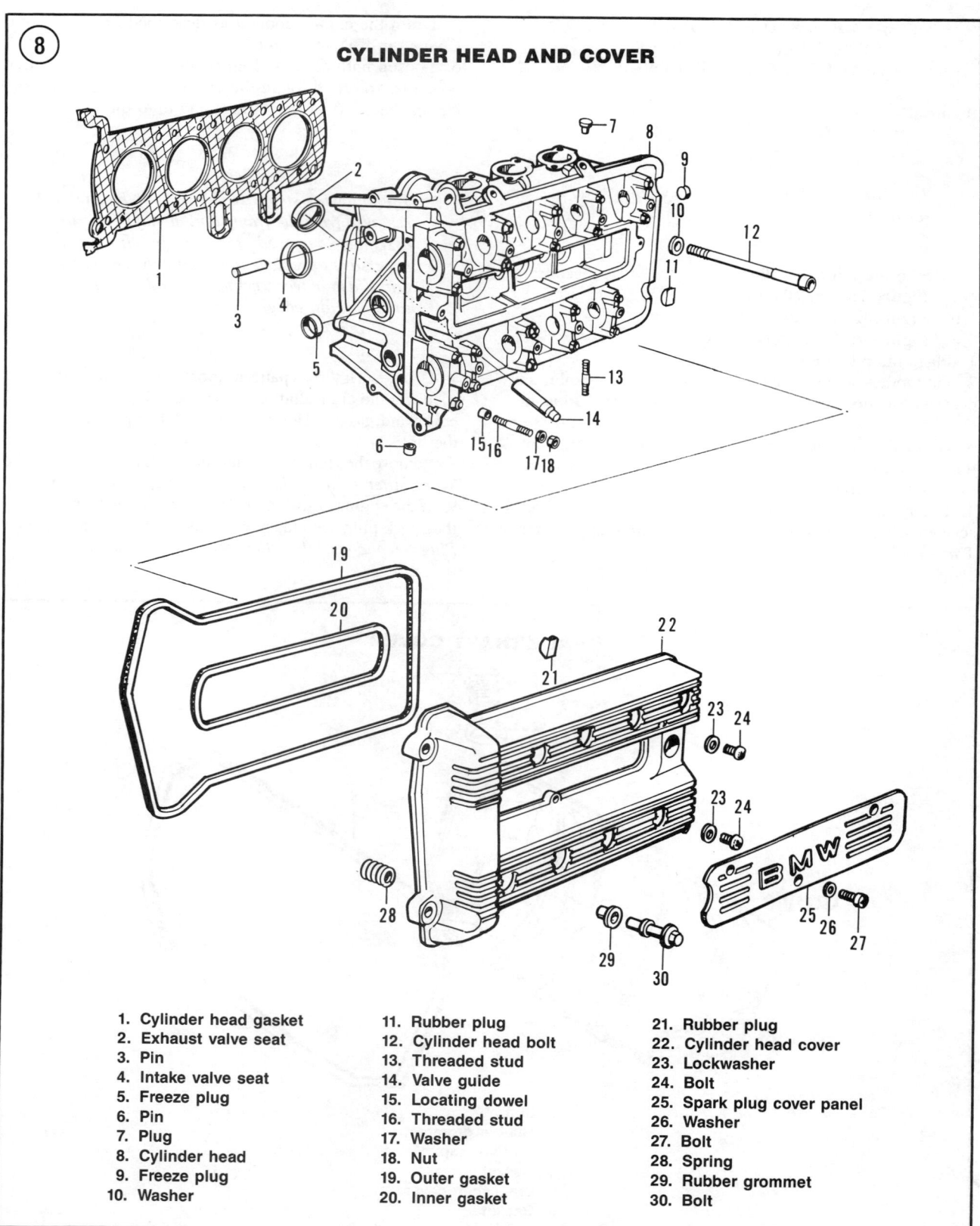

⑧   **CYLINDER HEAD AND COVER**

1. Cylinder head gasket	11. Rubber plug	21. Rubber plug
2. Exhaust valve seat	12. Cylinder head bolt	22. Cylinder head cover
3. Pin	13. Threaded stud	23. Lockwasher
4. Intake valve seat	14. Valve guide	24. Bolt
5. Freeze plug	15. Locating dowel	25. Spark plug cover panel
6. Pin	16. Threaded stud	26. Washer
7. Plug	17. Washer	27. Bolt
8. Cylinder head	18. Nut	28. Spring
9. Freeze plug	19. Outer gasket	29. Rubber grommet
10. Washer	20. Inner gasket	30. Bolt

⑨ TIMING CHAIN COVER

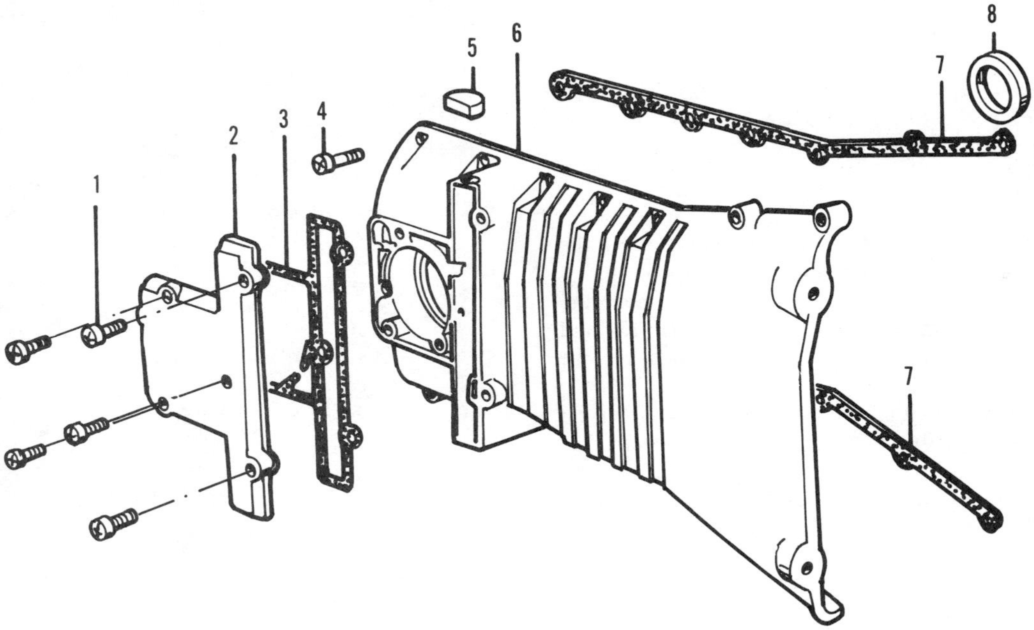

1. Bolt
2. Hall transmitter cover
3. Gasket
4. Bolt
5. Rubber plug
6. Timing chain cover
7. Gasket (models so equipped)
8. Oil seal

4

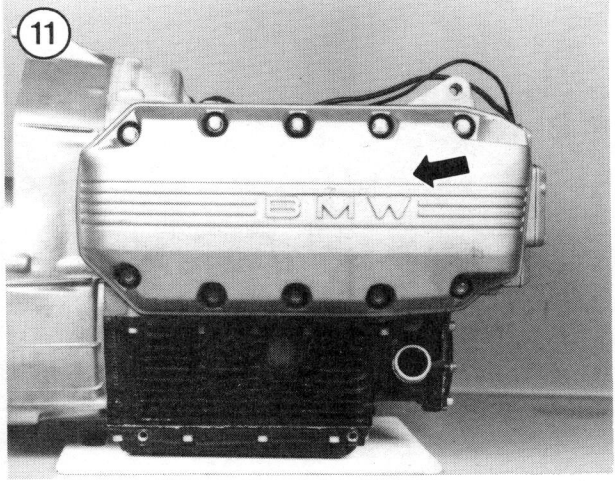

10. Using a crisscross pattern, loosen then remove the bolts securing the cylinder head cover (**Figure 12**) and remove the cover and gaskets. Don't lose the rubber grommets under the bolts or the single ground spring (**Figure 13**) on one of the camshaft bearing caps.

NOTE
Some early models were equipped with a gasket under the cover on each side. If so equipped, discard the gaskets as they must be replaced.

11. Unhook the rubber grommet (**Figure 14**) securing the oil pressure warning light wire to the cover.

12. Using a crisscross pattern, loosen, then remove the bolts securing the timing chain cover (**Figure 15**) and partially remove the cover. On models so equipped, remove the gaskets.

13. Carefully pull the oil pressure warning light electrical wire through the opening in the timing chain cover (**Figure 16**).

14. Pull the timing chain cover straight forward and off of the crankshaft boss and remove the cover from the engine. Don't lose the locating dowels. It is not necessary to remove them if they are secure in either the cover or the cylinder block.

Installation

1. Remove all old sealant or gasket residue from the mating surfaces of the timing chain cover (**Figure 17**) and engine. Finish off by cleaning the surfaces with an aerosol electrical contact cleaner and wipe with lint-free cloth.

2A. On models without gaskets, apply Three Bond No. 1216 gasket sealer to gasket surfaces of the timing chain cover following the manufacturer's instructions.

2B. On models equipped with gaskets, install new gaskets onto the timing chain cover.

3. Be sure to install the oil pressure warning light electrical wire through the opening in the timing chain cover (**Figure 16**).

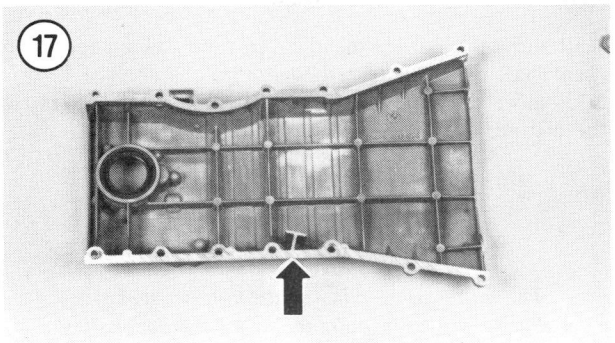

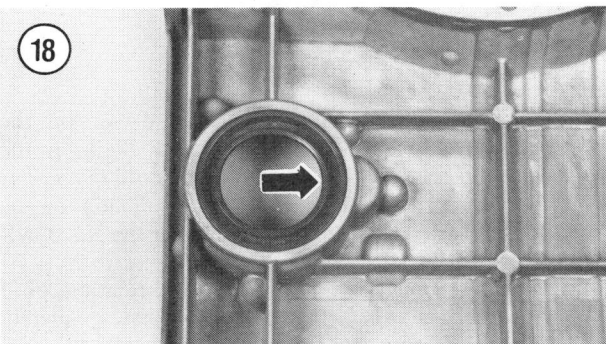

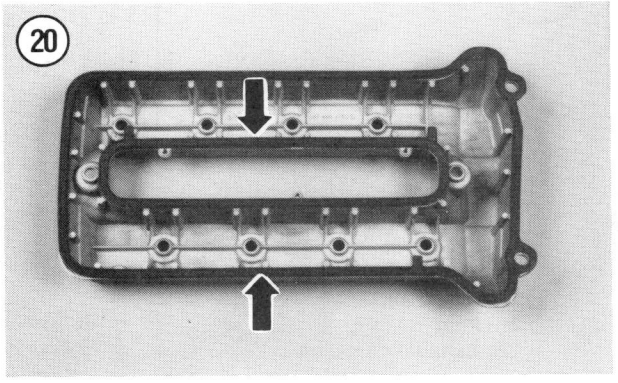

4. Apply a light coat of clean engine oil to the crankshaft boss oil seal (**Figure 18**) on the timing chain cover.

5. Make sure the locating dowels (**Figure 19**) are in place, then install the timing chain cover straight onto the engine. Do not damage the oil seal during cover installation onto the crankshaft boss.

6. Install the bolts and using a crisscross pattern, tighten the bolts to the torque specification listed in **Table 3**.

7. Install the Hall transmitter unit as described under *Hall Transmitter Unit Replacement* in Chapter Eight.

8. Inspect the rubber gaskets (**Figure 20**) around the inner and outer perimeter of the cylinder head cover. If they are starting to harden or deteriorate they should be replaced as a set. Replace as a set even if only one is bad.

9. Make sure the single ground spring (**Figure 13**) is still installed on one of the camshaft bearing caps. It can be installed on any one of the bearing caps.

10. Install the cylinder head cover, rubber grommets and bolts. Be sure to install the rubber grommet under each bolt or there will be an oil leak.

11. Using a crisscross pattern, tighten the bolts to the torque specification listed in **Table 3**.

12. If the engine is still in the frame, install and connect the spark plug secondary wires as described under *Spark Plug Secondary Wires Replacement* in Chapter Eight.

13. Remove all old sealant residue from the mating surfaces of the crankshaft cover and the engine. Finish off by cleaning the surfaces with an aerosol electrical contact cleaner and wipe with a lint-free cloth.

14. Apply Three Bond No. 1216 gasket sealer to gasket surfaces where the cylinder block meets the intermediate housing (A, **Figure 21**) and where it meets the timing chain cover (B, **Figure 21**). This is to prevent an oil leak where these parts meet.

NOTE
While the crankshaft cover is removed, inspect the coolant hose that runs through it for damage or deterioration. Replace if necessary.

15. Inspect the rubber gasket around the outer perimeter of the crankshaft cover. If it is starting to deteriorate or harden it should be replaced.

16. Install the crankshaft cover, the bolts and the rubber grommets. Be sure to install the rubber grommet under each bolt or there will be an oil leak.

17. Using a crisscross pattern, tighten the bolts securing the crankshaft cover (**Figure 11**). Tighten the bolts securely.

18. Install the front coolant hose onto the fittings and move the clamps (**Figure 10**) into position. Tighten the hose clamps securely.

19. Refill the engine coolant as described under *Coolant Change* in Chapter Three.

20. Refill the engine oil as described under *Engine Oil and Filter Change* in Chapter Three.

21. On models so equipped, install the lower sections of the front fairing and/or the radiator trim panel as described in Chapter Thirteen.

22. On models so equipped, install the engine spoiler as described under *Engine Spoiler Removal/Installation* in Chapter Thirteen.

CAMSHAFTS, TIMING CHAIN AND CHAIN TENSIONER ASSEMBLY

Refer to **Figure 22** for this procedure.

Removal

1. Remove the cylinder head cover, timing chain cover and crankshaft cover as described in this chapter.

2. Remove all spark plugs. This will make it easier to rotate the engine.

NOTE
The following step is not absolutely necessary, but it will even out the stress placed on the camshafts during removal. The engine must be at this location during camshaft installation.

3A. On K75 models, using an Allen driver on the crankshaft bolt (A, **Figure 23**), rotate the engine in the normal *counterclockwise* forward rotation until the rear or No. 3 cylinder is at top dead center (TDC) on its compression stroke. To determine TDC for the No. 3 cylinder, perform the following:

   a. Rotate the engine, in normal forward rotation, until the intake camshaft (upper camshaft) has completely opened the *intake valve* and then allowed it to close.

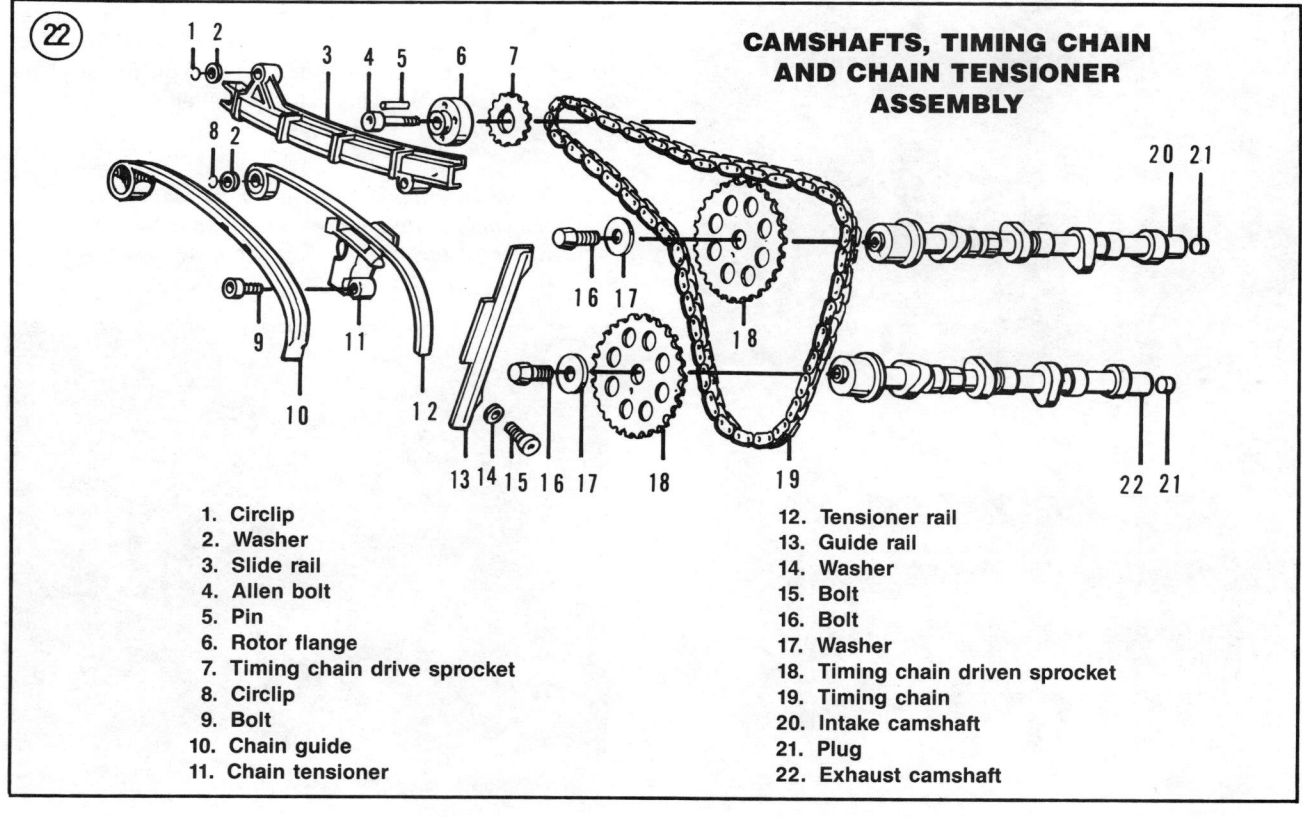

CAMSHAFTS, TIMING CHAIN AND CHAIN TENSIONER ASSEMBLY

1. Circlip
2. Washer
3. Slide rail
4. Allen bolt
5. Pin
6. Rotor flange
7. Timing chain drive sprocket
8. Circlip
9. Bolt
10. Chain guide
11. Chain tensioner
12. Tensioner rail
13. Guide rail
14. Washer
15. Bolt
16. Bolt
17. Washer
18. Timing chain driven sprocket
19. Timing chain
20. Intake camshaft
21. Plug
22. Exhaust camshaft

b. Using a small flashlight, direct the light into the spark plug hole to observe the piston as it moves up in the cylinder.

c. Continue to rotate the engine until the No. 3 cylinder's piston reaches the top of its stroke. This will be TDC on the compression stroke.

d. At this point the pin (B, **Figure 23**) on the timing chain drive sprocket will align with the "OT" index mark (C, **Figure 23**) on the cylinder block.

3B. On K100 models, using an Allen driver on the crankshaft bolt (A, **Figure 23**), rotate the engine in the normal *counterclockwise* forward rotation until the front or No. 1 cylinder is at top dead center (TDC) on its compression stroke. To determine TDC for the No. 1 cylinder, perform the following:

a. Rotate the engine, in normal forward rotation, until the intake camshaft (upper camshaft) has completely opened the *intake valve* and then allowed it to close.

b. Using a small flashlight, direct the light into the spark plug hole to observe the piston as it moves up in the cylinder.

c. Continue to rotate the engine until the No. 1 cylinder's piston reaches the top of its stroke. This will be TDC on the compression stroke.

d. At this point the pin (B, **Figure 23**) on the timing chain drive sprocket will align with the "OT" index mark (C, **Figure 23**) on the cylinder block.

4. Remove the Torx bolts (A, **Figure 24**) securing the timing chain guide rail and remove the guide rail (B, **Figure 24**).

5. Remove the bolts securing the timing chain tensioner (A, **Figure 25**). Pivot the tensioner counterclockwise and disengage it from the tensioner rail (B, **Figure 25**). Remove the tensioner assembly.

6. Remove the clip (**Figure 26**) and washer (**Figure 27**) securing the timing chain tensioner rail and guide to the cylinder block.

7. Remove the timing chain tensioner rail and guide (**Figure 28**) from the cylinder block.

8. Remove the upper E-clip (**Figure 29**) and lower E-clip (**Figure 30**) securing the timing chain guide rail to the cylinder block.

9. Remove the timing chain guide rail (**Figure 31**) from the cylinder block.

10. Insert the ends of a clean shop cloth into the oil return openings (**Figure 32**) in the cylinder head to prevent small parts from falling into the crankcase.

> *NOTE*
> *Each camshaft bearing cap has its own cast number that relates to the same number that is cast into the cylinder head (**Figure 33**). Each bearing cap must be reinstalled in the same location.*

11. First loosen, then remove the nuts and lockwashers securing both camshaft front thrust bearing caps (A, **Figure 34**). Remove these bearing caps and their locating dowels. The front bearing caps take up the thrust movement (end play) of the camshafts and must be removed first.

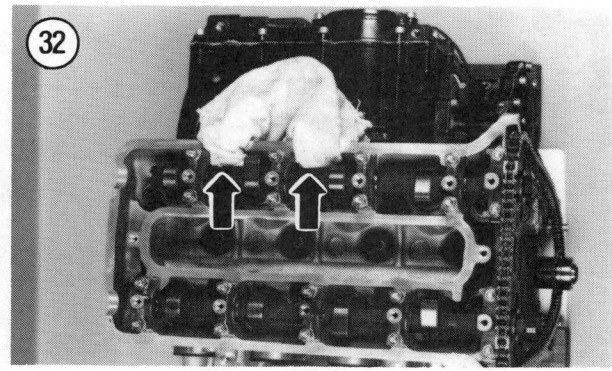

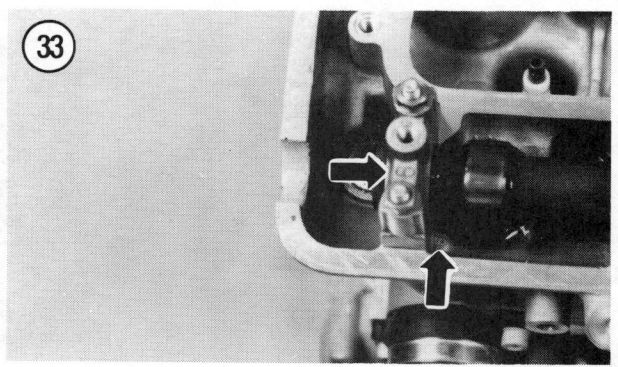

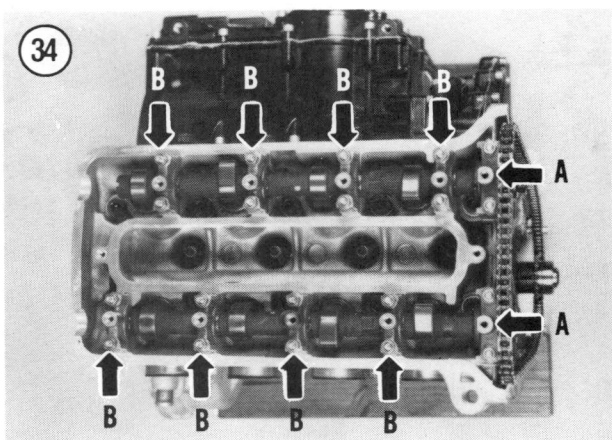

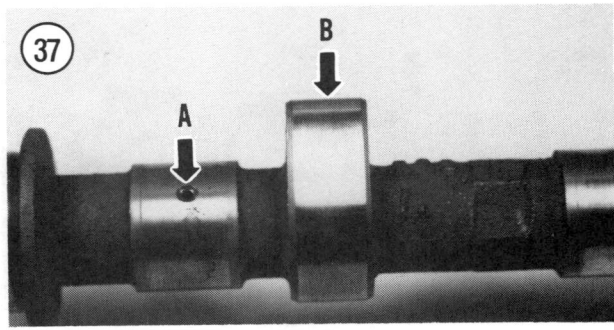

12. Using a crisscross pattern, loosen then remove the nuts securing the remaining camshaft bearing caps (B, **Figure 34**) on both camshafts.

13. Remove the remaining bearing caps from both camshafts. Don't lose the locating dowels in each cap.

14. Lift up on the exhaust camshaft (A, **Figure 35**), disengage the timing chain from the camshaft driven sprocket (B, **Figure 35**) and remove the exhaust camshaft.

15. Lift up on the intake camshaft (A, **Figure 36**), disengage the timing chain from the camshaft driven sprocket (B, **Figure 36**) and remove the exhaust camshaft.

16. Remove the timing chain from the drive sprocket attached to the end of the crankshaft and remove the timing chain.

17. Inspect all components as described in this chapter.

Inspection

1. Clean all parts in solvent and dry with compressed air. Blow out the oil flow holes (A, **Figure 37**) in both camshafts.

2. Inspect the bearing journals and lobes (**Figure 38**) for wear or damage.

3. Measure the camshaft thrust bearing journal with a micrometer (**Figure 39**) for wear and scoring. Compare to the dimensions given in **Table 1** or **Table 2**. If worn to the service limit or less the camshaft(s) must be replaced.

4

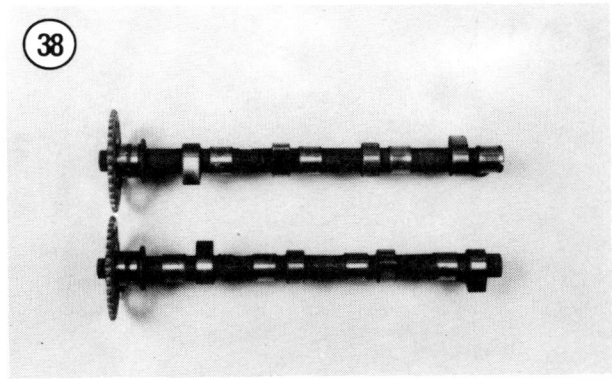

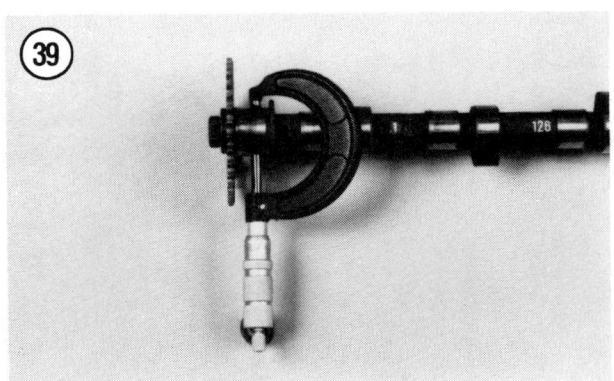

4. Measure the remaining camshaft bearing journals with a micrometer (**Figure 40**) for wear and scoring. Compare to the dimensions given in **Table 1** or **Table 2**. If worn to the service limit or less the camshaft(s) must be replaced.

5. Check the camshaft lobes (B, **Figure 37**) for wear. The lobes should show no signs of scoring and the edges should be square. Slight damage may be removed with a silicon carbide oilstone. Use No. 100-120 grit initially, then polish with a No. 280-320 grit.

6. Even though the camshaft lobe surface appears to be satisfactory, with no visible signs of wear, the camshaft lobes must be measured with a micrometer (**Figure 41**). Compare to the dimensions given in **Table 1** or **Table 2**. If worn to the service limit or less the camshaft(s) must be replaced.

7. Inspect the camshaft bearing surfaces in the cylinder head (**Figure 42**) and camshaft bearing caps (**Figure 43**). They should not be scored or excessively worn. Replace the cylinder head and camshaft bearing caps if the bearing surfaces are worn or scored.

8. Inspect the camshaft bearing cap mounting holes (**Figure 44**). They should not be elongated or excessively worn. Replace the cylinder head and camshaft bearing caps if the mounting holes are worn or damaged.

9. To remove the driven sprockets, perform the following:

   a. Hold onto the cast-in flats (**Figure 45**) on the camshaft with an open-end wrench.

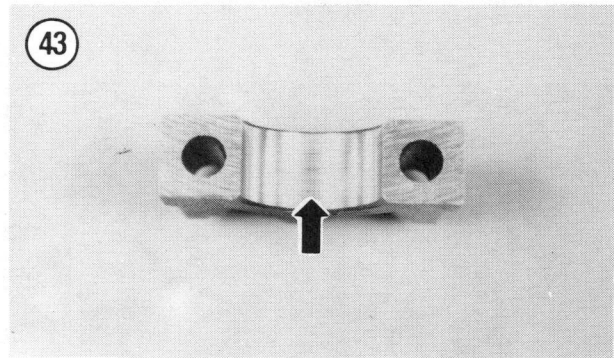

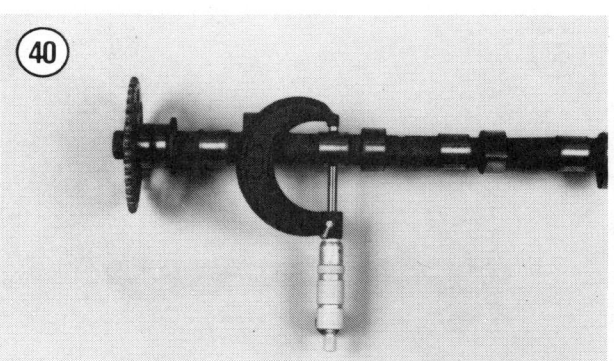

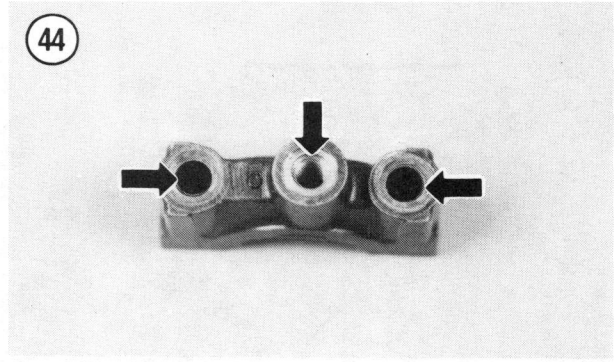

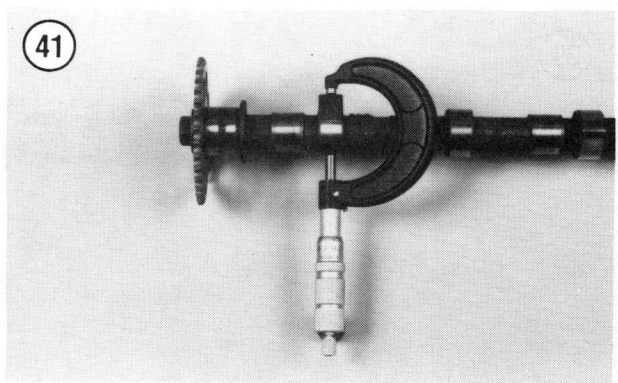

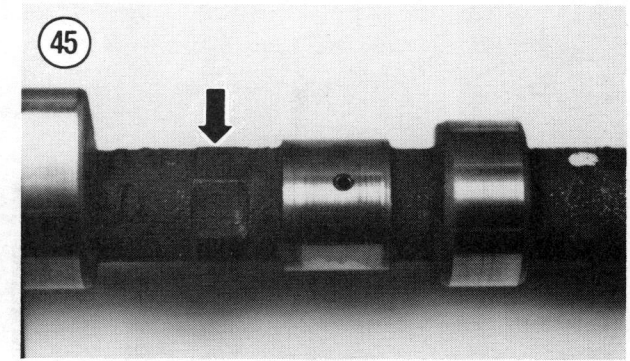

b. Unscrew the bolt securing the driven sprocket. Remove the bolt and washer (**Figure 46**) and the driven sprocket.

10. Inspect the camshaft sprocket teeth (**Figure 47**) for wear; replace if necessary.

11. Inspect the locating groove (**Figure 48**) in the end of the camshaft for wear or damage; replace if necessary.

12. To install the driven sprockets, perform the following:

   a. Align the locating pin (A, **Figure 49**) on the backside of the driven sprocket with the locating notch (B, **Figure 49**) and install the driven sprocket onto the camshaft.

   b. Make sure the locating pin is properly aligned (**Figure 50**).

   c. Apply a light coat of blue Loctite Threadlocker No. 242 to the bolt prior to installation.

   d. Install the bolt and washer (**Figure 46**) onto the driven sprocket and camshaft.

   e. Hold onto the cast-in flats (**Figure 44**) on the camshaft with an open-end wrench.

   f. Tighten the driven sprocket securing bolt (**Figure 51**) to the torque specification listed in **Table 3.**

13. Separate the tensioner assembly and thoroughly clean in solvent. Dry with compressed air.

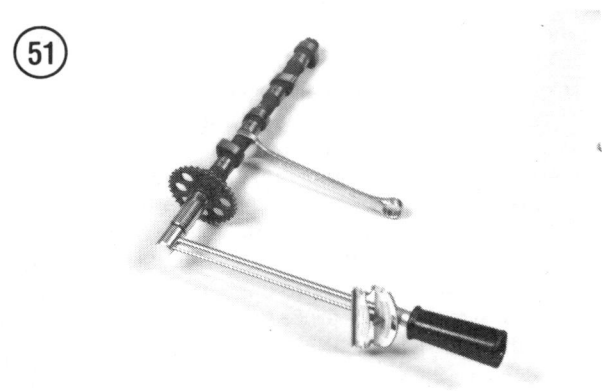

4

14. Inspect the timing chain rubbing surface of the guide rail (**Figure 52**) and the tensioner chain guide for wear or damage. Replace if necessary.

15. If the chain guide requires replacing, carefully pry it free from the tensioner rail (**Figure 53**) and install a new guide. Make sure the new guide is correctly seated in the tensioner rail.

16. Inspect the timing chain (**Figure 54**) for wear or damage. BMW does not provide service specifications for the length of the chain between any given number of pins as some manufacturers do. If the pins and plates look scuffed or worn or if the chain is noisy during normal engine operation, the chain should be replaced.

17. Disassemble the tensioner assembly (**Figure 55**) and thoroughly clean all parts with solvent. Inspect for wear or damage. If any part is damaged the entire assembly must be replaced—replacement parts are not available.

Camshaft Bearing Radial Running Clearance Measurement

> *NOTE*
> *Each camshaft bearing cap has its own number that relates to the number in the cylinder head (**Figure 33**). Each bearing cap must be installed in its correct location.*

1. Install all camshaft bearing caps in their correct location in the cylinder head. Refer to **Figure 56** for K75 models or **Figure 57** for K100 models for location numbers.

2. Install the lockwashers and nuts. Tighten the nuts finger-tight at first, then tighten in 2-3 stages to the torque specification listed in **Table 3**.

3. Insert a bore gauge into the bearing receptacle in the front thrust bearing bore (bearing caps No. 1 and No. 2) in the cylinder head. Write down the dimensions for each bearing bore.

4. Insert a bore gauge into the bearing receptacle in the remaining bearing bores (bearing caps No. 3 through No. 8 for K75 models or No. 3 through No. 0 for K100 models) in the cylinder head. Write down the dimensions for each bearing bore.

5. Compare to the thrust bearing and all other bearing bore dimension specifications listed in **Table 1** or **Table 2**. If within the specifications the parts are okay.

6. If the dimensions are not within specifications perform the following:

   a. Subtract the camshaft bearing journal outside diameter dimensions taken in *Inspection*, Step 3 and Step 4 from the bearing bore dimensions take in Step 3 and Step 4 of this procedure.

   b. This dimension will give the oil clearance.

   c. Refer to the camshaft oil clearance and wear limit dimensions listed in **Table 1** and **Table 2**.

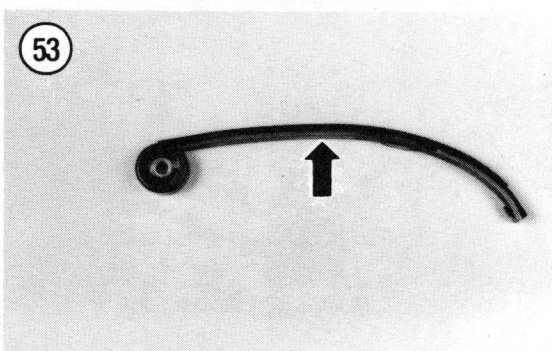

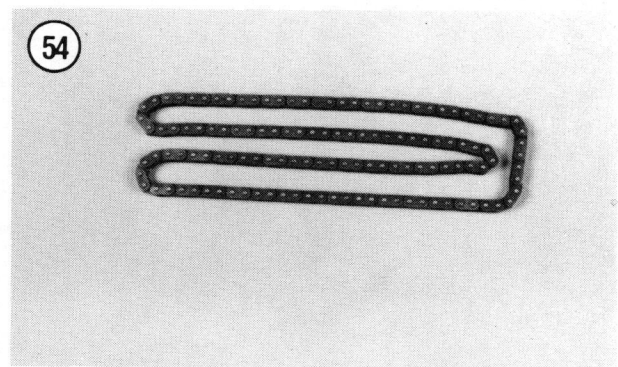

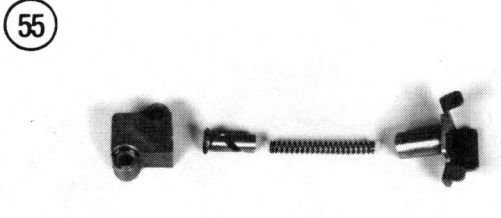

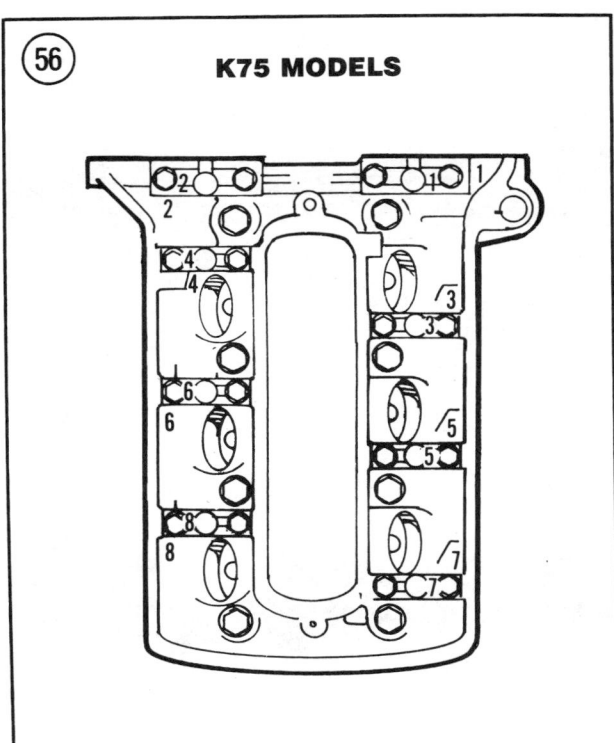

56

K75 MODELS

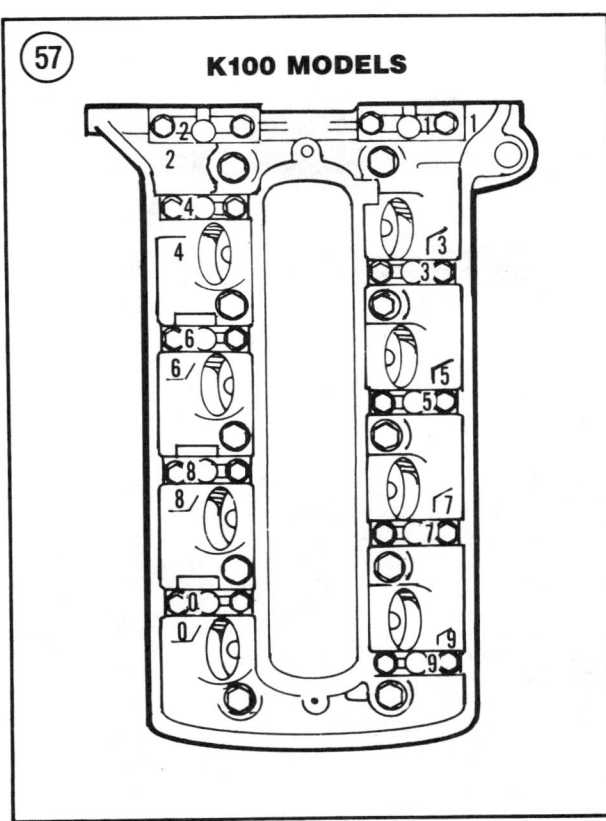

57

K100 MODELS

d. If worn to the wear limit replace the worn part—either the camshaft, or the cylinder head and bearing caps as an assembly. Individual replacement bearing caps are not available.

7. Remove the nuts, lockwashers and bearing caps.

Installation

1. Make sure the engine is still at top dead center (TDC).

2A. On K75 models, to determine if the No. 3 (rear) cylinder is at TDC, perform the following:

    a. Using a small flashlight, direct the light into the No. 3 cylinder spark plug hole to observe if the top of the piston as visible in the cylinder.

    b. Using an Allen driver on the crankshaft bolt (A, **Figure 58**), slightly rotate the engine back and forth to make sure the piston is at TDC. If the piston is at TDC, proceed to Step 3. If the No. 3 cylinder is not at TDC, rotate the engine in the normal *counterclockwise* forward rotation until the No. 3 cylinder is at top dead center (TDC).

    c. At this point the pin (B, **Figure 58**) on the timing chain drive sprocket must align with the "OT" index mark (C, **Figure 58**) on the cylinder block.

    d. The cylinder is now at TDC.

2B. On K100 models, to determine if the No. 1 (front) cylinder is at TDC, perform the following:

    a. Using a small flashlight, direct the light into the No. 1 cylinder spark plug hole to observe if the top of the piston as visible in the cylinder.

    b. Using an Allen driver on the crankshaft bolt (A, **Figure 58**), slightly rotate the engine back and forth to make sure the piston is at TDC. If the piston is at TDC, proceed to Step 3. If the No. 1 cylinder is not at TDC, rotate the engine in the normal *counterclockwise* forward rotation until the No. 1 cylinder is at top dead center (TDC).

    c. At this point the pin (B, **Figure 58**) on the timing chain drive sprocket must align with the "OT" index mark (C, **Figure 58**) on the cylinder block. If so, the cylinder is now at TDC.

4

58

3. Apply a light, but complete, coat of molybdenum disulfide grease to each camshaft bearing journal. Coat all bearing surfaces in the cylinder head and each bearing cap with clean engine oil.

CAUTION
The camshafts must be installed in their correct location in the cylinder head so that they will align with the valve lifters.

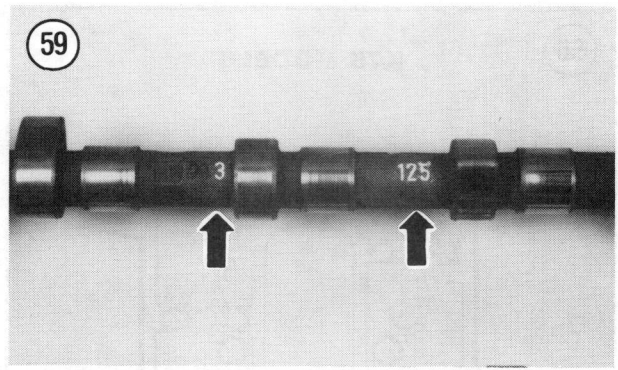

4. The camshafts are marked as follows:
  a. Intake camshaft: 125 M3 (**Figure 59**).
  b. Exhaust camshaft: 126 M1 (**Figure 60**).
5. The lobes on the different camshafts are offset. The set of lobes on the intake camshaft (A, **Figure 61**) are positioned closer to the driven sprocket than those on the exhaust camshaft (B, **Figure 61**).
6. Install the intake camshaft into the cylinder head. Position the notch in one of the circle cutouts in the driven sprocket so that it is aligned with the top surface of the cylinder head and is facing *away from the centerline* of the cylinder head.
7. Install the timing chain onto the drive sprocket (A, **Figure 62**) on the end of the crankshaft.
8. Mesh the timing chain onto the driven sprocket on the intake camshaft and install the camshaft into the cylinder head. Make sure the driven sprocket does not move.
9. Partially install the exhaust camshaft into the cylinder head. Position the notch in one of the circle cutouts in the driven sprocket so that is aligned with the top surface of the cylinder head and is facing *toward the intake camshaft* in the cylinder head.
10. Mesh the timing chain onto the driven sprocket on the exhaust camshaft and install the camshaft into the cylinder head.
11. After the exhaust camshaft is installed, recheck alignment. Make sure that both driven sprocket notches (**Figure 63**) are aligned with the top surface of the cylinder head. Also both notches must face toward the intake side of the cylinder head.

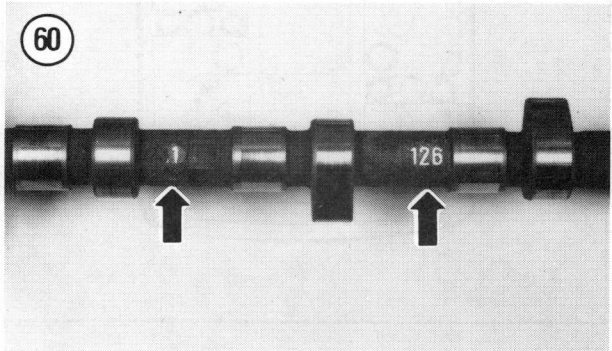

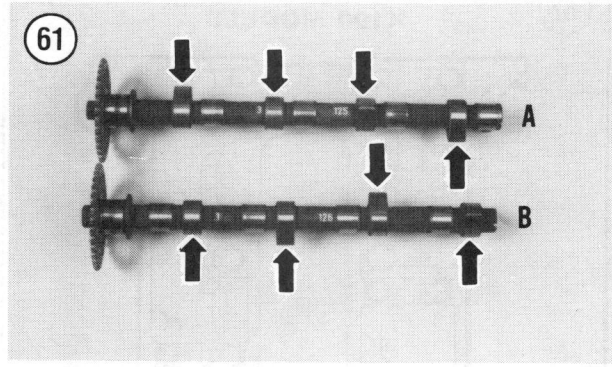

CAUTION
Very expensive damage could result from improper camshaft timing chain to camshafts alignment. Recheck your work several times to be sure alignment is correct.

12. Recheck the following:
  a. Refer to Step 2 and make sure the pin (B, **Figure 62**) on the timing chain drive sprocket is still aligned with the "OT" index mark (C, **Figure 62**) on the cylinder block.
  b. Make sure that both driven sprocket notches (**Figure 63**) are still aligned with the top surface of the

cylinder head and that both notches face toward the centerline of the cylinder head.

c. If alignment is incorrect, reposition the timing chain on the driven sprockets and again recheck the alignment.

NOTE
*Each camshaft bearing cap has its own number that relates to the same number that is cast into the cylinder head (**Figure 64**). Each bearing cap must be reinstalled in its correct location.*

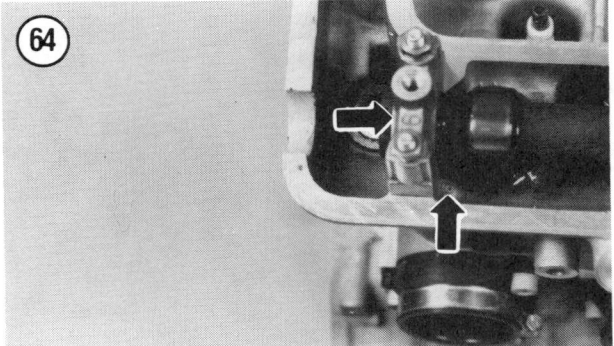

13. Make sure the locating dowels are in place on the threaded studs for the front thrust bearing caps. These are the only bearing caps equipped with locating dowels.

14. Install all camshaft bearing caps in their correct location in the cylinder head. Refer to **Figure 56** for K75 models or **Figure 57** for K100 models for location numbers.

CAUTION
Tighten the bearing caps evenly so that the camshafts are moved down into position evenly, avoiding any undue stress.

15. Install the lockwashers and nuts. Tighten the nuts finger-tight at first, then tighten in 2-3 stages in a crisscross pattern, working from the center of the camshaft toward each end. Tighten to the torque specification listed in **Table 3**.

16. Remove the shop cloth from the oil return openings in the cylinder head.

17. Install the timing chain guide rail (**Figure 65**) onto the mounting studs on the cylinder block.

18. Install the upper E-clip (**Figure 66**) and lower E-clip (**Figure 67**) securing the timing chain guide rail to the studs on the cylinder block. Make sure the clips are correctly seated in the stud grooves.

19. Install the timing chain tensioner rail and guide (**Figure 68**) onto the cylinder block.

CAUTION
The following step is very important as a final check for correct camshaft timing.

20. Push in on the timing chain tensioner rail and guide in the area where the tensioner assembly applies pressure. Make sure that both driven sprocket notches (**Figure 63**) are aligned with the top surface of the cylinder head. If alignment is not correct, repeat this procedure and correct the alignment at this time.
21. Install the washer (**Figure 69**) and clip (**Figure 70**) securing the timing chain tensioner rail and guide to the cylinder block.
22. Reassemble the timing chain tensioner as follows:
    a. Install the spring into the plunger (**Figure 71**).
    b. Install this assembly into the housing (**Figure 72**).
    c. Push the tensioner foot onto the spring (**Figure 73**) and index the pin on the foot with the groove in the plunger. Rotate the foot clockwise while pushing in to compress the spring until the foot bottoms out. Hold the foot in this position.

23. While holding the tensioner foot in place in the housing, install the tensioner assembly onto the cylinder block.
24. Correctly position the tensioner foot onto the tensioner rail and install the mounting bolts. Tighten the bolts to the torque specification listed in **Table 3**.
24. Install the guide rail and the Torx bolts. Tighten the Torx bolts to the torque specification listed in **Table 3**.

CAUTION
In the next step, if there is any binding while rotating the crankshaft, stop. Determine the cause before proceeding.

25. After installation is complete, *slowly* rotate the crankshaft in the normal *counterclockwise* direction several times using an Allen wrench on the timing chain bolt on the end of the crankshaft. Make sure the engine rotates smoothly with no interference.
26. If removed, apply a light coat of Three Bond 1216 gasket sealer to the rubber plugs and install the rubber plugs (**Figure 74**) into their receptacles at the rear of the cylinder head.
27. Install the spark plugs.
28. Install the cylinder head cover, timing chain cover and crankshaft cover as described in this chapter.
29. Adjust the valves as described under *Valve Clearance Measurement and Adjustment* in Chapter Three.

CYLINDER HEAD

Removal

> *NOTE*
> *This procedure is shown with the engine removed from the frame for clarity. It is not necessary to remove the engine to perform this procedure.*

> *CAUTION*
> *To prevent any warpage and damage, remove the cylinder head only when the engine has been at room temperature for a minimum of 12 hours.*

1. Remove the fuel injection throttle housing and plenum chamber as described under *Throttle Housing and Intake Manifold Removal/Installation* in Chapter Seven.
2. Remove the exhaust system as described under *Exhaust System Removal/Installation* in Chapter Seven.
3. Remove the camshafts, timing chain and chain tensioner assembly as described in this chapter.

> *NOTE*
> *The No. 1 cylinder is at the front (timing chain end) of the engine. Cylinders are numbered from front to rear of the engine (1-3 on K75 models; 1-4 on K100 models).*

4. To avoid losing or misplacing the valve lifters and spacers, remove them from the cylinder head at this time. Perform the following:
   a. Mark the top of each spacer with the cylinder from which it was removed. Mark the intake spacer with just the cylinder number (A, **Figure 75**). On the exhaust spacers, add an additional "X" for exhaust (B, **Figure 75**).
   b. Use a magnetic tool and remove the spacers. Place in an egg carton or similar container and keep them in order.
   c. Use a magnetic tool and remove the valve lifters. Mark each one as it is removed with its cylinder number and type (intake or exhaust). Place the lifters in the same egg carton or similar container as their spacers. Be sure to match them up with their respective spacers.
5. Loosen the cylinder head bolts (**Figure 76**) in 2-3 stages in the pattern shown in **Figure 77** for K75 models or **Figure 78** for K100 models. Work from the center out.
6. Remove the bolts and washers.
7. Loosen the cylinder head by tapping around the perimeter with a rubber or soft faced mallet. If necessary, *gently* pry the head loose with a broad-tipped screwdriver.

8. Lift the cylinder head (**Figure 79**) straight up and off the cylinder block.

9. Remove the cylinder head gasket and discard it. Don't lose the locating dowels.

10. If necessary, remove the bolts securing the rubber intake manifolds (**Figure 80**) and remove the manifolds.

Cylinder Head Inspection

1. Remove all traces of gasket material from the cylinder head mating surfaces on the cylinder head and the cylinder block (**Figure 81**).

2. *Without removing the valves*, remove all carbon deposits from the combustion chambers (**Figure 82**) and valve ports with a wire brush. A blunt screwdriver or chisel may be

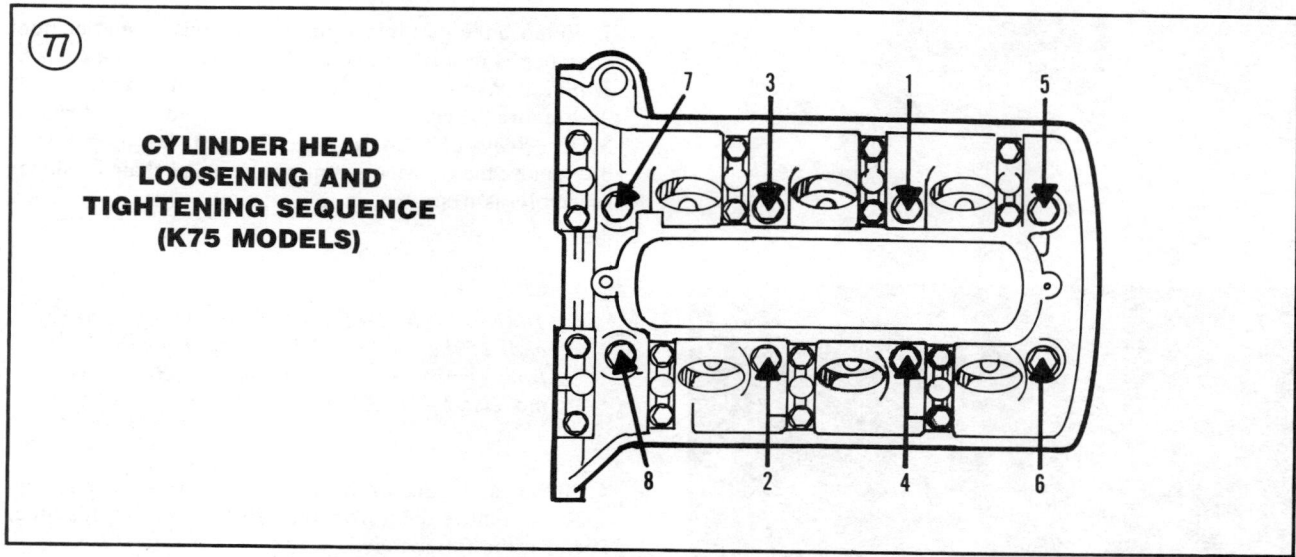

CYLINDER HEAD LOOSENING AND TIGHTENING SEQUENCE (K75 MODELS)

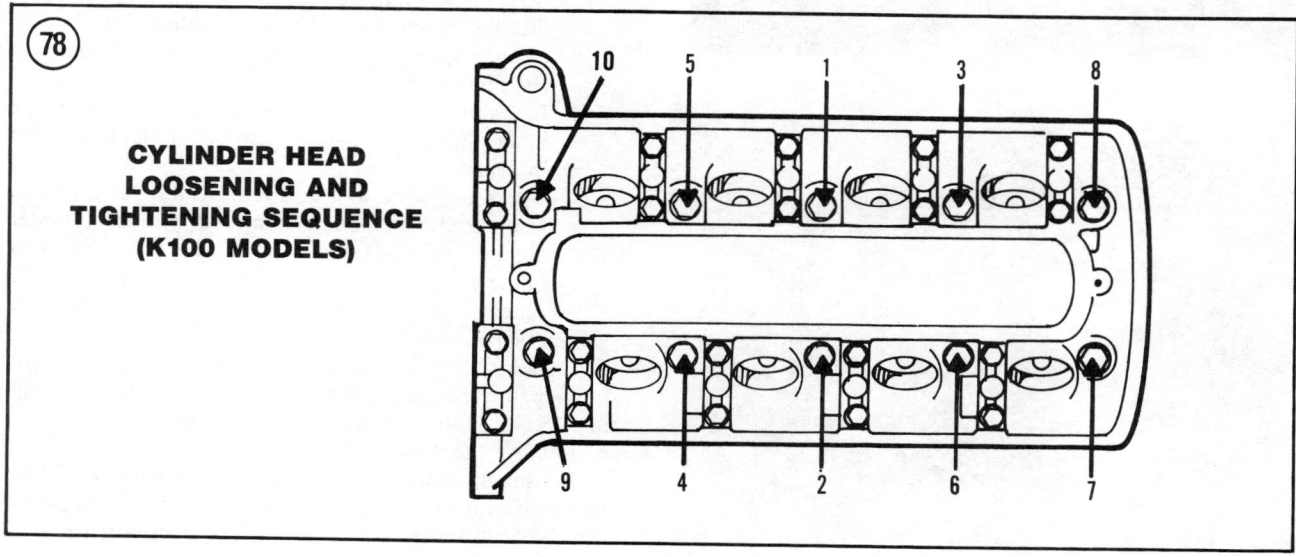

CYLINDER HEAD LOOSENING AND TIGHTENING SEQUENCE (K100 MODELS)

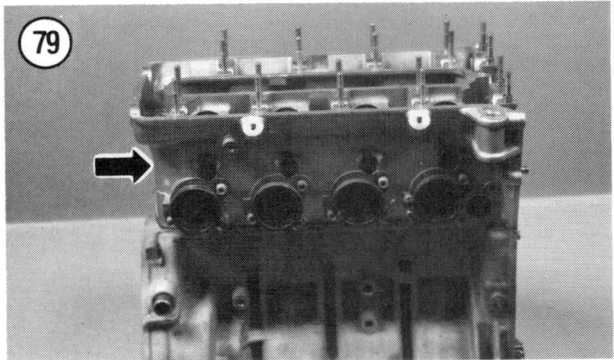

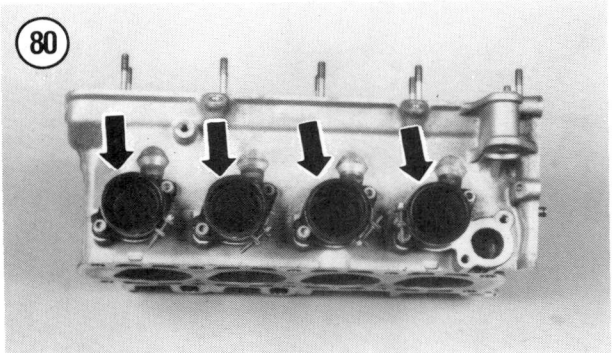

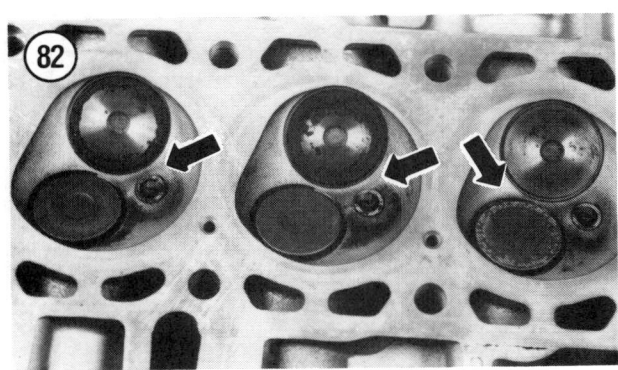

used if care is taken not to damage the head, valves and spark plug threads.

3. After the carbon is removed from the combustion chambers and the valve intake and exhaust ports (**Figure 83**), clean the entire head in cleaning solvent. Blow dry with compressed air.

4. Clean away all carbon from the piston crowns. Do not remove the carbon ridge at the top of the cylinder bore.

5. Check for cracks in the combustion chamber and exhaust ports. A cracked head must be replaced.

6. After the head has been thoroughly cleaned, place a straightedge across the cylinder head/cylinder gasket surface at several points. Measure the warp by inserting a flat feeler gauge between the straightedge and the cylinder head at each location. There should be no warpage; if a small amount is present, it can be resurfaced by a dealer or qualified machine shop. BMW does not provide service limit specifications for the maximum allowable amount of cylinder head distortion.

7. Check the valves and valve guides as described in this chapter.

8. Inspect the oil return channels (**Figure 84**) in the cylinder head. Make sure they are open and clean.

4

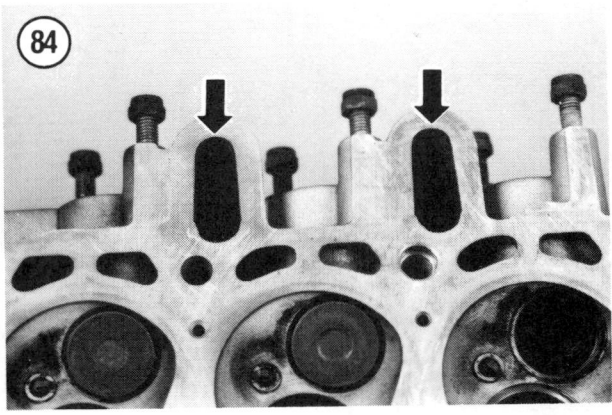

9. Make sure the oil control orifice (**Figure 85**) in each camshaft front bearing surface is clean and open. If clogged in any way, clean out with solvent and a piece of wire, then blow out with compressed air.

10. Inspect the freeze plugs for damage or leakage. Refer to **Figure 86**, **Figure 87** and **Figure 88**. Replace any freeze plug that looks suspect. It's a good idea to replace all as a set—if one is bad it's quite possible that some of the others may also leak in the future.

11. Make sure the timing chain slide rail mounting stud (**Figure 89**) is in good condition and is secure in the cylinder head. Replace if necessary.

12. Check that the camshaft bearing cap threaded studs (**Figure 90**) are secure in the cylinder head. Tighten if necessary or replace.

Valve Lifter Inspection

1. Remove the valve lifters from the cylinder head as described in this chapter.

2. Inspect the outside surface of the valve lifter (**Figure 91**) for wear or scratches. Replace as necessary.

3. Using a micrometer, measure the outside diameter of the valve lifter (**Figure 92**). Compare to the dimension listed in **Table 1** or **Table 2**. If worn to the wear limit or less, replace the valve lifter.

4. Inspect the spacer recess in the valve lifter. Make sure the oil hole (**Figure 93**) is open; clean out if necessary.

5. Inspect the inside surface of the valve lifter (**Figure 94**) for wear or scratches. Replace as necessary.

6. Insert the spacer (**Figure 95**) in the valve lifter and rotate it with your finger. It must rotate smoothly with no hesitation or binding. If it does not rotate freely, replace the faulty part.

7. Using a bore gauge, measure the inside diameter of each valve lifter receptacle in the cylinder head. Compare to the dimension listed in **Table 1** or **Table 2**. If worn to the wear limit or more, replace the valve lifter.

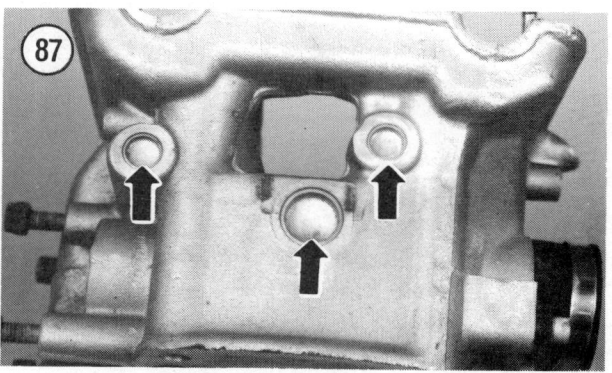

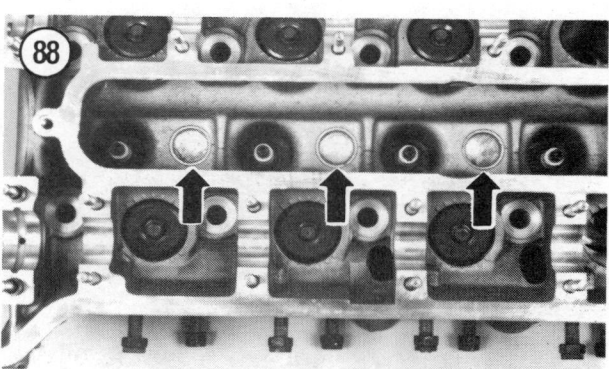

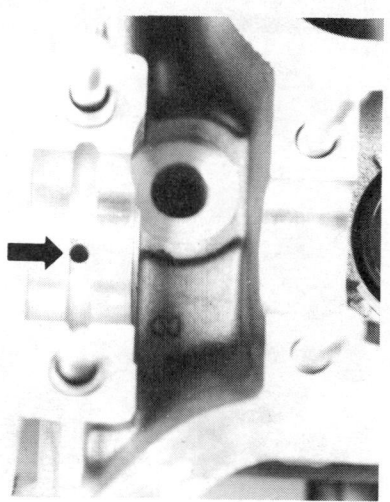

8. There is a specified oil or radial clearance between the valve lifter and the valve lifter receptacle in the cylinder head. To determine the clearance, perform the following:

  a. Subtract the valve lifter outside diameter dimension from the valve lifter receptacle bore dimension.
  b. This dimension will give the oil or radial clearance.
  c. Refer to the valve lifter oil or radial clearance wear limit dimensions listed in **Table 1** or **Table 2**.
  d. If worn to the wear limit replace the worn part (either the valve lifter or the cylinder head assembly).

9. Install the valves into the cylinder head as described in this chapter.

4

Installation

NOTE
Step 1 will make camshaft installation easier if the pistons are in their correct position before installing the cylinder head.

1A. On K75 models, before installing the cylinder head, make sure that the pistons are in the correct position. The No. 3, rear piston, should be at the top of its stroke.

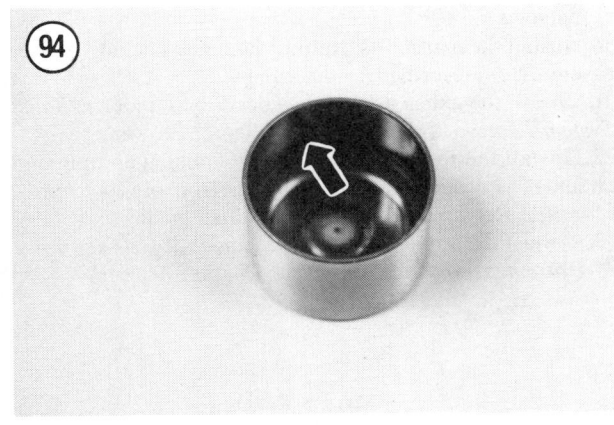

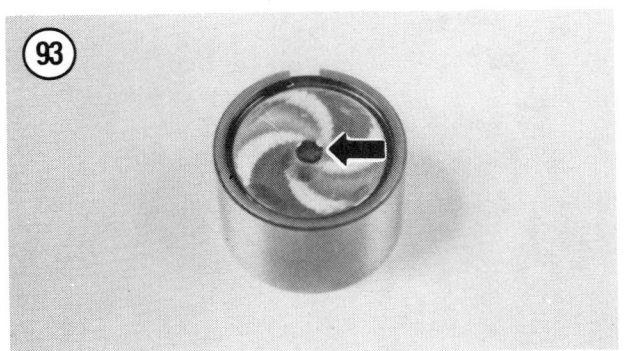

1B. On K100 models, before installing the cylinder head, make sure that the pistons are in the correct position. The No. 1, front piston, and No. 4, rear piston, should be at the top of their stroke (**Figure 96**).

2. If removed, install the locating dowel (**Figure 97**) at each end of the cylinder block.

3. Install a new cylinder head gasket (**Figure 98**) onto the cylinder block. Make sure that all of the holes in the gasket align with the holes in the cylinder block and that no holes are blocked.

4. Carefully slide the cylinder head onto the cylinder block. Make sure the locating dowels seat correctly in their receptacles in the cylinder head.

5. Apply oil to the threads and to the underside of the bolt heads of the cylinder head bolts.

6. Install the cylinder head bolts and washers (**Figure 76**).

7. Tighten the cylinder head bolts in 2-3 stages in the pattern shown in **Figure 77** for K75 models or **Figure 78** for K100 models. Work from the center out and tighten to the preliminary torque specification listed in **Table 3**.

8. Wait for 20 minutes, then retighten the bolts in the same torque pattern used in Step 7. Tighten to the final torque specification listed in **Table 3**.

9. Install the valve lifters and spacers into the cylinder head. Refer to marks made in Step 4, *Removal* and make sure to install them in their correct locations in the cylinder head receptacles.

10. Install the camshafts, timing chain and chain tensioner assembly as described in this chapter.

11. Install the exhaust system as described under *Exhaust System Removal/Installation* in Chapter Seven.

12. Install the fuel injection throttle housing and plenum chamber as described under *Throttle Housing and Intake Manifold Removal/Installation* in Chapter Seven.

13. Adjust the valves as described under *Valve Clearance Measurement and Adjustment* in Chapter Three.

VALVES AND VALVE COMPONENTS

General practice among those who do their own service is to remove the cylinder head and take it to a machine shop or dealer for inspection and service. Since the cost is low relative to the required effort and equipment, this is the best approach, even for the experienced mechanics.

This procedure is included for those who choose to do their own valve service.

Refer to **Figure 99** for this procedure.

Valve Removal

1. Remove the cylinder head and valve lifters as described in this chapter.

CAUTION
To avoid loss of spring tension, do not compress the springs any more than necessary to remove the keepers.

2. Compress the valve springs with a valve compressor tool (**Figure 100**). Remove the valve keepers and release the compression. Remove the valve compressor tool.

3. Remove the valve spring retainer and valve spring.

4. Before removing the valve, remove any burrs from the valve stem (**Figure 101**). Otherwise the valve guide will be damaged.

99

VALVE ASSEMBLY
1
2
3
4
5
6
7
8
9
1. Exhaust valve
2. Intake valve
3. Oil seal
4. Spring seat
5. Spring
6. Spring retainer
7. Keepers
8. Valve lifter
9. Spacer

100

101

Deburr
Valve stem

4

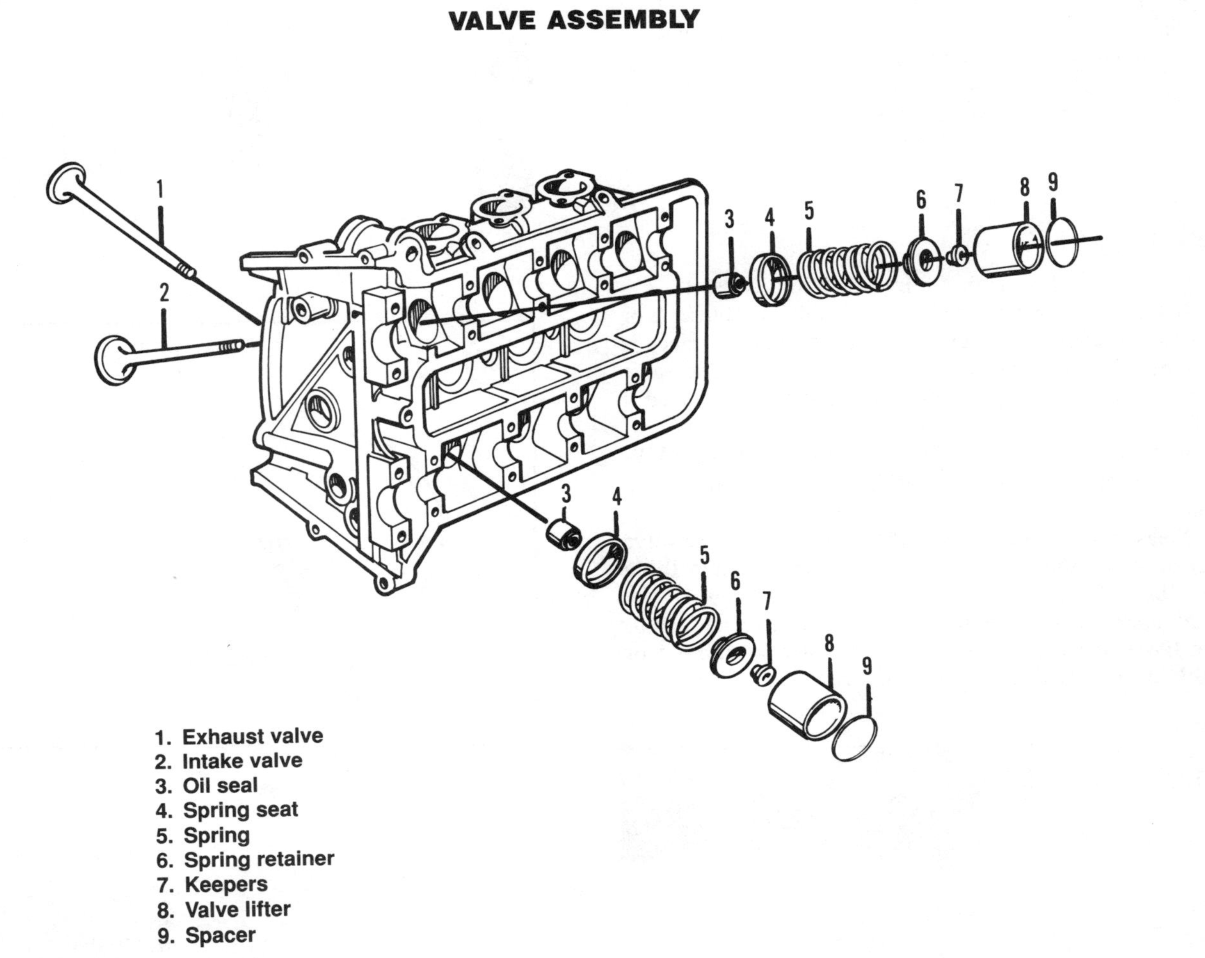

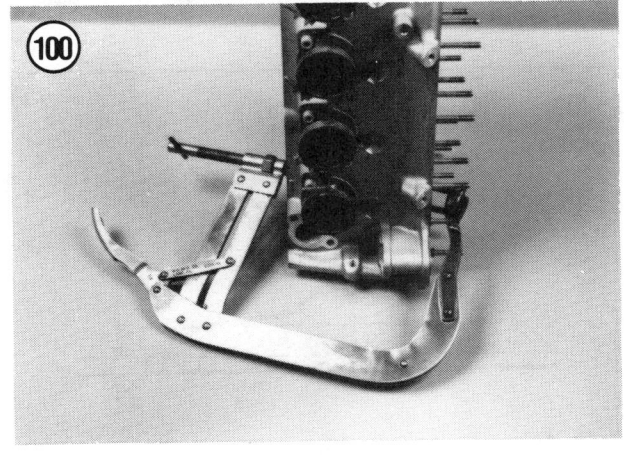

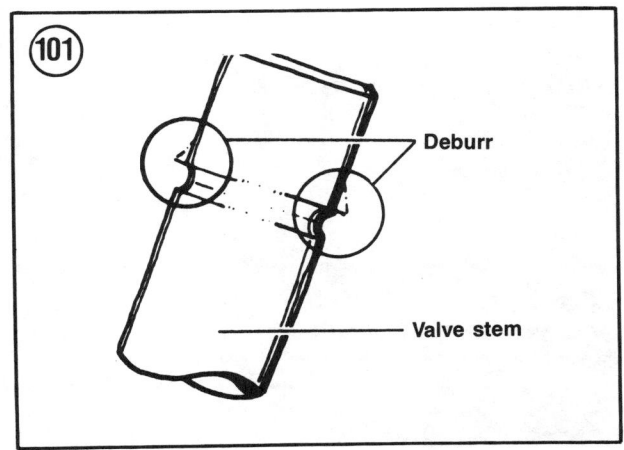

5. Remove the valve and the spring seat.

6. Repeat for all intake and exhaust valves.

7. Mark all parts (**Figure 102**) as they are disassembled so that they will be installed in their same locations.

8. Using BMW special tool (part No. 11 1 250) (**Figure 103**) or equivalent, remove the oil seal (**Figure 104**) from each valve guide.

Valve Inspection

1. Clean the valves with a wire brush and solvent.

2. Inspect the contact surface of each valve for burning or pitting (**Figure 105**). Unevenness of the contact surface is an indication that the valve is not serviceable. The valve contact surface can *not* be ground and must be replaced if defective.

3. Inspect each valve stem for wear and roughness. BMW does not provide service specifications for valve stem runout.

4. Measure the overall length of each valve from the valve face to end of stem. If worn to the wear limit listed in **Table 1** or **Table 2** or less, the valve must be replaced.

5. Measure the outside diameter of each valve stem (**Figure 106**)). If worn to the wear limit listed in **Table 1** or **Table 2** or less, the valve must be replaced.

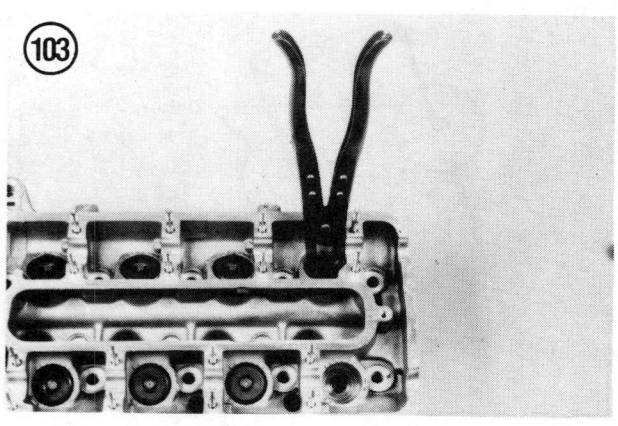

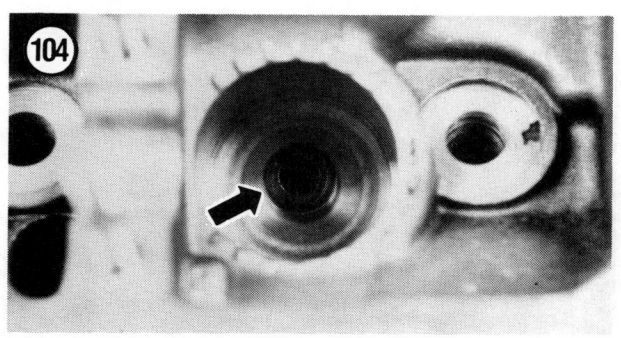

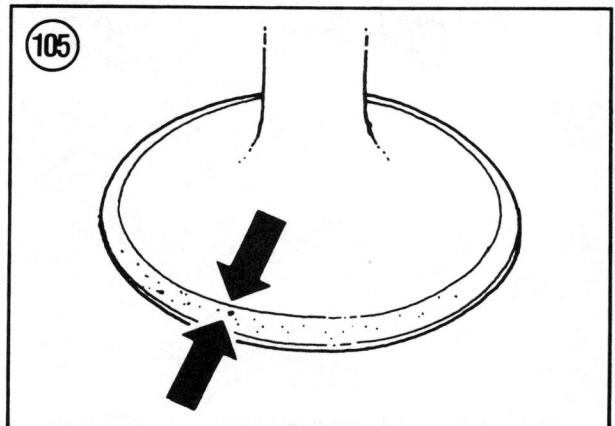

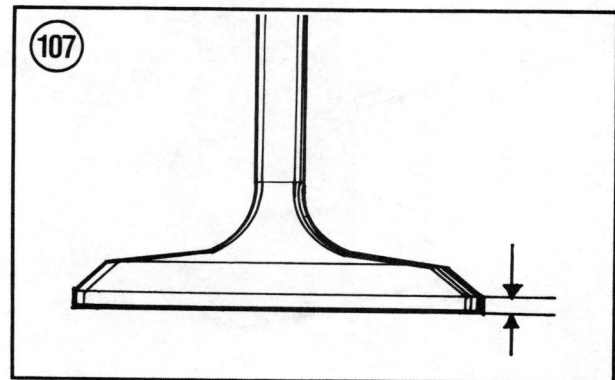

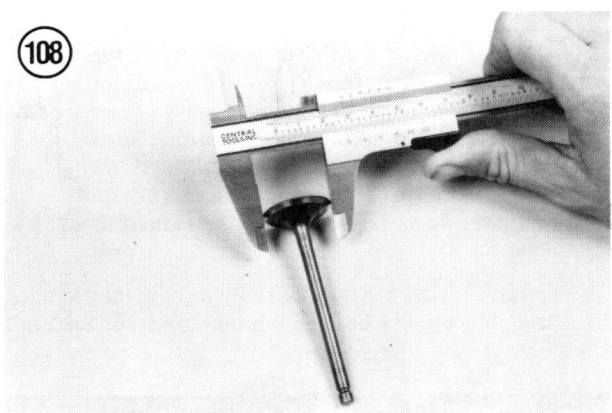

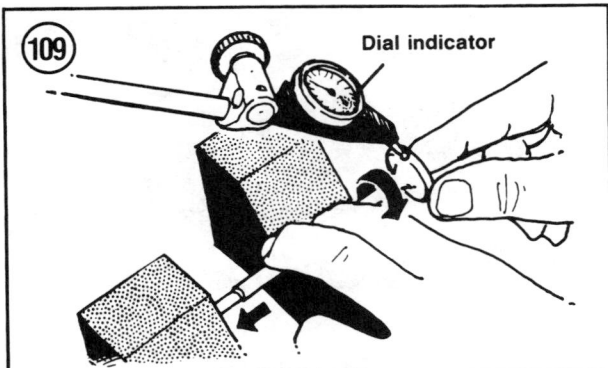

Dial indicator

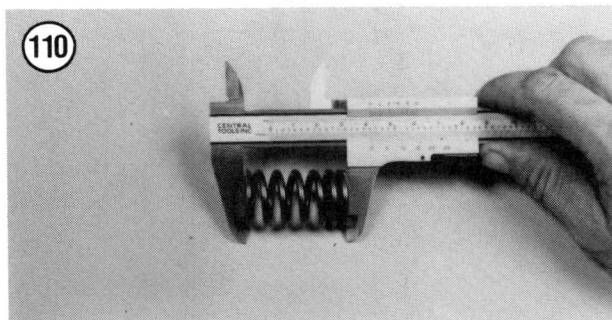

6. Measure each valve head edge thickness (**Figure 107**). If worn to the wear limit listed in **Table 1** or **Table 2** or less, the valve must be replaced.

7. Measure the outside diameter of each valve head (**Figure 108**). If worn to the wear limit listed in **Table 1** or **Table 2** or less, the valve must be replaced.

8. Place a valve in V-blocks. Using a dial indicator, measure the valve head runout as shown in **Figure 109**. If it exceeds the wear limit listed in **Table 1** or **Table 2** the valve must be replaced.

9. Remove all carbon and varnish from each valve guide with a stiff spiral wire brush.

10. Using a small bore gauge, measure the inside diameter of the valve guide. If worn to the wear limit listed in **Table 1** or **Table 2** or more, the valve guide must be replaced.

11. Measure the free length of each valve spring with a vernier caliper (**Figure 110**). All should be within the length specified in **Table 1** or **Table 2** with no signs of bends or distortion (**Figure 111**). Replace defective springs.

12. Check the valve stem grooves and the valve keepers (**Figure 112**). If they are in good condition they may be reused; replace as necessary.

13. Inspect the valve seats. If worn or burned, they must be reconditioned as described in this chapter.

Valve Installation

1. Coat the valve stems with molybdenum disulfide grease. To avoid damage to the valve stem seal, turn the valve slowly while inserting the valve into the cylinder head (**Figure 113**).

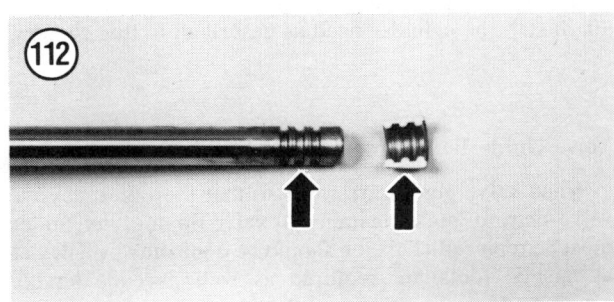

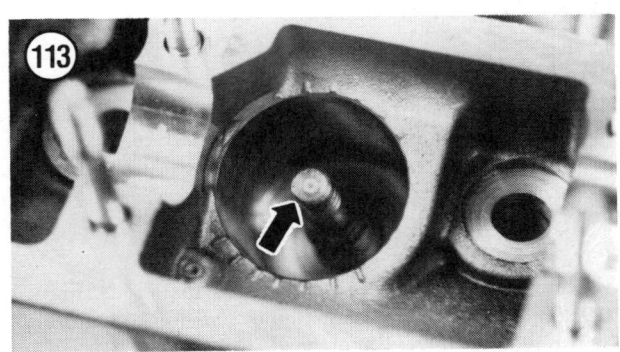

2. Install a new seal (**Figure 104**) on each valve guide as follows:

    a. Install BMW special tool (part No. 11 1 350) onto the valve stem.

    b. Install the new seal onto the valve stem and valve guide.

    c. Install BMW special tool (part No. 11 1 940) onto the valve stem and seal.

    d. Tap on the special tool with a hammer until the tool bottoms out on the cylinder head.

    e. Remove both special tools.

3. Position the spring seat with the flange side (**Figure 114**) facing up and install the spring seat (**Figure 115**).

4. Install the valve spring (**Figure 116**). The spring is *not* progressively wound so either end can go in first.

5. Install the valve spring retainer (**Figure 117**) on top of the valve spring.

> *CAUTION*
> *To avoid loss of spring tension, do not compress the springs any more than necessary to install the keepers.*

6. Compress the valve spring with a compressor tool (**Figure 100**) and install the valve keepers. Make sure the keepers fit snugly into the grooves in the valve stem.

7. Remove the compression tool.

8. After the spring has been installed, gently tap the end of the valve stem with a soft aluminum or brass drift and hammer. This will ensure that the keepers are properly seated (**Figure 118**).

9. Repeat for all valve assemblies.

10. Install the cylinder head as described in this chapter.

Valve Guide Replacement

When valve guides are worn so that there is excessive valve stem-to-guide clearance or valve tipping, the guides must be replaced. This job should be done only by a dealer as special tools are required as well as considerable expertise. If a valve guide is replaced, also replace its valve.

The following procedure is provided in case you choose to perform this task yourself.

> *CAUTION*
> *There **may** be a residual oil or solvent odor left in the oven after heating the cylinder head. If you use a household oven, check first with the person who uses the oven for food preparation to avoid getting into trouble.*

1. Remove the bolts securing the intake manifolds (**Figure 119**) onto the cylinder head. Remove all intake manifolds before placing the cylinder head in the oven.

> *CAUTION*
> *Do not heat the cylinder head with a torch (propane or acetylene); never bring a flame into contact with the cylinder head or valve guides. The direct heat will destroy the case hardening of the valve guides and will likely cause warpage of the cylinder head. The entire cylinder head assembly must be heated as a unit.*

2. The valve guides are installed with a slight interference fit. Place the cylinder head in a heated oven (or on a hot

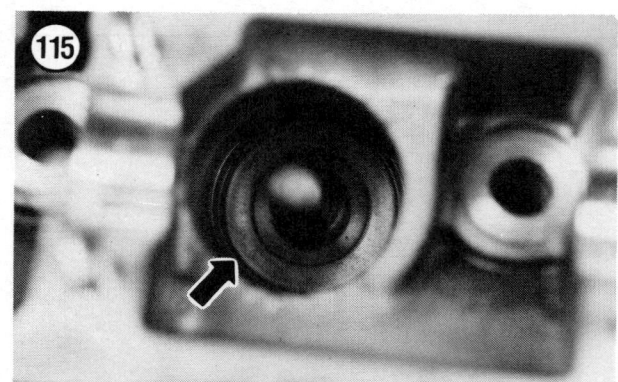

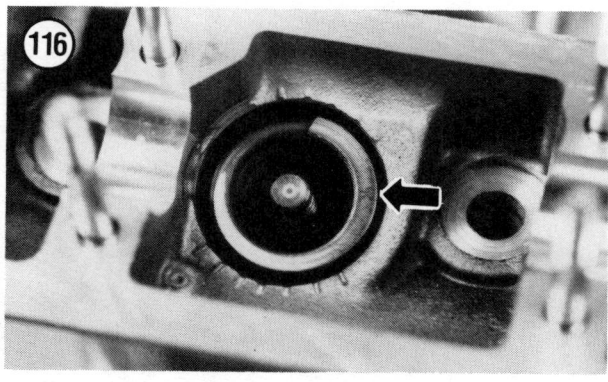

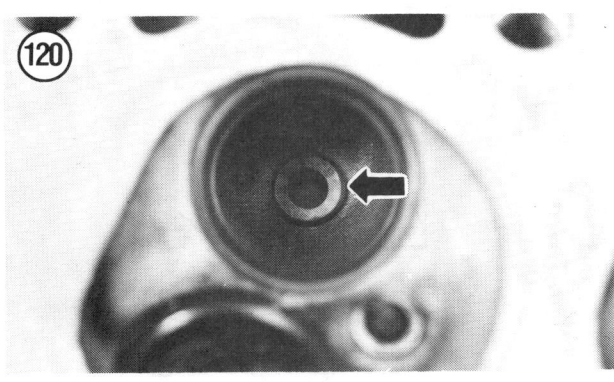

plate). Heat the cylinder head to a temperature between 222-240° C (428-465° F).

3. While heating up the cylinder head, place the new valve guides in a freezer for 30 minutes. Chilling them will slightly reduce their overall diameter while the hot cylinder head is slightly larger due to heat expansion. This will make valve guide installation much easier.

4. Remove the cylinder head from the oven and hold onto it with kitchen pot holders, heavy gloves or heavy shop cloths. It is very *hot*.

5. Turn the cylinder head upside down on wood blocks. Make sure the cylinder is properly supported on the wood blocks.

6. From the combustion chamber side of the cylinder head, drive out the old valve guide (**Figure 120**) with a hammer and BMW valve guide remover. Remove the special tool.

7. Remove and discard the valve guide and the ring. *Never* reinstall a valve guide or ring that has been removed as it is no longer true nor is it within tolerances.

8. Install a new ring onto the valve guide.

CAUTION
Failure to apply fresh engine oil to both the valve guide and the valve guide hole in the cylinder head will result in damage to the cylinder head and/or the new valve guide.

9. Reheat the cylinder head as previously described.

10. Apply fresh engine oil to the new valve guide and the valve guide hole in the cylinder head.

11. From the top side (camshaft side) of the cylinder head, drive in the new valve guide with a hammer and BMW valve guide installer. Drive the valve guide in until it completely seats in the cylinder head. Remove the special tool.

12. After installation, ream the new valve guide with the BMW special tool.

13. If necessary, repeat Steps 1-12 for any other valve guides.

14. Thoroughly clean the cylinder head and valve guides with solvent to wash out all metal particles. Dry with compressed air.

15. Reface the valve seats as described in this chapter.

16. Install the intake manifolds and bolts (**Figure 119**). Tighten all bolts securely.

Valve Seat Inspection

1. Remove the valves as described in this chapter.

2. The most accurate method for checking the valve seal is to use Prussian blue or machinist's dye, available from auto parts stores or machine shops. To check the valve seal with Prussian blue or machinist's dye, perform the following:

   a. Thoroughly clean off all carbon deposits from the valve face with solvent or detergent, then thoroughly dry.

4

b. Spread a thin layer of Prussian blue or machinist's dye evenly on the valve face.

c. Moisten the end of a suction cup valve tool (**Figure 121**) and attach it to the valve. Insert the valve into the guide.

d. Using the suction cup tool, tap the valve up and down in the cylinder head. Do *not* rotate the valve or a false indication will result.

e. Remove the valve and examine the impression left by the Prussian blue or machinist's dye. If the impression left in the dye (on the valve or in the cylinder head) is not even and continuous and the valve seat width is not within specified tolerance listed in **Table 1** or **Table 2**, the cylinder head valve seat must be reconditioned.

3. Closely examine the valve seat (**Figure 122**) in the cylinder head. It should be smooth and even with a polished seating surface.

4. If the valve seat is okay, install the valves as described in this chapter.

5. If the valve seat is not correct, recondition the valve seat as described in this chapter.

Valve Seat Reconditioning

Special valve cutter tools and considerable expertise are required to properly recondition the valve seats in the cylinder head. You can save considerable money by removing the cylinder head and taking just the cylinder head to a dealer or machine shop and have the valve seats ground.

The following procedure is provided in you choose to perform this task yourself.

The BMW valve seat cutter tool (part No. 00 3 520) is available from BMW dealers or from machine shop supply outlets. Follow the manufacturer's instructions for operating the cutter.

The intake and exhaust valve seats are machined to the same angles. See **Table 1** or **Table 2**.

Refer to **Figure 123** for valve seat diameter and valve seat width. The valve seat diameter and seat width are listed in **Table 1** or **Table 2**.

1. Use the special tool and descale and clean the valve seat with one or two turns.

CAUTION
Measure the valve seat contact area in the cylinder head after each cut to make sure the contact area is correct and to prevent removing too much material. If too much material is removed, the valve seat inserts will have to be replaced.

2. If the seat is still pitted or burned, turn the cutter additional turns until the surface is clean. Refer to the previous CAUTION to avoid removing too much material from the cylinder head.

3. Inspect the valve seat-to-valve face impression as follows:

a. Spread a thin layer of Prussian blue or machinist's dye evenly on the valve face.

b. Moisten the end of a suction cup valve tool (**Figure 121**) and attach it to the valve. Insert the valve into the guide.

c. Using the suction cup tool, tap the valve up and down in the cylinder head. Do *not* rotate the valve or a false indication will result.

d. Remove the valve and examine the impression left by the Prussian blue or machinist's dye.

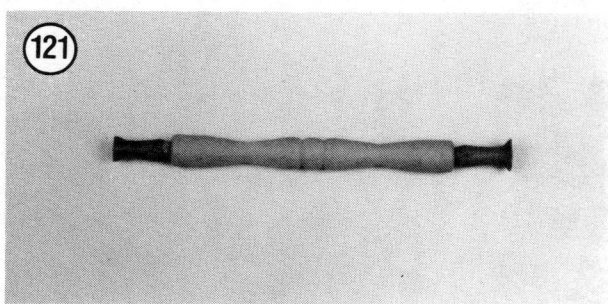

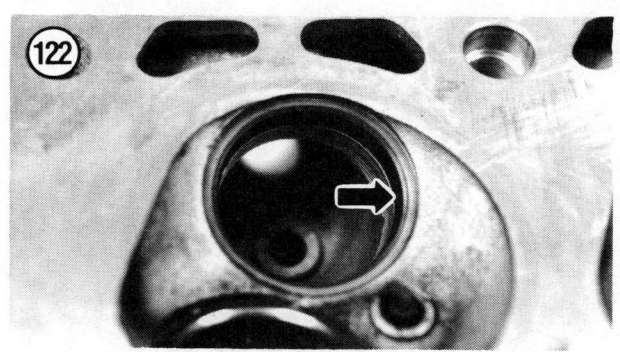

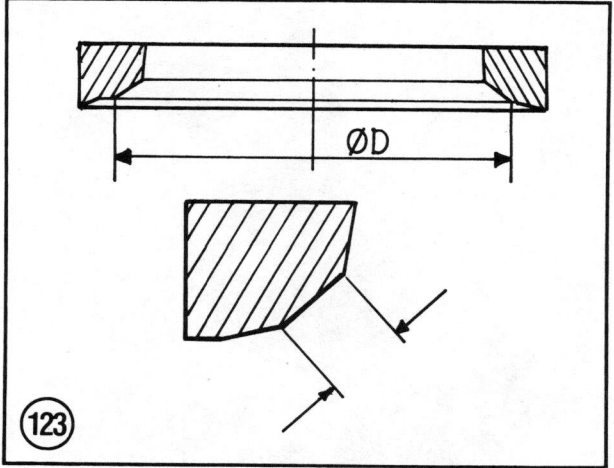

e. Measure the valve seat width. Refer to **Table 1** or **Table 2** for the seat width.

CAUTION
There must not be any tool chatter marks on the valve seat face as this will cause leaking.

4. Check that the finish has a smooth and velvety surface; it should *not* be shiny or highly polished. The final seating will take place when the engine is first run.
5. Repeat Steps 1-4 for all remaining valve seats.
6. Thoroughly clean the cylinder head and all valve components in solvent or detergent and hot water.
7. Install the valve assemblies as described in this chapter and fill the ports with solvent to check for leaks. If any leaks are present, the valve seats must be inspected for foreign matter or burrs that may be preventing a proper seal.

8. If the cylinder head and valve components were cleaned in detergent and hot water, apply a light coat of engine oil to all bare metal surfaces to prevent any rust formations.

OIL/WATER PUMP

Removal

The oil/water pump can be removed with the engine in the frame. This procedure is shown with the engine removed for clarity.
Refer to **Figure 124** for this procedure.
1. On models so equipped, remove the engine spoiler as described under *Engine Spoiler Removal/Installation* in Chapter Thirteen.
2. Drain the engine oil as described under *Engine Oil and Filter Change* in Chapter Three.

4

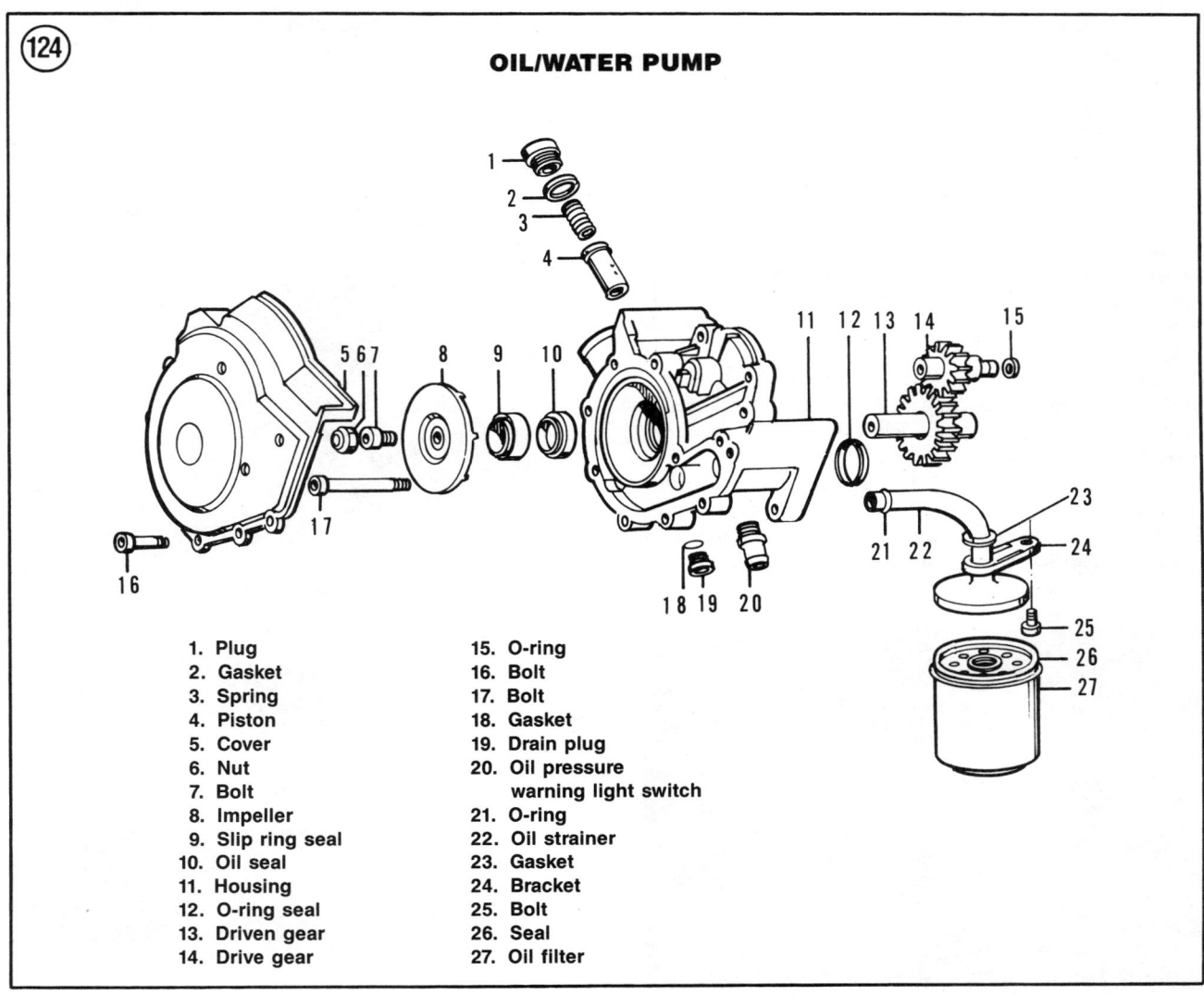

OIL/WATER PUMP

1. Plug
2. Gasket
3. Spring
4. Piston
5. Cover
6. Nut
7. Bolt
8. Impeller
9. Slip ring seal
10. Oil seal
11. Housing
12. O-ring seal
13. Driven gear
14. Drive gear
15. O-ring
16. Bolt
17. Bolt
18. Gasket
19. Drain plug
20. Oil pressure warning light switch
21. O-ring
22. Oil strainer
23. Gasket
24. Bracket
25. Bolt
26. Seal
27. Oil filter

3. Drain the cooling system as described under *Coolant Change* in Chapter Three.

4. Loosen the hose clamp (**Figure 125**) on the lower hose at the oil/water pump inlet. Slide the clamp off of the pump inlet and remove the hose from the inlet.

5. Remove the screws securing the cover (**Figure 126**) and remove the cover.

6. Disconnect the electrical connector (**Figure 127**) from the oil pressure warning light switch.

7. Remove the bolts (**Figure 128**) securing the pump assembly to the cylinder block and remove the pump assembly.

8. Remove the O-ring seal (**Figure 129**) from the lower crankcase. Discard the O-ring seal as a new one must be installed every time the pump is removed.

9. Inspect the pump assembly as described in this chapter.

Installation

> *NOTE*
> *If oil has been leaking from the oil/water pump sealing surface at the 2:00 position (looking straight on at the pump assembly) the oil return channel in the lower crankcase is probably clogged either with oil sludge or old gasket sealant. This channel provides an oil return path so that excess oil can be channeled back into the crankcase.*

1. Clean off all old gasket material from both mating surfaces of the pump assembly, the pump cover and the cylinder block. Make sure the U-shaped groove where the cylinder block and the lower crankcase meet is clear (**Figure 130**).

2. Install a new O-ring seal (**Figure 129**) into the receptacle in the lower crankcase. Apply a light coat of cold grease to hold the O-ring in place while installing the pump assembly.

3. Apply a thin even coat of Three Bond 1216 gasket sealer to the mating surfaces of the pump assembly as shown in **Figure 131**. Do not apply sealant where it will enter into the U-channel when the pump assembly is installed.

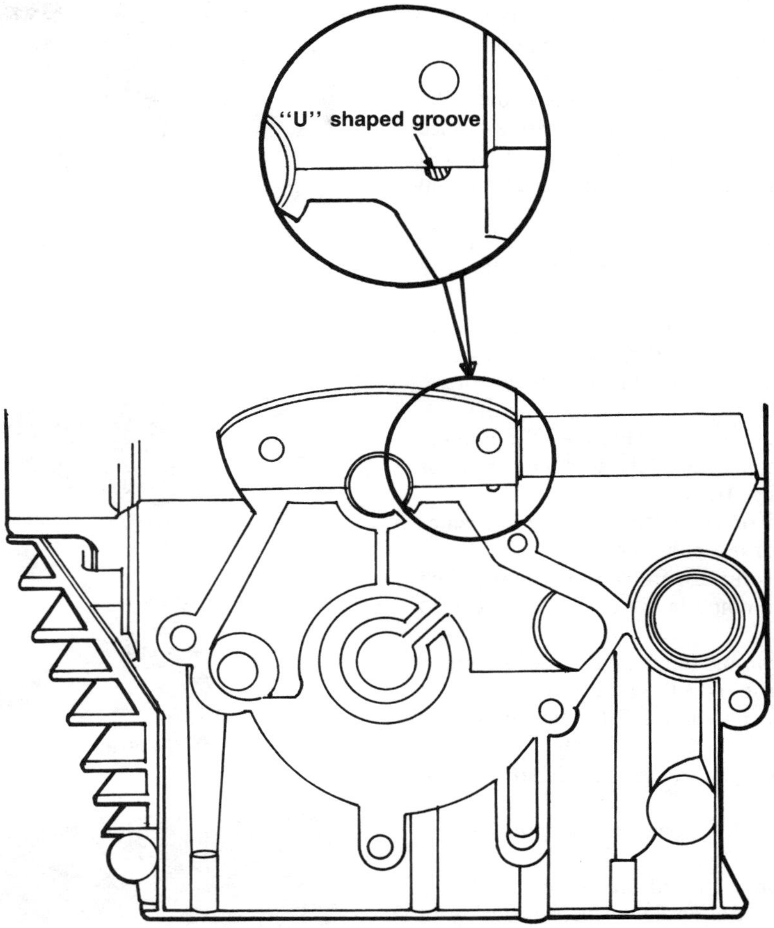

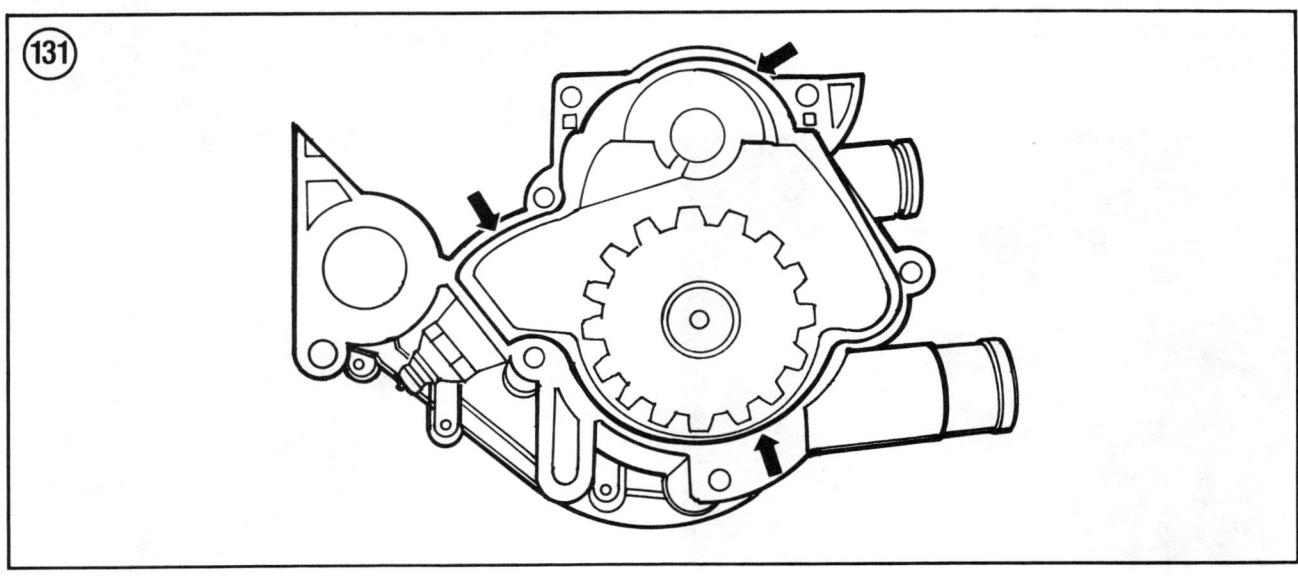

4. Align the locating tab (**Figure 132**) with the groove (**Figure 133**) in the output shaft and install the pump assembly. It may be necessary to slightly rotate the impeller (**Figure 134**) back and forth for final alignment.

5. Push the pump assembly on until it bottoms out. The pump should go on until it is flush against the mating surface of the cylinder block. Do not install the mounting bolts to try to pull the pump on the rest of the way. Remove the pump and solve the problem before proceeding any farther.

6. Install the mounting bolts. Install the long bolts (L, **Figure 128**) in the correct locations. Tighten the bolts only finger-tight at this time.

7. Tighten the bolts in a crisscross pattern. While tightening the bolts, have an assistant rotate the crankshaft in order to center the oil pump gears. Tighten the bolts to the torque specification listed in **Table 3**.

8. Connect the electrical connector (**Figure 127**) onto the oil pressure warning light switch. Make sure the connector is free of corrosion and is tight.

9. Apply a thin even coat of Three Bond 1216 gasket sealer to the mating surfaces of the pump cover.

10. Correctly locate the oil pressure warning light switch electrical wire under the notch in the cover (**Figure 135**) and install the cover.

11. Install the cover screws and tighten the screws securely.

12. Slide the coolant hose onto the pump inlet.

13. Slide the clamp into position and tighten the clamp securely.

14. Refill the cooling system as described under *Coolant Change* in Chapter Three.

15. Refill the engine oil as described under *Engine Oil and Filter Change* in Chapter Three.

16. On models so equipped, install the engine spoiler as described under *Engine Spoiler Removal/Installation* in Chapter Thirteen.

Disassembly/Inspection/Assembly

1. Remove the drive gear (**Figure 136**) from the backside of the pump housing.

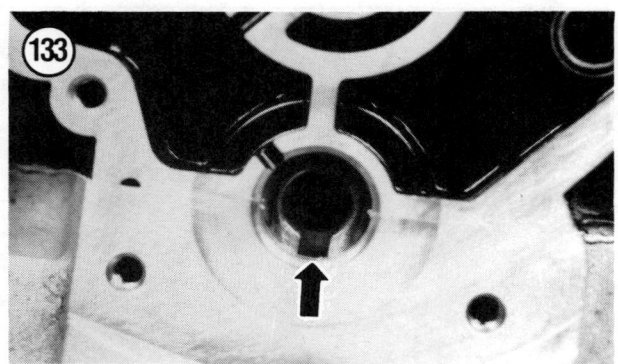

2. Install an Allen wrench into the end of the driven gear (**Figure 137**).

NOTE
Some early models are equipped with a bolt instead of a nut to secure the impeller to the driven gear.

3. Hold onto the Allen wrench and remove the nut (or bolt) (A, **Figure 138**) securing the impeller.
4. Remove the impeller (B, **Figure 138**).
5. Turn the pump over and remove the driven gear (**Figure 139**). If necessary, gently tap on the end of the driven gear shaft with a plastic or soft faced mallet.
6. Clean all parts in solvent and dry with compressed air.
7. If necessary, replace the slip ring seal and the oil seal as described in this chapter.
8. Inspect the housing for cracks or any visible damage. Refer to **Figure 140** and **Figure 141**.
9. If necessary, unscrew the oil pressure warning light switch (**Figure 142**) from the housing.

4

10. If necessary, unscrew the oil pressure relief valve (A, **Figure 143**) from the housing. Remove the plug, gasket, spring and piston from the housing.

11. Inspect the coolant inlet fitting (B, **Figure 143**) for damage or deterioration. If damaged to the point where the coolant hose will no longer fit on securely, replace the housing.

12. Inspect the vanes (**Figure 144**) on the impeller for wear or damage. Check the entire impeller for damage or deterioration and replace if necessary.

13. Inspect the teeth (**Figure 145**) on the driven gear. Replace the driven gear if the teeth are damaged or any are missing.

14. Inspect the shaft and the threads (**Figure 146**) on the driven gear. Replace the driven gear if the teeth are damaged or any are missing.

15. Inspect the teeth (**Figure 147**) on the drive gear. Replace the drive gear if the teeth are damaged or any are missing.

16. Install a new O-ring seal (**Figure 148**) on the drive gear.

CAUTION
Do not damage the slip ring and oil seals when installing the driven gear through them.

17. Install the driven gear (**Figure 139**). If necessary, gently tap on the end of the driven gear shaft with a plastic or soft faced mallet until the shaft is completely installed.

NOTE
Some early models are equipped with a bolt instead of a nut to secure the impeller to the driven gear.

18. Install the impeller (B, **Figure 138**) and bolt or nut.

19. Install an Allen wrench into the end of the driven gear (**Figure 137**).

CAUTION
*When tightening either a bolt or nut in Step 20, be sure to refer to the correct fastener in **Table***

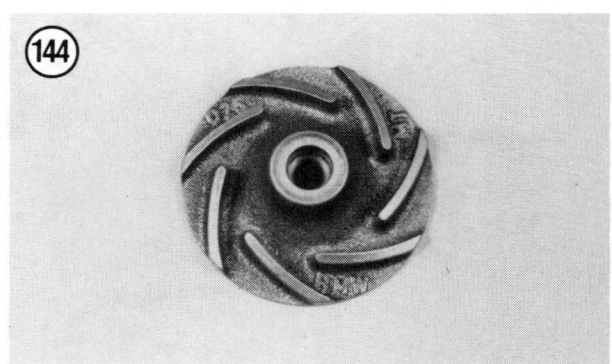

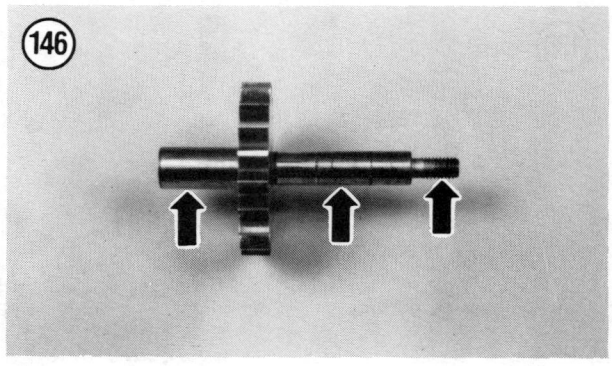

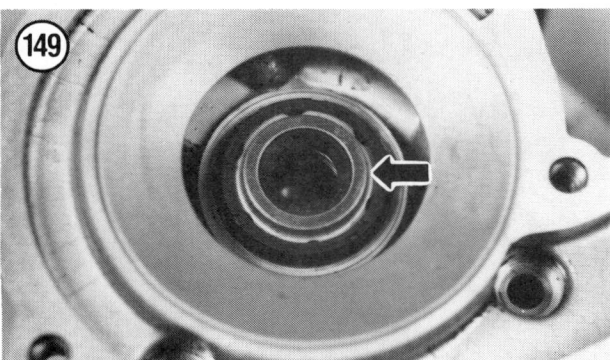

3 since the bolt is tightened a to a higher torque value than the nut.

20. Hold onto the Allen wrench and tighten the bolt or nut (A, **Figure 138**) securing the impeller. Tighten to the torque specification listed in **Table 3**. Remove the Allen wrench.

21. Install the drive gear (**Figure 136**) into the backside of the pump housing.

Seal Replacement

1. Carefully withdraw the slip ring seal (**Figure 149**) from the front side of the pump housing. Be careful not to damage the pump housing during seal removal.

2. Turn the pump housing over and carefully drive the oil seal (**Figure 150**) out of the pump housing from the backside. Be careful to not damage the pump housing during seal removal.

3. Clean the housing in solvent and dry with compressed air.

4. Make sure the weep hole (**Figure 151**) is open and free of any oil sludge. Clean out and blow out with compressed air.

5. Make sure the oil seal and slip ring seal area (**Figure 152**) in the housing are clean prior to installing the new seals.

6. Position the oil seal with the lip facing out (**Figure 153**).

7. Place the oil seal into position and drive it in with a socket that matches the outer diameter of the oil seal (**Figure 154**). Drive the seal in until it bottoms out.

8. Position the slip ring seal with the metal collar facing out (**Figure 155**).

9. Place the slip ring seal into position and drive it in with a socket that matches the outer diameter of the oil seal (**Figure 156**). Drive the seal in until it bottoms out.

INTERMEDIATE HOUSING

Removal/Inspection/Installation

1. Remove the frame from the engine as described in this chapter.

2. Remove the transmission housing as described under *Transmission Housing Removal* in Chapter Six.

3. Remove the clutch assembly as described under *Clutch Removal* in Chapter Five.

4. Using a T-30 Torx wrench, in a crisscross pattern remove the Torx bolts securing the intermediate housing (**Figure 157**) to the engine.

5. Pull the intermediate housing straight back and off of the engine. Don't lose the locating dowels on the backside of the housing. It is not necessary to remove the locating dowels if they are secure.

6. Rotate the starter intermediate shaft bearing (**Figure 158**) with your fingers. It must rotate smoothly with no binding. If necessary, replace the bearing as described in this chapter.

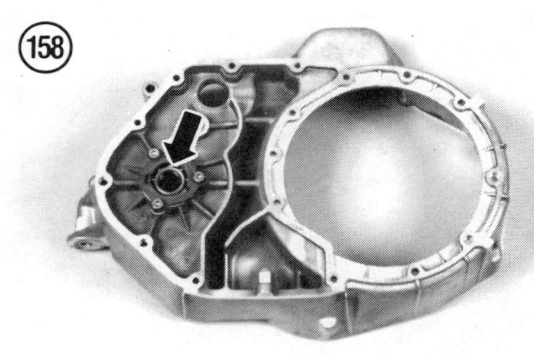

7. Inspect the intermediate housing for cracks or damage. Carefully inspect the ribs and bosses for damage. Refer to **Figure 159** and **Figure 160**.

8. Install by reversing these removal steps, noting the following.

9. Make sure the locating dowels are in place on the backside of the housing prior to installation.

10. Using a T-30 Torx wrench, in a crisscross pattern tighten the Torx bolts securing the intermediate housing to

the engine. Tighten the bolts to the torque specification listed in **Table 3**.

**Intermediate Shaft
Bearing Replacement
in Intermediate Housing**

Refer to **Figure 161** for this procedure.
1. Remove the bolts (A, **Figure 162**) securing the thrust plate and remove the thrust plate (B, **Figure 162**).

4

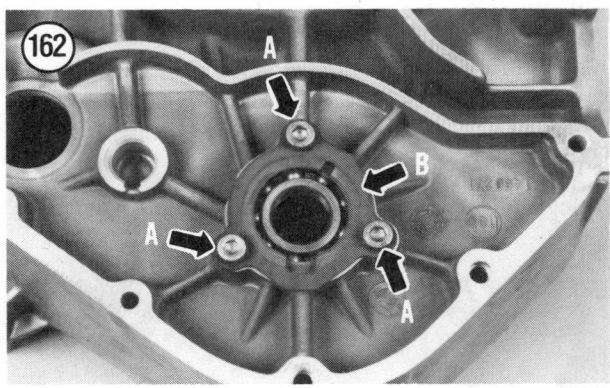

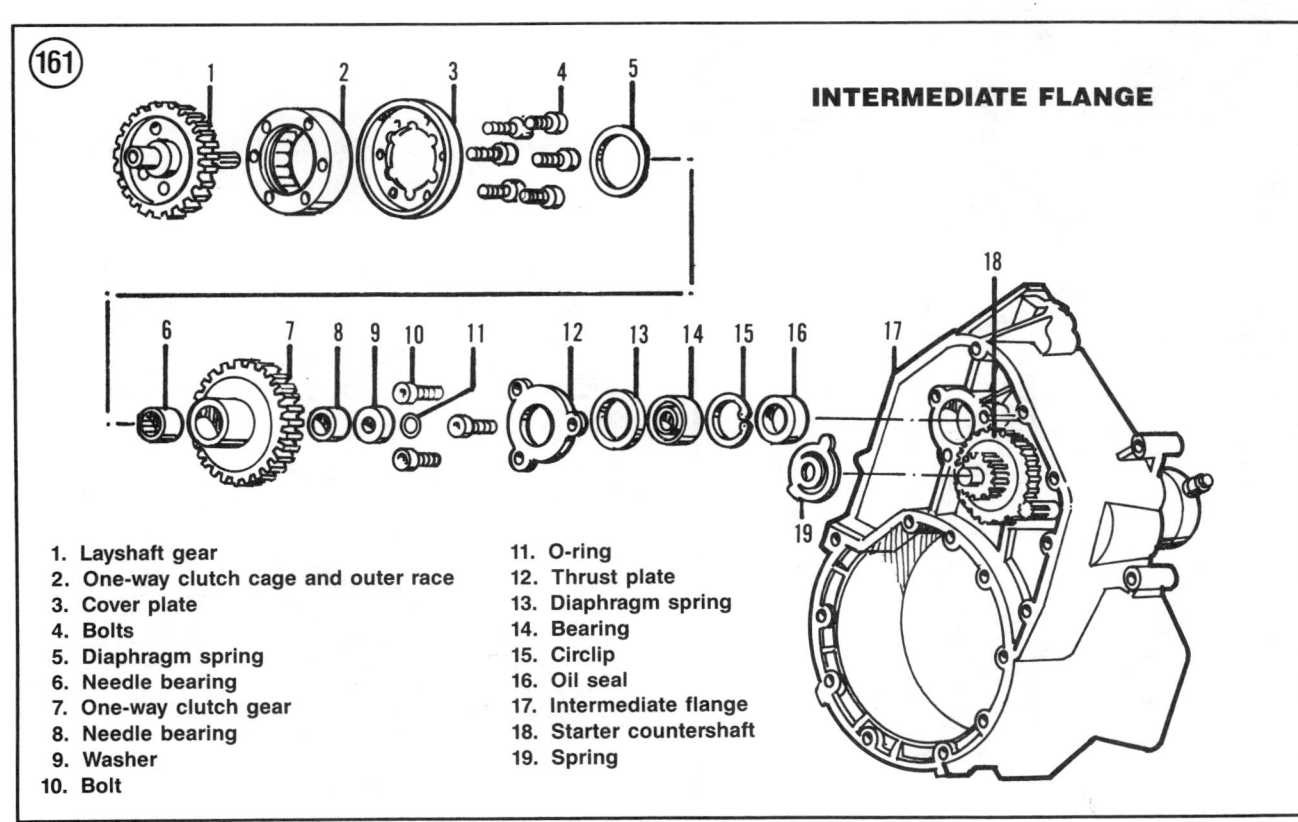

INTERMEDIATE FLANGE

1. Layshaft gear
2. One-way clutch cage and outer race
3. Cover plate
4. Bolts
5. Diaphragm spring
6. Needle bearing
7. One-way clutch gear
8. Needle bearing
9. Washer
10. Bolt
11. O-ring
12. Thrust plate
13. Diaphragm spring
14. Bearing
15. Circlip
16. Oil seal
17. Intermediate flange
18. Starter countershaft
19. Spring

2. Remove the diaphragm spring.

3. Heat the intermediate housing to 100-120° C (215-250° F).

4. Install BMW special tool (part No. 00 7 500) into the bearing and withdraw the bearing from the housing.

5. Carefully pry the oil seal out of the housing. Do not damage the surrounding area of the housing.

6. If necessary, remove the circlip with circlip pliers.

7. If removed, install the circlip.

8. Using a suitable size socket, carefully tap the new oil seal into the housing. Tap the new seal (**Figure 163**) in until it bottoms out against the circlip.

9. Place the new bearing in a freezer for 30 minutes. This will reduce the size of the bearing and make installation easier.

10. Install the bearing into the housing. If necessary tap it into place squarely using a hammer and socket that matches the outer race of the bearing. Tap the bearing in until it bottoms out against the circlip.

11. Position the diaphragm spring with the convex side facing out (**Figure 164**) and install the diaphragm spring.

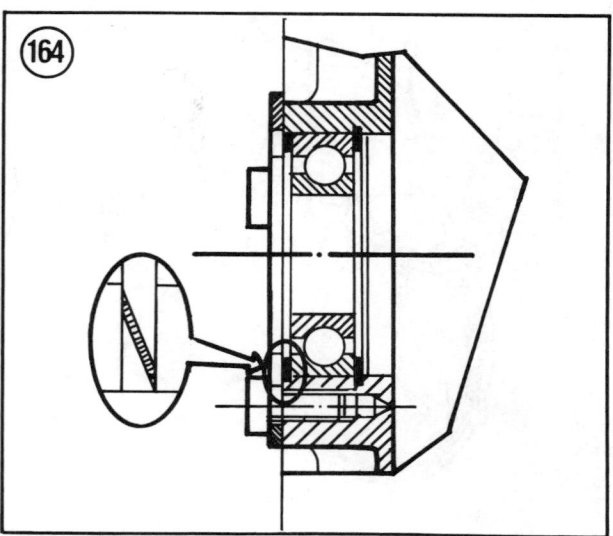

12. Install the thrust flange.

13. Apply blue Loctite Threadlocker No. 242 to the bolt threads prior to installation.

14. Install the bolts and tighten to the torque specification listed in **Table 3**.

**STARTER CLUTCH
AND GEARS**

Removal/Installation

1. Remove the intermediate housing as described in this chapter.

2. If not already removed, remove the bolt (A, **Figure 165**) and remove the alternator drive dog (B, **Figure 165**).

3. Remove the starter countershaft and spring (**Figure 166**).

4. Remove the starter one-way clutch assembly (**Figure 167**).

5. Install the starter one-way clutch assembly (**Figure 167**) and push it in until it bottoms out.

6. Apply a coat of cold grease to the cylinder block where the countershaft spring is installed (**Figure 168**). This will help hold the spring in place while installing the countershaft.

7. Install the spring as shown in **Figure 169**.

8. Install the starter countershaft (**Figure 166**). Make sure the spring is still in place when installing the countershaft. Push the countershaft in until it bottoms out.

9. Apply red Loctite Threadlocker No. 271 to the bolt threads prior to installation. Install the alternator drive dog (B, **Figure 165**) and the bolt (A, **Figure 165**). Tighten the bolt to the torque specification listed in **Table 3**.

10. Install the intermediate housing as described in this chapter.

Disassembly

Refer to **Figure 170** for this procedure.

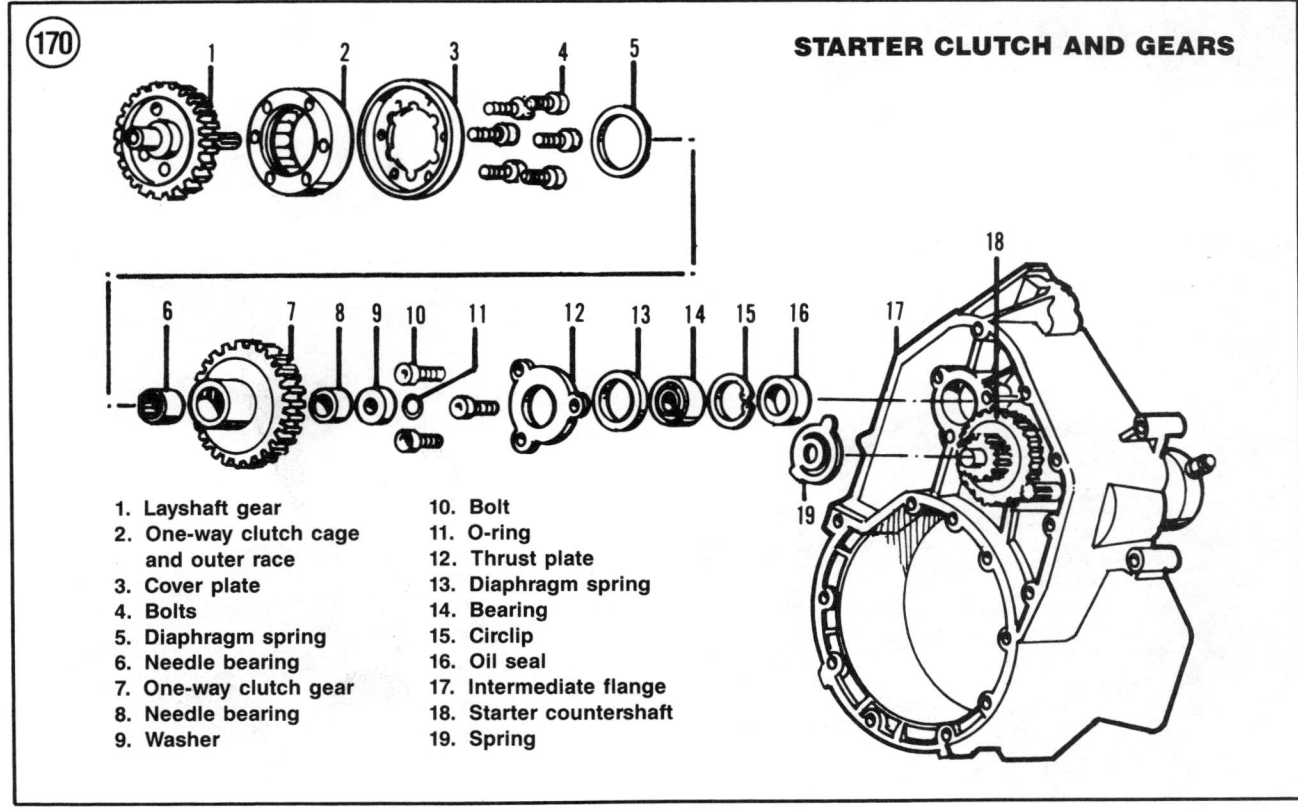

STARTER CLUTCH AND GEARS

1. Layshaft gear
2. One-way clutch cage and outer race
3. Cover plate
4. Bolts
5. Diaphragm spring
6. Needle bearing
7. One-way clutch gear
8. Needle bearing
9. Washer
10. Bolt
11. O-ring
12. Thrust plate
13. Diaphragm spring
14. Bearing
15. Circlip
16. Oil seal
17. Intermediate flange
18. Starter countershaft
19. Spring

NOTE
*A handy "tool" that should be used for this disassembly procedure is a large egg flat (the type that restaurants get their eggs in). As you remove a part from the shaft set it in one of the depressions in the same position from which it was removed (**Figure 171**). This is an easy way to remember the correct relationship of all parts.*

1. Remove the O-ring (**Figure 172**) and the thrust washer (**Figure 173**).

2. Remove the one-way clutch gear (**Figure 174**).

3. Remove the bolts (**Figure 175**) securing the cover plate and remove the cover plate (**Figure 176**).

4. Rotate the one-way clutch cage (**Figure 177**) *clockwise* and remove it from the outer race.

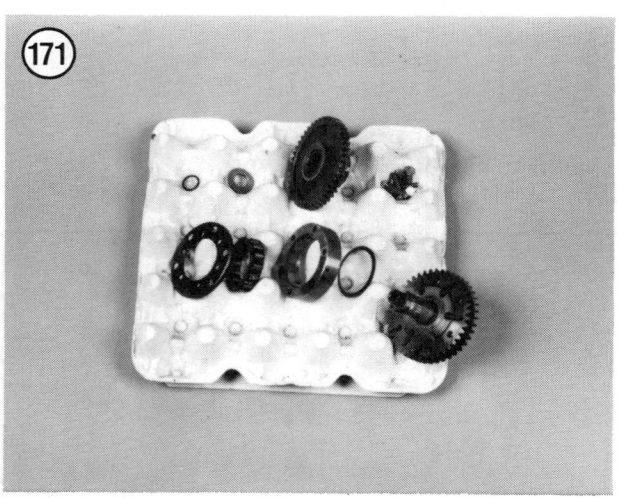

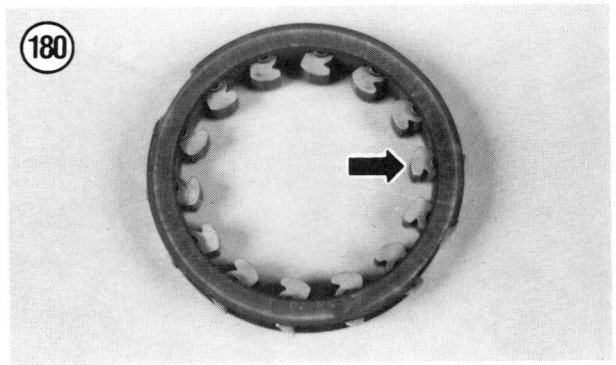

5. Remove the outer race (**Figure 178**) and diaphragm spring (**Figure 179**) from the layshaft.

6. Inspect all parts as described in this chapter.

Inspection

1. Check the rollers in the one-way clutch cage. Refer to **Figure 180** and **Figure 181**. Check for smooth operation. Check the rollers for uneven or excessive wear, galling and pitting.

2. Insert the one-way clutch cage into the outer race and rotate it with your fingers. Check for smooth operation in the *clockwise* direction and make sure it will not rotate *counterclockwise*. If the one-way clutch cage does not operate correctly, replace the faulty part.

3. Inspect the roller riding surface (**Figure 182**) of the outer race for wear or abrasion. If damaged, both the outer race and one-way clutch cage must be replaced as a set.

4

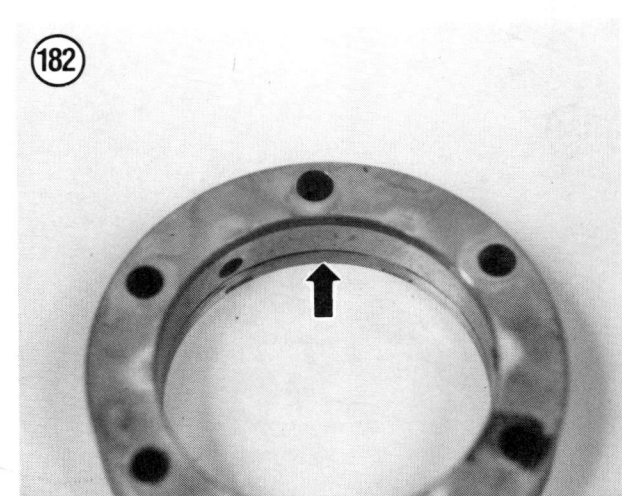

4. Inspect the outer race (**Figure 183**) for wear or damage. If damaged, both the outer race and one-way clutch cage must be replaced as a set.

5. Inspect the layshaft gear (**Figure 184**) for chipped or missing teeth. Look for uneven or excessive wear on the gear faces. If damaged, replace the layshaft gear.

6. Inspect the oil hole (A, **Figure 185**) in the layshaft gear. Make sure it is open. If necessary, clean out with solvent and blow out with compressed air.

7. Inspect the alternator drive dog splines (B, **Figure 185**) on the layshaft gear for damage. If damage is severe, replace the layshaft gear.

8. Inspect the oil grooves (**Figure 186**) on the layshaft gear for damage. If damage is severe, replace the layshaft gear.

9. Inspect the one-way clutch gear (**Figure 187**) for chipped missing teeth. Look for uneven or excessive wear on the gear faces. If found, replace the one-way clutch gear.

10. Inspect the roller riding surface of the one-way clutch for wear or abrasion. If damaged, both the one-way clutch gear and one-way clutch cage must be replaced as a set.

11. Inspect the one-way clutch gear needle bearings (**Figure 188**). Rotate each bearing with your fingers. Check for smooth operation. If necessary, replace the bearings as described in this chapter.

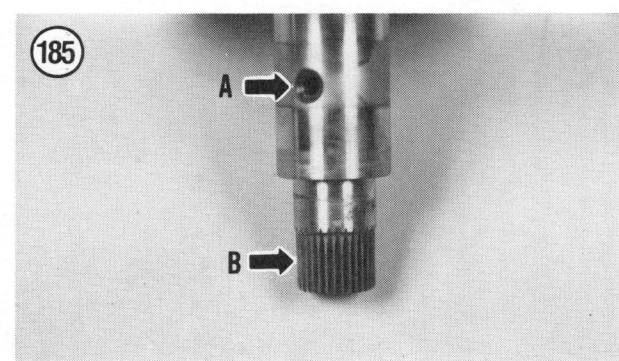

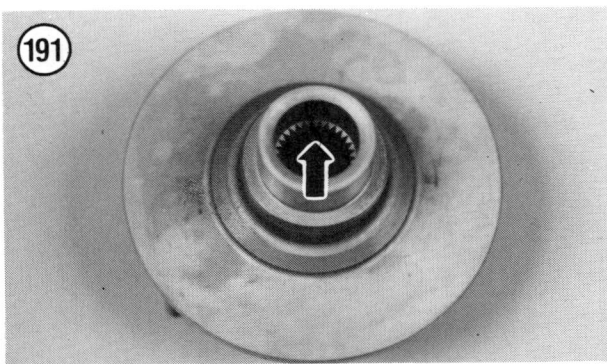

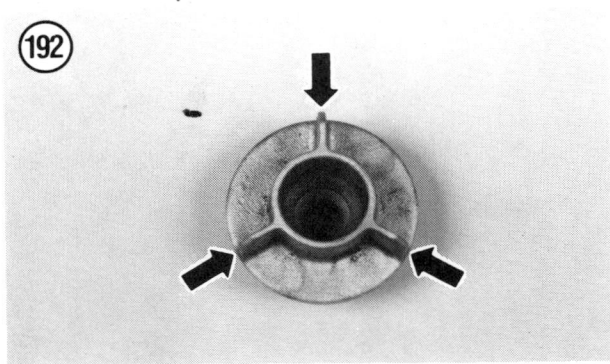

12. Inspect the starter countershaft gear for chipped or missing teeth. Refer to **Figure 189** and **Figure 190**. Look for uneven or excessive wear on the gear faces. If damaged, replace the starter countershaft gear.

13. Inspect the alternator drive dog inner splines (**Figure 191**). If damage is severe, replace the layshaft gear.

14. Inspect the raised tabs (**Figure 192**) on the alternator drive dog for wear or damage. Replace if necessary.

One-way Clutch Gear
Needle Bearing Replacement

1. Using BMW special tool (part No. 00 8 570) pull the bearing out of each side of the gear.

2. Clean out the inner surface of the gear with solvent and wipe dry with a lint free cloth.

3. Place the new bearings in a freezer for 30 minutes. This will reduce their overall size and will make installation easier.

4. Position the new bearing with the lettering facing toward the outside.

5. Using a socket that matches the outer diameter of the bearing, carefully tap or press the bearing into the gear. The bearing must *not* be installed flush with the gear shoulder. The bearing must be installed so that it is 0.2-0.6 mm (0.008-0.024 in.) past the outer surface of the gear shoulder as shown in **Figure 193**.

6. Repeat Step 5 for the other bearing.

7. After the bearings are installed, rotate each bearing with your fingers. Check for smooth operation.

8. Apply fresh engine oil to the bearings.

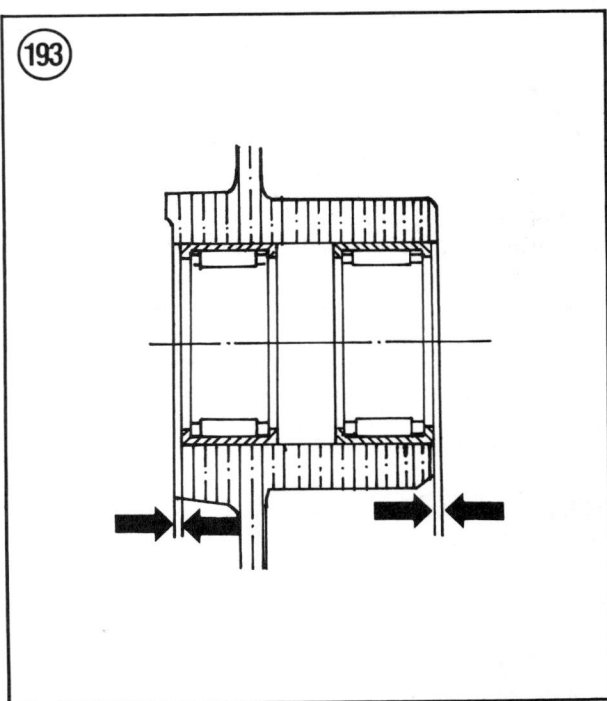

Assembly

1. Position the diaphragm spring (**Figure 194**) with the convex side facing up and install the diaphragm spring onto the layshaft gear.
2. Install the outer race (**Figure 178**) onto the layshaft and align the mounting holes with the layshaft gear.
3. Apply fresh engine oil to the one-way clutch cage.
4. Position the one-way clutch cage with the flange side (**Figure 195**) facing up.
5. Hold onto the outer race and insert the one-way clutch cage into the outer race while rotating it *clockwise* with your fingers (**Figure 177**).
6. Continue to rotate the one-way clutch cage and push down until the one-way clutch cage has bottomed out in the outer race.
7. Make sure the mounting holes are aligned and install the cover plate and the bolts (**Figure 175**). Tighten the bolts to the torque specification listed in **Table 3**.
8. Install the one-way clutch gear into the assembly while rotating it *clockwise*. Continue to rotate and push down until the one-way clutch gear bottoms out (**Figure 174**).
9. After the one-way clutch gear is installed, rotate it *clockwise* and check for smooth operation in this direction. Try to rotate the gear *counterclockwise;* the gear should not rotate. If the gear does not rotate as described, the one-way clutch is installed backwards. Remove the gear and repeat Steps 4-9 and check for correct operation.
10. Install the thrust washer (**Figure 173**).
11. Install a new O-ring (**Figure 172**).

OIL PAN, LOWER CRANKCASE HALF AND OUTPUT SHAFT

NOTE
If there is a distinct noise coming from somewhere between the crankshaft and the output shaft gears there could be a problem with the springs in the output shaft. The noise may vary between a whine, to a knock or rattle. These noises vary with engine speed but the noise usually occurs at low engine rpm. If you are experiencing this noise problem, take the bike to a BMW dealer and have them check it out. This problem was defined in BMW Service-Information Bulletin—October 1988, No. 11 037 88 (2289), Revision.

Removal

1. Remove the frame from the engine as described in this chapter.
2. Remove the intermediate flange as described in this chapter.
3. Remove the bolts securing the oil pan (**Figure 196**) and remove the oil pan.

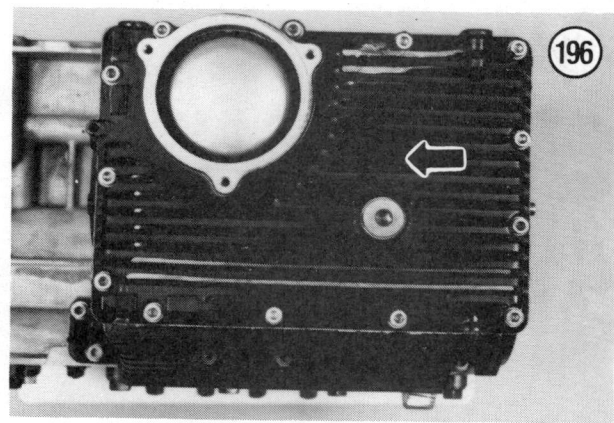

4. Unscrew the oil filter (**Figure 197**).

5. Remove the bolts (**Figure 198**) securing the lower crankcase half and remove the lower crankcase half (**Figure 199**) from the cylinder block. Don't lose the locating dowels in the cylinder block. It is not necessary to remove them if they are secure.

6. Remove the thrust washer and oil seal from the rear of the output shaft.

> *CAUTION*
> *On K75 models, the gear at the front of the shaft and the needle bearing at the rear of the shaft are loose and can slide off of the output shaft ends. Hold onto the gear and needle bearing while removing the output shaft from the cylinder block to avoid dropping them.*

7. Lift up and remove the output shaft (**Figure 200**) from the cylinder block.

8. Remove the O-ring seals (**Figure 201**) from the cylinder block. Discard the O-rings as they must be replaced.

9. Inspect the lower crankcase half and the output shaft as described in this chapter.

Installation

1. Remove all old sealant or gasket residue from the mating surfaces of the cylinder block, each side of the lower crankcase half and oil pan. Finish off by cleaning the surfaces with an aerosol electrical contact cleaner and wipe with lint-free cloth.

2. Make sure the locating dowels (**Figure 202**) are in place in the cylinder block.

3. Install new O-ring seals (**Figure 201**) into their receptacles in the cylinder block.

CAUTION
On K75 models, remember that the gear on the front of the output shaft and the needle bearing at the rear of the shaft are loose and can slide off of the output shaft ends. Hold onto the gear and needle bearing while installing the output shaft into the cylinder block.

CAUTION
On K75 models, the output shaft also includes a balancer weight. When the output shaft is installed into the cylinder block it must be aligned correctly with the crankshaft. This alignment must be correct or there will be severe engine vibration that could lead to engine damage.

4A. On K75 models, perform the following:
a. Rotate the crankshaft until the index mark (A, **Figure 203**) is visible.

b. Partially install the output shaft into the cylinder block.
c. Align the notch (B, **Figure 203**) on the output shaft gear with the index mark (A, **Figure 203**) on the crankshaft and mesh the output shaft gear with the crankshaft gear.
d. Push the output shaft down into the cylinder block.

4B. On K100 models, install the output shaft (**Figure 200**) into the cylinder block and mesh it with the crankshaft gear.

5. Make sure the circlips are correctly seated in the grooves in the cylinder block. These control output shaft end float. Refer to **Figure 204** and **Figure 205**.

6. Rotate the circlips so that one end of the circlip is flush with the cylinder block mating surface.

7. Apply Three Bond No. 1216 gasket sealant to the cylinder block mating surface of the lower crankcase half following the manufacturer's instructions.

8. Install the lower crankcase half onto the cylinder block.

9. Push the lower crankcase half all the way down until it bottoms out. The lower crankcase half should go on until it is flush against the mating surface of the cylinder block. Do not install the mounting bolts to try to pull the lower crankcase half the rest of the way down. Remove the lower crankcase half and solve the problem before proceeding any farther.

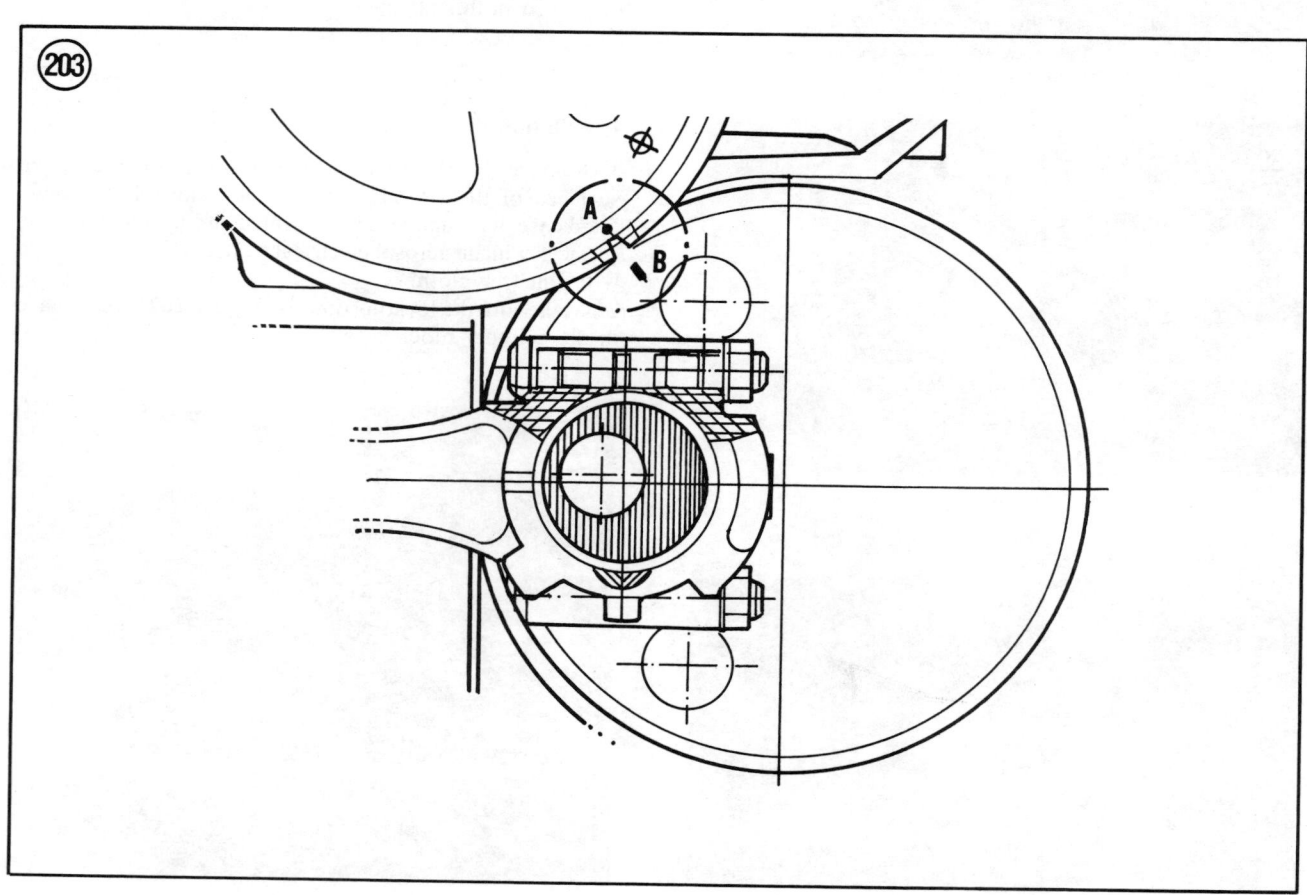

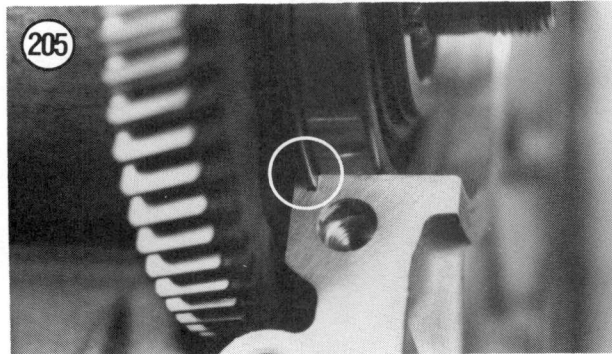

10. Install the bolts (**Figure 198**) securing the lower crankcase half. Tighten the bolts to the torque specification listed in **Table 3**.

11. Install a new oil seal (**Figure 206**) and thrust washer (**Figure 207**). Push the thrust washer in until it bottoms out (**Figure 208**).

12. Unscrew the oil filter (**Figure 197**).

13. Apply Three Bond No. 1216 gasket sealer to the sealing surface of the oil pan (**Figure 209**) following the manufacturer's instructions.

14. Install the oil pan (**Figure 196**) and bolts. Tighten the bolts in a crisscross pattern to the torque specification listed in **Table 3**.

15. Install the intermediate flange as described in this chapter.

16. Install the frame onto the engine as described in this chapter.

Oil Pan and Crankcase Lower Half Inspection

1. Thoroughly clean all parts in solvent and dry with compressed air.

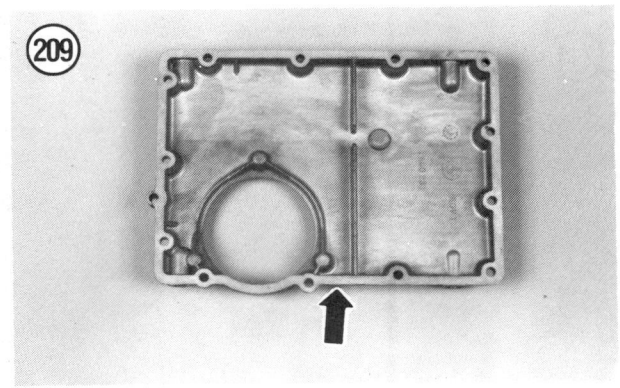

2. Inspect the oil pan for damaged cooling fins (**Figure 210**). If damage is slight and will not cause an oil leak there is no need to replace the oil pan. If there are any fractures that could lead to an oil leak, replace the oil pan.

3. Make sure the oil pan sealing surface (**Figure 209**) is free of any damage which could lead to an oil leak. Replace the oil pan if necessary.

4. Check the grooves for the output shaft bearing set rings. They must be clear and free of dirt in order for the rings to properly seat.

5. Make sure the oil return channel (A, **Figure 211**) is clear. This channel must be open to provide a flow path for excess oil from the oil pump. This will allow the oil to flow back into the crankcase.

6. Inspect the crankcase lower half for damage. Make sure the sealing surface on each side is free of any damage which could lead to an oil leak. Refer to B, **Figure 211** and **Figure 212**. Replace the crankcase lower half if necessary.

7. Make sure all oil flow channels in the crankcase lower half are open and clean. Blow out with compressed air.

Output Shaft
Preliminary Inspection

1. Clean the assembly in solvent and dry thoroughly.

2. Rotate the bearing (**Figure 213**) on the front end of the shaft. It should rotate freely with no signs of binding.

3. Inspect the gear and idle gear (**Figure 214**) for chipped or missing teeth. Look for uneven or excessive wear on the

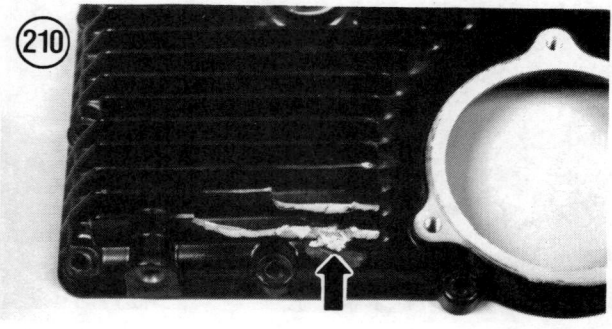

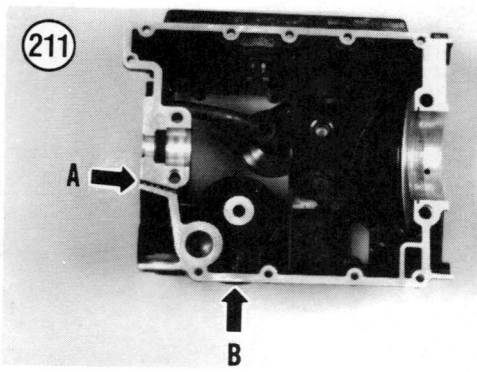

gear faces. If damaged, replace the gears as described in this chapter.

4. Slide off the needle bearing and inspect the needles (**Figure 215**) for wear or damage. Replace if necessary.

5. Make sure the large circlip (**Figure 216**) on the front end bearing is in good condition. If bent or damaged, replace with a new one.

6. Inspect the inner bearing ring (**Figure 217**) at the rear of the shaft. It should rotate freely with no signs of binding. Replace if necessary.

Output Shaft
Disassembly/Assembly (K75 Models)

Refer to **Figure 218** for this procedure.

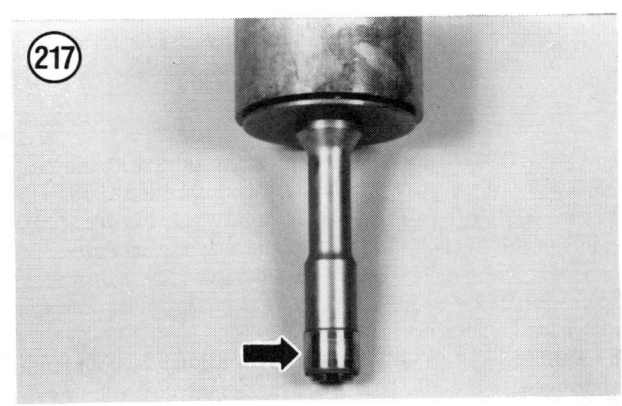

4

OUTPUT SHAFT (K75)

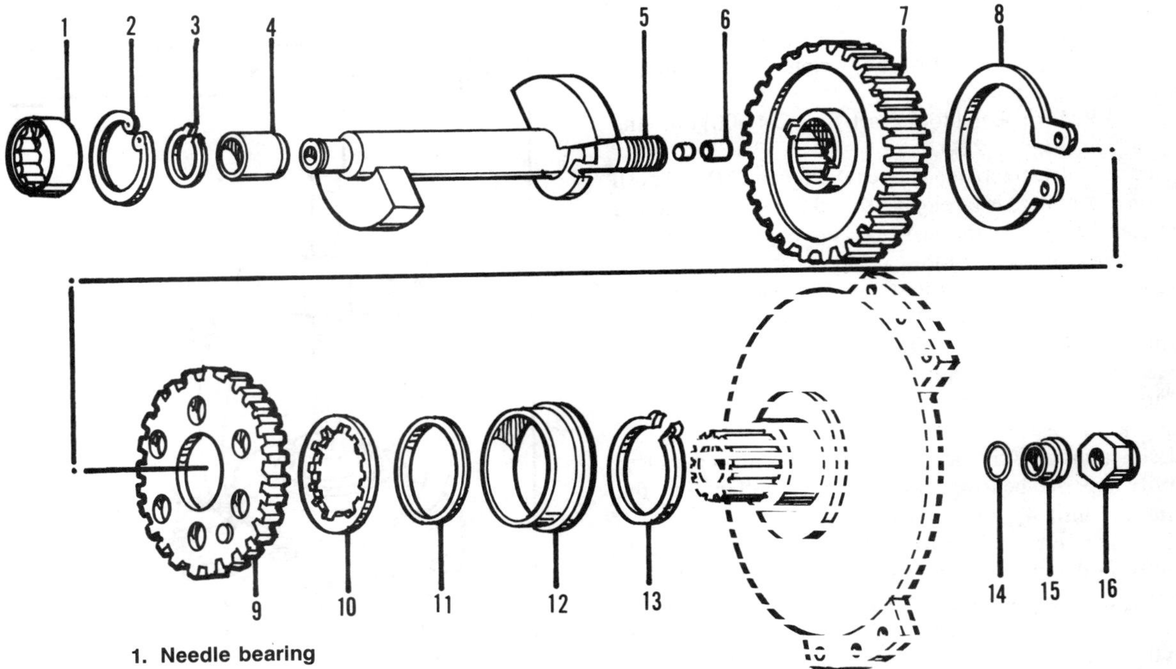

1. Needle bearing
2. Circlip
3. Circlip
4. Inner bearing race
5. Output shaft
6. Clutch release pushrod pilot bushing
7. Gear
8. Spring
9. Idle gear
10. Spring washer
11. Shim
12. Bearing
13. Circlip
14. O-ring
15. Compression ring
16. Nut

1. From the front end of the shaft, slide off the needle bearing and remove the circlips. Slide off the inner bearing ring.

2. From the rear end of the shaft, remove the nut and compression ring, then slide off the gear assembly.

3. Position the gear assembly with the bearing side up. Place the gear assembly in a vise equipped with soft jaws.

4. Remove the circlip securing the bearing (**Figure 219**).

NOTE
Step 5 is shown on a K100 model. The K75 procedure is the same except that the K100 is a larger unit.

5. Using BMW special tools (part No. 00 8 400 and No. 33 1 307) (A, **Figure 220**) carefully pull the bearing (B, **Figure 220**) off of the gear assembly (C, **Figure 220**). Remove the bearing and the spring washer or shim.

6. Leave the gear assembly in the vise.

7. Install BMW special tool (part No. 12 4 600) onto the idle gear (A, **Figure 221**).

8. Turn the special tool *clockwise* (B, **Figure 221**) and pull up to release the idle gear from the spring and other gear.

9. Remove the special tool and the idle gear.

10. Remove the spring and the gear from the vise.

11. Install the gear and spring in the vise with soft jaws.

12. Looking down onto the spring, make sure the left-hand end of the spring is indexed into the hole in the gear.

13. Align the pin on the backside of the idle gear with the hole in the right-hand end of the spring. Engage the pin with the spring hole.

14. Install BMW special tool (part No. 12 4 600) onto the idle gear (A, **Figure 221**).

15. Turn the special tool *clockwise* (B, **Figure 221**) and push down on the idle gear to engage the idle gear pin into the other gear. Make sure the two gears are engaged properly, then remove the special tool.

16. On models equipped with the spring washer, position the spring washer with the convex side facing up and install the spring washer. On all other models, install the shim.

17. Heat the bearing to 80° C (175° F).

18. Install the bearing onto the shaft with the groove for the circlip closest to the gear.

19. Using a suitable size socket that matches the inner race, carefully tap the bearing onto the gear collar. Tap the bearing on until it bottoms out.

20. Install the circlip (**Figure 222**) and make sure it seats correctly in the groove. This circlip carries the full axial load of the output shaft and must be installed correctly.

21. After the bearing has cooled down, apply clean engine oil to the bearing and rotate it. Make sure it is thoroughly lubricated.

22. Onto the front end of the shaft, install the following:
   a. Slide on the inner bearing ring.
   b. Install the circlip and slide on the needle bearing.

23. Install the gear assembly onto the rear end of the output shaft.

Output Shaft Disassembly/Assembly (K100 Models)

Refer to **Figure 223** for this procedure.

1. From the front end of the shaft, slide off the needle bearing and remove the circlips. Slide off the inner bearing ring.

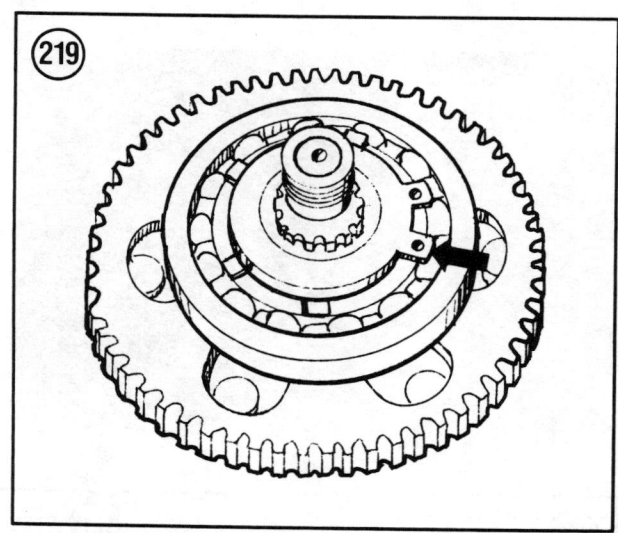

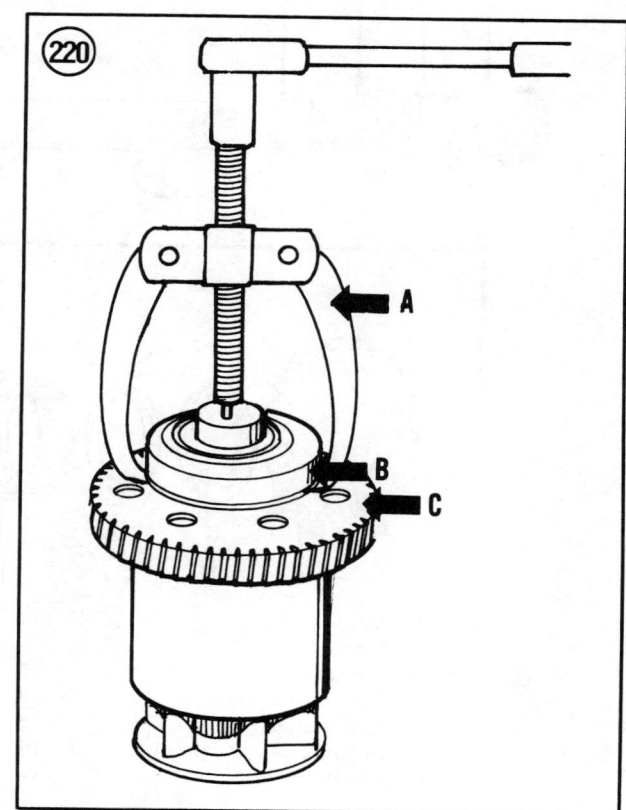

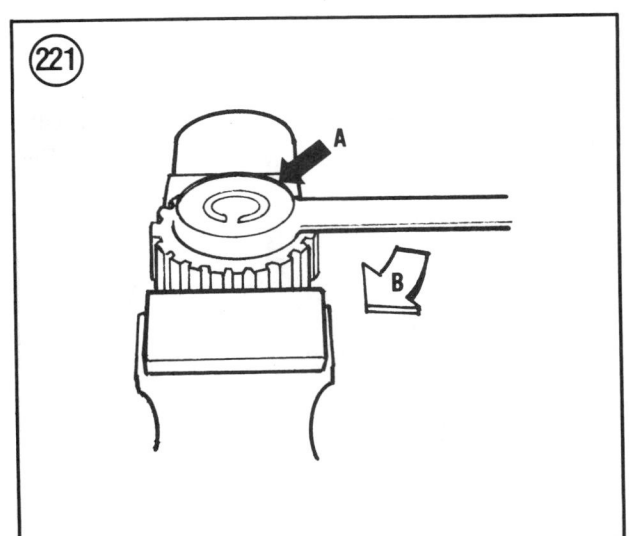

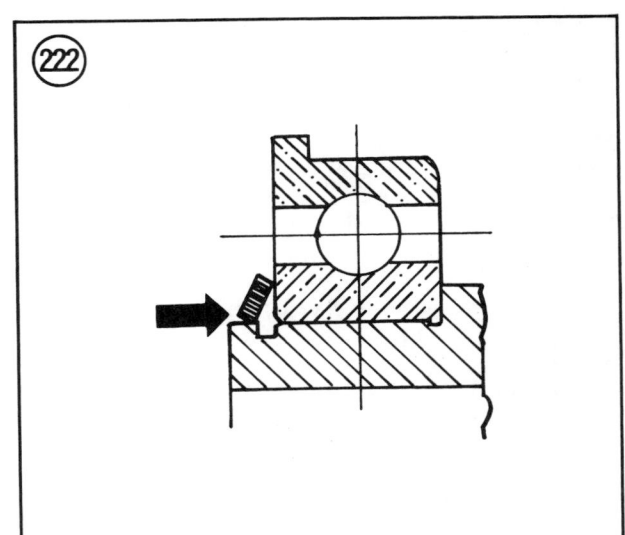

4

223

OUTPUT SHAFT (K100)

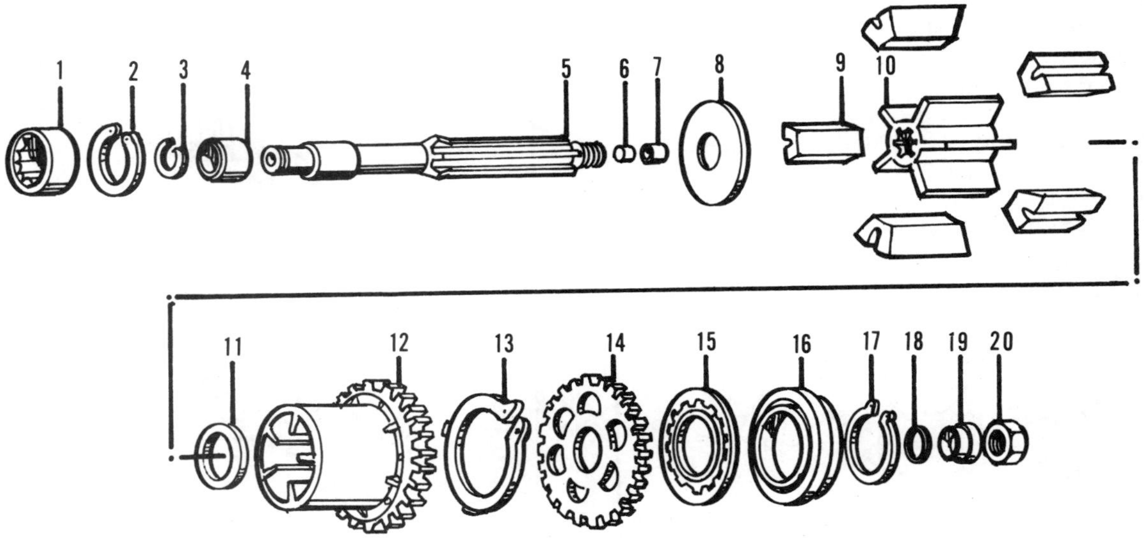

1. Needle bearing
2. Circlip
3. Circlip
4. Inner bearing ring
5. Output shaft
6. Locking plug
7. Clutch release pushrod
   pilot bushing
8. Bracket
9. Rubber dampers
10. Absorber

11. Thrust washer
12. Absorber gear
13. Spring
14. Idle gear
15. Damper spring
16. Bearing
17. Circlip
18. O-ring
19. Compression ring
20. Nut

2. Position the shaft assembly with the bearing side up. Place the gear assembly in a vise equipped with soft jaws.

3. Remove the circlip securing the bearing (**Figure 219**).

4. Using BMW special tools (part No. 00 8 400 and No. 33 1 307) (A, **Figure 220**) carefully pull the bearing (B, **Figure 220**) off of the gear assembly (C, **Figure 220**).

5. Remove the bearing and the diaphragm spring.

6. Leave the shaft assembly in the vise.

> *WARNING*
> *Sandwiched between the 2 gears is a spring that looks like a large circlip. It has a tab at each end and each tab is located in a hole in the absorber gear. When the idle gear is removed, the spring tabs may work loose from the absorber gear and fly off when the idle gear is removed. Protect yourself accordingly.*

7. Remove the idle gear from the absorber gear.

8. If necessary, using circlip pliers, remove the spring from the absorber gear.

9. Using a soft faced mallet or plastic hammer, carefully tap the output shaft out of the absorber gear assembly.

10. Remove the output shaft.

11. Remove the bracket, absorber, rubber dampers and thrust washer from the absorber gear.

12. Inspect the rubber dampers for wear or deterioration. If any are damaged, replace as a set.

13. Install the thrust washer and the rubber dampers into the absorber gear (**Figure 224**).

14. Install the bracket (A, **Figure 225**) and the absorber (B, **Figure 225**) onto the output shaft (C, **Figure 225**).

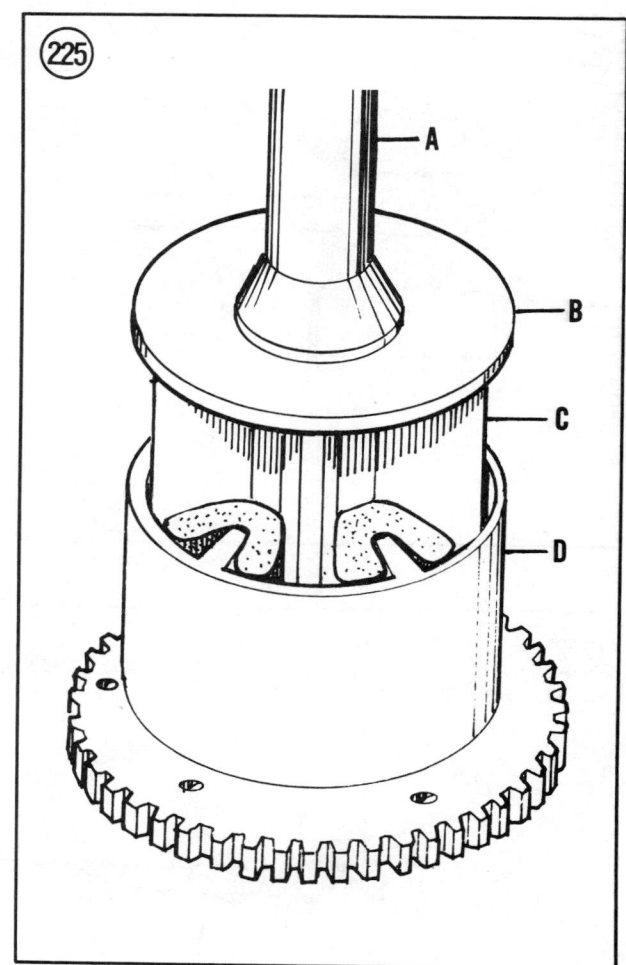

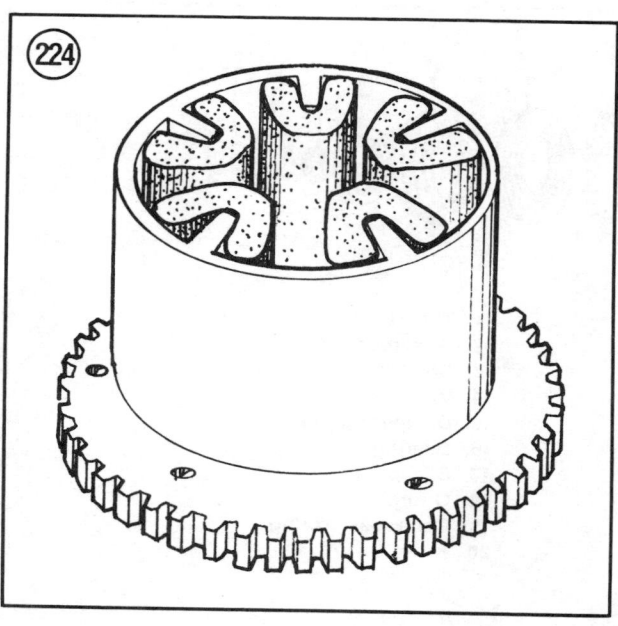

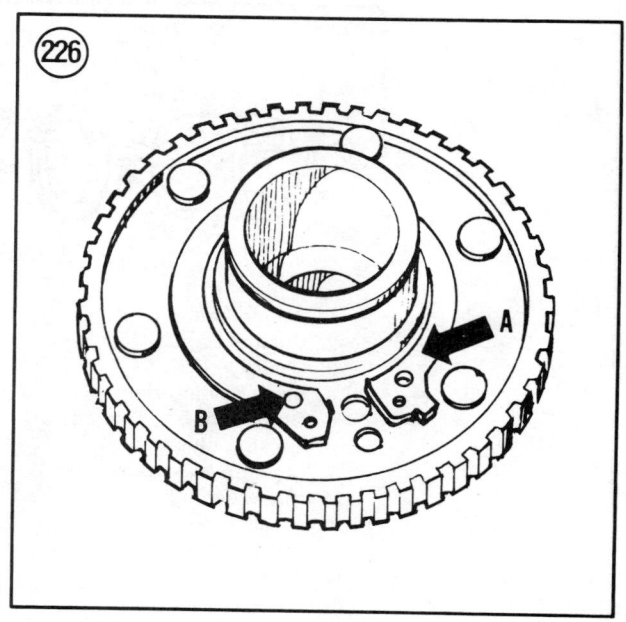

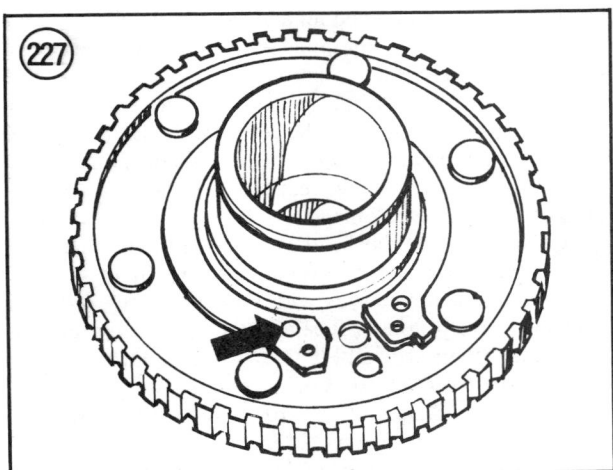

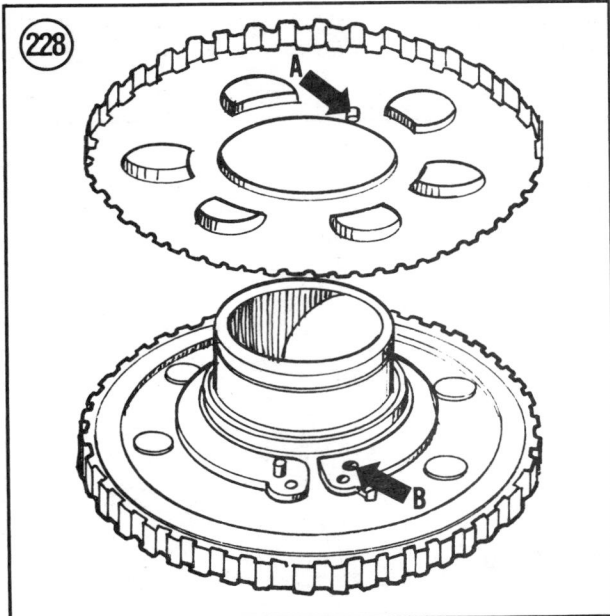

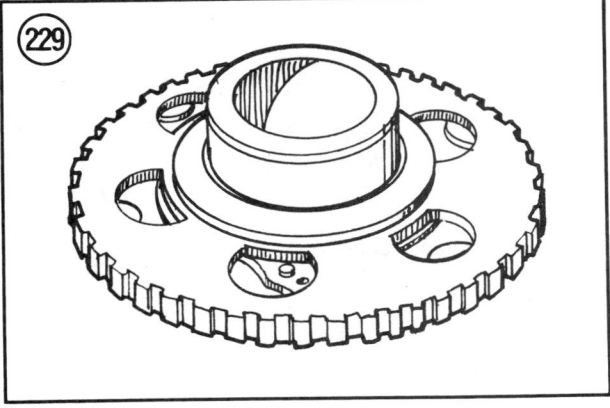

15. Install this assembly into the absorber gear (D, **Figure 225**). Push the assembly in until it bottoms out.

16. If removed, install the spring (A, **Figure 226**) onto the absorber gear.

17. Install the left-hand spring end onto the raised pin (B, **Figure 226**). Push it on and make sure it is correctly installed.

18. With the left-hand end secured (**Figure 227**) on the pin, carefully pull the right-hand end over and insert the tab into the hole in the absorber gear. Push the spring down and make sure it is properly seated on the absorber gear.

19. Align the pin (A, **Figure 228**) on the backside of the idle gear with the hole (B, **Figure 228**) in the right-hand end of the spring. Engage the pin with the spring hole.

20. Push down on the idle gear to engage the idle gear pin into the other gear. Make sure the two gears are engaged properly.

21. Install the diaphragm spring (**Figure 229**) with the convex side facing up and install the diaphragm spring (**Figure 230**).

22. Heat the bearing to 80° C (175° F).

23. Install the bearing onto the shaft with the groove for the circlip closest to the gear.

24. Using a suitable size socket that matches the inner race, carefully tap the bearing onto the gear collar. Tap the bearing on until it bottoms out.

25. Install the circlip (**Figure 222**) and make sure it seats correctly in the groove. This circlip carries the full axial load of the output shaft and must be installed correctly.

26. After the bearing has cooled down, apply clean engine oil to the bearing and rotate it. Make sure it is thoroughly lubricated.

27. Onto the front end of the shaft, install the following:
   a. Slide on the inner bearing ring.
   b. Install the circlip and slide on the needle bearing.

4

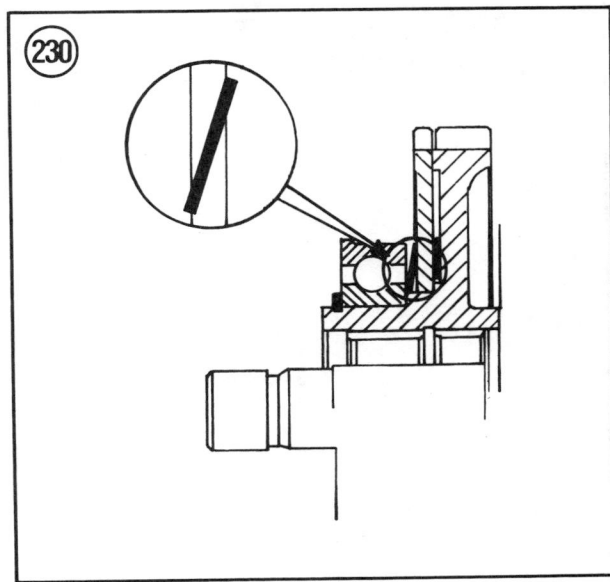

PISTONS AND
CONNECTING RODS

The pistons are made of an aluminum alloy. The piston pins are made of steel and are a precision fit in the piston pin bore in the piston. The piston pin is held in place by a clip at each end.

The pistons and connecting rods can be removed with the engine in the frame and with the crankshaft in place. The pistons come out through the top of the cylinder bores.

This procedure is shown with the engine removed for clarity.

Piston and Connecting Rod
Removal/Installation

Refer to **Figure 231** for this procedure.

A BMW special tool is required for this procedure to tighten the bearing cap nuts. The BMW special tool is part No. 11 2 110 (**Figure 232**) and it fits onto both cap nuts at the same time. After the cap nut is tightened to the initial torque it is then tightened an additional 80 degrees. This tool, or a similar tool equipped with a degree wheel, must be used to measure nut rotation.

The connecting rod bolts must be replaced every time the bearing cap is removed. The bolts stretch when tightened and must be replaced as described in this chapter. Do not try to reuse the bolts as they may fracture and break leading to expensive engine damage.

1. Remove the cylinder head as described in this chapter.
2. Remove the crankshaft cover as described in this chapter.
3. Mark the piston crowns with their respective cylinder numbers so the pistons will be reinstalled in the correct cylinder. Mark them with a "1", "2", "3" and on K100 models "4" starting from the front of the engine and working toward the back. Also add an arrow indicating the front of the piston. Refer to **Figure 233**.
4. Using an Allen wrench on the crankshaft end bolt (**Figure 234**) rotate the engine in the normal *counterclockwise* direction until the piston that is going to be removed is at bottom dead center (BDC). This will position the connecting rod end cap for easy access to the cap nuts.

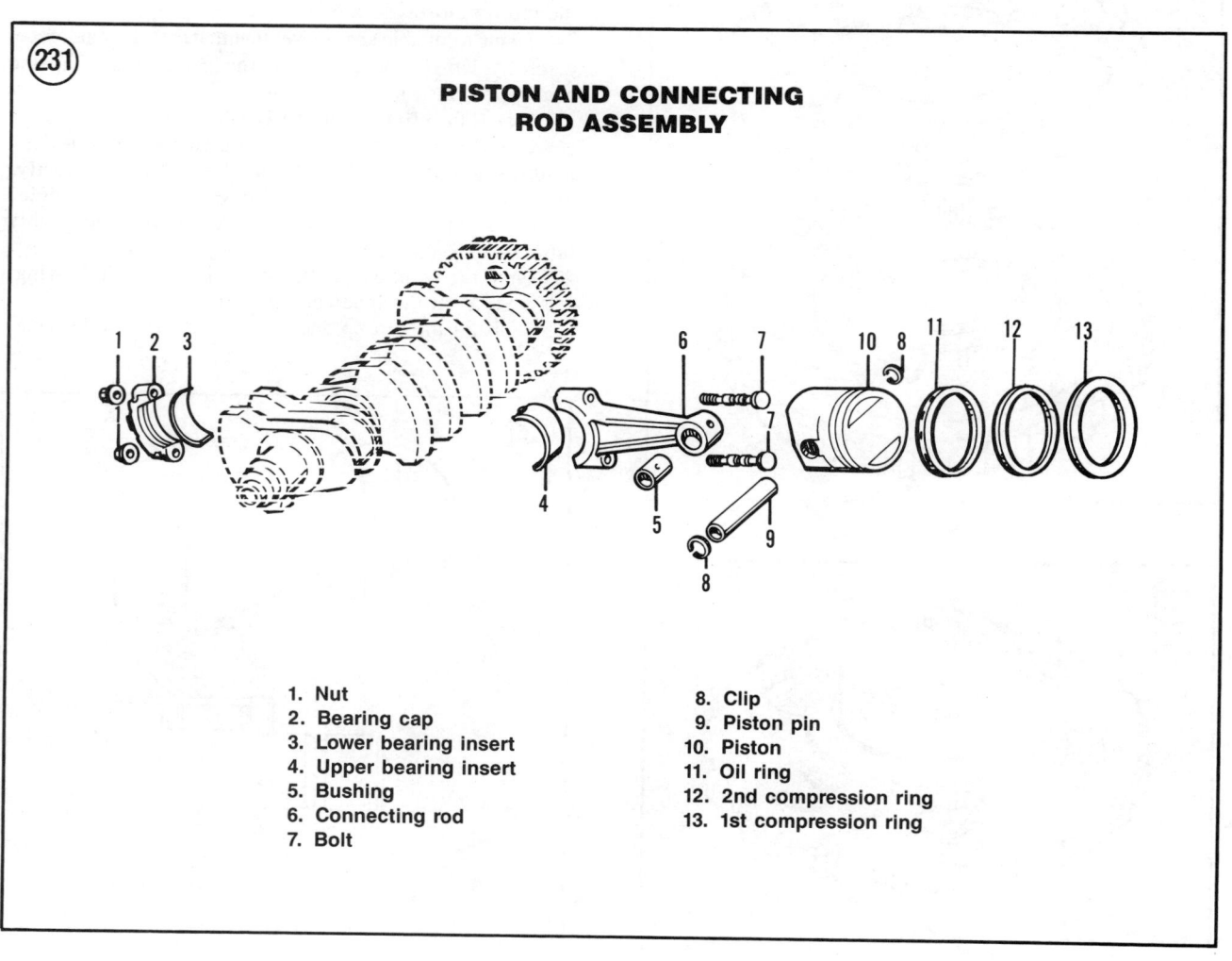

(231)

PISTON AND CONNECTING
ROD ASSEMBLY

1. Nut
2. Bearing cap
3. Lower bearing insert
4. Upper bearing insert
5. Bushing
6. Connecting rod
7. Bolt
8. Clip
9. Piston pin
10. Piston
11. Oil ring
12. 2nd compression ring
13. 1st compression ring

NOTE
Before disassembling the connecting rods, mark the rods and caps with a ''1'', ''2'', ''3'' and on K100 models ''4'' starting from the front of the engine and working toward the back. Use a centerpunch and hammer and carefully mark both the connecting rod and cap with the correct number of marks for each cylinder.

5. Remove the connecting rod cap nuts (**Figure 235**) and separate the rod cap (**Figure 236**) from the crankshaft. Keep each cap with its original rod with the weight mark on the end of the cap matching the mark on the rod.

NOTE
Keep each bearing insert in its original place on the rod or rod cap. If you are going to assemble the engine with the original inserts, they must be installed exactly as removed in order to prevent rapid wear.

6. Place a piece of rubber or vinyl hose over both rod studs (**Figure 237**). This is to protect the crankshaft bearing journal and the cylinder wall from being damaged during piston and rod removal.

NOTE
Due to the cylinder wall construction that is very hard, there will probably not be a wear ridge at the top of the bore. This is even true in high-mileage engines. To play it safe, feel around the top of the bore and check for a wear ridge prior to piston removal. If there is a slight ridge be careful removing the piston and connecting rod assembly.

7. Push the piston and connecting rod out through the top of the cylinder bore.

8. Repeat Steps 4-7 for the remaining piston and rod assemblies.

9. Install by reversing these removal steps, noting the following.

10. Replace the connecting rod studs as described in this chapter.

11. Make sure the arrow on the piston crown is pointed in the right direction—toward the front of the engine—and that it is the correct cylinder number (**Figure 238**).

12. If removed, place a piece of rubber or vinyl hose over both rod studs (**Figure 239**). This is to protect the crankshaft bearing journal and the cylinder wall from being damaged during piston and rod installation.

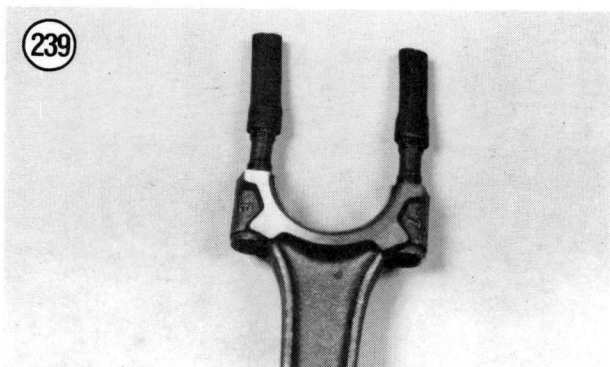

13. Make sure that the bearing inserts are locked into place in the connecting rod and the rod cap. Make sure the locking tab fits correctly into the groove in the rod or cap.

14. Install a piston ring compressor over the piston and rings.

15. Carefully install the piston and connecting rod assembly into the correct cylinder (**Figure 240**).

16. Carefully push the piston out through the ring compressor and into the cylinder bore.

17. Guide the connecting rod through the cylinder bore so the bore surface will not be damaged by the connecting rod during installation.

18. If new bearing inserts are going to be installed, check the bearing clearance as described in this chapter.

19. Apply a light even coat of molybdenum disulfide grease to the connecting rod bearing journals and to the connecting rod bearing inserts.

20. Install the connecting rod onto the crankshaft, being careful not to damage the bearing surface of the crankshaft with the rods' threaded studs.

21. Remove the pieces of hose (**Figure 237**) from the connecting rod studs.

NOTE
Figure 241 is shown with the piston and connecting rod removed for clarity.

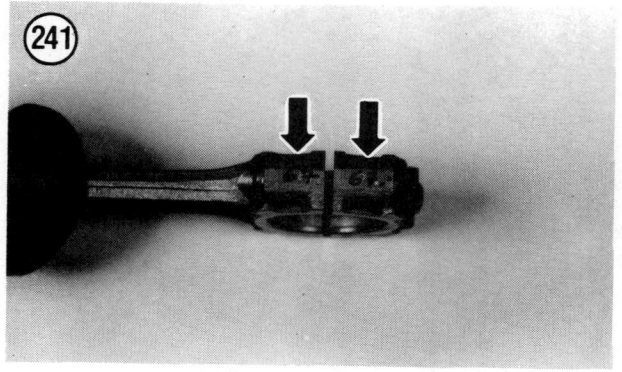

22. Match the weight mark on the end of the cap with the mark on the rod (**Figure 241**) and install the cap (**Figure 236**).

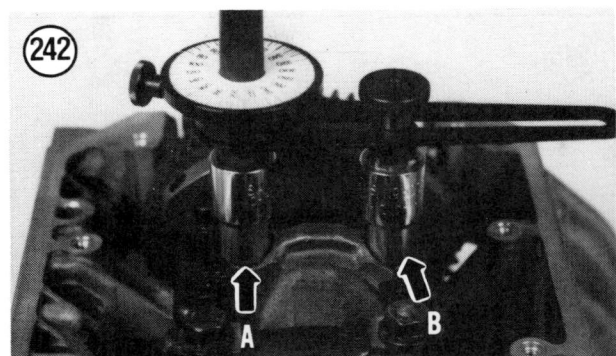

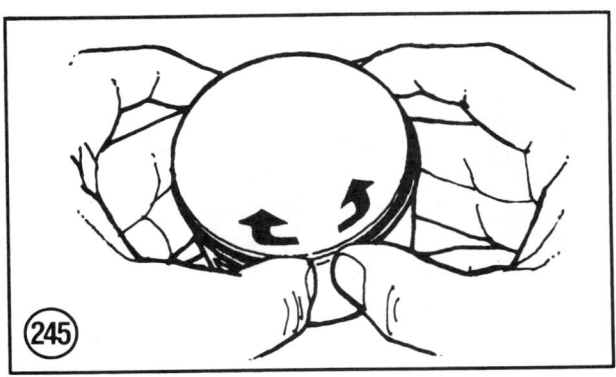

23. Install the cap nuts (**Figure 235**).

> *CAUTION*
> *The cap nuts must be tightened using the following procedure. Do **not** try to sidestep this procedure as the connecting rod studs or bearings will fail, leading to expensive engine damage.*

4

> *NOTE*
> *Do **not** rotate the crankshaft after the initial torque specification; wait until the cap nuts are tightened to the final tightening angle, then the crankshaft can be rotated.*

24. Tighten the cap nuts as follows:
  a. Using a torque wrench, tighten the cap nuts in 2-3 stages to the torque specification listed in **Table 3**.
  b. Install BMW special tool (part No. 11 2 110) onto the rod cap nuts. Place the socket attached to the degree wheel onto the nut to be tightened (A, **Figure 242**) and the other socket onto the other nut (B, **Figure 242**).
  c. Once the socket is installed onto the nut to be tightened, zero the dial indicator (**Figure 243**).
  d. Using a socket wrench on the special tool, tighten the nut an additional 77-83° (**Figure 244**).
  e. Remove the special tool from the cap nuts, turn it 180° and reinstall it on the cap nuts. Tighten the other cap nut in a similar manner.
  f. Remove the special tool.
25. After the connecting rods are installed and the cap nuts tightened to the correct torque, rotate the crankshaft several times and check that the bearings are not too tight. Make sure there is no binding.

Piston Disassembly

> *WARNING*
> *The edges of all piston rings are very sharp. Be careful when handling them to avoid cutting fingers.*

1. Remove the top ring with a ring expander tool or by spreading the ends with your thumbs just enough to slide the ring up over the piston (**Figure 245**). Repeat for the remaining rings.
2. Before removing the piston, place the crankshaft end of the connecting rod in a vise with soft jaws. Rock the piston

as shown in **Figure 246**. Any rocking motion (do not confuse with the normal sliding motion) indicates wear on the piston pin, piston pin bore or connecting rod small-end bore (more likely a combination of these).

NOTE
Have a small parts box for each piston assembly. As the piston is disassembled, place the parts for that piston and rod assembly into one box. If the parts all check out okay, they must be reassembled in the same set since the parts have taken a unique wear pattern as a set.

3. Remove the clip from each side of the piston pin bore (**Figure 247**) with a small screwdriver or scribe. Hold your thumb over one edge of the clip when removing it to prevent the clip from springing out.
4. Use a proper size wooden dowel or socket extension and push out the piston pin. Mark the piston pin in relation to the piston so that they will be reassembled into the same set.

CAUTION
Be careful when removing the pin to avoid damaging the connecting rod. If it is necessary to gently tap the pin to remove it, be sure that the piston is properly supported so that lateral shock is not transmitted to the lower connecting rod bearing.

5. If the piston pin is difficult to remove, heat the piston and pin with a hair drier. The pin will probably push right out. Heat the piston to only about 140 degrees F (60 degrees C), i.e., until it is too warm to touch, but not excessively hot. If the pin is still difficult to push out, use a homemade tool as shown in **Figure 248**.
6. Lift the piston off the connecting rod.
7. Repeat Steps 1-7 for the remaining pistons.

Piston Inspection

1. Carefully clean the piston as follows:
   a. Clean the carbon from the piston crown with a chemical remover or with a soft scraper.
   b. Be sure to remove all deposits from the valve reliefs in the piston crown.
   c. Do not remove or damage the carbon ridge around the circumference of the piston above the top ring.
   d. If the pistons, rings and cylinders are found to be dimensionally correct and can be reused, removal of the carbon ring from the top of the piston or the carbon ridge from the top of the cylinder wall will promote excessive oil consumption in this cylinder.

CAUTION
Do not wire brush the piston skirts.

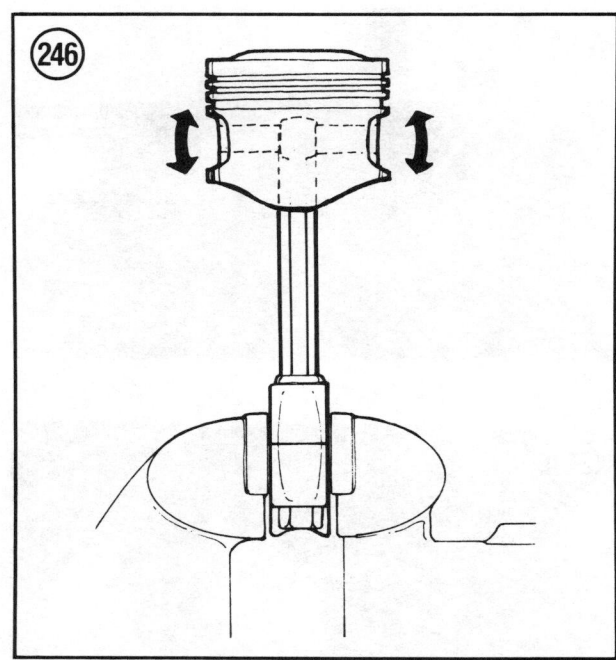

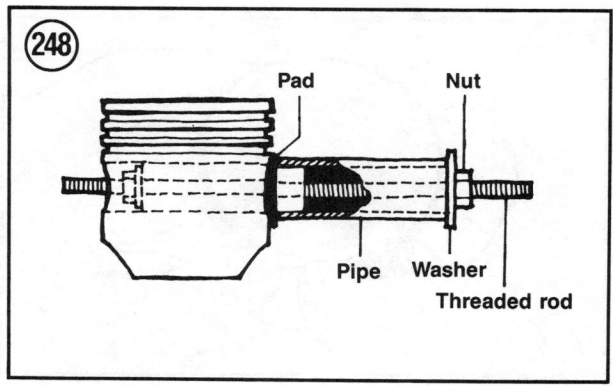

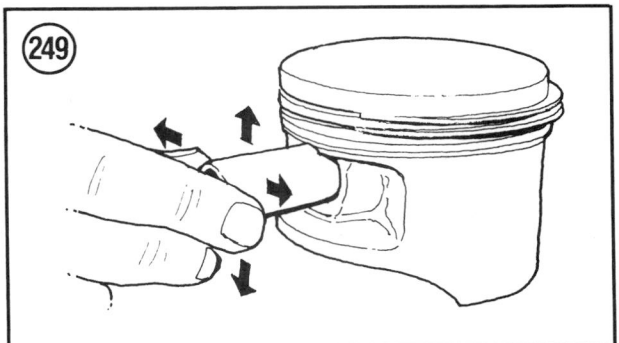

2. Examine each ring groove for burrs, dented edges and wide wear. Pay particular attention to the top compression ring groove as it usually wears more than the other grooves.

3. If damage or wear indicates piston replacement, select a new piston as described under *Piston Clearance* in this chapter.

4. Oil the piston pin and install it in the connecting rod. Slowly rotate the piston pin and check for play (**Figure 249**). If any play exists, the piston pin should be replaced, providing the connecting rod bore is in good condition.

5. Measure the inside diameter of the piston pin bore with a snap gauge (**Figure 250**) and measure the outside diameter of the piston pin with a micrometer (**Figure 251**). Compare with dimensions given in **Table 1** or **Table 2**. Replace the piston and piston pin as a set if either or both are worn. The piston and pin are a matched set—never replace only one of the parts.

6. Check the piston skirt (**Figure 252**) for galling and abrasion which may have been caused by piston seizure. If a piston(s) shows signs of partial seizure (bits of aluminum build-up on the piston skirt), the pistons should be replaced and the cylinder bores inspected by a BMW dealer. The cylinder bores *cannot* be rebored.

7. Check the oil control holes in the piston pin area (**Figure 253**) for carbon or oil sludge build-up. Clean the holes with a piece of wire or small diameter drill bit and blow out with compressed air.

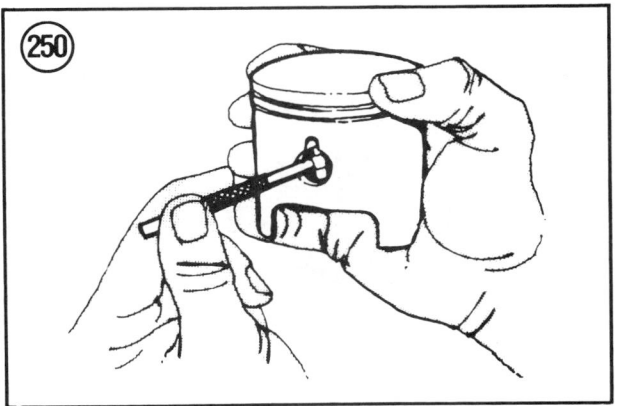

4

Piston Clearance

1. Make sure the pistons and cylinder walls are clean and dry.

2. Measure the inside diameter of the cylinder bore at a point 13 mm (1/2 in.) from the upper edge with a bore gauge.

3. Measure the outside diameter of each piston across the skirt (**Figure 254**) at right angles to the piston pin. Measure

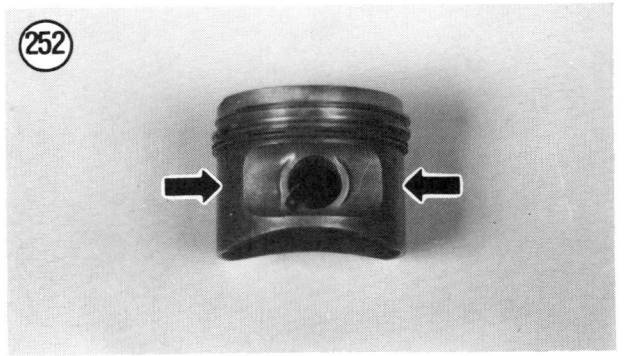

at a distance up from the bottom of the piston skirt as follows:

   a. MS pistons: 12.0 mm (0.472 in.).
   b. Mahle pistons: 7.6 mm (0.299 in.).

NOTE
Table 1 and Table 2 list piston outer dimensions in 2 categories ("A" or "B"). Either an "A" or "B" is stamped on the piston crown. These letters relate to the grade or finished outer dimension of the piston. It is virtually impossible to manufacture all pistons to the same exact dimensions.

4. Piston clearance is the difference between the maximum piston diameter and the minimum cylinder diameter. Subtract the dimension of the piston from the cylinder dimension and compare to the dimension listed in **Table 1** or **Table 2**. If the clearance exceeds that specified, and the piston is within specifications, the cylinder block must be replaced as it *cannot* be rebored.

Piston Assembly

1. Apply molybdenum disulfide grease to the inside surface of the connecting rod.

NOTE
New piston pin clips must be installed during assembly. Install the clips with the gap away from the cutout in the piston.

2. Install one piston pin clip in each piston on one side.
3. Oil the piston pin with assembly oil or fresh engine oil and install the piston pin in the piston until its end extends slightly beyond the inside of the boss.

NOTE
If installing new connecting rods, the connecting rod must be positioned correctly in relation to the engine. The upper side, or intake side, of the connecting rod has the grooves for the bearing insert tangs to index into.

4A. If reusing the same pistons and connecting rods, perform the following:
   a. Match the piston to the rod from which it came.
   b. The arrow on top of the piston must point toward the front of the engine. This will also position the piston with the larger intake valve relief (**Figure 255**) in the piston crown at the top.
   c. Position the connecting rod with the grooves for the bearing insert tangs at the top.

4B. If installing new pistons and/or connecting rods, perform the following:
   a. The arrow on top of the piston must point toward the front of the engine. This will also position the piston with the larger intake valve relief (**Figure 255**) in the piston crown at the top.
   b. Position the connecting rod with the grooves for the bearing insert tangs at the top.

CAUTION
When installing the piston pin in Step 5, do not push the pin in too far, or the piston pin clip

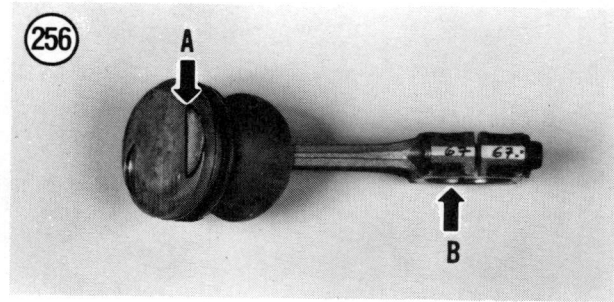

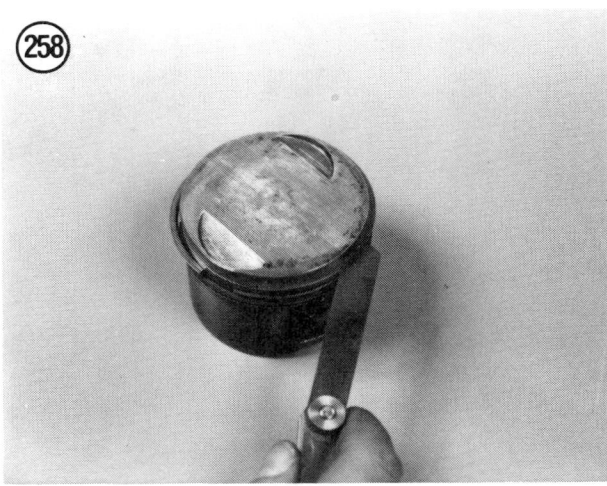

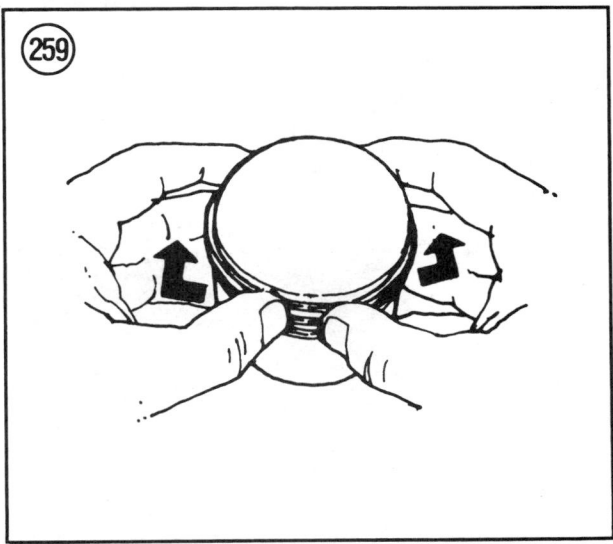

installed in Step 2 will be forced into the piston metal, destroying the clip groove and loosening the clip.

5. Line up the piston pin with the hole in the connecting rod. Push the piston pin into the connecting rod. It may be necessary to move the piston around until the piston pin enters the connecting rod. Do not use force during installation or damage may occur. Push the piston pin in until it touches the pin clip on the other side of the piston.

6. If the piston pin does not slide easily, use the homemade tool used during removal but eliminate the piece of pipe. Pull the piston pin in until it stops.

7. After the piston is installed, perform the following:
   a. Recheck and make sure that the arrow on top of the piston is pointing toward the front of the engine.
   b. The larger intake valve relief (A, **Figure 256**) in the piston crown must be at the top.
   c. The connecting rod (B, **Figure 256**) must have the grooves for the bearing insert tangs at the top.

NOTE
*New piston pin clips must be installed during assembly. Install the clips with the gap away from the cutout in the piston (**Figure 257**).*

8. Install the second piston pin clip in the groove in the piston. Make sure both piston pin clips are seated in the grooves in the piston.

9. Check the installation by rocking the piston back and forth around the pin axis and from side to side along the axis. It should rotate freely back and forth but not from side to side.

10. Repeat Steps 1-9 for the remaining pistons.

11. Install the piston rings as described in this chapter.

Piston Ring Replacement

WARNING
The edges of all piston rings are very sharp. Be careful when handling them to avoid cutting fingers.

1. Measure the side clearance of each ring in its groove with a flat feeler gauge (**Figure 258**) and compare to dimensions given in **Table 1** or **Table 2**. If the clearance is greater than specified, the rings must be replaced. If the clearance is still excessive with the new rings, the piston(s) must also be replaced.

2. Remove the old top ring by spreading the ends with your thumbs just enough to slide the ring up over the piston (**Figure 259**). Repeat for the other compression ring.

3. The oil ring is a 2-piece ring and must be removed as follows:
   a. Remove the outer wiper part in the same manner as the compression rings. Do not remove the coil spring spacer at the same time.
   b. Remove the coil spring spacer.

4. Carefully remove all carbon build-up from the ring grooves with a broken piston ring (**Figure 260**). Inspect the grooves carefully for burrs, nicks or broken and cracked lands. Recondition or replace the piston if necessary.

5. Roll each ring around its piston groove as shown in **Figure 261** to check for binding. Minor binding may be cleaned up with a fine-cut file.

6. Place each ring, one at a time, into the cylinder (**Figure 262**) and push it in about 20 mm (3/4 in.) with the crown of the piston (**Figure 263**) to ensure that the ring is square in the cylinder bore.

7. Measure the gap with a flat feeler gauge (**Figure 264**) and compare to dimensions in **Table 1** or **Table 2**. If the gap is greater than specified, the rings should be replaced.

8. When installing new rings, measure their end gap as described in Step 5 and Step 6 and compare to dimensions given in **Table 1** or **Table 2**. If the end gap is greater than specified, return the rings to the dealer for another set(s).

NOTE
Install the 1st and 2nd compression rings with the TOP mark facing up.

NOTE
*Install the piston rings as shown in **Figure 265**.*

9. The oil ring is a 2-piece ring and must be installed as follows:
   a. Install the coil spring spacer.

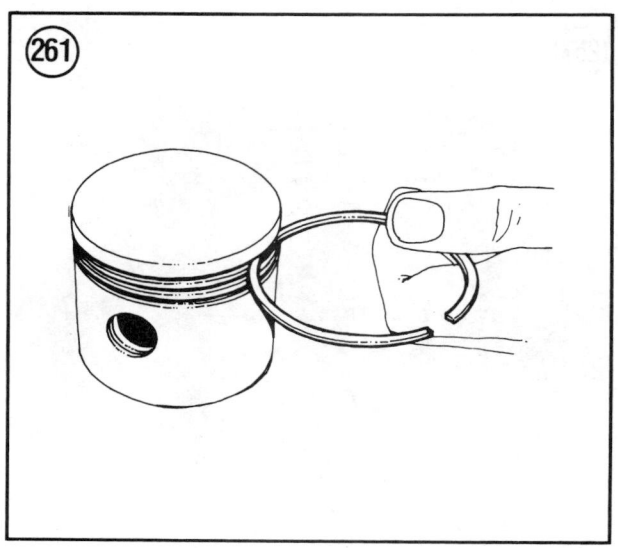

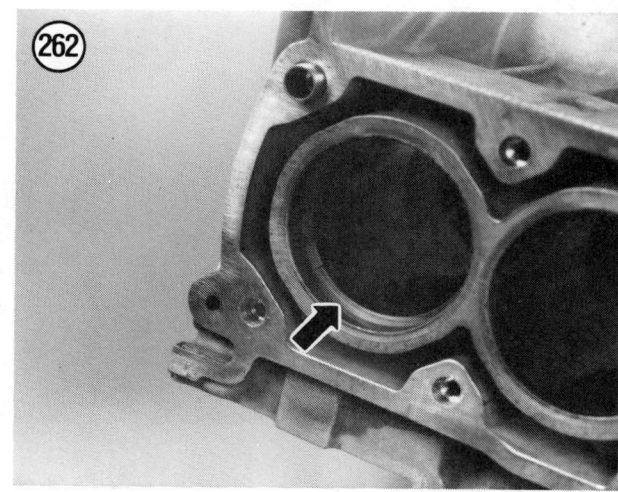

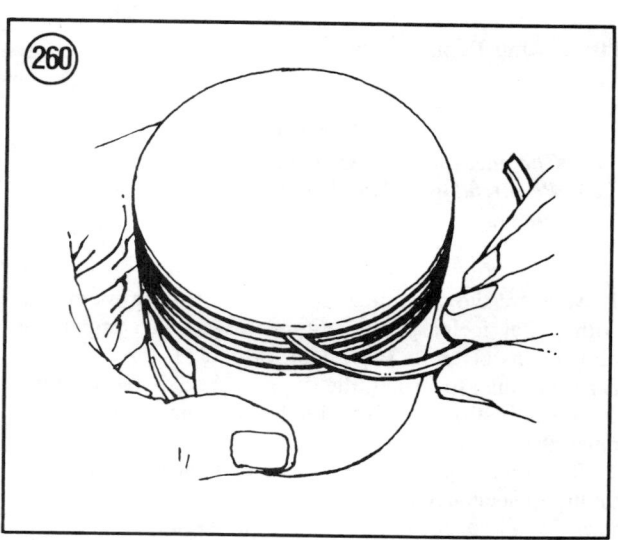

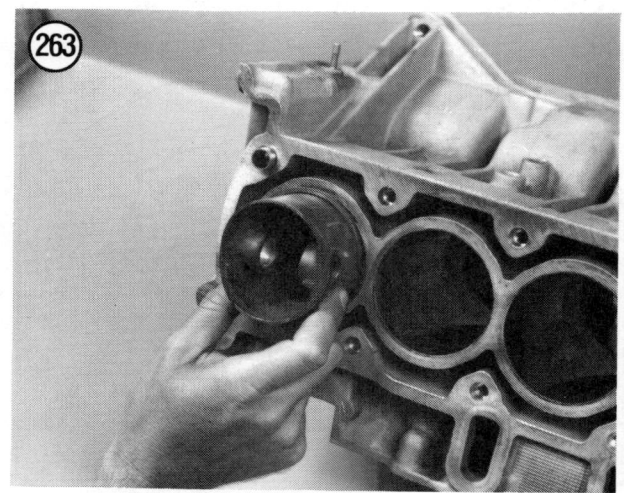

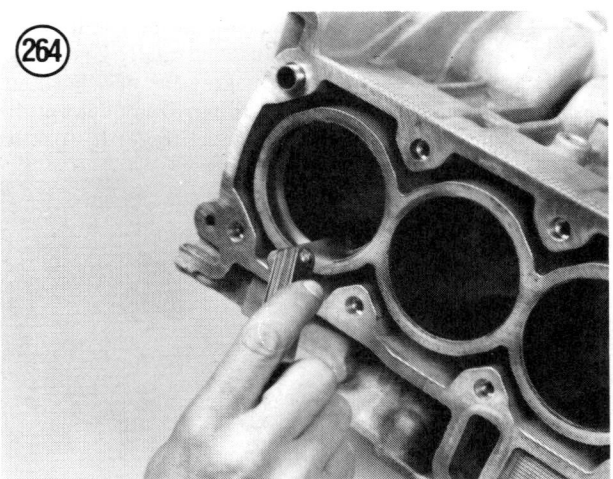

PISTON RINGS

1. 1st compression ring
2. 2nd compression ring
3. Oil ring

b. Install the outer wiper (A, **Figure 266**) part over the coil spring spacer in the same manner as the compression rings. Make sure the outer wiper is correctly seated over the coil spring spacer.

10. The second compression ring has an inner chamfer and must be installed in the 2nd groove (B, **Figure 266**)—by carefully spreading the ends of the ring with your thumbs and slipping the ring over the top of the piston. Remember that the mark on the piston ring is toward the top of the piston.

11. Install the top compression ring in the first groove (C, **Figure 266**) by carefully spreading the ends of the ring with your thumbs and slipping the ring over the top of the piston. Remember that the mark on the piston ring is toward the top of the piston.

12. Make sure the rings are seated completely in their grooves all the way around the piston and that the ends are distributed around the piston as shown in **Figure 267**. The important thing is that the ring gaps are not aligned with each other when installed to prevent compression pressure from escaping past them.

13. Follow the *Break-in Procedure* in this chapter if new pistons or new piston rings have been installed.

Connecting Rod Inspection

NOTE
If any of the connecting rods require replacement, they must be replaced with ones of the

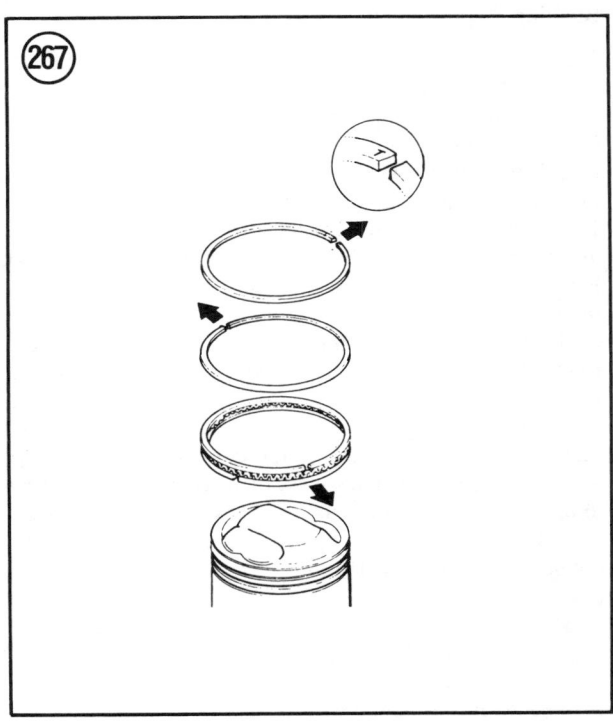

same weight tolerance. Each of the seven weight tolerance groups is color coded and marked. If the marking has worn off, the old connecting rods must be weighed in order to correctly match the new connecting rods. The allowable weight deviation between any one of the connecting rods in the set is ±4 grams.

1. Remove the piston and connecting rod assembly as described in this chapter.
2. Check each connecting rod for obvious damage such as cracks and burns.
3. Check the piston pin bushing for wear or scoring.
4. Take the connecting rods to a machine shop and check the alignment for twisting and bending.
5. Examine the bearing inserts for wear, scoring, or burning. They are reusable if in good condition. Examine the bearings as described under *Connecting Rod Big End Bearing Clearance Measurement* in this chapter.
6. Oil the piston pin and install it in the connecting rod. Slowly rotate the piston pin and check for play (**Figure 268**). If any play exists, measure the piston pin as described in this chapter. If the piston pin is okay, measure the connecting rod small end.
7. Measure the inside diameter of the piston pin bushing (**Figure 269**) with an inside micrometer or snap gauge. Compare with dimensions given in **Table 1** or **Table 2**. Replace the bushing if worn to the service limit or more as described in this chapter.

Connecting Rod Piston Pin Bushing Replacement

The bushing is pressed into place and must be removed and installed with a press and suitable size tool. After the new bushing is pressed into place it must be reamed out. Compare the cost of performing this procedure or having it performed by a BMW dealer. This procedure is included in case you choose to perform it yourself.
1. Using a suitable size socket or piece of pipe and a hydraulic press, press the bushing out of the connecting rod. Protect the connecting rod so it does not get damaged while removing the bushing.
2. Thoroughly clean out the inner surface of the connecting rod where the bushing was located. Make sure the oil hole is open and free of sludge.
3. Position the gap of the new bushing so it is 60° on either side of the centerline of the connecting rod.
4. Using a suitable size socket or piece of pipe and a hydraulic press, press the bushing back into the connecting rod. The bushing must be flush with each side of the connecting rod so it will not interfere with the inside bosses of the piston.
5. Drill an oil hole in the new bushing as follows:
   a. Using the oil hole in the side of the connecting rod as a guide for placement and hole size, drill an oil hole in the new bushing.

   b. Place a piece of wood or metal on the inside of the bushing so the drill will not accidentally go through and hit the other side, damaging the new bushing.
   c. Do not press hard while drilling. Don't deform the bushing in the oil hole area. Let the drill work its way through easily.

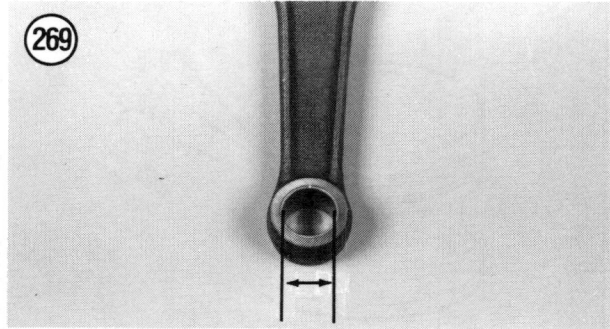

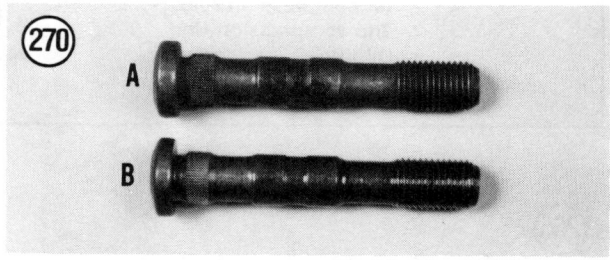

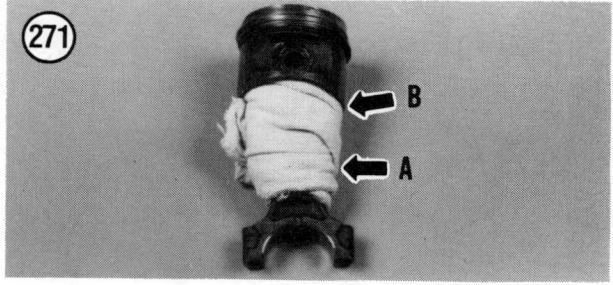

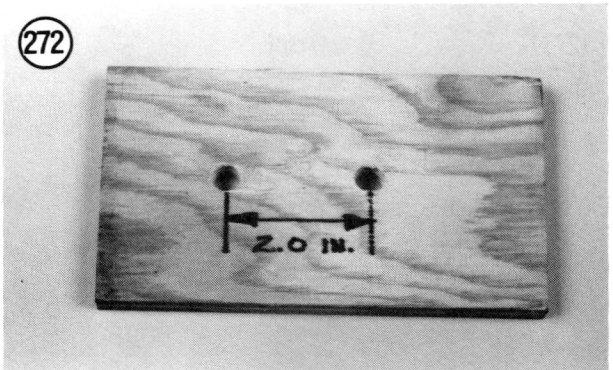

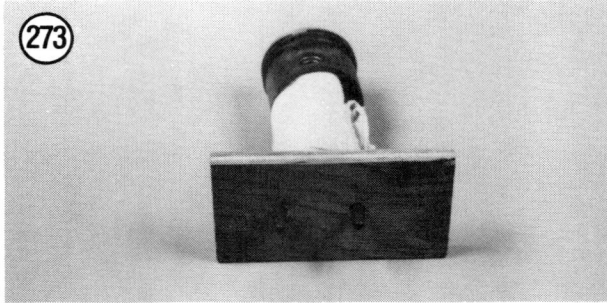

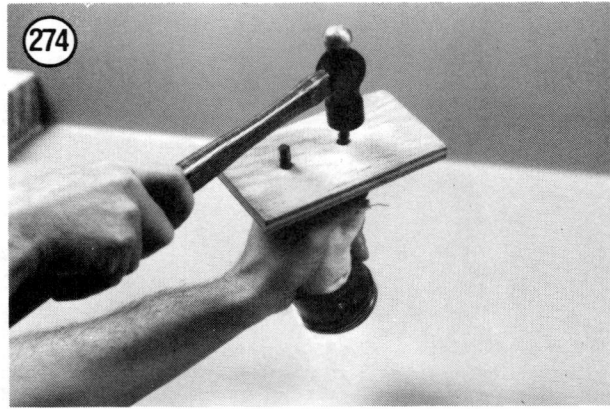

d. Carefully deburr the oil hole in the inner surface of the bushing.

6. Using a suitable size reamer, ream out the inner diameter of the bushing. Refer to **Table 1** or **Table 2** for the inside diameter of the piston pin bushing.

7. Thoroughly clean the connecting rod, especially the oil hole, in solvent and dry with compressed air. Make sure there are no metal particles left in the bore from the drilling operation. If any are left in, they will destroy the bushing or other components in the engine if they get into the oil and circulate in the engine.

4

Connecting Rod Cap Bolt Replacement

The connecting rod bolts must be replaced every time the bearing cap is removed. The bolts stretch when tightened and must be replaced. It is very difficult to see the difference between a new rod cap bolt (A, **Figure 270**) and a used one (B, **Figure 270**). When measured with a vernier caliper the difference was difficult to calculate. Do not try to reuse the bolts as they may fracture and break which could lead to expensive engine damage.

The connecting rod bolts must be carefully tapped out of the connecting rod. Be careful not to damage the piston and piston pin during this procedure. Always hold onto the connecting rod, not the piston.

1. Wrap a clean shop cloth around the connecting rod (A, **Figure 271**) and tightly stuff the cloth up under the piston skirt (B, **Figure 271**). This will keep the piston skirt from hitting against the connecting rod and being damaged.

2. Cut a piece of 3/8 in. plywood approximately 4 in. x 6 in. and drill 2 holes (slightly larger than the bearing cap bolts) 2 in. apart (**Figure 272**).

3. Push this piece of wood onto the lower end of the connecting rod over the connecting rod bolts (**Figure 273**).

CAUTION
*Hold the connecting rod and piston assembly in your hand in the air. Do **not** rest or set the piston on anything in order to stabilize the piston and connecting rod. As you are hammering on the bolt the connecting rod and piston must be able to move freely to avoid taking any shock. If you set the piston on something and hammer on the bolt, the hammer shock will apply pressure on the piston pin and connecting rod small end bushing and damage both of them, resulting in costly parts replacement.*

4. Carefully tap one bolt at a time out of the connecting rod (**Figure 274**). Tap the bolt until it is almost flush with the piece of plywood (**Figure 275**).

5. Repeat for the other bolt, then remove the piece of plywood.

6. Using Vise Grips, pull the cap bolt *straight out* of the connecting rod. Do not twist the bolt as it has longitudinal splines in it that have gouged into the connecting rod.

7. Remove both cap bolts and the shop cloth.

8. Thoroughly clean out both bolt holes (**Figure 276**) in the connecting rod with solvent and dry with compressed air.

9. Again wrap a clean shop cloth around the connecting rod (A, **Figure 271**) and tightly stuff the cloth up under the piston skirt (B, **Figure 271**). This will keep the piston skirt from hitting against the connecting rod and being damaged.

10. Wrap another cloth around the connecting rod and the piston (**Figure 277**).

11. Tightly wrap the end of the shop cloth with duct tape. This will hold the cloth against the connecting rod, allowing room to tap the new cap bolts into place.

12. Insert the new cap bolts into the connecting rod. Push them in by hand as far as they will go (**Figure 278**).

CAUTION
*Hold the connecting rod and piston assembly in your hand in the air. Do **not** rest or set the connecting rod or the piston on anything in order to stabilize the part. As you are hammering the bolt into the connecting rod both the connecting rod and the piston must be able to move freely to avoid taking any of the shock. If you set the piston on something and hammer on the bolt, the hammer shock will apply pressure on the piston pin and connecting rod small end bushing and damage both of them.*

13. Using a medium sized hammer, carefully tap one of the cap bolts partially into place (**Figure 279**). Do not try to hammer it all the way in.

14. Hammer the cap bolt in just far enough so it will protrude past the bearing cap when it is installed (**Figure 280**) later in this procedure.

15. Repeat Step 13 and Step 14 for the other bolt (**Figure 281**).

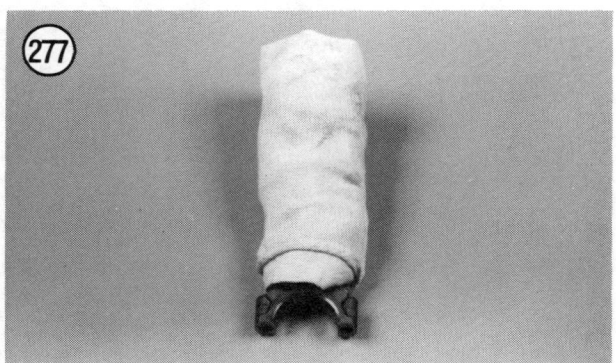

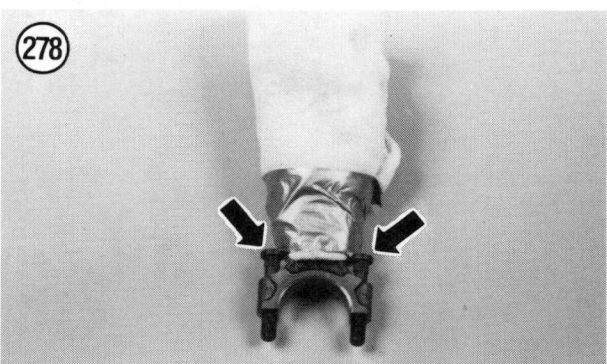

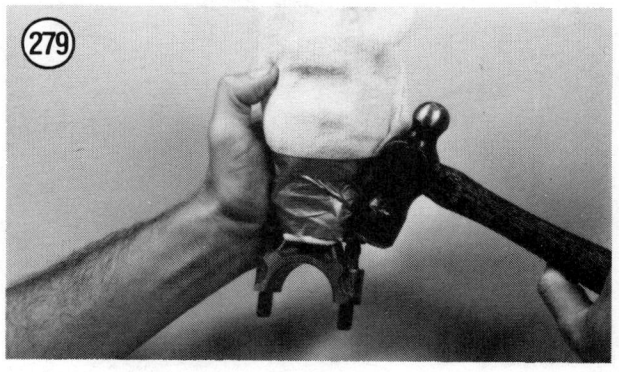

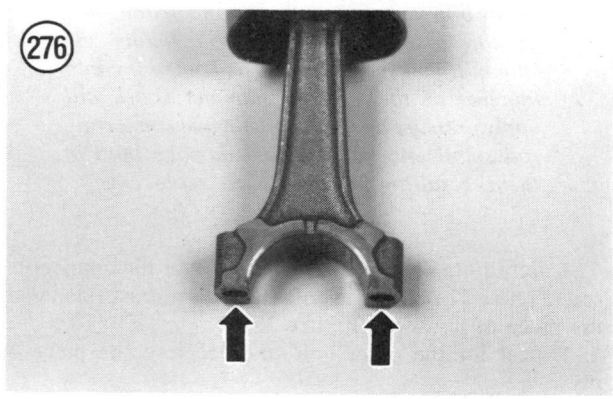

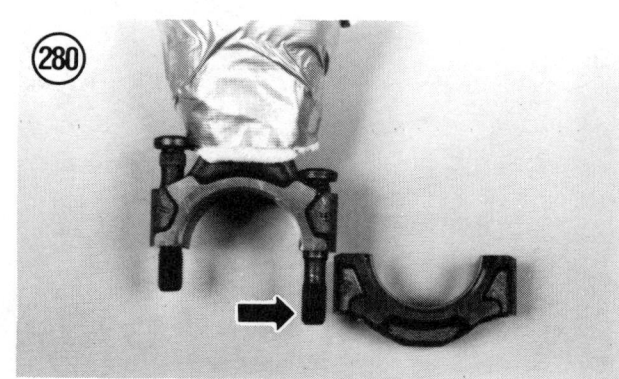

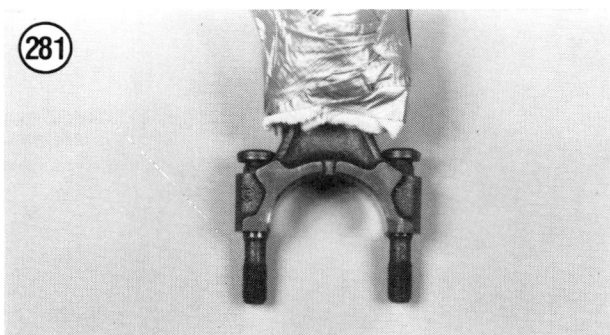

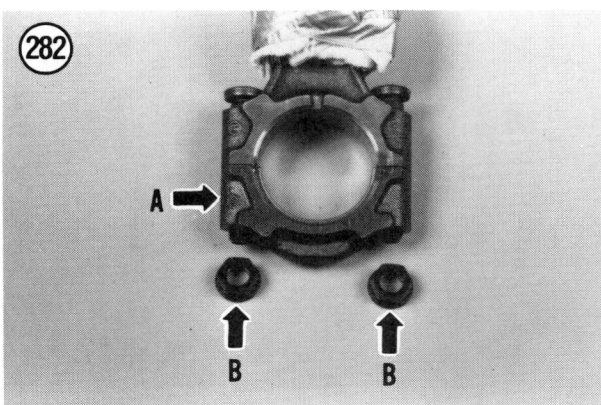

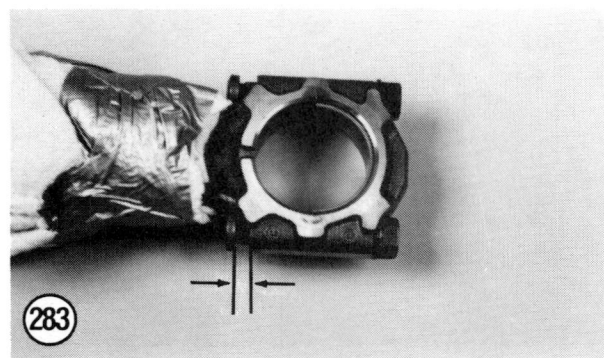

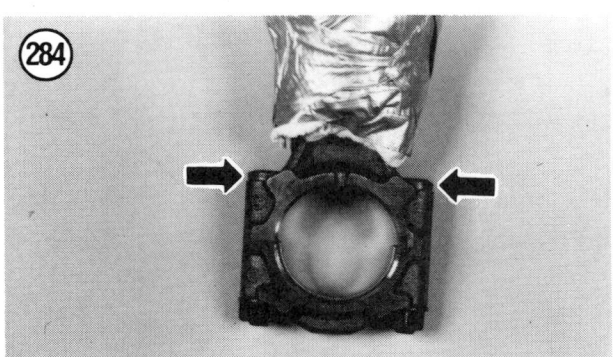

16. Install the bearing cap (A, **Figure 282**) and cap nuts (B, **Figure 282**). Tightening the cap nuts will pull the bolts the rest of the way into the connecting rod.

17. At this point the bolts will have to be pulled in the amount shown in **Figure 283**.

18. Working from side to side, tighten the cap nuts until the bolts are seated against the connecting rod (**Figure 284**). Tighten the nuts to a torque value *less* than that specified in **Table 3**. If they are tightened to the specified torque value in **Table 3**, the bolts will stretch and will have to be replaced.

19. Remove the cap nuts and the bearing cap from the connecting rod.

20. Remove the duct tape and shop cloths from the connecting rod and piston assembly.

21. Repeat Steps 1-20 for all connecting rods.

Connecting Rod Big End Bearing Clearance Measurement

1. Check each rod bearing insert for evidence of wear, abrasion, and scoring. If the bearings are good, they may be reused. If any insert is questionable, replace as a set.

2. Clean the bearing surfaces of the crankshaft; also clean the connecting rod bearing inserts.

3. Install the rod bearing inserts in the connecting rod and bearing cap. Make sure they are locked in place correctly.

4. Install the connecting rod onto the crankshaft, being careful to not damage the bearing surface of the crankshaft with the rods' threaded studs.

5. Place a piece of Plastigage over the rod bearing journal parallel to the crankshaft. Do not place the Plastigage material over an oil hole in the crankshaft.

CAUTION
Do not rotate the crankshaft while the Plastigage is in place.

6. Install the cap.

7. Apply a light coat of molybdenum disulfide grease to the connecting rod threaded studs and install the cap nuts (**Figure 285**).

8. Tighten the cap nuts as follows:
   a. Using a torque wrench, tighten the cap nuts in 2-3 stages to the torque specification listed in **Table 3**.
   b. Install BMW special tool (part No. 11 2 110) onto the rod cap nuts. Place the socket attached to the degree wheel onto the nut to be tightened (A, **Figure 286**) and the other socket onto the other nut (B, **Figure 286**).
   c. Once the socket is installed onto the nut to be tightened, zero the dial indicator (**Figure 287**).
   d. Using a socket wrench on the special tool, tighten the nut an additional 77-83° (**Figure 288**).
   e. Remove the special tool from the cap nuts, turn the special tool 180° and tighten the other cap nut in a similar manner.
   f. Remove the special tool.

9. Loosen the cap nuts and carefully remove the cap from the connecting rod.

10. Measure the width of the flattened Plastigage according to manufacturer's instructions. Measure at both ends of Plastigage strip (**Figure 289**). A difference of 0.025 mm (0.001 in.) or more indicates a tapered journal. Confirm with a micrometer (**Figure 290**). Bearing clearance for new connecting rod bearings is listed in **Table 1** or **Table 2**.

11. Remove the Plastigage strips from the bearing journals.

12. If the bearing clearance is greater than specified, select new bearings as described in this chapter.

13. Replace the connecting rod cap bolts as described in this chapter. They must be replaced every time the bolts are tightened to the torque specification described in this procedure.

Connecting Rod-to-Crankshaft Bearing Selection

The connecting rod bearings are color coded with paint. Those marked with yellow paint are the standard size. There are two additional undersize bearing inserts available from BMW and they are listed in **Table 4**. The undersize inserts are marked with green or white paint.

Refer to **Table 4** and select new bearing inserts to achieve the correct amount of bearing clearance listed in **Table 1** or **Table 2**.

After new bearing inserts have been installed, recheck the clearance by repeating the *Connecting Rod Bearing Clearance Measurement* procedure in this chapter. If the clearance is still out of specifications, either the connecting rod or the crankshaft is worn beyond the service limit and requires replacement.

CRANKSHAFT

Removal/Installation

Refer to **Figure 291** for this procedure.

1. Remove the pistons and connecting rods as described in this chapter.

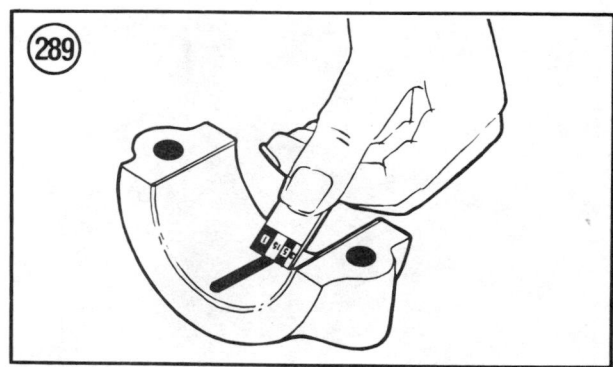

NOTE
*Before removing the main bearing caps, mark the caps with a ''1'', ''2'', ''3,'' ''4'' and on K100 models ''5'' starting from the front of the engine and working toward the back (**Figure 292**). Use a centerpunch and hammer and carefully mark the bearing cap with the correct number of marks for each journal.*

2. Loosen, then remove the bolts securing the crankshaft bearing caps. Remove all main bearing caps.

3. Carefully pull the crankshaft (**Figure 293**) straight up and out of the cylinder block.

4. If the main bearing inserts are going to be removed for cleaning, perform the following;

4

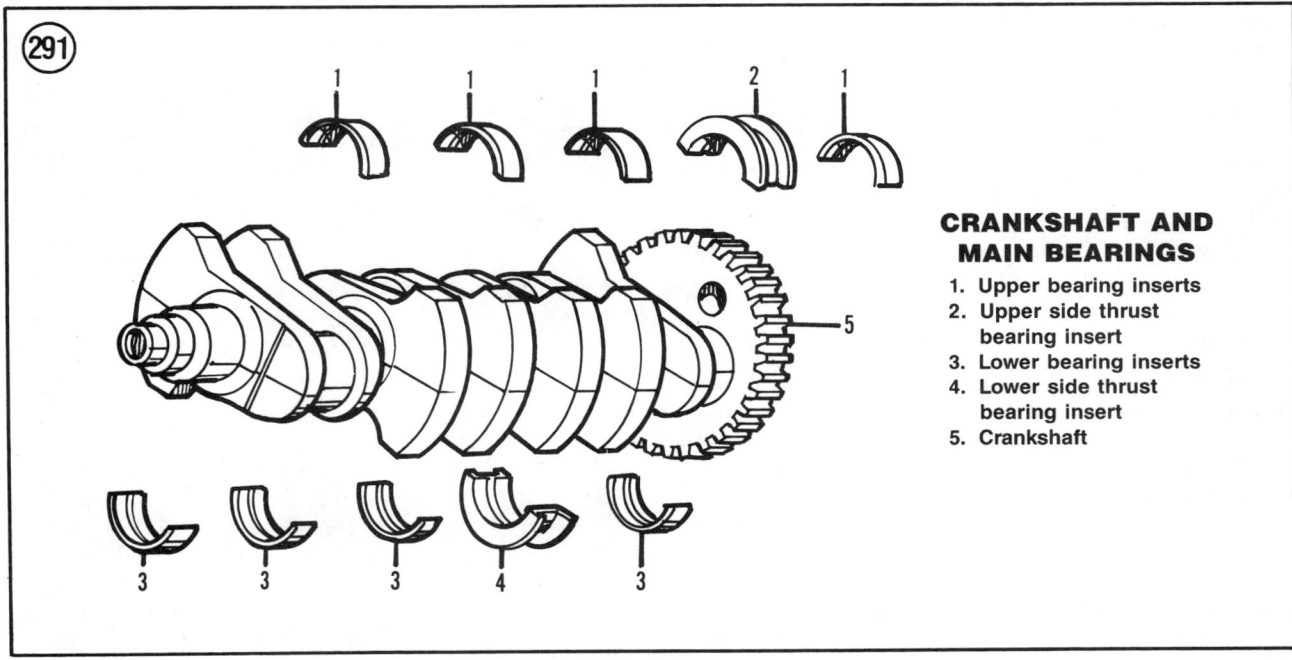

CRANKSHAFT AND MAIN BEARINGS
1. Upper bearing inserts
2. Upper side thrust bearing insert
3. Lower bearing inserts
4. Lower side thrust bearing insert
5. Crankshaft

a. Remove the main bearing inserts from the cylinder block (**Figure 294**) and from the main bearing caps.

b. Mark the backside of the inserts with a 1, 2, 3, 4 and on K100 models, 5 and "U" (upper—cylinder block) or "L" (lower—bearing cap).

> *CAUTION*
> *If the old bearings are reused, be sure that they are installed in their exact original locations because they have taken on a unique wear pattern.*

5. Inspect the crankshaft and main bearings as described in this chapter.

6. If removed, install the main bearing inserts in the cylinder block and the bearing caps. Make sure they are locked in place properly (**Figure 295**).

7. Carefully install the crankshaft (**Figure 293**) straight down into the cylinder block.

8. Install the main bearing caps in their correct locations, refer to marks made prior to Step 2.

9. Install the bolts (**Figure 296**) securing the crankshaft bearing caps. Tighten all bolts finger-tight.

10. Use a crisscross pattern and start from the center and work to each end. Tighten the main bearing cap bolts to the torque specification listed in **Table 3**.

Inspection

BMW does *not* recommend grinding the crankshaft since the crankshaft is hardened. It can be ground but then it has to be re-hardened and hardening specifications are not available from the BMW factory. If the journals are damaged, the crankshaft must be replaced.

1. Clean crankshaft thoroughly with solvent. Clean oil holes (**Figure 297**) with rifle cleaning brushes; flush thoroughly and dry with compressed air. Lightly oil all bearing journal surfaces immediately to prevent rust.

2. Carefully inspect each main bearing journal (**Figure 298**) for scratches, ridges, scoring, nicks, etc. Very small nicks and scratches may be removed with crocus cloth. If the damage is more serious, replace the crankshaft.

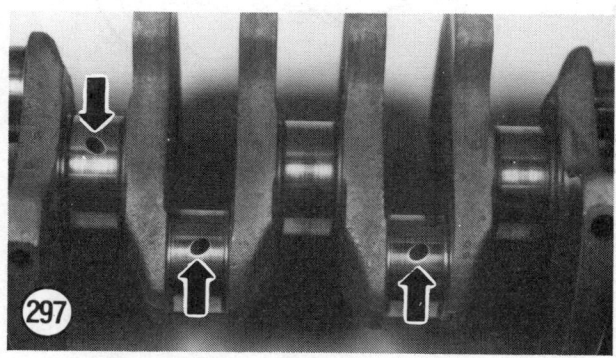

(299)

3. Inspect the camshaft chain sprocket teeth (**Figure 299**). If damaged, replace the sprocket as follows:

CAUTION
Do not completely remove the sprocket or place the puller on the end of the crankshaft as the crankshaft may be damaged.

a. Loosen, but do not remove, the Allen bolt (A, **Figure 300**) securing the camshaft sprocket to the end of the crankshaft. Loosen the Allen bolt sufficiently to allow the sprocket to be loosened from the crankshaft.
b. Install a small gear puller onto the sprocket. Place the threaded portion of the puller on the Allen bolt.
c. Gradually tighten the puller and withdraw the sprocket (B, **Figure 300**) from the end of the crankshaft.
d. Remove the Allen bolt, the puller and the sprocket.
e. Align the sprocket with the locating pin (C, **Figure 300**) on the crankshaft and install the new sprocket.
f. Carefully tap the sprocket onto the crankshaft with a soft faced mallet, then pull it on the rest of the way with the Allen bolt.
g. Tighten the bolt to the torque specification listed in **Table 3**.

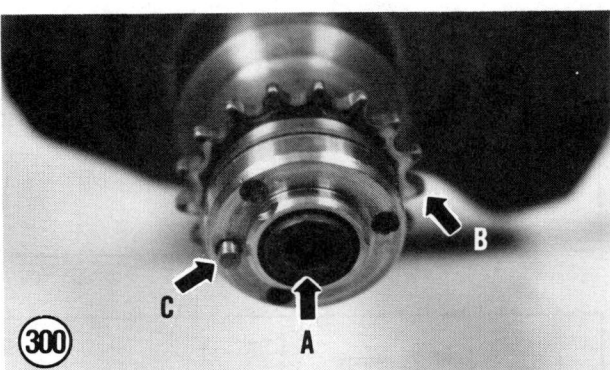

(300)

4. Inspect the output shaft gear teeth (**Figure 301**). If damaged, the crankshaft must be replaced.

5. If the surface finish on all journals (**Figure 302**) is satisfactory, measure the journals with a micrometer (**Figure 303**) and check out-of-roundness, taper, and wear on the journals. Check against measurements given in **Table 1** or **Table 2**.

(301)

Crankshaft Main Bearing Clearance Measurement

1. Check each main bearing insert for evidence of wear, abrasion, and scoring. If the bearings are good, they may be reused. If any insert is questionable, replace the entire set.

(302)

(303)

2. Clean the bearing surfaces of the crankshaft; also clean the main bearing inserts.

3. Install the existing main bearing inserts in the cylinder block and in the bearing caps in their original positions.

4. Install the crankshaft into the cylinder block (**Figure 293**).

5. Place a piece of Plastigage over each main bearing journal parallel to the crankshaft (**Figure 304**). Do not place the Plastigage material over an oil hole in the crankshaft.

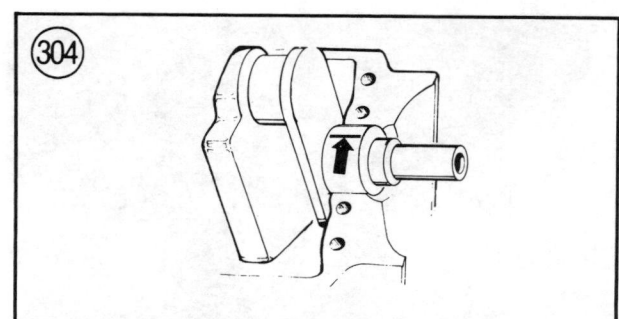

CAUTION
Do not rotate the crankshaft while the Plastigage is in place.

6. Install the main bearing caps in their correct location. Refer to marks made in Step 2, *Crankshaft Removal/Installation*.

7. Install the bolts (**Figure 296**) securing the crankshaft bearing caps. Tighten all bolts finger-tight.

8. Use a crisscross pattern and start from the center and work to each end. Tighten the main bearing cap bolts to the torque specification listed in **Table 3**.

9. Loosen, then remove the bolts securing the main bearing caps and remove the caps.

10. Measure the width of the flattened Plastigage according to manufacturer's instructions. Measure at both ends of Plastigage strip (**Figure 305**). A difference of 0.025 mm (0.001 in.) or more indicates a tapered journal. Confirm with a micrometer. Bearing clearance for new bearings is listed in **Table 1** or **Table 2**.

11. Remove the Plastigage strips from the main bearing journals.

12. If the bearing clearance is greater than specified, select new bearings as described in this chapter.

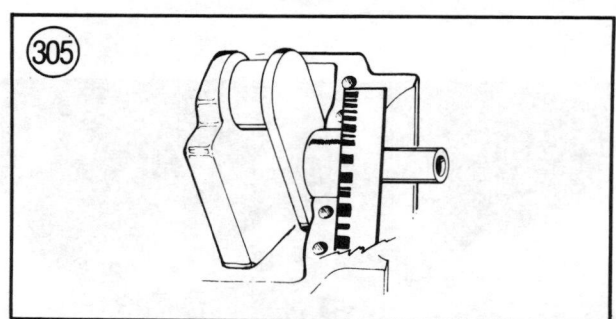

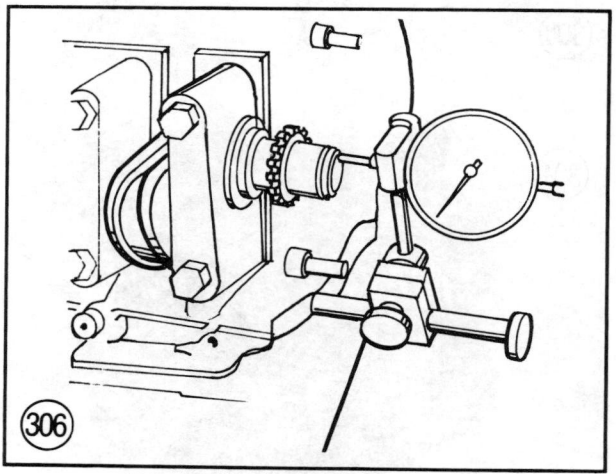

Crankshaft-to-Cylinder Block
Main Bearing Selection

Refer to **Figure 291** for this procedure.

The crankshaft main bearings are color coded with paint. Those marked with yellow paint are the standard size. There are two additional undersize bearing inserts available from BMW and they are listed in **Table 5**. The undersize inserts are marked with green or white paint.

Refer to **Table 5** and select new bearing inserts to achieve the correct amount of bearing clearance listed in **Table 1** or **Table 2**.

After new bearing inserts have been installed, recheck the clearance by repeating the *Crankshaft Bearing Clearance Measurement* procedure in this chapter. If the clearance is still out of specifications, the crankshaft is worn beyond the service limit and requires replacement.

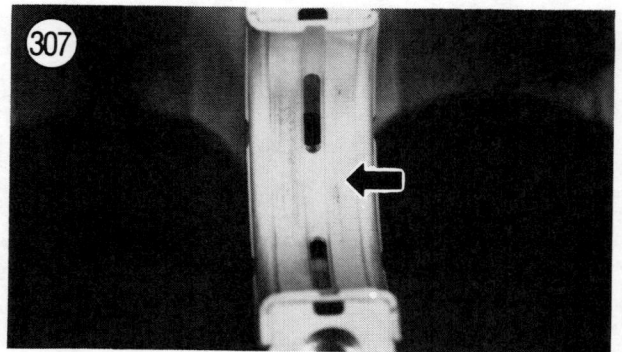

Crankshaft End Float Measurement

The crankshaft must be installed in the cylinder block and the main bearings correctly installed; bearing cap bolts must be tightened to the correct torque specification.

1. Attach a dial indicator to the front of the cylinder block as shown in **Figure 306**.
2. Using a large flat-bladed screwdriver, move the crankshaft all the way toward the *rear* of the cylinder block until it bottoms out.
3. Zero the dial indicator.
4. Using a large flat-bladed screwdriver, move the crankshaft all the way toward the *front* of the cylinder block until it bottoms out.
5. Note the distance the crankshaft traveled on the dial indicator.
6. Double check by repeating Steps 2-5 and note the distance traveled this time. It should be the same. If not, repeat Steps 2-5 until you get the same reading.
7. Refer to specifications listed in **Table 1** or **Table 2**. If the end float has worn to the specification or greater, the

side thrust bearing set (**Figure 307**) must be replaced with a wider set. There are 2 additional thrust bearing sets available from a BMW dealer. BMW does not provide the width specifications for these 2 additional bearings. Confer with a BMW dealer in order to obtain the correct width.
8. Remove the dial indicator.

CYLINDER BLOCK

Disassembly/Assembly

Refer to **Figure 308** for this procedure.
1. Remove the frame from the engine as described in this chapter.
2. Remove all external components as described in this chapter.
3. Install all external components as described in this chapter.
4. Install the frame onto the engine as described in this chapter.

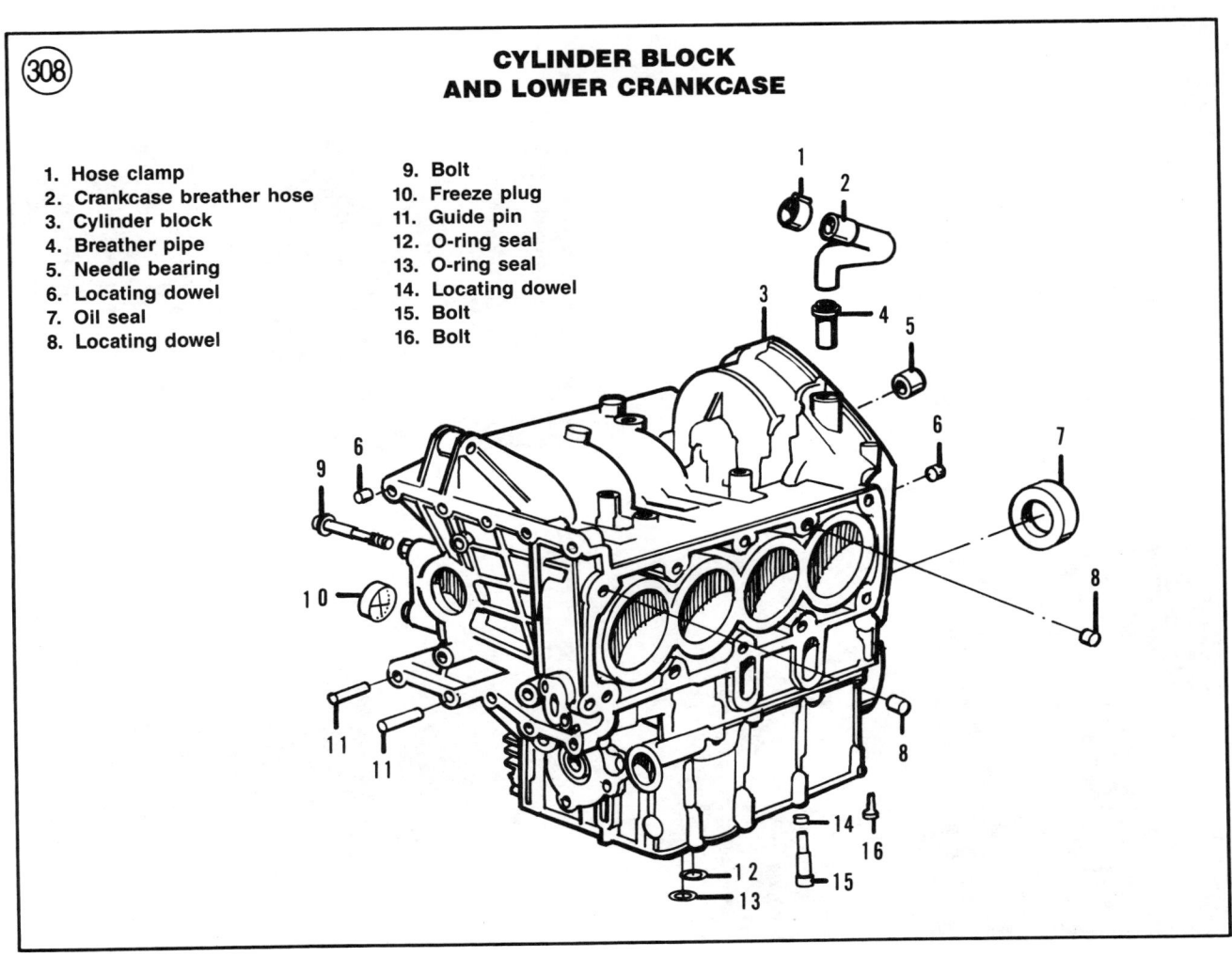

(308)

**CYLINDER BLOCK
AND LOWER CRANKCASE**

1. Hose clamp
2. Crankcase breather hose
3. Cylinder block
4. Breather pipe
5. Needle bearing
6. Locating dowel
7. Oil seal
8. Locating dowel
9. Bolt
10. Freeze plug
11. Guide pin
12. O-ring seal
13. O-ring seal
14. Locating dowel
15. Bolt
16. Bolt

Cylinder Bore Inspection

The following procedure requires the use of highly specialized and expensive measuring instruments. If such equipment is not readily available, have the measurements performed by a dealer or qualified machine shop.

The cylinder bores *cannot* be rebored. The cylinder bores are *not* equipped with steel liners. The cylinders instead are electrically plated with a very hard nickel/silicone carbide layer that is machined to the correct bore size. This surface is so hard that it will wear out a diamond hone if used. There are many well maintained K-Series bikes with close to 200,000 miles on them that rarely require any major engine service (e.g. cylinder bore out of specification). This type of extended service depends greatly on how well the bike is maintained. Don't forget to maintain the correct oil level and change the oil at the recommended intervals.

1. Soak with solvent any old cylinder head gasket material on the cylinder block. If necessary, use a broad-tipped *dull* chisel and gently scrape off all gasket residue. Do not gouge the sealing surface (**Figure 309**) as an oil or coolant leak will result.

2. Measure the cylinder bore with a cylinder gauge or inside micrometer at the 3 locations shown in **Figure 310**. Measure in 2 axes—in line with the piston-pin and at 90° to the pin. If the taper or out-of-round is 0.05 mm (0.002 in.) or greater in one cylinder, the cylinder block must be replaced as it *cannot* be rebored.

3. Check the cylinder walls (**Figure 311**) for scratches. If evident, the cylinder block may have to be replaced.

NOTE
*The maximum wear limit on the cylinders is listed in **Table 1** or **Table 2**. If any cylinder is worn to this limit, the cylinder block must be replaced.*

NOTE
Table 1 and Table 2 lists cylinder bore dimensions in 2 categories ("A" or "B"). Either an "A" or "B" is stamped on the cylin-

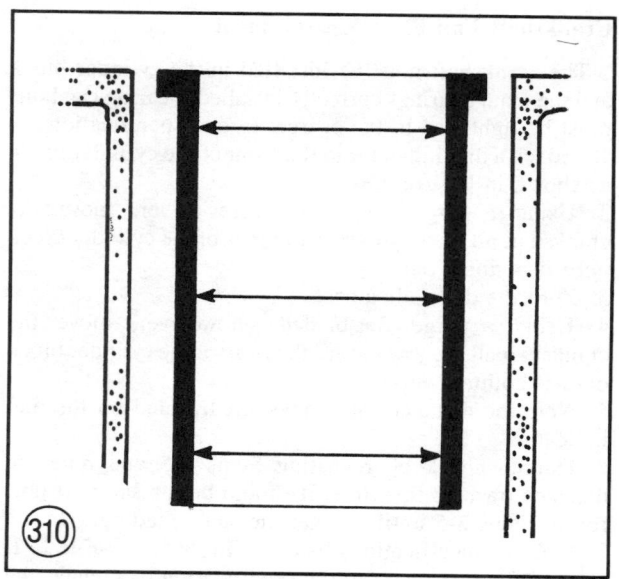

der block. These letters relate to the grade or finished inner dimension of the cylinder bore. It is virtually impossible to manufacture all cylinder bores to the same exact dimension.

Cylinder Block Inspection

1. Carefully inspect the cylinder block for cracks and fractures. Also check the areas around the stiffening ribs (**Figure 312**), around bearing bosses and threaded holes. If damage is found, have it repaired by a shop specializing in the repair of precision aluminum castings or replace the cylinder block.

2. Inspect the starter countershaft bearing (**Figure 313**) for wear or damage. Rotate the bearing with your finger. It should rotate smoothly with no roughness. Replace if necessary.

3. Make sure the oil channel (**Figure 314**) for the timing chain tensioner is clean. If necessary, clean out with solvent and dry with compressed air.

4. Make sure the oil return channels (**Figure 315**) for the timing chain tensioner are clean. If necessary, clean out with solvent and dry with compressed air.

5. Check the grooves for the output shaft bearing set rings. Refer to **Figure 316** and **Figure 317**. They must be clear and free of dirt in order for the rings to properly seat.

6. Check the bearing surfaces for the output shaft bearings (**Figure 318**). Make sure they are not gouged or damaged in any way. Replace the cylinder block if necessary.

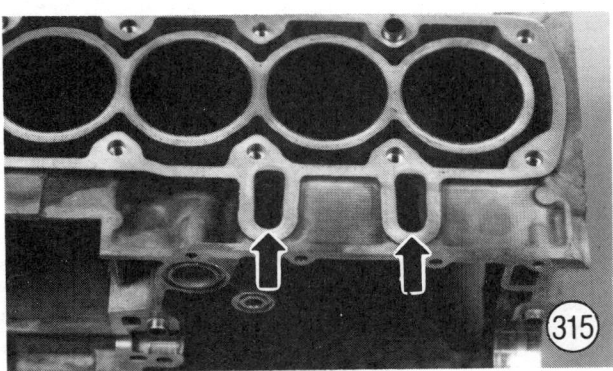

7. Make sure the timing chain tensioner studs (**Figure 319**) are tight.

8. Make sure the crankcase breather outlet fitting (**Figure 320**) and on models so equipped, the evaporative emission fitting (**Figure 321**) are clean. If necessary, clean out with solvent and dry with compressed air.

BREAK-IN

Following cylinder servicing (new pistons, new rings, etc.) and major lower end work, the engine should be broken in just as though it were new. The performance and service life of the engine depend greatly on a careful and sensible break-in.

For the first 800 km (500 miles), no more than one-third throttle should be used and speed should be varied as much as possible within the one-third throttle limit. Prolonged, steady running at one speed, no matter how moderate, is to be avoided, as is hard acceleration.

Following the 800 km (500-mile) service, increasingly more throttle can be used but full throttle should not be used until the motorcycle has covered at least 1,600 km (1,000 miles) and then it should be limited to short bursts until 2,410 km (1,500 miles) have been logged.

During this period, oil consumption will be higher than normal. It is therefore important to frequently check and correct the oil level. At no time, during break-in or later, should the oil level be allowed to drop below the bottom line on the sightglass; if the oil level is low, the oil will become overheated resulting in insufficient lubrication and increased wear.

800 km (500 Mile) Service

It is essential that oil and filter be changed after the first 800 km (500 miles). In addition, it is a good idea to change the oil and filter at the completion of break-in (about 2,410 km/1,500 miles) to ensure that all of the particles produced during break-in are removed from the lubrication system. The small added expense may be considered a smart investment that will pay off in increased engine life.

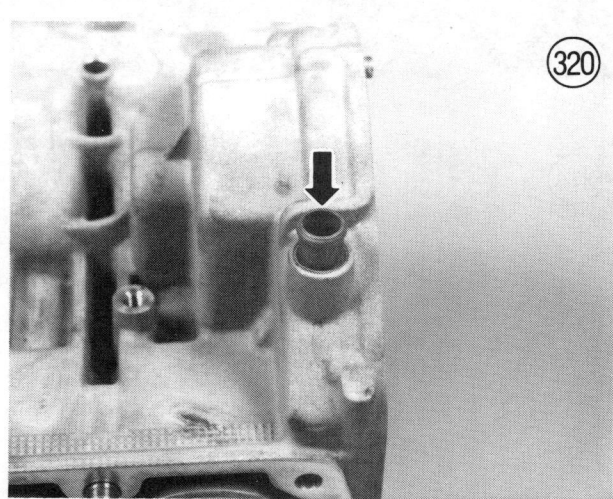

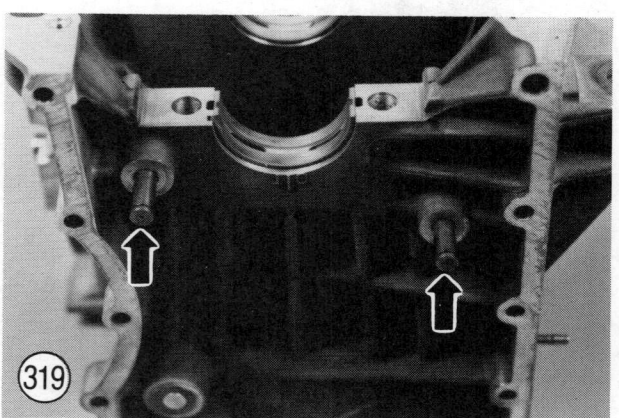

Table 1 ENGINE SPECIFICATIONS (3-CYLINDER K75 MODELS)

Item	Specification	Wear limit
General		
Engine type	Water cooled, 4-stroke longitudinal inline 3 cylinder. Four main bearings with dual overhead camshafts and 2 valves per cylinder	
Bore and stroke	67 x 70 mm (2.638 x 2.756 in.)	
Displacement	740 cc (45.1 cu. in.)	
Compression ratio	10.5 to 1	
Maximum constant engine speed	8,600 rpm	
Maximum engine speed	8,700 rpm	
Engine rotation	Counterclockwise as viewed from front of engine	
Firing order	3-1-2	
Maximum engine torque	68 N·m (49 ft.-lb.) at 6,750 rpm	
Compression pressure		
Good: more than 1012 kPa (145 psi)		
Normal: 848-1012 kPa (123-145 psi)		
Poor: less than 848 kPa (123 psi)		
Idle speed 900-1,000 rpm		
Engine lubrication		
Output shaft driven oil pump with wet sump		
Full flow oil filter		
Oil bypass valve opens at 151 kPa (22 psi)		
Oil pressure warning light comes on at 20-50 kPa (3-7 psi)		
Oil pressure relief valve opens at 537 kPa (78 psi)		
Maximum oil consumption per 62 miles (100 km): 0.15 liter (0.32 pt.)		
Valves		
Valve clearance (cold)		
Intake: 0.15-0.20 mm (0.006-0.008 in.)		
Exhaust: 0.25-0.30 mm (0.010-0.012 in.)		
Valve timing		
Intake opens: 5 degrees ATDC		
Intake closes: 27 degrees ABDC		
Exhaust opens: 28 degrees BBDC		
Exhaust closes: 5 degrees BTDC		
Valve total length		
Intake: 111 mm (4.370 in.)		
Exhaust: 110.61-110.81 mm (4.355-4.363 in.)		
Head diameter		
Intake: 34 mm (1.338 in.)		
Exhaust: 30 mm (1.181 in.)		
Stem diameter		
Intake	6.960-6.975 mm (0.2740-0.2746 in.)	6.950 mm (0.2736 in).
Exhaust	6.945-6.960 mm (0.2734-0.2740 in.)	6.935 mm (0.2730 in.)
Valve head edge thickness		
Intake and exhaust	1.36-1.65 mm (0.053-0.065 in.)	1.0 mm (0.039 in.)
Valve head runout		
Intake and exhaust	—	0.03 mm (0.0012 in.)

(continued)

4

Table 1 ENGINE SPECIFICATIONS (3-CYLINDER K75 MODELS) (continued)

Item	Specification	Wear limit
Valve seat angle		
Intake and exhaust	44° 10'-44° 30'	—
Valve seat width		
Intake	0.090-1.40 mm (0.035-0.055 in.)	2.50 mm (0.098 in.)
Exhaust	1.10-1.60 mm (0.043-0.063 in.)	3.00 mm (0.118 in.)
Valve guide		
Total length	45 mm (1.772 in.)	
Outside diameter	12.982-13.044 mm (0.5104-0.5135 in.)	—
Inside diameter	7.000-7.015 mm (0.2756-0.2762 in.)	7.100 mm (0.2795 in.)
Bore in cylinder head	13.000-13.018 mm (0.5118-0.5125 in.)	—
Repair size	13.200-13.218 mm (0.5197-0.5204 in.)	—
Valve stem clearance		
Intake	0.025-0.050 mm (0.0010-0.0020 in.)	0.150 mm (0.0059 in.)
Exhaust	0.040-0.070 mm (0.0016-0.0027 in.)	0.165 mm (0.0065 in.)
Valve springs		
Wire gauge	4.25 mm (0.167 in.)	
Coil winding direction	Clockwise	
Total number of coils	6.3	
Spring free length	44.5 mm (1.752 in.)	43.0 mm (1.693 in.)
Camshaft		
Thrust bearing O.D.	29.993-29.980 mm (1.1731-1.1808 in.)	29.95 mm (1.1791 in.)
All other bearings O.D.	23.997-23.999 mm (0.9419-9441 in.)	23.95 mm (0.9429 in.)
Thrust bearing bore in cylinder head I.D.	30.020-30.041 mm (1.1819-1.1827 in.	—
All other bearing bores in cylinder head I.D.	24.020-24.041 mm (0.9457-0.9465 in.)	—
Oil clearance		
Thrust bearing	0.027-0.061 mm (0.0011-0.0024 in.)	0.150 mm (0.0059 in.)
All other bearings	0.027-0.061 mm (0.0011-0.0024 in.)	0.150 mm (0.0059 in.)
Lobe height		
Intake	39.3617-39.4237 mm (1.5496-1.5520 in.)	39.10 mm (1.5494 in.)
Exhaust	39.3509-39.4129 mm (1.5493-1.5517 in.)	39.05 mm (1.5374 in.)
Valve lifters		
Outside diameter	33.475-33.491 mm (1.3179-1.3186 in.)	33.465 mm (1.3175 in.)
Receptacle in cylinder head	33.500-35.025 mm (1.3189-1.3199 in.)	33.615 mm (1.3234 in.)

(continued)

Table 1 ENGINE SPECIFICATIONS (3-CYLINDER K75 MODELS) (continued)

Item	Specification	Wear limit
Oil clearance	0.009-0.050 mm (0.0003-0.0020 in.)	0.150 mm (0.0059 in.)
Crankshaft		
Thrust bearing width	23.020-23.053 mm (0.9063-0.9076 in.)	—
Main bearing diameter	44.976-45.024 mm (1.7707-1.7716 in.)	—
Connecting rod bearing diameter	37.976-38.000 mm (1.4952-1.4961 in.)	—
Bearing bore diameter in cylinder block	49.000-49.160 mm (1.9291-1.9354 in.)	—
Main bearing journal oil clearance	0.020-0.056 mm (0.008-0.0022 in.)	0.110 mm (0.0043 in.)
Connecting rod journal oil clearance	0.030-0.066 mm (0.0012-0.0026 in.)	0.130 mm (0.0051 in.)
Crankshaft end float	0.080-0.183 mm (0.0031-0.0072 in.)	0.250 mm (0.0098 in.)
Connecting rods		
Big end bore I.D.	41.000-41.016 mm (1.6142-1.6148 in.)	—
Big end width	21.883-21.935 mm (0.8615-0.8636 in.)	—
Thrust journal width	22.065-22.195 mm (0.8684-0.8586 in.)	—
Oil clearance	0.130-0.312 mm (0.0051-0.0123 in.)	0.400 mm (0.0157 in.)
Small end bore I.D.	20.000-20.021 mm (0.7874-0.7882 in.)	—
Maximum weight deviation between rods	± 4 grams	
Cylinder block		
Bore I.D.		
Grade A	66.995-67.005 mm (2.6376-2.6380 in.)	67.05 mm (2.6397 in.)
Grade B	67.005-67.015 mm (2.6380-2.6384 in.)	67.06 mm (2.6401 in.)
Pistons		
Outer diameter		
KS grade A	66.966-66.980 mm (2.6364-2.6370 in.)	62.92 mm (2.6346 in.)
KS grade B	66.976-66.990 mm (2.6368-2.6374 in.)	62.93 mm (2.6350 in.)
Mahle grade A	66.963-66.977 mm (2.6363-2.6369 in.)	62.92 mm (2.6346 in.)
Mahle grade B	66.973-66.987 mm (2.6367-2.6373 in.)	62.93 mm (2.6350 in.)
Piston-to-cylinder clearance	0.015-0.039 mm (0.0006-0.0015 in.)	0.130 mm (0.0051 in.)

(continued)

Table 1 ENGINE SPECIFICATIONS (3-CYLINDER K75 MODELS) (continued)

Item	Specification	Wear limit
Piston pin bore I.D.	18.002-18.006 mm (0.7087-0.7089 in.)	—
Piston pin O.D.	17.996-18.004 mm (0.7085-0.7086 in.)	17.96 mm (0.7071 in.)
Pin-to-piston clearance	0.002-0.010 mm (0.00008-0.00039 in.)	—
Pin-to-connecting rod bushing clearance	0.006-0.021 mm (0.00024-0.00083 in.)	0.060 mm (0.0024 in.)
Piston rings		
1st compression ring Thickness	1.178-1.190 mm (0.0464-0.0468 in.)	1.10 mm (0.0433 in.)
End clearance (installed)	0.25-0.45 mm (0.098-0.0177 in.)	1.50 mm (0.059 in.)
Side clearance Mahle	0.050-0.082 mm (0.0020-0.0032 in.)	0.30 mm (0.012 in.)
KS	0.040-0.072 mm (0.0016-0.0028 in.)	0.30 mm (0.012 in.)
2nd compression ring Thickness	1.478-1.490 mm (0.0586-0.0581 in.)	1.40 mm (0.0551 in.)
End clearance (installed)	0.25-0.45 mm (0.098-0.0177 in.)	1.50 mm (0.059 in.)
Side clearance Mahle	0.040-0.072 mm (0.0016-0.0028 in.)	0.30 mm (0.012 in.)
KS	0.030-0.062 mm (0.0016-0.0028 in.)	0.30 mm (0.012 in.)
Oil ring Thickness	2.975-2.990 mm (0.1177-0.1171 in.)	2.90 mm (0.1142 in.)
End clearance (installed)	0.25-0.45 mm (0.098-0.0177 in.)	1.50 mm (0.059 in.)
Side clearance	0.020-0.055 mm (0.0008-0.0022 in.)	0.30 mm (0.012 in.)

Table 2 ENGINE SPECIFICATIONS (4-CYLINDER K100 MODELS)

Item	Specification	Wear limit
General		
Engine type	Water cooled, 4-stroke longitudinal inline 4 cylinder. Five main bearings with dual overhead camshafts and 2 valves per cylinder	
Bore and stroke	67 x 70 mm (2.638 x 2.756 in.)	
Displacement	980 cc (59.8 cu. in.)	
Compression ratio	10.2 to 1	
Maximum constant engine speed	8,500 rpm	
Maximum engine speed	8,600 rpm	
Engine rotation	Counterclockwise as viewed from front of engine	
Firing order	1-3-4-2	
Maximum engine torque	86 N·m (62 ft.-lb.) at 8,000 rpm	
Compression pressure		
Good: more than 1012 kPa (145 psi)		
Normal: 848-1012 kPa (123-145 psi)		
Poor: less than 848 kPa (123 psi)		
Idle speed 900-1,000 rpm		
Engine lubrication		
Output shaft driven oil pump with wet sump		
Full flow oil filter		
Oil bypass valve opens at 151 kPa (22 psi)		
Oil pressure warning light comes on at 20-50 kPa (3-7 psi)		
Oil pressure relief valve opens at 537 kPa (78 psi)		
Maximum oil consumption per 62 miles (100 km): 0.15 liter (0.32 pt.)		
Valves		
Valve clearance (cold)		
Intake: 0.15-0.20 mm (0.006-0.008 in.)		
Exhaust: 0.25-0.30 mm (0.010-0.012 in.)		
Valve timing		
Intake opens: 5 degrees ATDC		
Intake closes: 27 degrees ABDC		
Exhaust opens: 28 degrees BBDC		
Exhaust closes: 5 degrees BTDC		
Valve total length		
Intake: 111 mm (4.370 in.)		
Exhaust: 110.61-110.81 mm (4.355-4.363 in.)		
Head diameter		
Intake: 34 mm (1.338 in.)		
Exhaust: 30 mm (1.181 in.)		
Stem diameter		
Intake	6.960-6.975 mm (0.2740-0.2746 in.)	6.950 mm (0.2736 in).
Exhaust	6.945-6.960 mm (0.2734-0.2740 in.)	6.935 mm (0.2730 in.)
Valve head edge thickness		
Intake and exhaust	1.36-1.65 mm (0.053-0.065 in.)	1.0 mm (0.039 in.)
Valve head runout		
Intake and exhaust	—	0.03 mm (0.0012 in.)

(continued)

4

Table 2 ENGINE SPECIFICATIONS (4-CYLINDER K100 MODELS) (continued)

Item	Specification	Wear limit
Valve seat angle		
Intake and exhaust	44° 10'-44° 30'	—
Valve seat width		
Intake	0.090-1.40 mm (0.035-0.055 in.)	2.50 mm (0.098 in.)
Exhaust	1.10-1.60 mm (0.043-0.063 in.)	3.00 mm (0.118 in.)
Valve guide		
Total length	45 mm (1.772 in.)	—
Outside diameter	12.982-13.044 mm (0.5104-0.5135 in.)	—
Inside diameter	7.000-7.015 mm (0.2756-0.2762 in.)	7.100 mm (0.2795 in.)
Bore in cylinder head	13.000-13.018 mm (0.5118-0.5125 in.)	—
Repair size	13.200-13.218 mm (0.5197-0.5204 in.)	—
Valve stem clearance		
Intake	0.025-0.050 mm (0.0010-0.0020 in.)	0.150 mm (0.0059 in.)
Exhaust	0.040-0.070 mm (0.0016-0.0027 in.)	0.165 mm (0.0065 in.)
Valve springs		
Wire gauge	4.25 mm (0.167 in.)	
Coil winding direction	Clockwise	
Total number of coils	6.3	
Spring free length	44.5 mm (1.752 in.)	43.0 mm (1.693 in.)
Camshaft		
Thrust bearing O.D.	29.993-29.980 mm (1.1731-1.1808 in.)	29.95 mm (1.1791 in.)
All other bearings O.D.	23.997-23.999 mm (0.9419-9441 in.)	23.95 mm (0.9429 in.)
Thrust bearing bore in cylinder head I.D.	30.020-30.041 mm (1.1819-1.1827 in.	—
All other bearing bores in cylinder head I.D.	24.020-24.041 mm (0.9457-0.9465 in.)	—
Oil clearance		
Thrust bearing	0.027-0.061 mm	0.150 mm (0.0059 in.) (0.0011-0.0024 in.)
All other bearings	0.027-0.061 mm (0.0011-0.0024 in.)	0.150 mm (0.0059 in.)
Lobe height		
Intake	39.3617-39.4237 mm (1.5496-1.5520 in.)	39.10 mm (1.5494 in.)
Exhaust	39.3509-39.4129 mm (1.5493-1.5517 in.)	39.05 mm (1.5374 in.)
Valve lifters		
Outside diameter	33.475-33.491 mm (1.3179-1.3186 in.)	33.465 mm (1.3175 in.)
Receptacle in cylinder head	33.500-35.025 mm (1.3189-1.3199 in.)	33.615 mm (1.3234 in.)

(continued)

Table 2 ENGINE SPECIFICATIONS (4-CYLINDER K100 MODELS) (continued)

Item	Specification	Wear limit
Oil clearance	0.009-0.050 mm (0.0003-0.0020 in.)	0.150 mm (0.0059 in.)
Crankshaft		
Thrust bearing width	23.020-23.053 mm (0.9063-0.9076 in.)	—
Main bearing diameter	44.976-45.024 mm (1.7707-1.7716 in.)	—
Connecting rod bearing diameter	37.976-38.000 mm (1.4952-1.4961 in.)	—
Bearing bore diameter in cylinder block	49.000-49.160 mm (1.9291-1.9354 in.)	—
Main bearing journal oil clearance	0.020-0.056 mm (0.008-0.0022 in.)	0.110 mm (0.0043 in.)
Connecting rod journal oil clearance	0.030-0.066 mm (0.0012-0.0026 in.)	0.130 mm (0.0051 in.)
Crankshaft end float	0.080-0.183 mm (0.0031-0.0072 in.)	0.250 mm (0.0098 in.)
Connecting rods		
Big end bore I.D.	41.000-41.016 mm (1.6142-1.6148 in.)	—
Big end width	21.883-21.935 mm (0.8615-0.8636 in.)	—
Thrust journal width	22.065-22.195 mm (0.8684-0.8586 in.)	—
Oil clearance	0.130-0.312 mm (0.0051-0.0123 in.)	0.400 mm (0.0157 in.)
Small end bore I.D.	20.000-20.021 mm (0.7874-0.7882 in.)	—
Maximum weight deviation between rods	± 4 grams	
Cylinder block		
Bore I.D.		
Grade A	66.995-67.005 mm (2.6376-2.6380 in.)	67.05 mm (2.6397 in.)
Grade B	67.005-67.015 mm (2.6380-2.6384 in.)	67.06 mm (2.6401 in.)
Pistons		
Outer diameter		
KS grade A	66.966-66.980 mm (2.6364-2.6370 in.)	62.92 mm (2.6346 in.)
KS grade B	66.976-66.990 mm (2.6368-2.6374 in.)	62.93 mm (2.6350 in.)
Mahle grade A	66.963-66.977 mm (2.6363-2.6369 in.)	62.92 mm (2.6346 in.)
Mahle grade B	66.973-66.987 mm (2.6367-2.6373 in.)	62.93 mm (2.6350 in.)
Piston-to-cylinder clearance	0.015-0.039 mm (0.0006-0.0015 in.)	0.130 mm (0.0051 in.)

(continued)

Table 2 ENGINE SPECIFICATIONS (4-CYLINDER K100 MODELS) (continued)

Item	Specification	Wear limit
Piston pin bore I.D.	18.002-18.006 mm (0.7087-0.7089 in.)	—
Piston pin O.D.	17.996-18.004 mm (0.7085-0.7086 in.)	17.96 mm (0.7071 in.)
Pin-to-piston clearance	0.002-0.010 mm (0.00008-0.00039 in.)	—
Pin-to-connecting rod bushing clearance	0.006-0.021 mm (0.00024-0.00083 in.)	0.060 mm (0.0024 in.)
Piston rings		
1st compression ring		
Thickness	1.178-1.190 mm (0.0464-0.0468 in.)	1.10 mm (0.0433 in.)
End clearance (installed)	0.25-0.45 mm (0.098-0.0177 in.)	1.50 mm (0.059 in.)
Side clearance	0.013-0.027 mm (0.0005-0.0011 in.)	0.30 mm (0.012 in.)
2nd compression ring		
Thickness	1.478-1.490 mm (0.0586-0.0581 in.)	1.40 mm (0.0551 in.)
End clearance (installed)	0.25-0.45 mm (0.098-0.0177 in.)	1.50 mm (0.059 in.)
Side clearance	0.012-0.026 mm (0.00047-0.0010 in.)	0.30 mm (0.012 in.
Oil ring		
Thickness	2.975-2.990 mm (0.1177-0.1171 in.)	2.90 mm (0.1142 in.)
End clearance (installed)	0.25-0.45 mm (0.098-0.0177 in.)	1.50 mm (0.059 in.)
Side clearance	0.020-0.055 mm (0.0008-0.0022 in.)	0.30 mm (0.012 in.)

Table 3 ENGINE TORQUE SPECIFICATIONS

Item	N·m	ft.-lb.
Engine-to-frame bolts	39-45	28-32
Timing chain cover bolts	6-8	4.5-6
Cylinder head cover bolts	7-9	5.5-6.5
Crankshaft cover bolts	7-9	5.5-6.5
Camshaft driven sprocket bolt	48-60	35-43
Camshaft bearing cap bolts	8-10	6-7
Timing chain tensioner bolts	8-10	6-7
Timing chain guide rail		
Torx bolts	8-10	6-7
Cylinder head bolts		
Preliminary torque	26-34	19-25
Final torque	40-50	30-36

(continued)

Table 3 ENGINE TORQUE SPECIFICATIONS (continued)

Item	N·m	ft.-lb.
Water/oil pump		
Mounting bolts	6-8	4.5-6
Impeller nut	19-23	13.5-16.5
Impeller bolt	29-37	21-27
Intermediate housing		
Thrust plate bolts	8-10	6-7
Torx mounting bolts	8-10	6-7
Starter one-way clutch		
cover plate mounting bolts	8-10	6-7
Alternator drive dog bolt	29-37	21-27
Lower crankcase half bolts	8-10	6-7
Oil pan bolts	8-10	6-7
Connecting rod cap nuts		
Initial torque value	27-33	20-24
Final torque angle 77-83°		
Crankshaft main bearing		
cap bolts	44-56	32-40
Camshaft drive sprocket bolt		
on crankshaft	44-56	32-40

4

Table 4 CONNECTING ROD BEARING INSERT THICKNESS AND COLOR

Shaft diameter	Bearing wall thickness	Color
38.000-37.992 mm (1.4961-1.4957 in.)	1.479-1.485 mm (0.0582-0.0584 in.)	Yellow
37.992-37.984 mm (1.4957-1.4954 in.)	1.483-1.489 mm (0.0584-0.0586 in.)	Green
37.984-37.976 mm (1.4954-1.4951 in.)	1.487-1.493 mm (0.0585-0.0587 in.)	White

Table 5 CRANKSHAFT BEARING INSERT THICKNESS AND COLOR

Shaft diameter	Bearing wall thickness	Color
45.000-44.992 mm (1.7716-1.7713 in.)	1.987-1.993 mm (0.0782-0.0784 in.)	Yellow
44.992-44.984 mm (1.7713-1.7710 in.)	1.991-1.997 mm (0.0784-0.0786 in.)	Green
44.984-44.976 mm (1.7710-1.7707 in.)	1.995-2.001 mm (0.0785-0.0787 in.)	White

CHAPTER FIVE

CLUTCH

This chapter provides complete service procedures for the clutch and clutch release mechanism.

The clutch is a dry single-plate type that is mounted at the rear portion of the engine. The clutch design is basically an automotive type clutch instead of the usual wet multi-plate type found on most Japanese motorcycles. The clutch friction plate is splined to the transmission input shaft and is sandwiched between the clutch pressure plate and the clutch housing cover. The forged alloy clutch housing is splined and bolted to the end of the engine output shaft. The housing cover is equipped with locating pins that go through mounting holes in the pressure plate and this assembly is then bolted to the clutch housing. The clutch housing, pressure plate and the housing cover rotate with the engine and when the clutch is engaged, the friction plate also turns with this assembly, thus turning the transmission shaft.

The outer circumference of the diaphragm spring rides on a steel ring that is positioned against the inner surface of the clutch housing. This steel ring protects the alloy clutch housing from constant contact with the diaphragm spring.

The clutch release pushrod, which is a light alloy, rides within the hollow channel in the transmission's input shaft. It is controlled by the cable operated clutch release lever that is mounted on the rear of the transmission housing. When the clutch lever on the handlebar is pulled in, the clutch cable actuates the clutch release lever on the transmission housing and pushes the release pushrod forward. A pressure piston, ball bearing and bearing race accommodate the rotation of the release pushrod as it touches the rotating diaphragm spring. The forward end of the release push rod has a conical steel tip that rides against the center of the diaphragm spring. As the release pushrod moves forward, it releases the spring pressure allowing the clutch housing assembly to rotate freely without touching or rotating the friction plate and transmission input shaft.

> *NOTE*
> *The friction plate is **free of asbestos**.*

In order to maintain smooth clutch operation, BMW suggests that the clutch be disassembled and certain parts be lubricated at least once a year. Refer to *Clutch Lubrication* in Chapter Three.

This type of clutch *does* require routine adjustment as the cable will stretch with use. Refer to Chapter Three for adjustment procedures.

Specifications for the clutch are listed in **Table 1**. **Table 1** and **Table 2** are located at the end of this chapter.

CLUTCH

Removal

Refer to **Figure 1** for K75 models or **Figure 2** for K100 models for this procedure.

The clutch assembly can be removed with the engine in the frame but the transmission housing must be removed.

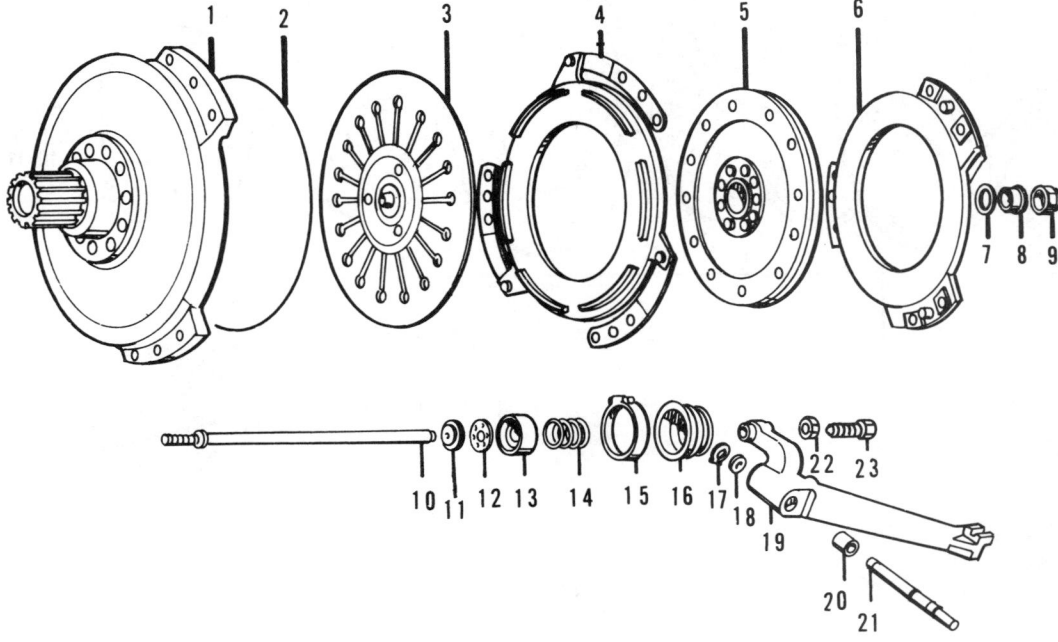

CLUTCH ASSEMBLY (K75)

1. Clutch housing
2. Wire ring
3. Diaphragm spring
4. Pressure plate
5. Friction plate
6. Housing cover
7. O-ring
8. Thrust ring
9. Clutch nut
10. Release pushrod
11. Bearing race
12. Ball bearing

13. Pressure piston
14. Spring
15. Clamp
16. Rubber boot
17. Circlip
18. Washer
19. Clutch release lever
20. Needle bearing
21. Pin
22. Locknut
23. Adjust bolt

5

②

CLUTCH ASSEMBLY (K100)

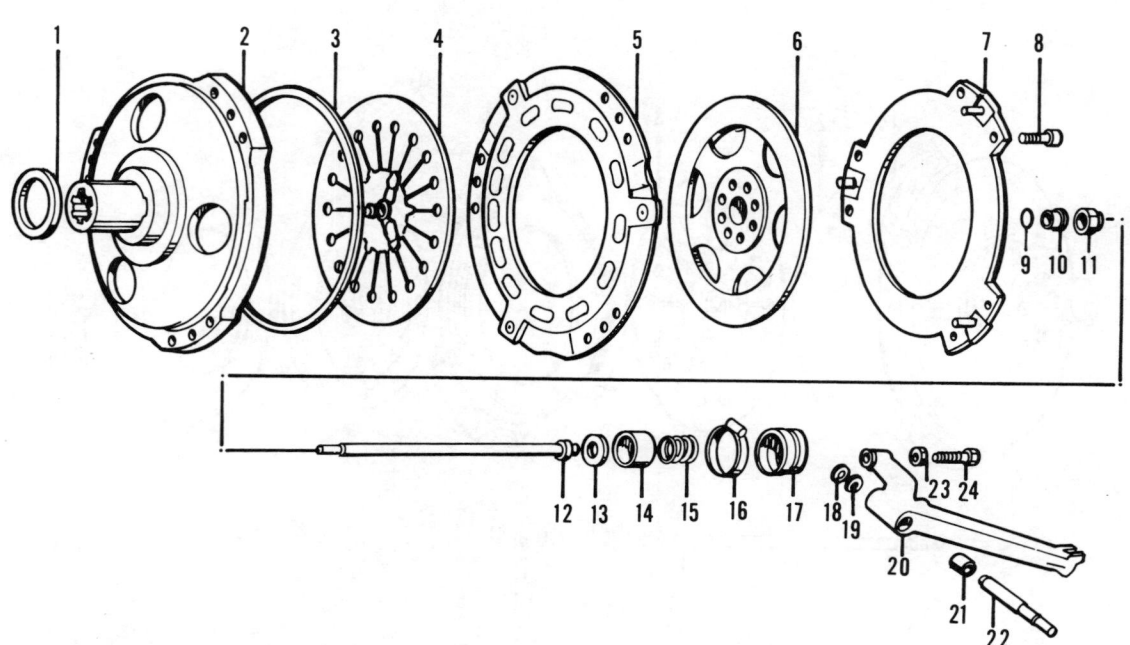

1. Thrust washer
2. Clutch housing
3. Wire ring
4. Diaphragm spring
5. Pressure plate
6. Friction plate
7. Housing cover
8. Bolt
9. O-ring
10. Thrust ring
11. Clutch nut
12. Release pushrod
13. Ball bearing
14. Pressure piston
15. Spring
16. Clamp
17. Rubber boot
18. Circlip
19. Washer
20. Clutch release lever
21. Needle bearing
22. Pin
23. Locknut
24. Adjust bolt

This procedure is shown with the engine removed for clarity.

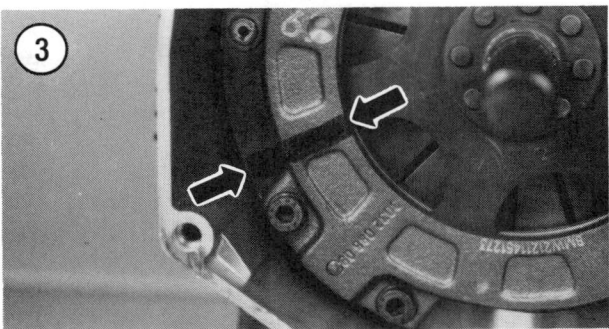

are basically the same. Where differences occur they are identified.

1. Remove the transmission housing as described under *Transmission Housing Removal/Installation* in Chapter Six.

CAUTION
*The housing cover, pressure plate and clutch housing are installed as a balanced assembly. The relationship of these 3 parts must remain the same or **severe vibration** may result. Prior to performing Step 2, check to see if there is a yellow or white factory paint balance mark on each of these 3 parts. These parts are not symmetrical in shape or weight and the marks are placed at the **heaviest portion** of each part. The parts are installed with the balance marks spaced 120° apart from each other. This spreads out the weight imbalance in order to equalize the assembly into a **balanced assembly**.*

NOTE
*If these balance marks are not visible, and there was no appreciable vibration coming from the engine, it is then presumed that the 3 parts were previously installed correctly. Using a permanent marking pen, make a straight line (**Figure 3**) across the housing cover, the pressure plate and the clutch housing. These marks can then be used during the reassembly alignment procedure.*

2. Using a crisscross pattern, loosen, then remove the clutch assembly mounting bolts (**Figure 4**).
3. Remove the housing cover, friction plate and pressure plate as an assembly.
4. Remove the diaphragm spring and the wire ring.
5A. On K75 models, install special BMW tool to keep the clutch housing from rotating in the following step. The BMW special tool is part No. 21 21 000 and is held in place with 2 of the Allen bolts removed in Step 2.

NOTE
The special tool is not necessary on K100 models.

5B. On K100 models, to loosen the clutch nut *without* the BMW special tool, perform the following:
   a. To keep the clutch housing from rotating while loosening the clutch nut insert a piece of wood, a hammer handle or large metal rod (e.g. socket extension or torque bar) through one of the holes in the clutch housing (**Figure 5**). Rest the end of the bar on one of the ribs of the intermediate housing.

5

b. Loosen the clutch nut (**Figure 6**) with a 30 mm socket.

c. Remove and discard the clutch nut (**Figure 7**). It must be replaced every time it is removed.

d. Remove the thrust ring (**Figure 8**).

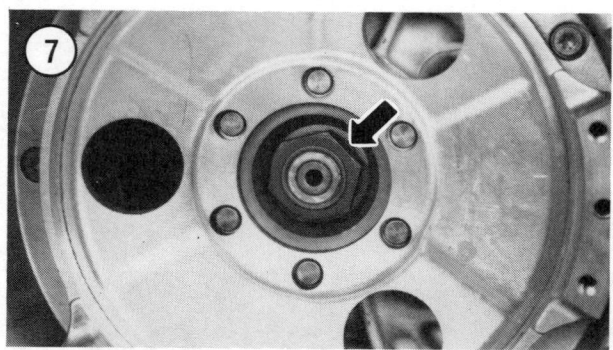

NOTE
The splines on the clutch housing are quite long, therefore there is a long contact surface between the clutch housing splines and the output shaft splines. If the clutch housing was previously removed and was not correctly lubricated with the recommended grease during assembly, it may be difficult to remove the clutch housing. This was the case on the engine used for this procedure. If you are unable to pull the clutch housing off of the output shaft, on K100 models attach a 3-leg bearing puller to the 3 holes in the clutch housing and to the end of the output shaft. Withdraw the clutch housing. On K75 models, carefully pry around the circumference of the clutch housing until the housing has moved out.

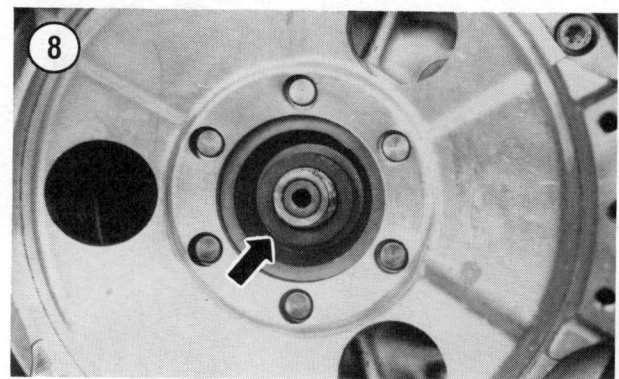

6. Carefully pull, then push back the clutch housing on the output shaft until the O-ring seal works its way out of the recess in the clutch housing.

7. Use an X-acto knife and cut the O-ring, then remove the O-ring seal (**Figure 9**) from the output shaft. Discard the O-ring seal as it must be replaced every time it is removed.

8. Carefully slide the clutch housing (**Figure 10**) and on models so equipped, the thrust washer (**Figure 11**) off of the output shaft.

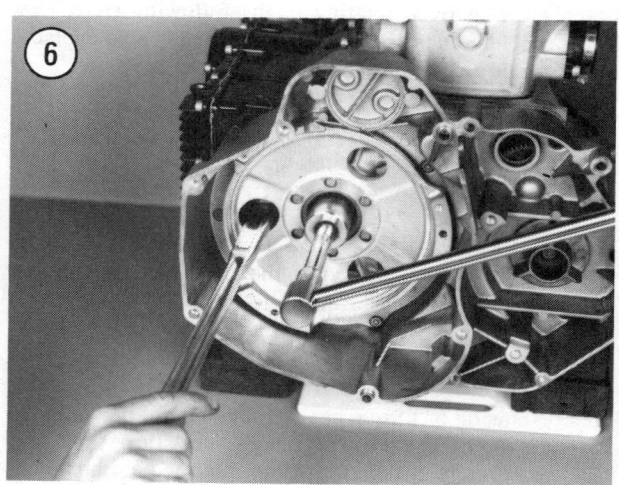

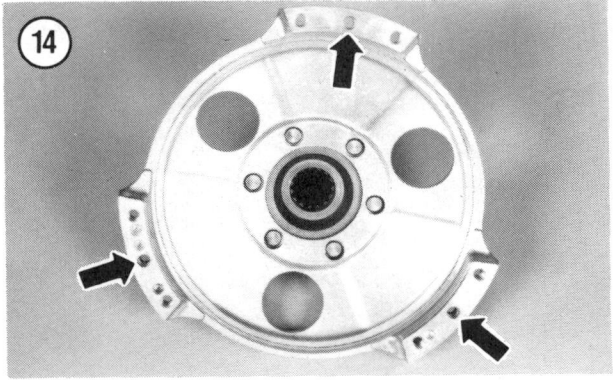

9. Inspect all clutch components as described in this chapter.

Inspection

Refer to **Table 1** for clutch specifications.

1. Check all parts for oil or grease contamination. If the friction plate is fouled with oil or grease it must be replaced. It is impossible to remove *all* oil or grease residue from the friction material.

2. If the housing cover, pressure plate, diaphragm spring or clutch housing are contaminated with oil and/or grease, perform the following:

   a. Thoroughly clean in solvent and dry with compressed air.

   b. After cleaning in solvent, clean the surfaces of the housing cover and pressure plate that contact the friction disc with lacquer thinner and/or aerosol electrical contact cleaner to remove any petroleum-based solvent residue.

   c. Dry with a lint-free cloth.

3. If there is oil and/or grease contamination on the clutch parts, inspect the oil seals in the transmission housing and the output shaft oil seal (**Figure 12**) on the engine. Replace the oil seals if necessary.

4. Inspect the locating pins (**Figure 13**) on the housing cover and the locating pin holes in the pressure plate and clutch housing (**Figure 14**) for wear or damage. Replace any defective part.

5. Inspect the friction plate for damage or wear. If the friction material has worn close to the rivet head, replace the friction plate.

6. Measure the friction plate at several places around the plate with a micrometer (**Figure 15**) or vernier caliper. Compare to the specifications listed in **Table 1**. Replace the friction plate if it is worn to the service limit or less.

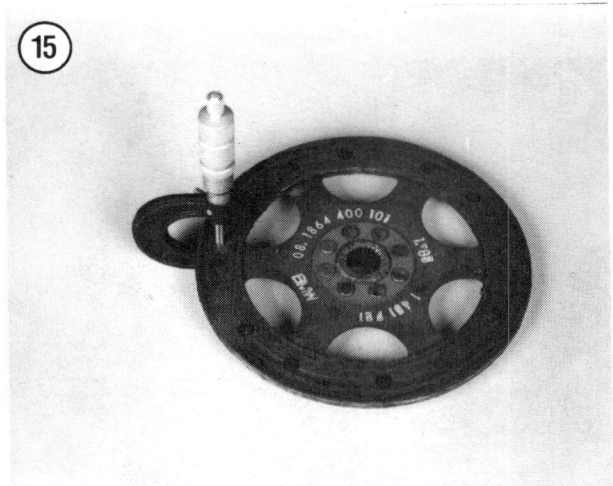

7. Inspect the inner splines (**Figure 16**) in the friction plate for cracks, nicks or galling where they come in contact with the transmission shaft. If any severe damage is evident, the friction plate must be replaced. If the splines are damaged, the clutch action may be erratic. Replace the friction plate. Also inspect the transmission input shaft splines for wear or damage that may have been caused by the friction plate or vice versa. If the transmission input shaft is damaged, refer to Chapter Six for transmission shaft replacement procedures.

8. Inspect the rivets securing the inner spline portion to the friction disc and the rivets securing the friction material to each side of the disc (**Figure 17**). If any of the rivets are loose or appear to be damaged, replace the friction disc.

9. Inspect the friction plate contact surface of both the pressure plate (**Figure 18**) and the housing cover (**Figure 19**). Check for wear, cracks or scoring (friction disc rivet contact). If any of these conditions are found, replace either or both parts.

10. Inspect the diaphragm spring as follows:

   a. Check the center portion (A, **Figure 20**) where the release pushrod makes contact for wear or damage.

   b. Check the outer portion (**Figure 21**) where the spring makes contact with the pressure plate for wear or damage.

   c. Check the spring for any cracked or broken spring fingers (B, **Figure 20**).

   d. Check the spring for weakness. BMW does not provide any specifications for the spring height in order to determine spring sag. If the clutch has been slipping and the clutch release mechanism is properly adjusted, the spring may have sagged to the point where it is no longer exerting sufficient pressure on the friction plate.

   e. Replace the diaphragm spring if any of these faults are found.

In order to maintain maximum performance from the clutch assembly, replace any part(s) that is questionable. Do not try to clean up unserviceable parts that should be replaced.

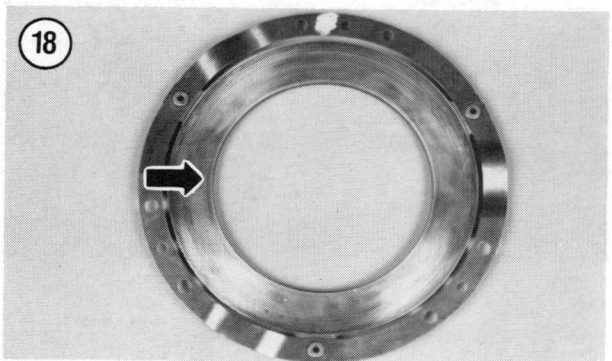

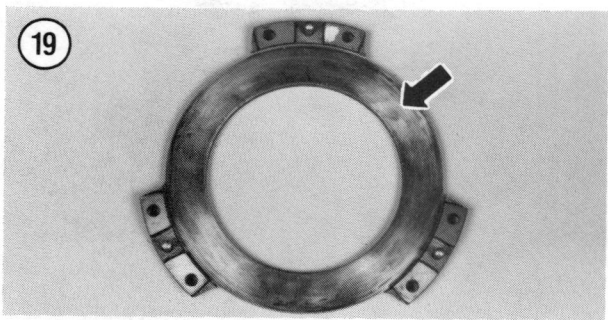

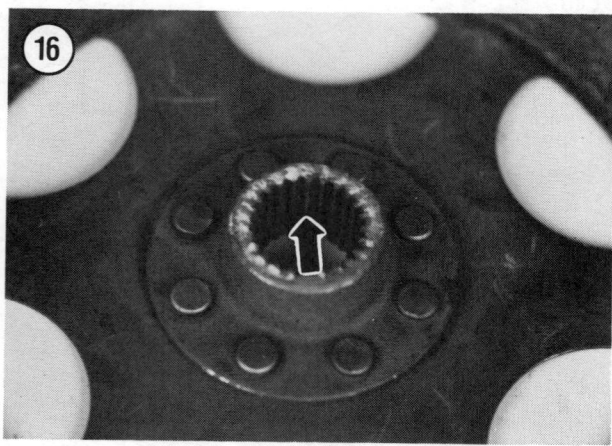

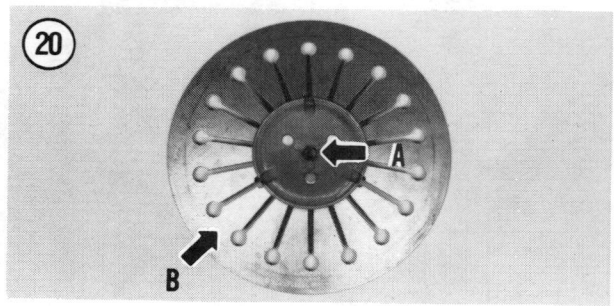

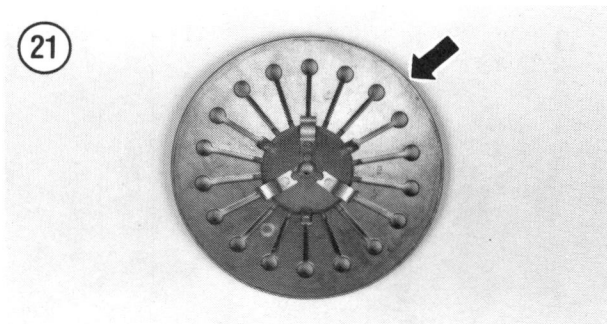

11. Inspect the inner splines (**Figure 22**) in the clutch housing for cracks, nicks or galling where they come in contact with the output shaft. If any severe damage is evident, the clutch housing must be replaced. Also inspect the output shaft splines (**Figure 23**) for wear or damage. If the output shaft is damaged, refer to Chapter Four for output shaft replacement procedures.

Installation

Refer to **Figure 1** or **Figure 2** for this procedure.

> *CAUTION*
> *Staburags NBU 30 PTM (**Figure 24**) was originally recommended for light lubrication of the splines joining the clutch friction plate and transmission input shaft. BMW Lubricant #10 is the latest recommendation. The lubricant is available from a BMW dealership.*

> *CAUTION*
> *When applying the special lubricant, **apply only a thin coat** and only to the designated areas. If too much lubricant is used or is applied in the wrong place it will be thrown off and may contaminate the clutch friction plate.*

1. Make sure the pilot bushing (**Figure 25**) is in place in the receptacle in the rear of the output shaft. Carefully tap it into place if necessary. Apply a light coat of Staburags NBU grease or an equivalent to the inner surface of the pilot bushing.

2A. On K75 models, carefully slide the clutch housing onto the transmission output shaft. Push it on until it bottoms out.

5

2B. On K100 models, install the thrust washer (**Figure 26**) onto the end of the output shaft, then carefully slide the clutch housing onto the transmission output shaft. Push it on until it bottoms out.

3. Install a *new* O-ring seal onto the output shaft and carefully push the O-ring seal in until it stops (**Figure 27**).

4. Position the thrust ring with the raised shoulder side (**Figure 28**) going on first and slide the thrust ring in until it stops (**Figure 29**).

5. Install a *new* clutch nut with the raised section (**Figure 30**) facing out and install the nut (**Figure 31**).

6. Use the same tool set-up used during Step 5, *Removal* to keep the clutch housing from turning while tightening the clutch nut.

7A. On K75 models, tighten the clutch nut to the torque specification listed in **Table 2**.

7B. On K100 models, perform the following:
   a. Tighten the clutch nut to the initial torque specification listed in **Table 2** to seat the O-ring seal.
   b. Completely loosen the clutch nut.
   c. Retighten to the final torque specification listed in **Table 2**.

CAUTION
As noted during removal, the housing cover, pressure plate and clutch housing must be installed in a specific arrangement in order to

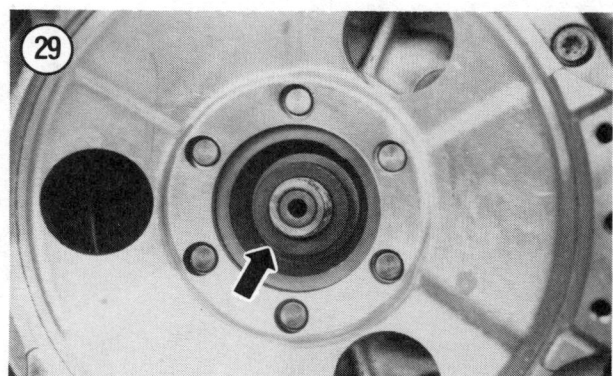

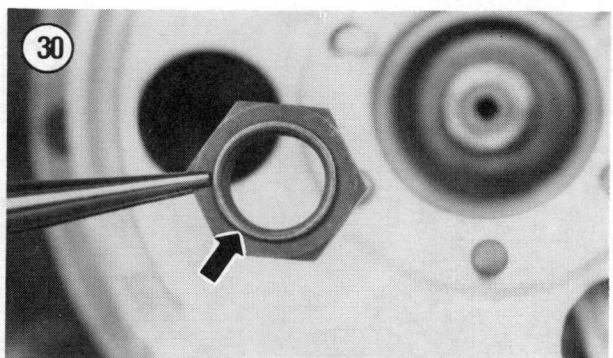

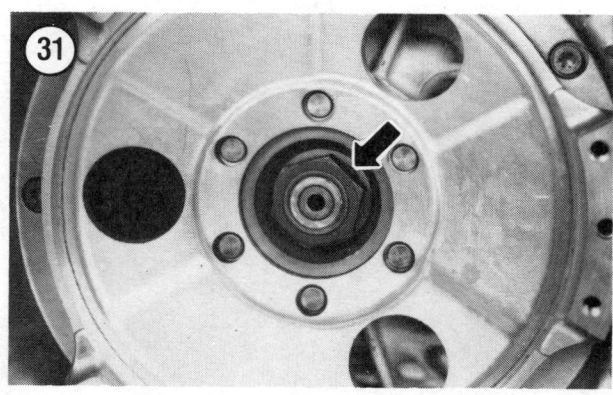

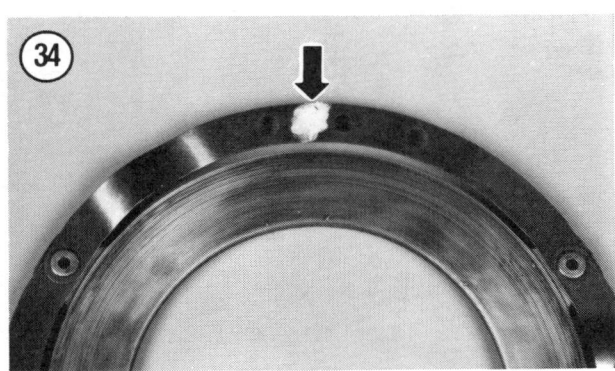

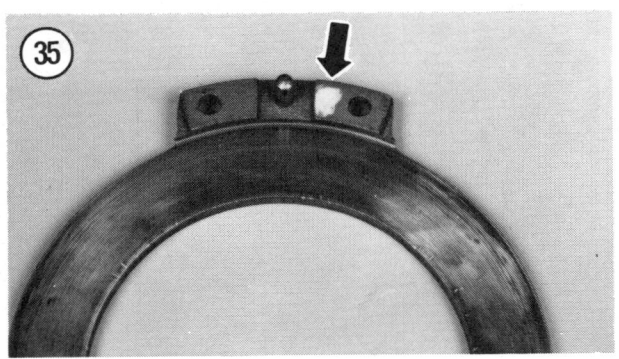

form a balanced assembly. The relationship of these three parts must be correct or severe vibration will result, leading to costly clutch and/or engine damage.

NOTE
*Refer to the factory balance paint marks noted prior to Step 2, **Removal** or the marks that you made.*

8. Install the wire ring (**Figure 32**) into the clutch housing. Make sure it is correctly seated.

9. Apply a light coat of Staburags NBU 30 PTM grease, or an equivalent, to the perimeter and the raised portions (**Figure 33**) on the diaphragm spring where they make contact with the pressure plate.

NOTE
*The balance mark on the pressure plate (**Figure 34**) can be positioned 120° apart, either clockwise or counterclockwise, from the balance mark on the clutch cover (**Figure 35**). If there were no factory marks, refer to the marks made in Step 2, **Removal** as shown in **Figure 36**.*

10. Place the clutch cover on your work bench with the locating pins facing up (**Figure 37**).

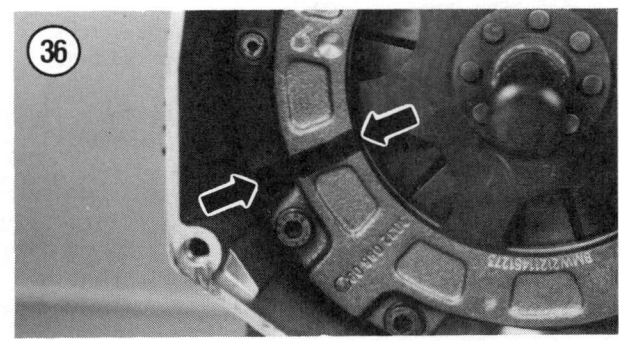

5

11. Position the clutch friction disc with the long side of the spline section facing down so that the flush side is up (A, **Figure 38**) and install the clutch friction plate (B, **Figure 38**) onto the clutch cover.

12. Install the clutch pressure plate as follows:
   a. Apply a light coat of multipurpose grease to the locating pins on the housing cover to prevent corrosion. This will make it easier the next time the housing cover is removed.
   b. Referring to the NOTE preceding Step 10, align the factory paint marks 120° apart.
   c. Align the mounting holes in the pressure plate with the locating pins on the housing cover.
   d. Install the clutch pressure plate (**Figure 39**) onto the housing cover and friction disc.
   e. Push the clutch pressure plate onto the locating dowels and make sure it is completely seated.

13. Pick up the clutch assembly and from the backside, install the friction plate centering tool (BMW special tool part No. 21 6 670) into the center of the friction plate (**Figure 40**). This will correctly center the friction disc within the clutch assembly.

14. Position the diaphragm spring with the concave side facing up (A, **Figure 41**) and install the diaphragm spring onto the clutch assembly and onto the special tool (B, **Figure 41**).

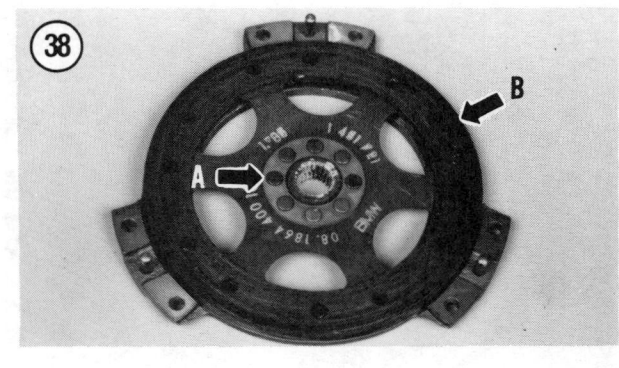

NOTE
*Do **not** try to reassemble and install the clutch assembly without the clutch plate centering tool (BMW special tool part No. 21 6 670). The alignment of the friction plate-to-pilot bushing is very critical. During transmission assembly installation, the transmission's input shaft slides through the friction plate's center splines and into the pilot bushing in the end of the output shaft. If this alignment is not correct you will **not** be able to install the transmission assembly.*

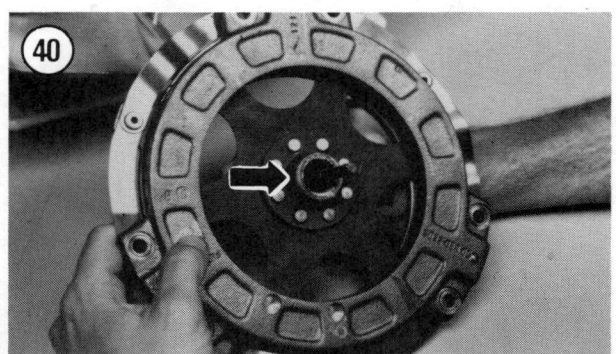

15. Install the clutch assembly (A, **Figure 42**) onto the engine. Carefully insert the end of the BMW special tool (B, **Figure 42**) into the pilot bushing in the end of the output shaft.

16. Align the mounting bolt holes of the clutch assembly with the holes in the clutch housing.

17. Install the clutch assembly mounting bolts (**Figure 43**) finger-tight at this time.

18. Using a crisscross pattern, tighten the clutch housing mounting bolts in 2-3 stages to the torque specification listed in **Table 2**.

19. Remove the special tool (B, **Figure 42**) from the friction plate.

20. Prior to installing the transmission, apply a light coat of Staburags NBU 30 PTM grease, or an equivalent, to the following areas:
   a. The release pushrod end.
   b. Inner splines of the friction plate.
   c. Outer splines of the transmission input shaft where it rides in the friction plate.
21. Install the transmission as described under *Transmission Installation* in Chapter Six.

CLUTCH RELEASE MECHANISM

Refer to **Figure 44** for this procedure.

Removal

The clutch release bearing can be removed with the engine and transmission gear box in the frame. Most of this procedure is shown with the engine/transmission assembly removed for clarity.

5

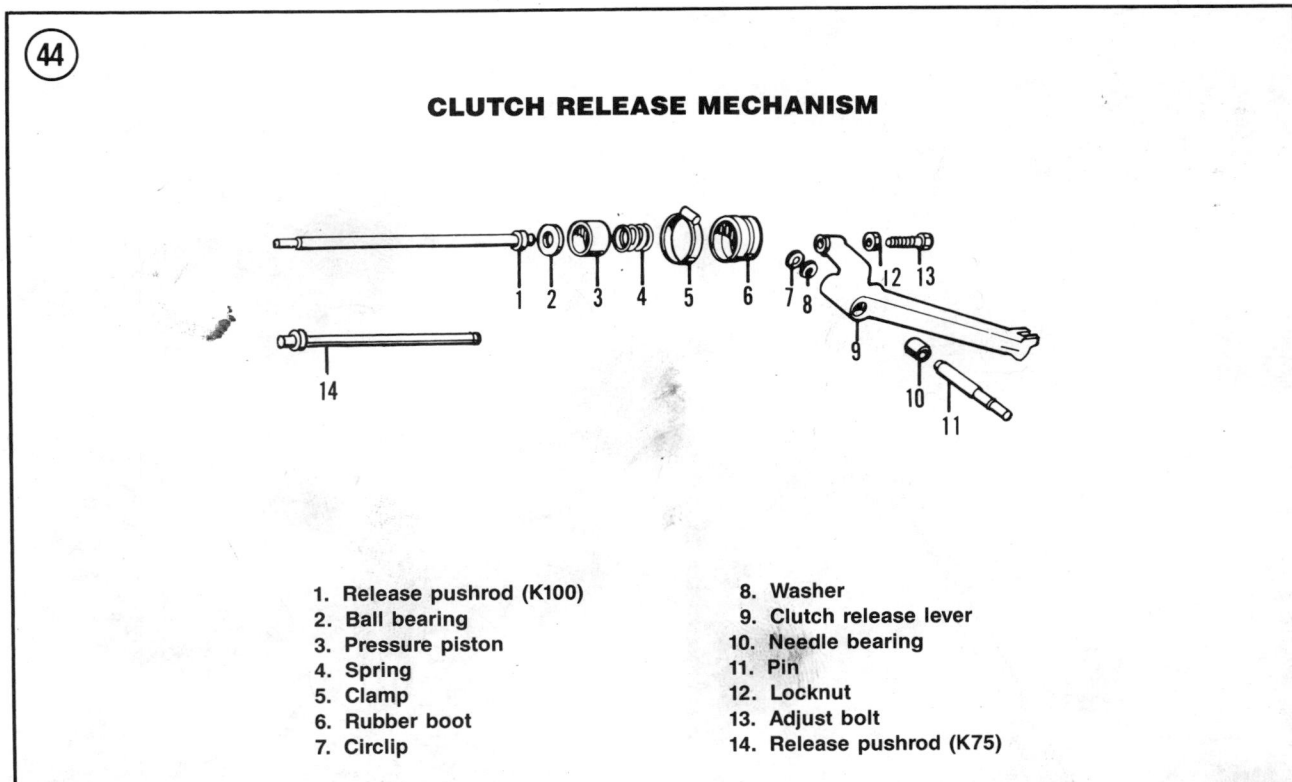

CLUTCH RELEASE MECHANISM

1. Release pushrod (K100)
2. Ball bearing
3. Pressure piston
4. Spring
5. Clamp
6. Rubber boot
7. Circlip

8. Washer
9. Clutch release lever
10. Needle bearing
11. Pin
12. Locknut
13. Adjust bolt
14. Release pushrod (K75)

1. Place the bike on the center stand.

2. At the clutch hand lever on the handlebar, loosen the locknut (A, **Figure 45**) and turn the adjuster (B, **Figure 45**) all the way in to provide maximum amount of clutch cable slack.

3. Disconnect the clutch cable from the clutch release lever (**Figure 46**) at the rear of the transmission housing.

4. Remove the muffler as described under *Exhaust System Removal/Installation* in Chapter Seven.

5. On K100 models, remove the rear wheel as described under *Rear Wheel Removal/Installation* in Chapter Eleven.

6. On models so equipped, disconnect the sidestand retracting rod link, then remove the return spring (**Figure 47**).

7. Loosen the clamp screw securing the rubber boot (**Figure 48**) to the transmission housing boss.

8. Remove the circlip and shim (**Figure 49**) securing the clutch lever.

9. Carefully tap out the pivot rod (A, **Figure 50**) sufficiently to remove the clutch release lever. It is not necessary to completely remove the pivot rod or the sidestand retracting rod link (models so equipped) from the rear of the transmission housing. If necessary, the pivot rod (A, **Figure 51**) and retracting rod link (B, **Figure 51**) can be removed.

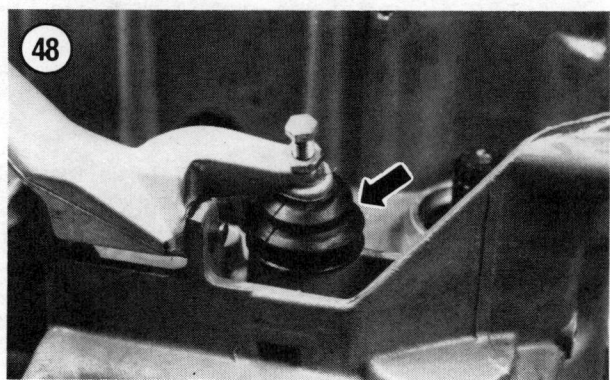

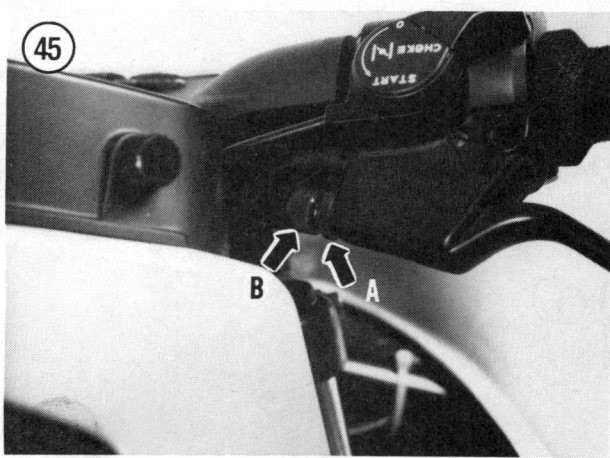

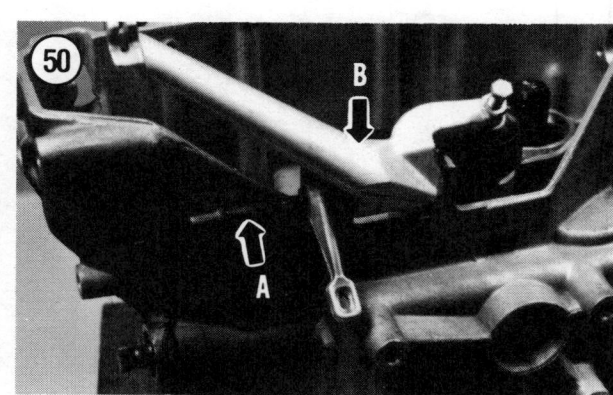

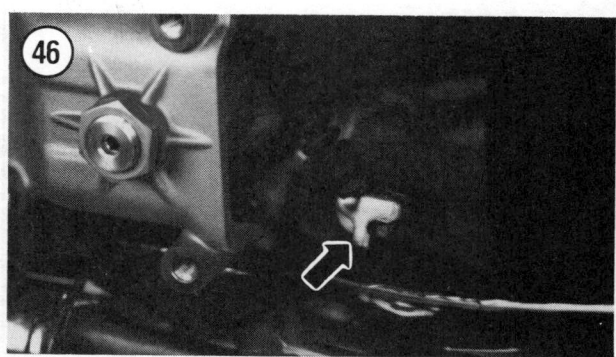

10. Remove the clutch release lever (B, **Figure 50**).

11. Remove the spring (**Figure 52**), the pressure piston (**Figure 53**) and the bearing (**Figure 54**).

12A. On K75 models, perform the following:

    a. Remove the transmission as described under *Transmission Removal* in Chapter Six.

    b. Using a suitable size punch, drive the clutch release rod, from the rear, out of the transmission input shaft.

    c. Remove the rod from the front of the transmission input shaft.

    d. Remove the bearing race.

12B. On K100 models, pull the clutch release pushrod from the transmission input shaft.

Inspection

1. Inspect the rubber boot (**Figure 55**) for damage or deterioration; replace if necessary.

2. Inspect the spring for sagging or damage. BMW does not provide a service limit dimension for the spring free length. Replace the spring if it is questionable.

3. Lay the release pushrod on a piece of plate glass and check for straightness. Replace if the rod is warped the slightest amount as it may hang up in the hollow portion of the transmission input shaft.

4. Inspect the release pushrod end where it makes contact with the diaphragm spring. Make sure it is not damaged or rough. Replace if necessary.

5. Inspect the bearing (**Figure 56**). Turn it by hand; it must rotate smoothly with no signs of wear or damage.

5

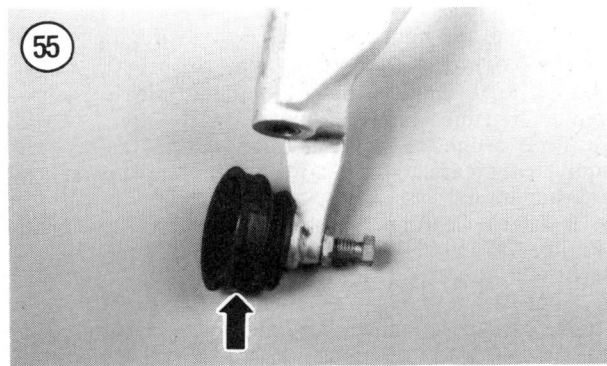

6. Insert the pivot rod into the clutch release lever. Slowly rotate the rod and check for needle bearing wear or damage. If the needle bearing is damaged and requires replacement, remove the pivot end and perform the following:

   a. Heat the clutch release lever in the area of the needle bearing with a hair dryer or hot water.

   b. Carefully tap the needle bearing (**Figure 57**) out of the lever from the inside surface.

   c. Use solvent and thoroughly clean out the pivot area of the lever prior to installing a new needle bearing. Dry with compressed air.

   d. Apply a light coat of Staburags NBU 30 PTM or an equivalent grease to the inner surface of the needle bearing.

   e. Carefully tap the new needle bearing into the lever until it is flush with the outer surface (**Figure 57**).

   f. Apply a light coat of Staburags NBU 30 PTM, or an equivalent grease, to the inner surface of the needle bearing.

7. Inspect the clutch release lever where the clutch cable attaches (**Figure 58**) for wear or damage. Replace if necessary.

8. Inspect the clutch release lever adjustment bolt and locknut (**Figure 59**) for wear or damage. Replace if necessary.

Installation

1A. On K75 models, perform the following:

   a. Insert the rod into the front of the transmission input shaft. Push it in all the way.

   b. Install the bearing race and tap it into place with a suitable size socket.

   c. Install the transmission as described under *Transmission Installation* in Chapter Six.

1B. On K100 models, push the clutch release pushrod into the transmission input shaft.

2. Apply a light coat of Staburags NBU 30 PTM, or an equivalent grease, to the bearing and pressure piston prior to installation.

3. Install the bearing (**Figure 60**) and the pressure piston (**Figure 53**).

4. Install the spring (**Figure 52**).

5. Apply a light coat of Staburags NBU 30 PTM or an equivalent grease to the pivot rod prior to installation.

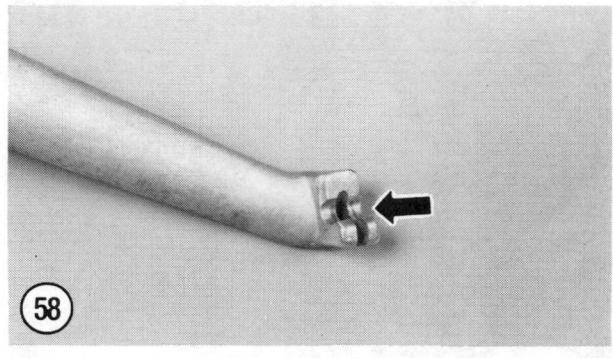

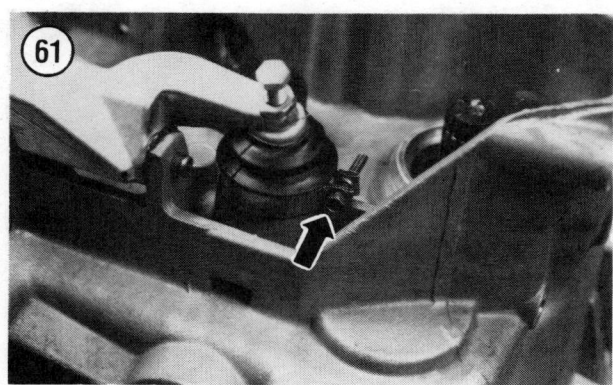

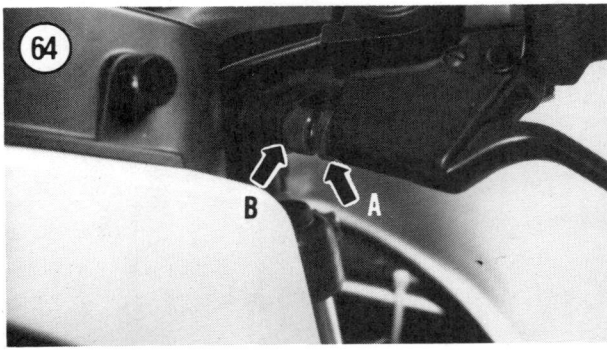

6. If removed, install the pivot rod (A, **Figure 51**) into the retracting rod link (B, **Figure 51**) and install them on the transmission housing.

7. Install the clutch release lever (B, **Figure 50**) into position and install the pivot rod (A, **Figure 50**). Push the pivot rod in until it stops.

8. On models so equipped, install the sidestand retracting rod link return spring (**Figure 47**).

9. Install the rubber boot onto the transmission housing boss. Tighten the clamp screw securely (**Figure 61**).

10. Install the shim (**Figure 62**) and the circlip (**Figure 63**) securing the clutch lever. Make sure the circlip is properly seated in the groove in the pivot rod.

11. On models so eqipped, connect the sidestand retracting rod link.

12. On K100 models, install the rear wheel as described under *Rear Wheel Removal/Installation* in Chapter Eleven.

13. Install the muffler as described under *Exhaust System Removal/Installation* in Chapter Seven.

14. Connect the clutch cable onto the clutch release lever (**Figure 46**).

15. Adjust the clutch hand lever free play as described under *Clutch Adjustment* in Chapter Three.

5

CLUTCH CABLE

Replacement

In time the clutch cable will stretch to the point where it is no longer useful and must be replaced.

1. Place the bike on the center stand.

2. Remove the fuel tank as described under *Fuel Tank Removal/Installation* in Chapter Seven.

3. At the clutch hand lever on the handlebar, loosen the locknut (A, **Figure 64**) and turn the adjuster (B, **Figure 64**) all the way in to provide the maximum amount of clutch cable slack.

4. Disconnect the clutch cable from the clutch release lever (**Figure 65**) on the rear of the transmission housing.

5. Remove any straps securing the clutch cable to the frame.

NOTE
Before removing the cable, make a drawing of the cable routing through the frame. It is very easy to forget how it was, once it has been removed. Replace the cable exactly as it was, avoiding any sharp turns.

6. Pull the clutch cable out from behind the steering head area and out of the frame.

7. Remove the cable and replace it with a new cable.

8. Install by reversing these removal steps, noting the following.

9. Adjust the clutch as described under *Clutch Adjustment* in Chapter Three.

Table 1 CLUTCH SPECIFICATIONS

Item	Specification	Wear limit
Friction plate thickness	5.05-5.55 mm (0.198-0.218 in.)	4.5 mm (0.177 in.)
Clutch lever free play	3.5-4.5 mm (0.14-0.18 in.)	—
Clutch cable length at release lever	74-76 mm (2.9-3.0 in.)	—

Table 2 CLUTCH TORQUE SPECIFICATIONS

Item	N•m	ft.-lb.
Clutch housing cover mounting bolts	17-21	12.5-15.5
Clutch nut		
K75	135-145	97-105
K100		
Initial	140	103
Final	90-114	65-82
K1100		
Initial	140	103
Final	50-100	37-74

CHAPTER SIX

TRANSMISSION AND
GEARSHIFT MECHANISMS

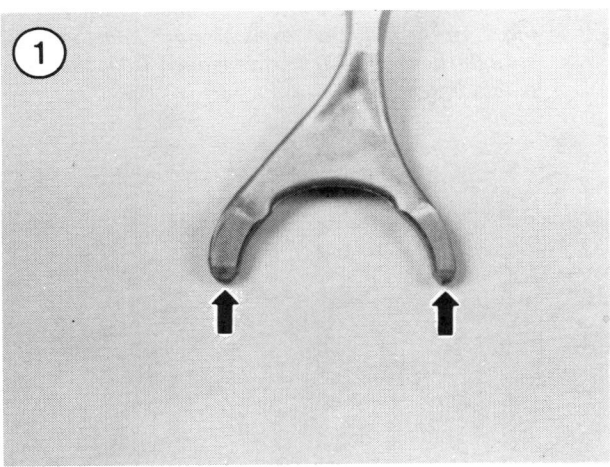

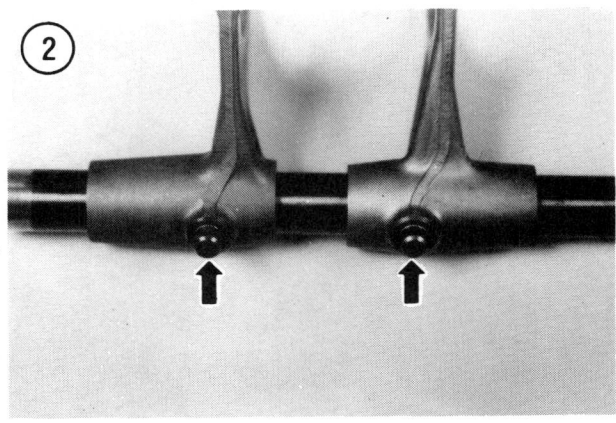

This chapter provides complete service procedures for the transmission shaft assemblies and the gearshift mechanism.

The transmission shafts and the gearshift mechanism are all located within a transmission housing that is bolted directly to the back of the engine. The transmission input shaft runs on tapered roller bearings at each end while the intermediate shaft and the output shaft are equipped with a ball bearing at each end.

The input shaft (engine driven shaft) is splined to the clutch friction plate and is equipped with a shock damper to dampen out engine-to-transmission shock loads. The rear end of the input shaft has a helical-cut gear that mates to a similar gear on the intermediate shaft. The intermediate shaft transmits engine power from the input shaft to the output shaft. With the exception of the one helical-cut gear on the input and intermediate shaft all other gears are straight-cut.

Refer to **Table 1** for transmission and gearshift mechanism specifications. **Table 1** and **Table 2** are located at the end of this chapter.

TRANSMISSION AND
GEARSHIFT OPERATION

Each sliding transmission gear has a deep groove machined around its outside. The curved shift fork fingers (**Figure 1**) ride in this groove, controlling the side-to-side sliding of the gear on its shaft. This movement determines the selection of the different gear ratios. Each shift fork slides back and forth on its shift fork shaft. Each shift fork has a peg and roller (**Figure 2**) that rides in the machined grooves in the shift drum. When the foot-operated gear change pedal operates the selector shaft, which in turn rotates the gearshift drum, the zigzag grooves (**Figure 3**) in the shift drum move the shift forks, thus sliding the gears back and forth. This action shifts the transmission from one gear to another.

Gear changing is accomplished by 2 sliding gears on the output shaft and one gear on the layshaft. The sliding gears on the output shaft ride either on a needle bearing or on a bronze bushing.

TRANSMISSION HOUSING

The transmission housing can be removed from the engine in the frame or separated from the engine after the engine and transmission housing assembly are removed as a complete unit.

Removal/Installation
(Engine in Frame)

1. Place the bike on the center stand.
2. If the transmission is going to be disassembled, drain the transmission oil as described under *Transmission Oil Change* in Chapter Three.
3. Remove the battery as described under *Battery Removal, Electrolyte Level Check and Installation* in Chapter Three.
4. Remove the exhaust system as described under *Exhaust System Removal/Installation* in Chapter Seven.
5. Remove the rear wheel as described under *Rear Wheel Removal/Installation* in Chapter Eleven.
6. Remove the swing arm and drive shaft as described under *Swing Arm and Drive Shaft Removal/Installation* in Chapter Eleven.
7. Remove the rear fender as described under *Rear Fender Removal/Installation* in Chapter Thirteen.
8. Remove the right-hand and the left-hand footpeg assemblies as described under *Footpeg Assembly Removal/Installation* in Chapter Thirteen.
9. Remove the clutch release lever as described under *Clutch Release Mechanism Removal* in Chapter Five.
10. On disc brake models, remove the rear master cylinder reservoir as described under *Rear Master Cylinder Removal/Installation* in Chapter Twelve.
11. Disconnect the electrical connector from the rear brake light switch. Remove any straps securing the electrical wire to the frame and move the wire out of the way.
12. Remove the coolant reserve tank as described under *Coolant Reserve Tank Removal/Installation* in Chapter Nine.
13. Remove the screws securing the ignition coil cover and remove the cover.
14. Disconnect and remove all spark plug secondary wires as described under *Spark Plug Secondary Wires Replacement* in Chapter Eight.
15. Remove the fuel injection control unit as described under *Fuel Injection Control Unit Removal/Installation* in Chapter Eight.

16. Remove the bolts securing the alternator cover and remove the cover.
17. Remove the starter as described under *Starter Motor Removal/Installation* in Chapter Eight.
18. Disconnect the electrical connector from the transmission gear position switch.
19. Place a suitable size jack under the engine oil pan. Place a piece of wood between the jack and the oil pan to protect the cooling fins in the oil pan.
20. Apply jack pressure and lift the bike up sufficiently to raise the center stand off of the ground.
21. Remove the bolts securing the center stand assembly to the transmission housing and remove the center stand assembly.
22. Place wood blocks or a small floor jack under the transmission housing.
23. Remove the side bolts and washers securing the transmission to the frame.
24. Remove the bolts and washers securing the transmission to the engine.

CAUTION
In the following step, to prevent damage to the transmission input shaft and clutch release push rod, pull the transmission housing straight back until it is disengaged from the clutch assembly.

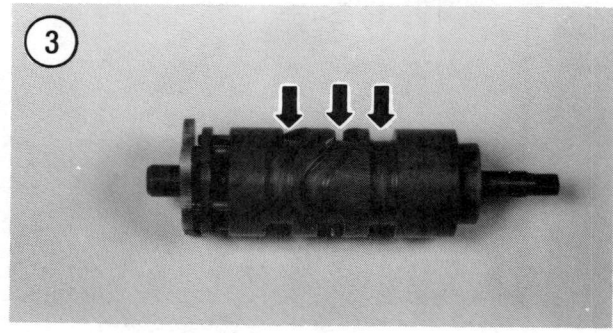

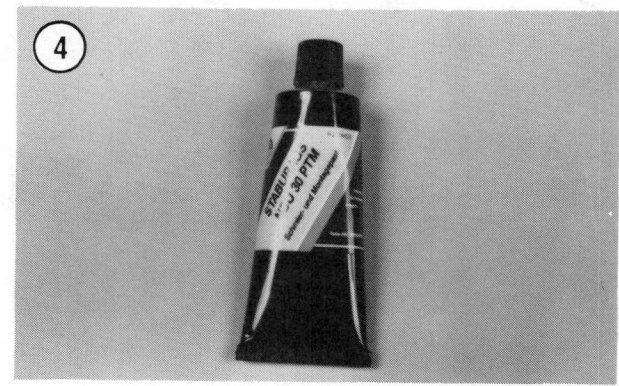

25. Using a soft faced mallet, tap around the perimeter of the transmission housing to break it loose from the rear of the engine.

NOTE
The transmission housing should separate easily from the engine. If it won't, first check that all external components have been removed that would hinder separation. If the bike has a lot of miles on it or if it has been subjected to salt solutions (either salt water or road salt) the 4 locating pins may be corroded at the engine-to-transmission mounting bolts. Apply Liquid Wrench, or equivalent penetrating oil, to the locating pins and let it sit for 15 minutes.

26. Pull the transmission housing straight back until it is free of the engine and clutch assembly.

27. Lower the transmission housing and take to workbench for further disassembly.
28. Install by reversing these removal steps, noting the following.
29. If the transmission shaft assemblies were disassembled, rotate the input shaft and shift the transmission through all 5 gears. Make sure all shafts rotate smoothly.
30. Prior to installing the transmission, apply a light coat of Staburags NBU 30 PTM grease (**Figure 4**), or an equivalent, to the following areas:
   a. The release pushrod end.
   b. Inner splines of the clutch friction plate.
   c. Outer splines of the transmission input shaft where it rides in the clutch friction plate.
31. Clean the mating surfaces of both the engine and the transmission housing of any corrosion. Make sure the locating pins are in place and are clean. Apply a light coat of multipurpose grease to both the locating pins and their receptacles to prevent any further corrosion.
32. Raise the transmission housing and align it with the back surface of the engine.

CAUTION
To prevent damage to the transmission input shaft and clutch release pushrod, push the transmission housing straight forward until it is properly engaged into the clutch assembly.

33. Push the transmission housing forward and align the input shaft splines with the inner splines of the clutch friction plate. If necessary, shift the transmission into 5th gear and slightly wiggle or rotate the output shaft at the rear of the transmission housing until alignment is achieved. Also align the locating pins on the engine-to-transmission housing.
34. Push the transmission housing forward until it has bottomed out. Install the mounting bolts and tighten to the torque specification listed in **Table 2**.
35. Install and tighten the following bolts and tighten to the torque specification listed in **Table 2**.
   a. Transmission housing side bolts.
   b. Center stand assembly bolts.
36. If the transmission was disassembled, refill the transmission oil as described under *Transmission Oil Change* in Chapter Three.

Removal/Installation (Engine Removed from Frame)

1. Remove the engine and transmission housing as an assembly as described under *Engine Removal/Installation* in Chapter Four.
2. Remove the bolts and washers securing the transmission to the engine. Refer to **Figure 5** and **Figure 6**.

CAUTION
In the following step, to prevent damage to the transmission input shaft and clutch release pushrod, pull the transmission housing straight back until it is disengaged from the clutch assembly.

3. Using a soft faced mallet, tap around the perimeter of the transmission housing to break it loose from the rear of the engine.

NOTE
The transmission housing should separate easily from the engine. If it won't, first check that all external components have been removed that would hinder separation. If the bike has a lot of miles on it or if it has been subjected to salt solutions (either salt water or road salt) the 4 locating pins may be corroded at the engine-to-transmission mounting bolts. Apply Liquid Wrench, or equivalent penetrating oil, to the locating pins and let it sit for 15 minutes.

4. Pull the transmission housing straight back until it is free of the engine and clutch assembly.

5. Install by reversing these removal steps, noting the following:

6. If the transmission shaft assemblies were disassembled, rotate the input shaft and shift the transmission through all 5 gears. Make sure all shafts rotate smoothly.

7. Before installing the transmission, apply a light coat of Staburags NBU 30 PTM grease (**Figure 4**), or an equivalent, to the following areas:
   a. The release pushrod end.
   b. Inner splines of the clutch friction plate.
   c. Outer splines of the transmission input shaft when it rides in the clutch friction plate.

8. Clean the mating surfaces of both the engine and the transmission housing of any corrosion. Make sure the locating pins (**Figure 7**) are in place and are clean. Apply a light coat of multipurpose grease to both surfaces to prevent any further corrosion.

9. Raise the transmission housing and align it with the back surface of the engine.

CAUTION
To prevent damage to the transmission input shaft and clutch release pushrod, push the transmission housing straight forward until it is properly engaged into the clutch assembly.

10. Push the transmission housing forward and align the input shaft splines with the inner splines of the clutch friction plage. If necessary, shift the transmission into 5th gear and slightly wiggle or rotate the output shaft at the rear of the transmission housing until alignment is achieved. Also align the locating pins on the engine-to-transmission housing.

11. Push the transmission housing froward until it has bottomed out. Install the mounting bolts and tighten to the torque specification listed in **Table 2**.

12. If the transmission was disassembled, refill the transmission oil as described under *Transmission Oil Change* in Chapter Three.

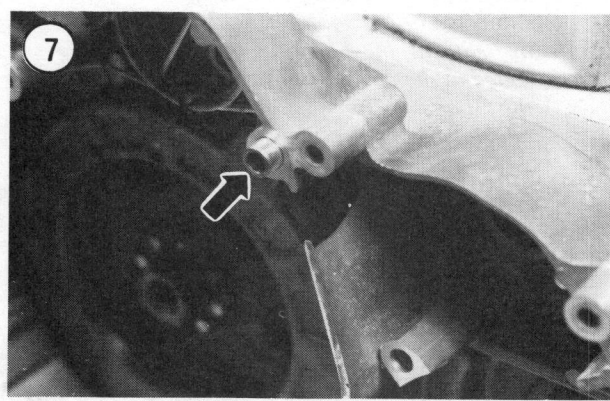

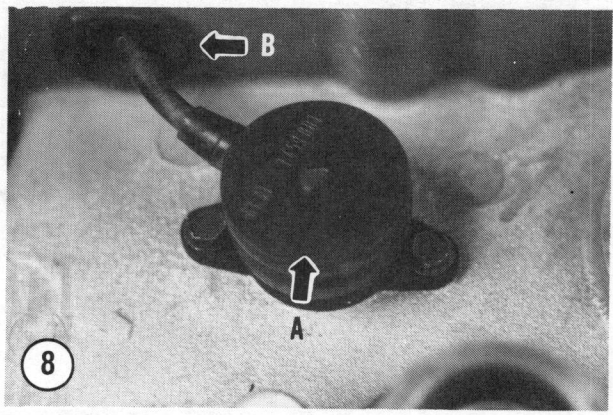

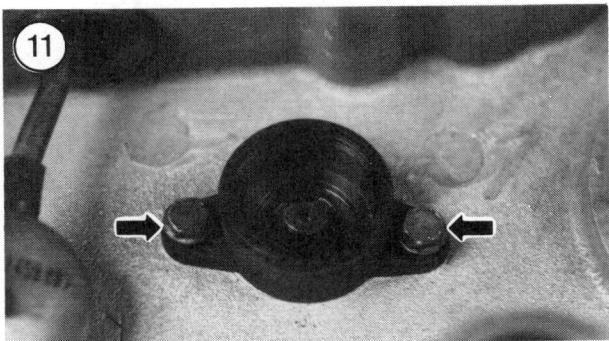

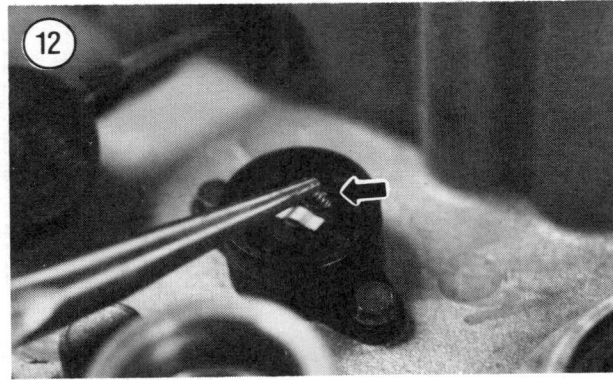

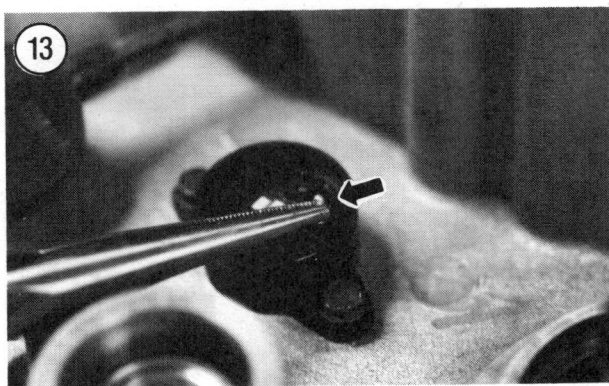

Gear Position Switch
Removal/Installation

1. Remove the electrical connector cap (A, **Figure 8**) from the switch on the rear of the transmission housing. If necessary, remove the electrical connector cap and wiring harness from the transmission housing. Don't lose the rubber grommet (B, **Figure 8**).

2. Remove all 3 contacts (**Figure 9**) and springs from the switch housing.

3. Remove the switch rotor (**Figure 10**) from the switch housing.

4. Remove the bolts (**Figure 11**) securing the switch to the rear of the transmission housing and remove the switch.

5. Install the switch onto the transmission housing and install the bolts (**Figure 11**). Tighten the bolts securely.

6. Install the switch rotor (**Figure 10**) into the switch housing.

7. Install all 3 springs (**Figure 12**) and all 3 contacts (**Figure 13**) into the switch housing.

8. If removed, install the electrical connector cap and wiring harness into the opening in the transmission housing. Be sure to install the rubber grommet (B, **Figure 8**).

9. Install the electrical connector cap (A, **Figure 8**) onto the switch.

Housing Cover
Removal/Installation

Refer to **Figure 14** for this procedure.

1. Remove the neutral detent Allen bolt plug (**Figure 15**). Using a small magnetic tool remove the spring and ball from the receptacle in the cover.

2. Using a crisscross pattern, loosen then remove the bolts and lockwashers securing the housing cover (A, **Figure 16**).

3. Using a soft faced mallet, carefully tap around the perimeter of the housing cover to loosen it from the housing.

> *NOTE*
> *BMW recommends that the cover be heated to 100° C (212° F) to aid in the removal of the cover. If you are unable to remove the cover in Step 5, heat the cover with rags and hot water. We found that this was not necessary as the cover slipped off easily.*

> *CAUTION*
> *Do **not** heat the cover with a torch (propane or acetylene); never bring a flame into contact with the cover. The direct heat will cause warpage of the cover.*

> *NOTE*
> *When the cover is removed from the transmission housing, you will hear a loud click or thump. This is not a problem, it is only*

6

⑭ **TRANSMISSION HOUSING**

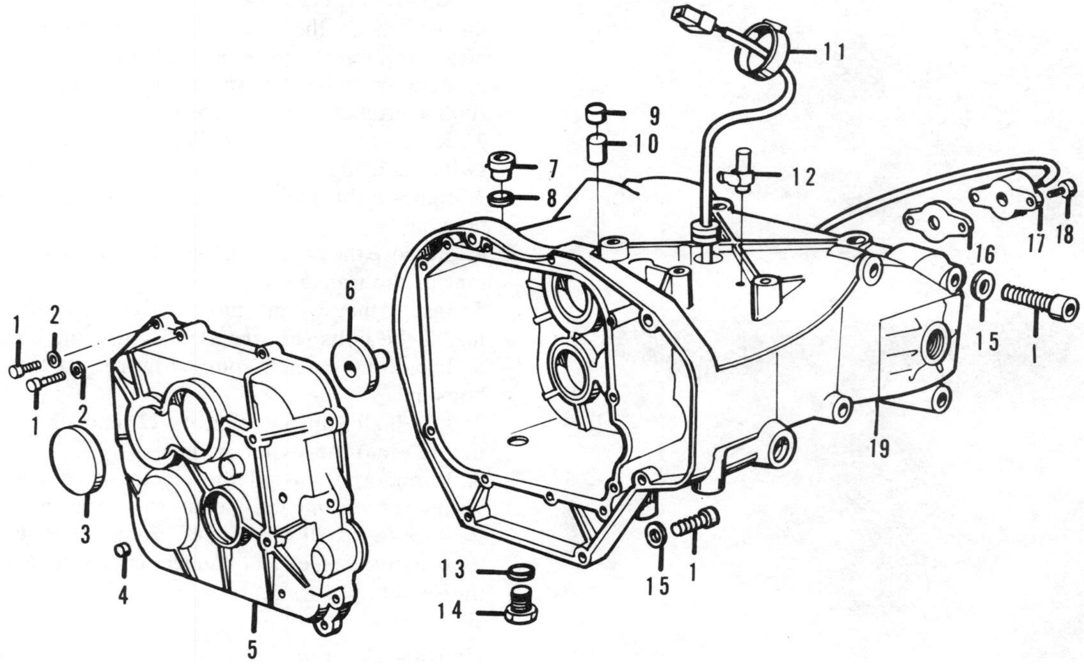

1. Bolt
2. Washer
3. Cover
4. Plug
5. Housing cover
6. Oil guide
7. Plug

8. Gasket
9. Cap
10. Sleeve
11. Strap
12. Clamp
13. Gasket

14. Drain plug
15. Washer
16. Gasket
17. Gear position switch
18. Bolt
19. Transmission housing

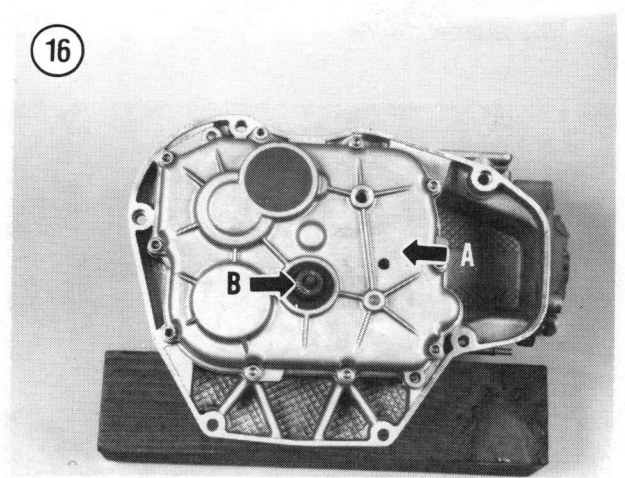

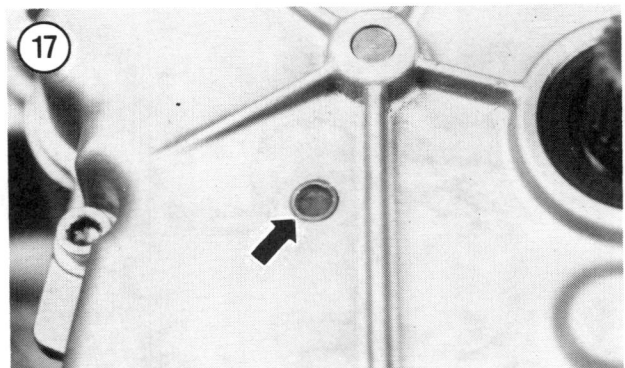

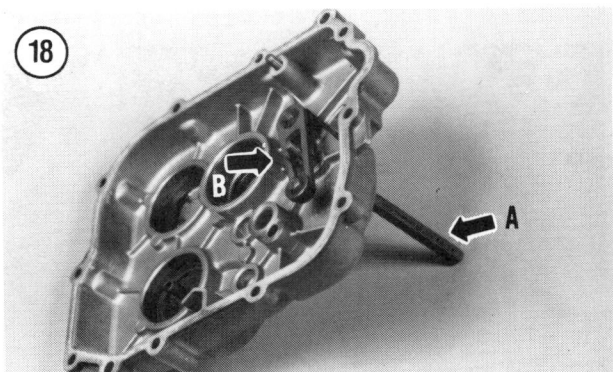

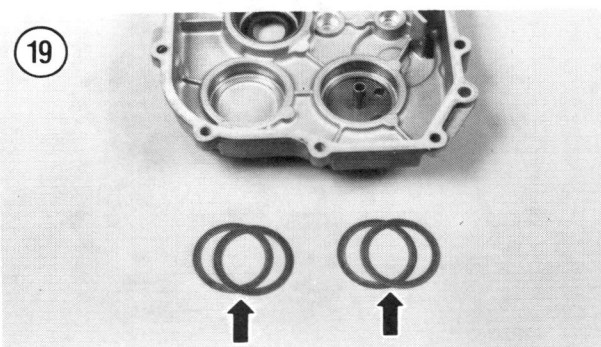

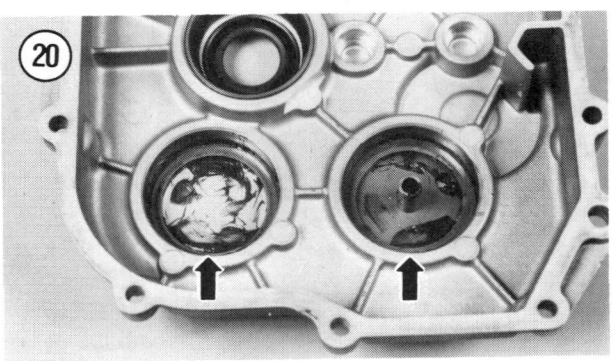

the spring loaded gearshift mechanism detent arm moving over and hitting against a stop in the cover.

5. If necessary use a broad tipped screwdriver and *carefully* pry off the cover. Also tap on the end of the input shaft (B, **Figure 16**) with a soft faced mallet to aid in removal. Remove the cover from the housing. Don't lose any of the end float shims that will either stay on the end of the transmission shafts or in the bearing recesses in the cover. They must be reinstalled on the same transmission shafts during assembly.

6. After the cover is removed, use a drift and hammer and drive out the plug (**Figure 17**) from the inside surface of the cover. Save the plug as it will be driven back in after the cover is reinstalled.

7. Thoroughly clean and inspect the cover as described in this chapter.

8. Clean off all old gasket sealer from the mating surface of the cover and the transmission housing with solvent. Thoroughly dry with compressed air.

9. Move the detent arm over toward the outer surface of the cover and hold it in this position.

10. After the surfaces have been cleaned, clean once again with aerosol electrical contact cleaner and a lint-free cloth to remove any traces of solvent.

11. From the outside surface of the cover, insert a drift into the hole where the plug was removed (A, **Figure 18**). Let go of the detent arm and let it rest against the drift (B, **Figure 18**). Keep the drift in place until the cover is completely installed.

12. Apply a light even coat of Three Bond No. 1216 gasket sealer to the mating surface of the cover.

13. Apply a light coat of grease to the end float shims (**Figure 19**) and place them in their proper receptacles in the cover (**Figure 20**). They must reinstalled on the same transmission shafts.

14. Apply a light coat of transmission gear oil or engine oil to the outer surfaces of the transmission shaft ball bearings and to the gearshift drum where it rides in the transmission cover. This will make cover installation easier.

15. Position the cover onto the transmission housing and start it down into place. If necessary, move the ends of the transmission shaft assemblies so that the bearings are aligned with their respective receptacles in the cover.

16. Push the cover down until the bearings have started to enter the cover. After you are sure the bearings are properly started, *carefully* tap the cover into place with a soft faced mallet. Tap on the cover directly over the bearing locations and around the perimeter until the cover is completely seated against the transmission housing.

17. Remove the drift from the cover and listen for the detent arm to come into contact with the selector cam on the end of the shift drum.

18. Install the cover bolts and lockwashers. Using a crisscross pattern, tighten the bolts to the torque specification listed in **Table 2**.

6

19. Install the neutral detent ball (**Figure 21**) and spring (**Figure 22**).

20. Apply blue Loctite Threadlocker No. 242 to the neutral detent Allen bolt plug threads prior to installation.

21. Install the neutral detent Allen bolt plug (**Figure 15**) and tighten to the torque specification listed in **Table 2**.

CAUTION
Don't forget to install the plug in the cover. If it is not installed there will be an oil leak and possibly the total loss of transmission oil, leading to a costly transmission repair bill.

22. Install the plug (**Figure 23**), removed in Step 6, into the cover. Tap it into place and make sure it is completely installed to prevent an oil leak.

Cover Inspection and Input Shaft Seal Replacement

1. Thoroughly clean the cover in solvent and dry with compressed air.

2. Inspect the cover for any cracks or damage. Check around the ribs and the transmission sealing surface. If damaged, replace the cover.

3. Check the movement of the detent arm (A, **Figure 24**). It should move freely and the return spring should move the arm back to its normal position.

4. To replace the detent arm, perform the following:
   a. Lift the leg of the return spring (B, **Figure 24**) up and off of the boss in the cover. This will relieve the spring pressure.
   b. Remove the circlip (C, **Figure 24**) and remove the detent arm (A, **Figure 24**) from the post on the cover.
   c. Install a new detent arm and circlip. Make sure the circlip is correctly seated in the post groove.
   d. Move the leg of the return spring back onto the correct position on the boss.

5. Inspect the input shaft oil seal (**Figure 25**) in the cover. If it is worn or if the sealing lips are damaged in any way, replace the seal as follows:

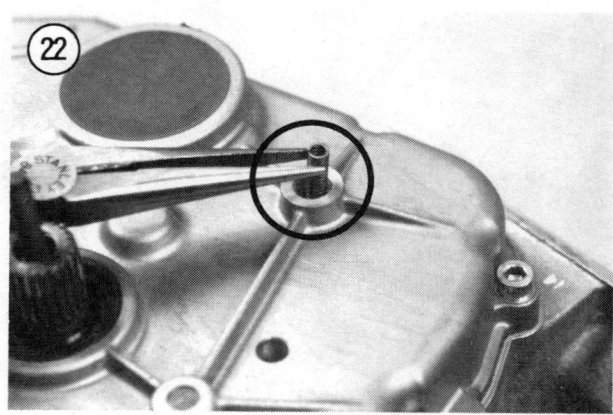

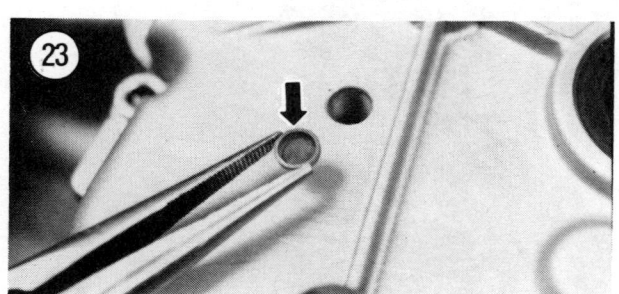

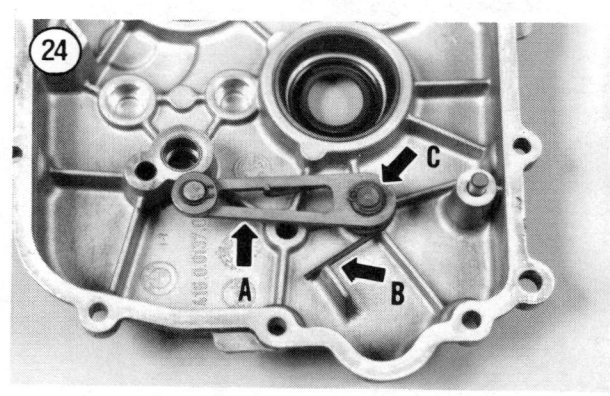

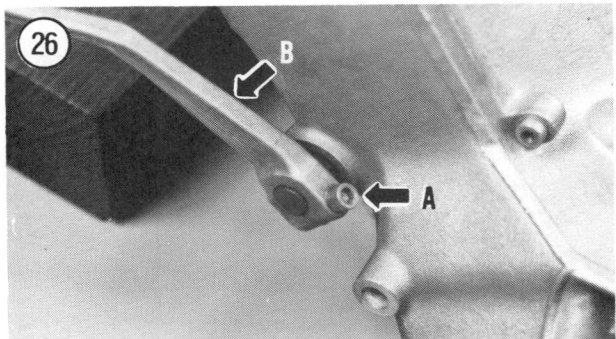

a. Use a suitable size socket and hammer; drive out the old seal from the *inside* surface of the cover.

b. Thoroughly clean out the seal receptacle in the cover with solvent and dry with compressed air.

c. Apply a light coat of multipurpose grease to the outer surface of the new seal and the seal receptacle in the cover.

d. Position the new seal with the open side facing in toward the inside.

NOTE
In the following step BMW special tools can be used to install the oil seal but a carefully used socket will perform the same job for a lot less money. If you choose to use the special tools, use BMW part No. 23 1 770 and 00 5 500 for oil seal installation.

e. Using a suitable size socket that matches the outer diameter of the seal and hammer, carefully tap the new seal into the cover from the *outside* surface of the cover. Tap the seal in squarely and evenly until it bottoms out in the cover.

f. Apply a light coat of multipurpose grease to the sealing lips of the new seal.

TRANSMISSION SHAFTS AND GEARSHIFT MECHANISM

Removal

1. Remove the transmission housing as described in this chapter.

2. Remove the transmission housing cover as described in this chapter.

3. Remove the bolt (A, **Figure 26**) securing the gearshift lever and remove the lever (B, **Figure 26**) from the pivot shaft.

4. Withdraw the shift fork shafts (**Figure 27**).

NOTE
Don't lose the individual roller on each shift fork pin during removal in Step 4 and Step 7.

5. Pivot the 2 top shift forks (1st/2nd gears and 3rd/4th gears) out of mesh with the shift drum.

6. Tilt the input shaft away from the shift drum.

7. Pivot the lower shift fork (5th gear) out of mesh with the shift drum.

8. Move the shift pawl (A, **Figure 28**) out of the way and hold it back to the transmission housing with a piece of wire.

9. Withdraw the shift drum (B, **Figure 28**).

10. Remove all 3 shift forks (**Figure 29**).

11. Withdraw the input shaft (A, **Figure 30**).

> *CAUTION*
> *In the following step, do not try to remove one shaft without the other shaft as the bevel gears (5th gear) will be damaged. The shafts **must be withdrawn as an assembly.***

12. Withdraw the intermediate shaft (B, **Figure 30**) and the output shaft (C, **Figure 30**) as an assembly.

13. Inspect the transmission shaft assemblies as described under *Transmission Shafts, Preliminary Inspection* in this chapter.

> *NOTE*
> *The following steps are for removal of the gearshift mechanism. Continue to Step 14 only if this mechanism is to be removed and serviced.*

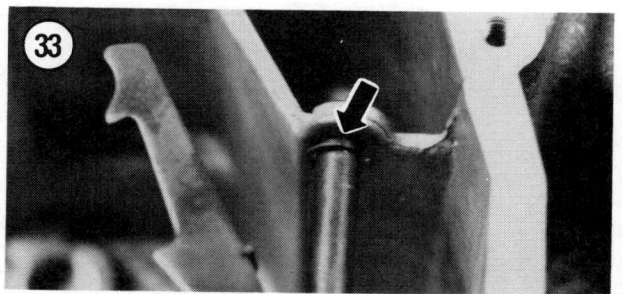

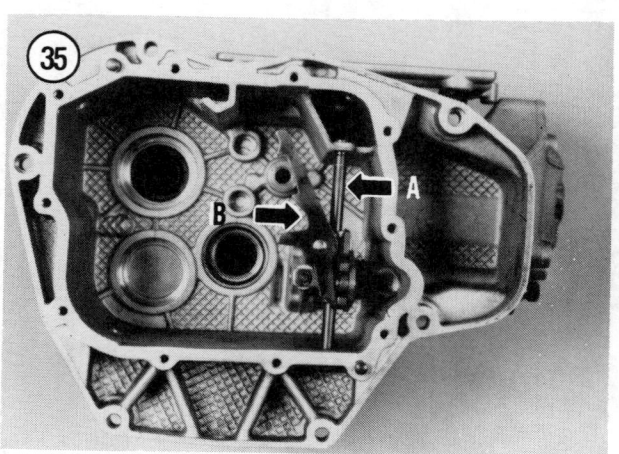

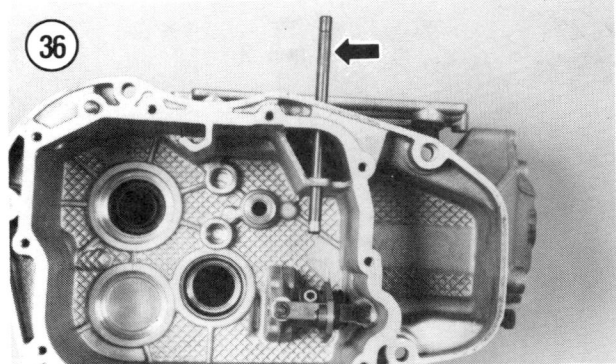

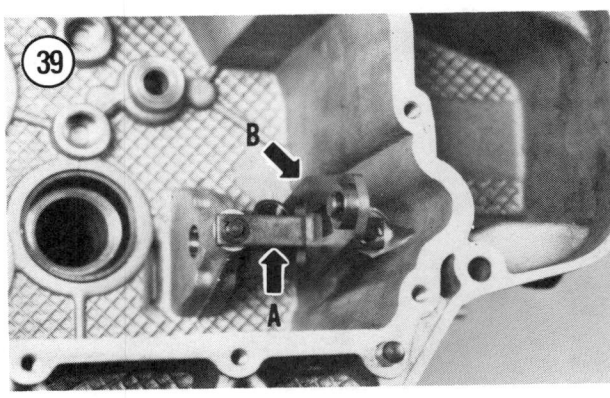

14. Remove the cap (**Figure 31**) from the transmission housing breather.

15. Use a drift and hammer and tap out the transmission housing breather sleeve (**Figure 32**) from the *inside* surface of the housing. Remove the breather sleeve.

16. Remove the circlip (**Figure 33**) securing the guide rod.

17. Remove the circlip securing the roller (**Figure 34**) and remove the roller from the pin on the shift arm.

18. Partially withdraw the guide rod (A, **Figure 35**) and remove the shift pawl and shift pawl holder (B, **Figure 35**).

19. Withdraw the guide rod out through the breather receptacle in the housing (**Figure 36**).

20. Remove the Allen bolt (**Figure 37**) securing the shift shaft.

21. Remove the E-clips (**Figure 38**) securing the shift arm stop.

22. Partially withdraw the shift shaft sufficiently to remove the shift arm.

23. Remove the stop (A, **Figure 39**) and remove the shift arm (B, **Figure 39**).

24. Remove the spring and shim (**Figure 40**).

25. Withdraw the shift shaft (**Figure 41**) from the transmission housing.

6

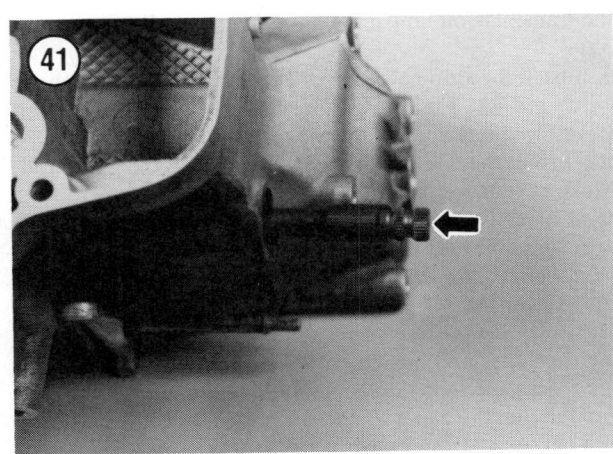

26. To separate the shift pawl from the shift pawl holder, perform the following:

    a. Remove the E-clip (A, **Figure 42**) securing the shift pawl to the shift pawl holder.

    b. Remove the shift pawl (B, **Figure 42**), spring and spacer.

27. Inspect the gearshift mechanism as described under *Gearshift Mechanism Inspection* in this chapter.

Installation

NOTE
If the gearshift mechanism was removed, perform Steps 1-13. If the mechanism was not removed, proceed to Step 14.

1. To assemble the shift pawl onto the shift pawl holder, perform the following:

    a. Install the shift pawl (B, **Figure 42**), spring and spacer onto the holder.

    b. Install the E-clip (A, **Figure 42**) securing the shift pawl to the shift pawl holder. Make sure the E-clip is correctly seated in the groove.

2. Partially insert the shift shaft into the transmission housing (**Figure 41**).

3. Install the shim (**Figure 40**) onto the shift shaft.

4. Install the shift arm (B, **Figure 39**) and spring and push the shift shaft the rest of the way in.

5. Install the shift arm stop (A, **Figure 39**) and install the E-clips (**Figure 38**). Make sure the E-clips are properly seated in the grooves in the raised studs.

6. Rotate the shift shaft until the detent in the shaft aligns with the hole (**Figure 43**) in the shift arm.

7. Apply blue Loctite Threadlocker No. 242 to the shift shaft Allen bolt prior to installation, then install the Allen bolt (**Figure 37**). Tighten the Allen bolt to the torque specification listed in **Table 2**.

8. Insert the guide rod through the breather receptacle in the transmission housing and push it partially in (**Figure 36**).

9. Install the shift pawl holder (B, **Figure 35**) and push the guide rod (A, **Figure 35**) through the shift pawl holder. Push the guide rod all the way in until it stops.

10. Install the circlip (**Figure 33**) securing the guide rod. Make sure the circlip is correctly seated in the groove.

11. Correctly position the roller (**Figure 34**) on the shift arm stud and into the yoke of the shift pawl holder, then install the E-clip. Make sure the E-clip is correctly seated in the groove.

12. From the *outside* surface of the housing carefully tap the transmission housing breather sleeve (**Figure 32**) into the receptacle in the housing. Tap the breather in only far enough that the cap will not touch the housing. Install the cap (**Figure 31**) and push it on firmly.

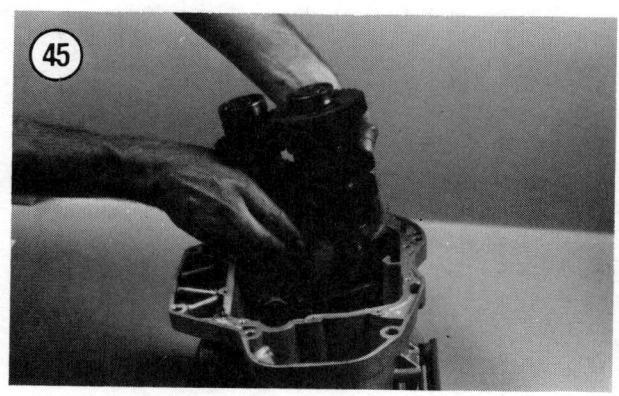

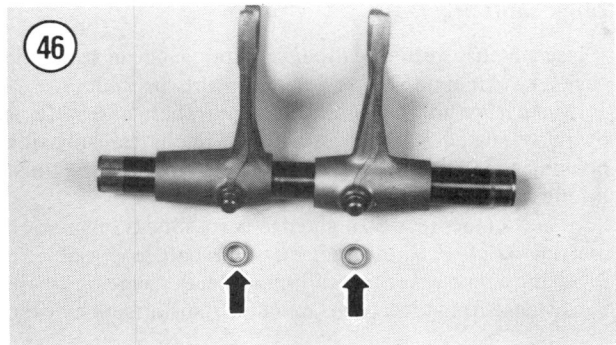

13. Correctly position the shift shaft so the shift lever is facing toward the front of the transmission housing. Install the lever and bolt and tighten the bolt securely.

14. Place the intermediate and output transmission shaft assemblies in a freezer for 30 minutes. This will reduce the overall size of the roller bearings and will make transmission shaft assembly installation much easier.

15. Apply the specified type and viscosity of clean gear oil to the bearings at each end of all 3 transmission shafts and to the bearing receptacles (**Figure 44**) in the end of the transmission housing. Refer to **Table 1** for the recommended gear oil. This will make transmission shafts installation easier.

> *CAUTION*
> *In the following step, do not try to install one shaft without the other shaft as the bevel gears (5th gear) will be damaged. The shafts must be installed as an assembly.*

16. Properly mesh the intermediate shaft and the output shaft together as an assembly. Install them into the transmission housing (**Figure 45**) as an assembly.

17. Make sure the bearings are properly aligned with their respective bearing receptacles in the transmission housing. Carefully tap on the ends of the transmission shaft assemblies with a plastic or soft-faced mallet. Tap on the shaft assemblies until they are completely seated.

18. Spin each transmission shaft and make sure it rotates freely. If it binds or does not spin at all, correct the problem at this time.

19. Install the input shaft with the helical cut gear end going in first. Tilt the input shaft slightly away from the shaft assemblies already installed.

20. If either transmission shaft assembly was disassembled (even for bearing replacement), perform *Transmission Shaft Preload and End Float Measurement and Adjustment* as described in this chapter. This procedure is necessary if any component has been removed, since the overall length of the transmission shaft(s) has changed.

21. Apply a light coat of multipurpose grease to each roller (**Figure 46**) and install them onto each gear shift fork. The grease will help to hold the roller in place during installation.

22. Install the 3rd/4th gear shift fork as follows:
   a. Position the 3rd/4th gear shift fork with the short guide end facing down.
   b. Partially pull up on the output shaft (A, **Figure 47**) to make room for the shift fork (B, **Figure 47**) to be installed in the intermediate shaft.
   c. Install the 3rd/4th gear shift fork into the groove in the 3rd/4th gear (**Figure 48**).
   d. Push the output shaft back down into position.

23. Position the 5th gear shift fork with the short guide end facing up and install the shift fork into the 5th gear (**Figure 49**).

24. Position the 1st/2nd gear shift fork with the short guide end facing down and install the shift fork into the 1st/2nd gear (**Figure 50**).

25. Apply a liberal coat of transmission gear oil to the shift drum and install the shift drum assembly (**Figure 51**).

26. Make sure the rollers are still in place on all shift fork cam pin followers. Move the cam pin followers into the grooves in the shift drum (**Figure 52**).

27. Apply a liberal coat of transmission gear oil onto the shift fork shaft holes in each shift fork and to each shift fork shaft.

28. Insert the 1st/2nd gear and the 5th gear shift fork shaft (**Figure 53**).

29. Insert the 3rd/4th gear shift fork shaft (**Figure 54**).

30. Install the housing cover as described in this chapter but do not install the bolts until after Step 31.

31. Spin the transmission shafts and shift through all 5 gears using the shift lever. Make sure you can shift into all gears. This is the time to find that something may be installed incorrectly—not after the transmission is completely assembled and installed onto the engine.

32. If the transmission shifts through all gears correctly, install the housing cover bolts and tighten to the torque specification listed in **Table 2**.

33. Install the transmission housing as described in this chapter.

Transmission Shaft Preload and End Float Measurement and Adjustment

The transmission preload (input shaft) and end float (output and intermediate shaft(s) must be checked whenever the transmission shafts have been serviced or removed from the transmission housing.

The preload is the amount of pressure applied to the input shaft tapered roller bearings after the transmission housing and cover are assembled. This type of bearing requires some preload or pressure to maintain a correct roller-to-race relationship. If the preload is not correct, the bearings will wear prematurely.

The end float is the play or free space between the end of the transmission output shaft and the intermediate shaft and the transmission housing cover. The ball bearings do not require a preload, as do tapered roller bearings, and must have a certain amount of freedom or end float. If the end float is not correct, the bearings will wear prematurely.

The transmission shaft rear bearings must be completely seated in the transmission housing in order for this adjustment to be correct. If they are not completely seated, the transmission shaft will sit up too high and throw off the measurements taken in this procedure.

The BMW special tool (part No. 23 1 660) can be used as shown in **Figure 55** but it is expensive and is not necessary. A machined straightedge can be used at a substantial cost savings.

Input shaft preload

Use a metric vernier caliper or depth gauge as it will be easier to calculate shim selection in this procedure.

1. Make sure the transmission input shaft assembly is properly seated in the bearing race in the transmission housing and is sitting perfectly upright—it cannot be tilted to one side.

2. Place a machined straightedge across the transmission housing as close to the transmission shaft as possible.

3. Using a metric vernier caliper or depth gauge, measure the distance from the top surface of the transmission housing

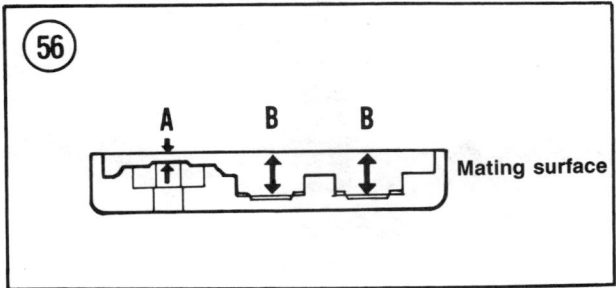

A   B   B

Mating surface

to the top surface of the input transmission shaft bearing shoulder. Write down this dimension (dimension A).

4. If removed, install the front bearing outer race into the transmission housing cover. Make sure it is properly seated.

5. Place the bearing inner race into the outer race. Make sure it is correctly seated.

6. Using a vernier caliper or depth gauge, measure the distance from the top surface of the transmission housing cover to the top surface of the bearing inner race (A, **Figure 56**). Write down this dimension (dimension B).

7. For correct shim(s) selection proceed as follows:

NOTE
For calculations use the mid-point of the specified preload. For instance, if the specified amount of preload is 0.03-0.08 mm, the mid-point is 0.05 mm.

NOTE
The following numbers are for examples only. Use the numbers written down during this procedure.

Example:

Actual measured distance	
Measurement B	11.30 mm
Subtract measurement A	-9.90 mm
Equals excess clearance (without any shims)	=1.40 mm
Specified preload	+0.05 mm
Equals required shim thickness (round off to the nearest shim thickness)	=1.45 mm

NOTE
Shims are available from BMW dealers in the following thicknesses: 0.3, 0.4, 0.5, 1.42, 1.44, 1.46, 1.48 and 1.50 mm. Use the correct thickness of one shim or a combination of shims to achieve the specified preload.

8. The shim(s) is placed between the front bearing inner race and the transmission shaft bearing shoulder.

Output shaft and intermediate shaft

Use a metric vernier caliper or depth gauge as it will be easier to calculate shim selection in this procedure.

1. Make sure the transmission shaft assemblies are properly seated in the transmission housing and are sitting perfectly upright—they cannot be tilted to one side.

2. Place a machined straightedge across the transmission bearing and hold it level.

NOTE
To avoid confusion, measure and calculate one shaft assembly at a time.

3. Using a metric vernier caliper or depth gauge, measure the distance from the top surface of the transmission housing to the top surface of the intermediate transmission shaft bearing (**Figure 57**). Write down this dimension (dimension A).
4. Place a machined straightedge across the housing cover (**Figure 58**).
5. Using a vernier caliper (**Figure 59**) or depth gauge, measure the distance from the top surface of the transmission housing cover to the shoulder (**Figure 60**) where the shaft's rear bearing bottoms out in the cover (B, **Figure 56**). Write down this dimension (dimension B).
6. For correct shim(s) selection proceed as follows:

NOTE
The specified amount of free play load is 0.05-0.15 mm. For calculations use the low-point of the specified preload—i.e., 0.05 mm.

NOTE
The following numbers are for examples only. Use the numbers written down during this procedure.

Example:

Actual measured distance	
Measurement B	36.90 mm
Subtract measurement A	-36.05 mm
Equals excess clearance (without any shims)	=0.85 mm
Specified free play	-0.05 mm
Equals required shim thickness (round off to the nearest shim thickness)	=0.80 mm

NOTE
Shims are available from BMW dealers in the following thicknesses: 0.3, 0.4 and 0.5 mm. Use the correct thickness of one shim or a combination of shims to achieve the specified preload.

7. The shim(s) is placed between the front bearing outer race and the transmission housing cover.
8. Repeat Steps 3-7 for the output shaft and refer to **Figure 61**.

Gearshift Mechanism Inspection

Refer to **Figure 62** and **Figure 63** for this procedure.
1. Clean all parts in solvent and thoroughly dry.

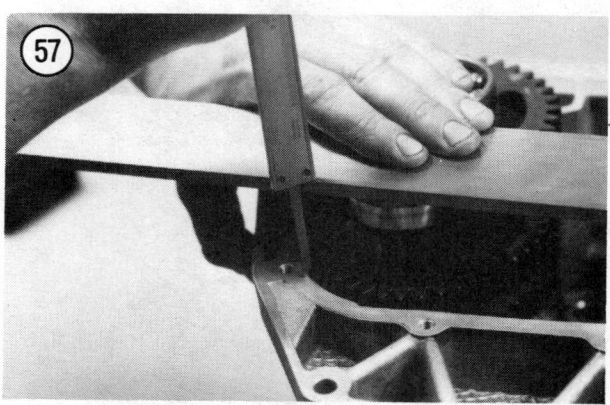

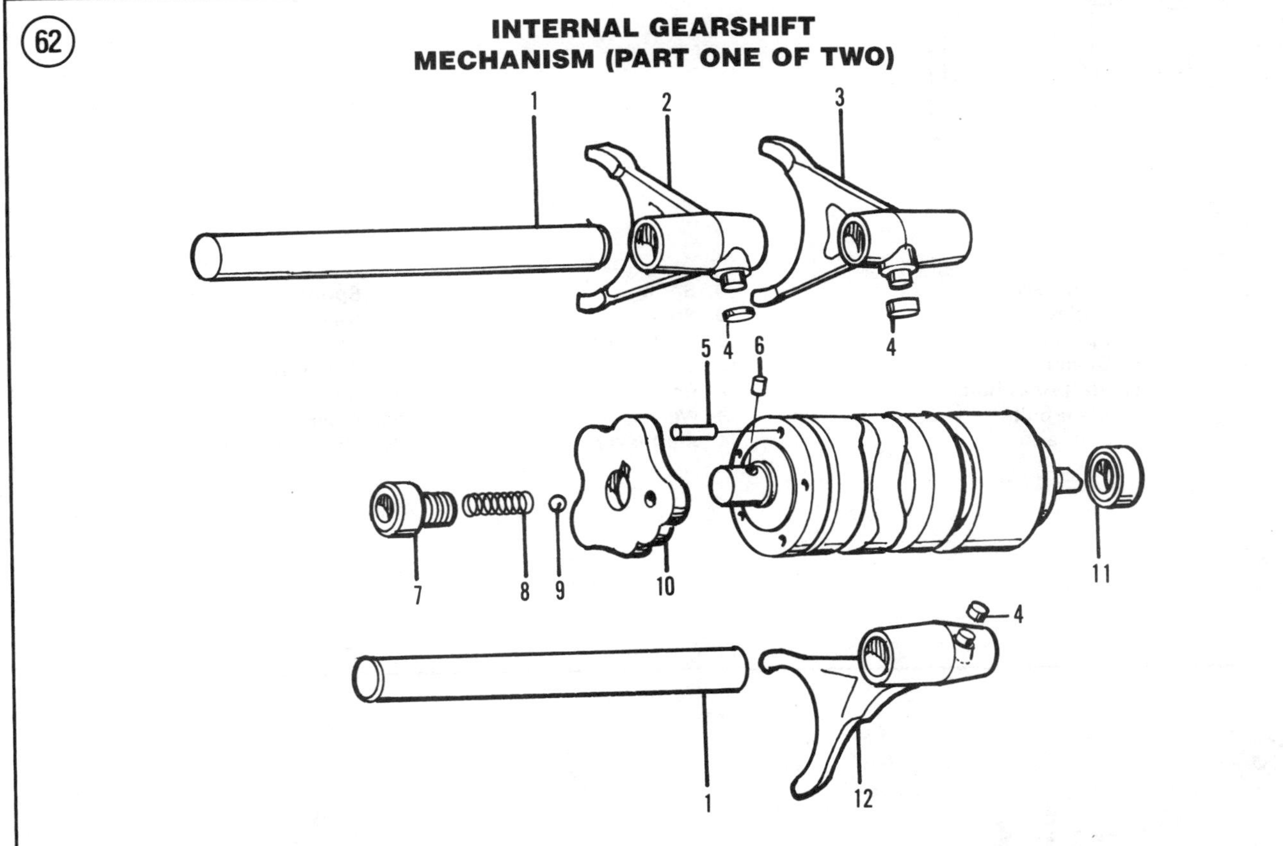

6

INTERNAL GEARSHIFT
MECHANISM (PART ONE OF TWO)

1. Shift fork shaft
2. 1st/2nd gear shift fork
3. 5th gear shift fork
4. Roller
5. Roll pin
6. Antirattle pin

7. Allen bolt
8. Spring
9. Ball
10. Selector cam
11. Bearing
12. 3rd/4th gear shift fork

63

INTERNAL GEARSHIFT
MECHANISM (PART TWO OF TWO)

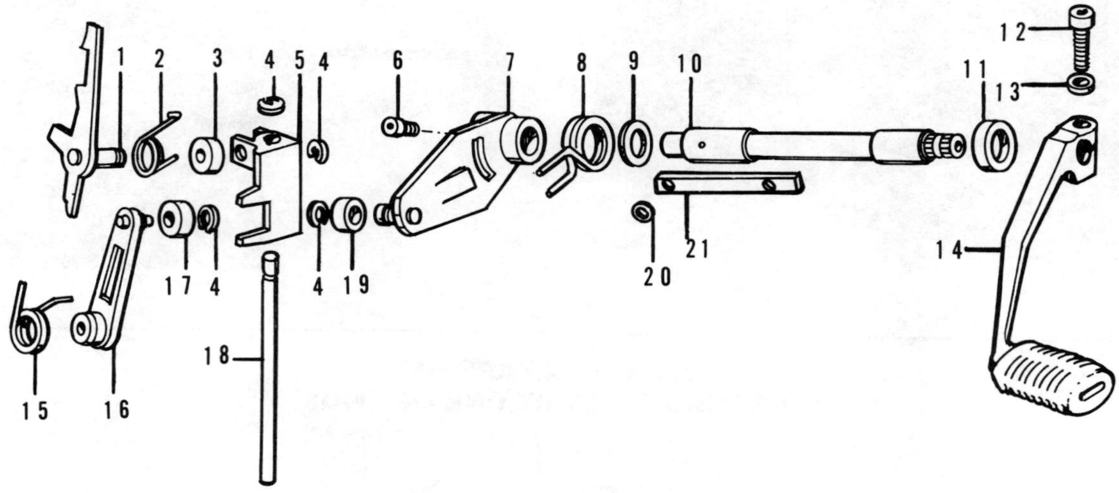

1. Shift pawl
2. Spring
3. Spacer
4. Circlip
5. Shift pawl holder
6. Allen bolt
7. Shift arm

8. Spring
9. Shim
10. Shift shaft
11. Oil seal
12. Bolt
13. Washer
14. Shift lever

15. Spring
16. Detent arm
17. Roller
18. Guide rod
19. Roller
20. E-clip
21. Shift arm stop

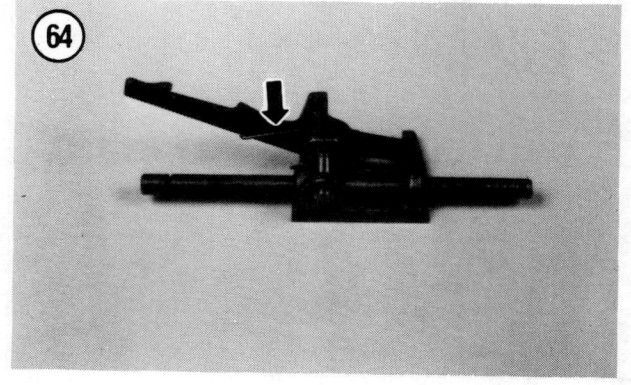

64

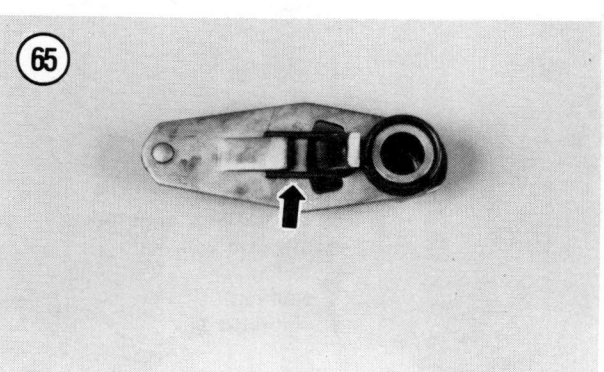

65

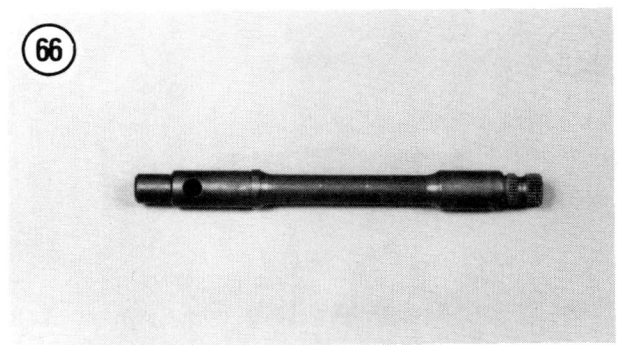

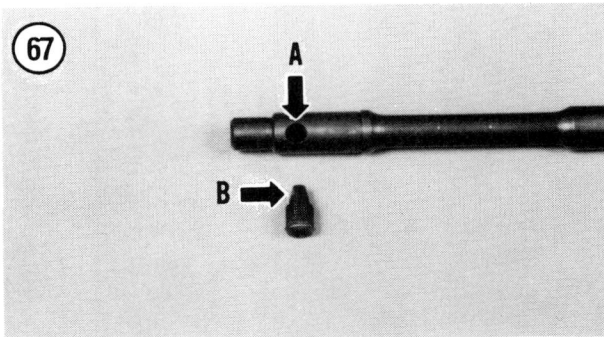

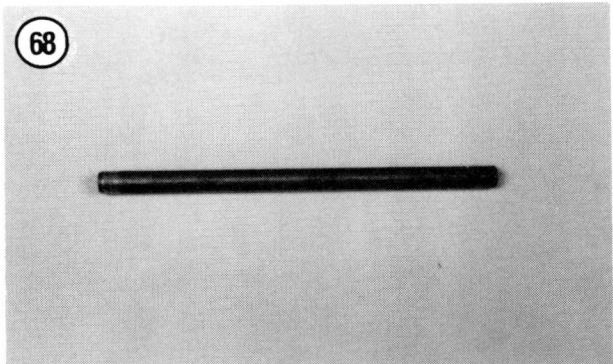

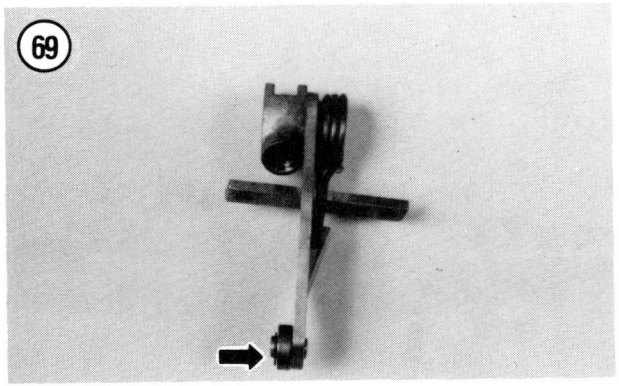

2. Inspect the return spring on the following parts:
   a. Detent arm.
   b. Shift pawl (**Figure 64**).
   c. Shift arm (**Figure 65**).
   If broken or weak, replace the spring.

3. Inspect the gearshift shaft (**Figure 66**) for bending, wear or other damage. Roll the shaft on a flat surface such as a piece of plate glass and check for any bends. If the shaft is bent, it must be replaced.

4. Inspect the Allen bolt receptacle (A, **Figure 67**) in the gearshift shaft for damage or wear. Also inspect the tapered end of the Allen bolt (B, **Figure 67**) where it engages the gearshift shaft for wear or damage. If necessary, replace either or both parts.

5. Inspect the guide rod (**Figure 68**). Roll the rod on a flat surface such as a piece of plate glass and check for any bends. If the rod is bent, it must be replaced.

6. Inspect the roller (**Figure 69**) on the shift arm. If worn or damaged, remove the circlip and replace the roller.

7. Inspect the roller on the detent arm. If worn or damaged, remove the circlip and replace the roller.

8. Insert the shift arm onto the shift shaft and check for excessive play. BMW does not provide specifications for the inside diameter of the shift arm or the outside diameter of the shift shaft. If play is noticeable, replace the worn part.

9. Inspect the shift pawl holder (**Figure 70**) for wear or damage. Make sure there are no cracks or other damage to the mounting bosses or fingers. Replace if necessary.

10. Inspect the ramps (**Figure 71**) on the selector cam for wear or damage. Replace the selector cam if necessary.

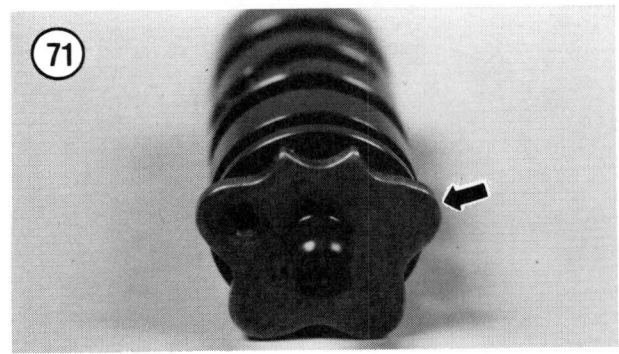

6

11. Inspect the roller pins in the end of the shift drum. Make sure they are a tight fit in the shift drum. If the pins are loose, replace all of them as a set.

12. Inspect the end of the shift drum (**Figure 72**) where it rides in the transmission housing for wear or damage. Replace if necessary.

13. Inspect each shift fork for signs of wear or cracking. Check for bending and make sure each fork slides smoothly on the shaft (**Figure 73**). Replace any worn or damaged forks.

14. Check for any arc-shaped wear or burn marks on the shift fork fingers (**Figure 74**). This indicates that the shift fork has come in contact with the gear. The fork fingers have become excessively worn and the fork must be replaced.

15. Check the grooves in the shift drum (**Figure 75**) for wear or roughness. If any of the groove profiles have excessive wear or damage, replace the shift drum.

16. Check the cam pin followers (**Figure 76**) and roller on each shift fork that rides in the shift drum for wear or damage. Replace the shift fork(s) as necessary.

17. Roll each shift fork shaft on a flat surface such as a piece of plate glass (**Figure 77**) and check for any bends. If the shaft is bent, it must be replaced.

CAUTION
Marginally worn shift forks should be replaced. Worn forks can cause the transmission to slip out of gear, leading to more serious and expensive damage.

TRANSMISSION SHAFTS

Preliminary Inspection

After the transmission shaft assemblies have been removed from the transmission housing, clean and inspect the assemblies prior to disassembling them. Place the assembled shaft into a large can or plastic bucket and thoroughly clean with a petroleum based solvent such as

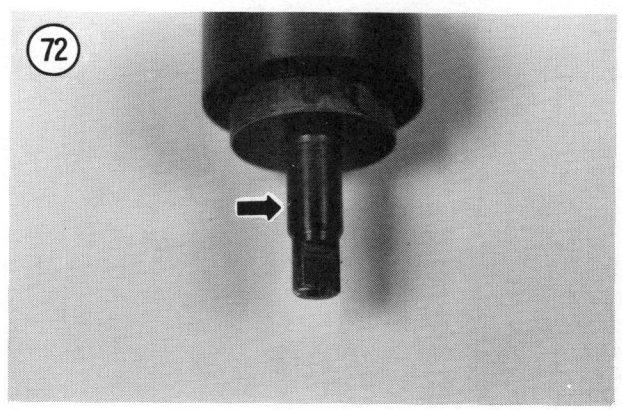
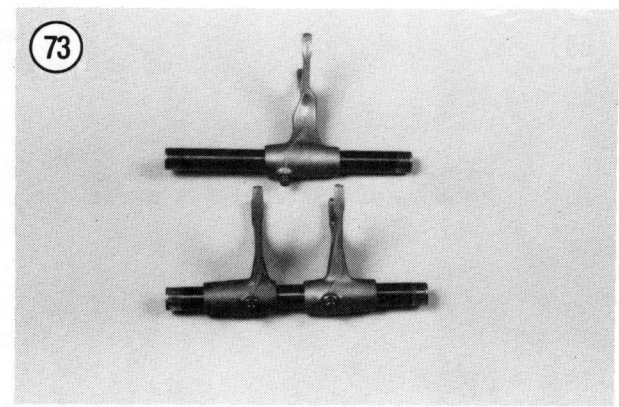
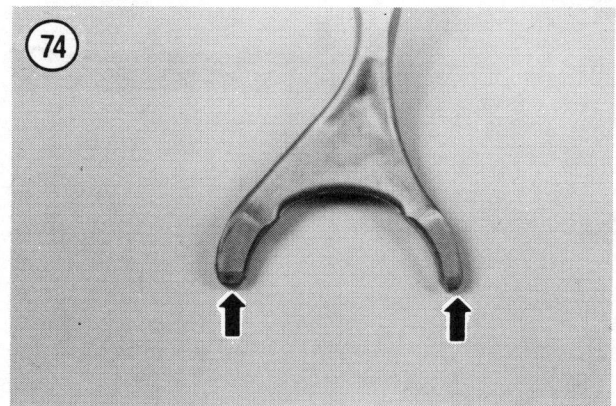

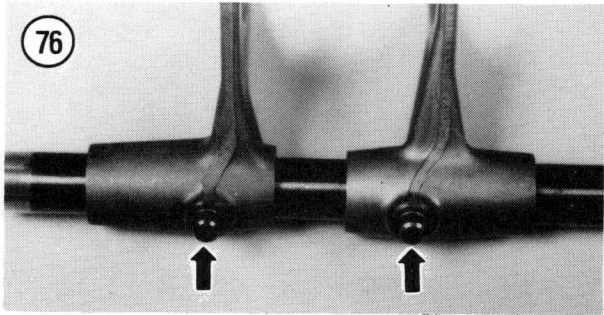

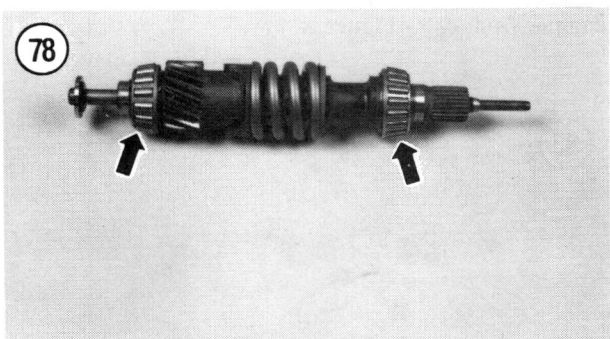

kerosene and a stiff brush. Dry with compressed air or let it sit on rags to drip dry. Repeat for the other shaft assemblies.

1. After they have been cleaned, visually inspect the components of the assemblies for excessive wear. Any burrs, pitting or roughness on the teeth of a gear will cause wear on the mating gear. Minor roughness can be cleaned up with an oilstone but there's little point in attempting to remove deep scars.

NOTE
Defective gears should be replaced. It's a good idea to replace the mating gear on the other shaft even though it may not show as much wear or damage.

2. Carefully check the engagement dogs. If any are chipped, worn, rounded or missing, the affected gear must be replaced.

3. Rotate the transmission bearings by hand. Refer to **Figures 78-81**. Check for roughness, noise and radial play. Any bearing that is suspect should be replaced as described in this chapter.

4. If the transmission shafts are satisfactory and are not going to be disassembled, apply clean gear oil to all components and reinstall them in the transmission housing as described in this chapter.

NOTE
If disassembling a used, well run-in (high mileage) transmission for the first time by yourself, pay particular attention to any additional shims that may have been added by a previous owner. These may have been added to take up the tolerance of worn components or thrust washers and must be reinstalled in the same position since the shims have devel-

6

*oped a wear pattern. If new parts are going to be installed these shims may be eliminated. This is something you will have to determine upon reassembly. Do **not** confuse this statement with the end float and preload adjustment that must be done prior to installing the shaft assembles as noted in this chapter.*

Input Shaft
Disassembly/Inspection

Disassembly of the input shaft requires the use of a hydraulic press (**Figure 82**), an insert (**Figure 83**) and a bearing puller.

Refer to **Figure 84** for this procedure.

NOTE
*A helpful ''tool'' that should be used for transmission disassembly is a large egg flat (the type that restaurants get their eggs in) as shown in **Figure 85**. As you remove a part from the shaft, set it in one of the depressions in the same position from which it was removed. This is an easy way to remember the correct relationship of all parts.*

1. If not cleaned in the *Preliminary Inspection* sequence, place the assembled shaft into a large can or plastic bucket and thoroughly clean with solvent and a stiff brush. Dry with compressed air or let it sit on rags to dry.
2. Attach a bearing puller to the input shaft as shown in **Figure 86**. Place the puller fingers on the ledge of the shock damper front cam (**Figure 87**).

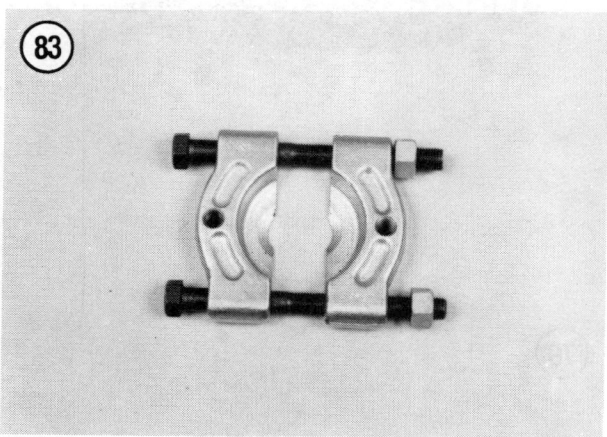

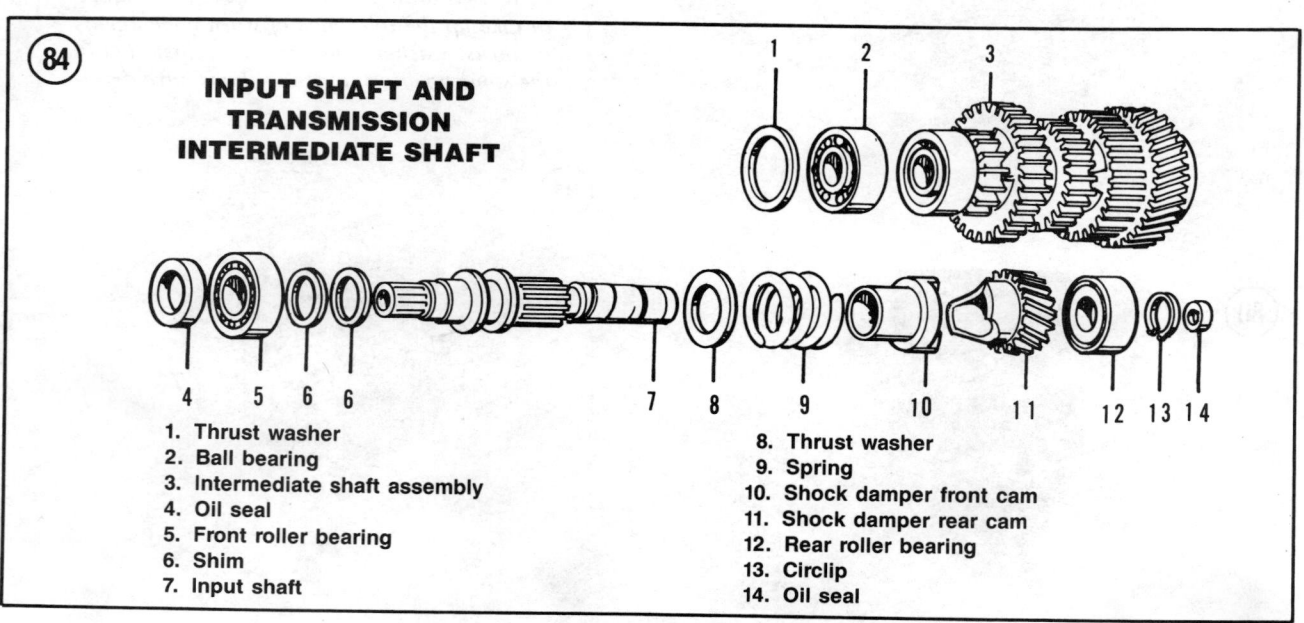

INPUT SHAFT AND TRANSMISSION INTERMEDIATE SHAFT

1. Thrust washer
2. Ball bearing
3. Intermediate shaft assembly
4. Oil seal
5. Front roller bearing
6. Shim
7. Input shaft
8. Thrust washer
9. Spring
10. Shock damper front cam
11. Shock damper rear cam
12. Rear roller bearing
13. Circlip
14. Oil seal

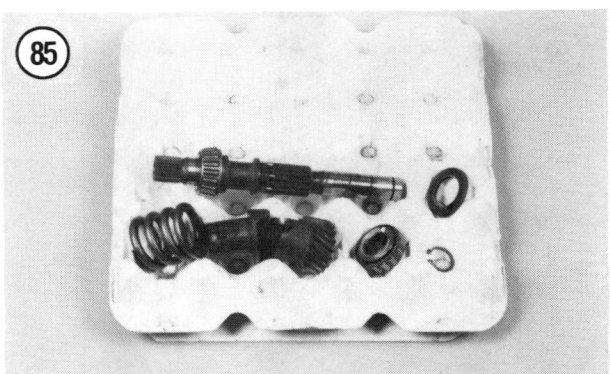

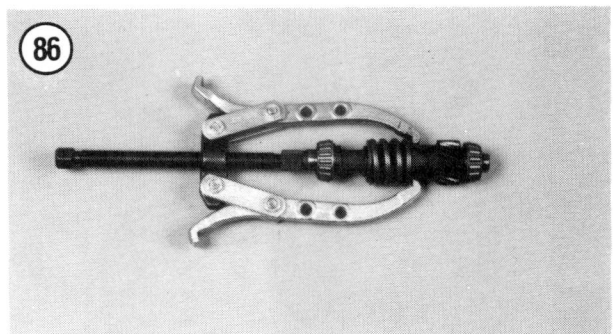

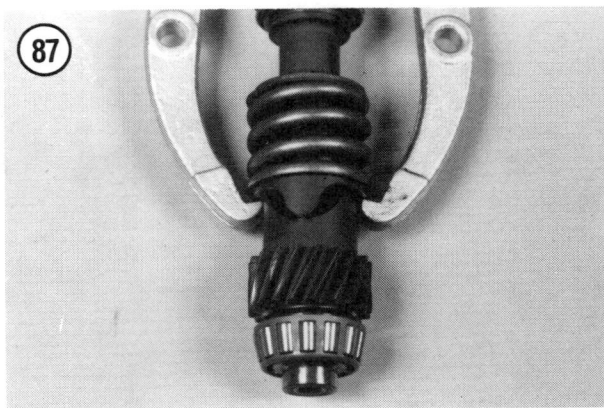

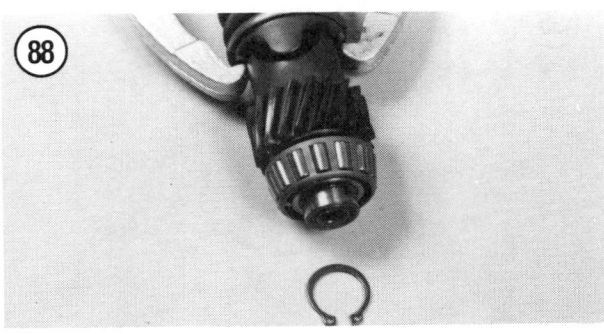

3. Tighten the bearing puller and compress the spring sufficiently to take the spring pressure off the shock damper rear cam.

4. Remove the circlip (**Figure 88**) from the rear of the shaft.

5. Install the insert under the rear bearing (**Figure 89**).

6. Install the input shaft and bearing puller assembly in the hydraulic press (**Figure 90**).

7. Place a suitable size socket (**Figure 91**) on the rear end of the shaft. The socket must be small enough to pass through the inner race of the roller bearing being pressed off.

6

8. While holding onto the input shaft and bearing puller assembly, slowly press the bearing off of the shaft.

9. Release the hydraulic pressure and remove the shaft and bearing puller assembly from the hydraulic press.

10. Gradually loosen the bearing puller and remove it from the shaft assembly.

11. Slide off the rear shock damper, the front shock damper, the spring and the thrust washer.

12. If the front bearing requires removal, perform the following:

   a. Install the insert under the front bearing (**Figure 92**).

   b. Install the input shaft assembly in the hydraulic press.

   c. Place a suitable size socket on the front end of the shaft. The socket must be small enough to pass through the inner race of the roller bearing being pressed off.

   d. While holding onto the input shaft assembly, slowly press the bearing off of the shaft. Remove the shaft assembly from the hydraulic press.

13. Inspect the ramps of both the front and rear shock dampers (**Figure 93**). Check for excessive wear, burrs, pitting or chipped areas. Replace if necessary.

14. Inspect the inner splines of the front shock damper for wear or damage. Replace if necessary.

15. Inspect the splines for the front shock damper (A, **Figure 94**) and the clutch friction disc (B, **Figure 94**) on the input shaft for wear or damage. If worn or damaged, replace the shaft.

16. Make sure that the shock dampers slide smoothly on the input shaft splines and sliding surfaces.

17. Inspect the spring. If broken or weak, replace the spring. BMW does not provide specifications for the overall length of the spring in the relaxed position.

18. Rotate the input shaft bearings (**Figure 95**) by hand. Check for roughness, noise and radial play. Any bearing that is suspect should be replaced.

Input Shaft Assembly

1. Apply a light coat of clean engine oil to all sliding surfaces prior to installing any parts.

2. If the front bearing was removed, perform the following:

   a. Position the front bearing on the front end of the input shaft.

   b. Install the input shaft assembly into the hydraulic press and set the rear end of the shaft on the press plates. Have an assistant hold the shaft in place.

CAUTION
*Do **not** press the bearing into place using the bearing outer race as the bearing will be damaged.*

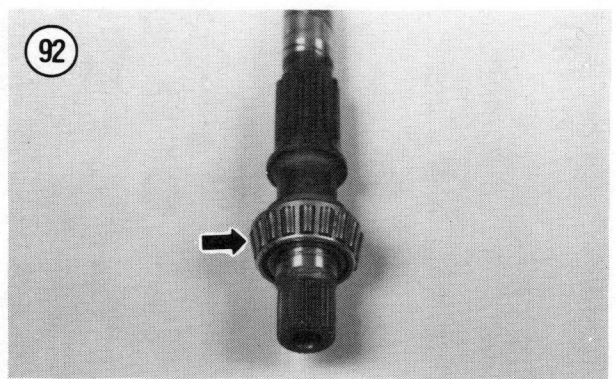
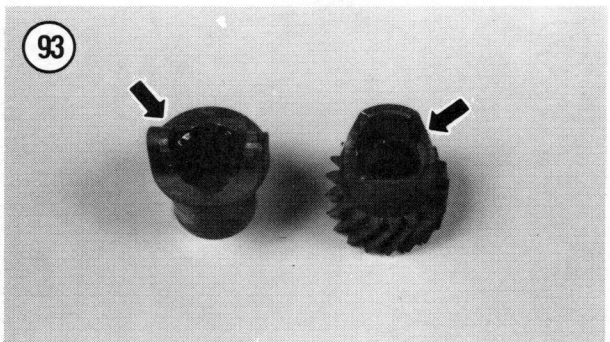
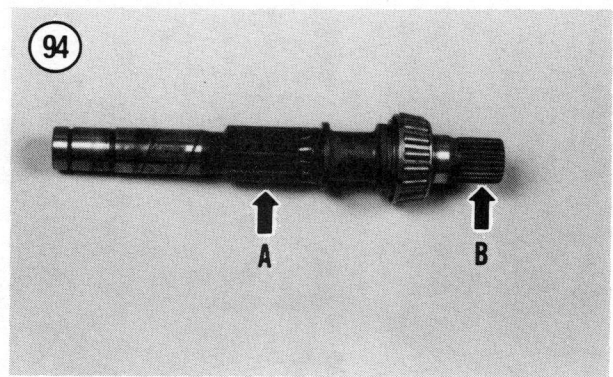

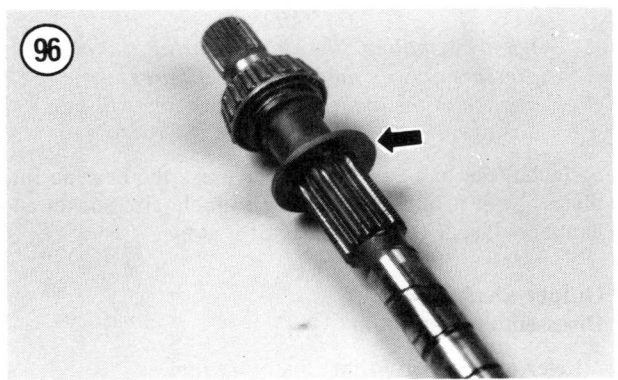

c. Place a suitable size socket on the inner race of the front bearing. The socket must fit the inner race only and must also be large on the inside to clear the splines on the input shaft. If the inner surface of the socket touches the shaft splines the splines will be damaged and the socket may get pressed onto the shaft by mistake.

d. Slowly press the front bearing onto the shaft. Press it on until it bottoms out.

e. Release the hydraulic pressure and remove the socket and the input shaft from the hydraulic press.

f. Rotate the bearing (**Figure 92**) by hand to make sure it rotates freely and was not damaged during installation.

3. Slide the thrust washer (**Figure 96**) and spring (**Figure 97**) onto the input shaft.

4. Slide the front shock damper (**Figure 98**) onto the input shaft, carefully aligning the splines in both parts.

5. Install the rear shock damper and rear bearing onto the rear end of the shaft.

6. Install the input shaft assembly into the hydraulic press and set the front end of the shaft on the press plates (**Figure 99**). Have an assistant hold the shaft in place.

CAUTION
*Do **not** press the bearing into place using the bearing outer race as the bearing will be damaged.*

7. Place a suitable size socket (A, **Figure 100**) on the inner race of the rear bearing. The socket must fit the inner race only.

8. Slowly press the rear bearing (B, **Figure 100**) and the rear shock damper (C, **Figure 100**) onto the shaft. Press it on until it bottoms out.

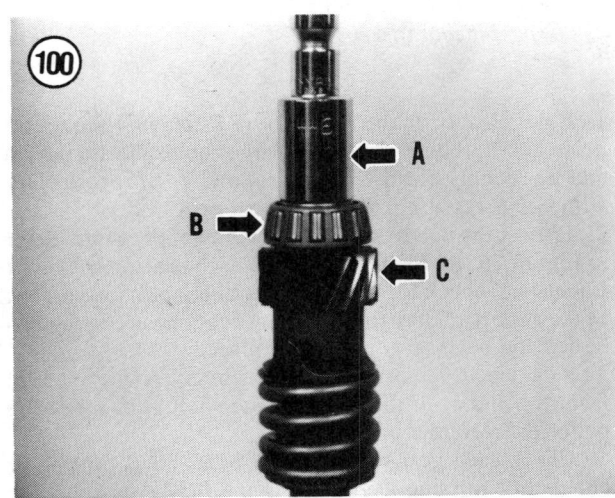

9. Release the hydraulic pressure and remove the socket from the input shaft.

10. Check that the circlip groove in the shaft is visible above the rear bearing. If necessary, press the bearing on farther until the circlip groove is visible and can accept the circlip.

NOTE
The circlip should be replaced every time the transmission is disassembled to ensure proper bearing alignment. When installing circlips, slide them onto the shaft with the rounded side going on first. This will position the sharp side outward to take the gear thrust correctly. Do not expand a circlip more than necessary to slide it over the shaft.

11. Rotate the bearing (**Figure 92**) by hand to make sure it rotates freely and was not damaged during installation.

12. Install the circlip (**Figure 101**). Make sure the circlip is properly seated in the groove in the input shaft.

13. After the input shaft is assembled, refer to **Figure 102** for correct component placement.

Intermediate Shaft
Inspection and Bearing Replacement

Refer to **Figure 84** for this procedure.

The intermediate shaft is one assembly with no removable parts except for the ball bearing. If any portion of the shaft is defective, except for the ball bearing, the entire shaft assembly must be replaced.

NOTE
In the following procedure, the ball bearing at each end of the shaft can be removed either with a gear puller or with a hydraulic press and a special tool insert.

1. If not cleaned in the *Preliminary Inspection* sequence, place the shaft assembly into a large can or plastic bucket and thoroughly clean with solvent and a stiff brush. Dry with compressed air or let it sit on rags to dry.

2. Inspect the ball bearing on each end of the shaft. Refer to **Figure 79** and **Figure 80**. Rotate each bearing with your fingers and check for roughness, pitting, galling and play. Make sure it rotates freely. If any roughness or play can be felt the bearing(s) must be replaced.

3. If damaged, remove the ball bearing(s) (A, **Figure 103**) from the end(s) of the intermediate shaft with a bearing puller or hydraulic press.

4. Check each gear for excessive wear, burrs, pitting or chipped or missing teeth (B, **Figure 103**).

CAUTION
*When installing the ball bearing, apply pressure only on the **inner race**. If pressure is applied to the outer race, the bearing will be damaged.*

5. Install the ball bearing. Either press the bearing into place or tap it into place with a suitable size socket and hammer. Install the bearing until it stops.

Output Shaft
Disassembly/Inspection

Refer to **Figure 104** for this procedure.

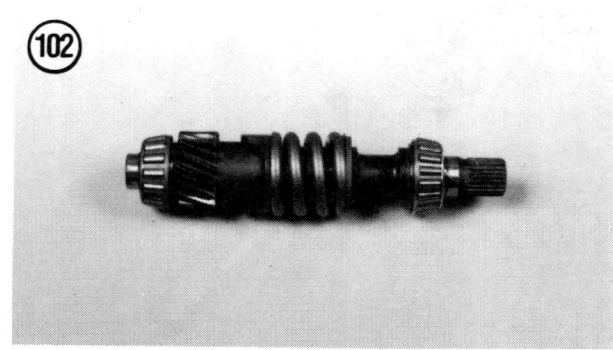

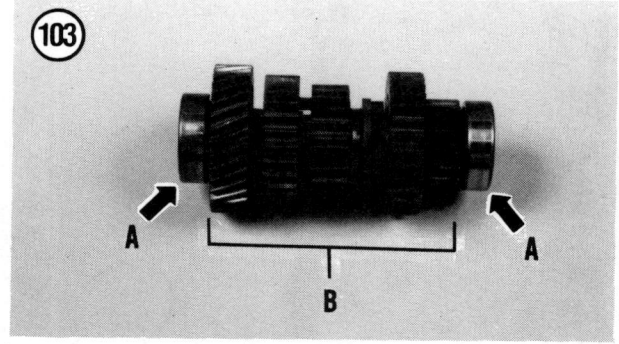

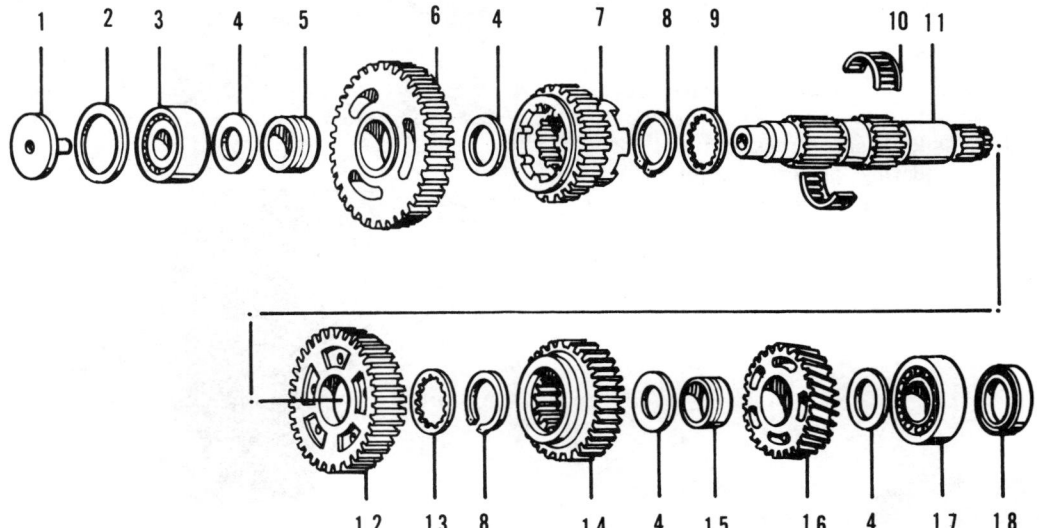

TRANSMISSION OUTPUT SHAFT

1. Oil trap
2. Shim
3. Ball bearing
4. Thrust washer
5. Bushing
6. 1st gear
7. 4th gear
8. Circlip
9. Splined washer
10. Split needle bearing
11. Output shaft
12. 2nd gear
13. Splined washer
14. 3rd gear
15. Bushing
16. 5th gear
17. Ball bearing
18. Oil seal

NOTE
*A helpful "tool" that should be used for transmission disassembly is a large egg flat (the type that restaurants get their eggs in) as shown in **Figure 105**. As you remove a part from the shaft, set it in one of the depressions in the same position from which it was removed. This is an easy way to remember the correct relationship of all parts.*

Disassembly of the output shaft requires the use of a hydraulic press (**Figure 82**) and an insert (**Figure 83**).

1. If not cleaned in the *Preliminary Inspection* sequence, place the assembled shaft into a large can or plastic bucket and thoroughly clean with solvent and a stiff brush. Dry with compressed air or let it sit on rags to dry.

2. To remove the rear bearing, perform the following:
   a. Install the insert (A, **Figure 106**) under the bearing at the front end of the shaft.
   b. Place the transmission assembly in the hydraulic press.

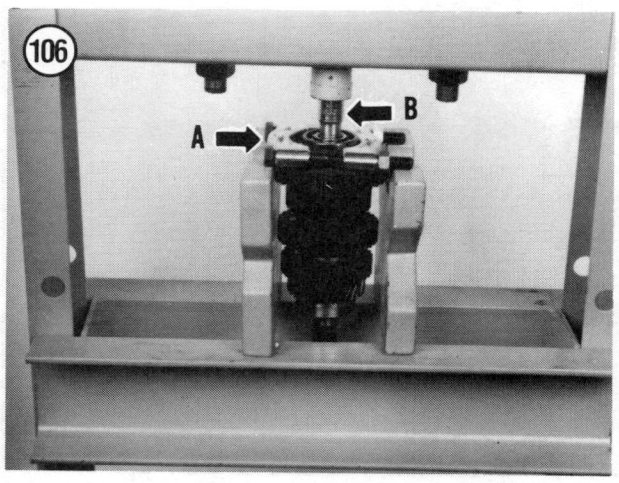

c. Place a suitable size socket (B, **Figure 106**) on the rear end of the shaft. The socket must be small enough to pass through the inner race of the roller bearing being pressed off.

d. While holding onto the output shaft assembly, slowly press the bearing off of the shaft.

e. Release the hydraulic pressure and remove the shaft assembly from the hydraulic press.

3. To remove the front bearing, perform the following:

a. Install the insert (A, **Figure 107**) under the bearing at the front end of the shaft.

b. Place the transmission assembly in the hydraulic press.

c. Place a suitable size socket (B, **Figure 107**) on the front end of the shaft. The socket must be small enough to pass through the inner race of the roller bearing being pressed off.

d. While holding onto the output shaft assembly, slowly press the bearing off of the shaft.

e. Release the hydraulic pressure and remove the shaft assembly from the hydraulic press.

4. Slide off the thrust washer (**Figure 108**).

5. Slide off the 1st gear (**Figure 109**).

6. To remove the 1st gear bushing, perform the following:

a. Install the insert under the 4th gear.

b. Place the transmission assembly in the hydraulic press.

c. While holding onto the output shaft assembly, slowly press the 4th gear off of the shaft sufficiently for the 1st gear bushing to be released from the shaft.

d. Release the hydraulic pressure and remove the shaft assembly from the hydraulic press.

e. Slide off the 1st gear bushing (**Figure 110**) and thrust washer (**Figure 111**).

7. Slide off the 4th gear (**Figure 112**).

8. Remove the circlip (**Figure 113**) and slide off the splined washer (**Figure 114**).

9. Slide off the 2nd gear (**Figure 115**) and remove the split needle bearing (**Figure 116**).

10. Slide off the splined washer (**Figure 117**) and remove the circlip (**Figure 118**).

11. Slide off the 3rd gear (**Figure 119**).

12. From the other end of the shaft, slide off the thrust washer (A, **Figure 120**) and the 5th gear (B, **Figure 120**).

13. To remove the 5th gear bushing and thrust washer, perform the following:

   a. Install the insert under the thrust washer.

   b. Place the transmission assembly in the hydraulic press.

   c. While holding onto the output shaft assembly, slowly press the 5th gear bushing off of the shaft.

   d. Release the hydraulic pressure and remove the shaft assembly from the hydraulic press.

   e. Slide off the 5th gear bushing (A, **Figure 121**) and thrust washer (B, **Figure 121**).

NOTE
Defective gears should be replaced. It is a good idea to replace the intermediate shaft assembly

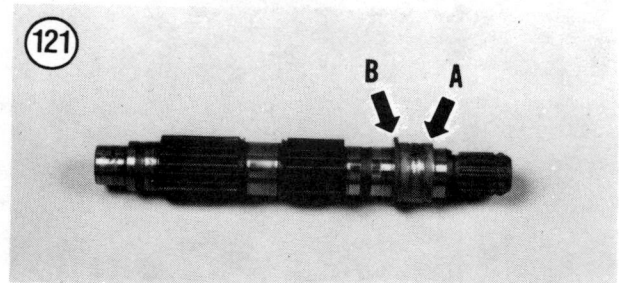

even though it may not show as much wear or damage. If you feel that the intermediate shaft requires replacement, discuss it with a BMW dealer and get their opinion as this shaft is very expensive.

14. Check each gear for excessive wear, burrs, pitting or chipped or missing teeth (A, **Figure 122**).

15. Make sure the lugs on the gears are in good condition. Refer to **Figure 123** and A, **Figure 124**.

16. Inspect the lug receptacles in each gear. Refer to B, **Figure 122** and **Figure 125**.

17. Check the inner splines of the 3rd and 4th gears (B, **Figure 124**) for excessive wear or burrs.

18. Inspect the machined groove (**Figure 126**) for the gearshift forks in the respective gears. Check for wear, gouges or other damage. Replace the gear if necessary.

19. Check the 1st and 5th gear bushings for excessive wear, pitting or damage. BMW does not provide specifications for either the inside or outside diameter of the bushings.

20. Make sure that all gears and bushings slide smoothly on the output shaft.

21. Inspect the splines and circlip grooves (**Figure 127**) on the output shaft. If any are damaged, the shaft must be replaced.

6

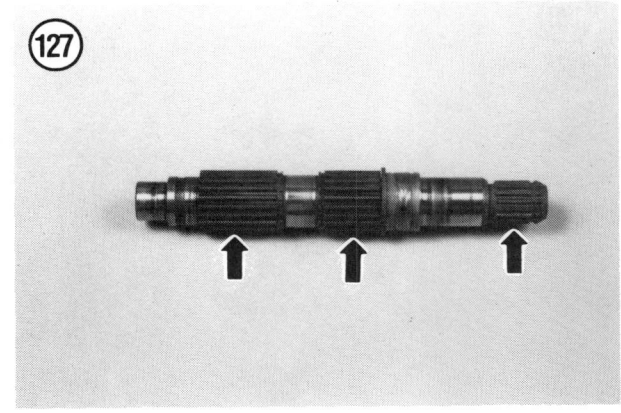

22. Inspect the ball bearings (**Figure 128**). Rotate the bearing with your fingers (**Figure 129**) and check for roughness, pitting, galling and play. Make sure it rotates freely. If any roughness or play can be felt the bearing(s) must be replaced.

23. Inspect the split roller bearing. Check the bearing cage for cracks at the corners of the needle slots and inspect the needles themselves for cracking. If any cracks are found, the split bearing must be replaced.

Output Shaft Assembly

NOTE
All circlips should be replaced every time the transmission is disassembled to ensure proper gear alignment. Transmission circlips become worn with use and increase gear side play. For this reason, it is always better to use new circlips whenever the transmission shaft is being reassembled. When installing circlips, slide them onto the shaft with the rounded side going on first. This will position the sharp side outward to take the gear thrust correctly. Do not expand a circlip more than necessary to slide it over the shaft. If the circlip is expanded too far it will become distorted and will not grip the shaft sufficiently, resulting in a loose fit.

1. Apply a light coat of clean gear oil to all sliding surfaces of the gears, bushings and shaft prior to installing any parts.

2. To install the 5th gear bushing, perform the following:
   a. Slide the thrust washer and the 5th gear bushing (A, **Figure 130**) onto the end of the output shaft.
   b. Place the insert (B, **Figure 130**) on the plates of the hydraulic press.
   c. Place the transmission shaft assembly (C, **Figure 130**) into the hydraulic press.
   d. Slowly apply pressure and press the 5th gear bushing onto the output shaft.

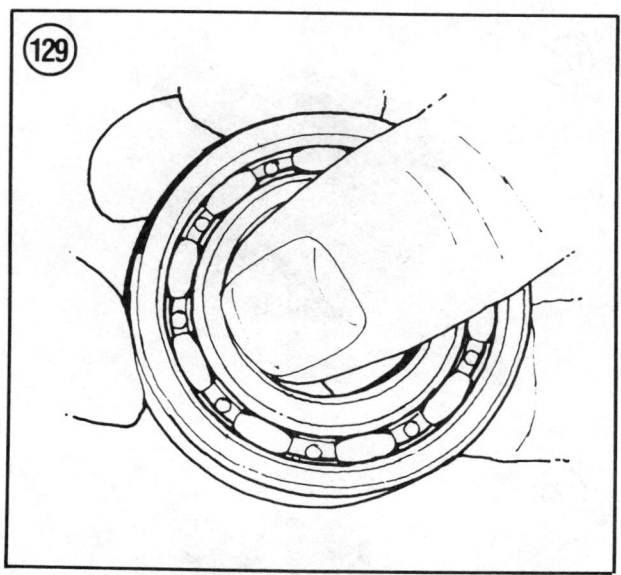

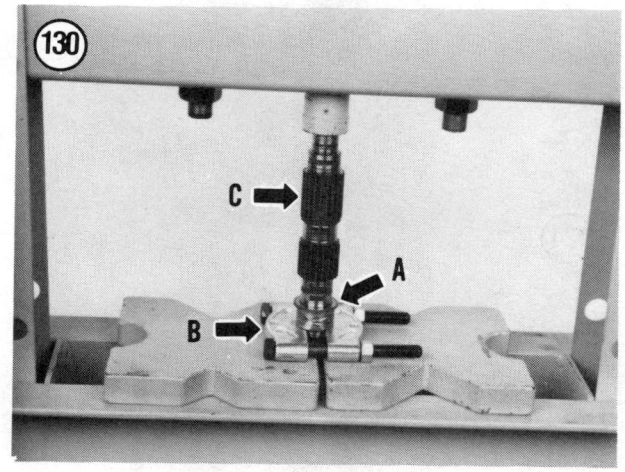

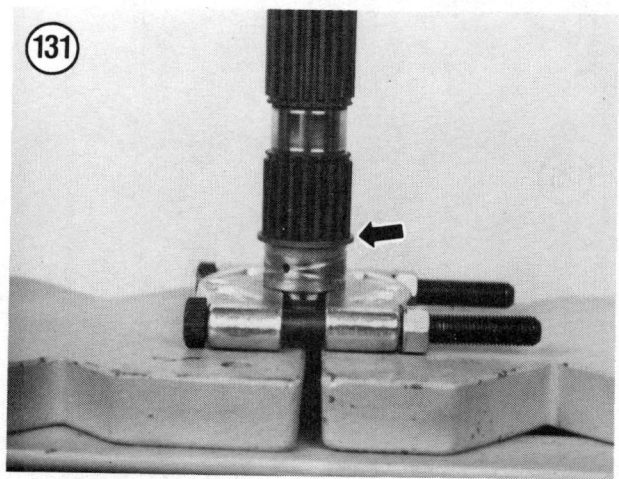

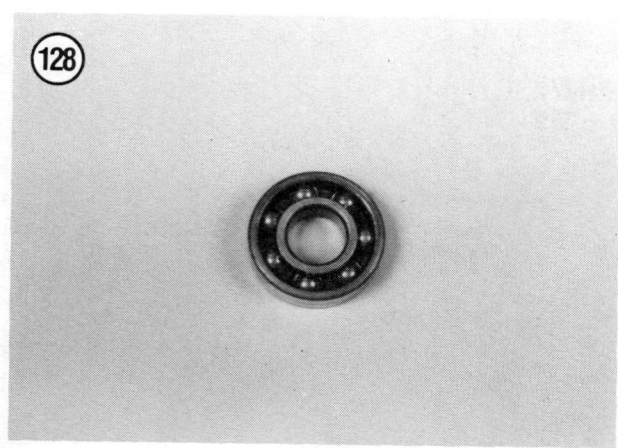

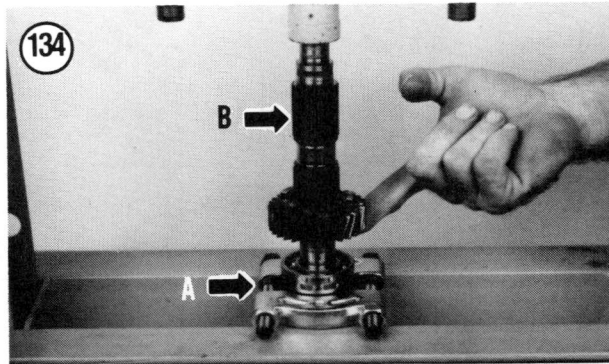

e. Press the bushing and thrust washer on until they bottom out (**Figure 131**) on the raised spline shoulder on the shaft.

f. Release the pressure and remove the output shaft assembly from the press.

3. Position the 5th gear with the engagement dog side going on first and slide on the 5th gear (**Figure 132**).

4. Slide on the thrust washer (A, **Figure 133**).

CAUTION
*When installing the ball bearing, apply pressure only on the **inner race**. If pressure is applied to the outer race the balls and the inner and outer races will be damaged.*

5. Install the ball bearing (B, **Figure 133**) onto the end of the output shaft.

6. To install the ball bearing, perform the following:

a. Place the insert (A, **Figure 134**) on the plates of the hydraulic press.

b. Place the transmission shaft assembly (B, **Figure 134**) into the hydraulic press.

c. Hold the 5th gear up away from the ball bearing.

d. Slowly apply pressure and press the ball bearing onto the output shaft.

e. Press the bearing on until it bottoms out (**Figure 135**).

f. Relax the hydraulic pressure and remove the shaft assembly from the hydraulic press.

7. After the bearing (**Figure 136**) has been pressed into place, spin it with your fingers to make sure it rotates freely with no binding.

8. Position the 3rd gear with the shift fork groove side going on last and slide on the 3rd gear (**Figure 119**).

9. Install a *new* circlip (**Figure 118**) and slide on the splined washer (**Figure 117**). Make sure the circlip is correctly seated in the countershaft groove.

10. Install the split needle bearing and hold it in place (**Figure 116**).

6

11. Position the 2nd gear with the receptacles for the engagement dogs side going on last and slide the 2nd gear (**Figure 115**) onto the split needle bearings.

12. Slide on the splined washer (**Figure 114**) and install a *new* circlip (**Figure 113**). Make sure the circlip is correctly seated in the countershaft groove.

13. Position the 4th gear with the engagement dogs side going on first and slide on the 4th gear (**Figure 112**).

14. Slide on the thrust washer (**Figure 111**).

15. To install the 1st gear bushing, perform the following:
   a. Install the 1st gear bushing on the end of the shaft (**Figure 110**).
   b. Place the transmission shaft assembly (A, **Figure 137**) on the plates (B, **Figure 137**) of the hydraulic press.
   c. Install the thrust washer (A, **Figure 138**) on top of the 1st gear bushing.
   d. Place a suitable size socket (B, **Figure 138**) on the thrust washer. The socket must fit the thrust washer and must also be large on the inside to clear the splines on the output shaft. If the inner surface of the socket touches the shaft splines the splines will be damaged and the socket may get pressed onto the shaft by mistake.
   e. Slowly press the 1st gear bushing onto the shaft. Press it on until it bottoms out (**Figure 139**).
   f. Relax the hydraulic pressure and remove the socket, thrust washer and the input shaft from the hydraulic press.

16. Position the 1st gear with the flush side going on last and slide on the 1st gear (**Figure 109**).

17. Slide off the thrust washer (**Figure 108**).

CAUTION
*When installing the ball bearing, apply pressure only on the **inner race**. If pressure is applied to the outer race the bearing will be damaged.*

18. To install the ball bearing, perform the following:
   a. Position the ball bearing with the closed side (**Figure 140**) of the bearing cage going on first.
   b. Install the ball bearing onto the end of the shaft (A, **Figure 141**).
   c. Place the transmission shaft assembly (B, **Figure 141**) on the plates (C, **Figure 141**) of the hydraulic press.
   d. Place a suitable size socket (D, **Figure 141**) onto the ball bearing. The socket must fit the inner race and must also be large on the inside to clear the splines on the output shaft. If the inner surface of the socket touches the shaft splines the splines will be damaged and the socket may get pressed onto the shaft by mistake.
   e. Slowly press the ball bearing onto the shaft. Press it on until it bottoms out (**Figure 142**).
   f. Relax the hydraulic pressure and remove the socket and the output shaft from the hydraulic press.

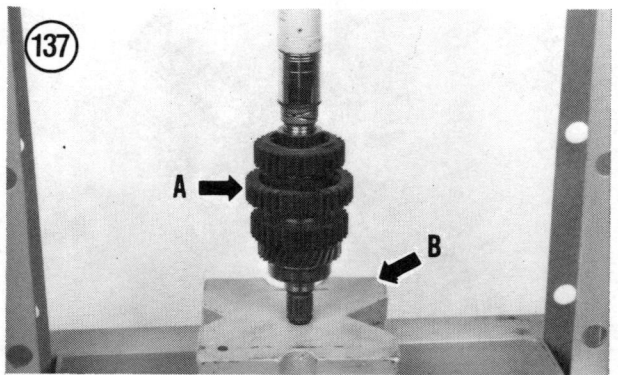

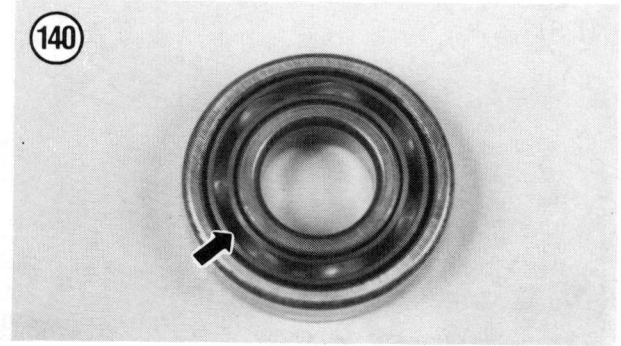

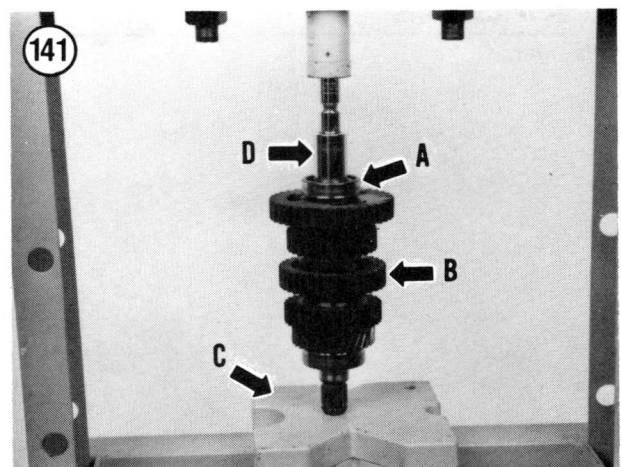

19. After the bearing (**Figure 143**) has been pressed into place, spin it with your fingers to make sure it rotates freely with no binding.

20. Refer to **Figure 144** for correct placement of all gears. Make sure all circlips are seated correctly in the output shaft grooves.

21. Make sure each gear engages properly to the adjoining gear where applicable.

22. After the output shaft assembly has been assembled, mesh the output shaft and the intermediate shaft together in their correct position (**Figure 145**). Check that all gears meet correctly. This is your last check prior to installing both assemblies into the transmission housing.

6

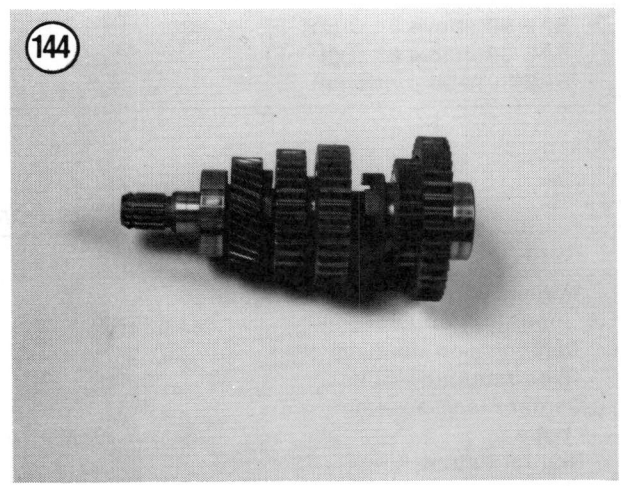

Tables are on the following page.

Table 1 TRANSMISSION SPECIFICATIONS

5-speed constant mesh transmission with integral spring damper.
Claw-type shift fork shifting mechanism.
Foot operated shift lever.
Gear ratios:
  1st gear: 4.50
  2nd gear: 2.96
  3rd gear: 2.30
  4th gear: 1.88
  5th gear: 1.67
Intermediate shaft end float: 0.05-0.15 mm (0.002-0.006 in.)
Output shaft end float: 0.05-0.15 mm (0.002-0.006 in.)
Transmission oil
  Capacity: 0.85 liter (1.8 pt.)
  Hypoid gear oil GL5
  SAE 90 above 5° C (41° F)
  SAE 80 below 5° C (41° F)
  SAE 80W-90 (optional)

Table 2 TRANSMISSION TORQUE SPECIFICATIONS

Item	N·m	ft.-lb.
Transmission housing-to-engine mounting bolts	15-17	11-12
Transmission housing side mounting bolts	39-45	28-32
Center stand assembly bolts	36-46	27-33
Neutral detent Allen bolt plug	11-15	8-10
Transmission housing cover bolts	8-10	6-7
Shift shaft Allen bolt	15-19	11-13

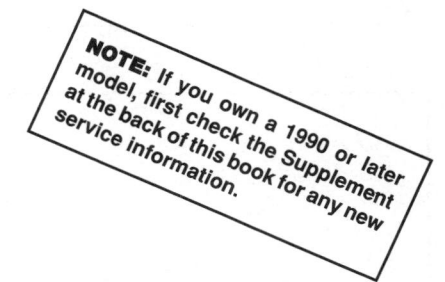

CHAPTER SEVEN

FUEL INJECTION SYSTEM, EMISSION CONTROLS AND EXHAUST SYSTEM

This chapter includes all fuel injection service procedures practical for home mechanics. It describes how the fuel injection system works, how to maintain it and how to replace some of the parts. Some of the components must be serviced by a BMW dealer either due to any applicable warranty or because they require expensive, complicated electronic troubleshooting equipment and a thorough knowledge of the fuel injection system. Some of these components are very expensive and could be damaged by someone unfamiliar with the test equipment or the components.

CAUTION
*Servicing the electronic fuel injection requires special precautions to prevent damage to the expensive electronic control units. Common electrical system service procedures acceptable on other bikes may damage several parts of the fuel injection system. Be sure to read **Fuel Injection Precautions** in this chapter.*

This chapter also includes service procedures for the emission control systems and the exhaust system. Fuel injection system specifications are listed in **Table 1**. **Table 1** and **Table 2** are at the end of this chapter.

Air filter service is covered in Chapter Three but service to the air filter case is covered in this chapter.

FUEL INJECTION SYSTEM DESCRIPTION

The electronic fuel injection system consists of a fuel pump and filter, 1 fuel injector per cylinder, fuel delivery pipe, fuel pressure regulator, throttle housing assembly, air filter assembly and all of the electronic support hardware. **Figure 1** is a basic layout of the fuel injection system.

The fuel injection system is electronically controlled and is known as the "LE-Jetronic" system. This system is similar in design to many of the fuel injection systems manufactured by Bosch and sold to various automobile manufacturers. The "L" stands for the German word "Luft" (air). The system measures the incoming air and supplies fuel in the correct ratio to the air flow. The "E" means it is the European version of the system and "Jetronic" is the trade name for the total fuel injection system. The system consists of three sub-systems: air flow system, fuel flow system and the electronic control systems.

Air Flow System

The air for the fuel/air mixture is drawn into the engine by engine vacuum. The volume of air is controlled by throttle butterflies within the throttle housing assembly and is measured by the air flow meter.

The incoming air travels through the air flow meter and passes a spring-loaded pivoting baffle plate. As engine speed increases, so does air flow, causing the pivoting baffle

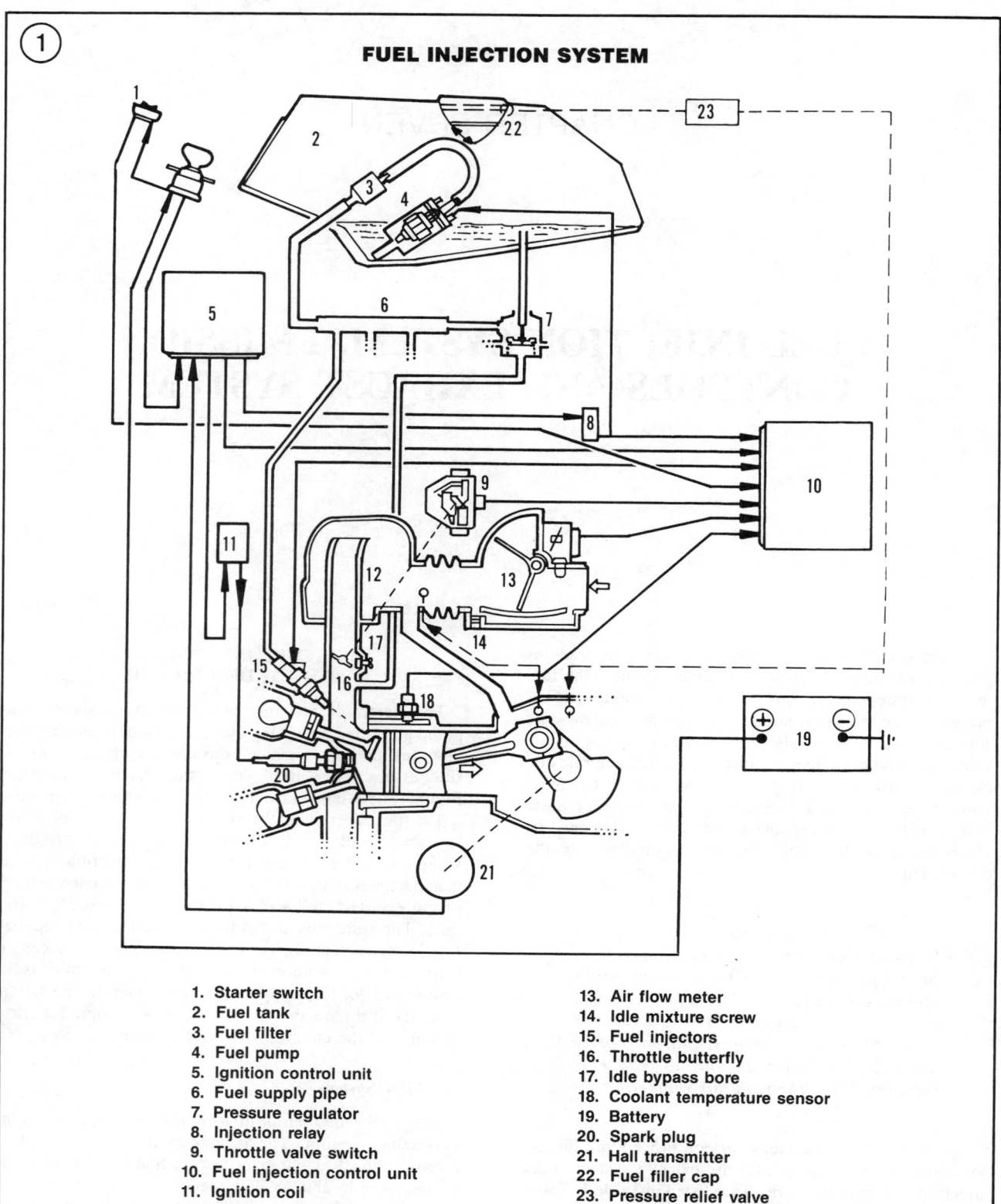

FUEL INJECTION SYSTEM

1. Starter switch
2. Fuel tank
3. Fuel filter
4. Fuel pump
5. Ignition control unit
6. Fuel supply pipe
7. Pressure regulator
8. Injection relay
9. Throttle valve switch
10. Fuel injection control unit
11. Ignition coil
12. Intake manifold
13. Air flow meter
14. Idle mixture screw
15. Fuel injectors
16. Throttle butterfly
17. Idle bypass bore
18. Coolant temperature sensor
19. Battery
20. Spark plug
21. Hall transmitter
22. Fuel filler cap
23. Pressure relief valve
    (models so equipped)

to move. Attached to one end of the pivoting baffle shaft is a variable resistor which transmits the baffle's position to the control unit for use in fuel mixture ratio, etc.

After passing the air flow meter baffle, the incoming air is then distributed to the throttle pipes within the throttle housing assembly. The throttle butterfly within the throttle pipe is attached to the throttle linkage which interconnects all throttle pipes. At one end of the throttle linkage is the throttle butterfly switch. This switch controls the fuel over-run fuel shutoff and the full-load mixture enrichment systems.

The air flow system measures the incoming air and meters it to achieve maximum fuel/air mixture for the cylinders. This system also provides controls for adjusting the CO content of the exhaust and the engine idle speed.

Fuel Flow System

The fuel flow system consists of the fuel tank, fuel pump, fuel filter, fuel supply pipe, pressure regulator and individual fuel injectors.

After the fuel leaves the fuel tank and the fuel pump, the fuel passes through a fuel filter and then flows to the fuel supply pipe to which the fuel injectors are attached. The fuel supply pipe is large enough to store a sufficient amount of pressurized fuel to help maintain a constant fuel pressure at all times while injection is actually taking place. This helps maintain an even flow and prevents fluctuations of fuel to the fuel injectors.

The fuel pump supplies pressurized fuel to the fuel injectors at a constant pressure. The pressure regulator maintains a constant fuel pressure of 248 kPa (36 psi). If the specified pressure is exceeded, the pressure regulator valve opens, allowing the fuel to return automatically to the fuel tank via a separate hose.

A vacuum hose connects the pressure regulator and the throttle pipe to the last cylinder (either No. 3 or No. 4). This enables a constant pressure differential to be maintained at the fuel injectors even with changes in engine vacuum. This helps maintain a near-perfect fuel/air ratio and eliminates a "too-rich" or "too-lean" fuel/air mixture that could lead either to excessive exhaust emissions or engine damage from burned valves.

The fuel is injected in all cylinders at the same time at each complete crankshaft rotation. Due to the safeguard built into the system, the fuel is injected only when there is an ignition pulse. The volume of fuel injected is controlled by the injector open time period.

Electronic Control System

The electronic control system consists of the electronic ignition control unit, throttle butterfly switch, fuel injection control unit, air flow meter, fuel injectors, coolant temperature sensor and the Hall transmitter assembly.

The system controls the length of time the fuel injectors are open to maintain optimum fuel economy, to keep the exhaust emissions low and to make sure the bike is responsive under all speed ranges and load conditions.

Engine temperature information is always fed into the fuel injection control unit. The control unit knows if the engine is cold or hot and compensates for this to obtain the optimum fuel/air mixture in relation to engine temperature. For cold starts, the mixture enrichment system is used to provide the engine with a "fuel-rich" mixture to aid in starting. The initial enrichment percentage is used only when the starter button is depressed and held in during engine cranking. After the starter button is released, a follow-up mixture enrichment system maintains a "fuel rich" mixture until the engine starts to warm up. After the engine reaches normal operating temperature the fuel percentage changes to the normal idle setting.

During rapid acceleration, the increased incoming air flow travels through the air flow meter and raises the spring-loaded pivoting baffle plate. The variable resistor attached to one end of the air flow meter pivoting baffle shaft sends a signal voltage to the fuel injection control unit, which initiates a rich fuel/air mixture for acceleration. When acceleration is slowed down, enrichment is reduced to the normal fuel/air mixture.

At full load, throttle opening of ⅔ or more, the air flow meter pivoting baffle sends a signal voltage to the fuel injection control unit which initiates a rich fuel/air mixture for this type of riding situation. When riding speed is slowed down, enrichment is reduced and the fuel/air mixture returns to normal.

When the throttle is closed during deceleration (overrun condition—throttle closed but engine rpm and ignition output still high), the fuel injection control unit shuts off signals to the fuel injectors if the engine speed is above 2,000 rpm. To prevent an engine stall situation, the fuel injectors are reactivated again once the engine slows down to 2,000 rpm.

The fuel injection control unit has 2 safety features to help avoid engine damage due to either mechanical or human error. The first feature shuts off the fuel pump if the engine suddenly stops running due to an ignition failure or other mechanical failure. The second feature is an "over-rev protection" that shuts off the fuel supply once the engine speed reaches 8,770 rpm. This second feature is also tied in with the ignition system, which automatically lowers the ignition advance curve at 8,650 rpm.

FUEL INJECTION SYSTEM COMPONENTS

This is a brief description of the fuel injection system components. It will help familiarize you with the system and the function of each component. An understanding of the function of each of the fuel injection system components and their relation to one another is a valuable aid for pinpointing a source of fuel injection problems. **Figure 1** shows the basic layout of all of the components.

7

Fuel Injection Control Unit

The fuel injection control unit does the following:
a. Receives signals from all of the support sensors to inject fuel into the cylinders in the correct amount and at the correct time. The control unit signals the injectors to one of their two basic discharge memories; one for small throttle openings and the other for large throttle openings. The fuel injector opening is fixed in the full open position. The fuel mixture is controlled by the length of time the injectors are open.
b. Controls the fuel pump.
c. Determines the optimum ignition timing based on the signals it receives from the various sensors.

Hall Transmitter

The Hall transmitter is located at the front of the crankshaft. The transmitter or pickup coil assembly is mounted to the engine cylinder block and the rotor is attached to the end of the crankshaft. This unit is part of the ignition system and provides ignition information to the ignition control unit.

Coolant Temperature Sensor

This sensor is located on the cylinder block and measures the engine coolant temperature. This information is sent to the fuel injection control unit.

Air Flow Meter

The incoming air flow travels through the air flow meter and passes a spring-loaded pivoting baffle plate. As engine speed increases, so does air flow, causing the pivoting baffle to move. Attached to one end of the pivoting baffle shaft is a variable resistor which transmits its position to the fuel injection control unit for use in fuel mixture ratio, etc.

Idle Mixture Screw

The idle mixture adjust screw is located on the base of the air flow meter. Adjusting this screw changes the bypass cross section, thus altering the fuel/air mixture at idle speed, which affects CO content of the exhaust.

Throttle Butterflies

The air for the fuel/air mixture is drawn into the engine by engine vacuum. The volume of air is controlled by throttle butterflies within the throttle housing assembly and is measured by the air flow meter.

The throttle butterfly within the throttle pipe is attached to the throttle linkage which interconnects all throttle pipes. At one end of the throttle linkage is the throttle butterfly switch. This switch controls the over-run (deceleration) fuel shutoff and the full-load mixture enrichment systems.

Fuel Pump and Filter

The fuel pump and filter are located within the fuel tank. The electric fuel pump is a roller-cell type and has an output rate of 45 liters/hour (11.9 gal./hour). The fuel pump is protected by a fine mesh inlet screen and the fuel is filtered again after leaving the fuel pump. The fuel pump supplies pressurized fuel to the fuel injectors at a constant pressure.

Pressure Regulator

The pressure regulator maintains a constant fuel pressure of 248 kPa (36 psi). If this specified pressure is exceeded, the pressure regulator valve opens, allowing the fuel to automatically return to the fuel tank via a separate hose.

The pressure regulator maintains a constant fuel pressure to the injectors.

Fuel Injectors

The fuel injectors are a solenoid-actuated constant-stroke pintle type consisting of a solenoid, plunger, needle valve and housing. When electrical current is applied to the solenoid coil, the valve is lifted and fuel is injected into the intake passageway adjacent to the intake valve. The fuel injectors are in a parallel circuit and the fuel is injected in all cylinders at the same time at each complete crankshaft rotation. Due to the safeguard built into the system, the fuel is injected only when there is an ignition pulse.

The size of the fuel injector's opening is fixed and fuel pressure is constant at all times. The amount of fuel injected is controlled by the length of time the injector is open, somewhere between 1.5-9 ms. The opening duration is controlled by the fuel injection control unit and depends on engine speed and air intake volume.

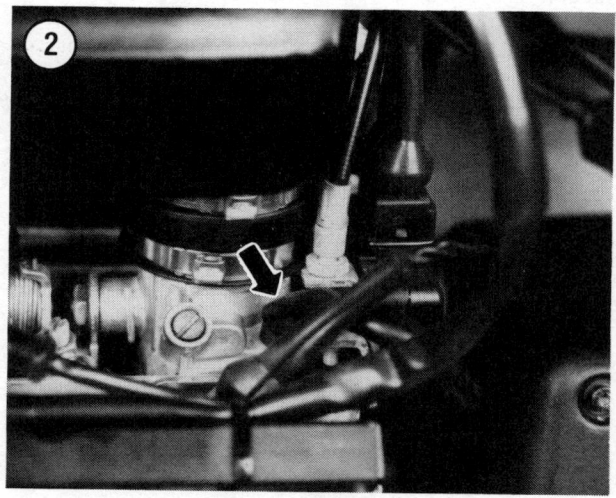

Ignition Control Unit

The ignition control unit receives signals from the Hall transmitter and the ignition switch. The unit interprets this information and signals the fuel injection control unit, the ignition coils and the injection relay.

It determines the optimum ignition timing based on the signals it receives from the various components.

DEPRESSURIZING
THE FUEL SYSTEM

The fuel system is pressurized at 248 kPa (36 psi) while the engine is running. This pressure is maintained for some time after the engine is shut off. The system *must be depressurized* before any fuel hose is disconnected.

There are several ways to depressurize the fuel system; 3 ways are presented in this procedure.

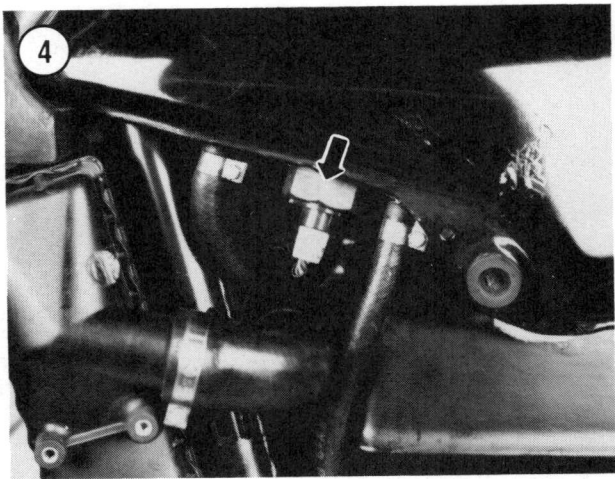

1. Relieving the fuel pressure via the pressure regulator:
   a. Disconnect the pressure regulator vacuum hose (**Figure 2**) from the throttle body on the last cylinder.
   b. Apply vacuum to the vacuum hose either by mouth or a hand operated vacuum pump like the Mity-Vac (used for brake system bleeding).
   c. Applying the vacuum will relieve the fuel pressure by opening the valve, thus allowing the fuel to recirculate back into the fuel tank until the pressure is relieved.
2. Relieving the fuel pressure by emptying the fuel system down-stream from the fuel pump:
   a. Remove the right-hand frame side cover.
   b. Start the engine and let it idle.
   c. Disconnect the fuel pump electrical connector from the main wiring harness. Refer to **Figure 3** for K75 models or **Figure 4** for K100 models.
   d. Allow the engine to idle until the fuel is exhausted within the fuel line from the fuel filter to the fuel supply pipe and fuel injectors. When the engine stops running, the fuel is exhausted and the pressure is relieved.
   e. After the engine has stopped, turn the ignition switch to the OFF position and then reconnect the fuel pump electrical connector.

> *WARNING*
> *Before attempting to depressurize the fuel system in Step 3, be sure to have a fire extinguisher rated for gasoline or chemical fires within reach. Do not smoke or allow anyone to smoke or work where there are any open flames (e.g., water heater or clothes dryer gas pilots). The work area must be well-ventilated.*

> *WARNING*
> *This step is the only dangerous one of the 3 presented here. Only perform this step if the bike is allowed to cool overnight at room temperature (not run for at least 12 hours). This will allow the fuel system to partially depressurize by itself due to pressure leakage (not fuel leakage). Do **not** perform this step on a bike that has a warm engine and a hot exhaust system. If any of the fuel should spill on a hot component it would present a hazardous fire condition.*

3. Relieving the fuel pressure by disconnecting the fuel hose from the fuel tank:
   a. Remove the frame left-hand side cover.
   b. Disconnect the battery negative lead as described under *Battery* in Chapter Three.

7

c. On models so equipped, remove any body panels from the front left-hand side of the fuel tank.

d. Wrap a clean shop rag around the fuel line at the fuel tank to catch the fuel that will be expelled when the fuel line is disconnected.

> *WARNING*
> *Wear eye protection to protect your eyes from any fuel that may spurt out of the fuel line when it is disconnected.*

e. Slowly disconnect the fuel line (**Figure 5**) from the fuel tank outlet pipe.

f. Place a golf tee into the fuel line to prevent the entry of foreign matter.

g. Discard the gasoline-soaked shop rag properly.

h. Wipe up any spilled fuel immediately.

FUEL INJECTION PRECAUTIONS

> *CAUTION*
> *Servicing the electronic fuel injection system requires special precautions to prevent damage to the expensive fuel injection control unit. Common electrical system service procedures acceptable on other bikes may damage several parts of the fuel injection system.*

Fuel Injection Control Unit Precautions

1. Unless otherwise specified in a procedure, do not start the bike while any electrical connectors are disconnected. Do not disconnect the battery cables or any electrical connector while the ignition switch is ON. The fuel injection control unit will be ruined.

2. Before disconnecting any electrical connectors, turn the ignition switch OFF.

3. When repairs are completed, do not try to start the engine without double checking to make sure all fuel injection electrical connectors are connected; faulty connectors may damage the control unit and its related components.

4. Do not disconnect the battery while the engine is running.

5. Do not apply anything other than a 12-volt battery to the bike's electrical system. The bike's battery must be removed before attaching a battery charger.

6. Do not use any piece of electrical test equipment that has its own power supply (ohmmeter, multimeter, megger

or homemade battery and test lamp unit) as the applied voltage, minimal as it is, may destroy a portion of the very sensitive circuits in the system. Use only the specified BMW test equipment suggested in the test procedures.

Fuel System Precautions

1. The fuel system is pressurized so wear eye protection whenever working on the fuel system, especially when disconnecting fuel lines.

2. The fuel pump is cooled and its bearings are lubricated by the fuel it is pumping. Refill the fuel tank when there is a minimum of 1/4 tank remaining. If the pump is operated without fuel, its bearings may be damaged. The fuel pump cannot be disassembled; if damaged, it must be replaced.

3. Do not add any lubricants, preservatives or additives to the gasoline as fuel system corrosion or clogging may result.

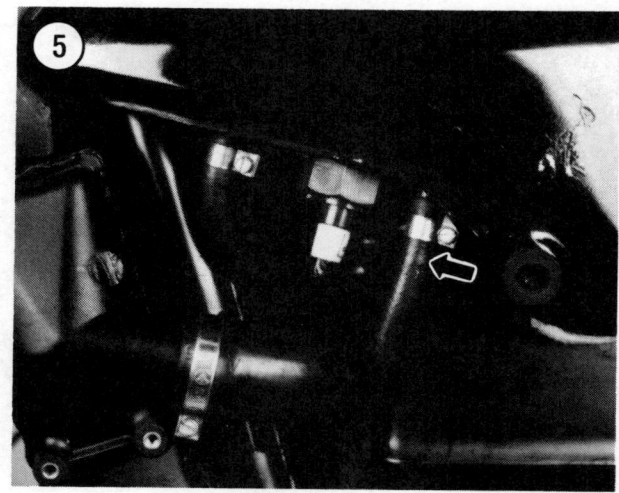

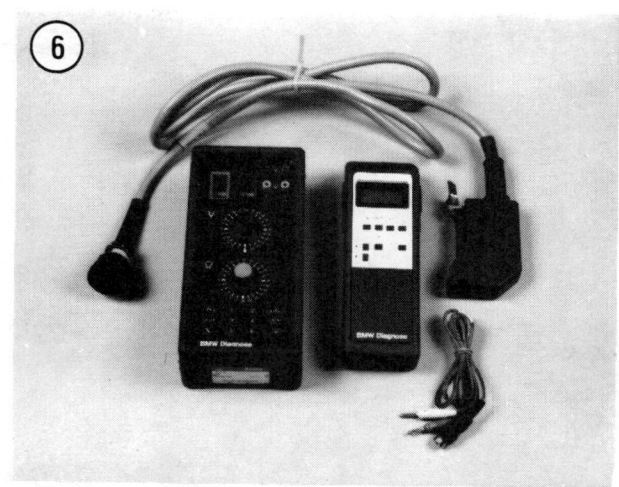

TROUBLESHOOTING

The control unit is a very complex and *expensive* piece of electronic hardware, therefore entrust any service work on the control unit to a BMW dealer. If you perform any service work on the control unit yourself, it will void any applicable BMW warranty.

The special BMW troubleshooting equipment shown in **Figure 6** is priced in the thousands of dollars and is not a practical purchase for home mechanics. The service charge to troubleshoot the fuel injection system by a BMW dealer will be minimal compared to the purchase price of this equipment.

FUEL INJECTORS AND FUEL SUPPLY PIPE

Removal/Installation

Refer to **Figure 7** for K75 models or **Figure 8** for K100 models for this procedure.

1. Remove the fuel tank as described in this chapter.

2. Remove the frame left-hand side cover.

3. Disconnect the battery negative lead as described under *Battery* in Chapter Three.

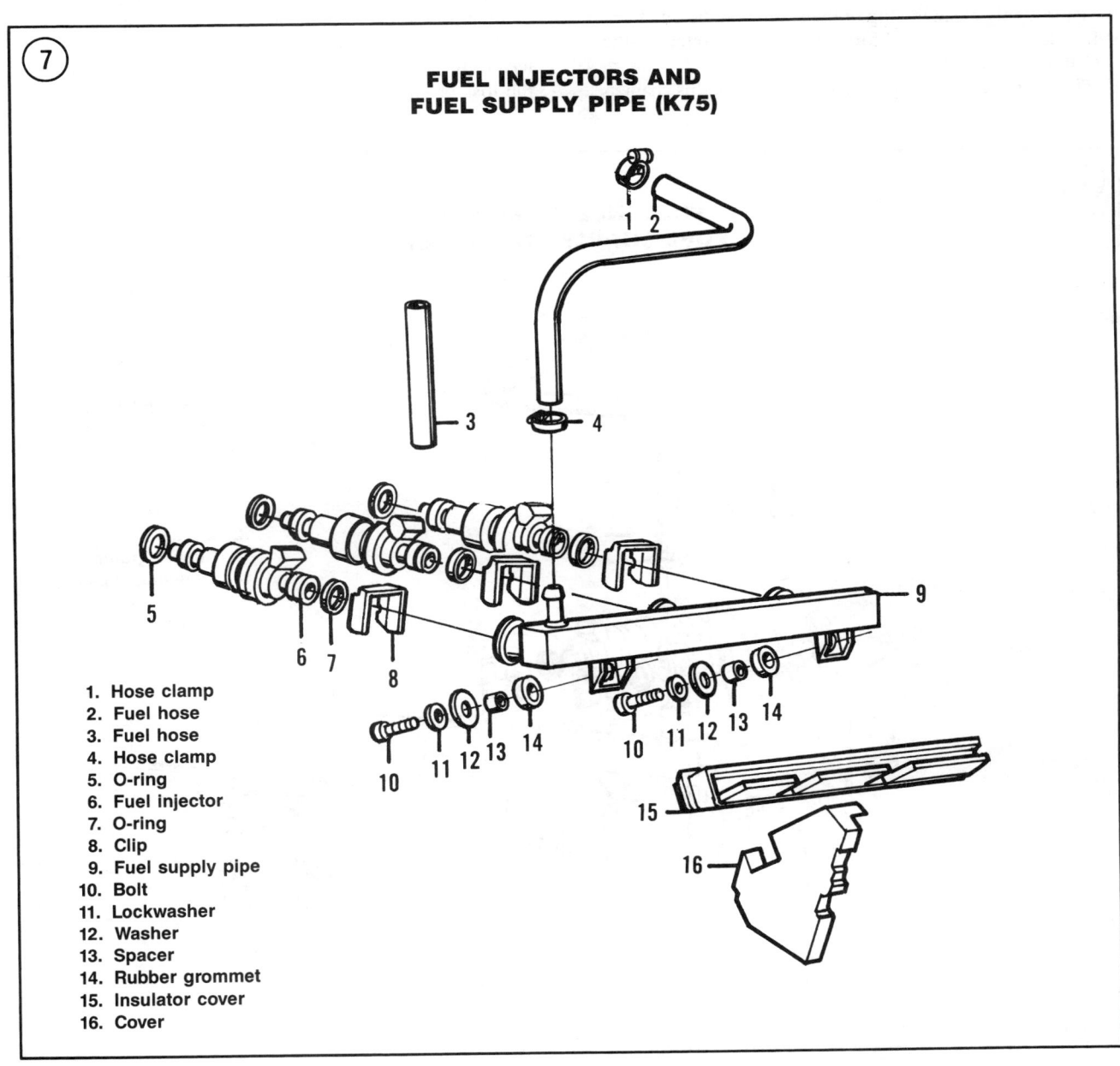

FUEL INJECTORS AND FUEL SUPPLY PIPE (K75)

1. Hose clamp
2. Fuel hose
3. Fuel hose
4. Hose clamp
5. O-ring
6. Fuel injector
7. O-ring
8. Clip
9. Fuel supply pipe
10. Bolt
11. Lockwasher
12. Washer
13. Spacer
14. Rubber grommet
15. Insulator cover
16. Cover

4. Remove the front fairing knee pads (K100 models) or lower panels (K75 models) as described under *Front Fairing Removal/Installation* in Chapter Thirteen.

CAUTION
All dirt and foreign matter must be removed from the cylinder head prior to removing the fuel injectors. If any dirt or foreign matter falls into the fuel injector opening in the cylinder head it will cause internal engine damage.

5. Thoroughly clean the top of the engine on the left-hand side. Blow off all dirt and foreign matter surrounding the fuel injectors and fuel supply pipe.
6. Depressurize the fuel system as described in this chapter.

7. Disengage the wire clip securing the electrical connector to each fuel injector.
8. Carefully disconnect the electrical connector (A, **Figure 9**) from each fuel injector. If necessary, remove any tie wraps securing the electrical wires to the fuel supply pipe. Carefully move the electrical wires out of the way.

NOTE
Place a shop cloth under the following hoses before disconnecting them and catch any remaining fuel.

9. Disconnect the fuel supply hose (**Figure 10**) at the front and the pressure regulator hose (**Figure 11**) at the rear of the fuel supply pipe. Plug the ends of both hoses with golf tees to prevent the entry of foreign matter and to prevent the loss of any residual fuel.

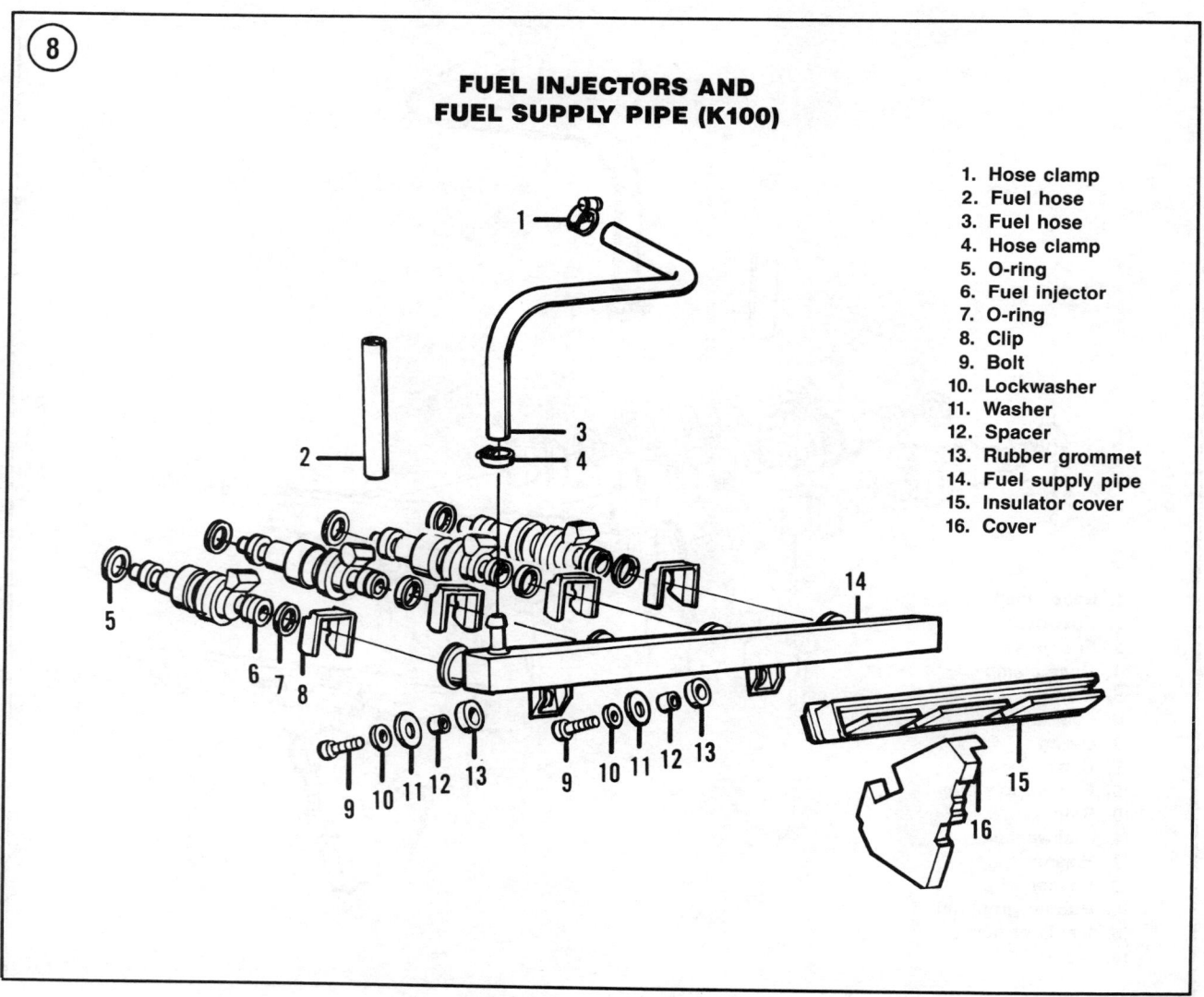

⑧

FUEL INJECTORS AND FUEL SUPPLY PIPE (K100)

1. Hose clamp
2. Fuel hose
3. Fuel hose
4. Hose clamp
5. O-ring
6. Fuel injector
7. O-ring
8. Clip
9. Bolt
10. Lockwasher
11. Washer
12. Spacer
13. Rubber grommet
14. Fuel supply pipe
15. Insulator cover
16. Cover

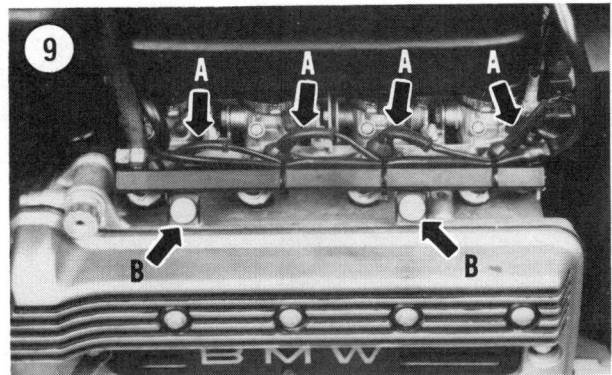

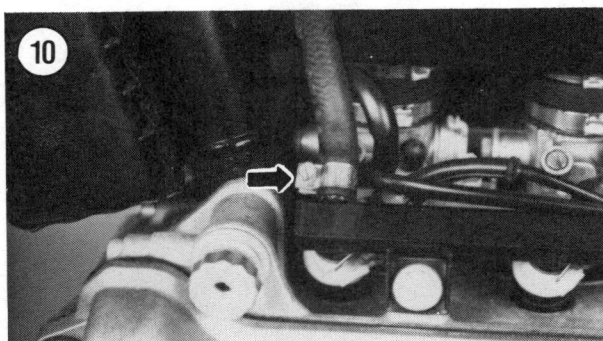

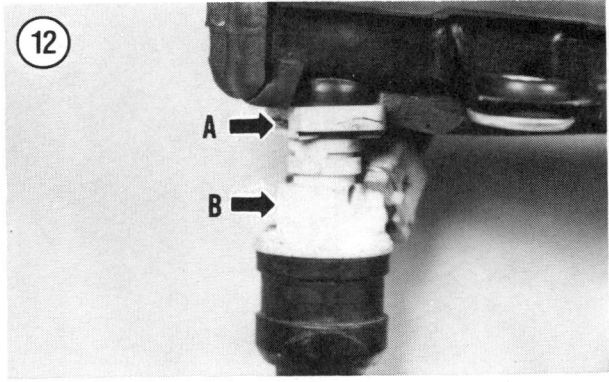

10. On models so equipped, remove the insulating cover.

NOTE
Place shop cloths under the fuel supply pipe to absorb the gasoline remaining in the fuel pipe.

11. Slowly loosen the bolts (B, **Figure 9**) securing the fuel supply pipe to the cylinder head. Remove the bolts, lockwashers and washers. Don't lose the spacer in the rubber grommet in the mounting tabs.
12. Carefully pull straight out and remove the fuel injectors and fuel supply pipe assembly from the cylinder head. Allow the remaining gasoline to drain out of the fuel supply pipe onto the shop cloths. Discard or wash out the shop cloths. Do not store the shop cloths that are saturated with gasoline.
13. To prevent the entry of dirt or foreign matter, cover the fuel injector holes in the cylinder head with pieces of duct tape or stuff a clean lint-free cloth into each opening.

NOTE
If the existing fuel injectors are going to be reinstalled, mark them so they will be reinstalled on the fuel supply pipe in the same location. The No. 1 cylinder is at the front of the engine.

14. Using a pair of pliers, carefully remove the clip (A, **Figure 12**) securing the fuel injector to the fuel supply pipe and remove the fuel injector.
15. Carefully remove each fuel injector (B, **Figure 12**) from the fuel supply pipe.
16. Remove and discard the O-ring seal from each end of the fuel injectors (**Figure 13**). The O-rings must be replaced every time the fuel injector is removed to maintain a leak-free installation.

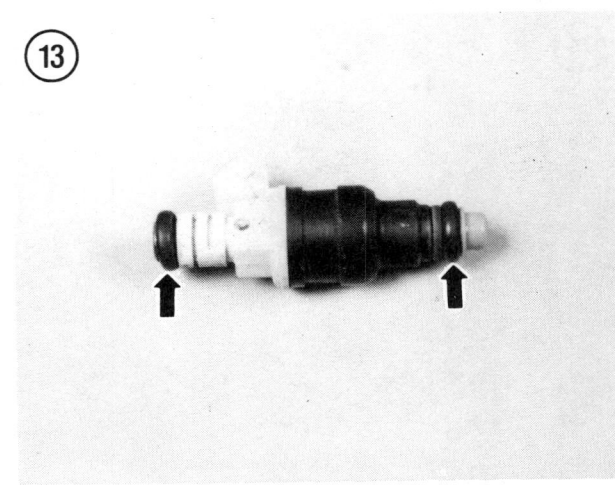

7

17. Make sure each end of each fuel injector is open and clean. Refer to **Figure 14** and **Figure 15**.

18. Inspect each fuel injector receptacle in the fuel supply pipe. Clean off any rust or corrosion and apply a light coat of clean engine oil to the receptacle.

19. Install by reversing these removal steps, noting the following.

20. Coat the new O-ring seal with clean engine oil and install the new O-rings onto each end of the fuel injectors. Refer to **Figure 16** and **Figure 17**.

21. Install the fuel injector carefully and squarely (to avoid damage to the O-ring seal) into the fuel supply pipe.

22. Hold the fuel injectors securely into the fuel supply pipe and install this assembly onto the cylinder head.

23. Tighten the retaining bolts in a staggered pattern and in 2-3 stages. Tighten the bolts securely.

24. Make sure the fuel injector electrical connectors (**Figure 18**) are free of corrosion. Push them onto the fuel injector and make sure the connection is tight. Make sure the wire clip holds the connector on securely.

WARNING
In the following step, do not allow the engine to start up in case there is a gasoline leak.

25. After all of the hoses and lines are attached, turn the ignition ON, but do not operate the starter. After the fuel pump runs for approximately 2 seconds the fuel pressure in the fuel line will rise. Turn the ignition switch OFF.

WARNING
*Do **not** start or ride the bike if there is the slightest fuel leak. Any type of fuel leak can lead to a dangerous fire that could result in rider body burns and the possible total loss of the bike.*

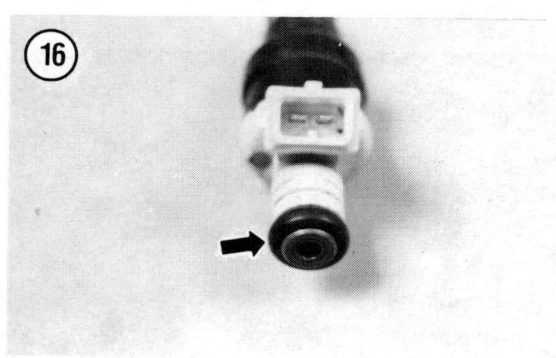

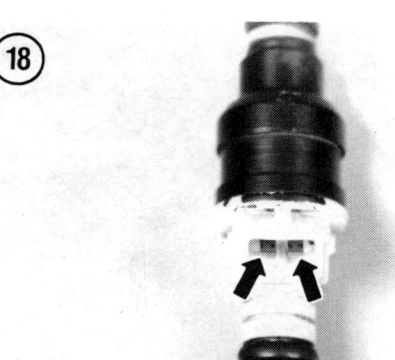
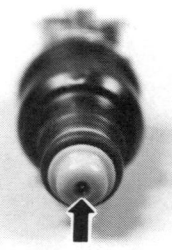

26. Repeat Step 25 two or three times and check for gasoline leaks. Fix any leakage before starting the engine.
27. Start the engine and recheck for gasoline leakage.

THROTTLE HOUSING AND INTAKE MANIFOLD

The throttle body is extremely complicated and tampering with it may void any applicable BMW emission control warranty. The only procedures recommended for the home mechanic are removal and installation of the throttle housing from the cylinder head. The only replacement parts are the ones shown removed from the main assembly in the exploded view drawings relating to this procedure.

Removal/Installation

Refer to **Figure 19** (K75 throttle housing) **Figure 20** (K100 throttle housing) and **Figure 21** (air plenum chamber and inlet tubes) for this procedure.
1. Depressurize the fuel system as described in this chapter.
2. Remove the air filter housing as described in this chapter.

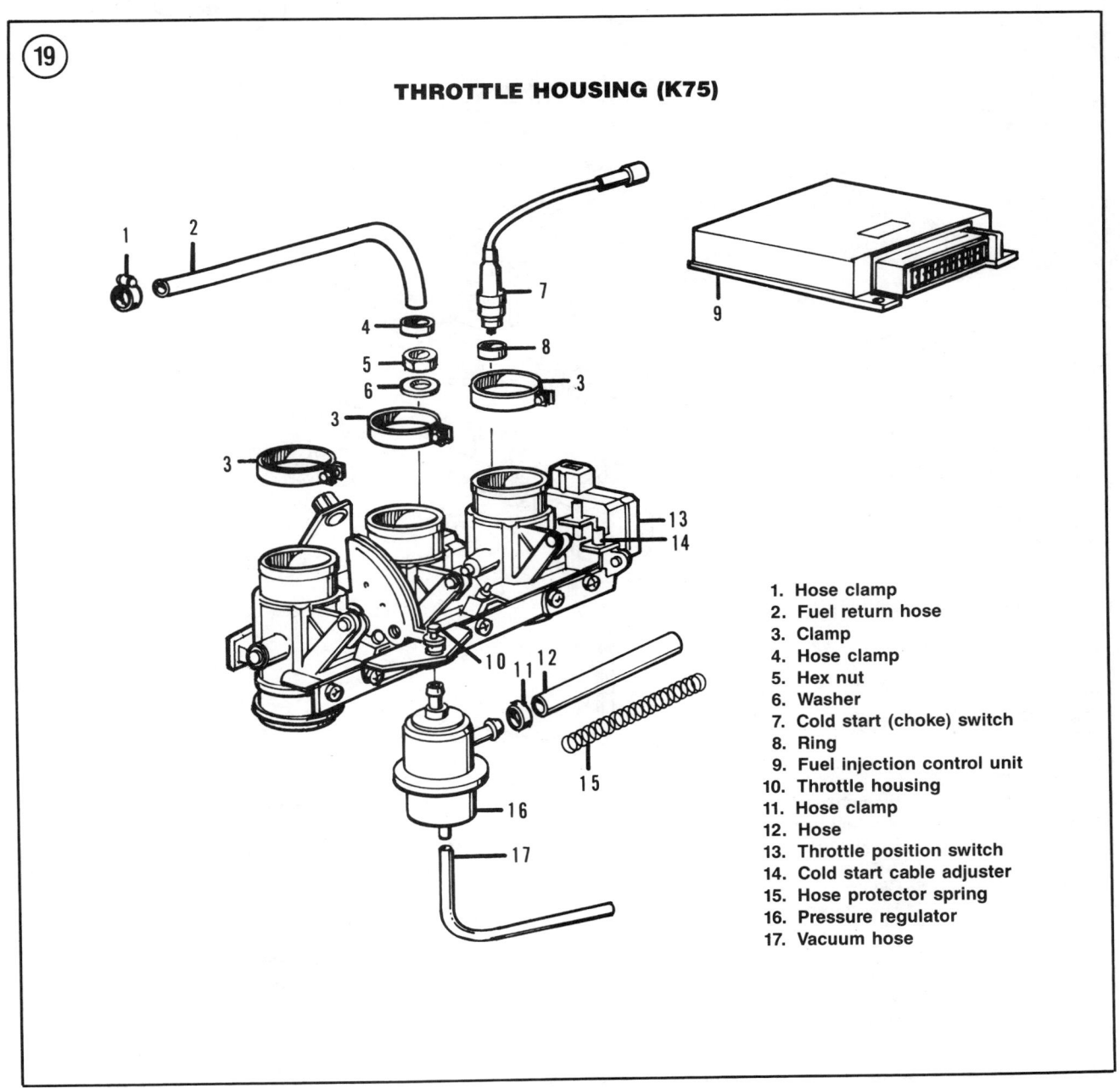

(19)

THROTTLE HOUSING (K75)

1. Hose clamp
2. Fuel return hose
3. Clamp
4. Hose clamp
5. Hex nut
6. Washer
7. Cold start (choke) switch
8. Ring
9. Fuel injection control unit
10. Throttle housing
11. Hose clamp
12. Hose
13. Throttle position switch
14. Cold start cable adjuster
15. Hose protector spring
16. Pressure regulator
17. Vacuum hose

7

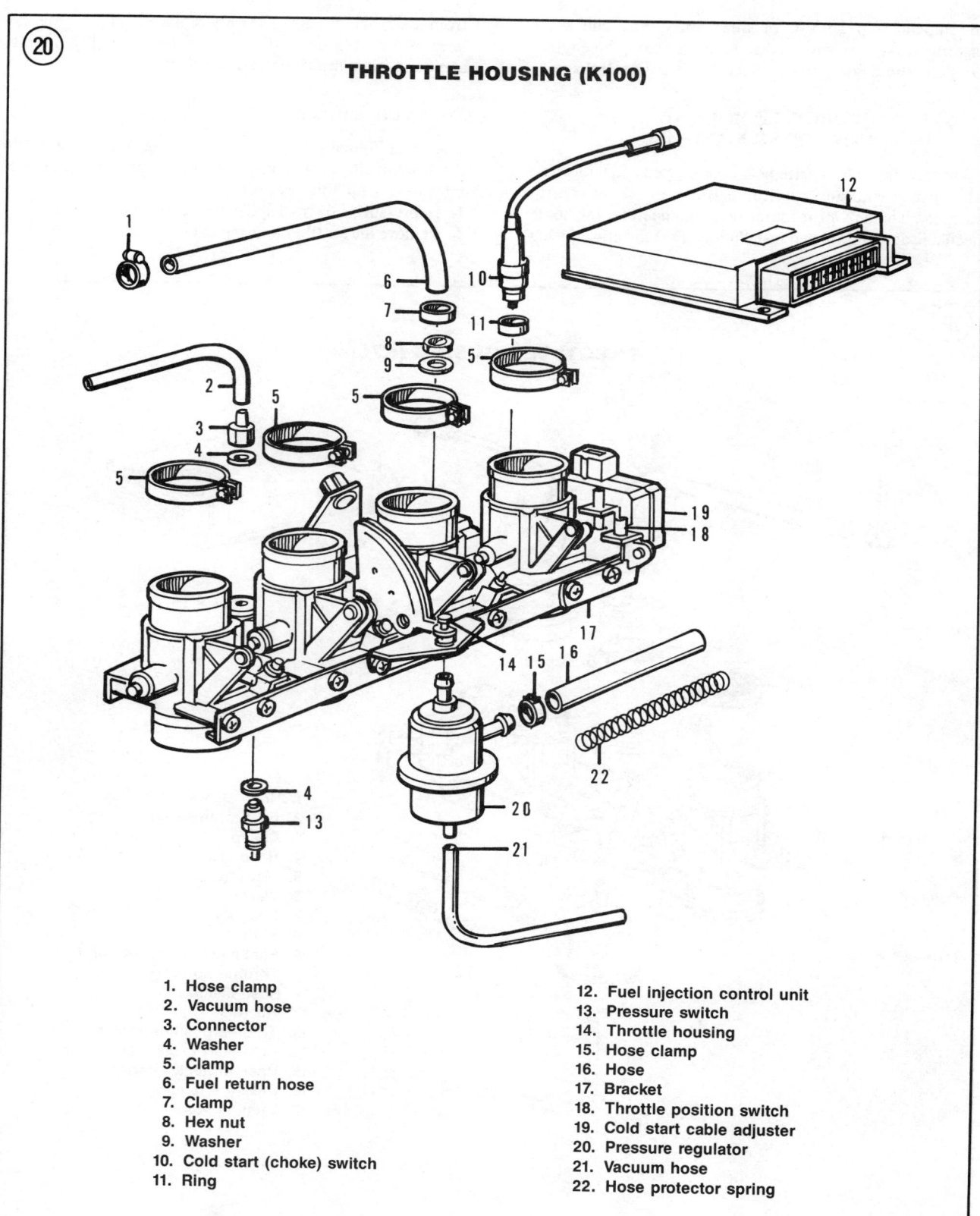

THROTTLE HOUSING (K100)

1. Hose clamp
2. Vacuum hose
3. Connector
4. Washer
5. Clamp
6. Fuel return hose
7. Clamp
8. Hex nut
9. Washer
10. Cold start (choke) switch
11. Ring
12. Fuel injection control unit
13. Pressure switch
14. Throttle housing
15. Hose clamp
16. Hose
17. Bracket
18. Throttle position switch
19. Cold start cable adjuster
20. Pressure regulator
21. Vacuum hose
22. Hose protector spring

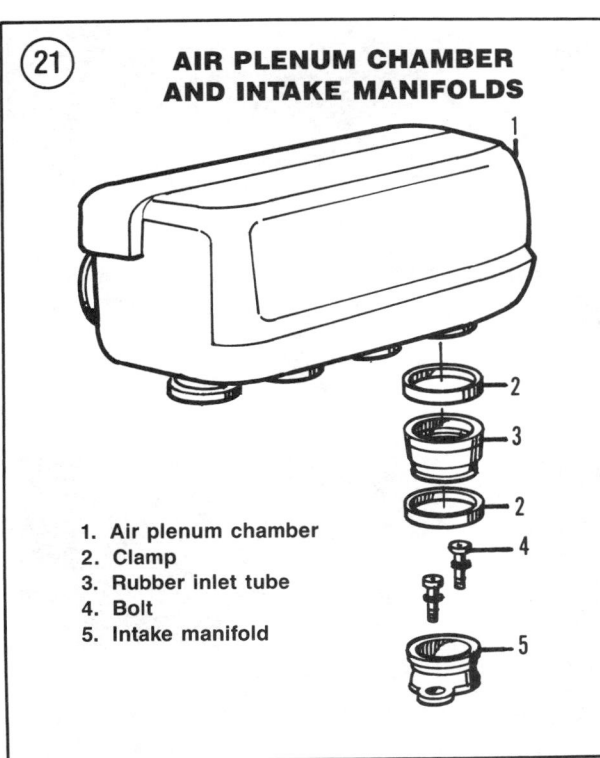

AIR PLENUM CHAMBER AND INTAKE MANIFOLDS

1. Air plenum chamber
2. Clamp
3. Rubber inlet tube
4. Bolt
5. Intake manifold

3. Disconnect the pressure regulator vacuum hose (**Figure 22**) from the throttle body on the last cylinder.

4. Remove the fuel injectors and fuel supply pipe assembly as described in this chapter.

5. Loosen the clamp screw securing the crankcase breather hose (**Figure 23**) to the intake manifold. Disconnect the hose from the intake manifold.

6. Disconnect the throttle cable (**Figure 24**) from the throttle wheel.

7. Disconnect the choke cable (**Figure 25**) from the throttle housing.

8. Disconnect the throttle position switch electrical connector (**Figure 26**).

7

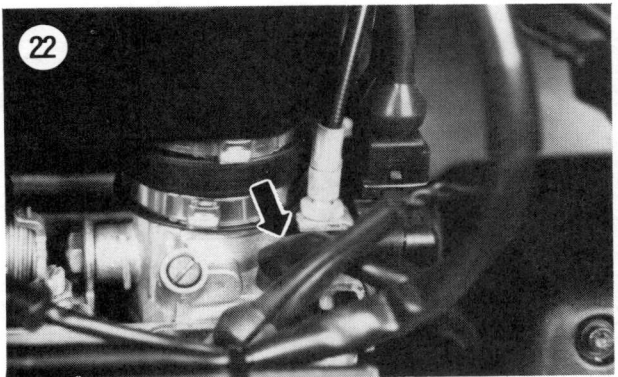

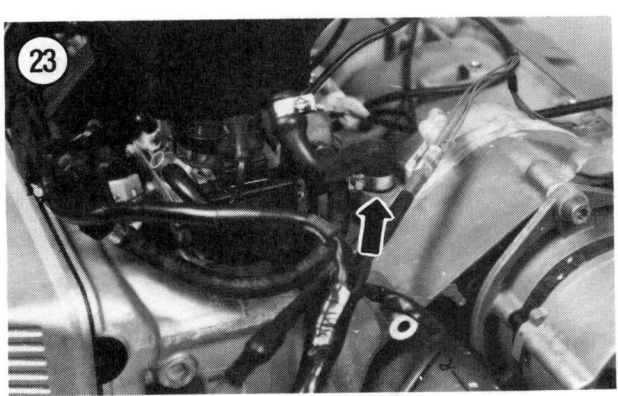

9. Disconnect the choke warning lamp switch electrical connector.

10. Loosen the clamp screws on the individual intake manifolds securing the rubber inlet tubes to the intake manifolds.

11. Carefully pull the throttle housing and air plenum chamber assembly up and off of the intake manifolds (**Figure 27**).

12. Place duct tape over, or place a clean lint-free cloth into, each throat of the intake manifolds to prevent the entry of foreign matter.

13. If necessary, loosen the locknut (**Figure 28**) securing the pressure regulator to the throttle housing and remove the pressure regulator.

14. On California models, if necessary, remove the screws (**Figure 29**) securing the pressure relief valve to the throttle housing and remove the pressure relief valve.

15. Install by reversing these removal steps, noting the following.

16. Apply a light coat of rubber lube or Armor All to the inside surfaces of the intake manifolds. This will make installation of the throttle housing throats easier.

NOTE
If the pressure regulator vacuum hose has come loose from its fitting, make sure it is free of oil prior to installing it onto the fitting.

17. Make sure the pressure regulator vacuum hose (**Figure 22**) and fitting on the throttle body are free of any oil. If necessary, clean with aerosol electrical contact cleaner.

18. Be sure to tighten the clamping screws securely to avoid an air leak in the system which would lead to a too-lean fuel/air mixture, resulting in engine damage.

19. Adjust the throttle cable as described under *Throttle Cable Adjustment* in Chapter Three.

Inspection

1. Inspect the intake manifolds (A, **Figure 30**) for cracks or damage. To replace, remove the bolts (B, **Figure 30**)

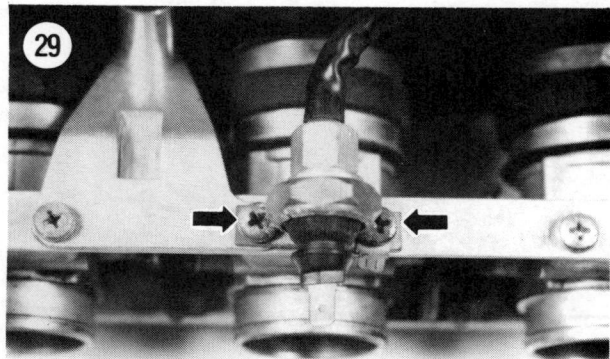

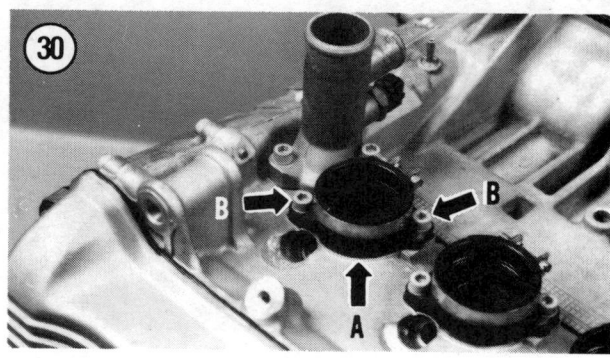

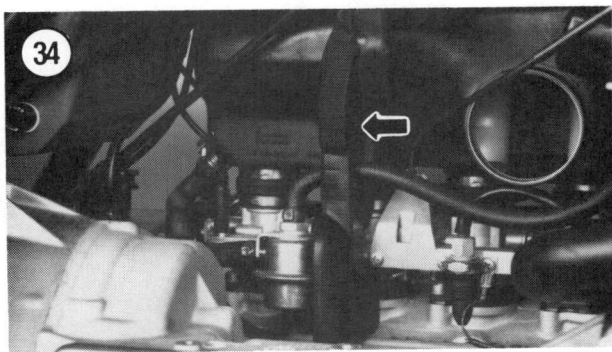

securing the intake manifolds and remove the manifolds. Reinstall and tighten the bolts securely.

2. Make sure the screws securing the throttle housings to the mounting bracket (**Figure 31**) are tight. Tighten if necessary.

3. Inspect the throttle plate (**Figure 32**) in each throttle housing for wear or damage. If any are damaged, the throttle housing assembly must be replaced.

4. If necessary, remove the air plenum chamber assembly as follows:

    a. Use BMW special tool (part No. 13 1 500) and loosen the hose clamps (A, **Figure 33**) securing the rubber inlet tube to each throttle housing.

    b. Carefully separate the air plenum chamber assembly (B, **Figure 33**) from the throttle housing assembly.

PRESSURE REGULATOR

Removal/Installation

Refer to **Figure 19** (K75 models) or **Figure 20** (K100 models) for this procedure.

1. Depressurize the fuel system as described in this chapter.
2. Remove the air filter case as described in this chapter.
3. Remove the rubber heat shield (**Figure 34**).

NOTE
Before removing the hoses in the following steps, mark them and the fittings on the pressure regulator so the hoses will be reinstalled onto the correct fittings.

4. Carefully remove the vacuum hose (A, **Figure 35**) from the base of the pressure regulator.

5. Loosen the clamping screw (B, **Figure 35**) and carefully slide off the fuel supply hose from the side of the pressure regulator.

6. Loosen the clamping screw and carefully slide off the fuel return hose (C, **Figure 35**) from the top of the pressure regulator.

7. Unscrew the hex nut (D, **Figure 35**) and washer securing the pressure regulator to the mounting bracket on the throttle housing assembly.

8. Install by reversing these removal steps, noting the following.

WARNING
If the fuel supply hose requires replacement, be sure to use a BMW replacement fuel hose that is rated for the pressure requirements of the fuel system. If a lesser rated hose is used it may burst under the system pressure and will spray fuel over a hot engine leading to a serious fire.

7

9. Inspect the vacuum and fuel hoses for cracks and deterioration. Replace if necessary.

10. Inspect the pressure regulator for cracks or damage.

11. Connect a vacuum line to the bottom fitting. Apply vacuum to the pressure regulator and check for any signs of vacuum leakage (a slight hissing sound). If the unit fails this test, it must be replaced.

12. Tighten the hex nut securing the pressure regulator to the torque specification listed in **Table 2**.

13. Be sure to attach the hoses to the correct fittings on the pressure regulator.

14. Tighten the hose clamps securely.

AIR FLOW METER

Removal/Inspection/Installation

1. Perform Steps 1-9 of *Air Filter Case Removal/ Installation* in this chapter and remove the air filter upper case half.

2. Remove the Allen screws (A, **Figure 36**) securing the air flow meter to the upper case half.

3. Loosen the clamping screw (B, **Figure 36**) securing the air flow meter to the air outlet hose.

4. Note the placement of the electrical cable within the air filter case.

5. If not already disconnected, remove the wire clip and disconnect the electrical connector from the air flow meter.

6. Carefully remove the air flow meter (**Figure 37**) from the air outlet hose and remove the air flow meter.

7. Inspect the exterior of the air flow meter (**Figure 38**) for damage. Do not attempt to work on the air flow meter as there are no replacement parts available.

8. Check the air temperature sensor (**Figure 39**) for damage or deterioration.

9. Install by reversing these removal steps, noting the following.

10. There are no test procedures for the air flow meter that can be performed by the home mechanic. If you believe the meter to be faulty, have the meter tested by a BMW dealer.

11. Make sure to route the electrical cable correctly so that it won't get pinched or damaged in any way.

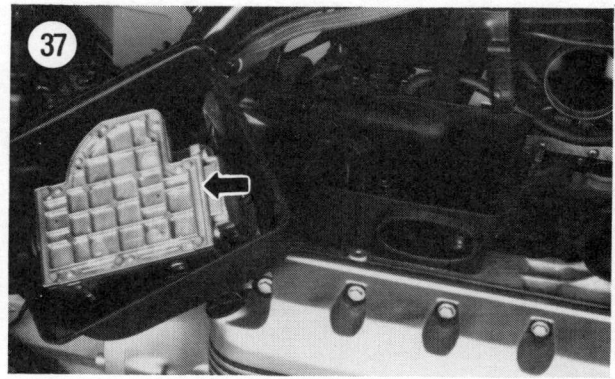

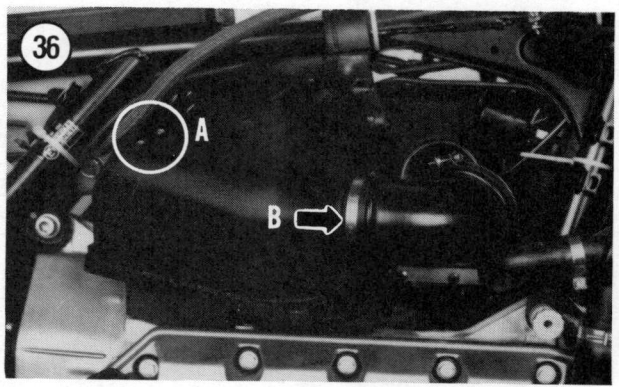

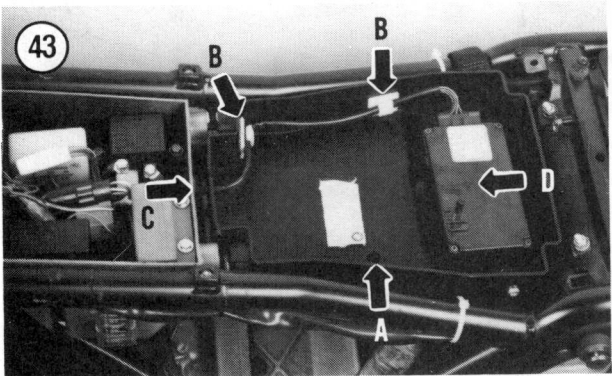

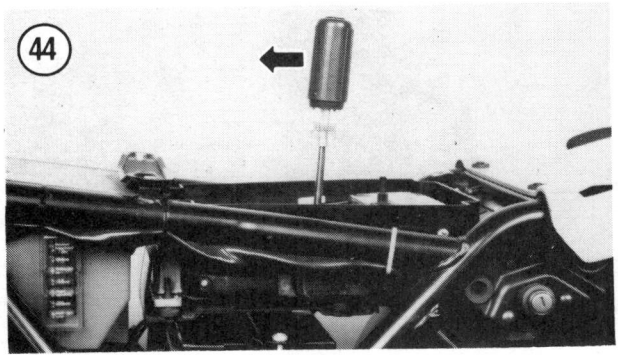

12. Make sure the electrical connector is free of corrosion and is tight.

FUEL INJECTION CONTROL UNIT

Removal/Installation

1. Raise or remove the seat.
2. Remove the left-hand frame side cover (**Figure 40**).
3. Remove the storage tray cover (**Figure 41**).
4. Carefully pull out on the front edge and remove the protective cover (**Figure 42**) from the fuel injection control unit.
5. Insert a long screwdriver through the hole (A, **Figure 43**) in the storage compartment tray. Insert the screwdriver blade into the keeper on the electrical connector and move the handle toward the front of the bike (**Figure 44**).
6. Release the keeper, pull the electrical connector (**Figure 45**) toward the rear and disconnect it from the fuel injection control unit.
7. On models equipped with the BMW electronic alarm system, perform the following:
   a. Remove the screws (A, **Figure 46**) securing the alarm unit to the storage tray.

7

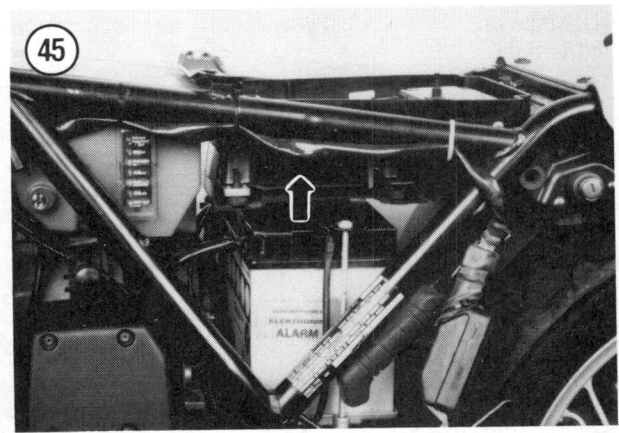

b. Unhook the electrical wires from the clips (B, **Figure 43**) on the side of the storage tray.

c. Pull the alarm wires out of the notch and grommet (C, **Figure 43**) at the front of the storage tray.

d. Remove the alarm unit (D, **Figure 43**).

8. Pull the storage tray (along with the fuel injection unit) up and out of the frame (B, **Figure 46**) and remove it.

9. To remove the control unit from the storage tray, perform the following:

a. Remove the locking pins securing the control unit to the storage tray. Refer to **Figure 47** and **Figure 48**.

b. Slide the control unit out of the storage tray.

c. Reinstall the control unit into the storage tray.

d. Insert the locking pins (**Figure 49**) in from the bottom and make sure they go all the way into the rubber holders at the front and rear of the control unit.

10. Inspect the bottom surface of the storage tray (**Figure 50**) for damage. If damaged, replace the storage tray as it must be able to securely hold the control unit to protect it from damage.

11. Install by reversing these removal steps, noting the following.

12. There are no test procedures for the fuel injection control unit that can be performed by the home mechanic. Have the unit tested by a BMW dealer.

13. Make sure to route the electrical cable correctly so that it won't get pinched or damaged in any way.

14. Make sure the electrical connector is free of corrosion and is tight.

THROTTLE VALVE SWITCH

Removal/Installation and Adjustment

1. On models so equipped, remove the left-hand knee pads as described under *Front Fairing Removal/Installation* in Chapter Thirteen.

2. Unhook the clip securing the electrical connector in place.

3. Disconnect the electrical connector (A, **Figure 51**).

4. Remove the mounting screws securing the throttle valve switch (B, **Figure 51**).

5. Carefully pull the throttle valve switch off of the throttle shaft.

6. Reinstall the throttle valve switch onto the throttle shaft and install the screws only finger-tight.

7. Make sure the throttle cable is properly adjusted as described in this chapter. The cable slack must be correct before adjusting the throttle valve switch.

8. Rotate the switch on the throttle shaft so that as soon as the throttle is opened, and the cable slack is taken up, you hear a "click."

9. Hold the switch in that position and tighten the mounting screws securely.

10. On models so equipped, install the left-hand knee pads as described under *Front Fairing Removal/Installation* in Chapter Thirteen.

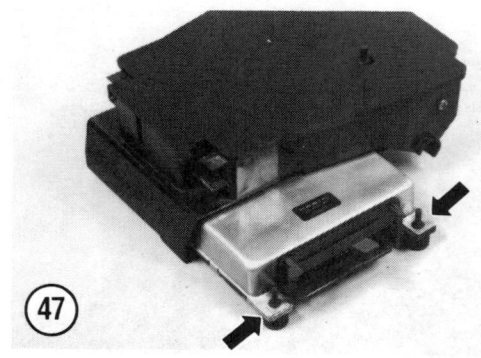

(47)

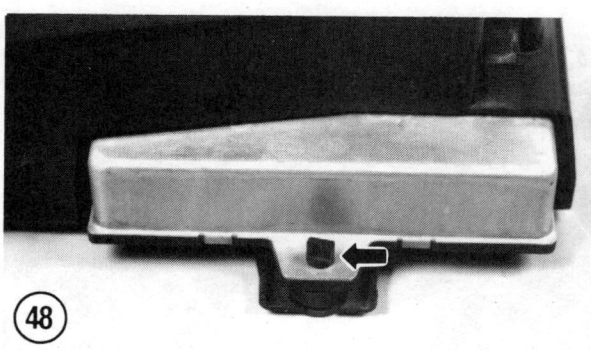

(48)

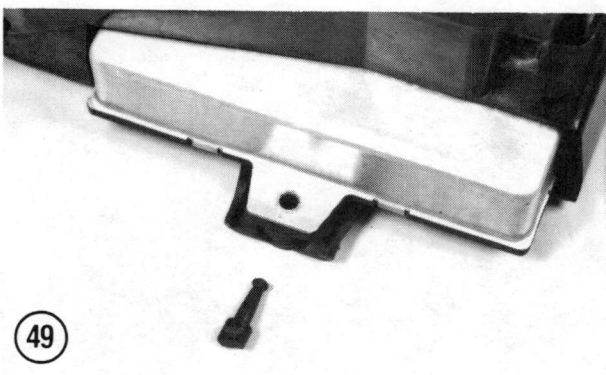

(49)

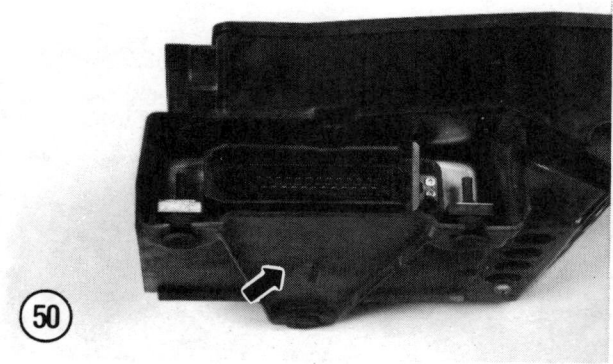

(50)

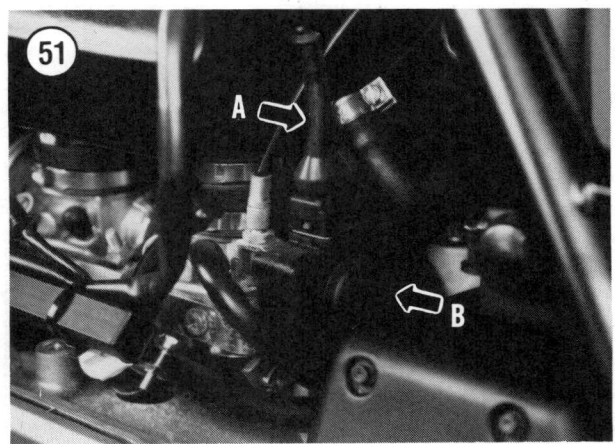

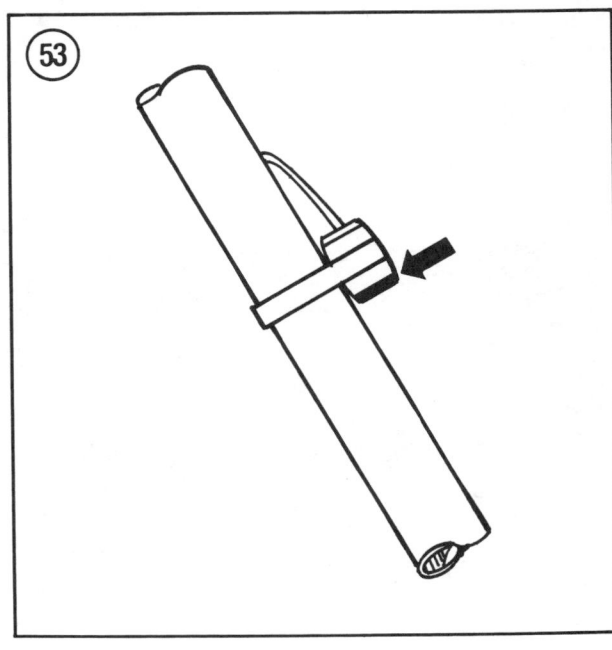

FUEL INJECTION
SYSTEM ADJUSTMENTS

Throttle Cable Adjustment

The throttle cable should have 0.5-1.0 mm (0.02-0.04 in.) of free play. If adjustment is necessary, perform the following.

1. The engine idle speed must be correct before adjusting the throttle cable. Refer to *Idle Speed Adjustment* in Chapter Three.

2. On models so equipped, remove the left-hand knee pads as described under *Front Fairing Removal/Installation* in Chapter Thirteen.

3. Slide back the rubber boot on the throttle cable at the throttle grip.

4. At the throttle grip, loosen the locknut and turn the adjuster in either direction until the correct amount of free play (0.5-1.0 mm/0.02-0.04 in.) is achieved.

5. Tighten the locknut (A).

6. If the proper amount of adjustment cannot be achieved using this procedure, the throttle cable has stretched to the point where it needs replacing as described in this chapter.

7. Check the throttle cable from the throttle grip to the throttle housing. Make sure it is not kinked or chafed. Replace as necessary.

8. Make sure the throttle grip rotates freely from a fully closed to fully open position. Check with the handlebar at center, at full right and at full left. If necessary, remove the throttle grip and apply a lithium base grease to the rotating surfaces.

WARNING
*With the engine idling, move the handlebar from side to side. If idle speed increases during this movement, the throttle cable may need adjusting or may be incorrectly routed through the frame. Correct this problem immediately. Do **not** ride the bike in this unsafe condition.*

High Altitude Adjustment

If the bike is going to be ridden for any sustained period of time at high elevations (1,200 m/4,000 ft.) the fuel system must be modified electronically to improve performance and decrease exhaust emissions. A small wire loop, available at BMW dealers, is added to the electronic circuit to compensate for altitude change.

1. Remove the frame left-hand side cover (**Figure 40**).

2. Located on the frame left-hand down tube is a portion of the main wiring harness with a cap on it (**Figure 52**).

3. Remove the cap (**Figure 53**) from the end of the wire harness. Save the cap as it must be reinstalled once the bike is returned to a lower elevation and the loop is disconnected.

4. Plug in the high altitude loop (**Figure 54**). Make sure the loop is pushed in all the way in order to make good contact and to prevent any entry of moisture.

5. When the bike is returned to lower elevations (near sea level), remove the high elevation loop and reinstall the original cap. Push the cap on tightly to prevent the entry of moisture.

6. Install the frame left-hand side cover.

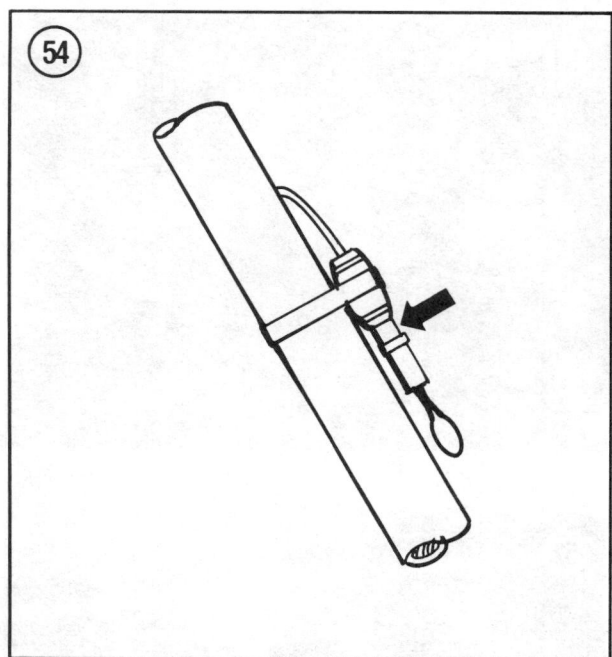

Throttle Housing Butterfly Synchronization

This test requires the use of a special tool. It is a mercury manometer, or dial gauge set. This special tool is also used for carburetor synchronizing. Due to the intricacy of the fuel injection system, it is suggested that this procedure be performed with the special BMW tools designed for this purpose. These special tools are the mercury manometer (part No. 13 0 700) and adapters (part No. 13 0 702 and part No. 13 0 703). Aftermarket mercury manometers are available and are less expensive but are not as accurate as the BMW unit. This procedure is shown with an aftermarket dial gauge set to show how it is to be connected and used.

The mercury manometer and its adapters are expensive pieces of equipment and this adjustment is required infrequently. You should compare the purchase price of the test equipment to the cost of having the throttle housing butterflies synchronized by a BMW dealer.

The following procedure is provided if you choose to perform this procedure yourself. Follow the manufacturer's instructions provided with the special tool.

Prior to synchronizing the throttle housing butterflies the following conditions must exist.

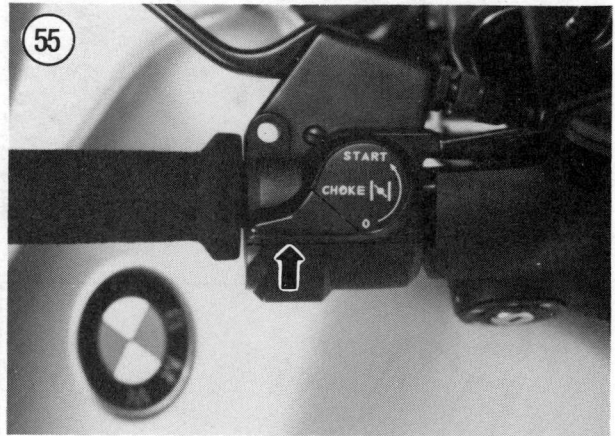

a. Ignition timing must be correct.

b. Spark plugs must be new or fairly new.

c. Valve clearances must be correctly adjusted.

d. The air filter element must be clean.

e. The choke lever (**Figure 55**) must be in the OFF position (parallel to the hand grip). This is the position for an engine at normal operating temperature.

f. The intake and exhaust systems must be free of all leaks.

g. The engine idle speed must be correct.

h. Engine must be at normal operating temperature (approximately 10-15 minutes of stop-and-go riding is usually sufficient).

1. Start the engine and let it reach normal operating temperature. Approximately 10-15 minutes of stop-and-go riding is usually sufficient.

2. Place the bike on the center stand and shut off the engine.

3. On models so equipped, remove the right-hand knee pads as described under *Front Fairing Removal/Installation* in Chapter Thirteen.

4. Remove the rubber cap (**Figure 56**) from the vacuum fittings on the throttle housing assembly.

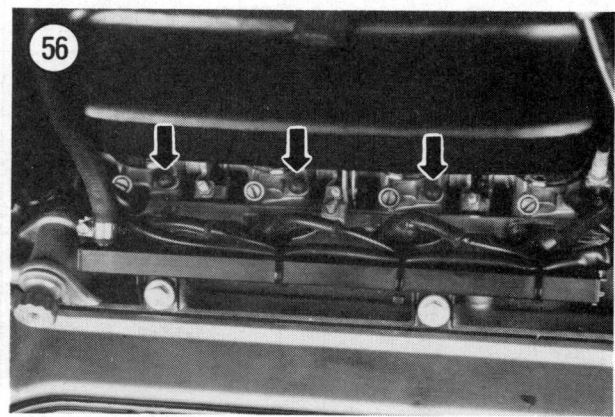

5. Attach the mercury manometer following the manufacturer's instructions. Refer to **Figure 57** and **Figure 58**. Be sure to install the "T" fitting onto the pressure regulator's vacuum hose (**Figure 59**). The pressure regulator must be connected during this procedure, but vacuum must also be drawn off from this hose connection.

6. Start the engine and let it idle.

NOTE
If the manometer is equipped with damping adjusters, adjust them so that the fluctuations are just removed. If adjusted too far, the instrument will not be able to read small changes in vacuum.

7. Note the level of the mercury in all columns (or gauge dials). The level should be *exactly* the same for all cylinders.

CAUTION
*Do not turn the throttle shaft screws linking the throttle butterflies (**Figure 60**). If any of these are upset the throttle housing will have to be replaced.*

8A. If the levels *are* correct, turn the engine off, disconnect the special tool and its adapters. Install the rubber caps onto the vacuum ports.

8B. If the levels are *not* correct, *slowly* turn the air bypass screw(s) (**Figure 61**) in either direction until the mercury level is exactly the same for all cylinders. Once this is achieved, turn the engine off, disconnect the special tool and its adapters. Install the rubber caps onto the vacuum ports.

9. Adjust the engine idle speed as described under *Idle Speed Adjustment* in Chapter Three.

10. On models so equipped, install the right-hand knee pads as described under *Front Fairing Removal/Installation* in Chapter Thirteen.

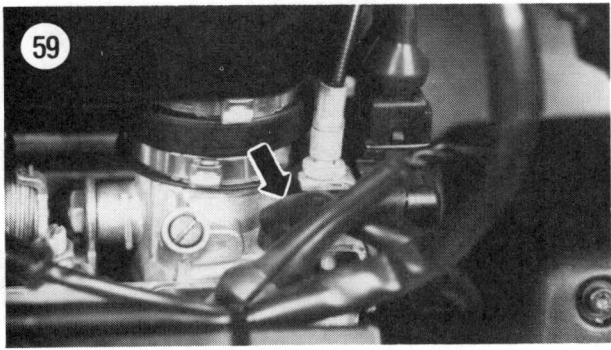

7

CO (Carbon Monoxide) Level
Inspection and Adjustment

This test requires the use of a special tool called an exhaust gas analyzer. The exhaust gas analyzer determines the composition of the exhaust gases—mainly the carbon monoxide level. This level must be maintained to the correct percentage to conform with environmental laws.

The exhaust gas analyzer is an expensive piece of equipment, and this adjustment is required infrequently. You should compare the purchase price of the test equipment to the cost of having the CO level tested and adjusted by a BMW dealer.

The following procedure is provided if you choose to perform this procedure yourself. Follow the manufacturer's instructions provided with the special tool.

If adjustment is necessary, carry it out in small increments. A minimal amount of adjustment can make quite a difference in the end result. Also after an adjustment has been made, wait a few minutes for the system to stabilize after the adjustment has been made. On models equipped with the evaporative emission control system, make sure the engine is thoroughly warmed up to normal operating temperature. The fuel vapors stored in the crankcase on these models must be thoroughly burned off after the engine is started and run. If a reading is made too soon the exhaust composition will not be normal.

Before adjusting the CO (carbon monoxide) level the following conditions must exist.

   a. Ignition timing must be correct.
   b. Spark plugs must be new or fairly new.
   c. Valve clearances must be correct.
   d. The air filter element must be clean.
   e. The choke lever must be in the off position (parallel to the hand grip). This is the position for a normal operating temperature engine.
   f. The intake and exhaust systems must be free of all leaks.
   g. The throttle housing butterflies must be synchronized.
   h. The engine idle speed must be correct.
   i. Engine must be at normal operating temperature (approximately 10-15 minutes of stop-and-go riding is usually sufficient).
   j. The exhaust gas analyzer probe or sensor must be inserted at least 3 mm (12 in.) into the muffler opening. This is necessary to prevent outside air (oxygen rich) from coming in contact with the analyzer probe and giving a false meter reading.

1. Start the engine and let it reach normal operating temperature. Approximately 10-15 minutes of stop-and-go riding is usually sufficient.
2. Place the bike on the center stand and shut off the engine.
3. On models so equipped, remove the right-hand knee pads as described under *Front Fairing Removal/Installation* in Chapter Thirteen.

4. Install the exhaust gas analyzer probe or sensor into the muffler opening a minimum of 3 mm (12 in.). Make sure the probe is secure and that it stays in the desired position.
5. Start the engine and let idle for a few minutes to allow the analyzer to stabilize.
6. Follow the manufacturer's instructions and observe the needle movement. When it stabilizes, note the reading. The specified maximum amount of CO (carbon monoxide) is 2 ± 0.5 %.

NOTE
If you want to inspect the condition of the air filter element, perform **Air Filter Element Test**

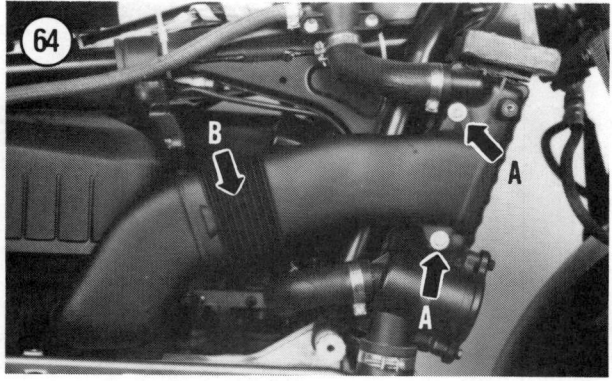

as described in this chapter. If so desired, perform this test at this time while the analyzer is installed.

7A. If the reading is within specification, shut off the engine and disconnect the analyzer.

7B. If the CO is outside of the specification, let the engine continue to idle and perform the following:

   a. Remove the plug (**Figure 62**) from the front left-hand side of the air filter case upper half.

   b. Insert a 5 mm Allen wrench (**Figure 63**) into the hole and into the adjuster in the air flow meter bypass screw.

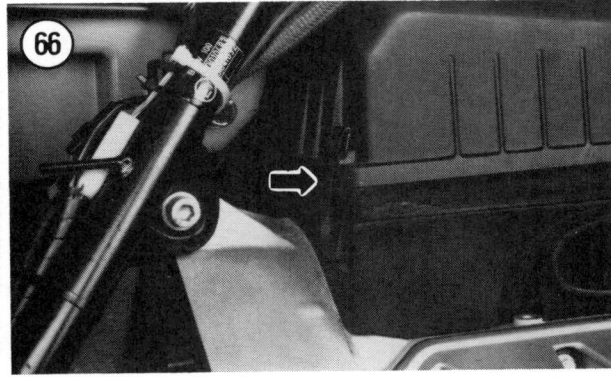

NOTE
After an adjustment has been made, wait a few minutes for the system to stabilize. Don't be in a hurry. This procedure requires patience and time. Different types of analyzers respond differently and some take a little longer to settle down and give an accurate reading.

   c. Slowly rotate the adjuster in either direction until the percentage of CO is within specification.

   d. After the CO level percentage is correct, shut off the engine and disconnect the analyzer.

   e. Remove the Allen wrench and install the plug with the index mark toward the rear. Make sure the plug is correctly installed so that it will be an air-tight seal.

8. On models so equipped, install the right-hand knee pads as described under *Front Fairing Removal/Installation* in Chapter Thirteen.

7

Air Filter Element Testing

1. Perform Steps 1-6 of *CO (Carbon Monoxide) Level Inspection and Adjustment* in this chapter.

2. Increase engine speed to about 2/3 of the maximum speed (approximately 5,500 rpm). Note the exact engine rpm and analyzer needle position. Write down both numbers.

3. Remove the air guide as follows:

   a. Remove the bolts (A, **Figure 64**) securing the front section of the air guide to the radiator.

   b. Pull the lower section of the air guide channel (B, **Figure 64**) out of the air filter air box.

   c. Remove the air guide channel.

4. Unhook the spring clamps securing the upper case to the lower case. Refer to **Figure 65** and **Figure 66**.

5. Raise the upper case away from the lower case and withdraw the air filter element (**Figure 67**) out through the right-hand side.

6. Increase engine speed again to the exact same rpm noted in Step 2. The engine rpm must be exact (± 100 rpm) or the test result will not be valid.

7. Note the exact engine rpm and analyzer needle position. Write down both numbers.

8. If the analyzer needle position reading in Step 7 was lower than that noted in Step 2, the air filter is clogged (even if it looks okay) and is not allowing sufficient air into the intake system. Install a new air filter element.

9. Apply a light coat of multipurpose grease to the sealing edges of the new air filter element. This will assure an air-tight fitting of the element to the air filter case.

10. Position the air filter element with the "TOP-OBEN" arrow (**Figure 67**) facing *UP*.

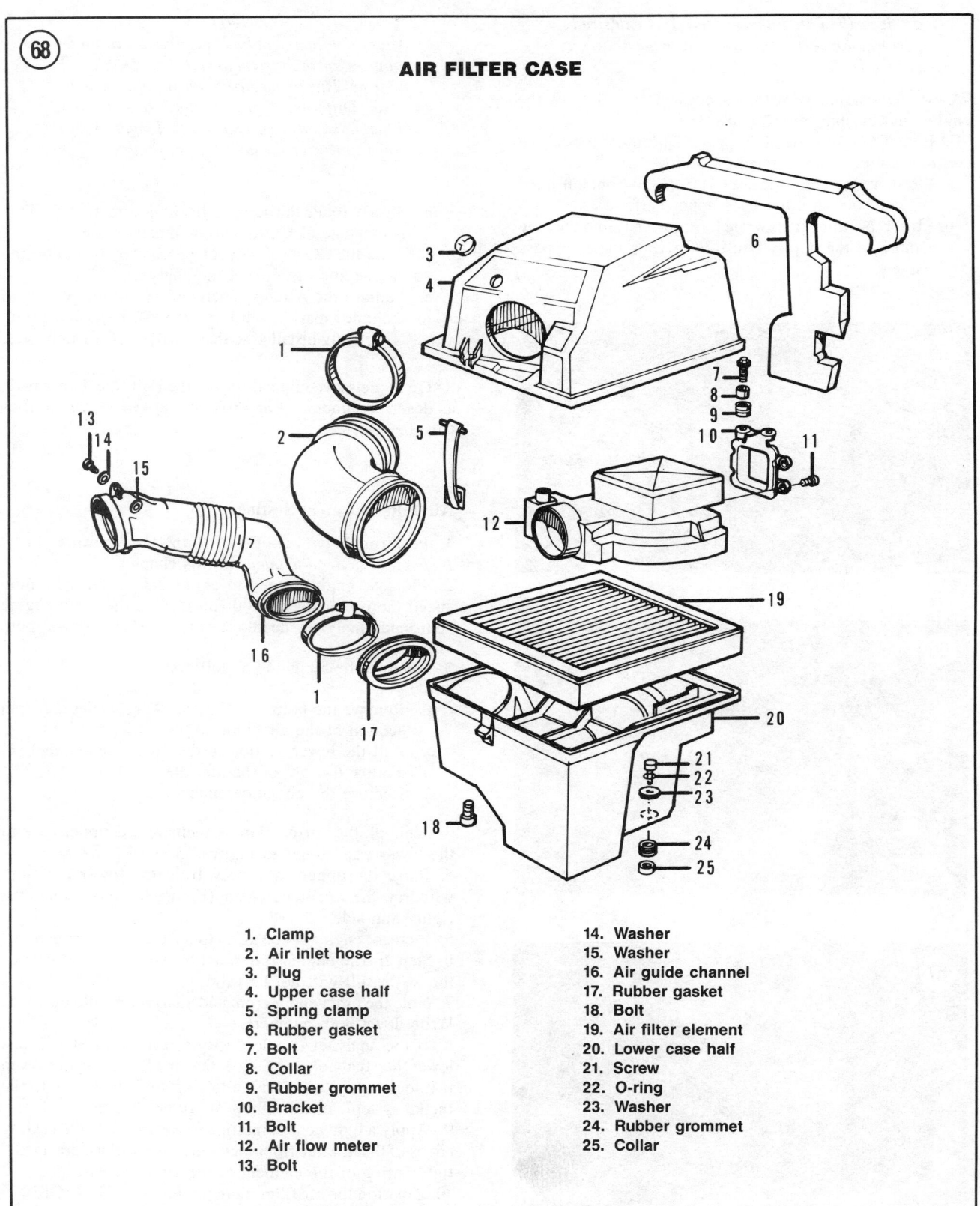

AIR FILTER CASE

1. Clamp
2. Air inlet hose
3. Plug
4. Upper case half
5. Spring clamp
6. Rubber gasket
7. Bolt
8. Collar
9. Rubber grommet
10. Bracket
11. Bolt
12. Air flow meter
13. Bolt
14. Washer
15. Washer
16. Air guide channel
17. Rubber gasket
18. Bolt
19. Air filter element
20. Lower case half
21. Screw
22. O-ring
23. Washer
24. Rubber grommet
25. Collar

11. Install the air filter into the lower case and press it down to make sure it seats correctly. Make sure the element is correctly seated into the air box so the sealing surface is tight up against the air box surfaces.

12. Install the upper case onto the lower case and make sure it is correctly seated all the way around the perimeter. Secure the upper case to the lower case with the spring clamps. Make sure the spring clamps have snapped over-center and are holding tightly.

13. Apply a light coat of rubber lube or Armor All to the lower section of the air guide channel where it fits into the

gasket on the air filter lower case. This will make installation easier.

14. Install the air guide as follows:
    a. Install the lower section of the air guide channel (B, **Figure 64**) into the air filter air box.
    b. Move the air guide channel into position.
    c. Install the bolts (A, **Figure 64**) securing the front section of the air guide to the radiator. Tighten the bolts securely—but not too tightly, as the plastic mounting tabs may be damaged.

15. Install all body panels removed as described in Chapter Thirteen.

AIR FILTER CASE

Removal/Installation

Refer to **Figure 68** for this procedure.

1. Place the bike on the center stand.

2. On models so equipped, remove the radiator trim panel as described under *Radiator Trim Panel Removal/Installation* in Chapter Thirteen.

3. On models so equipped, remove the left-hand knee pads and lower panel on the right-hand side as described under *Front Fairing Removal/Installation* in Chapter Thirteen.

4. Remove the fuel tank as described in this chapter.

5. Remove the air guide as follows:
    a. Remove the bolts (A, **Figure 64**) securing the front section of the air guide to the radiator.
    b. Pull the lower section of the air guide channel (B, **Figure 64**) out of the air filter air box.
    c. Remove the air guide channel.

6. Move the coolant recovery tank hose (A, **Figure 69**) out of the rubber air dam (B, **Figure 69**) and move the rubber air dam out of the way.

7. Unhook the spring clamps securing the upper case to the lower case. Refer to **Figure 65** and **Figure 66**.

8. Raise the upper case away from the lower case and withdraw the air filter element (**Figure 67**) out through the right-hand side.

NOTE
In Step 9, if you are unable to get a screwdriver on the clamping screw, use a 7 mm nut driver and ratchet.

9. Loosen the clamping screw (**Figure 70**) on the air outlet elbow where it attaches to the air plenum chamber.

10. Remove the Allen screws (A, **Figure 71**) securing the air flow meter to the upper case half.

11. Loosen the clamping screw (B, **Figure 71**) securing the air flow meter to the air outlet hose.

12. Note the placement of the electrical cable within the air filter case.

13. If not already disconnected, remove the wire clip and disconnect the electrical connector from the air flow meter.

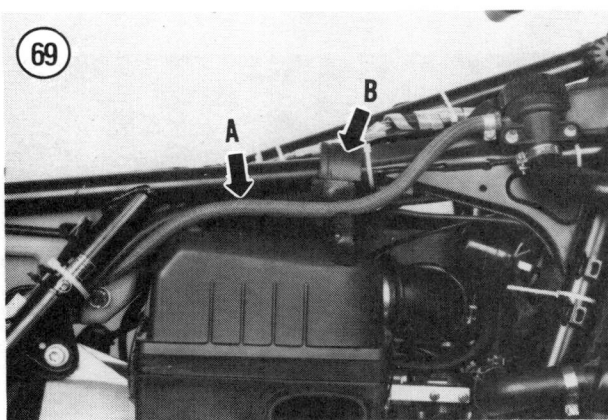

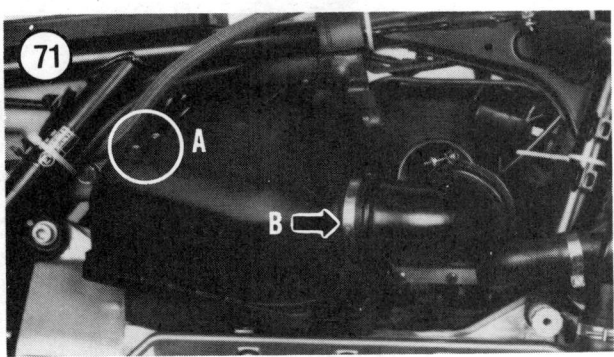

7

14. Carefully remove the air flow meter (**Figure 72**) from the air outlet hose and remove the air flow meter.

15. Carefully pull the electrical connector and cable out of the rubber grommet in the air filter upper case half.

16. Remove the upper case half.

17. Remove the bolts and washers securing the lower case half (**Figure 73**) to the cylinder block.

18. Remove the lower case half. Don't lose the collar in the rubber grommet in each mounting bolt hole.

19. Install by reversing these removal steps, noting the following.

20. Position the clamping screw (**Figure 74**) on the air outlet elbow as shown in **Figure 70** so that it will be easy to reach if you need to repeat this procedure.

21. Install the upper case onto the lower case and make sure it is correctly seated all the way around the perimeter. Secure the upper case to the lower case with the spring clamps. Make sure the spring clamps have snapped over-center and are holding tightly.

22. Apply a light coat of rubber lube or Armor All to the lower section of the air guide channel where it fits into the gasket on the air filter lower case. This will make installation easier.

23. Install the air guide as follows:

    a. Install the lower section of the air guide channel (B, **Figure 64**) into the air filter air box.

    b. Move the air guide channel into position.

    c. Install the bolts (A, **Figure 64**) securing the front section of the air guide to the radiator. Tighten the bolts securely—but not too tight as the plastic mounting tabs may be damaged.

24. Install all body panels removed as described in Chapter Thirteen.

THROTTLE CABLE REPLACEMENT

1. Remove the seat as described under *Seat Removal/Installation* in Chapter Thirteen.

2. Remove the fuel tank as described in this chapter.

3. On models so equipped, remove the front fairing as described under *Front Fairing Removal/Installation* in Chapter Thirteen.

4. Remove the air filter case as described in this chapter.

> *NOTE*
> *When the throttle cable cover is removed, the throttle grip becomes loose and may fall off of the end of the handlebar. Either secure the throttle grip in place or remove it from the handlebar.*

5. Remove the screw (A, **Figure 75**) securing the throttle cable cover (B, **Figure 75**) and remove the cover.

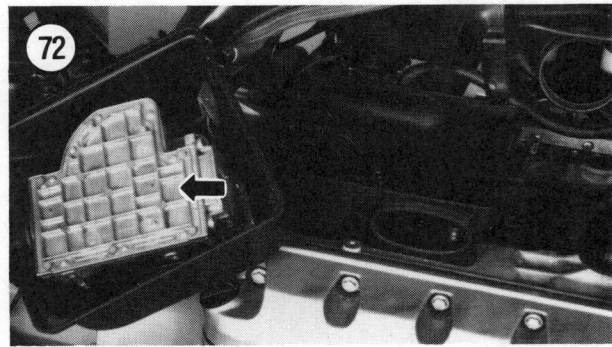

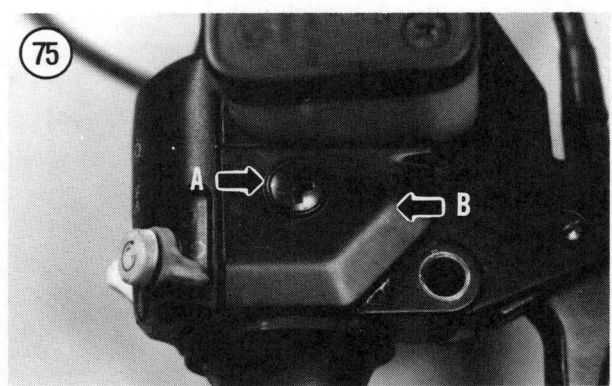

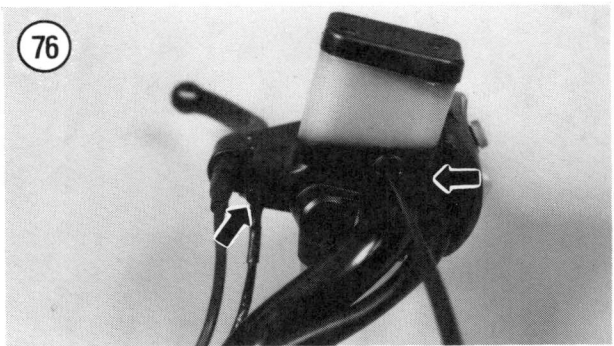

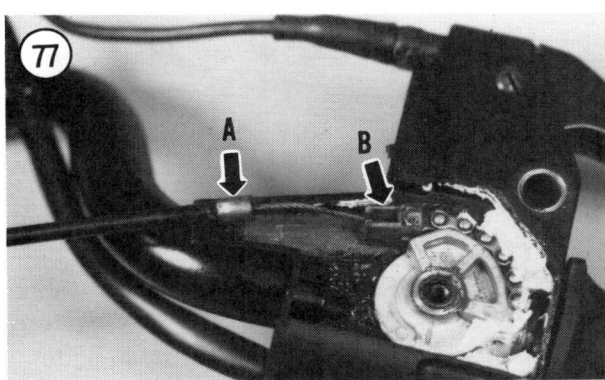

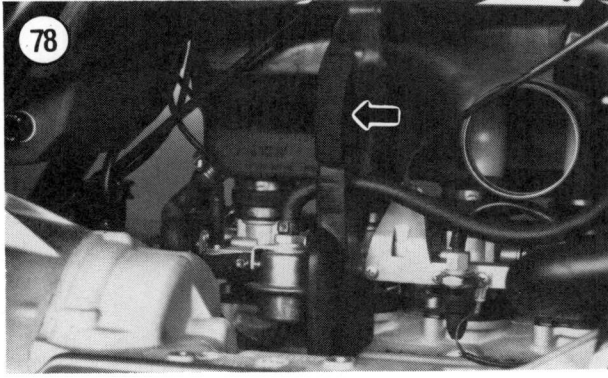

CAUTION
Cover the instrument cluster, front fairing (models so equipped) and frame with a heavy cloth or plastic tarp to protect it from accidental spilling of brake fluid. Wash any spilled brake fluid off any painted or plated surface immediately, as it will destroy the finish. Use soapy water and rinse thoroughly.

6. Remove the bolts (**Figure 76**) securing the master cylinder assembly to the throttle housing. Carefully move the master cylinder out of the way and lay it over the frame. Keep the reservoir in the upright position to minimize loss of brake fluid and to keep air from entering into the brake system. It is not necessary to disconnect the hydraulic brake line.
7. Pull up and disengage the cable end cap (A, **Figure 77**), then disengage the throttle cable end (B, **Figure 77**) from the throttle wheel chain.
8. Remove the rubber heat shield (**Figure 78**).
9. Remove the screws securing the throttle cable bracket (**Figure 79**) to the back of the throttle housing assembly.
10. Remove the throttle cable from the cable bracket and disconnect the cable from the throttle wheel on the throttle housing assembly.

NOTE
The piece of string attached in the next step will be used to pull the new throttle cable back through the frame so it will be routed in exactly the same position as the old cable.

11. Tie a piece of heavy string or cord (approximately 6-8 ft./1.8-2.4 m long) to the throttle housing end of the throttle cable. Wrap this end with masking or duct tape. Do not use an excessive amount of tape as it must be pulled through the frame during removal. Tie the other end of the string to the frame or air box.
12. At the throttle grip end of the cable, carefully pull the cable (and attached string) out through the frame. Make sure the attached string follows the same path as the cable through the frame.
13. Remove the tape and untie the string from the old cable.
14. Lubricate the new cable as described under *Throttle and Choke Control Cable Lubrication* in Chapter Three.
15. Tie the string to the new throttle cable and wrap it with tape.
16. Carefully pull the string back through the frame, routing the new cable through the same path as the old cable.
17. Remove the tape and untie the string from the cable and the frame.
18. Attach the end of the throttle cable onto the throttle wheel and into the cable bracket.
19. Move the throttle cable bracket (**Figure 79**) into position and install the mounting screws securing the throttle cable bracket to the back of the throttle housing assembly. Tighten the screws securely.

20. Install the rubber heat shield (**Figure 78**).

21. Attach the throttle cable (B, **Figure 77**) onto the throttle wheel chain and place the cable end (A, **Figure 77**) into the receptacle in the throttle housing lower half.

22. Install the master cylinder assembly onto the throttle housing and install the bolts (**Figure 76**). Tighten the bolts securely.

23. Make sure the throttle cable end is still engaged properly in the throttle wheel chain (**Figure 80**).

24. Apply a coat of lithium-based grease to the end of the throttle grip (**Figure 81**) and insert the throttle grip into the housing. Align the index marks of the throttle grip and the throttle chain gear (**Figure 82**).

25. Hold the throttle grip in place and install the throttle cable cover (B, **Figure 75**). Install the screw (A, **Figure 75**) and tighten securely.

26. Operate the throttle grip and make sure the throttle housing throttle linkage is operating correctly, with no binding. If operation is incorrect or there is binding, carefully check that the cable is attached correctly and there are no tight bends in the cable.

27. Install the air filter case as described in this chapter.

28. On models so equipped, install the front fairing as described under *Front Fairing Removal/Installation* in Chapter Thirteen.

29. Install the fuel tank as described in this chapter.

30. Adjust the throttle cable as described in this chapter.

31. Test ride the bike slowly at first and make sure the throttle is operating correctly.

CHOKE CABLE REPLACEMENT

NOTE
The choke mechanism increase engine idle speed during cold starting. It does not work like a choke mechanism used on carburetors.

1. Remove the fuel tank as described in this chapter.

2. On models so equipped, remove the front fairing as described under *Front Fairing Removal/Installation* in Chapter Thirteen.

3. Carefully pry off the cover on the choke operating lever.

4. Unscrew the large flat screw (**Figure 83**) and remove the special washer (**Figure 84**).

5. Remove the lever (A, **Figure 85**) from the housing and disconnect the cable (B, **Figure 85**) from the lever.

6. Push the cable sleeve out and remove the cable from the slot (C, **Figure 85**) in the cable housing.

7. Loosen the locknut (A, **Figure 86**) completely and remove the choke cable from the bracket (B, **Figure 86**) on the throttle housing.

8. Disconnect the choke cable end from the choke lever on the throttle housing and remove the choke cable.

NOTE
The piece of string attached in the next step will be used to pull the new choke cable back

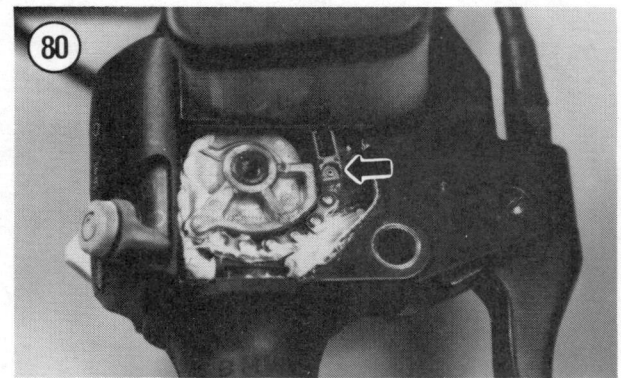

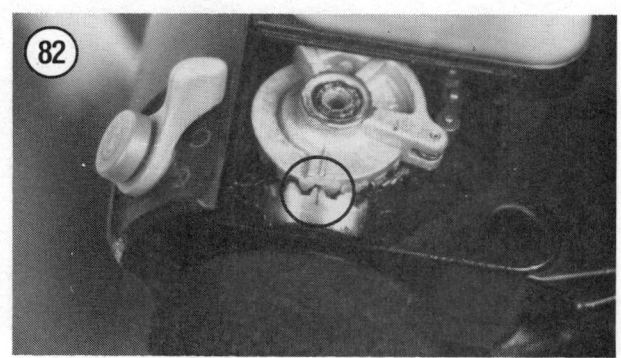

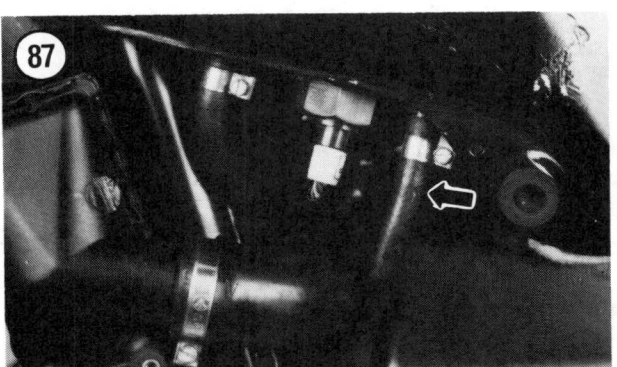

through the frame so it will be routed in the same position as the old cable.

9. Tie a piece of heavy string or cord (approximately 6-8 ft./1.8-2.4 m long) to the throttle housing end of the choke cable. Wrap this end with masking or duct tape. Do not use an excessive amount of tape as it must be pulled through the frame during removal. Tie the other end of the string to the frame or air box.

10. At the choke lever end of the cable, carefully pull the cable (and attached string) out through the frame. Make sure the attached string follows the same path that the cable does through the frame.

11. Remove the tape and untie the string from the old cable.

12. Lubricate the new cable as described under *Throttle and Choke Control Cable Lubrication* in Chapter Three.

13. Tie the string to the new choke cable and wrap it with tape.

14. Carefully pull the string back through the frame, routing the new cable through the same path as the old cable.

15. Remove the tape and untie the string from the cable and the frame.

16. Connect the choke cable end onto the choke lever on the throttle housing.

17. Insert the choke cable into the bracket (B, **Figure 86**) on the throttle housing.

18. Temporarily tighten the locknut (A, **Figure 86**) to hold the cable in place.

19. Install the cable and sleeve into the slot (C, **Figure 85**) in the cable housing.

20. Install the cable end into the lever (B, **Figure 85**) and install the lever onto the housing (A, **Figure 85**).

21. Install the special washer (**Figure 84**) and the large flat screw (**Figure 83**). Tighten the flat screw securely.

22. Install the cover onto the choke operating lever.

23. Operate the choke lever and make sure the choke linkage is operating correctly, with no binding. If operation is incorrect or there is binding carefully check that the cable is attached correctly and there are no tight bends in the cable.

24. Adjust the choke cable as described in this chapter.

FUEL PUMP

Pressure Test

1. On models so equipped, remove the radiator trim panel as described under *Radiator Trim Panel Removal/Installation* in Chapter Thirteen.

2. Depressurize the fuel system as described in this chapter.

3. Disconnect the fuel feed hose (**Figure 87**) from the fuel tank on the front left-hand corner.

4. Connect a pressure gauge between the fuel feed hose and the fuel tank outlet fitting. Any type of pressure gauge can be used. BMW offers one (part No. 16 1 500) and it is available at BMW dealers.

7

WARNING
Make sure all fuel hoses are tightly secured to avoid a fuel leak while the engine is running.

NOTE
The fuel pressure is constant throughout all engine speeds, therefore it is not necessary to increase engine speed during this test.

5. Start the engine and let it idle. Note the fuel pressure and compare to the specification listed in **Table 1**. Shut off the engine.

6. If the indicated pressure is *less* than specified, make sure all fuel and vent hoses are open (not clogged or knocked) and that the fuel filter is clear. Before replacing the fuel pump, replace the fuel filter as described under *Fuel Filter Replacement* in Chapter Three. Recheck the fuel pressure. If the pressure is still low, replace the fuel pump as described in this chapter.

7. If the indicated pressure is *greater* than specified, the fuel pressure regulator may be faulty. Inspect the fuel pressure regulator as described in this chapter. If the fuel pressure regulator is faulty, replace it as described in this chapter. Recheck the fuel pressure. If the pressure is still high, replace the fuel pump as described in this chapter.

8. Disconnect the pressure gauge and reconnect the fuel feed hose to the fuel tank. Make sure the hose clamp is tight.

9. Before installing the body panels, start the engine and check for fuel leaks. If present, correct immediately.

10. On models so equipped, install the radiator trim panel as described under *Radiator Trim Panel Removal/ Installation* in Chapter Thirteen.

Removal/Installation

Refer to **Figure 88** for this procedure. The fuel pump is located within the fuel tank.

WARNING
Before attempting this procedure, be sure to have a fire extinguisher rated for gasoline or chemical fires within reach. Do not smoke or allow anyone to smoke or work where there are any open flames (e.g., water heater or clothes dryer gas pilots). The work area must be well-ventilated.

NOTE
If you have large hands this job will be very difficult. You must work down inside the filler cap opening in the fuel tank and disconnect

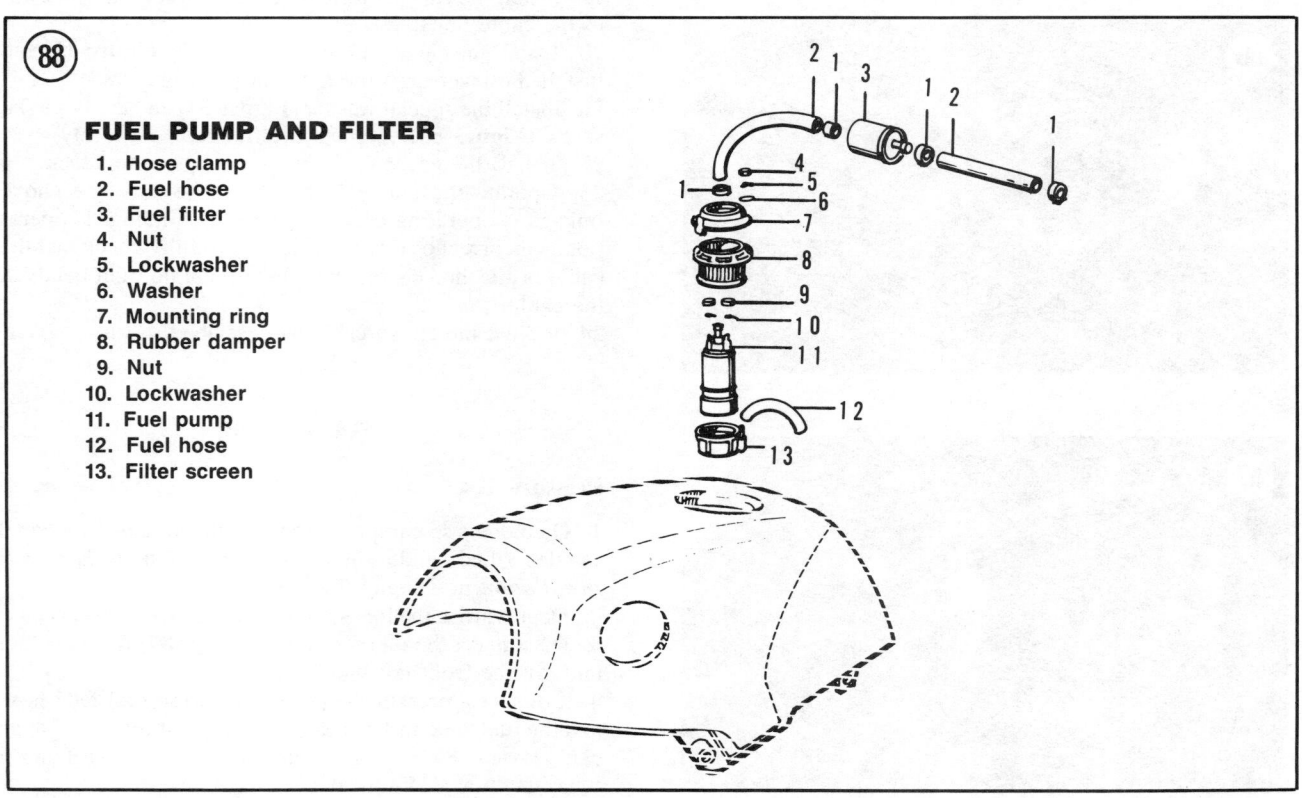

(88)

FUEL PUMP AND FILTER
1. Hose clamp
2. Fuel hose
3. Fuel filter
4. Nut
5. Lockwasher
6. Washer
7. Mounting ring
8. Rubber damper
9. Nut
10. Lockwasher
11. Fuel pump
12. Fuel hose
13. Filter screen

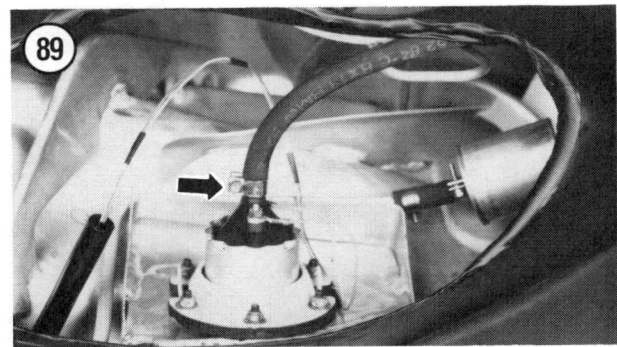

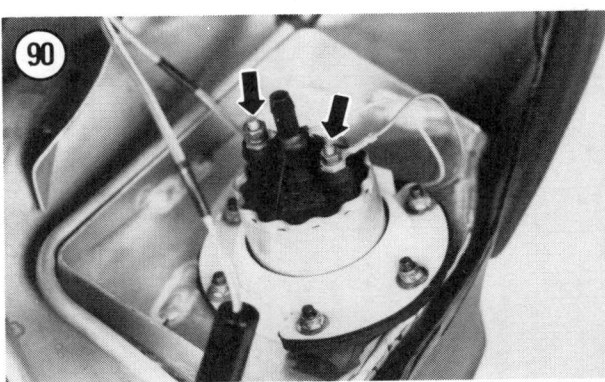

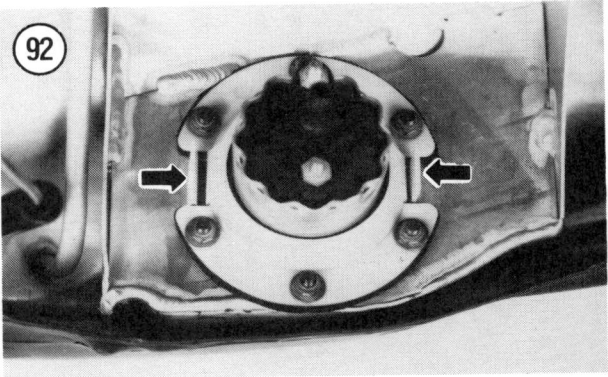

electrical wires, a fuel hose, etc. If your hands are large, you may have to find someone with small hands to perform this procedure for you.

1. Remove the frame left-hand side cover.
2. Disconnect the battery negative lead as described under *Battery* in Chapter Three.

NOTE
The fuel pump can be removed with the fuel tank installed on the bike or removed. This procedure is shown with the fuel tank removed; also, the left-hand side of the tank has been cut away for clarity.

3. Open the fuel tank filler cap.
4. Siphon off all fuel in the tank and store it in a suitable sealed metal container.
5. If compressed air is available, blow out the interior of the fuel tank to evacuate most of the fumes.
6. Protect the painted surface of the fuel tank with heavy cloths or apply duct tape around the filler cap area.
7. Remove the fuel filler cap assembly as described in this chapter.
8. Disconnect the fuel hose (**Figure 89**) from the top of the fuel pump.
9. Within the fuel tank, use a long-handled nut driver to remove the nuts (**Figure 90**) securing the electrical connectors to the fuel pump.

NOTE
*The electrical terminals (**Figure 91**) on the fuel pump are different sizes. The positive terminal is smaller (4 mm nut) while the larger terminal is larger (5 mm nut). The **original** electrical wire connectors have corresponding sized holes to help avoid the intermixing of the wires during installation. If you are working on an older bike, someone may have modified the wiring and connectors. Take note of the electrical wire colors and the terminals to which they are attached prior to removal. Make sure they are attached to the correct terminals during assembly.*

10. Remove the nuts, lockwashers and washers from the electrical terminals. Remove the electrical wires from the connectors on the fuel pump. Note which side the *larger electrical terminal* is located on. Reinstall the fuel pump in the same orientation so that reconnecting the electrical wires will be easier.
11. Squeeze the mounting tabs (**Figure 92**) securing the fuel pump to the mounting platform in the fuel tank and remove the fuel pump from the mounting platform.
12. Withdraw the fuel pump assembly from the fuel tank.
13. Inspect the fuel pump as described in this chapter.

7

14. Install by reversing these removal steps, noting the following.

15. If the electrical leads are long enough, attach the electrical wires to the fuel pump prior to installing the fuel pump into the fuel tank (**Figure 93**).

16. Be sure to attach the correct electrical wire to the correct terminal on the fuel pump (**Figure 94**).

CAUTION
Make sure the fuel pump is securely attached to the mounting platform in the fuel tank. If the fuel pump works loose it may damage the tank.

17. Install the fuel pump with the wires attached into the fuel tank and push the fuel pump into place. Make sure the mounting tabs (**Figure 92**) are completely locked into place on the mounting platform. You will hear a click when each one is locked in completely.

18. Route the fuel pump electrical wires *in front of* the rear slosh panel (**Figure 95**). The backside of the slosh panel has a sharp edge at the top and may cut though the wiring insulation, causing a short.

19. Make sure the fuel hose (**Figure 89**) is properly attached to the outlet of the fuel pump.

20. Install the filler cap assembly as described in this chapter.

21. After installation is complete, thoroughly check for fuel leaks.

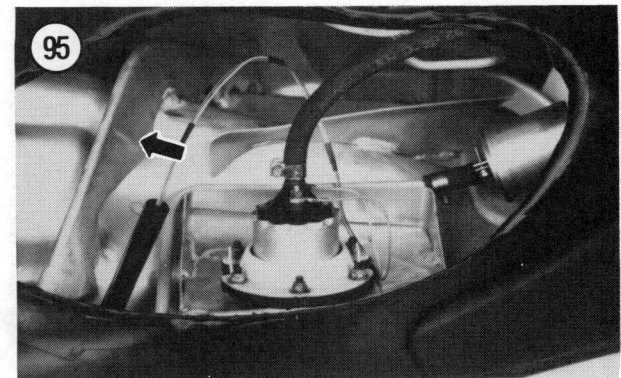

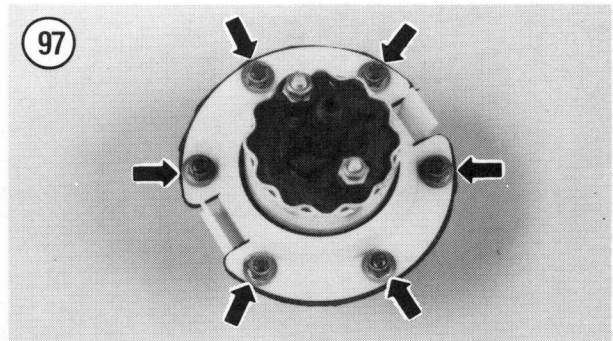

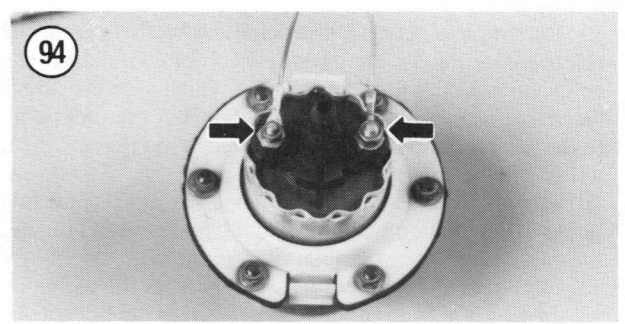

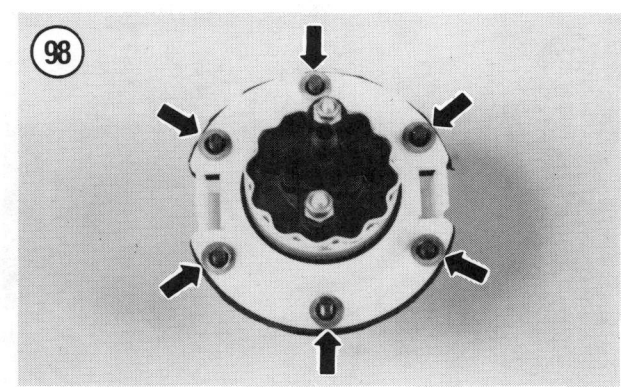

Disassembly/Inspection/
Filter Replacement/Assembly

Refer to **Figure 88** for this procedure.
1. Slide the filter screen (**Figure 96**) off of the base of the fuel pump.
2. Remove the nuts (**Figure 97**) securing the mounting ring to the rubber damper assembly.
3. Remove the washers (**Figure 98**) and the mounting ring (**Figure 99**).
4. Slide the rubber damper assembly (**Figure 100**) off of the base of the fuel pump.
5. Inspect the rubber damper assembly (**Figure 101**) for deterioration, tears or damage. Replace if necessary.
6. Clean the filter screen (**Figure 102**) with solvent and a soft toothbrush to remove any dirt and debris trapped in the screen.
7. Inspect the filter screen for tears or holes. If the filter screen is damaged in any place, replace it with a new one.
8. Check the fuel pump body (**Figure 103**) for any signs of damage. If damaged, replace with a new one.
9. Make sure the fuel inlet opening (**Figure 104**) in the base of the fuel pump is open and clear. Clean out any foreign matter that may have collected in the hole.
10. Inspect the locking ring for cracks or damage. Replace if necessary.
11. Slide the rubber damper assembly onto the base of the fuel pump. Slide it on until it stops on the shoulder of the fuel pump.

7

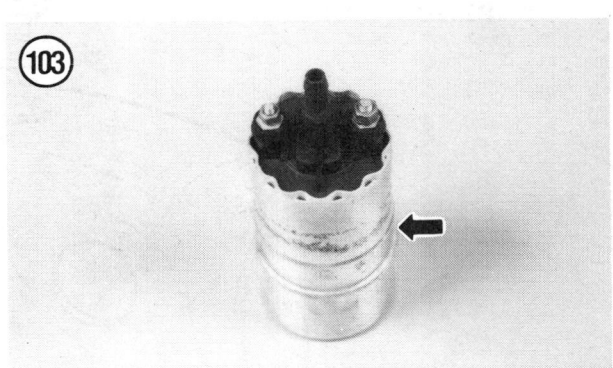

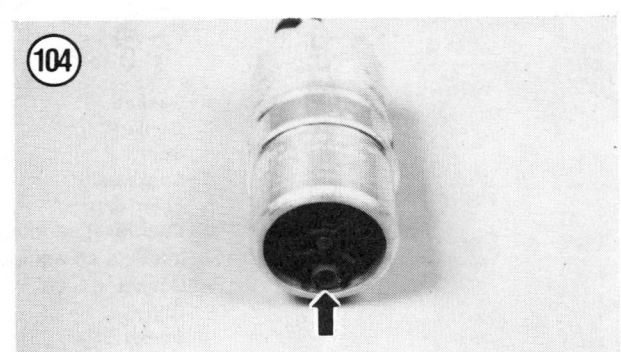

12. Position the notches in the rubber damper assembly so they are 90° from the electrical terminals (**Figure 105**). This alignment is necessary so the electrical wires can be properly connected when the fuel pump is installed in the fuel tank.
13. Install the mounting ring and the washers (**Figure 98**).
14. Install the nuts (**Figure 97**) securing the mounting ring to the rubber damper assembly. Tighten the nuts securely.
15. Slide the filter screen (**Figure 96**) onto the base of the fuel pump.

105
90°

FUEL FILLER CAP

Removal/Installation

Refer to **Figure 106** for this procedure.
1. Protect the painted surface of the fuel tank with heavy cloths or apply duct tape around the filler cap area.

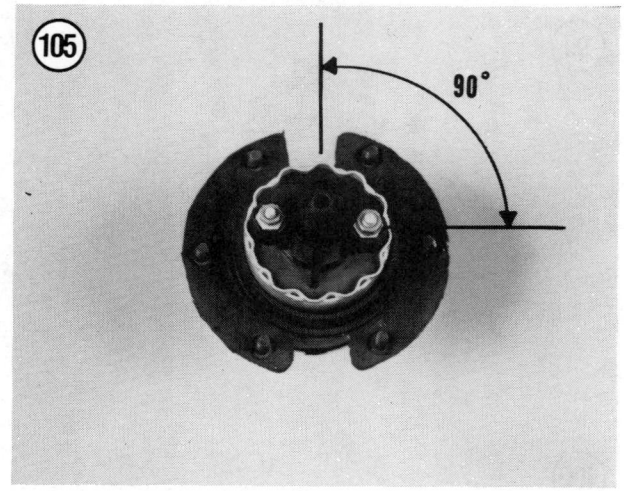

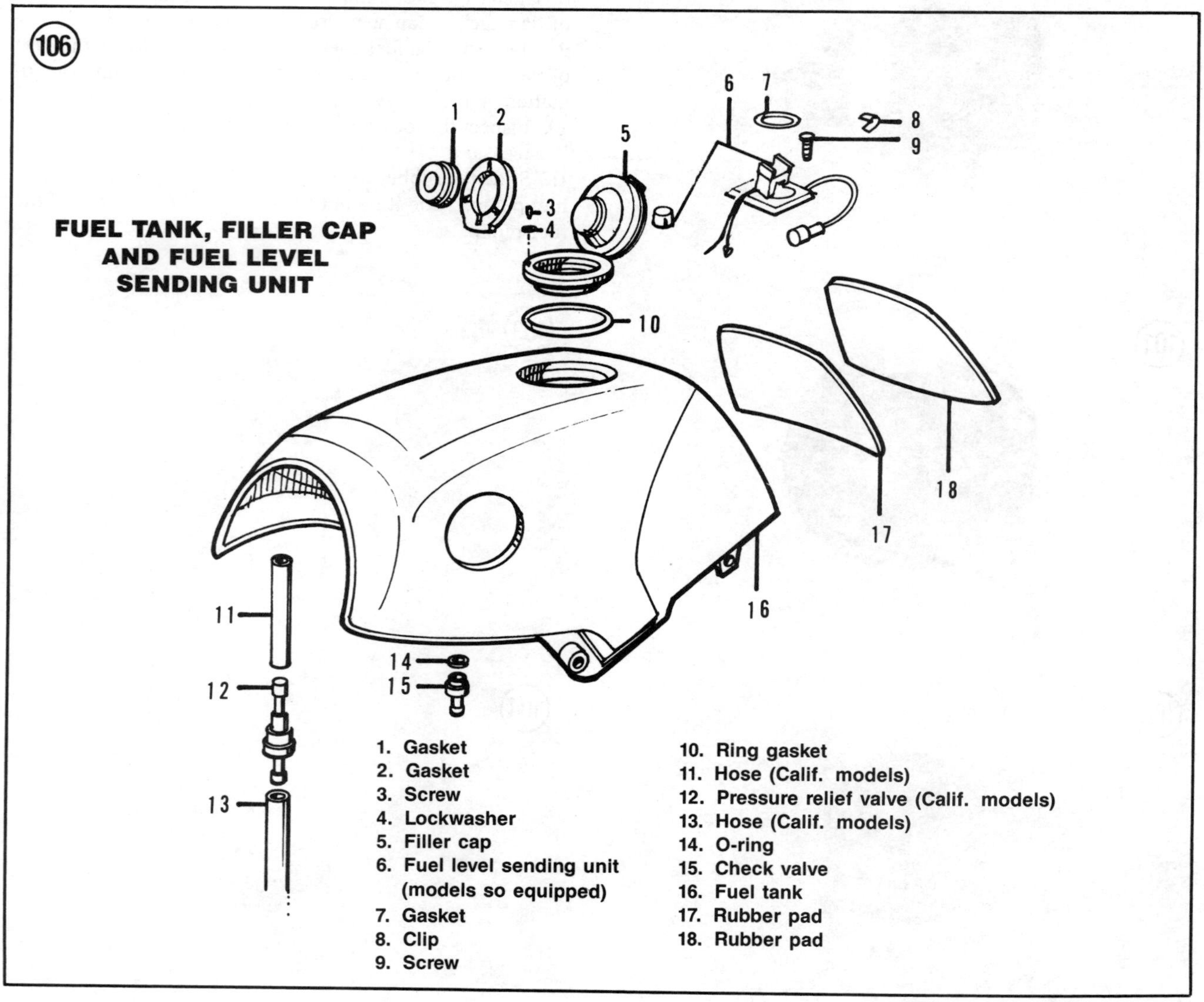

106
FUEL TANK, FILLER CAP AND FUEL LEVEL SENDING UNIT
1
2
3
4
5
6
7
8
9
10
11
12
13
14
15
16
17
18
1. Gasket
2. Gasket
3. Screw
4. Lockwasher
5. Filler cap
6. Fuel level sending unit (models so equipped)
7. Gasket
8. Clip
9. Screw
10. Ring gasket
11. Hose (Calif. models)
12. Pressure relief valve (Calif. models)
13. Hose (Calif. models)
14. O-ring
15. Check valve
16. Fuel tank
17. Rubber pad
18. Rubber pad

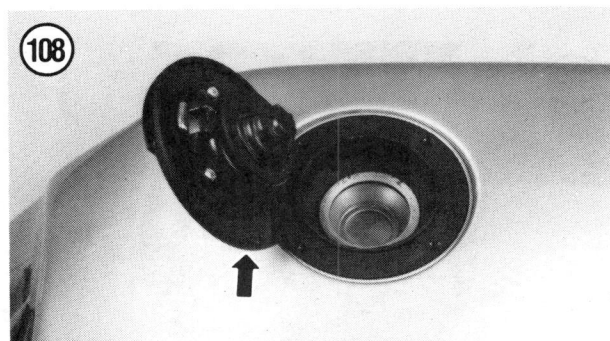

2. Remove the screws and lockwashers (**Figure 107**) securing the filler cap assembly.
3. Remove the fuel filler cap assembly (**Figure 108**) and ring gasket.
4. Inspect the ring gasket on the fuel filler cap assembly; replace if necessary.
5. On California models, perform the following:
   a. Align the vent cutout (A, **Figure 109**) in the ring gasket with the tank vent hole (B, **Figure 109**) and install the ring gasket.
   b. After the ring gasket is installed, recheck the alignment (**Figure 110**).
6. Install the filler cap assembly, lockwashers and screws. Tighten the mounting screws securely.

Gasket Replacement

1. Remove the screws (**Figure 111**) securing the lower plate and remove the lower plate.
2. Remove the old gasket and discard.
3. Install a new gasket (**Figure 112**) and reinstall the lower plate. Tighten the screws securely.

7

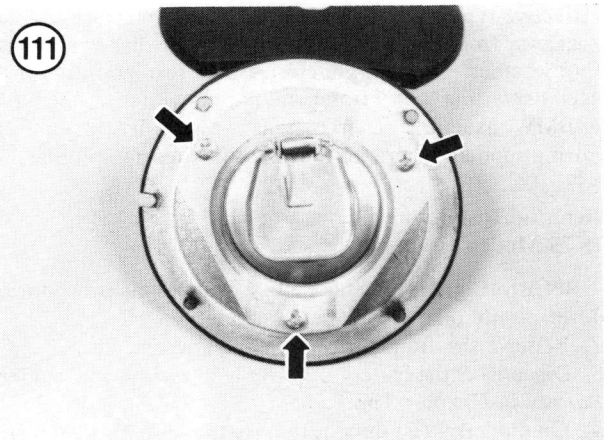

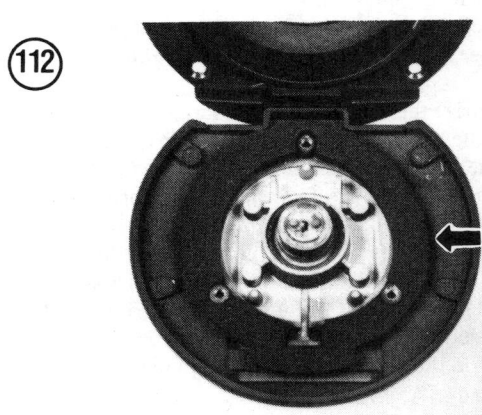

4. Remove the screws (**Figure 113**) securing the locking plate assembly to the cap and remove the assembly.

5. Inspect the cap button assembly (**Figure 114**). If faulty, the filler cap assembly must be replaced.

6. Inspect the locking plate assembly for wear or damage. Refer to **Figure 115** and **Figure 116**. If faulty, the filler cap assembly must be replaced.

7. Install the locking plate assembly and screws. Tighten the screws securely.

FUEL TANK

The fuel filler neck on California models is equipped with a flapper assembly that is used in conjunction with the evaporative emission control system. Do not modify this flapper assembly as it could lead to engine damage.

Never fill the fuel tank all the way to the top as there has to be room for expansion of the air and fuel in hot temperatures. If the tank is overfilled, liquid fuel instead of fuel vapor may be routed into the crankcase via the vent tube. This could result in severe engine damage.

The bottom of the fuel tank is covered with a heat reflective type of insulation. This is to help direct engine heat away from the fuel tank under adverse riding conditions (hot weather, stop-and-go, etc.). If this insulation is damaged or starting to deteriorate, replace it with the same type of BMW insulating material. This is especially true on full fairing models where air flow in this area is minimal.

Removal/Installation
(K75 Models)

Refer to **Figure 106** and **Figure 117** for this procedure.
1. Place the bike on the center stand.
2. Remove the frame left-hand side cover.
3. Disconnect the battery negative lead as described under *Battery* in Chapter Three.
4. On models so equipped, remove the radiator trim panel as described under *Radiator Trim Panel Removal/Installation* in Chapter Thirteen.
5. On models so equipped, remove the lower panels as described under *Front Fairing Removal/Installation* in Chapter Thirteen.
6. Depressurize the fuel system as described in this chapter.
7. Lift up the seat and lock it in the UP position.
8. Disconnect the fuel feed and return hoses (**Figure 118**) from the fuel tank on the front left-hand corner.
9. Install a golf tee into the fuel hose to prevent the entry of foreign matter. Also install a golf tee into the fuel line fittings on the fuel tank to prevent fuel from dribbling out.
10. Using a pair of pliers, remove the clip (**Figure 119**) on each side securing the tank at the rear.
11. Pull up on the rear of the tank and place a wood block under the tank (A, **Figure 120**).
12. Disconnect the fuel pump electrical connector (B, **Figure 120**).

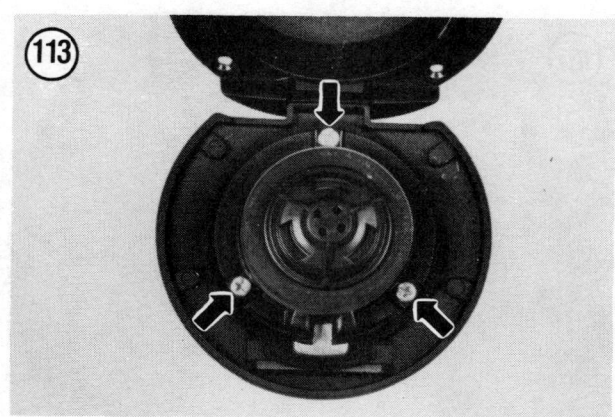

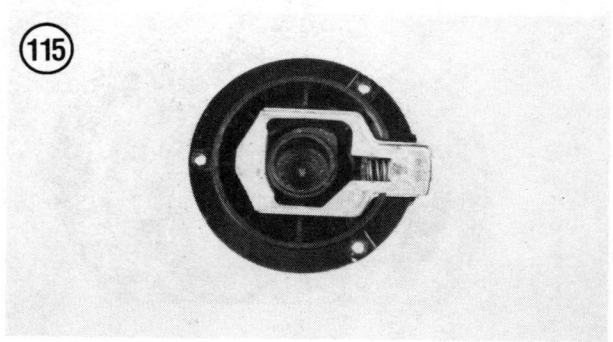

117

**FUEL TANK INSULATION
AND MOUNTING GASKET**

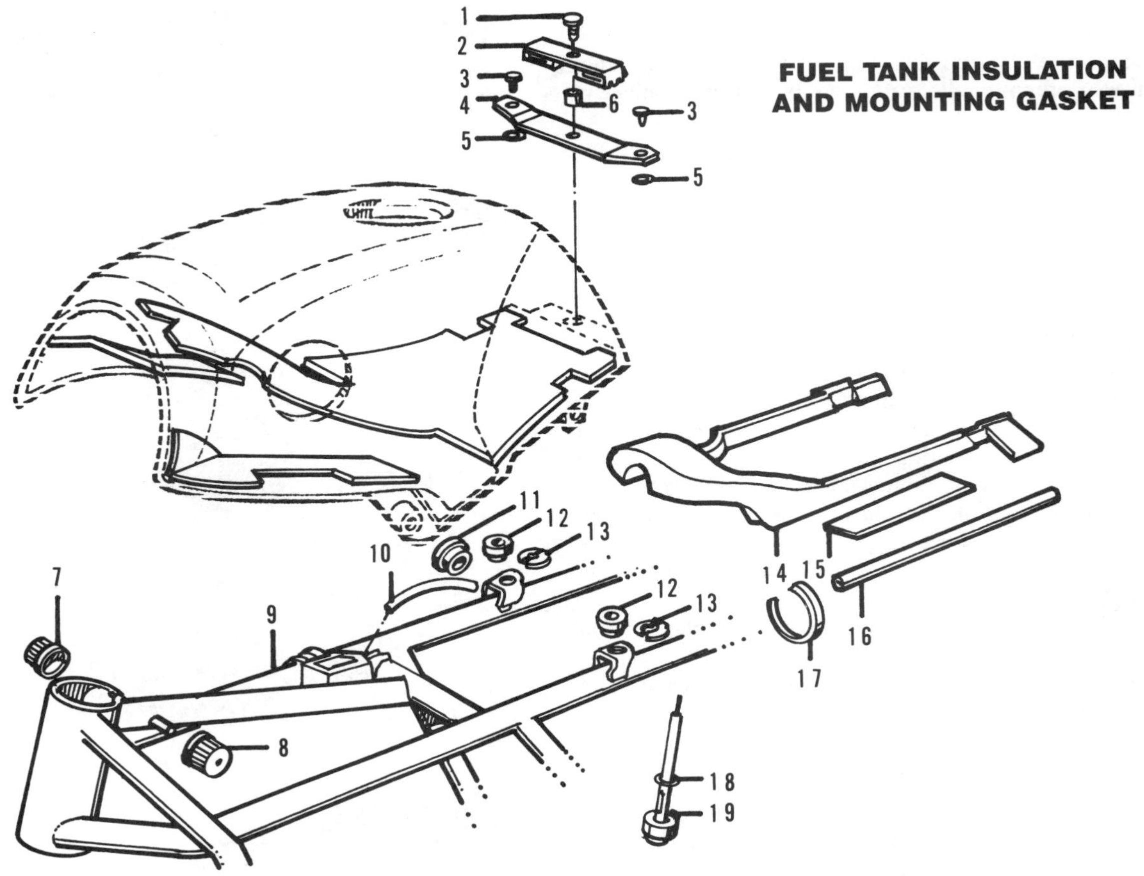

7

1. Bolt (K100)
2. Pad (K100)
3. Bolt (K100)
4. Bracket (K100)
5. Nut (K100)
6. Collar (K100)
7. Rubber cushion

8. Rubber cushion
9. Frame
10. Hose
11. Bracket
12. Rubber bushing (K75)
13. Retaining clip (K75)

14. Rubber pad (K100)
15. Adhesive strip
16. Hose
17. Cable strap
18. O-ring seal
19. Fuel gauge sensor

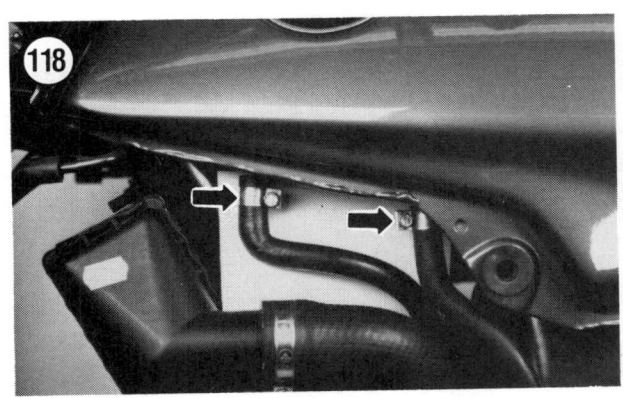

118

119

13. On models so equipped, disconnect the vent hoses from the fuel tank. Install a golf tee into the vent hoses to prevent the entry of foreign matter.

14. On California models, disconnect the pressure relief valve (**Figure 121**) from the vent line fitting on the fuel tank. Leave the pressure relief valve and its vent line in place in the frame.

15. Lift up on the rear of the tank and carefully pull the tank to the rear and remove it.

16. Install by reversing these removal steps, noting the following.

17. Inspect the rubber pad at the rear (**Figure 122**). Replace if damaged or starting to deteriorate.

18. Inspect the rubber mounting cushions at the front (**Figure 123**) and rear (**Figure 124**). Replace if they are damaged or starting to deteriorate.

19. Apply rubber lube, Armor All or equivalent to the rubber front mounting cushions on the frame. This will make fuel tank installation easier.

20. Make sure the vent and fuel hoses are installed correctly and not kinked. If the fuel hose is kinked, the fuel flow will be restricted. If the vent hose is kinked, abnormal pressure will buildup in the fuel tank which could damage the system.

21. Make sure the electrical connector is free of corrosion and tight.

22. After installation is complete, start the engine and thoroughly check for fuel leaks.

Removal/Installation
(K100 Models)

Refer to **Figure 106** and **Figure 117** for this procedure.
1. Place the bike on the center stand.
2. Remove the frame left-hand side cover.
3. Disconnect the battery negative lead as described under *Battery* in Chapter Three.
4. On models so equipped, remove the radiator trim panel as described under *Radiator Trim Panel Removal/Installation* in Chapter Thirteen.

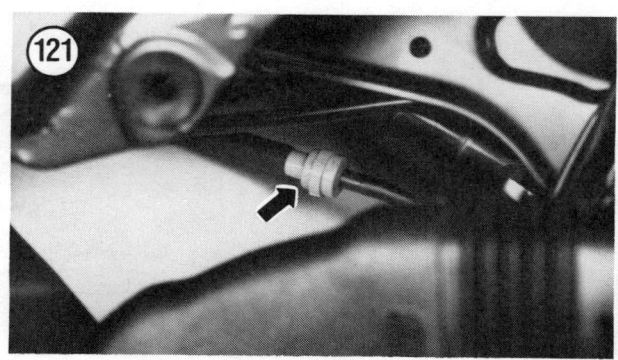
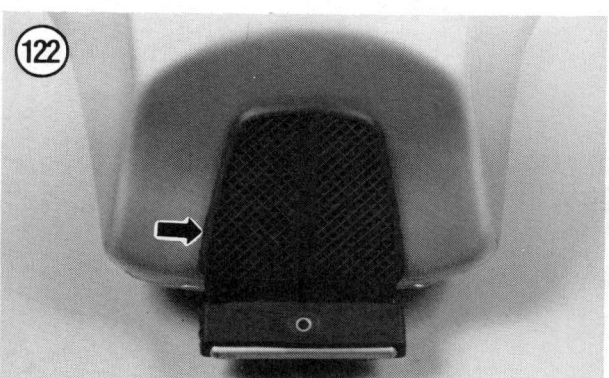

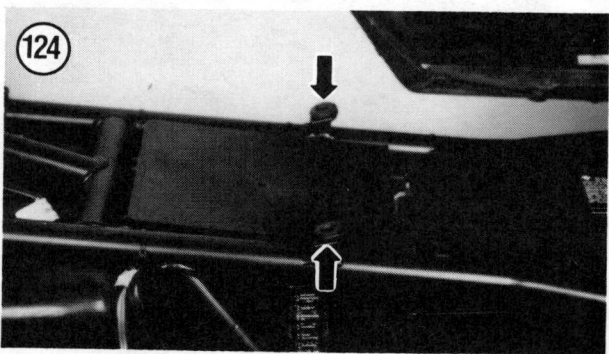

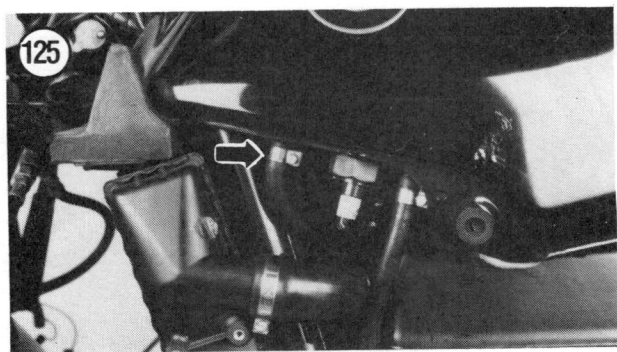

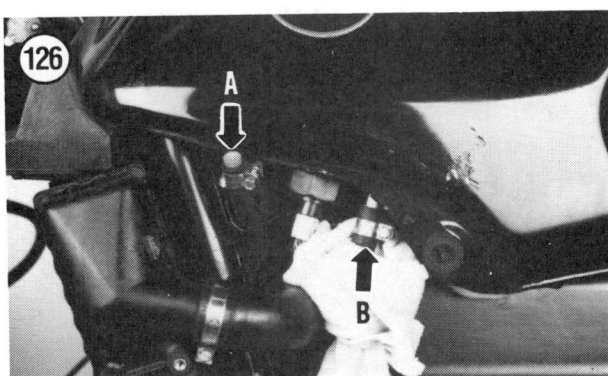

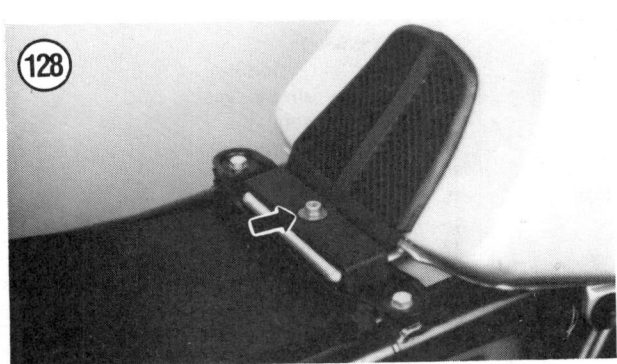

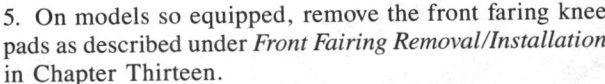

5. On models so equipped, remove the front faring knee pads as described under *Front Fairing Removal/Installation* in Chapter Thirteen.

6. Depressurize the fuel system as described in this chapter.

7. Disconnect the fuel return hose (**Figure 125**) from the fuel tank on the front left-hand corner. Install a golf tee (A, **Figure 126**) into the fuel hose to prevent the entry of foreign matter.

8. Wrap a shop rag around the fuel feed hose and disconnect the fuel feed hose (B, **Figure 126**) from the fuel tank. Install a golf tee into the fuel hose to prevent the entry of foreign matter.

9. Install a golf tee into the fuel line fittings (A, **Figure 127**) on the fuel tank to prevent fuel from dribbling out.

10. Disconnect the fuel pump and the fuel level sensor (models so equipped) electrical connector (B, **Figure 127**).

11. Remove the bolt (**Figure 128**) at the rear of the tank. Don't lose the metal spacer in the rubber cushion.

12. Pull up on the rear of the tank and place a wood block under the tank (**Figure 129**).

13. On models so equipped, disconnect the vent hoses (**Figure 130**) from the fuel tank. Install a golf tee into the vent hoses to prevent the entry of foreign matter.

14. On California models, disconnect the pressure relief valve (**Figure 121**) from the vent line fitting on the fuel tank. Leave the pressure relief valve and the vent line attached to it in place in the frame.

7

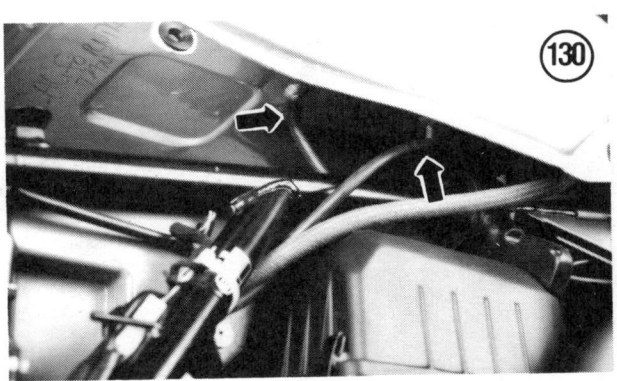

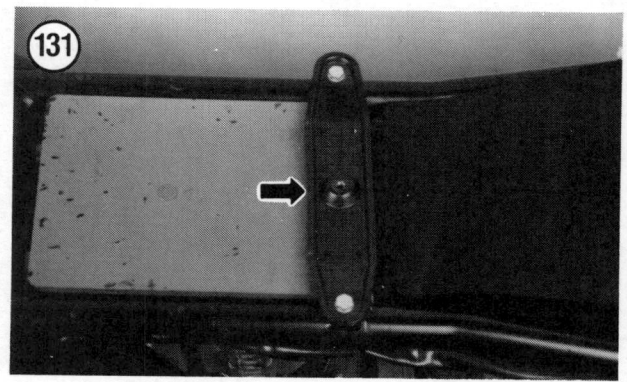

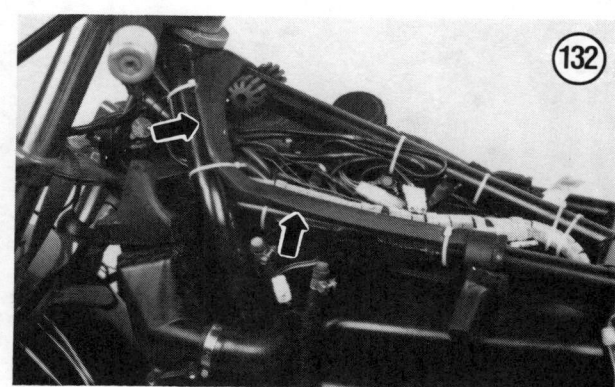

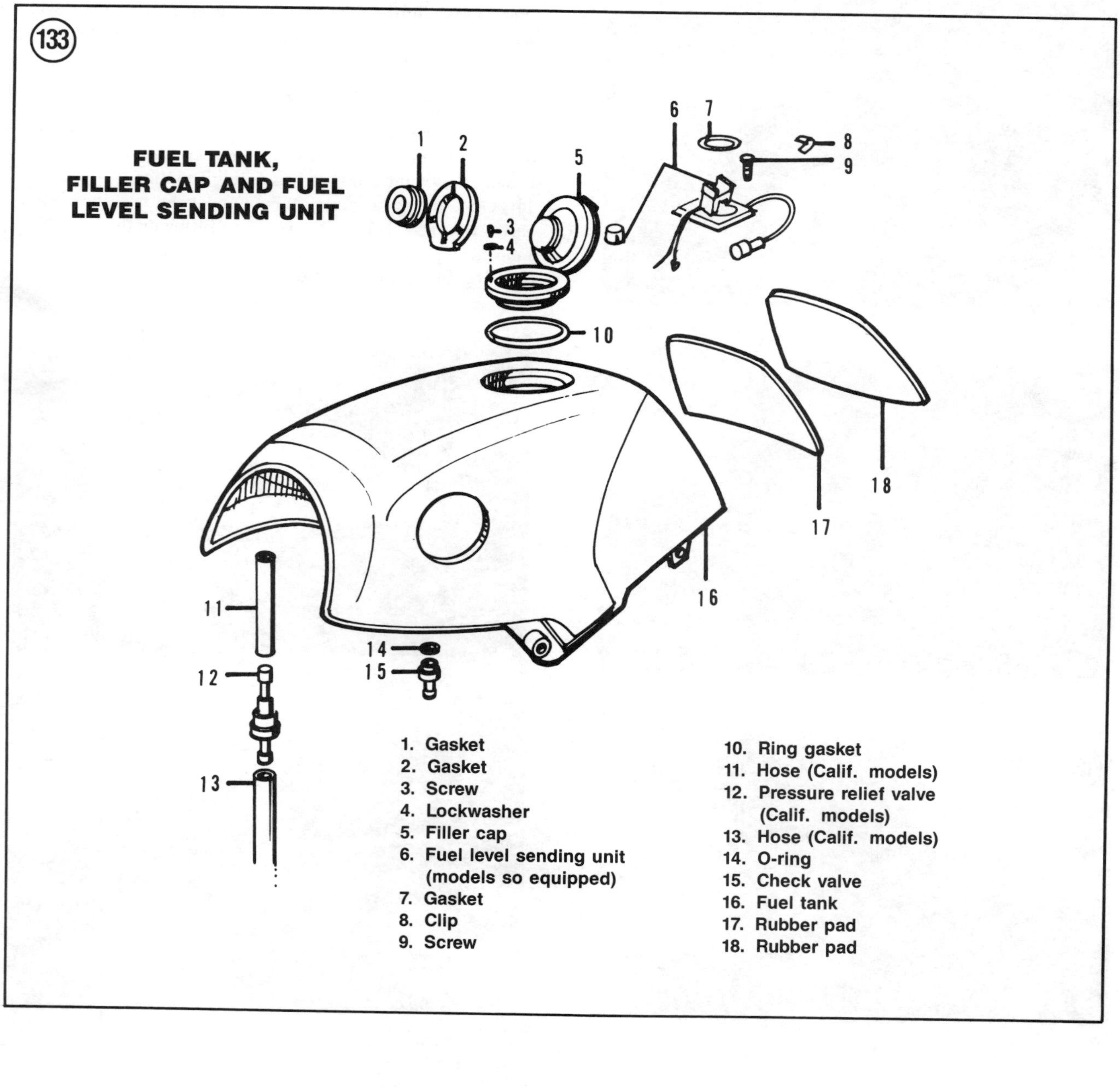

FUEL TANK, FILLER CAP AND FUEL LEVEL SENDING UNIT

1. Gasket
2. Gasket
3. Screw
4. Lockwasher
5. Filler cap
6. Fuel level sending unit (models so equipped)
7. Gasket
8. Clip
9. Screw
10. Ring gasket
11. Hose (Calif. models)
12. Pressure relief valve (Calif. models)
13. Hose (Calif. models)
14. O-ring
15. Check valve
16. Fuel tank
17. Rubber pad
18. Rubber pad

15. Lift up on the rear of the tank and carefully pull the tank to the rear and remove it.

16. If necessary, remove the bolts securing the seat support bracket (**Figure 131**) and remove the bracket.

17. Install by reversing these removal steps, noting the following.

18. Inspect the rubber mounting cushions at the front. Replace if they are damaged or starting to deteriorate.

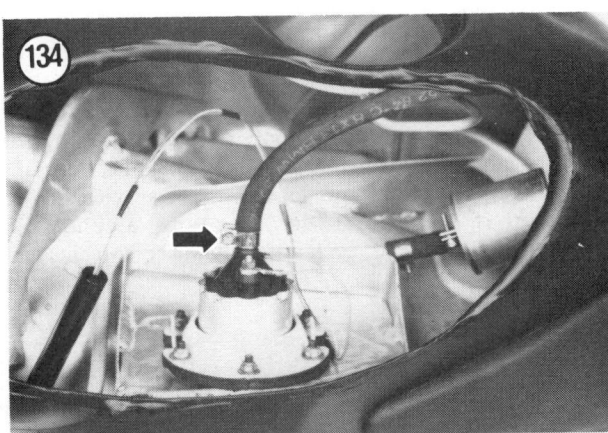

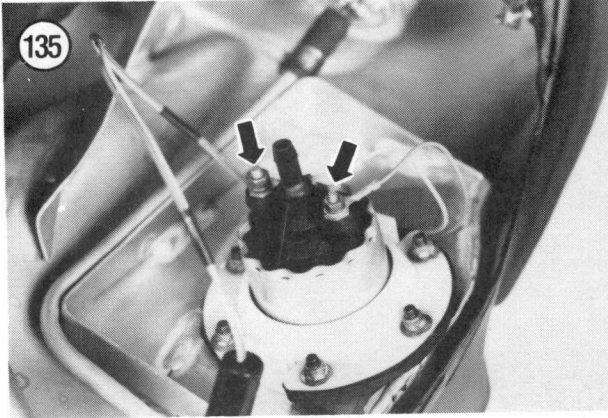

19. Inspect the horseshoe shaped rubber cushion that surrounds the frame (**Figure 132**). Remove the tie wraps and replace if it is damaged or starting to deteriorate.

20. Apply rubber lube, Armor All or equivalent to the rubber mounting cushions at the front of the frame. This will make fuel tank installation easier.

21. Make sure the vent and fuel hoses are installed correctly and not kinked. If the fuel hose is kinked, the fuel flow will be restricted. If the vent hose is kinked, abnormal pressure will build up in the fuel tank which could damage the system.

22. Make sure the electrical connector is free of corrosion and tight.

23. After installation is complete, start the engine and thoroughly check for fuel leaks.

FUEL GAUGE SENSOR

Removal/Installation

Refer to **Figure 133** for this procedure.

1. Remove the fuel tank as described in this chapter.

2. Place a thick blanket or shop cloths on the work bench to protect the fuel tank finish.

3. Remove the fuel filler cap as described in this chapter.

4. Siphon off all fuel in the tank and store it in a suitable sealed metal container.

5. If compressed air is available, blow out the interior of the fuel tank to evacuate most of the fumes.

6. Protect the painted surface of the fuel tank with heavy cloths or apply duct tape around the filler cap area.

7. Disconnect the fuel hose (**Figure 134**) from the top of the fuel pump.

8. Within the fuel tank, using a long-handled nut driver, remove the nuts (**Figure 135**) securing the electrical connectors to the fuel pump.

NOTE
*The electrical terminals (**Figure 136**) on the fuel pump are different sizes. The positive terminal is smaller (4 mm nut) while the negative terminal is larger (5 mm nut). The **original** electrical wire connectors have corresponding sized holes to help avoid intermixing the wires during installation. If you are working on an older bike, someone may have modified the wiring and connectors. Take note of the electrical wires' colors and the terminals to which they are attached prior to removal. Make sure they are attached to the correct terminals during assembly.*

9. Remove the nuts, lockwashers and washers from the electrical terminals. Remove the electrical wires from the connectors on the fuel pump. Note which side the *larger electrical terminal* is located on.

10. Turn the fuel tank upside down on the blanket or shop cloths (**Figure 137**).

11. If necessary, remove any insulating material from the left-hand side of the fuel tank to gain access to the fuel gauge sensor.

12. Unscrew the fuel gauge sensor (**Figure 138**) from the base of the fuel tank.

13. Carefully withdraw the fuel gauge sensor assembly and electrical wires from the opening in the base of the fuel tank.

14. Remove and discard the gasket seal from under the large nut (**Figure 139**) that secures the sensor to the fuel tank. To prevent a fuel leak, the gasket seal must be replaced every time the fuel gauge sensor is removed.

15. Install by reversing these removal steps, noting the following.

16. Install a *new* gasket seal in the large nut of the sensor.

17. Carefully insert the electrical wires into the fuel tank opening and install the fuel gauge sensor. Securely tighten the nut.

18. Be sure to attach the correct electrical wire to the correct terminal on the fuel pump (**Figure 135**).

19. Route the fuel pump electrical wires in *front* of the rear slosh panel (**Figure 140**). The backside of the slosh panel has a sharp edge at the top and may cut though the wiring insulation, causing a short.

20. Make sure the fuel hose (**Figure 134**) is properly attached to the outlet of the fuel pump.

21. Install the filler cap assembly as described in this chapter.

22. After installation is complete, thoroughly check for fuel leaks.

FUEL LEVEL SENDER
(MODELS SO EQUIPPED)

When the fuel level in the tank drops to 5 liters (1.3 gal.) the low fuel warning light, mounted on the instrument cluster, comes on. The warning light is activated by the fuel level sensor mounted within the fuel tank.

Removal/Installation

Refer to **Figure 133** for this procedure.

1. Remove the fuel tank as described in this chapter.

2. Remove the fuel pump as described in this chapter.

3. Place a thick blanket or shop cloths on the work bench to protect the fuel tank finish.

4. Turn the fuel tank upside down on the blanket or shop cloths.

5. If necessary, remove any insulating material from the center portion of the fuel tank to gain access to the fuel level sensor.

6. Remove the screws securing the fuel level sensor to the base of the fuel tank.

7. Carefully remove the fuel level sensor assembly from the opening in the base of the fuel tank. Do not bend the float arm during removal.

8. Remove and discard the O-ring seal from the mounting plate. To prevent a fuel leak, the O-ring seal must be replaced every time the fuel level sensor is removed.

9. Install by reversing these removal steps, noting the following.

10. Install a *new* O-ring seal and the fuel level sensor.

11. Install the fuel level sensor so the float mechanism is pointing toward the front of the fuel tank.

12. Tighten the mounting screws securely.

GASOLINE/ALCOHOL
BLEND TEST

Gasoline blended with alcohol is available in many areas. Most states and most fuel suppliers require labeling of gasoline pumps that dispense gasoline containing a certain percentage of alcohol. If in doubt, ask the service station operator if their fuel contains any alcohol. A gasoline/alcohol blend, even if it contains co-solvents and

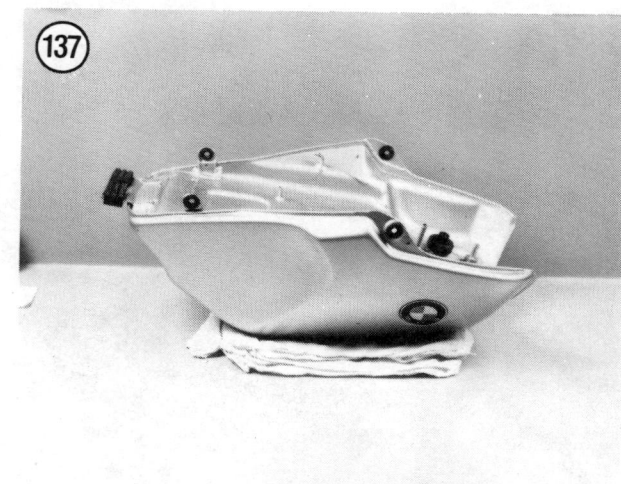

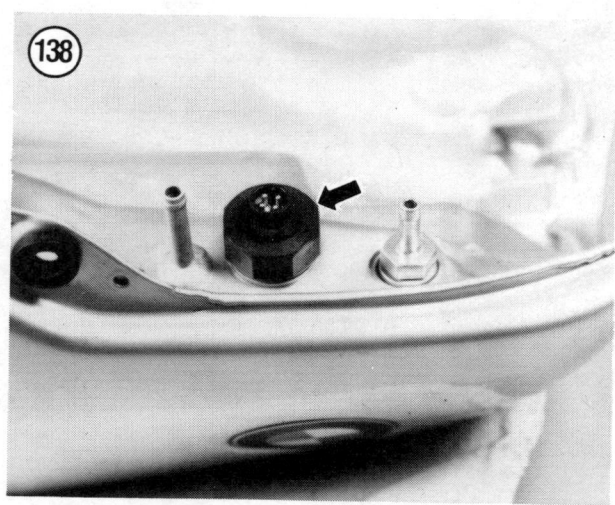

corrosion inhibitors for methanol, may damage the fuel system. It may also cause poor performance, hot-engine restart or hot-engine running problems.

If you are not sure if the fuel you purchased contains alcohol, run this simple and effective test. A blended fuel doesn't look any different from straight gasoline so it must be tested.

WARNING
Gasoline is very volatile and presents an extreme fire hazard. Be sure to work in a well-

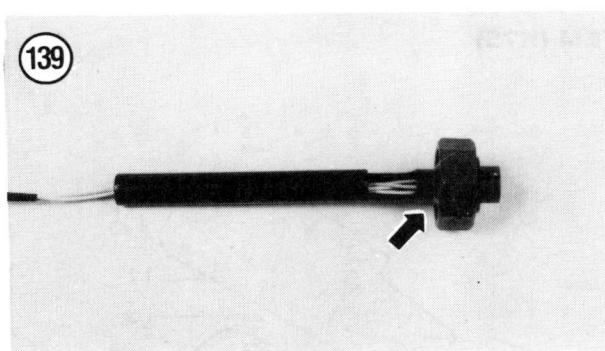

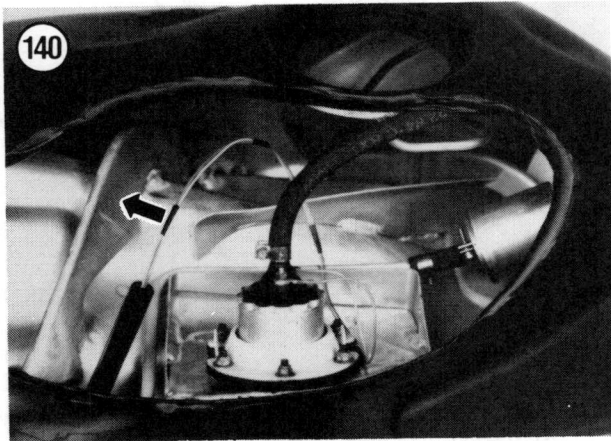

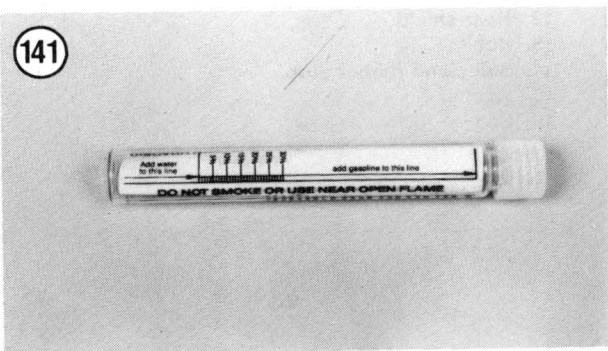

ventilated area away from any open flames (including pilot lights on household appliances). Do not allow anyone to smoke in the area and have a fire extinguisher rated for gasoline fires handy.

During this test keep the following facts in mind:
   a. Alcohol and gasoline mix together.
   b. Alchohol mixes *easier* with water.
   c. Gasoline and water do *not* mix.

NOTE
If co-solvents have been used in the gasoline, this test may not work with water. Repeat this test using automotive antifreeze instead of water.

NOTE
A very handy item is now available at some motorcycle dealers and motorcycle supply houses that is designed specifically for this test. It is a glass vial with a screw-on cap (**Figure 141**). There are instructions for performing the test printed on the side of the glass. If you purchase one of these items, follow the manufacturer's instructions.*

Use an 8 oz. transparent baby bottle with a sealable cap.
1. Set the baby bottle on a level surface and add water up to the 1.5 oz mark. Mark this line on the bottle with a fine-line permanent marking pen. This will be the reference line used later in this test.
2. Add the suspect fuel into the baby bottle up to the 8 oz. mark.
3. Install the sealable cap and shake the bottle vigorously for about 10 seconds.
4. Set the baby bottle upright on the level surface used in Step 1 and wait for a few minutes for the mixture to settle down.
5. If there is *no* alcohol in the fuel the gasoline/water separation line will be exactly on the 1.5 oz reference line made in Step 1.
6. If there *is* alcohol in the fuel the gasoline/water separation line will be *above* the 1.5 oz. reference line made in Step 1. The alcohol has separated from the gasoline and mixed in with the water (remember it is easier for the alcohol to mix with water than gasoline).

WARNING
*After the test, discard the baby bottle or place it out of reach of small children. There will always be a gasoline and alcohol residue in it and it should **not** be used to drink out of.*

CRANKCASE BREATHER SYSTEM
(U.S. ONLY)

To comply with air pollution standards, the BMW K-series bikes are equipped with a crankcase breather system. The system draws blowby gases from crankcase and recirculates them into the fuel/air mixture and thus into the engine to be burned.

Make sure all hose clamps are tight. Check all hoses for deterioration and replace as necessary.

EVAPORATIVE EMISSION CONTROL SYSTEM
(CALIFORNIA MODELS)

When the bike is stopped after a ride the fuel and fuel vapor in the fuel tank expands due to engine heat (or ambient temperature). When the pressure within the fuel tank reaches 20 kPa (2.9 psi) the pressure relief valve (**Figure 121**) opens, allowing the fuel vapor to enter the engine crankcase via a vent hose where it is stored.

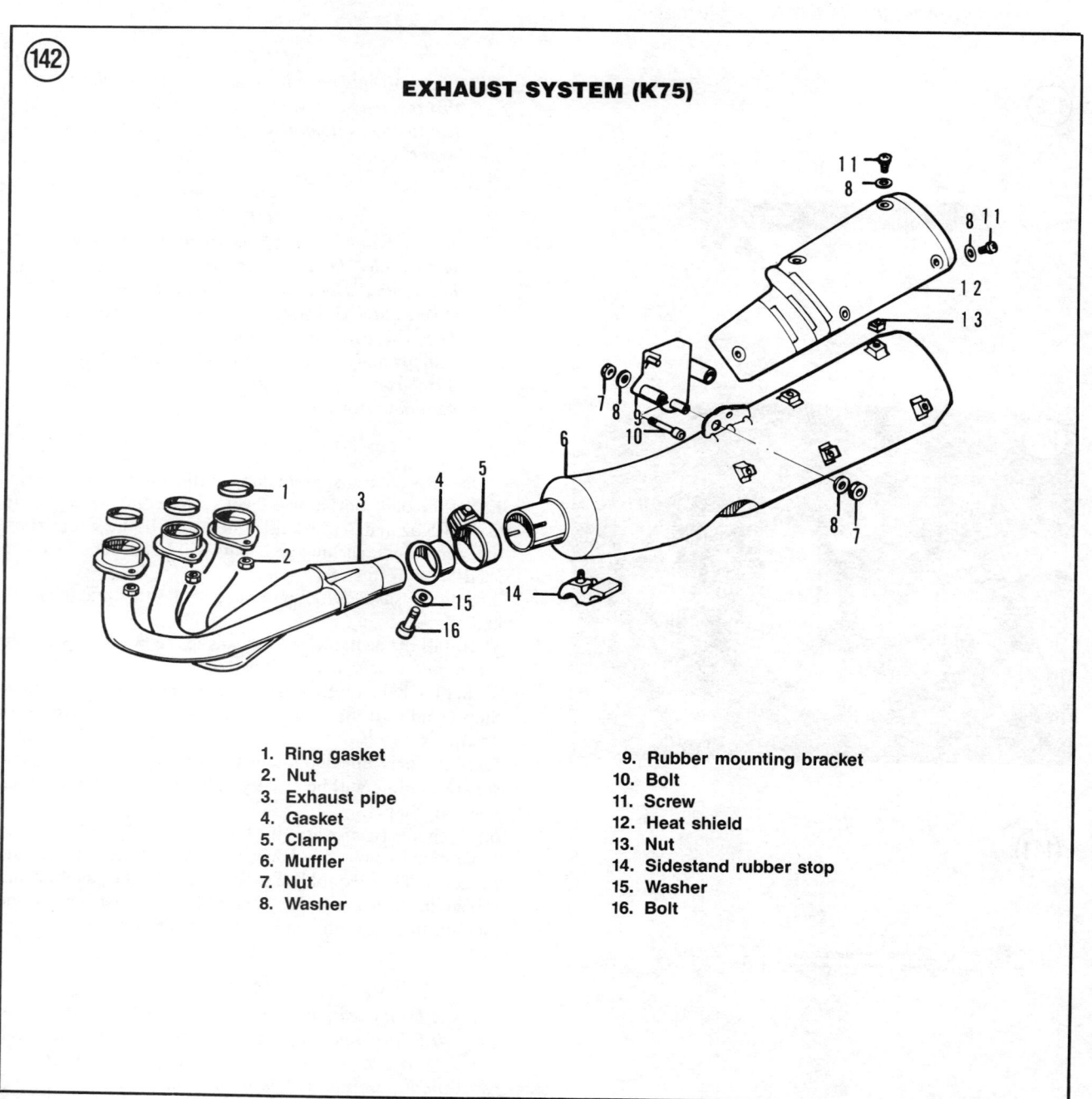

(142)

EXHAUST SYSTEM (K75)

1. Ring gasket
2. Nut
3. Exhaust pipe
4. Gasket
5. Clamp
6. Muffler
7. Nut
8. Washer
9. Rubber mounting bracket
10. Bolt
11. Screw
12. Heat shield
13. Nut
14. Sidestand rubber stop
15. Washer
16. Bolt

When the bike is restarted, the vacuum in the air collector of the air intake system pulls the fuel vapor from the crankcase and mixes it with the incoming fresh air to be burned in the engine.

There is no routine maintenance on the evaporation emission control system other than to inspect the hoses and the pressure relief valve whenever the fuel tank is removed. Make sure the hoses are not kinked or damaged.

Make sure all vapor hoses are correctly routed and attached. Inspect the hoses and replace any if necessary.

EXHAUST SYSTEM

The exhaust system consists of an exhaust pipe and a single muffler. The complete exhaust system is made of stainless steel and should last a long time if well maintained. Protect the finish with a good grade of stainless steel polish and wax.

The mounting flanges on the K75 models are an integral part of the exhaust pipe while those on the K100 models are separate.

Refer to **Figure 142** for K75 models or **Figure 143** for K100 models for this procedure.

7

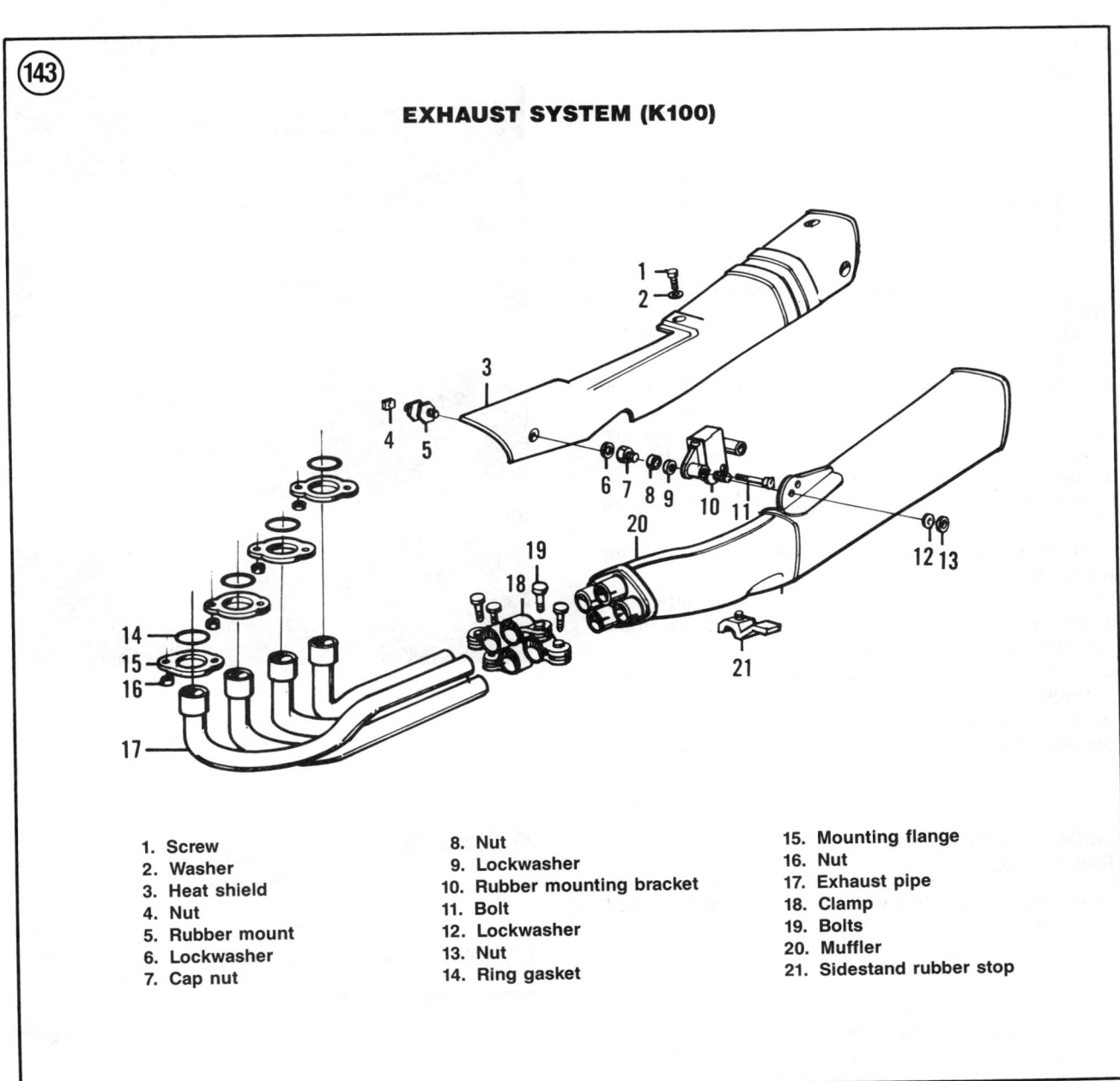

(143)

EXHAUST SYSTEM (K100)

1. Screw
2. Washer
3. Heat shield
4. Nut
5. Rubber mount
6. Lockwasher
7. Cap nut
8. Nut
9. Lockwasher
10. Rubber mounting bracket
11. Bolt
12. Lockwasher
13. Nut
14. Ring gasket
15. Mounting flange
16. Nut
17. Exhaust pipe
18. Clamp
19. Bolts
20. Muffler
21. Sidestand rubber stop

Muffler Removal/Installation (K75 Models)

WARNING
Do not work on the exhaust system when it is hot. Allow the system to cool down prior to performing any service procedures.

1. Place the bike on the center stand. Lower the sidestand to get it out of the way.
2. Loosen the clamping bolt (**Figure 144**) securing the muffler to the exhaust pipe.
3. Remove the bolts (**Figure 145**) securing the muffler to the left-hand rear foot peg assembly.
4. Pull the muffler off of the footpeg assembly.

NOTE
If difficult to remove, spray some WD-40 or equivalent on the clamping bolt(s) to help loosen the muffler from the exhaust pipe outlet(s).

5. Carefully pull the muffler back and out of the exhaust pipe outlet(s).
6. Inspect the heat shield for damage and deterioration. Replace if necessary as follows:
   a. Remove the bolts and washers securing the heat shield to the muffler and remove the heat shield.
   b. Reinstall the heat shield and tighten the bolts securely.
7. Inspect the rubber stopper for the side stand. Replace if worn or starting to deteriorate.
8. Install a new gasket between the muffler and the exhaust pipe.
9. Make sure the clamp is in place on the muffler prior to installation.
10. Install the muffler onto the exhaust pipe outlet.
11. Install the muffler onto the footpeg assembly and install the bolts only finger-tight at this time.
12. Tighten the clamp bolts to the torque specification listed in **Table 2**.
13. Tighten the bolts securing the muffler to the footpeg assembly to the torque specification listed in **Table 2**.

Muffler Removal/Installation (K100 Models)

This procedure is shown with the exhaust system removed for clarity.

WARNING
Do not work on the exhaust system when it is hot. Allow the system to cool down prior to performing any service procedures.

1. Place the bike on the center stand. Also lower the sidestand to get it out of the way.

NOTE
Prior to loosening the clamping bolts, note the location of the clamps so they will be reinstalled in the same position. With 4 clamps located in such a small area they have to be

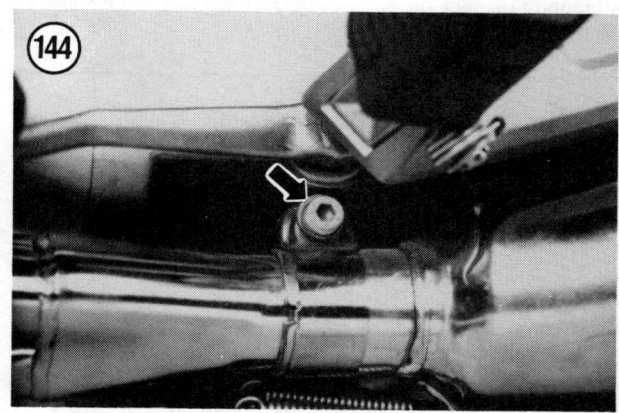

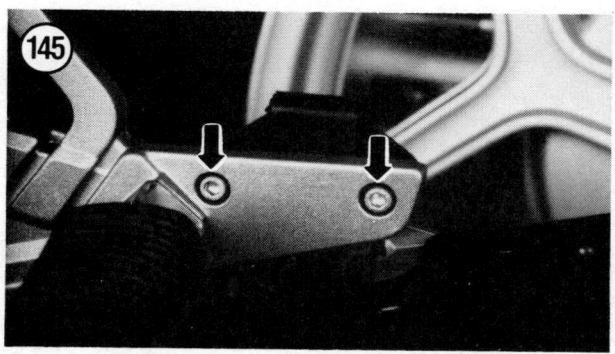

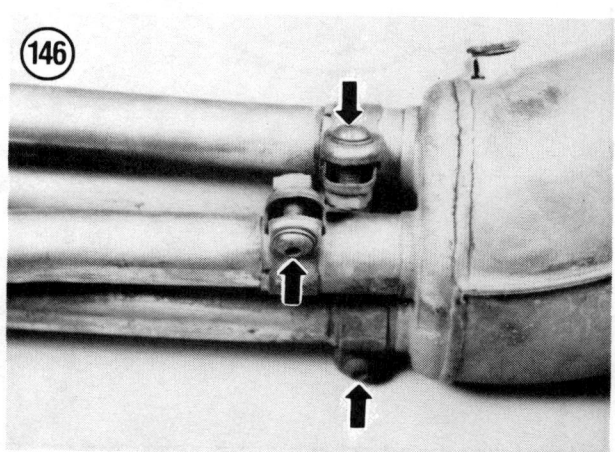

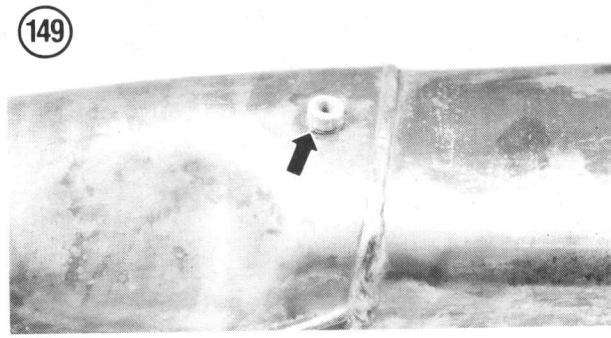

positioned correctly, otherwise there will be an exhaust leak.

2. Loosen the clamping bolt (**Figure 146**) on each clamp securing the muffler to the exhaust pipe.
3. Remove the bolts (**Figure 147**) securing the muffler to the left-hand rear footpeg assembly.
4. Pull the muffler off of the footpeg assembly.

> *NOTE*
> *If difficult to remove, spray some WD-40 or equivalent on the clamping bolt(s) to help loosen the muffler from the exhaust pipe outlet(s).*

5. Carefully pull the muffler back and out of the exhaust pipe outlet(s).
6. Inspect the heat shield for damage and deterioration. Replace if necessary as follows:
    a. Remove the cap nut (A, **Figure 148**) and lockwasher at the front of the heat shield.
    b. Remove the bolts (B, **Figure 148**) and lockwashers securing the heat shield.
    c. Remove the heat shield. Don't lose the spacers (**Figure 149**) at each bolt hole.
    d. Reinstall the spacers and heat shield. Tighten the bolts and cap nut securely.
7. Inspect the rubber stopper for the sidestand. Replace if worn or starting to deteriorate.
8. Make sure the clamp(s) are in place on the muffler prior to installation.
9. Install the muffler onto the exhaust pipe outlets.
10. Install the muffler onto the footpeg assembly and install the bolts only finger-tight at this time.
11. Locate the clamps as noted during removal.
12. Tighten the clamp bolts to the torque specification listed in **Table 2**.
13. Tighten the bolts securing the muffler to the footpeg assembly to the torque specification listed in **Table 2**.

**Exhaust Pipe
Removal/Installation**

> *WARNING*
> *Do not work on the exhaust system when it is hot. Allow the system to cool down prior to performing any service procedures.*

1. On models so equipped, remove the engine fairing as described under *Engine Fairing Removal/Installation* in Chapter Thirteen.
2. Remove the muffler as described in this chapter.
3A. On K75 models, loosen the nuts (**Figure 150**) on the mounting flanges securing the exhaust pipe to the cylinder head.

7

3B. On K100 models, loosen the nuts (**Figure 151**) on the mounting flanges securing the exhaust pipe to the cylinder head.

4. Remove the mounting flange nuts.

5. Pull the exhaust pipe free of the cylinder head and remove it.

6. Remove the ring gaskets either from the cylinder head port or the exhaust pipe. Discard all ring gaskets—they must be replaced every time the exhaust pipe is removed in order to maintain a leak-free seal.

7. Inspect the exhaust pipe for wear, rust, damage (**Figure 152**) or slight "burn through areas." Replace the exhaust pipe if necessary.

8. Inspect the exhaust pipes where they enter the cylinder head (**Figure 153**) for damage. Replace the exhaust pipe if necessary.

9. Install a new ring gasket in each exhaust port in the cylinder head.

10. Install the exhaust pipe onto the cylinder head and install the nut only finger-tight at this time.

11. Install the muffler as described—*but* do not tighten the bolts and nuts at this time.

12. After both the exhaust pipe and muffler are installed, then tighten the exhaust flange nuts to the torque specification listed in **Table 2**. This will minimize the chances of an exhaust leak at the cylinder head.

13. Tighten all bolts and nuts to the torque specification listed in **Table 2**.

14. After installation is complete, make sure there are no exhaust leaks.

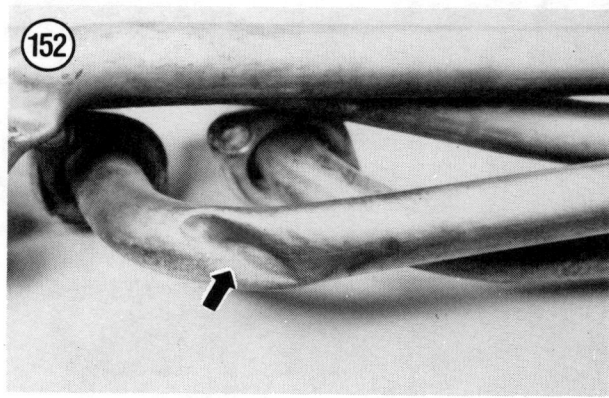

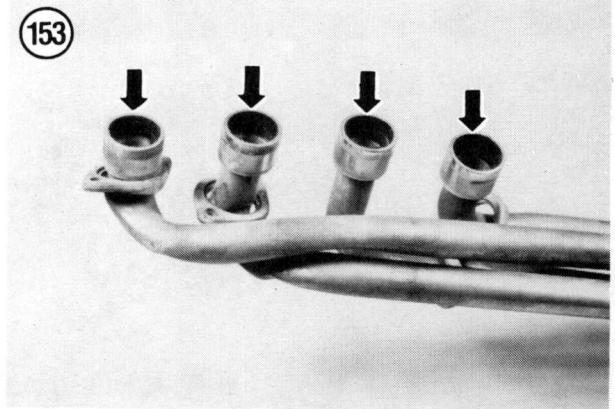

Table 1 FUEL SYSTEM SPECIFICATIONS

Recommended fuel type	Regular unleaded
Fuel tank capacity	
K75 models	21 liters (5.5 U.S. gal.)
K100 and K1100 models	22 liters (5.8 U.S. gal.)
Fuel pump (Bosch)	
Roller cell type	12-volt
Delivery rate	47 liters/hr (45 U.S. qts./hr)
Fuel pressure	36 psi (248 kPa)

Table 2 FUEL AND EXHAUST SYSTEM TORQUE SPECIFICATIONS

Item	N•m	ft.-lb.
Pressure regulator hex nut	22-28	16-20
Air filter lower case half		
mounting bolts	19-22	14-16
Muffler-to-exhaust pipe		
clamp bolts	19-22	14-16
Muffler-to-footpeg assembly bolts	8-10	6-7
Exhaust pipe mounting flange nuts		
K75	19-22	14-16
K100	16.5	11.5

7

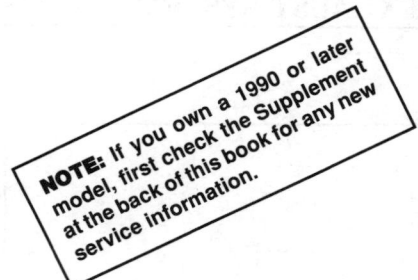
NOTE: If you own a 1990 or later model, first check the Supplement at the back of this book for any new service information.

CHAPTER EIGHT

ELECTRICAL SYSTEM

The electrical system consists of the following:
a. Charging system.
b. Ignition system.
c. Lighting system.
d. Directional signal system.
e. Switches.
f. Electrical components.

Tables 1-4 are located at the end of this chapter.
Wiring diagrams are at the end of the book.
For complete spark plug and battery information and service procedures, refer to Chapter Three.

CHARGING SYSTEM

The charging system consists of the battery and a 3-phase, 12-volt alternator with an integral voltage regulator/rectifier.

Alternating current generated by the alternator is rectified to direct current. The voltage regulator maintains the voltage to the battery and additional electrical loads (lights, ignition, etc.) at a constant voltage regardless of variations in engine speed and load.

The alternator is driven by the auxiliary shaft of the engine. Since the auxiliary shaft rotates faster than the crankshaft (1:1.5) the alternator achieves approximately 1/3 of its maximum output of 460 watts when the engine is at idle speed. This enables the alternator to maintain the charging system even at low speed.

Leakage Test

Perform this test prior to performing the output test.
1. Remove the frame left-hand side cover.
2. Turn the ignition to the OFF position.

3. Refer to *Battery* in Chapter Three and disconnect the battery negative (-) lead.
4. Connect a voltmeter between the battery ground cable and the negative terminal on the battery.
5. The voltmeter should read 0 volts.
6. If there is a voltage reading, this indicates a voltage drain in the system that will drain the battery.
7. Check all components of the charging system for any bare wires that may be shorting out which could cause the drain.

Output Test

Whenever charging system trouble is suspected, make sure the battery is fully charged and in good condition before going any further. Clean and test the battery as described under *Battery* in Chapter Three.
1. Turn the ignition switch on. The charge light on the instrument cluster should come on. If the light does not come on, refer to *Instrument Cluster* in this chapter and see if the charge light bulb is burned out.
2. Start the bike and increase idle speed. The charge light should now go off. If the light does not go off, shut off the engine. Check the alternator brushes, as they are usually the primary problem. Refer to *Alternator Brush Replacement* in this chapter.
3. Start the bike and let it reach normal operating temperature. Usually 10-15 minutes of stop-and-go riding is sufficient. Shut off the engine.
4. Remove the right- and left-hand side covers.
5. Refer to *Battery* in Chapter Three and make sure that the battery cables are securely attached to the battery terminals and that the terminals are clean. If necessary remove the battery cables, clean the terminals and cables and reconnect the battery cables.

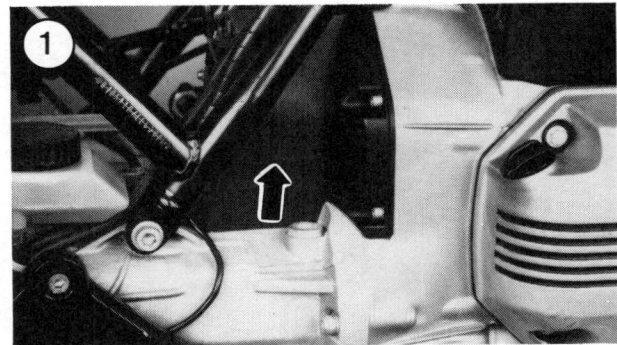

6. Leave the battery terminal protective covers hinged up as the terminals must be accessible.

7. Connect a portable tachometer following the manufacturer's instructions.

8. Start the engine and let it run at a fast idle of approximately 1,400 rpm.

9. Connect a 0-20 volt voltmeter to the battery terminals. The reading should be between 13-14 volts.

10. Turn on all lights and accessories. The voltage reading should remain between 13-14 volts.

11. If the voltage is less than specified, inspect the alternator brushes and commutator as described in this chapter.

12. If the voltage is more than specified, the voltage regulator is probably faulty and must be replaced as described in this chapter.

13. Shut the engine off and disconnect the voltmeter and portable tachometer.

14. Hinge the battery terminal protective covers down to the closed position.

15. Install the right- and left-hand side covers.

ALTERNATOR

The alternator is a form of electrical generator in which a rotor, which produces a magnetic field, revolves within a set of stationary coils called a stator assembly. As the rotor revolves, alternating current is induced in the stator coils. The current is then rectified to direct current and is used to operate the electrical systems on the motorcycle and to keep the battery charged.

Removal/Installation

1. Remove both frame side covers.

2. Remove the fuel injection control unit and storage tray as described under *Fuel Injection Control Unit Removal/Installation* in Chapter Seven.

3. Remove the battery as described under *Battery Removal/Installation* in Chapter Three.

4. Remove the coolant recovery tank as described under *Coolant Recovery Tank Removal/Installation* in Chapter Nine.

5. Remove the screws securing the alternator side cover (**Figure 1**) and remove the cover.

6. Pull the electrical connector (**Figure 2**) straight back and disconnect it from the rear of the alternator.

NOTE
Figure 3 is shown with the engine removed for clarity.

7. Remove the bolts (**Figure 3**) securing the alternator to the back of the engine.

8. Pull the alternator straight back out and disengage it from the drive dog on the backside of the intermediate flange on the engine. Don't lose the rubber dampers (**Figure 4**) located in the clutch housing.

8

9. Install by reversing these removal steps, noting the following.

10. Install the rubber dampers so they fit between the raised ribs in the clutch housing (**Figure 5**).

11. Make sure all of the rubber dampers (**Figure 4**) are installed in the clutch housing. Apply a light coat of rubber lube or Armor All to the slots in the rubber dampers to make installation easier.

12. Install the alternator and align the slots in the rubber dampers onto the raised tabs on the drive dog on the engine. Push the alternator in until it bottoms out.

13. Install the mounting bolts and tighten to the torque specification listed in **Table 1**.

14. Make sure the electrical connector is free of corrosion and is securely attached the alternator.

ALTERNATOR

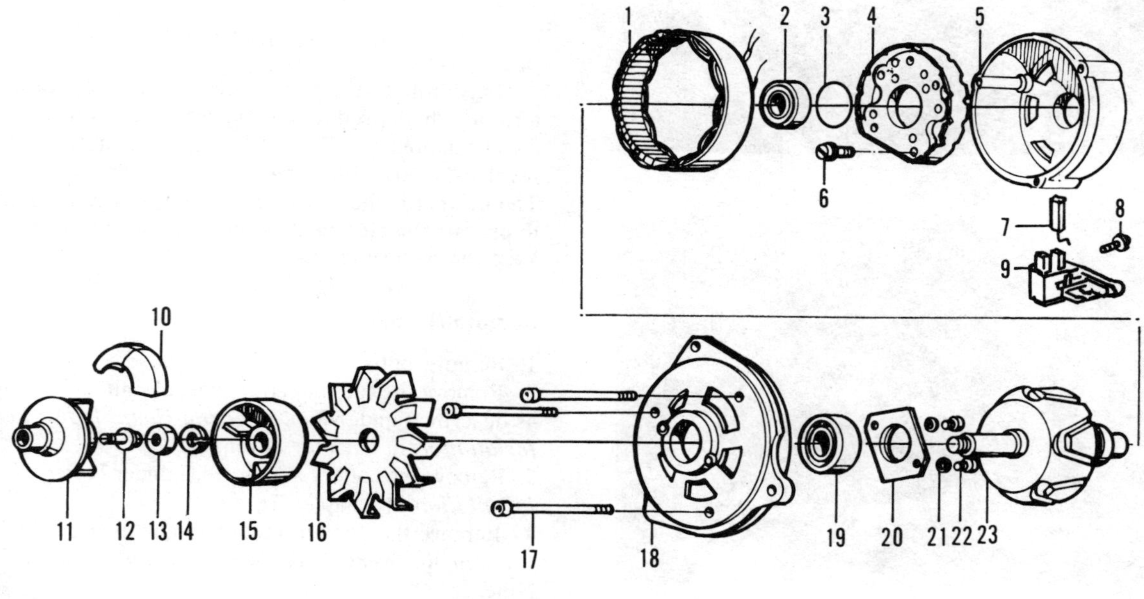

1. Stator assembly
2. Bearing
3. O-ring
4. Rectifier assembly
5. Housing
6. Bolt
7. Brush
8. Bolt
9. Voltage regulator/brush assembly
10. Rubber dampers
11. Drive dog
12. Bolt
13. Nut
14. Lockwasher
15. Clutch housing
16. Fan
17. Bolt
18. Cover
19. Bearing
20. Bearing plate
21. Lockwasher
22. Bolt
23. Rotor assembly

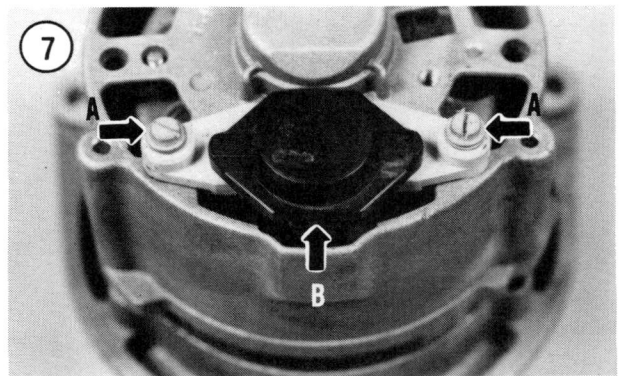

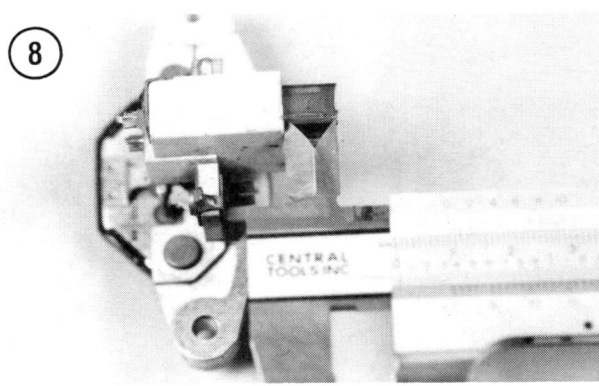

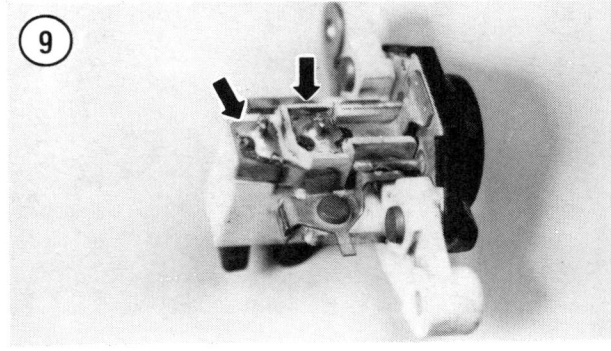

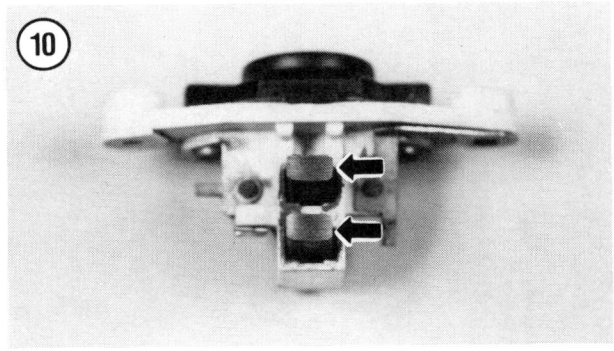

Brush Replacement

The brushes can be replaced without disassembling the alternator unit. The brush assembly can be removed with the alternator installed in the engine, but alternator removal is very simple.

Refer to **Figure 6** for this procedure.

1. Remove the alternator as described in this chapter.

2. Remove the screws (A, **Figure 7**) securing the voltage regulator and brush assembly (B, **Figure 7**) and withdraw the unit from the rear of the alternator.

3. Measure the length of the brushes with a vernier caliper (**Figure 8**). If worn to the service limit projection listed in **Table 2**, the brushes must be replaced.

> *CAUTION*
> *The individual brushes are soldered in place in the voltage regulator and brush assembly. While using the soldering gun, be careful not to overheat the assembly, as excessive heat will damage the voltage regulator portion of the assembly.*

4. Using a soldering gun on the low heat range unsolder the individual brush from the assembly (**Figure 9**). Remove the brush and repeat for the other brush. Replace the brushes as a set even if only one is worn to the service limit.

> *CAUTION*
> *The new brushes must move freely after they are installed. If they do not move freely they will not make contact with the slip rings and will make the alternator inoperative.*

5. Install the new brushes as follows:
   a. Insert the brushes and solder them in place. Avoid excessive heat.
   b. Make sure that the solder *does not* run down the brush leads during installation. If the solder runs down onto the brush and its channel, it will inhibit brush movement.
   c. The brushes (**Figure 10**) must move freely in order to maintain contact on the slip rings.
   d. Remove any excessive solder from the brush channels.

6. Install the voltage regulator and brush assembly into the rear of the alternator. Install the screws and tighten securely.

7. Install the alternator as described in this chapter.

Disassembly/Assembly

Alternator overhaul is best left to an expert. This procedure shows how to detect a defective alternator.

Refer to **Figure 6** for this procedure.

1. Remove the alternator as described in this chapter.
2. Remove the screws (A, **Figure 7**) securing the voltage regulator and brush assembly (B, **Figure 7**) and withdraw the unit from the rear of the alternator.
3. Make a mark on the cover and the case (**Figure 11**) to assure proper alignment during assembly.
4. If not already removed, remove the rubber dampers (**Figure 4**) from the clutch housing.
5. Remove the nut (**Figure 12**) and lockwasher (**Figure 13**) securing the clutch housing and fan.
6. Remove the clutch housing (A, **Figure 14**) and the fan (B, **Figure 14**).
7. Remove the Woodruff key (**Figure 15**).
8. Remove the long screws (**Figure 16**) securing the cover to the housing.
9. Remove the cover and rotor assembly (A, **Figure 17**) from the housing (B, **Figure 17**).
10. Remove the screws (**Figure 18**) securing the stator and rectifier assembly in the housing.
11. Make a mark on the stator/rectifier assembly and the housing (**Figure 19**) to assure proper alignment during assembly.

12. Remove the stator and rectifier assembly.

13. Inspect the components as described in this chapter.

14. Assemble by reversing these disassembly steps, noting the following.

15. Be sure to align the mark on the stator/rectifier assembly and the housing (**Figure 19**).

16. Be sure to install the Woodruff key (**Figure 15**).

17. Be sure to align the cutout (**Figure 20**) for the Woodruff key with the Woodruff key when installing the fan.

18. Be sure to align the mark on the cover and the case (**Figure 11**).

19. Be sure to install the Woodruff key before installing the clutch housing.

20. Tighten all screws and the nut securely.

Inspection

1. Make sure the rotor bearings (**Figure 21**) rotate freely. If necessary, press the old bearing off and install a new one.

2. Inspect the rubber dampers (**Figure 22**) for wear, damage or deterioration. Replace as a set of 3 if any are damaged.

3. Inspect the housing (**Figure 23**) for cracks or damage. Replace if necessary.
4. Inspect the windings (**Figure 24**) of the stator assembly for wear or damage. Replace the stator assembly if necessary.
5. Inspect the slip rings (**Figure 25**) for wear or corrosion. Clean off with solvent. If corrosion is severe, carefully clean off with 600 wet and dry sandpaper. Then clean with aerosol electrical contact cleaner. Wipe clean with a lint-free cloth.
6. Check the O-ring seal (**Figure 26**) in the housing for wear or damage. Replace if necessary.
7. Inspect the fan (**Figure 27**) for cracks or damage. Replace if necessary.
8. Inspect the rubber damper ribs (**Figure 28**) in the clutch housing for cracks or damage. Replace if necessary.
9. Inspect the Woodruff keyway (**Figure 29**) in the clutch housing for wear or damage. Replace if necessary.

Rotor Testing

BMW does not provide any service specifications for the rotor assembly (**Figure 30**). If defective, the rotor must be replaced; it cannot be serviced.

Stator Testing

BMW does not provide any service specifications for the stator assembly. If defective, the stator must be replaced; it cannot be serviced.

VOLTAGE RECTIFIER

Test

The voltage rectifier is built into the alternator and can be tested while still attached to the stator assembly.

Use an analog ohmmeter (one with an indicator needle) for this test. The test current of digital ohmmeters is so small that it will flow both ways through a diode, indicating falsely that the diode is bad.

In this test when using the ohmmeter, the current must flow through each diode in one direction only. With the ohmmeter leads connected one way there should be current flow (low resistance) and with the test leads reversed there should be no current flow (infinite resistance) through each diode.

1. Remove the alternator and disassemble it as described in this chapter.
2. Use an ohmmeter set at R × 1 and check continuity between the rectifier's electrical connector terminals.
3. Connect the ohmmeter leads to the D+ terminal and to each of the 3 wires coming from the stator assembly and note the readings. Reverse the ohmmeter leads and note the readings. The second reading should be opposite the first reading.
4. Connect the ohmmeter leads to the B+ terminal and to each of the 3 wires coming from the stator assembly and note the readings. Reverse the ohmmeter leads and note the

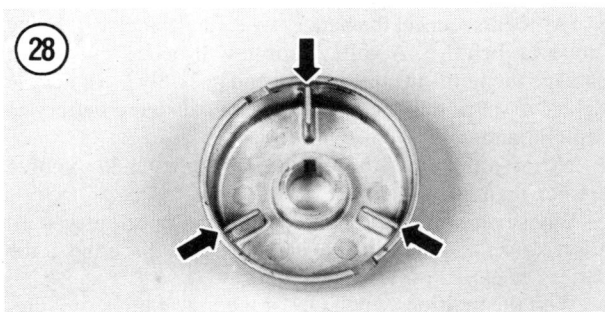

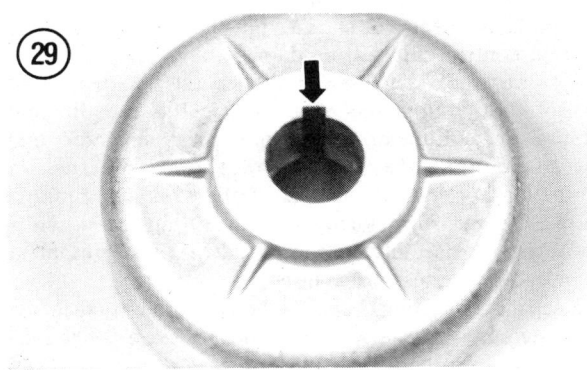

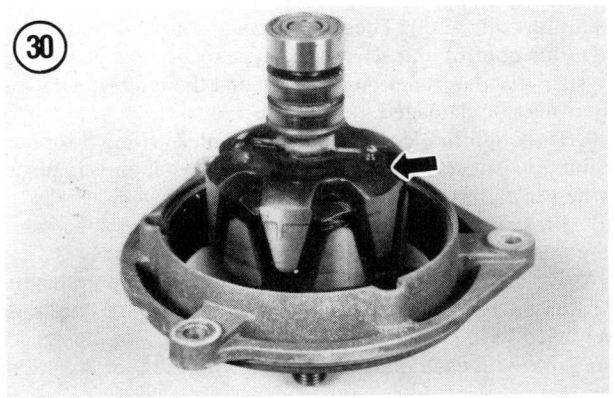

readings. The second reading should be opposite the first reading.

5. Connect the ohmmeter leads to the diode plate and to each of the 3 wires coming from the stator assembly and note the readings. Reverse the ohmmeter leads and note the readings. The second reading should be opposite the first reading.

6. If the rectifier portion of the voltage regulator/rectifier fails any of these tests, the unit is faulty and must be replaced as described in this chapter.

Rectifier Replacement

Refer to **Figure 6** for this procedure.
1. Remove the alternator as described in this chapter.
2. Disassemble the alternator as described in this chapter.

> *CAUTION*
> *The rectifier leads are soldered in place in the stator windings. While using the soldering gun, be careful to not overheat the assembly as excessive heat will damage the surrounding wiring and destroy the diodes.*

> *NOTE*
> *Before unsoldering the electrical wires, note where each wire is attached. They must be reattached to the same connector in order for the alternator to operate correctly.*

3. Using a soldering gun on the low heat range, unsolder the individual wires connected to the rectifier assembly (**Figure 31**). Remove the rectifier assembly from the stator assembly.
4. Install the new rectifier assembly and solder each wire in place using the same caution relating to excessive heat. Make sure that any excess solder *does not* run down onto the stator assembly as it may short out any exposed wires.
5. Assemble the alternator as described in this chapter.
6. Install the alternator as described in this chapter.

8

IGNITION SYSTEMS

All BMW K-series models are equipped with a solid state transistorized ignition system that uses no breaker points. This system provides a longer life for the components and delivers a more efficient spark throughout the entire speed range of the engine than breaker point systems.

The ignition system consists of an ignition control unit (computer); a trigger assembly or Hall-effect transmitter; 3 individual ignition coils on K75 models or 2 dual ignition coils on K100 models; and either 3 spark plugs (K75 models) or 4 spark plugs (K100 models). Refer to **Figure 32**.

The Hall transmitter is attached to the front end of the crankshaft and the rotor turns at crankshaft speed. The ignition signal is triggered by this transmitter and is sent to the ignition control unit. The ignition control unit then evaluates this information in addition to engine rpm and builds up the voltage on the primary side of the ignition coils.

The ignition control unit is pre-programmed to decide whether to advance or retard the spark according to engine speed. Below an engine speed of 1,300 rpm the basic ignition timing is 6 degrees before top dead center (BTDC). Above this engine speed, the ignition timing is varied electronically by the ignition control unit. There are 2 characteristic ignition curves programmed into the ignition control unit. One is the par-load curve and the other is the full-load curve. The system chooses one of these curves, and relates this information to the fuel injection control unit to determine the correct amount of fuel to achieve fuel savings when applicable. Ignition timing is not fixed, but is to be adjusted only to one setting as described in this chapter. If ignition timing is incorrect, the Hall transmitter base plate probably has moved or an ignition system part is faulty.

The ignition control unit has several built-in safety features for engine protection. One of these prevents engine over-revving. When engine speed reaches 8,770 rpm the fuel injection system is automatically shut off to prevent engine damage. The fuel injection shutoff is controlled in 2 stages to prevent slowing down engine speed too rapidly.

A lockout feature is also included to prevent the starter motor from operating if the engine is running. Power to the starter relay is shut off by the ignition control unit if engine speed is greater than 711 rpm.

To prevent flooding if the engine has stopped suddenly for some reason, the ignition control unit shuts off the fuel pump via the fuel pump relay. Also the primary current is shut off within one second to the output-stage resistors and the ignition coils.

Ignition System Precautions

Certain measures must be taken to protect the transistorized ignition system. Damage to the semiconductors in the system may occur if the following precautions are not observed.

WARNING
*This ignition system produces a very high electrical output that could be **very dangerous or even fatal** if any of the components or any uninsulated electrical connections are touched while the engine is running or if the ignition switch is the ON position. Be very careful even if you are using a pair of insulated pliers—the best advice is **hands off**.*

1. Always keep the battery fully charged and at the correct electrolyte level. Refer to *Battery* in Chapter Three.
2. Never connect the battery backwards. If the connected battery polarity is wrong, the components in the ignition system will be damaged.
3. Do not disconnect the battery when the engine is running (not even briefly). A voltage surge will occur which will damage the ignition components and possibly burn out the lights. A spark may occur which can cause the battery to explode and spray acid.
4. Never jump start the engine with an outside source greater than 16 volts.
5. Whenever working on any part of the ignition system, always turn the ignition switch OFF or disconnect the battery negative (-) lead.
6. With the ignition switch ON or with the engine running, *never* disconnect the ignition coil(s) electrical connectors (primary or secondary). Not only will you receive severe (maybe fatal) electrical shocks, but the ignition coil and ignition control unit will be damaged.
7. Never try to test either the Hall transmitter or the ignition control unit with a piece of electrical test equipment (ohmmeter, multimeter, megger or homemade battery and test lamp unit) that has its own power source (internal 1.5 volt battery, or equivalent). The applied voltage, minimal as it is, may destroy a portion of the very sensitive circuits in the system. Use only the specified BMW test equipment suggested in the test procedures.
8. Keep all connections between the various units clean and tight. Be sure that the wiring connections are pushed together firmly to help keep out moisture.
9. Use only genuine BMW components whenever replacing any faulty component (e.g. spark plugs, spark plug wires, ignition coils, etc.). These components are matched to the ignition control unit. If another type or brand is used, the system may not function properly and the ignition control unit may be damaged.
10. If the ignition component is mounted within a rubber vibration isolator, always be sure that the isolator is in place when installing component units in the system.
11. Make sure all ground wires are properly attached and are free of oil and corrosion.
12. Do not try to modify or change any of the components within the ignition system. The original ignition system is a closed loop system where all components are designed to work with each other as well as with the fuel injection system.

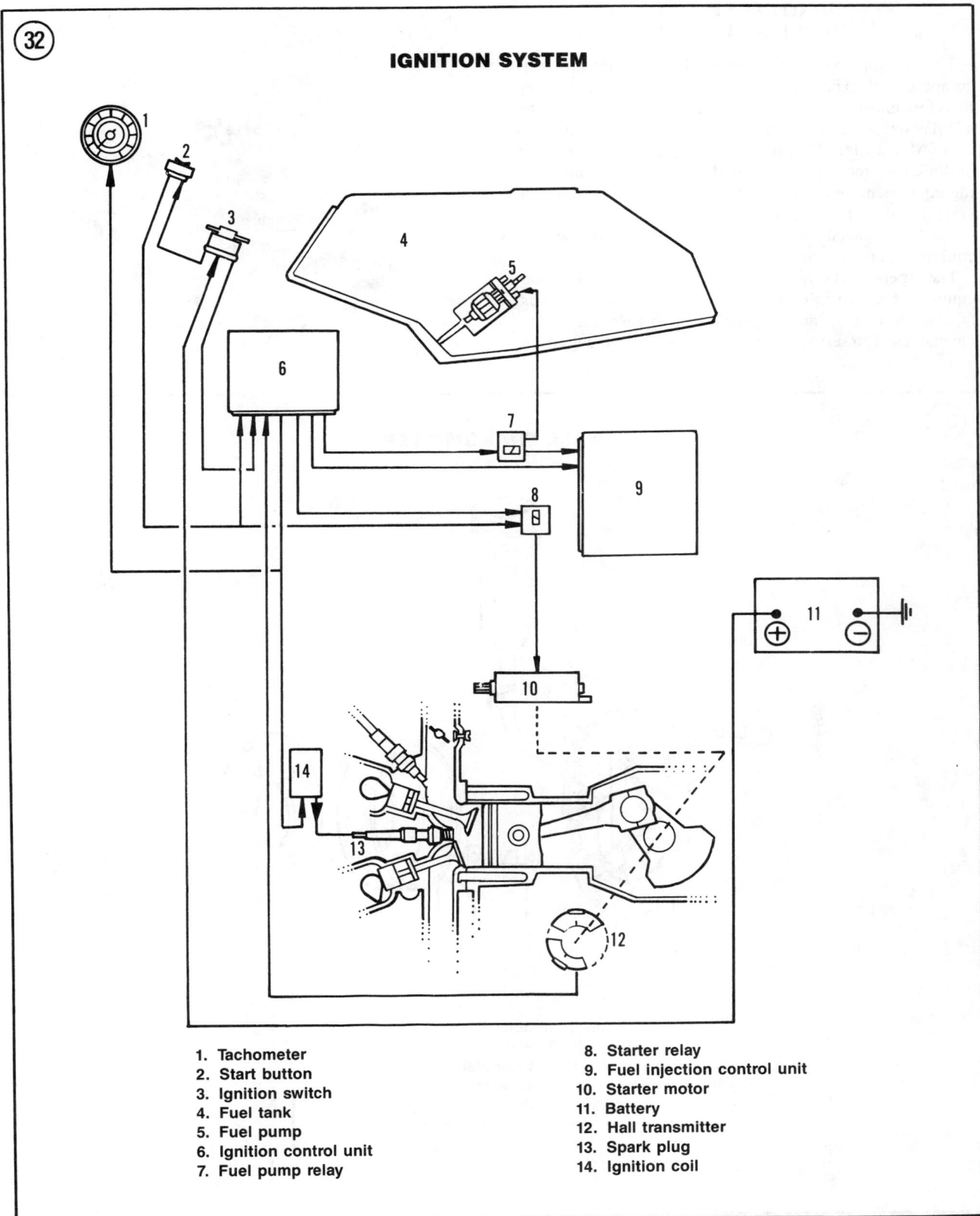

IGNITION SYSTEM

1. Tachometer
2. Start button
3. Ignition switch
4. Fuel tank
5. Fuel pump
6. Ignition control unit
7. Fuel pump relay
8. Starter relay
9. Fuel injection control unit
10. Starter motor
11. Battery
12. Hall transmitter
13. Spark plug
14. Ignition coil

8

IGNITION SYSTEM TROUBLESHOOTING

The ignition control unit and Hall transmitter are very complex and *expensive* pieces of electronic hardware, therefore entrust any service work on these components to a BMW dealer. Some of the components must be serviced by a BMW dealer either due to any applicable warranty or because they require complicated electronic troubleshooting equipment and a thorough knowledge of the ignition system. Some of these components are very expensive and could be damaged by someone unfamiliar with the test equipment or the components.

The special BMW ignition system troubleshooting equipment shown in **Figure 33** is priced in the thousands of dollars and is not a practical purchase for home mechanics. The service charge to troubleshoot the ignition

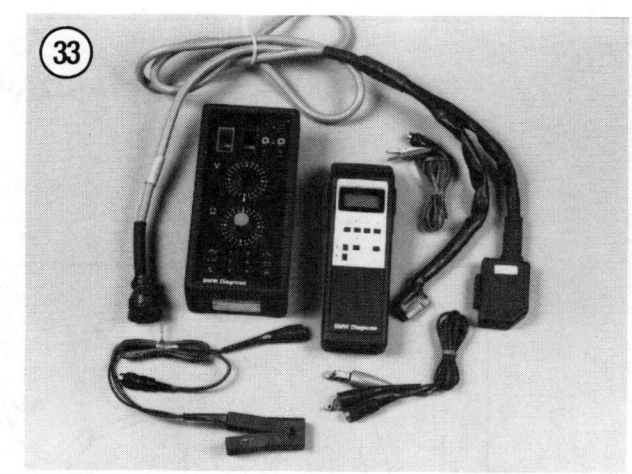

HALL TRANSMITTER

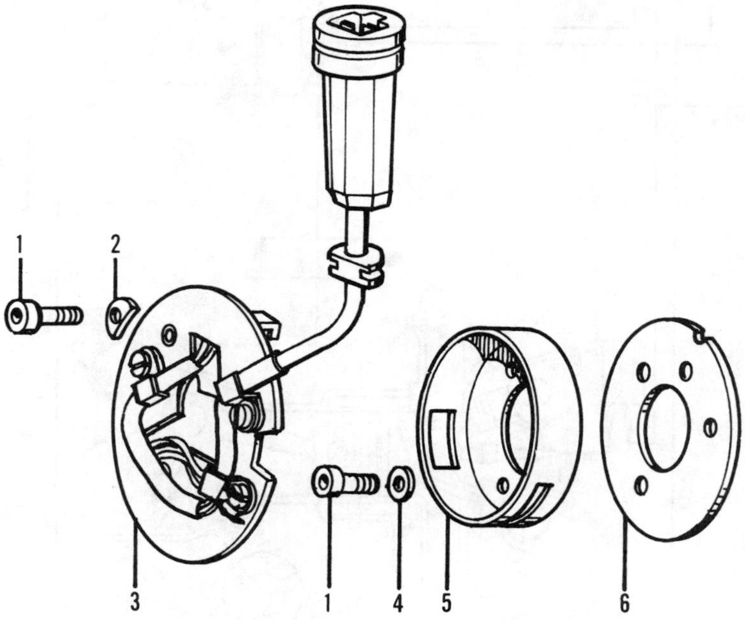

1. Bolt
2. Washer
3. Base plate
4. Washer
5. Rotor
6. Timing plate

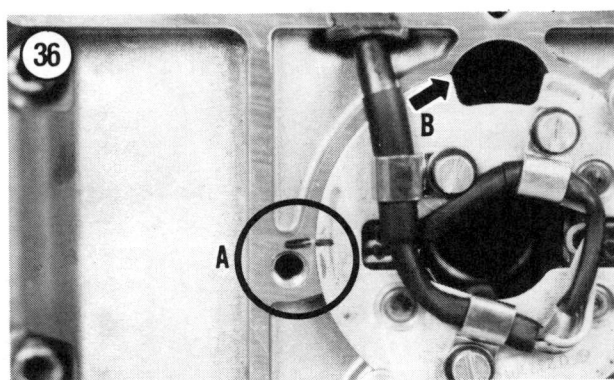

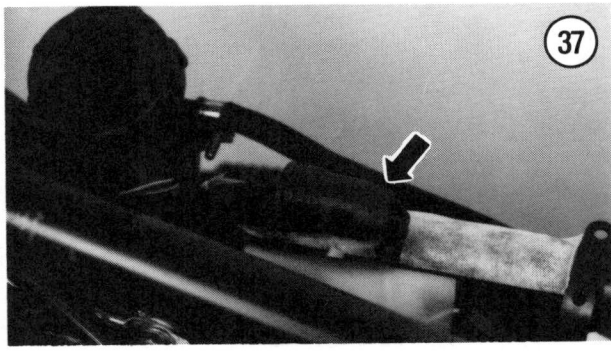

system by a BMW dealer will be minimal compared to the purchase price of this expensive equipment.

> *CAUTION*
> *Servicing the electronic ignition system requires special precautions to prevent damage to the expensive electronic control units. Common electrical system service procedures acceptable on other bikes may damage several parts of the ignition system. Be sure to read **Ignition System Precautions** in this chapter.*

HALL TRANSMITTER UNIT

Testing

Testing of the Hall transmitter unit requires special precautions to prevent damage to the unit. Common electrical system service procedures acceptable on other bikes may cause damage to this unit.

This component must be serviced by a BMW dealer due to any applicable warranty and because it requires complicated electronic troubleshooting equipment and a thorough knowledge of the ignition system. This component is expensive and could be damaged by someone unfamiliar with the test equipment or the components.

8

Replacement

Refer to **Figure 34** for this procedure.

> *NOTE*
> *This procedure is shown with the engine removed from the frame for clarity. The Hall transmitter can be removed with the engine in place.*

1. Remove the fuel tank as described under *Fuel Tank Removal/Installation* in Chapter Seven.
2. Disconnect the battery negative lead as described under *Battery* in Chapter Three.
3. On models so equipped, remove the engine spoiler as described under *Engine Spoiler Removal/Installation* in Chapter Thirteen.
4. Remove the screws securing the Hall transmitter cover (**Figure 35**) and remove the cover and gasket.
5. Make an alignment mark on the edge of the base plate and on the engine (A, **Figure 36**). This will ensure that the base plate is reinstalled in its original position.
6. Pull back the rubber boot (**Figure 37**) and disconnect the Hall transmitter electrical connector from the main wiring harness.
7. Remove the screws and washers (A, **Figure 38**) securing the base plate to the engine.
8. Carefully pull the base plate assembly (B, **Figure 38**) and rubber grommet (C, **Figure 38**) out of the receptacle in the engine.

9. Remove the screws and washers (**Figure 39**) securing the rotor and timing plate to the crankshaft. Remove the rotor (**Figure 40**) and timing plate (A, **Figure 41**).

10. When the No. 1 cylinder is at top dead center (TDC) the notch on the timing plate will align with the pointer on the engine (B, **Figure 41**).

11. Align the dowel pin on the end of the crankshaft with the locating hole in the timing plate (C, **Figure 41**) and install the timing plate.

12. Install the rotor, washers and screws. Tighten the screws securely.

NOTE
*If alignment marks were not made prior to disassembly, align the cutout in the base plate with the cutout in the engine (B, **Figure 36**). This is only a **preliminary** setting and the ignition timing must be adjusted as described in Chapter Three.*

13. Align the marks on the edge of the base plate and on the engine (A, **Figure 36**) and install the base plate assembly. Install the screws and washers and tighten securely. After the screws are tightened, recheck the alignment marks and readjust if necessary.

14. Make sure the electrical cable rubber grommet (C, **Figure 38**) is positioned correctly in the receptacle on the engine.

15. Connect the Hall transmitter electrical connector to the main wiring harness. Make sure the electrical connector is tight and free of corrosion. Pull the rubber boot back over the connector.

16. Install a new gasket (**Figure 42**) on the Hall transmitter cover.

17. Install the Hall transmitter cover, the screws and washers and tighten securely.

18. On models so equipped, install the engine spoiler as described under *Engine Spoiler Removal/Installation* in Chapter Thirteen.

19. Connect the battery negative lead.

20. Install the fuel tank as described under *Fuel Tank Removal/Installation* in Chapter Seven.

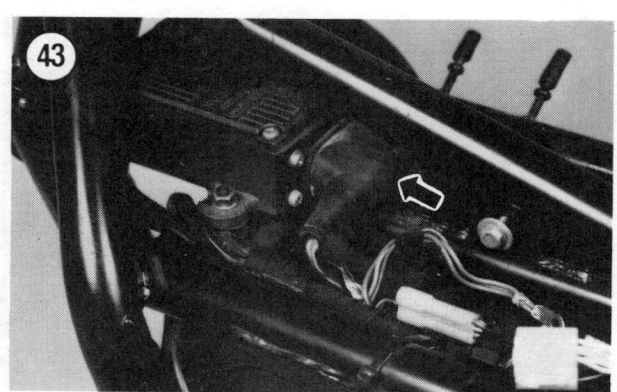

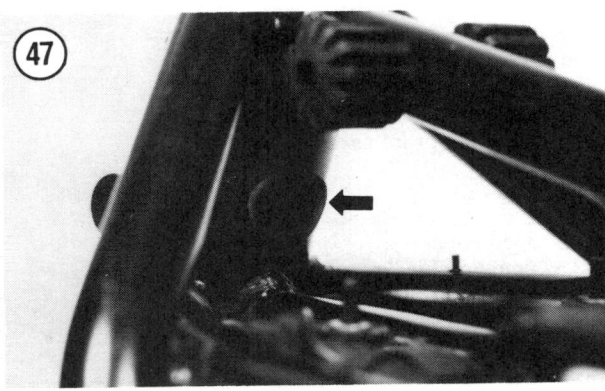

IGNITION CONTROL UNIT

Testing

Testing of the electronic ignition control unit requires special precautions to prevent damage to the unit. Common electrical system service procedures acceptable on other bikes may cause damage to this unit.

This component must be serviced by a BMW dealer because of any applicable warranty and because it requires complicated electronic troubleshooting equipment and a thorough knowledge of the ignition system. This component is very expensive and could be damaged by someone unfamiliar with the test equipment or the components.

Replacement

1. Remove the fuel tank as described under *Fuel Tank Removal/Installation* in Chapter Seven.
2. Disconnect the battery negative lead as described under *Battery* in Chapter Three.
3. Carefully pull back the rubber boot (**Figure 43**).
4. Disconnect the electrical connector (**Figure 44**) from the ignition control unit.
5. Loosen the nuts and washers (**Figure 45**) securing the ignition control unit to the frame. It is not necessary to remove the nuts and washers since the mounting tabs on the ignition control unit are slotted with the front end open.
6. Carefully pull the ignition control unit toward the rear (**Figure 46**) and out of the mounts on the frame.
7. Carefully pull the ignition control unit out through the side of the frame and remove it.
8. Inspect the rubber locating grommet (**Figure 47**) on the frame for damage or deterioration. Replace if necessary.
9. Inspect the exterior of the ignition control unit (A, **Figure 48**) on the frame for damage or deterioration. Make sure the side mounting tabs and front post are in good condition. Replace if necessary.
10. Inspect the contacts of the electrical connector on the ignition control unit (B, **Figure 48**) for damage or corrosion. Clean off the contacts with an aerosol electrical contact cleaner. Replace if necessary.
11. Install by reversing these removal steps. Make sure the electrical connector is tight and free of corrosion and that the rubber boot is securely in place.

8

IGNITION COILS

There are 3 individual ignition coils on K75 models and 2 dual ignition coils on K100 models.

The ignition coil is a form of transformer which develops the high voltage required to jump the spark plug gaps. The only maintenance required is that of keeping the electrical connections clean and tight and occasionally checking to see that the coils are mounted securely.

Dynamic Test

Disconnect the high voltage lead from one of the spark plugs. Remove the spark plug from the cylinder head. Connect a new or known good spark plug to the high voltage lead and place the spark plug base on a good ground like the engine cylinder head. Position the spark plug so you can see the electrodes (**Figure 49**).

IGNITION COIL ASSEMBLY (K75)

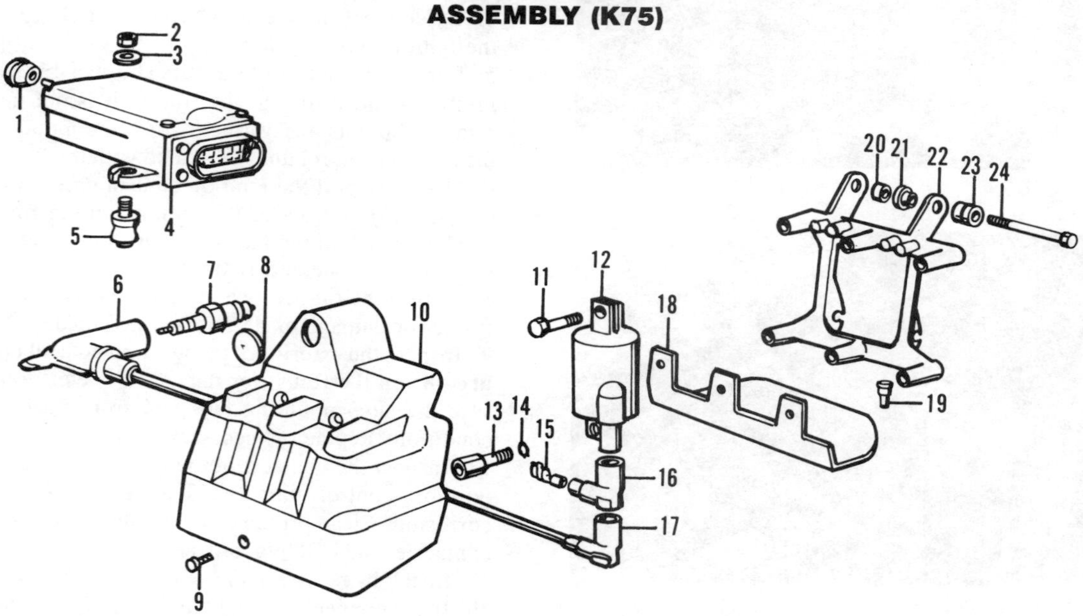

1. Rubber grommet	13. Spacer bolt
2. Nut	14. Lockwasher
3. Lockwasher	15. Cable socket
4. Ignition control unit	16. Suppressor socket
5. Rubber isolator	17. Spark plug wire assembly
6. Spark plug cap	18. Cover
7. Spark plug	19. Plug
8. Plug	20. Nut
9. Screw	21. Metal collar
10. Cover	22. Mounting bracket
11. Bolt	23. Rubber grommet
12. Ignition coil	24. Bolt

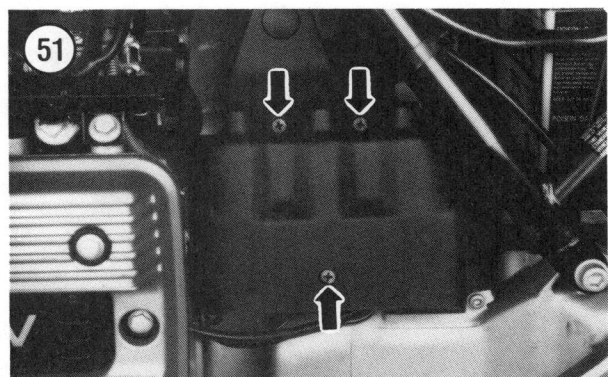

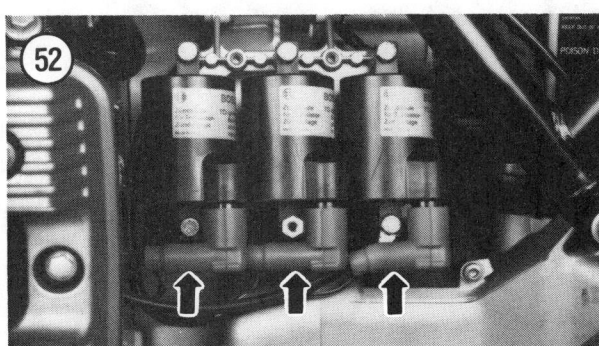

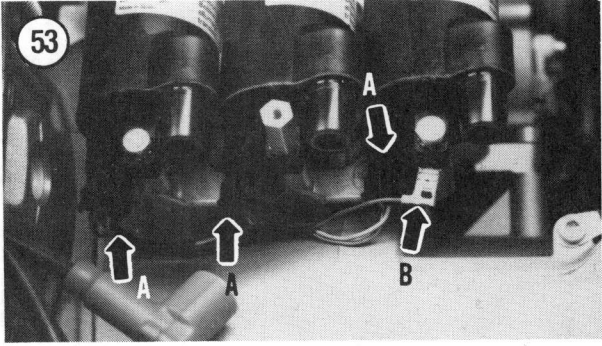

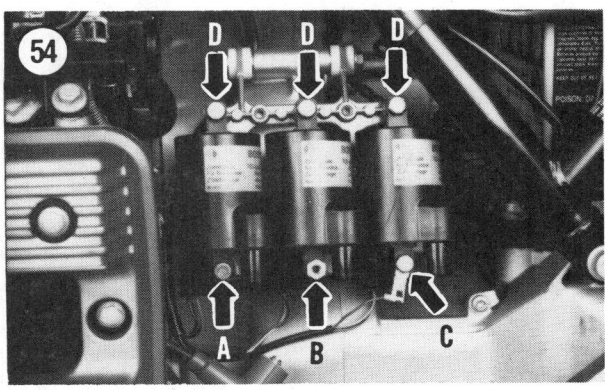

WARNING
If it is necessary to hold the high voltage lead, do so with an insulated pair of pliers. The high voltage generated could produce serious or fatal shocks.

Push the starter button to turn the engine over a couple of times. If a fat blue spark occurs the coil is in good condition; if not it must be replaced. Make sure that you are using a known good spark plug for this test. If the spark plug used is defective the test results will be incorrect.

Reinstall the spark plug in the cylinder head and reconnect the spark plug lead.

Testing

BMW does not provide any test procedures or resistance values for checking the primary and secondary side of the ignition coils. If a coil(s) is suspect have it tested by a BMW dealer using a spark gap tester.

Removal/Installation
(K75 Models)

Refer to **Figure 50** for this procedure.
1. Disconnect the battery negative lead as described under *Battery* in Chapter Three.
2. Remove the screws (**Figure 51**) securing the ignition coil cover and remove the cover.
3. Disconnect each secondary wire (**Figure 52**).
4. Disconnect each primary wire electrical connector (A, **Figure 53**).
5. Disconnect the ground wire connector (B, **Figure 53**).
6. Remove the front bolt (A, **Figure 54**), the special threaded head middle bolt (B, **Figure 54**) and the rear bolt and ground wire (C, **Figure 54**) securing the ignition coils to the mounting bracket.
7. Remove the upper bolts (D, **Figure 54**), one at a time, securing the ignition coil to the mounting bracket. Remove each ignition coil from the bracket.
8. Remove the bolts and nuts (A, **Figure 55**) securing the ignition coil mounting bracket (B, **Figure 55**) to the engine intermediate housing.

8

9. Remove the ignition coil bracket assembly. Don't lose the rubber grommets or the metal collars.

10. Install by reversing these removal steps, noting the following.

11. Be sure to install the rubber grommets or metal collars along with the mounting bolts. Tighten the bolts and nuts securely.

12. Make sure that the mounting surfaces of each ignition coil and the post on the mounting bracket are clean and free of oil. There must be good metal-to-metal contact at all contact points.

13. Be sure to install the lower middle special bolt (B, **Figure 54**) in the correct place. This bolt is unique in that it has a threaded hole in the end. This is used to accept the ignition coil cover mounting bolt. Be sure to reinstall this bolt in the exact same location.

---

(57)

IGNITION COIL ASSEMBLY (K100)

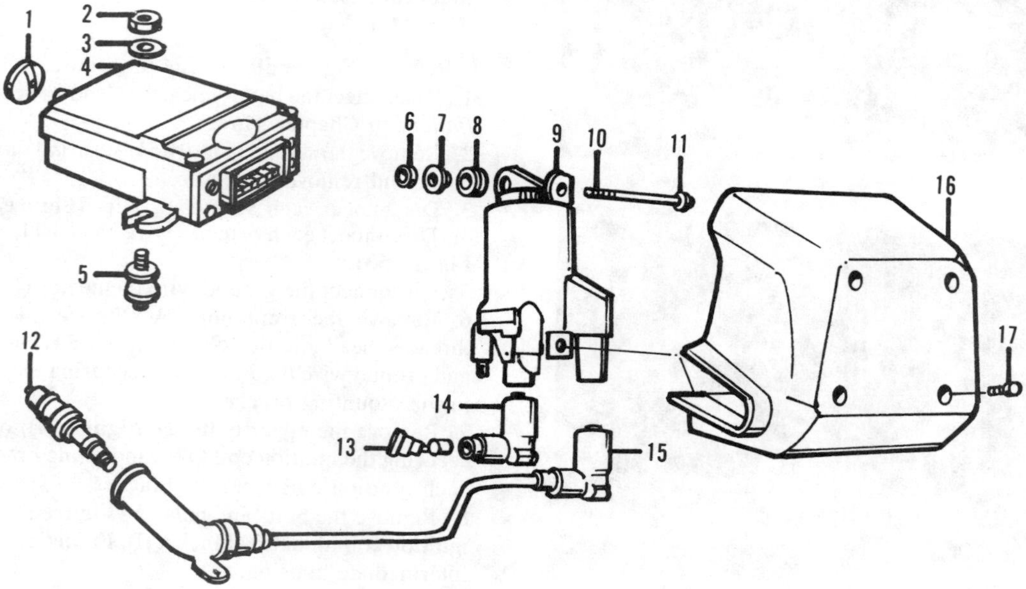

1. Rubber grommet
2. Nut
3. Lockwasher
4. Ignition control unit
5. Rubber isolator
6. Nut
7. Metal collar
8. Rubber grommet
9. Ignition coil
10. Bolt
11. O-ring
12. Spark plug
13. Cable socket
14. Suppressor socket
15. Spark plug wire assembly
16. Cover
17. Screw

14. Make sure all electrical connections are tight and free of corrosion.

15. Route the spark plug wires to the correct cylinder. Each spark plug wire is numbered next to the spark plug rubber boot (**Figure 56**). The cylinders are numbered starting with the No. 1 cylinder at the front of the engine and working toward the back with No. 2 and No. 3 cylinders.

**Removal/Installation
(K100 Models)**

Refer to **Figure 57** for this procedure.

1. Disconnect the battery negative lead as described under *Battery* in Chapter Three.

2. Remove the screws (**Figure 58**) securing the ignition coil cover and remove the cover.

3. Write down the primary wire colors and the terminal to which each is attached (**Figure 59**). This will ensure correct installation of each wire during installation.

4. Disconnect the No. 1 cylinder (A, **Figure 60**) and the No. 2 cylinder (B, **Figure 60**) secondary wires.

5. Disconnect the No. 3 cylinder (**Figure 61**) secondary wire.

6. Disconnect each primary wire (**Figure 62**).

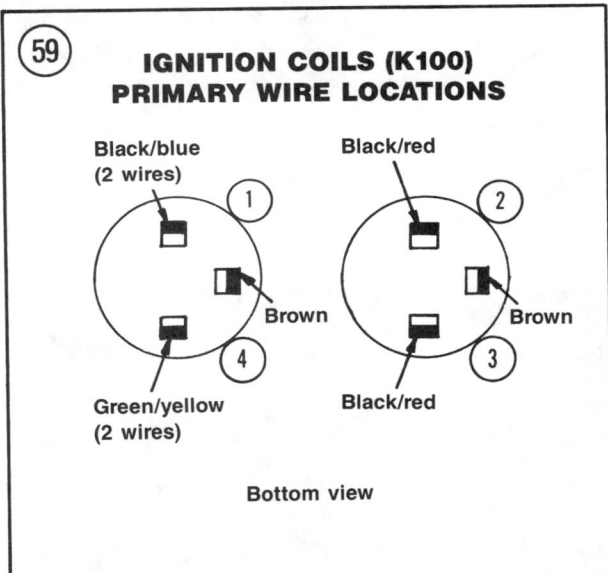

8

7. Disconnect the No. 4 cylinder (**Figure 63**) secondary wire.

8. Remove the bolts and nuts (**Figure 64**) securing the lower portion of the ignition coils to the mounting boss on the engine intermediate housing.

9. Remove the bolts and nuts (**Figure 65**) securing the upper portion of the ignition coils to the mounting boss on the engine intermediate housing.

10. Remove the individual ignition coils from the mounting boss on the engine intermediate housing. Don't lose the rubber grommets or metal collars.

11. Install by reversing these removal steps, noting the following.

12. Make sure that the mounting surfaces of each ignition coil and the mounting boss on the engine intermediate housing are clean and free of oil. There must be good metal-to-metal contact at all contact points.

13. Be sure to install the rubber grommets or metal collars along with the mounting bolts. Tighten the bolts and nuts securely.

14. Make sure all electrical connections are tight and free of corrosion. If you are in doubt of the location of the primary wire colors-to-terminals, refer to **Figure 59** for correct location. The front ignition coil is for the No. 1 and No. 4 cylinders while the rear ignition coil is for the No. 2 and No. 3 cylinders.

15. Route the spark plug wires to the correct cylinder. Each spark plug wire is numbered next to the spark plug rubber boot (**Figure 56**). The cylinders are numbered starting with the No. 1 cylinder at the front of the engine and working toward the back with No. 2, No. 3 and No. 4 cylinders.

SPARK PLUG SECONDARY WIRES

Replacement

Refer to **Figure 50** for K75 models or **Figure 57** for K100 models for this procedure.

1. Disconnect the battery negative lead as described under *Battery* in Chapter Three.

2. Remove the screws securing the ignition coil cover and remove the cover. Refer to **Figure 51** for K75 models or **Figure 58** for K100 models.

3. Identify each secondary wire and the coil terminal to which it is attached. Each spark plug wire is numbered next to the spark plug rubber boot (**Figure 56**). This will ensure correct installation of each wire during installation.

4. Remove the screws and lockwashers securing the spark plug cover panel and remove the panel. Refer to **Figure 66** for K75 models or **Figure 67** for K100 models.

5. Before removing the spark plug wires, note the routing of the wires within the cylinder head cavity. Refer to **Figure 68** for K75 models or **Figure 69** for K100 models. The wires must be rerouted in this manner to keep from being damaged.

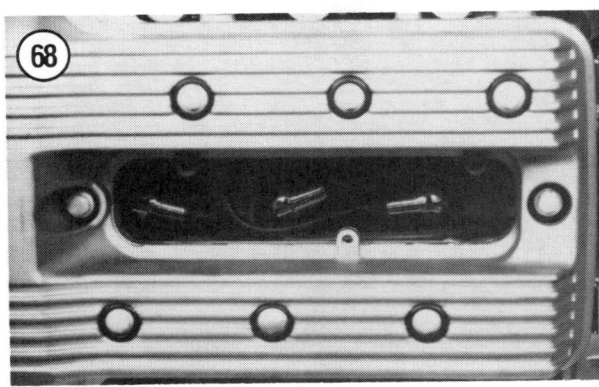

CAUTION
If the wires are being removed and not replaced with new ones, pull on the wires carefully so as to not damage them in any way during removal.

6. Using a pair of slip joint pliers, pull on the metal suppressor cap on the spark plug wire and carefully remove the spark plug suppressor cap from one spark plug (A, **Figure 70**).

7. Disconnect the same spark plug secondary wire from the ignition coil (B, **Figure 70**).

NOTE
Pull the ignition coil end of the spark plug wire assembly out through the opening in the cylinder head. The suppressor caps are too large to go through the opening.

8. Carefully pull that spark plug wire out through the opening at the rear of the cylinder head (C, **Figure 70**).

9. Remove only one wire at a time.

10. Repeat Steps 6-9 for the remaining spark plug wires.

NOTE
*Be sure to use genuine original BMW spark plug wires as they have the correct wire resistance, the correct resistance suppressors within the caps and the correct length. The genuine original BMW wires are also marked with the cylinder number (**Figure 56**).*

11. Install new spark plug wires, one at a time, and route them correctly into the cylinder head cavity.

12. Be sure to route the spark plug wires within the cylinder head cavity the same as they were as noted during removal. Refer to **Figure 68** for K75 models or **Figure 69** for K100 models.

13. Using a pair of slip joint pliers, install the spark plug wire and metal suppressor cap. Push hard and make sure all wires are on tight. Push until the suppressor cap bottoms out on the spark plug.

14. Connect each secondary wire onto the ignition coils.

15. Install the spark plug cover panel and secure with the screws and lockwashers. Tighten the screws securely.

16. Install the ignition coil cover and screws. Tighten the screws securely.

17. Connect the battery negative lead.

18. Start the bike and make sure it idles smoothly. If there is a miss, the probable cause is that one of the wires is not pushed on all the way and is not making good electrical contact.

8

STARTING SYSTEM

The starting system consists of the starter motor, starter gears, starter relay, load shedding relay and the starter button.

When the starter button is pressed, it allows current flow through the starter relay and load shedding relay. The starter and load shedding relays allow electricity to flow from the battery to the starter motor.

CAUTION
Do not operate the starter for more than 5 seconds at a time. Let it rest approximately 10 seconds, then use it again.

The starter gears are covered in Chapter Four.

Table 3, at the end of the chapter, lists possible starter problems, probable causes and most common remedies.

STARTER

Removal/Installation

1. Remove both frame side covers.
2. Remove the battery as described under *Battery* in Chapter Three.
3. Remove the fuel injection control unit as described under *Fuel Injection Control Unit Removal/Installation* in Chapter Seven.
4. Remove the protective cap (**Figure 71**) and disconnect the electric starter cable (A, **Figure 72**) from the starter.
5. Remove the bolts (B, **Figure 72**) securing the starter to the intermediate housing of the engine.
6. Carefully withdraw the starter toward the rear and out of the intermediate housing of the engine.
7. Install by reversing these removal steps, noting the following.
8. Make sure the O-ring seal (A, **Figure 73**) is in good condition and is in place on the starter. Apply a light coat of clean engine oil to the O-ring. This will make starter installation a little easier.
9. Make sure the electrical wire connection is tight and free of corrosion.

Preliminary Inspection

Starter motor overhaul is best left to an expert. This procedure shows how to detect a defective starter.

Inspect the O-ring seal (A, **Figure 73**). O-ring seals tend to harden after prolonged use and heat and therefore lose their ability to seal properly. Replace as necessary.

Inspect the gear (B, **Figure 73**) for chipped or missing teeth. If damaged, the starter assembly must be replaced.

Disassembly

Refer to **Figure 74** for this procedure.
1. Mark alignment marks between the front cover and body and rear cover and body (**Figure 75**). This will assure correct placement during assembly.
2. Remove the case screws and washers (**Figure 76**) securing the assembly together.
3. Separate the front cover from the body.
4. Carefully separate the rear cover and brush holder plate as an assembly from the body. Don't damage the brush assembly during rear cover removal.

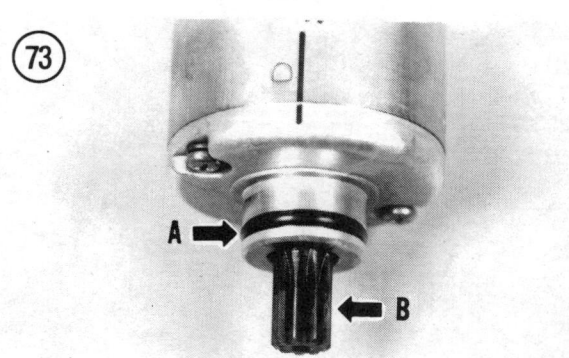

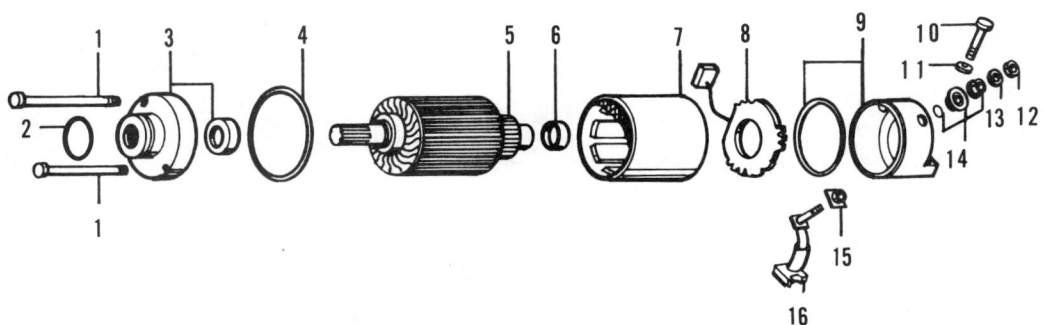

STARTER MOTOR

1. Bolt
2. O-ring
3. Front cover and oil seal
4. O-ring
5. Armature
6. Shim
7. Field coil and body
8. Brush holder plate
9. Rear cover and O-ring
10. Bolt
11. Lockwasher
12. Outer nut
13. Lockwasher
14. Insulator assembly
15. Insulator
16. Brush terminal set

8

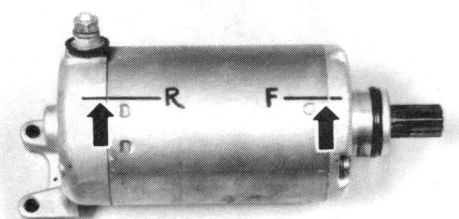

NOTE
Write down the number of shim(s) used on the armature shaft next to the commutator. Be sure to install the same number when reassembling the starter.

5. Remove the shim(s) (**Figure 77**) from the rear cover end of the shaft.
6. Withdraw the armature coil assembly (**Figure 78**) from the body.

NOTE
Before removing the nuts and washers, write down their description and order. They must be reinstalled in the same order to insulate this set of brushes from the body.

7. Remove the outer nut (A, **Figure 79**) and washer (B, **Figure 79**).
8. Remove the nut (A, **Figure 80**) and insulator assembly (B, **Figure 80**).
9. Using a small scribe or dental tool, remove the O-ring seal (**Figure 81**) from the threaded stud on brush/terminal set. Remove the brush/terminal set.

CAUTION
Do not immerse the wire windings in the case or the armature coil in solvent as the insulation may be damaged. Wipe the windings with a cloth lightly moistened with solvent and thoroughly dry.

10. Clean all grease, dirt and carbon from all components.

Inspection

1. Release the brush retaining springs (**Figure 82**) and remove the brushes (**Figure 83**) from their holders in the brush holder plate.
2. BMW does not provide wear limit length specifications for the brushes. A good rule of thumb is to replace a brush

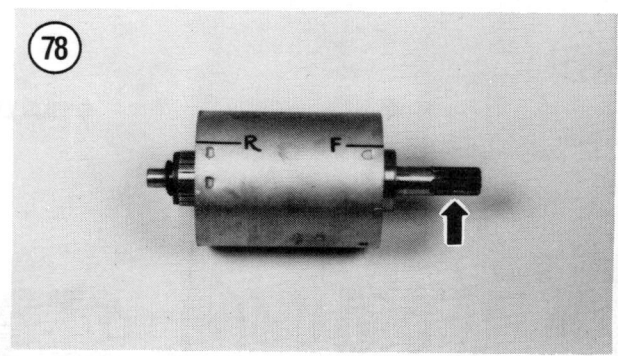

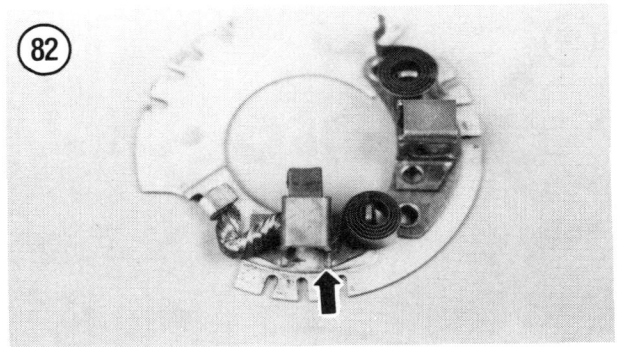

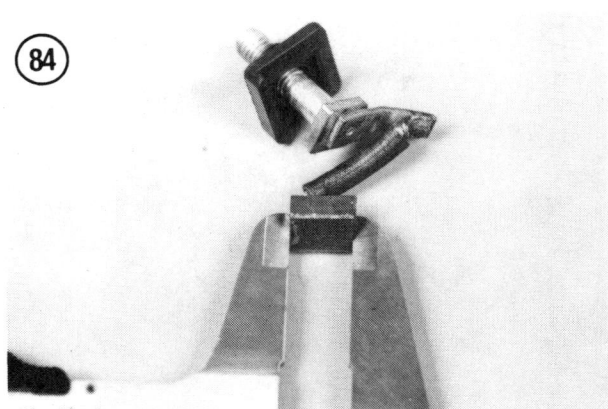

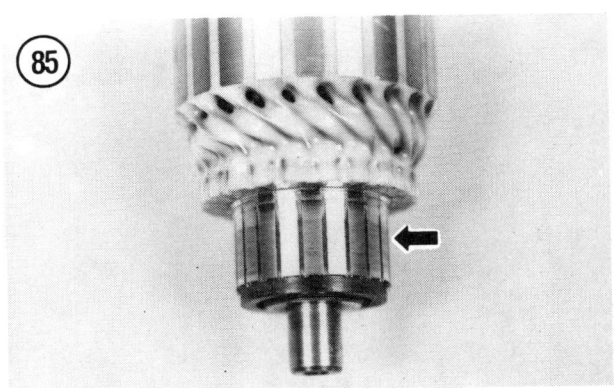

that is worn half way. The approximate length of a new brush is 12 mm (0.47 in.) so the brushes should be replaced when worn to 6 mm (0.24 in.). Measure the length of each brush (**Figure 84**) with a vernier caliper.

3. The brushes cannot be replaced individually but must be replaced along with the part to which they are attached. One brush is attached to the brush holder plate and the other is attached to the brush terminal set.

4. Inspect the commutator (**Figure 85**). The mica in a good commutator is below the surface of the copper bars as shown in **Figure 86**. On a worn commutator the mica and copper bars may be worn to the same level (**Figure 86**). If necessary, have the commutator serviced by a dealer or electrical repair shop.

5. Inspect the commutator copper bars for discoloration. If a pair of bars are discolored, grounded armature coils are indicated.

6. Use an ohmmeter and perform the following:

    a. Check for continuity between the commutator bars (**Figure 87**); there should be continuity (indicated resistance) between pairs of bars.

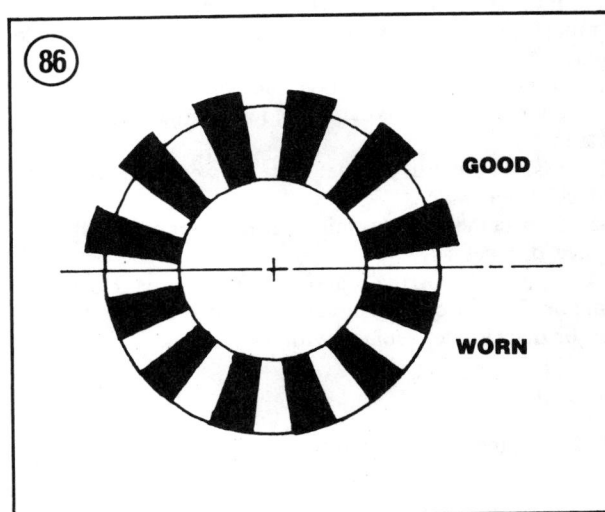

GOOD

WORN

8

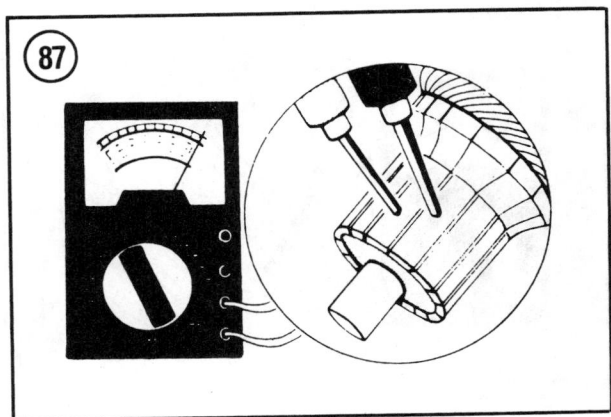

b. Check for continuity between the commutator bars and the shaft (**Figure 88**); there should be *no* continuity (infinite resistance).

c. If the unit fails either of these tests, replace the armature.

7. Temporarily install the brush/terminal set in the rear cover. Be sure to install the nuts, washers and O-ring (**Figure 89**) in the order noted in Step 7 of *Disassembly*. Use an ohmmeter and perform the following:

a. Check for continuity between the starter cable terminal and the starter rear cover; there should be *no* continuity (infinite resistance).

b. Check for continuity between the starter cable terminal and the brush wire terminal; there should be continuity (indicated resistance).

c. If the unit fails either of these tests, the brush/terminal set is not properly insulated and must be replaced.

8. Inspect the bushing (**Figure 90**) in the rear cover for wear or damage. If either is damaged, replace the rear cover.

9. Inspect the oil seal (**Figure 91**) in the front cover for wear or damage. If it is damaged, replace the oil seal or the front cover.

10. Inspect the front bearing (**Figure 92**) on the armature. It must rotate freely with no signs of wear or damage. Replace if necessary.

11. Inspect the field coil/body assembly (**Figure 93**) for wear or damage. If it is damaged, replace the field coil/body assembly.

12. Inspect the brush holder plate for wear or damage. Replace if necessary.

13. Inspect the brush/terminal set for wear or damage. Replace if necessary.

14. Inspect the O-ring seal on the front cover (**Figure 94**) and on the rear cover (**Figure 95**). If it is starting to harden or deteriorate, replace with a new one.

Assembly

1. Install the brushes into their receptacles (**Figure 83**).

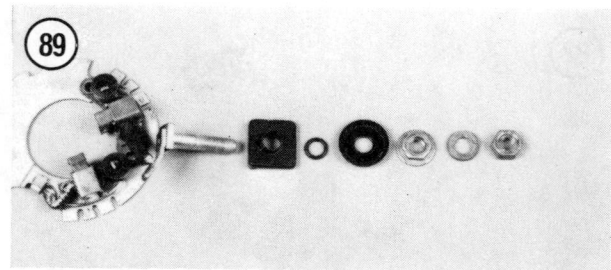

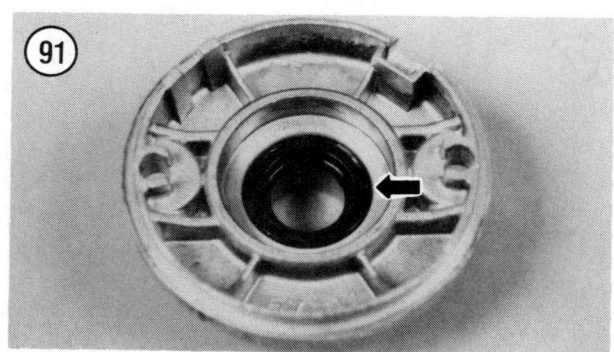

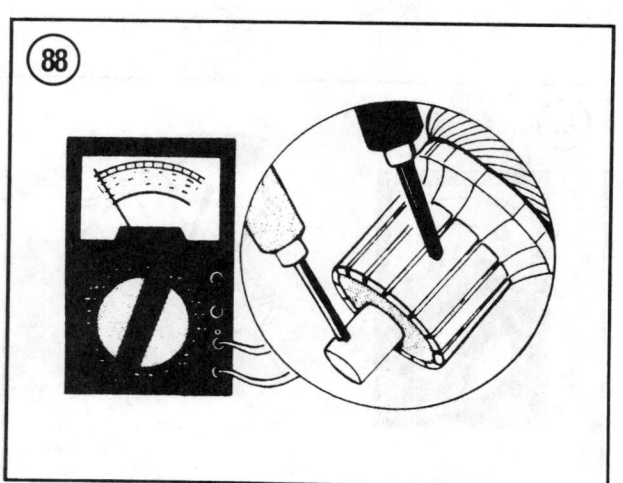

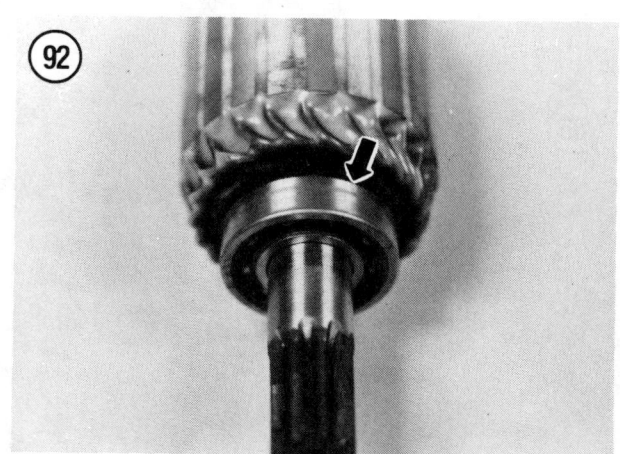

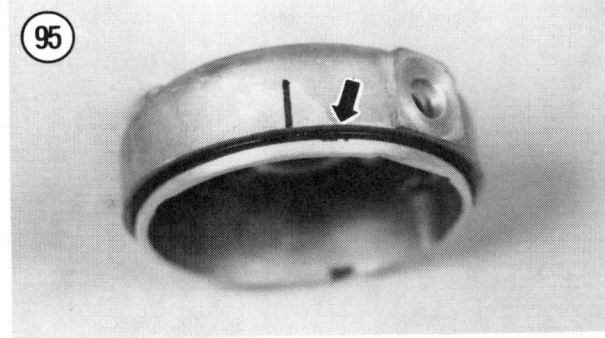

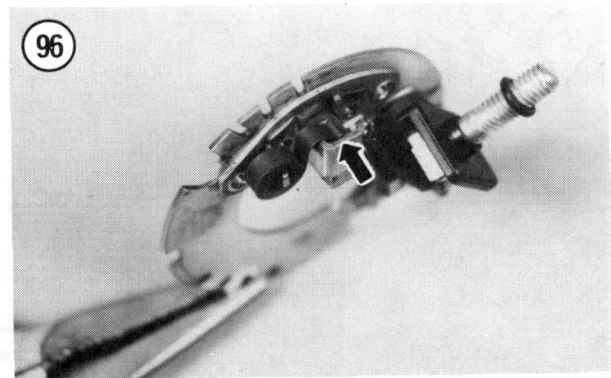

2. Using needlenose pliers, rotate the spring *counterclockwise* and place it on top of the brush in its receptacle. Make sure the spring is correctly seated on top of the brush (**Figure 96**).

3. Install the brush/terminal assembly (A, **Figure 97**) into the rear cover.

NOTE
In Step 4 and Step 5, reinstall all parts in the same order as noted during removal. This is essential in order to insulate this set of brushes from the rear cover.

4. Install the O-ring seal (B, **Figure 97**) onto the threaded stud. Push the O-ring in until it is seated in the rear cover (**Figure 81**).

5. Install the insulator assembly (B, **Figure 80**) and the nut (A, **Figure 80**).

6. Position the armature coil assembly with the gear end (A, **Figure 98**) toward the front of the case (B, **Figure 98**). Insert the armature coil assembly into the case from either end of the case (**Figure 78**).

8

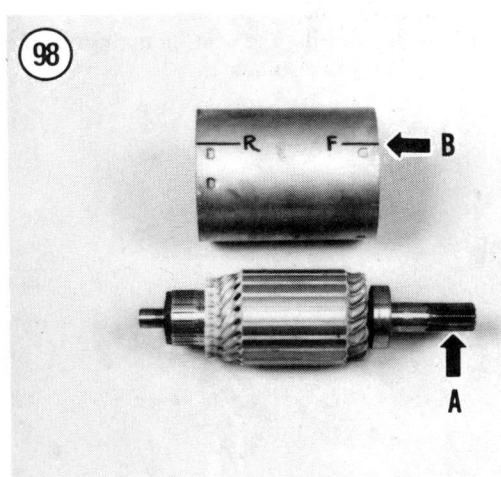

7. Install the front cover and align the marks made during disassembly (**Figure 99**).

8. Install the shim(s) (**Figure 77**) onto the armature.

CAUTION
Do not damage the brushes during this step.

9. Carefully install the rear cover onto the armature. Help guide the brushes onto the armature with a small scribe or dental tool. Push the cover on all the way until it stops.

NOTE
*If alignment marks were not made prior to disassembly, align the rear cover raised marks with the depressed square on the case (**Figure 100**). Rotate the front cover to align the screw holes.*

10. Align the marks on the rear cover and case (**Figure 75**) made during disassembly.

11. Install the case screws and washers (**Figure 76**). Make sure the marks are still aligned (**Figure 75**). Tighten the screws securely.

STARTER RELAY

Testing

BMW does not provide any test procedures or resistance values for the starter relay. If a starter relay is suspect, have it tested by a BMW dealer.

Removal/Installation

1. Remove the seat as described in Chapter Thirteen.
2. Remove the right-hand side cover.
3. Disconnect the negative battery lead as described under *Battery* in Chapter Three.
4. Remove the fuel tank as described under *Fuel Tank Removal/Installation* in Chapter Seven.
5. Remove the bolts securing the seat mounting bracket (**Figure 101**) and remove the bracket.

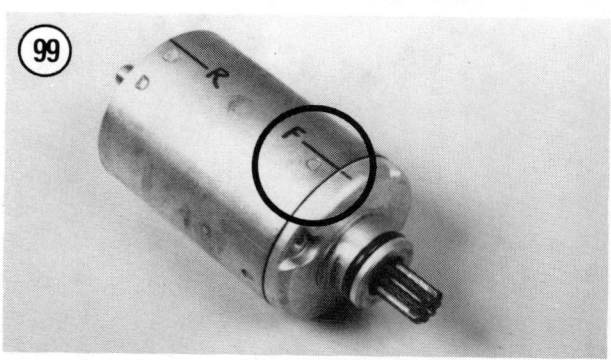

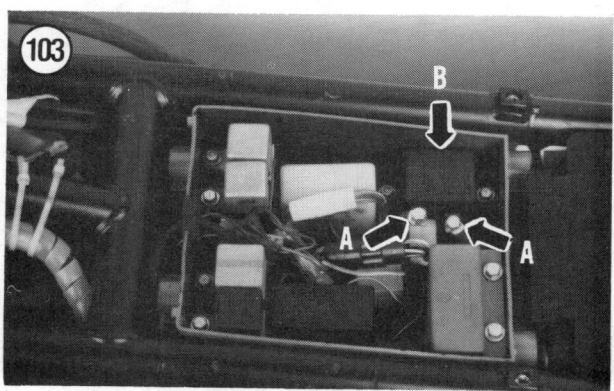

6. Remove the cover (**Figure 102**) from the electric control box.

7. Remove the screws (A, **Figure 103**) securing the electrical wires to the starter relay.

8. Remove the screws securing the starter relay (B, **Figure 103**) and remove the relay.

9. Install by reversing these removal steps, noting the following.

10. Make sure the electrical connectors are tight and free of corrosion.

LIGHTING SYSTEM

The lighting system consists of a headlight, taillight/brake light combination, license plate light, turn signals, indicator lights and illumination lights for the speedometer and tachometer. **Table 4** lists replacement bulbs for these components.

Always use the correct wattage bulb as indicated in this section. The use of a larger wattage bulb will give a dim light and a smaller wattage bulb will burn out prematurely.

HEADLIGHT

The headlight on all models is equipped with an H4 quartz halogen bulb. Special handling of the quartz halogen bulb is required in order to prolong bulb life. The bulb has 3 side prongs where it fits into the headlight reflector. These prongs are offset so the bulb can only be installed one way. When fitting the bulb, if it will not go into the reflector receptacle, rotate the bulb until the prongs align with the cutouts in the reflector receptacle and push it in.

CAUTION
Carefully read all instructions shipped with the replacement quartz halogen bulb. Do not touch the bulb glass with your fingers because of oil on your skin. Any traces of oil on the glass will drastically reduce the life of the bulb. Clean any traces of oil from the bulb with a cloth moistened in alcohol or lacquer thinner.

Headlight and Parking Light Bulb Replacement (K75T, K75C, K75 Low Seat and Base K100 Models)

Refer to **Figure 104** for this procedure.

8

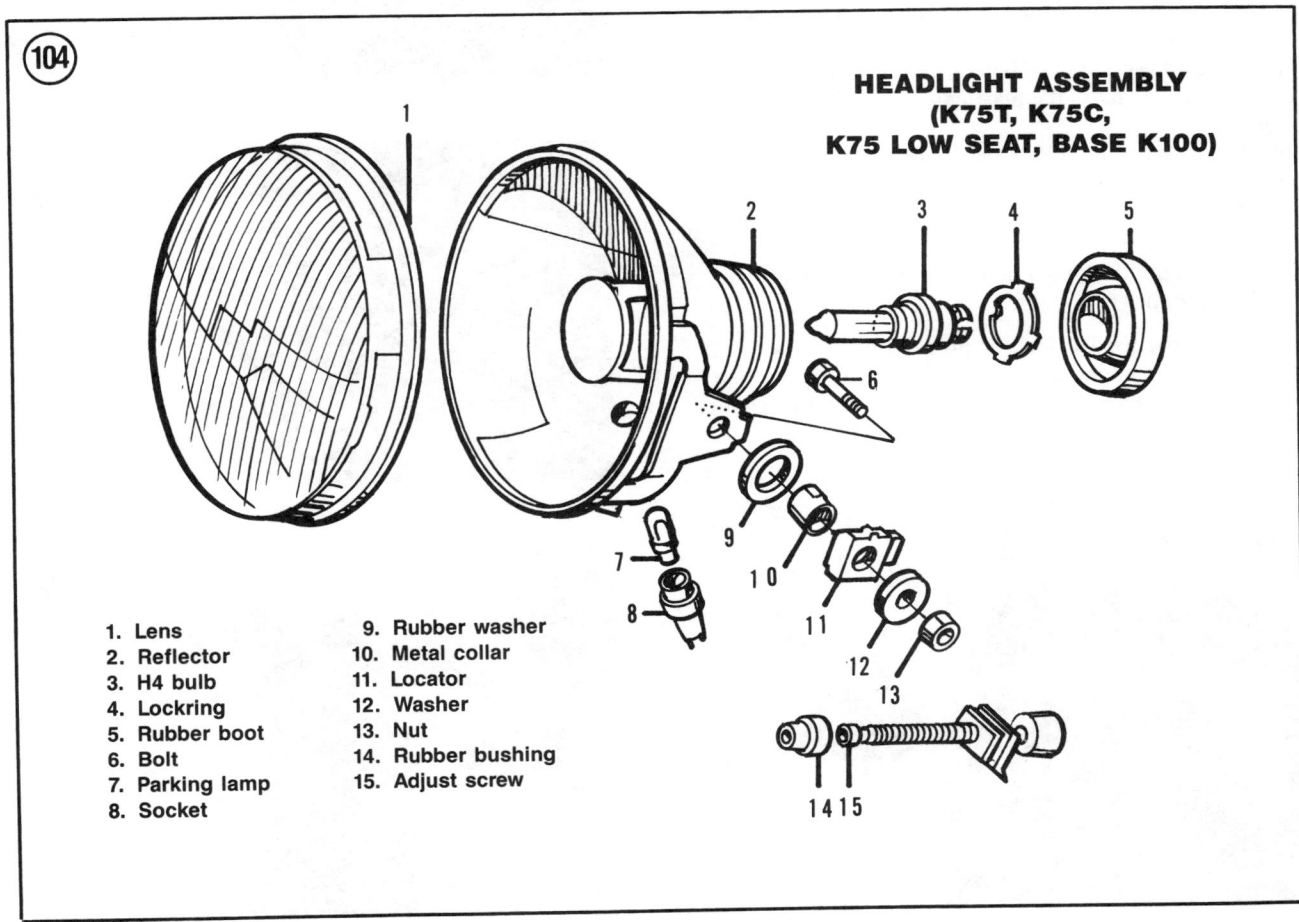

HEADLIGHT ASSEMBLY (K75T, K75C, K75 LOW SEAT, BASE K100)

1. Lens
2. Reflector
3. H4 bulb
4. Lockring
5. Rubber boot
6. Bolt
7. Parking lamp
8. Socket
9. Rubber washer
10. Metal collar
11. Locator
12. Washer
13. Nut
14. Rubber bushing
15. Adjust screw

1. Remove the frame left-hand side cover.

2. Disconnect the battery negative lead as described under *Battery* in Chapter Three.

3A. On all K75 models, remove the Phillips head screws and Allen screws and washers on the backside of the fairing.

3B. On K100 models, remove the screws and lockwashers (**Figure 105**) on each side of the backside of the fairing mounting panel.

4. Carefully pull the headlight fairing and trim panel (**Figure 106**) off of the mounting panel and headlight assembly.

5. Carefully pull the headlight assembly (**Figure 107**) forward and out of the mounting panel.

6. Disconnect the electrical connector (**Figure 108**) from the base of the lens assembly.

7. Remove the rubber boot from the reflector.

8. Unhook the set spring and remove the bulb assembly.

9. Replace with a new bulb assembly. Do not touch the bulb with your fingers (refer to CAUTION at the beginning of this procedure).

10. Carefully withdraw the parking light bulb from the reflector and install a new one. Push the socket in until it seats completely.

11. Install by reversing these removal steps, noting the following.

12. Install the headlight assembly and align the arrow with the arrow on the mounting tab (**Figure 109**) on each side. This is to maintain correct horizontal headlight aim.

13. Tighten the screws and bolts securely. Don't overtighten the screws or bolts as the plastic mounting bosses may be damaged.

14. Make sure the electrical connectors are free of corrosion and are tight.

15. Adjust the headlight as described in this chapter.

Headlight and Parking Light Bulb Replacement (K75S Model)

Refer to **Figure 110** for this procedure.

1. Remove the frame left-hand side cover.

2. Disconnect the battery negative lead as described under *Battery* in Chapter Three.

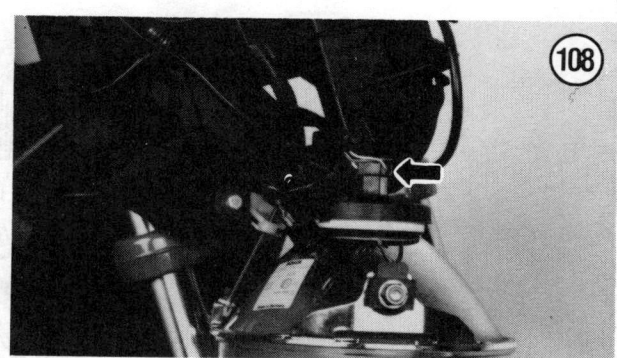

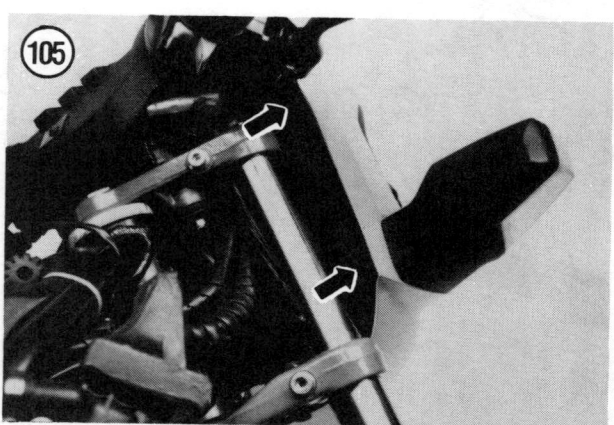

3. Remove the screws and washers securing the windshield and remove the windshield and the gasket on each side.

4. Remove the screws securing the radiator trim panel and remove the trim panel.

5. At the front center of both side panels, remove the screw and collar holding both side panels together.

6. Remove the screws securing the side panels to the center panel.

7. Remove the screw securing the turn signal housing and pull the housing out of the side panel. Disconnect the electrical connector and remove the turn signal housing.

8. Unscrew the side panel upper mounting screw in the turn signal area.

9. Remove the screw and washer on each side securing the center cover to the side panel.

NOTE
It is only necessary to remove one of the front fairing side panels to gain access to the headlight bulb. If the parking light is going to be replaced, remove the right-hand side panel. If the bulb is not going to be replaced, removal of either side is okay.

10. Remove the screw securing the lower trim panel to the side panel and remove the lower trim panel.

11. Remove the bolt securing the side panel to the side panel mounting bracket.

12. Remove the side panel. Don't lose the rubber grommet and metal collar from the mounting hole in the side panel.

13. Disconnect the electrical connector from the base of the headlight.

14. Remove the rubber boot from the base of the lens assembly.

15. Rotate the locking clip and remove it.

16. Remove the bulb assembly.

17. Replace with a new bulb assembly—do not touch the bulb with your fingers. Refer to CAUTION at the beginning of this procedure.

18. Carefully withdraw the parking light bulb from the lens assembly and install a new one. Push the socket in until it seats completely.

19. Install by reversing these removal steps, noting the following.

20. Be sure to use the metal collar in the plastic mounting boss on the lower mount of the side panel on each side. If the collar is not in place and the bolt and nut are tightened, the plastic mounting boss will be damaged and the side panel will have to be replaced. Don't overtighten the bolts as the plastic mounting bosses may be damaged even with the metal collars in place.

21. Tighten the screws, bolts and nuts securing the components securely.

22. Adjust the headlight as described in this chapter.

8

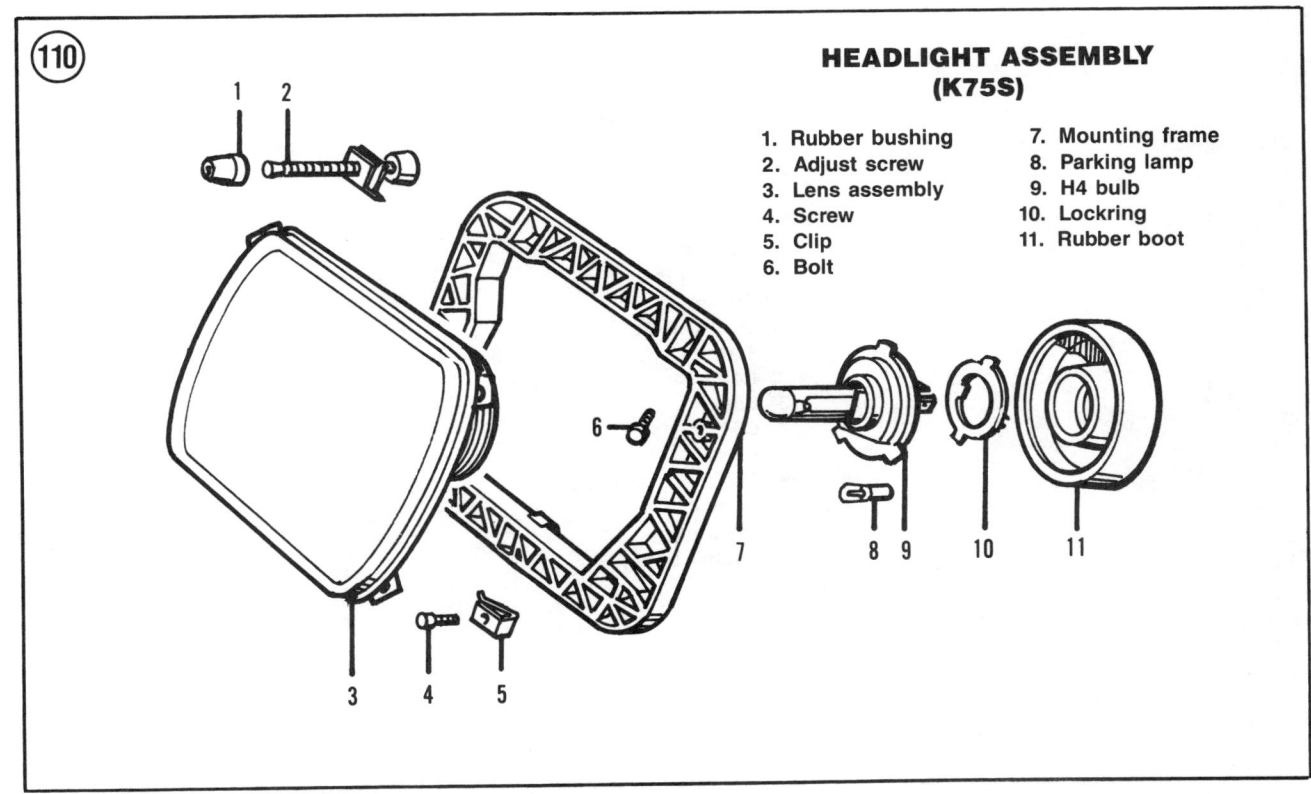

(110)

HEADLIGHT ASSEMBLY
(K75S)

1. Rubber bushing
2. Adjust screw
3. Lens assembly
4. Screw
5. Clip
6. Bolt
7. Mounting frame
8. Parking lamp
9. H4 bulb
10. Lockring
11. Rubber boot

(111)

HEADLIGHT ASSEMBLY
(K100RS, K100RT, K100LT)

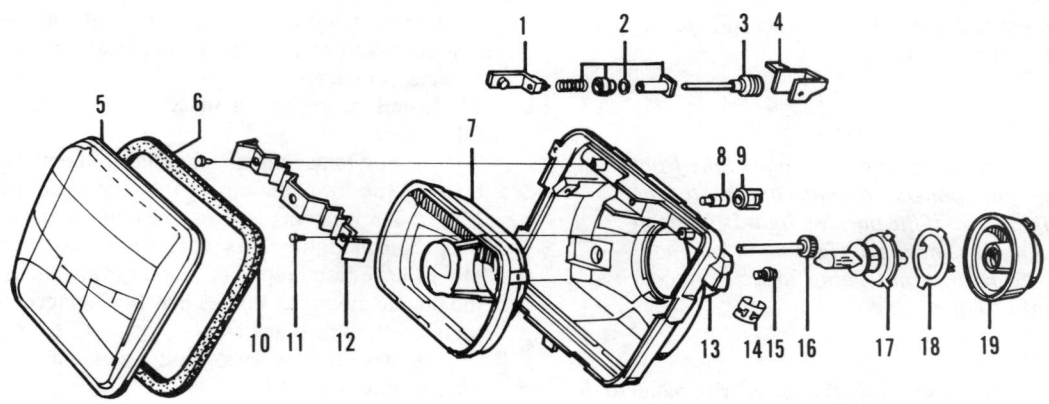

1. Bracket
2. Adjuster assembly
3. Adjust screw
4. Bracket
5. Lens
6. Gasket
7. Reflector
8. Parking lamp
9. Socket
10. Lens gasket
11. Screw
12. Reflector
13. Base
14. Clip
15. Screw
16. Horizontal adjust screw
17. H4 bulb
18. Lockring
19. Rubber boot

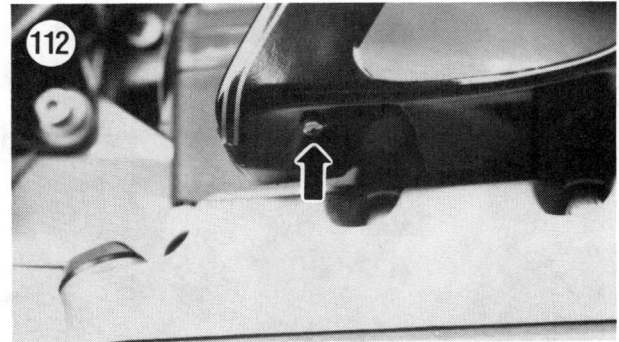

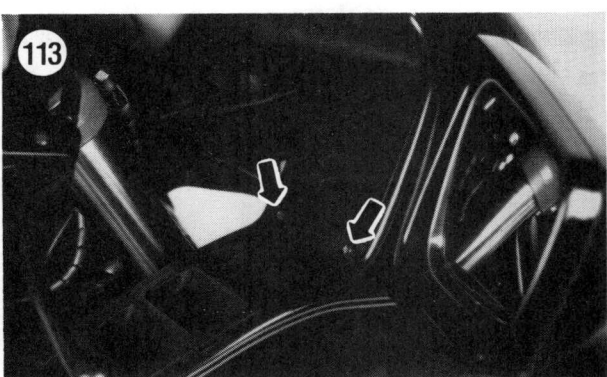

Headlight Replacement
(K100RS Model)

Refer to **Figure 111** for this procedure.

1. Remove the frame left-hand side cover.

2. Disconnect the battery negative lead as described under *Battery* in Chapter Three.

3. Remove the knee pads as follows:

   a. Remove the single screw (**Figure 112**) at the bottom of the knee pad.

   b. Remove the screws (**Figure 113**) at the top of the knee pad.

   c. Unhook the clip at the mid-point of the knee pad, then carefully remove the knee pad (**Figure 114**) from the front fairing upper portion and lower side panel.

   d. Repeat for the knee pad on the other side.

4. Carefully lift up on the small upper covers (**Figure 115**) and unhook them from the center cover.

5. Remove the bolts securing the wing panel (**Figure 116**) and remove the wing panel. Repeat for the other side.

6. Remove the bolts securing the center cover (**Figure 117**) and remove the center cover.

8

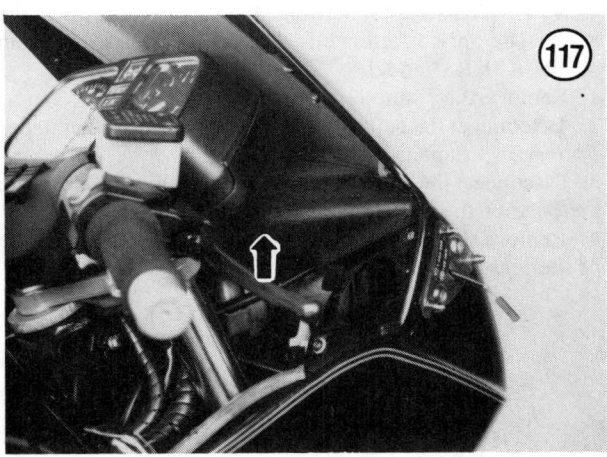

7. Disconnect the electrical connector (A, **Figure 118**) from the base of the headlight.

8. Remove the rubber boot (B, **Figure 118**) from the base of the lens assembly.

NOTE
Figure 119 and Figure 120 are shown with the headlight assembly removed from the front fairing for clarity.

9. Rotate the locking clip and remove it. Refer to A, **Figure 121** and **Figure 119**.

10. Remove the bulb assembly. Refer to B, **Figure 121** and **Figure 120**.

11. Replace with a new bulb assembly—do not touch the bulb with your fingers. Refer to CAUTION at the beginning of this procedure.

12. To replace the parking light bulb, perform the following:

   a. Push in and rotate the parking light bulb socket *counterclockwise*.

   b. Carefully pull the bulb from the socket assembly (**Figure 122**) and install a new one.

   c. Push the socket assembly in and rotate it *clockwise*.

13. Install by reversing these removal steps, noting the following.

14. Tighten the screws and nuts securely. Don't overtighten the screws or nuts as the plastic mounting bosses may be damaged.

15. Make sure all electrical connectors are free of corrosion and are tight.

16. Adjust the headlight as described in this chapter.

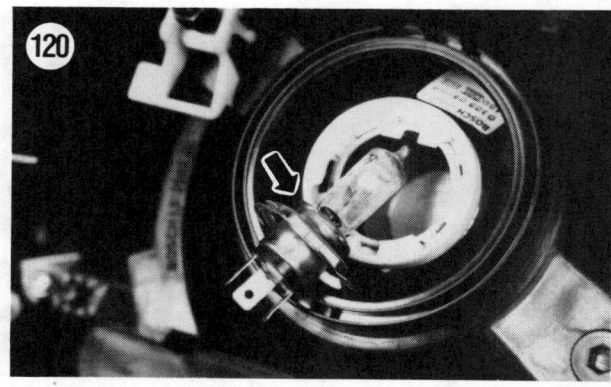

**Headlight Replacement
(K100RT and K100LT Model)**

Refer to **Figure 111** for this procedure.

It is not necessary to remove any body components on these models as there is sufficient room between the instrument cluster and the windshield. This procedure is shown on a K100RS model since the basic procedure is the same. The only difference is that there is less work room on the K100RS model.

1. Remove the frame left-hand side cover.

2. Disconnect the battery negative lead as described under *Battery* in Chapter Three.

3. Disconnect the electrical connector (A, **Figure 118**) from the base of the headlight.

4. Remove the rubber boot (B, **Figure 118**) from the base of the lens assembly.

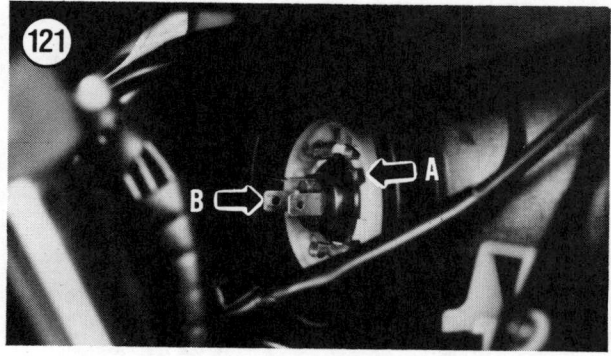

NOTE
Figure 119 and Figure 120 are shown with the headlight assembly removed from the front fairing for clarity.

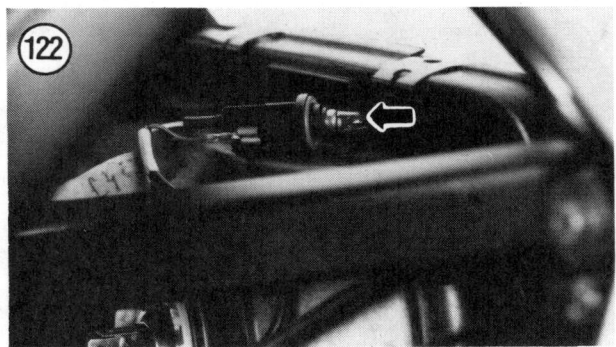

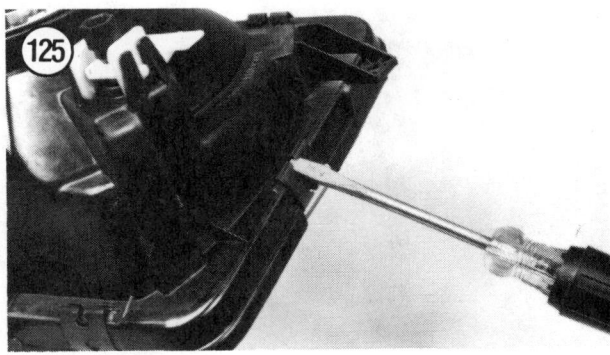

5. Rotate the locking clip and remove it. Refer to A, **Figure 121** and **Figure 119**.

6. Remove the bulb assembly. Refer to B, **Figure 121** and **Figure 120**.

7. Replace with a new bulb assembly—do not touch the bulb with your fingers. Refer to CAUTION at the beginning of this procedure.

8. To replace the parking light bulb, perform the following:
   a. Push in and rotate the parking light bulb socket *counterclockwise*.
   b. Carefully pull the bulb from the socket assembly (**Figure 122**) and install a new one.
   c. Push the socket assembly in and rotate it *clockwise*.

9. Install by reversing these removal steps, noting the following.

10. Tighten the screws and nuts securely. Don't overtighten the screws or nuts as the plastic mounting bosses may be damaged.

11. Make sure all electrical connectors are free of corrosion and are tight.

12. Adjust the headlight as described in this chapter.

Headlight Lens Replacement
(K100RS, K100RT and K100LT Models)

1. Remove the front fairing as described under *Front Fairing Removal/Installation, K100RS* or *Front Fairing Removal/Installation, K100RT and K100LT* in Chapter Thirteen.

2. To remove the headlight assembly from the front fairing upper panel, remove the screws (A, **Figure 123**) securing the headlight assembly (B, **Figure 123**) and remove the headlight assembly.

3. Remove the headlight gasket (**Figure 124**) from the perimeter of the lens.

4. Using a flat-bladed screwdriver (**Figure 125**), pry loose the clips (**Figure 126**) loose securing the headlight lens to the base. Remove all of the clips.

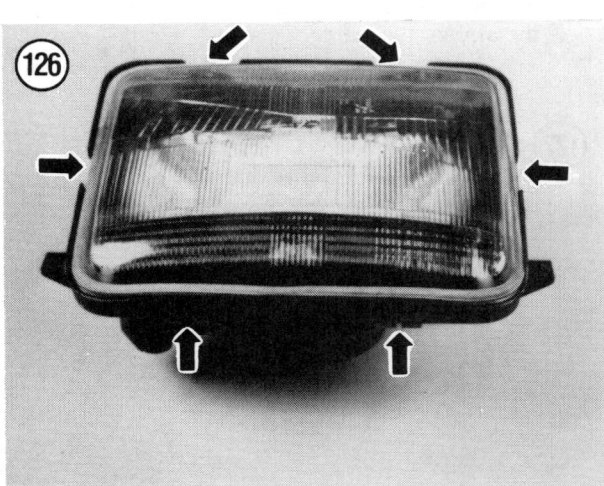

8

5. Separate the lens (**Figure 127**) from the base.

6. Inspect the lens gasket (**Figure 128**) for damage or deterioration; replace if necessary.

7. Wash the inside and outside of the lens with a mild detergent and wipe dry.

8. Inspect the reflectors for the headlight (A, **Figure 129**) and the parking lamp (B, **Figure 129**).

9. Wash both reflectors with a mild detergent and wipe dry.

10. If necessary, remove the screws (A, **Figure 130**) securing the parking lamp reflector (B, **Figure 130**) and remove the reflector. Install the reflector and tighten the screws securely.

11. If necessary, remove the vertical adjust knob assembly (A, **Figure 131**) and the horizontal adjust knob assembly (B, **Figure 131**).

12. Assemble by reversing these disassembly steps, noting the following.

13. Make sure all clips (**Figure 126**) are in place and are secure. This is necessary to keep moisture from entering the headlight assembly.

Headlight Adjustment

Adjust the headlight horizontally and vertically according to Department of Motor Vehicles regulations in your area.

K75T, K75C, K75 Low Seat and K100 models

1. For horizontal adjustment, perform the following:

   a. Remove the screws and lockwashers (**Figure 132**) on each side of the backside of the fairing mounting panel.

   b. Carefully pull the headlight fairing and trim panel (**Figure 133**) off of the mounting panel and headlight assembly.

   c. Check that the headlight assembly arrow is aligned with the arrow on the mounting tab (**Figure 134**) on each side. This is to maintain correct horizontal headlight aim.

   d. If the alignment is not correct, loosen the headlight mounting bolt (**Figure 135**) on each side and realign the arrows.

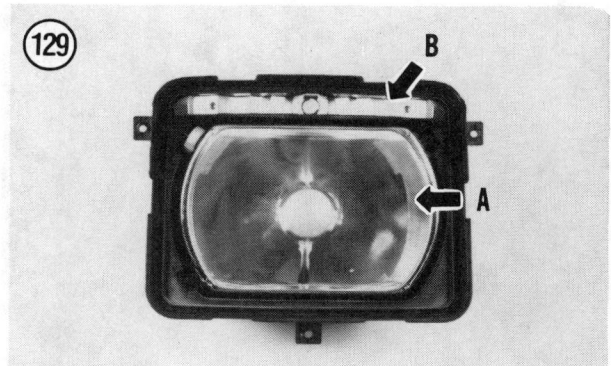

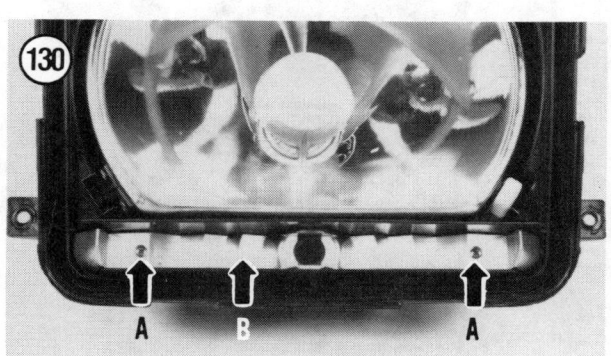

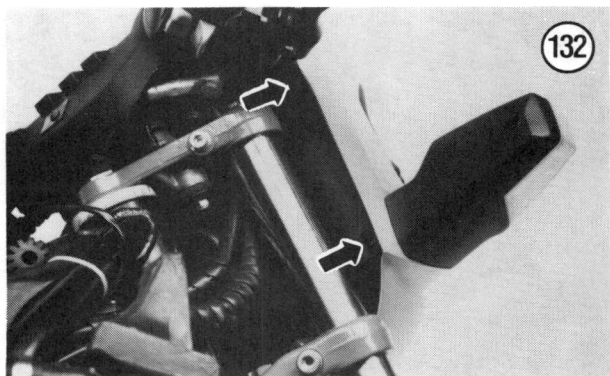

e. Tighten the mounting bolts securely.

f. Install the headlight fairing and trim panel onto the mounting panel and headlight assembly.

g. Install the lockwashers and screws (**Figure 132**) on each side of the backside of the fairing mounting panel. Tighten the screws securely.

NOTE
Figure 136 is shown with the headlight assembly removed from the bike for clarity. It is not necessary to remove this assembly in order to adjust the headlight.

2. For vertical adjustment, perform the following:

a. Turn the vertical adjust knob (**Figure 136**) located on the left-hand side of the headlight fairing mounting panel.

b. Turning the knob counterclockwise turns the light downward; turning it clockwise will direct the light upward.

K75S models

The vertical and horizontal adjust knobs are accessible from the underside of the front fairing adjacent to the fork tubes.

To adjust the headlight horizontally, turn the adjust knob on the right-hand side. Turning the knob clockwise turns the light toward the right-hand side of the rider; turning it counterclockwise will direct the light to the left-hand side of the rider.

To adjust the headlight vertically, turn the adjust knob on the left-hand side. Turning the knob clockwise turns the light upward and counterclockwise will direct the light downward.

8

K100RS, K100RT and K100LT models

To adjust the headlight horizontally, turn the adjust knob (A, **Figure 137**) on the left-hand side of the front fairing next to the fork tube. Turning the adjust knob clockwise turns the light toward the left-hand side of the rider; turning it counterclockwise will direct the light to the right-hand side of the rider.

The vertical adjustment on these models consists of a quick change lever (**Figure 138**) located on the right-hand side of the front fairing next to the fork tube. A change in the vehicle load will drastically change the headlight beam's vertical adjustment.

For major vertical adjustment changes use the change lever (B, **Figure 137**) and for minor adjustments use the special hex bolt (C, **Figure 137**) located within the change lever. For vertical adjustments, perform the following:
1. Remove the right-hand knee pad as follows:
   a. Remove the single screw (**Figure 139**) at the bottom of the knee pad.
   b. Remove the screws (**Figure 140**) at the top of the knee pad.
   c. Unhook the clip at the mid-point of the knee pad, then carefully remove the knee pad from the front fairing upper portion and lower side panel.
2. For vertical adjustments, perform the following:
   a. Move the lever to the top position. This will move the beam upward.
   b. Move the lever to the center position. This will move the beam to the middle or neutral position.

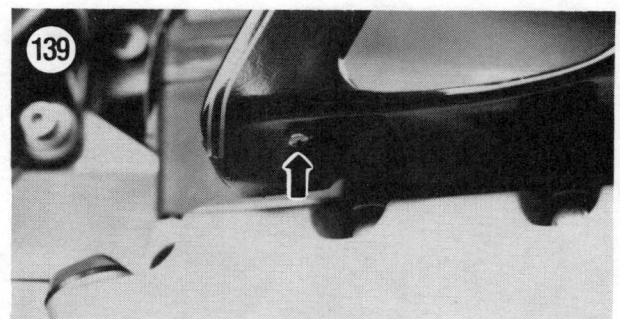

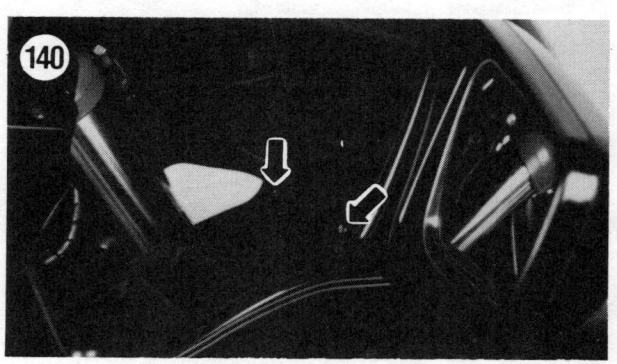

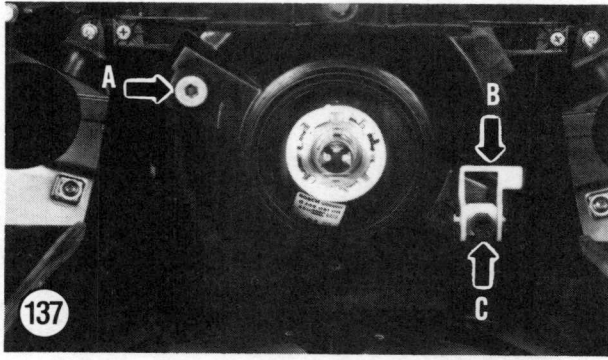

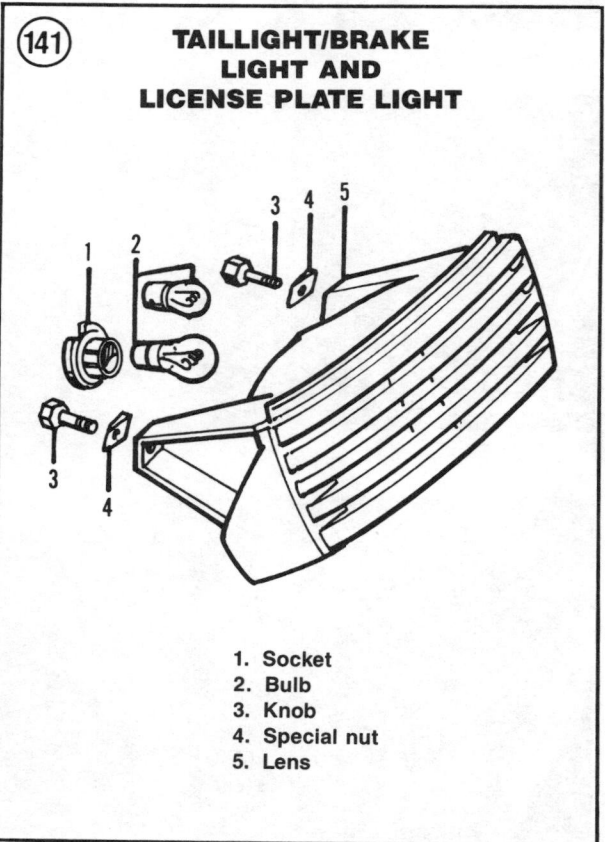

TAILLIGHT/BRAKE LIGHT AND LICENSE PLATE LIGHT

1. Socket
2. Bulb
3. Knob
4. Special nut
5. Lens

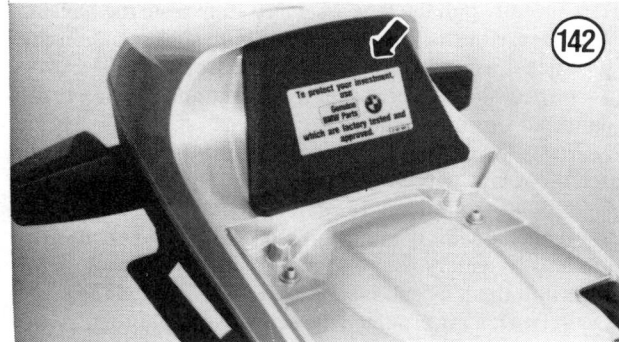

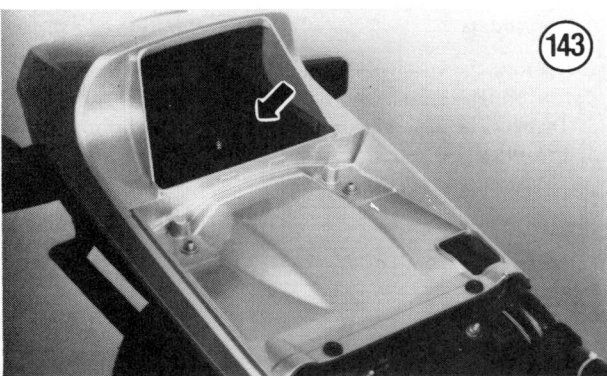

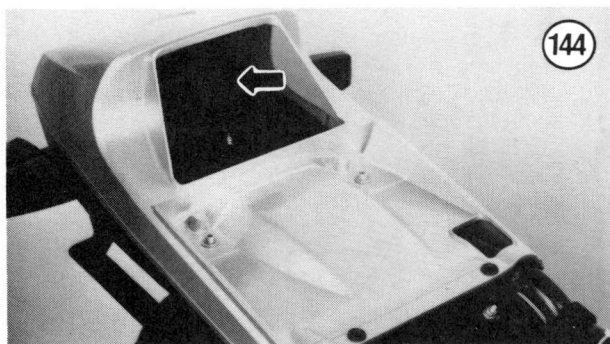

c. Move the lever to the lower position. This will move the beam downward.

TAILLIGHT/BRAKE LIGHT AND LICENSE PLATE LIGHT

Light Replacement

Refer to **Figure 141** for this procedure.

1. Remove the seat as described in Chapter Thirteen.
2. Remove the storage compartment lid (**Figure 142**).
3. Within the underseat storage box, perform the following:
   a. Remove the factory tool kit, owner's manual and anything else that may be stored in the compartment.
   b. On ABS models, remove the electronic control unit from the rubber isolators and move the control unit out of the way.
   c. Remove the rubber mat (**Figure 143**).
4. Unscrew the black plastic knobs (**Figure 144**) securing the light assembly to the rear cowl.
5. Pull the light assembly out from the rear cowl.
6. To remove the taillight/brake light bulb, squeeze the locking tabs on the bulb socket (A, **Figure 145**) and remove the socket assembly from the light assembly.
7. To remove the license plate light bulb, squeeze the locking tabs on the bulb socket (B, **Figure 145**) and remove the socket assembly from the light assembly.
8. Remove the light assembly.
9. Wash the inside and outside of the light assembly with a mild detergent and wipe dry.
10. Inspect the light assembly for damage or deterioration. Refer to **Figure 146** and **Figure 147**.

8

---

11. Inspect the socket assembly(ies) and replace if damaged or deteriorated.

12. Assemble by reversing these disassembly steps, noting the following.

13. Replace the bulb and install the socket assembly. Push the socket assembly in until it clicks and locks securely in the lens assembly. If not tightened correctly, water will enter the lens area.

TURN SIGNALS

Front Turn Signal
Light Replacement

K75T, K75C, K75 Low Seat and K100 models

Refer to **Figure 148** for this procedure.

1. Remove the screw (**Figure 149**) on the backside of the turn signal housing, securing the lens assembly.

2. Carefully pull the lens assembly away from the housing.

3. Squeeze the locking tabs on the bulb socket and remove the socket assembly from the lens assembly.

4. Inspect the socket assembly gasket and replace if it is damaged or deteriorated.

5. Wash the inside and outside of the lens with a mild detergent and wipe dry.

6. Replace the bulb and install the socket assembly. Push the socket assembly in until it clicks and locks securely in the lens assembly.

7. Install the lens and install the screw. Tighten the screw securely. Don't overtighten the screw as the plastic lens may be damaged.

K75S models

1. Remove the screw securing the lens to the front fairing.

2. Carefully remove the lens and gasket.

3. Inspect the lens gasket and replace if it is damaged or deteriorated.

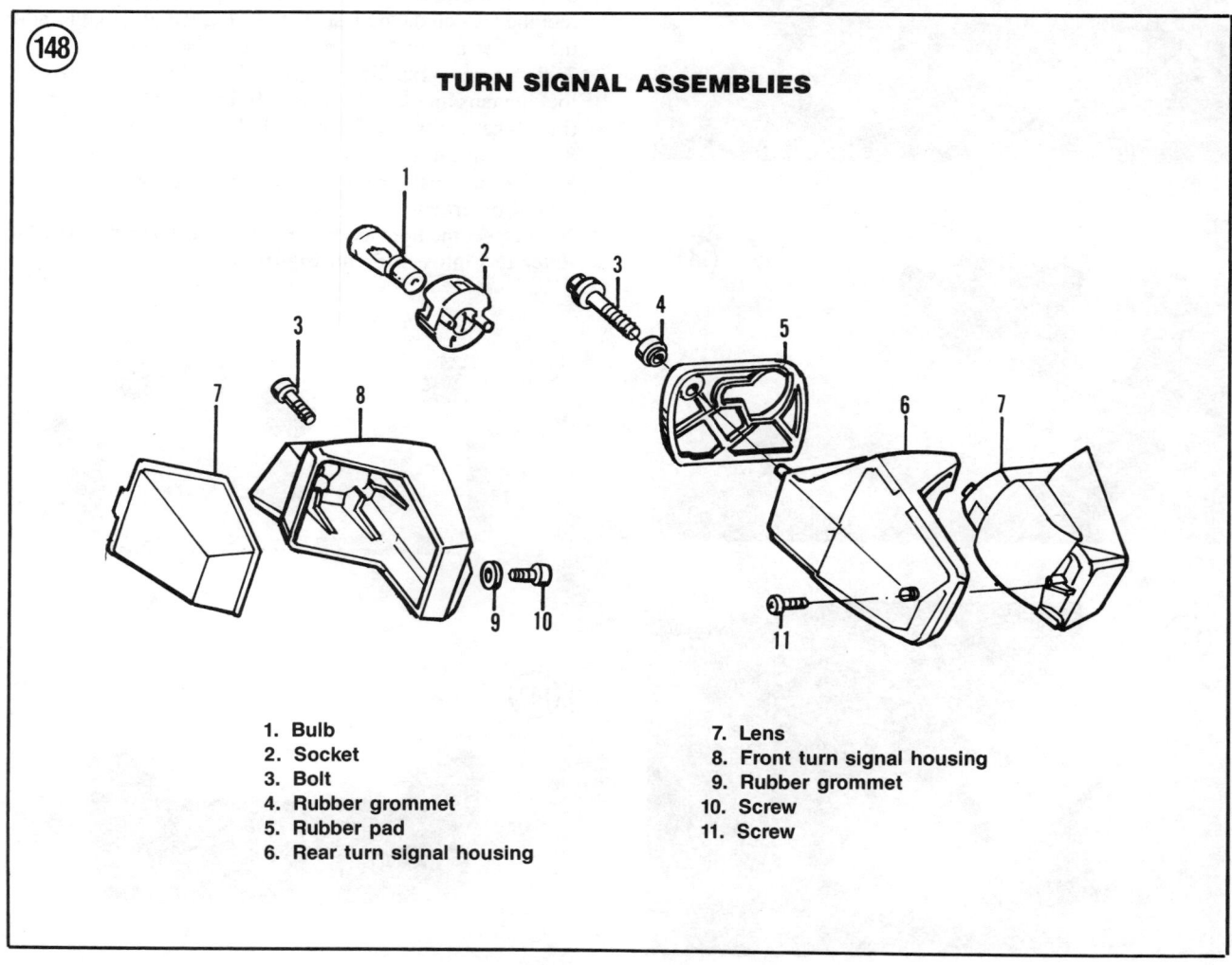

(148)

TURN SIGNAL ASSEMBLIES

1. Bulb
2. Socket
3. Bolt
4. Rubber grommet
5. Rubber pad
6. Rear turn signal housing
7. Lens
8. Front turn signal housing
9. Rubber grommet
10. Screw
11. Screw

4. Wash the inside and outside of the lens with a mild detergent and wipe dry.
5. Carefully remove the bulb from the socket.
6. Replace the bulb.
7. Install the lens and gasket and install the screw. Tighten the screw securely. Don't overtighten the screws as the plastic lens may be damaged.

K100 RS models

1. Remove the screw (**Figure 150**) securing the lens to the rear view mirror.
2. Carefully remove the lens and gasket.

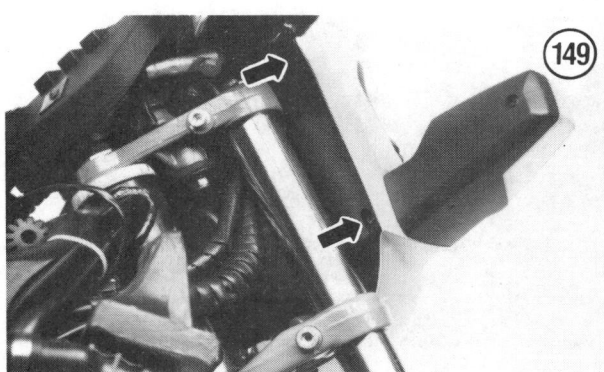

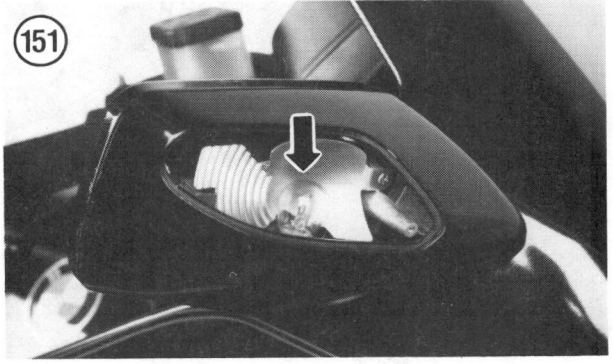

3. Inspect the lens gasket and replace if it is damaged or deteriorated.
4. Wash the inside and outside of the lens with a mild detergent and wipe dry.
5. Carefully remove the bulb (**Figure 151**) from the socket.
6. Replace the bulb.
7. Install the lens and gasket and install the screw. Tighten the screw securely. Don't overtighten the screws as the plastic lens may be damaged.

K100 RT and K100 LT models

1. Turn the handlebar all the way to the opposite side, away from the bulb to be replaced (e.g. turn to the left to gain access to the right-hand bulb).
2. On the inside surface of the front fairing, turn the socket assembly counterclockwise and remove the assembly from the front fairing.
3. Replace the bulb and install the socket assembly. Push the socket assembly in and rotate it clockwise until it locks securely in place.

Rear Turn Signal
Light Replacement
(All Models)

Refer to **Figure 148** for this procedure.
1. Remove the screw on the backside of the turn signal housing, securing the lens assembly.
2. Carefully pull the lens assembly away from the housing.
3. Squeeze the locking tabs on the bulb socket and remove the socket assembly from the lens assembly.
4. Inspect the socket assembly gasket and replace if it is damaged or deteriorated.
5. Wash the inside and outside of the lens with a mild detergent and wipe dry.
6. Replace the bulb and install the socket assembly. Push the socket assembly in until it clicks and locks securely in the lens assembly.
7. Install the lens and install the screw. Tighten the screw securely. Don't overtighten the screws as the plastic lens may be damaged.

Rear Turn Signal Assembly
Removal/Installation
(All Models)

Refer to **Figure 148** for this procedure.
1. Remove the rear cowl as described under *Rear Cowl Removal/Installation* in Chapter Thirteen.
2. Remove the screw on the backside of the turn signal housing, securing the lens assembly.
3. Carefully pull the lens assembly away from the housing.
4. Disconnect the electrical connectors from the socket assembly.

8

5. Remove the bolt and rubber grommet (A, **Figure 152**) securing the housing to the rear cowl.

6. Remove the housing (B, **Figure 152**) and the rubber pad from the rear cowl.

7. To remove the wiring harness, perform the following:

   a. Remove the screws securing the electrical connector (A, **Figure 153**) to the rear cowl.

   b. Carefully pull the electrical wires out through the rubber grommet (B, **Figure 153**) in the rear cowl.

   c. Remove the wiring harness and electrical connector from the rear cowl.

8. Install by reversing these removal steps, noting the following.

9. Be sure to install the rubber pad between the housing and the rear cowl.

10. Install the housing and install the rubber grommet and bolt. Tighten the bolt securely. Don't overtighten the bolt as the mounting post may be damaged.

11. Make sure the electrical connectors are free of corrosion and are tight.

SWITCHES

Ignition and Combination Switch Testing

BMW does not provide test information for these control switches on the bike. If you suspect a faulty switch, perform the following test.

1. Remove the switch as described in this chapter.

2. Refer to the electrical diagrams at the end of this manual and locate the switch and switch electrical wire colors.

3. To check continuity of the switch, use an ohmmeter and perform the following:

   a. Connect the ohmmeter test leads to the indicated color wires and check for continuity (indicated resistance) in all switch positions.

   b. Also check for continuity (indicated resistance) of all related electrical wires.

   c. If the switch fails any portion of this test, replace the switch.

Ignition Switch Removal/Installation

1. Disconnect the battery negative lead as described under *Battery* in Chapter Three.

2. Remove the fuel tank as described under *Fuel Tank Removal/Installation* in Chapter Seven. This is necessary to gain access to the switch electrical connections located on the frame under the fuel tank.

3. Remove the screws (**Figure 154**) securing the impact pad.

4. Carefully remove the ignition switch trim disc (**Figure 155**) surrounding the switch.

5. Insert a narrow flat-bladed screwdriver down on each side of the switch to release the locking tabs on the switch.

6. Partially pull the impact pad (**Figure 156**) up and off of the handlebar assembly.

7. With both locking tabs released, press down on the center of the switch and push it out of the impact pad.

8. Follow the electrical wires from the ignition switch back to its electrical connectors at the main wiring harness. If necessary, remove any tie wrap(s) (**Figure 157**) securing the electrical wires to the frame.

9. Pull the electrical wire away from the frame and disconnect the electrical connector.

10. If necessary, test the switch as described in this chapter.

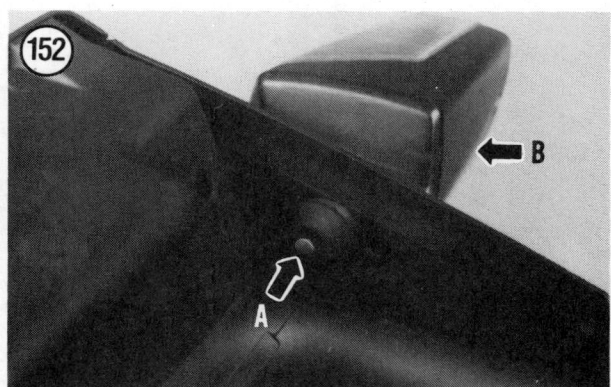

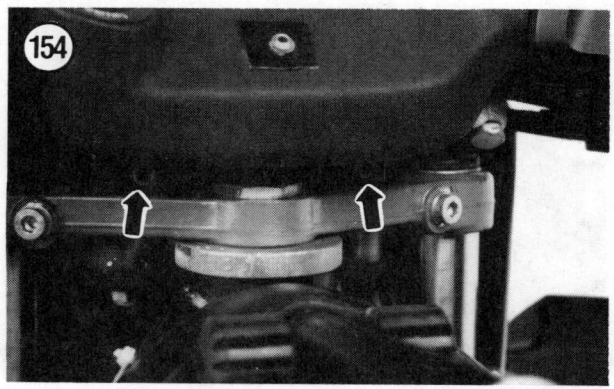

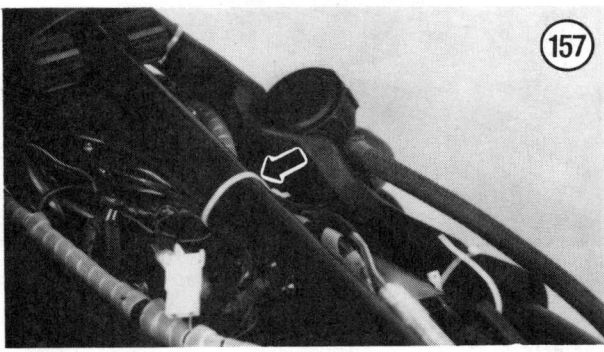

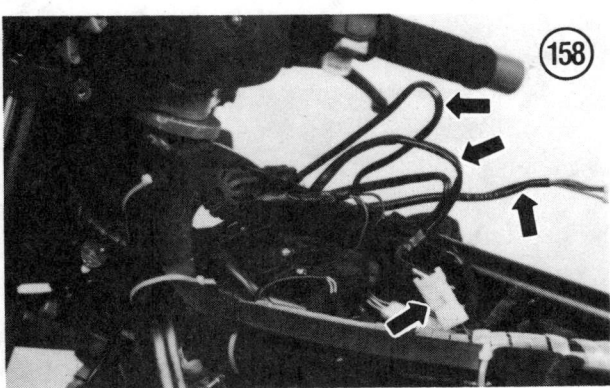

11. Install by reversing these removal steps.

12. Make sure all electrical connections are free of corrosion and are tight.

13. Move the electrical wires back into position and secure with tie wrap(s) (**Figure 157**). Make sure the wires are not above the frame members as they may be damaged by the fuel tank when it is installed.

Right-hand and Left-hand Combination Switch Removal/Installation

The right-hand combination switch assembly contains the engine stop switch, starter button and right-hand turn signal switch. The left-hand combination switch assembly contains the headlight switch, the horn button and the left-hand turn signal switch.

All of the switches are an integral part of their respective combination switch assemblies and if any portion of the switch is faulty the entire switch assembly must be replaced.

1. Disconnect the battery negative lead as described under *Battery* in Chapter Three.

2. Remove the fuel tank as described under *Fuel Tank Removal/Installation* in Chapter Seven. This is necessary to gain access to the switch electrical connections located on the frame under the fuel tank.

3. Remove the screws (**Figure 154**) securing the impact pad.

NOTE
It is necessary to remove the impact pad in order to gain access to the area behind it for electrical wire and connector removal.

4A. On models with no auxiliary switches, remove the impact pad.

4B. On models equipped with auxiliary switches, perform the following:

    a. Partially pull up on the impact pad (**Figure 156**) and move it out of the way. Don't move the pad too far as there is very little slack in the electrical wires at this time.

    b. Follow the electrical wires from the impact pad back to their electrical connectors at the main wiring harness. If necessary, remove any tie wrap(s) (**Figure 157**) securing the electrical wires to the frame.

    c. Pull the electrical wires away from the frame (**Figure 158**) to allow slack in wires.

    d. Pull the impact pad up and away from the steering head area. It is not necessary to completely remove the impact pad, just move it out of the way.

NOTE
On some models it is necessary to remove the instrument cluster in order to gain access to the area in front of it for electrical wire and connector removal.

8

5. If necessary, remove the instrument cluster as described in this chapter.

6A. To remove the right-hand combination switch assembly (**Figure 159**), remove the screw securing the switch to the handlebar. Move the switch up and off of the handlebar.

6B. To remove the left-hand combination switch assembly (**Figure 160**), remove the screw securing the switch to the handlebar. Move the switch up and off of the handlebar.

7. Unhook any tie wraps securing the switche's electrical wires and any other wires to the handlebar.

> *NOTE*
> *It may be necessary to remove the electrical wire spiral protective wrap from the wire (**Figure 161**). This switch wire may be wrapped along with another group of wires as it passes the front of the steering stem area.*

8. Carefully pull on the switch and electrical wire assembly and follow the electrical wires down in front of the steering stem and the frame to where the electrical connector is located.

9. Disconnect the electrical connector.

10. Carefully pull the switch and electrical wire assembly out from in front of the steering stem and the frame.

11. If necessary, test the switch as described in this chapter.

12. Install a new switch by reversing these removal steps, noting the following.

13. Make sure all electrical connections are tight and free of corrosion.

14. Move the electrical wires back into position and secure with tie wrap(s) (**Figure 157**). Make sure the wires are not above the frame members as they may be damaged by the fuel tank when it is installed.

Front Brake Light Switch
Testing

1. Disconnect the battery negative lead as described under *Battery* in Chapter Three.

2. Remove the fuel tank as described under *Fuel Tank Removal/Installation* in Chapter Seven. This is necessary to gain access to the switch electrical connections located on the frame under the fuel tank.

3. Disconnect the front brake light switch 2-pin electrical connector (containing 2 yellow wires). The connector is located on the right-hand side of the frame center tube that runs back from the steering head.

4. Use an ohmmeter and check for continuity between the 2 terminals on the brake light switch electrical connector. There should be no continuity (infinite resistance) with the brake lever released. With the brake lever applied there should be continuity (low resistance). If the switch fails either of these tests the switch must be replaced as described in this chapter.

Removal/installation

1. If not already removed, perform the following:
    a. Disconnect the battery negative lead as described under *Battery* in Chapter Three.
    b. Remove the fuel tank as described under *Fuel Tank Removal/Installation* in Chapter Seven. This is necessary to gain access to the switch electrical connections located on the frame under the fuel tank.

2. Disconnect the front brake light switch 2-pin electrical connector (containing 2 yellow wires). The connector is located on the right-hand side of the frame center tube that runs back from the steering head.

3. Remove the screws (**Figure 154**) securing the impact pad.

> *NOTE*
> *It is necessary to remove the impact pad in order to gain access to the area behind it for electrical wire and connector removal.*

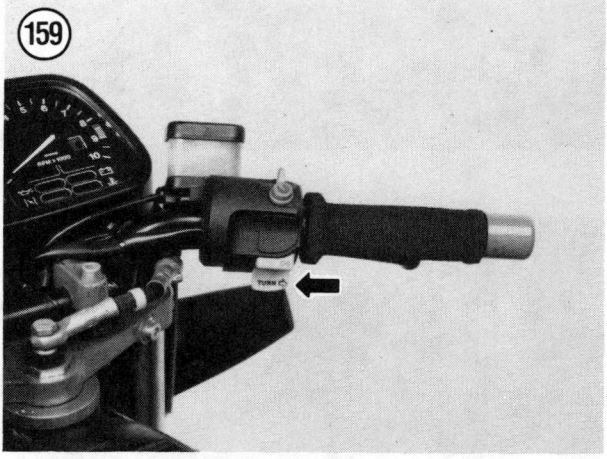

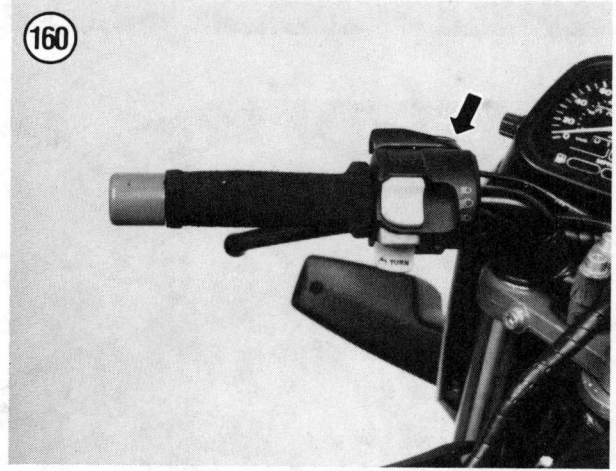

4A. On models with no auxiliary switches, remove the impact pad.

4B. On models equipped with auxiliary switches, perform the following:

a. Partially pull up on the impact pad (**Figure 156**) and move it out of the way. Don't move the pad too far as there is very little slack in the electrical wires at this time.

b. Follow the electrical wires from the impact pad back to their electrical connectors at the main wiring harness. If necessary, remove any tie wrap(s) (**Figure 157**) securing the electrical wires to the frame.

c. Pull the electrical wires away from the frame (**Figure 158**) to allow slack in wires.

d. Pull the impact pad up and away from the steering head area. It is not necessary to completely remove the impact pad, just move it out of the way.

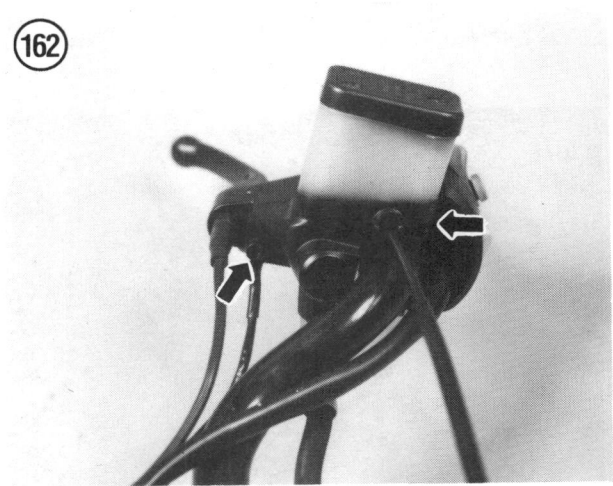

NOTE
On some models it is necessary to remove the instrument cluster in order to gain access to the area in front of it for electrical wire and connector removal.

5. If necessary, remove the instrument cluster as described in this chapter.

NOTE
*If the plastic pin on the end of the switch is bent, refer to **Brake Lever Modification** following this procedure to eliminate this problem in the future.*

6. Unscrew the brake light switch (**Figure 162**) from the master cylinder.

7. Unhook any tie wraps securing the switch's electrical wires and any other wires to the handlebar.

NOTE
*It may be necessary to remove the electrical wire spiral protective wrap from the wire (**Figure 161**). This switch wire may be wrapped along with another group of wires as it passes the front of the steering stem area.*

8. Carefully pull on the switch and electrical wire assembly and follow the electrical wires down in front of the steering stem and the frame to where the electrical connector is located on the right-hand side.

9. Disconnect the front brake light switch 2-pin electrical connector (containing 2 yellow wires). The connector is located on the right-hand side of the frame center tube that runs back from the steering head.

10. Carefully pull the switch and electrical wire assembly out from in front of the steering stem and the frame.

11. Install a new switch by reversing these removal steps, noting the following.

12. Make sure all electrical connections are tight and free of corrosion.

13. Move the electrical wires back into position and secure with tie wrap(s) (**Figure 157**). Make sure the wires are not above the frame members as they may be damaged by the fuel tank when it is installed.

Brake lever modification

If the plastic pin on the end of the brake light switch is bent, the switch will not function properly. BMW has determined that a slight modification to the brake lever will eliminate this problem. The sharp corner on the hand lever tends to snag the plastic pin and bend it as the lever moves past the pin during full brake application.

8

1. Remove the screw (**Figure 163**) securing the front brake lever and remove the lever.

2. File or grind off the *sharp* corner of the lever shown in **Figure 164**. Only remove the sharp corner as shown.

3. Do not remove any material in the area where the lever normally contacts the brake switch. This area is used to push the switch to the OFF position. If material is removed from this area the brake switch will not work in the OFF position.

4. Make sure all burrs are removed and that all surfaces are smooth.

5. Install the front brake lever and screw. Tighten the screw securely.

Rear Brake Light Switch

Testing

1. Remove the frame right-hand side cover.

2. Disconnect the electrical connector (**Figure 165**) going to the rear brake light switch.

3. Use an ohmmeter and check for continuity between the 2 terminals on the brake light switch. There should be no continuity (infinite resistance) with the brake pedal released. With the brake pedal down or applied there should be continuity (low resistance). If the switch fails either of these tests the switch must be replaced as described in this chapter.

Removal/installation—disc brake models

1. If not already removed, perform the following:
   a. Remove the frame right-hand side cover.
   b. Disconnect the electrical connector (**Figure 165**) going to the rear brake light switch.

2. Unhook the small return spring from the frame.

3. On models so equipped, remove the bolts (**Figure 166**) securing the luggage rack carrier to the right-hand footpeg assembly.

4. Remove the bolts (**Figure 167**) securing the right-hand footpeg assembly to the frame and carefully pull the top portion of the assembly away from the frame.

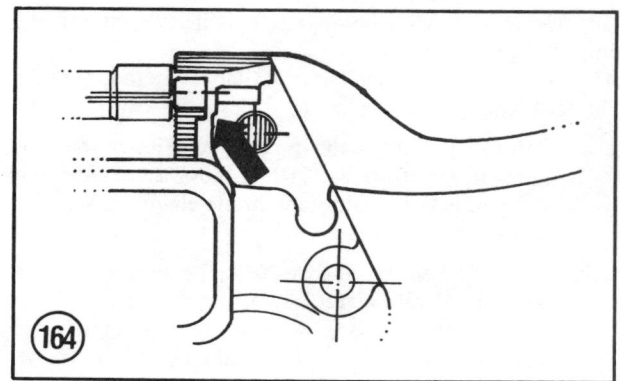

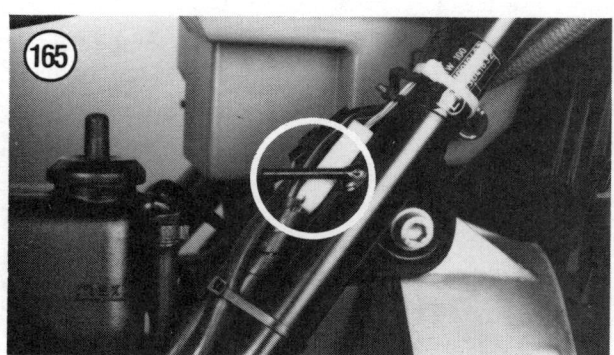

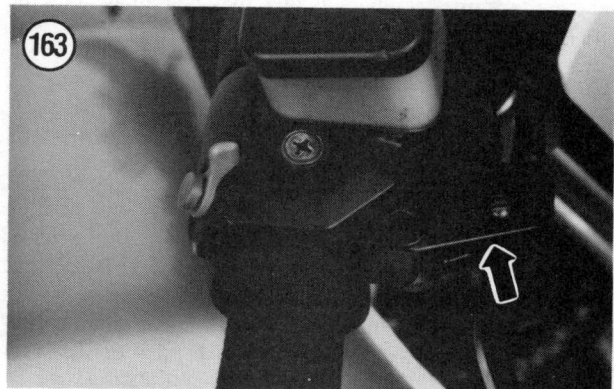

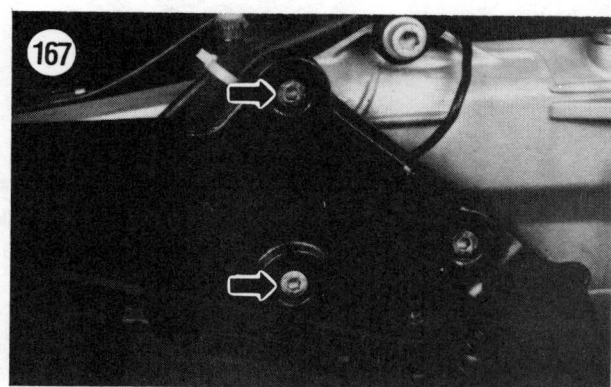

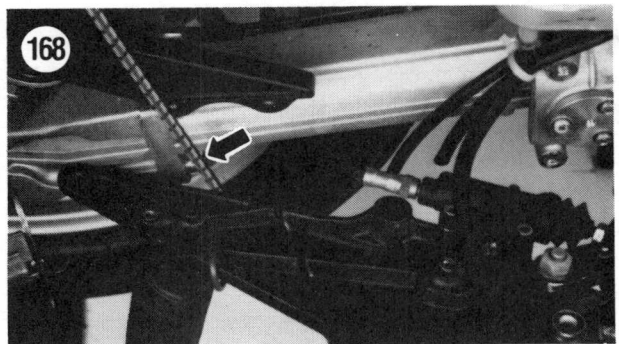

5. Secure the rear of the assembly with a Bungee cord (**Figure 168**) to take the strain off of the flexible brake hoses.
6. Unscrew the brake switch (**Figure 169**) from the footpeg assembly.

NOTE
If the plastic pin on the end of the switch is bent, refer to **Brake Pedal Modification** *following this procedure to eliminate this problem in the future.*

7. Remove any clips securing the electrical wires to the footpeg assembly.
8. Unhook any tie wraps securing the electrical wires to the frame.
9. Carefully pull the switch and electrical wire assembly out of the frame.
10. Install a new switch by reversing these removal steps, noting the following.
11. Make sure all electrical connections are tight and free of corrosion.
12. Move the electrical wires back into position and secure with tie wrap(s).

Removal/installation—drum brake models

1. If not already removed, perform the following:
   a. Remove the frame right-hand side cover.
   b. Disconnect the electrical connector (**Figure 165**) going to the rear brake light switch.
2. On models so equipped, remove the bolts (**Figure 166**) securing the luggage rack carrier to the right-hand footpeg assembly.
3. Completely unscrew the adjust nut (**Figure 170**) from the end of the brake rod.
4. Depress the brake pedal and withdraw the brake rod from the brake lever.
5. Remove the pivot pin (**Figure 171**) from the brake lever.
6. Install the pivot pin and adjust nut (**Figure 172**) onto the brake rod to avoid misplacing them.

8

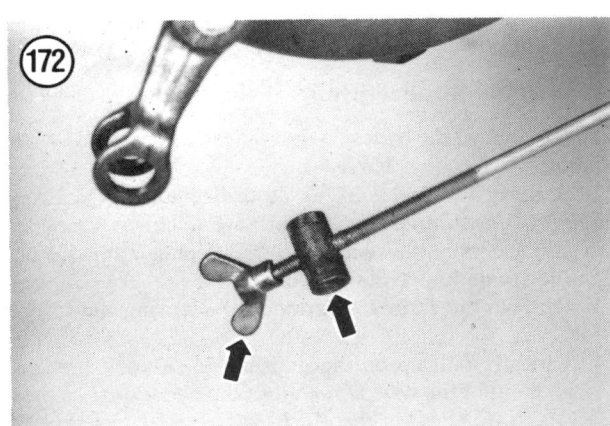

7. Remove the bolts (**Figure 173**) securing the right-hand footpeg assembly to the frame and carefully pull the top portion of the assembly away from the frame.

8. Secure the rear of the assembly with a Bungee cord.

9. Remove the screw and washer (A, **Figure 174**) securing the brake switch to the footpeg assembly.

NOTE
*If the plastic pin on the end of the switch is bent, refer to **Brake Pedal Modification** following this procedure to eliminate this problem in the future.*

10. Remove any clips securing the electrical wires to the footpeg assembly.

11. Remove the rear brake switch (B, **Figure 174**) from the footpeg assembly.

12. Unhook any tie wraps securing the electrical wires to the frame.

13. Carefully pull the switch and electrical wire assembly out of the frame.

14. Install a new switch by reversing these removal steps, noting the following.

15. Make sure all electrical connections are tight and free of corrosion.

16. Move the electrical wires back into position and secure with tie wrap(s).

17. Tighten the bolts securing the right-hand footpeg assembly to the torque specification listed in **Table 1**.

Brake pedal modification

If the plastic pin on the end of the brake light switch is bent, the switch will not function properly. BMW has determined that adding a plastic cap to the brake light switch bolt on the brake pedal will eliminate this problem.

1. Remove the brake light switch as described in this chapter.

2. Add a plastic cap (BMW part No. 35 21 1 244 520) to the bolt head as shown in **Figure 175**.

3. Install the brake light switch as described in this chapter.

4. Adjust the bolt (with cap) so there is 3.5 mm (0.138 in.) clearance between the plastic cap and the brake switch.

Impact Pad Auxiliary Switch Replacement

1. Disconnect the battery negative lead as described under *Battery* in Chapter Three.

2. Remove the fuel tank as described under *Fuel Tank Removal/Installation* in Chapter Seven. This is necessary to gain access to the switch electrical connections located on the frame under the fuel tank.

3. Remove the screws (**Figure 154**) securing the impact pad.

4. Partially pull up on the impact pad (**Figure 156**) and move it out of the way. Don't move the pad too far as there is very little slack in the electrical wires at this time.

5. Follow the electrical wires from the impact pad back to their electrical connectors at the main wiring harness. If necessary, remove any tie wrap(s) (**Figure 157**) securing the electrical wires to the frame.

6. Pull the electrical wires away from the frame (**Figure 158**) to allow slack in wires. Disconnect all electrical wires going to the impact pad electrical switches.

7. Pull the impact pad up and away from the steering head area.

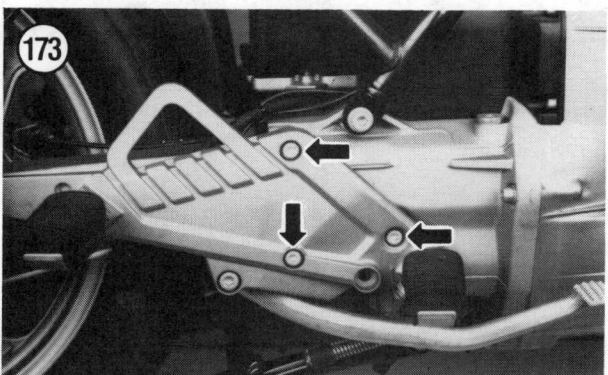

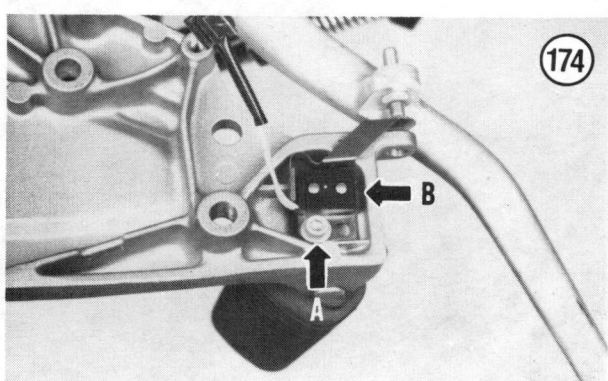

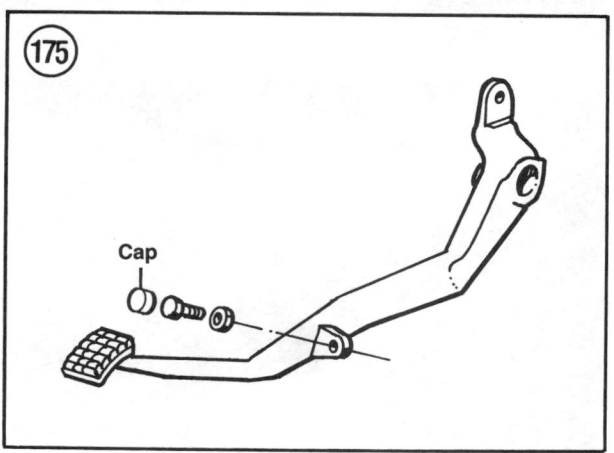

8. Carefully pull all switch electrical wires out from in front of the steering stem and the frame.

9. Remove the impact pad.

10. Insert a narrow flat-bladed screwdriver (**Figure 176**) into each locking tab (**Figure 177**) of the switch. Push the tabs in toward the switch to release them from the impact pad.

11. Pull the switch assembly (**Figure 178**) out through the front of the impact pad.

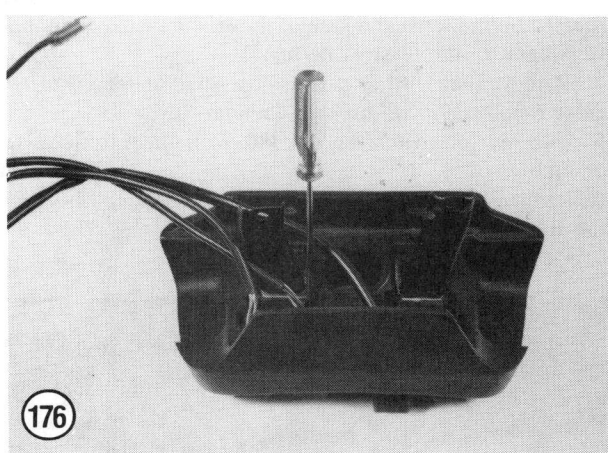

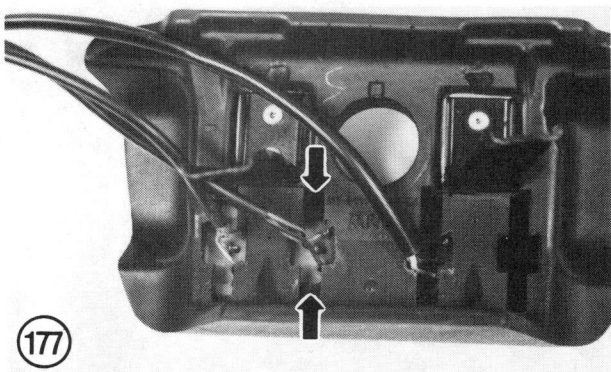

12. Repeat for any additional switches that require replacement.

13. Install a new switch by reversing these removal steps, noting the following.

14. Make sure the locking tabs are locked correctly in place.

15. Make sure all electrical connections are tight and free of corrosion.

16. Move the electrical wires back into position and secure with tie wrap(s) (**Figure 157**). Make sure the wires are not above the frame members as they may be damaged by the fuel tank when it is installed.

Clutch Switch

Testing

1. Disconnect the battery negative lead as described under *Battery* in Chapter Three.

2. Remove the fuel tank as described under *Fuel Tank Removal/Installation* in Chapter Seven. This is necessary to gain access to the switch electrical connections located on the frame under the fuel tank.

3. Disconnect the clutch switch 2-pin electrical connector (containing 2 yellow wires). The connector is located on the left-hand side of the frame center tube that runs back from the steering head.

4. Use an ohmmeter and check for continuity between the 2 terminals on the clutch switch electrical connector. There should be no continuity (infinite resistance) with the clutch lever released. With the clutch lever pulled there should be continuity (low resistance). If the switch fails either of these tests the switch must be replaced.

Removal/installation

1. If not already removed, perform the following:
   a. Disconnect the battery negative lead as described under *Battery* in Chapter Three.
   b. Remove the fuel tank as described under *Fuel Tank Removal/Installation* in Chapter Seven. This is necessary to gain access to the switch electrical connections located on the frame under the fuel tank.

2. Disconnect the clutch switch 2-pin electrical connector (containing 2 yellow wires). The connector is located on the left-hand side of the frame center tube that runs back from the steering head.

3. Remove the screws (**Figure 154**) securing the impact pad.

NOTE
It is necessary to remove the impact pad in order to gain access to the area behind it for electrical wire and connector removal.

4A. On models with no auxiliary switches, remove the impact pad.

8

4B. On models equipped with auxiliary switches, perform the following:

   a. Partially pull up on the impact pad (**Figure 156**) and move it out of the way. Don't move the pad too far as there is very little slack in the electrical wires at this time.

   b. Follow the electrical wires from the impact pad back to their electrical connectors at the main wiring harness. If necessary, remove any tie wrap(s) (**Figure 157**) securing the electrical wires to the frame.

   c. Pull the electrical wires away from the frame (**Figure 158**) to allow slack in wires.

   d. Pull the impact pad up and away from the steering head area. It is not necessary to completely remove the impact pad, just move it out of the way.

NOTE
On some models it is necessary to remove the instrument cluster in order to gain access to the area in front of it for electrical wire and connector removal.

5. If necessary, remove the instrument cluster as described in this chapter.
6. Unscrew the clutch switch (**Figure 179**) from the clutch lever assembly.
7. Unhook any tie wraps securing the switch's electrical wires and any other wires to the handlebar.

NOTE
*It may be necessary to remove the electrical wire spiral protective wrap from the wire (**Figure 161**). This switch wire may be wrapped along with another group of wires as it passes the front of the steering stem area.*

8. Carefully pull on the switch and electrical wire assembly and follow the electrical wires down in front of the steering stem and the frame to where the electrical connector is located on the right-hand side.
9. Disconnect the clutch switch 2-pin electrical connector (containing 2 yellow wires). The connector is located on the left-hand side of the frame center tube that runs back from the steering head.
10. Carefully pull the switch and electrical wire assembly out from in front of the steering stem and the frame.
11. Install a new switch by reversing these removal steps, noting the following.
12. Make sure all electrical connections are tight and free of corrosion.
13. Move the electrical wires back into position and secure with tie wrap(s) (**Figure 157**). Make sure the wires are not above the frame members as they may be damaged by the fuel tank when it is installed.

Cold Start (Choke) Switch
Removal/Installation

1. Disconnect the battery negative lead as described under *Battery* in Chapter Three.
2. Remove the fuel tank as described under *Fuel Tank Removal/Installation* in Chapter Seven. This is necessary to gain access to the switch electrical connections located on the frame under the fuel tank.
3. Disconnect the cold start switch 2-pin electrical connector (containing 2 yellow wires). The connector is located on the left-hand side of the frame center tube that runs back from the steering head.
4. Remove the air filter case as described under *Air Filter Case Removal/Installation* in Chapter Seven.
5. Unscrew the switch (**Figure 180**) from the throttle valve assembly.
6. Remove the switch and electrical wire assembly from the frame.

(179)

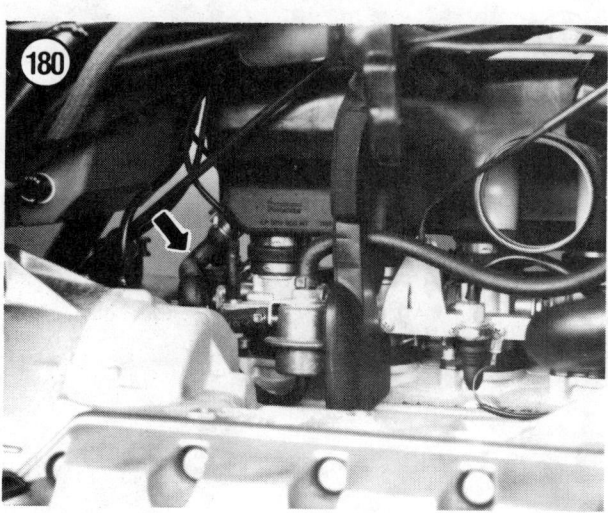

(180)

7. Install a new switch by reversing these removal steps, noting the following.

8. Make sure all electrical connections are tight and free of corrosion.

9. Move the electrical wires back into position and secure with tie wrap(s) (**Figure 157**). Make sure the wires are not above the frame members as they may be damaged by the fuel tank when it is installed.

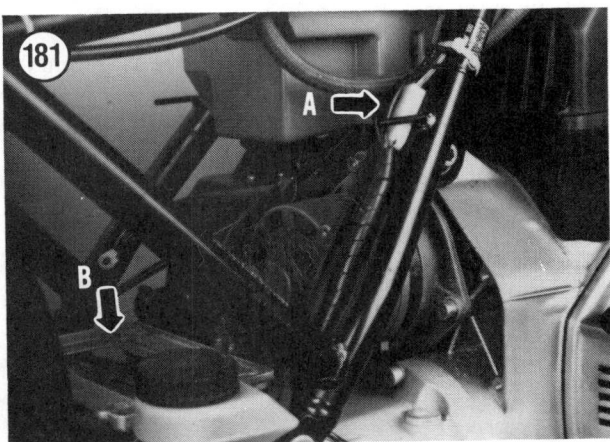

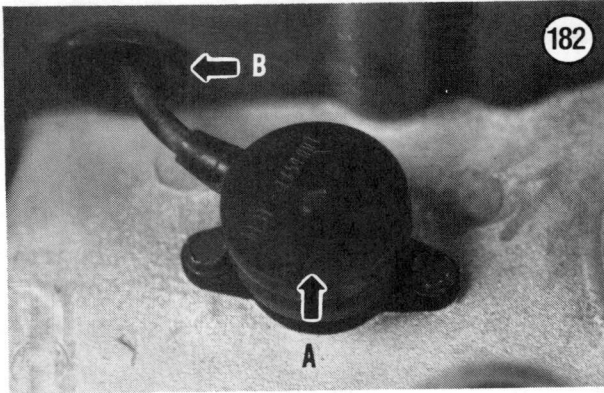

Gear Indicator Switch
Removal/Installation

The gear indicator switch is located on the backside of the transmission housing. There is no test procedure for this switch. If the gear indicator on the instrument cluster is incorrect or is not working at all, check all electrical connections. If the electrical connections are okay, replace the switch.

The switch can be removed with the engine and transmission assembly in the frame. It is shown removed in this procedure for clarity.

1. Remove the battery as described under *Battery* in Chapter Three.

2. Remove the swing arm as described under *Swing Arm Removal/Installation* in Chapter Eleven.

3. Disconnect the electrical connector (A, **Figure 181**) going to the gear indicator switch.

4. Remove the bolts securing the switch (A, **Figure 182**) to the transmission housing.

5. Remove the gear indicator electrical wires and electrical connector from the frame.

6. Pull the electrical wires and electrical connector through the battery holder (B, **Figure 181**) and out through the rubber grommet (B, **Figure 182**) on the top surface of the transmission housing.

7. Remove the switch assembly from the backside of the transmission housing.

8. Install by reversing these removal steps, noting the following.

9. Make sure the rubber grommet is installed correctly in the groove in the transmission housing.

10. Make sure the electrical connector is free of corrosion and is tight.

Oil Pressure Warning Switch
Testing/Replacement

The oil pressure warning light on the instrument cluster is designed to come on when the ignition is turned on, before starting the engine. As soon as the engine is started and the oil pressure rises to the correct level, the warning light should go out.

If the light fails to come on, check the bulb as described under *Instrument Cluster* in this chapter. Replace the bulb if necessary.

If the oil warning light stays on while the engine is running, stop the engine and check the oil level as described under *Engine Oil Level* in Chapter Three. If the oil level is correct the oil pressure switch may be faulty.

The oil pressure warning switch is located on the lower left-hand side of the water/oil pump assembly at the front of the engine.

1. On models so equipped, remove the engine spoiler as described under *Engine Spoiler Removal/Installation* in Chapter Thirteen.

2. Pull back the rubber boot (**Figure 183**) and remove the screw securing the electrical connector to the switch.

8

3. Turn the ignition switch on.

4. Have an assistant observe the oil pressure warning light on the instrument cluster.

5. Briefly touch the electrical connector to a bare metal spot on the engine. The warning light should come on. If the light comes on, the switch is faulty and must be replaced. If the light does not come on, the bulb is faulty and must be replaced.

6. Unscrew the oil pressure warning light from the water/oil pump assembly.

7. Install the new oil pressure warning light into the water/oil pump assembly. Tighten the switch to the torque specification listed in **Table 1**.

8. Attach the electrical wire. Make sure the connection is free from oil and corrosion.

9. Slide the rubber boot back into position and make sure it is on tight. This is very important, especially if the bike is not equipped with the engine spoiler. The rubber boot must keep out road oil and water that would lead to electrical connector corrosion. If the warning light flickers in the ON mode, this is an indication of corrosion or a poor electrical connection at the switch.

Coolant Temperature Warning and Fan Control Switch Testing/Replacement

The switch controls the radiator fan according to engine coolant temperature. This switch is attached to the coolant pipe on the top front left-hand corner of the cylinder block.

When the coolant reaches 103° C (185° F) the radiator coolant fan starts to run. When the coolant reaches 111° C (232° F) the coolant warning on the instrument cluster comes on.

1. Remove the air filter case as described under *Air Filter Case Removal/Installation* in Chapter Seven.

> *NOTE*
> *If the cooling fan is not operating correctly, make sure that the cooling fan fuse has not blown prior to starting this test. Also clean off any rust or corrosion from the electrical terminals on the switch.*

2. Remove the clip and disconnect the electrical connector (**Figure 184**) from the switch.

3. Place a jumper wire between the two electrical terminals in the electrical connector.

4. Turn the ignition switch on. The cooling fan should start running.

5A. If the fan now runs, the switch is defective and must be replaced.

5B. If the fan does not run under any circumstances either the fan or the wiring to the fan is faulty. Connect the fan motor directly to a 12-volt battery. If the fan runs the wiring

is faulty. Replace the fan motor if the wiring checks out okay.

6. Drain the cooling system as described under *Coolant Change* in Chapter Three.

> *NOTE*
> *Figure 185 is shown with the coolant pipe removed from the engine for clarity. It is not necessary to remove the coolant pipe to remove the switch.*

7. Unscrew and remove the switch (**Figure 185**) from the coolant pipe.

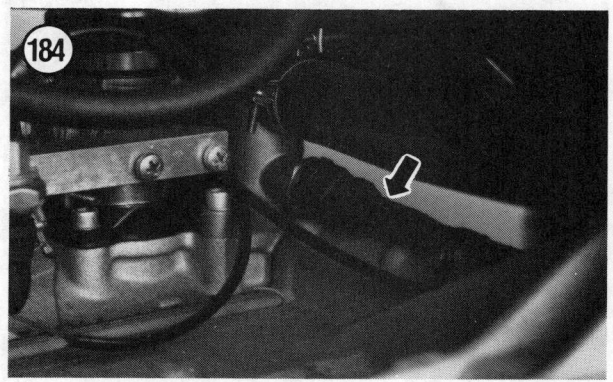

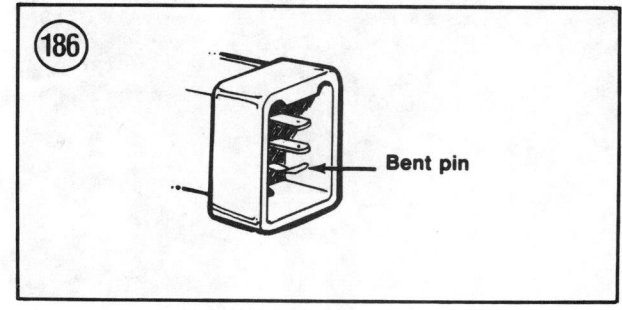

Bent pin

8. Apply a silicone-based sealant to the threads of the switch and install the switch in the coolant pipe. Tighten the switch securely.

9. Refill the cooling system with the recommended type and quantity of coolant. Refer to Chapter Three.

10. Attach the electrical wires to the switch. Make sure the connections are tight and free from oil and corrosion.

11. Install the air filter case as described under *Air Filter Case Removal/Installation* in Chapter Seven.

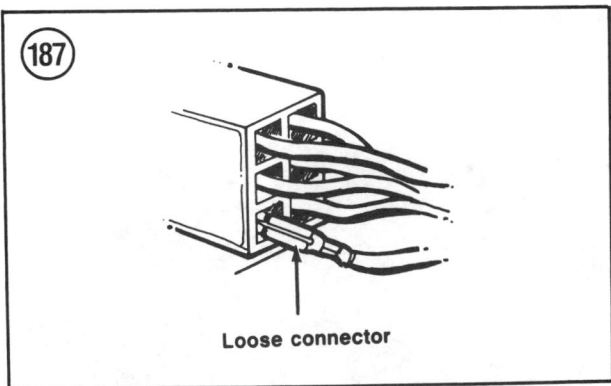

Loose connector

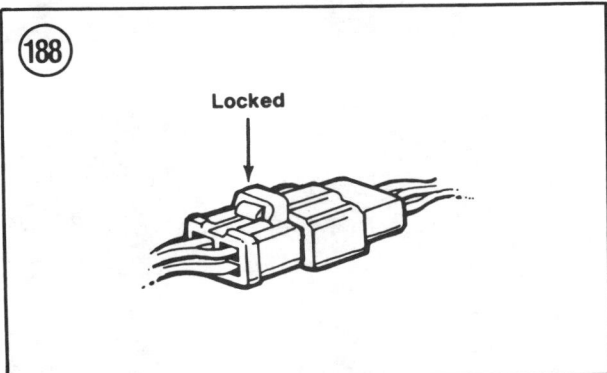

Locked

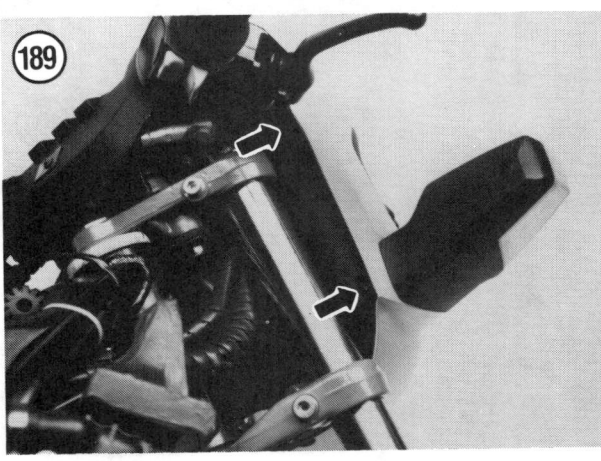

ELECTRICAL CONNECTORS

Connector problems may cause trouble in any part of the electrical system. If you are having trouble with some of these components, some quick preliminary checks may save a lot of time.

1. Disconnect each electrical connector and check that there are no bent metal pins on the male side of the electrical connector (**Figure 186**). A bent pin will not connect to its mating receptacle in the female end of the connector, causing an open circuit.

2. Check each female end of the connector. Make sure that the metal connector on the end of each wire (**Figure 187**) is pushed in all the way into the plastic connector. If not, carefully push them in with a narrow bladed screwdriver.

3. Check all electrical wires where they enter the individual metal terminals in both the male and female plastic connector.

4. After all is checked out, push the connectors together and make sure they are fully engaged and locked together (**Figure 188**).

INSTRUMENT CLUSTER

BMW has determined that there may be problems with the instrument cluster due to various causes. The following are some of the problems that you may encounter with the instrument cluster and the BMW Service Information Bulletin relating to each specific problem:

  a. Fogging of the inside surface of the instrument lens: BMW Service Information Bulletin July 1987, 62 004 87 (2264A).
  b. Fogging of the inside of the instruments: BMW Service Information Bulletin July 1987, 62 004 87 (2264B).
  c. Speedometer fails to operate and/or operates intermittently after riding over a severe bump(s) or railroad tracks: BMW Service Information Bulletin July 1987, 62 004 87 (2264C).
  d. Speedometer and/or tachometer readings are intermittent or not working at all: BMW Service Information Bulletin July 1987, 62 004 87 (2264D).
  e. Fuel gauge flickers or flashes intermittently: BMW Service Information Bulletin July 1987, 62 004 87 (2264E).

If you have encountered any of these problems, take the bike to a BMW dealer and have them check it out. It *may* be covered under any applicable warranty.

Removal/Installation
(K75C, K75T and K100 Models)

1. Remove the frame left-hand side cover.
2. Disconnect the battery negative lead as described under *Battery* in Chapter Three.
3. Remove the screws and lockwashers (**Figure 189**) on each side of the backside of the fairing mounting panel.

8

4. Carefully pull the headlight fairing and trim panel off of the mounting panel and headlight assembly.

5. Disconnect the electrical connectors for the turn signals and remove headlight fairing and trim panel.

6. Loosen the headlight mounting bolt (**Figure 190**) on each side.

7. Carefully pull the headlight assembly forward and out of the mounting panel.

8. Disconnect the electrical connector (A, **Figure 191**) from the base of the headlight and remove the headlight.

9. Disconnect the electrical connector to each horn.

10. Remove the bolts (B, **Figure 191**) securing each horn and remove the horns.

11. Remove the screw securing the electrical connector cover panel (**Figure 192**) and remove the cover panel.

12. Carefully disconnect the electrical connectors (**Figure 193**) from the instrument cluster.

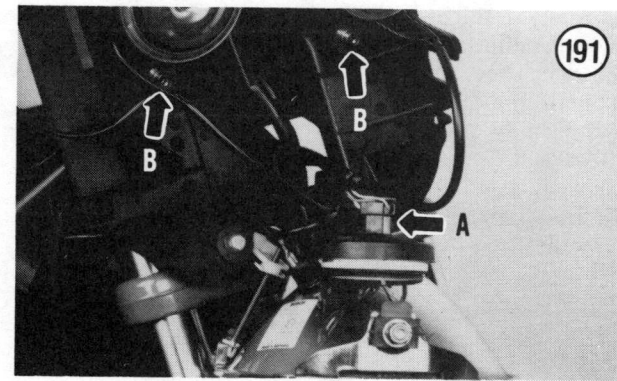

NOTE
The mounting panel can be removed with the
instrument cluster attached or removed.

13. If necessary, remove the bolts and washers (A, **Figure 194**) securing the instrument cluster to the mounting panel and remove the instrument cluster (B, **Figure 194**).

14. Install by reversing these removal steps, noting the following.

15. Install the headlight assembly and align the arrow with the arrow on the mounting tab (**Figure 195**) on each side. This is to maintain correct horizontal headlight aim.

16. Tighten the screws and bolts securely. Don't overtighten the screws or bolts as the plastic mounting bosses may be damaged.

17. Make sure the electrical connectors are free of corrosion and are tight.

Removal/Installation
(K75S Models)

1. Remove the front fairing as described under *Front Fairing (K75S) Removal/Installation* in Chapter Thirteen.

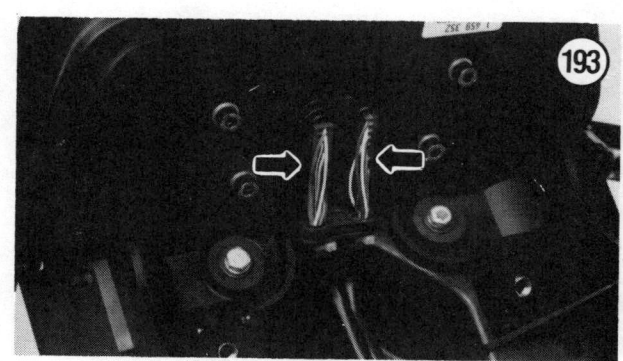

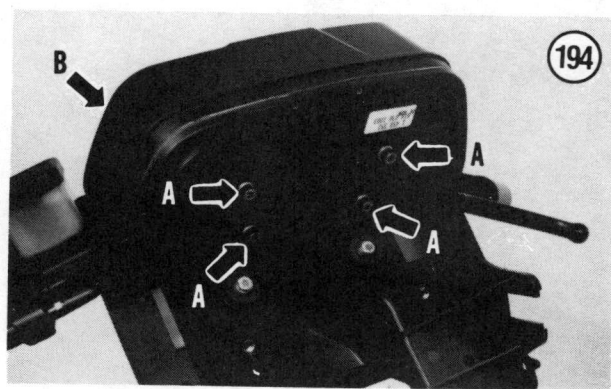

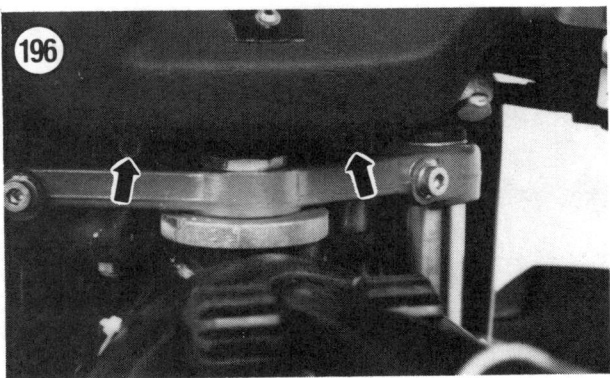

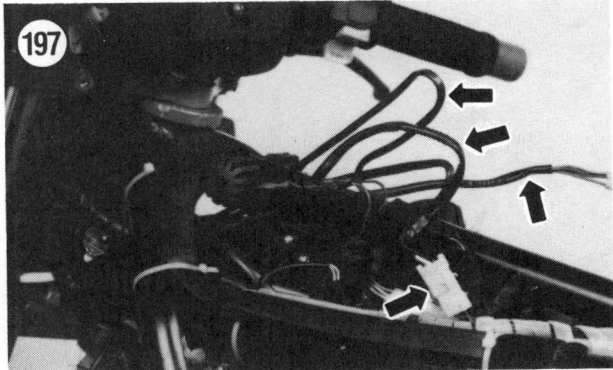

2. Remove the screw securing the electrical connector cover panel and remove the cover panel.

3. Carefully disconnect the electrical connectors from the instrument cluster.

4. Remove the bolts and washers securing the instrument cluster and lower panel to the mounting panel and remove the instrument cluster.

5. Install by reversing these removal steps, noting the following.

6. Tighten the bolts securely. Don't overtighten the bolts as the plastic mounting bosses may be damaged.

7. Make sure the electrical connectors are free of corrosion and are tight.

Removal/Installation
(K100RS Models)

1. Remove the right-hand side cover.

2. Disconnect the battery negative lead as described under *Battery* in Chapter Three.

3. Remove the fuel tank as described under *Fuel Tank Removal/Installation* in Chapter Seven.

4. Remove the screws (**Figure 196**) securing the impact pad.

5A. On models with no auxiliary switches, remove the impact pad.

5B. On models equipped with auxiliary switches, perform the following:

    a. Partially pull up on the impact pad and move it out of the way. Don't move the pad too far as there is very little slack in the electrical wires at this time.

    b. Follow the electrical wires from the impact pad back to their electrical connectors at the main wiring harness. If necessary, remove any tie wrap(s) securing the electrical wires to the frame.

    c. Pull the electrical wires away from the frame (**Figure 197**) and disconnect them.

    d. Pull the impact pad up and away from the steering head area. It is not necessary to completely remove the impact pad, just move it out of the way.

6. Remove the screw securing the electrical connector cover panel (**Figure 198**) and remove the cover panel.

7. Carefully disconnect the electrical connectors (**Figure 199**) from the instrument cluster.

8

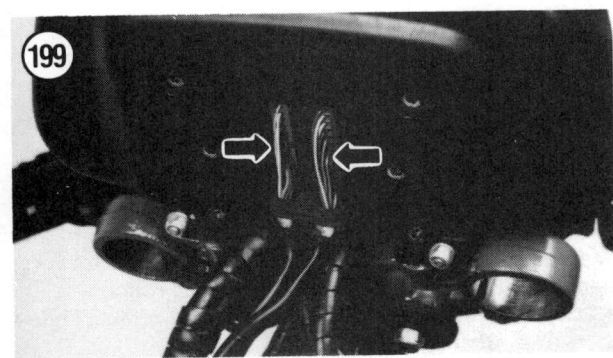

8. Remove the bolts and washers (**Figure 200**) securing the instrument cluster to the upper fork bridge.

9. Carefully pull the instrument cluster up and away from its mounting area.

10. Remove the instrument cluster assembly.

11. Install by reversing these removal steps, noting the following.

12. Tighten the bolts securely.

13. Make sure the electrical connectors are free of corrosion and are tight.

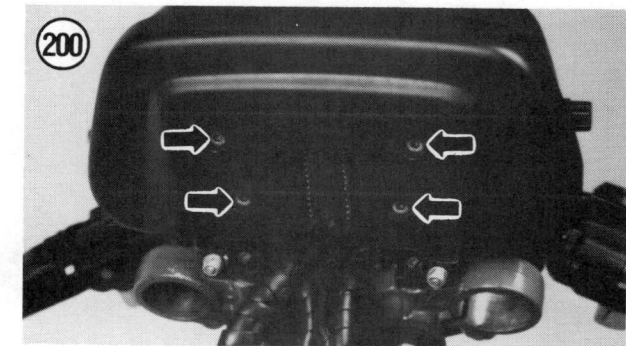

Removal/Installation
(K100RT and K100LT Models)

1. Remove the right-hand side cover.

2. Disconnect the battery negative lead as described under *Battery* in Chapter Three.

3. Remove the fuel tank as described under *Fuel Tank Removal/Installation* in Chapter Seven.

4. Remove the screws (**Figure 196**) securing the impact pad.

5A. On models with no auxiliary switches, remove the impact pad.

5B. On models equipped with auxiliary switches, perform the following:

  a. Partially pull up on the impact pad and move it out of the way. Don't move the pad too far as there is very little slack in the electrical wires at this time.

  b. Follow the electrical wires from the impact pad back to their electrical connectors at the main wiring harness. If necessary, remove any tie wrap(s) securing the electrical wires to the frame.

  c. Pull the electrical wires away from the frame (**Figure 197**) and disconnect them.

  d. Pull the impact pad up and away from the steering head area. It is not necessary to completely remove the impact pad, just move it out of the way.

6. Remove the knee pads, center cover and both storage boxes as described under *Front Fairing (K100RT and K100LT Models) Removal/Installation* in Chapter Thirteen.

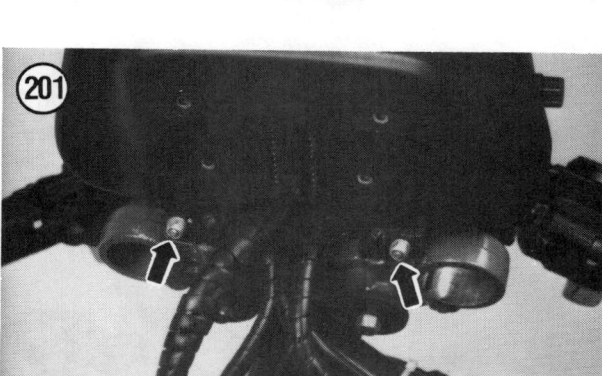

NOTE
The following steps are shown with the front fairing and front forks removed for clarity. It is not necessary to remove either of these assemblies for this procedure.

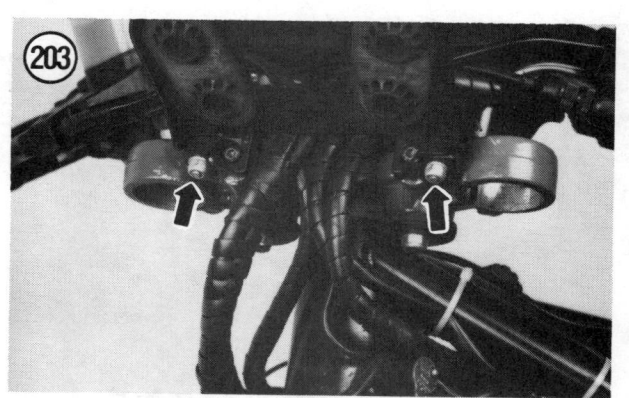

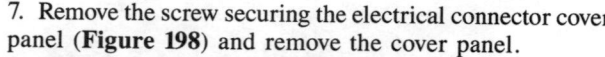

7. Remove the screw securing the electrical connector cover panel (**Figure 198**) and remove the cover panel.

8. Carefully disconnect the electrical connectors (**Figure 199**) from the instrument cluster.

9A. To remove the instrument cluster and mounting bracket, remove the nuts and washers (**Figure 200**) and remove the instrument cluster assembly.

9B. To remove only the instrument cluster, perform the following:

    a. Remove the bolts and washers (**Figure 201**) and remove the instrument cluster.

    b. Remove the lower section (**Figure 202**) from the mounting bracket.

    c. If necessary, remove the nuts and washers (**Figure 203**) securing the mounting bracket to the upper fork bridge and remove the mounting bracket.

10. Install by reversing these removal steps, noting the following.

11. Tighten the bolts and/or nuts securely. Don't overtighten the bolts and/or nuts as the plastic mounting bosses may be damaged.

12. Make sure the electrical connectors are free of corrosion and are tight.

**Disassembly/Assembly,
Component Replacement
and Lamp Replacement**

    Refer to **Figure 204** and **Figure 205** for this procedure.

1. Remove the instrument cluster as described in this chapter.

2. If the entire assembly was removed, remove the screws and washers (A, **Figure 206**) securing the lower section and remove the lower section (B, **Figure 206**).

3. Remove the screws securing the rear cover (**Figure 207**) and remove the rear cover.

8

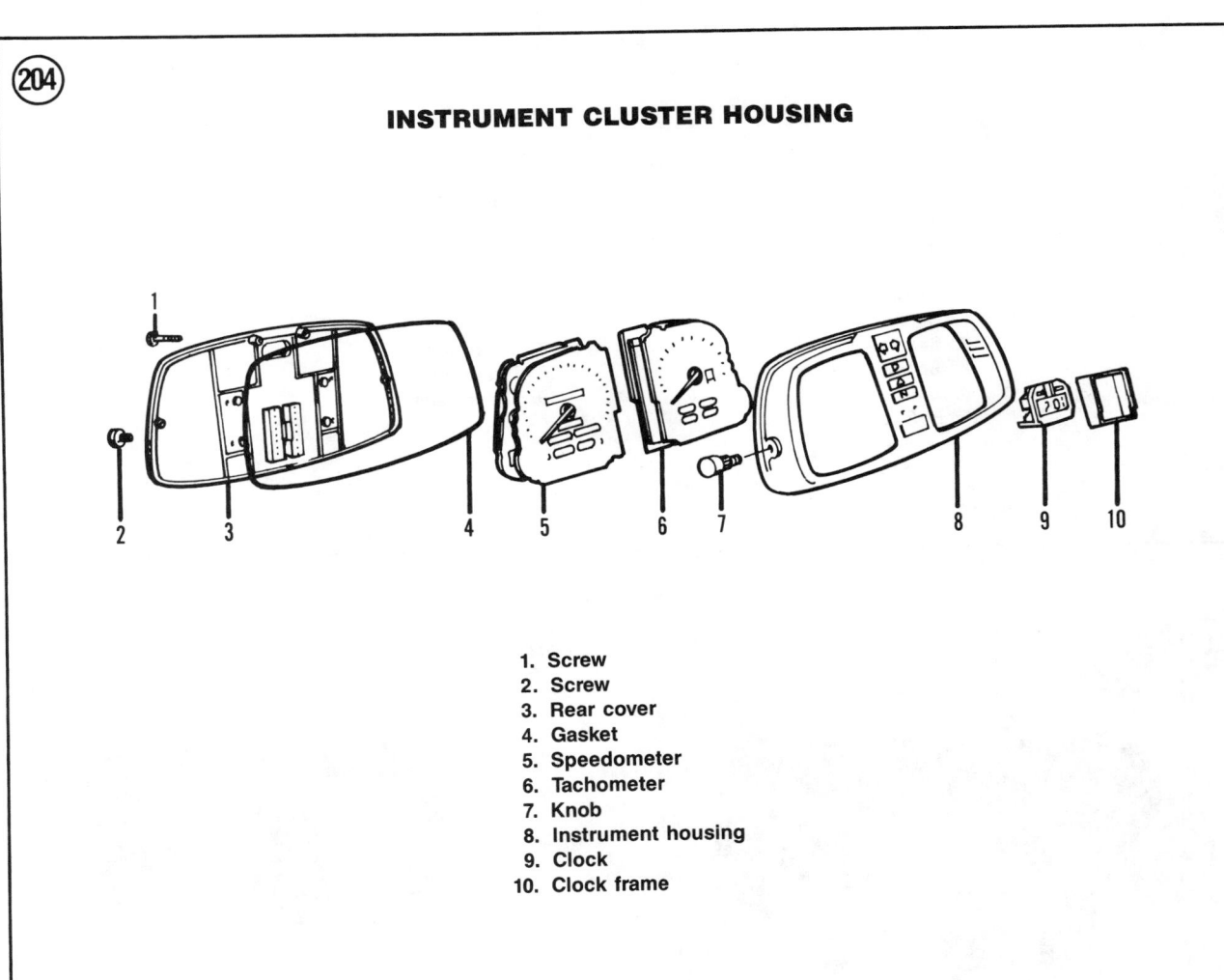

(204)

INSTRUMENT CLUSTER HOUSING

1. Screw
2. Screw
3. Rear cover
4. Gasket
5. Speedometer
6. Tachometer
7. Knob
8. Instrument housing
9. Clock
10. Clock frame

205

INSTRUMENT CLUSTER COMPONENTS

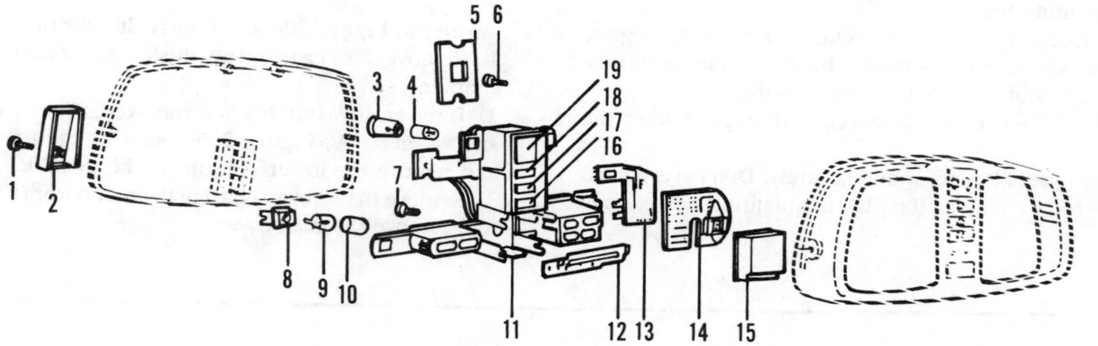

1. Screw
2. Electrical connector cover
3. Socket
4. Bulb
5. Gasket
6. Screw
7. Screw
8. Socket
9. Bulb
10. Bulb cover
11. Conductor plate
12. Conductor plate
13. Conductor plate
14. Conductor plate
15. Cover
16. Red lens
17. Green lens
18. Blue lens
19. Green lens

206

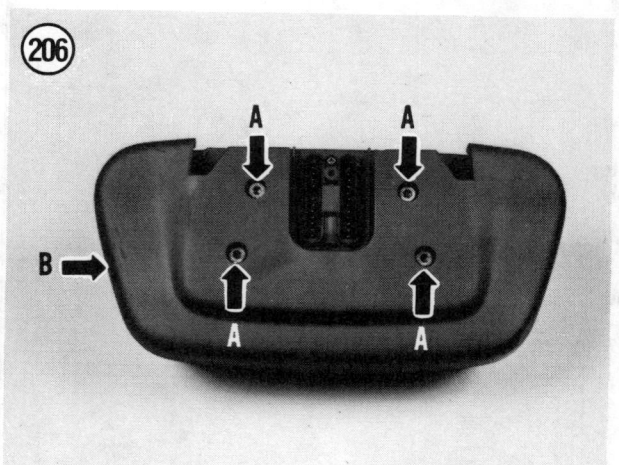

207

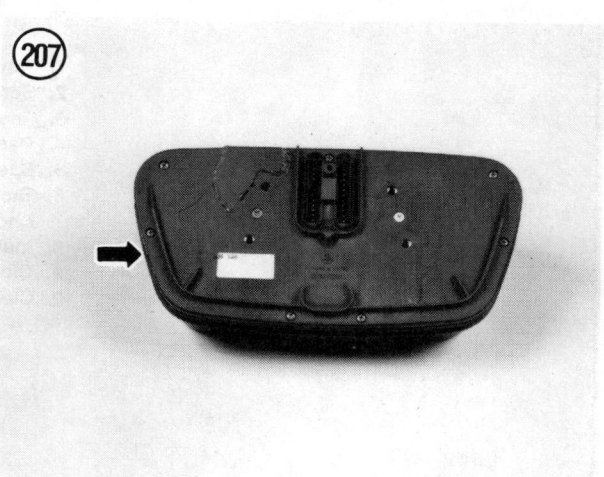

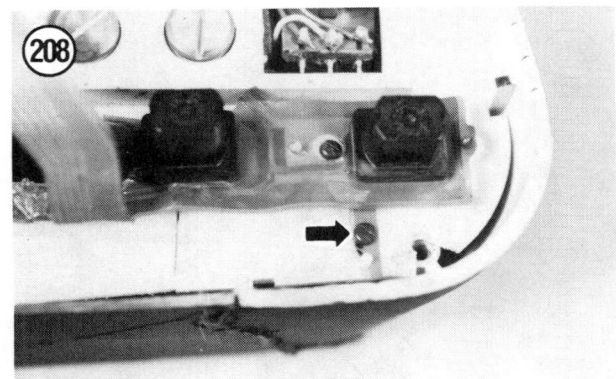

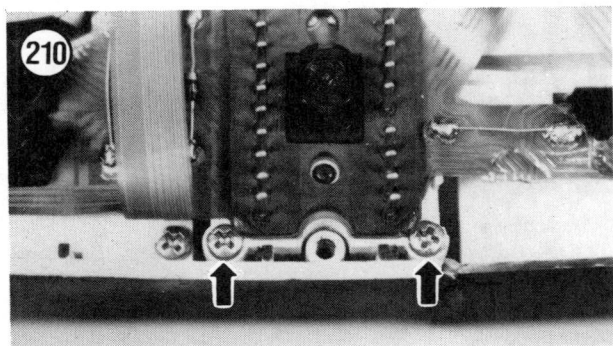

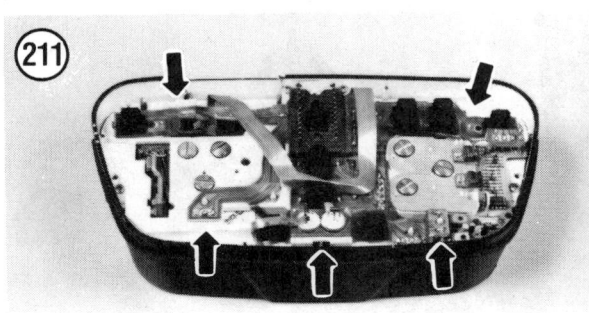

4. To remove and install the printed circuit board, perform the following:
   a. Remove the right-hand screw (**Figure 208**) and the left-hand screw (**Figure 209**) securing the printed circuit board.
   b. Remove the center screws (**Figure 210**) securing the printed circuit board.
   c. Using a flat-bladed screwdriver, carefully pry the printed circuit board loose from its various contact points (**Figure 211**).
   d. Carefully remove the printed circuit board and its related components from the housing.
   e. Carefully install the printed circuit board and its related components into the housing.
   f. Carefully align the printed circuit board contact pins with their receptacles (**Figure 212**) and push in completely. Make sure not to bend any of the contact pins during installation.
   g. Install the screw and tighten securely. Do not overtighten as the plastic mounting bosses may be damaged.

5. To remove and install the tachometer (A, **Figure 213**) and/or speedometer (B, **Figure 213**) assembly(ies), perform the following:

8

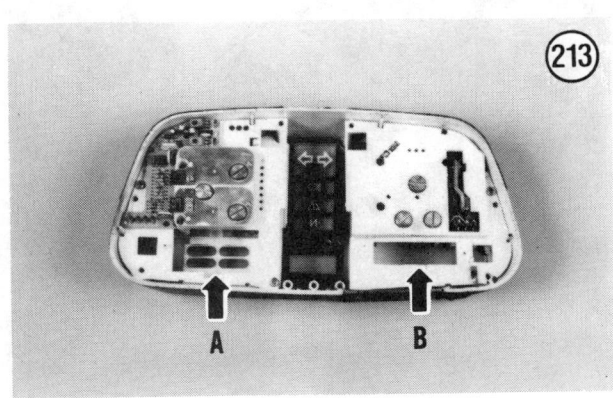

a. Remove the screws securing the assembly(ies) to the housing and remove the assembly(ies) (**Figure 214**).

b. To replace the dial face, carefully pull the needle off of the post, then remove the screws securing the face. Replace the face with a new one and install the screws and the needle.

6. To remove and install the digital clock, perform the following:

a. Carefully pry the clock frame (**Figure 215**) off of the mounting posts.

b. Carefully unhook the top mounting hooks (A, **Figure 216**), then the lower mounting hooks (B, **Figure 216**) securing the clock assembly (C, **Figure 216**).

c. Remove the clock assembly.

d. Carefully align the contact pins (**Figure 217**) with their receptacles in the clock and push the clock down completely. Be sure not to bend either of the contact pins during installation. Make sure the clock snaps securely into place in the mounting posts at all 4 corners.

e. Install the clock frame and make sure the frame snaps securely into place.

7. To remove and install the warning light lens covers and replace the bulbs, perform the following:

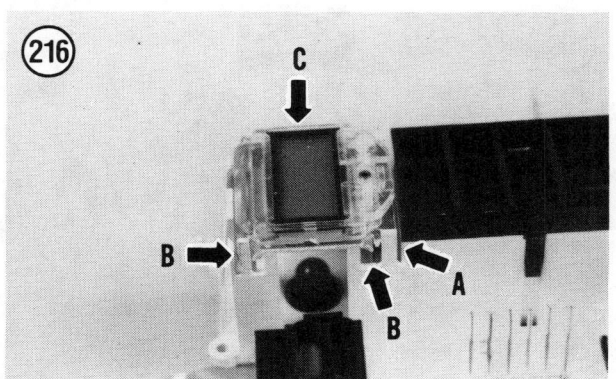

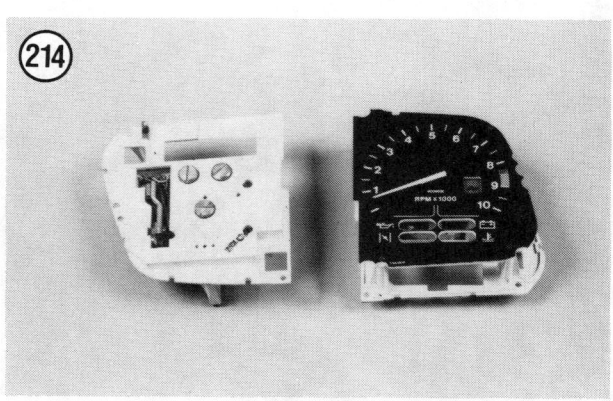

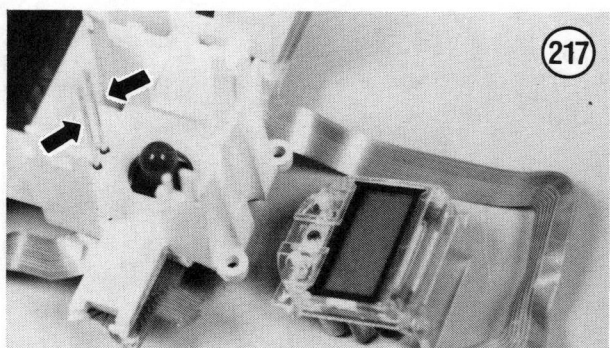

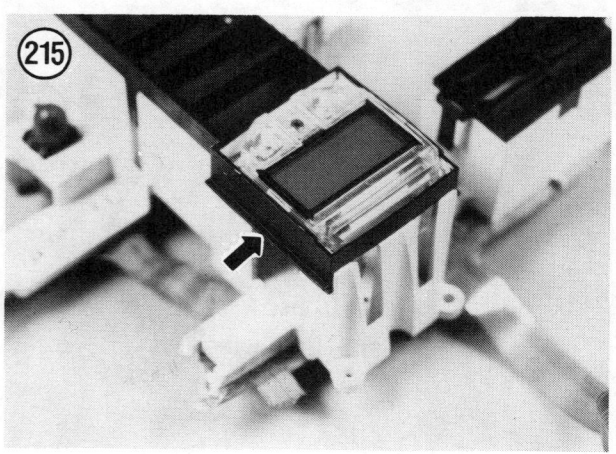

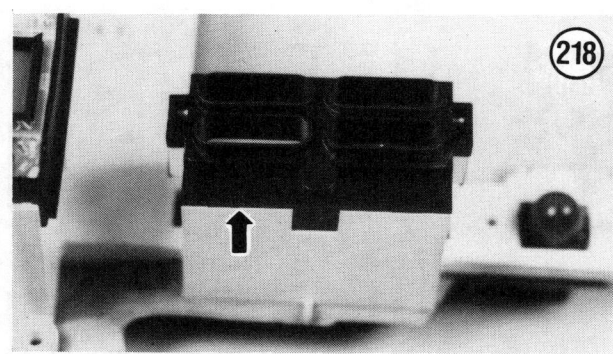

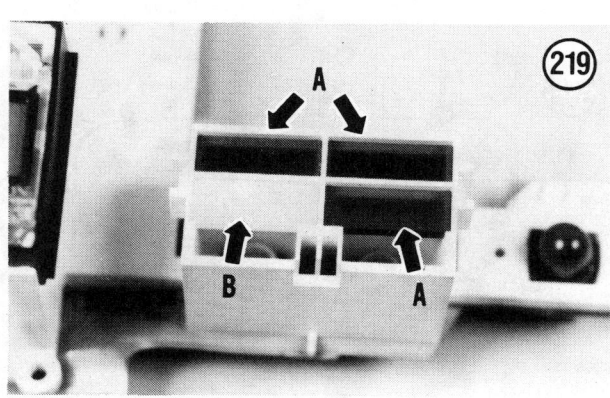

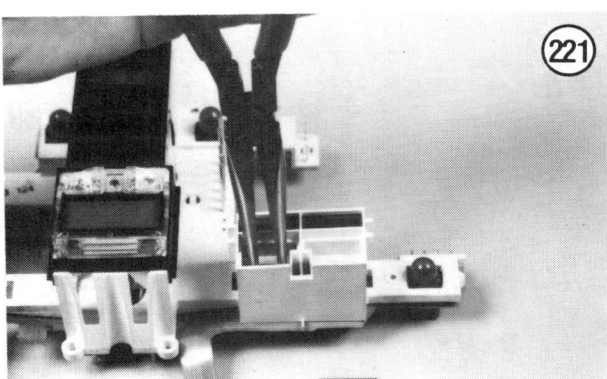

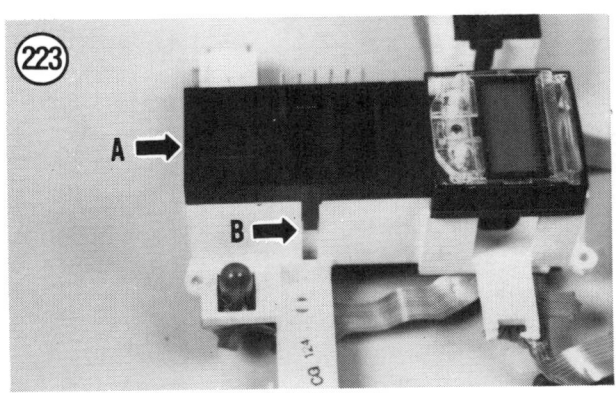

a. Unhook the lens cover frame (**Figure 218**) and remove it.
b. Remove the red colored lens (A, **Figure 219**) and yellow lens (B, **Figure 219**) from their receptacles.
c. To remove the bulb(s) (**Figure 220**), use a pair of needlenose pliers (**Figure 221**) and pull the bulb(s) out of their sockets.
d. Install a new bulb(s) with needlenose pliers and push it into place with a wooden dowel or pencil. Be sure to push the bulb in all the way to make good electrical contact.
e. Install the red colored lens (A, **Figure 219**) and yellow lens (B, **Figure 219**) in their correct locations.
f. Install the lens cover frame and make sure the hooks (**Figure 222**) snap into place.

8. To remove and install the high beam, taillight monitor and neutral indicator light lens covers and replace the bulbs, perform the following:

a. Unhook the lens cover frame (A, **Figure 223**) and remove it.
b. Remove the blue colored lens (A, **Figure 224**), green colored lens (B, **Figure 224**) and red lens (C, **Figure 224**) from their receptacles.
c. To remove the bulb(s) (**Figure 225**), use a pair of needlenose pliers (**Figure 226**) and pull the bulb(s) out of their sockets.

8

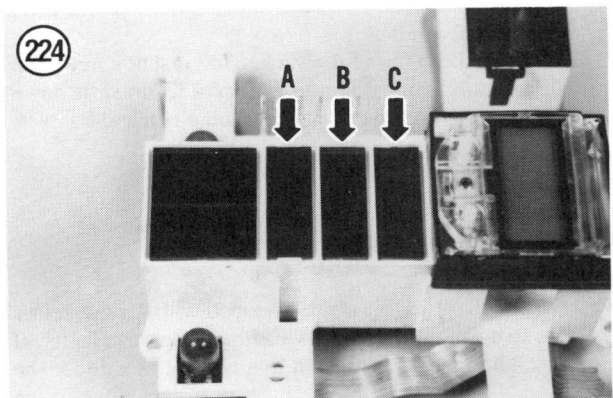

d. Install a new bulb(s) with needlenose pliers and push it into place with a wooden dowel or pencil. Be sure to push the bulb in all the way to make good electrical contact.

e. Install the blue colored lens (A, **Figure 224**), green colored lens (B, **Figure 224**) and red lens (C, **Figure 224**) into the correct locations.

f. Install the lens cover frame and make sure the hooks (B, **Figure 223**) snap into place.

9. To replace the turn signal indicator lights, perform the following:

a. Disconnect the electrical connector (**Figure 227**) from the socket assembly.

b. Carefully withdraw the socket assembly (**Figure 228**).

c. Pull the bulb out of the socket (**Figure 229**) and install a new one.

d. Push the socket assembly back into the receptacle.

e. Reconnect the electrical connector. Push it down all the way in order to make good electrical contact.

10. To replace other bulbs, perform the following:

a. Using a flat-bladed screwdriver (**Figure 230**), carefully pry the socket assembly up and out of the printed circuit board.

b. Pull the bulb out of the socket (**Figure 231**) and install a new one.

c. Push the socket assembly back into the printed circuit board. Push it down all the way in order to make good electrical contact.

d. Pull the bulb out of the socket and install a new one. Refer to **Figure 232** and **Figure 233**. Push it down all the way in order to make good electrical contact.

RELAYS

The BMW K-series bikes are equipped with various relays that are used in conjunction with the different electrical systems. The relays are located in a control box under the seat and fuel tank. BMW does not provide service information for the relays. If you are having troubles within a specific system that has a relay in the circuit, check the circuit thoroughly prior to replacing the relay. Don't purchase a new relay prematurely without checking out the circuit, as this may lead to the unnecessary purchase of an expensive electrical part that cannot be returned for a refund. Most dealers and parts houses will not accept any returns on electrical parts.

Circuit Inspection

NOTE
If the bike was involved in a fire, the chemical compounds used in some fire extinguishers will severely corrode electrical connectors.

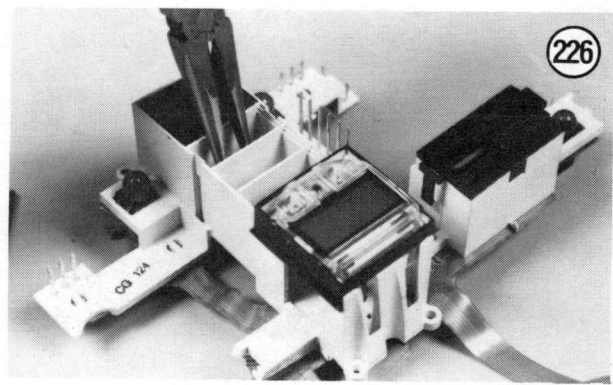

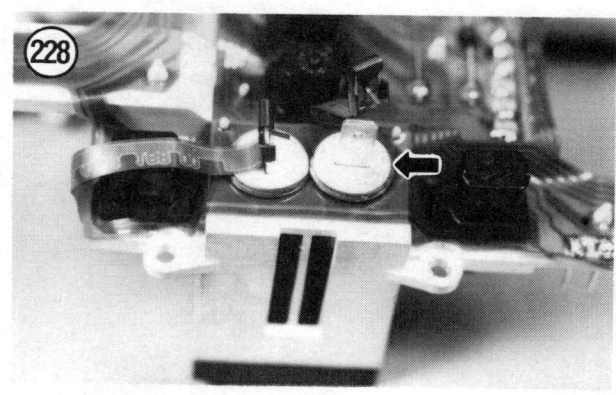

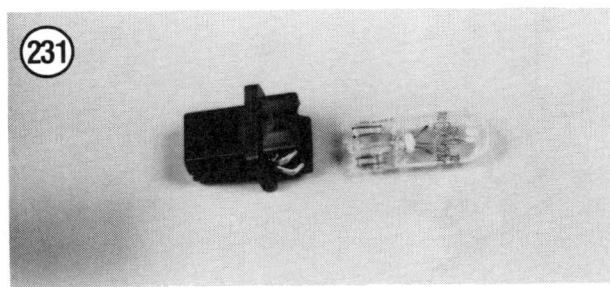

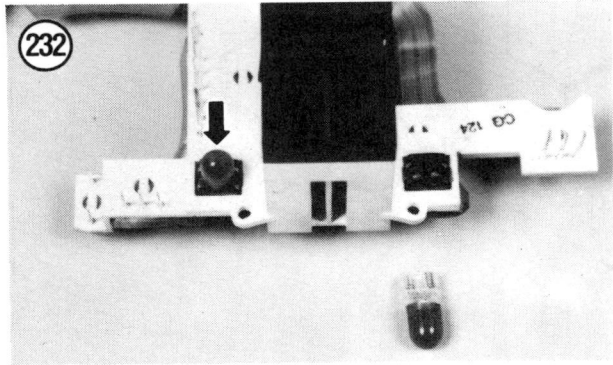

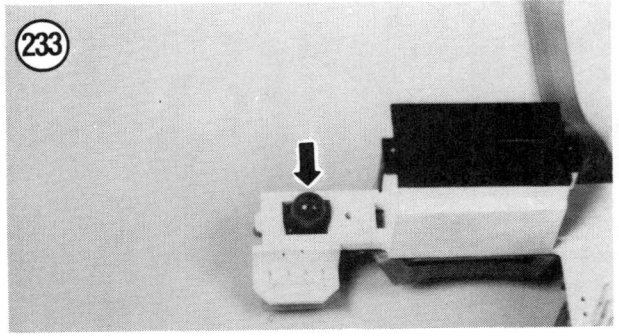

1. Inspect all electrical connections for corrosion. Clean off all corrosion and do a final cleaning with an aerosol electrical contact cleaner.
2. Make sure all electrical connections are tight. If possible, use a pair of pliers to tighten the male portion of the connector.
3. Where possible, check out the continuity of the electrical wire from one end to the other. Connect one test lead of an ohmmeter to one end of the wire in the electrical connector and attached the other end to the wire in the electrical connector. There should be continuity (indicated low or no resistance). If there is no continuity (infinite resistance) there is an open in the wire or electrical connector and it must be replaced. Disconnect the ohmmeter.
4. If a light bulb is used in the circuit, make sure the bulb has not blown. If so replace the bulb.
5. If a fuse is used in the circuit, make sure the fuse has not blown. If it has, replace the fuse as described in this chapter.
6. Make sure a switch in the circuit is functioning properly. Refer to *Switches* in this chapter.
7. If all of these simple tests prove to be okay, then replace the relay.

Relay Replacement

Refer to **Figure 234** for relay location in the control box.
1. Remove the fuel tank as described under *Fuel Tank Removal/Installation* in Chapter Seven.
2. Remove the bolts securing the fuel tank mounting bracket (**Figure 235**) and remove the bracket.
3. Remove the cover (**Figure 236**) from the control box.
4. Prior to removing and disconnecting any electrical wires from a relay, mark the wire and to which relay terminal it is attached. This will ensure a correct wire connection when the new relay is installed.
5. Remove the relay (**Figure 237**) from the control box.
6. Install by reversing these removal steps, noting the following.
7. Make sure the electrical connectors are free of corrosion and are tight.

HORN

Removal/Installation

The horn(s) is located within the front fairing assembly.

Removal/Installation
(K75C, K75T and K100 Models)

1. Remove the frame left-hand side cover.
2. Disconnect the battery negative lead as described under *Battery* in Chapter Three.
3. Remove the screws and lockwashers on each side of the backside of the fairing mounting panel.

8

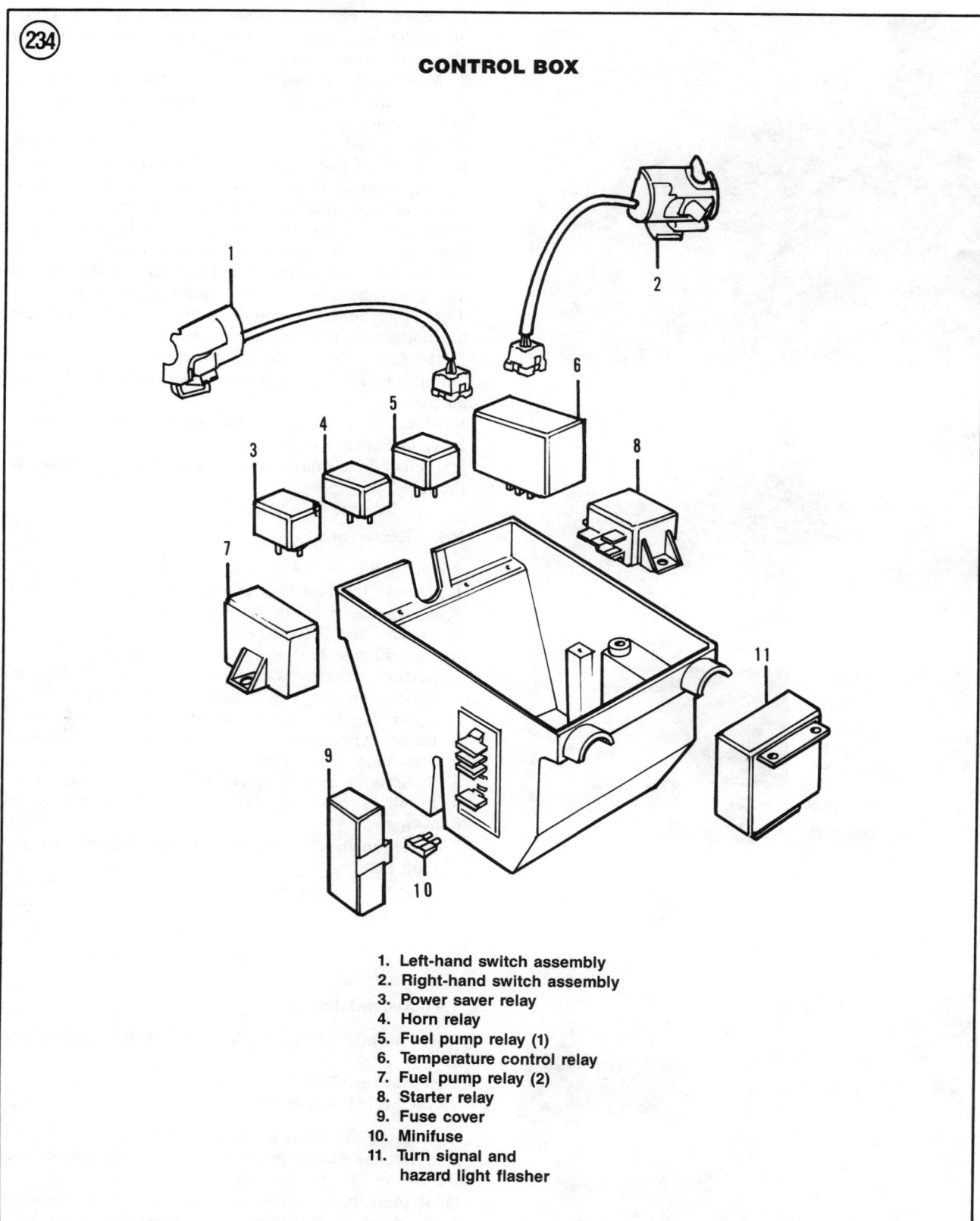

CONTROL BOX

1. Left-hand switch assembly
2. Right-hand switch assembly
3. Power saver relay
4. Horn relay
5. Fuel pump relay (1)
6. Temperature control relay
7. Fuel pump relay (2)
8. Starter relay
9. Fuse cover
10. Minifuse
11. Turn signal and
    hazard light flasher

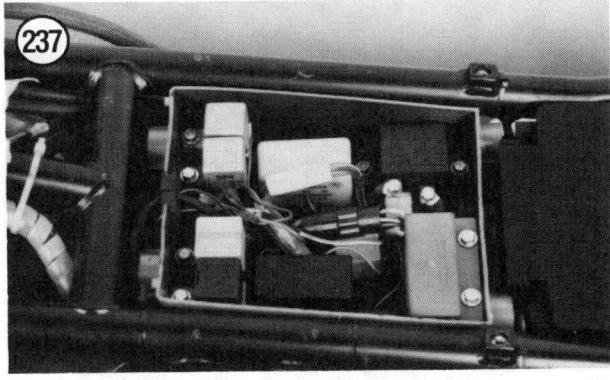

4. Carefully pull the headlight fairing and trim panel off of the mounting panel and headlight assembly.

5. Disconnect the electrical connectors for the turn signals and remove headlight fairing and trim panel.

6. Loosen the headlight mounting bolt on each side.

7. Carefully pull the headlight assembly forward and out of the mounting panel.

8. Disconnect the electrical connector (A, **Figure 238**) from the base of the headlight and remove the headlight.

9. Disconnect the electrical connector to each horn.

10. Remove the bolts (B, **Figure 238**) securing each horn and remove the horns.

11. Install by reversing these removal steps, noting the following.

12. Install the headlight assembly and align the arrow with the arrow on the mounting tab on each side. This is to maintain correct horizontal headlight aim.

13. Tighten the screws and bolts securely. Don't overtighten the screws or bolts as the plastic mounting bosses may be damaged.

14. Make sure the electrical connectors are free of corrosion and are tight.

Removal/Installation (K75S Models)

1. Remove the right-hand side panel of the front fairing as described under *Front Fairing (K75S) Removal/Installation* in Chapter Thirteen.

2. Disconnect the electrical connector.

3. Remove the nut and washer securing the horn to the mounting bracket.

4. Remove the horn.

5. Repeat Steps 2-4 for the other horn if so equipped and if necessary.

6. Install by reversing these removal steps, noting the following.

7. Tighten the nut securely.

8. Make sure the electrical connector is tight and free of corrosion.

Removal/Installation (K100 Models)

1. Remove the right-hand side cover.

2. Disconnect the battery negative lead as described under *Battery* in Chapter Three.

3. Remove the fuel tank as described under *Fuel Tank Removal/Installation* in Chapter Seven.

4. Remove the screws securing the impact pad.

5A. On models with no auxiliary switches, remove the impact pad.

5B. On models equipped with auxiliary switches, perform the following:

    a. Partially pull up on the impact pad and move it out of the way. Don't move the pad too far as there is very little slack in the electrical wires at this time.

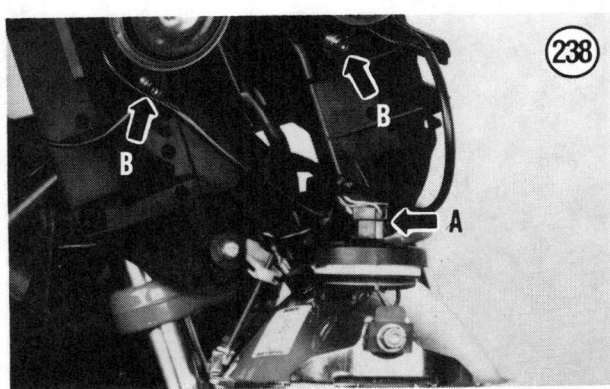

8

b. Follow the electrical wires from the impact pad back to their electrical connectors at the main wiring harness. If necessary, remove any tie wrap(s) securing the electrical wires to the frame.

c. Pull the electrical wires away from the frame and disconnect them.

d. Pull the impact pad up and away from the steering head area. It is not necessary to completely remove the impact pad, just move it out of the way.

6. Remove the knee pads, center cover and both storage boxes as described under *Front Fairing Removal/Installation* in Chapter Thirteen.

7. Disconnect the electrical connector.

8. Remove the nut and washer securing the horn to the mounting bracket.

9. Remove the horn.

10. Repeat Steps 7-9 for the other horn if so equipped and if necessary.

11. Install by reversing these removal steps, noting the following.

12. Tighten the nut securely.

13. Make sure the electrical connector is tight and free of corrosion.

Horn Testing

Remove the horn as described in this chapter. Connect a 12-volt battery to the horn. If the horn is good, it will sound. If not, replace it.

FUSES

The number of fuses vary among the various models. They are located in the fuse panel located under the frame left-hand side cover.

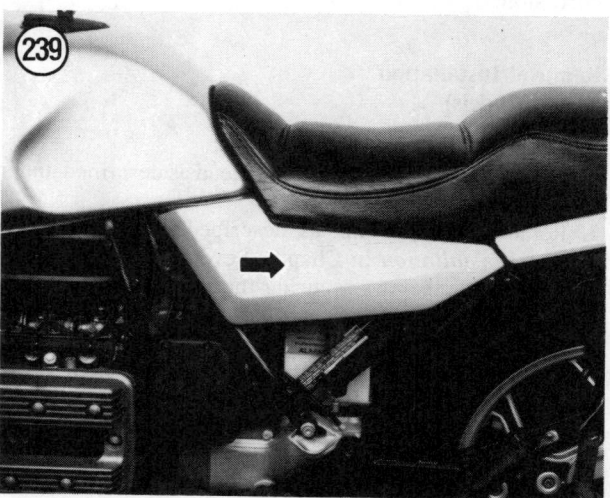

CAUTION
When replacing a fuse, make sure the ignition switch is in the OFF position. This will lessen the chance of a short circuit.

Fuse Replacement

The following procedure should be performed if a fuse in the fuse holder blows.

1. Remove the frame left-hand side cover (**Figure 239**).

2. Gently press in on each side of the clear plastic cover (**Figure 240**) and remove the cover.

NOTE
The fuses are not the typical glass tube with metal ends. Carry extra fuses in your tool box.

3. Remove the old fuse (**Figure 241**) and install a new one.

Whenever a fuse blows, find out the reason for the failure before replacing the fuse. Usually the trouble is a short circuit in the wiring. This may be caused by worn-through insulation or a disconnected wire shorted to ground.

CAUTION
Never substitute aluminum foil or wire for a fuse. Never use a higher amperage fuse than specified. An overload could cause a fire and complete loss of the motorcycle.

CHASSIS WIRING HARNESS

Figure 242 shows the chassis wiring harness and the electrical connections for the various electrical systems and components. Refer to this and the wiring diagrams at the end of this book when working on the wiring system.

WIRING DIAGRAMS

Wiring diagrams are located at the end of this book.

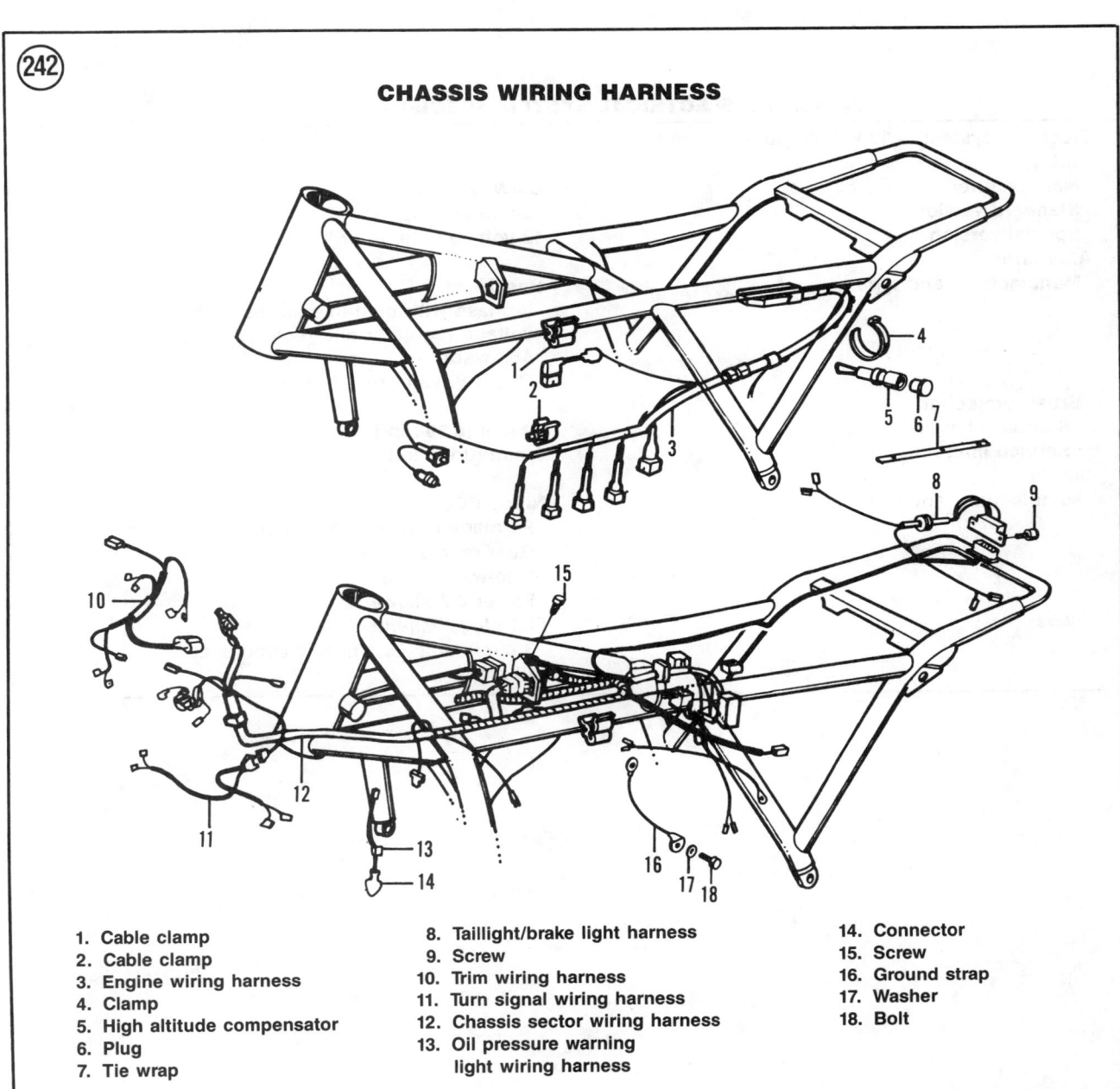

(242)

CHASSIS WIRING HARNESS

1. Cable clamp	8. Taillight/brake light harness	14. Connector
2. Cable clamp	9. Screw	15. Screw
3. Engine wiring harness	10. Trim wiring harness	16. Ground strap
4. Clamp	11. Turn signal wiring harness	17. Washer
5. High altitude compensator	12. Chassis sector wiring harness	18. Bolt
6. Plug	13. Oil pressure warning	
7. Tie wrap	light wiring harness	

8

Table 1 ELECTRICAL SYSTEM TORQUE SPECIFICATIONS

Item	N·m	ft.-lb.
Alternator mounting bolts	19-25	14-18
Footpeg mounting bolts	13-17	10-12
Oil pressure switch	35-45	26-33

Table 2 ELECTRICAL SYSTEM SPECIFICATIONS

Electrical system is 12-volt negative ground.
Battery
  Manufacturer   BMW (Mareg)
  Standard version   12-volt/25 amp. hour
  Special version   12-volt/30 amp. hour
Alternator
  Manufacturer and type   Bosch
                                              3-phase with built-in solid state
                                              voltage regulator and rectifier
                                              460 watts
                                              Direct drive (1 to 1.5 ratio)
  Brush projection
    Standard length   10 mm (0.394 in.)
    Service limit   5 mm (0.197 in.)
Starter
  Manufacturer and type   Nippon Denso
                                              Permanent magnet field coil
                                            Gear ratio 27 to 1
                                            One-way clutch
                                            Power 0.7 kilowatts
Fuses   Flat plug "Minifuse"
                                            3 circuits at 7.5 amps, 4 circuits at
                                            15 amps

Table 3 STARTER TROUBLESHOOTING

Symptom	Probable cause	Remedy

Starter does not work	Low battery
	Worn brushes
	Defective relay
	Defective switch
	Defective wiring
	  connection
	Internal short circuit
		Recharge battery
		Replace brushes
		Repair or replace
		Repair or replace
		Repair wire or clean
		  connection
		Repair or replace defective
		  component

Starter action
  is weak
	Low battery
	Pitted relay contacts
	Worn brushes
	Defective connection
	Short circuit in
	  commutator
		Recharge battery
		Clean or replace
		Replace brushes
		Clean and tighten
		Replace armature

Starter runs continuously	Stuck relay	Replace relay

Starter turns;
  does not
  turn engine
	Defective starter
	  clutch
		Replace starter
		  clutch

8

Table 4 BULB REPLACEMENT

Item	Voltage/wattage	Number designation
Headlight	12 volt 60/55 watt	H4-halogen (Phillips)
Parking lamp	12 volt 4 watt	T 8/4
Taillight	12 volt 10 watt	R 19/10
Brakelight	12 volt 21 watt	R 25/1
Turn signals	12 volt 21 watt	P25-1
Instrument cluster		
Turn signal indicator	12 volt 4 watt	T8/4
All others	12 volt 3 watt	W 10/3

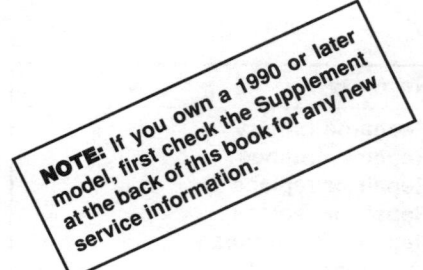
NOTE: If you own a 1990 or later model, first check the Supplement at the back of this book for any new service information.

CHAPTER NINE

COOLING SYSTEM

The pressurized cooling system consists of a radiator, a combination water and oil pump, thermostat, electric cooling fan and a coolant recovery tank. **Figure 1** shows the major components of the cooling system.

The system uses a coolant filler cap with a designed relief pressure of 110kPa (16 psi). The cap is designed to operate with an 85° C (185° F) thermostat. It is important to keep the coolant level to the UPPER mark (**Figure 2**) on the coolant recovery tank. Always add coolant to the recovery tank, not to the coolant filler cap adjacent to the radiator. The radiator is not equipped with a fill cap.

> *CAUTION*
> *Drain and flush the cooling system at least every 2 years. Refer to **Coolant Change** in Chapter Three. Refill with a mixture of ethylene glycol antifreeze (formulated for aluminum engines) and purified water. Do not reuse the old coolant as it deteriorates with use. **Do not** operate the cooling system with only purified water (even in climates where antifreeze protection is not required). This is important because the cylinder block and head are aluminum; they will not rust but will oxidize internally and have to be replaced. Refer to **Coolant Change** in Chapter Three.*

This chapter describes repair and replacement of the cooling system components. The water pump is combined with the oil pump as a single unit and is covered in Chapter Four.

Table 1 at the end of this chapter lists all of the cooling system specifications. For routine maintenance of the system, refer to Chapter Three.

The cooling system must be cool before removing any component of the system.

> *WARNING*
> *Do not remove the coolant filler cap (**Figure 3**) when the engine is hot. The coolant is very hot and is under pressure. Severe scalding could result if the coolant comes in contact with your skin.*

HOSES AND HOSE CLAMPS

The small diameter coolant hoses are very stiff and are sometimes difficult to install onto the fittings of the various cooling system parts. Before installing the hoses, soak the ends in hot water to make them pliable and they will slide on much easier. Do not apply any type of lubricant to the inner surfaces of the hoses as the hose may slip off even with the hose clamp in place.

Always use screw adjusting type hose clamps. This type of clamp is superior in its holding ability and is easily released with a screwdriver.

1. Be sure the cooling system is cool before replacing the hoses.

COOLING SYSTEM LAYOUT

①

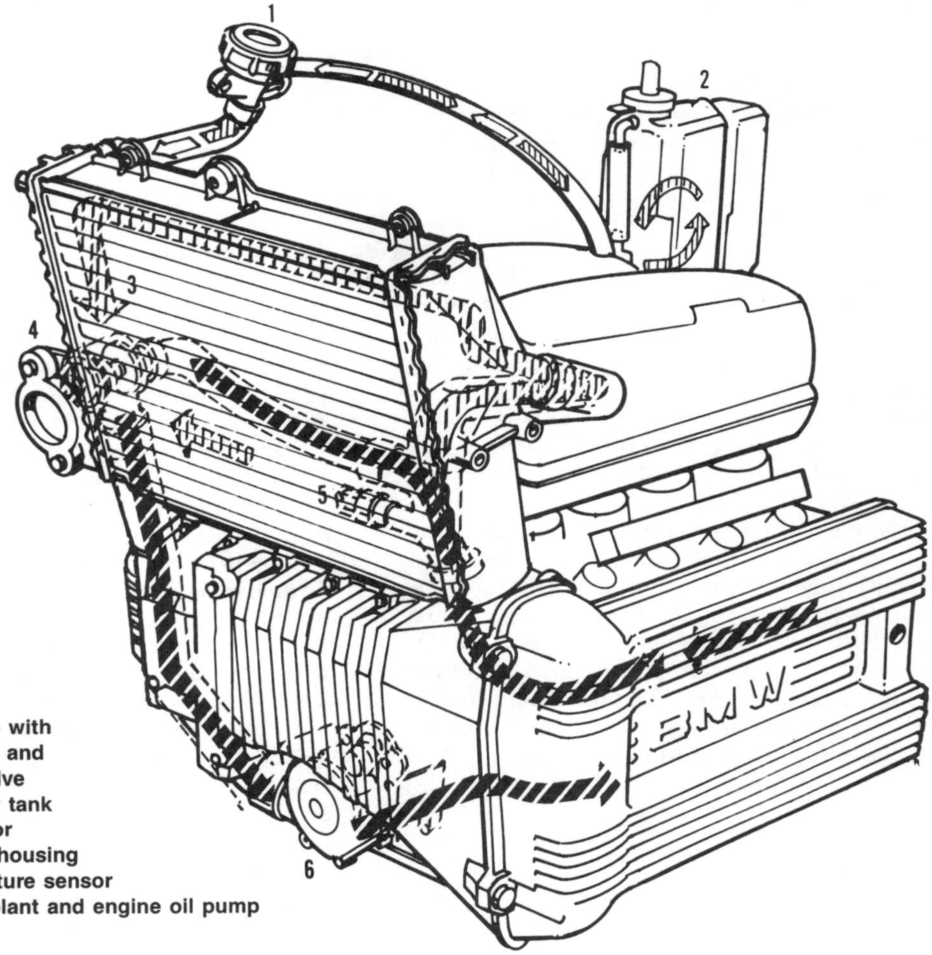

1. Coolant filler cap with
   integral pressure and
   vacuum relief valve
2. Coolant recovery tank
3. Crossflow radiator
4. Thermostat and housing
5. Coolant temperature sensor
6. Combination coolant and engine oil pump

9

2. Be sure to replace the hoses with BMW replacement hoses since they are formed to a specific shape and are of the correct length and inner diameter to fit correctly.
3. Loosen the hose clamps on the hose that is to be replaced. Slide the clamps back off of the fittings.

CAUTION
In trying to remove a stubborn hose from the fittings, especially the radiator inlet and outlet fittings, do not twist too hard or the fittings may be damaged, leading to expensive repair.

4. Twist the hose to release it from the fitting. If the hose has been on for some time, it will probably be difficult to break loose. If so, carefully cut the hose parallel to the fitting with a knife. Carefully pry the hose from the fitting with a broad-tipped screwdriver.
5. Examine the fittings for cracks or other damage. Repair or replace as necessary. If the fitting is okay, use sandpaper and clean off any hose residue that may have transferred to the fitting. Wipe clean with a cloth.
6. Inspect the hose clamps; replace if necessary. The hose clamps are as important as the hoses. If they do not hold the hose in place tightly there will be a coolant leak. For best results, always use screw adjusting type hose clamps.
7. With the hose installed correctly on the each fitting, position each hose clamp back away from the end of the hose by about 1/2 inch. Make sure the hose clamps are still positioned over the fitting and tighten the clamps securely, but not so much that the hose will be damaged.

COOLING SYSTEM CHECK

Two checks should be made before disassembly if a cooling system fault is suspected.
1. Run the engine until it reaches operating temperature. While the engine is running, a pressure surge should be felt when the upper hose (left-hand side) is squeezed.
2. If a substantial coolant loss is noted, the head gasket may be blown. In extreme cases sufficient coolant will leak into a cylinder(s) when the bike is left standing for several hours so the engine cannot be turned over with the starter. White smoke (steam) might also be observed at the muffler when the engine is running. Coolant may also find its way into the oil. Check the dipstick; if the oil is foamy or milky there is coolant in the oil system. If so, repair the cooling system immediately.

CAUTION
After the cooling system is repaired, drain and thoroughly flush the engine oil system to eliminate all coolant residue. Refill with fresh engine oil; refer to Chapter Three.

PRESSURE CHECK

If the cooling system requires repeated refilling, there is probably a leak somewhere in the system. Perform *Cooling System Inspection* in Chapter Three.

RADIATOR

Removal/Installation

Refer to **Figure 4** and **Figure 5** for this procedure.
1. Remove the fuel tank as described under *Fuel Tank Removal/Installation* in Chapter Seven.
2. On models so equipped, remove the radiator trim panel as described under *Radiator Trim Panel Removal/Installation* in Chapter Thirteen.
3. On models so equipped, remove the front fairing side panels as described under *Front Fairing Removal/Installation* in Chapter Thirteen.
4. Drain the cooling system as described under *Coolant Change* in Chapter Three.
5. Remove the frame left-hand side cover.
6. Disconnect the battery negative lead as described under *Battery* in Chapter Three.
7. Remove bolts and washers (A, **Figure 6**) securing the air intake pipe to the radiator.
8. Pull the lower section of the air intake pipe (B, **Figure 6**) out of the air filter air box and remove the air intake pipe.
9. Loosen the screw (A, **Figure 7**) on the upper hose clamp of the lower hose. Move the clamp back onto the lower hose and off of the neck of the thermostat housing.
10. Loosen the screw (B, **Figure 7**) on the bypass hose clamp at the front end of the bypass hose. Move the clamp back onto the hose and off of the neck of the thermostat housing fitting.
11. Loosen the screw (**Figure 8**) on the filler neck hose clamp at the front end of the filler neck hose. Move the clamp back onto the hose and off of the neck of the radiator right-hand outlet fitting.
12. Loosen the screw (**Figure 9**) on the upper hose clamp at the front end of the bypass hose. Move the clamp back onto the hose and off of the neck of the radiator left-hand inlet fitting.
13. Disconnect the cooling fan electrical connector.
14. Remove the nut and washer (**Figure 10**) securing the radiator at the top.
15. Pull the radiator slightly forward and disengage all radiator hoses from the radiator and thermostat housing.
16. Remove the radiator from the frame.
17. Inspect the radiator as described in this chapter.
18. Install by reversing these removal steps, noting the following.
19. Replace all radiator hoses if they are starting to deteriorate or are damaged in any way as described in this chapter.
20. Make sure the cooling fan electrical connection is free of corrosion and is tight.

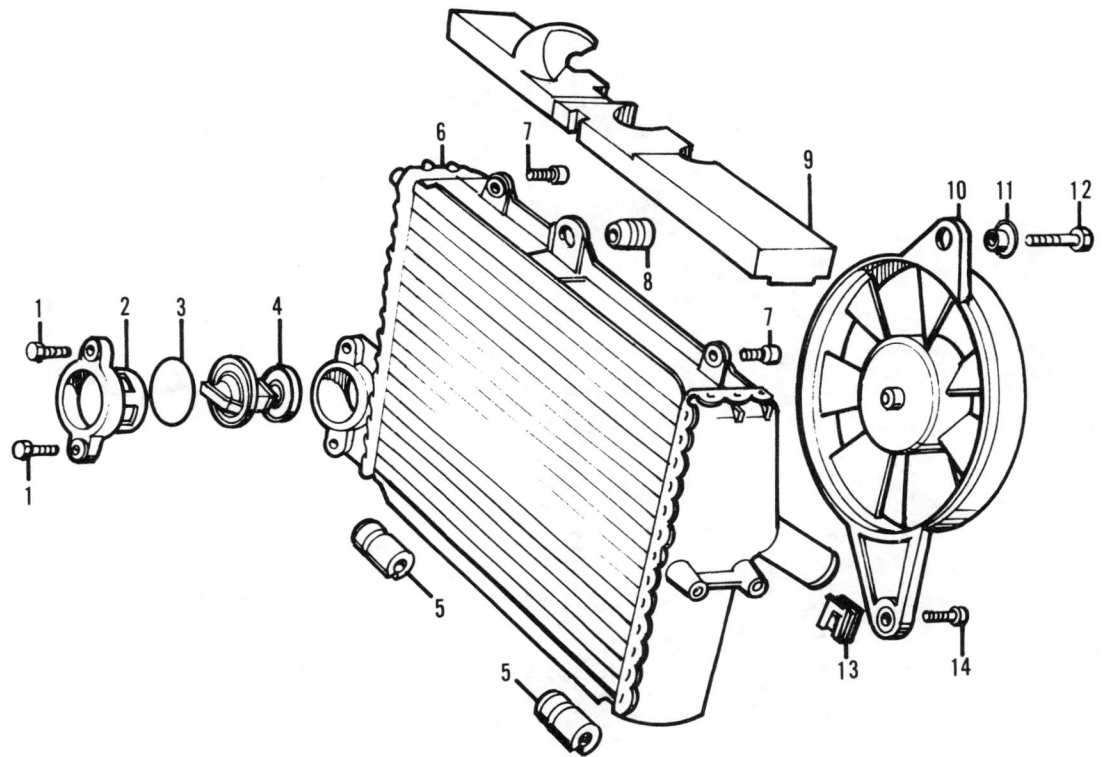

④

RADIATOR AND FAN ASSEMBLY

1. Bolt
2. Thermostat cover
3. O-ring seal
4. Thermostat
5. Rubber cushion
6. Crossflow radiator
7. Bolt
8. Rubber mount
9. Rubber dam
10. Cooling fan
11. Collar
12. Bolt
13. Special nut
14. Bolt

9

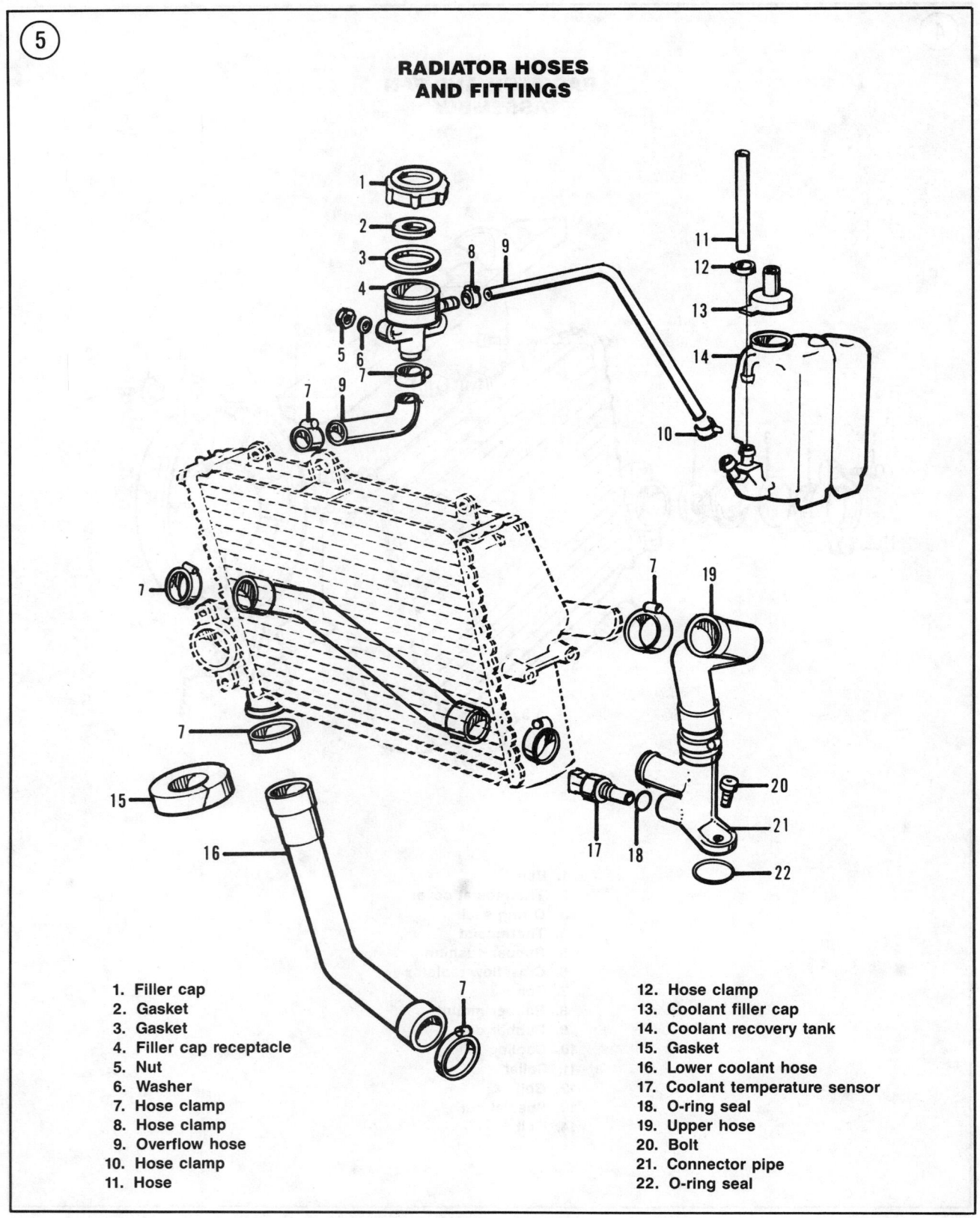

⑤

**RADIATOR HOSES
AND FITTINGS**

1. Filler cap
2. Gasket
3. Gasket
4. Filler cap receptacle
5. Nut
6. Washer
7. Hose clamp
8. Hose clamp
9. Overflow hose
10. Hose clamp
11. Hose

12. Hose clamp
13. Coolant filler cap
14. Coolant recovery tank
15. Gasket
16. Lower coolant hose
17. Coolant temperature sensor
18. O-ring seal
19. Upper hose
20. Bolt
21. Connector pipe
22. O-ring seal

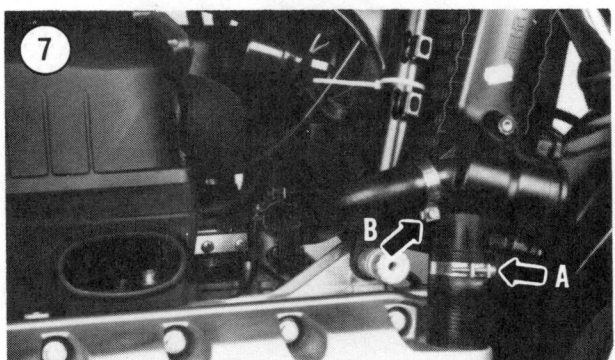

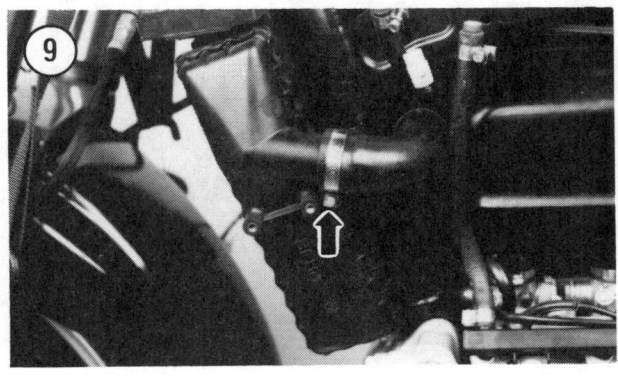

21. Refill the cooling system with the recommended type and quantity of coolant as described under *Coolant Change* in Chapter Three.

Radiator Inspection

1. Remove the screws (**Figure 11**) securing the radiator fan assembly to the radiator at the base of the radiator. Pivot the fan assembly up to allow access to entire back surface of the radiator core.
2. If compressed air is available, use short spurts of air directed to the backside of the radiator core and blow out dirt and bugs.
3. Flush off the exterior of the radiator (A, **Figure 12**) with a garden hose on low pressure. Spray both the front and

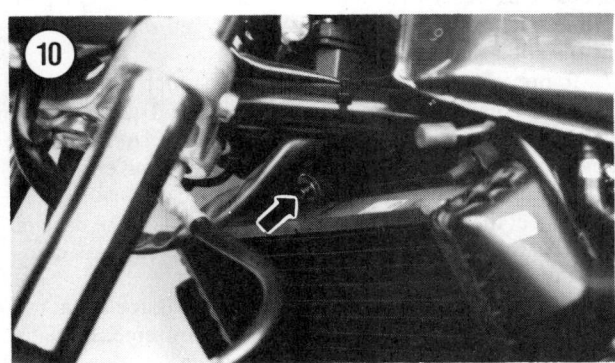

9

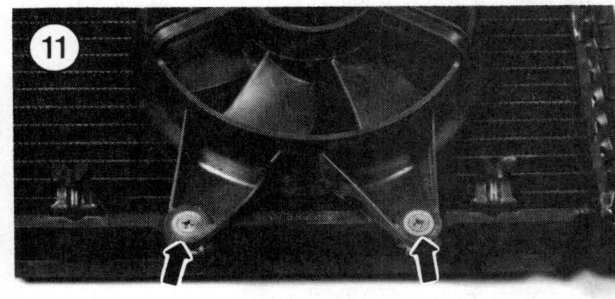

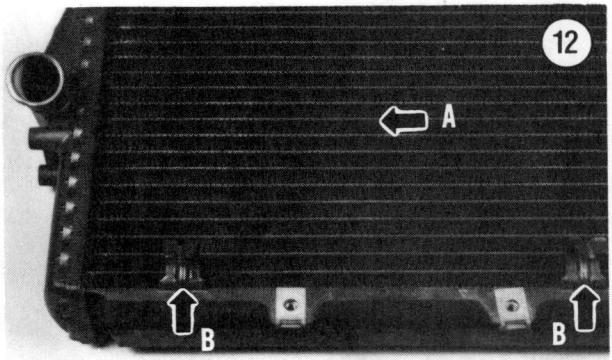

the back to remove all road dirt and bugs. Carefully use a whisk broom or stiff paint brush to remove any stubborn dirt from the cooling fins.

CAUTION
Do not press too hard or the cooling fins and tubes may be damaged, causing a leak.

4. Carefully straighten out any bent cooling fins with a broad tipped screwdriver or putty knife.
5. Check for cracks or leakage (usually a moss-green colored residue) at the inlet hose fitting (A, **Figure 13**) and outlet hose fitting (A, **Figure 14**) and both side tank seams. Refer to B, **Figure 13** and B, **Figure 14**.
6. If the condition of the radiator is doubtful, have it checked as described under *Pressure Check* in Chapter Three. The radiator can be pressure checked while removed or installed on the bike.
7. To prevent oxidation of the radiator, touch up any area where the black paint is worn off. Use a good quality spray paint and apply several *light* coats of paint. Do not apply heavy coats as this will cut down on the cooling efficiency of the radiator.
8. Inspect the metal hangers (B, **Figure 12**) on the base of the radiator where it fits onto the engine. If either is damaged or worn, replace the radiator.
9. Inspect the center rubber cushion (A, **Figure 15**) at the top of the radiator where it attaches to the frame. Replace if it is damaged or starting to deteriorate.
10. Inspect the rubber stoppers (B, **Figure 15**) at the top of the radiator where it touches the frame. Replace if they are damaged or starting to deteriorate.

COOLING FAN

Removal/Installation

Replacement parts for the fan assembly are not available. If the fan motor is defective the entire fan assembly must be replaced.
Refer to **Figure 4** for this procedure.
1. Remove the radiator as described in this chapter.
2. Remove the bolts (**Figure 11**) securing the fan shroud. Carefully detach the fan assembly from the radiator at the top (**Figure 16**) and remove the assembly from the radiator. Don't lose the collar on the upper mounting tab.
3. Test the cooling fan as described under *Cooling Fan Inspection* in Chapter Eight.
4. Install by reversing these removal steps, noting the following.
5. Be sure to install the collar (**Figure 16**) on the upper mount and bolt.
6. Install the fan motor and shroud assembly and tighten the bolts securely.

THERMOSTAT

Removal/Installation

The thermostat is located on the right-hand side of the radiator.
Refer to **Figure 4** for this procedure.
1. On models so equipped, remove the radiator trim panel as described under *Radiator Trim Panel Removal/Installation* in Chapter Thirteen.

2. On models so equipped, remove the front fairing right-hand side panel as described under *Front Fairing Removal/ Installation* in Chapter Thirteen.

3. Drain the cooling system as described under *Coolant Change* in Chapter Three.

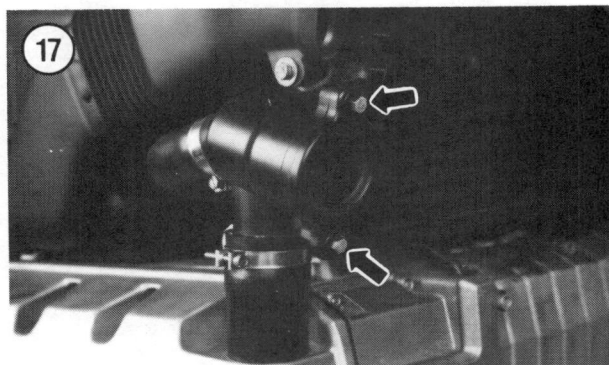

4. Remove the screws (**Figure 17**) securing the thermostat cover and remove the cover and O-ring seal.

5. Remove the thermostat from the thermostat housing on the radiator.

6. If necessary, test the thermostat as described in this chapter.

7. Install by reversing these removal steps, noting the following.

8. Inspect the O-ring seal on the cover. If is damaged or starting to harden or deteriorate, replace it with a new O-ring seal.

9. Install a new O-ring seal in the thermostat housing cover. Apply a light coat of cold multipurpose grease to hold the O-ring in place during installation.

10. Refill the cooling system with the recommended type and quantity of coolant as described in Chapter Three.

Testing

Test the thermostat to ensure proper operation. The thermostat should be replaced if it remains open at normal room temperature or stays closed after the specified temperature has been reached during the test procedure.

Place the thermostat on a small piece of wood in a pan of water (**Figure 18**). Place a thermometer in the pan of water (use a cooking or candy thermometer that is rated higher than the test temperature). Gradually heat the water and continue to gently stir the water until it reaches 80-85° C (176-185° F). At this temperature the thermostat valve should open.

NOTE
Valve operation is sometimes sluggish; it usually takes 3-5 minutes for the valve to operate properly and to open completely.

If the valve fails to open, the thermostat should be replaced (it cannot be serviced). Be sure to replace it with one of the same temperature rating.

CONNECTOR PIPE

Removal/Inspection/Installation

Inspect the connector pipe attached to the cylinder head for leakage. If there are signs of leakage, perform the following.

1. Remove the air filter case as described under *Air Filter Case Removal/Installation* in Chapter Seven.

2. Remove the coolant hoses going to the connector pipe as described under *Hoses* in this chapter.

NOTE
Figure 19 is shown with the engine removed and partially disassembled for clarity. The connector pipe can be removed with the engine in the frame.

9

3. Remove the bolts (**Figure 19**) securing the connector pipe to the cylinder head.

4. Remove the connector pipe and O-ring seal.

5. Remove and replace the O-ring seal (**Figure 20**). Apply a light coat of cold multipurpose grease to the O-ring seal to hold it in place during installation.

6. If necessary, unscrew the temperature sensor (**Figure 21**) and O-ring seal from the connector pipe. Discard the O-ring seal as it must be replaced every time the temperature sensor is removed.

7. If removed, install the temperature sensor and O-ring seal. Tighten securely.

8. Install the connector pipe and bolts and tighten the bolts securely.

9. Install the coolant hoses going to the connector pipe as described under *Hoses* in this chapter.

COOLANT RECOVERY TANK

Removal/Installation

1. Remove the frame right-hand side cover.

2. Loosen the screw on the hose clamp (**Figure 22**) at the base of the coolant recovery tank.

3. Pull the coolant recovery tank (**Figure 23**) up and out of the locating receptacles in the battery holder base.

4. Remove the hose from the base of the tank. Place your finger over the tank fitting as the coolant within the tank will drain out.

> *NOTE*
> *On some models a dark black residue will come out while draining the coolant. The inside surface of the water pump cover was painted black on some models and this paint has come off, has entered the cooling system and usually settles in the coolant recovery tank. Thoroughly rinse out the inside of the coolant recovery tank to remove this residue prior to installation.*

5. Drain the coolant from the tank.

6. Install by reversing these removal steps, noting the following.

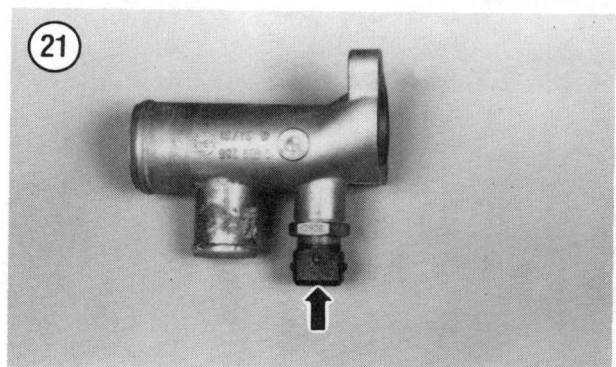

7. Make sure the locating tabs on the coolant recovery tank are properly indexed into the receptacles in the battery holder base.

HOSES

Hoses deteriorate with age and should be replaced periodically or whenever they show signs of cracking or leakage. To be safe, replace the hoses every 2 years. The spray of hot coolant from a cracked hose can injure the rider and passenger. Loss of coolant can also cause the engine to overheat, resulting in damage.

Whenever any component of the cooling system is removed, inspect the hoses and determine if replacement is necessary.

Refer to **Figure 24** for this procedure.

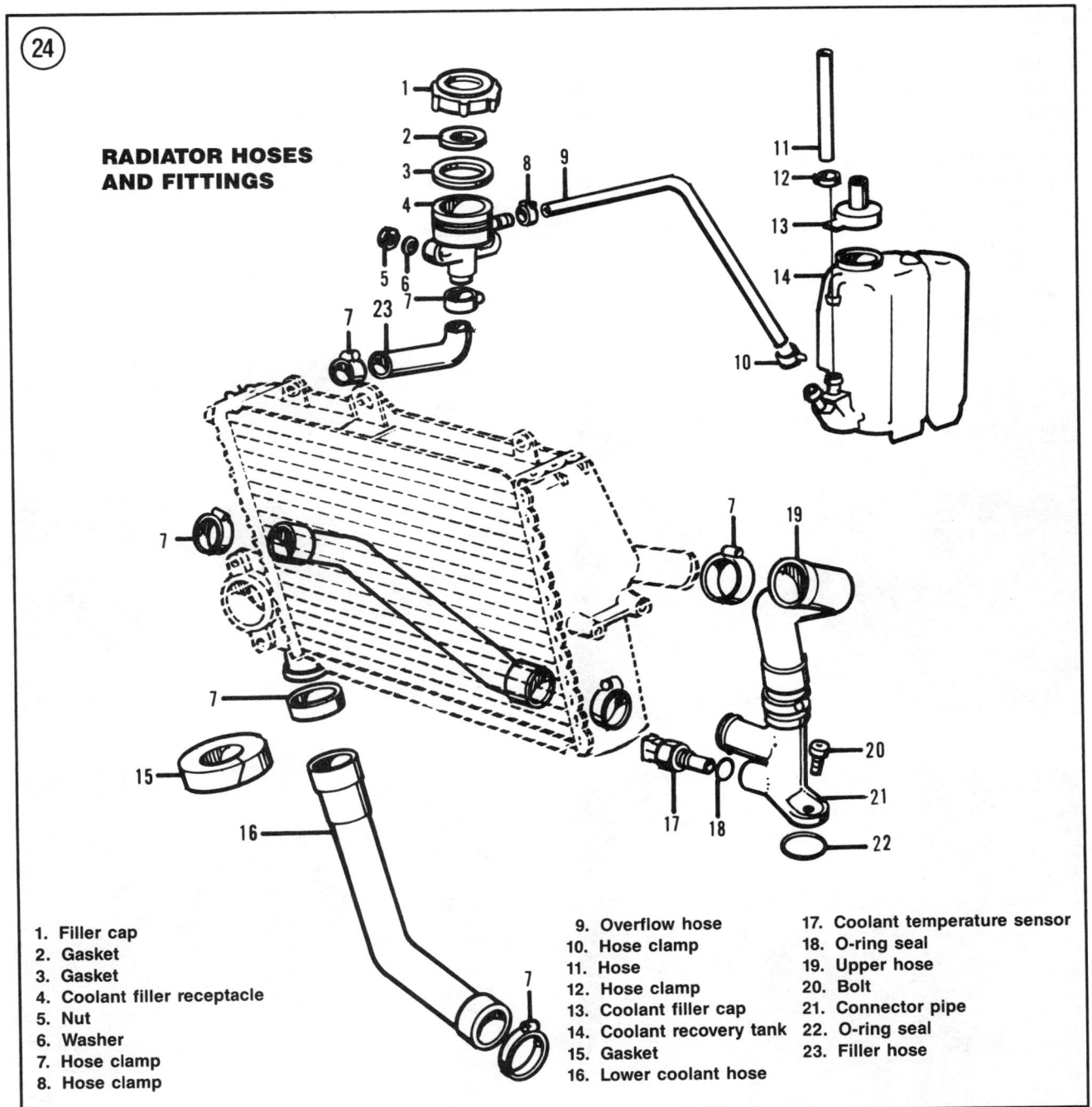

RADIATOR HOSES AND FITTINGS

1. Filler cap
2. Gasket
3. Gasket
4. Coolant filler receptacle
5. Nut
6. Washer
7. Hose clamp
8. Hose clamp
9. Overflow hose
10. Hose clamp
11. Hose
12. Hose clamp
13. Coolant filler cap
14. Coolant recovery tank
15. Gasket
16. Lower coolant hose
17. Coolant temperature sensor
18. O-ring seal
19. Upper hose
20. Bolt
21. Connector pipe
22. O-ring seal
23. Filler hose

9

1. On models so equipped, remove the radiator trim panel as described under *Radiator Trim Panel Removal/Installation* in Chapter Thirteen.

2. On models so equipped, remove the front fairing side panels as described under *Front Fairing Removal/Installation* in Chapter Thirteen.

3. Drain the cooling system as described under *Coolant Change* in Chapter Three.

4. Remove the frame left-hand side cover.

5. Disconnect the battery negative lead as described under *Battery* in Chapter Three.

6. Remove bolts and washers (A, **Figure 25**) securing the air intake pipe to the radiator.

7. Pull the lower section of the air intake pipe (B, **Figure 25**) out of the air filter air box and remove the air intake pipe.

8. To remove the lower hose, perform the following:
   a. Loosen the screws on the upper and lower hose clamps (**Figure 26**).
   b. Move the upper clamp off of the hose at the top.
   c. Move the lower clamp back onto the hose and off of the neck of the water/oil pump.
   d. Pull the lower hose down and out of the engine crankcase cover. This may be difficult if there is

corrosion within the crankcase cover. Carefully pull the hose down and out from the cover. If necessary, apply Armor All, liquid detergent or another liquid that may help ease the hose out of the cover. Remove the lower hose.

9. To remove the bypass hose, perform the following:
   a. Loosen the screws on the bypass hose clamps (A, **Figure 27**) at each end of the bypass hose.
   b. Move the clamps back onto the hose and off of the neck of the thermostat housing fitting and the connector pipe.
   c. Remove the bypass hose (B, **Figure 27**) from the radiator and engine.

10. To remove the upper hose, perform the following:
   a. Loosen the screws on the upper hose clamps (A, **Figure 28**).
   b. Move the clamp back onto the hose and off of the neck of the connector pipe and the radiator left-hand inlet fitting.
   c. Remove the upper hose (B, **Figure 28**) from the radiator and engine.

11. To remove the coolant filler neck hose, perform the following:

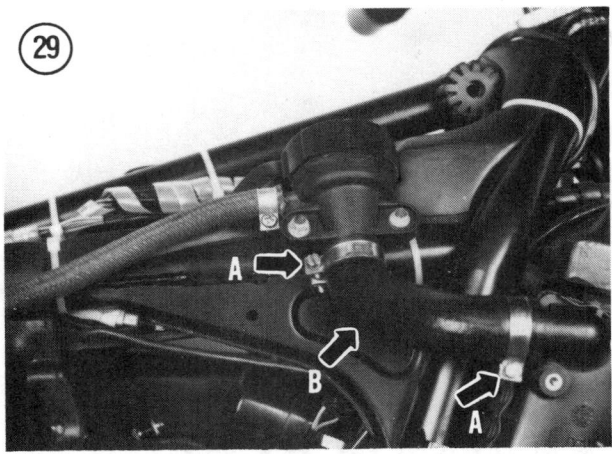

a. Loosen the screws on the filler neck hose clamps (A, **Figure 29**).

b. Move the clamps back onto the hose and off of the neck of the radiator right-hand outlet fitting and filler neck.

c. Remove the filler neck hose (B, **Figure 29**) from the radiator and the filler neck.

12. Install all hoses by reversing these removal steps, noting the following.

a. Before installing the hoses, soak the ends in hot water to make them pliable and they will slide on much easier. Do not apply any type of lubricant to the inner surfaces of the hoses.

b. Always use clamping screw type hose clamps. This type of clamp is superior in its holding ability and is easily released with a screwdriver.

Table 1 COOLING SYSTEM SPECIFICATIONS

Capacity	
Engine and radiator	
K75	2.5 liters (2.6 qts.)
K100 and K1100	3.0 liters (3.2 qts.)
Recovery tank	0.4 liters (0.8 qt.)
Antifreeze/distilled water ratio	
Temperature down to -28° C	60% distilled water
(-18° F)*	40% BMW antifreeze
Temperature below -36° C	50% distilled water
(-31° F)*	50% BMW antifreeze
Thermostat opens at 85° C (185° F)	
Cooling fan starts to run at 103° C	
(217° F)	
Coolant temperature warning lamp comes on	
at 111° C (232° F)	
Filler neck cap	
Pressure relief valve opens at 100-114 kPa	
(14.5-16.5 psi)	
Vacuum valve opens at 10.34 kPa (1.5 psi)	

*BMW does not provide antifreeze mixture specifications for temperatures between -28° and -36° C.

9

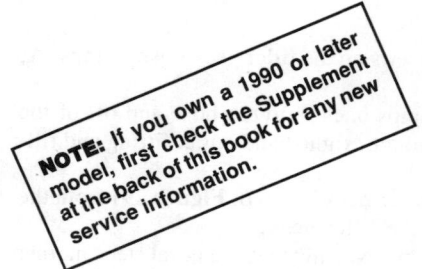

NOTE: If you own a 1990 or later model, first check the Supplement at the back of this book for any new service information.

CHAPTER TEN

FRONT SUSPENSION AND STEERING

This chapter describes procedures for the repair and maintenance of the front wheel, front forks and the steering components.

Front suspension torque specifications are covered in **Table 1**. **Tables 1-3** are at the end of this chapter.

FRONT WHEEL

Removal

1. On models so equipped, remove the engine spoiler as described under *Engine Spoiler Removal/Installation* in Chapter Thirteen.
2. Place the bike on the center stand or place wood blocks under the engine oil pan to support it securely with the front wheel off the ground.
3A. On ABS equipped models, perform the following:

> *CAUTION*
> *The ABS electronic trigger sensor is attached to the right-hand caliper assembly. Do not damage the sensor during caliper removal.*

  a. Remove the front fender (A, **Figure 1**) as described under *Front Fender (1-Piece Type) Removal/Installation* in Chapter Thirteen.

  b. Remove the brake caliper assembly mounting bolts (B and C, **Figure 1**) from the front fork on each side. Both caliper assemblies must be removed on these models.

  c. Slide both caliper assemblies off of the brake discs. The 2 calipers are interconnected by a U-shaped brake line. Do not kink or damage this brake line assembly.

  d. Tie the caliper assemblies and brake line up with a Bungee cord to take the strain off the hydraulic brake line.

3B. On all other models, perform the following:

  a. Remove the brake caliper assembly mounting bolts (**Figure 2**) from the front fork.

  b. Remove the bolt (**Figure 3**) securing the brake hose to the fork slider.

  c. Slide the caliper assembly off of the brake disc and tie the caliper assembly up with a Bungee cord to take the strain off the flexible hydraulic brake hose.

  d. Repeat for the other brake caliper assembly.

4. Insert a piece of vinyl tubing or wood in the calipers in place of the brake disc. That way if the brake lever is inadvertently squeezed, the pistons will not be forced out of the cylinders. If this does happen, the calipers may have to be disassembled to reseat the pistons and the system will have to be bled.

5. Loosen the front axle clamping bolts (**Figure 4**) on the left-hand fork leg.

6. Remove the bolt (A, **Figure 5**) and special washer (B, **Figure 5**) from the left-hand side of the front axle.

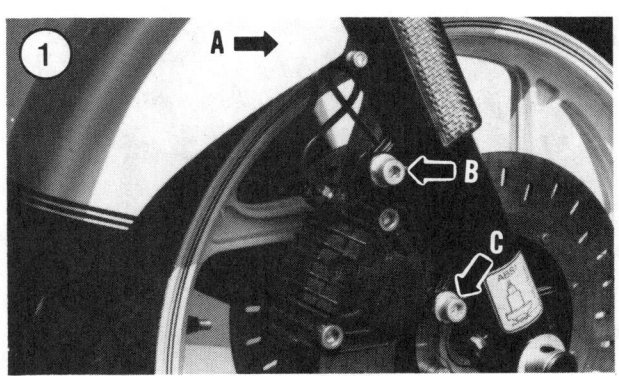

7. Loosen the front axle clamping bolts (**Figure 6**) on the right-hand fork leg.

NOTE
*Before removing the front wheel, note the direction of the tire rotation arrow (**Figure 7**). If the tire is not marked, mark a rotation arrow either on the tire or wheel. The wheel must be reinstalled the same way so the arrow will be pointing in the correct direction.*

10

8. Insert a drift or Allen wrench into the hole (**Figure 8**) in the right-hand side of the front axle.

9. Rotate the axle back and forth and withdraw the front axle from both fork legs.

10. Let the wheel come down and forward and remove it. Don't lose the spacer on each side of the front hub. Don't intermix them as they must be reinstalled on the correct side of the wheel during installation.

> *CAUTION*
> *Do not set the wheel down on the disc surface as it may get scratched or warped. Set the tire sidewalls on 2 wood blocks as shown in Figure 9.*

11. Inspect the front wheel as described in this chapter.

Installation

1. Make sure the axle bearing surfaces of both fork sliders and the axle are free from burrs and nicks.

2. Apply a small amount of cold grease to the inner surface of the spacers. This will help hold them in place.

3. Position the spacers onto the correct side of the wheel hub. The narrow spacer goes on the right-hand side. Refer to **Figure 10** for the right-hand side and **Figure 11** for the left-hand side.

4. Make sure the front wheel tire rotation arrow (**Figure 7**) is pointing in the correct direction.

5. Apply a light coat of multipurpose grease to the front axle prior to installation.

6. Roll the wheel into position. Lift the wheel up and install the front axle from the right-hand side (**Figure 12**). Push the axle all the way in until it bottoms out on the left-hand fork leg. Make sure the axle spacers (**Figure 13**) are still in place.

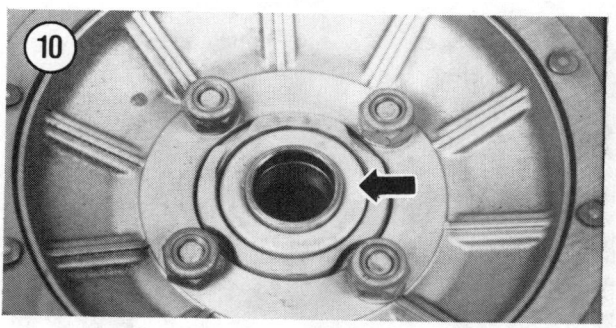

7. Install the special washer (B, **Figure 5**) and the Allen bolt (A, **Figure 5**) into the front axle.

8. Install a drift or Allen bolt wrench into the hole in the right-hand end of the front axle. This is to prevent the axle from turning while tightening the Allen bolt on the opposite end.

9. Tighten the Allen bolt to the torque specification listed in **Table 1**.

10. Remove the vinyl tubing or pieces of wood from both brake calipers.

11A. On ABS equipped models, perform the following:

> *NOTE*
> *The ABS electronic trigger sensor is attached to the right-hand caliper assembly. Do not damage the sensor during caliper installation.*

a. Carefully install the caliper assemblies onto the disc. Be careful not to damage the leading edge of the pads during installation. Do not kink or damage the brake line assembly.

b. Install the brake caliper assembly mounting bolts. Be sure to install the bolt with the special shoulder at the top (B, **Figure 1**). This bolt properly locates the caliper assembly onto the front fork. This location is necessary to properly maintain the distance between the ABS sensor on the caliper assembly and the pulse generating wheel attached to the front wheel.

c. Tighten the caliper mounting bolts to the torque specifications listed in **Table 1**.

d. Install the front fender (A, **Figure 1**) as described under *Front Fender (1-Piece Type) Removal/Installation* in Chapter Thirteen.

> *WARNING*
> *If the distance between the trigger sensor and pulse generating wheel is not maintained correctly, the ABS system will **not** function properly.*

e. After the wheel is installed, inspect the distance between the ABS sensor and the pulse generating wheel as described under *Trigger Sensor-to-Pulse Generating Wheel Clearance, Measurement and Adjustment (Front Trigger Sensor)* in Chapter Twelve.

11B. On all other models, perform the following:

a. Carefully install the caliper assembly onto the disc. Be careful not to damage the leading edge of the pads during installation.

b. Install the caliper mounting bolts (**Figure 2**) and tighten to the torque specifications listed in **Table 1**.

c. Install the bolt (**Figure 3**) securing the brake hose to the fork slider. Tighten the bolt securely.

d. Repeat for the other brake caliper assembly.

12. Remove the wood block(s) from under the engine oil pan and take the bike off the center stand.

13. Apply the front brakes and pump the front forks up and down several times to seat and center the front axle within the fork tubes.

14. Tighten the front axle clamp bolts on each fork leg to the torque specification listed in **Table 1**.

15. After the wheel is completely installed, rotate it several times and apply the brakes a couple of times to make sure the wheel rotates freely and that the brake pads are against the discs correctly.

16. On models so equipped, install the engine spoiler as described under *Engine Spoiler Removal/Installation* in Chapter Thirteen.

Inspection

Install the wheel in a wheel truing stand (**Figure 14**). Measure the axial and radial runout of the wheel with a dial indicator. The maximum axial and radial runout is 2.0 mm (0.08 in.). If the runout exceeds this dimension, check the wheel bearing condition.

If the wheel bearings are okay, the alloy wheel will have to be replaced as it cannot be serviced. Inspect the wheel for signs of cracks, fractures, dents or bends. If it is damaged in any way, it must be replaced.

> *WARNING*
> *Do not try to repair any damage to the BMW or any alloy wheel as it will result in an unsafe riding condition.*

10

Check axle runout as described under *Front Hub Inspection* in this chapter.

FRONT HUB

Inspection

Inspect each wheel bearing prior to removing it from the wheel hub.

> *CAUTION*
> *Do not remove the wheel bearings for inspection purposes as they will be damaged during the removal process. Remove wheel bearings only if they are to be replaced.*

1. Remove the front wheel as described in this chapter.
2. Turn each bearing by hand. Make sure bearings turn smoothly. Replace the bearing(s) if they are noisy or have excessive play.
3. On non-sealed bearings, check the balls for evidence of wear, pitting or excessive heat (bluish tint). Replace the bearings if necessary; always replace as a complete set. When replacing the bearings, be sure to take your old bearings along to ensure a perfect match.

> *NOTE*
> *Fully sealed bearings are available from many bearing specialty shops. Fully sealed bearings*

provide better protection from dirt and moisture that may get into the hub.

4. Check the axle for wear and straightness. Use V-blocks and a dial indicator as shown in **Figure 15**. If the runout is 0.2 mm (0.01 in.) or greater, the axle should be replaced.

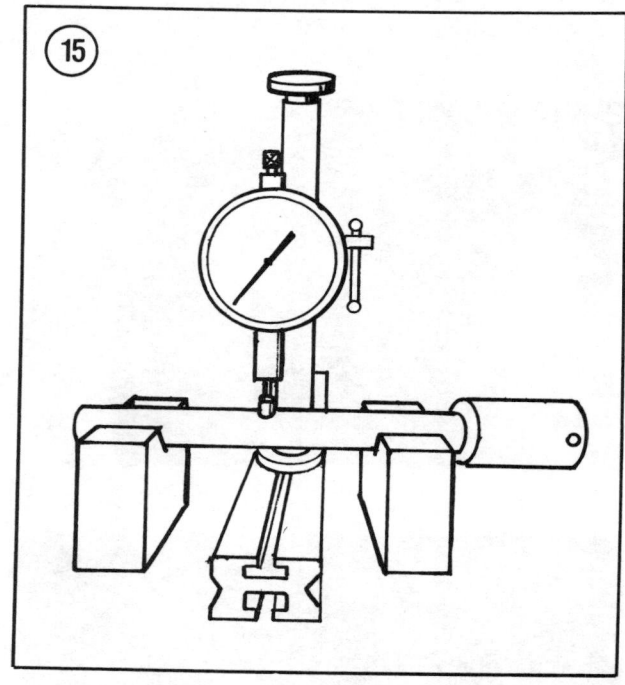

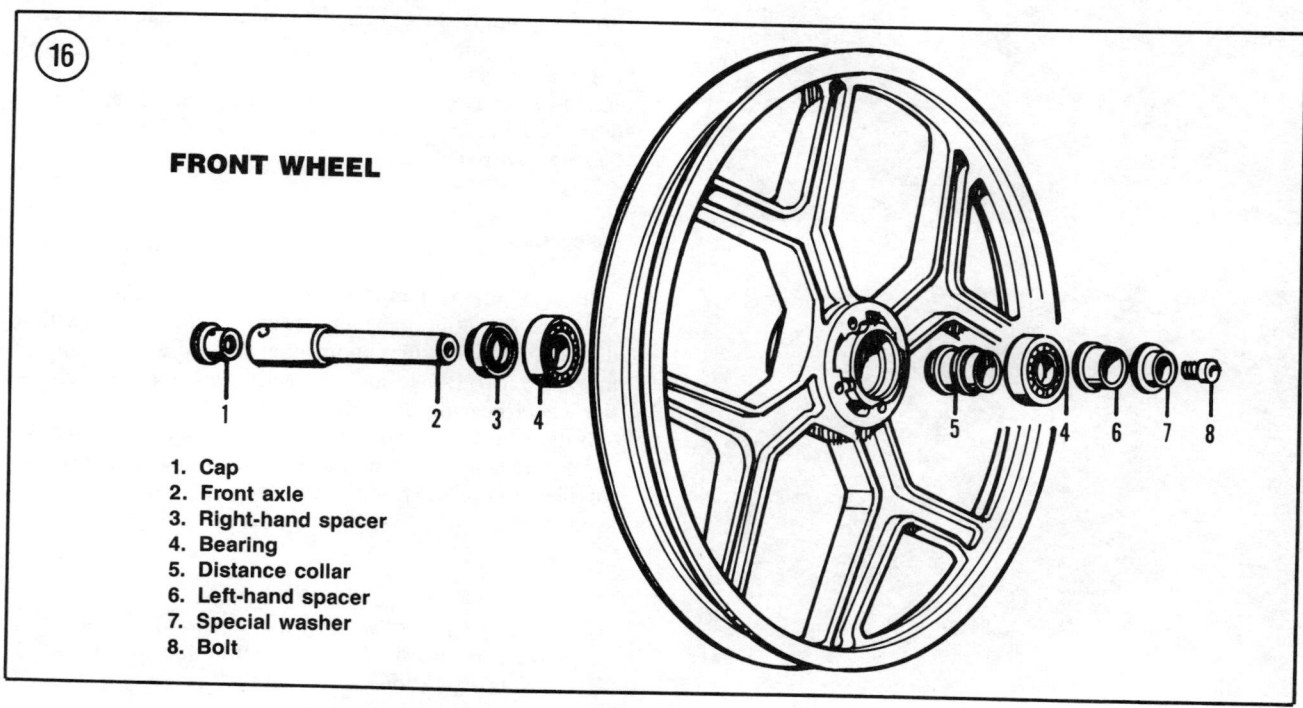

FRONT WHEEL

1. Cap
2. Front axle
3. Right-hand spacer
4. Bearing
5. Distance collar
6. Left-hand spacer
7. Special washer
8. Bolt

Disassembly

The distance collar is a very tight fit between both bearings. There is a shoulder at each end of the distance collar and it covers the inner bearing race. This shoulder makes it impossible to move the distance collar over to one side in order to tap the first bearing out with a drift and hammer. A special BMW tool is required.

Refer to **Figure 16** for this procedure.

1. Remove the front wheel as described in this chapter.

2. Inspect the wheel bearings as described in this chapter. If they must be replaced, proceed as follows.

> *NOTE*
> *The disc mounting bolts go through both brake discs and the wheel hub.*

> *NOTE*
> *If working on a well run-in bike (high mileage), mark the brake discs with an "R" (Figure 17) and an "L" (on an attached piece of masking tape) so they will be reinstalled on the same side of the wheel from where they were removed. Older parts tend to form a wear pattern and should be reinstalled in the same location. The BMW discs are not marked in regard to right-hand or left-hand side placement.*

3. To remove the brake discs, perform the following:
   a. Hold onto the nut (**Figure 18**) on the right-hand side of the wheel and loosen the Allen bolt (**Figure 19**) on the left-hand side. Loosen all bolts and nuts.
   b. Remove all but one of the bolts, washers and nuts.
   c. Place the wheel in the horizontal position on wood blocks.
   d. Hold onto the lower brake disc and remove the remaining bolt, washers and nut.
   e. Remove the lower brake disc then the upper brake disc.

4. To remove the right- and left-hand bearings and distance collar, perform the following:
   a. Install BMW special tool (part No. 008 570) onto either wheel bearing.
   b. Tighten the special tool and withdraw the wheel bearing from that side of the front hub.
   c. Remove the distance collar from the front hub.

> *NOTE*
> *After the first wheel bearing and distance collar are removed, it is then possible to drive out the opposite bearing with a drift and hammer if you so desire.*

   d. Turn the wheel over and install the BMW special tool onto the other wheel bearing.
   e. Tighten the special tool and withdraw the wheel bearing from that side of the front hub.

5. Clean the inside and the outside of the hub with solvent. Dry with compressed air.

Assembly

The wheel bearings are such a tight fit that BMW recommends the front hub be heated to 100° C (212° F)

10

in order to expand the hub bearing receptacle. The entire wheel is so large that it is very difficult for a home mechanic to find a large enough oven. If the entire wheel is heated, the tire, valve stem, brake discs and balance weights must be removed first.

An alternate way is to heat only the bearing receptacle area of the hub with rags and boiling hot water. Also place the wheel bearings in a freezer for approximately 30 minutes. This will reduce their overall size and will make installation easier.

CAUTION
Do not heat the hub area with a torch (propane or acetylene); never bring a flame into contact with the bearing receptacle of the front hub. The direct heat will destroy the painted finish, remove any case hardening and could lead to wheel warpage.

1. On non-sealed bearings, pack the bearings with a good quality bearing grease. Work the grease in between the balls thoroughly; turn the bearing by hand a couple of times to make sure the grease is distributed evenly inside the bearing.
2. Blow any dirt or foreign matter out of the hub before installing the bearings.
3. Place the new wheel bearings in a freezer if possible. Chilling them will slightly reduce their overall diameter while the hot wheel hub is slightly larger due to heat expansion. This will make installation easier.
4. Wrap both sides of the hub center with shop cloths or a small bath towel. Secure the cloths or towel(s) with a Bungee cord to hold them in place since you will be pouring boiling hot water on both sides of the hub.

WARNING
Protect yourself accordingly in the next step as you will be working with boiling water. Wear long pants and shoes (no shorts and sandals). Use pot holders to handle the hot pans containing the boiling water.

5. Heat about 2-3 pans (4-5 qt. capacity pan) of water until it boils. You will want to heat the hub sufficiently to enable installation of *both bearings* without reheating the hub. You don't want to reheat the hub after the first bearing and the distance collar have already been installed. If this is done some water is bound to be trapped in the hub, leading to bearing rust and premature bearing failure.
6. Slowly and carefully pour the boiling water onto *both sides* of the hub. Try to heat both sides to the same approximate temperature.

WARNING
Do not operate the electric hair drier or heat gun in the area where there is residual water that was used to heat the wheel hub.

NOTE
While installing the bearing on the one side, try to keep the other side of the hub warm with a portable hair drier or heat gun.

CAUTION
Install the bearings with the single sealed side facing outward (Figure 20).

7. Correctly position the bearing into the hub and tap it squarely into place on the outer race only. Use a socket (**Fig-**

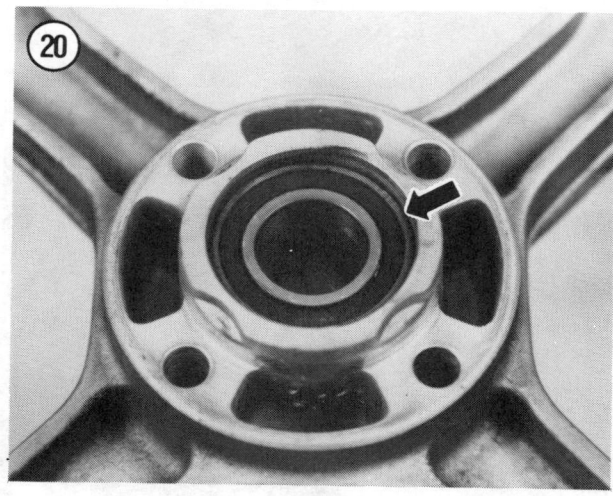

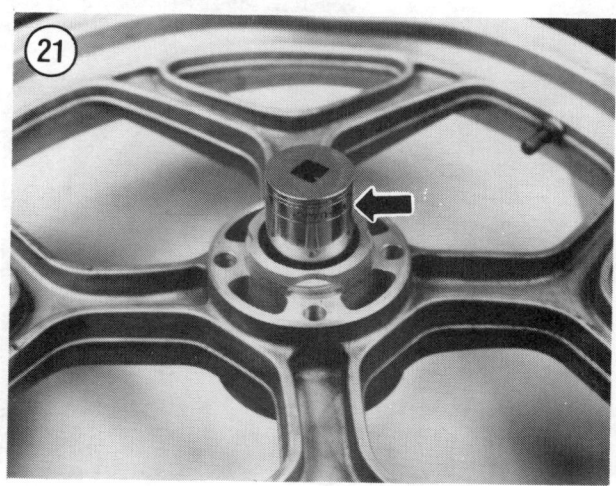

ure **21**) that matches the outer race diameter. Do not tap on the inner race or the bearing might be damaged. Be sure that the bearing is completely seated in the hub receptacle.

8. Turn the wheel over and install the distance collar.

9. Correctly position the bearing into the hub and tap it squarely into place on the outer race only. Use a socket (**Figure 21**) that matches the outer race diameter. Do not tap on the inner race or the bearing might be damaged. Be sure that the bearing is completely seated in the hub and that the distance collar is correctly positioned between the 2 bearings.

10. Use compressed air and thoroughly dry the wheel on both sides.

11. Position the brake discs on the correct side. Refer to marks made in Step 3, *Disassembly*.

12. Be sure to place a washer under the bolt head and between the brake disc and the nut. Install the bolt from the left-hand side and install the washer and nut.

13. Tighten the brake disc bolts and nuts to the torque specification listed in **Table 1**.

14. Install the front wheel as described in this chapter.

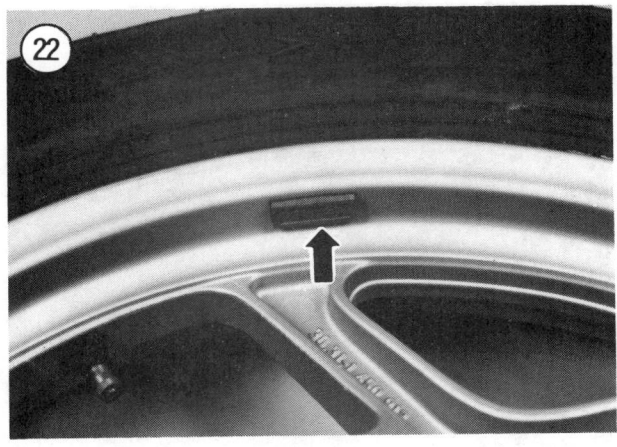

WHEEL BALANCE

An unbalanced wheel is unsafe. Depending on the degree of unbalance and the speed of the motorcycle, the rider may experience anything from a mild vibration to a violent shimmy which may even result in loss of control.

On alloy wheels, weights are attached to the rim (**Figure 22**). A kit of adhesive-backed weights may be purchased from most BMW dealers or motorcycle supply stores. This kit contains test weights and strips of adhesive-backed weights that can be cut to the desired weight and attached directly to the rim.

Before you attempt to balance the wheel, check to be sure that the wheel bearings are in good condition and properly lubricated and that the brakes do not drag. The wheel must rotate freely.

1. Remove the wheel as described in this chapter or Chapter Eleven.

2. Mount the wheel on a fixture such as the one shown in **Figure 14** so it can rotate freely.

3. Give the wheel a spin and let it coast to a stop. Mark the tire at the lowest point.

4. Spin the wheel several more times. If the wheel keeps coming to rest at the same point, it is out of balance.

5. Tape a test weight to the upper (or light) side of the wheel.

6. Experiment with different weights until the wheel, when spun, comes to a rest at a different position each time.

7. Remove the test weight and install the correct size adhesive-backed or clamp-on weight.

10

TIRE CHANGING

The rim of the alloy wheel is aluminum and the exterior appearance can easily be damaged. Special care must be taken with tire irons when changing a tire to avoid scratches and gouges to the outer rim surface. Insert scraps of leather between the tire iron and the rim to protect the rim from gouges. All models are factory-equipped with tubeless tires and wheels designed specifically for use with tubeless tires.

> *WARNING*
> *Do not install tubeless tires on wheels designed for use only with tube-type tires. Personal injury and tire failure may result from rapid tire deflation while riding. Some wheels for use with tubeless tires are so marked.*

Removal

1. Remove the valve cap (**Figure 23**) and core and deflate the tire.

2. Press the entire bead on both sides of the tire into the center of the rim. Lubricate the beads with soapy water.

3. Insert the tire iron under the bead next to the valve (**Figure 24**). Force the bead on the opposite side of the tire into the center of the rim and pry the bead over the rim with the tire iron.

4. Insert a second tire iron next to the first to hold the bead over the rim. Then work around the tire with the first tire iron, prying the bead over the rim (**Figure 25**).

5. Stand the tire upright. Insert the tire iron between the second bead and the side of the rim that the first bead was pried over (**Figure 26**). Force the bead on the opposite side from the tire iron into the center of the rim. Pry the second bead off the rim, working around as with the first.

6. It is recommended that the tire valve stem be replaced whenever the tire is removed from the wheel.

Installation

1. Carefully inspect the tire for any damage, especially inside.

2. A new tire may have balancing rubbers inside. These are not patches and should not be disturbed. A colored spot

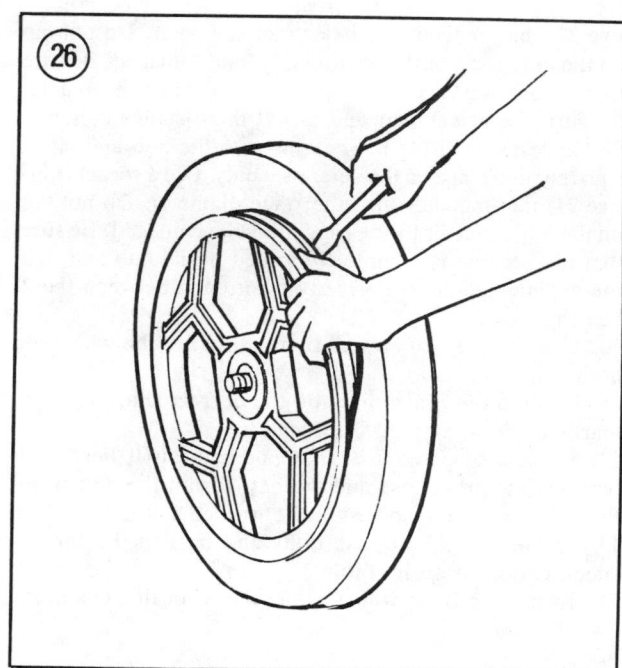

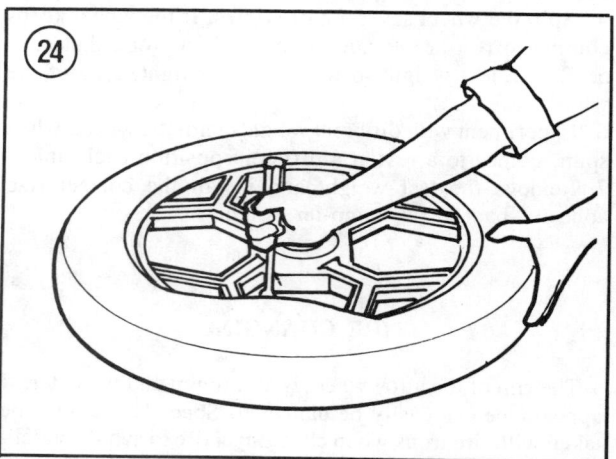

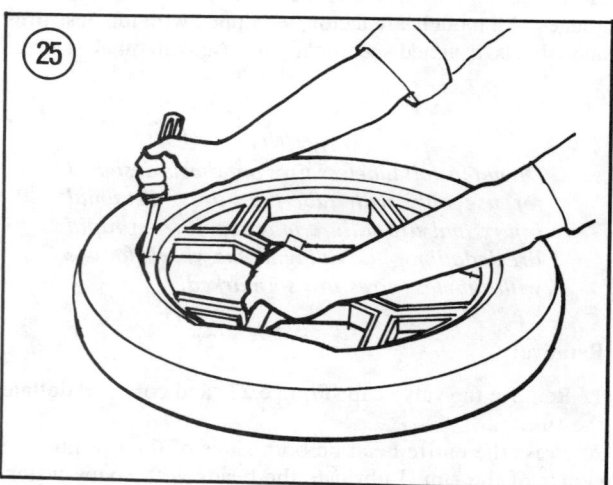

(A, **Figure 27**) near the bead indicates a lighter point on the tire. This spot should be placed next to the valve stem (B, **Figure 27**).

3. Install the tire so that it revolves in the proper direction. The tire is marked with an arrow and "Rotation" or "Drive" on the side wall. Refer to **Figure 28** for the front wheel or **Figure 29** for the rear wheel.

4. Lubricate both beads of the tire with soapy water.

5. Place the backside of the tire into the center of the rim. The lower bead should go into the center of the rim and the upper bead outside. Work around the tire in both directions (**Figure 30**). Use a tire iron for the last few inches of bead (**Figure 31**).

6. Press the upper bead into the rim opposite the valve (**Figure 32**). Pry the bead into the rim on both sides of the initial point with a tire iron, working around the rim to the valve (**Figure 33**).

7. Check the bead on both sides of the tire for even fit around the rim.

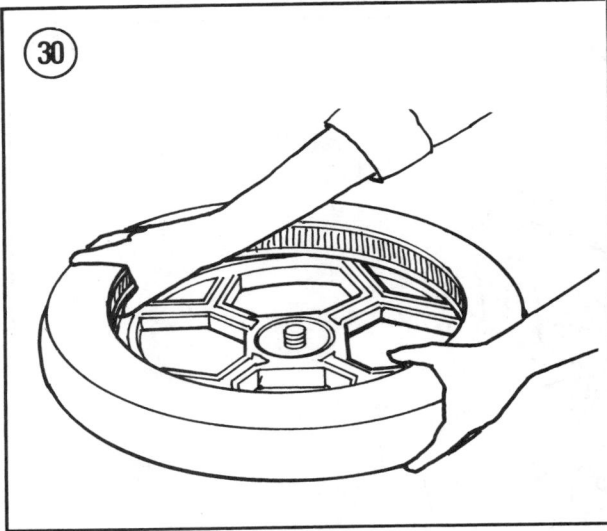

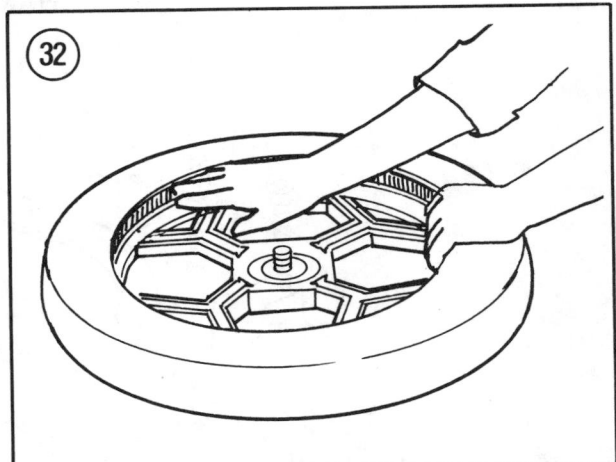

10

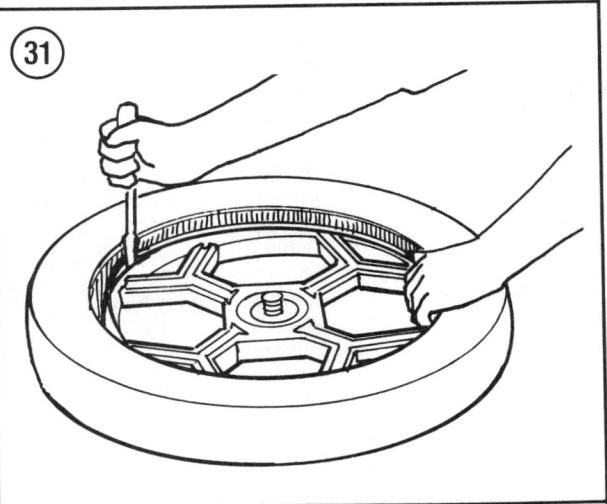

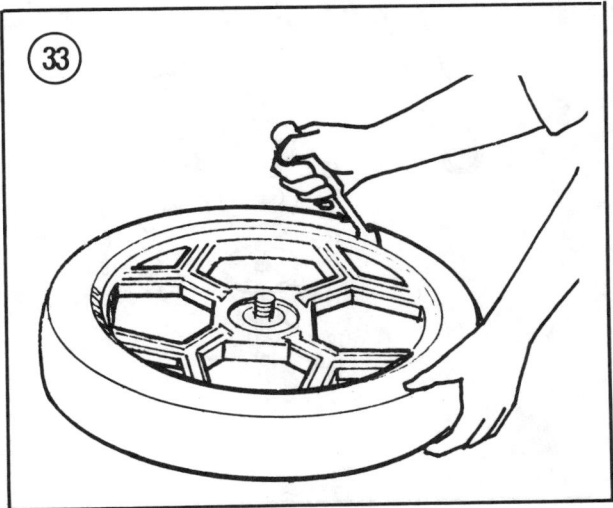

8. Bounce the wheel several times, rotating it each time. This will force the tire beads against the rim flanges. After the tire beads are in contact with the rim evenly, inflate the tire to seat the beads.

NOTE
If you are unable to get an airtight seal this way, install an inflatable band around the circumference of the tire. Slowly inflate the band until the beads are seated against the rim flanges, then inflate the tire. If you still encounter trouble, deflate the inflation band and the tire. Apply additional lubricant to the beads and repeat the inflation procedure. Also try rolling the tire back and forth while inflating it.

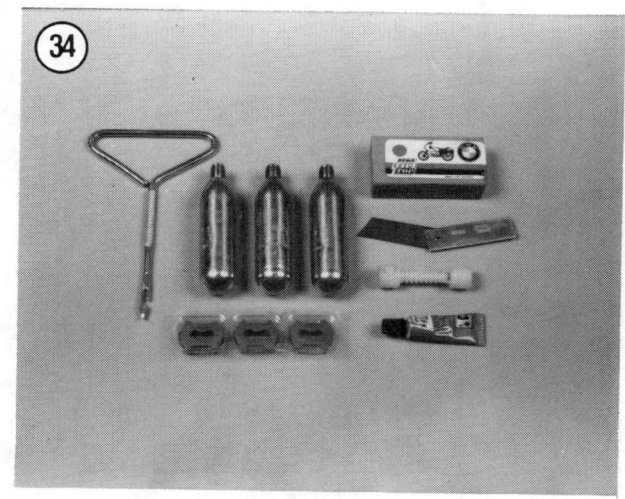

HANDLEBAR

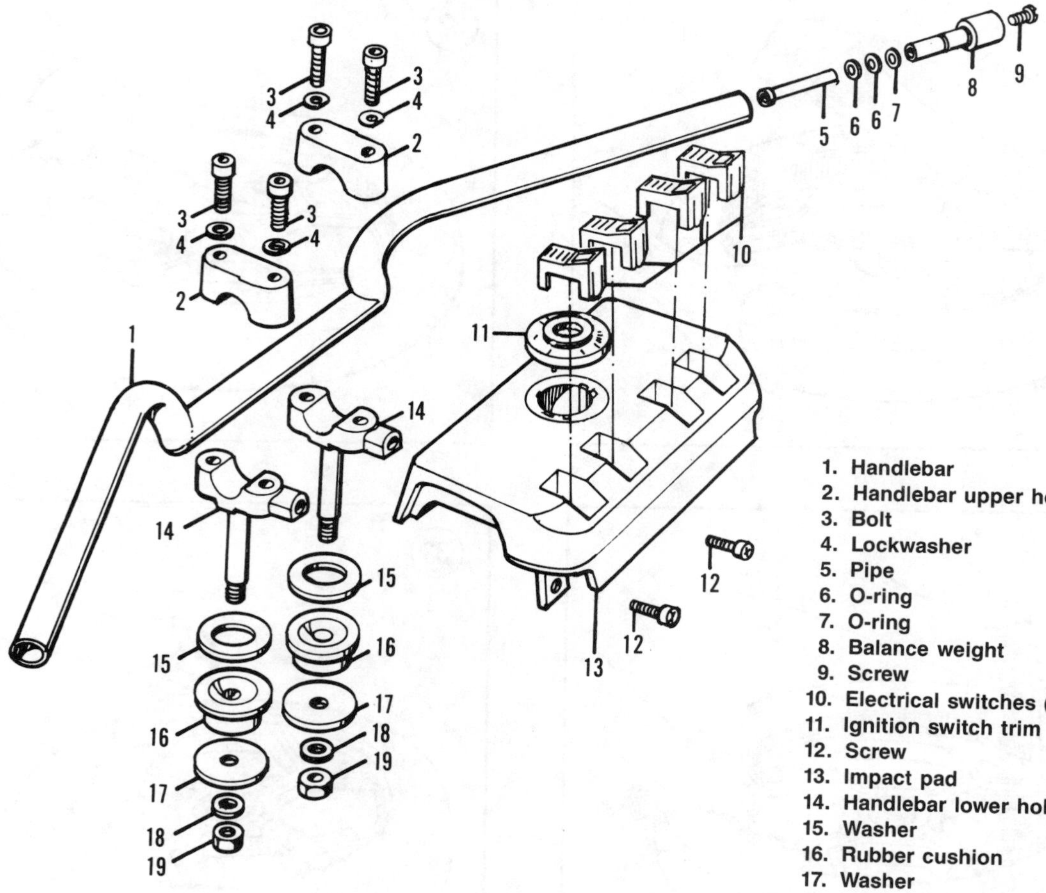

1. Handlebar
2. Handlebar upper holder
3. Bolt
4. Lockwasher
5. Pipe
6. O-ring
7. O-ring
8. Balance weight
9. Screw
10. Electrical switches (optional)
11. Ignition switch trim ring
12. Screw
13. Impact pad
14. Handlebar lower holder
15. Washer
16. Rubber cushion
17. Washer
18. Lockwasher
19. Nut

WARNING
Never exceed 40 kPa (56 psi) inflation pressure in Step 9 as the tire could burst, causing severe injury. Never stand directly over the tire while inflating it.

9. Inflate the tire to more than the recommended inflation pressure for the initial seating of the rim flanges. Once the beads are seated correctly, deflate the tire to the correct pressure. Refer to **Table 2**.

10. Be sure to reinstall the valve stem cap. The cap prevents small pebbles and dirt from collecting in the valve stem; this could allow air leakage or result in incorrect tire pressure readings.

TIRE REPAIRS

Patching a tubeless tire on the road is very difficult. If both beads are still in place against the rim, a can of pressurized tire sealant may inflate the tire and seal the hole. The beads must be against the wheel for this method to work.

BMW does offer a emergency tire repair kit (**Figure 34**) that can be used on a nail hole puncture of up to 4 mm (0.16 in.) in diameter. This is only a temporary fix and the tire must be replaced as soon as possible.

WARNING
After fixing a flat tire with a temporary patch, do not ride the bike faster than 37 mph (60 km/h) or farther than 250 miles (400 km).

Another solution is to carry a spare inner tube that could be temporarily installed and inflated. This will enable you to get to a tire dealer or motorcycle shop where the tire can be replaced. Be sure that the tube is designed for use with a tubeless tire.

Due to the variations of material supplied with different tubeless tire repair kits, follow the instructions and recommendations supplied with the repair kit.

BMW recommends that the valve stem be replaced each time the tire is removed from the wheel.

HANDLEBAR

Removal

Refer to the following illustrations for this procedure.
  a. **Figure 35**.
  b. **Figure 36**.

1. Remove the right-hand side cover.
2. Disconnect the battery negative lead as described under *Battery* in Chapter Three.

10

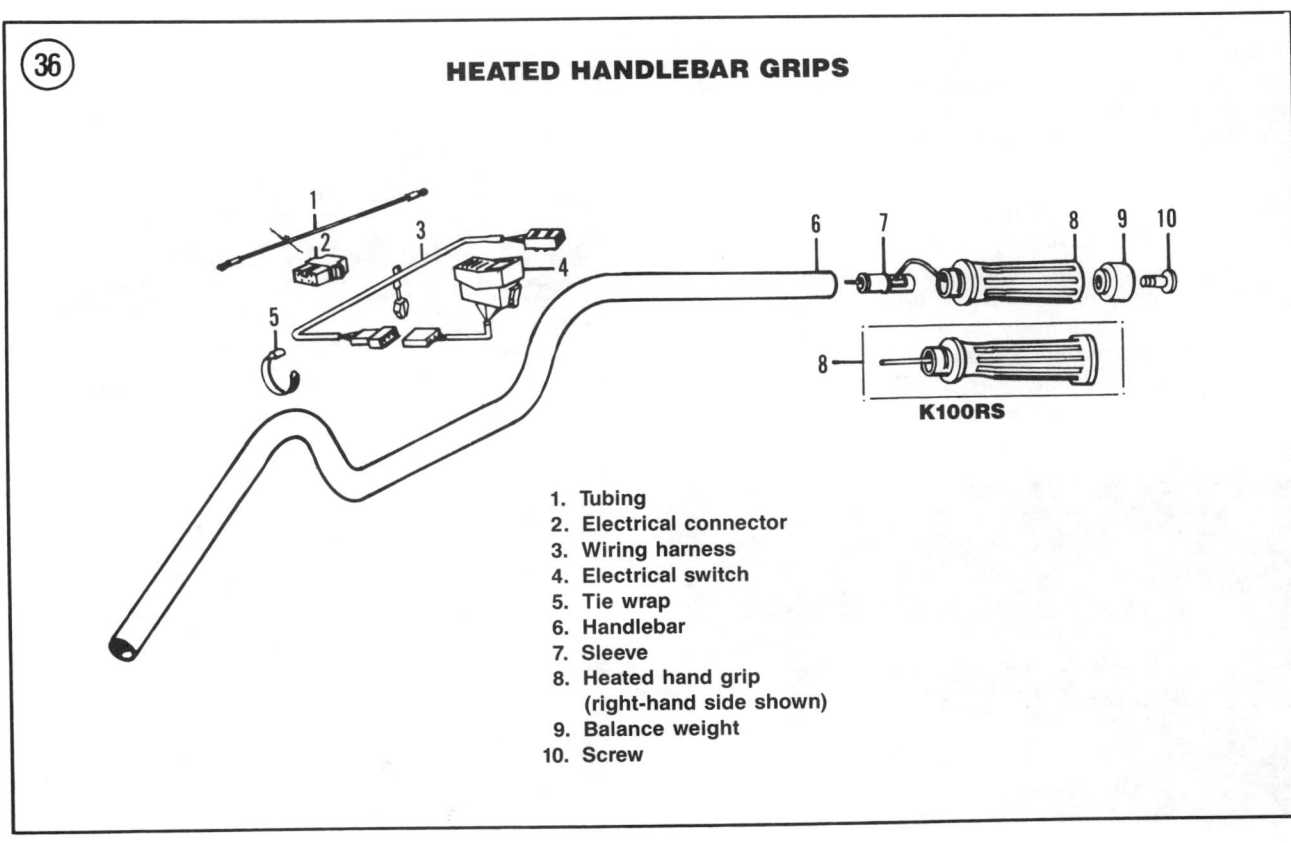

HEATED HANDLEBAR GRIPS

K100RS

1. Tubing
2. Electrical connector
3. Wiring harness
4. Electrical switch
5. Tie wrap
6. Handlebar
7. Sleeve
8. Heated hand grip
   (right-hand side shown)
9. Balance weight
10. Screw

3. Remove the fuel tank as described under *Fuel Tank Removal/Installation* in Chapter Seven.

4. Remove the screws (**Figure 37**) securing the impact pad.

5A. On models with no auxiliary switches, remove the impact pad.

5B. On models equipped with auxiliary switches, perform the following:

    a. Partially pull up on the impact pad (**Figure 38**) and move it out of the way. Don't move the pad too far as there is very little slack in the electrical wires at this time.

    b. Follow the electrical wires from the impact pad back to their electrical connectors at the main wiring harness. If necessary, remove any tie wrap(s) (**Figure 39**) securing the electrical wires to the frame.

    c. Pull the electrical wires away from the frame (**Figure 40**) and disconnect them.

    d. Pull the impact pad up and away from the steering head area. It is not necessary to completely remove the impact pad, just move it out of the way.

6. On models so equipped, unscrew the rear view mirrors (**Figure 41**) from the handlebar switch assemblies.

NOTE
When the throttle cable cover is removed, the throttle grip becomes loose and may fall off of the end of the handlebar.

7. Disconnect the throttle cable as follows:

    a. Remove the screw (A, **Figure 42**) securing the throttle cover (B, **Figure 42**) and remove the cover.

    b. Remove the throttle grip from the end of the handlebar.

CAUTION
Cover the instrument cluster, front fairing (models so equipped) and frame with a heavy cloth or plastic tarp to protect it from accidental spilling of brake fluid. Wash any spilled brake fluid off any painted or plated surface immediately, as it will destroy the finish. Use soapy water and rinse thoroughly.

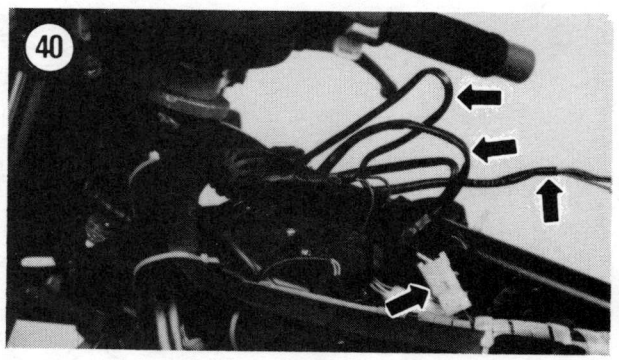

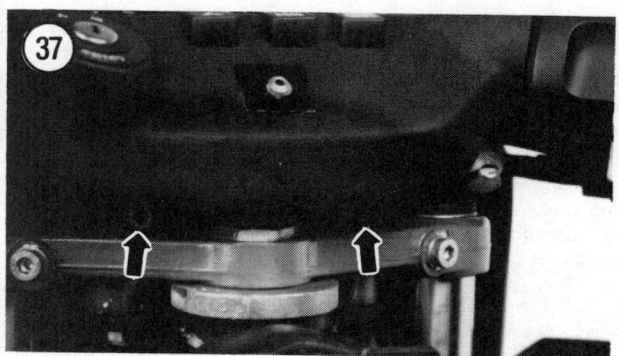

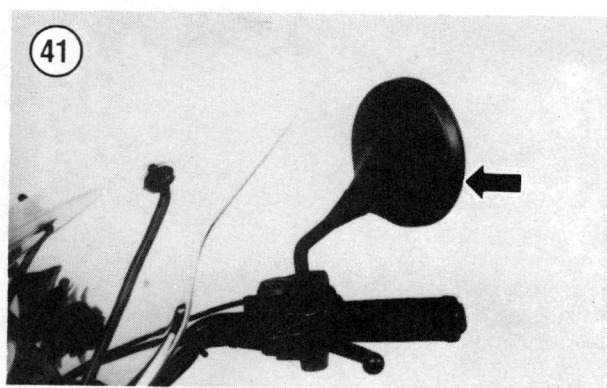

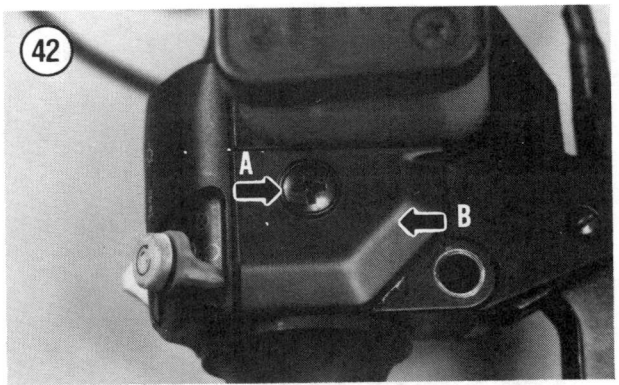

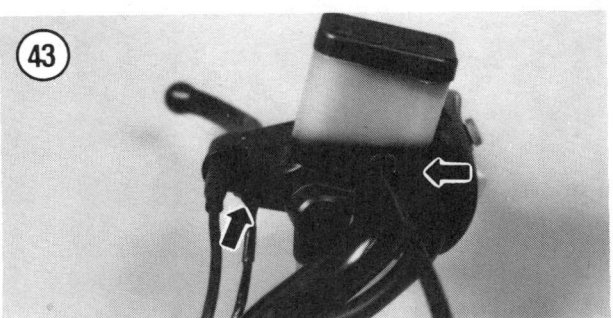

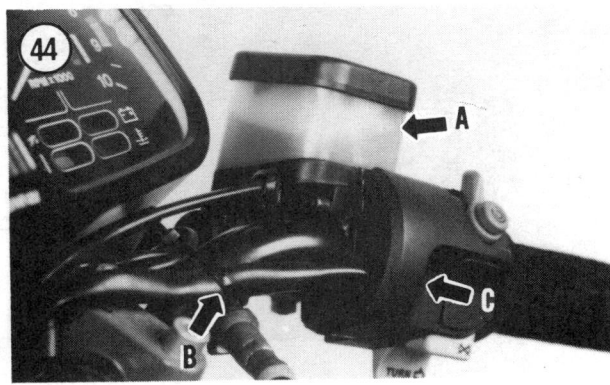

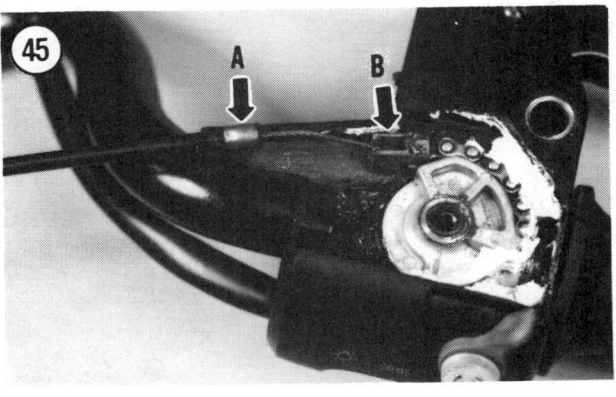

c. Remove the screws (**Figure 43**) securing the master cylinder. Carefully move the master cylinder (A, **Figure 44**) out of the way and lay it over the frame. Keep the reservoir in the upright position to minimize loss of brake fluid and to keep air from entering the brake system. It is not necessary to remove the hydraulic brake line.

d. Remove the throttle cable (A, **Figure 45**) from the locator within the right-hand switch housing and disconnect the cable from the chain end (B, **Figure 45**) on the throttle wheel.

e. Disconnect the throttle cable from the throttle housing.

8. Remove the tie wrap(s) (B, **Figure 44**) securing the electrical cables to the handlebar.

9. Remove the screw securing the right-hand switch assembly (C, **Figure 44**) and remove the switch assembly.

10. Disconnect the clutch cable as follows:

a. Loosen the locknut (A, **Figure 46**) and turn the adjuster (B, **Figure 46**) in all the way. This will allow slack in the clutch cable.

b. Disconnect the clutch cable and nipple (**Figure 47**) from the underside of the clutch lever. Remove the clutch cable (**Figure 48**).

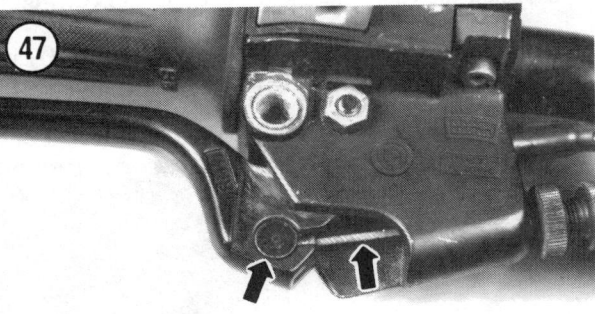

10

11. Disconnect the choke cable as follows:

    a. Carefully pry off the cover on the choke operating lever.

    b. Unscrew the large flat screw (**Figure 49**) and special washer (**Figure 50**).

    c. Remove the lever (A, **Figure 51**) from the housing and disconnect the cable (B, **Figure 51**) from the lever.

    d. Push the cable sleeve out and remove the cable from the slot (C, **Figure 51**) in the cable housing.

12. Apply compressed air to the left-hand hand grip (A, **Figure 52**) and blow it off of the handlebar. If the compressed air does not work, cut along the length of the grip with a knife and remove it from the handlebar.

13. Remove the tie wrap(s) (B, **Figure 52**) securing the electrical cables to the handlebar.

14. Loosen the bolt securing the left-hand switch assembly (C, **Figure 52**) and slide if off of the handlebar.

15. Loosen all Allen bolts securing the handlebar upper holders (**Figure 53**).

16. Remove the Allen bolts, lockwashers and handlebar upper holders, then remove the handlebar.

Installation

1. Position the handlebar onto the lower holder and install the upper holders, lockwashers and Allen bolts.

2. Align the index mark on the handlebar with the top surface of the handlebar lower holders (**Figure 54**).

3. Tighten the Allen bolts to the torque specification listed in **Table 1**. After the bolts are tightened, recheck the alignment of the handlebar index mark. Readjust if necessary.

4. Slide on the left-hand switch assembly (C, **Figure 52**) and tighten the bolt clamping bolt.

5. Install new tie wrap(s) (B, **Figure 52**) securing the electrical cables to the handlebar.

6. Apply a contact cement (Loctite No. 469 or equivalent) to the handlebar area for the left-hand grip. Install the left-hand grip (A, **Figure 52**) and move it into position.

7. Connect the choke cable as follows:

    a. Install the cable and sleeve into the slot (C, **Figure 51**) in the cable housing.

    b. Install the cable end into the lever (B, **Figure 51**) and install the lever onto the housing (A, **Figure 51**).

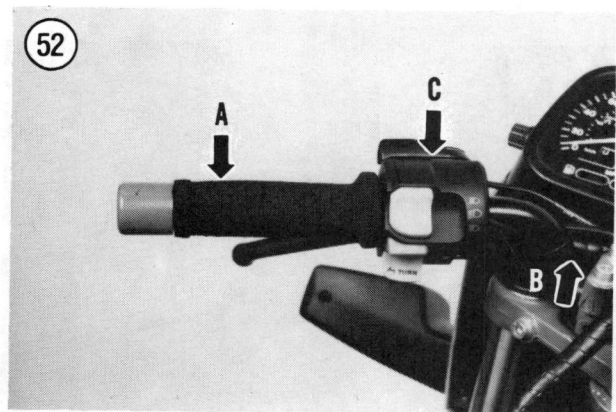

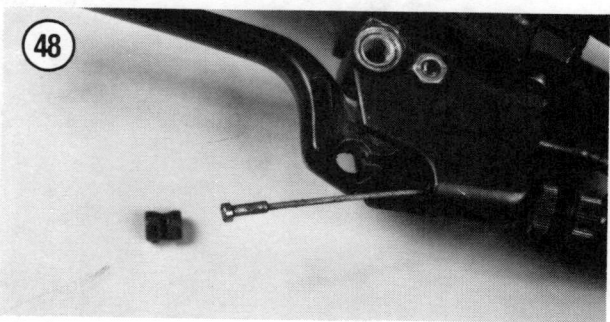

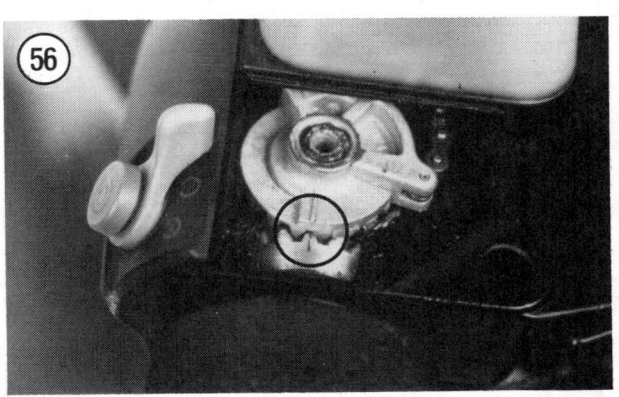

c. Install the special washer (**Figure 50**) and the large flat screw (**Figure 49**). Tighten the flat screw securely.

d. Install the cover onto the choke operating lever.

8. Connect the clutch cable and nipple (**Figure 47**) onto the underside of the clutch lever.

9. Install the right-hand switch assembly and tighten the screw securing the right-hand switch assembly (C, **Figure 44**).

10. Install the tie wrap(s) (B, **Figure 44**) securing the electrical cables to the handlebar.

11. Connect the throttle cable as follows:

a. Apply a light coat of multipurpose grease to the throttle grip area on the handlebar prior to installing the throttle grip assembly.

b. Install the throttle grip (**Figure 55**) onto the end of the handlebar. Align the index marks (**Figure 56**) on the throttle grip and the throttle wheel.

c. Install the throttle cable onto the throttle housing.

d. Install the throttle cable (A, **Figure 45**) and the locator in the right-hand switch housing and connect the cable into the chain end (B, **Figure 45**) of the throttle wheel.

e. Install the master cylinder and tighten the screws (**Figure 43**) securing the master cylinder.

f. Make sure the throttle cable is still attached to the chain end (**Figure 57**).

g. Install the throttle cover (B, **Figure 42**) and the screw (A, **Figure 42**) securing it. Tighten the screw securely.

WARNING
After installation is completed, make sure the brake lever does not come in contact with the throttle grip assembly when it is pulled on fully. If it does, the brake fluid may be low in the reservoir; refill as necessary. Refer to Chapter Twelve. Do not ride the bike until the problem has been corrected.

12. On models so equipped, screw the rear view mirrors (**Figure 41**) onto the handlebar switch assemblies.

13A. On models with no auxiliary switches, install the impact pad.

10

13B. On models equipped with auxiliary switches, perform the following:

   a. Connect the electrical wires going to the switches (**Figure 40**).

   b. Move the electrical wires back into position and secure with tie wrap(s) (**Figure 39**). Make sure the wires are not above the frame members as they may be damaged by the fuel tank when it is installed.

   c. Push the impact pad back into position and install the mounting screws (**Figure 37**). Tighten the screws securely.

14. Install the fuel tank as described under *Fuel Tank Removal/Installation* in Chapter Seven.

15. Connect the battery negative lead as described under *Battery* in Chapter Three.

16. Install the right-hand side cover.

STEERING HEAD AND STEM

Disassembly

Refer to **Figure 58** for this procedure.

1. Remove the front wheel as described in this chapter.

2. Remove the fuel tank as described under *Fuel Tank Removal/Installation* in Chapter Seven.

3. On models so equipped, remove the front fairing as described under *Front Fairing Removal/Installation* in Chapter Thirteen. Be sure to remove the fairing mounting bracket and headlight assemblies also.

4. Remove the instrument cluster as described under *Instrument Cluster Removal/Installation* in Chapter Eight.

5. Remove the front fork assemblies as described in this chapter.

6. Remove the union bolt and sealing washer (A, **Figure 59**) securing the master cylinder flexible brake hose to the brake pipe running through the center of the steering stem. Place the loose end of the brake hose in a resealable plastic bag. Zip the bag closed around the brake hose.

7. Remove the plastic nut (B, **Figure 59**) securing the brake pipe to the steering stem.

8. Withdraw the brake pipe down and out of the steering stem. Remove the brake pipe and lower flexible brake hose(s) as an assembly.

9. Remove the hex nut (C, **Figure 59**) securing the upper fork bridge to the steering stem.

10. Remove the upper fork bridge (D, **Figure 59**).

11. On models so equipped, remove the plastic nut (**Figure 60**) from the top of the steering stem.

NOTE
Some K75 models are fitted with a steering damper (Fluidbloc) within the steering head. If the bike is fitted with the steering damper

there will be 2 small bolt heads located on the steering head portion of the frame. The damper unit is rubber that is packed with a special silicone grease. Other types of grease will contaminate the damper unit and the special grease, therefore the steering stem must be free of all grease during removal and installation.

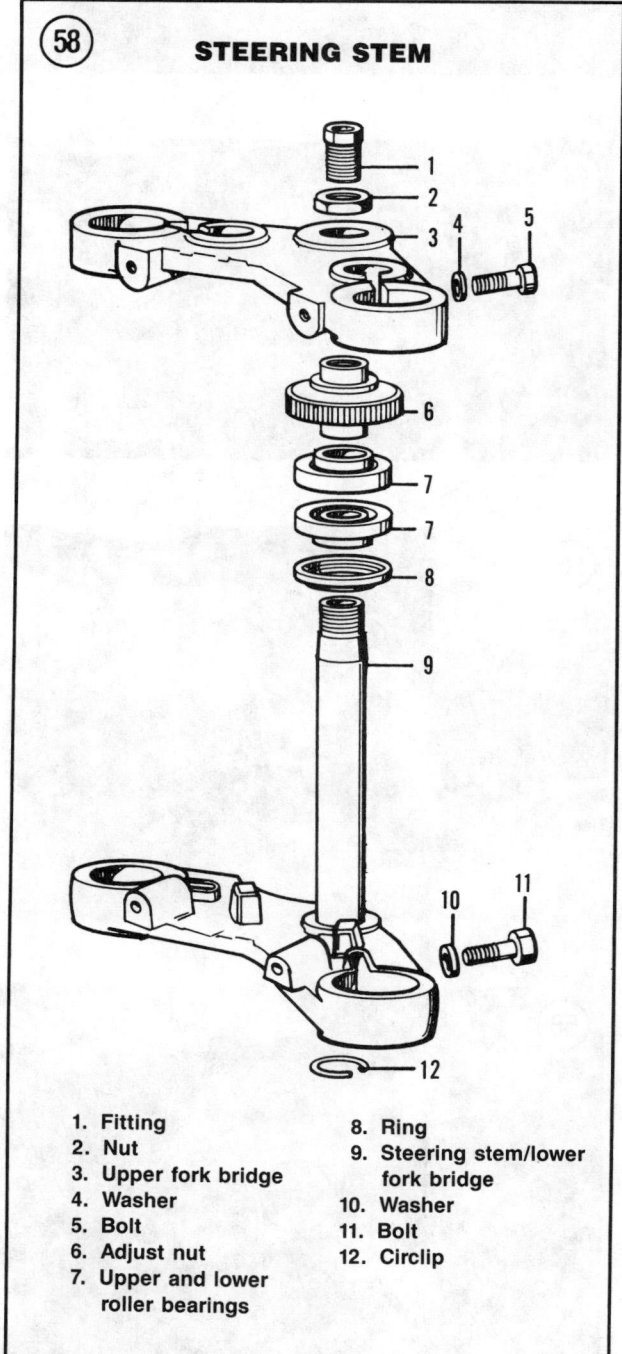

58 STEERING STEM

1. Fitting
2. Nut
3. Upper fork bridge
4. Washer
5. Bolt
6. Adjust nut
7. Upper and lower roller bearings
8. Ring
9. Steering stem/lower fork bridge
10. Washer
11. Bolt
12. Circlip

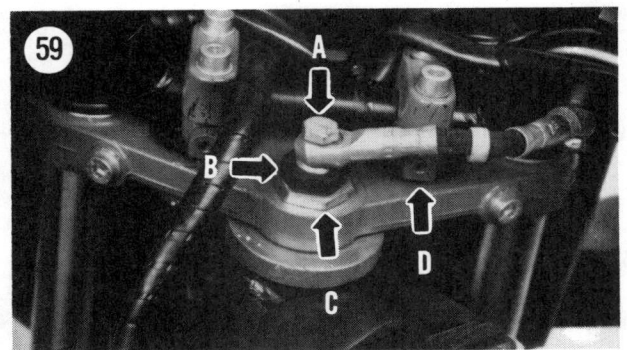

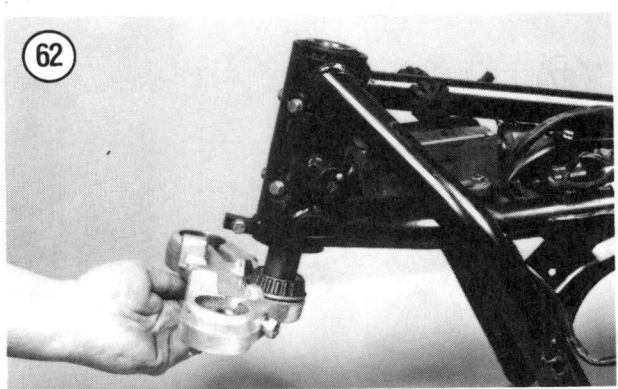

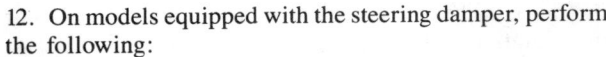

12. On models equipped with the steering damper, perform the following:

   a. Wipe the exposed portion of the steering stem clean of all grease or foreign matter.

   b. Use a smooth tape (e.g. 3M Magic Mending Tape, black electrical tape or equivalent) and wrap the threads of the steering stem with 1-2 layers. This will avoid damage to the steering damper as the steering stem passes through it.

13. Remove the steering stem adjust nut (**Figure 61**).

14. Have an assistant hold onto the steering stem and, using a soft-faced mallet or plastic hammer, carefully tap the steering stem down (**Figure 62**) and out of the steering stem bearings. Don't worry about catching any loose steel balls as the steering stem is equipped with assembled roller bearings.

15. Remove the upper roller bearing (**Figure 63**) from the steering head.

Inspection

1. Clean the bearing races in the steering head and the bearings with solvent and wipe dry.

2. Check the welds (**Figure 64**) around the steering head for cracks and fractures. If any are found, have them repaired by a competent frame shop or welding service.

10

3. Check the bearings (**Figure 65**) for pitting, scratches or discoloration indicating wear or corrosion. Replace as necessary.
4. Check the races (**Figure 66**) for pitting, galling and corrosion. If any of these conditions exist, replace the races as described in this chapter.

CAUTION
If the steering stem must be replaced on a K75 model equipped with the steering damper unit, use only the specified steering stem. Install steering stem BMW part No. 31 42 1 475 220. This steering stem part number has the correct outer diameter tolerance to work effectively with the steering damper unit.

5. Check the steering stem (**Figure 67**) for cracks, damage or wear. Replace if necessary.
6. Thread the steering stem adjust nut onto the steering stem. Make sure it screws on easily with no roughness. Unscrew the steering stem adjust nut. If necessary, clean the threads on the steering stem (**Figure 68**) and the adjust nut (**Figure 69**) with a wire brush or tap and die of the correct thread type and size.

Steering Damper Unit
(K75 Models)
Removal/Installation

The steering damper (Fluidbloc) is a firm rubber donut with receptacles that hold the special silicone grease. This rubber donut is secured to the frame's steering head and rides against the steering stem. It provides friction to damp any steering and fork action over 1° of movement.

The steering damper is installed on some K75 models. The damper can be installed on any K75 that is not presently equipped with one. The damper *cannot* be installed on K100 models since the damper unit will only work in conjunction with a steering stem having an outer diameter of a specific dimension. This specific dimension is controlled on K75 models but is *not* controlled on K100 models.

1. Remove the steering stem as described in this chapter.
2. Remove the steering stem upper bearing outer race as described in this chapter.
3. Remove the bolts securing the damper unit to the frame steering head.
4. From the bottom, carefully tap the damper unit out from the steering head. Use a hardwood dowel and hammer.

CAUTION
Use only the specified silicone grease that has the specific properties to provide the required friction between the damper unit and the steering stem.

5A. If reinstalling the existing damper unit, it must be repacked with silicone grease. Perform the following:
 a. Use only "Heavy Duty Silicone Grease" (BMW part No. 07 58 9 058 193). Other types of grease, even other types of silicone grease, will not provide the correct friction values designed into the system.
 b. Pack the inner receptacles of the damper unit with the specified silicone grease. All receptacles *must* be completely filled.

NOTE
A new steering damper comes from the factory properly packed with the specified silicone grease and does not have to be repacked.

5B. If installing a new damper unit, perform the following:
   a. An installation alignment line must be made on the side of the damper unit. This line must align with the existing bolt holes in the frame's steering head.
   b. Measure down 7 mm (0.28 in.) from the top surface of the larger diameter portion of the damper unit (**Figure 70**).
   c. Run a line around the circumference of the damper with a fine point permanent marking pen. Make sure this line is visible as it must be visible through the bolt holes in the steering stem.

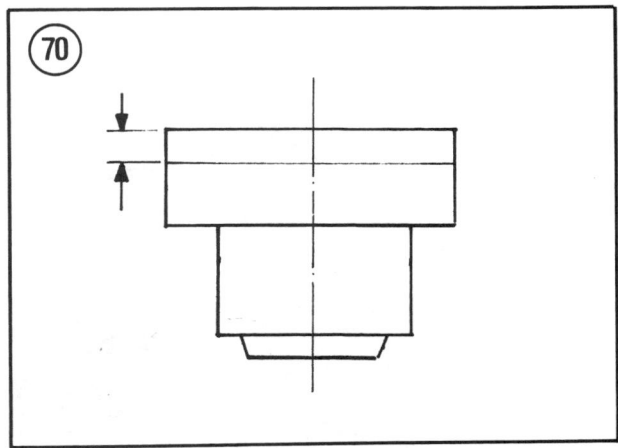

NOTE
If reinstalling the existing steering damper unit, align the bolt hole depressions in the damper unit with the bolt holes in the frame steering head.

6. Install the damper unit into the top of the steering head.

CAUTION
Do not substitute a different type of bolt in Step 7. This bolt has a pointed end that penetrates into the damper unit and secures it in place. A bolt with the normal flat end will not work for this purpose.

7A. If installing the existing damper unit, perform the following:
   a. Using a wood dowel and hammer, carefully tap the damper unit down until the existing bolt hole depressions align with the bolt holes in the steering head.
   b. Install the tapered bolts and tighten to the torque specification listed in **Table 1**.
7B. If installing a new damper unit, perform the following:
   a. Using a wood dowel and hammer, carefully tap the damper unit down until the alignment line made in Step 5B aligns with the bolt holes in the steering head.
   b. Install the tapered bolts and tighten to the torque specification listed in **Table 1**.
8. Install the steering stem upper bearing outer race as described in this chapter.
9. Install the steering stem as described in this chapter.

10

Assembly

Refer to **Figure 58** for this procedure.
1. Make sure both steering head bearing outer races are properly seated in the steering head tube.
2. Pack the bearing cavities of the lower roller bearings with bearing grease. Coat the outer bearing races, within the steering head, with bearing grease also.
3. Pack the upper bearing with bearing grease and install it in the steering head (**Figure 63**).
4. On models equipped with the steering damper, perform the following:
   a. Wipe the entire length of the steering stem clean of all grease or foreign matter.
   b. If not already wrapped, use a smooth tape (e.g. 3M Magic Mending Tape, black electrical tape or equivalent) and wrap the threads of the steering stem with 1-2 layers. This will avoid damage to the steering damper as the steering stem passes through it.
5. Install the steering stem (**Figure 62**), with the lower bearing in place, into the steering head and hold it firmly in place. If necessary, using a soft-faced mallet or plastic hammer, carefully tap the steering stem up and into the steering stem bearings.

6. On models equipped with the steering damper, remove the tape from the threads of the steering stem.

7. Apply a coat of grease to the threads of the steering stem and steering stem adjust nut.

8. Install the steering stem adjust nut (**Figure 61**). Tighten the adjust nut firmly by hand to preload the bearings, then loosen the adjust nut until the bearing free play is all but eliminated.

9. On models so equipped, install the plastic nut (**Figure 60**) onto the top of the steering stem.

10. Install the upper fork bridge (D, **Figure 59**).

11. Install the hex nut (C, **Figure 59**) securing the upper fork bridge to the steering stem. Do not tighten the nut at this time.

12. Install the brake pipe up and into the steering stem. Align the tab on the lower end of the brake pipe with the locating notch in the steering head.

13. Install the nut (B, **Figure 59**) securing the brake pipe to the steering stem. Do not tighten the nut at this time.

14. Install a new sealing washer and install the union bolt (A, **Figure 59**) securing the master cylinder flexible brake hose to the steering stem brake pipe. Tighten the union bolt to the torque specification listed in **Table 1**.

15. Install the front fork assemblies as described in this chapter.

16. Tighten the hex nut (C, **Figure 59**) securing the upper fork bridge to the steering stem to the torque specification listed in **Table 1**.

17. Securely tighten the nut securing the brake pipe to the steering stem.

18. Install the instrument cluster as described under *Instrument Cluster Removal/Installation* in Chapter Eight.

19. On models so equipped, install the front fairing as described under *Front Fairing Removal/Installation* in Chapter Thirteen. Be sure to remove the fairing mounting bracket and headlight assemblies also.

20. Install the fuel tank as described under *Fuel Tank Removal/Installation* in Chapter Seven.

21. Reconnect the battery negative lead as described under *Battery* in Chapter Three.

22. Install the front wheel as described in this chapter.

Steering Stem Adjustment

If play develops or there is binding in the steering system, it may only require adjustment. However, don't take a chance on it. Disassemble the steering stem assembly and look for possible damage as described in this chapter.

STEERING HEAD BEARING RACE

The headset and steering stem bearing races are pressed into place. Because they are easily bent, do not remove them unless they are worn and require replacement. The top and bottom bearings and bearing races are identical, both having the same BMW part number.

Steering Head Bearing Outer Race Replacement

1. To remove the headset race, insert a hardwood stick or soft punch into the head tube (**Figure 71**) and carefully tap the race out from the inside. After it is started, tap around the race so that neither the race nor the steering head tube is damaged. Repeat for the other bearing race if necessary.

2. Thoroughly clean out the steering head of all old grease.

3. To install the upper bearing race, perform the following:

    a. Place the upper bearing race in a freezer for 30 minutes. This will reduce the overall size of the race for easier installation.

    b. Tap it in slowly with a block of wood (**Figure 72**), a suitable size socket or piece of pipe.

    c. Make sure that the race is squarely seated in the steering head race bore before tapping it into place.

d. Tap the race in until it is flush with the steering head surface and make sure it has bottomed out.

NOTE
On K75 models equipped with the steering damper, if the steering damper was removed, be sure to install the damper after one of the bearing races is installed. The damper cannot be installed after both of the races have been installed.

4. To install the lower bearing race, perform the following:
   a. Place the upper bearing race in a freezer for 30 minutes. This will reduce the overall size of the race for easier installation.
   b. Tap it in slowly with a block of wood, a suitable size socket or piece of pipe.
   c. Make sure that the race is squarely seated in the steering head race bore before tapping it into place.
   d. Tap the race in until it is flush with the steering head surface and make sure it has bottomed out.

Steering Stem Lower Bearing Assembly Removal/Installation

NOTE
*Do **not** remove the steering stem lower bearing unless it is going to be replaced with a new bearing. Do **not** reinstall a bearing that has been removed as it is no longer true to alignment.*

In order to remove the lower bearing, the steering stem must be pressed out of the lower fork bridge with a press.
1. Before removing the steering stem, make a mark (A, **Figure 73**) on the lower fork bridge in alignment with the

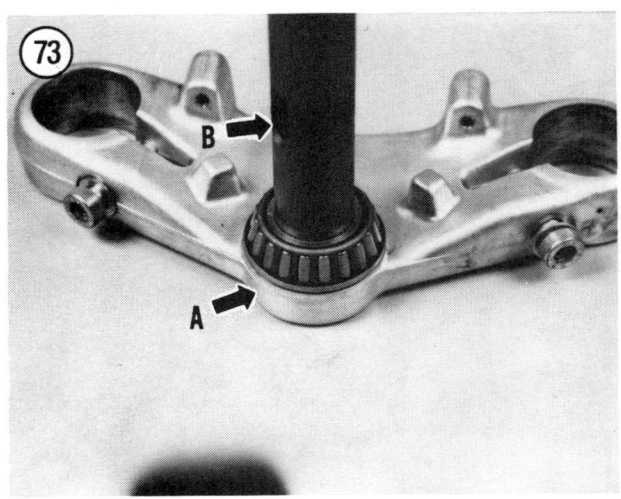

steering lock receptacle (B, **Figure 73**) in the steering stem. These 2 parts must align after assembly.
2. Heat the steering stem assembly to 120-130° C (250-265° F).

WARNING
Use insulated gloves or thick pot holders to hold onto the steering stem after it has been heated.

NOTE
It is not necessary to completely remove the steering stem from the lower fork bridge unless either part is going to be replaced.

3. Place the steering stem in a hydraulic press and press the steering stem partially out of the lower fork bridge until the bearing assembly can be removed from the steering stem.
4. Remove the bearing assembly and the dust seal on models so equipped.
5. While the steering stem is still hot, turn the assembly over in the press and using a 30 mm (1.2 in.) drift, press the steering stem back into the lower fork bridge. Check the alignment marks made in Step 1 during the installation procedure. These marks must align in order for the steering lock to operate properly.
6. Press the steering stem into the lower fork bridge until the circlip on the steering stem bottoms out on the lower surface of the lower fork bridge.
7. Heat the new lower roller bearing to 80° C (176° F) for easy installation.
8. On models so equipped, slide a new dust seal over the steering stem.
9. Install the new roller bearing onto the steering stem.
10. Use a long piece of pipe that matches the inner race diameter and tap the bearing down the steering stem and into place. Make sure it is seated squarely and is all the way down.
11. After the lower bearing has cooled down, pack it with bearing grease.

FRONT FORK

The front suspension uses a spring controlled, hydraulically damped, telescopic fork. Before suspecting major trouble, drain the front fork oil and refill with the proper type and quantity; refer to *Front Fork Oil Change* in Chapter Three. If you still have trouble such as poor damping, a tendency to bottom or top out or leakage around the rubber oil seals, follow the service procedures in this section.

To simplify fork service and to prevent the mixing of parts, the legs should be removed, serviced and installed individually.

10

Optional Air Scoops
(K100RS ABS Models)

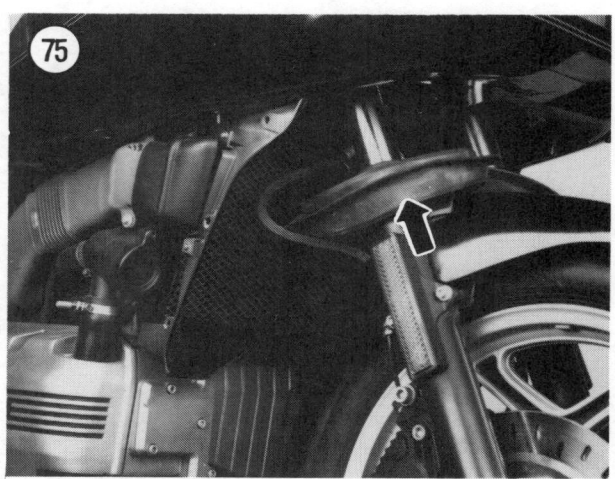

BMW offers an optional air scoop set that fits onto the fork legs where they enter the lower portion of the front fairing. These air scoops bring in additional fresh air during hot weather riding. The air scoop part numbers are as follows: part No. 31 42 1 455 333 and part No. 31 42 1 455 334.

The air scoops take the place of the large rubber boots that attach to the front fairing and wrap around the fork tubes.

1. Remove the screws securing the rubber boots (**Figure 74**) and slide the boots down the fork tubes (**Figure 75**).

CAUTION
In the next step, cut the rubber boots carefully as they can be reinstalled for cooler weather riding.

2. Carefully cut the rubber boot on the inner surface where the boots face each other as follows:
   a. Using side cutting pliers or metal shears, cut the metal armature that runs around the outer perimeter of the rubber boot.
   b. Using a sharp razor blade, carefully cut the rubber boot in a straight line (**Figure 76**) from the metal armature up to where the boot contacts the fork tube.
3. Carefully remove the rubber boots from the fork sliders. Place the rubber boots and their attachment screws in a resealable plastic bag and store them for use during cooler weather.
4. Install the air scoop and screws. Tighten the screws securely.
5. To reinstall the rubber boots, perform the following:
   a. Remove the air scoops and place them and their attachment screws in a resealable plastic bag and store them.
   b. Reinstall the rubber boots onto the fork tube.

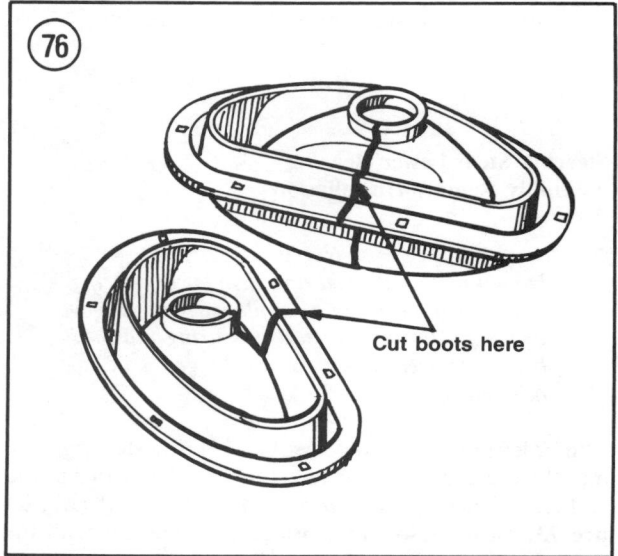

Cut boots here

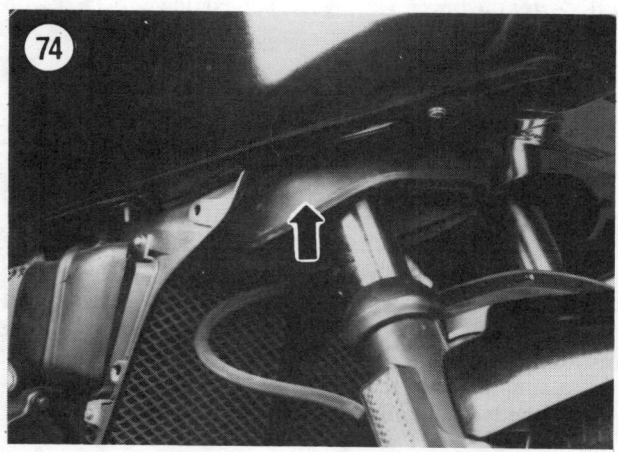

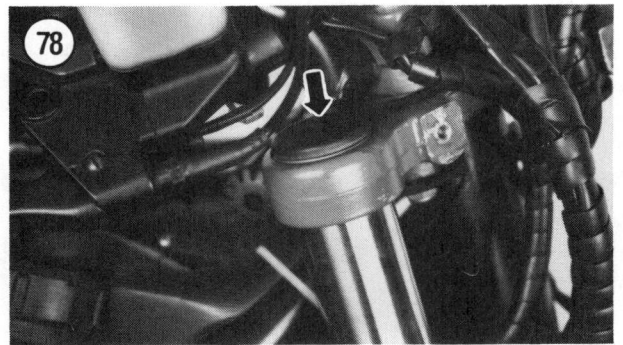

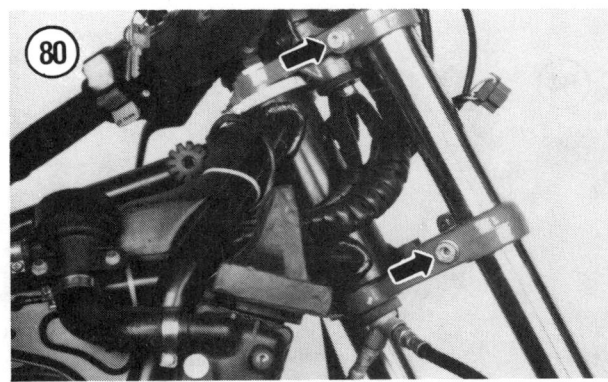

c. Secure the inner portion of the rubber boot to the fork tube with a plastic tie wrap.

d. Slide the fork boot up and onto the front fairing. Install and tighten the screws securely.

Removal

1. Remove the fuel tank as described under *Fuel Tank Removal/Installation* in Chapter Seven.

2A. On models equipped with a full front fairing, remove the inner sections of the fairing (e.g. knee pads) in order to gain access to the lower fork bridge clamping bolts. Refer to *Front Fairing Removal/Installation* in Chapter Thirteen.

2B. On K75 C models, remove the front fairing as described under *Front Fairing Removal/Installation* in Chapter Thirteen.

3. Remove the front wheel as described in this chapter.

> *NOTE*
> *On models with a 2-piece front fender be sure to remove the fork brace (**Figure 77**) that bridges both fork legs.*

4. Remove the front fender as described under *Front Fender Removal/Installation* in Chapter Thirteen.

5. Carefully pry off the top trim cap (**Figure 78**).

6. Remove the bolt (**Figure 79**) securing the brake line to the fork slider. Tie the brake calipers up with a Bungee cord to take the strain off of the flexible brake hose.

7. Loosen the upper and lower (**Figure 80**) fork bridge clamp bolts.

8. Lower the fork assembly (**Figure 81**) down and out of the upper and lower fork bridge. It may be necessary to slightly rotate the fork tube while pulling it down and out.

Installation

1. Clean off any corrosion or dirt on the upper and lower fork bridge fork receptacles.

> *NOTE*
> *The fork assemblies must be reinstalled on the correct side of the bike so the brake calipers and front fender can be installed. If the fork assemblies are installed on the wrong side these components cannot be installed onto the fork sliders.*

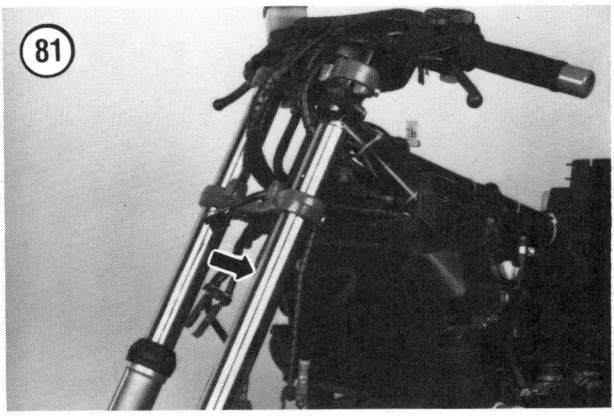

2. Install the right-hand fork assembly so that the front fender mounting boss is positioned as shown in **Figure 82**. The left-hand is just the opposite.

10

3. Install the fork tube up through the lower and upper fork bridges (**Figure 83**).

4. Push the fork tube up until the top surface is 180 mm (7.087 in.) above the top surface of the upper fork bridge (**Figure 84**). In this position, the top surface of the fork tube is almost even with the top surface of the upper fork bridge.

5. Tighten the upper and lower fork bridge bolts to the torque specification listed in **Table 1**.

6. Install the top trim cap.

7. Install the brake line to the fork slider and tighten the bolt securely.

8. Install the front fender as described under *Front Fender Removal/Installation* in Chapter Thirteen.

9. Install the front wheel as described in this chapter.

10. Apply the front brake and pump the front forks several times to seat the forks and front wheel.

11. On models so equipped, install and tighten the fork brace bolts to the torque specification listed in **Table 1**.

12A. On models equipped with a full front fairing, install the inner sections of the fairing (e.g. knee pads). Refer to *Front Fairing Removal/Installation* in Chapter Thirteen.

12B. On K75 C models, install the front fairing as described under *Front Fairing Removal/Installation* in Chapter Thirteen.

13. Install the fuel tank as described under *Fuel Tank Removal/Installation* in Chapter Seven.

Disassembly

To simplify fork service and to prevent the mixing of parts, the legs should be disassembled and assembled individually. Some models have some different internal components in the right-hand fork assembly than those installed in the left-hand fork assembly.

Refer to **Figure 85** for this procedure.

1. Using the front brake caliper mounting bosses, clamp the slider in a vise with soft jaws.

2. Loosen the Allen screw (**Figure 86**) on the bottom of the slider. Remove the fork slider from the vise.

3. If not already removed, remove the plastic trim cap (**Figure 87**) from the fork tube.

NOTE
This Allen screw has been secured with a locking compound and is often very difficult to remove because the damper rod will turn inside the slider. It sometimes can be removed with an air impact driver. If you are unable to remove it, take the fork tubes to a dealer and have the screws removed.

4. Hold onto the fork top cap (A, **Figure 88**) with an open end wrench and remove the oil fill plug (B, **Figure 88**).

5. Pour the fork oil out and discard it. Pump the fork several times by hand to expel most of the remaining oil.

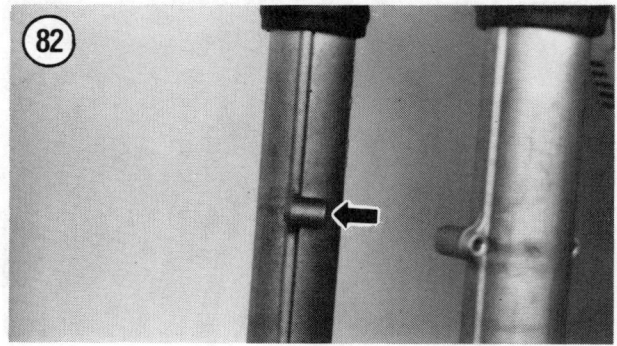

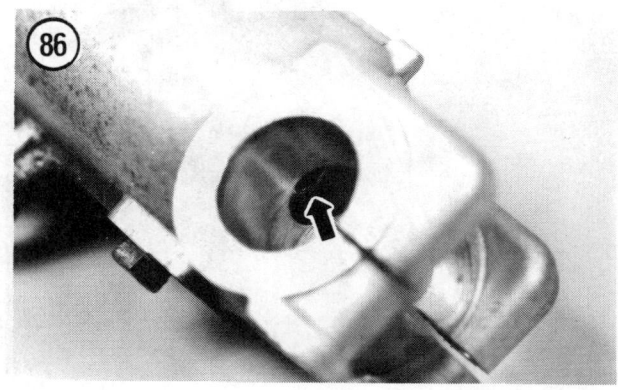

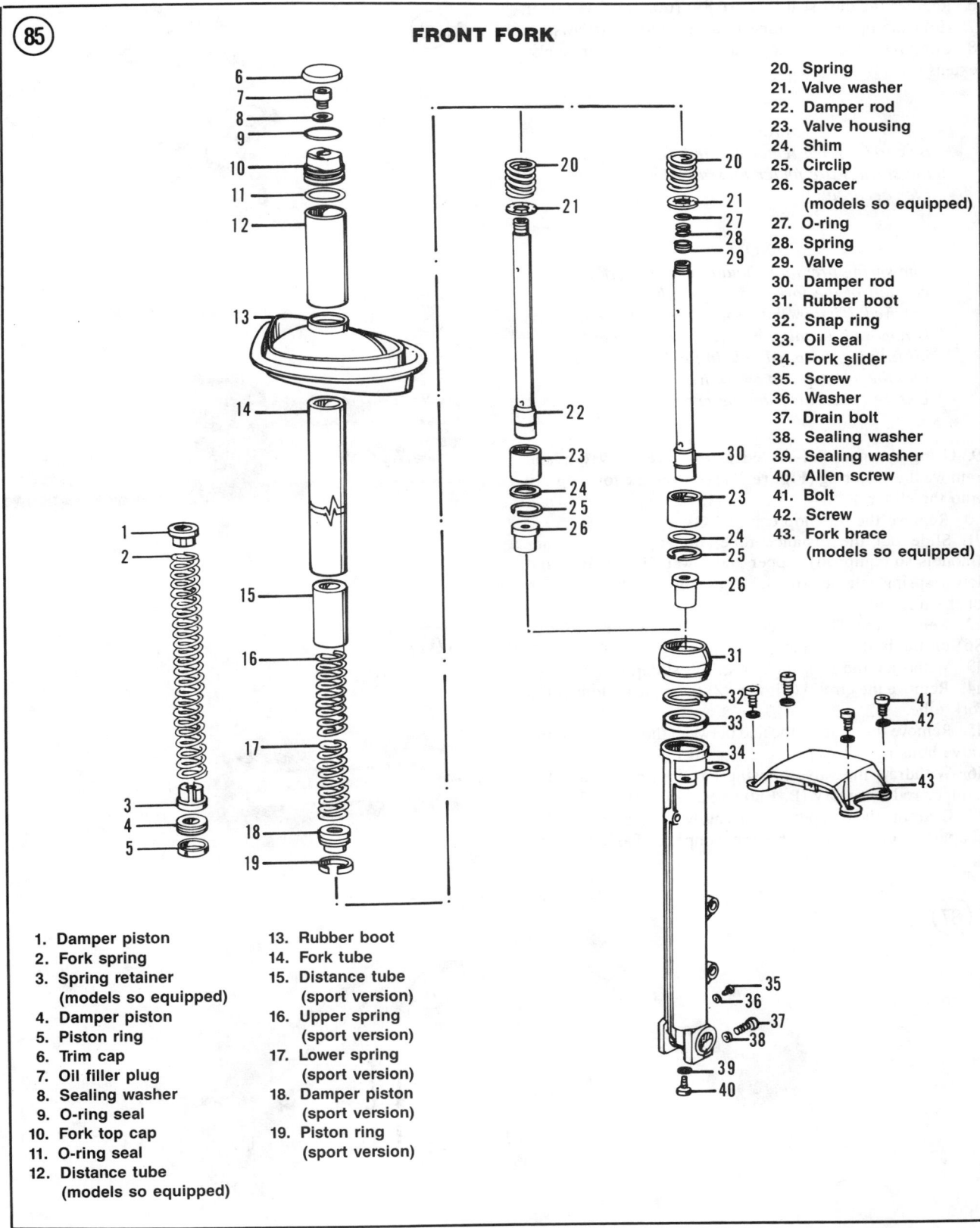

85 **FRONT FORK**

20. Spring
21. Valve washer
22. Damper rod
23. Valve housing
24. Shim
25. Circlip
26. Spacer
   (models so equipped)
27. O-ring
28. Spring
29. Valve
30. Damper rod
31. Rubber boot
32. Snap ring
33. Oil seal
34. Fork slider
35. Screw
36. Washer
37. Drain bolt
38. Sealing washer
39. Sealing washer
40. Allen screw
41. Bolt
42. Screw
43. Fork brace
   (models so equipped)

10

1. Damper piston
2. Fork spring
3. Spring retainer
   (models so equipped)
4. Damper piston
5. Piston ring
6. Trim cap
7. Oil filler plug
8. Sealing washer
9. O-ring seal
10. Fork top cap
11. O-ring seal
12. Distance tube
   (models so equipped)
13. Rubber boot
14. Fork tube
15. Distance tube
   (sport version)
16. Upper spring
   (sport version)
17. Lower spring
   (sport version)
18. Damper piston
   (sport version)
19. Piston ring
   (sport version)

6. Remove the dust seal (**Figure 89**) from the fork slider.

7. Hold the upper fork tube in a vise with soft jaws.

8. Compress the fork top cap with a drift or socket extension.

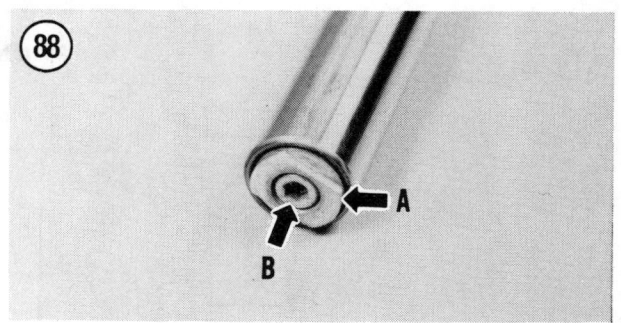

> *WARNING*
> *Be careful when removing the fork top cap as the springs are under pressure. Protect your eyes accordingly.*

> *NOTE*
> *The spring pressure should push the fork top cap out of the fork slider after the circlip is removed. If it does not come out after the circlip is removed, install a bolt (Figure 90) into the oil fill plug threaded hole in the fork top cap. Pull the fork top cap out with a pair of pliers. Unscrew the bolt from the cap.*

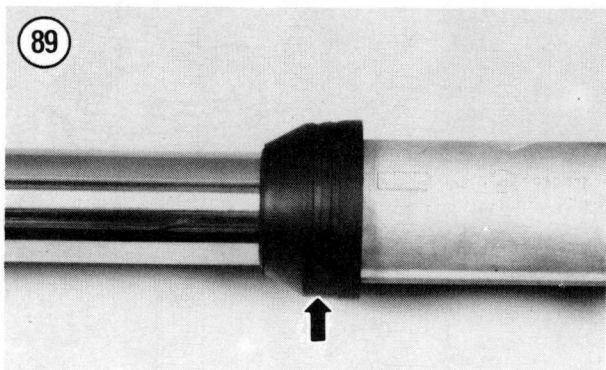

9. Using a small flat-bladed screwdriver, pry out and remove the snap ring (**Figure 91**) securing the fork top cap into the slider.

10. Remove the fork top cap and O-ring.

11. Slide out the distance tube, upper spring retainer (models so equipped), upper and lower fork springs and lower spring retainer (models so equipped) from the top of the fork tube.

12. Remove the Allen screw and sealing washer (**Figure 86**) on the bottom of the slider.

13. Withdraw the fork tube from the slider.

14. Remove the circlip (**Figure 92**) from the bottom of the fork tube.

15. Remove the shim(s) located between the circlip and the valve housing.

16. Withdraw the valve housing (A, **Figure 93**) and the damper rod assembly (B, **Figure 93**) from the fork tube.

17. Examine the damper rod assembly as described in this chapter. Do not disassemble the damper rod assembly for

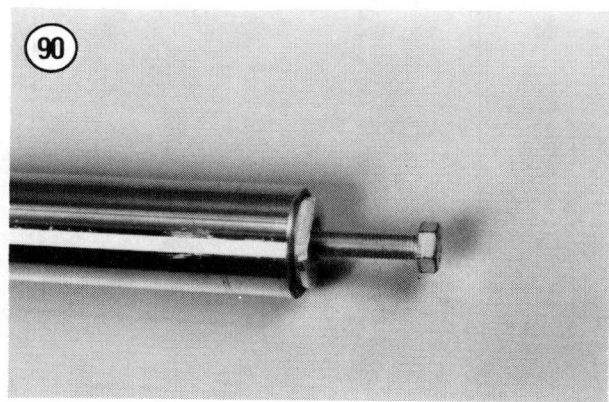

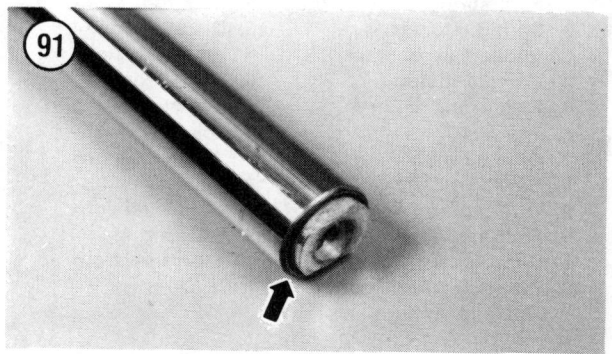

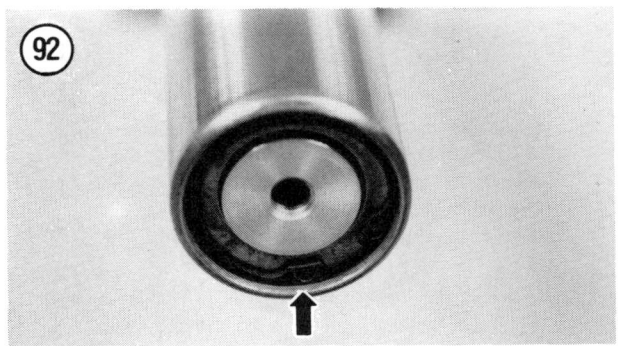

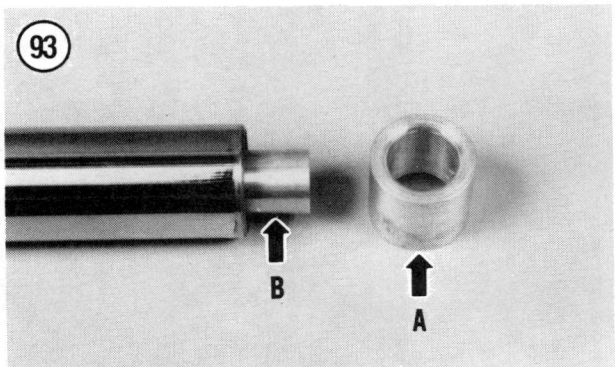

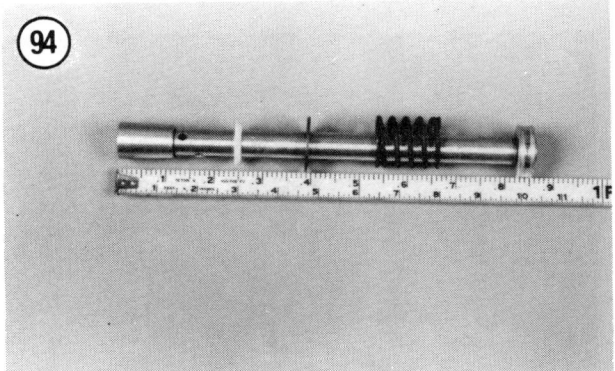

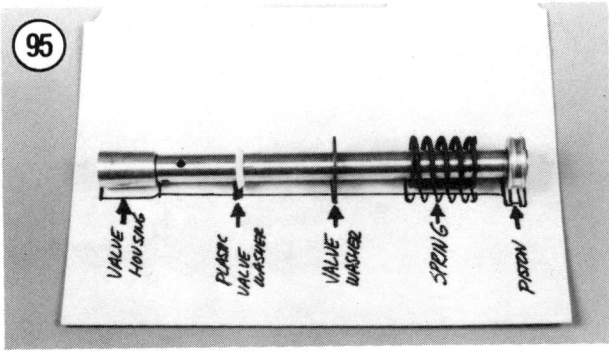

inspection purposes. If one of the components is faulty, disassemble it as follows:

a. Thoroughly clean the assembly in solvent and dry with compressed air.

b. Wash the assembly in soap and hot water to remove all traces of cleaning solvent and fork oil.

WARNING
Make sure all traces of solvent are removed from the damper rod assembly. The damper rod is going to be heated and must be thoroughly free of all solvent residue to avoid a fire hazard.

c. Measure the overall length of the damper rod assembly (**Figure 94**) and write it down. The specified length is listed in **Table 3**.

d. Lay the damper rod on a piece of paper or cardboard and make an outline around each part and identify each part so that they will be reinstalled in the same location (**Figure 95**).

NOTE
The damper piston has been secured to the damper rod with a locking compound and is very difficult to remove without first heating the damper piston.

e. Place the damper rod in a vise with soft jaws so the damper piston is sticking out to one side.

f. Using a propane torch, heat the damper piston (**Figure 96**) until the Loctite starts to burn (approximate temperature of 250° C/482° F).

g. Using a pair of pliers, unscrew the damper piston from the end of the damper rod.

h. Remove the components from the damper rod.

10

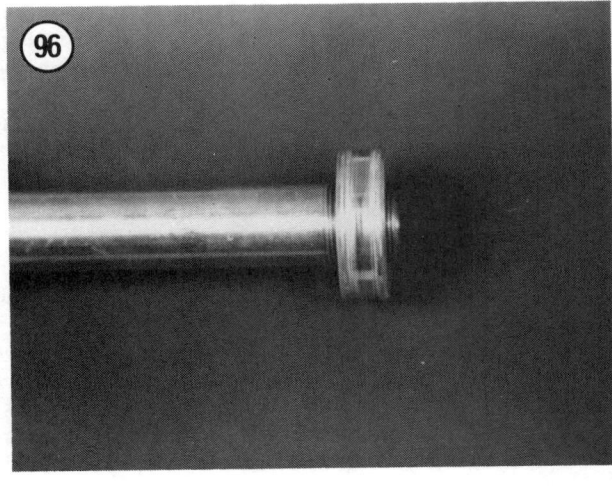

18. Using a broad-tipped screwdriver, carefully pry the oil seal (**Figure 97**) out of the fork slider. Protect the edge of the fork slider with a piece of wood or plastic to keep the screwdriver from making contact with the slider while prying out the oil seal.

19. On K75 S models, remove the spacer from the slider.

20. Inspect all parts as described in this chapter.

Assembly

Refer to **Figure 85** for this procedure.

1. On K75 S models, install the spacer into the slider.

2. Apply fork oil to the inner surface of the fork slider and to the outer surface of the oil seal.

> *CAUTION*
> *Do **not** install the oil seal into the fork slider any farther than specified as the seal will be distorted resulting in an oil leak.*

3. Using a hammer and a socket that matches the outer diameter of the fork oil seal, carefully tap the oil seal squarely into the fork slider. Tap it in until it is flush with the top surface of the slider.

4. Install the dust seal (**Figure 97**) into the fork slider.

5. If the damper rod assembly was disassembled, assemble it as follows:

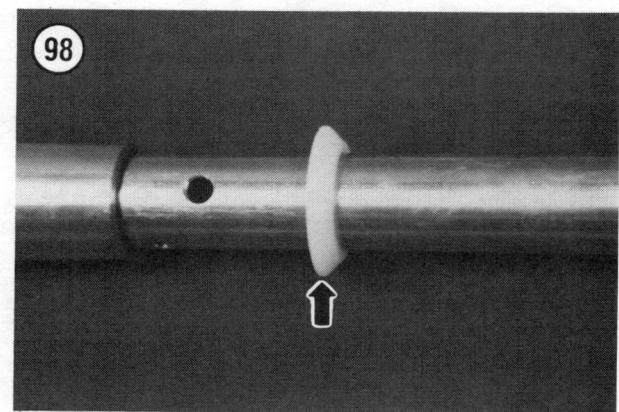

> *NOTE*
> *If an outline was made of the damper rod assembly, lay it down and refer to it during the assembly procedure.*

a. On K75 C models, slide the valve with the O-ring end going on first, then install the spring, O-ring seal and compression spring onto the damper rod.

b. On all other models, install the plastic valve washer (**Figure 98**) (chamfer side on last), valve washer (**Figure 99**) and compression spring (**Figure 100**) onto the damper rod.

c. Apply one drop of Loctite Threadlocker No. 638 or No. 273 to the threads on the end of the damper rod and install the damper piston (**Figure 96**).

d. Screw the damper piston onto the damper rod until the overall length is the same as noted in *Disassembly* (Step 17, substep c). This dimension must be exact in order to maintain maximum fork performance. The specified length is also listed in **Table 3**.

e. Apply heat to the damper piston with a heat gun *or* allow the Loctite on the piston assembly threads to cure at room temperature for a minimum of 24 hours. Do not allow fork oil to come in contact with the piston assembly until the Loctite is completely cured.

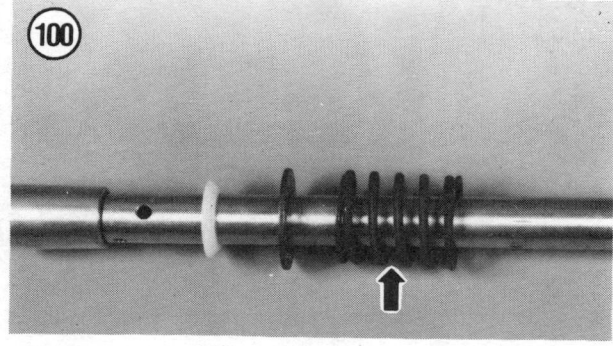

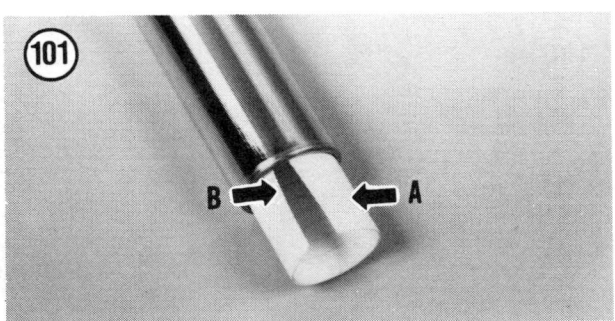

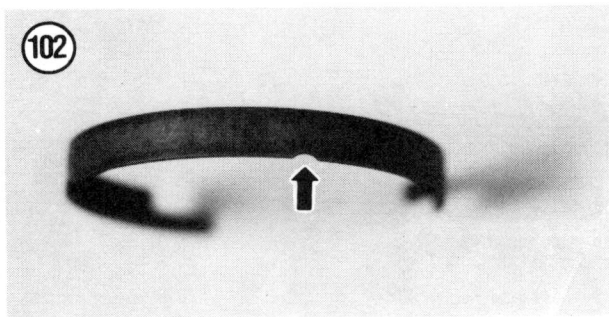

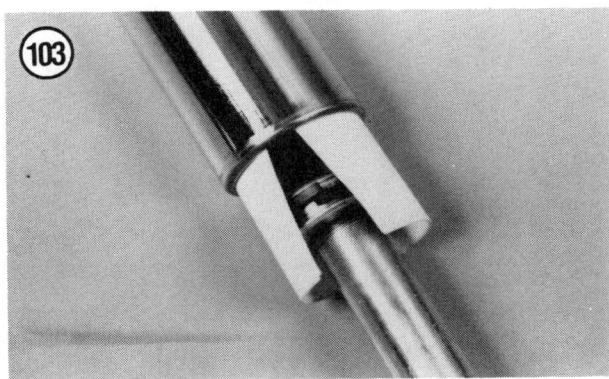

NOTE
There is a shoulder on the inner surface of the lower end of the fork slider. The valve housing bottoms out on this shoulder when it is installed later in this procedure. A shim material must be temporarily installed into the lower end of the fork slider to fill in the lower area, thus eliminating the shoulder. Don't try to install the damper rod assembly without adding this shim material as the piston ring will snag on the shoulder and "pop off" during installation.

6. Install the damper rod assembly as follows:
   a. Cut three 3 × 5 index cards so they are only 4 inches long. The thickness of the 3 cards is sufficient to fill in the area, thus eliminating the fork slider shoulder.
   b. Wrap the long side of the 3 × 4 cards around the exterior of the fork slider so that they take on the natural curve of the slider. Continue to contour the cards so that they have a natural curve that follows the fork slider.
   c. Insert the three 3 × 4 cards into the fork slider (A, **Figure 101**). The cards were trimmed down from 5 inches to 4 inches so there will be a gap (B, **Figure 101**) that will allow you to see the piston ring in the next step.
   d. Apply some fork oil to the piston ring, then position the piston ring onto the damper piston with its notched end facing down (**Figure 102**). Install the piston ring onto the damper piston.
   e. Hold the piston ring onto the damper piston and partially insert the damper rod into the 3 × 4 cards in the fork slider (**Figure 103**). The piston ring ends must be visible so position the ring ends facing upward the gap in the cards.
   f. Make sure the piston ring ends are meshed properly and that the piston ring is correctly seated in the damper piston groove (**Figure 104**).
   g. Slowly push the damper rod assembly into the fork slider and past the shoulder (**Figure 105**). You will

10

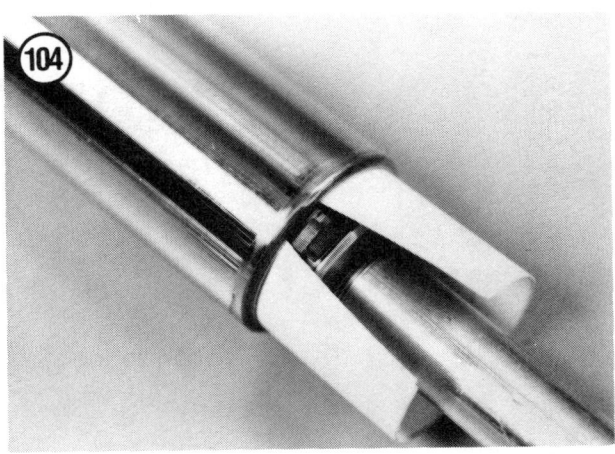

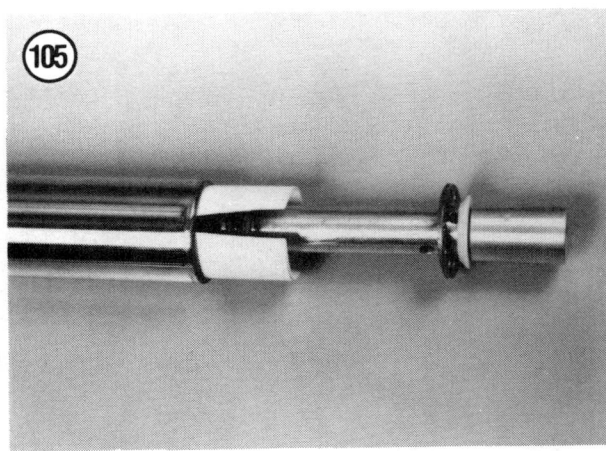

feel a slight hesitation when the piston ring slides past the 3 × 4 cards and into the fork slider. Once you have passed the shoulder, move the damper rod assembly farther in, then carefully move it in and out to make sure the piston ring stayed in place within the piston groove.

h. Hold onto the damper rod assembly and the fork slider and turn this assembly up to a vertical position with the damper rod end facing down. If the piston ring did not stay in the piston groove it will slide down the damper rod assembly. If this has happened, repeat this procedure until the damper rod is installed correctly with the piston ring in place in the piston groove.

i. Hold the damper rod in place and remove the 3 × 4 cards from the fork slider.

NOTE
In the following step, do not allow the damper rod assembly to come out far enough so that the piston ring travels past the fork slider shoulder or you will have to start all over again.

j. Move the damper rod in and out (**Figure 106**) to make sure the piston ring is properly seated within the piston groove.

7. Push the damper rod assembly the rest of the way into the fork slider (**Figure 107**).

8. Position the valve housing with the recessed end (**Figure 108**) going on first.

9. Install the valve housing (**Figure 109**) onto the end of the damper rod assembly, then push the assembly into the fork tube until it stops.

10. Install the same number of shims (A, **Figure 110**) that were located between the circlip and the valve housing noted during disassembly.

NOTE
If the damper rod assembly was disassembled and reassembled, the overall length may be

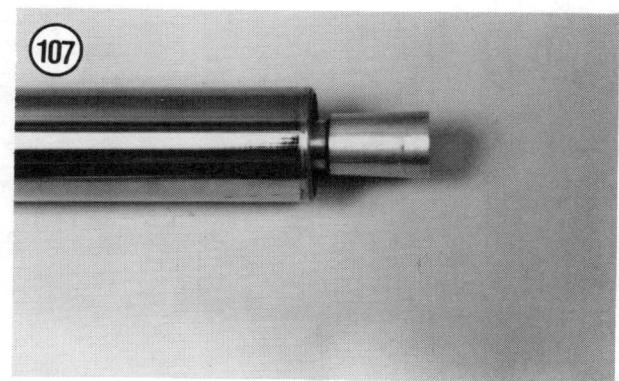
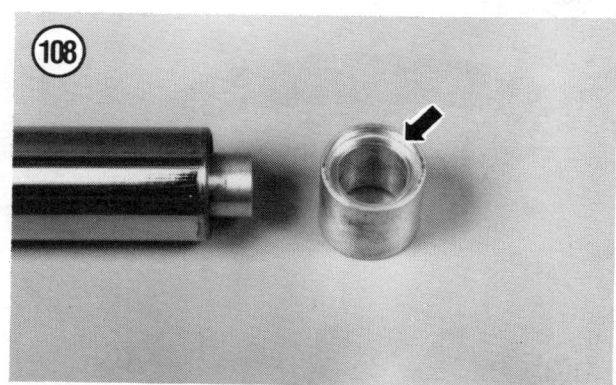

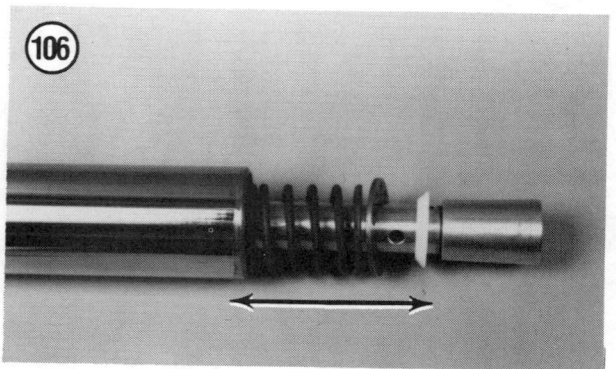
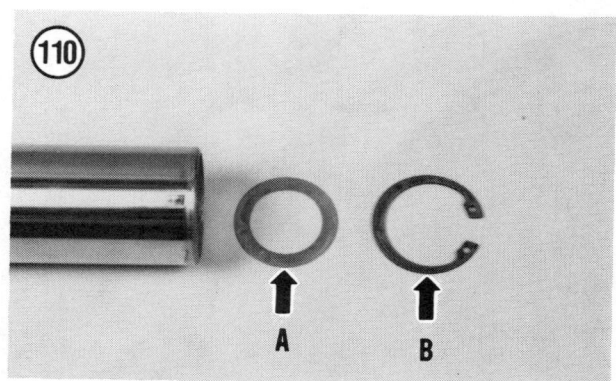

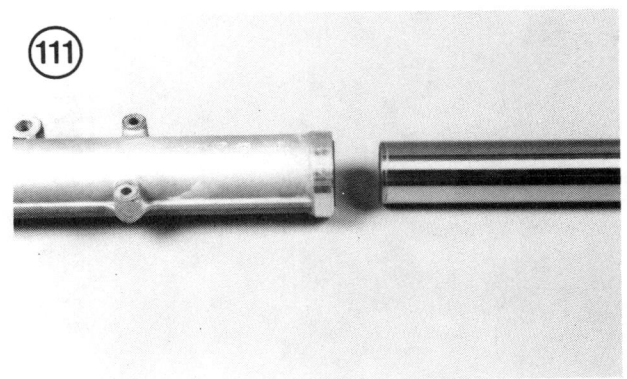

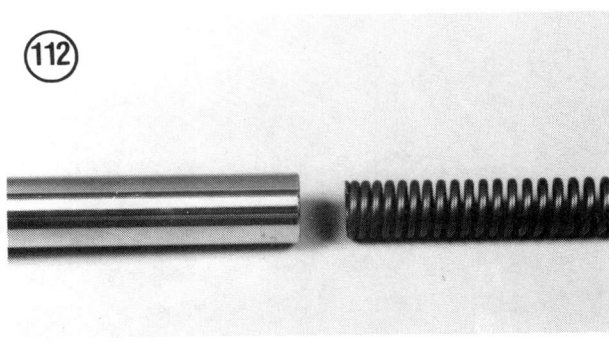

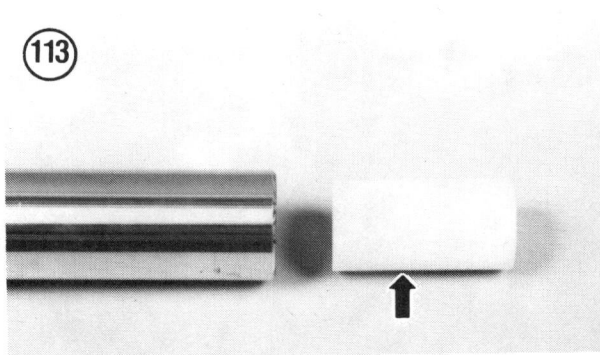

slightly different than the original length. If so, the number of shims used between the valve housing and the circlip may be different from those originally used.

11. Position the circlip (B, **Figure 110**) with the sharp side facing out.

12. Install the circlip (**Figure 92**) securing the valve housing and damper rod assembly in the fork tube. If the circlip will not seat correctly, one or more of the shims, installed in Step 10, may have to be removed to make additional room. Reinstall the circlip.

13. After the circlip is correctly seated, push down on the valve housing. There should be no play between the bottom surface of the circlip and the top surface of the valve housing. If there is play between the 2 parts, additional shim(s) must be added. The shims are available from BMW dealers.

14. Apply a coat of fork oil to the outer surface of the fork tube and install the fork tube into the slider (**Figure 111**).

NOTE
Steps 15-18 are necessary to help hold the damper rod from turning while installing and tightening the Allen screw at the base of the slider.

15A. On models equipped with a single fork spring, install the fork spring (**Figure 112**) and spring retainers and the distance tube (**Figure 113**) into the fork slider.

15B. On all other models, install the lower spring retainer (models so equipped), the lower and upper fork springs, upper spring retainer (models so equipped) and the distance tube into the top of the fork tube.

16. Hold the upper fork tube in a vise with soft jaws.

17. Inspect the O-ring seal (**Figure 114**) on the fork top cap; replace if necessary.

18. Install the fork top cap and O-ring (**Figure 115**).

10

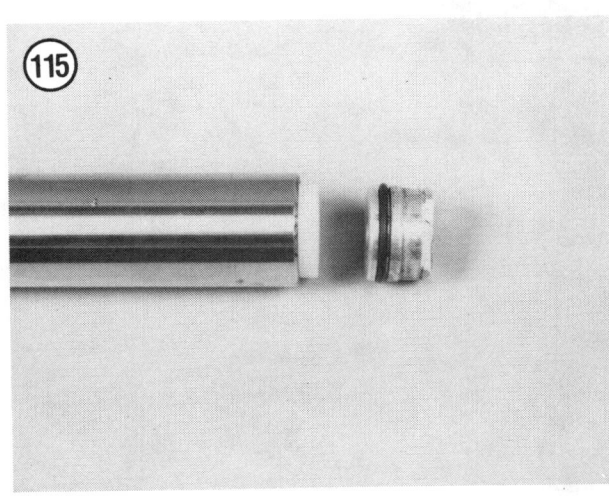

19. Press down on the fork top cap with a drift or socket extension. While holding the fork top cap down, install the snap ring (**Figure 116**). Make sure the snap ring is correctly seated in the fork tube groove.

20. Make sure the sealing washer (**Figure 117**) is in place on the Allen screw.

21. Install the Allen screw and sealing washer (**Figure 118**) in the bottom of the slider. Tighten the Allen screw (**Figure 119**) to the torque specification listed in **Table 1**.

22. Insert a small funnel in the opening in the fork top cap.

23. Add the recommended type and specified amount of fork oil through the small opening in the fork top cap. Refer to **Table 3** for fork oil capacity.

24. Make sure the sealing washer (**Figure 120**) is in place on the Allen screw.

25. Hold onto the fork top cap with an open end wrench and install the oil fill plug (**Figure 121**). Tighten the plug securely.

NOTE
*Models produced since November 5, 1987 are equipped with a newly designed dust seal. The new dust seal has a sharper upper edge which enables it to seat better against the fork tube. The contours of the old and new seals are shown in **Figure 122**. If the bike has the old design seal, replace it with the new dust seal (BMW part No. 31 42 1 451 829). The new dust seal requires the addition of a spacer ring (BMW part No. 31 42 1 548 327) (**Figure 123**) under the seal to prevent the fork oil seal from*

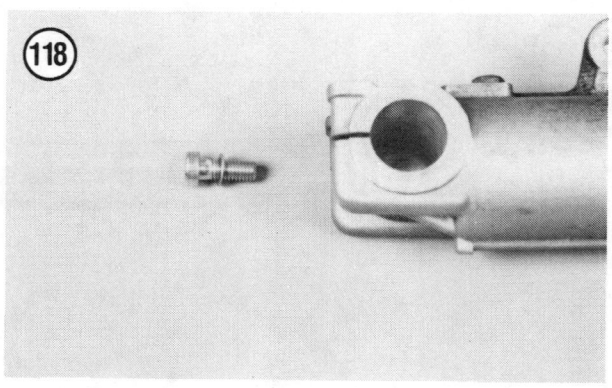

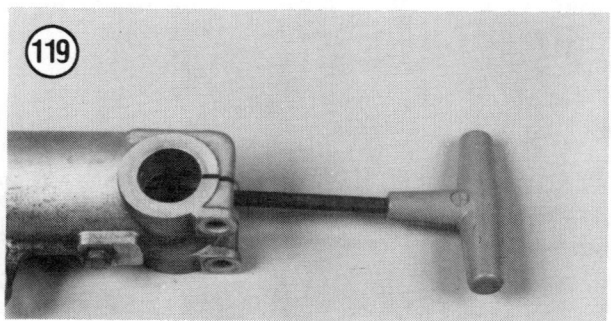

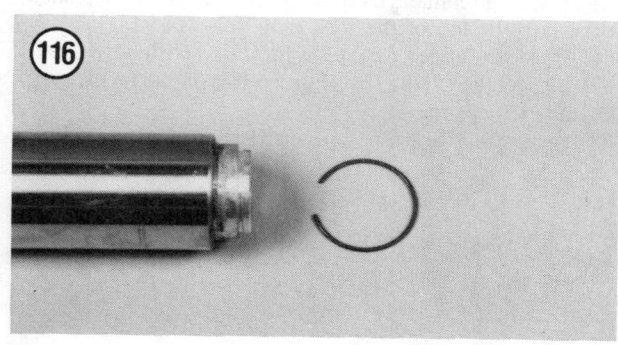

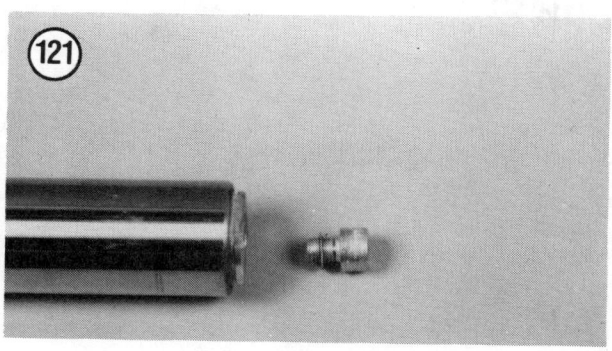

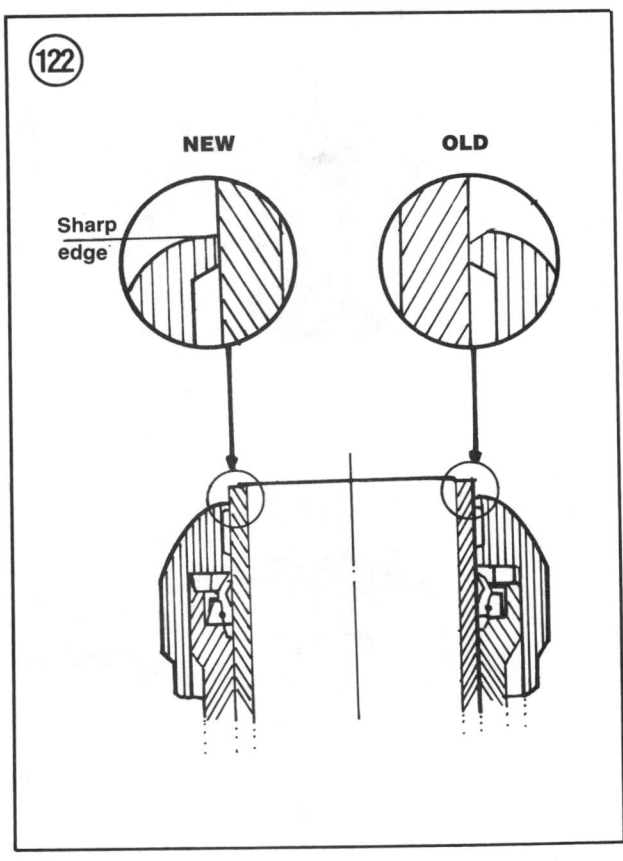

coming in contact with the lower lip of the dust seal.

26. Clean the inside of the fork seal in solvent and thoroughly dry. Make sure all old grease is removed from the grease pocket.

27. Slide the dust seal onto the fork tube and slide it back and forth. It must slide back and forth but still be tight. There is to be no clearance between the fork tube and the dust seal. Make sure the sharp edge of the seal is tight up against the fork tube and that it is straight without any distortion. Replace if necessary.

28. Fill the grease pocket in the dust seal with Shell Retinax A grease, or equivalent.

29. Install the spacer ring (**Figure 123**).

30. Slide the dust seal (**Figure 124**) down the fork tube. Push it down until it snaps into place on the fork slider.

31. Install the fork assembly as described in this chapter.

32. Repeat for the other fork assembly.

Inspection

1. Thoroughly clean all parts in solvent and dry them.

Check the fork tube for signs of wear or scratches.

2. Check the damper rod for straightness. If the damper rod assembly was disassembled, roll it on a piece of plate glass and check for any runout. BMW does not provide service limit specifications for runout.

3. Carefully check the damper piston (**Figure 125**) and piston ring (**Figure 126**) for wear or damage. Replace if necessary.

10

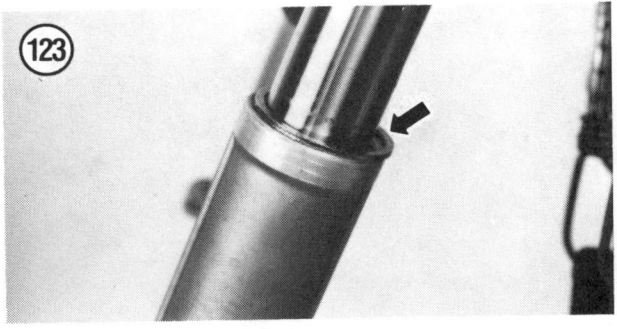

4. Make sure the oil passage holes (**Figure 127**) in the damper rod are clean. If clogged or congested, clean out with solvent and dry with compressed air.

5. Inspect the threads in the valve housing (**Figure 128**) for wear or damage. Clean out the threads with the correct size thread tap or replace the valve housing if necessary.

6. To determine the clearance between the fork tube and the fork slider, perform the following:

   a. Measure the outside diameter of the fork tube with a micrometer or vernier caliper (**Figure 129**). Compare to the dimensions listed in **Table 3**.

   b. Measure the inside diameter of the fork slider with a bore gauge, inside micrometer or vernier caliper (**Figure 130**). Compare to the dimensions listed in **Table 3**.

   c. Subtract the dimension of the fork tube from the fork slider. This will give you the clearance between the 2 parts. Compare to the dimensions listed in **Table 3**. If the clearance is greater than specified, replace the worn part(s).

7. Inspect the fork oil seal (**Figure 131**) for wear or deterioration. Replace if necessary,

8. Check the fork tube for straightness (**Figure 132**). If bent or severely scratched, it should be replaced.

9. Check the slider (**Figure 133**) for dents or exterior damage that may cause the fork tube to hang up during riding. Replace if necessary.

10. Check the slider in the area where the fork seal is installed for wear or damage. Replace if necessary.

11. Inspect the snap ring groove (**Figure 134**) in the fork tube for wear, corrosion or damage. Clean out the groove if necessary so that the snap ring can seat correctly during assembly.

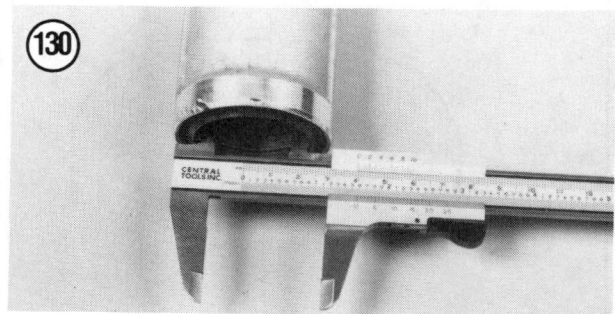

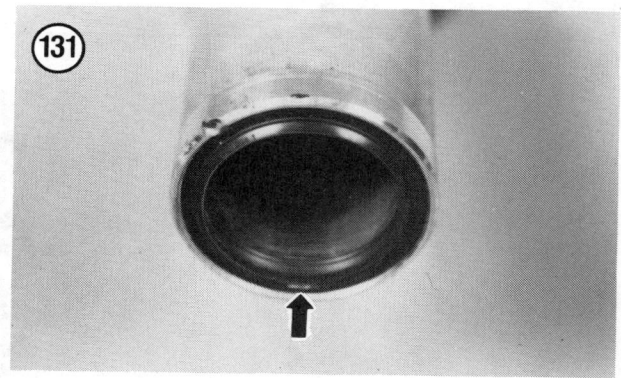

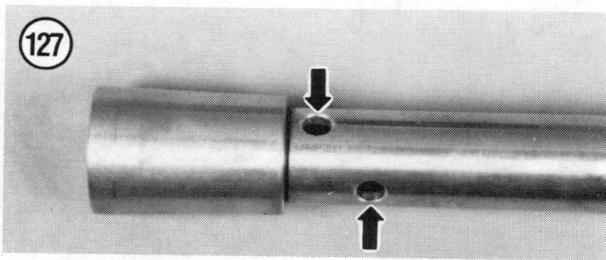

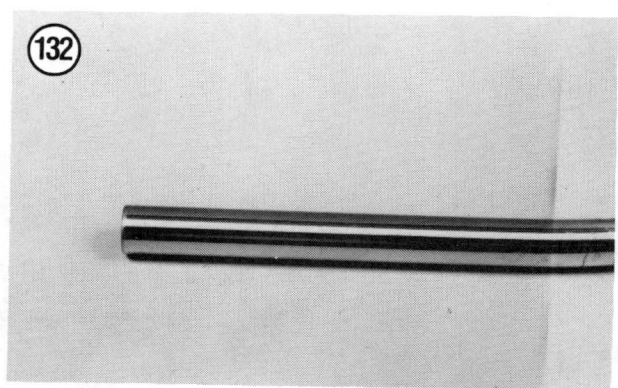

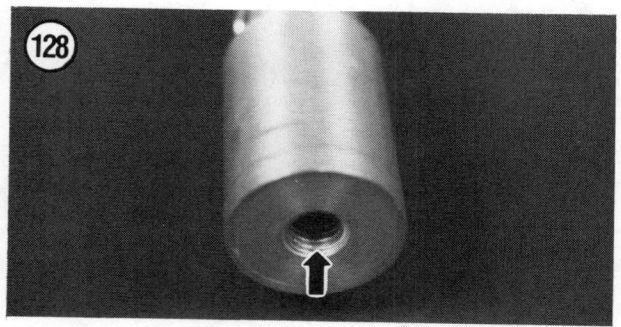

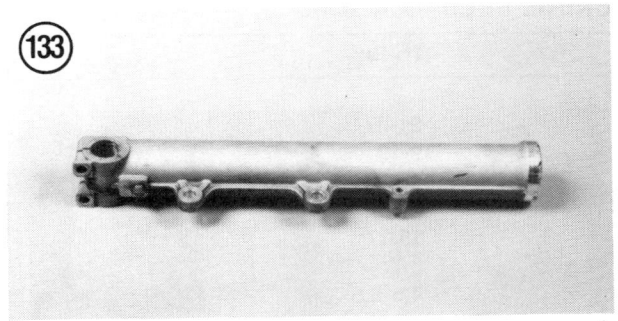

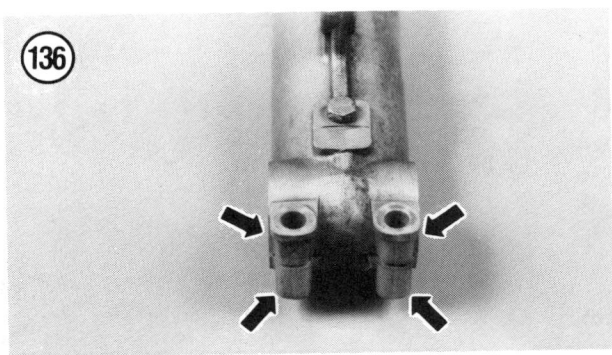

12. Check the axle bearing surfaces of the slider (**Figure 135**) for wear or gouges. Clean up the surfaces or replace the slider if necessary.

13. Inspect the axle clamping lugs (**Figure 136**) on the slider for cracks or fractures from overtightening the clamping bolts. If any evidence of cracks is found, replace the fork slider.

14. Inspect the rubber boot for cracks or deterioration. Replace if necessary.

15. Inspect the distance tube (**Figure 137**) for wear or damage. Replace if necessary.

16. Inspect the valve housing (**Figure 138**) for wear or damage. Replace if necessary.

17. Measure the uncompressed length of the fork lower main spring as shown in **Figure 139**. If the spring has sagged to the minimum dimension listed in **Table 3** the spring must be replaced.

18. Any parts that are worn or damaged should be replaced. Simply cleaning and reinstalling unserviceable components will not improve performance of the front suspension.

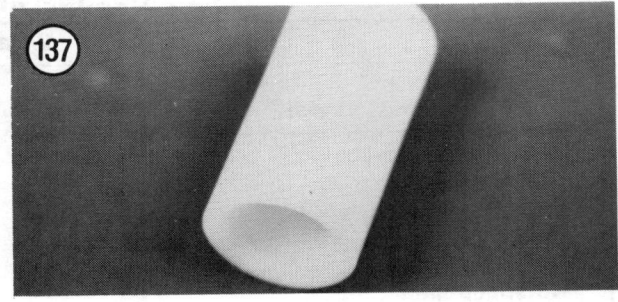

10

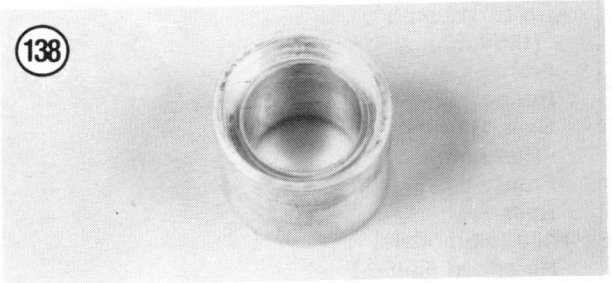

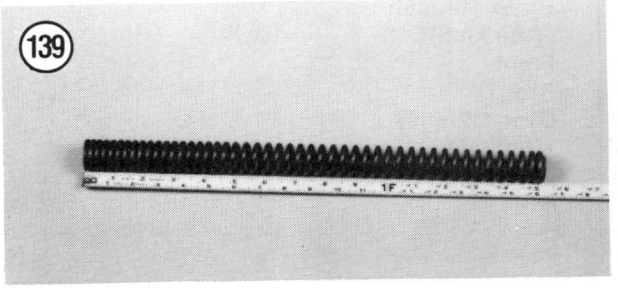

Table 1 FRONT SUSPENSION TORQUE SPECIFICATIONS

Item	N·m	ft.-lb.
Front axle		
Allen bolt	29-37	21-27
Clamp bolts	12-16	9-13
Front caliper mounting bolts	30-34	21-25
Brake disc mounting bolts	29	21
Handlebar holder bolts	20-24	15-17
Steering damper tapered bolts	8-10	6-7
Brake hose union bolts	6-8	4.5-5.5
Steering stem hex nut	42-48	31-35
Fork bridge clamping bolts		
Upper	19-23	14-16
Lower	40-46	29-33
Front fork brace bolts	19-23	14-16
Fork slider Allen screw	18-22	13-15
Fork oil drain bolt	8-10	6-7

Table 2 TIRE INFLATION PRESSURE (COLD) *

	V-Rated Tires				
	Rider only			**Rider and passenger**	
Model	psi	kPa		psi	kPa
K75, K75C					
No speed limit					
Front	29	200		33	230
Rear	36	250		42	290
K75S					
No speed limit					
Front	32.5	225		—	—
Rear	36	250		—	—
Up to 112 mph					
(180 kmh)					
Front	—	—		32.5	225
Rear	—	—		39	270
Over 112 mph					
(180 kmh)					
Front	—	—		39	270
Rear	—	—		42	290
K100 (all models)					
No speed limit					
Front	32.5	225		—	—
Rear	36	250		—	—
Up to 112 mph					
(180 kmh)					
Front	—	—		32.5	225
Rear	—	—		39	270
Over 112 mph					
(180 kmh)					
Front	—	—		39	270
Rear	—	—		42	290

(continued)

Table 2 TIRE INFLATION PRESSURE (COLD)* (continued)

	Rider only		Rider and passenger	
Model	psi	kPa	psi	kPa
K100 (all models)				
No speed limit				
Front	37	255	—	—
Rear	40.5	280	—	—
Up to 112 mph (180 kmh)				
Front	—	—	37	255
Rear	—	—	43.5	300
Over 112 mph (180 kmh)				
Front	—	—	43.5	300
Rear	—	—	46	320

* Tire inflation pressure for factory equipped tires. Aftermarket tires may require different inflation pressure.
** VR-rated tires not recommended by BMW for installation on K75 models.

Table 3 FRONT SUSPENSION SPECIFICATIONS

Front wheel caster	101 mm (3.976 in.)
Handlebar lock-to-lock	
K75, K75C, K100	40°
K75S, K100RS, K100RT, K100LT	35°
Spring travel with 75 kg (165 lb.) of load	185 mm (7.283 in.)
Fork tube outer diameter	41.325-41.397 mm (1.6270-1.6277 in.)
Fork slider inner diameter	41.400-41.439 mm (1.6299-1.6314 in.)
Clearance between fork tube and slider	0.050-0.114 m (0.0020-0.0045 in.)
Fork tube runout (maximum)	0.1 mm (0.004 in.)
Fork spring	
Free length	395-401 mm (15.551-15.787 in.)
Wire gauge size	4.4-5.0 mm (0.1838-0.1862 in.)
Damper rod overall length	253-263 mm (10.043-10.081 in.)
Front fork oil	
K75 models	
Standard	320-330 cc (10.7-11 oz.)
Sport Suspension	270-290 cc (9.23-9.8 oz.)
K100	320-330 cc (10.7-11 oz.)
K100RS, K100RT, K100LT	
Standard	350-360 cc (11.7-12 oz.)
Sport suspension	270-290 cc (10.7-11 oz.)
Recommended type	Bel-Ray SAE 5, Castrol Extra Light Castrol DB Hydraulic Fluid, Castrol Shock Absorber Oil 1/318, Castrol LMH, Golden Spectro Very Light, Mobil Aero HFA, Mobil DTE 11, Shell Aero Fluid 4, Shell 4001

10

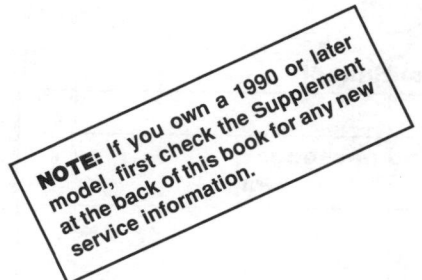

CHAPTER ELEVEN

REAR SUSPENSION AND FINAL DRIVE

This chapter includes repair and replacement procedures for the rear wheel, the rear suspension components and the final drive unit. Power from the engine is transmitted to the rear wheel via a drive shaft and a final drive unit similar to an automobile differential.

The swing arm is known as the BMW Monolever and it carries the final drive unit and rear wheel on the right-hand side only. The swing arm is made of a high-strength alloy casting that pivots on the frame in tapered roller bearings. The drive shaft runs through the hollow swing arm and has a splined universal joint at the front end where it attaches to the engine. The universal joint and splines allow for the up-and-down movement of the swing arm and the slight in-and-out movement of the drive shaft.

The single shock absorber has a progressively wound coil and is hydraulically damped. The spring pre-load can be adjusted to any one of 3 positions to compensate for additional load (passenger and/or luggage). The shock is matched to the spring and damping rate of the front forks.

The self-leveling Nivomat shock absorber is an option on some K100 models. This shock is unique in that it will automatically return the bike to the correct height after a short ride regardless of additional weight. This allows a consistent ground clearance and headlight aim. It also maintains the same spring rate.

Tire changing, tire repair and wheel balancing are covered in Chapter Ten.

Refer to **Table 1** for rear suspension torque specifications. **Table 1** and **Table 2** are located at the end of this chapter.

REAR WHEEL

Removal/Installation

Refer to **Figure 1** for disc brake models or **Figure 2** for drum brake models.

1. Place the bike on the center stand or block up the engine so that the rear wheel clears the ground.
2. On disc brake models, use a flat-bladed screwdriver and carefully remove the hub cap (**Figure 3**).
3. Either shift the transmission into 5th gear or have an assistant apply the rear brake to prevent the rear wheel from rotating.
4. Using a crisscross pattern, loosen the bolts securing the rear wheel to the final drive unit. Refer to **Figure 4** for disc brake models or **Figure 5** for drum brake models.
5. Remove the bolts and special steel washers.

NOTE
On disc brake models, don't lose the metal shim between the wheel mating surface and the final drive unit. It may stay on the final drive unit or rear wheel or it may fall off.

NOTE
Depending on tire size and the area in which you are performing the tire removal, it may be necessary to remove the license plate bracket

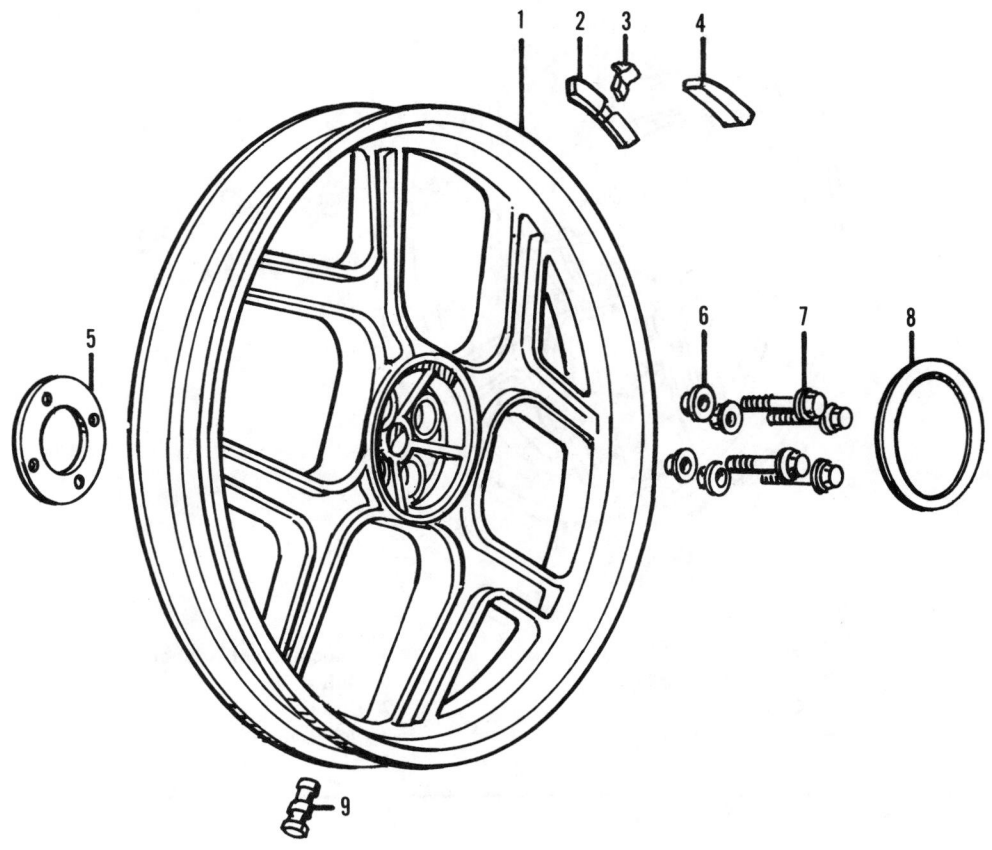

REAR WHEEL
(DISC BRAKE MODELS)

1. Wheel
2. Balance weight
3. Clip
4. Balance weight
5. Shim
6. Special steel washer
7. Bolt
8. Hub cap
9. Valve stem

11

② **REAR WHEEL
(DRUM BRAKE MODELS)**

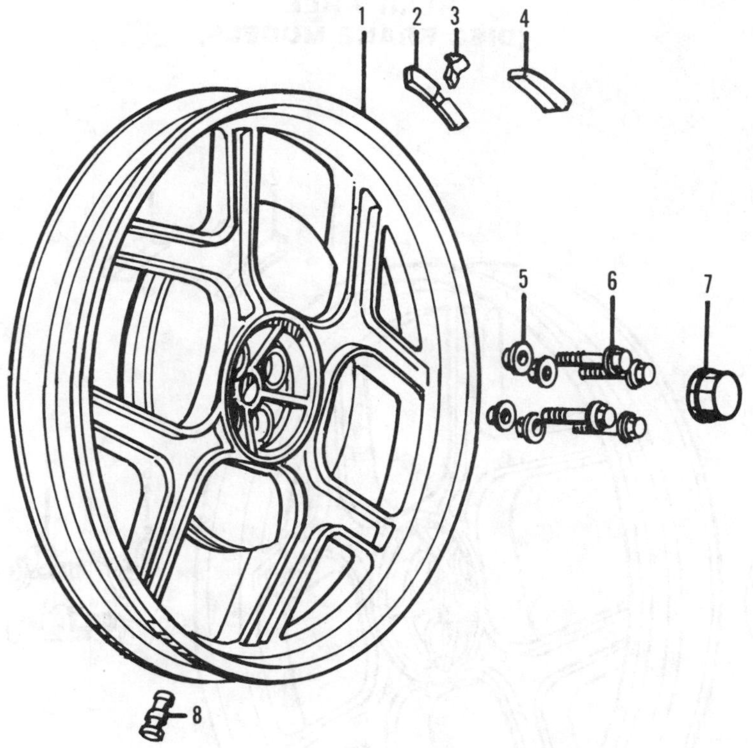

1. Wheel
2. Balance weight
3. Clip
4. Balance weight
5. Special steel washer
6. Bolt
7. Hub cap
8. Valve stem

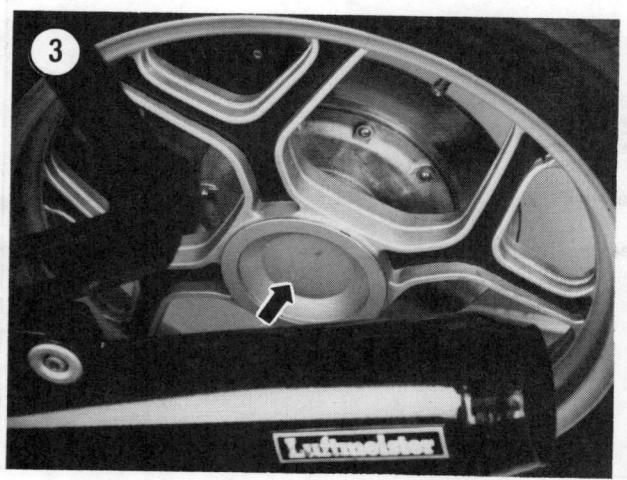

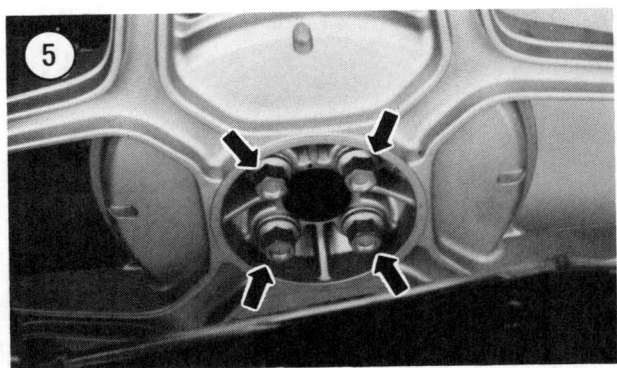

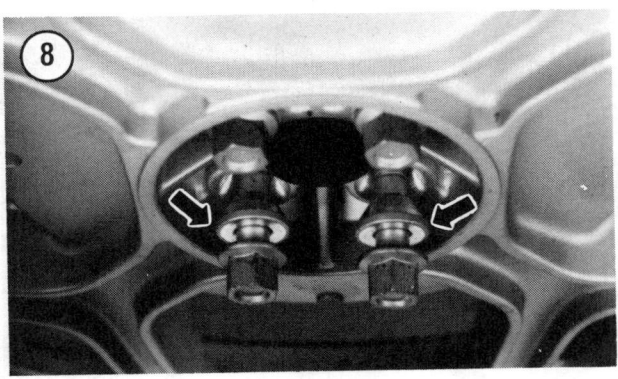

assembly to allow the rear wheel to be removed out through the back of the fender area. If necessary, refer to **License Plate Bracket Removal/Installation** in Chapter Thirteen.

6. Pull the rear wheel toward the left-hand side to disengage it from the final drive unit and roll the wheel toward the rear and remove it.

7. Inspect the rear wheel as described in this chapter.

8. Make sure the mating surface of the rear wheel and the final drive unit are clean. They must be free of road dirt and grease. If necessary wipe clean with a cloth and cleaning solvent. Dry thoroughly prior to installation.

9. Make sure the tapered recesses (**Figure 6**) in the wheel are free of dirt and any gouges or burrs. Clean all surfaces so the steel washers will seat properly.

10. On disc brake models, install the metal shim (**Figure 7**) on the rear wheel shoulder and align the bolt holes.

11. Correctly position the rear wheel next to the final drive unit and align the bolt holes.

> *NOTE*
> *Make sure the correct bolts are used to mount the rear wheel. Drum brake models use longer bolts that are 60 mm long while disc brake models use shorter bolts that are 55 mm long. The bolt length is marked into the bolt head during manufacture.*

> *CAUTION*
> *Always use the special steel washer (**Figure 8**) along with the wheel bolt. The taper on the washer matches the bolt hole taper in the wheel and correctly locates the rear wheel onto the final drive unit.*

> *WARNING*
> ***Never** install the bolts without the special steel washers (**Figure 9**). The bolts cannot correctly*

11

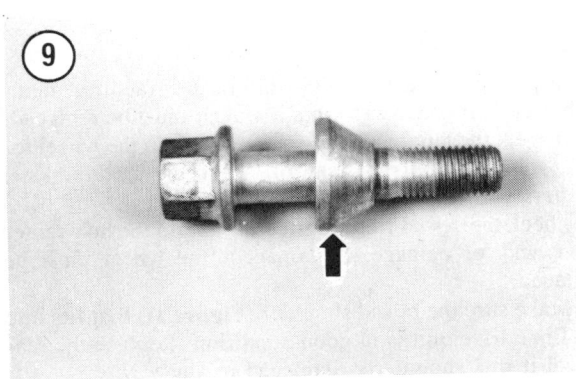

*locate the wheel to the final drive unit without these washers. The wheel will **not** be centered on the final drive unit and will vibrate severely, leading to an unsafe ride and probable accident.*

12. Install the bolts and special steel washers.
13. If not already done, either shift the transmission into 5th gear or have an assistant apply the rear brake to prevent the rear wheel from rotating.

NOTE
*If you are on the road and have to remove and install the rear wheel, tighten the bolts as securely as possible with the tools in the factory tool kit. As soon as possible, check and retighten the bolts with a torque wrench to the correct torque specification. Refer to **Table 1**.*

14. Using a crisscross pattern, tighten the bolts to the torque specification listed in **Table 1**.
15. On disc brake models, install the hub cap (**Figure 3**). Carefully tap it into place and make sure it is on completely so it won't be lost the first rough road you come across.
16. If removed, install the license plate bracket assembly.
17. If used, remove the block(s) from under the engine.

Inspection

The rear wheel is not equipped with any wheel bearings. The bearings for the rear wheel are located within the final drive unit and all service procedures for this unit are also covered in this chapter.

WARNING
Do not try to repair any damage to the alloy wheel as it will result in an unsafe riding condition.

1. Inspect the wheel for signs of cracks, fractures, dents or bends. If it is damaged in any way, it must be replaced.
2. Inspect the tapered recesses (**Figure 6**) in the wheel for dirt, gouges or burrs. Clean off all surfaces so the steel washers will seat properly.
3. Check the raised ribs (**Figure 10**) within the hub center for cracks or damage. If damaged, the wheel must be replaced.
4. Make sure the raised shoulder (**Figure 11**) that fits into the final drive unit is in good condition. Replace the rear wheel if this shoulder is damaged in any way.

Runout Check

Rear wheel runout must be checked with the wheel installed on the final drive unit in the bike.
1. Place the bike on the center stand so the rear wheel clears the ground.
2. Shift the transmission into neutral.
3. Attach a dial indicator to the right-hand side of the swing arm and measure the runout at the rim surface.
4. Slowly rotate the wheel and measure the axial and radial runout of the wheel with a dial indicator. The maximum axial and radial runout is 0.5 mm (0.02 in.). If the runout exceeds this dimension, the wheel will have to be replaced, as it cannot be serviced.

SHOCK ABSORBER

The single shock absorber is mounted to the swing arm on the right-hand side.

Spring Pre-load Adjustment (Non-Nivomat Shocks)

The spring pre-load setting can be adjusted to any of 3 settings as follows:

a. Normal spring setting: Solo rider with no luggage.
b. Medium spring setting: With a passenger or heavy luggage.
c. Hard spring setting: Maximum loads (do not exceed the vehicle's maximum weight limit listed in **Table 2**).
Using the spanner wrench (**Figure 12**) and extension provided in the factory tool kit, rotate the adjuster (**Figure 13**) at the top of the spring to the desired position. Rotating the ring *counterclockwise* achieves the normal or softest setting. Rotating the ring *clockwise* achieves the hardest setting.

NOTE
The Nivomat shock absorber is not adjustable.

Removal/Installation

Refer to **Figure 14** for this procedure.
1. Place the bike on level ground on the center stand.
2. Place wood block(s) under the rear wheel to maintain the swing arm in the at-rest position.
3. Remove the frame right-hand side cover.

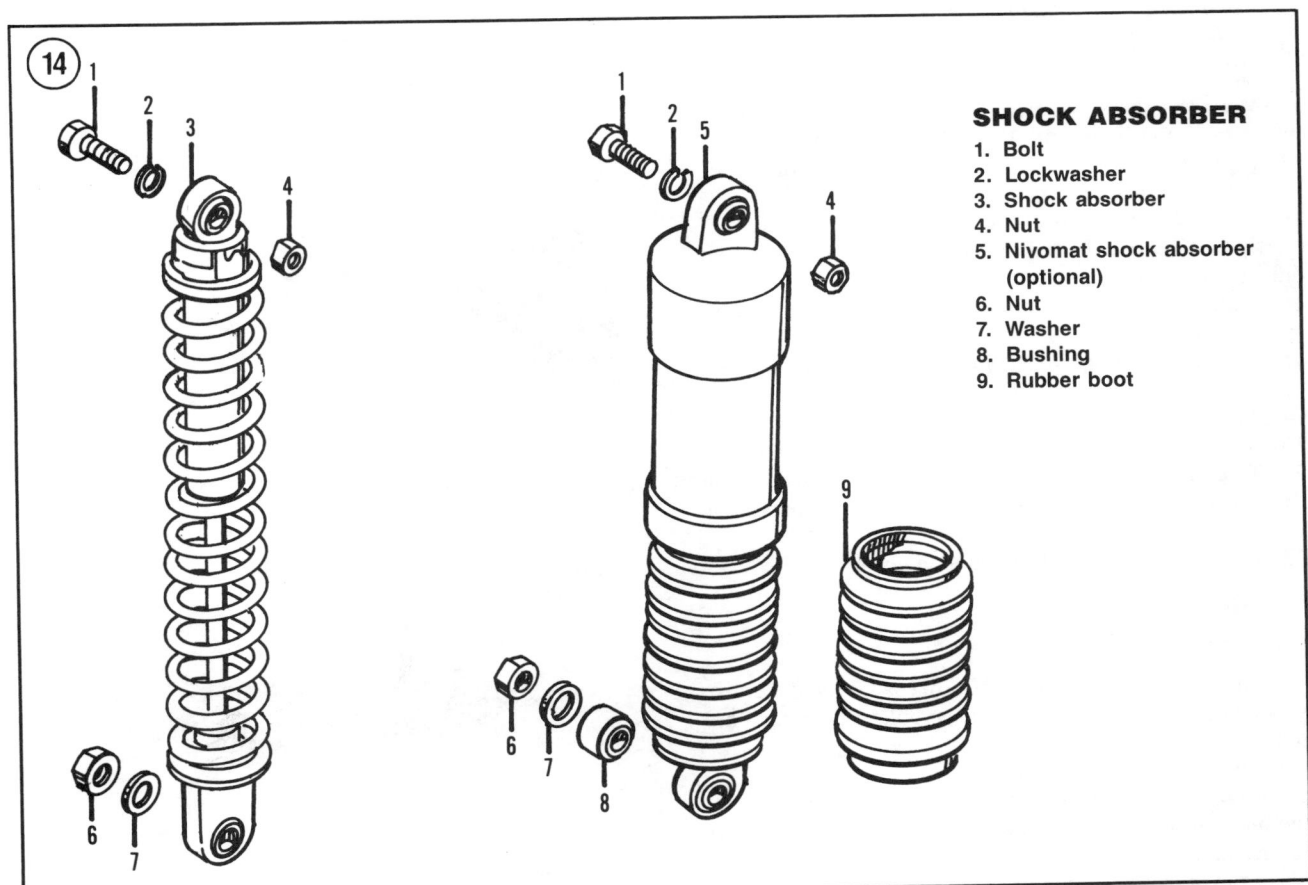

SHOCK ABSORBER
1. Bolt
2. Lockwasher
3. Shock absorber
4. Nut
5. Nivomat shock absorber (optional)
6. Nut
7. Washer
8. Bushing
9. Rubber boot

11

4. On models so equipped, remove the luggage and rack on the right-hand side as described under *Luggage and Rack* in Chapter Thirteen.

5. Remove the upper mounting bolt, lockwasher and nut (A, **Figure 15**) securing the shock absorber to the frame.

6. Remove the lower nut and washer (B, **Figure 15**) securing the shock absorber to the final drive unit.

7. Remove the shock absorber from the mounting stud on the final drive unit.

8. Pull the upper end of the shock absorber out of the mounting area in the frame and remove the shock absorber.

9. Inspect the shock absorber unit as described in this chapter.

10. Apply a light coat of molybdenum disulfide paste grease to the upper and lower rubber bushings on the shock absorber.

> *WARNING*
> *All bolts and nuts used on the Monolever suspension must be replaced with parts of the same type. Do **not** use a replacement part of lesser quality or substitute design, as this may affect the performance of the system or result in failure of the part which will lead to loss of control of the bike. Torque values listed in **Table 1** must be used during installation to assure proper retention of these parts.*

11. Move the shock absorber into position and align the upper mounting hole with the hole in the frame.

12. Install the bolt, lockwasher and nut securing the upper portion to the frame.

13. Install the shock absorber onto the mounting stud on the final drive unit. Install the washer and nut and tighten only finger-tight at this time.

14. Tighten the bolt and nuts to the torque specification listed in **Table 1**.

15. On models so equipped, install the luggage and rack on the right-hand side as described under *Luggage and Rack* in Chapter Thirteen.

16. Remove the wood block(s) from under the rear wheel.

17. Take the bike off of the center stand and push down on the rear of the bike and make sure the rear suspension is operating properly.

18. Install the frame right-hand side cover.

Inspection

If any portion of the shock absorber is faulty, the entire shock absorber must be replaced as replacement parts are not available.

Refer to **Figure 14** for this procedure.

1. Inspect the upper (**Figure 16**) and lower (**Figure 17**) mounting bushings of the shock absorber where it attaches to the frame and final drive unit. If they are damaged, replace the shock absorber unit.

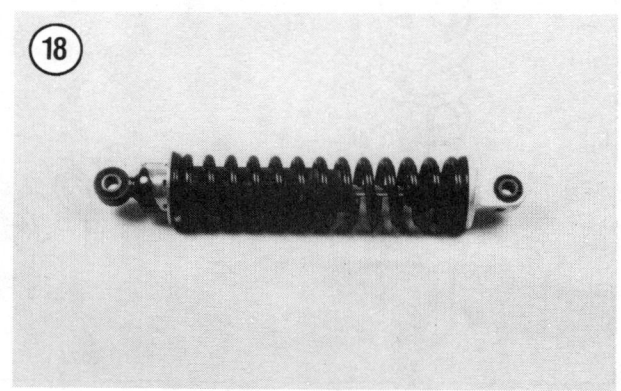

2. Clean the mounting bushings with solvent. Thoroughly dry and apply molybdenum disulfide grease to the mounting bushings.
3. Check the damper unit (**Figure 18**) for leakage.
4. Make sure the damper rod (**Figure 19**) is straight and that the rubber guide (**Figure 20**) is not damaged or worn. If either is faulty, the shock absorber must be replaced.
5. On Nivomat models, if the rubber boot is torn or deteriorated, carefully pull the rubber boot from the damper unit and replace with a new one.

SWING ARM
AND DRIVE SHAFT

In time, the pivot roller bearings will wear and will have to be replaced. The condition of the bearings can greatly affect handling performance and if worn parts are not replaced they can produce erratic and dangerous handling. Common symptoms are wheel hop, pulling to one side during acceleration and pulling to the other side during braking.

Refer to **Figure 21** for these procedures.

Removal

1. Place the bike on the center stand.
2. Remove the muffler as described under *Muffler Removal/Installation* in Chapter Seven.
3. Remove the rear wheel as described in this chapter.
4. Grasp the rear end of the swing arm and try to move it from side to side in a horizontal arc. There should be

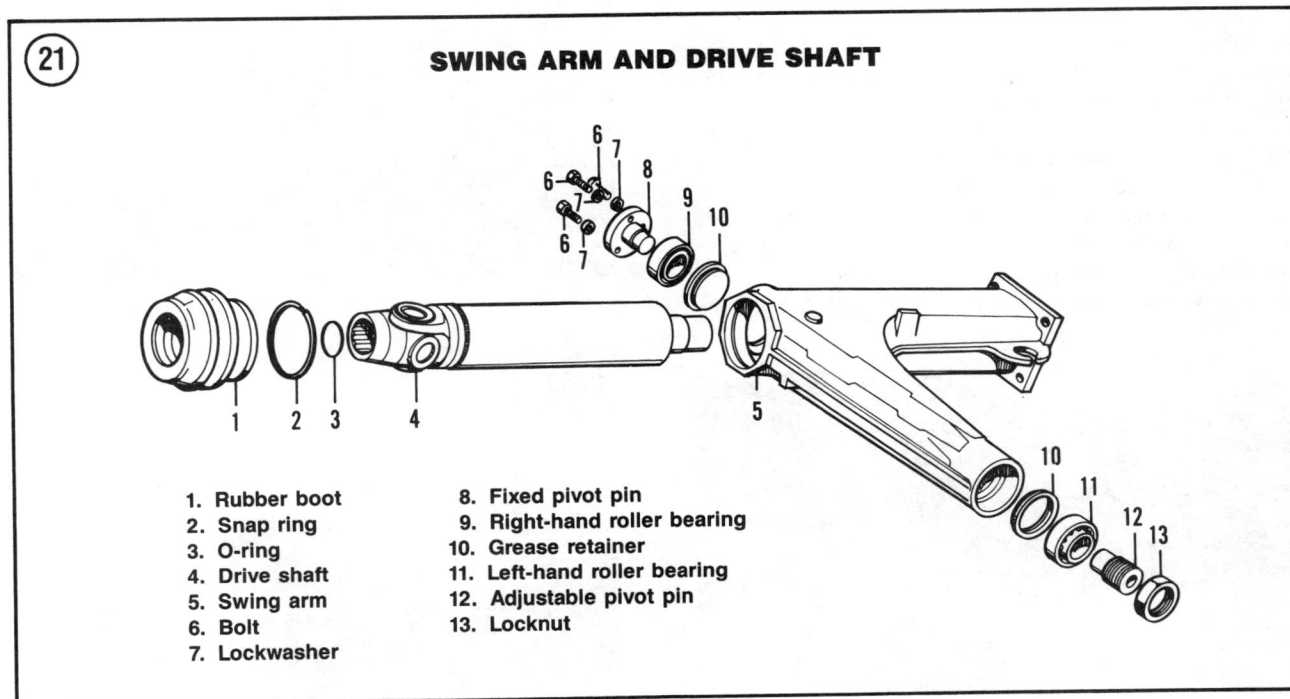

SWING ARM AND DRIVE SHAFT

1. Rubber boot
2. Snap ring
3. O-ring
4. Drive shaft
5. Swing arm
6. Bolt
7. Lockwasher
8. Fixed pivot pin
9. Right-hand roller bearing
10. Grease retainer
11. Left-hand roller bearing
12. Adjustable pivot pin
13. Locknut

11

no noticeable side play. If play is evident and the adjustable pivot pin is tightened correctly, the bearings should be replaced.

5. Remove the rear brake caliper assembly and the final drive unit as described in this chapter.

6. Remove the right-hand and left-hand footpeg assemblies as described under *Footpeg Assembly Removal/Installation* in Chapter Thirteen.

7. Disconnect the clutch cable from the release lever as follows:

    a. At the clutch hand lever on the handlebar, loosen the locknut (A, **Figure 22**) and turn the adjuster (B, **Figure 22**) all the way in to provide maximum amount of clutch cable slack.

    b. Disconnect the clutch cable from the clutch release lever (**Figure 23**) at the rear of the transmission housing.

8. Place wood block(s) under the swing arm at the rear to hold the swing arm in position after the pivot pins are removed.

9. At the left-hand pivot point, loosen the locknut (A, **Figure 24**) and unscrew the adjustable pivot pin (B, **Figure 24**).

NOTE
*In the following step, if you are unable to withdraw the fixed pivot pin, install one of the mounting bolts into the center threaded hole and pull the pivot pin out with a pair of pliers. If necessary, **carefully** pry the pivot pin away from the transmission housing with a broad-tipped screwdriver.*

10. At the right-hand pivot point, remove the bolts (A, **Figure 25**) and lockwashers securing the fixed pivot pin (B, **Figure 25**) and remove the pivot pin.

11. Pull the swing arm toward the rear and remove it from the frame. The rubber boot will usually stay on the transmission case—but may come off with the swing arm.

12. Using a slight jerking motion, pull on the drive shaft and disengage it from small circlip on the transmission output shaft. Remove the drive shaft assembly.

13. Inspect the swing arm as described in this chapter.

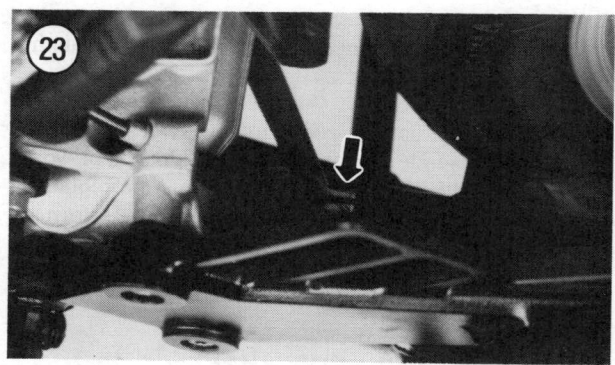

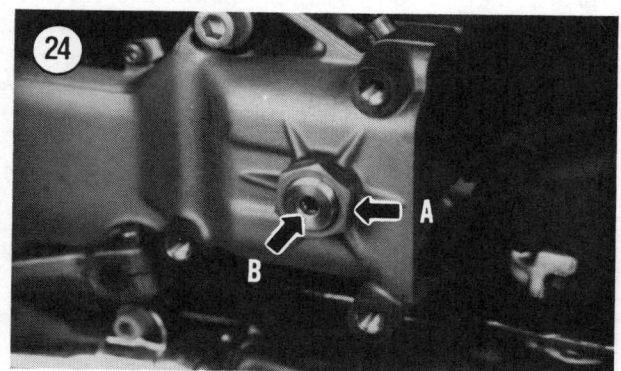

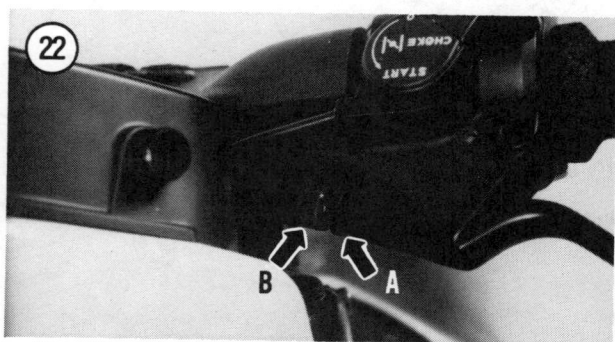

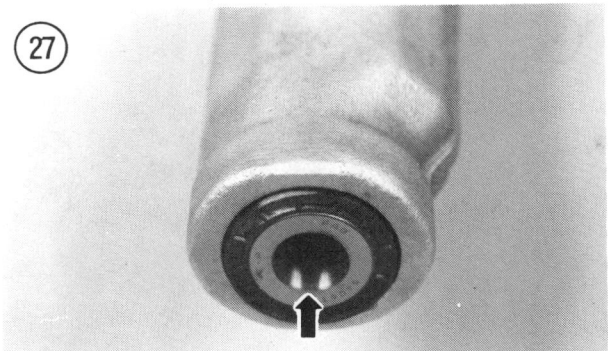

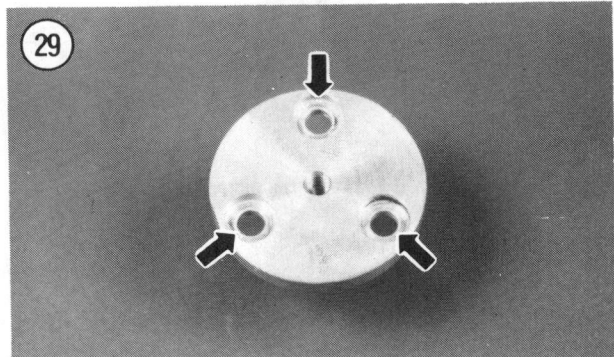

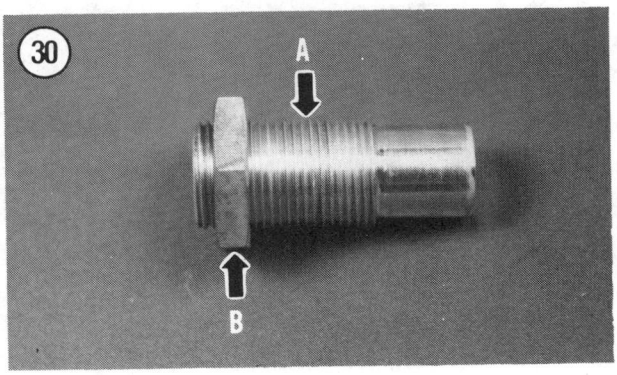

Swing Arm Inspection

1. Inspect the swing arm for wear, cracks or damage. Replace if necessary.

2. Inspect the pivot bearings for wear or damage. Refer to **Figure 26** for the right-hand side and **Figure 27** for the left-hand side. Rotate them with your fingers. They should rotate freely with no signs of drag or roughness. Replace if necessary as described in this chapter.

3. Inspect the fixed pivot pin (**Figure 28**) for wear, cracks or damage. Replace if necessary.

4. Inspect the mounting holes (**Figure 29**) in the fixed pivot pin for wear or damage. Replace if necessary.

5. Inspect the adjustable pivot pin (A, **Figure 30**) and locknut (B, **Figure 30**) for wear, cracks or damage. If the threads are damaged, clean out the threads with the correct size and pitch thread tap or die or replace if necessary.

6. Inspect the rubber boot (**Figure 31**) for cracks or damage. If any cracks or damage are evident, replace the rubber boot.

7. Inspect the final drive unit mounting flange (**Figure 32**) of the swing arm for wear, damage or distortion. This flange must be free of any damage or distortion to enable the final drive unit to fit correctly for proper alignment. If any damage is found, replace the swing arm.

11

Drive Shaft Inspection

1. Inspect the inner splines (**Figure 33**) of the drive shaft where it attaches to the final drive unit. If they are damaged or worn, the drive shaft must be replaced.

> *NOTE*
> *If the splines are damaged, also check the splines of the final drive unit; it may also have to be replaced.*

2. Inspect the inner splines (**Figure 34**) of the universal joint end of the drive shaft. If they are damaged or worn, the drive shaft must be replaced. The universal joint cannot be replaced separately.

> *NOTE*
> *If the splines are damaged, also check the splines of the transmission output shaft; it may also have to be replaced.*

3. Inspect the universal joint pivot points for play (**Figure 35**). Rotate the joint in both directions. If there is noticeable side play the universal joint must be replaced.

Installation

> *NOTE*
> *Even though the drive shaft was the last item to be removed, it will be installed after the swing arm has been installed. This is necessary so that the rubber boot can be installed correctly.*

1. Apply a light coat of Staburags NBU 30 PTM grease (**Figure 36**), or an equivalent, to the outer splines of the transmission output shaft, the inner splines of the drive shaft and the inner surface of the rubber boot.
2. Install the rubber boot onto the end of the swing arm.
3. Install the snap ring into the inner surface of the rubber boot securely to the swing arm.

> *CAUTION*
> *The rubber boot must be installed correctly on both the swing arm and the transmission*

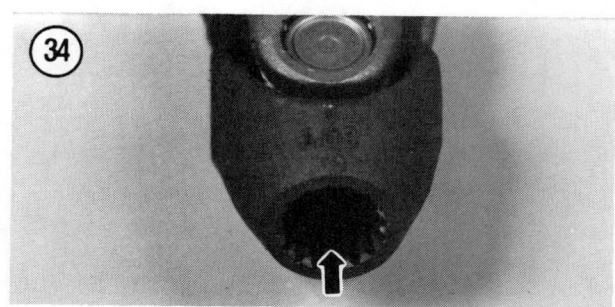

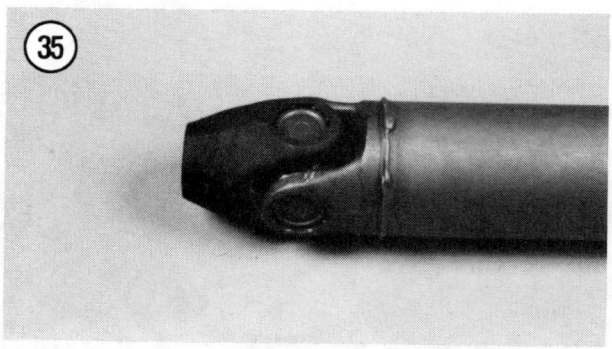

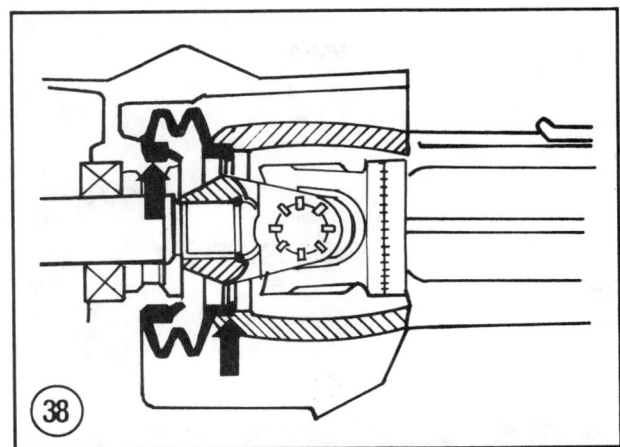

housing flange. This boot protects the universal joint from moisture and foreign matter. If the boot is not installed correctly, the universal joint will wear out prematurely.

4. Position the swing arm into the mounting area of the frame (**Figure 37**). Slightly move the swing arm in and out until the rubber boot is correctly engaged on the transmission housing flange (**Figure 38**). Using your fingers, feel around the circumference of the rubber boot to make sure it is correctly seated both on the swing arm and on the transmission housing.

5. After the boot is seated on both parts, gently pull the swing arm toward the rear to make sure the boot is properly seated.

6. Apply a coat of anti-seize lubricant (Permatex Anti-Seize part No. 133K, or equivalent) (**Figure 39**) to the fixed pivot pin and to the adjustable pivot pin prior to installation.

7. Align the holes in the swing arm with the holes in the frame. Position the loose end of the swing arm on the wood block(s) used during removal.

8. Install the fixed pivot pin (**Figure 40**) to the right-hand side of the frame and swing arm. Install the bolts and lockwashers (**Figure 41**) and tighten only finger-tight at this time.

9. Install the adjustable pivot pin (**Figure 42**) into the left-hand side of the frame and swing arm. Screw the pin until it stops.

10. Carefully move the swing arm up and down a couple of times to make sure the swing arm is correctly seated before tightening the pivot pins.

11. Tighten the bolts securing the fixed pivot pin to the torque specification listed in **Table 1**.

12. Tighten the adjustable pivot pin securely to seat the bearings, then loosen it. Then retighten it to the torque specification listed in **Table 1**.

11

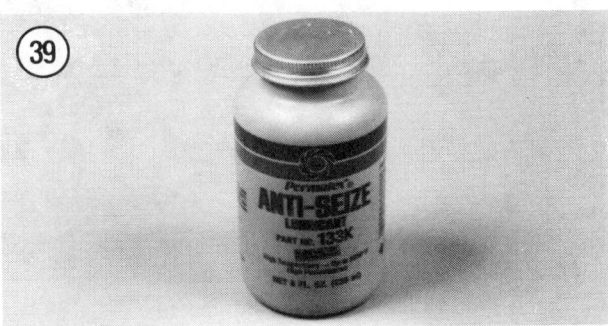

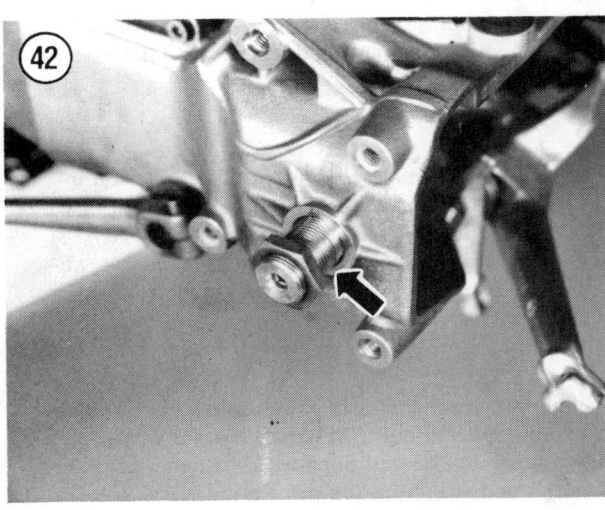

CAUTION
In Step 13, make sure the adjusting pivot pin does not rotate and tighten while tightening the locknut against it.

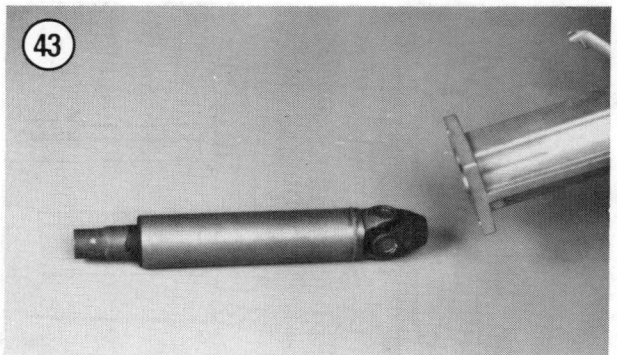

13. Hold the adjustable pivot pin with an Allen wrench and tighten the locknut to the torque specification listed in **Table 1**.

14. Position the drive shaft with the universal joint going in first (**Figure 43**) and insert the drive shaft into the swing arm.

15. Slightly rotate the drive shaft to align the splines of the transmission output shaft and the universal joint. Once the splines are aligned, push the drive shaft forward until you hear a click. This click indicates that the circlip has snapped into its groove.

16. After the circlip snaps into the groove, pull slightly back on the drive shaft to make sure it is properly seated.

17. Connect the clutch cable onto the release lever as follows:

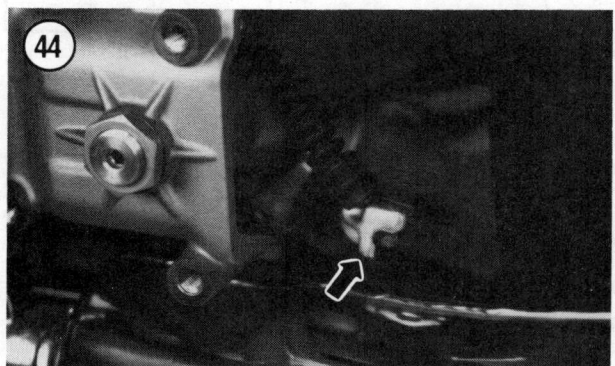

  a. Connect the clutch cable onto the clutch release lever (**Figure 44**) at the rear of the transmission housing.

  b. Adjust the clutch as described under *Clutch Adjustment* in Chapter Three.

18. Install the right-hand and left-hand footpeg assemblies as described under *Footpeg Assembly Removal/Installation* in Chapter Thirteen.

19. Install the rear brake caliper assembly and the final drive unit as described in this chapter.

20. Install the muffler as described under *Muffler Removal/Installation* in Chapter Seven.

21. Install the rear wheel as described in this chapter.

Bearing and Grease Retainer Replacement

The swing arm is equipped with a roller bearing on each side of the swing arm.

A special tool is required to remove the bearing assembly from the swing arm and is described in this procedure.

CAUTION
Do not remove the bearing for inspection purposes. Never reinstall a bearing that has been removed. During removal it becomes slightly damaged and is no longer true to alignment. If installed, it will create an unsafe riding condition.

1. Remove the swing arm as described in this chapter.

2. Using special tool (BMW part No. 00 8 572 or Kukko Extractor No. 21/3 and Support 22-1) withdraw the roller bearing and seal from the pivot point.

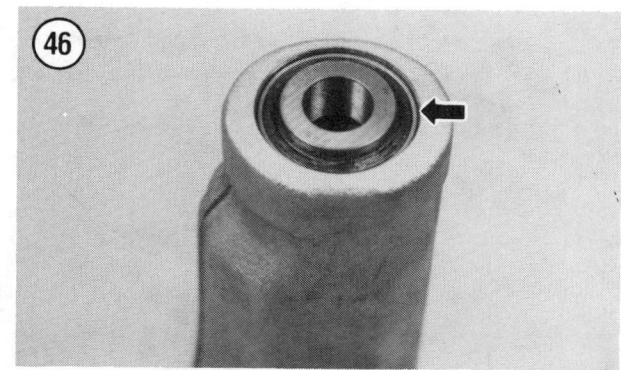

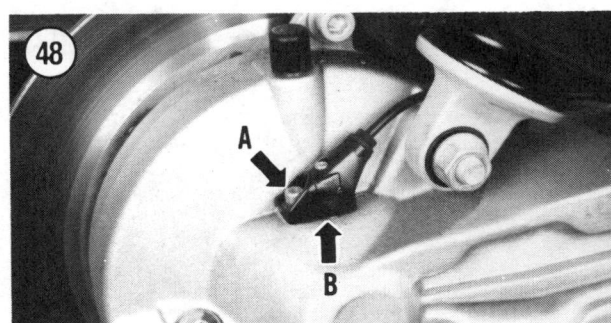

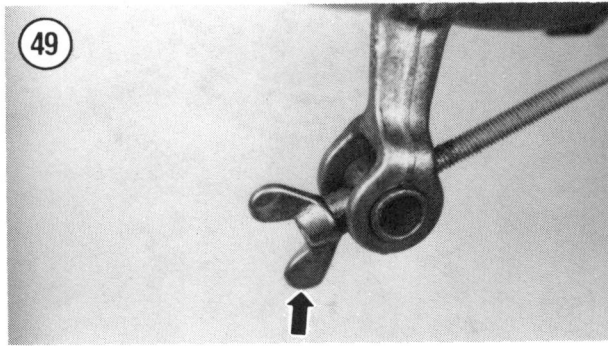

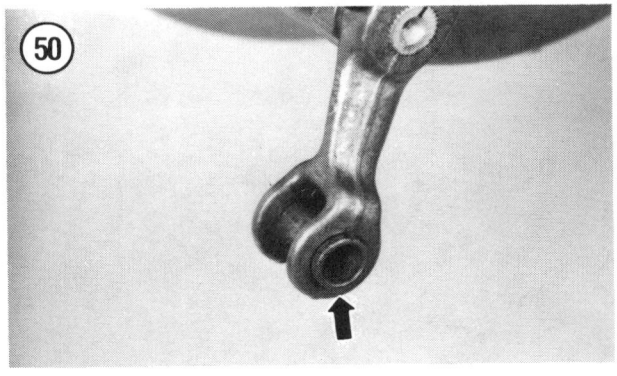

3. Repeat Step 2 for the bearing on the other side.

4. If necessary, remove the grease retainer located behind the roller bearing as follows:

    a. Remove the rubber boot from the swing arm.

    b. Insert a drift through the drive shaft opening on the right-hand side and tap out the right-hand grease retainer.

    c. Insert a long drift through the right-hand bearing area and tap out the left-hand grease retainer.

5. Thoroughly clean out the inside surfaces of the pivot portions of the swing arm with solvent and dry with compressed air.

6. If removed, install new grease retainers on each side. Tap the retainers in squarely and evenly until they bottom out. Their fit is not critical in that they do not affect the bearing. They only retain the grease and keep it from going into the inner portion of the swing arm.

7. Pack the new roller bearings and the inner surface of both grease retainers with Staburags NBU 30 PTM grease (**Figure 36**), available from BMW dealers.

CAUTION
In order to prevent damage to the swing arm, place the opposite end of the swing arm on a piece of soft wood when installing the bearing into the other side.

8. Install the new bearing into the swing arm. Use a suitable size socket that matches the *outer race* of the bearing (**Figure 45**). Tap the bearing in slowly and squarely until it seats completely (**Figure 46**). Make sure it is properly seated.

9. Repeat Step 8 for the bearing on the other side.

10. On models so equipped, install the grease seal onto each bearing.

11. Install the rubber boot.

12. Install the swing arm as described in this chapter.

11

FINAL DRIVE UNIT

Removal

1. Remove the rear wheel (A, **Figure 47**) as described in this chapter.

2. Remove the bolt (A, **Figure 48**) securing the speedometer sensor. Carefully pry the sensor (B, **Figure 48**) out of the final drive unit.

3A. On drum brake models, perform the following:

    a. Completely unscrew the brake adjuster nut (**Figure 49**).

    b. Depress the brake pedal to withdraw the brake rod from the actuating arm.

    c. Remove the pivot pin (**Figure 50**) from the brake actuating arm.

d. Reinstall the pivot pin and the adjuster nut (**Figure 51**) on the brake rod to prevent their accidental loss.

3B. On disc brake models, remove the rear caliper assembly and brake disc as described in Chapter Twelve.

4. Place a wood block under the swing arm to support it after the shock absorber is removed.

5. Loosen the shock absorber upper mounting bolt and nut (B, **Figure 47**). Do not remove the bolt or nut.

6. Remove the shock absorber lower mounting nut and washer (C, **Figure 47**).

7. Pull the shock absorber off of the mounting stud on the final drive unit.

8. Pivot the shock absorber up and tie it up and out of the way.

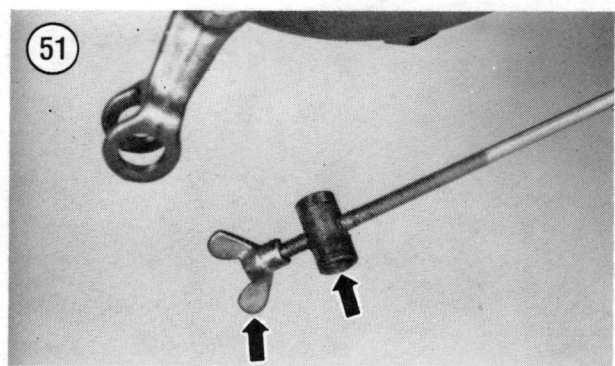

NOTE
Figure 52 is shown with the swing arm and final drive unit assembly removed for clarity. It is not necessary to remove the swing arm for final drive unit removal.

9. Unscrew the bolts (**Figure 52**) securing the final drive unit to the swing arm.

10. Pull back on the final drive unit and separate it from the drive shaft and swing arm. If necessary, gently tap on the final drive unit with a soft-faced mallet or plastic hammer to separate it. Remove the final drive unit and take it to your workbench for inspection or disassembly. Don't lose the locating dowels. It is not necessary to remove them if they are secure and are in good condition.

11. Inspect all parts as described in this chapter.

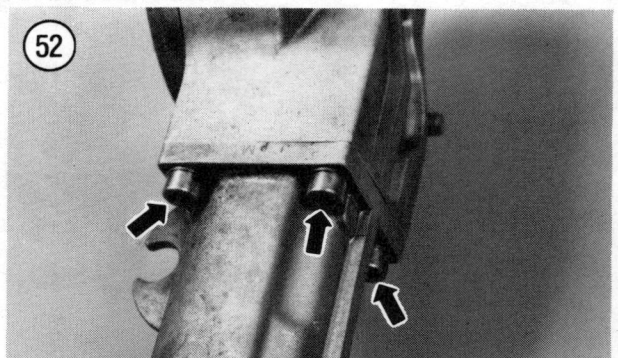

Inspection

1. Inspect the exterior of the final drive unit housing for cracks or damage. Replace if necessary as described under *Final Drive Overhaul* in this chapter.

2. Check the rear brake caliper mounting tabs (**Figure 53**) on the final drive unit cover for cracks, damage or hole elongation. Replace the final drive unit cover if necessary.

3. Inspect the exterior of the final drive unit housing cover for cracks or damage. Replace if necessary as described under *Final Drive Overhaul* in this chapter.

4. Inspect the splines of the drive unit (**Figure 54**). If the splines are worn or damaged the ring gear assembly must be replaced as described under *Final Drive Overhaul* in this chapter.

NOTE
If the splines are worn or damaged, also inspect the splines on the end of the drive shaft for damage as described in this chapter; it may also need to be replaced.

5. Check for any signs of oil leakage at the spline portion. If the oil seal has been leaking it must be replaced as described under *Final Drive Overhaul* in this chapter.

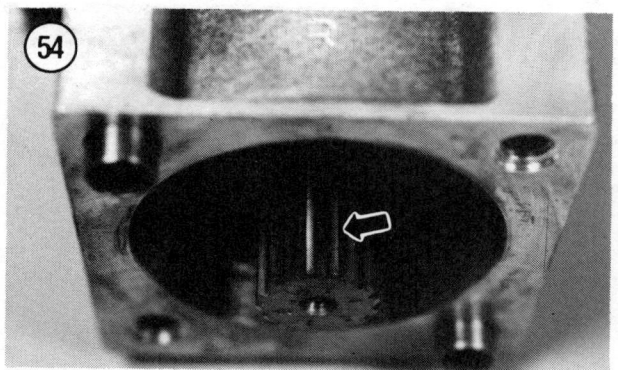

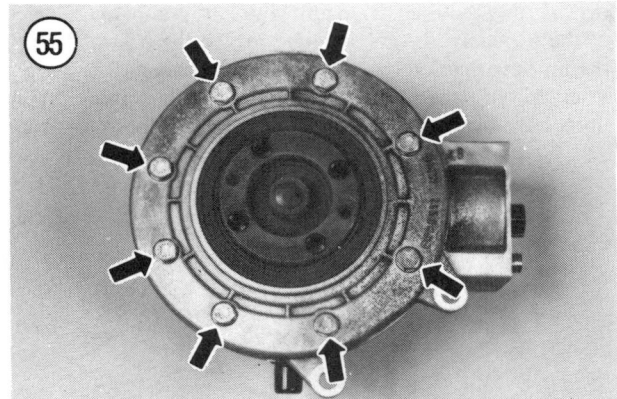

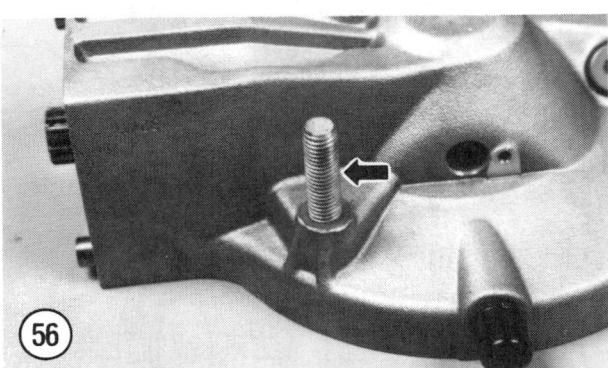

6. Make sure the cover mounting bolts (**Figure 55**) are tight. Refer to **Table 1** for torque specifications.

7. Inspect the shock absorber lower mounting stud (**Figure 56**) for wear or damage. If necessary, clean out the threads with the correct size and pitch thread die or replace if necessary.

Installation

1. If there was any moisture present when the final drive unit was removed, apply a light coat of Three Bond No. 1216 gasket sealer to the mating surface of the final drive unit prior to installation.

2. Make sure the locating dowels (**Figure 57**) are in place.

3. Apply a thick coat of Staburags NBU 30 PTM grease (**Figure 58**), or an equivalent, to the final drive unit splines and to the drive shaft splines.

4. Make sure the swing arm is in the correct height position.

> *CAUTION*
> *The final drive unit must bottom out on the mating surface of the swing arm before installing the mounting bolts. Do not install or tighten any mounting bolts to try to pull the 2 assemblies together. If there is any interference, pulling the 2 parts together will only damage internal parts, leading to costly parts replacement.*

5. Install the final drive unit onto the swing arm If necessary, slightly rotate the ring gear until the splines align with the drive shaft. Push the final drive unit on until it completely bottoms out. If the 2 parts will not seat correctly, remove the final drive unit and correct the problem.

6. Install the bolts (**Figure 52**) securing the final drive unit to the swing arm. Using a crisscross pattern, tighten the bolts to the torque specification listed in **Table 1**.

7. Pivot the shock absorber down and install it on the stud on the final drive unit.

8. Install the shock absorber lower mounting nut and washer (C, **Figure 47**) and tighten to the torque specification listed in **Table 1**.

9. Tighten the shock absorber upper mounting bolt and nut (B, **Figure 47**) to the torque specification listed in **Table 1**.

10. Remove the wood block from under the swing arm.

11A. On drum brake models, perform the following:
  a. Completely unscrew the brake adjuster nut (**Figure 51**) from the brake rod and remove the pivot pin also.
  b. Install the pivot pin (**Figure 50**) into the brake actuating lever.
  c. Depress the brake pedal and reinstall the brake rod into the pivot pin in the actuating arm.
  d. Reinstall the adjuster nut on the brake rod loosely.
  e. Adjust the rear brake as described under *Rear Drum Brake Height and Freeplay Adjustment* in Chapter Three.

11

11B. On disc brake models, install the rear brake disc and caliper assembly as described in Chapter Twelve.

12. Install the speedometer speed sensor as follows:
   a. Inspect the O-ring seal (**Figure 59**) for damage; replace if necessary.
   b. Clean off all dirt and grease from the end of the sensor that is down in the final drive unit.
   c. Make sure the O-ring seal is in place and install the speedometer sensor into the final drive unit.
   d. Install the screw and tighten securely—do not overtighten as the plastic housing may fracture.

13. Install the rear wheel (A, **Figure 47**) as described in this chapter.

Overhaul

Overhauling the final drive unit requires many BMW special tools along with a heat gun or hot plate. Before overhauling the final drive unit yourself, compare the price of the expensive BMW special tools to the cost of having the unit overhauled by a BMW dealer. This unit is almost "bulletproof" and rarely requires any type of service. Many units have over 150,000 miles on them without any prob-

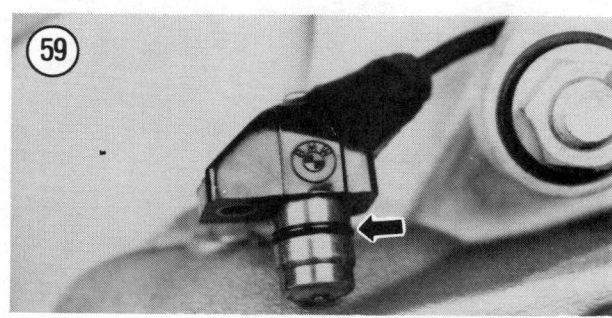
(59)

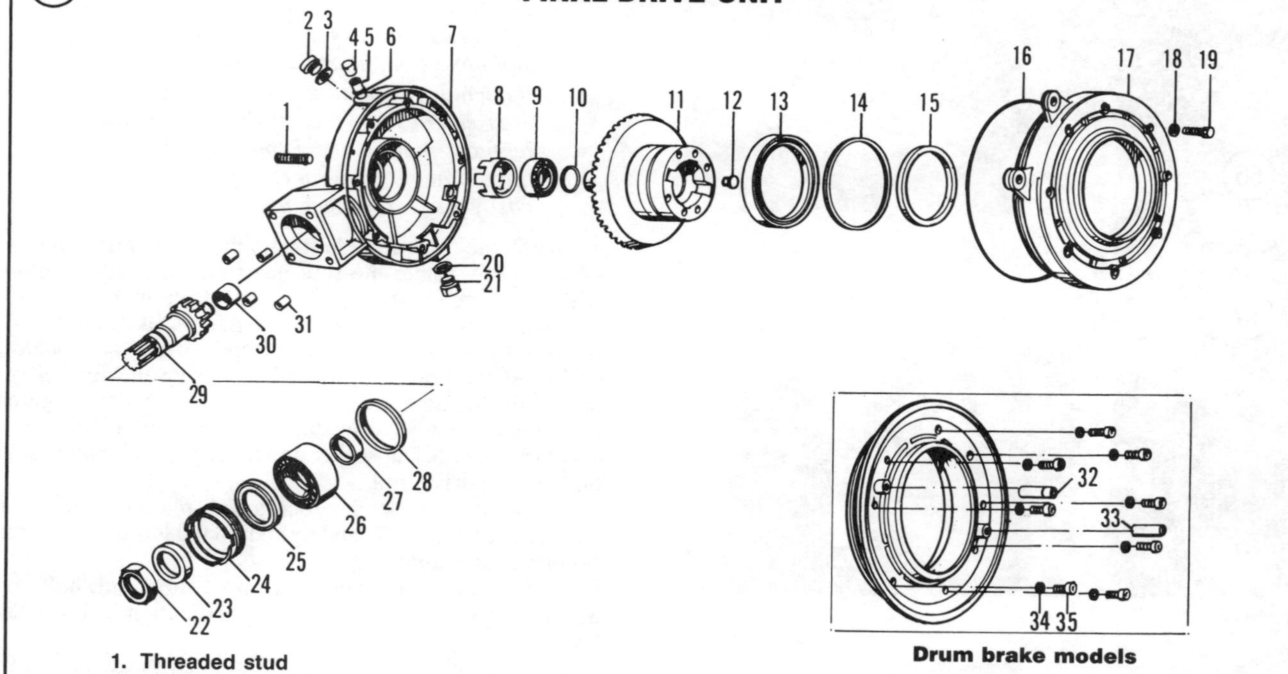

---

(60)   **FINAL DRIVE UNIT**

Drum brake models

1. Threaded stud
2. Filler cap
3. Sealing washer
4. Cap
5. Vent sleeve
6. O-ring
7. Case
8. Speedometer sensing wheel
9. Tapered roller bearing
10. Shim
11. Ring gear (part of ring and pinion gear set)
12. Cover cap
13. Ball bearing
14. Shim
15. Oil seal
16. O-ring
17. Cover
18. Washer
19. Bolt
20. Sealing washer
21. Drain plug
22. Nut
23. Compression ring
24. Threaded ring
25. Oil seal
26. Bearing
27. Inner race
28. Shim
29. Pinion gear (part of ring and pinion gear set)
30. Needle sleeve
31. Locating dowels
32. Brake shoe pivot pin
33. Pipe
34. Washer
35. Allen bolt

lems. To maintain the final drive unit in good condition the gear oil should be changed at the intervals recommended in Chapter Three.

The following procedure is provided if you choose to perform this procedure yourself.

This procedure is presented as a complete, step-by-step, major overhaul of the final drive unit that should be followed if a final drive unit is to be completely reconditioned. However, if you are replacing a part that you know has failed, the disassembly should be carried out only until the failed part is accessible; there is no need to disassemble the final drive unit beyond that point so long as you know the remaining components are in good condition and that they were not affected by the failed part.

Before starting on this procedure, carefully read the entire procedure. Disassembling the unit is complicated but not nearly as complicated as reassembling it. During assembly there are many tolerances that must be calculated. Also the

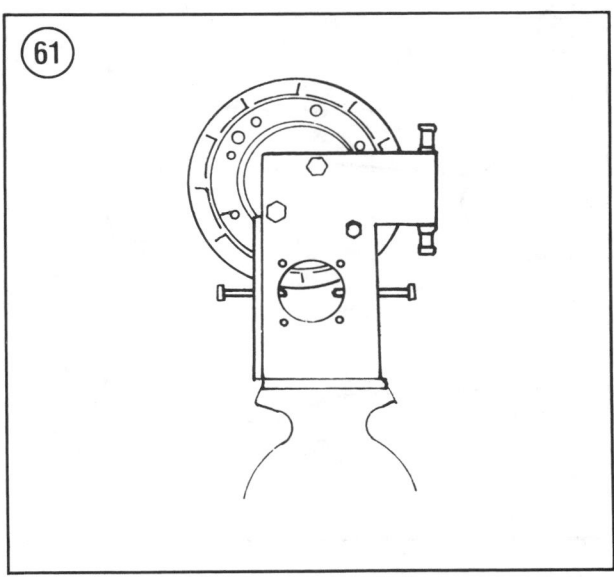

proper gear backlash between the ring and pinion gear must be achieved in order to have the correct gear tooth contact between the 2 parts. If the gear backlash is incorrect, the ring and pinion gears will wear prematurely and will also emit a "howl" when riding.

The following BMW special tools are required for the overhaul procedure:

   a. Case holding fixture (part No. 33 1 500).
   b. Cover oil seal mandrel and driver (part Nos. 33 1 860 and 00 5 500).
   c. Bearing puller and insert (part Nos. 33 1 830 and 33 1 307).
   d. Threaded ring remover (part No. 33 1 700).
   e. Needle bearing remover (part No. 40 0 151 / T2 or 00 8 570).
   f. Tapered roller bearing remover (part No. 00 8 560).
   g. Shaft seal installer (part No. 33 1 760).
   h. Drive pinion ball bearing puller (part No. 00 7 500).
   i. Backlash adjuster (special dial indicator) (part No. 33 2 600).
   j. Gear holding tool (part No. 33 2 630).
   k. Distance (or depth) gauge (part No. 00 2 550).
   l. Drum brake models only—sleeve remover (part No. 33 2 640).
   m. Special drift (drum brake only) (part No. 33 2 640).

Also needed is a hot plate or a heat gun with a heat capacity of approximately 130° C (266° F).

Disassembly

Refer to **Figure 60** for this procedure.

> *WARNING*
> *During this procedure many of the components must be heated for removal. Protect your hands when handling hot components. Either wear thick gloves or use heavy household pot holders to hold onto hot parts.*

1A. On disc brake models, if not already removed, remove the screws securing the rear brake disc. Remove the disc from the final drive unit.

1B. On drum brake models, if not already removed, remove the brake shoes as described under *Rear Drum Brake* in Chapter Twelve.

2. If not already drained, remove the drain plug and the filler cap. Drain out all of the gear oil, then reinstall the drain plug and filler cap and tighten both securely.

3. Secure the final drive unit in the BMW special tool (part No. 33 1 500) and secure the special tool in a vise as shown in **Figure 61**. Tighten the mounting bolts to the torque specification listed in **Table 1**.

4. Using a heat gun, heat the pinion gear nut (A, **Figure 62**) to 100° C (215° F).

11

5. Using a suitable size socket, completely unscrew the gear nut (**Figure 63**).

6. Using a heat gun, heat the final drive unit neck to 120° C (250° F).

7. Using BMW special tool (part No. 33 1 700), completely unscrew the threaded ring and oil seal. Refer to B, **Figure 62** and **Figure 64**.

8. To remove the oil seal from the threaded ring, perform the following:

    a. Using a suitable size socket, press the oil seal out of the threaded ring.

    b. Position the new oil seal with the lettering facing toward the outside surface of the threaded ring.

    c. Using BMW special tool (part No. 33 1 760 and part No. 00 5 500) drive the new oil seal into place in the threaded ring (**Figure 65**).

    d. Remove the special tools.

9. Using a heat gun, heat the final drive unit neck (surrounding the ball bearing outer race) to 125° C (260° F).

CAUTION
Do not damage the splines on the pinion gear while removing the pinion gear and ball bearing from the final drive unit neck.

10. Use a pair of slip joint pliers or Vise Grips and carefully withdraw the pinion gear and the ball bearing from the final drive unit neck (**Figure 66**). Remove the compression ring from the shaft.

11. To remove the bearing assembly from the pinion gear, perform the following:

    a. Secure the pinion gear and ball bearing in a vise with soft jaws to protect the gears.

    b. Install BMW special tools (part No. 00 7 500) onto the pinion gear and bearing assembly (**Figure 67**).

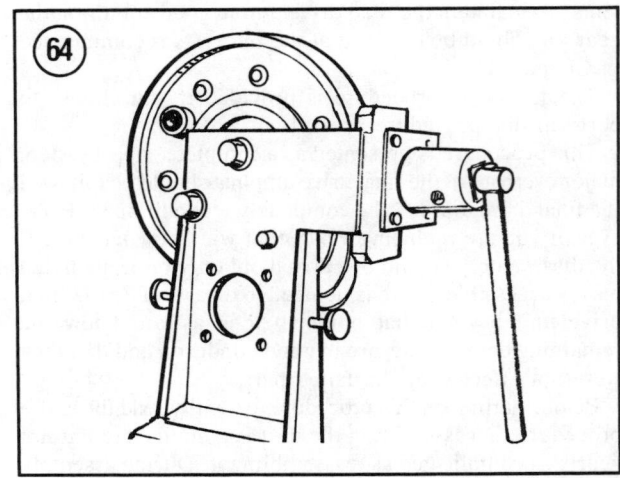

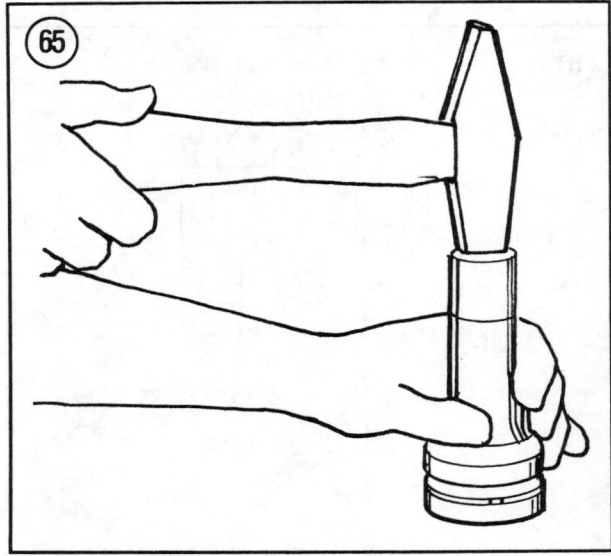

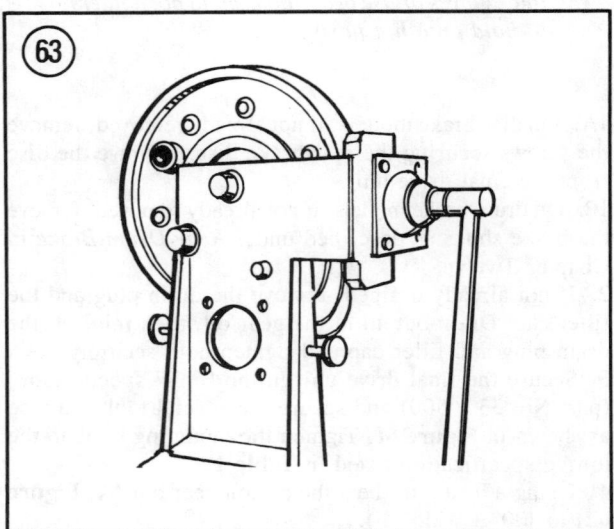

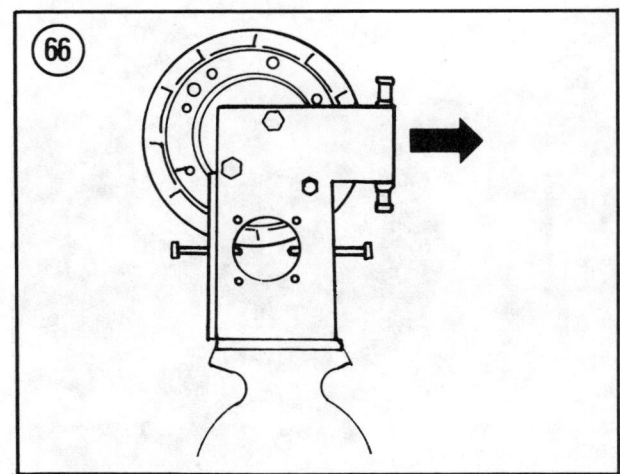

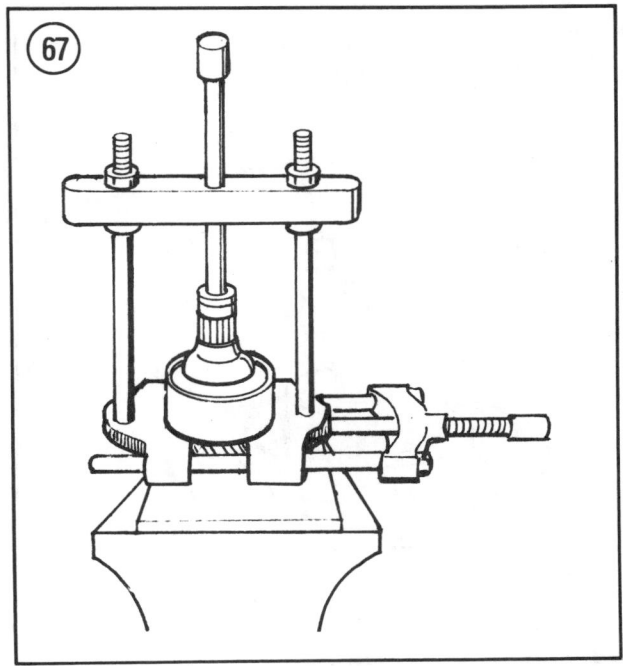

c. Hold a pan under the vise as the bearing assembly may separate during removal and the loose bearing balls may fall out.

d. Withdraw the bearing assembly from the pinion gear.

e. Disassemble the bearing assembly and place all parts in a box to keep all the small parts together.

12. Make alignment marks (**Figure 68**) on the case and cover. This will ensure correct alignment of the 2 parts during assembly.

NOTE
Figure 69 is shown on a disc brake model. Cover removal on a drum brake model is the same. The only difference is that the covers are different in appearance.

13. Remove the screws (**Figure 69**) securing the cover to the case.

14. Using a plastic hammer or soft-faced mallet, tap around the perimeter of the cover until it is loose.

15. Remove the cover and the ring gear from the case.

16. On drum brake models, perform the following:

a. Using a heat gun, heat the final drive case to about 80° C (175° F).

b. Using BMW special tool (part No. 33 2 640), or a suitable size drift, carefully tap the pipe out of the case (**Figure 70**).

17. Using a heat gun, heat the final drive cover to about 80° C (175° F).

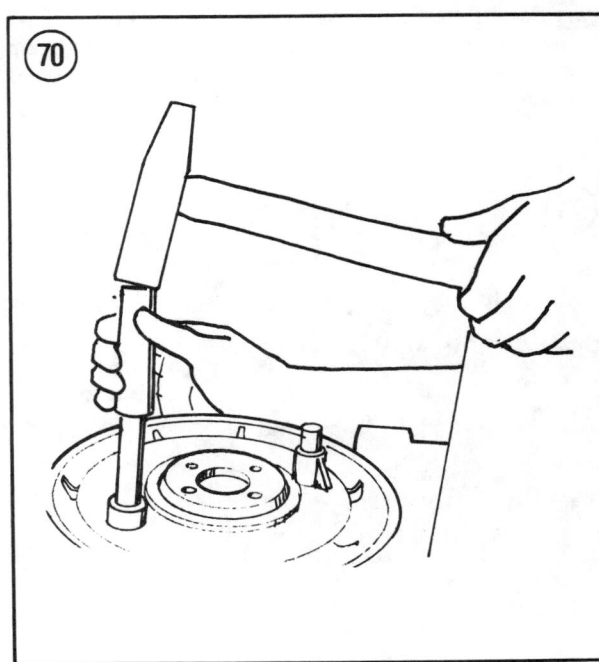

11

18. Using thick gloves or heavy pot holders, separate the ring gear (A, **Figure 71**) from the cover (B, **Figure 71**). Don't lose the shim between the ring gear and the cover. It must be reinstalled.

19. To replace the ring gear oil seal in the cover, perform the following:

    a. Use a hammer and drift and work around the perimeter of the oil seal and carefully tap the seal out of the cover. Discard the oil seal. Be careful not to damage the cover in the area of the oil seal.

    b. Clean out the oil seal area of the cover with solvent and thoroughly dry.

    c. Apply a light coat of oil to the outer surface of the new oil seal.

    d. Using BMW special tools (part No. 33 1 860 and 00 5 500), carefully tap the new oil seal into the case (**Figure 72**). Be sure to tap the oil seal in squarely and tap it in until it bottoms out in the cover.

20. To remove the pinion gear needle bearing from the case, perform the following:

    a. Insert BMW special tool (part No. 00 8 570 or 40 0 151/T2) into the neck of the case and position it behind the needle bearing (A, **Figure 73**). Turn the special tool end to expand it behind the needle bearing.

    b. Attach a suitable size commercial bearing puller (B, **Figure 73**) onto the backside of the BMW special tool.

    c. Using a heat gun, heat the final drive unit neck (surrounding the needle bearing) to 120° C (250° F).

    d. Carefully and slowly tighten the bearing puller and withdraw the tapered roller bearing from the case.

21. To remove the ring gear tapered roller bearing outer race (**Figure 74**) from the case, perform the following:

    a. Secure the final drive unit in a vise with soft jaws with the open portion of the case facing up to gain access to the ring gear tapered roller bearing outer race.

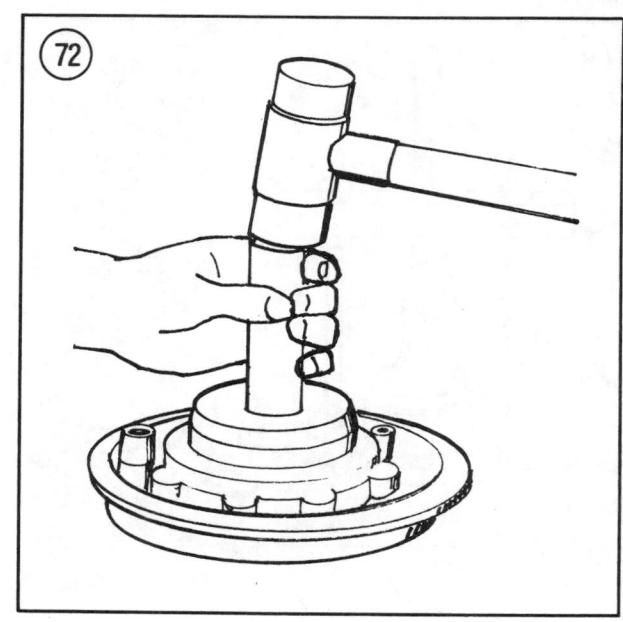

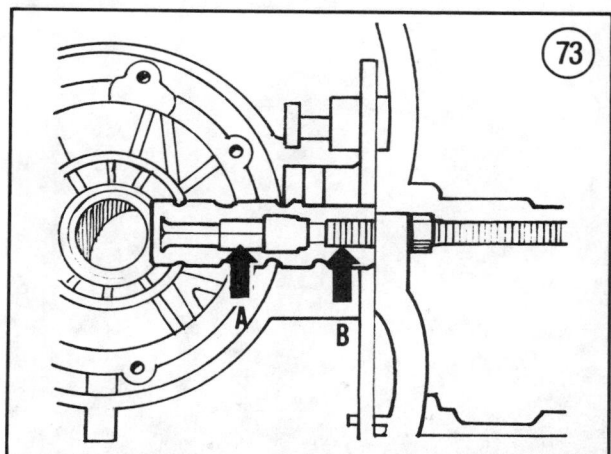

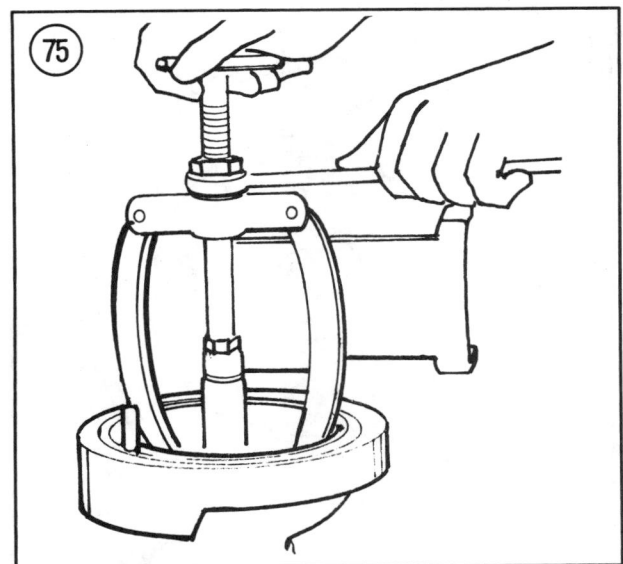

b. Install the bearing puller, BMW special tool (part No. 00 8 560) onto the outer race (**Figure 75**).

c. Carefully and slowly tighten the bearing puller and withdraw the outer race from the case.

d. Remove the final drive case from the vise.

22. To remove the ball bearing on the ring gear, perform the following:

   a. Secure the ring gear, ball bearing side up, in a vise with soft jaws.

   b. Insert BMW special tool (part No. 33 1 307) into the center of the ring gear (A, **Figure 76**).

   c. Install the bearing puller, BMW special tool (part No. 33 1 830) onto the ball bearing (B, **Figure 76**).

   d. Carefully and slowly tighten the bearing puller and withdraw the ball bearing from the ring gear.

   e. Remove the special tools from the ring gear.

23. To remove the tapered roller bearing, inner race (**Figure 77**) and shim from the ring gear, perform the following:

   a. Secure the ring gear, tapered roller bearing side up, in a vise with soft jaws.

   b. Install the bearing puller, BMW special tool (part No. 00 7 500) onto the tapered roller bearing (A, **Figure 78**).

   c. Carefully and slowly tighten the bearing puller (B, **Figure 78**) and withdraw the tapered roller bearing from the ring gear.

   d. Remove the tapered roller bearing, inner race and shim from the ring gear.

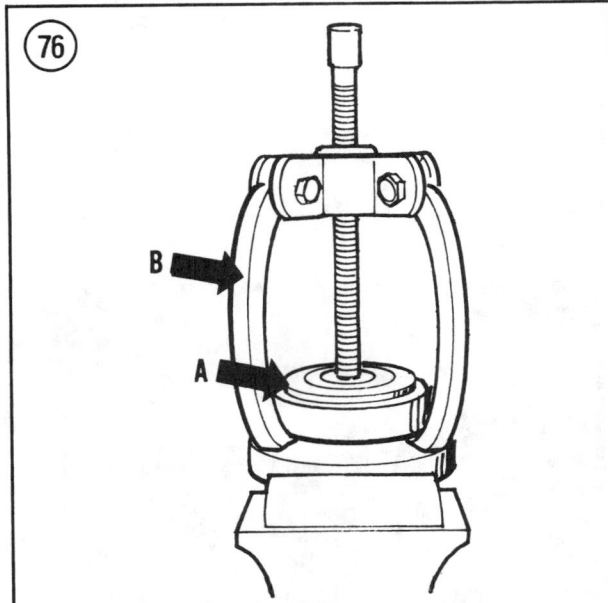

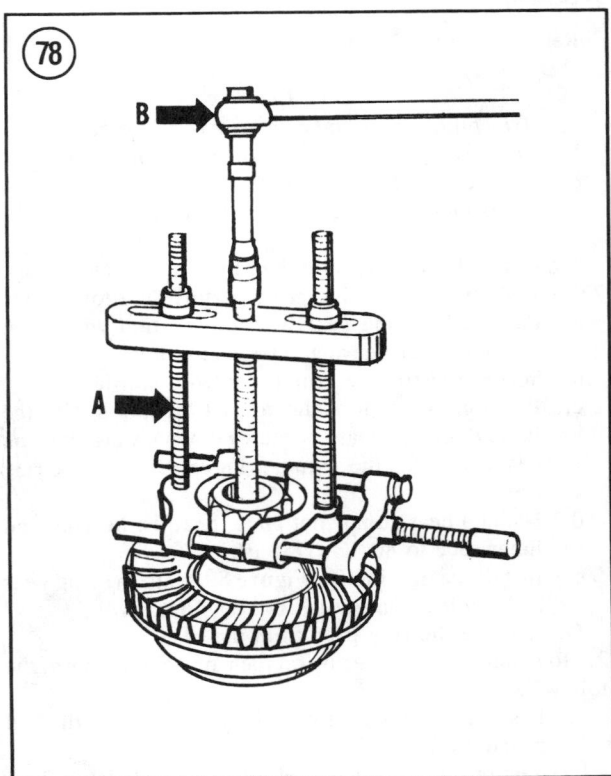

11

Inspection

1. Wash all parts in solvent and dry thoroughly with compressed air.

> *NOTE*
> *The ring and pinion gear must be replaced as a set and are marked with a pair code on each gear (Figure 79).*

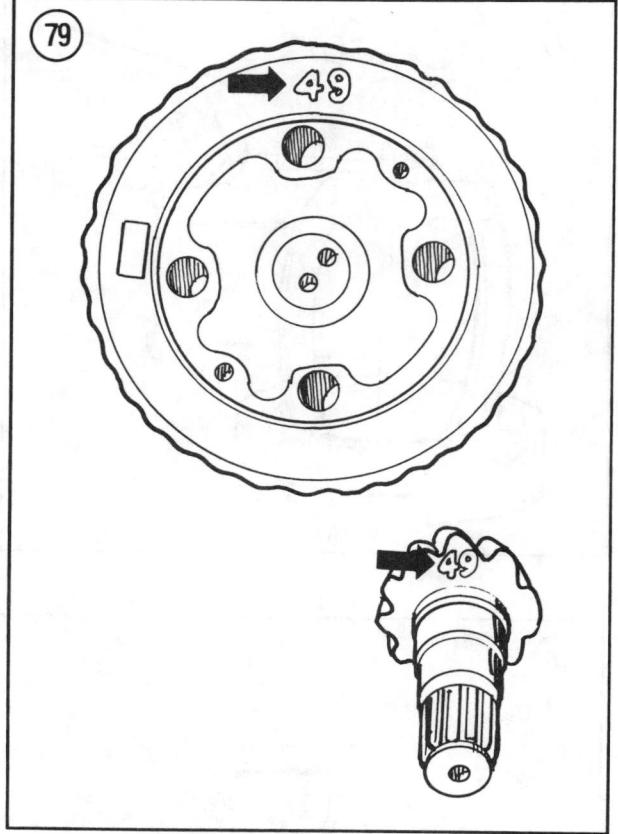

2. Inspect the teeth on the ring gear (**Figure 80**) and the pinion gear set (**Figure 81**). If the teeth are worn or damaged on either of the gears, both gears must be replaced as a set (the only way they are sold is as a set).
3. Inspect the case and the cover for cracks or other damage. Make sure all ribs and bosses are not damaged or missing. Replace either or both parts.
4. Inspect the threads on the threaded ring for wear or damage. Clean out the threads with the correct size and pitch thread tap or replace if necessary.
5. On disc brake models, inspect the threaded holes (A, **Figure 82**) for the disc mounting screws. Check for wear or damage. If necessary, clean out the threads with the correct size and pitch thread tap or replace if necessary.
6. On all models, inspect the threaded holes (B, **Figure 82**) for the wheel mounting bolts. Check for wear or damage. Clean out the threads with the correct size and pitch thread tap or replace if necessary.

Assembly

Refer to **Figure 60** for this procedure.

> *NOTE*
> *If the pinion gear and ring gear were replaced with a new gear set, or any of the bearings were replaced, perform **Pinion Gear-to-Ring Gear Adjustment** as described in this chapter.*

1. To install the tapered roller bearing, inner race (**Figure 77**) and shim onto the ring gear, perform the following:
   a. Position the ring gear with the portion where the tapered roller bearing rides facing up.
   b. Secure the ring gear in a vise with soft jaws.
   c. Position the shim of the correct thickness with the inner diameter chamfer facing down toward the ring gear and install the shim (A, **Figure 83**) onto the ring gear.
   d. Using a heat gun or hot plate, heat the bearing and inner race to 80° C (175° F).
   e. Install the bearing (B, **Figure 83**) onto the ring gear and tap it down until it bottoms out.
   f. Remove the ring gear from the vise.
2. To install the ball bearing on the ring gear, perform the following:
   a. Position the ring gear with the portion where the ball bearing rides facing up.
   b. Secure the ring gear in a vise with soft jaws.

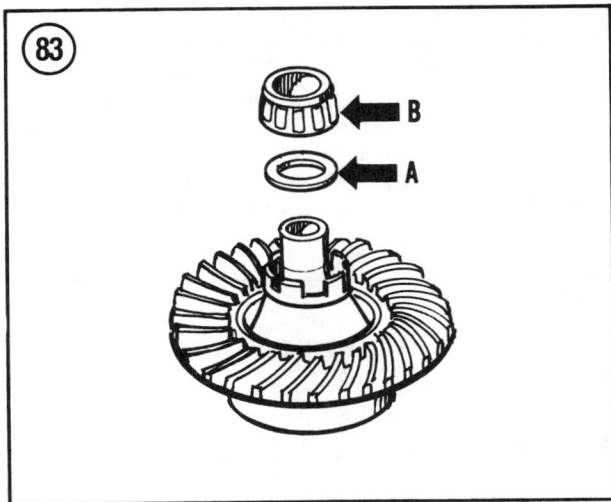

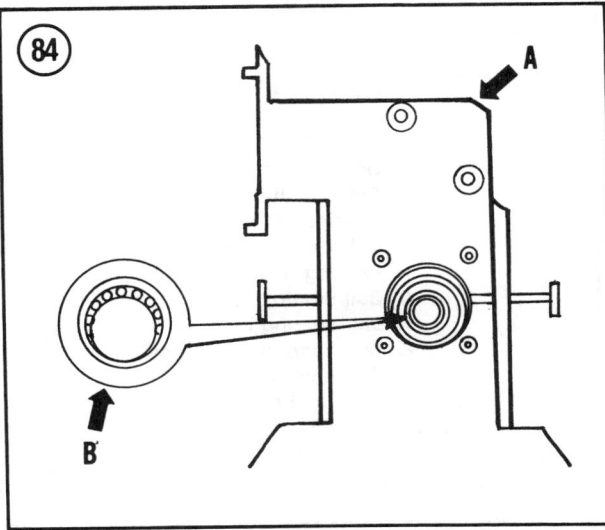

c. Install a shim of the correct thickness onto the ring gear.

d. Using a heat gun or hot plate, heat the bearing assembly to 80° C (175° F).

e. Install the bearing onto the ring gear and tap it down until it bottoms out.

f. Remove the ring gear from the vise.

3. To install the ring gear tapered roller bearing outer race into the case, perform the following:

a. Place the tapered roller bearing outer race in a freezer for 10-15 minutes. This will reduce its overall size.

b. Using a heat gun or hot plate, heat the case to 120° C (250° F).

c. Set the case on wood blocks with the open portion of the case facing up.

d. Install the tapered roller bearing outer race into the case and tap it down in until it bottoms out in the case. Make sure the outer race is installed straight down and that it does not get cocked during installation.

4. To install the pinion gear needle bearing into the case, perform the following:

a. Clamp the final drive case in the BMW special tool (part No. 33 1 630) (A, **Figure 84**).

b. Place the pinion gear needle bearing in a freezer for 10-15 minutes. This will reduce its overall size.

c. Using a heat gun, heat the case in the area where the needle bearing is to be located. Heat the case to 120° C (250° F).

d. Position the needle bearing with the identification marks facing out (B, **Figure 84**).

e. Install the needle bearing into the case and tap it in with a suitable size socket or use the pinion gear. Tap it in until it bottoms out in the case. Make sure the needle bearing is installed straight in and that it does not get cocked in the case during installation.

5. Place the ring gear assembly in a freezer for about 15-30 minutes. This will reduce its overall size.

6. Install the shim on the cover.

7. Install the ring gear (A, **Figure 71**) into the cover (B, **Figure 71**).

8. Install a new O-ring seal (**Figure 85**) into the groove in the cover.

11

9. Install the cover and the ring gear onto the case.

10. Using a plastic hammer or soft-faced mallet, tap around the perimeter of the cover until it bottoms out.

11. Install the screws (**Figure 69**) securing the cover to the case. Tighten the screws to the torque specification listed in **Table 1**.

12. On drum brake models, perform the following:

   a. Place the pipe in a freezer for about 15 minutes. This will reduce its overall size.

   b. Using BMW special tool (part No. 33 2 640), or a suitable size drift, carefully tap the pipe into the case until it bottoms out.

13. To install the bearing assembly (**Figure 86**) onto the pinion gear, perform the following:

   a. Place the pinion gear in a freezer for about 30 minutes. This will reduce its overall size.

   b. Using a heat gun or hot plate, heat the cylindrical roller bearing inner race to 120° C (250° F) and install the bearing inner race onto the pinion gear shaft.

   c. Carefully tap the cylindrical roller bearing inner race into place until it bottoms out.

   d. Install the cylindrical needle bearing outer race and the cylindrical roller bearing cage into place on the inner race.

   e. Using a heat gun or hot plate, heat the ball bearing inner race to 120° C (250° F) and install the bearing inner race onto the pinion gear shaft.

   f. Carefully tap the ball bearing inner race into place until it bottoms out.

   g. Install the ball bearing cage in place over the inner race and install each individual ball bearing into place in these 2 parts. Install all ball bearings.

   h. Using a heat gun or hot plate, heat the compression ring to 120° C (250° F) and install the compression ring onto the pinion gear shaft.

   i. Install a shim of the correct thickness.

   j. Place the ball bearing outer race in a freezer for about 30 minutes. This will reduce its overall size.

   k. Using a heat gun, heat the final drive unit neck (surrounding the ball bearing outer race) to 120° C (250° F).

   l. Install the ball bearing outer race into the final drive unit neck and over the ball bearings in the bearing cage.

14. Thoroughly clean the threaded ring of all oil and/or grease.

15. Secure the final drive unit in the BMW special tool (part No. 33 1 500) and secure the special tool in a vise as shown in **Figure 61**. Tighten the mounting bolts to the torque specification listed in **Table 1**.

16. Coat the threaded ring with a coat of Hylomar SQ 37 grease and place it in a freezer for about 15 minutes. This will reduce its overall size.

17. Using a heat gun, heat the final drive unit neck (surrounding the ball bearing outer race) to between 80-100° C (175-215° F).

CAUTION
Do not damage the new oil seal in the threaded ring during installation. After the threaded ring is installed, make sure the oil seal lip is seated correctly around the pinion gear shaft. This is necessary to prevent an oil leak.

18. Start the threaded ring by hand, then using BMW special tool (part No. 33 1 700), screw in the threaded ring. Refer to B, **Figure 62** and **Figure 60**. Tighten the threaded ring to the torque specification listed in **Table 1**.

19. Apply about 0.1 gram of Loctite No. 273 to the gear nut and install the nut (A, **Figure 62**).

20. Using a suitable size socket, tighten the gear nut to the torque specification listed in **Table 1**.

21. Install the drain plug and new sealing washer. Tighten the drain plug to the torque specification listed in **Table 1**.

22A. On disc brake models, install the rear brake disc and mounting screws. Tighten the screws to the torque specification listed in **Table 1**.

22B. On drum brake models, install the brake shoes as described under *Rear Drum Brake* in Chapter Twelve.

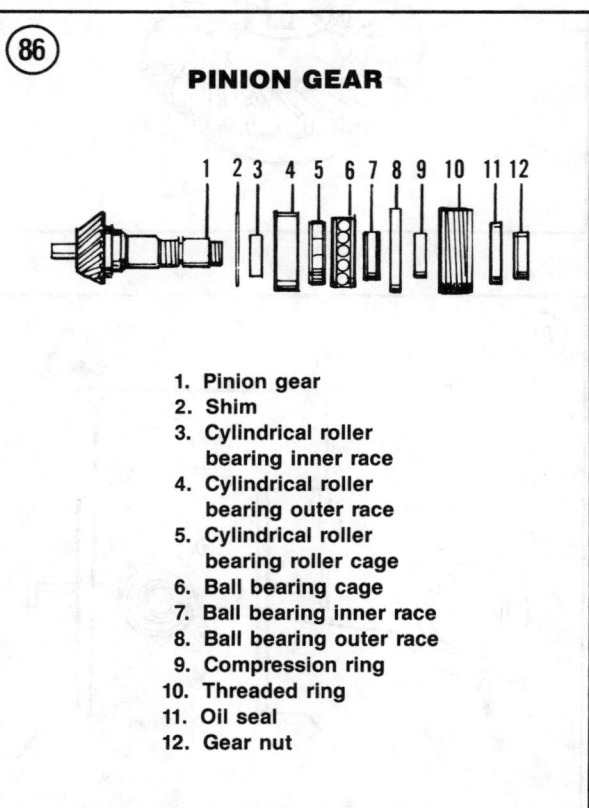

(86)

PINION GEAR

1. Pinion gear
2. Shim
3. Cylindrical roller bearing inner race
4. Cylindrical roller bearing outer race
5. Cylindrical roller bearing roller cage
6. Ball bearing cage
7. Ball bearing inner race
8. Ball bearing outer race
9. Compression ring
10. Threaded ring
11. Oil seal
12. Gear nut

23. Refill the final drive unit with the recommended type and quantity of oil. See Chapter Three.

PINION GEAR-TO-RING GEAR ADJUSTMENT

If the ring and pinion gear set is being replaced, make sure they are from the same pair that was tested together and "designated as a compatible pair" at the BMW factory. The gears are run on a factory test stand and paired up in sets. This is to provide smooth running and the correct amount of backlash. After testing they are then given a *pair code mark* that appears on both gears (**Figure 79**). Only

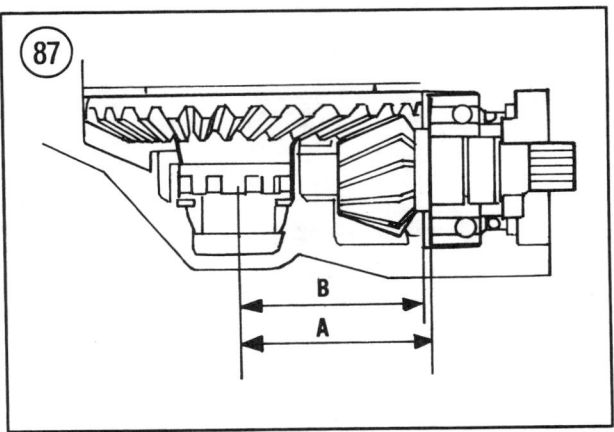

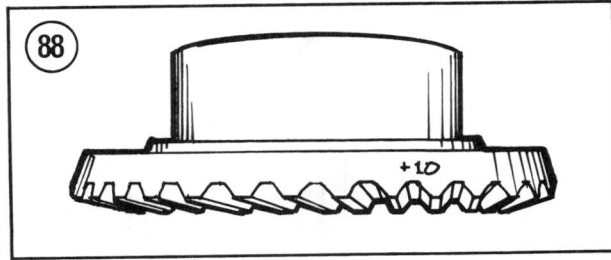

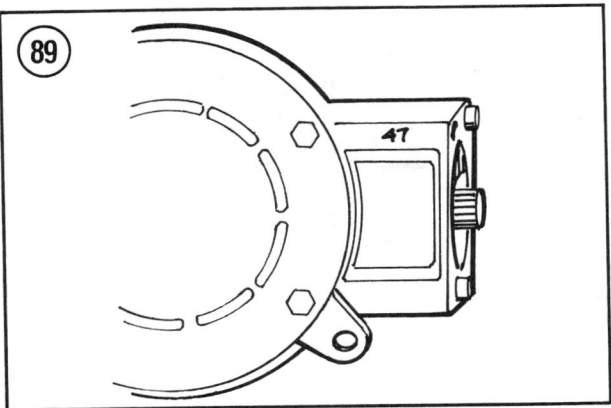

accept a ring and pinion gear set from a BMW dealer with matching numbers—don't accept a set with 2 different numbers.

If a *new* ring and pinion gear set is going to be installed into a used case or a *new* case is going to be used with the used ring and pinion set, the tolerance between these parts must be checked. There is a specified distance that provides the correct relation of the ring gear to the pinion gear.

The pinion gear is installed in the case and the ring gear is installed in the cover. When the cover and case are attached to each other the relationship between the ring gear and pinion gear must be correct.

NOTE
If any of the bearings have been replaced within the final drive unit, all of the following procedures must be followed.

The *first section* of the procedure is for the pinion gear adjustment. This adjustment is made to correctly locate the pinion gear in relation to the case. A shim is used to achieve the in-and-out location of the pinion gear in the case and to correctly align it to the center of the ring gear.

The *second section* of the procedure is the adjustment of the ring gear backlash to the pinion gear. This adjustment is made to correctly locate the ring gear to the pinion gear. A shim is used to achieve the up-and-down location of the ring gear in the cover and to correctly align it with the pinion gear.

The *third section* is the tooth contact pattern or how the pinion gear and ring gear teeth mate to each other. The gear contact must be centered, otherwise there will be abnormal stress placed on the gear teeth causing premature wear.

11

Pinion Gear-to-Case Adjustment

There is a specified distance for the location of the pinion gear within the case. This dimension is the distance from the inner surface of the pinion gear roller bearing to the centerline of the ring gear axis once the case and cover are assembled. The specified *drive pinion basic distance* is 77.50 mm; refer to dimension "A" in **Figure 87**. If the drive gear pinion is *not within specification* it is so marked on the outer surface of the ring gear as shown in **Figure 88**. This number (e.g. +10) is a metric dimension in 1/100 of a mm and it is to be substituted for the standard number (e.g. +10 changes 77.50 mm to 77.60 mm).

Within the case is a shoulder where the pinion gear roller bearing stops during installation. This is called the "case basic distance" and it is 75.50 mm (3.022 in.); refer to dimension "B" in **Figure 87**. If the case has the exact finished distance there will be no marking on it. If the case is *not within specification* it is so marked on the inner surface with a number (e.g. 47) as shown in **Figure 89**. This number (e.g. 47) is a metric dimension in 1/100 of a mm and it is to be substituted for the standard number (e.g. 47 changes 75.50 mm to 75.47 mm).

Shims are available from a BMW dealer in increments of 0.005 mm and range from 1.500-2.500 mm.

To determine the thickness of the shim required, perform the following:

If both the case and the pinion gear are within specification, subtract the case basic distance from the pinion gear basic distance:

$$\begin{array}{r} 77.50 \text{ mm} \\ -75.50 \text{ mm} \\ \hline 2.00 \text{ mm} \end{array}$$ shim required

If the case is *not* within specification, but the pinion is, subtract the case basic distance (minus any dimensional deviation—e.g. 47 = 75.47 mm) from the pinion gear basic distance:

$$\begin{array}{r} 77.50 \text{ mm} \\ -75.47 \text{ mm} \\ \hline 2.03 \text{ mm} \end{array}$$ shim required

If the case is within specification, but the pinion gear is *not* within specification, subtract the case basic distance from the pinion gear basic distance (plus any dimensional deviation—e.g. +10 = 77.60 mm):

$$\begin{array}{r} 77.60 \text{ mm} \\ -75.50 \text{ mm} \\ \hline 2.10 \text{ mm} \end{array}$$ shim required

Backlash Adjustment

To check and adjust the backlash, several BMW special tools are required. They are as follows:
a. Gear holding tool (part No. 33 2 630).
b. Backlash adjuster (special dial indicator) (part No. 33 2 600).
1. If the ring gear's tapered roller bearing outer race was removed from the case, perform the following:
a. Heat the final drive case to about 80° C (175° F).
b. Install the bearing outer race. Install the bearing race until it bottoms out.
2. For a preliminary backlash adjustment, install a 2.35 mm shim between the roller bearing and the ring gear.
3. Position the shim with the inner chamfer facing toward the ring gear and install the shim onto the ring gear (A, **Figure 83**).

4. Heat the tapered roller bearing to about 80° C (175° F).
5. Install the tapered roller bearing (B, **Figure 83**) onto the ring gear. Make sure it is completely seated on the ring gear.

NOTE
Before proceeding, allow the case and the bearing to cool down to room temperature. If they are still hot it will affect the following readings and give a false reading.

6. Install the ring gear into the case and into mesh with the pinion drive gear.

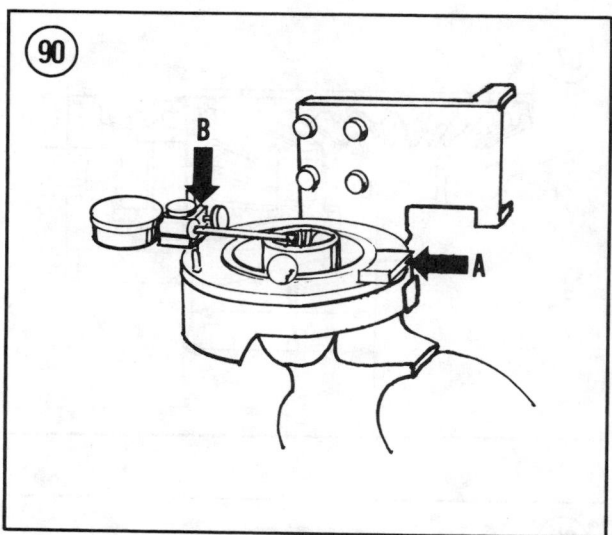

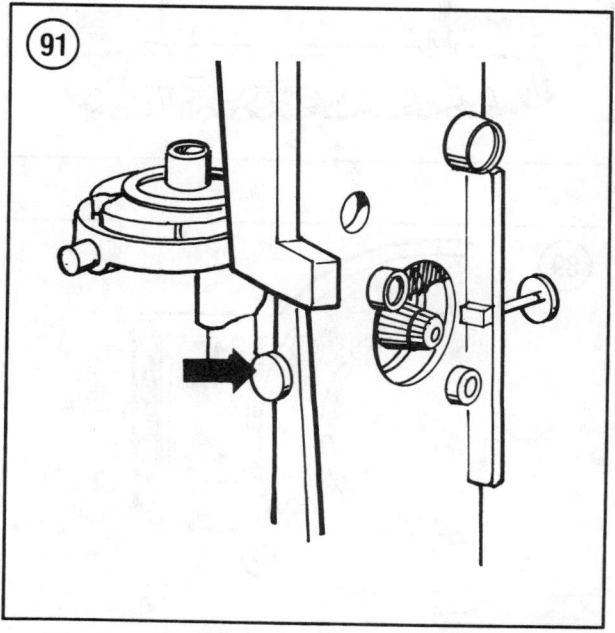

7. Attach the gear holding tool (part No. 33 2 630) (A, **Figure 90**) so the pinion gear cannot rotate. The gear must remain stationary during this procedure, otherwise the results will be incorrect.

8. Attach the backlash adjuster (special dial indicator) (part No. 33 2 600) (B, **Figure 90**) to the final drive unit case.

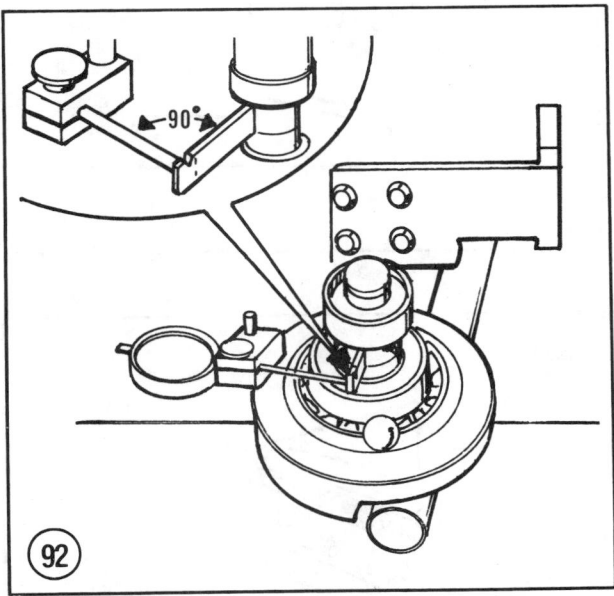

9. Tighten the arresting screw (**Figure 91**) so that the pinion gear will not move.

10. Adjust the tool so that the dial gauge point is 90° to the rod on the special tool (**Figure 92**).

11. Adjust the dial gauge to zero.

12. Slightly rotate the ring gear back and forth and note the dial gauge reading.

13. Reposition the special tool and check the backlash 120° from the point tested in Step 12. Note the reading.

14. Again reposition the special tool and check the backlash 120° from the point tested in Step 13. Note the reading. The specified backlash is listed in **Table 2**.

15A. If the backlash is within specification, remove the special tools from the final drive unit case.

15B. If the backlash is incorrect, remove the special tools from the final drive unit case and perform the following:

    a. Remove the ring gear from the final drive case.

    b. Remove the shim and replace it with a thicker or thinner one. Remember to position the shim with the inner chamfer facing toward the ring gear.

    c. Install the ring gear into the case and into mesh with the pinion drive gear.

    d. Repeat Steps 7-15A until the correct amount of backlash is obtained.

16. Inspect the tooth contact pattern as described in this chapter.

Tooth Contact Pattern

After completing the *Backlash Adjustment* the tooth contact pattern must be checked.

1. Remove the ring gear from the final drive case.

2. Apply a light coat of gear marking compound to both sides of a couple of teeth on the pinion gear.

3. Install the ring gear into the final drive case and pinion gear.

4. Press down firmly on the ring gear and rotate it back and forth several times so the marking compound will transfer onto the ring gear teeth.

5. Remove the ring gear from the final drive case.

6. Observe the pattern on the pinion gear. If it looks like that in **Figure 93** the tooth contact pattern is correct. If so, wipe off all marking compound residue from each gear.

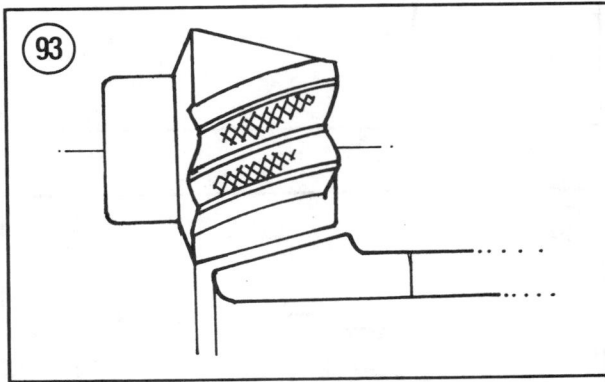

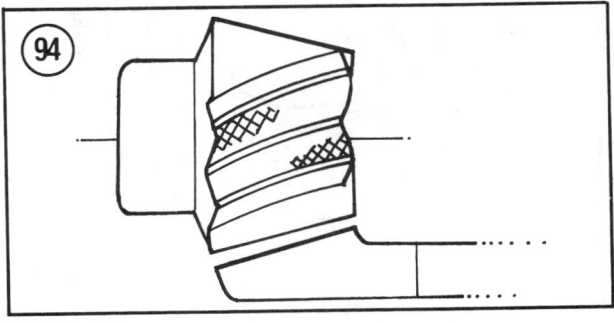

NOTE
Perform Steps 7-14 only if the tooth contact pattern is not correct and requires shim replacement.

7. If the pattern does not look like **Figure 93**, compare to the following illustrations:

    a. **Figure 94**: pinion gear must be moved farther out in the final drive case. Replace the existing shim with a *thicker* shim between the pinion gear and the final drive case.

11

b. **Figure 95**: pinion gear must be moved farther back into the final drive case. Replace the existing shim with a *thinner* shim between the pinion gear and the final drive case.

8. Replace the shim between the pinion gear and the final drive case as described in this chapter.

9. Reapply a light coat of gear marking compound to both sides of a couple of teeth on the pinion gear.

10. Install the ring gear into the final drive case and pinion gear.

11. Press down firmly on the ring gear and rotate it back and forth several times so the gear marking compound will transfer onto the ring gear teeth.

12. Remove the ring gear from the final drive case.

13. Observe the pattern on the pinion gear. If it looks like that in **Figure 93** the tooth contact pattern is correct. If not, repeat this procedure until the tooth contact pattern is correct.

14. After the tooth contact pattern is correct in the loaded condition, check in the unloaded condition as follows:

a. Reapply a light coat of gear marking compound to both sides of a couple of teeth on the pinion gear.

b. Install the ring gear into the final drive case and pinion gear.

c. *Press down firmly* on the ring gear and rotate it back and forth several times so the marking compound will transfer onto the ring gear teeth.

d. This time do *not* press down firmly on the ring gear, just rotate it back and forth with no pressure, several times so the ink or paint will form an additional pattern within the one made in substep 14c. The new pattern should be centered (A, **Figure 96**) on the forward side of the gear and should be toward the larger end of the gear on the reverse side of the gear (B, **Figure 96**).

15. Remove the ring gear from the final drive case. Wipe off all gear marking compound residue from both gears.

TAPER ROLLER BEARING PRELOAD

The preload on the taper roller bearing, located on the right-hand side of the ring gear, is controlled by the shim placed between the ball bearing, located on the left-hand side of the ring gear, and the case cover. The correct spacing of this ball bearing determines the preload on the tapered roller bearing. A specific amount of preload is necessary for the tapered roller bearing to seat correctly and operate properly. The preload thickness is listed in **Table 2** and the shims are available from BMW dealers in the following thicknesses: 0.180, 0.280, 0.380, 0.500, 0.630, 0.750 and 0.880 mm.

1. Place the case cover on the workbench with the inner surface facing up.

2. Place the BMW special tool (distance or depth gauge—part No. 00 2 550) (A, **Figure 97**) on spacers (B, **Figure 97**) on the case-to-cover mating surface of the cover.

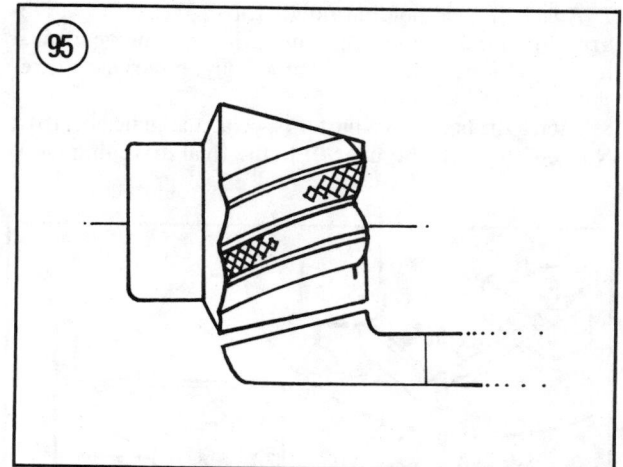
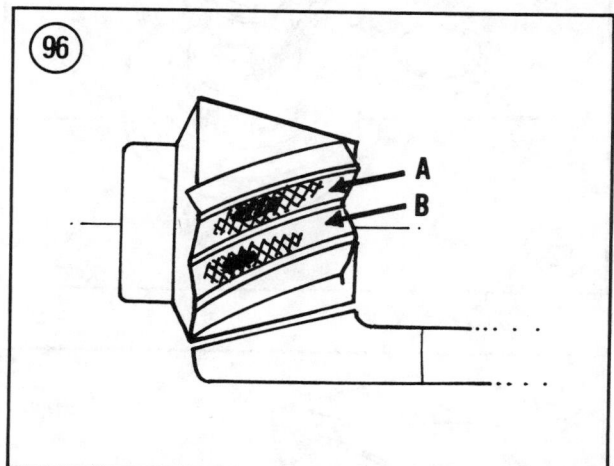
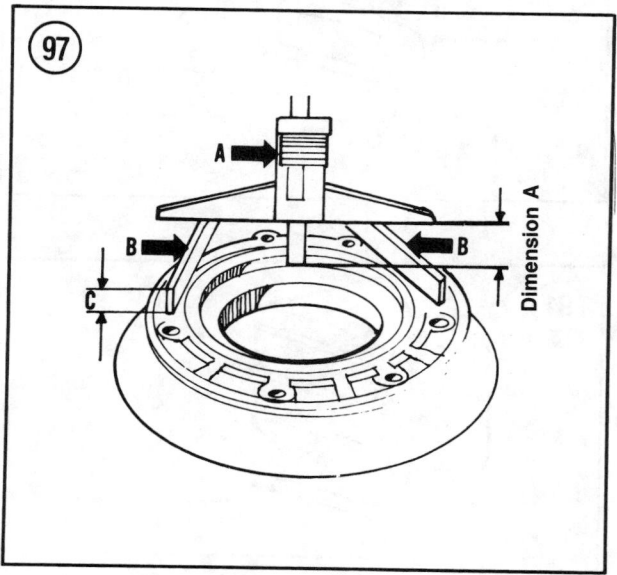

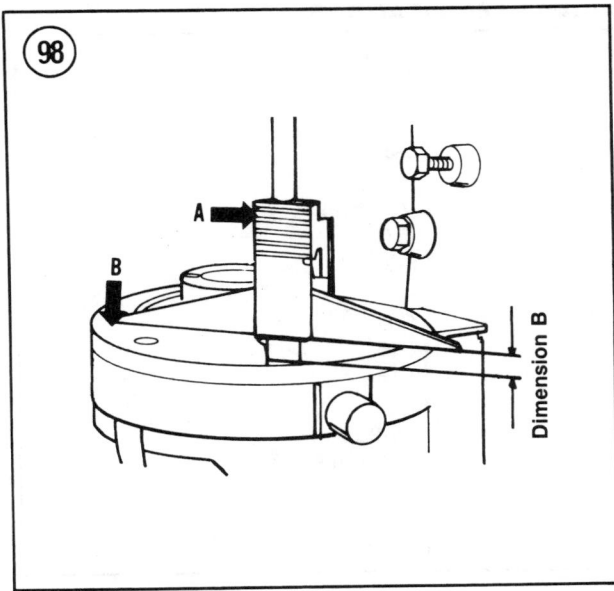

3. Measure the distance from the mating surface down to the ball bearing seating shoulder of the cover. Subtract the thickness of the spacers (C, **Figure 97**) from this dimension. This is dimension "A."

4. Install the ring gear into the final drive case and pinion gear.

5. Install the ball bearing onto the ring gear.

6. Place the BMW special tool (distance or depth gauge—part No. 00 2 550) (A, **Figure 98**) on the upper surface of the ball bearing on the ring gear. Place the special tool in the opening in the gauge ring (B, **Figure 98**).

7. Measure the distance from the ball bearing upper surface to the case mating surface. This is dimension "B" (**Figure 98**).

8. Subtract dimension "B" from dimension "A." This dimension is the shim thickness required *without preload*.

9. Add the thickness of the dimension without preload, determined in Step 8, to the specified preload listed in **Table 2**. This will give you the dimension for the shim thickness to provide the correct amount of preload.

10. Remove the special tool.

Tables are on the following page.

11

Table 1 REAR SUSPENSION TORQUE SPECIFICATIONS

Item	N·m	ft.-lb.
Rear wheel mounting bolts	105	77
Shock absorber mounting		
bolts and nuts	48-54	35-39
Swing arm		
Fixed pivot pin mounting bolts	8-10	6-7
Adjustable pivot pin	6.8-7.8	5-5.6
Adjustable pivot pin locknut	39-44	28-32
Final drive unit		
Mounting bolts	37-43	27-31
Cover screws	19-23	14-16
Oil filler plug	18-22	13-16
Drain plug	22-28	16-20
Threaded ring	106-130	76.5-93.5
Pinion gear nut	180-220	130.5-159.5
Final drive unit-to-BMW		
special tool (33-1 500)	100	72
Brake disc mounting bolt	19-23	13.5-16.5

Table 2 REAR SUSPENSION SPECIFICATIONS

Maximum vehicle weight rating	
K75	450 kg (992 lb.)
K100	480 kg (1058 lb.)
Vehicle unloaded weight (road ready with all	
liquids on board)	
K75C	227 kg (500 lb.)
K75S, K75T	229 kg (505 lb.)
K100RS, K100RT	253 kg (558 lb.)
K100LT	283 kg (624 lb.)
Final drive unit	
Manufacturer	Klingeinberg ring and pinion type
Ring gear backlash	0.07-0.16 mm (0.0027-0.0063 in.)
Tapered roller bearing	
pre-load	0.05-0.10 mm (0.002-0.004 in.) with 600-1,600 N·m (132-353 lb.) of pre-load force
Oil capacity	0.26 liter (0.5 pt.)
Oil type	Hypoid gear oil GL5
Oil weight	SAE 90 above 5° C (41° F) SAE 80 below 5° C (41° F) SAE 80W/90 (optional)
Drive shaft	Located within the swing arm. Universal joint at front end of shaft.
Rear suspension travel	110 mm (4.331 in.)

NOTE: If you own a 1990 or later model, first check the Supplement at the back of this book for any new service information.

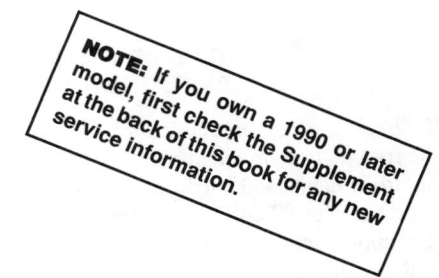

CHAPTER TWELVE

BRAKES

All models use dual disc brakes on the front. K100 and K75S models use a single disc brake on the rear. All other models use a drum brake on the rear.

The disc brakes are actuated by hydraulic fluid and are controlled by the right-hand hand lever for the front brakes or right-hand foot pedal for the rear brake. The brake pedal is connected to the master cylinder. As the brake pads wear, the caliper pistons move out automatically to keep lever or pedal freeplay constant. Over a period of time, this gradual repositioning of the pistons in response to brake pad wear will drop the level of the hydraulic fluid in the reservoir.

The rear drum brake is controlled by the right-hand foot pedal and rod that is attached to the drum brake lever.

When working on hydraulic brake systems, it is necessary that the work area and all tools be absolutely clean. Any tiny particles of foreign matter and grit in the caliper assembly or the master cylinder can damage the components.

Refer to **Table 1** for brake specifications and **Table 2** for torque specifications. **Table 1** and **Table 2** are located at the end of this chapter.

Disc Brake System Service Hints

Consider the following when servicing the front and rear disc brake systems.

1. Disc brake components rarely require disassembly, so do not disassemble them unless necessary.

2. Use only DOT 4 brake fluid from a sealed container.

WARNING
Do not intermix silicone based (DOT 5) brake fluid as it can cause brake component damage leading to brake system failure.

3. Do not allow disc brake fluid to contact any plastic, painted or plated surfaces or surface damage will occur.
4. Always keep the master cylinder's reservoir cover closed to prevent dust or moisture from entering.
5. Use only DOT 4 brake fluid to wash parts. Never clean any internal brake components with solvent or any other petroleum-based cleaners. Solvents will cause the seals to swell and distort and require replacement.
6. Whenever *any* component has been removed from the brake system, the system is considered "opened" and must be bled to remove the air bubbles. Also, if the brake feels "spongy," this usually means there is air in the system and it must be bled. For safe brake operation, refer to *Bleeding the System* as described in this chapter.

WARNING
*When working on the brake system, do **not** inhale brake dust. It may contain asbestos, which can cause lung injury and cancer. Wear a disposable face mask and wash your hands thoroughly after completing the work.*

12

FRONT BRAKE PAD REPLACEMENT

There is no recommended mileage interval for changing the friction pads in the disc brake. Pad wear depends greatly on riding habits and conditions. The pads should be checked for wear every 7,240 km (4,500 miles) and replaced when the lining thickness reaches 1.5 mm (1/16 in.) from the brake pad backing plate. To maintain an even brake pressure on the disc always replace both pads in both calipers at the same time. Always use brake pads from the same manufacturer in both front calipers—never intermix different brands.

CAUTION
Watch the pads more closely when the wear line approaches the disc. On some pads the wear line is very close to the metal backing plate.

If pad wear happens to be uneven for some reason the backing plate may come in contact with the disc and cause damage.

Refer to **Figure 1** for this procedure.

NOTE
It is not necessary to remove the caliper assembly in order to replace the brake pads.

1. To prevent accidental application of the front brake lever, place a spacer between the front brake lever and the hand grip. Hold the spacer in place with a large rubber band, a tie wrap or a piece of tape.
2. Using a large flat-bladed screwdriver, carefully remove the brake caliper cover (**Figure 2**).
3. Using a drift and small hammer, carefully tap the top lockpin (**Figure 3**) out from the backside of the caliper.

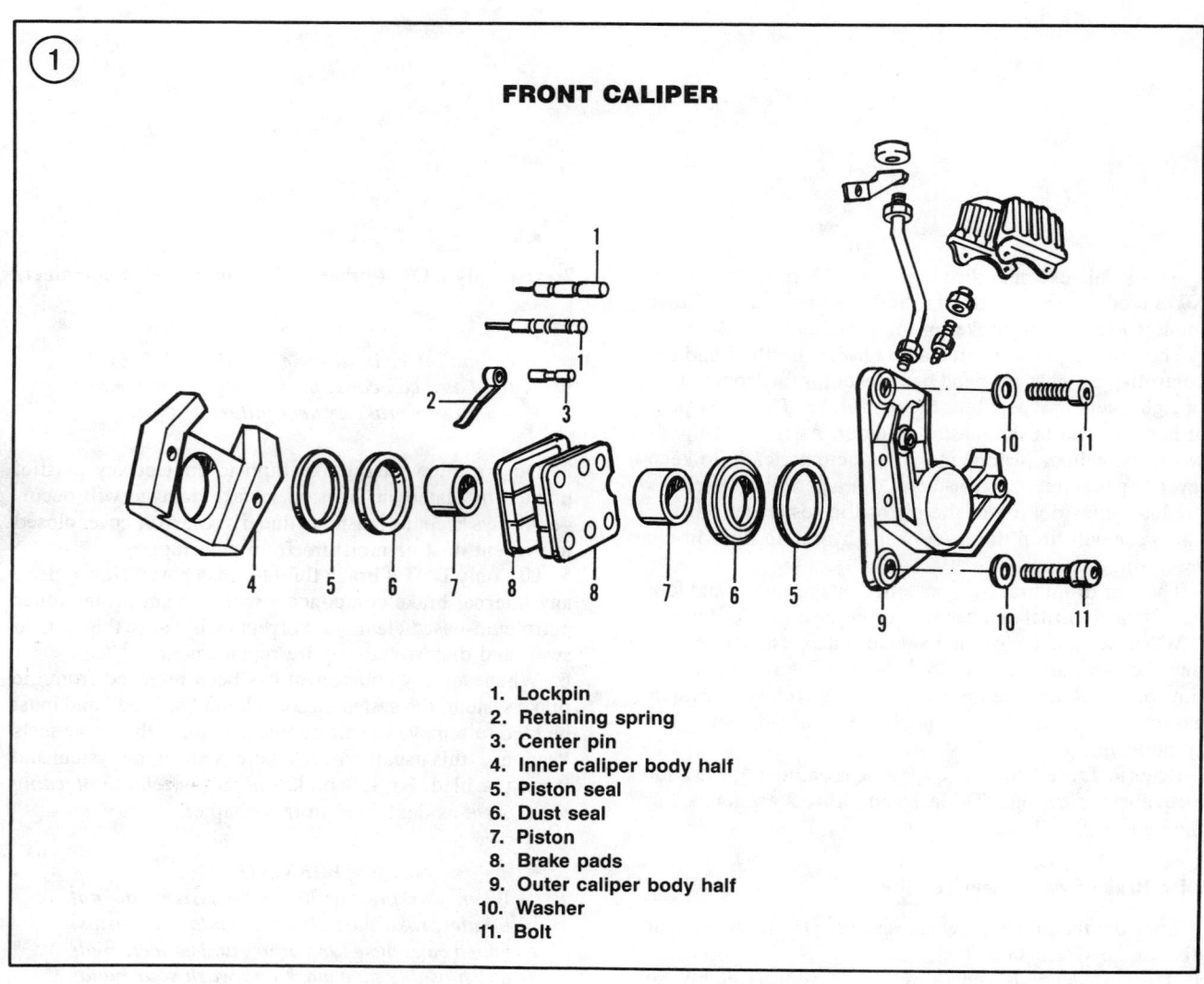

FRONT CALIPER

1. Lockpin
2. Retaining spring
3. Center pin
4. Inner caliper body half
5. Piston seal
6. Dust seal
7. Piston
8. Brake pads
9. Outer caliper body half
10. Washer
11. Bolt

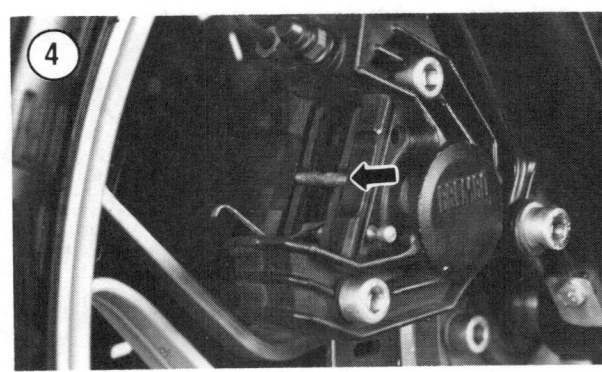

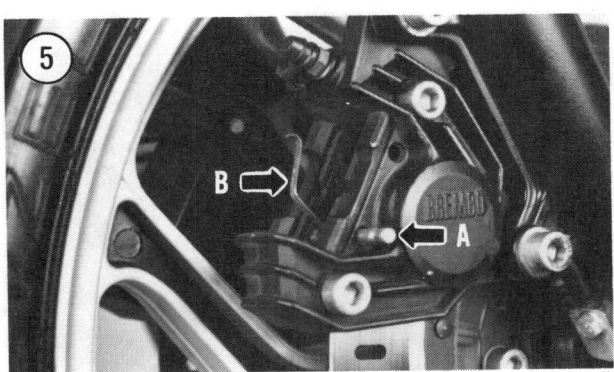

4. Hold a finger over the center pin and retaining spring and remove the upper lockpin.

5. Remove the center pin (**Figure 4**).

6. Use a drift and small hammer, carefully tap the lower lockpin (A, **Figure 5**) out from the backside of the caliper. Remove the spring retainer (B, **Figure 5**) and the lower lockpin.

7. The pistons must be repositioned within the caliper assembly before installing the new *thicker* brake pads. The front master cylinder brake fluid level will rise as the caliper pistons are being repositioned. Perform the following:

    a. Clean the top of the front master cylinder of all dirt and foreign matter.

    b. Remove the screws securing the top cover (**Figure 6**) and remove the top cover, the spacer and the rubber diaphragm from the master cylinder.

    c. Note the brake fluid level in the reservoir. If it is up to, or close to, the top surface of the reservoir, siphon off some of the fluid at this time.

    d. First push the caliper assembly toward the brake disc until it stops. This will reposition the outboard piston into the caliper cylinder.

    e. Then pull the caliper assembly toward the brake disc until it stops. This will reposition the inboard piston into the caliper cylinder.

    f. Constantly check the reservoir to make sure the brake fluid does not overflow. Remove brake fluid, if necessary, before it overflows.

    g. The pistons should move freely during repositioning. If they don't, and there is evidence of them sticking in the cylinders, the caliper should be removed and serviced as described under *Front Caliper Rebuilding* in this chapter.

8. Remove both brake pads.

WARNING
*When working on the brake system, do **not** inhale brake dust. It may contain asbestos, which can cause lung injury and cancer. Wear a disposable face mask and wash your hands thoroughly after completing the work.*

12

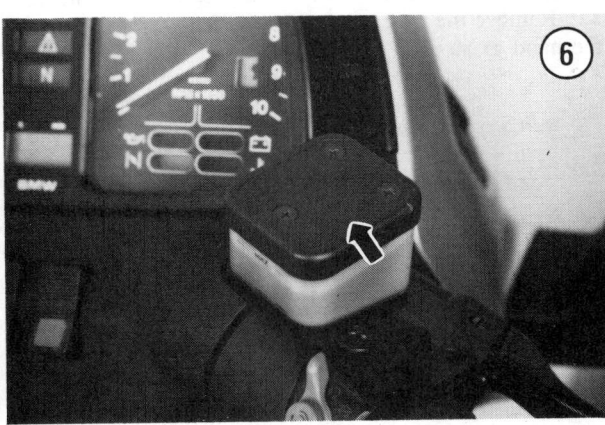

9. Clean the pad recess and the end of the pistons (**Figure 7**) with a soft brush. Do not use solvent, a wire brush or any hard tool which would damage the pistons or disc.

10. Carefully remove any rust or corrosion from the disc.

11. Lightly coat the end of the pistons and the backs of the new pads *(not the friction material)* with disc brake lubricant.

NOTE
When purchasing new pads, check with your dealer to make sure the friction compound of the new pad is compatible with the disc material. Remove any roughness from the backs of the new pads with a fine-cut file; wipe them clean with a lint-free cloth.

12. Install the inboard pad (**Figure 8**) and then the outboard pad (**Figure 9**). The pads will slide down within the caliper assembly until they stop.

13. Pull both brake pads up until the lockpin holes align with the brake pads and caliper assembly.

14. Partially install the lower lockpin (A, **Figure 5**) through the outboard brake pad.

15. Install the retaining spring with the arched side facing *up* (B, **Figure 5**). Push the lower lockpin through the retaining spring, inboard brake pad and the caliper assembly. Tap it in until it stops and locks in place.

16. Install the center pin (**Figure 4**) into the notch in both brake pads.

17. Pivot the retaining spring down over the center pin (**Figure 10**).

18. Press the retaining spring down (A, **Figure 11**) and partially install the upper lockpin (B, **Figure 11**). Push the upper lockpin in, over the retaining spring end and through the inboard brake pad and caliper. Tap it in until it stops and locks in place.

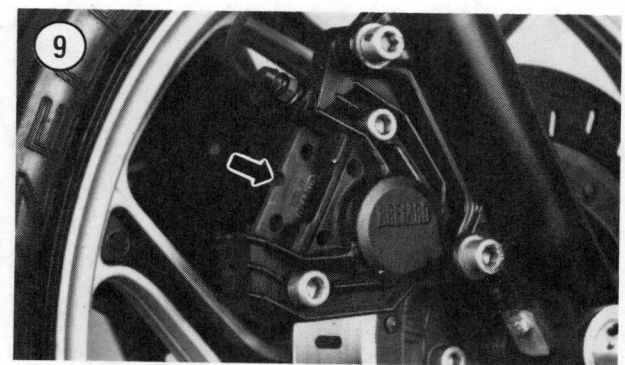

19. Make sure the retaining spring is correctly hooked under the top lockpin and is located within the lockpin recess. Make sure both lockpins (**Figure 12**) are completely seated.

20. Install the brake caliper cover (**Figure 2**) and push it down until it locks in place.

21. Repeat Steps 2-20 for the other caliper assembly.

22. Remove the spacer between the front brake lever and the hand grip.

CAUTION
In Step 23, don't come to fast stops as the brake fluid may slosh out of the open master cylinder reservoir.

23. Carefully roll the bike back and forth and activate the brake lever as many times as it takes to refill the cylinders in both calipers and correctly locate all pads.

WARNING
Use brake fluid clearly marked DOT 4 from a sealed container. Other types may vaporize and

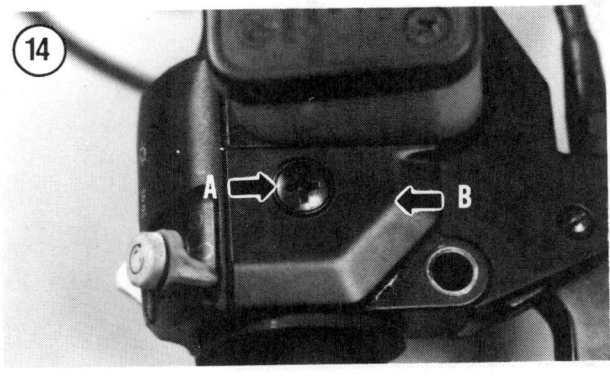

cause brake failure. Always use the same brand name; do not intermix silicone based (DOT 5) brake fluid as it can cause brake component damage leading to brake system failure.

24. Refill the master cylinder reservoir, if necessary, to maintain the correct fluid level.

25. Install the rubber diaphragm, spacer and top cover. Install the screws and tighten securely.

WARNING
Do not ride the motorcycle until you are sure the brakes are operating correctly with full hydraulic advantage. If necessary, bleed the brake as described in this chapter.

26. Bed the pads in gradually for the first 80 km (50 miles) by using only light pressure as much as possible. Immediate hard application will glaze the new friction pads and greatly reduce the effectiveness of the brake.

FRONT MASTER CYLINDER

Removal/Installation

CAUTION
Cover the fuel tank, instrument cluster and front fairing with a heavy cloth or plastic tarp to protect them from accidental brake fluid spills. Wash brake fluid off any painted or plated surfaces immediately, as it will destroy the finish. Use soapy water and rinse completely.

1. Place a couple of shop cloths under the union bolt and remove the union bolt and sealing washer (**Figure 13**) securing the brake hose to the master cylinder. Remove the brake hose. Tie the brake hose up and cover the end with a resealable plastic bag to prevent the entry of foreign matter.

2. Remove the screw (A, **Figure 14**) securing the throttle cable cover (B, **Figure 14**) and remove the cover.

3. Remove the bolts (**Figure 15**) securing the master cylinder assembly to the throttle housing and remove the master cylinder.

12

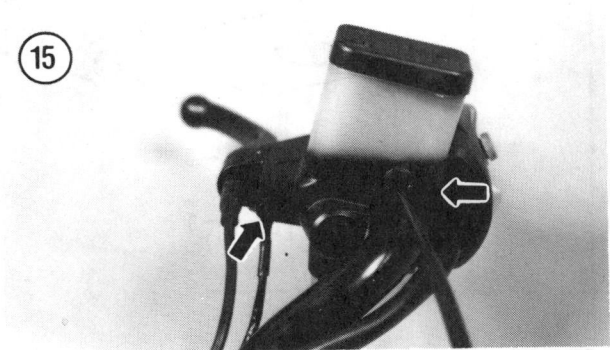

4. Install by reversing these removal steps, noting the following.

5. Make sure the throttle cable is routed properly in the throttle housing (A, **Figure 16**) and is attached to the throttle wheel receptacle (B, **Figure 16**).

6. Install the brake hose onto the master cylinder. Be sure to place a sealing washer on each side of the fitting and install the union bolt. Tighten the union bolt to the torque specifications listed in **Table 2**.

7. Bleed the brake as described in this chapter.

Disassembly

Refer to **Figure 17** for this procedure.

1. Remove the master cylinder as described in this chapter.

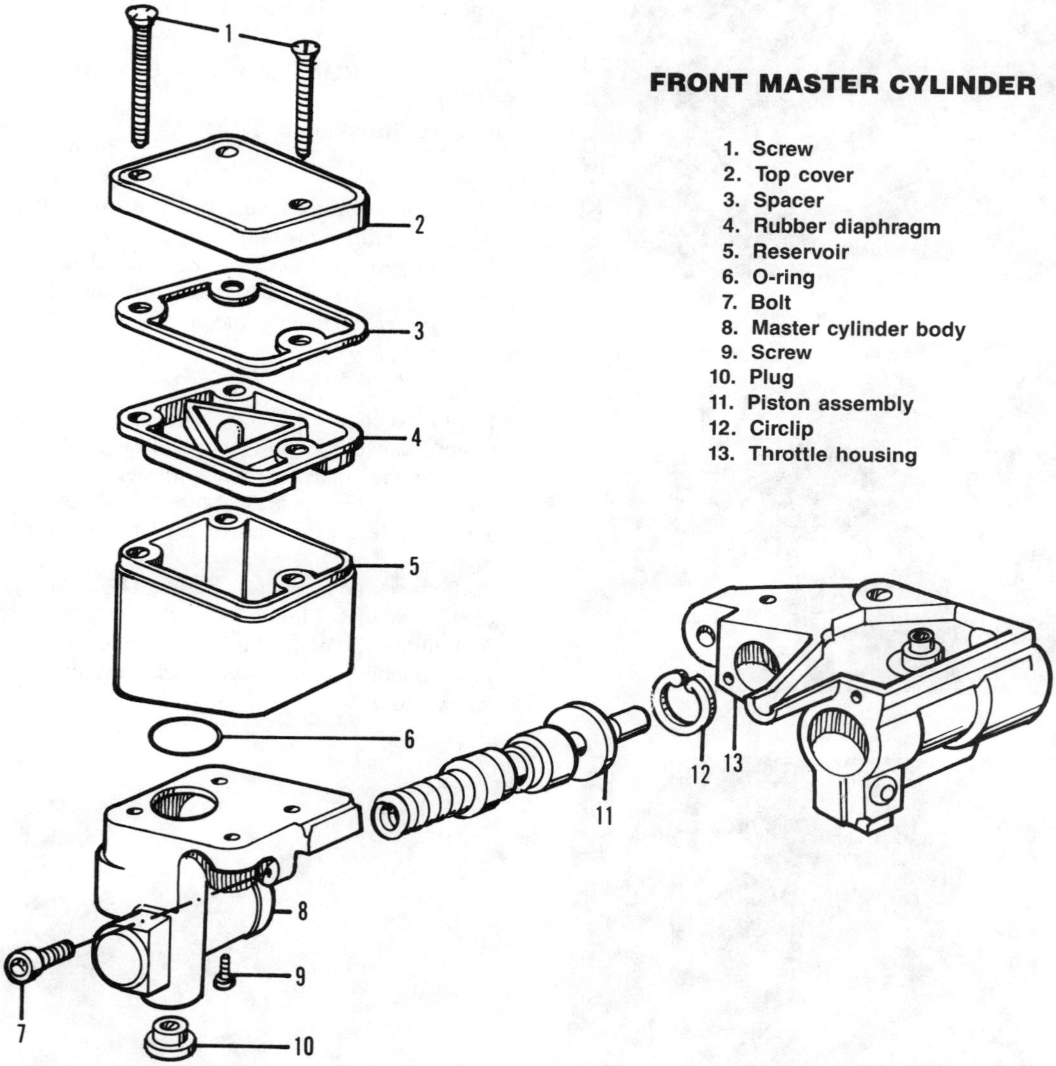

FRONT MASTER CYLINDER

1. Screw
2. Top cover
3. Spacer
4. Rubber diaphragm
5. Reservoir
6. O-ring
7. Bolt
8. Master cylinder body
9. Screw
10. Plug
11. Piston assembly
12. Circlip
13. Throttle housing

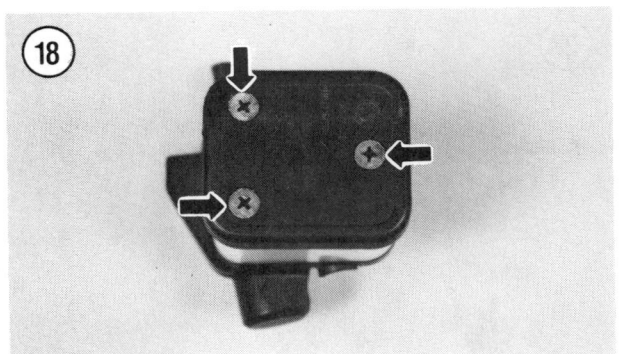

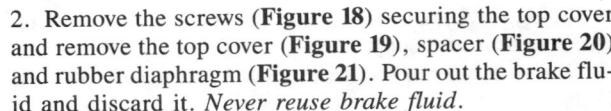

2. Remove the screws (**Figure 18**) securing the top cover and remove the top cover (**Figure 19**), spacer (**Figure 20**) and rubber diaphragm (**Figure 21**). Pour out the brake fluid and discard it. *Never reuse brake fluid.*

3. To remove the reservoir from the master cylinder body, perform the following:

   a. Remove the screw (**Figure 22**) securing the reservoir to the body.

   b. Carefully pull up and rotate the reservoir (**Figure 23**). Remove it from the body.

   c. Remove the O-ring seal (**Figure 24**) from the recess in the body. Discard the O-ring seal as it must be replaced every time the reservoir is removed regardless of the condition of the O-ring.

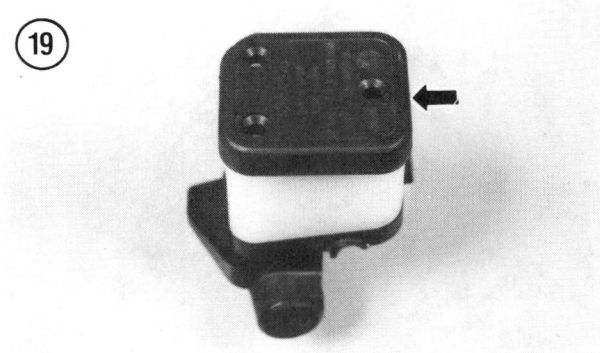

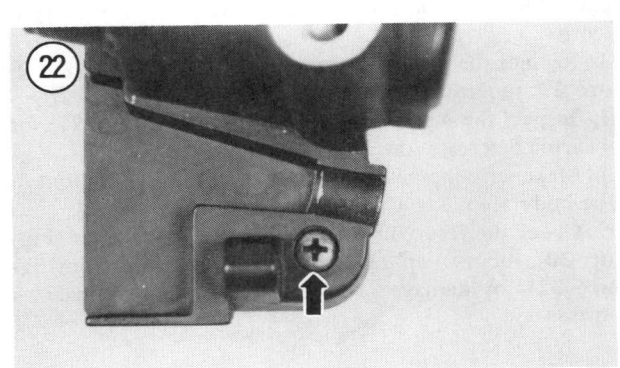

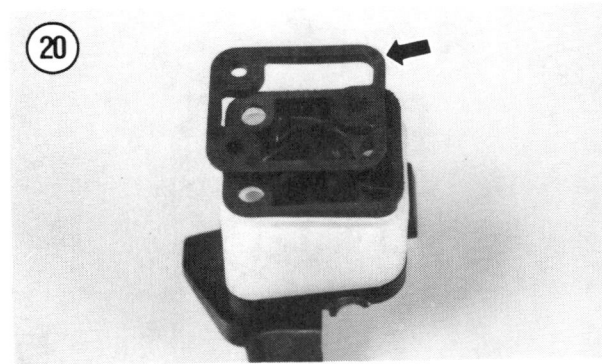

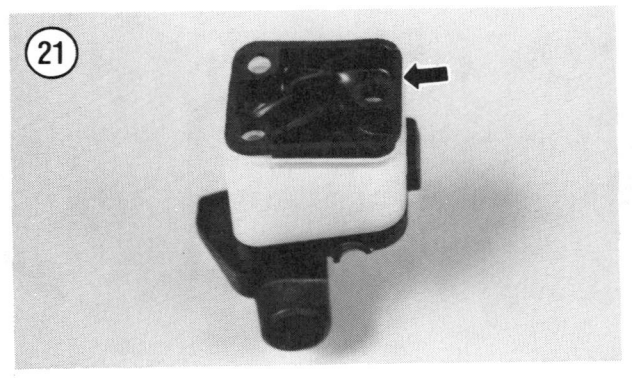

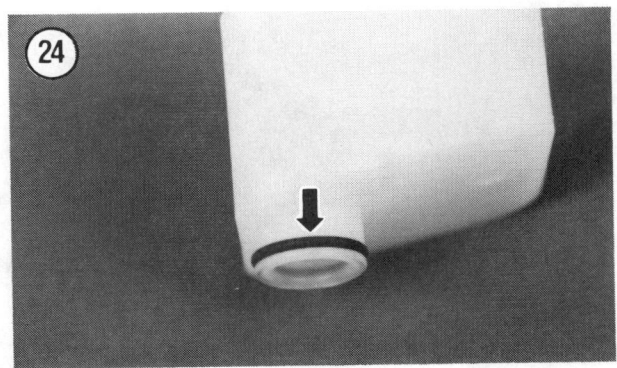

12

4. Using circlip pliers, remove the internal circlip (**Figure 25**) from the body.

5. Withdraw the piston assembly (**Figure 26**) from the body.

Inspection

BMW does not provide any specifications for wear limits on any of the master cylinder components. Replace any parts that appear to be damaged or worn.

1. Clean all parts in denatured alcohol or fresh brake fluid. Inspect the cylinder bore and piston contact surfaces for signs of wear and damage. If either part is less than perfect, replace it.

2. Check the end of the piston (A, **Figure 27**) for wear caused by the hand lever. Replace the piston assembly if worn.

3. Replace the piston assembly if the piston cups (B, **Figure 27**) require replacement.

4. Inspect the piston assembly spring (C, **Figure 27**) for wear or deterioration. Replace if necessary.

5. Make sure the passages (**Figure 28**) on the bottom of the body are clear. Clean out if necessary.

6. Check the reservoir top cap (**Figure 29**), spacer (**Figure 30**), rubber diaphragm (**Figure 31**) and reservoir (**Figure 32**) for damage and deterioration and replace as necessary.

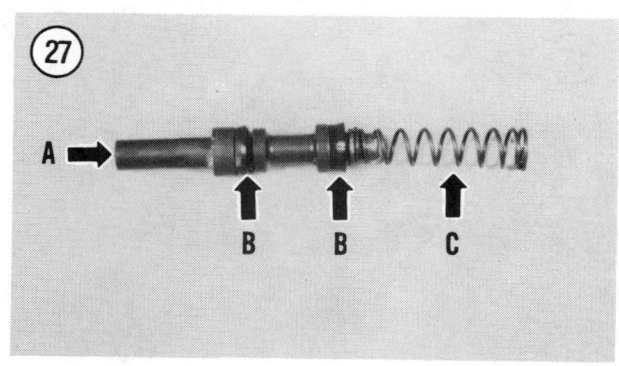

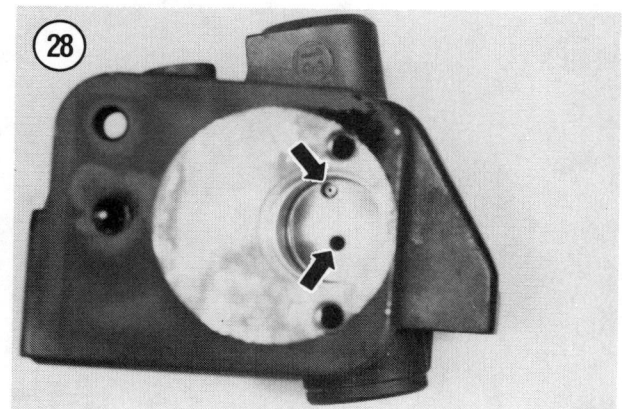

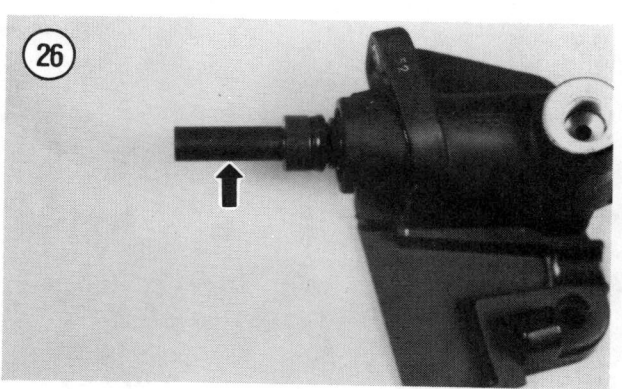

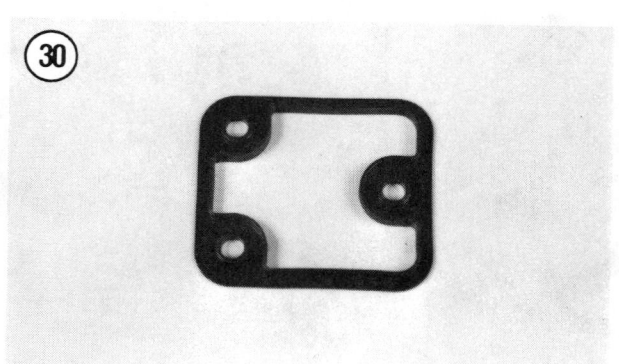

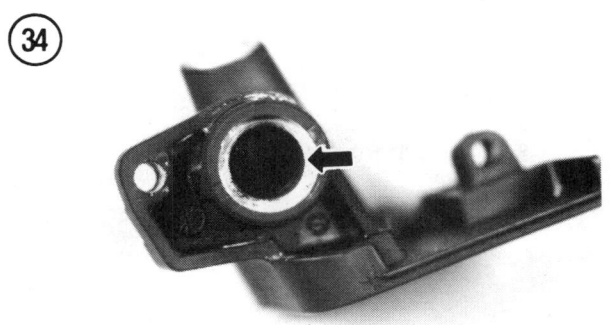

7. Inspect the threads and hole (**Figure 33**) in the bore for the brake hose union bolt. If the threads are slightly damaged, clean them up with a proper size thread tap. If the threads are worn or damaged beyond a "thread clean up," replace the master cylinder body.

8. Inspect the piston bore (**Figure 34**) in the body for wear, corrosion or damage. Replace the body if necessary.

9. Make sure the fluid passage hole (**Figure 35**) on the union bolt is clear. Clean out if necessary.

Assembly

1. Soak the new piston assembly in fresh brake fluid for at least 15 minutes to make the cups pliable. Coat the inside of the cylinder bore with fresh brake fluid before assembling parts.

CAUTION
When installing the piston assembly, do not allow the cups to turn inside out as they will be damaged and allow brake fluid leakage within the cylinder bore.

2. Install the piston assembly and spring into the reservoir cylinder (**Figure 36**).

3. Push the piston assembly in and install the circlip (**Figure 25**). Make sure it is correctly seated in the cylinder groove.

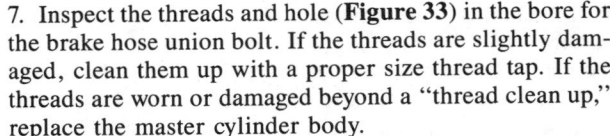

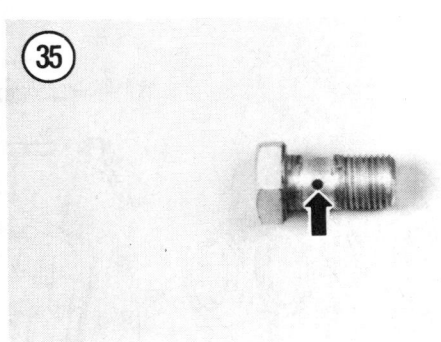

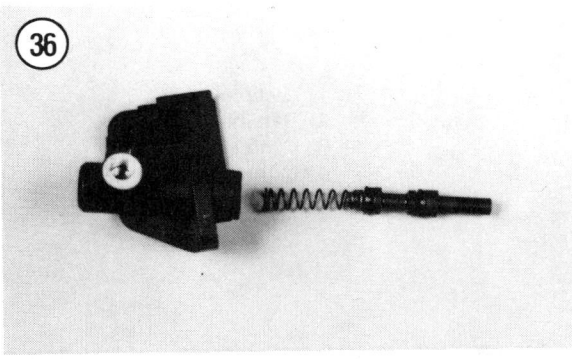

12

4. To install the reservoir onto the master cylinder body, perform the following:

   a. Install a new O-ring seal (**Figure 24**) into the recess in the body. Coat the new O-ring seal with fresh DOT 4 brake fluid.

   b. Coat the inner surface of the reservoir where it contacts the O-ring seal with fresh DOT 4 brake fluid.

   c. Carefully push down and rotate the reservoir and install it onto the body. Make sure that the reservoir is completely seated around the entire perimeter prior to installing the screw in the next step.

   d. Align the reservoir to the body and install the screw (**Figure 22**) securing the reservoir to the body. Tighten the screw securely.

5. Install the rubber diaphragm (**Figure 21**), the spacer (**Figure 20**) and top cover (**Figure 19**). Loosely install, but do not tighten the cover screws (**Figure 18**) at this time as fluid will have to be added later.

6. Install the master cylinder as described in this chapter.

FRONT CALIPER

Removal
(ABS Equipped Models)

Refer to **Figure 37** for this procedure.

It is not necessary to remove the front wheel in order to remove either or both caliper assemblies.

CAUTION
Do not spill any brake fluid on the painted portion of the front wheel or front fork slider. Wash any spilled brake fluid immediately, as it will destroy the finish. Use soapy water and rinse completely.

1. Drain the hydraulic brake fluid from the front brake system as follows:

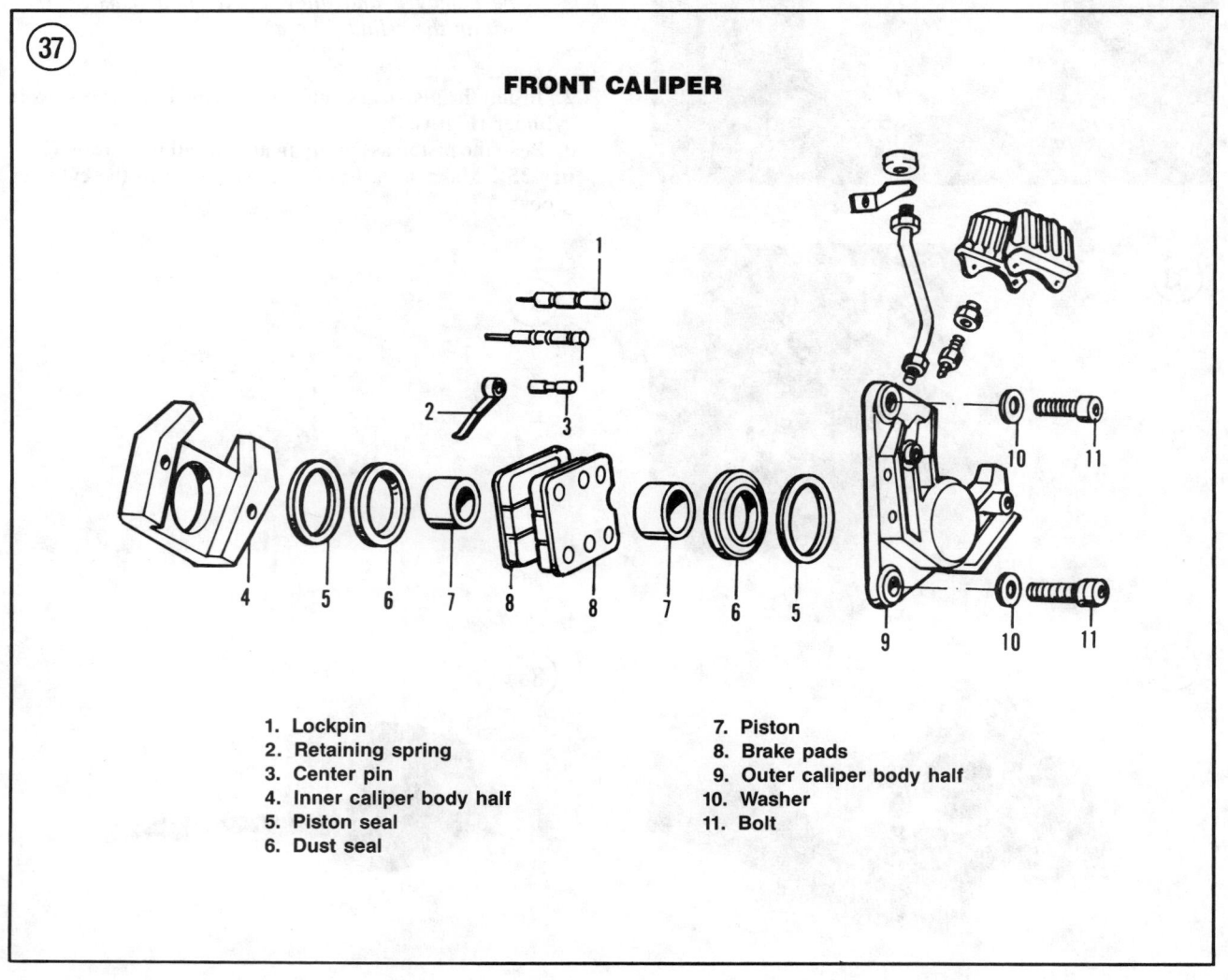

FRONT CALIPER

1. Lockpin
2. Retaining spring
3. Center pin
4. Inner caliper body half
5. Piston seal
6. Dust seal
7. Piston
8. Brake pads
9. Outer caliper body half
10. Washer
11. Bolt

a. Attach a hose to the bleed valve on the caliper assembly.
b. Place the loose end of the hose in a container to catch the brake fluid.
c. Open the bleed valve and continue to apply the front brake lever until the brake fluid is pumped out of the system.
d. Disconnect the hose and tighten the bleed valve.
e. Dispose of this brake fluid—*never* reuse brake fluid. Contaminated brake fluid may cause brake failure.

2. Remove the front fender (A, **Figure 38**) as described under *Front Fender (1-Piece Type) Removal/ Installation* in Chapter Thirteen.

> *CAUTION*
> *The ABS electronic trigger sensor is attached to the right-hand caliper assembly. Do not damage the sensor during caliper removal.*

3. Disconnect the electrical connector from the trigger sensor (**Figure 39**) on the right-hand caliper.
4. Remove the brake caliper assembly mounting bolts (B, and C, **Figure 38**) from the front fork.

> *NOTE*
> *If the caliper assembly is going to be disassembled for service, loosen the Allen bolts securing the caliper assembly halves together. The fork slider makes a good holding fixture.*

5. On the right-hand caliper, using a brake flare nut wrench, loosen both brake line nuts (**Figure 40**) securing the brake lines to the caliper assembly. Completely unscrew the brake line nuts from the caliper.
6. Slide the caliper assembly off of the brake discs.
7. To prevent the entry of moisture and dirt, cap the end of the brake line.
8. Repeat Steps 4-7 for the other caliper assembly.

Installation
(ABS Equipped Models)

> *CAUTION*
> *The ABS electronic sensor is attached to the right-hand caliper assembly. Do not damage the sensor during caliper installation.*

1. Carefully install the right-hand caliper assembly onto the disc. Be careful not to damage the leading edge of the pads during installation. Do not kink or damage the brake line assembly.
2. Install the brake caliper assembly mounting bolts. Be sure to install the bolt with the special shoulder at the top (B, **Figure 38**). This bolt properly locates the caliper assembly onto the front fork. This location is necessary to properly maintain the distance between the ABS sensor on the caliper assembly and the pulse generating wheel attached to the front wheel.
3. Tighten the caliper mounting bolts to the torque specifications listed in **Table 2**.

> *NOTE*
> *If the caliper assembly was disassembled for service, securely tighten the Allen bolts securing the caliper assembly halves together.*

12

4. Connect the electrical connector to the trigger sensor (**Figure 39**) on the right-hand caliper.

> *WARNING*
> *If the distance between the trigger sensor and pulse generating wheel is not maintained correctly, the ABS system will **not** function properly.*

5. After the right-hand brake caliper is installed, inspect the distance between the ABS trigger sensor and the pulse generating wheel as described under *Trigger Sensor-to-Pulse Generating Wheel Clearance, Measurement and Adjustment (Front Trigger Sensor)* in this chapter.

6. Carefully install the left-hand caliper assembly onto the disc. Be careful not to damage the leading edge of the pads during installation. Do not kink or damage the brake line assembly.

7. Install the brake caliper assembly mounting bolts. Tighten the caliper mounting bolts to the torque specifications listed in **Table 2**.

8. Attach the brake lines to both caliper assemblies. Using a brake flare nut wrench, tighten the brake line nuts to the torque specification listed in **Table 2**.

9. Install the front fender (A, **Figure 38**) as described under *Front Fender (1-Piece Type) Removal/Installation* in Chapter Thirteen.

10. Refill the system and have the brakes bled by a BMW dealer as described in this chapter.

> *WARNING*
> *Do not ride the motorcycle until you are sure that the brakes are operating properly.*

Removal
(Non-ABS Models)

Refer to **Figure 37** for this procedure.

It is not necessary to remove the front wheel in order to remove either or both caliper assemblies.

> *CAUTION*
> *Do not spill any brake fluid on the painted portion of the front wheel or front fork slider. Wash any spilled brake fluid immediately, as it will destroy the finish. Use soapy water and rinse completely.*

1. Drain the hydraulic brake fluid from the front brake system as follows:
   a. Attach a hose to the bleed valve (**Figure 41**) on the caliper assembly.
   b. Place the loose end of the hose in a container to catch the brake fluid.
   c. Open the bleed valve and continue to apply the front brake lever until the brake fluid is pumped out of the system.
   d. Disconnect the hose and tighten the bleed valve.
   e. Dispose of this brake fluid—*never* reuse brake fluid. Contaminated brake fluid may cause brake failure.

2. Using a brake flare nut wrench, loosen the brake line nut securing the brake line (A, **Figure 42**) to the caliper assembly. Completely unscrew the brake line nut from the caliper.

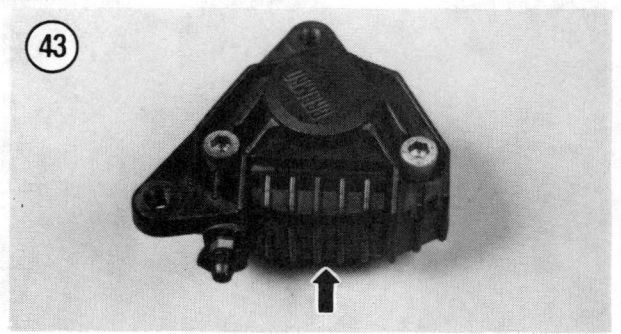

3. To prevent the entry of moisture and dirt, cap the end of the brake hose.

NOTE
If the caliper assembly is going to be disassembled for service, loosen the Allen bolts (B, Figure 42) securing the caliper assembly halves together. The fork slider makes a good holding fixture.

4. Remove the Allen bolts (C, **Figure 42**) securing the caliper to the fork slider.

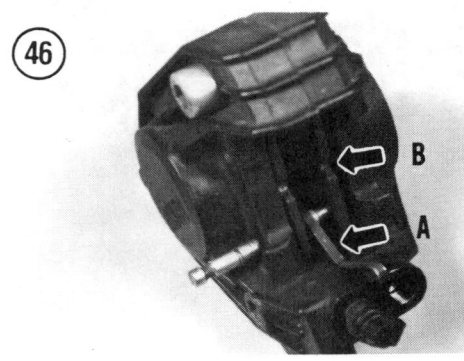

5. Pivot the caliper assembly up and off the disc and remove the caliper assembly.
6. Repeat for the other brake caliper assembly.

**Installation
(Non-ABS Models)**

1. Carefully install the caliper assembly onto the disc. Be careful not to damage the leading edge of the pads during installation.
2. Install the caliper mounting bolts (C, **Figure 42**) and tighten to the torque specifications listed in **Table 2**.

NOTE
If the caliper assembly was disassembled for service, securely tighten the Allen bolts (B, Figure 42) securing the caliper assembly halves together.

3. Connect the brake line(s) to the caliper assembly. Tighten the flare nuts to the torque specification listed in **Table 2**.
4. Refill the system and bleed the brake as described in this chapter.

WARNING
Do not ride the motorcycle until you are sure that the brakes are operating properly.

Rebuilding

Refer to **Figure 37** for this procedure.
BMW does not provide any specifications for wear limits on any of the front caliper components. Replace any parts that appear to be damaged or worn.
1. Remove the caliper assembly as described in this chapter.
2. On ABS equipped right-hand caliper assembly, perform the following:
   a. Remove the screws securing the trigger sensor assembly.
   b. Remove the assembly and the shim from the caliper. Don't lose the shim as it must be reinstalled.
3. Remove the brake pads as follows:
   a. Using a large flat-bladed screwdriver, carefully remove the brake caliper cover (**Figure 43**).
   b. Using a drift and small hammer, carefully tap one of the lockpins (**Figure 44**) out from the backside of the caliper.
   c. Hold a finger over the center pin and retaining spring and remove that lockpin.
   d. Remove the center pin (**Figure 45**).
   e. Use a drift and small hammer, carefully tap the other lockpin partway out of the caliper and remove the retaining spring (A, **Figure 46**).
   f. Remove the inboard brake pad (B, **Figure 46**).

12

g. Remove the lockpin (**Figure 47**) from the caliper.

h. Remove the outboard brake pad (**Figure 48**).

4. Remove the Allen bolts (**Figure 49**) securing the caliper assembly halves together.

5. Separate the caliper halves.

6. Remove the small O-ring seal (**Figure 50**) from the inboard caliper half. Discard the O-ring seal as it must be replaced.

CAUTION
In the following step, do not use a sharp tool to remove the dust seals from the caliper body. Do not damage the cylinder surfaces.

7. Remove the dust seal (**Figure 51**) from each caliper body half. Discard the dust seals. They cannot be reused after removal as they will no longer seal effectively.

8. Withdraw the piston (**Figure 52**) from each caliper body half. If you cannot remove the piston easily, perform the following:

a. Either wrap the caliper half and piston with a heavy cloth or place a shop cloth or piece of soft wood over the end of the piston.

b. Perform this step over and close down to a workbench top. Hold the caliper body with the piston facing away from you.

WARNING
*In the next step, the piston may shoot out of the caliper body like a bullet. Keep your fingers out of the way. Wear shop gloves and apply air pressure gradually. Do **not** use high pressure air or place the air hose nozzle directly against the hydraulic fluid passageway in the caliper body. Hold the air nozzle away from the inlet, allowing some of the air to escape during the procedure.*

c. Apply the air pressure in short spurts to the hydraulic fluid passageway (**Figure 53**) and force the piston out of the caliper body. Place your finger over the other fluid passageways to prevent the air from escaping. Use a service statoin air hose if you don't have an air compressor.

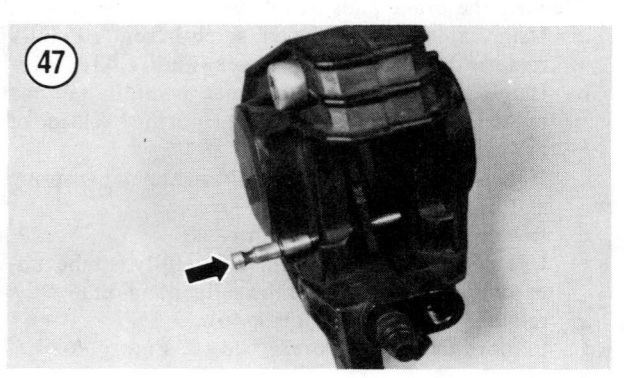

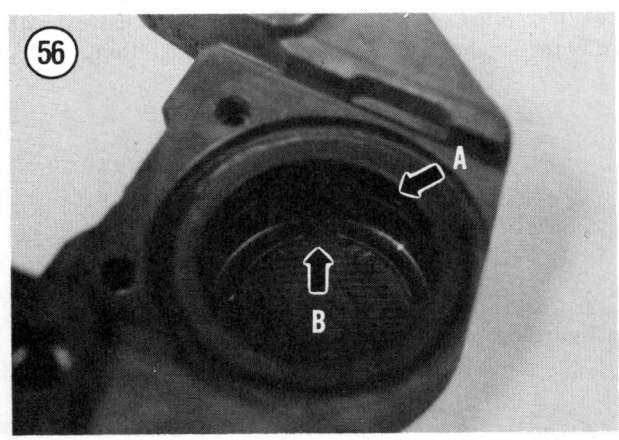

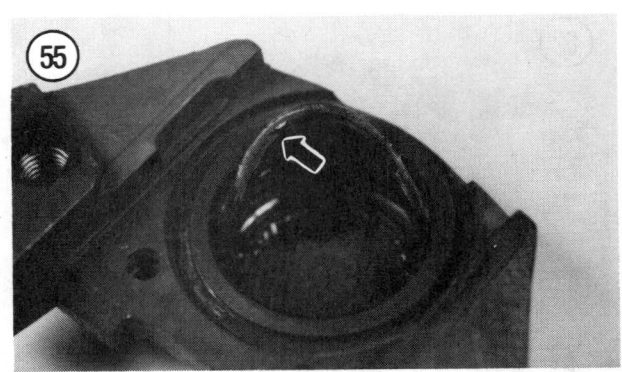

CAUTION
In the following step, do not use a sharp tool to remove the piston seals from the caliper cylinders. Do not damage the cylinder surfaces.

9. Use a piece of plastic or wood and carefully push the piston seal (**Figure 54**) in toward the caliper cylinder and out of its groove. Remove the piston seal (**Figure 55**) from each caliper body half. Discard the piston seals. They cannot be reused after removal as they will no longer seal effectively.

10. Inspect the seal groove in each caliper body half (A, **Figure 56**) for damage. If damaged or corroded, replace the caliper assembly.

NOTE
The caliper body cannot be replaced separately. If it is damaged in any way the entire caliper assembly must be replaced.

11. Unscrew and remove the bleed screw and cap (**Figure 57**).

12

12. Inspect the caliper body halves (**Figure 58**) for damage; replace the caliper body if necessary.

13. Inspect the hydraulic fluid passageway (B, **Figure 56**) in the base of each cylinder bore. Make sure it is clean and open. Apply compressed air to the opening and make sure it is clear. Clean out, if necessary, with fresh brake fluid.

14. Inspect the cylinder walls (**Figure 59**) and the pistons (**Figure 60**) for scratches, scoring or other damage. If either is rusty or corroded, replace the caliper assembly. The pistons cannot be replaced separately.

15. Inspect the caliper mounting bolt holes. If the threads are slightly damaged, clean them up with a proper size thread tap. If the threads are worn or damaged beyond a "thread clean up," replace the caliper assembly.

16. Inspect the caliper halves' assembly bolt holes (**Figure 61**). If the threads are slightly damaged, clean them up with a proper size thread tap. If the threads are worn or damaged beyond a "thread clean up," replace the caliper assembly.

17. Inspect the union bolt hole threads (**Figure 62**). If the threads are slightly damaged, clean them up with a proper size thread tap. If the threads are worn or damaged beyond a "thread clean up," replace the caliper assembly.

18. Make sure the hole in the bleed screw is clean and open. Apply compressed air to the opening and make sure it is clear. Clean out if necessary with fresh brake fluid.

19. If serviceable, clean the caliper body halves with rubbing alcohol and rinse with clean brake fluid.

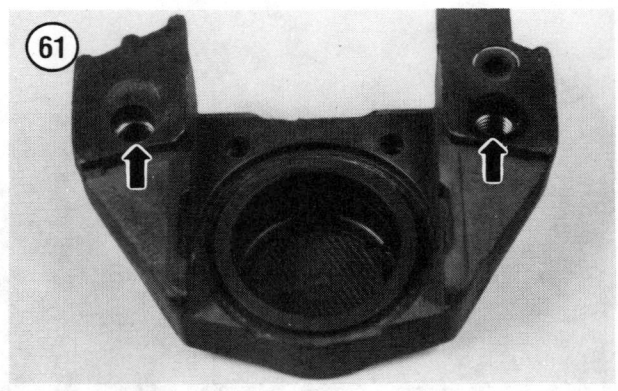

> *WARNING*
> *Never reuse a dust seal or piston seal that has been removed. Very minor damage or age deterioration can make the seals useless.*

20. Coat the new dust seals (**Figure 63**) and piston seals (**Figure 64**) with fresh DOT 4 brake fluid.

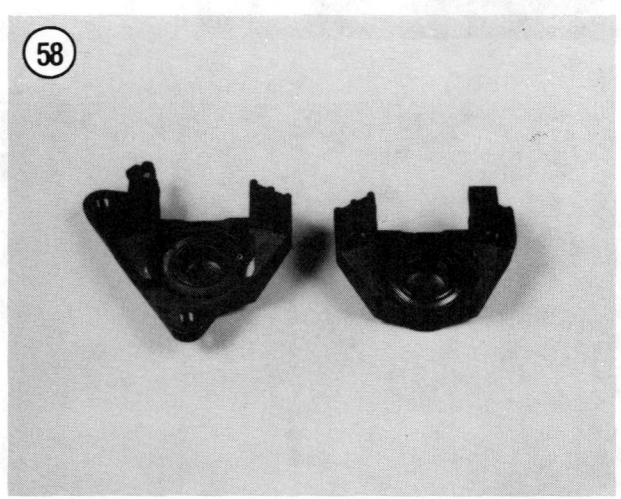

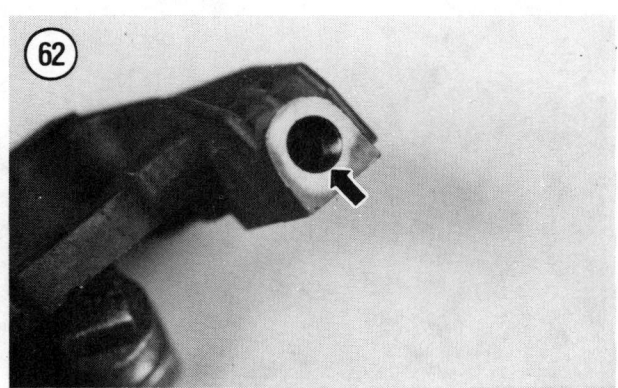

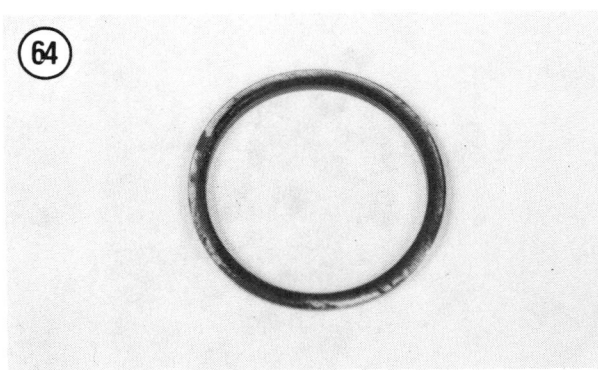

21. Carefully install the new piston seal (**Figure 55**) in the groove in each caliper cylinder. Make sure the seal is properly seated in the groove (**Figure 54**).

22. Coat the pistons and the caliper cylinders with fresh DOT 4 brake fluid.

23. Position the pistons with the *open end facing out* (**Figure 65**) toward the brake pads and install the piston into each caliper cylinder (**Figure 66**). Push the pistons in until they bottom out (**Figure 67**).

24. Carefully install the new dust seal (**Figure 68**) in the groove in each caliper cylinder. Make sure the seal is properly seated in the caliper half.

25. Install the bleed screw and cap (**Figure 57**).

26. Install a new O-ring seal (**Figure 50**) into the recess in the inboard caliper half.

27. Lay the inboard caliper half down and install the outboard half on top of it. This is to prevent the small O-ring seal from falling out during assembly.

NOTE
*There are 2 different length Allen bolts of the same diameter and thread size. The longer bolts (A, **Figure 69**) are used to assemble the*

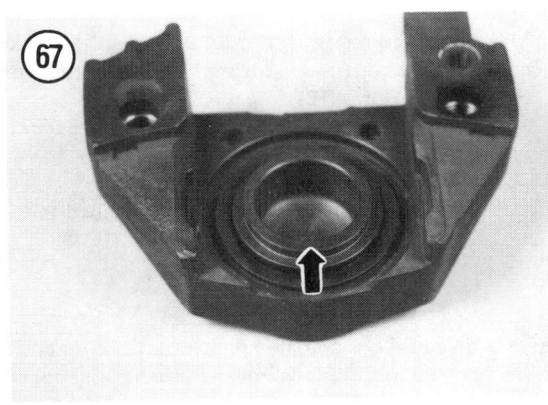

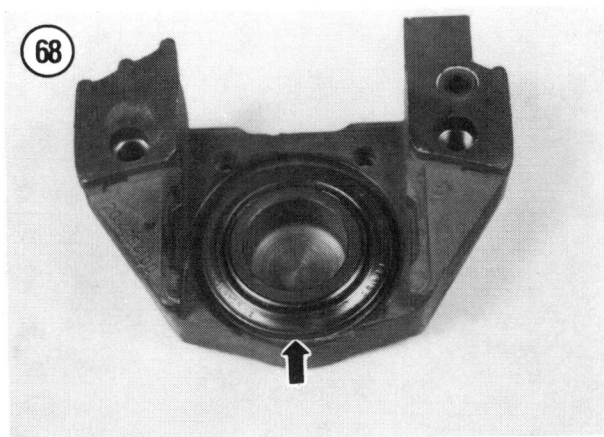

12

*2 caliper halves together and the shorter ones (B, **Figure 69**) are used as mounting bolts to hold the caliper assembly onto the fork slider.*

28. Install the Allen bolts (**Figure 49**) securing the caliper assembly halves together.
29. Install the brake pads as follows:
   a. Install the outboard brake pad (**Figure 48**).
   b. Partially install the lockpin (**Figure 47**) into the caliper and brake pad.
   c. Install the inboard brake pad (B, **Figure 46**).
   d. Install the retaining spring (A, **Figure 46**) onto the lockpin so the raised section will be facing upward away from the brake pads.
   e. Tap the lockpin in until it stops and locks in place.
   f. Install the center pin (**Figure 45**) into the notch in both brake pads.
   g. Move the retaining spring down and into position over the center pin.
   h. Partially install the other lockpin through the outer hole in the caliper and outboard brake pad.
   i. Press the retaining spring down and push the lockpin over the retaining spring end (**Figure 70**).
   j. Push the lockpin through the inboard brake pad and caliper (**Figure 71**). Tap it in until it stops and locks in place.
   k. Make sure the retaining spring is correctly hooked under the lockpin and is located over the center pin recess (A, **Figure 72**).
   l. Make sure both lockpins (B, **Figure 72**) are locked in place completely.
30. Install the brake caliper cover (**Figure 43**).
31. Install the brake caliper assembly as described in this chapter.

REAR DISC BRAKE

The rear disc brake is actuated by hydraulic fluid and is controlled by the right-hand foot-operated pedal that is linked to the master cylinder. As the brake pads wear, the brake fluid level drops in the reservoir and automatically adjusts for wear.

⑦⓪

⑦①

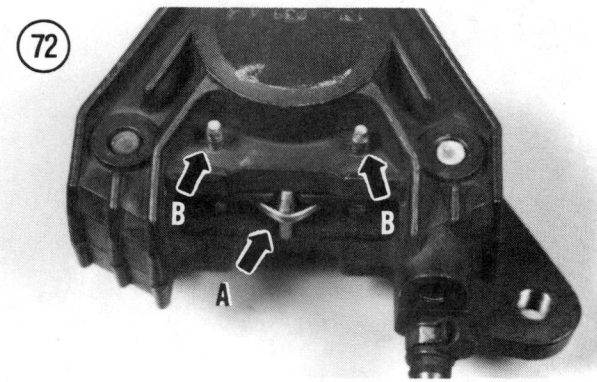

⑦②

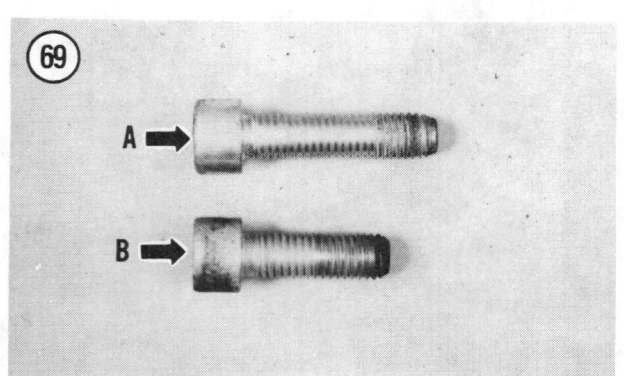

⑥⑨

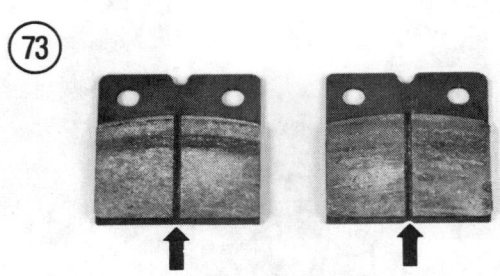

⑦③

REAR BRAKE PAD REPLACEMENT

There is no recommended mileage interval for changing the friction pads in the disc brake. Pad wear depends greatly on riding habits and conditions. The pads should be checked for wear every 7,240 km (4,500 miles) and replaced when the lining thickness reaches 1.5 mm (1/16 in.) from the brake pad backing plate. To maintain an even brake pressure on the disc, always replace both pads in both calipers at the same time.

CAUTION
*Watch the pads more closely when the wear line (**Figure 73**) approaches the disc. On some pads the wear line is very close to the metal backing plate. If pad wear happens to be uneven for some reason the backing plate may come in contact with the disc and cause damage.*

Refer to **Figure 74** for this procedure.

NOTE
It is not necessary to remove the caliper assembly in order to replace the brake pads.

1. To prevent accidental application of the rear brake pedal, tie the pedal up to the frame so it cannot be depressed.

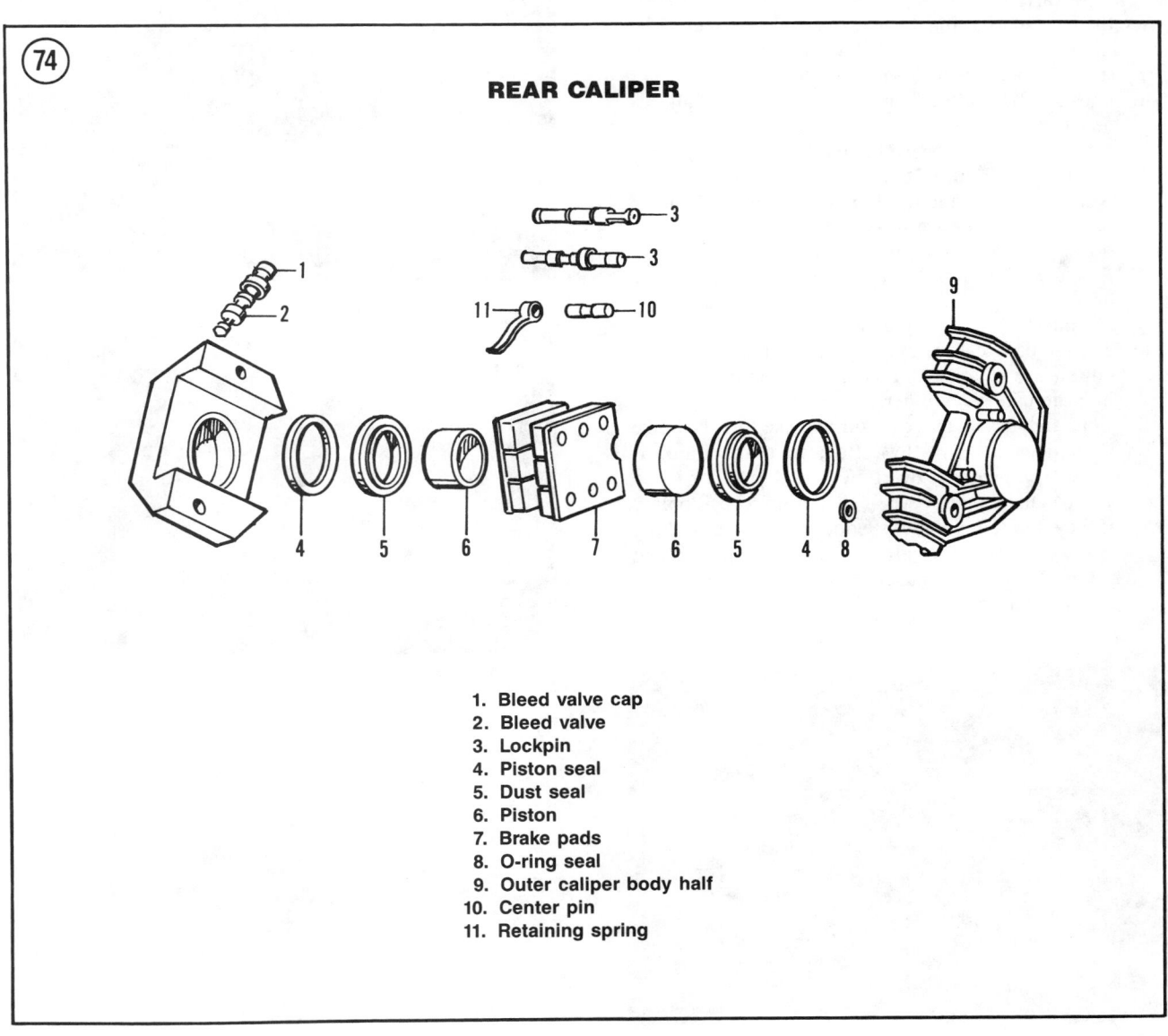

REAR CALIPER

1. Bleed valve cap
2. Bleed valve
3. Lockpin
4. Piston seal
5. Dust seal
6. Piston
7. Brake pads
8. O-ring seal
9. Outer caliper body half
10. Center pin
11. Retaining spring

12

2. Using a large flat-bladed screwdriver, carefully remove the brake caliper cover (**Figure 75**).

3. Rotate the rear wheel so that one of the open spaces between wheel spokes is opposite the brake caliper. This is necessary in order to work on the caliper assembly from the muffler side of the bike.

4. Use a drift and small hammer, carefully tap one of the lockpins loose from the backside of the caliper.

5. Hold a finger over the center pin and retaining spring and remove the lockpin that was loosened in Step 4 (A, **Figure 76**).

6. Remove the center pin and retaining spring (B, **Figure 76**).

7. Use a drift and small hammer, carefully tap the other lockpin out from the backside of the caliper. Remove the lockpin.

8. The pistons must be repositioned within the caliper assembly before installing the new *thicker* brake pads. The front master cylinder brake fluid level will rise as the caliper pistons are being repositioned. Perform the following:

   a. Clean the top of the front master cylinder of all dirt and foreign matter.

   b. Remove the top cover (**Figure 77**) and the rubber diaphragm (**Figure 78**) from the master cylinder.

   c. Note the brake fluid level in the reservoir. If it is up to, or close to, the top surface of the reservoir, siphon off some of the fluid at this time.

   d. First push the caliper assembly toward the brake disc until it stops. This will reposition the outboard piston into the caliper cylinder.

   e. Then pull the caliper assembly toward the brake disc until it stops. This will reposition the inboard piston into the caliper cylinder.

   f. Constantly check the reservoir to make sure the brake fluid does not overflow. Remove brake fluid, if necessary, before it overflows.

   g. The pistons should move freely during repositioning. If they don't, and there is evidence of them sticking in the cylinders, the caliper should be removed and serviced as described under *Front Caliper Rebuilding* in this chapter.

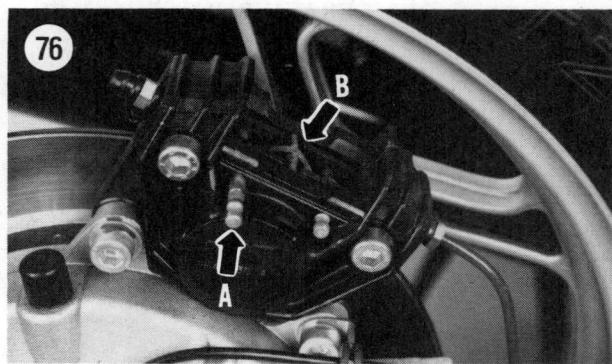

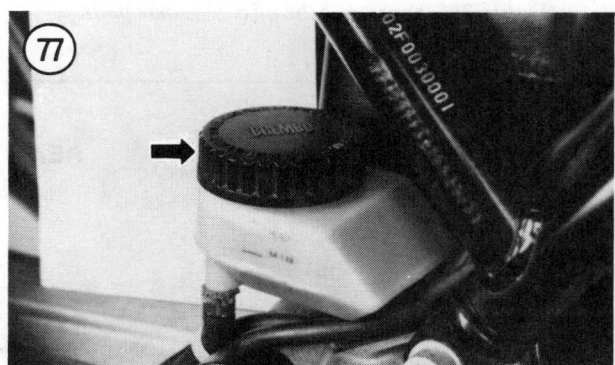

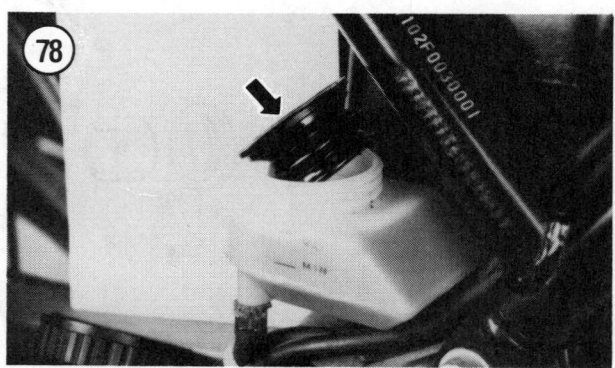

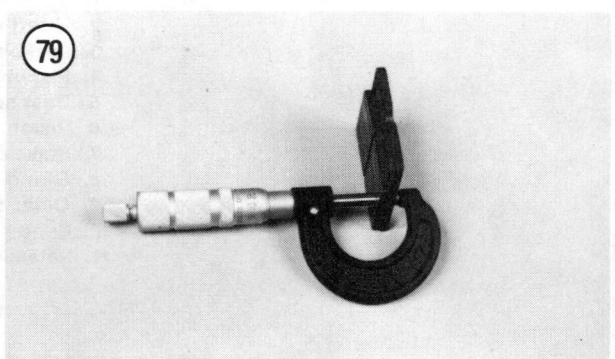

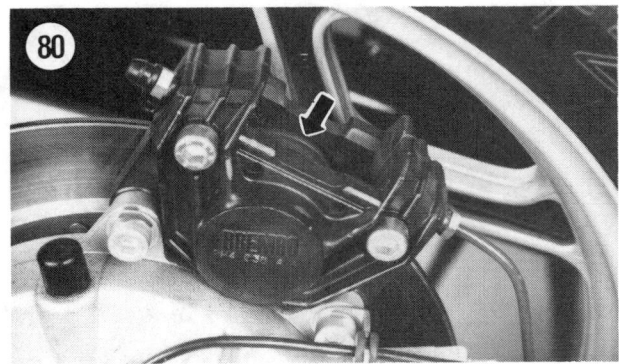

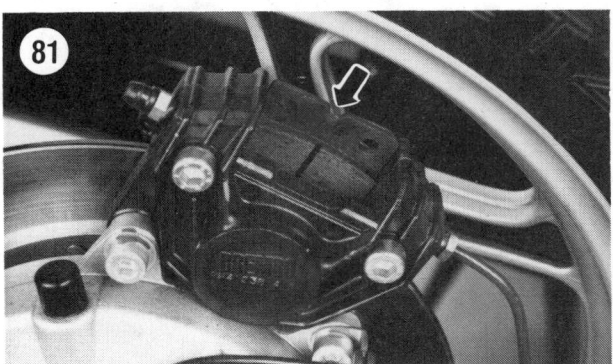

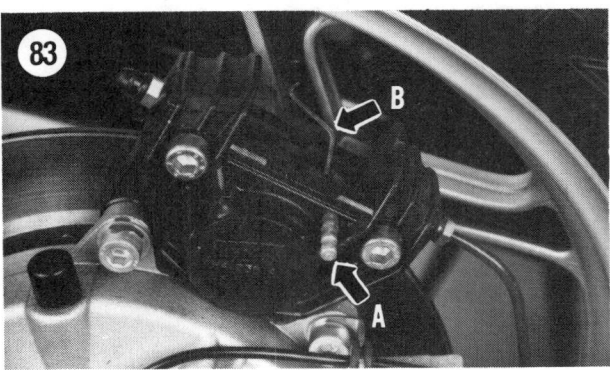

9. Remove both brake pads and measure them with a micrometer (**Figure 79**) or vernier caliper. Replace the pads if worn to the service limit listed in **Table 1** or less.

WARNING
*When working on the brake system, do **not** inhale brake dust. It may contain asbestos, which can cause lung injury and cancer. Wear a disposable face mask and wash your hands thoroughly after completing the work.*

10. Clean the pad recess and the end of the pistons (**Figure 80**) with a soft brush. Do not use solvent, a wire brush or any hard tool which would damage the pistons or disc.
11. Carefully remove any rust or corrosion from the disc.
12. Lightly coat the end of the pistons and the backs of the new pads (*not the friction material*) with disc brake lubricant.

NOTE
When purchasing new pads, check with your dealer to make sure the friction compound of the new pad is compatible with the disc material. Remove any roughness from the backs of the new pads with a fine-cut file; wipe them clean with a lint-free cloth.

13. Install the inboard pad (**Figure 81**) and then the outboard pad (**Figure 82**). The brake pads may slip down within the caliper assembly since there is no stop for them.
14. If necessary, pull the brake pads up until the holes align with the caliper assembly.
15. Install one lockpin (A, **Figure 83**) and the retaining spring (B, **Figure 83**) through the holes in the caliper and both brake pads. Tap it in until it stops and locks in place.
16. Install the center pin (**Figure 84**) into the notch in both brake pads.

12

17. Partially install the other lockpin through the outer hole in the caliper and outboard brake pad.

18. Press the retaining spring down and push the lockpin over the retaining spring end and through the inboard brake pad and caliper (**Figure 85**). Tap it in until it stops and locks in place. Make sure the retaining spring is correctly hooked under both lockpins and is located within the lockpin recess.

19. Install the brake caliper cover (**Figure 75**).

20. Remove the spacer between the front brake lever and the hand grip.

> *CAUTION*
> *In Step 21, don't come to fast stops as the brake fluid may slosh out of the open master cylinder reservoir.*

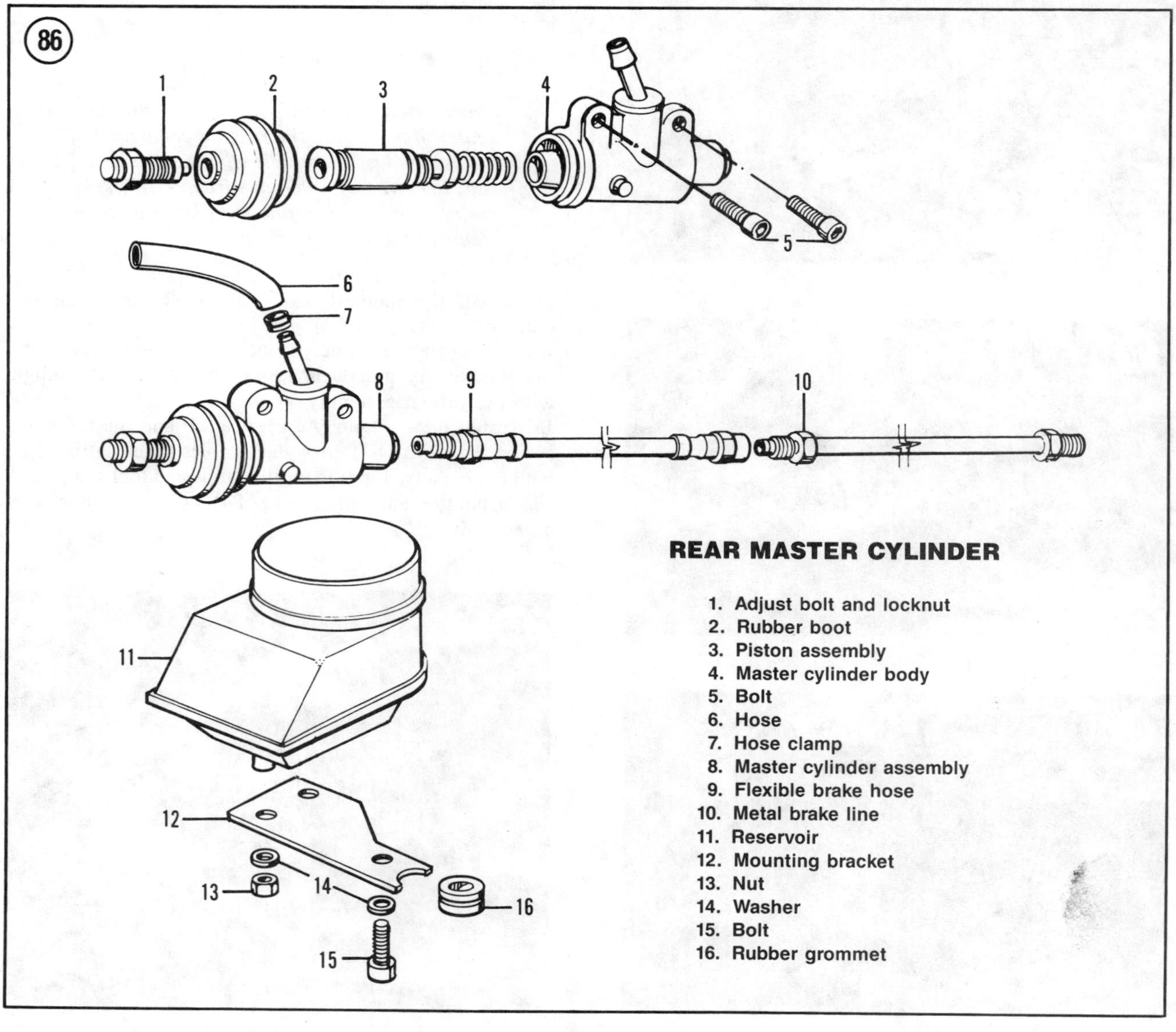

REAR MASTER CYLINDER

1. Adjust bolt and locknut
2. Rubber boot
3. Piston assembly
4. Master cylinder body
5. Bolt
6. Hose
7. Hose clamp
8. Master cylinder assembly
9. Flexible brake hose
10. Metal brake line
11. Reservoir
12. Mounting bracket
13. Nut
14. Washer
15. Bolt
16. Rubber grommet

21. Carefully roll the bike back and forth and activate the brake lever as many times as it takes to refill the cylinders in the caliper and correctly locate both brake pads.

> *WARNING*
> *Use brake fluid clearly marked DOT 4 from a sealed container. Other types may vaporize and cause brake failure. Always use the same brand name; do not intermix silicone based (DOT 5) brake fluid as it can cause brake component damage leading to brake system failure.*

22. Refill the master cylinder reservoir, if necessary, to maintain the correct fluid level.

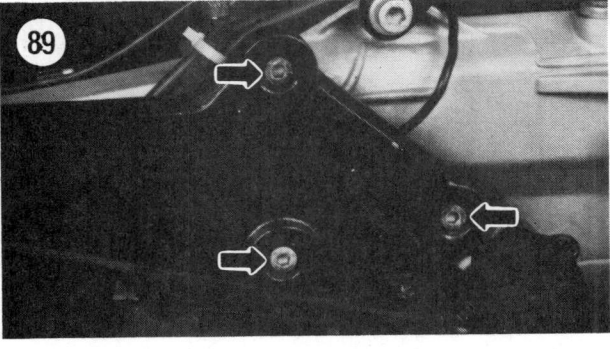

23. Install the rubber diaphragm and top cover.

> *WARNING*
> *Do not ride the motorcycle until you are sure the brakes are operating correctly with full hydraulic advantage. If necessary, bleed the brake as described in this chapter.*

24. Bed the pads in gradually for the first 80 km (50 miles) by using only light pressure as much as possible. Immediate hard application will glaze the new friction pads and greatly reduce the effectiveness of the brake.

REAR MASTER CYLINDER AND RESERVOIR

Removal/Installation

Refer to **Figure 86** for this procedure.

> *CAUTION*
> *Cover the surrounding area of the frame and the wheel with a heavy cloth or plastic tarp to protect them from accidental brake fluid spills. Wash brake fluid off any painted or plated surfaces immediately, as it will destroy the finish. Use soapy water and rinse completely.*

> *NOTE*
> *Drain the brake fluid from the hose and discard it—never reuse brake fluid. Contaminated brake fluid may cause brake failure.*

1. Drain the hydraulic brake fluid from the rear brake system as follows:
     a. Attach a hose to the bleed valve (**Figure 87**) on the caliper assembly.
     b. Place the loose end of the hose in a container to catch the brake fluid.
     c. Open the bleed valve and continue to apply the rear brake pedal until the brake fluid is pumped out of the system.
     d. Disconnect the hose and tighten the bleed valve.
     e. Dispose of this brake fluid—*never* reuse brake fluid. Contaminated brake fluid may cause brake failure.
2. On models so equipped, remove the bolts (**Figure 88**) securing the saddlebag rack to the right-hand footpeg assembly.
3. Remove the bolts (**Figure 89**) securing the right-hand footpeg assembly to the frame and carefully pull the top portion of the assembly away from the frame.

12

4. Secure the rear of the assembly with a Bungee cord (**Figure 90**) to take the strain off of the flexible brake hoses.

5. Disconnect the flexible brake hose (A, **Figure 91**) from the reservoir to the master cylinder. Insert a golf tee into the end of the hose and cover the end with a resealable plastic bag to prevent the entry of foreign matter.

6. Remove the Allen bolts (B, **Figure 91**) securing the master cylinder to the right-hand footpeg assembly.

7. Disconnect the flexible brake hose (C, **Figure 91**) from the rear of the master cylinder. Insert a golf tee into the end of the hose and cover the end with a resealable plastic bag to prevent the entry of foreign matter.

8. Remove the master cylinder and take it to your work bench for further disassembly.

9. To remove the master cylinder reservoir, perform the following:

    a. Loosen the hose clamp and disconnect the brake hose (A, **Figure 92**) from the reservoir.

    b. Remove the mounting bolt or nut securing the master cylinder reservoir (B, **Figure 92**) to the frame.

    c. Remove the reservoir from the frame.

10. Install by reversing these removal steps, noting the following.

11. Tighten the hose fittings to the torque specification listed in **Table 2**.

12. Fill the reservoir and bleed the brake as described in this chapter.

Disassembly

Refer to **Figure 86** for this procedure.

1. Remove the master cylinder as described in this chapter.

2. Remove the dust cover (**Figure 93**) from the front end of the master cylinder.

3. Remove the stopper (**Figure 94**) from the end of the piston assembly.

CAUTION
When the retaining screw is removed, the pushrod will be pushed out by the internal spring pressure. Protect yourself accordingly.

4. Remove the retaining screw (**Figure 95**) on the side of the master cylinder body securing the piston assembly.

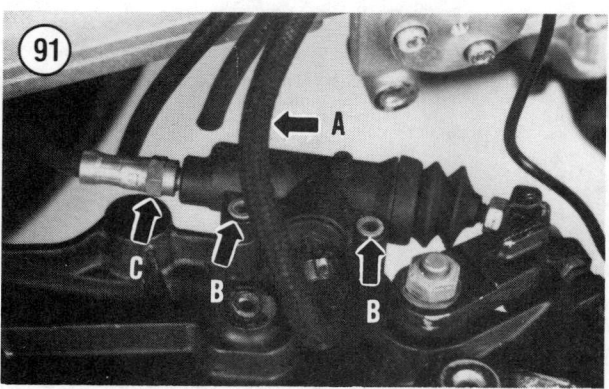

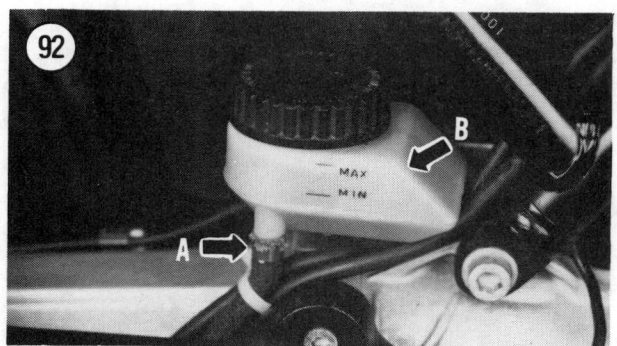

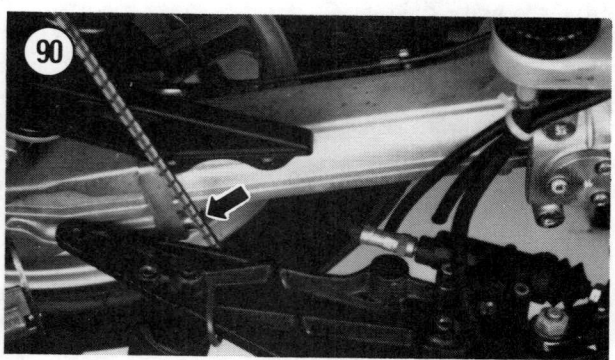

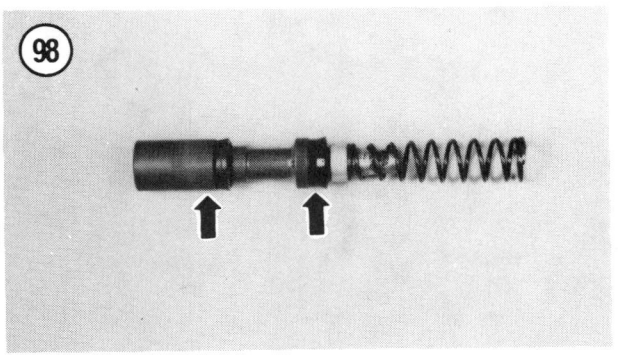

5. Withdraw the piston assembly (**Figure 96**) from the body.

NOTE
It may be necessary to apply a small amount of air pressure to the brake fluid outlet to remove the piston assembly. If necessary, apply the air in short spurts and catch the piston assembly as it comes out.

Inspection

BMW does not provide any specifications for wear limits on any of the master cylinder components. Replace any parts that appear to be damaged or worn.
1. Clean all parts in denatured alcohol or fresh brake fluid.
2. Apply compressed air to all openings in the master cylinder body to thoroughly dry it out.
3. Inspect the cylinder bore (**Figure 97**) and piston contact surfaces (**Figure 98**) for signs of wear and damage. If either part is less than perfect, replace it.
4. Replace the piston assembly if the cups require replacement. The cups can not be replaced individually.
5. Check the end of the stopper for wear caused by the adjust bolt. Replace stopper if worn.
6. Inspect the brake hoses (**Figure 99**) on the body. Remove and replace if necessary.
7. Inspect the rubber boot (**Figure 100**) for deterioration, cracking and wear. Replace boot if necessary.

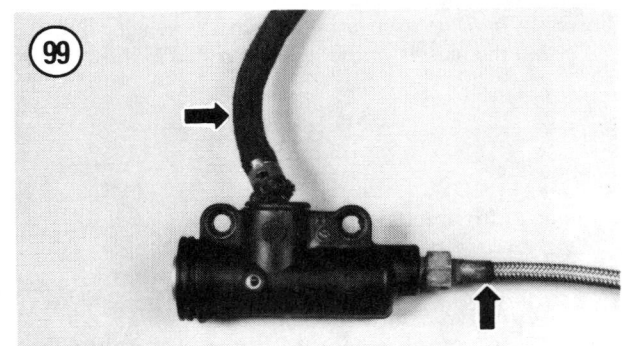

12

Assembly

1. Soak the piston assembly in fresh brake fluid for at least 15 minutes to make the primary cup pliable. Coat the inside of the cylinder with fresh brake fluid before assembling parts.

> *CAUTION*
> *When installing the piston assembly, do not allow the cups to turn inside out as they will be damaged and allow brake fluid leakage within the cylinder bore.*

2. Place the master cylinder in a vise with soft jaws. Do not tighten the jaws too much or the master cylinder may be distorted or damaged.
3. Install the piston assembly and spring (**Figure 101**) into the cylinder together.
4. Press the piston assembly into the master cylinder body and install the retaining screw (**Figure 95**). The piston assembly must be pressed in far enough so that the retaining screw can fit into the space between the primary and secondary cups in the piston assembly. Tighten the screw securely.
5. After the retaining screw has been tightened, push the piston assembly in and let the spring push it back out several times to make sure it is seated correctly and moves freely in the master cylinder bore.
6. Install the stopper (**Figure 102**) into the end of the piston assembly.
7. Install the dust boot (**Figure 93**) and make sure it snaps correctly into the groove in the master cylinder body.
8. Install the master cylinder as described in this chapter.

REAR CALIPER

Removal

Refer to **Figure 103** for this procedure.

> *CAUTION*
> *Do not spill any brake fluid on the painted portion of the rear wheel. Wash any spilled brake fluid immediately, as it will destroy the finish. Use soapy water and rinse completely.*

1. Remove the rear wheel (A, **Figure 104**) as described under *Rear Wheel Removal/Installation* in Chapter Eleven.
2. On ABS equipped models, remove the trigger sensor as described in this chapter.
3. Drain the hydraulic brake fluid from the rear brake system as follows:
  a. Attach a hose to the bleed valve (B, **Figure 104**) on the caliper assembly.
  b. Place the loose end of the hose in a container to catch the brake fluid.
  c. Open the bleed valve and continue to apply the rear brake pedal until the brake fluid is pumped out of the system.
  d. Disconnect the hose and tighten the bleed valve.
  e. Dispose of this brake fluid—*never reuse brake fluid. Contaminated brake fluid may cause brake failure.*
4. Use a brake flare nut wrench to loosen, then unscrew the flare nut (A, **Figure 105**) securing the brake line to the rear caliper.
5. To prevent the entry of moisture and dirt, cap the end of the brake line. Place the loose end in a resealable plastic bag and tie the loose end up to the frame.

> *NOTE*
> *If the caliper assembly is going to be disassembled for service, loosen the Allen bolts (B, **Figure 105**) securing the caliper assembly halves together. The fork slider makes a good holding fixture.*

6. Remove the caliper mounting bolts (C, **Figure 105**) securing the caliper assembly to the final drive unit.
7. Pull the caliper assembly up and off the brake disc.

(101)

(102)

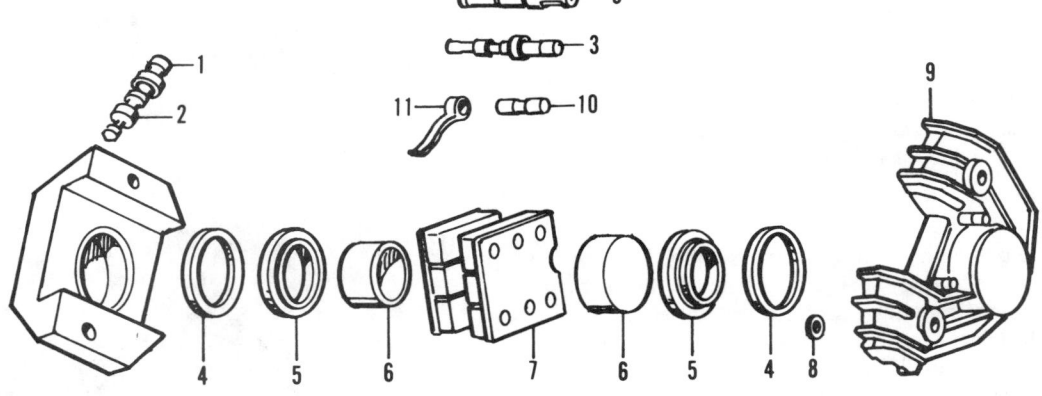

REAR CALIPER

1. Bleed valve cap
2. Bleed valve
3. Lockpin
4. Piston seal
5. Dust seal
6. Piston
7. Brake pads
8. O-ring seal
9. Outer caliper body half
10. Center pin
11. Retaining spring

12

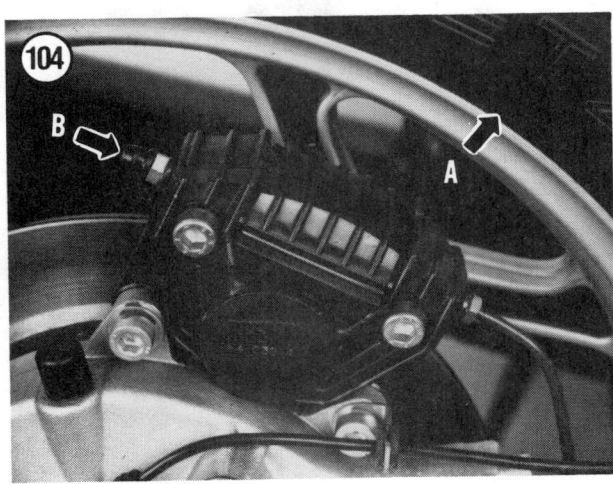

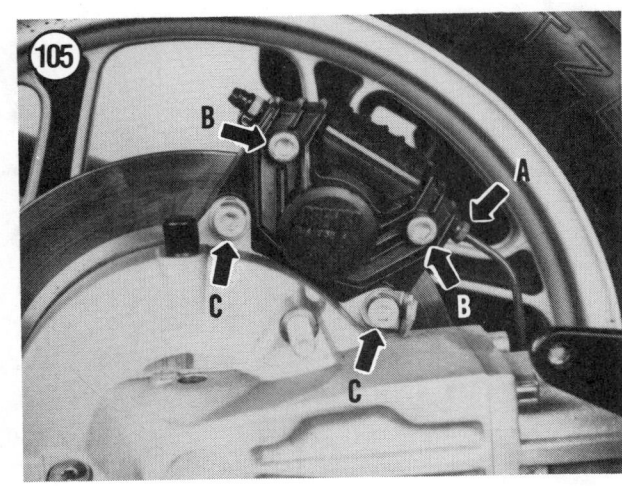

Installation

1. Attach the brake line to the rear caliper and tighten the flare nut to the torque specification listed in **Table 2**.
2. Carefully install the caliper assembly down onto the disc and final drive unit. Be careful not to damage the leading edge of the pads during installation.
3. Install the caliper mounting bolts (C, **Figure 105**). Tighten the bolts to torque specifications listed in **Table 2**.

> *NOTE*
> *If the caliper assembly was disassembled for service, securely tighten the Allen bolts (B, **Figure 105**) securing the caliper assembly halves together.*

4. Connect the brake line to the caliper assembly. Tighten the flare nuts to the torque specification listed in **Table 2**.
5. On ABS equipped models, perform the following:
   a. Install the trigger sensor as described in this chapter.
   b. Inspect, and adjust if necessary, the trigger sensor-to-pulse generating wheel clearance as described in this chapter.
6. Install the rear wheel as described under *Rear Wheel Removal/Installation* in Chapter Eleven.
7. Bleed the brake as described in this chapter.

> *WARNING*
> *Do not ride the motorcycle until you are sure that the brake is operating properly.*

Rebuilding

Refer to **Figure 103** for this procedure.
BMW does not provide any specifications for wear limits on any of the rear caliper components. Replace any parts that appear to be damaged or worn.
1. Remove the caliper assembly as described in this chapter.

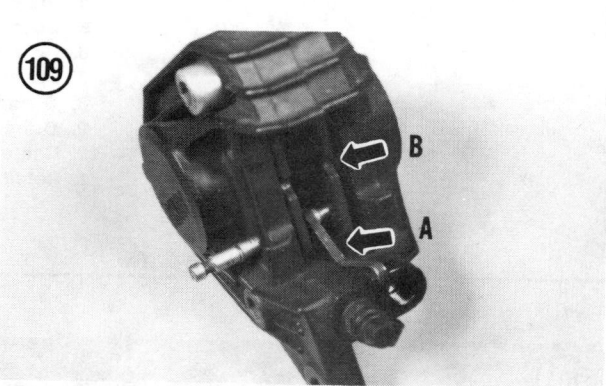

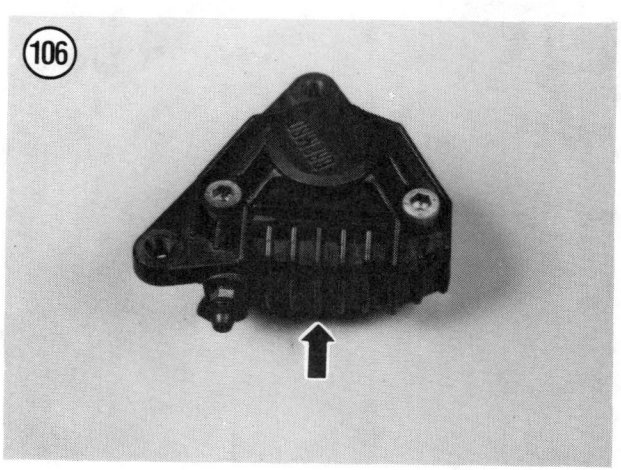

2. Remove the brake pads as follows:
   a. Using a large flat-bladed screwdriver, carefully remove the brake caliper cover (**Figure 106**).
   b. Using a drift and small hammer, carefully tap one of the lockpins (**Figure 107**) out from the backside of the caliper.
   c. Hold a finger over the center pin and retaining spring and remove that lockpin.
   d. Remove the center pin (**Figure 108**).
   e. Using a drift and small hammer, carefully tap the other lockpin partway out of the caliper and remove the retaining spring (A, **Figure 109**).
   f. Remove the inboard brake pad (B, **Figure 109**).
   g. Remove the lockpin (**Figure 110**) from the caliper.
   h. Remove the outboard brake pad (**Figure 111**).

3. Remove the Allen bolts (**Figure 112**) securing the caliper assembly halves together.

4. Separate the caliper halves.

5. Remove the small O-ring seal (**Figure 113**) from the inboard caliper half. Discard the O-ring seal as it must be replaced.

> *CAUTION*
> *In the following step, do not use a sharp tool to remove the dust seals from the caliper body. Do not damage the cylinder surfaces.*

6. Remove the dust seal (**Figure 114**) from each caliper body half. Discard the dust seals. They cannot be reused after removal as they will no longer seal effectively.

7. Withdraw the piston (**Figure 115**) from each caliper body half. If you cannot remove the piston easily, perform the following:
   a. Either wrap the caliper half and piston with a heavy cloth or place a shop cloth or piece of soft wood over the end of the piston.
   b. Perform this step over and close down to a workbench top. Hold the caliper body with the piston facing away from you.

12

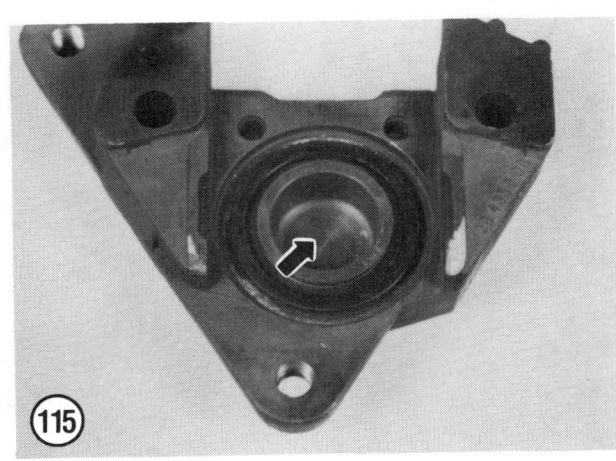

WARNING
*In the next step, the piston may shoot out of the caliper body like a bullet. Keep your fingers out of the way. Wear shop gloves and apply air pressure gradually. Do **not** use high pressure air or place the air hose nozzle directly against the hydraulic fluid passageway in the caliper body. Hold the air nozzle away from the inlet allowing some of the air to escape during the procedure.*

c. Apply the air pressure in short spurts to the hydraulic fluid passageway (**Figure 116**) and force the piston out of the caliper body. Place your finger over the other fluid passageways to prevent the air from escaping. Use a service station air hose if you don't have an air compressor.

CAUTION
In the following step, do not use a sharp tool to remove the piston seals from the caliper cylinders. Do not damage the cylinder surfaces.

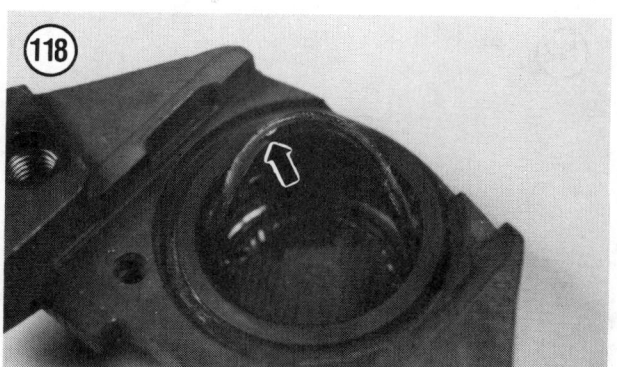

8. Use a piece of plastic or wood and carefully push the piston seal (**Figure 117**) in toward the caliper cylinder and out of its groove. Remove the piston seal (**Figure 118**) from each caliper body half. Discard the piston seals. They cannot be reused after removal as they will no longer seal effectively.

9. Inspect the seal groove in each caliper body half (A, **Figure 119**) for damage. If damaged or corroded, replace the caliper assembly.

NOTE
The caliper body cannot be replaced separately. If it is damaged in any way the entire caliper assembly must be replaced.

10. Unscrew and remove the bleed screw and cap (**Figure 120**).

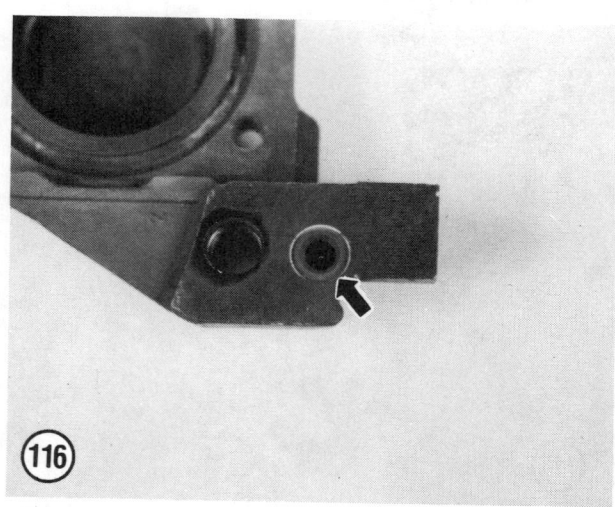

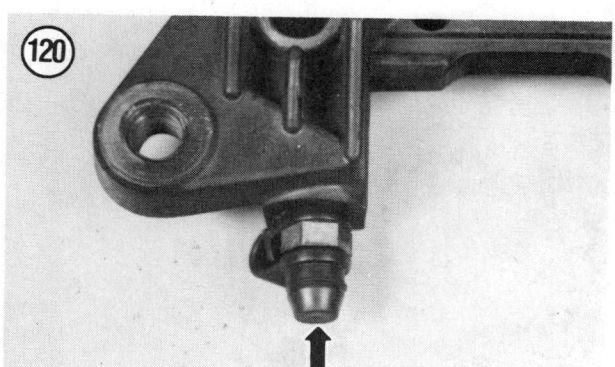

11. Inspect the caliper body halves (**Figure 121**) for damage. Replace the caliper body if necessary.

12. Inspect the hydraulic fluid passageway (B, **Figure 119**) in the base of each cylinder bore. Make sure it is clean and open. Apply compressed air to the opening and make sure it is clear. Clean out if necessary with fresh brake fluid.

13. Inspect the cylinder walls (**Figure 122**) and the pistons (**Figure 123**) for scratches, scoring or other damage. If either is damaged, rusty or corroded, replace the caliper assembly. The pistons cannot be replaced separately.

14. Inspect the caliper mounting bolt holes. If the threads are slightly damaged, clean them up with a proper size thread tap. If the threads are worn or damaged beyond a "thread clean up," replace the caliper assembly.

15. Inspect the caliper halves' assembly bolt holes (**Figure 124**). If the threads are slightly damaged, clean them up with a proper size thread tap. If the threads are worn or damaged beyond a "thread clean up," replace the caliper assembly.

16. Inspect the union bolt hole threads (**Figure 125**). If the threads are slightly damaged, clean them up with a proper size thread tap. If the threads are worn or damaged beyond a "thread clean up," replace the caliper assembly.

17. Make sure the hole in the bleed screw is clean and open. Apply compressed air to the opening and make sure it is clear. Clean out if necessary with fresh brake fluid.

18. If serviceable, clean the caliper body halves with rubbing alcohol and rinse with clean brake fluid.

WARNING
Never reuse a dust seal or piston seal that has been removed. Very minor damage or age deterioration can make the seals useless.

19. Coat the new dust seals (**Figure 126**) and piston seals (**Figure 127**) with fresh DOT 4 brake fluid.

20. Carefully install the new piston seal (**Figure 118**) in the groove in each caliper cylinder. Make sure the seal is properly seated in the groove (**Figure 117**).

12

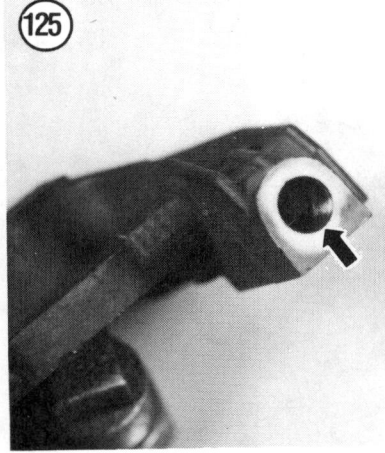

21. Coat the pistons and the caliper cylinders with fresh DOT 4 brake fluid.

22. Position the pistons with the *open end facing out* (**Figure 128**) toward the brake pads and install the piston into each caliper cylinder (**Figure 129**). Push the pistons in until they bottom out (**Figure 130**).

23. Carefully install the new dust seal (**Figure 131**) in the groove in each caliper cylinder. Make sure the seal is properly seated in the caliper half.

24. Install the bleed screw and cap (**Figure 120**).

25. Install a new O-ring seal (**Figure 113**) into the recess in the inboard caliper half.

26. Lay the inboard caliper half down and install the outboard half on top of it. This is to prevent the small O-ring seal from falling out during assembly.

NOTE
*There are 2 different length Allen bolts of the same diameter. The longer bolts (A, **Figure 132**) are used to assemble the 2 caliper halves together and the shorter ones (B, **Figure 132**) are used as mounting bolts to hold the caliper assembly onto the final drive unit.*

27. Install the Allen bolts (**Figure 112**) securing the caliper assembly halves together.

28. Install the brake pads as follows:
   a. Install the outboard brake pad (**Figure 111**).
   b. Partially install the lockpin (**Figure 110**) into the caliper and brake pad.
   c. Install the inboard brake pad (B, **Figure 109**).
   d. Install the retaining spring (A, **Figure 109**) onto the lockpin so the raised section will be facing upward away from the brake pads.
   e. Tap the lockpin in until it stops and locks in place.
   f. Install the center pin (**Figure 108**) into the notch in both brake pads.
   g. Move the retaining spring down and into position over the center pin.
   h. Partially install the other lockpin through the outer hole in the caliper and outboard brake pad.

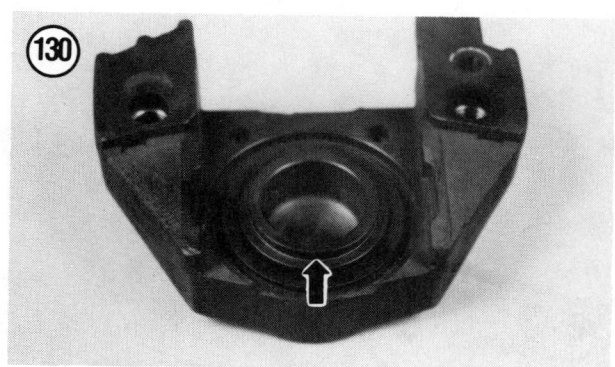

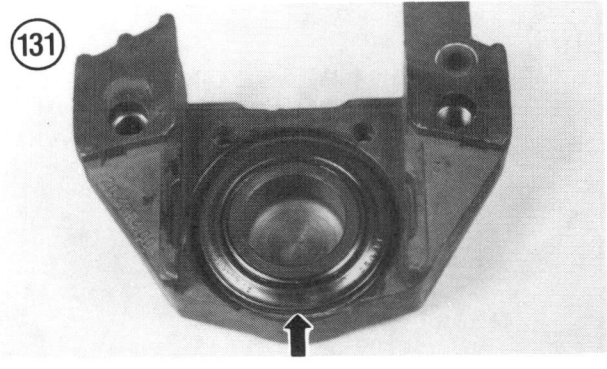

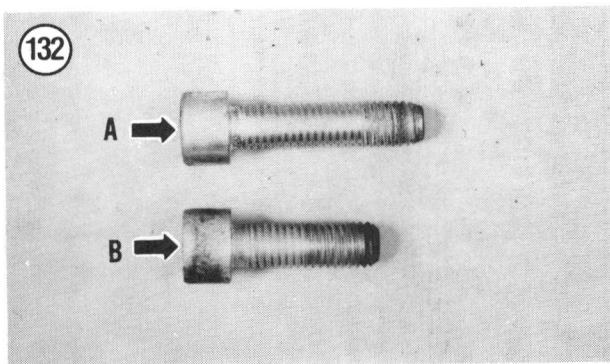

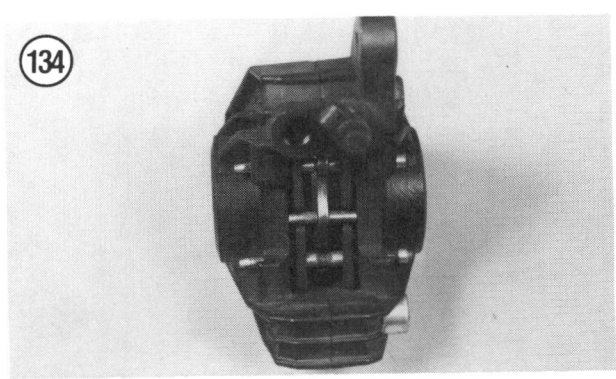

i. Press the retaining spring down and push the lockpin over the retaining spring end (**Figure 133**).

j. Push the lockpin through the inboard brake pad and caliper (**Figure 134**). Tap it in until it stops and locks in place.

k. Make sure the retaining spring is correctly hooked under the lockpin and is located over the center pin recess (A, **Figure 135**).

l. Make sure both lockpins (B, **Figure 135**) are locked in place completely.

29. Install the brake caliper cover (**Figure 106**).

30. Install the brake caliper assembly as described in this chapter.

BRAKE HOSE AND LINE REPLACEMENT (NON-ABS MODELS)

There is no factory-recommended replacement interval, but it is a good idea to replace all flexible brake hoses every four years or when they show signs of cracking or damage.

The metal brake lines do not require routine replacement unless they are damaged or the end fittings are leaking. While replacing the flexible brake hoses, inspect the metal brake lines for damage. If they have been hit, the line may be restricted, thus decreasing braking effectiveness.

CAUTION
Cover the fuel tank, front wheel, front fender, rear wheel and rear portion of the frame with a heavy cloth or plastic tarp to protect it from accidental spilling of brake fluid. Wash brake fluid off of any painted, plastic or plated surface immediately, as it will destroy the finish. Use soapy water and rinse completely.

12

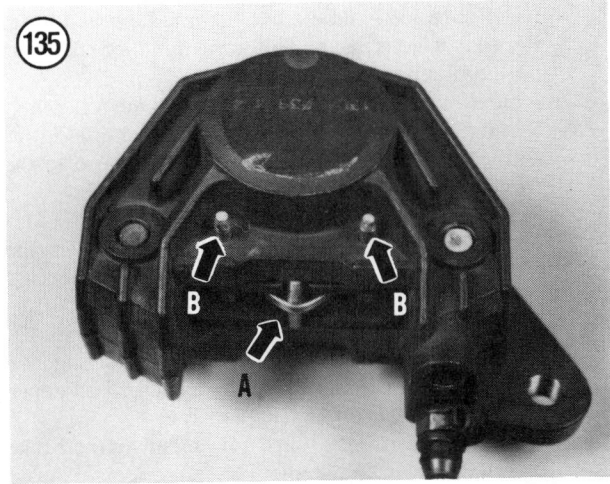

Front Hoses and Lines
Removal/Installation

Refer to **Figure 136** for this procedure.

1. On models so equipped, remove the front fairing as described under *Front Fairing Removal/Installation* in Chapter Thirteen.

2. Remove the front fender as described under *Front Fender Removal/Installation* in Chapter Thirteen.

> *NOTE*
> *To prevent the entry of moisture and dirt, cap the end of the brake hoses and lines that are not going to be replaced. Place the loose end in a plastic resealable bag and zip it closed around the hose or line.*

3. Drain the hydraulic brake fluid from the front brake system as follows:

   a. Attach a hose to the bleed valve (**Figure 137**) on each caliper assembly.

   b. Place the loose end of the hose in a container to catch the brake fluid.

   c. Open the bleed valve on each caliper and apply the front brake lever until the brake fluid is pumped out of the system.

   d. Disconnect the hoses and tighten the bleed valves.

   e. Dispose of this brake fluid—*never* reuse brake fluid. Contaminated brake fluid may cause brake failure.

4. Using a brake flare nut wrench, loosen, then unscrew the flare nut (**Figure 138**) securing the lower brake line to the front caliper.

5. To remove the middle brake hose, perform the following:

   a. Hold onto the fitting on the middle brake hose with a wrench and using an 11 mm brake flare nut wrench, loosen, then unscrew the flare nut (A, **Figure 139**) securing the lower brake line to the middle flexible hose. Remove the lower brake line.

   b. Unscrew the middle brake hose from the brake pipe (B, **Figure 139**) and remove the middle brake hose.

   c. Repeat substeps 5a and 5b for the middle brake hose on the other side.

6. To remove the upper brake hose, perform the following:

   a. Remove the union bolt and sealing washer (**Figure 140**) securing the upper flexible brake hose to the front master cylinder.

   b. Remove the union bolt and sealing washer (A, **Figure 141**) securing the upper flexible brake hose to the brake pipe running through the center of the steering stem.

   c. Remove the upper flexible brake hose (B, **Figure 141**).

7. To remove the brake pipe, perform the following:

   a. Remove the handlebar assembly as described under *Handlebar Removal* in Chapter Ten.

   b. Remove the nut (C, **Figure 141**) securing the brake pipe to the steering stem.

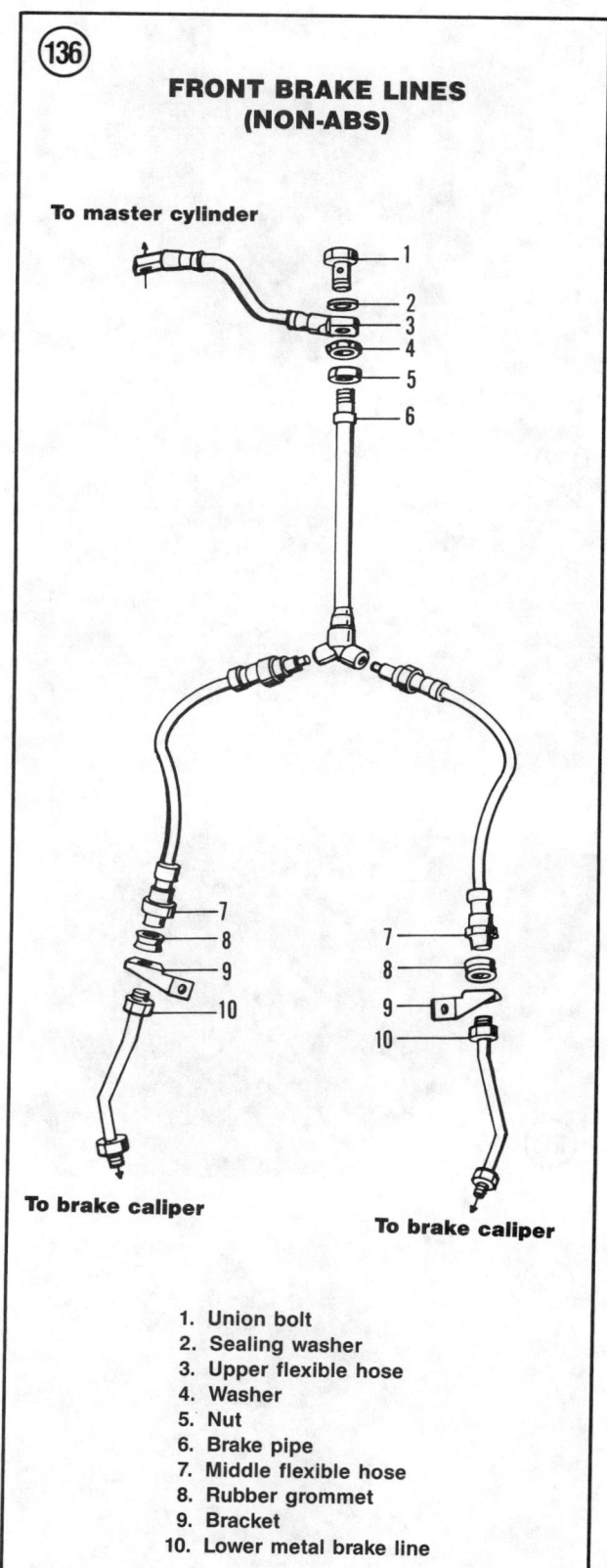

(136)

FRONT BRAKE LINES (NON-ABS)

To master cylinder

To brake caliper   To brake caliper

1. Union bolt
2. Sealing washer
3. Upper flexible hose
4. Washer
5. Nut
6. Brake pipe
7. Middle flexible hose
8. Rubber grommet
9. Bracket
10. Lower metal brake line

c. Withdraw the brake pipe down and out of the steering stem and remove the brake pipe.

8. Inspect the brake pipe as follows:

a. Check the brake pipe for any cracks or fractures (**Figure 142**).

b. Check the condition of the threads (**Figure 143**) at the upper end. Clean up with a proper size die or replace if severely damaged.

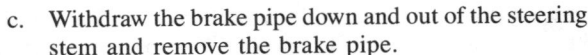

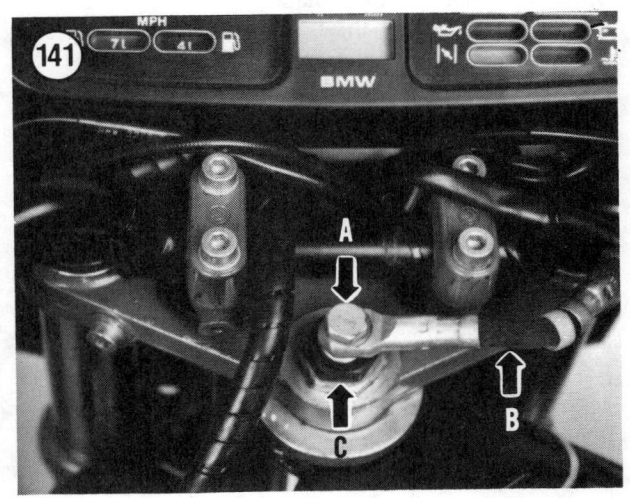

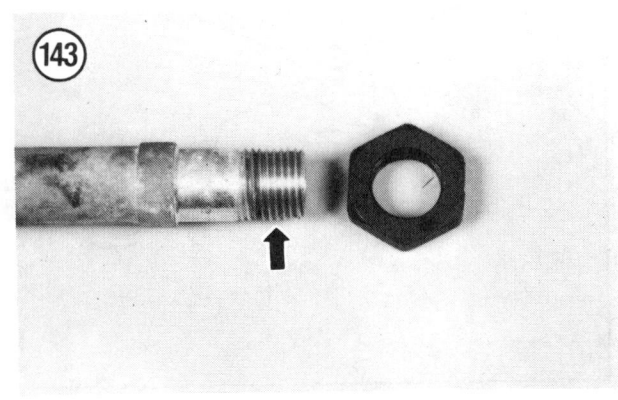

12

c. Check the condition of the threads (A, **Figure 144**) at the lower end. Clean up with a proper size tap or replace if severely damaged.

d. Make sure the rubber seal (B, **Figure 144**) is in good condition. Replace if it is starting to deteriorate.

9. Install new hoses, sealing washers and union bolts in the reverse order of removal. Be sure to install new sealing washers in the correct positions.

10. Tighten all union bolts and flare nut fittings to torque specifications listed in **Table 2**.

11. Refill the master cylinder with fresh brake fluid clearly marked DOT 4. Bleed the front brake system as described in this chapter.

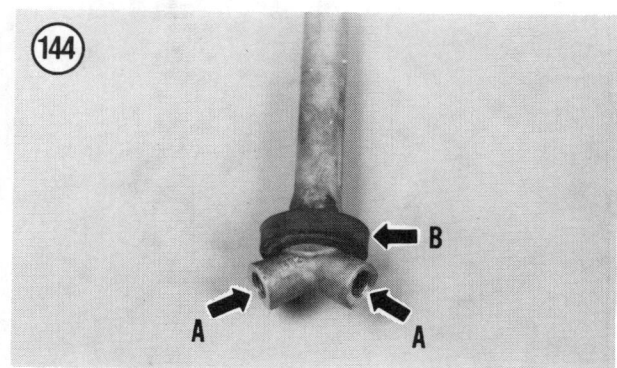

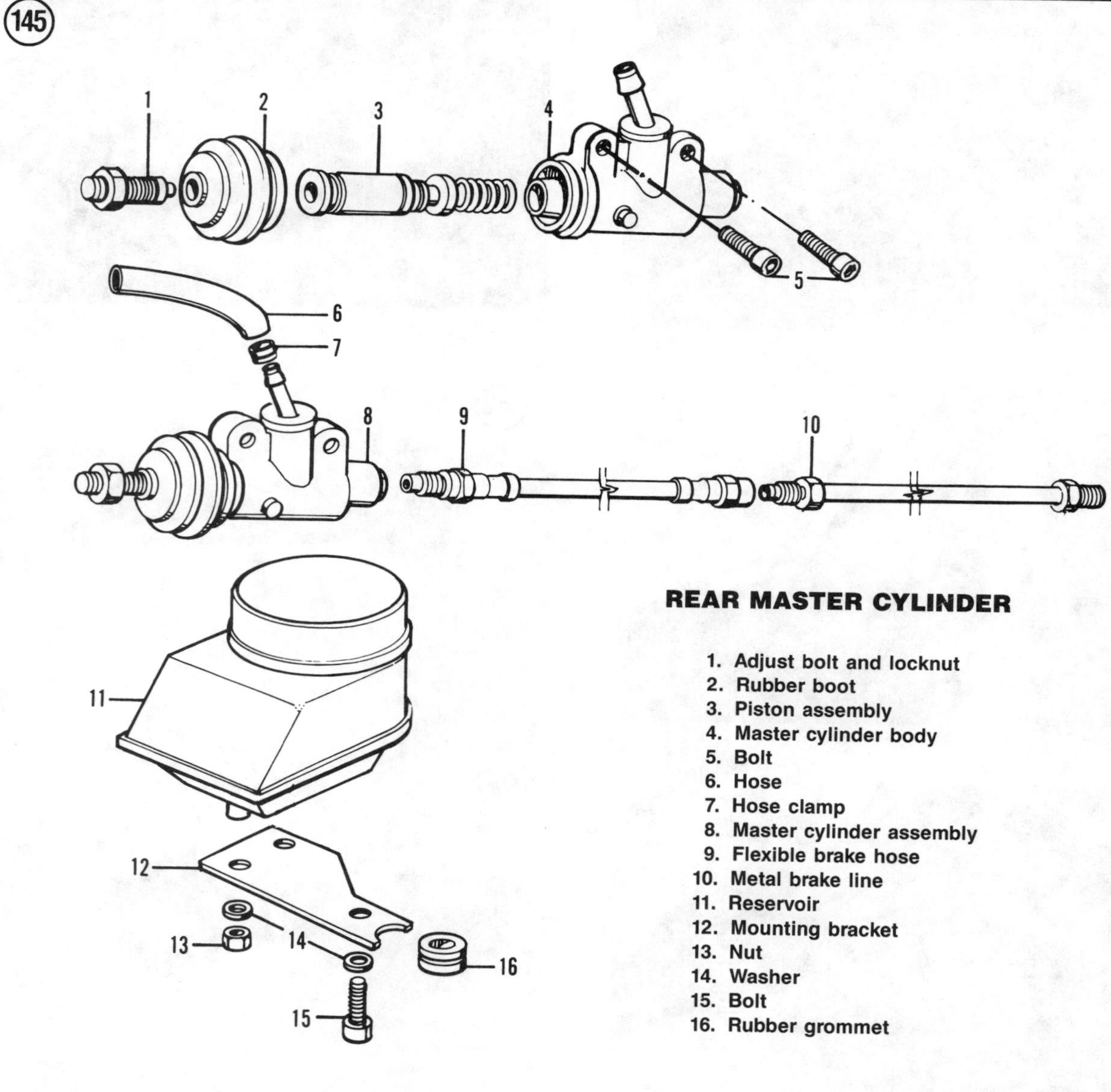

REAR MASTER CYLINDER

1. Adjust bolt and locknut
2. Rubber boot
3. Piston assembly
4. Master cylinder body
5. Bolt
6. Hose
7. Hose clamp
8. Master cylinder assembly
9. Flexible brake hose
10. Metal brake line
11. Reservoir
12. Mounting bracket
13. Nut
14. Washer
15. Bolt
16. Rubber grommet

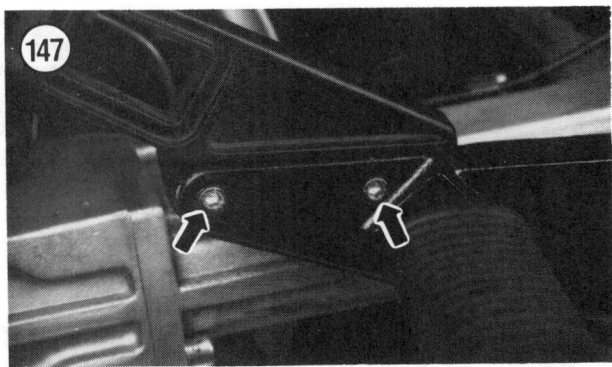

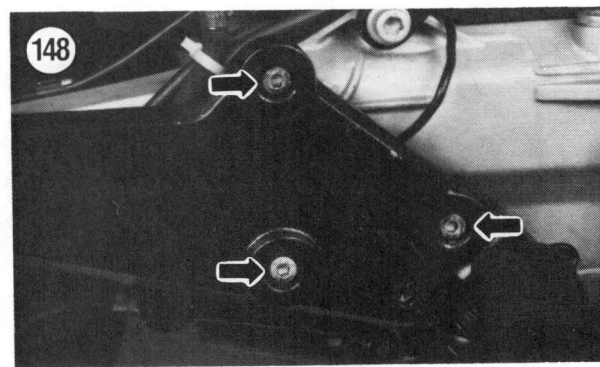

WARNING
*Do not ride the motorcycle until you are sure
that the brakes are operating properly.*

12. On models so equipped, install the front fairing as described in Chapter Thirteen.

**Rear Brake Hose
Removal/Installation**

Refer to **Figure 145** for this procedure.
1. Drain the hydraulic brake fluid from the rear brake system as follows:
   a. Attach a hose to the bleed valve (**Figure 146**) on the rear caliper assembly.
   b. Place the loose end of the hose in a container to catch the brake fluid.
   c. Open the bleed valve and continue to apply the rear brake pedal until the brake fluid is pumped out of the system.
   d. Disconnect the hose and tighten the bleed valve.
   e. Dispose of this brake fluid—*never* reuse brake fluid. Contaminated brake fluid may cause brake failure.
2. To replace the flexible brake hose, perform the following:
   a. Hold onto the fitting on the flexible brake hose with a wrench. Use a brake flare nut wrench to loosen, then unscrew the flare nut securing the brake line to the flexible brake hose.
   b. On models so equipped, remove the bolts (**Figure 147**) securing the saddlebag rack to the right-hand footpeg assembly.
   c. Remove the bolts (**Figure 148**) securing the right-hand footpeg assembly to the frame and carefully pull the top portion of the assembly away from the frame.
   d. Secure the rear of the assembly with a Bungee cord to take the strain off of the flexible brake hoses.
   e. Unscrew the flexible brake hose (**Figure 149**) from the master cylinder.
   f. Remove the flexible brake hose.
3. To replace the brake line, perform the following:
   a. Hold onto the fitting on the flexible brake hose with a wrench. Use a brake flare nut wrench to loosen, then unscrew the flare nut securing the brake line to the flexible brake hose.
   b. Use a brake flare nut wrench to loosen, then unscrew the flare nut (**Figure 150**) securing the brake line to the rear caliper assembly.
   c. Remove the brake line.
4. Install a new flexible brake hose and brake line in the reverse order of removal.
5. Tighten all hose and line connections to torque specifications listed in **Table 2**.
6. To replace the master cylinder-to-reservoir hose, perform the following:

12

a. Remove the hose clamp at the reservoir (A, **Figure 151**) and at the master cylinder (B, **Figure 151**).
b. Remove the hose (C, **Figure 151**) from both fittings.
c. Install a new hose and tighten the hose clamps securely.

7. Refill the master cylinder with fresh brake fluid clearly marked DOT 4 only. Bleed the brake as described in this chapter.

> *WARNING*
> *Do not ride the motorcycle until you are sure that the brakes are operating properly.*

BRAKE DISC
(FRONT AND REAR)

Removal/Installation

1. Remove the front or rear wheel as described in Chapter Ten or Chapter Eleven.

> *NOTE*
> *Place a piece of wood or vinyl tube in the caliper(s) in place of the disc(s). This way, if the brake lever is inadvertently squeezed, or the brake pedal depressed, the pistons will not be forced out of the cylinders. If this does happen, the caliper may have to be disassembled to reseat the pistons and the system will have to be bled.*

> *CAUTION*
> *Do not set the wheel down on the disc surface, as it may get scratched or warped. Set the tire sidewall on 2 blocks of wood (**Figure 152**).*

> *NOTE*
> *On the front wheel, the bolts go through both brake discs and through the wheel hub.*

> *NOTE*
> *On the front wheel, if working on a well run-in bike (high mileage), mark the brake discs with ''R'' and ''L'' (**Figure 153**) (on an attached piece of masking tape) so they will be reinstalled on the same side of the wheel from where they were removed. Older parts tend to form a wear pattern and should be reinstalled in the same location. The BMW discs are not*

marked to indicate to right-hand or left-hand sides.

2. On the front wheel, perform the following:
   a. Hold onto the nuts (**Figure 154**) on the right-hand side of the wheel and loosen the Allen bolts (**Figure 155**) on the left-hand side. Loosen all bolts and nuts.
   b. Remove all but one of the bolts, washers and nuts.

   c. Place the wheel in the horizontal position on wood blocks.
   d. Hold onto the lower brake disc and remove the remaining bolt, washers and nut. Discard the nuts as they should be replaced every time they are removed.
   e. Remove the lower brake disc, then the upper brake disc.

3. On the rear wheel, remove the countersunk Allen bolts securing the disc to the final drive unit. Refer to **Figure 156** and **Figure 157**. Remove the brake disc.

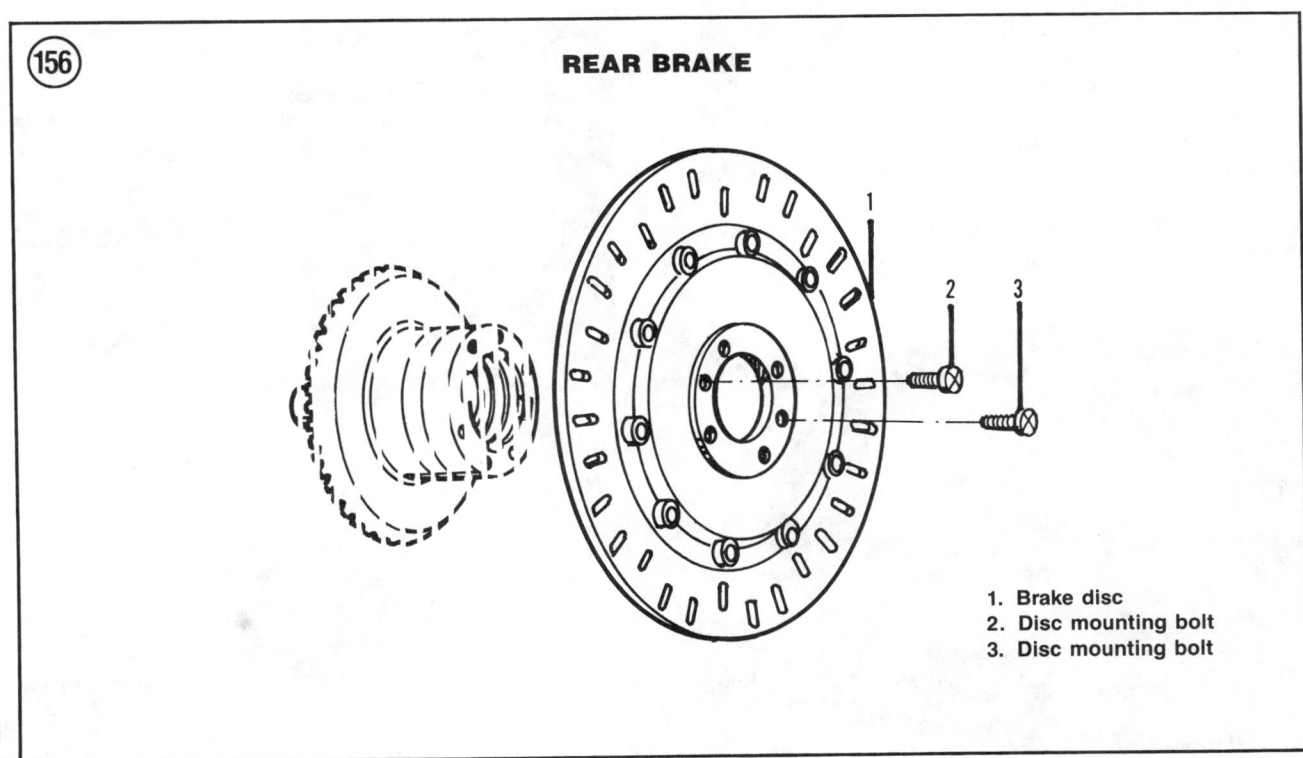

REAR BRAKE

1. Brake disc
2. Disc mounting bolt
3. Disc mounting bolt

12

4. Inspect the brake discs for wear or damage. Refer to **Figure 158** for the front brake and **Figure 159** for the rear brake. Make sure the attachment rivets (A, **Figure 160**) and the mounting holes (B, **Figure 160**) are not damaged. Replace the brake disc(s) if necessary.

5. Install by reversing these removal steps, noting the following.

6. On the front wheel, perform the following:

  a. Replace the self-locking nuts each time they are removed. During removal, the locking ring (**Figure 161**) may be damaged and its retention qualities lessened.

  b. Be sure to place a washer under the bolt head and between the brake disc and the nut.

  c. Install the bolts from the left-hand side.

  d. Tighten the bolts and nuts (front wheel) to the torque specification listed in **Table 2**.

7. On the rear wheel, be sure to use the special countersunk screws (**Figure 162**) to secure the disc to the final drive unit. Tighten the screws to the torque specification listed in **Table 2**.

Inspection

It is not necessary to remove the disc from the wheel to inspect it. Small marks on the disc are not important, but deep radial scratches, deep enough to snag a fingernail, reduce braking effectiveness and increase brake pad wear. If these grooves are found, the disc should be replaced.

1. Measure the thickness of the disc at several locations round the disc with a micrometer or vernier caliper. Refer to **Figure 163** for the front discs or **Figure 164** for the rear disc. The disc must be replaced if the thickness, in any area, is less than that specified in **Table 1**. Each disc is marked with its minimum allowable thickness. Refer to **Figure 165** for the front discs or **Figure 166** for the rear disc.

2. Make sure the disc bolts are tight before running this check.

3. Check the disc runout with a dial indicator mounted either to the front fork or to the swing arm.

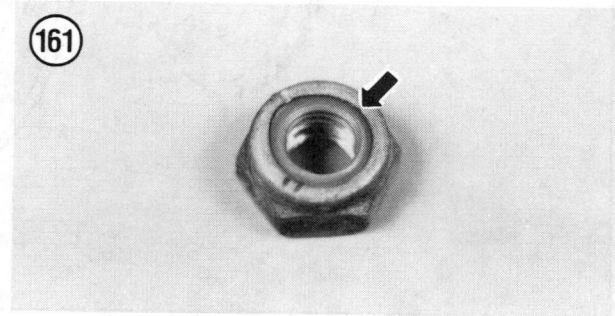

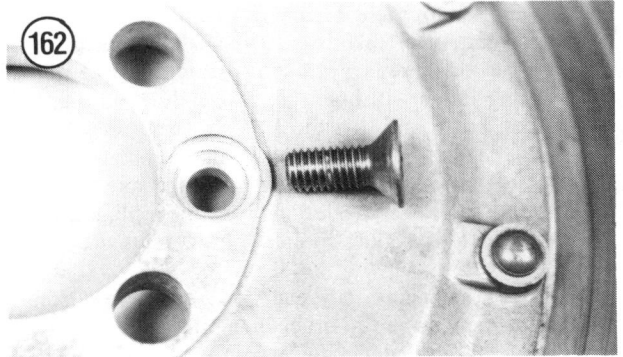

4. Slowly rotate the wheel and watch the dial indicator. On all models, if the runout exceeds that listed in **Table 1**, the disc(s) must be replaced.

5. Clean the disc of any rust or corrosion and wipe clean with lacquer thinner. Never use an oil-based solvent that may leave an oil residue on the disc.

ABS BRAKE SYSTEM

The ABS (Anti-lock Braking System) is designed to eliminate brake lock-up and skidding under wet or slippery conditions. The system is designed specifically for the K100LT/ABS and the K100RS/ABS; replacement parts for these specific bikes are available. However, the system is not designed as a retro-fit for prior models or to present models not originally designed and equipped with this system.

The system consists of the electronic control unit (ECU or computer) which manages the sensing and control functions of the entire system. The ECU is located in the rear cowl. The ECU receives information from the pulse generating inductive sensors (**Figure 167**) that are located at each wheel. The inductive sensors relay information

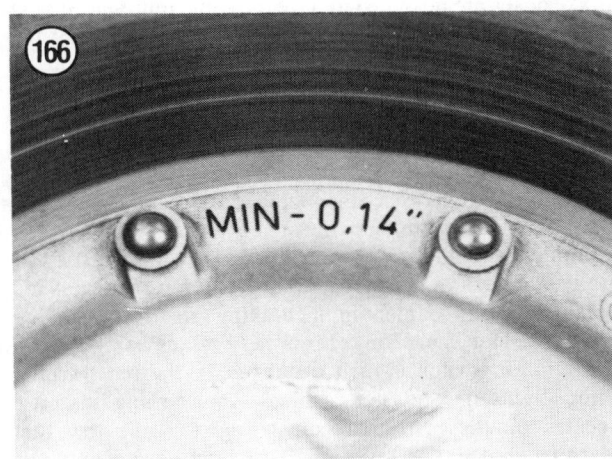

12

regarding wheel rotation speed from the 100 tooth pulse-generating ring that is attached to the backside of the brake disc. Refer to **Figure 168** for the front wheel and **Figure 169** for the rear wheel.

A pressure modulator is used for each wheel's individual brake system. The pressure modulators receive data (wheel speed rate, etc.) from the ECU and then regulate the brake pressure to the caliper assemblies. The pressure modulators regulate and interrupt brake pressure up to 7 times a second, depending on the specific traction situation. On wet, icy or slick surfaces the bike will come to a quicker and safer stop.

If either wheel approaches lock-up or decelerates quicker than the maximum rate programed into the ECU, the pressure modulators reduce the hydraulic pressure in that brake line. This allows the wheel that is near lockup to rotate again.

When the master cylinder lever or pedal is applied, the hydraulic fluid exits the master cylinder, travels to and goes through the pressure modulator and then travels to the caliper assembly for braking action.

Most of the brake system plumbing uses metal brake lines with a minimal use of flexible brake hoses. Since brake pressure is critical in an ABS system, the BMW flexible brake hoses are designed to have the same minimal flexing characteristics as the steel lines. When replacing the flexible brake hoses, be sure to install authorized BMW replacement hoses specifically designed for use with the ABS system. Using a flexible brake hose of an alternate design will drastically change the characteristics of the brake system.

A warning light system is included to let the rider know that the ABS system is operating correctly—or if there is a problem and it is not working at all. The rider must know if the system is working properly, or is not working, as the rider becomes confident in the braking effectiveness of the system and tends to change his or her braking habits. When the ignition switch is turned on, one of the red warning lamps lights up solid (not flashing). The warning lights are located on the instrument cluster next to the low fuel warning light. If the ABS system is operating correctly, the red warning light will go from solid to flashing after the

brake is applied for the first time. Both red lights will then go out as soon as the bike is traveling at 2.5 mph. If they don't go out, or there is a problem within the system, the red warning lights will begin to flash indicating that the system has failed and that the ECU has shut the system down. The regular brake system will still operate—*but with no ABS*. If the warning lights are flashing, take the bike to an authorized BMW dealer and have them plug in their test computer to the bike's computer to find out what went wrong.

The ABS system is simple yet complex. If there is a fault within the system, the test procedures must be done by an authorized BMW dealer with service school training and the assistance of an expensive test computer. *Do not try to work on any part of the ABS system* as it will void any applicable BMW warranty.

BRAKE HOSE AND LINE REPLACEMENT (ABS EQUIPPED MODELS)

There is no factory-recommended replacement interval, but it is a good idea to replace all flexible brake hoses every four years or when they show signs of cracking or damage.

The metal brake lines do not require routine replacement unless they are damaged or the end fittings are leaking. While replacing the flexible brake hoses, inspect the metal brake lines for damage. If they have been hit the line may be restricted, thus decreasing braking effectiveness.

WARNING
On models equipped with the ABS brake system, most of the brake system uses metal brake lines with a minimal use of flexible brake hoses. Since brake pressure is critical in an ABS system the BMW flexible brake hoses are designed to have the same minimal flexing characteristics as the steel lines. When replacing the flexible brake hoses be sure to install authorized BMW replacement hoses

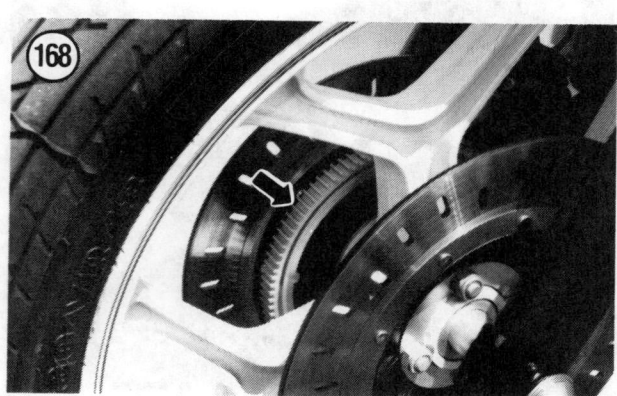

specifically designed for use with the ABS system. Using a flexible brake hose of an alternate design will drastically change the characteristics of the brake system.

CAUTION
Cover the fuel tank, front wheel, front fender, rear wheel and rear portion of the frame with a heavy cloth or plastic tarp to protect it from accidental spilling of brake fluid. Wash brake fluid off of any painted, plastic or plated surface immediately, as it will destroy the finish. Use soapy water and rinse completely.

Front Hoses and Lines
Removal/Installation

NOTE
*Since the ABS brake system **must** be bled with a power bleeder you may want to have the*

brake hoses replaced by a BMW dealer. If you choose to replace the brake hoses yourself, you will then have to trailer the bike to a BMW dealer to have the system bled after the hoses and lines are replaced.

Refer to **Figure 170** for this procedure.
1. Remove the front fairing as described under *Front Fairing Removal/Installation* in Chapter Thirteen.
2. Remove the front fender as described under *Front Fender Removal/Installation* in Chapter Thirteen.

NOTE
To prevent the entry of moisture and dirt, cap the ends of the brake hoses and lines that are not going to be replaced. Place the loose end in a resealable plastic bag and zip it closed around the hose or line.

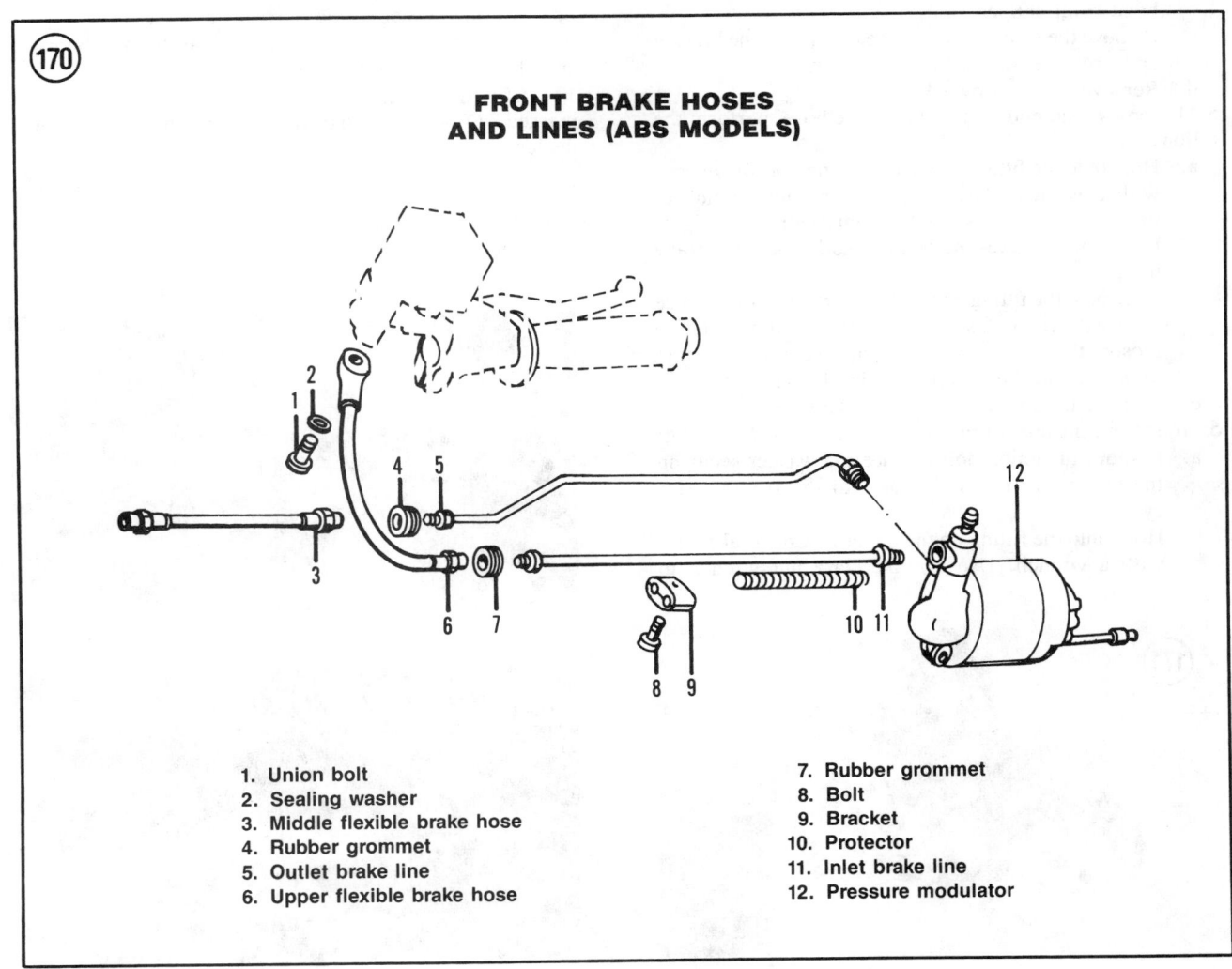

(170)

**FRONT BRAKE HOSES
AND LINES (ABS MODELS)**

1. Union bolt
2. Sealing washer
3. Middle flexible brake hose
4. Rubber grommet
5. Outlet brake line
6. Upper flexible brake hose
7. Rubber grommet
8. Bolt
9. Bracket
10. Protector
11. Inlet brake line
12. Pressure modulator

12

3. Drain the hydraulic brake fluid from the front brake system as follows:

a. Attach a hose to the bleed valve (A, **Figure 171**) on each caliper assembly.

b. Place the loose end of the hose in a container to catch the brake fluid.

c. Open the bleed valve on each caliper and apply the front brake lever until the brake fluid is pumped out of the system.

d. Disconnect the hoses and tighten the bleed valves.

e. Dispose of this brake fluid—*never* reuse brake fluid. Contaminated brake fluid may cause brake failure.

4. To remove the front lower and crossover brake lines, perform the following:

a. On the right-hand caliper, using a brake flare nut wrench, loosen then unscrew the flare nuts (**Figure 172**) securing the lower brake line and the crossover line to the right-hand front caliper.

b. On the left-hand caliper, using a brake flare nut wrench, loosen, then unscrew the flare nut securing the crossover brake line (B, **Figure 171**) to the left-hand front caliper.

c. Remove the screw securing the crossover line bracket and grommet to the fork assembly.

d. Remove the crossover line.

5. To remove the middle flexible brake hose, perform the following:

a. Hold onto the fitting on the middle flexible brake hose with a wrench. Use a brake flare nut wrench to loosen, then unscrew the flare nut securing the right-hand lower brake line to the middle flexible brake hose.

b. Hold onto the fitting on the middle flexible brake hose with a wrench. Use a brake flare nut wrench to loosen, then unscrew the flare nut securing the outlet brake line to the middle flexible brake hose.

c. Remove the middle flexible brake hose.

6. To remove the upper brake hose, perform the following:

a. Remove the union bolt and sealing washer securing the upper flexible brake hose to the front master cylinder.

b. Hold onto the fitting on the upper flexible brake hose with a wrench. Use a brake flare nut wrench to

loosen, then unscrew the flare nut securing the inlet brake line to the upper flexible brake hose.

c. Remove the upper flexible brake hose.

7. To remove the inlet and outlet brake lines, perform the following:

a. Hold onto the fitting on the upper flexible brake hose with a wrench. Use a brake flare nut wrench to loosen, then unscrew the flare nut securing the inlet brake line to the upper flexible brake hose.

b. Hold onto the fitting on the middle flexible brake hose with a wrench. Use a brake flare nut wrench to loosen, then unscrew the flare nut securing the outlet brake line to the middle flexible brake hose.

c. Using a brake flare nut wrench, loosen, then unscrew the flare nuts securing both the inlet and outlet brake lines to the pressure modulator (**Figure 173**).

d. Remove any tie wraps securing the brake lines to the frame and carefully remove the brake lines from the frame.

8. Install new hoses, brake lines, sealing washer and union bolt in the reverse order of removal. Be sure to install a new sealing washer in the correct position.

9. Tighten the union bolt and all flare nut fittings to torque specifications listed in **Table 2**.

10. Refill the master cylinder with fresh brake fluid clearly marked DOT 4. Have the front brake system bled by a BMW dealer.

WARNING
Do not ride the motorcycle until you are sure that the brakes are operating properly.

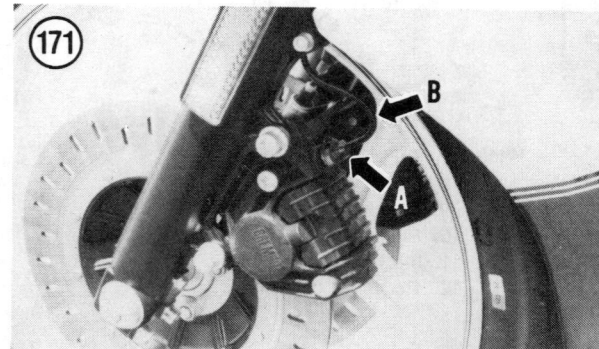

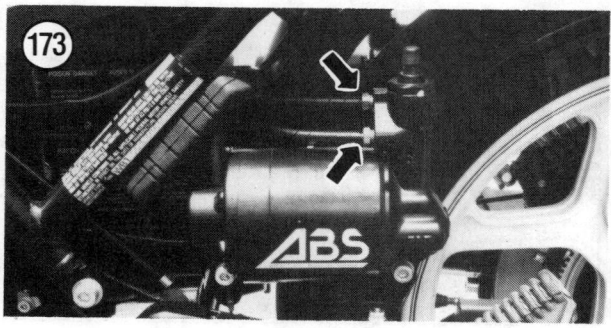

11. Install the front fairing as described in Chapter Thirteen.

Rear Brake Hose
Removal/Installation

Refer to **Figure 174** for this procedure.

NOTE
Since the ABS brake system must be bled with a power bleeder you may want to have the brake hoses replaced by a BMW dealer. If you choose to replace the brake hoses yourself, you will then have to trailer the bike to a BMW dealer to have the system bled after the hoses and lines are replaced.

NOTE
To prevent the entry of moisture and dirt, cap the ends of the brake hoses and lines that are not going to be replaced. Place the loose end in a resealable plastic bag and zip it closed around the hose or line.

1. Drain the hydraulic brake fluid from the rear brake system as follows:

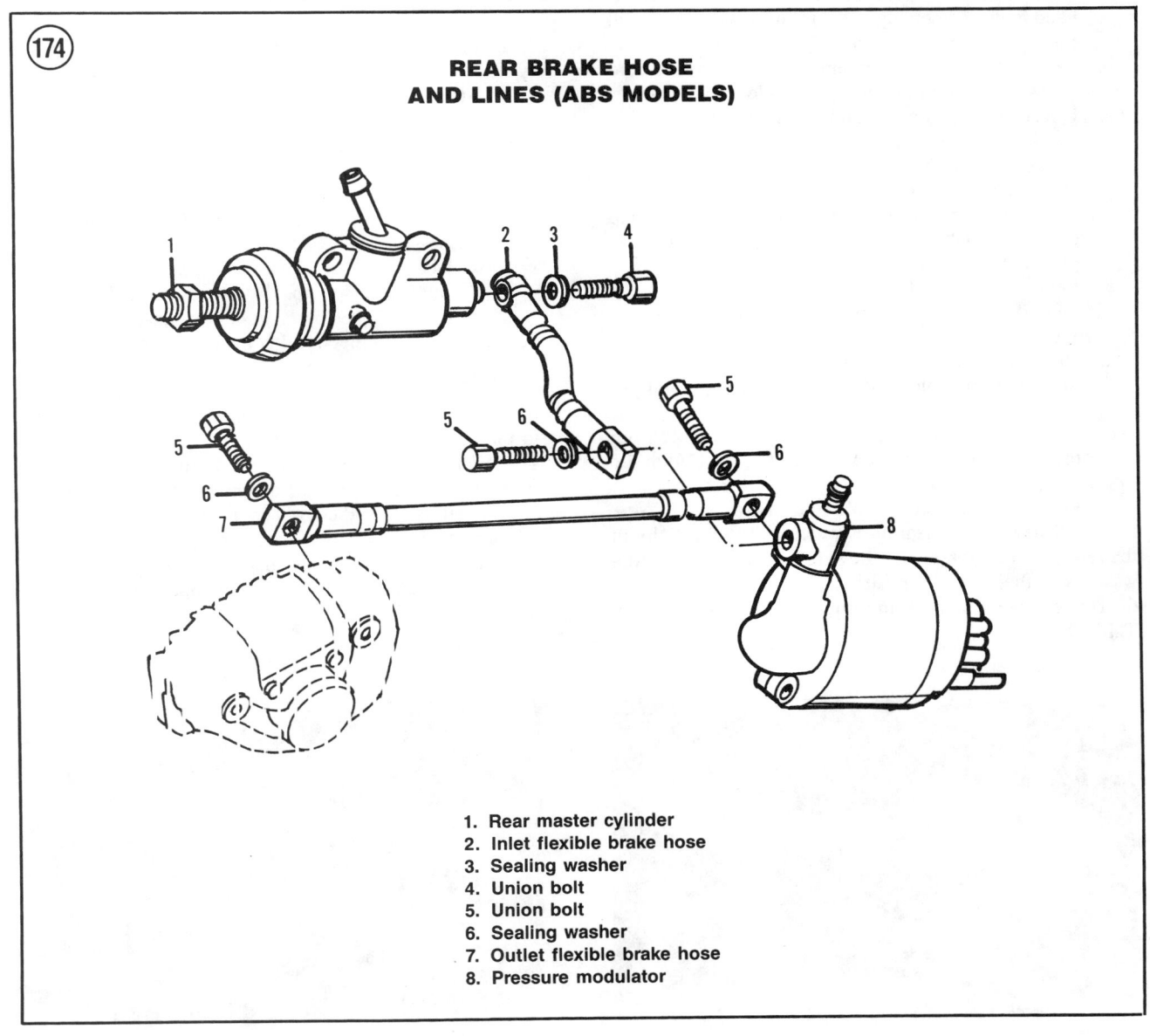

174

REAR BRAKE HOSE
AND LINES (ABS MODELS)

1. Rear master cylinder
2. Inlet flexible brake hose
3. Sealing washer
4. Union bolt
5. Union bolt
6. Sealing washer
7. Outlet flexible brake hose
8. Pressure modulator

12

a. Attach a hose to the bleed valve (**Figure 175**) on the rear caliper assembly.

b. Place the loose end of the hose in a container to catch the brake fluid.

c. Open the bleed valve and continue to apply the rear brake pedal until the brake fluid is pumped out of the system.

d. Disconnect the hose and tighten the bleed valve.

e. Dispose of this brake fluid—*never* reuse brake fluid. Contaminated brake fluid may cause brake failure.

2. On models so equipped, remove the bolts (**Figure 147**) securing the saddlebag rack to the right-hand footpeg assembly.

3. To remove the inlet flexible brake hose, perform the following:

a. Remove the bolts (A, **Figure 176**) securing the right-hand footpeg assembly to the frame and carefully pull the top portion of the assembly away from the frame.

b. Secure the rear of the assembly with a Bungee cord to take the strain off of the flexible brake hoses.

c. Unscrew the union bolt and sealing washer securing the inlet flexible brake hose to the rear of the master cylinder. Insert a golf tee into the end of the master cylinder to prevent the entry of foreign matter.

d. Unscrew the union bolt and sealing washer securing the inlet flexible brake hose (B, **Figure 176**) to the pressure modulator.

e. Remove the inlet flexible brake hose.

4. To remove the outlet flexible brake hose, perform the following:

a. Unscrew the union bolt and sealing washer securing the outlet flexible brake hose to the rear caliper assembly.

b. Unscrew the union bolt and sealing washer securing the outlet flexible brake hose (C, **Figure 176**) to the pressure modulator.

c. Remove the outlet flexible brake hose.

5. Install new hoses, sealing washers and union bolts in the reverse order of removal. Be sure to install new sealing washers in their correct position.

6. Tighten the union bolts to torque specification listed in **Table 2**.

7. Refill the master cylinder with fresh brake fluid clearly marked DOT 4. Have the rear brake system bled by a BMW dealer.

> *WARNING*
> *Do not ride the motorcycle until you are sure that the brakes are operating properly.*

PRESSURE MODULATOR AND MOUNTING BRACKET

Refer to **Figure 177** for this procedure.

Front Pressure Modulator Removal/Installation

1. Drain the hydraulic brake fluid from the front brake system as follows:

a. Attach a hose to the bleed valve on each caliper assembly.

b. Place the loose end of the hose in a container to catch the brake fluid.

c. Open the bleed valve on each caliper and apply the front brake lever until the brake fluid is pumped out of the system.

d. Disconnect the hoses and tighten the bleed valves.

e. Dispose of this brake fluid—*never* reuse brake fluid. Contaminated brake fluid may cause brake failure.

2. Disconnect the electrical connector from the backside of the pressure modulator.

3. Using a brake flare nut wrench, loosen, then unscrew the flare nuts securing both the inlet and outlet brake lines to the pressure modulator (A, **Figure 178**).

4. Remove the bolts and washers (B, **Figure 178**) securing the pressure modulator to the mounting bracket. The ground strap is attached to the front mounting bolt.

5. Remove the pressure modulator from the frame. Hold the unit in the upright position so the remaining brake fluid will not drain out of the brake line openings in the unit.

6. Install by reversing these removal steps, noting the following.

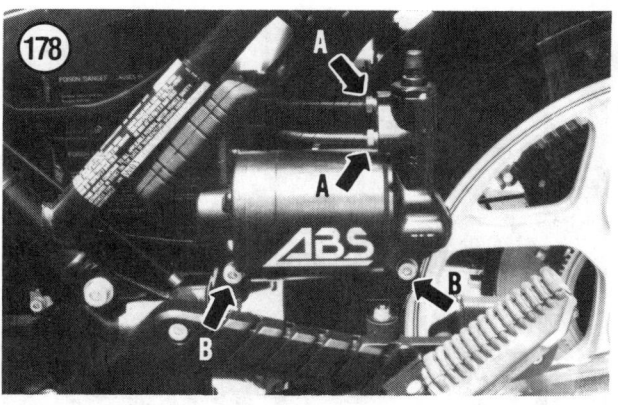

7. Install the pressure modulator onto the mounting bracket. Be sure to install the ground strap to the front mounting bolt. Tighten the bolts securely.

8. Install the lines and tighten the flare nut fittings to torque specifications listed in **Table 2**.

9. Refill the master cylinder with fresh brake fluid clearly marked DOT 4. Have the front brake system bled by a BMW dealer.

WARNING
Do not ride the motorcycle until you are sure that the brakes are operating properly.

10. Make sure the electrical connector is tight and free of corrosion.

PRESSURE MODULATOR AND MOUNTING BRACKET

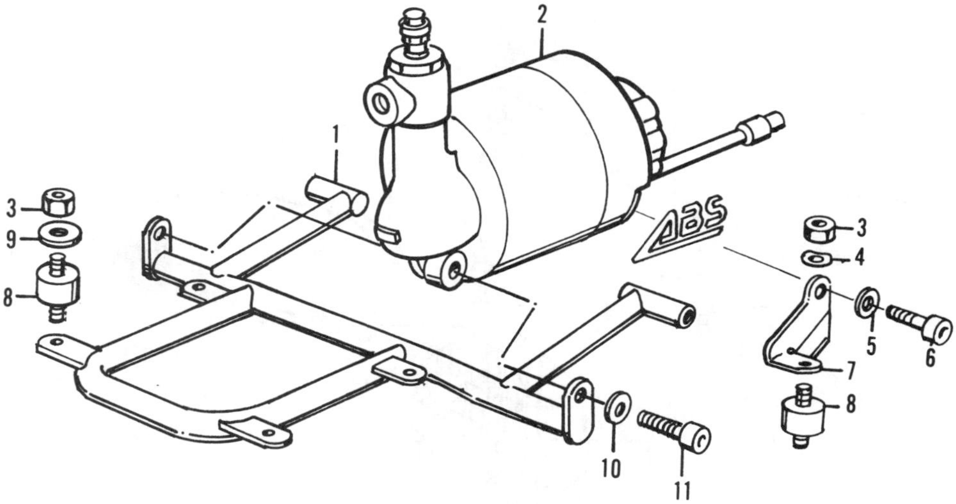

1. Mounting bracket
2. Pressure modulator
3. Nut
4. Lockwasher
5. Washer
6. Bolt
7. Bracket
8. Rubber mount
9. Washer
10. Washer
11. Bolt

12

Rear Pressure Modulator
Removal/Installation

1. Drain the hydraulic brake fluid from the rear brake system as follows:
   a. Attach a hose to the bleed valve (**Figure 175**) on the caliper assembly.
   b. Place the loose end of the hose in a container to catch the brake fluid.
   c. Open the bleed valve on each caliper and apply the rear brake pedal until the brake fluid is pumped out of the system.
   d. Disconnect the hose and tighten the bleed valve.
   e. Dispose of this brake fluid—*never* reuse brake fluid. Contaminated brake fluid may cause brake failure.

FRONT TRIGGER SENSOR

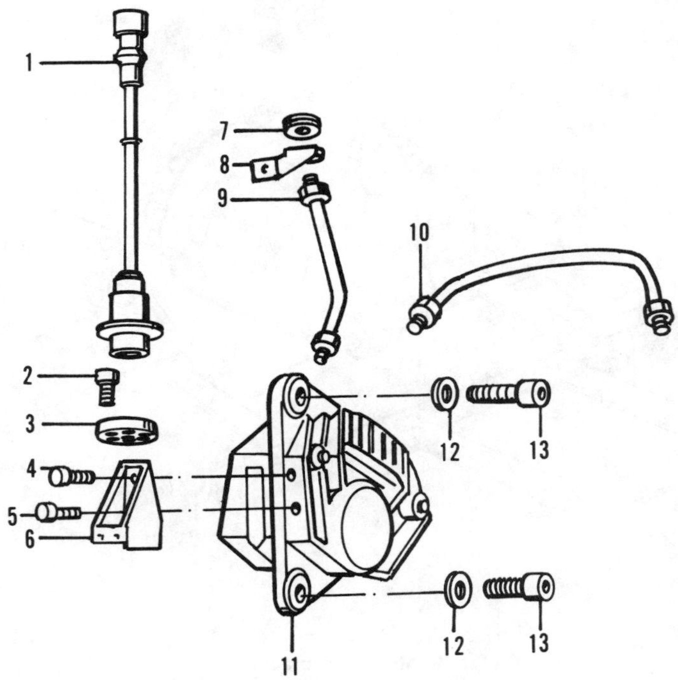

1. Trigger sensor assembly
2. Bolt
3. Shim
4. Bolt
5. Bolt
6. Bracket
7. Rubber grommet
8. Bracket
9. Lower metal brake line
10. Crossover pipe
11. Front caliper assembly
12. Washer
13. Bolt

2. Disconnect the electrical connector from the backside of the pressure modulator.

3. Using a brake flare nut wrench, loosen, then unscrew the flare nuts securing both the inlet (A, **Figure 179**) and outlet (B, **Figure 179**) brake lines to the pressure modulator.

4. Remove the bolts and washers (C, **Figure 179**) securing the pressure modulator to the mounting bracket. The ground strap is attached to the front mounting bolt.

5. Remove the pressure modulator from the frame. Hold the unit in the upright position so the remaining brake fluid will not drain out of the brake line openings in the unit.

6. Install by reversing these removal steps, noting the following.

7. Install the pressure modulator onto the mounting bracket. Be sure to install the ground strap to the front mounting bolt. Tighten the bolts securely.

8. Install the lines and tighten the flare nut fittings to torque specifications listed in **Table 2**.

9. Refill the master cylinder with fresh brake fluid clearly marked DOT 4. Have the front brake system bled by a BMW dealer.

WARNING
Do not ride the motorcycle until you are sure that the brakes are operating properly.

10. Make sure the electrical connector is free of corrosion and is tight.

Pressure Modulator
Mounting Bracket
Removal/Installation

1. Remove the rear wheel as described under *Rear Wheel Removal/Installation* in Chapter Eleven.

2. Remove the front and rear pressure modulators as described in this chapter.

3. Remove the nuts and washers securing the mounting bracket to the frame. Pull the mounting bracket toward the rear and remove it from the frame.

4. Install by reversing these removal steps, noting the following.

5. Make sure the rubber cushion mounts are in place before installing the mounting bracket.

6. Tighten the nuts securely.

TRIGGER SENSOR

Front and Rear
Removal/Installation

Refer to **Figure 180** for the front brake or **Figure 181** for the rear brake.

1. Disconnect the electrical connector going to the wiring harness.

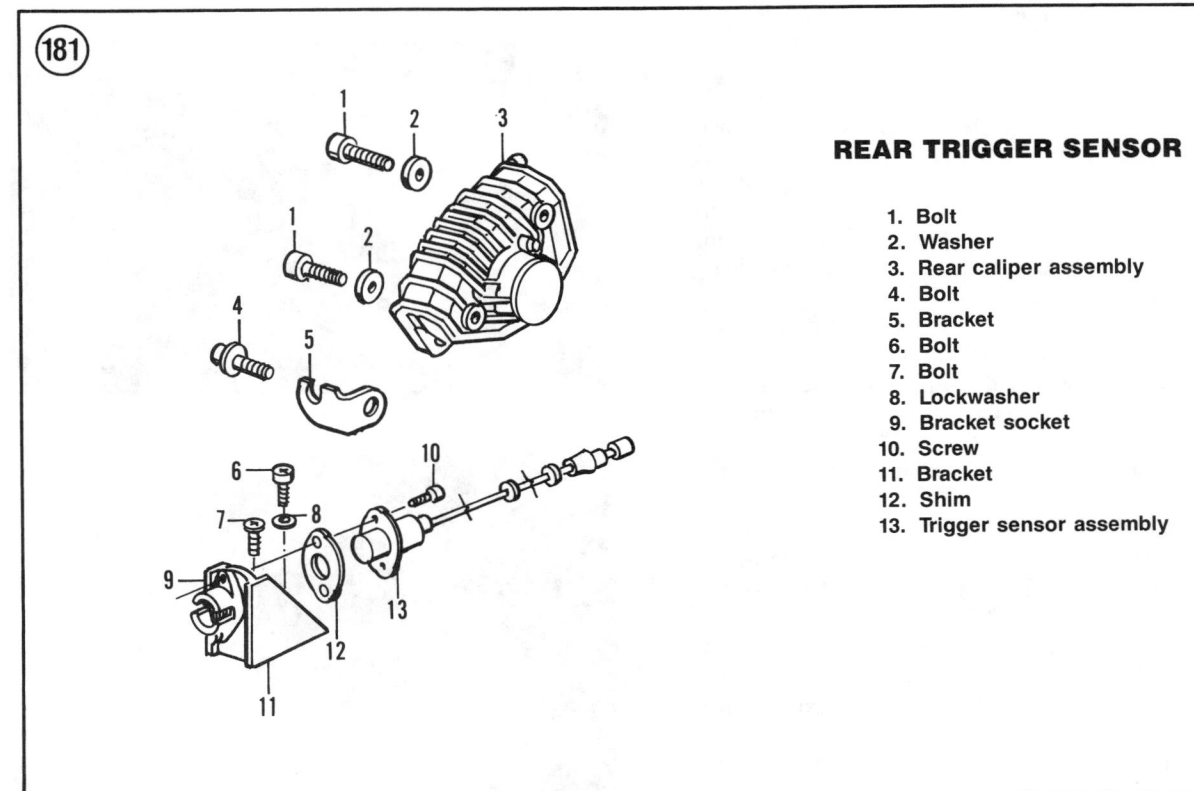

(181)

REAR TRIGGER SENSOR

1. Bolt
2. Washer
3. Rear caliper assembly
4. Bolt
5. Bracket
6. Bolt
7. Bolt
8. Lockwasher
9. Bracket socket
10. Screw
11. Bracket
12. Shim
13. Trigger sensor assembly

12

2. Remove the screws securing the trigger sensor to the mounting bracket. Refer to **Figure 182** for the front wheel or **Figure 183** for the rear wheel.

3. Remove the trigger sensor and shim from the mounting bracket or brake caliper.

4. Install by reversing these removal steps, noting the following.

5. Be sure to reinstall the shim between the trigger sensor and the mounting bracket.

6. Tighten the screws securely.

> *WARNING*
> *If the distance between the trigger sensor and pulse generating wheel is not maintained correctly, the ABS system will not function properly.*

7. Inspect the trigger sensor-to-pulse generating wheel clearance as described in this chapter.

Trigger Sensor-to-Pulse Generating Wheel Clearance Measurement and Adjustment

Front trigger sensor

> *WARNING*
> *If the distance between the trigger sensor and pulse generating wheel is not maintained correctly, the ABS system will not function properly.*

1. After the front wheel is installed, inspect the distance between the trigger sensor and the pulse generating wheel with a flat feeler gauge (**Figure 184**). The correct distance is 0.50-0.55 mm (0.020-0.022 in.) for model years to 1996. For 1997 models, the distance is 0.45-0.55 mm (0.018-0.022 in.). Rotate the wheel and check the clearance at 6 different places around the pulse generating wheel (60° apart). The maximum allowable difference between any of the 6 points is 0.2 mm (0.008 in.).

2. If the distance is greater than specified, the shim between the trigger sensor and the caliper assembly must be changed.

3. There are 4 shims of various thickness available as follows:
   a. 0.1 mm (0.004 in.): BMW part No. 34 51 1 458 406.
   b. 0.2 mm (0.008 in.): BMW part No. 34 51 1 458 407.
   c. 0.3 mm (0.012 in.): BMW part No. 34 51 1 458 408.
   d. 0.5 mm (0.020 in.): BMW part No. 34 51 1 458 409.

4. Remove the screws securing the trigger sensor assembly and remove the trigger contact assembly. The trigger sensor assembly is attached to the front right-hand caliper assembly (**Figure 182**).

5. Remove the existing shim and replace with one of the appropriate thickness to achieve the correct clearance.

6. Install the trigger sensor assembly and screw. Tighten the screws securely.

7. Repeat Step 1 and recheck the clearance. Repeat this procedure if the clearance is still not within specification.

Rear trigger sensor

The rear trigger sensor assembly is attached to the final drive unit. The rear wheel is attached to the final drive unit in such a way that very little dimensional change will occur during rear wheel removal and installation.

> *WARNING*
> *If the distance between the trigger sensor and pulse generating wheel is not maintained correctly, the ABS system will not function properly.*

The only time that the distance must be checked is when the trigger sensor assembly is removed from the final drive unit and reinstalled.

1. After the rear trigger sensor has been reinstalled, inspect the distance between the trigger sensor and the pulse generating wheel with a flat feeler gauge (**Figure 184**). The correct distance is 0.60-0.65 mm (0.024-0.026 in.) for model years to 1996. For 1997 models, the distance is 0.45-0.55 mm (0.018-0.022 in.). Rotate the rear wheel and check the clearance at 6 different places around the pulse generating wheel (60° apart). The maximum allowable difference between any of the 6 points is 0.2 mm (0.008 in.).

2. If the distance is greater than specified, the shim between the trigger sensor and the final drive unit must be changed.

3. There are 4 shims of various thickness available as follows:

    a. 0.1 mm (0.004 in.): BMW part No. 34 51 1 458 406.

    b. 0.2 mm (0.008 in.): BMW part No. 34 51 1 458 407.

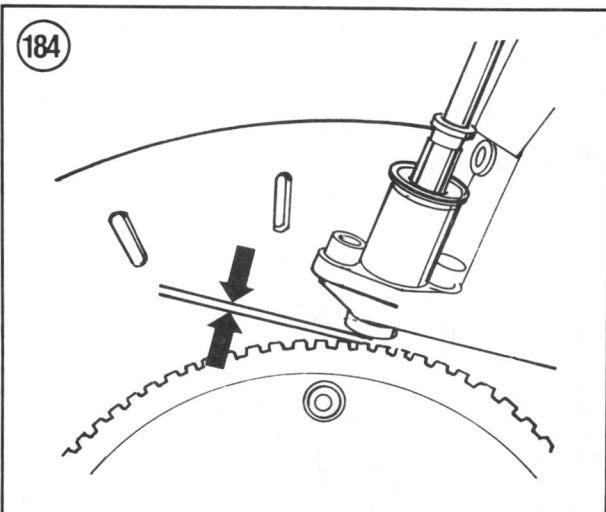

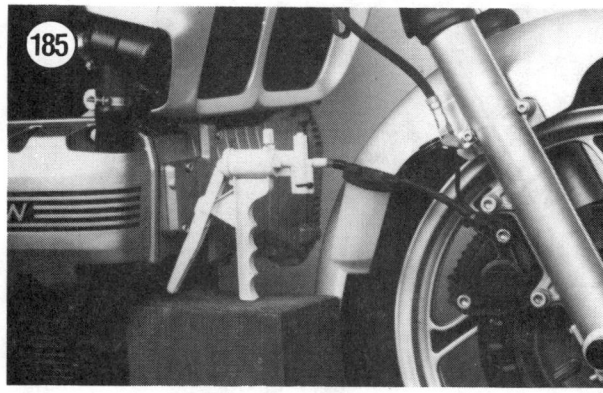

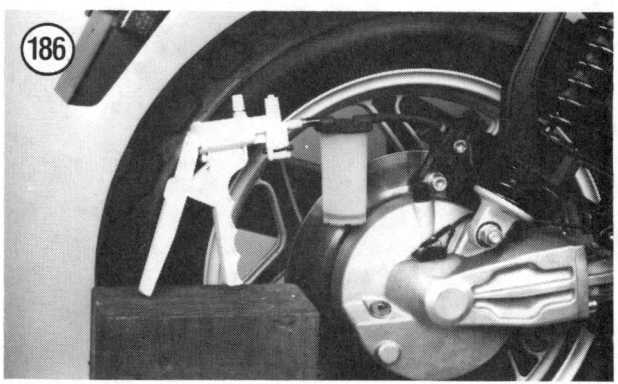

    c. 0.3 mm (0.012 in.): BMW part No. 34 51 1 458 408.

    d. 0.5 mm (0.020 in.): BMW part No. 34 51 1 458 409.

4. Remove the screws securing the trigger sensor assembly and remove the trigger contact assembly. The trigger sensor assembly is attached to the final drive unit (**Figure 183**).

5. Remove the existing shim and replace with one of the appropriate thickness to achieve the correct clearance.

6. Install the trigger sensor assembly and screws. Tighten the screws securely.

7. Repeat Step 1 and recheck the clearance. Repeat this procedure if the clearance is still not within specification.

BLEEDING THE SYSTEM

This procedure is not necessary unless the brakes feel spongy, there has been a leak in the system, a component has been replaced or the brake fluid has been replaced.

When bleeding the front brakes, bleed one caliper at a time. It doesn't make any difference which one is done first.

NOTE
*Bikes equipped with the ABS system **must** have the system bled by a BMW dealer using a power brake bleeder unit. This is necessary due to the number of pipes and hoses and the volume of brake fluid used with this system. It is impossible to remove all air bubbles from this system with hand bleeding, even using the hand-operated brake bleeder shown in this procedure for non-ABS models.*

Brake Bleeder Process
(Non-ABS System)

This procedure uses a brake bleeder that is available from motorcycle or automotive supply stores or from mail order outlets.

1. Remove the dust cap from the bleed valve on the caliper assembly.

2. Connect the brake bleeder to the bleed valve on the caliper assembly. Refer to **Figure 185** for the front caliper or **Figure 186** for the rear caliper.

CAUTION
Cover the front and rear wheels with a heavy cloth or plastic tarp to protect it from the accidental spilling of brake fluid. Wash any brake fluid off of any plastic, painted or plated surface immediately as it will destroy the finish. Use soapy water and rinse completely.

3. Clean the top of the master cylinder of all dirt and foreign matter.

12

4A. For the front caliper, remove the screws securing the master cylinder top cover (**Figure 187**) and remove the reservoir top cover, spacer and rubber diaphragm.
4B. For the rear caliper, unscrew the master cylinder cover (**Figure 188**) and remove the cover and diaphragm.
5. Fill the reservoir almost to the top lip. Insert the diaphragm and the cover loosely. Leave the cover in place during this procedure to prevent the entry of dirt.

WARNING
Use brake fluid from a sealed container marked DOT 4 only (specified for disc brakes). Other types may vaporize and cause brake failure. Do not intermix different brands or types as they may not be compatible. Do not intermix a silicone based (DOT 5) brake fluid as it can cause brake component damage leading to brake system failure.

6. Open the bleed valve about one-half turn and pump the brake bleeder.

NOTE
If air is entering the brake bleeder hose from around the bleed valve, apply several layers of Teflon tape to the bleed valve. This should make a good seal between the bleed valve and the brake bleeder hose.

7. As the fluid enters the system and exits into the brake bleeder, the level will drop in the reservoir. Maintain the level to just about the top of the reservoir to prevent air from being drawn into the system.
8. Continue to pump the lever on the brake bleeder until the fluid emerging from the hose is completely free of bubbles.
9. Tap on the brake hoses to help free any bubbles stuck to the walls of the hoses.

NOTE
Do not allow the reservoir to empty during the bleeding operation or more air will enter the system. If this occurs, the entire procedure must be repeated.

10. When the brake fluid is free of bubbles, tighten the bleed valve, remove the brake bleeder tube and install the bleed valve dust cap.
11. If necessary, add fluid to correct the level in the reservoir. It should be to the upper level line.
12A. For the front caliper, install the rubber diaphragm, spacer and top cover (**Figure 187**) and tighten the screws securely.

12B. For the rear caliper, install the diaphragm and screw on the master cylinder cover (**Figure 188**) securely.
13. Repeat Steps 1-12A for the other front caliper assembly.
14. Test the feel of the brake lever or pedal. It should be firm and should offer the same resistance each time it's operated. If it feels spongy, it is likely that there is still air in the system and it must be bled again. When all air has been bled from the system and the fluid level is correct in the reservoir, double-check for leaks and tighten all fittings and connections.

WARNING
Before riding the bike, make certain that the brake is operating correctly by operating the lever several times.

15. Test ride the bike slowly at first to make sure that the brakes are operating properly.

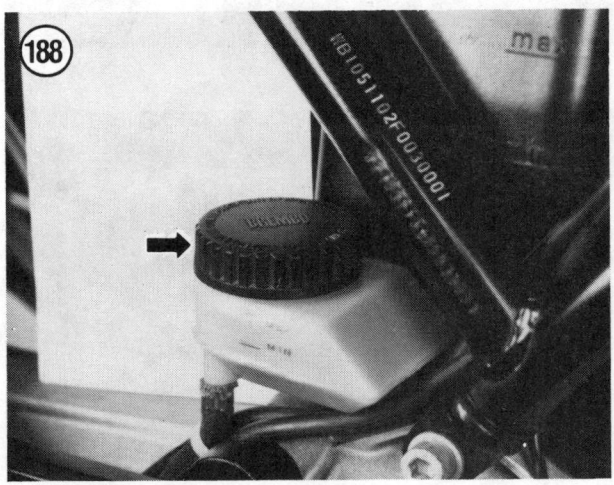

Without a Brake Bleeder
(Non-ABS System)

1. Remove the dust cap from the bleed valve on the caliper assembly(ies).

2. Connect a piece of clear tubing to the bleed valve on the caliper assembly. Refer to **Figure 189** for the front caliper or **Figure 190** for the rear caliper.

CAUTION
Cover the front and rear wheels with a heavy cloth or plastic tarp to protect them from the accidental spilling of brake fluid. Wash any brake fluid off of any plastic, painted or plated surface immediately as it will destroy the finish. Use soapy water and rinse completely.

3. Clean the top of the master cylinder of all dirt and foreign matter.

4A. For the front caliper, remove the screws securing the master cylinder top cover (**Figure 187**) and remove the reservoir top cover, spacer and rubber diaphragm.

4B. For the rear caliper, unscrew the master cylinder cover (**Figure 188**) and remove the cover and diaphragm.

5. Place the other end of the tube into a clean container. Fill the container with enough fresh brake fluid to keep the end submerged. The tube should be long enough so that a loop can be made higher than the bleed valve to prevent air from being drawn into the caliper during bleeding.

CAUTION
Cover the front fender and front wheel with a heavy cloth or plastic tarp to protect it from the accidental spilling of brake fluid. Wash any brake fluid off of any plastic, painted or plated surface immediately as it will destroy the finish. Use soapy water and rinse completely.

6. Fill the reservoir almost to the cover lip. Insert the diaphragm and the cover loosely. Leave the cover in place during this procedure to prevent the entry of dirt.

WARNING
Use brake fluid from a sealed container marked DOT 4 only (specified for disc brakes). Other types may vaporize and cause brake failure. Do not intermix different brands or types as they may not be compatible. Do not intermix a silicone based (DOT 5) brake fluid as it can cause brake component damage leading to brake system failure.

NOTE
During this procedure, all the hose junctions in the brake system will be bled of air. It is very important to check the fluid level in the brake master cylinder reservoir often. If the reservoir runs dry, you'll introduce more air into the system which will require starting over.

7. If the master cylinder was drained, it must be bled first. Remove the union bolt and hose from the master cylinder. Slowly apply the brake lever, or brake pedal, several times while holding your thumb over the opening in the master cylinder and perform the following:

   a. With the lever or pedal held depressed, slightly release your thumb pressure. Some of the brake fluid and air bubbles will escape.

   b. Apply thumb pressure and pump lever or pedal once more.

   c. Repeat this procedure until you can feel resistance at the lever or pedal.

12

8. Refill the master cylinder and quickly reinstall the hose, sealing washers and the union bolt.

9. Tighten the union bolt and pump the lever or pedal again and perform the following:

    a. Loosen the union bolt 1/4 turn. Some brake fluid and air bubbles will escape.

    b. Tighten the union bolt and repeat this procedure until no air bubbles escape.

10. If working on the front brakes, each union bolt or brake line fitting, all the way down to the caliper assembly, must be bled using the same procedure detailed in Step 7.

    a. Bleed the union bolt and fittings in this order: first the end of the upper flexible hose at the brake pipe; second, the fitting at the top of the middle flexible brake hose; third, the fitting at the lower metal brake line.

    b. Refill the master cylinder.

11. Tighten all brake line fittings and union bolts to the torque specification listed in **Table 2**.

12. Slowly apply the brake lever, or brake pedal, several times as follows:

    a. Pull the lever in or depress the pedal. Hold the lever in the applied position or the pedal in the depressed position.

    b. Open the bleed valve about one-half turn. Allow the lever or pedal to travel to its limit.

    c. When this limit is reached, tighten the bleed valve.

13. As the fluid enters the system, the level will drop in the reservoir. Maintain the level to just about the top of the reservoir to prevent air from being drawn into the system.

14. Continue to pump the lever and fill the reservoir until the fluid emerging from the hose is completely free of bubbles.

NOTE
Do not allow the reservoir to empty during the bleeding operation or more air will enter the system. If this occurs, the entire procedure must be repeated.

15. Hold the lever in, tighten the bleed valve, remove the bleed tube and install the bleed valve dust cap.

16. If necessary, add fluid to correct the level in the reservoir.

17. Repeat Steps 1-16 for the other front caliper assembly.

18A. For the front master cylinder, install the rubber diaphragm, spacer and top cover (**Figure 187**) and tighten the screws securely.

18B. For the rear master cylinder, install the diaphragm and screw on the master cylinder cover (**Figure 188**) securely.

19. Test the feel of the brake lever. It should be firm and should offer the same resistance each time it's operated. If it feels spongy, it is likely that there is still air in the system and it must be bled again. When all air has been bled from the system and the fluid level is correct in the reservoir, double-check for leaks and tighten all fittings and connections.

WARNING
Before riding the bike, make certain that the brakes are operating correctly by operating the lever or pedal several times.

20. Test ride the bike slowly at first to make sure that the brakes are operating properly.

REAR DRUM BRAKE
(K75C MODELS)

BMW has determined that under certain slow braking conditions the brake shoe spring will vibrate, emitting an annoying noise. A rubber damper (**Figure 191**) was added to the lower return spring and this solved some of the noise problems.

In some cases this rubber damper will not completely solve the noise problem. The next thing to do is to change to updated brake shoes. The part numbers are as follows:

   a. Upper brake shoe: BMW part No. 34 21 1 242 401.

   b. Lower brake shoe: BMW part No. 34 21 1 242 402.

These brake shoes have relocated brake spring attachment points. These make the return springs exert more pressure on the shoes, thus pressing them harder against the camshaft and pivot post. This along with the rubber damper should cut down on the noise.

The new brake shoes are marked with an "86" within a double circle containing 10 dots.

If you have had this noise problem, replace the brake shoes along with the springs as they have weakened due to the abnormal vibration.

Disassembly

Refer to **Figure 192** for this procedure.

1. Remove the rear wheel as described under *Rear Wheel Removal/Installation* in Chapter Eleven.

2. Using a vernier caliper, measure the thickness of the brake linings (**Figure 193**). They should be replaced if the lining portion is worn to the service limit listed in **Table 2**.

NOTE
If the brake linings are in good condition and are going to be reinstalled, place a clean shop cloth on the linings to protect them from oil and grease during removal.

3. Remove the circlip (**Figure 194**) securing the brake shoes to the pivot pin.

4. Pull up on the center of each brake shoe and remove the brake shoes from the backside of the final drive unit.

5. Remove the return springs (**Figure 195**) and separate the brake shoes.

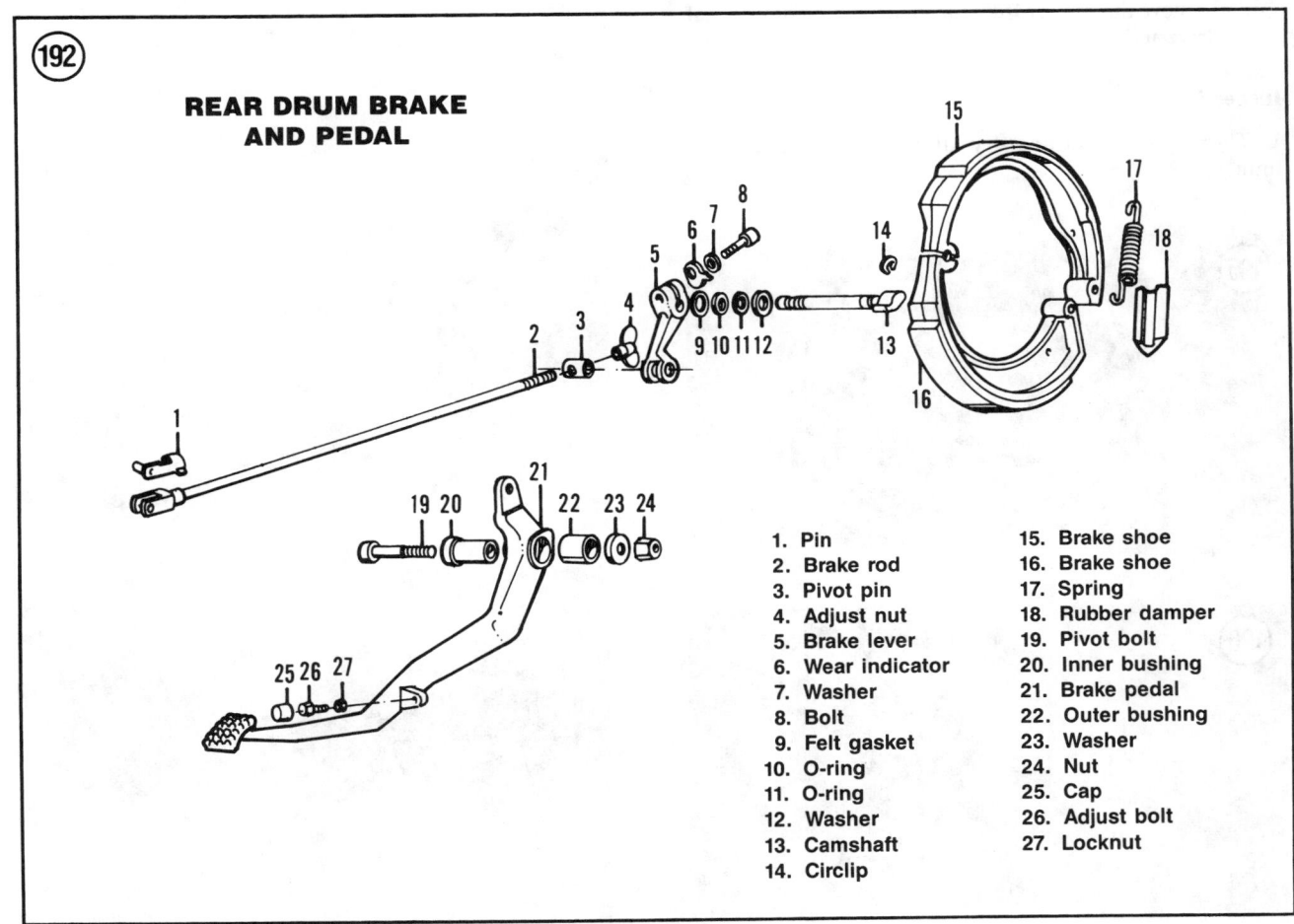

REAR DRUM BRAKE AND PEDAL

1. Pin	15. Brake shoe
2. Brake rod	16. Brake shoe
3. Pivot pin	17. Spring
4. Adjust nut	18. Rubber damper
5. Brake lever	19. Pivot bolt
6. Wear indicator	20. Inner bushing
7. Washer	21. Brake pedal
8. Bolt	22. Outer bushing
9. Felt gasket	23. Washer
10. O-ring	24. Nut
11. O-ring	25. Cap
12. Washer	26. Adjust bolt
13. Camshaft	27. Locknut
14. Circlip	

12

6. To remove the brake camshaft, perform the following:
   a. Completely unscrew the adjust nut (**Figure 196**) from the end of the brake rod.
   b. Depress the brake pedal and withdraw the brake rod from the brake lever.
   c. Remove the pivot pin (**Figure 197**) from the brake lever.
   d. Install the pivot pin and adjust nut (**Figure 198**) onto the brake rod to avoid misplacing them.

NOTE
*Use a centerpunch and hammer and make a small mark on the end of the camshaft next to the gap in the brake lever (**Figure 199**). This will ensure the correct alignment of these 2 parts during assembly.*

   e. Remove the bolt, washer and wear indicator (**Figure 200**) from the brake lever.
   f. Slide the brake lever off of the camshaft.
   g. Withdraw the camshaft and O-rings from the final drive unit.
   h. Remove the felt gasket from the outer surface of the final drive unit.
   i. Remove the washer from the inner surface of the final drive unit.

Inspection

1. Thoroughly clean and dry all parts except the brake linings.

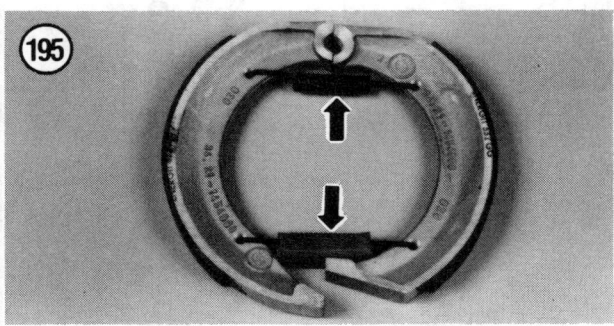

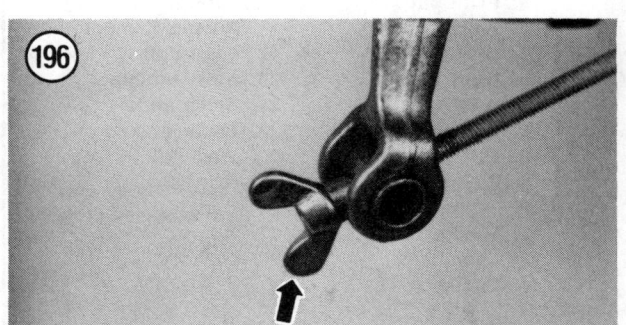

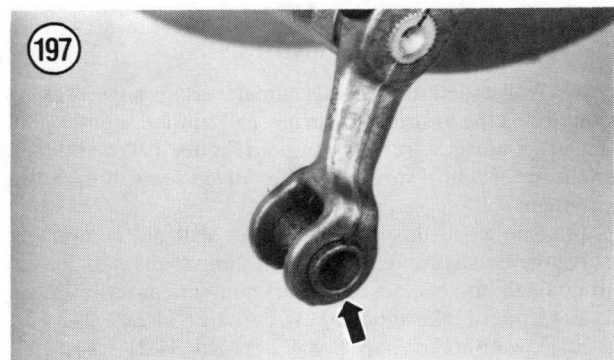

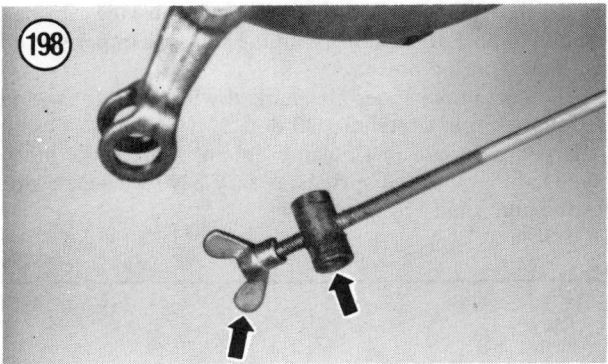

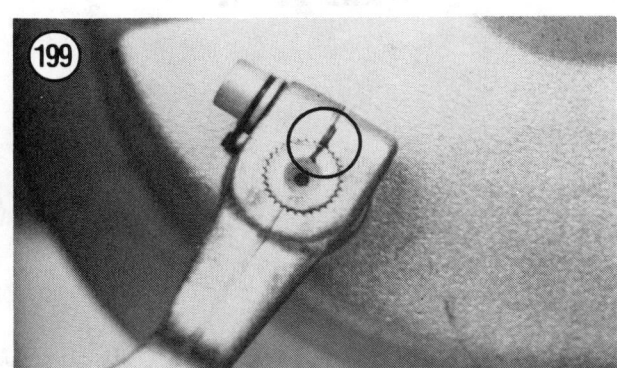

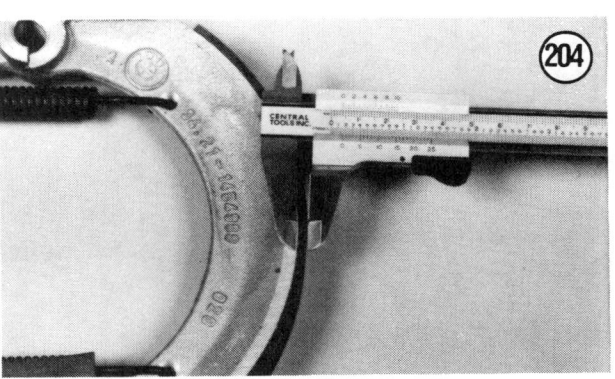

2. Check the contact surface of the brake drum (**Figure 201**) for scoring. If there are grooves deep enough to snag a fingernail the drum should be reground.

NOTE
*The maximum allowable inside diameter is cast into the brake drum as shown in **Figure 202**.*

3. Measure the inside diameter (**Figure 203**) of the brake drum with a vernier caliper. If the dimension is worn to or greater than the service limit listed in **Table 2**, the rear wheel must be replaced. The brake drum is an integral part of the wheel and cannot be replaced separately.

4. If the drum is scored or grooved, have it turned providing the finished dimension is still within the maximum service limit dimension diameter listed in **Table 2**.

5. If the drum is turned, the linings will have to be replaced and arced to conform to the new drum contour.

6. Inspect the linings for embedded foreign material. Dirt can be removed with a stiff wire brush. Check for any traces of oil or grease; if the linings are contaminated they must be replaced.

7. If not measured prior to removal, measure the thickness of the brake linings with a vernier caliper (**Figure 204**). They should be replaced if the lining portion is worn to the service limit listed in **Table 2**.

8. Inspect the camshaft lobe (A, **Figure 205**) and the pivot post (**Figure 206**) on the final drive unit for wear or corrosion. Minor roughness can be removed with fine emery cloth.

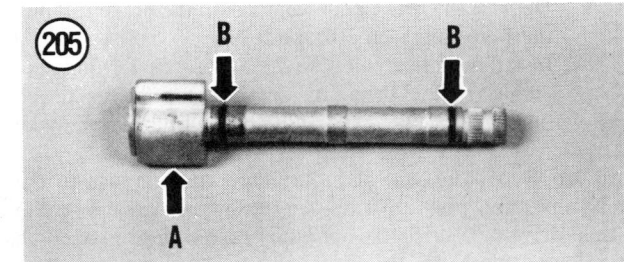

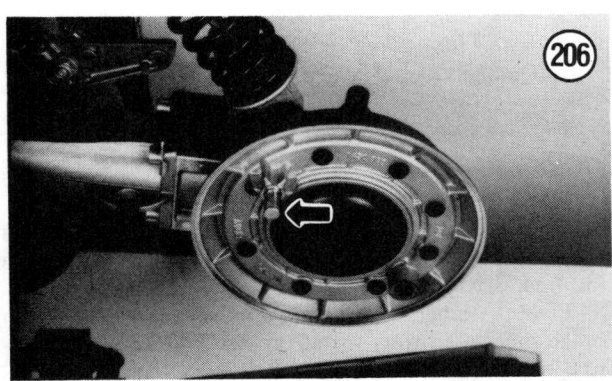

12

9. Inspect the O-ring seals (B, **Figure 205**) on the camshaft for wear or deterioration; replace if necessary.

10. Inspect the brake shoe return springs (**Figure 195**) for wear or weakness. If they are stretched, they will not fully retract the brake shoes, leading to premature wear. Replace the springs as a pair if necessary.

Assembly

1. If the brake camshaft was removed, install by performing the following:

   a. If removed, install the O-ring seals (B, **Figure 205**) onto the camshaft.

   b. Apply a light coat of molybdenum disulfide grease to the camshaft.

   c. Install the washer (**Figure 207**) onto the inside surface of the final drive unit.

   d. Position the camshaft with the index mark made during removal toward the top.

   e. Install the camshaft into the backside of the final drive unit. Push it in until it bottoms out.

   f. Install a new felt gasket (**Figure 208**) onto the outer surface of the final drive unit.

   g. Using the mark made during removal, align the brake lever with the camshaft and install the brake lever onto the camshaft (**Figure 199**).

   h. Install the bolt, washer and wear indicator (**Figure 209**) onto the brake lever. Tighten the bolt securely.

   i. Remove the adjust nut and the pivot pin from the brake rod.

   j. Install the pivot pin into the brake lever and align the hole to accept the brake rod.

   k. Depress the brake pedal and install the brake rod into the pivot pin in the brake lever.

   l. Install the adjust nut onto the brake rod. Tighten only enough to hold the adjust nut in place. If it is screwed on too far it may expand the brake linings and make rear wheel installation difficult.

2. Apply a light coat of high-temperature grease to the camshaft and pivot post; avoid getting any grease on the final drive unit surface where the brake linings may come in contact with it.

NOTE
If new linings are being installed, file off the leading edge of each shoe a little so that the brake will not grab when applied for the first few times.

3. Attach the brake shoes to the brake linings.

4. Hold the shoes in a "V" formation with the return springs attached and snap one of the shoes into place on the final drive unit.

5. Pivot the other shoe down into place. Make sure both brake shoes are firmly seated on the final drive unit (**Figure 210**).

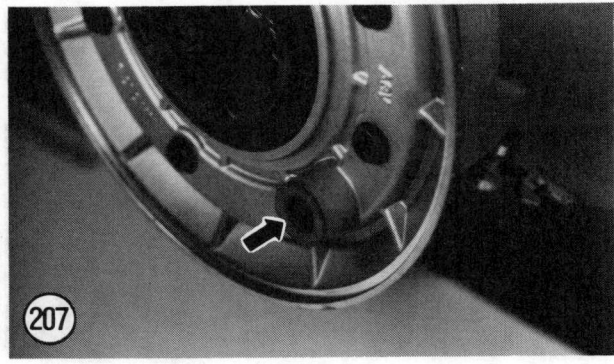

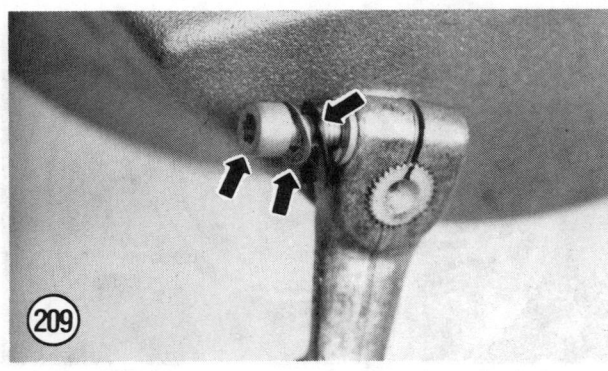

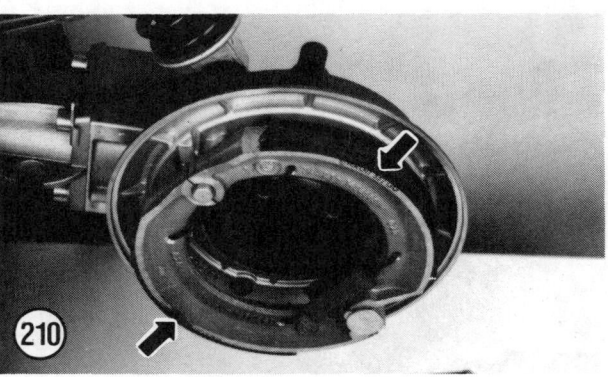

6. Make sure the rubber damper (**Figure 191**) is in place on the lower return spring.

7. Install the circlip (**Figure 194**) securing the brake shoes to the pivot pin.

8. Install the rear wheel as described under *Rear Wheel Removal/Installation* in Chapter Eleven.

9. Adjust the rear brake as described under *Rear Drum Brake Pedal Height and Freeplay Adjustment* in Chapter Three.

REAR BRAKE PEDAL

Removal/Inspection/Installation (Disc Brake Models)

Refer to **Figure 211** for this procedure.

1. Unhook the small return spring from the frame.

2. On models so equipped, remove the bolts securing the saddlebag rack to the right-hand footpeg assembly.

3. Remove the bolts (**Figure 212**) securing the right-hand footpeg assembly to the frame and carefully pull the top portion of the assembly away from the frame.

4. Secure the rear of the assembly with a Bungee cord (**Figure 213**) to take the strain off of the flexible brake hoses.

5. Hold onto the pivot bolt with an Allen wrench and remove the brake pedal pivot bolt nut and washer (A, **Figure 214**).

6. Withdraw the pivot bolt.

7. Carefully withdraw the adjust bolt from the rubber boot (B, **Figure 214**) on the master cylinder.

8. Remove the brake pedal (C, **Figure 214**) from the footpeg assembly.

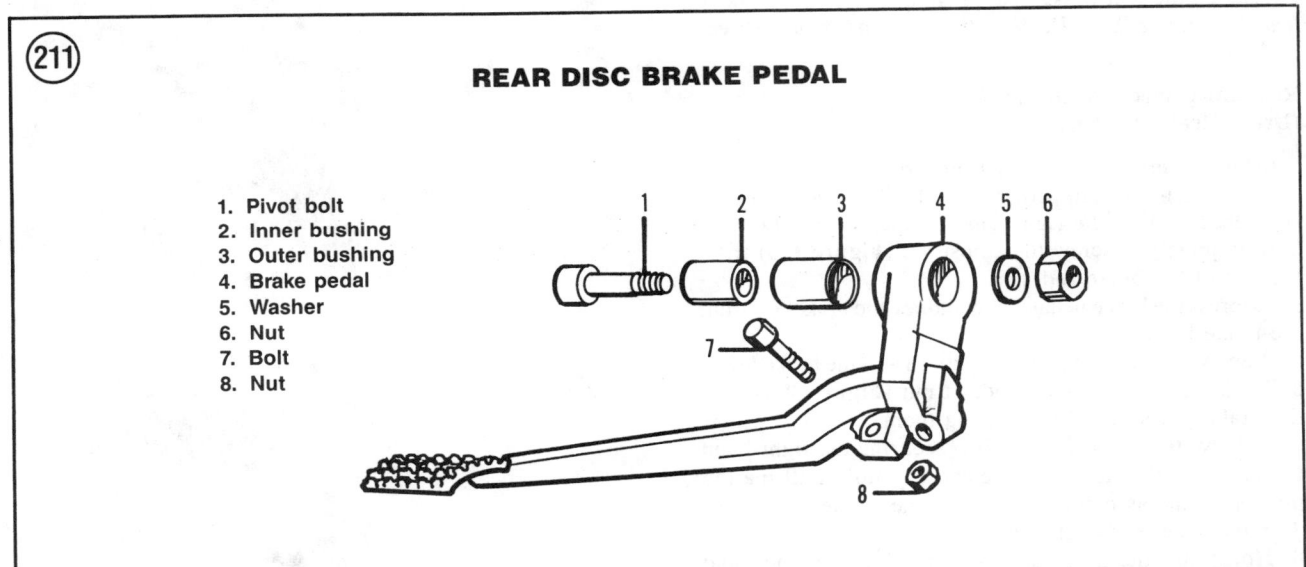

REAR DISC BRAKE PEDAL

1. Pivot bolt
2. Inner bushing
3. Outer bushing
4. Brake pedal
5. Washer
6. Nut
7. Bolt
8. Nut

12

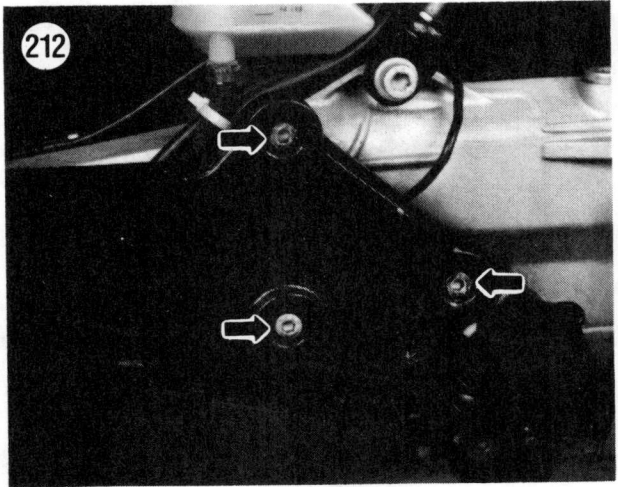

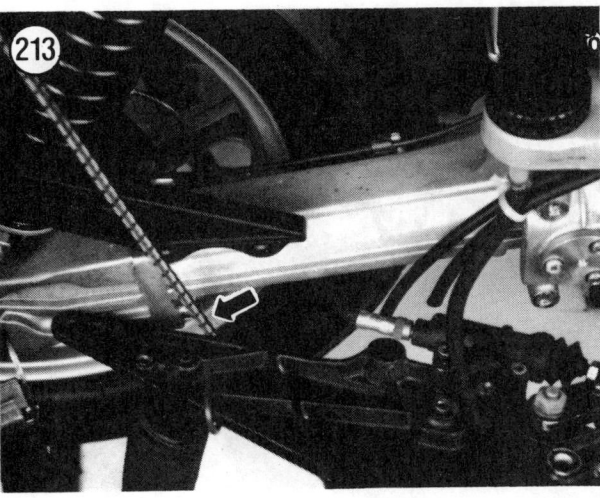

9. Remove the inner bushing (A, **Figure 215**) from the brake pedal.

10. Inspect the inner bushing (A, **Figure 215**) and outer bushing (B, **Figure 215**) for wear or damage; replace either or both if necessary.

11. Inspect the adjust bolt and locknut (A, **Figure 216**) for wear or damage. Replace if necessary.

12. Inspect the pedal height adjust bolt and locknut (**Figure 217**) for wear or damage. Replace if necessary.

13. Inspect the return spring (B, **Figure 216**) for sagging, wear or damage. Replace if necessary.

14. Install by reversing these removal steps, noting the following.

15. Apply a light coat of multi-purpose grease to all pivot areas prior to installing any components.

16. Tighten the pivot bolt and nut to the torque specification listed in **Table 2**.

17. Adjust the rear brake pedal height as described under *Rear Disc Brake Pedal Height Adjustment* in Chapter Three.

**Removal/Inspection/Installation
(Drum Brake Models)**

Refer to **Figure 192** for this procedure.

1. On models so equipped, remove the bolts securing the saddlebag rack to the right-hand footpeg assembly.

2. Completely unscrew the adjust nut (**Figure 196**) from the end of the brake rod.

3. Depress the brake pedal and withdraw the brake rod from the brake lever.

4. Remove the pivot pin (**Figure 197**) from the brake lever.

5. Install the pivot pin and adjust nut (**Figure 198**) onto the brake rod to avoid misplacing them.

6. Remove the bolts (**Figure 218**) securing the right-hand footpeg assembly to the frame and carefully pull the top portion of the assembly away from the frame.

7. Secure the rear of the assembly with a Bungee cord.

8. Hold onto the pivot bolt with an Allen wrench and remove the brake pedal pivot bolt nut and washer (A, **Figure 219**).

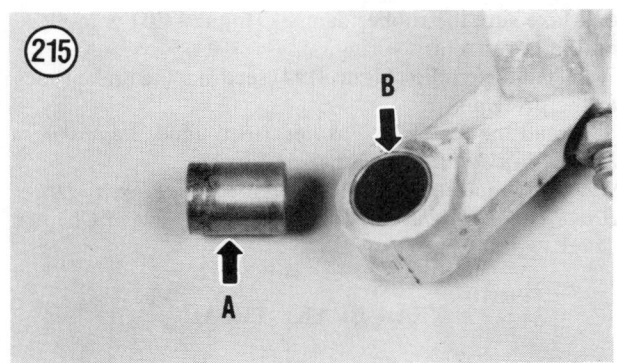

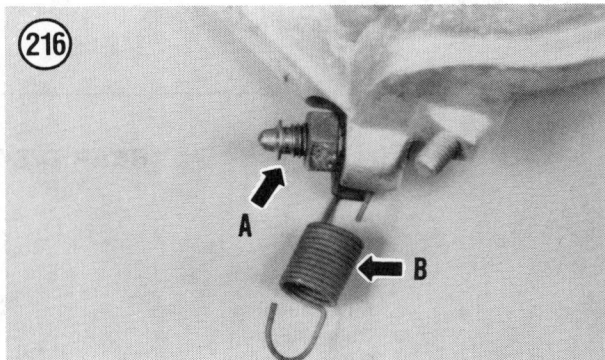

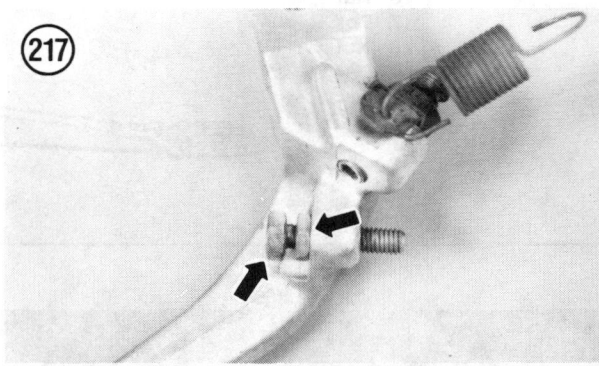

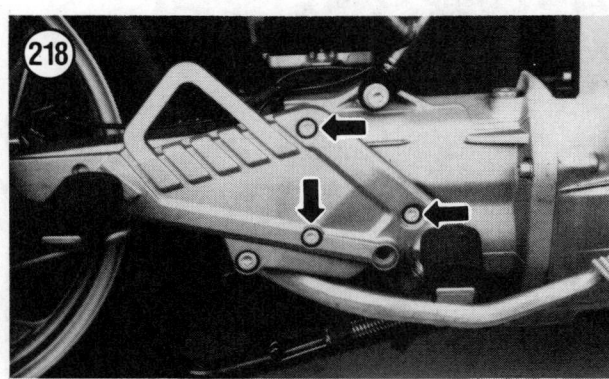

9. Withdraw the pivot bolt.

10. Remove the brake pedal (B, **Figure 219**) and brake rod assembly (C, **Figure 219**) from the footpeg assembly.

11. Remove the inner bushing from the brake pedal.

12. Inspect the inner bushing and outer bushing for wear or damage; replace either or both if necessary.

13. Install by reversing these removal steps, noting the following.

14. Apply a light coat of multi-purpose grease to all pivot areas before installing any components.

15. Tighten the pivot bolt and nut to the torque specification listed in **Table 2**.

16. Adjust the rear brake pedal height as described under *Rear Drum Brake Pedal Height and Freeplay Adjustment* in Chapter Three.

Tables are on the following page.

12

Table 1 BRAKE SPECIFICATIONS

Brake fluid	DOT 4 for disc brakes
Front brake disc	
Diameter	285 mm (11.220 in.)
Effective pad area	80 sq. cm. (12.5 sq. in.)
Thickness	
Standard	4.0-4.04 mm (0.157-0.173 in.)
Minimum	3.55 mm (0.140 in.)
Lateral runout (maximum)	0.2 mm (0.008 in.)
Brake pad minimum thickness	1.5 mm (0.059 in.)
Front caliper	
Piston O.D.	38 mm (1.496 in.)
Front master cylinder	
Piston O.D.	13 mm (0.512 in.)
Rear brake disc	
Diameter	285 mm (11.220 in.)
Effective pad area	40 sq. cm. (6.2 sq. in.)
Thickness	
Standard	4.0-4.04 mm (0.157-0.173 in.)
Minimum	3.55 mm (0.140 in.)
Lateral runout (maximum)	0.2 mm (0.008 in.)
Brake pad minimum thickness	1.5 mm (0.059 in.)
Rear caliper	
Piston O.D.	38 mm (1.496 in.)
Rear master cylinder	
Piston O.D.	13 mm (0.512 in.)
Rear drum brake	
Drum diameter	
Standard	200 mm (7.874 in.)
Maximum	201.16 mm (7.920 in.)
Effective brake area	89 sq. cm (13.8 sq. in.)
Brake lining minimum thickness	1.5 mm (0.059 in.)

Table 2 BRAKE SYSTEM TORQUE SPECIFICATIONS

Item	N·m	ft.-lb.
Brake hose union bolts	6-8	4.5-5.5
Brake caliper mounting bolts		
Front and rear	30-34	22-24
Flexible brake hose connections	6-8	4.5-5.5
Brake line flare nuts	6-8	4.5-5.5
Brake disc mounting bolts		
Front	27-31	19-23
Rear	19-23	14-16
Brake caliper bleed screw	6-8	4.5-5.5
Brake pedal pivot bolt and nut	22-28	16-20
Rear master cylinder		
mounting bolts	5-7	3.5-4.5

NOTE: If you own a 1990 or later model, first check the Supplement at the back of this book for any new service information.

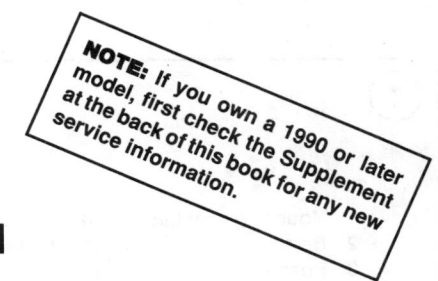

CHAPTER THIRTEEN

FRAME, BODY AND FRAME REPAINTING

This chapter includes replacement procedures for components attached to the frame that are not covered in the rest of the book. Also included are the body panels and luggage components for all models. Some of these components are optional. Torque specifications are listed in **Table 1**.

This chapter also describes procedures for completely stripping and repainting the frame.

KICKSTAND (SIDESTAND)

Removal/Installation

Refer to **Figure 1** and **Figure 2** for this procedure.
1. Place the bike on the center stand.
2. Raise the kickstand and disconnect the return spring from the pin on the frame with Vise Grips.
3. On models so equipped, remove the nut securing the kickstand retracting arm rod. Disconnect the rod from the actuating arm at the transmission housing.

NOTE

The following steps are shown with the center stand, the sidestand and the mounting bracket assembly removed from the transmission housing for clarity. It is not necessary to remove the entire assembly to remove the individual components.

4. Disconnect the return spring(s) from the studs on the kickstand (A, **Figure 3**).
5. On models so equipped, remove the return spring arm (B, **Figure 3**) and the pawl and rod assembly (C, **Figure 3**).
6. From under the frame, remove the pivot bolt (**Figure 4**) and remove the kickstand from the frame. Don't lose the pivot bolt bushing.
7. Install by reversing these removal steps, noting the following.
8. Apply a light coat of multipurpose grease to the pivot surfaces of the pivot bushing and bolt prior to installation.
9. Tighten the pivot bolt to the torque specification listed in **Table 1**.

CENTER STAND

Removal/Installation

Refer to **Figure 1** for this procedure.
1. On models so equipped, remove the engine spoiler as described in this chapter.
2. Place a wood block(s) under the engine oil pan to hold the bike securely in place.

NOTE

The following steps are shown with the center stand, the sidestand and the mounting bracket

13

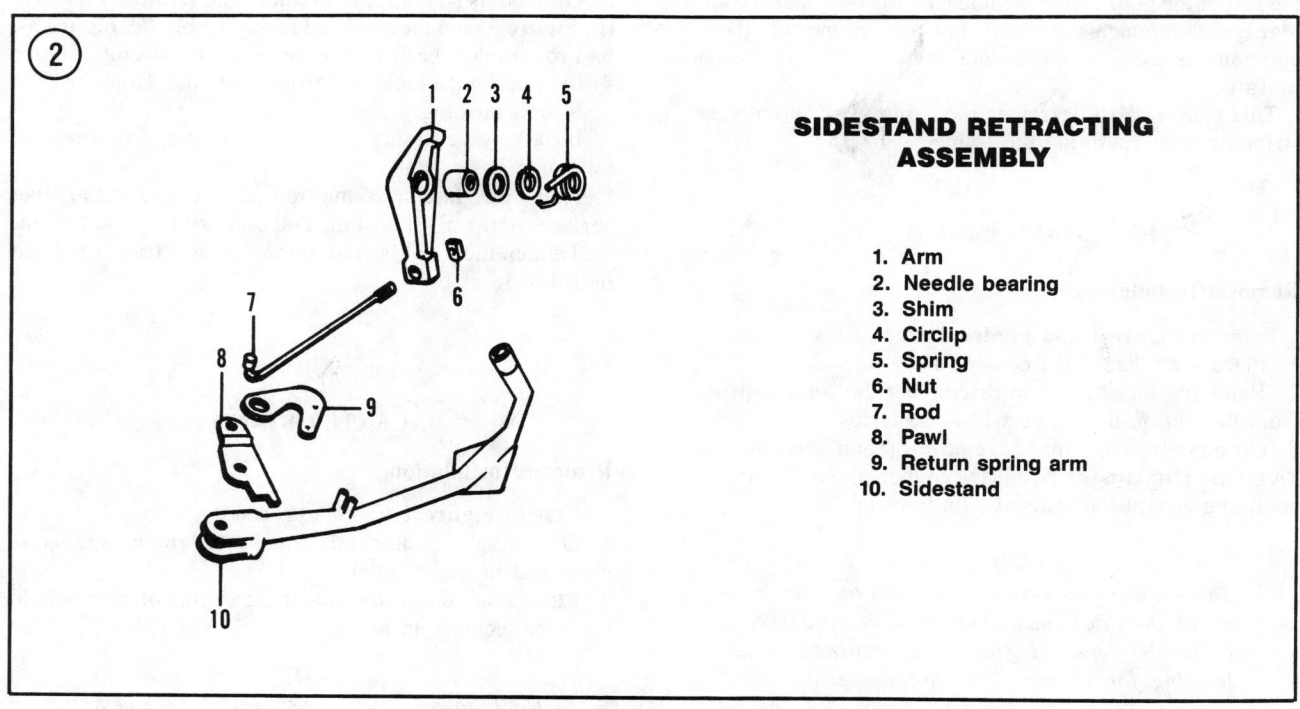

**CENTER STAND
AND SIDESTAND**

1. Mounting bracket
2. Bolt
3. Bushing
4. Sidestand
5. Return spring arm
6. Return spring
7. Tip
8. Screw
9. Rubber stop
10. Circlip
11. Bushing
12. Bolt
13. Return spring
14. Bolt
15. Rubber grommet
16. Center stand
17. Cap

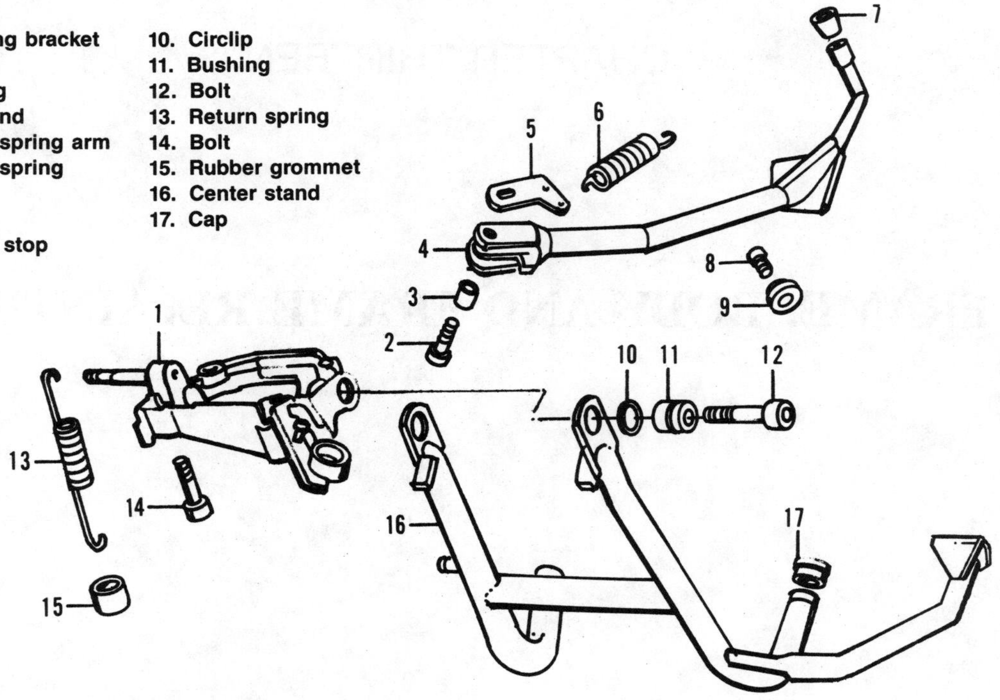

**SIDESTAND RETRACTING
ASSEMBLY**

1. Arm
2. Needle bearing
3. Shim
4. Circlip
5. Spring
6. Nut
7. Rod
8. Pawl
9. Return spring arm
10. Sidestand

assembly removed from the transmission housing for clarity. It is not necessary to remove the entire assembly to remove the individual components.

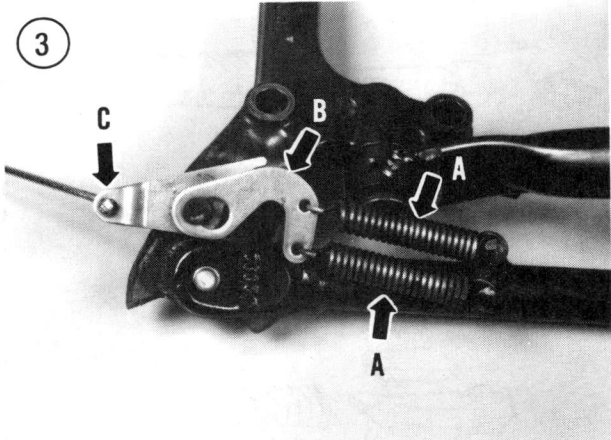

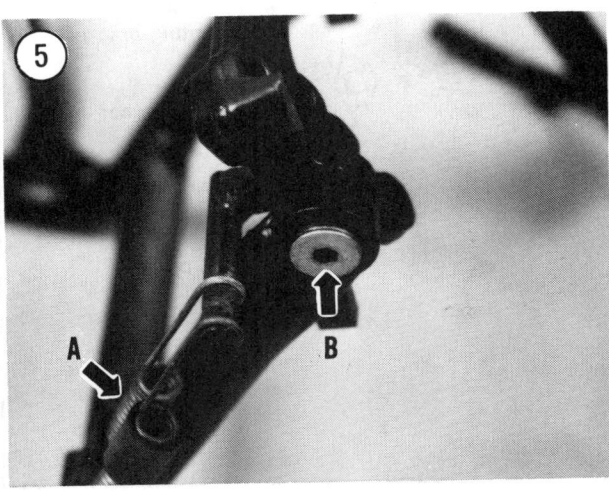

3. Raise the center stand and use Vise Grips to unhook the return springs (A, **Figure 5**) from the stud on the center stand.

4. Remove the bolts (B, **Figure 5**) on each side securing the center stand to the mounting bracket on the engine.

5. Remove the center stand from the mounting bracket.

6. To replace the bushings, perform the following:
   a. Remove the circlip securing the bushing into the mounting bracket and remove the bushing.
   b. Inspect the bushing for wear or damage and replace if necessary.
   c. Apply multipurpose grease to the pivot bushings and to the pivot areas of the mounting bracket where the pivot bushings ride.
   d. Install the bushings and install the circlips.

7. Install by reversing these removal steps, noting the following.

8. Apply multipurpose grease to the pivot bolts.

9. Tighten the pivot bolts to the torque specification listed in **Table 1**.

10. Be sure to install the rubber bushings on the return springs.

FOOTPEGS

Removal/Installation

Refer to **Figures 6-8** for this procedure. These illustrations show the left-hand footpeg assembly. The right-hand assembly is an exact mirror image and all parts are identical.

1. To remove individual footpegs, perform the following:
   a. Remove the cotter pin (A, **Figure 9**) and sleeve or washer securing the footpeg to the bracket on the footpeg bracket.
   b. Remove the pivot pin (B, **Figure 9**) and remove the footpeg and spring.
   c. Make sure the spring is in good condition and not broken. Replace as necessary.
   d. If necessary, slide off the rubber pad and replace with a new one.
   e. Lubricate the pivot point and pivot pin prior to installation. Install a new cotter pin and bend the ends over completely.

2. To remove the entire footpeg assembly, perform the following:
   a. On models so equipped, remove the bolts, nuts and washers (**Figure 10**) securing the footpeg assembly to the saddlebag rack. On the left-hand side the muffler is held in place with these bolts (**Figure 11**). Secure the muffler to the frame with wire or a Bungee cord.
   b. On models without a saddlebag rack, remove the bolts, nuts and washers securing the footpeg assembly. On the left-hand side the muffler is held in place with these bolts. Secure the muffler to the frame with wire or a Bungee cord.

13

FOOTPEG ASSEMBLY

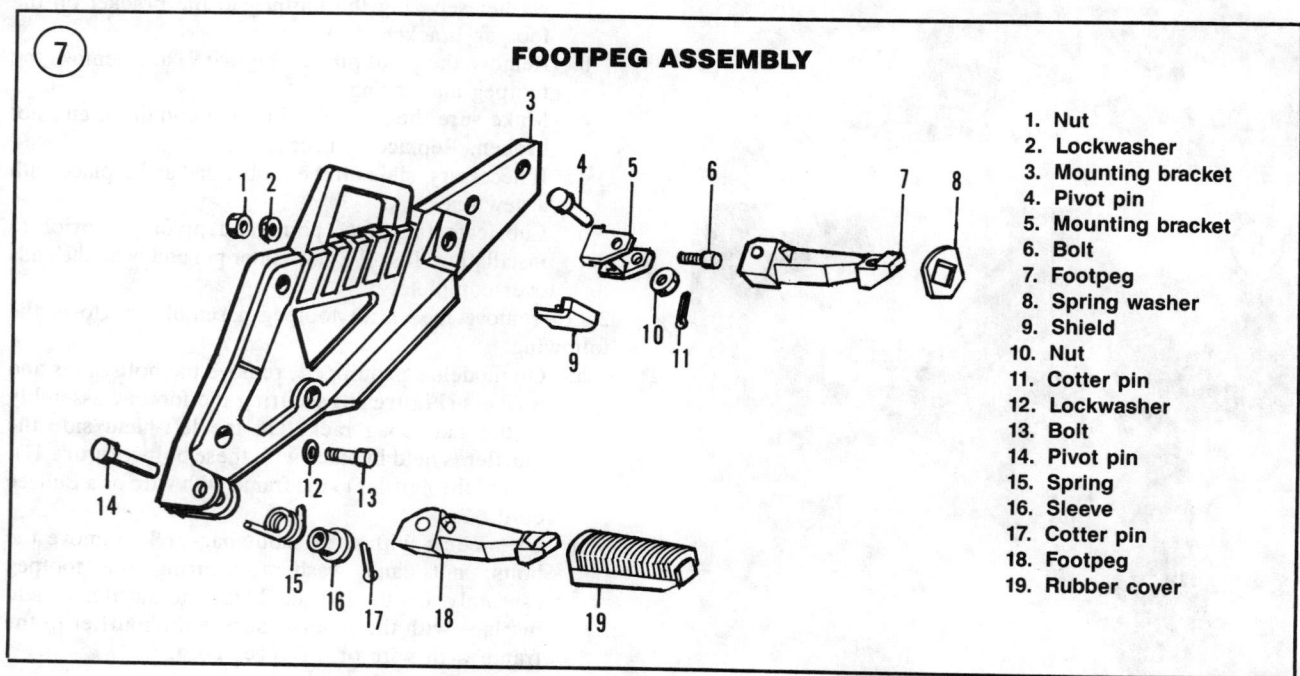

1. Pivot pin	8. Cotter pin	14. Mounting bracket
2. Bolt	9. Washer	15. Return spring
3. Footpeg	10. Bolt	16. Sleeve
4. Spring washer	11. Screw	17. Cotter pin
5. Rubber cover	12. Shield	18. Footpeg
6. Support bracket	13. Pivot pin	19. Rubber cover
7. Washer		

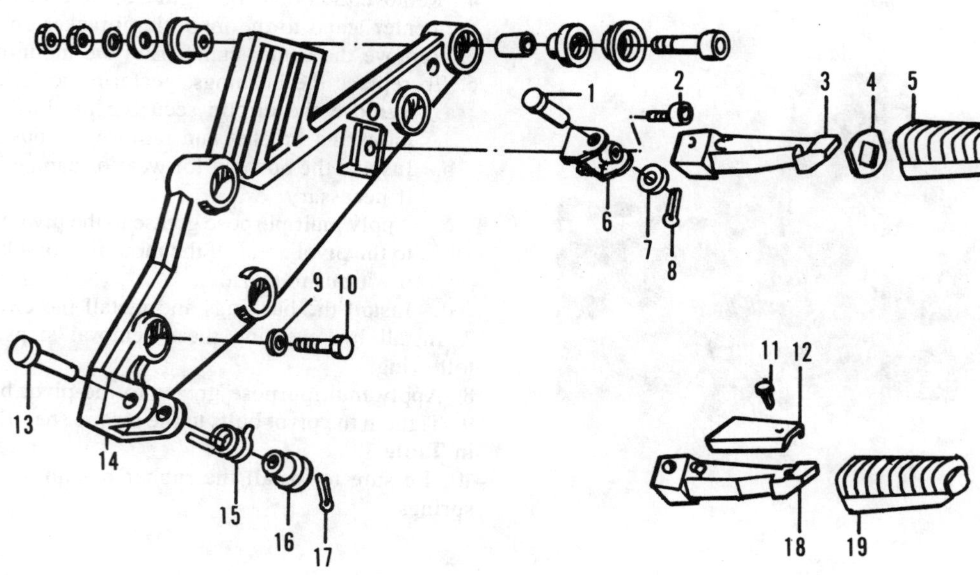

FOOTPEG ASSEMBLY

1. Nut
2. Lockwasher
3. Mounting bracket
4. Pivot pin
5. Mounting bracket
6. Bolt
7. Footpeg
8. Spring washer
9. Shield
10. Nut
11. Cotter pin
12. Lockwasher
13. Bolt
14. Pivot pin
15. Spring
16. Sleeve
17. Cotter pin
18. Footpeg
19. Rubber cover

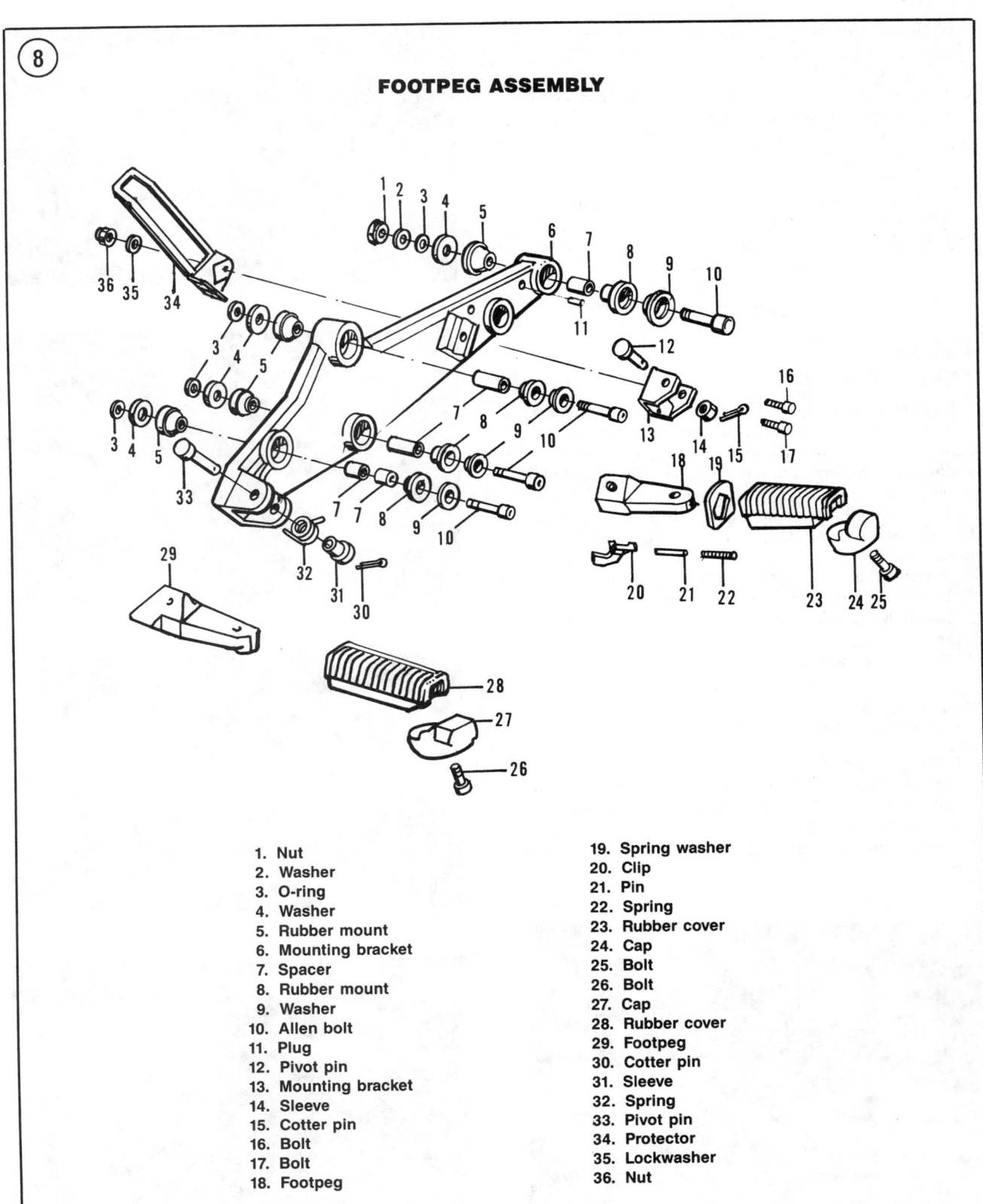

FOOTPEG ASSEMBLY

1. Nut
2. Washer
3. O-ring
4. Washer
5. Rubber mount
6. Mounting bracket
7. Spacer
8. Rubber mount
9. Washer
10. Allen bolt
11. Plug
12. Pivot pin
13. Mounting bracket
14. Sleeve
15. Cotter pin
16. Bolt
17. Bolt
18. Footpeg

19. Spring washer
20. Clip
21. Pin
22. Spring
23. Rubber cover
24. Cap
25. Bolt
26. Bolt
27. Cap
28. Rubber cover
29. Footpeg
30. Cotter pin
31. Sleeve
32. Spring
33. Pivot pin
34. Protector
35. Lockwasher
36. Nut

13

c. Remove the bolts securing the footpeg assembly to the transmission housing. Refer to **Figure 12** or **Figure 13**.

d. On the left-hand side, remove the footpeg assembly.

e. On the right-hand side, remove the footpeg assembly and the rear brake pedal assembly. If necessary, remove the rear brake pedal assembly from the footpeg assembly as described in Chapter Twelve.

f. Install by reversing these removal steps, noting the following.

g. Tighten the mounting bolts to the torque specifications listed in **Table 1**.

SAFETY BARS

Front Safety Bars
Removal/Installation

Refer to **Figure 14** and **Figure 15** for this procedure.
1. Remove the cap covering the upper mounting bolt.
2. Remove the bolts or nuts (depending on model) and lockwashers securing the lower portion of the safety bar to the engine.
3. Remove the bolts or nuts (depending on model) and lockwashers securing the upper portion of the safety bar to the engine.
4. Remove the safety bar from the engine.
5. Repeat for the other side if necessary.
6. Install by reversing these removal steps, noting the following.
7. Tighten the mounting bolts and nuts securely.

Rear Safety Bars
Removal/Installation

Refer to **Figure 16** for this procedure.
1. Remove the cap covering the rear lower mounting bolt.
2. Loosen the lower bolts securing the lower portion of the safety bar to the footpeg bracket.
3. Loosen the nuts securing the upper U-clamp to the frame.

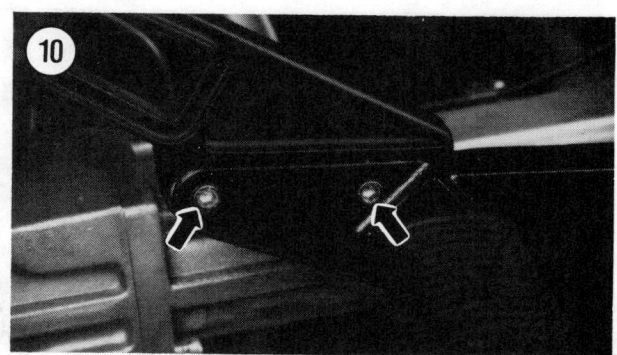

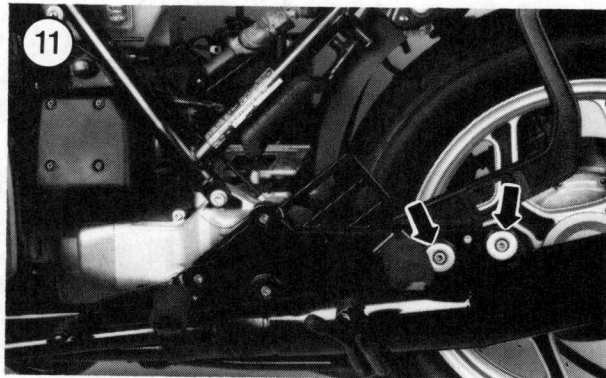

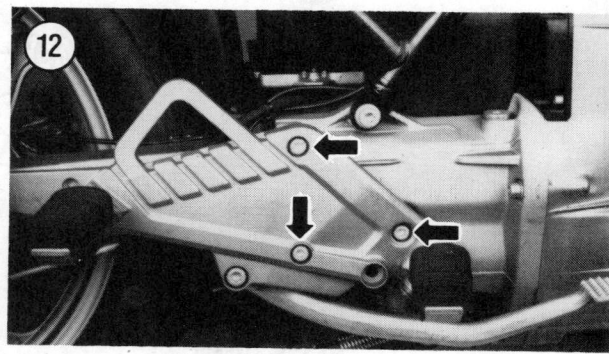

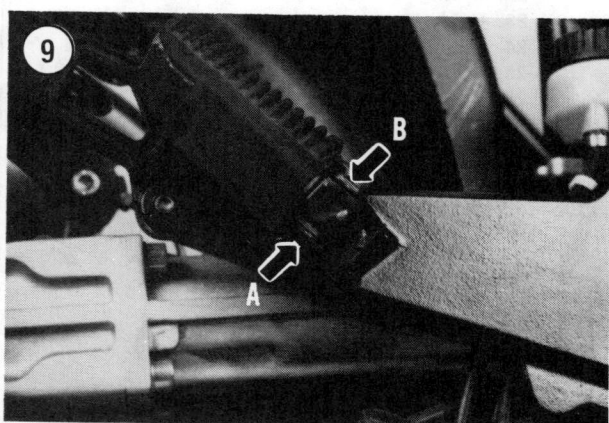

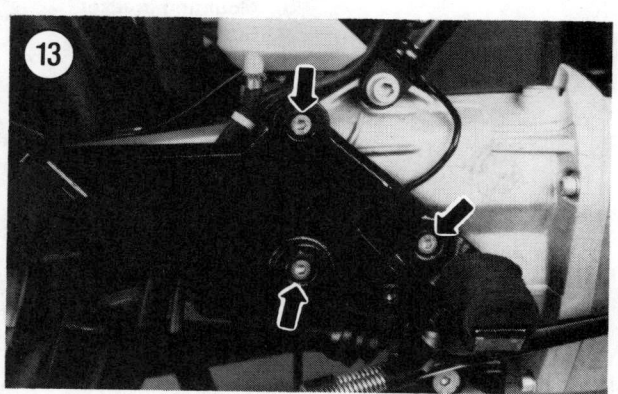

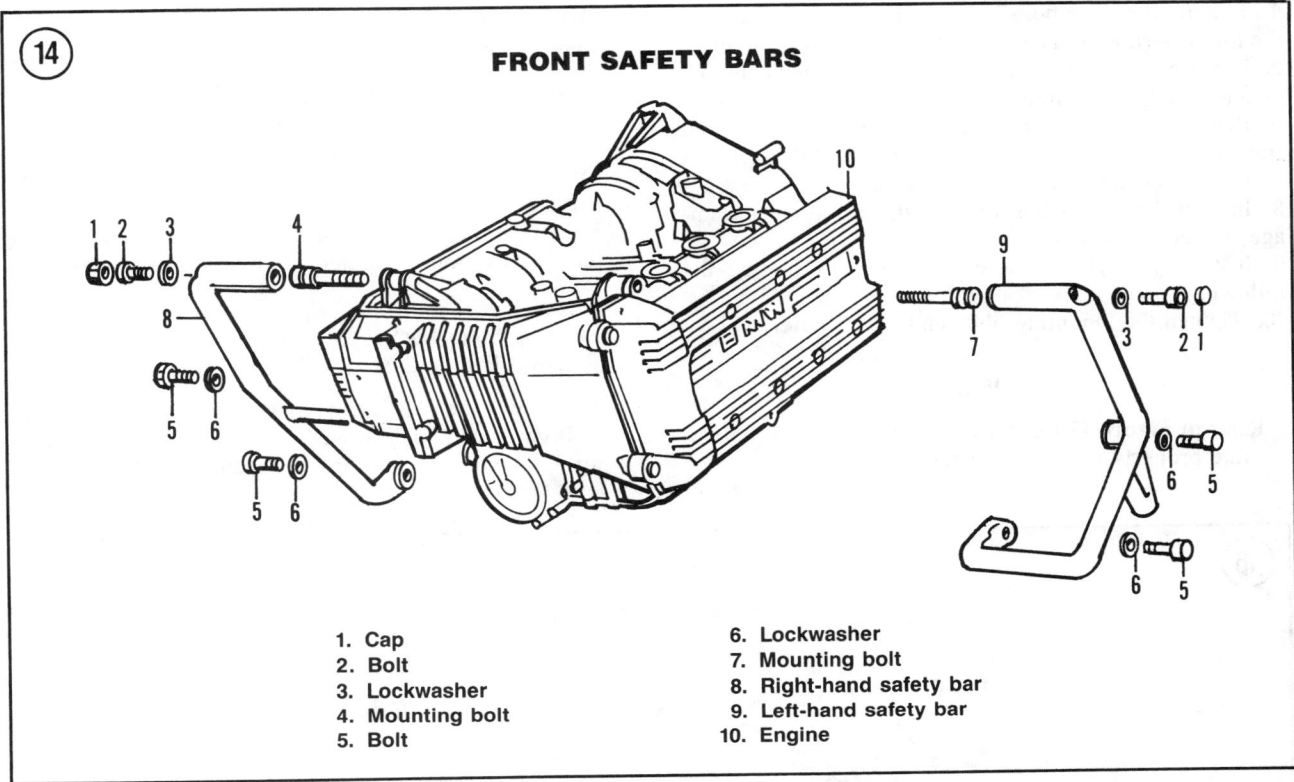

FRONT SAFETY BARS

14

1. Cap
2. Bolt
3. Lockwasher
4. Mounting bolt
5. Bolt
6. Lockwasher
7. Mounting bolt
8. Right-hand safety bar
9. Left-hand safety bar
10. Engine

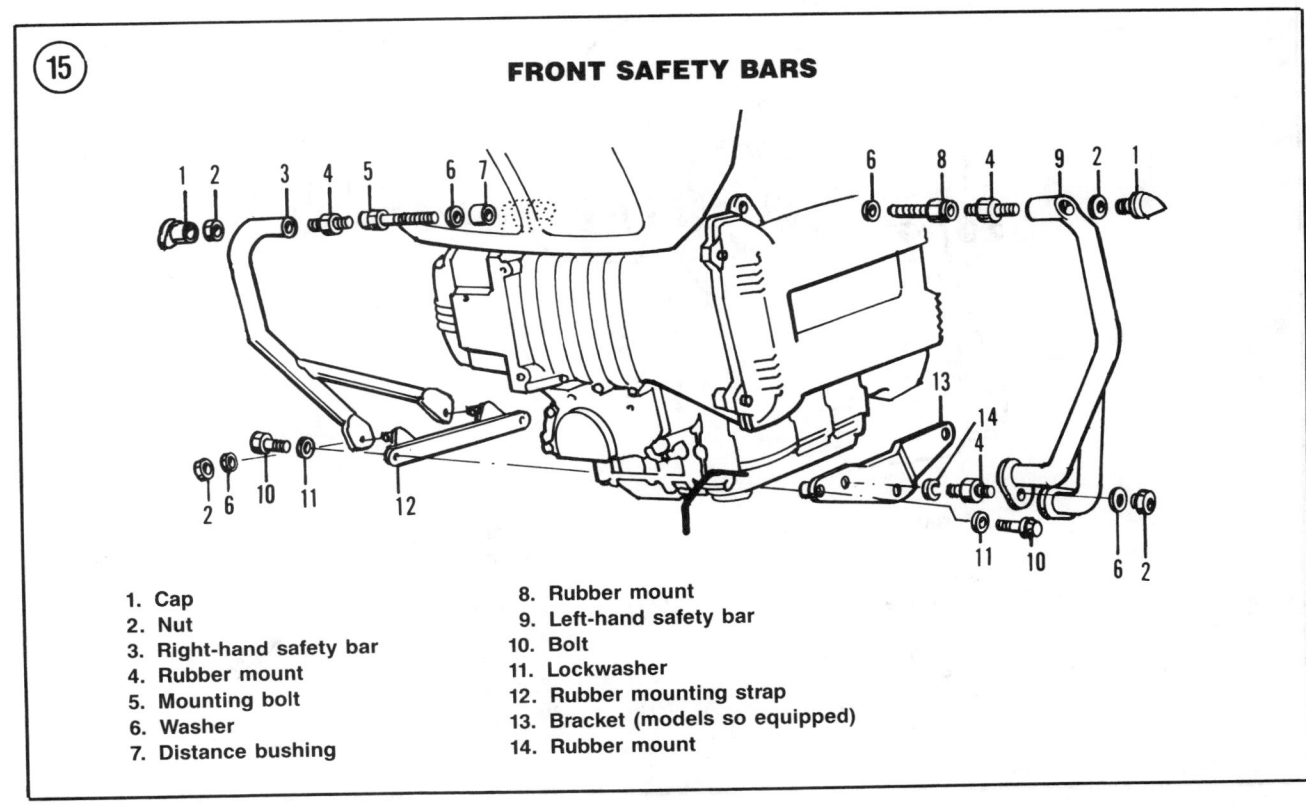

FRONT SAFETY BARS

15

1. Cap
2. Nut
3. Right-hand safety bar
4. Rubber mount
5. Mounting bolt
6. Washer
7. Distance bushing
8. Rubber mount
9. Left-hand safety bar
10. Bolt
11. Lockwasher
12. Rubber mounting strap
13. Bracket (models so equipped)
14. Rubber mount

13

4. Remove the lower bolts, nuts and lockwashers securing the lower portion of the safety bar to the footpeg bracket.
5. Remove the nuts and lockwashers securing the upper U-clamp to the frame. Remove the U-clamp.
6. Remove the safety bar from the footpeg bracket and frame.
7. Repeat for the other side if necessary.
8. Inspect the rubber bushings for deterioration or damage; replace if necessary.
9. Install by reversing these removal steps, noting the following.
10. Tighten the mounting bolts and nuts securely.

LOCKS

Refer to **Figure 17** for this procedure. If a lock fails to operate properly it must be replaced.

Helmet Lock
Removal/Installation

1. To remove the helmet lock, remove the mounting screws (**Figure 18**) securing the lock assembly.
2. Take the tumbler and the set of keys to a BMW dealer for replacement. They can match the new tumbler to your existing set of keys.
3. Install the helmet lock and the mounting screws securing the lock assembly. Tighten the screws securely.

Steering Stem Lock
Removal/Installation

1. Remove the plastic cover (A, **Figure 19**) on the lock. This cover will be destroyed when it is removed. There is no way to remove it so it can be reused.

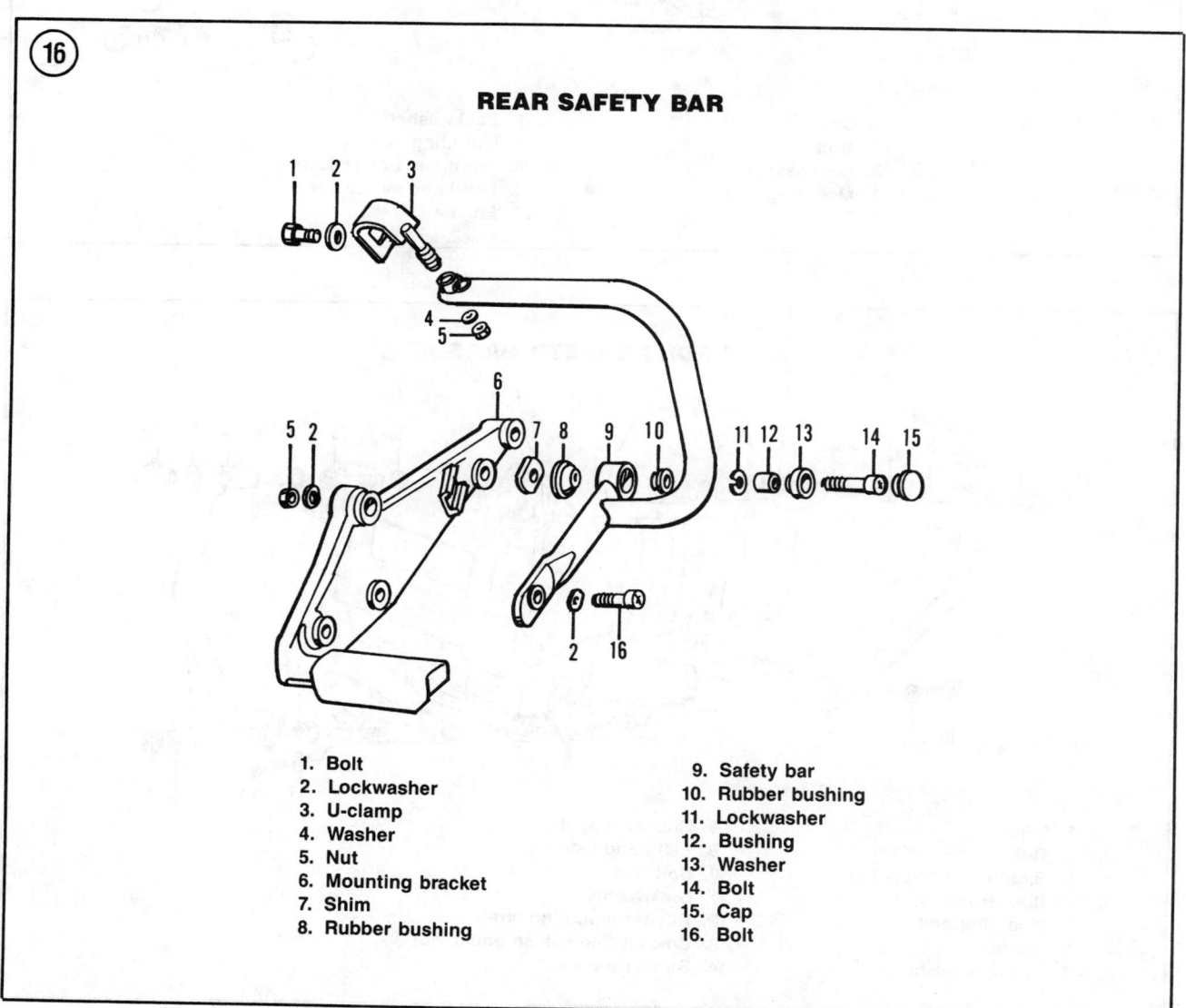

REAR SAFETY BAR

1. Bolt
2. Lockwasher
3. U-clamp
4. Washer
5. Nut
6. Mounting bracket
7. Shim
8. Rubber bushing
9. Safety bar
10. Rubber bushing
11. Lockwasher
12. Bushing
13. Washer
14. Bolt
15. Cap
16. Bolt

2. Using a pair of side cutting pliers, grab hold of the notched pin (B, **Figure 19**) and pull the pin and washers out of the frame boss.

3. Pry the metal cover off of the tumbler.

4. Insert the key into the tumbler, turn the key and withdraw the tumbler from the frame boss.

5. Take the tumbler and the set of keys to a BMW dealer for replacement. They can match the new tumbler to your existing set of keys.

6. Install the tumbler into the frame boss.

7. Install a new metal cover, plastic cover, washers and notched pin.

8. Tap the notched pin in until it bottoms out.

Ignition Switch
Removal/Installation

1. Disconnect the battery negative lead as described under *Battery* in Chapter Three.

---

(17) **LOCKS**

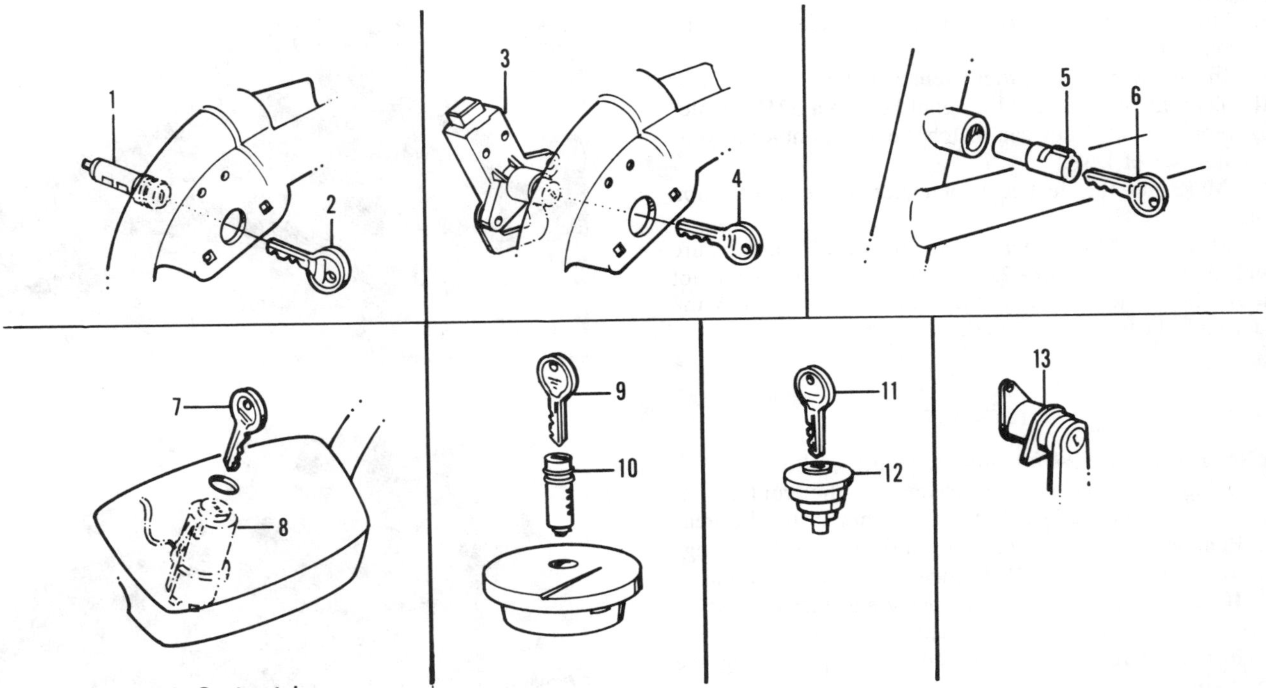

1. Seat catch
2. Key
3. Helmet lock
4. Key
5. Steering stem lock
6. Key
7. Key
8. Ignition switch
9. Key
10. Fuel filler cap lock
11. Key
12. Fuel filler cap lock
13. Seat lock (K75C only)

13

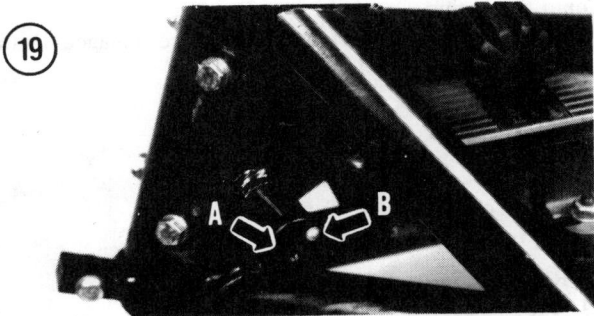

2. Remove the fuel tank as described under *Fuel Tank Removal/Installation* in Chapter Seven.

3. Remove the screws (**Figure 20**) securing the impact pad.

4. Carefully remove the ignition switch trim disc (**Figure 21**) surrounding the switch.

5. Insert a narrow flat-bladed screwdriver down on each side of the switch to release the locking tabs on the switch.

6. Partially pull the impact pad (**Figure 22**) up and off of the handlebar assembly.

7. With both locking tabs released, press down on the center of the switch and push it out of the impact pad.

8. Follow the electrical wires from the ignition switch back to its electrical connectors at the main wiring harness. If necessary, remove any tie wrap(s) (**Figure 23**) securing the electrical wires to the frame.

9. Pull the electrical wire away from the frame and disconnect it.

10. Install by reversing these removal steps.

11. Take the tumbler and the set of keys to a BMW dealer for replacement. They can match the new tumbler to your existing set of keys.

12. Make sure the electrical connector is free of corrosion and is tight.

13. Move the electrical wires back into position and secure with tie wrap(s) (**Figure 23**). Make sure the wires are not above the frame members as they may be damaged by the fuel tank when it is installed.

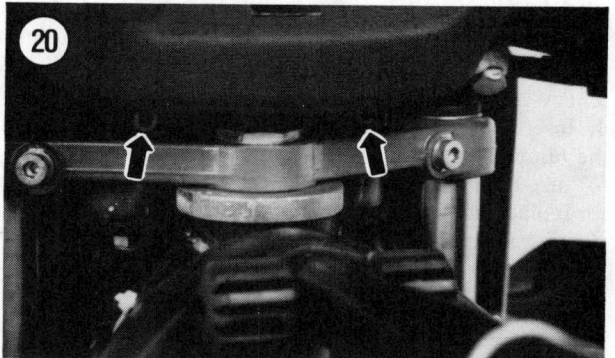

HANDLE

Refer to **Figure 24** for this procedure.

1. Using a flat-bladed screwdriver, pry the front spring retainer (A, **Figure 25**) and spring out from the handle area.

2. Remove the spring retainer from the end of the spring.

3. Remove the handle (B, **Figure 25**) from the frame.

4. If necessary, withdraw the spring and the rear spring retainer from the frame receptacle.

5. Install by reversing these removal steps, noting the following.

6. Apply a light coat of multipurpose grease to the pivot point on the handle and pivot post on the frame.

7. If removed, install the spring and the rear spring retainer into the frame receptacle. Make sure the spring retainer is properly hooked onto the spring.

8. Make sure the front spring retainer is properly hooked onto the spring.

9. Make sure both spring retainers are engaged in the grooves in the handle.

FENDERS

Front Fender (1-Piece Type)
Removal/Installation

Refer to **Figure 26** for this procedure.

1. Place the bike on the center stand.

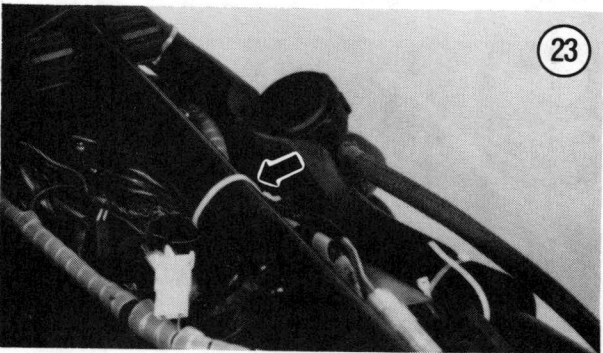

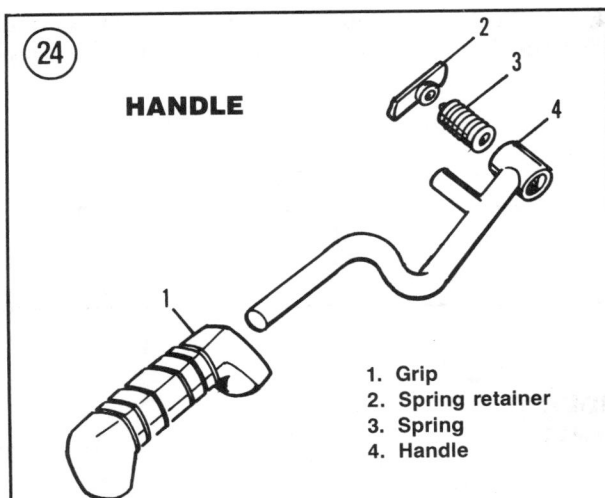

HANDLE

1. Grip
2. Spring retainer
3. Spring
4. Handle

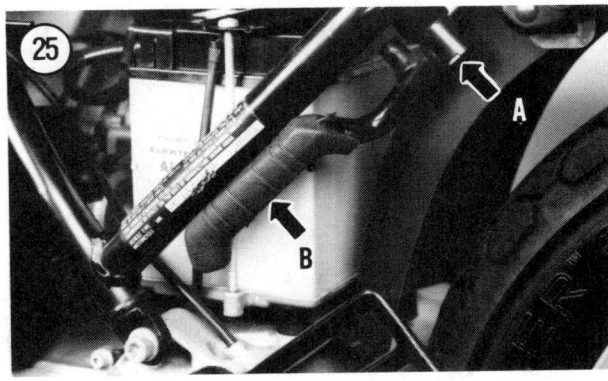

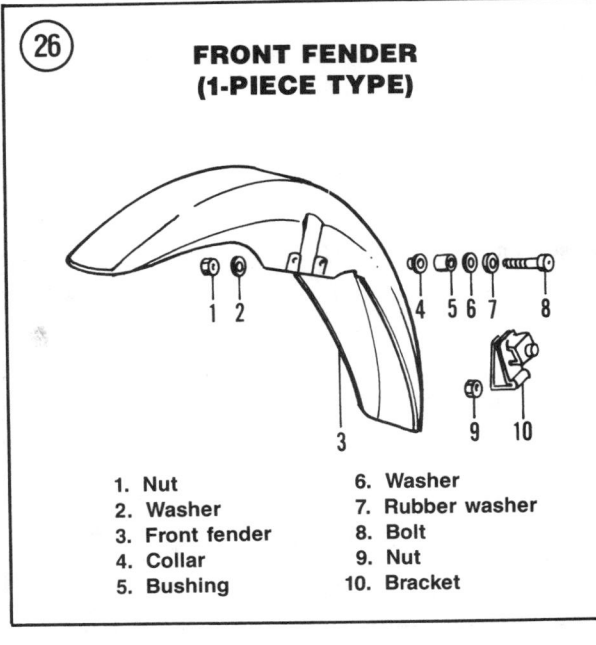

**FRONT FENDER
(1-PIECE TYPE)**

1. Nut
2. Washer
3. Front fender
4. Collar
5. Bushing
6. Washer
7. Rubber washer
8. Bolt
9. Nut
10. Bracket

2. Slide the front fork dust seals (**Figure 27**) up and off of the fork slider.

3. Remove the bolts (A, **Figure 28**), rubber washers, washers, bushings, metal collar, washers and nuts on each side securing the fender to the fork sliders.

4. Don't lose the special washers and bushings that fit into the mounting areas of the fender on each side.

5. Don't lose the hydraulic hose clamps (B, **Figure 28**) (if the hose has been removed) on the rear mounting bolts.

6. Pull the fender up past the fork sliders and then out toward the front and remove.

7. Install by reversing these removal steps, noting the following.

8. Be sure to use the special washers and bushings on the fender mounting bosses on the fender on each side. If the special washers and bushings are not in place and the bolt and nut are tightened, the fender mounting areas will be damaged and the fender will have to be replaced.

9. Apply a small amount of blue Loctite Threadlocker No. 242 to the fender mounting bolts prior to installation.

10. Tighten the bolts and nuts securing the fender securely. Don't overtighten the bolts as the fender mounting areas may be damaged even with the bushings and special washers in place.

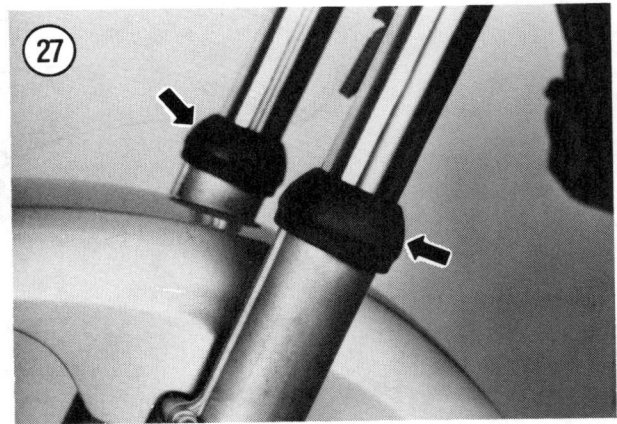

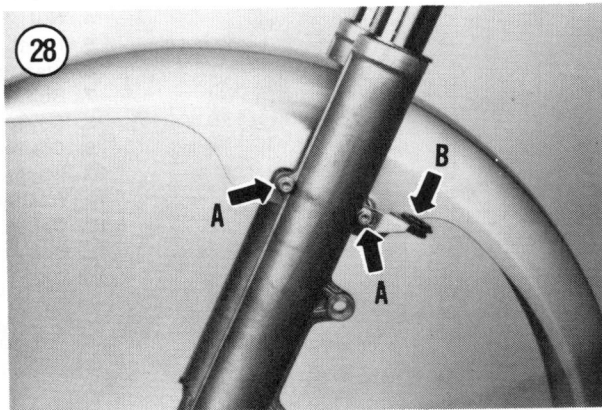

13

Front Fender (2-Piece Type)
Removal/Installation

Refer to **Figure 29** for this procedure.
1. Place the bike on the center stand.
2. Turn the front wheel completely to one side (either side, it doesn't make any difference).
3. Hinge the cover (**Figure 30**) down on the rear section of the fender and remove it.

4. Remove the bolt (**Figure 31**), washers and nut securing the fender front section to the fender rear section at the top of the fender.

CAUTION
The mounting tabs on the fenders where they attach to the fork sliders are an open-ended

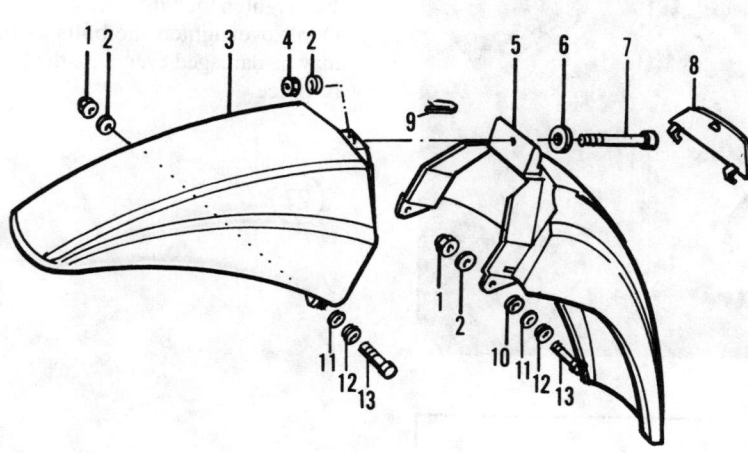

FRONT FENDER (2-PIECE TYPE)

1. Nut
2. Washer
3. Front fender front section
4. Nut
5. Front fender rear section
6. Washer
7. Bolt
8. Cover
9. Grommet
10. Washer
11. Washer
12. Collar
13. Bolt

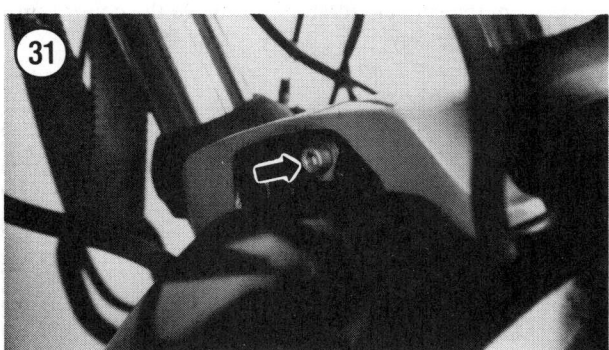

type that can slide up and off of the mounting bolts. Be careful when sliding the fenders up and off of these mounting bolts so that you do not break the mounting tabs. The tabs are only fiberglass with no metal reinforcement and will break off if too much force is applied.

5. To remove the front section, perform the following:
   a. Loosen the bolt, washers and nut (A, **Figure 32**) on each side securing the fender front section to the fork slider.
   b. Carefully pull up on the front section and free it from the mounting bolts on the fork slider.
   c. Remove the front section (**Figure 33**) from the fork assembly.

6. To remove the rear section, perform the following:
   a. Loosen the bolt, washers and nut (B, **Figure 32**) on each side securing the fender rear section to the fork slider.
   b. Carefully pull up on the rear section and free it from the mounting bolts on the fork slider.
   c. Remove the rear section (**Figure 34**) from the fork assembly.

7. If necessary, remove the bolt, metal collar, washers and nut used to secure the fender sections on each side. Don't lose the metal collar that fits into the mounting tabs of the fender on each side.

8. Install by reversing these removal steps, noting the following.

9. Be sure to use the metal collar in the plastic mounting tabs on the fender on each side. If the collar is not in place and the bolt and nut are tightened, the plastic mounting tabs will be damaged and the fender section will have to be replaced.

10. Tighten the bolts securing the fender sections securely. Don't overtighten the bolts as the fender mounting tabs may be damaged even with the metal collars in place.

Rear Fender
Removal/Installation

Refer to **Figure 35** for this procedure.

1. Place the bike on the center stand.

2. Remove the seat as described in this chapter.

3. Remove the rear cowl as described in this chapter.

4. Remove the license plate bracket as described in this chapter.

5. Remove the nuts and washers (A, **Figure 36**) securing the mid-point of the fender to the frame.

6. Pull the fender (B, **Figure 36**) up and out of the receptacles at the front where it is indexed into the frame.

7. Install by reversing these removal steps, noting the following.

8. Tighten the nuts securing the fender securely. Don't overtighten the nuts as the fender may be damaged.

LICENSE PLATE BRACKET

Removal/Installation

Refer to **Figure 37** for this procedure.
1. Remove the seat as described in this chapter.
2. Remove the storage compartment lid (**Figure 38**).
3. Within the underseat storage box, perform the following:
  a. Remove the factory tool kit, owner's manual and anything else that may be stored in the compartment.
  b. On ABS models, remove the electronic control unit from the rubber isolators and move the control unit out of the way.

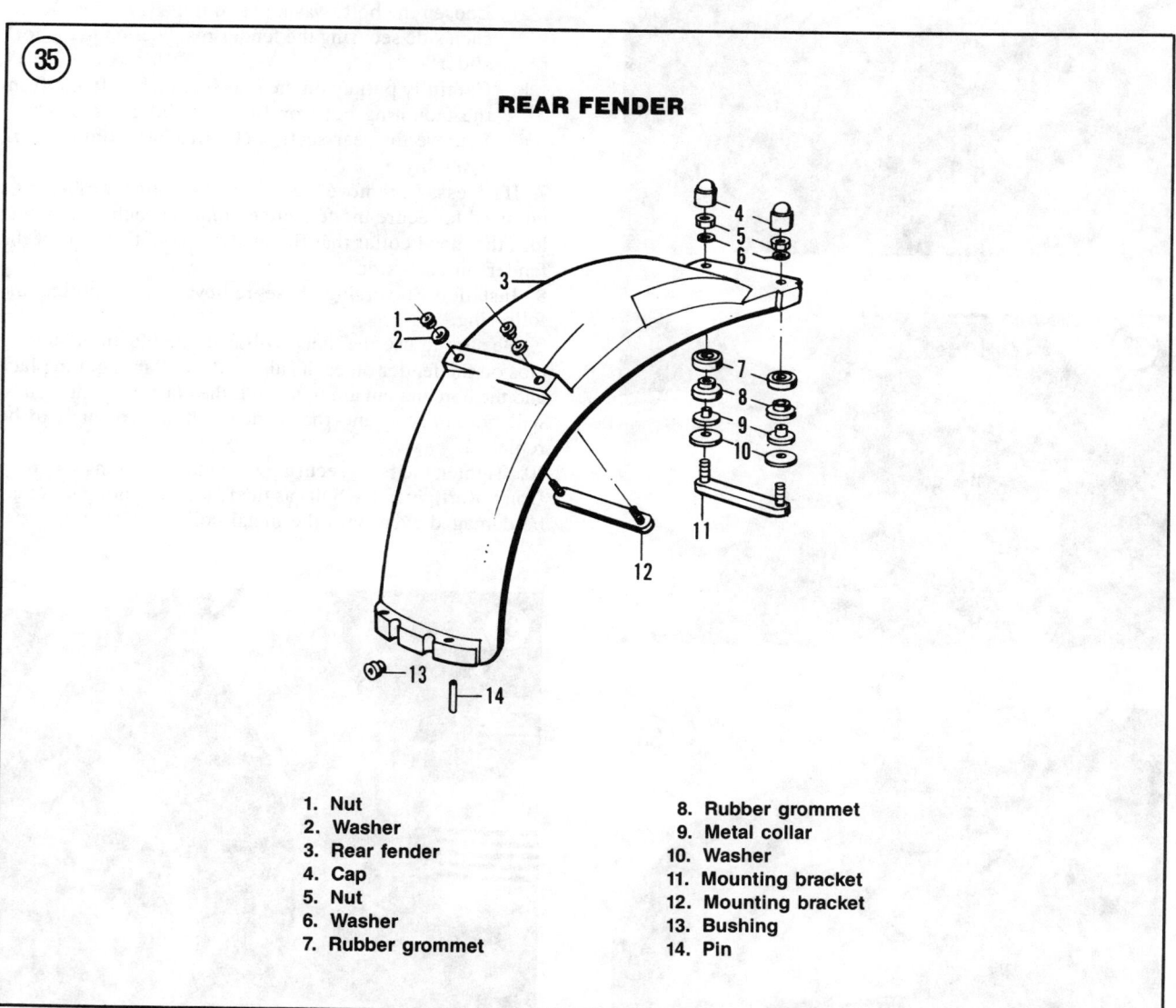

REAR FENDER

1. Nut
2. Washer
3. Rear fender
4. Cap
5. Nut
6. Washer
7. Rubber grommet

8. Rubber grommet
9. Metal collar
10. Washer
11. Mounting bracket
12. Mounting bracket
13. Bushing
14. Pin

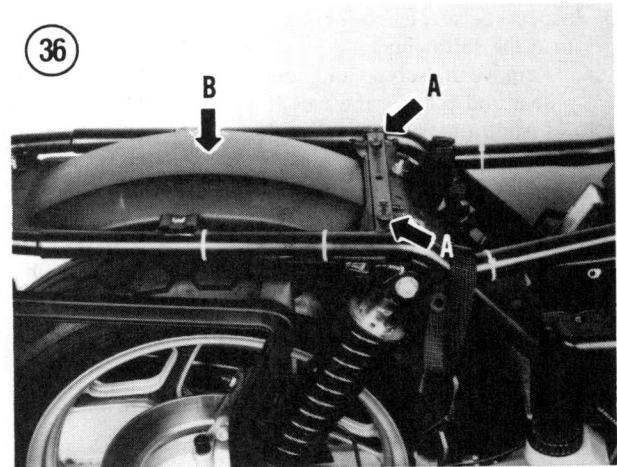

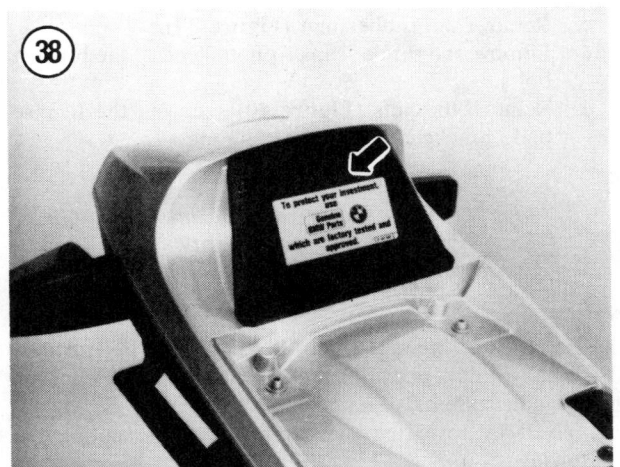

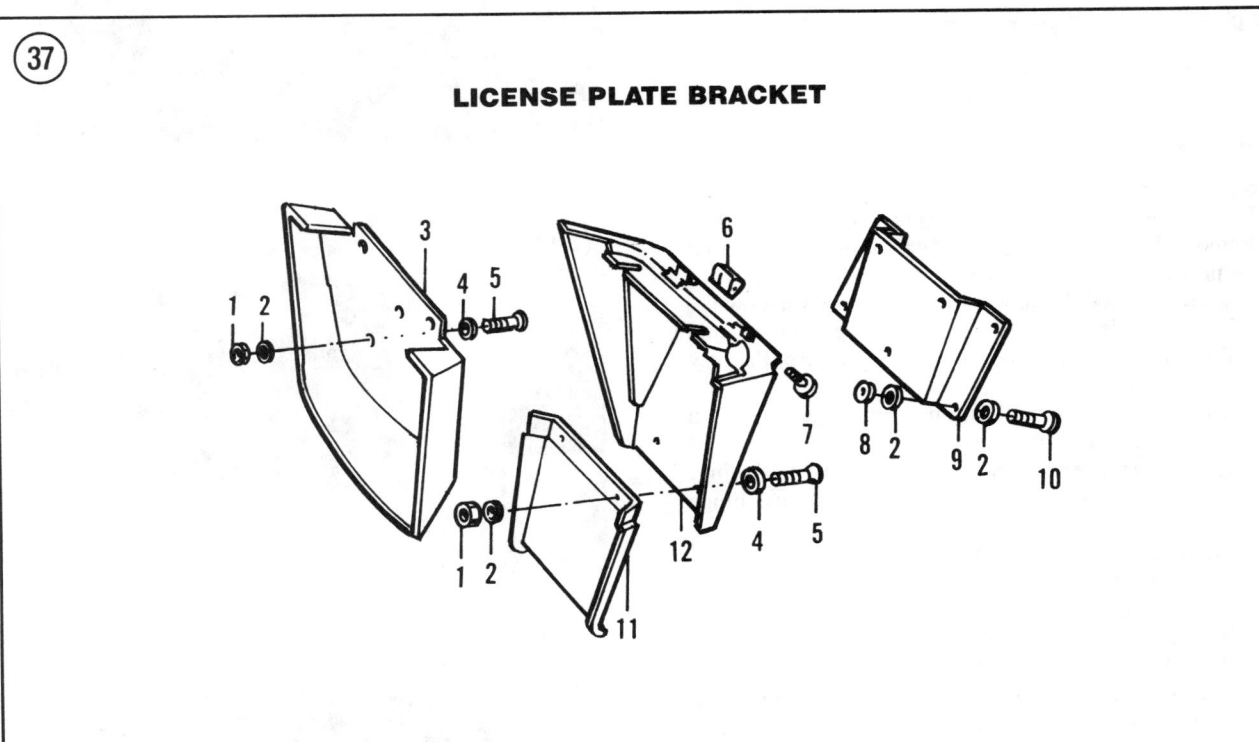

LICENSE PLATE BRACKET

1. Nut
2. Washer
3. Mud flap
4. Collar
5. Bolt
6. Special nut

7. Screw
8. Nut
9. Mounting plate
10. Bolt
11. Mud guard
12. License plate bracket

13

c. Remove the rubber mat (**Figure 39**).
d. Remove the rubber caps from the end of the bracket bolts.
e. Remove the nuts (**Figure 40**) securing the license plate bracket.

NOTE
Figure 41 is shown with the brake/taillight assembly removed for clarity. It is not necessary to remove the light assembly for this procedure.

4. Remove the screws (**Figure 41**) securing the license plate bracket assembly and slide the assembly out and off of the rear fender assembly.
5. Install by reversing these removal steps, noting the following.
6. Tighten the nuts and screws securing the license plate bracket securely. Don't overtighten the nuts or screws as the plastic mounting bosses may be damaged.

SEAT

Removal/Installation

Refer to **Figure 42** and **Figure 43** for this procedure.
1. Remove the frame right-hand side cover (**Figure 44**).
2. Remove the special clip (**Figure 45**) from the seat's front hinge point.
3A. On K75C models, move the seat lock lever down.
3B. On all models except K75C, insert the ignition key into the seat lock on the left-hand side and turn the key counterclockwise.
4A. On K75C models, pull up on front of the seat, then pull it forward and remove the seat.
4B. On all models except K75C, perform the following:
   a. Pull up on the left-hand side of the seat and hinge it open.
   b. Remove the special clip (**Figure 46**) from the seat support.
   c. Remove the special clip (**Figure 47**) from the seat's rear hinge point.
   d. Remove the pivot pin (**Figure 48**).
   e. Move the seat forward to clear the rear pivot pin and remove the seat.
5. Install by reversing these removal steps, noting the following.
6. Make sure the special clips are correctly installed. If they work loose and fall out the seat will become loose and unstable.

Inspection
(K75C Models)

1. Remove the seat as described in this chapter.
2. Inspect the rubber bumpers for wear or damage. If damaged, remove the screws, rubber bumper and plate. Install a new bumper and tighten the screws securely.

3. Inspect the seat catch for wear or damage. If damaged, perform the following:
   a. Remove the screws and nuts securing the catch to the seat and remove the catch.
   b. Install a new catch and tighten the screws and nuts securely.

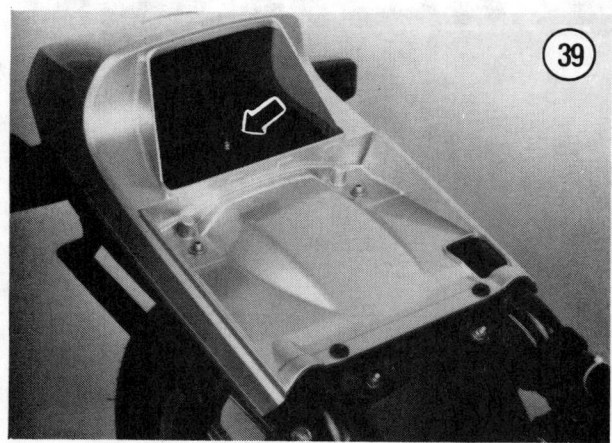

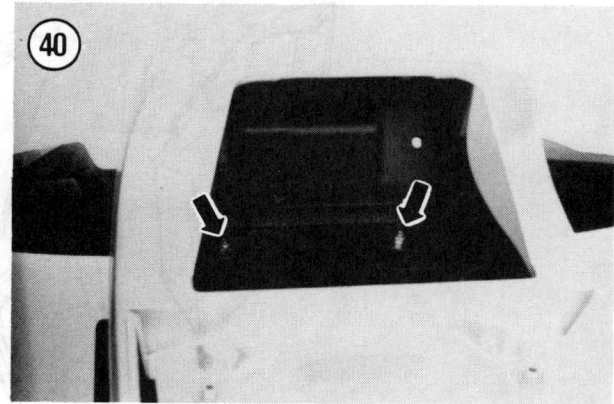

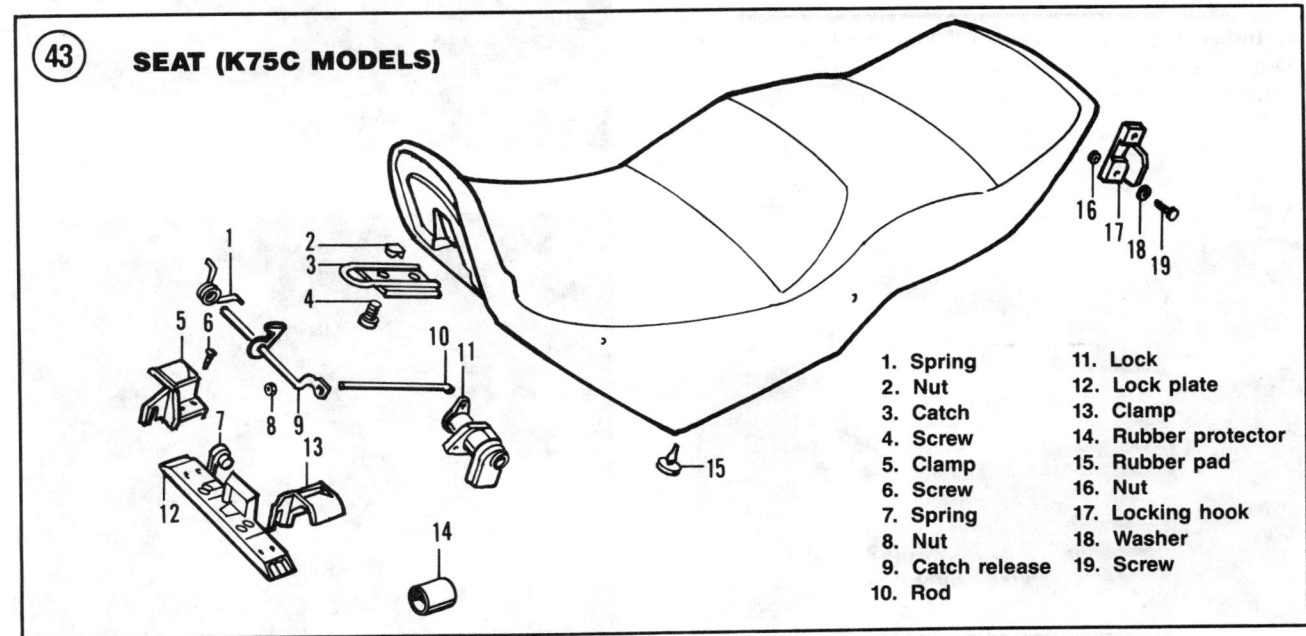

42   **SEAT (ALL MODELS EXCEPT K75C)**

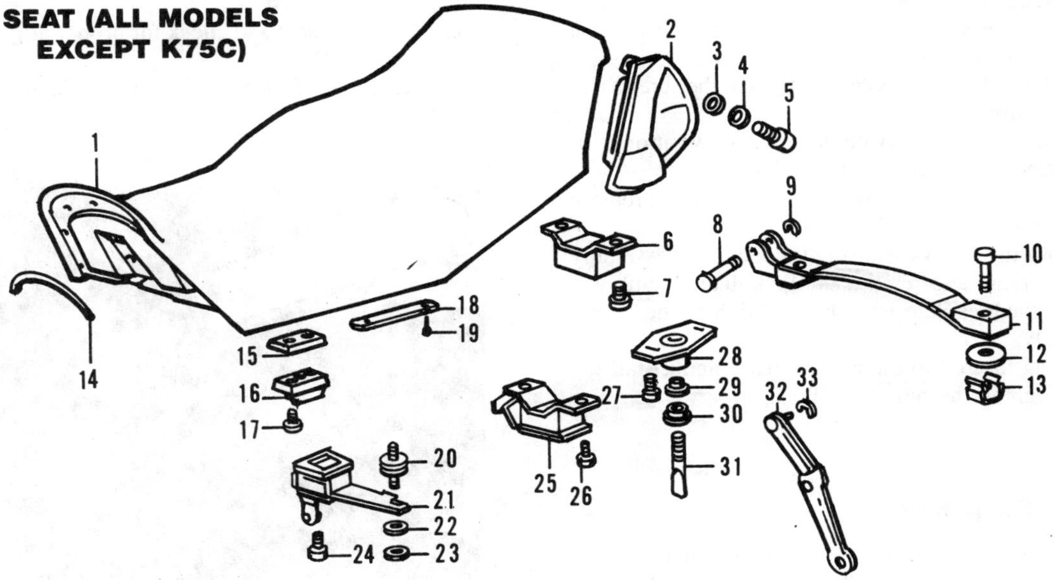

1. Seat	12. Washer	23. Nut
2. Rear hand hold	13. Special clip	24. Screw
3. Washer	14. Trim	25. Rear hinge
4. Lockwasher	15. Plate	26. Screw
5. Bolt	16. Rubber bumper	27. Screw
6. Rubber bumper	17. Screw	28. Rubber mount
7. Screw	18. Strap	29. Lockwasher
8. Pivot pin	19. Screw	30. Nut
9. Special clip	20. Rubber bushing	31. Catch
10. Bolt	21. Support hinge	32. Support
11. Hinge support	22. Washer	33. Clip

43   **SEAT (K75C MODELS)**

1. Spring	11. Lock
2. Nut	12. Lock plate
3. Catch	13. Clamp
4. Screw	14. Rubber protector
5. Clamp	15. Rubber pad
6. Screw	16. Nut
7. Spring	17. Locking hook
8. Nut	18. Washer
9. Catch release	19. Screw
10. Rod	

13

4. Inspect the seat locking hooks for wear or damage. If damaged, perform the following:
   a. Remove the screws and nuts securing the locking hooks and remove the locking hooks.
   b. Install new locking hooks and tighten the screws and nuts securely.
5. Inspect the catch assembly on the frame for wear or damage. If damaged, perform the following:
   a. Remove the nut securing the rod to the catch release mechanism.
   b. Remove the screws securing the lockplate assembly to the frame and remove the lockplate assembly.
   c. Install the lockplate assembly and tighten the screws securely.
   d. Connect the rod to the catch release and install the nut. Tighten the nut securely.

Inspection
(All Models Except K75C)

1. Remove the seat as described in this chapter.
2. Inspect the front rubber bumpers (**Figure 49**) for wear or damage. If damaged, remove the screws, rubber bumper and plate. Install a new bumper and tighten the screws securely.
3. Inspect the seat hinge and hinge support (A, **Figure 50**) for wear or damage. If damaged, perform the following:
   a. Remove the screws and the hinge and hinge support assembly.
   b. Install a new hinge and hinge support assembly and tighten the screws loosely at first.
   c. Close the seat and check for proper alignment of the hinge and hinge support assembly.
   d. Readjust if necessary, then tighten the screws securely.
4. Inspect the seat lock catch (B, **Figure 50**) for wear or damage. If damaged, perform the following:
   a. Remove the screws and the catch assembly.

b. Install a new catch assembly and tighten the screws loosely at first.
c. Close the seat and check for proper alignment of the catch to the lock.
d. Readjust if necessary, then tighten the screws securely.

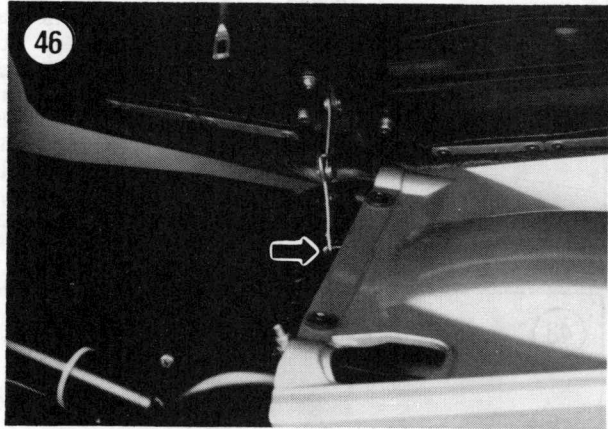

5. Inspect the rear hinge assembly (A, **Figure 51**) for wear or damage. If damaged, perform the following:
   a. Remove the screws and the rear hinge assembly.
   b. Install a new rear hinge assembly and tighten the screws securely.

6. Inspect the rear rubber bumpers (B, **Figure 51**) for wear or damage. If damaged, remove the screws and rubber bumper. Install a new bumper and tighten the screws securely.

7. Inspect the rear hand holds (A, **Figure 52**) for damage. If damaged, perform the following:
   a. Remove the screws, lockwashers and washers (B, **Figure 52**) securing the hand hold.
   b. Remove the hand hold from the seat.
   c. Install a new hand hold and tighten the screws securely.
   d. Repeat for the other side if necessary.

8. Install the seat as described in this chapter.

REAR COWL AND STORAGE TRAY

Rear Cowl
Removal/Installation

Refer to **Figure 53** and **Figure 54** for this procedure.
1. Remove the side covers and the seat as described in this chapter.

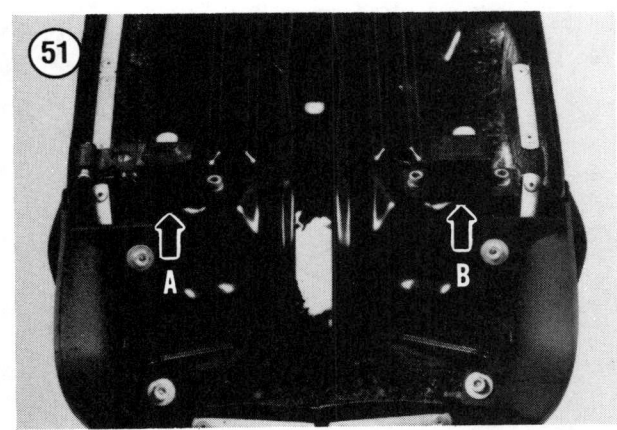

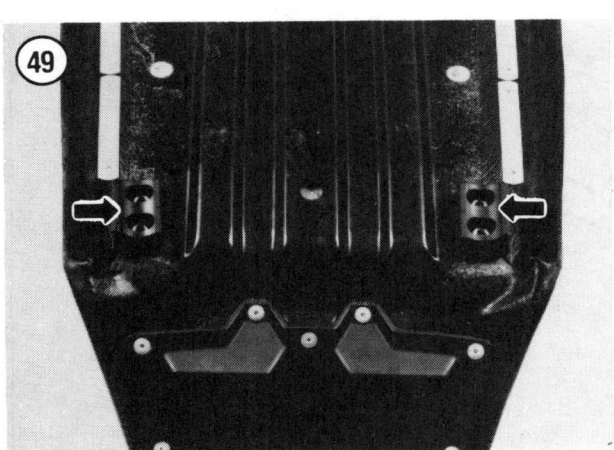

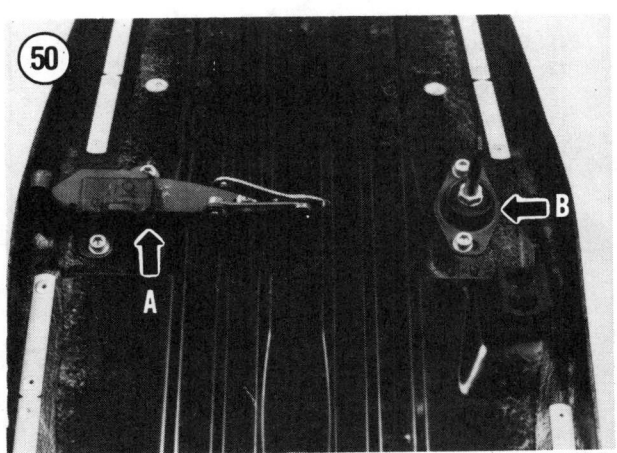

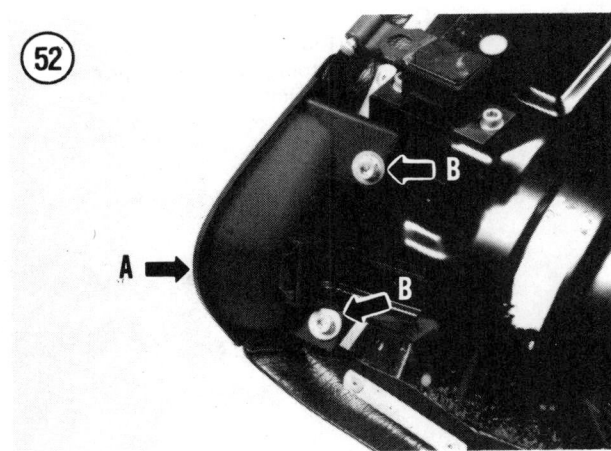

13

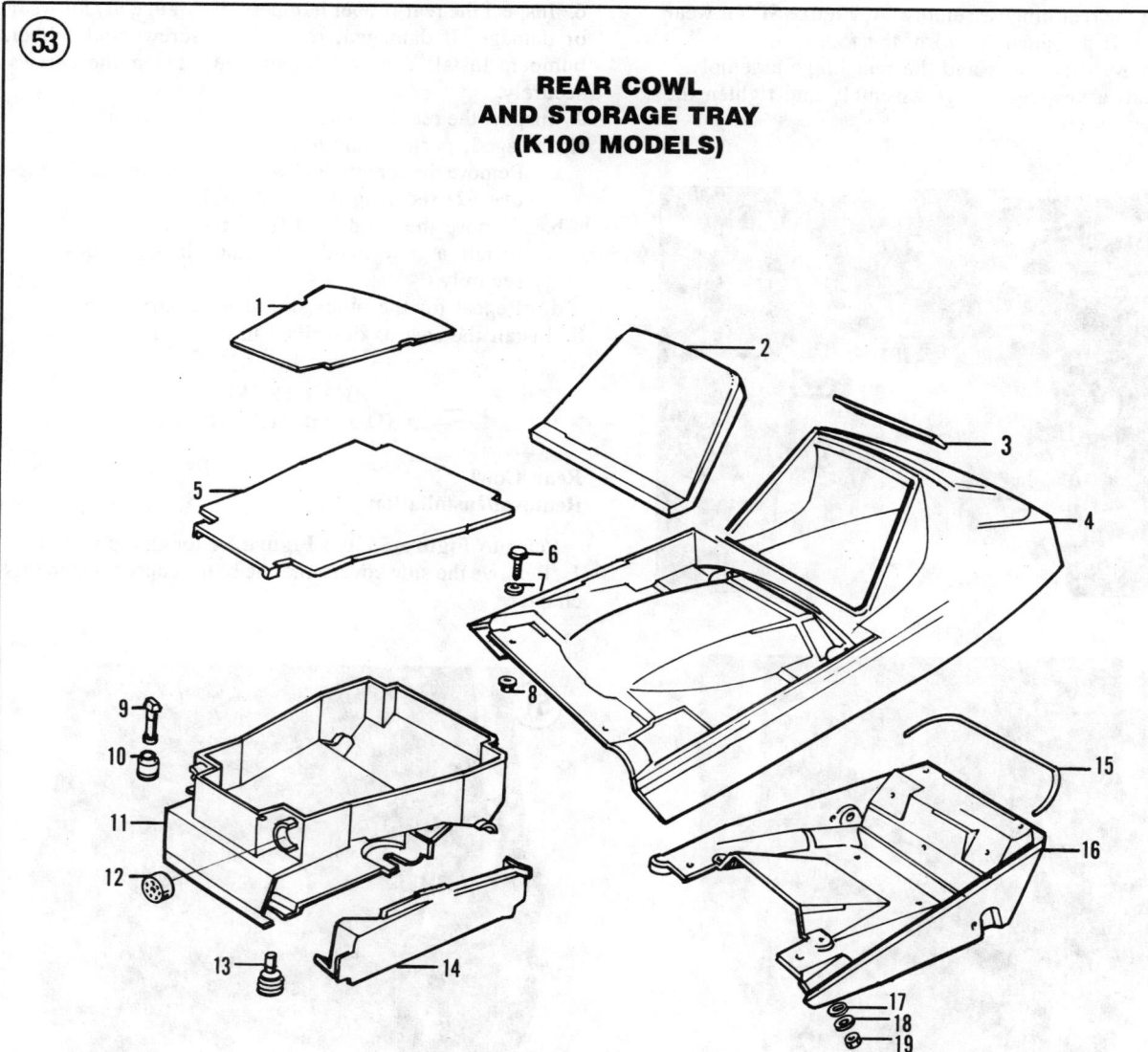

**REAR COWL
AND STORAGE TRAY
(K100 MODELS)**

53

1. Rubber mat
2. Storage compartment cover
3. Gasket
4. Rear cowl upper portion
5. Cover
6. Bolt
7. Washer
8. Nut
9. Pin
10. Rubber stopper
11. Storage tray
12. Rubber stopper
13. Rubber cushion
14. Side cover
15. Gasket
16. Rear cowl lower portion
17. Washer
18. Lockwasher
19. Nut

**REAR COWL
AND STORAGE TRAY
(K75 MODELS)**

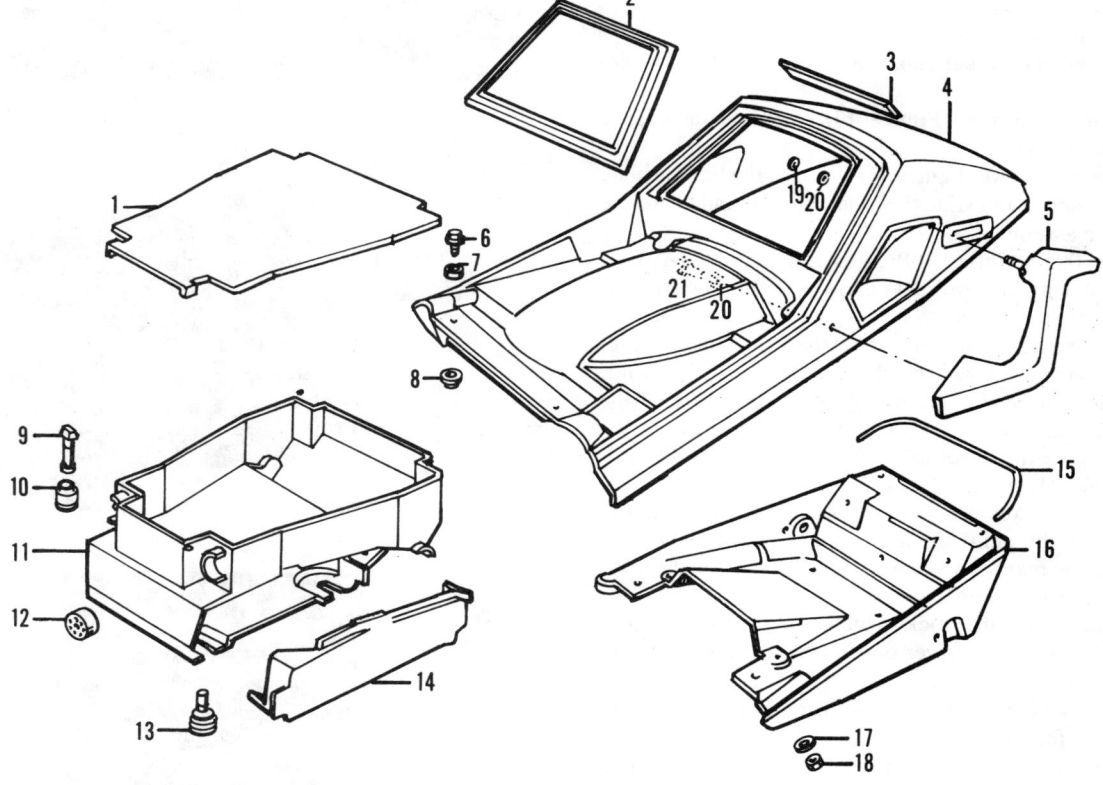

1. Cover
2. Storage compartment cover
3. Gasket
4. Rear cowl upper portion
5. Handle
6. Bolt
7. Washer
8. Nut
9. Pin
10. Rubber stopper
11. Storage tray

12. Rubber stopper
13. Rubber cushion
14. Side cover
15. Gasket
16. Rear cowl lower portion
17. Washer
18. Nut
19. Nut
20. Washer
21. Bolt

13

2. Remove the taillight/brake light assembly as described under *Taillight/Brake Light* in Chapter Eight.

3. Disconnect the electrical connector (**Figure 55**) for the rear turn signals.

4. Remove the storage compartment lid (**Figure 38**).

5. Within the underseat storage box, perform the following:
   a. Remove the factory tool kit, owner's manual and anything else that may be stored in the compartment.
   b. On ABS models, remove the electronic control unit from the rubber isolators and move the control unit out of the way.
   c. Remove the rubber mat (**Figure 39**).
   d. Remove the rubber caps from the end of the bracket bolts.
   e. Remove the nuts (**Figure 40**) securing the license plate bracket.

6. Remove the screws (**Figure 41**) securing the license plate bracket assembly and slide the assembly out and off of the rear fender assembly.

7. Remove the mounting bolts, washers and nuts (A, **Figure 56**) securing the rear cowl and the seat hinge support to the frame at the rear.

8. Remove the mounting screws, washers and nuts (B, **Figure 56**) securing the rear cowl to the frame at the front.

9. Pull the rear cowl assembly straight up and off of the frame and rear fender.

10. To separate the lower portion from the upper portion, perform the following:
   a. Lay a blanket or shop cloths on the workbench to protect the paint finish of the cowl assembly.
   b. Turn the rear cowl assembly upside down on the blanket or shop cloths.
   c. Remove the nuts, lockwashers and washers (**Figure 57**) securing the lower portion to the upper portion.
   d. Remove the lower portion.

11. To remove the rack (**Figure 58**) from the upper portion, perform the following:
   a. Turn the upper portion over in a blanket or shop cloths.
   b. Remove the nuts and washers (**Figure 59**) securing the rack.

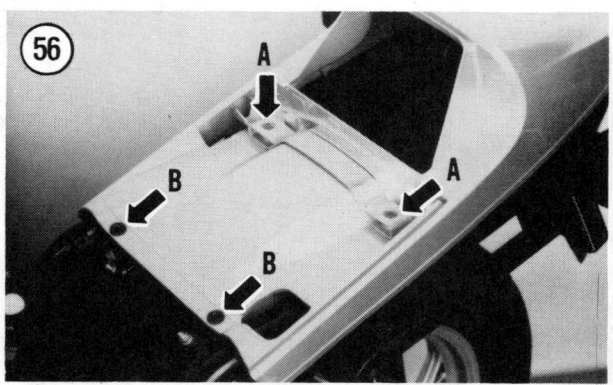

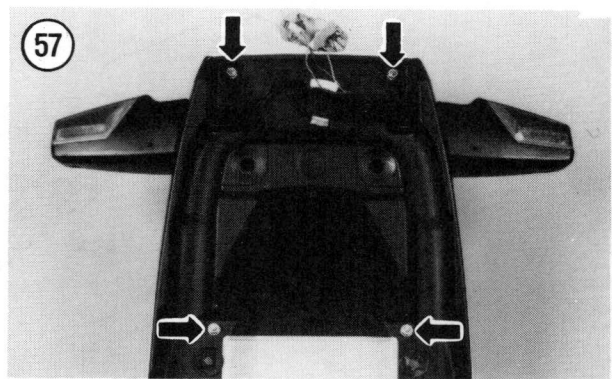

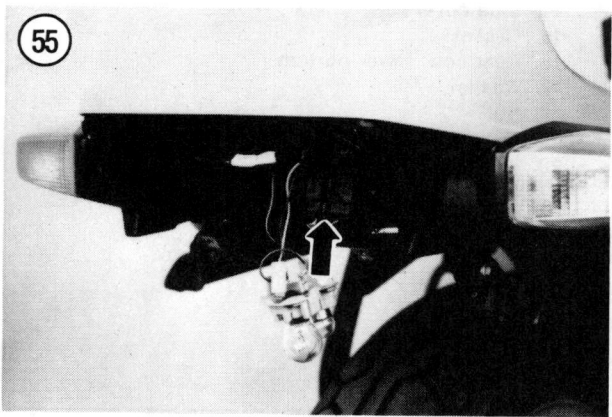

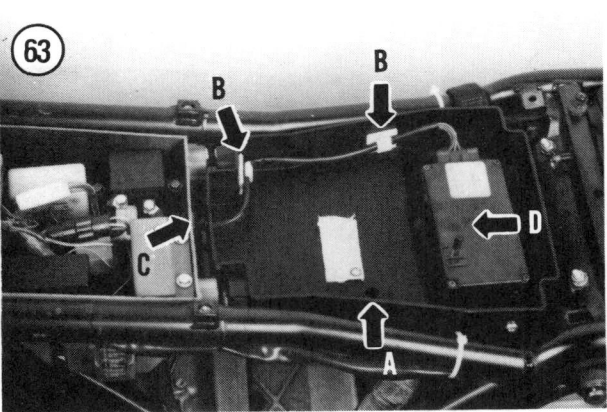

c. Remove the rack.

d. Install the rack and secure with the nuts and washers. Tighten the nuts securely.

12. Install by reversing these removal steps, noting the following.

13. Tighten the rear cowl fasteners. Don't overtighten the fasteners as the plastic mounting bosses may be damaged.

Storage Tray
Removal/Installation

1. Raise or remove the seat.
2. Remove the frame left-hand side cover (**Figure 60**).
3. Remove the storage tray cover (**Figure 61**).
4. Carefully pull out on the front edge and remove the protective cover (**Figure 62**) from the fuel injection control unit.
5. Insert a long screwdriver through the hole (A, **Figure 63**) in the storage compartment tray. Insert the screwdriver blade into the keeper on the electrical connector and move the handle toward the front of the bike (**Figure 64**).
6. Release the keeper, pull the electrical connector (**Figure 65**) toward the rear and disconnect it from the fuel injection control unit.

13

7. On models equipped with the BMW electronic alarm system, perform the following:

   a. Remove the screws (A, **Figure 66**) securing the alarm unit to the storage tray.

   b. Unhook the electrical wires from the clips (B, **Figure 63**) on the side of the storage tray.

   c. Pull the alarm wires out of the notch and grommet (C, **Figure 63**) at the front of the storage tray.

   d. Remove the alarm unit (D, **Figure 63**).

8. Pull the storage tray (along with the fuel injection unit) up and out of the frame (B, **Figure 66**) and remove it.

9. To remove the control unit from the storage tray, perform the following:

   a. Remove the locking pins securing the control unit to the storage tray. Refer to **Figure 67** and **Figure 68**.

   b. Slide the control unit out of the storage tray.

   c. Reinstall the control unit into the storage tray.

   d. Insert the locking pins (**Figure 69**) from the bottom and make sure they go all the way into the rubber holders at the front and rear of the control unit.

10. Inspect the bottom surface of the storage tray (**Figure 70**) for damage. If damaged, replace the storage tray as it must be able to securely hold the control unit to protect it from any damage.

11. Install by reversing these removal steps, noting the following.

12. Make sure to route the electrical cable correctly so that it won't get pinched or damaged in any way.

13. Make sure the electrical connector is free of corrosion and is tight.

BODY PANELS
(K75 MODELS)

Radiator Trim Panel
Removal/Installation

Refer to **Figure 71** for this procedure.

1. Carefully pull out at the rear corner (**Figure 72**) of the radiator trim panel on each side. This will disengage the tab on the trim panel from the rubber grommet on the fuel tank.

67

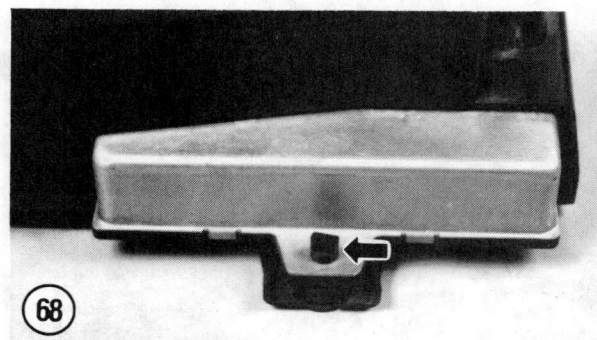

68

69

70

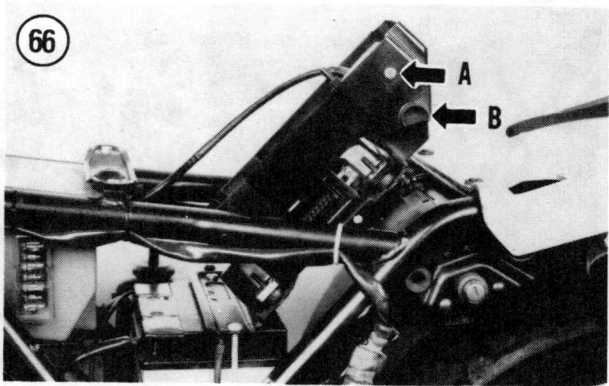

66

2. Pull the radiator trim panel forward to clear the frame and remove the panel out through one side of the frame.

3. To separate the radiator trim panel halves, perform the following:

a. Remove the mesh grille from the backside of the panels.

b. Remove the bolt, nut and washer securing the 2 halves together at the top.

c. Remove the clip at the bottom of the 2 halves.

d. Separate the 2 halves.

e. Assemble the 2 halves by reversing these steps.

4. Install by reversing these removal steps, noting the following.

5. Make sure the rubber grommets (**Figure 73**) are in place on the mounting tabs on the fuel tank.

6. Make sure to install the trim panel and engage the rubber grommets into the receptacles in the backside of the trim panel. This is necessary to support the front of the trim panel.

(71)

**RADIATOR TRIM PANEL
(K75 MODELS)**

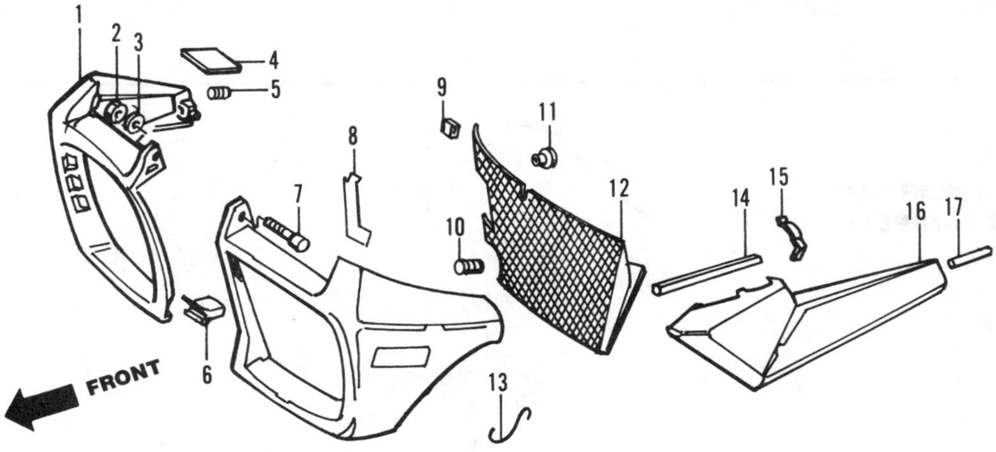

FRONT

1. Radiator trim panel
2. Nut
3. Washer
4. Foil patch
5. Grommet
6. Clip
7. Bolt
8. Grid
9. Clip
10. Grommet
11. Screw
12. Mesh grille
13. Hook
14. Edge trim
15. Spring
16. Cover
17. Bushing

13

Front Fairing (K75C)
Removal/Installation

Refer to **Figure 74** for this procedure. The illustrations show the left-hand cover panel and bracket. The right-hand components are an exact mirror image and both parts are the same.

1. Remove the frame left-hand side cover.
2. Disconnect the battery negative lead as described under *Battery* in Chapter Three.
3. Remove the Phillips head screws and Allen screws and washers on the backside of the fairing.
4. Carefully pull the front fairing out from the cover panels and disconnect the electrical connectors for the turn signals.
5. Remove the front fairing from the cover panels.
6. If necessary, remove the screws, washers and nuts securing the cover panels and brackets onto the fork tubes. Remove the cover panels and brackets.

7. Install by reversing these removal steps, noting the following.
8. Tighten the screws and nuts securely. Don't overtighten the screws or nuts as the plastic mounting bosses may be damaged.

Front Fairing (K75S)
Removal/Installation

Refer to **Figure 75** and **Figure 76** for this procedure. The illustrations show the left-hand side panel and lower trim panel. The right-hand components are an exact mirror image and both parts are the same.

1. Remove the frame left-hand side cover.
2. Disconnect the battery negative lead as described under *Battery* in Chapter Three.
3. Remove the screws and washers securing the windshield and remove the windshield and the gasket on each side.

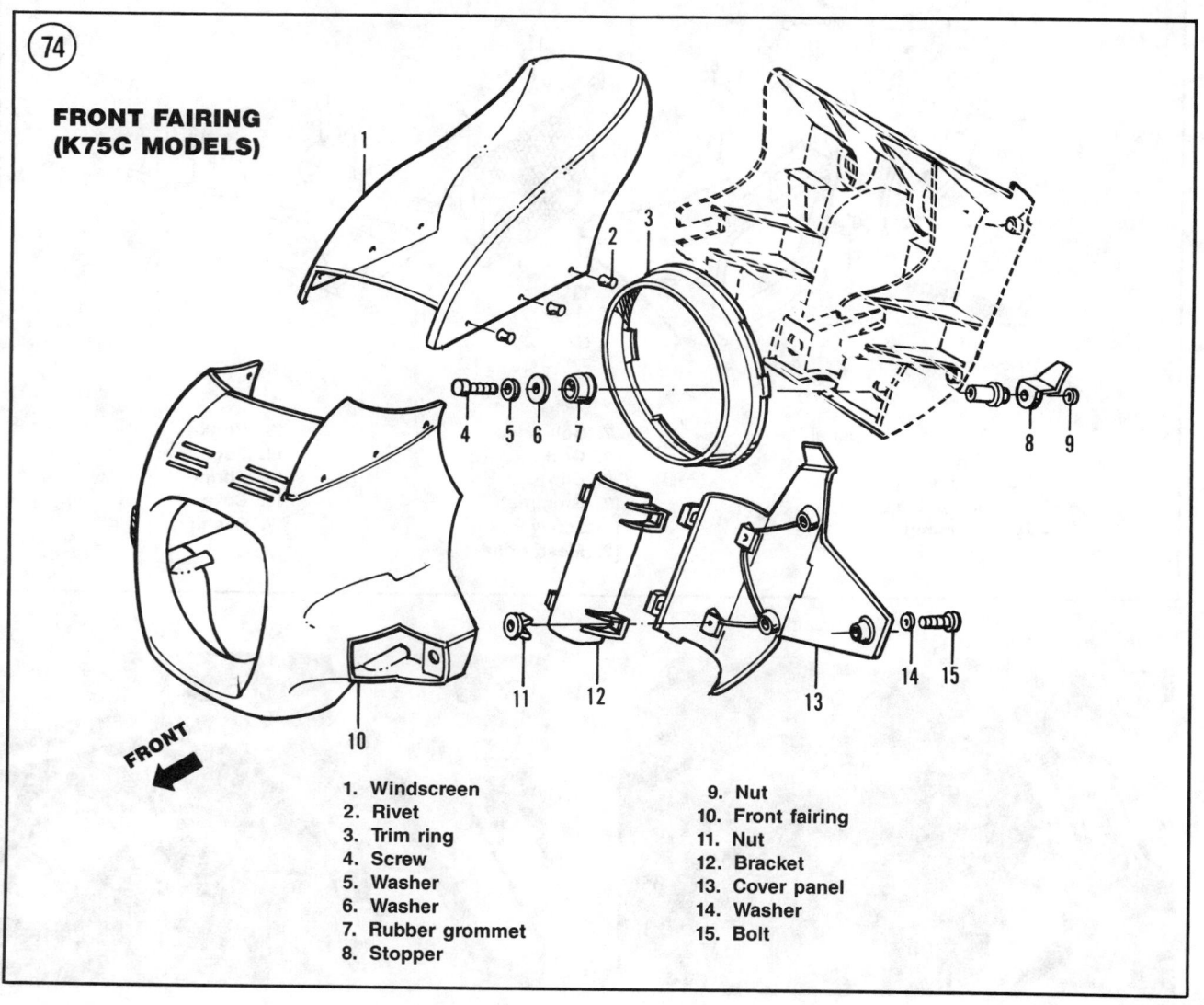

(74)

**FRONT FAIRING
(K75C MODELS)**

FRONT

1. Windscreen
2. Rivet
3. Trim ring
4. Screw
5. Washer
6. Washer
7. Rubber grommet
8. Stopper
9. Nut
10. Front fairing
11. Nut
12. Bracket
13. Cover panel
14. Washer
15. Bolt

4. Remove the screws securing the radiator trim panel and remove the trim panel.

5. At the front center of both side panels, remove the screw and collar holding both side panels together.

6. Remove the screws securing the side panels to the center panel.

7. Remove the screw securing the turn signal housing and pull the housing out of the side panel. Disconnect the electrical connector and remove the turn signal housing. Repeat for the other side.

8. Unscrew the side panel upper mounting screw in the turn signal area.

9. Remove the screw and washer on each side securing the center cover to the side panel.

10. Remove the screw securing the lower trim panel to the side panel and remove the lower trim panel. Repeat for the other side.

11. Remove the bolt securing the side panel to the side panel mounting bracket.

12. Remove the side panel. Don't lose the rubber grommet and metal collar from the mounting hole in the side panel. Repeat for the other side.

13. Remove the bolt and screw on each side securing the center panel and remove the center panel.

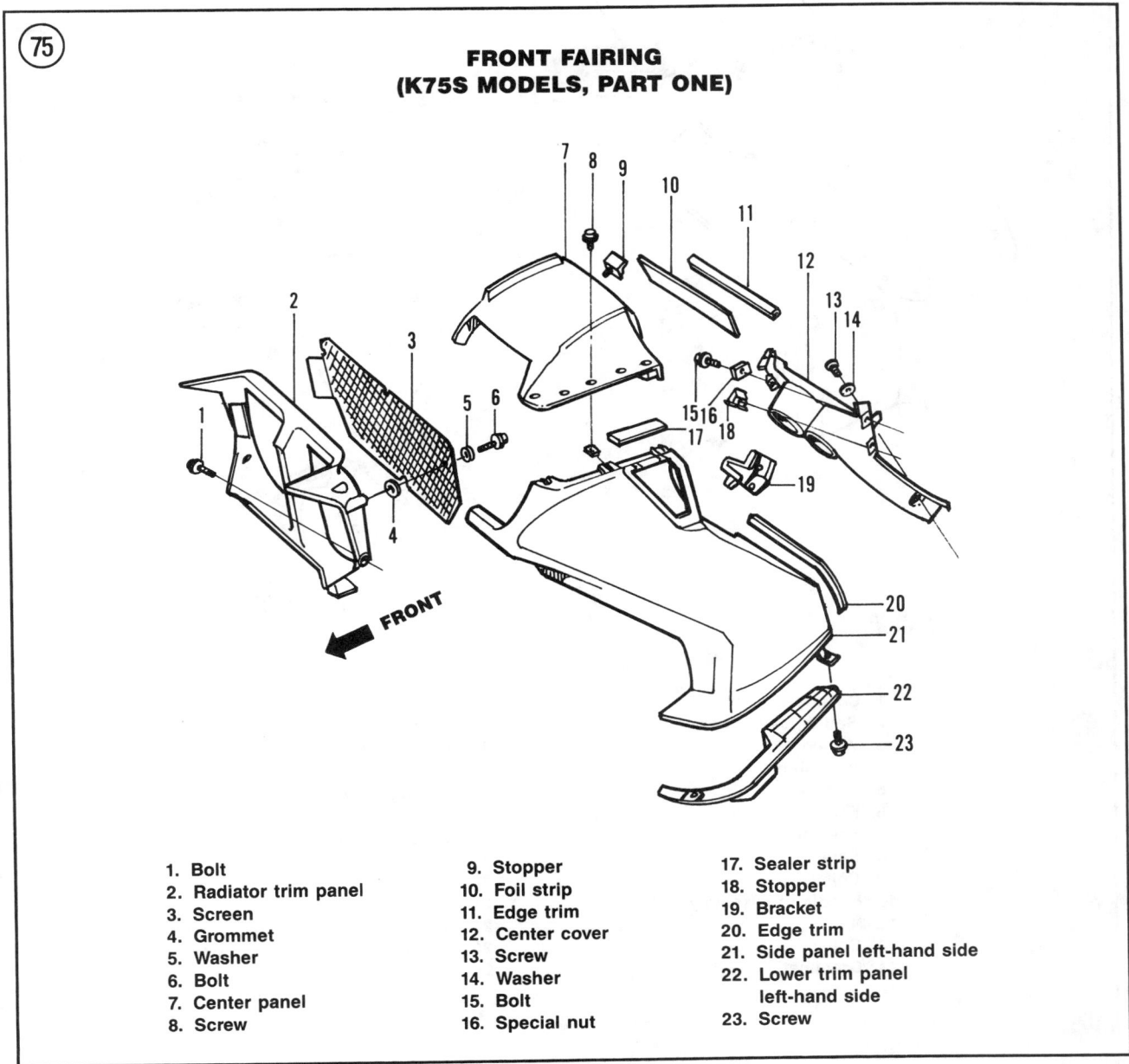

FRONT FAIRING (K75S MODELS, PART ONE)

1. Bolt
2. Radiator trim panel
3. Screen
4. Grommet
5. Washer
6. Bolt
7. Center panel
8. Screw
9. Stopper
10. Foil strip
11. Edge trim
12. Center cover
13. Screw
14. Washer
15. Bolt
16. Special nut
17. Sealer strip
18. Stopper
19. Bracket
20. Edge trim
21. Side panel left-hand side
22. Lower trim panel left-hand side
23. Screw

13

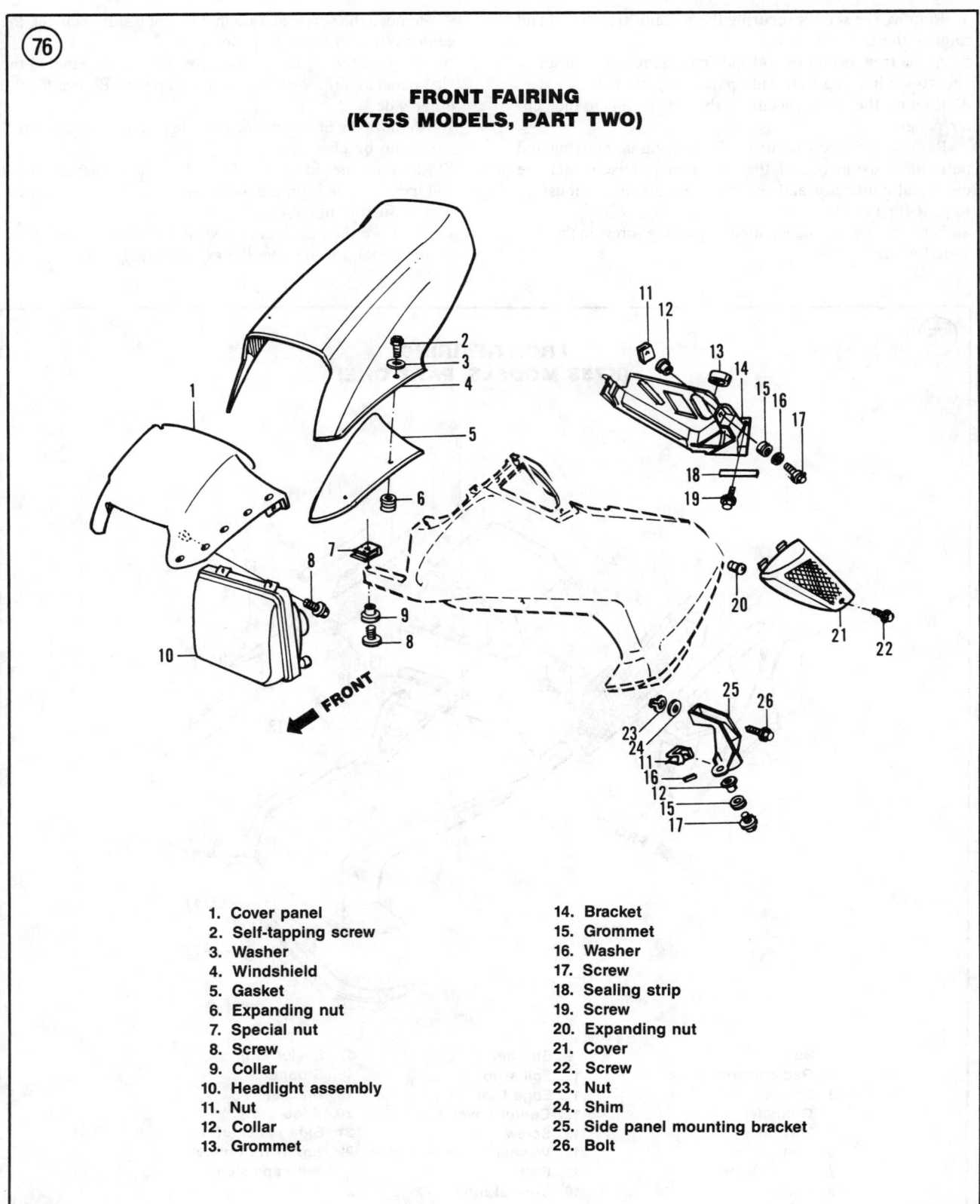

**FRONT FAIRING
(K75S MODELS, PART TWO)**

1. Cover panel
2. Self-tapping screw
3. Washer
4. Windshield
5. Gasket
6. Expanding nut
7. Special nut
8. Screw
9. Collar
10. Headlight assembly
11. Nut
12. Collar
13. Grommet
14. Bracket
15. Grommet
16. Washer
17. Screw
18. Sealing strip
19. Screw
20. Expanding nut
21. Cover
22. Screw
23. Nut
24. Shim
25. Side panel mounting bracket
26. Bolt

14. Install by reversing these removal steps, noting the following.

15. Be sure to use the metal collar in the plastic mounting boss on the lower mount of the side panel on each side. If the collar is not in place and the bolt and nut are tightened, the plastic mounting boss will be damaged and the side panel will have to be replaced. Don't overtighten the bolts as the plastic mounting bosses may be damaged even with the metal collars in place.

16. Tighten the screws, bolts and nuts securing the components securely.

Engine Spoiler (K75C)
Removal/Installation

Refer to **Figure 77** for this procedure. The illustration shows the left-hand engine spoiler panel. The right-hand component is an exact mirror image and the procedure is the same.

1. From underneath the front of the engine spoiler, remove the bolt, lockwasher and washer on each side securing the engine spoiler to the top of the engine.

2. Pull the engine spoiler assembly forward and disengage it from the rear mounting bracket.

3. Remove the engine spoiler from the engine.

4. To separate the engine spoiler, perform the following:
   a. Remove the screw on each side securing the mesh grille and remove the mesh grille from the backside of both panels.
   b. Remove the bolts and washers securing the 2 halves together at the front and rear.
   c. Separate the 2 halves.
   d. Assemble the 2 halves by reversing these steps.

5. Install by reversing these removal steps, noting the following.

6. Be sure to use the metal collar in the plastic mounting boss on the front mount of the engine spoiler on each side. If the collar is not in place and the bolt and nut are tightened, the plastic mounting boss will be damaged and the engine spoiler panel will have to be replaced. Don't overtighten the bolts as the plastic mounting bosses may be damaged even with the metal collars in place.

7. Tighten the bolts and nuts securing the components securely.

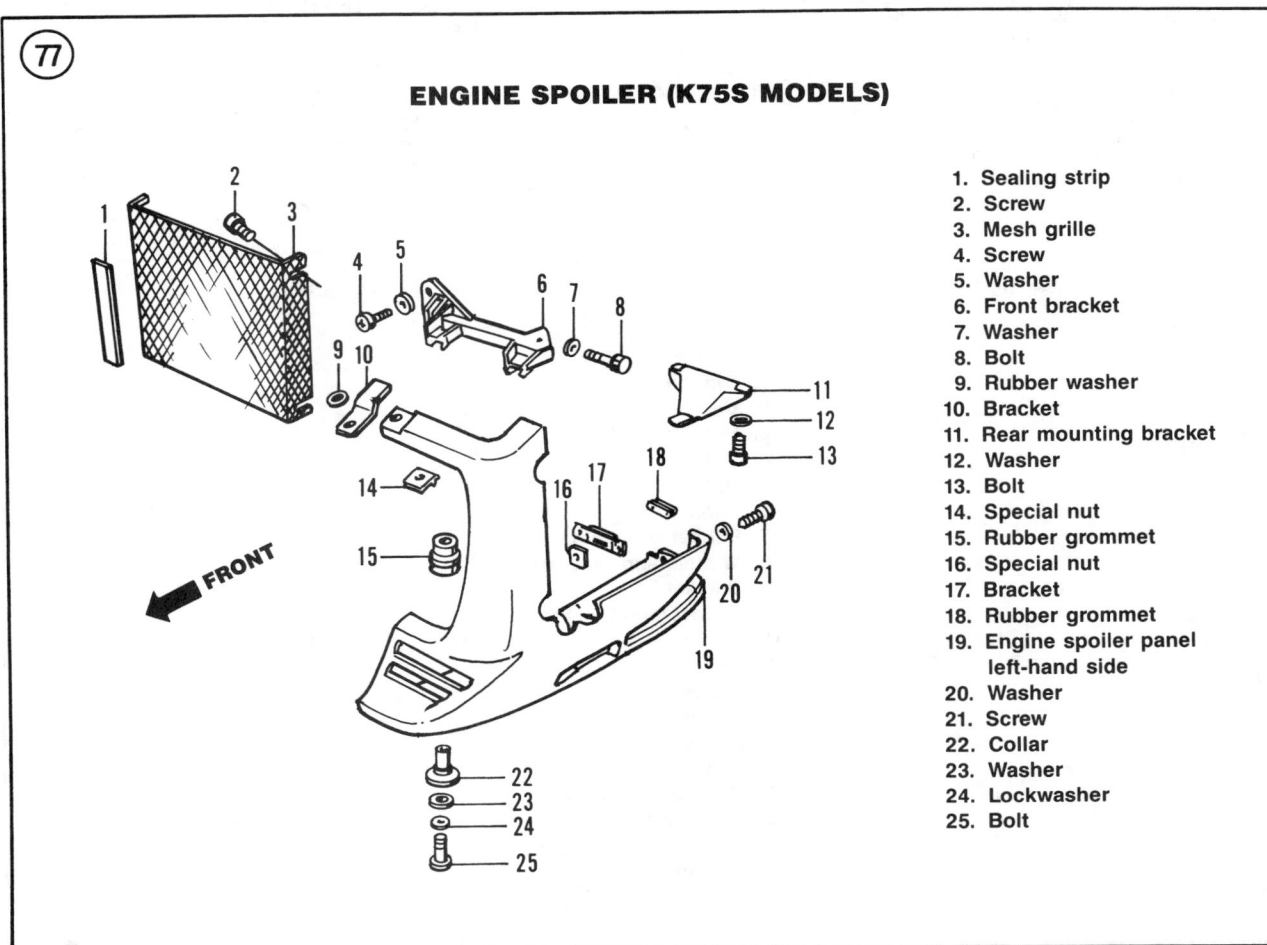

⑦

ENGINE SPOILER (K75S MODELS)

1. Sealing strip
2. Screw
3. Mesh grille
4. Screw
5. Washer
6. Front bracket
7. Washer
8. Bolt
9. Rubber washer
10. Bracket
11. Rear mounting bracket
12. Washer
13. Bolt
14. Special nut
15. Rubber grommet
16. Special nut
17. Bracket
18. Rubber grommet
19. Engine spoiler panel
    left-hand side
20. Washer
21. Screw
22. Collar
23. Washer
24. Lockwasher
25. Bolt

FRONT

13

HEADLIGHT FAIRING
(BASE K100 MODELS)

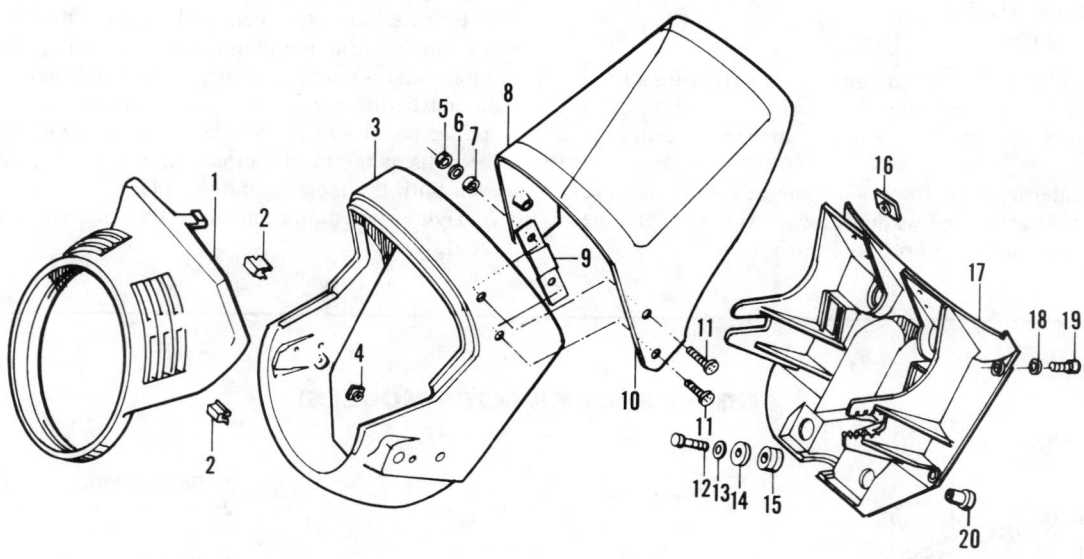

1. Trim piece
2. Clip
3. Headlight fairing
4. Nut
5. Nut
6. Bushing
7. Rubber grommet
8. Windscreen (optional)
9. Bracket
10. Windscreen bracket
11. Screw
12. Bolt
13. Lockwasher
14. Washer
15. Rubber grommet
16. Clip
17. Mounting bracket
18. Lockwasher
19. Bolt
20. Bushing

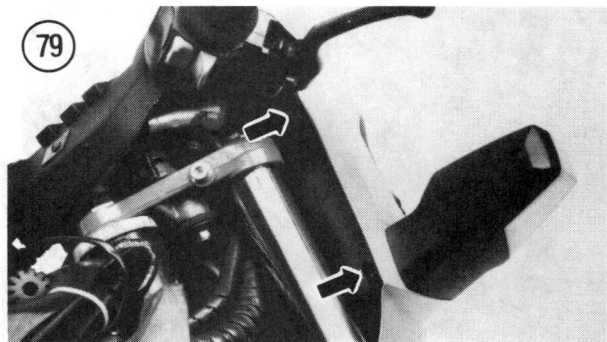

BODY PANELS
(K100 MODELS)

Headlight Fairing (Base K100)
Removal/Installation

Refer to **Figure 78** for this procedure.

1. Remove the frame left-hand side cover.

2. Disconnect the battery negative lead as described under *Battery* in Chapter Three.

3. Remove the screws and lockwashers (**Figure 79**) on each side of the backside of the fairing mounting panel.

4. Carefully pull the headlight fairing and trim panel (**Figure 80**) off of the mounting panel and headlight assembly.

5. Disconnect the electrical connectors for the turn signals and remove headlight fairing and trim panel.

6. Loosen the headlight mounting bolt (**Figure 81**) on each side.

7. Carefully pull the headlight assembly (**Figure 82**) forward and out of the mounting panel.

8. Disconnect the electrical connector (A, **Figure 83**) from the base of the headlight and remove the headlight.

9. Disconnect the electrical connector to each horn.

10. Remove the bolts (B, **Figure 83**) securing each horn and remove the horns.

11. Remove the screw securing the electrical connector cover panel (**Figure 84**) and remove the cover panel.

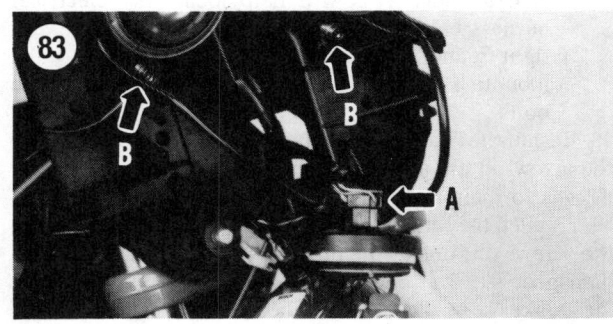

13

12. Carefully disconnect the electrical connectors (**Figure 85**) from the instrument cluster.

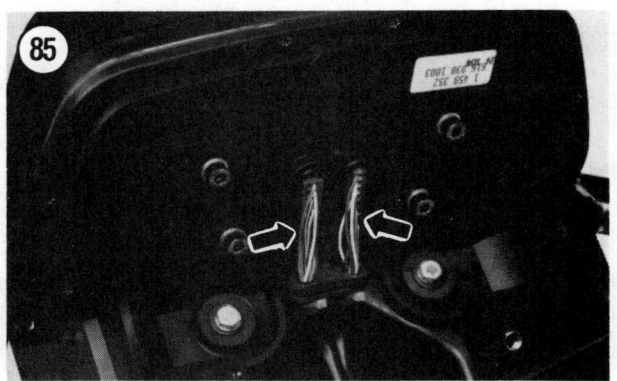

NOTE
The mounting panel can be removed with the
instrument cluster attached or removed.

13. If necessary, remove the bolts and washers (A, **Figure 86**) securing the instrument cluster to the mounting panel and remove the instrument cluster (B, **Figure 86**).

14. Remove the bolts, lockwashers and washers (A, **Figure 87**) securing the mounting panel to the upper and lower fork bridges.

15. Carefully pull the mounting panel away and feed the electrical wires out through the opening (B, **Figure 87**) in the mounting panel.

16. Install by reversing these removal steps, noting the following.

17. When installing the mounting panel to the upper and lower fork bridges, perform the following:

   a. Move the electrical harness to one side behind the mounting panel.

   b. Install the mounting bolts and washers and tighten in a crisscross pattern.

   c. While tightening the bolts, move the handlebar from side to side. This will help locate the electrical harness behind the mounting panel. This is a very tight fit and if the harness isn't properly located, the mounting panel may be damaged while tightening the bolts.

18. Install the headlight assembly and align the arrow with the arrow on the mounting tab (**Figure 88**) on each side. This is to maintain correct horizontal headlight aim.

19. Tighten the screws and bolts securely. Don't overtighten the screws or bolts as the plastic mounting bosses may be damaged.

20. Make sure the electrical connectors are free of corrosion and are tight.

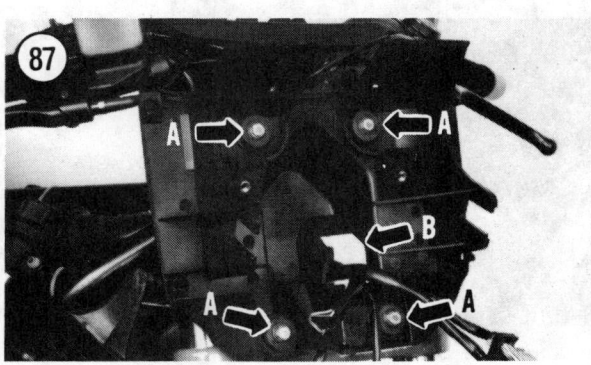

Radiator Trim Panel (K100)
Removal/Installation

Refer to **Figure 89** for this procedure.

1. Remove the screws and washers (A, **Figure 90**) securing the left-hand side panel to the radiator trim panel.

2. Carefully pull out at the rear corner (B, **Figure 90**) of the left-hand side panel. This will disengage the tab on the trim panel from the rubber grommet on the fuel tank.

3. Remove the left-hand side panel.

NOTE
The right-hand side panel remains attached to
the radiator trim panel during removal.

(89)

RADIATOR TRIM PANEL
(K100 MODELS)

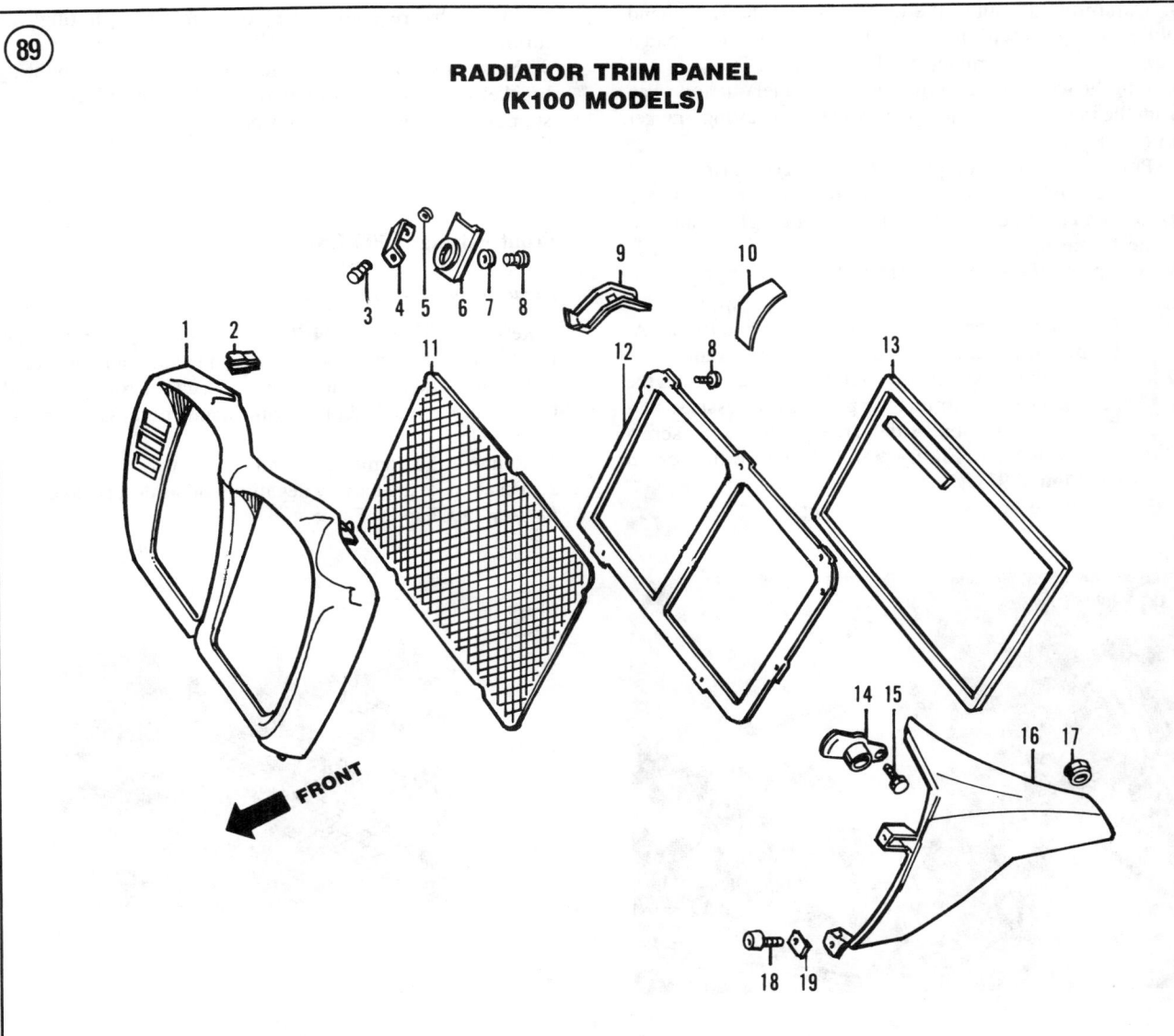

FRONT

1. Radiator trim panel
2. Clip
3. Screw
4. Bracket
5. Nut
6. Mounting bracket
7. Lockwasher
8. Screw
9. Bracket
10. Foil strip

11. Screen
12. Frame
13. Gasket
14. Mounting bracket
15. Screw
16. Side panel
    left-hand side
17. Rubber grommet
18. Screw
19. Special nut

13

4. Carefully pull out at the rear corner of the right-hand side panel. This will disengage the tab on the trim panel from the rubber grommet on the fuel tank.

5. Pull the front of the right-hand trim panel out and away from the radiator to disengage it from the mounting bracket on the radiator.

6. Pull the radiator trim panel (**Figure 91**) and right-hand side panel slightly forward to clear the radiator, then move it down and remove the panel out from the right-hand side of the frame.

7. To replace the screen, perform the following:

   a. Remove the screws securing the screen and frame (A, **Figure 92**) and remove the screen and frame.

   b. Inspect the gasket material (B, **Figure 92**) around the perimeter of the frame. Replace as necessary.

   c. To remove the small side screen, remove the screw and washer (A, **Figure 93**) and remove the screen (B, **Figure 93**).

   d. Assemble by reversing these steps.

8. Install by reversing the removal steps, noting the following.

9. Make sure to install the side panels onto the mounting brackets attached to the radiator. This is necessary to support the front of the trim panel.

Front Fairing (K100 RS)

Removal/installation

Refer to **Figures 94-96** for this procedure. The illustrations show mainly the left-hand panels and brackets. The right-hand components are an exact mirror image and both parts are attached in the same manner unless otherwise specified.

1. Remove the frame left-hand side cover.

2. Disconnect the battery negative lead as described under *Battery* in Chapter Three.

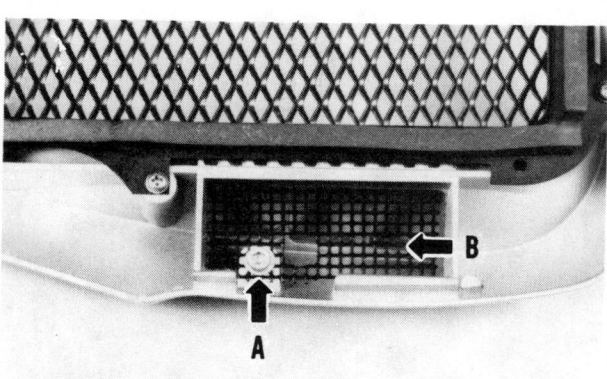

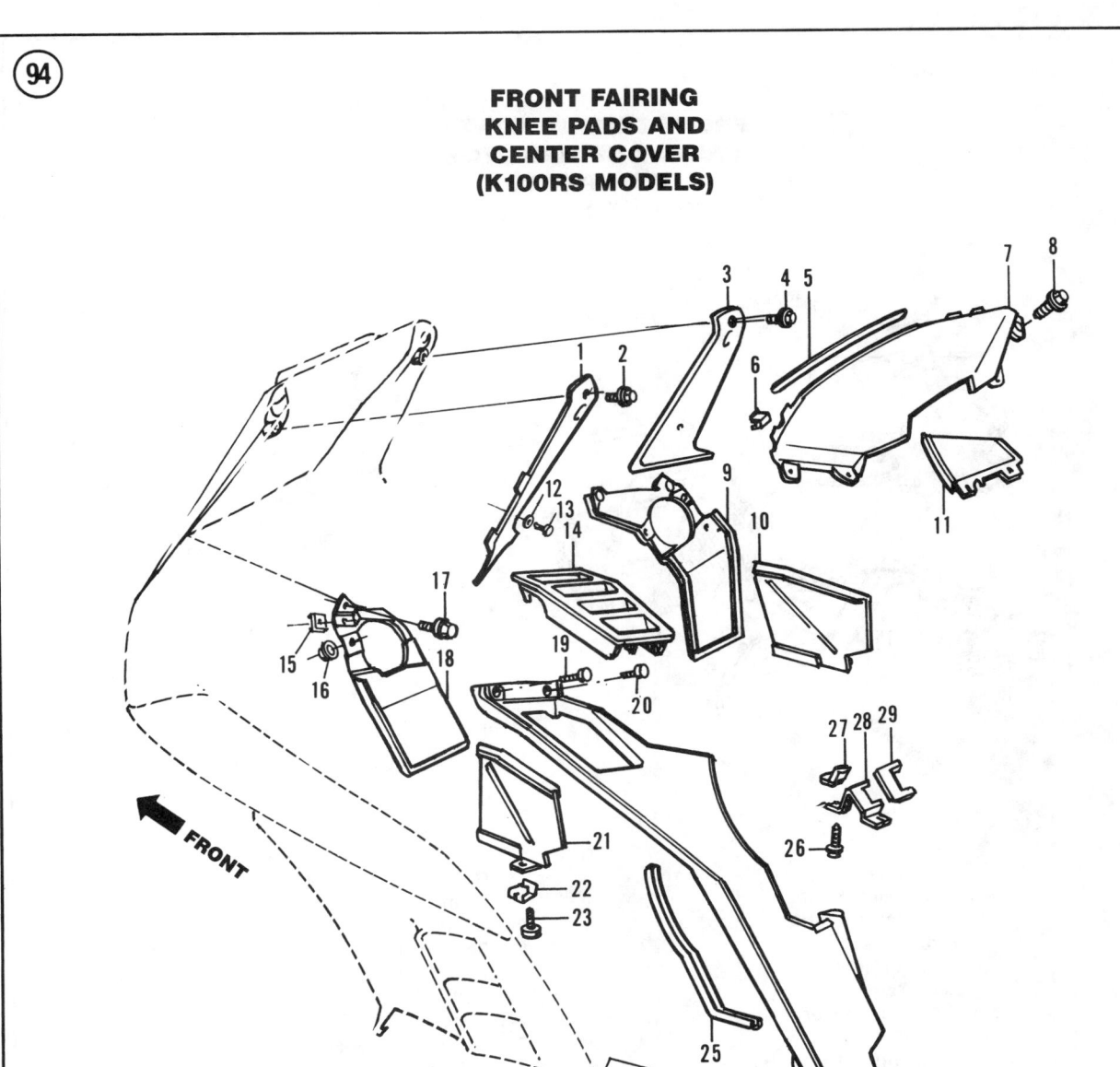

94

**FRONT FAIRING
KNEE PADS AND
CENTER COVER
(K100RS MODELS)**

FRONT

1. Wing panel	11. Upper cover	21. Inner trim panel
2. Screw	12. Washer	22. Special nut
3. Wing panel	13. Screw	23. Bolt
4. Screw	14. Cover	24. Screw
5. Gasket	15. Nut	25. Gasket
6. Clip	16. Nut	26. Screw
7. Center cover	17. Bolt	27. Special nut
8. Bolt	18. Inner trim panel	28. Bracket
9. Inner trim panel	19. Screw	29. Bracket
10. Inner trim panel	20. Screw	

13

FRONT FAIRING LOWER PANEL AND RADIATOR TRIM PANEL (K100RS MODELS)

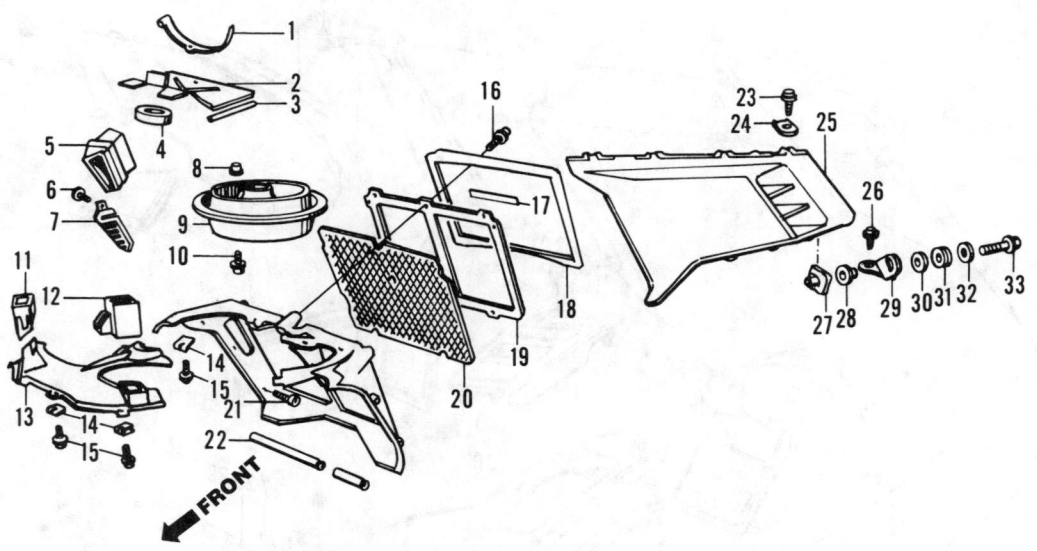

1. Cable strap	18. Gasket
2. Sealant panel	19. Frame
3. Sealant strip	20. Screen
4. Gasket	21. Radiator trim panel
5. Air intake	22. Gasket
6. Screw	23. Bolt
7. Side louver	24. Special nut
8. Nut	25. Lower side panel
9. Fork tube rubber boot	left-hand side
10. Screw	26. Screw
11. Horn guide channel	27. Special nut
12. Horn guide channel	28. Metal collar
13. Center panel	29. Bracket
14. Special nut	30. Rubber grommet
15. Screw	31. Rubber grommet
16. Screw	32. Washer
17. Foil strip	33. Bolt

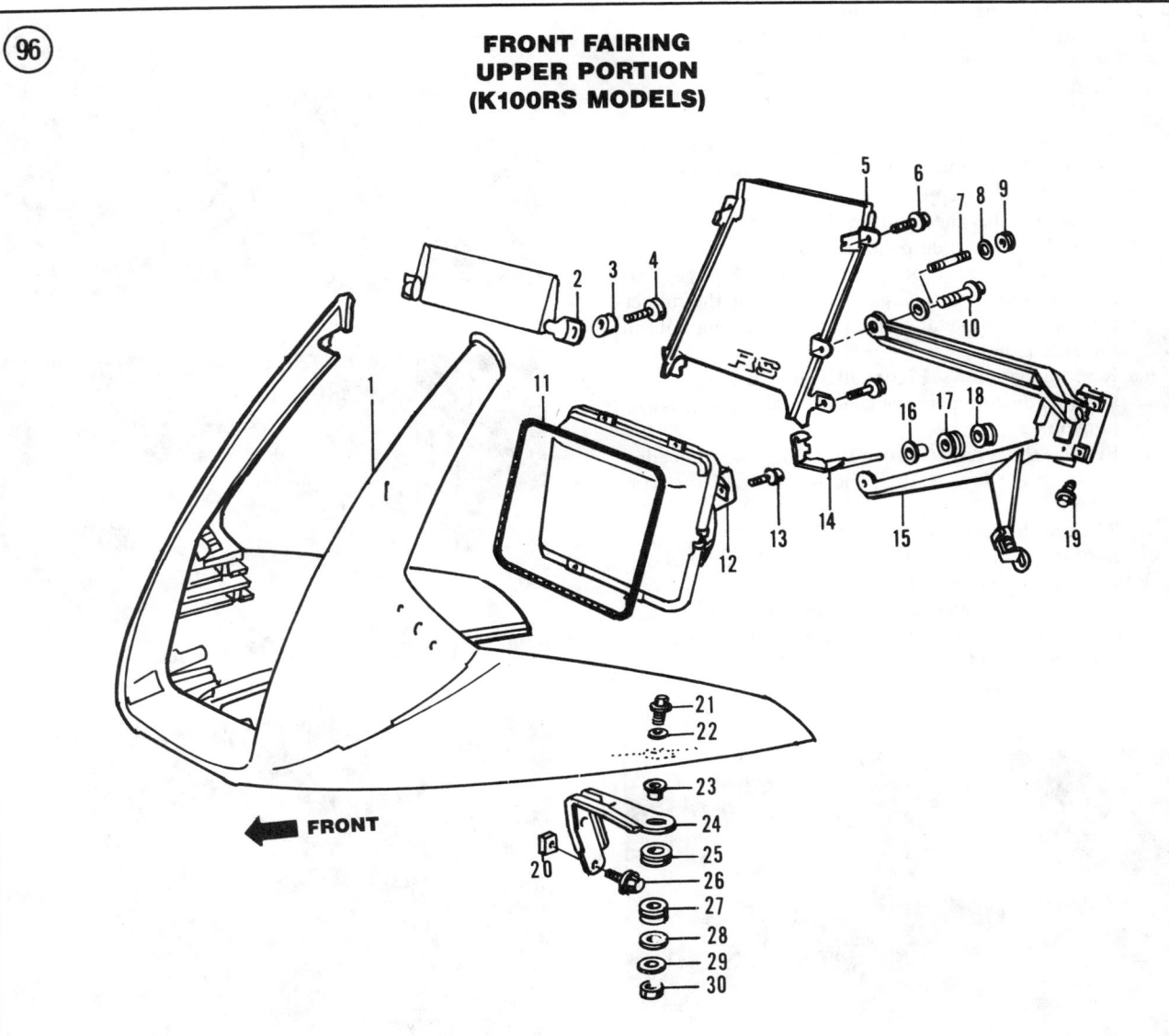

96

**FRONT FAIRING
UPPER PORTION
(K100RS MODELS)**

FRONT

1. Front fairing upper portion
2. Deflector
3. Clamp
4. Bolt
5. Windscreen
6. Bolt
7. Threaded stud
8. Washer
9. Nut
10. Bolt

11. Gasket
12. Headlight
13. Bolt
14. Bracket
15. Fairing mounting bracket
16. Bushing
17. Rubber grommet
18. Rubber grommet
19. Screw
20. Nut

21. Bolt
22. Washer
23. Bushing
24. Bracket
25. Rubber grommet
26. Bolt
27. Rubber grommet
28. Washer
29. Lockwasher
30. Nut

13

3. Remove the knee pads as follows:
   a. Remove the single screw (**Figure 97**) at the bottom of the knee pad.
   b. Remove the screws (**Figure 98**) at the top of the knee pad.
   c. Unhook the clip at the mid-point of the knee pad, then carefully remove the knee pad (**Figure 99**) from the front fairing upper portion and lower side panel.
   d. Repeat for the knee pad on the other side.
4. Remove the lower side panel as follows:
   a. Remove the lower bolt and washer (**Figure 100**) securing the lower side panel. Don't lose the rubber grommets and metal collar in the mounting hole in the side panel.
   b. Remove the screws (**Figure 101**) along the upper edge securing the lower side panel to the front fairing upper portion.
   c. Remove the screws (**Figure 102**) along the front edge securing the lower side panel to the radiator trim panel.
   d. Remove the lower side panel (**Figure 103**).
   e. Repeat for the lower trim panel on the other side.
5. Remove the radiator trim panel as follows:
   a. Remove the screws securing the front fork rubber boots (**Figure 104**) and slide the boots down (A, **Figure 105**) on the fork tubes and away from the radiator trim panel upper center panel.

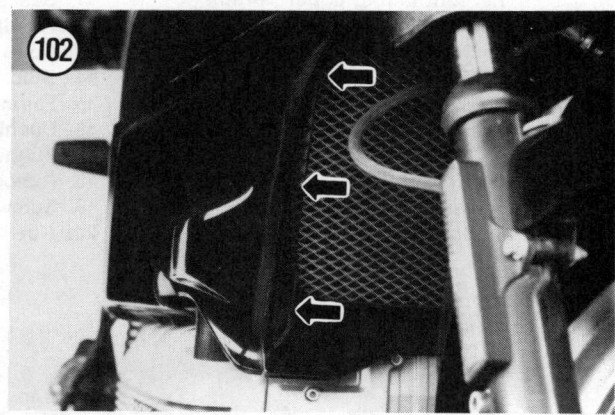

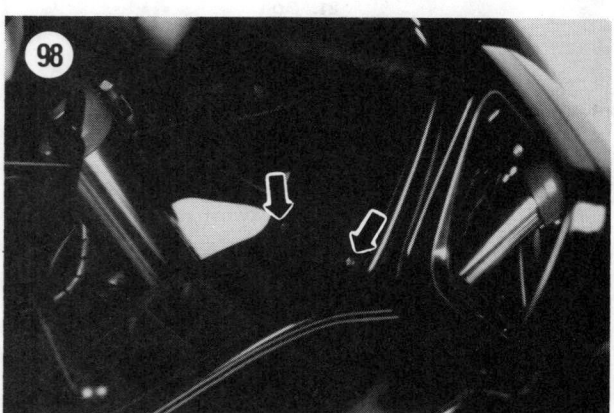

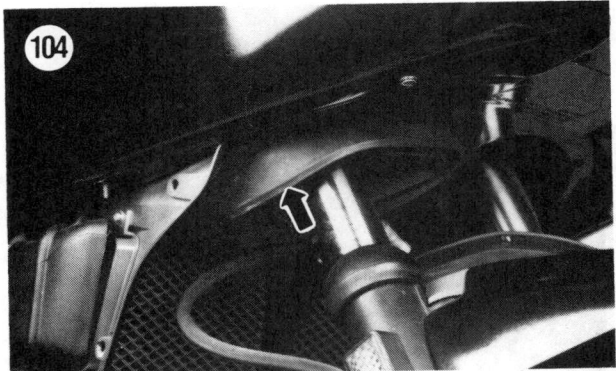

b. Hold onto the radiator trim panel and remove the screws securing the radiator trim panel to the front fairing upper portion (B, **Figure 105**).

c. Pull out on the lower portion of the radiator trim panel (**Figure 106**) and carefully remove the radiator trim panel.

NOTE
The mirrors are not attached mechanically (i.e. no bolts and nuts) and are designed to break away if hit hard enough. They are attached with rounded end studs on the outer mounting plate that fit into undersized holes in the housing rubber gasket.

6. Remove the rear view mirrors as described in this chapter.

7. Carefully lift up on the small upper covers (**Figure 107**) and unhook them from the center cover.

8. Remove the bolts securing the wing panel (**Figure 108**) and remove the wing panel. Repeat for the other side.

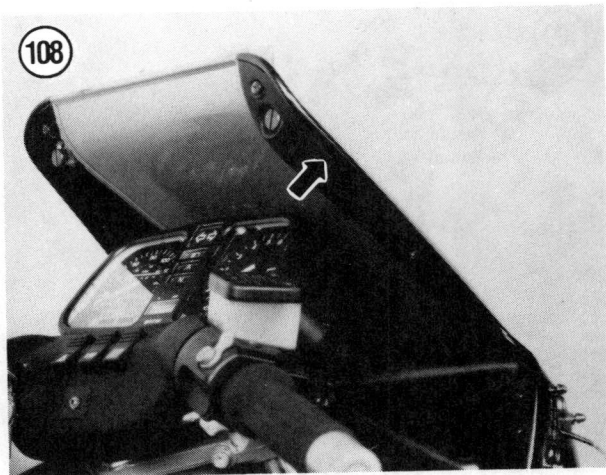

13

9. Remove the bolts securing the center cover (**Figure 109**) and remove the center cover.

10. Remove the bolts securing the inner trim panel (**Figure 110**) and remove the trim panel. Repeat for the other side.

11. Loosen the horn mounting nuts and pivot the horns up and out of the way.

12. Remove the screw securing the horn guide channel and remove the guide channel. Repeat for the other side.

13. Disconnect the headlight and turn signal electrical connectors from the main wiring harness.

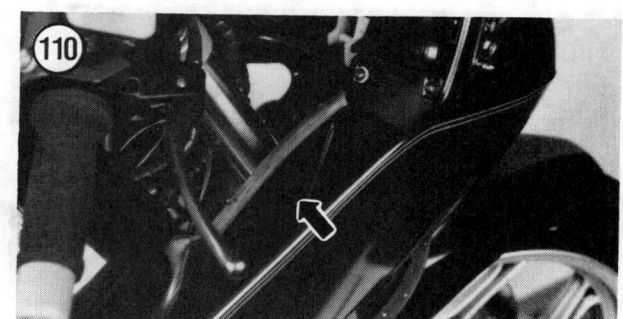

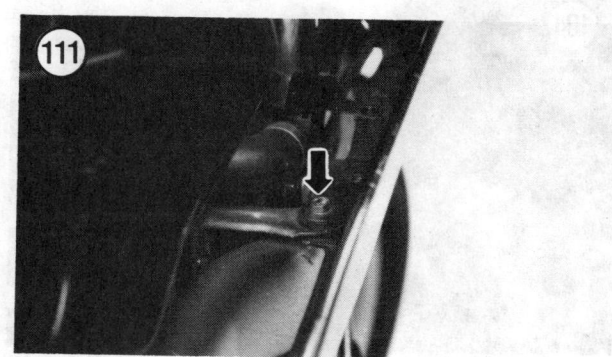

NOTE
The next step requires the aid of an assistant. The fairing is not heavy, but it is difficult to hold in place while removing the mounting bolts and nuts.

14. Have an assistant hold onto the front of the front fairing and perform the following:

   a. Remove the side bolt (**Figure 111**) on each side securing the front fairing upper portion to the side mounting bracket.

   b. Remove the upper bolt (**Figure 112**) on each side securing the front fairing upper portion to the mounting bracket.

   c. Remove the middle bolt on each side securing the front fairing middle portion to the mounting bracket.

   d. To protect the finish, place a couple of blankets on the workbench or floor for the front fairing to sit on after removal.

   e. Carefully pull the front fairing forward (**Figure 113**) and remove the front fairing from the mounting bracket and set in on the blankets.

15. If necessary, remove the bolts securing the mounting bracket (**Figure 114**) to the frame and remove the mounting bracket.

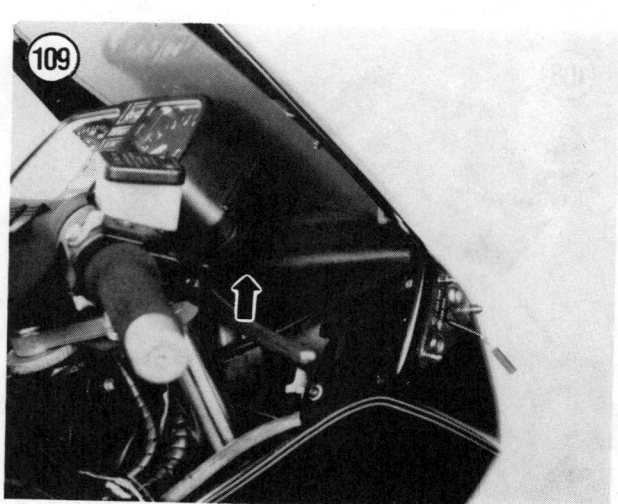

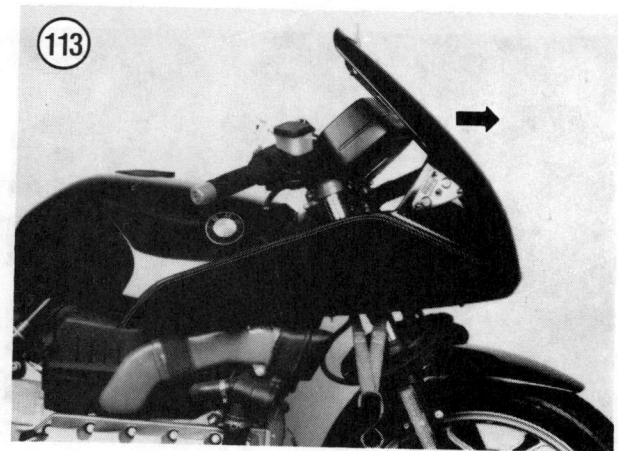

16. If any components require replacement, refer to *Component Removal/installation* in this chapter.

17. Install by reversing these removal steps, noting the following.

18. Tighten the screws and nuts securely. Don't overtighten the screws or nuts as the plastic mounting bosses may be damaged.

19. Make sure all electrical connectors are free of corrosion and are tight.

Component removal/installation

1. To replace the radiator trim panel screen, perform the following:
   a. Remove the screws securing the screen and frame (A, **Figure 115**) and remove the screen and frame.
   b. Inspect the gasket material (B, **Figure 115**) around the perimeter of the frame. Replace as necessary.
   c. Assemble by reversing these steps.

2. To remove the air intake side louver, remove the screws (**Figure 116**) securing the louver and remove the louver. Install and tighten the screws securely.

3. To remove the center panel from the front fairing upper panel, remove the screws (A, **Figure 117**) securing the center panel (B, **Figure 117**) and remove the center panel. Install and tighten the screws securely.

4. To remove the headlight assembly from the front fairing upper panel, remove the screws (A, **Figure 118**) securing the headlight assembly (B, **Figure 118**) and remove the headlight assembly. Install and tighten the screws securely.

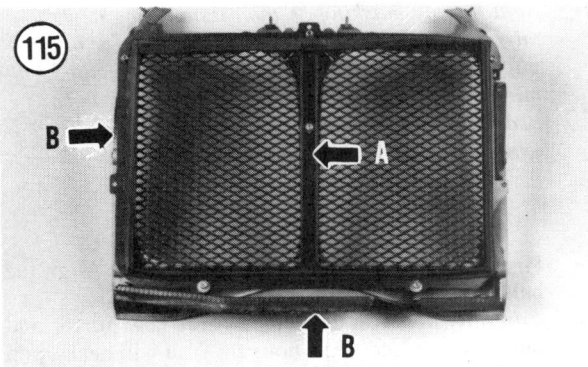

Front Fairing Mirror Assembly (K100RS) Removal/Installation

Refer to **Figure 119** for this procedure.

These illustrations show the left-hand mirror assembly. The right-hand components are an exact mirror image and the parts are attached in the same manner.

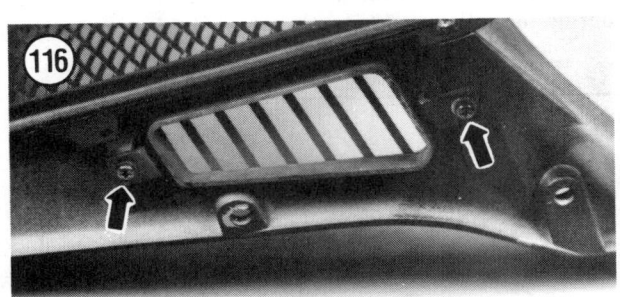

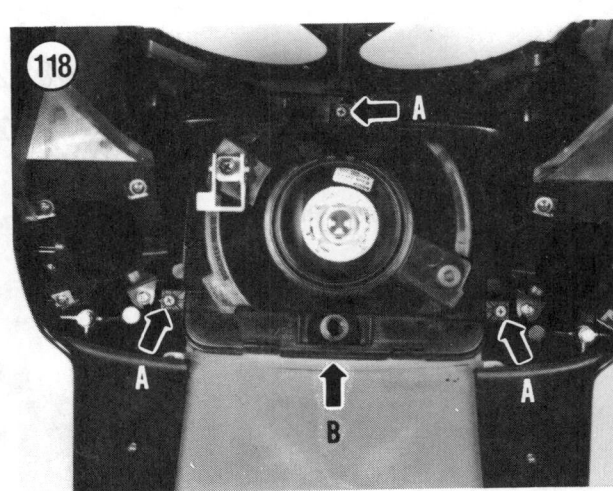

NOTE
The mirrors are not attached mechanically (i.e. no bolts and nuts) and are designed to break away if hit hard enough. They are attached with studs on the outer mounting plate that fit into mounting clips in the housing.

NOTE
If only the mirror portion of the assembly is to be replaced, do not remove the mirror assembly, as the front fairing is a great holding fixture. The mirror portion snaps into place in a socket in the housing. For mirror replacement only, refer to Step 1. To remove the complete assembly, refer to Step 2.

1. To replace only the mirror portion of the mirror assembly, perform the following.
   a. Push on the top portion of the glass mirror until it stops. This will leave a gap at the bottom of the glass.
   b. To protect the housing finish, place a doubled-over shop cloth (A, **Figure 120**) on the housing lower surface.

WARNING
*Apply masking or duct tape (B, **Figure 120**) to the mirror surface. This will lessen the chance of glass popping out during the removal step. Also wear eye protection and heavy gloves.*

Protect yourself accordingly while working with glass.

   c. Using a wide flat-bladed screwdriver or flat pry bar (C, **Figure 120**), *carefully* pry out on the bottom surface of the mirror until it pops out of the ball and socket. Remove the mirror from the housing.
   d. Don't apply any type of lubricant to the ball or socket joint as this may make the joint too loose to maintain the mirror in a fixed position while riding.

WARNING
Again apply masking or duct tape to the new mirror surface. This will lessen the chance of glass popping out during installation if the mirror breaks. Also wear eye protection and heavy gloves. Protect yourself accordingly while working with glass.

   e. Position the new mirror into the housing. Align the ball and socket.
   f. *Carefully* press on the center of the new mirror and push it into place in the housing. You will hear a pop when the ball and socket snap into place.
2. Place one hand over the mirror assembly to catch it during the following step.

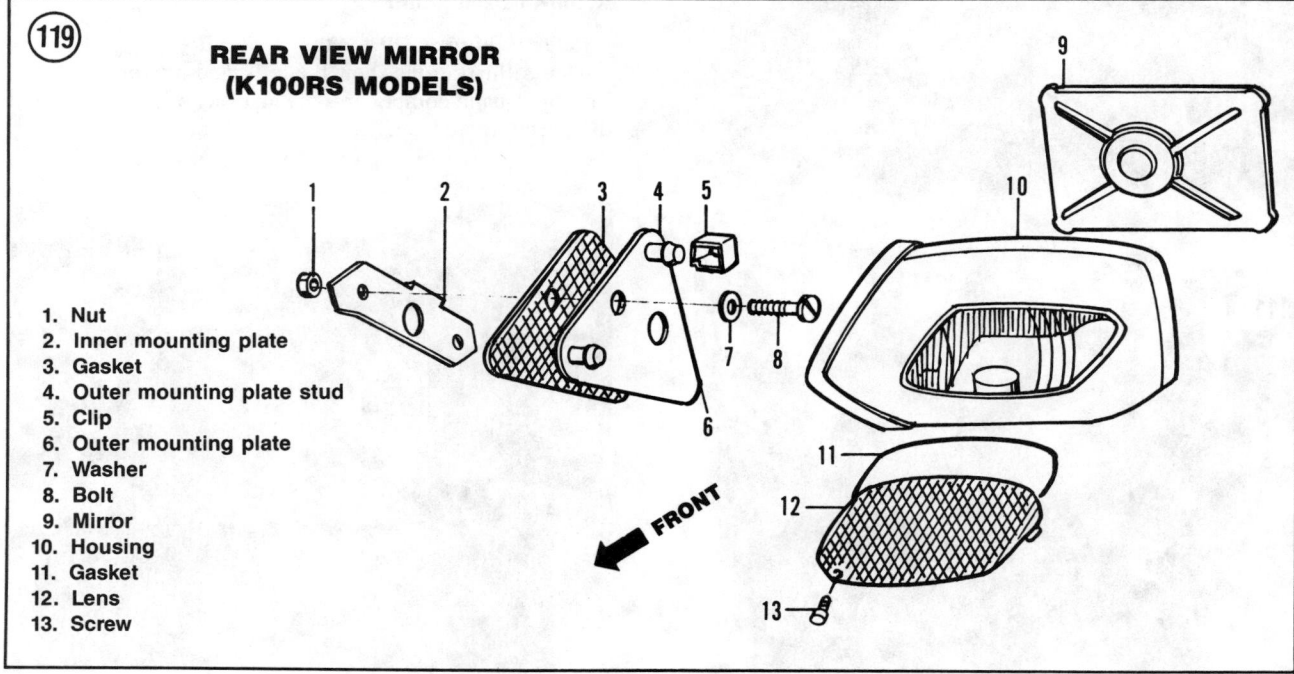

(119) **REAR VIEW MIRROR (K100RS MODELS)**

FRONT

1. Nut
2. Inner mounting plate
3. Gasket
4. Outer mounting plate stud
5. Clip
6. Outer mounting plate
7. Washer
8. Bolt
9. Mirror
10. Housing
11. Gasket
12. Lens
13. Screw

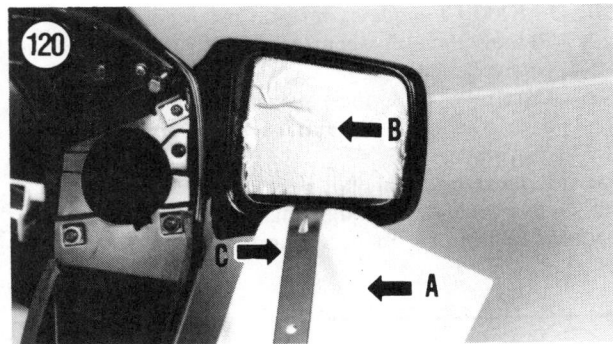

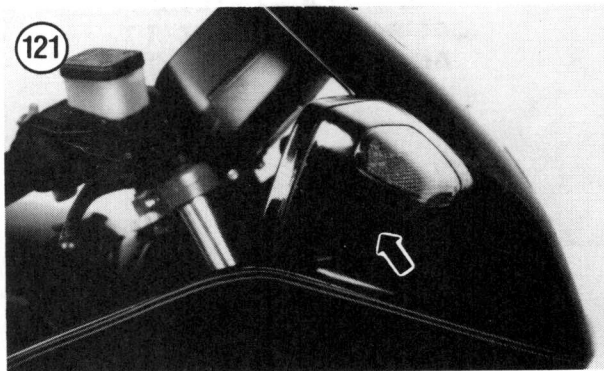

CAUTION
*In the next step, do **not** use any type of tool (e.g. mallet or plastic hammer) as it will not only damage the finish but could fracture the plastic housing—**use your hand only**.*

3. Apply small upward hits, or knocks, to the outer under side of the mirror housing (**Figure 121**) with the palm of your hand and break the mirror housing away from the outer mounting plate. Continue to hit the mirror until all studs are free from the housing mounting clips.

4. Carefully pull the mirror assembly away from the front fairing (**Figure 122**).

5. On K100 RS models, disconnect the turn signal electrical wire connectors (**Figure 123**).

6. Remove the rear view mirror assembly.

7. If necessary, remove the mounting bracket as follows:
   a. Remove the upper cover (**Figure 107**) or the storage compartment on each side. This is necessary to gain access to the nuts and the inner mounting brackets.
   b. Remove the bolts, washers (**Figure 124**) and nuts securing the mounting brackets to the front fairing.
   c. Remove the inner mounting bracket.
   d. Pull the outer mounting bracket and gasket off of the front fairing. On models so equipped, carefully pull the turn signal electrical wire through the opening in the outer bracket.
   e. Install by reversing these removal steps.

8. Repeat for the rear view mirror on the other side.

9. To install the mirror, perform the following.
   a. On K100 RS models, connect the turn signal electrical connector.
   b. Apply a light coat of engine oil or Armor All to the mounting clips in the mirror housing. This will make it easier to install the mirror housing onto the mounting studs.
   c. Position the mirror assembly onto the mounting bracket assembly on the front fairing. Align the mounting studs with the mirror clips.
   d. Again using the palm of your hand, tap the mirror housing into position. Make sure all studs are completely locked into the mounting clips in the mirror. When installed correctly, there should be no gap around the perimeter of the mirror housing.

13

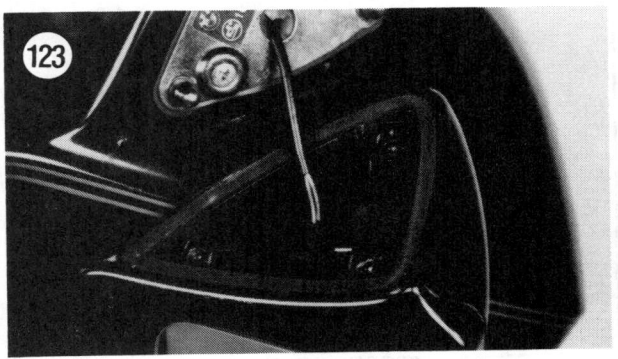

Front Fairing (K100 RT and K100 LT) Removal/Installation

Refer to **Figures 125-131** for this procedure. The illustrations show mainly the left-hand panels, brackets and the mounting hardware. The right-hand components are an exact mirror image and are attached in the same manner unless otherwise specified.

1. Remove the frame left-hand side cover.
2. Disconnect the battery negative lead as described under *Battery* in Chapter Three.
3. Remove the knee pads as follows:
   a. Remove the single screw at the bottom of the knee pad.
   b. Remove the screws at the top of the knee pad.
   c. Carefully remove the knee pad from the front fairing upper portion and lower side panel.
   d. Repeat for the knee pad on the other side.
4. Remove the storage compartment as follows:
   a. Remove the storage compartment cover panel.
   b. Remove the screws securing the storage compartment and remove the storage compartment.
   c. Repeat for the storage compartment on the other side.
5. Remove the fuel tank as described under *Fuel Tank Removal/Installation* in Chapter Seven.
6. Remove the radiator trim panel as follows:
   a. Remove the screws securing the front fork rubber boots and slide the boots up on the fork tubes and away from the radiator trim panel upper center panel.
   b. Remove the screws securing the radiator trim panel to the lower side panels on each side.
   c. Hold onto the radiator trim panel and remove the screws securing the radiator trim panel to the front fairing upper portion.
   d. Carefully remove the radiator trim panel.
   e. Remove the screws securing the upper center cover and remove the cover.
7. Remove the lower side panels as follows:
   a. Remove the rear bolts and washers securing the lower side panel. Don't lose the rubber grommets and metal collar in the mounting hole in the side panel.
   b. Remove the bolts along the upper edge securing the lower side panel to the front fairing upper portion.
   c. Remove the lower side panel and the metal inner panel.
   d. Repeat for the lower trim panel on the other side.
8. Remove the screws securing the windshield and remove the windshield.
9A. On K100 RT models, remove the bolts securing the inner trim panel and center panel and remove both panels.

NOTE
*If the bike is equipped with the optional instruments, refer to **Optional Instruments and Panel** in this chapter for removal procedures.*

9B. On K100 LT models, perform the following:
   a. Remove the bolts securing the instrument panel and center panel.
   b. Carefully pull the instrument panel out and disconnect the electrical connectors to the instruments.
   c. Remove both panels.
10. Disconnect the headlight and turn signal electrical connectors from the main wiring harness.

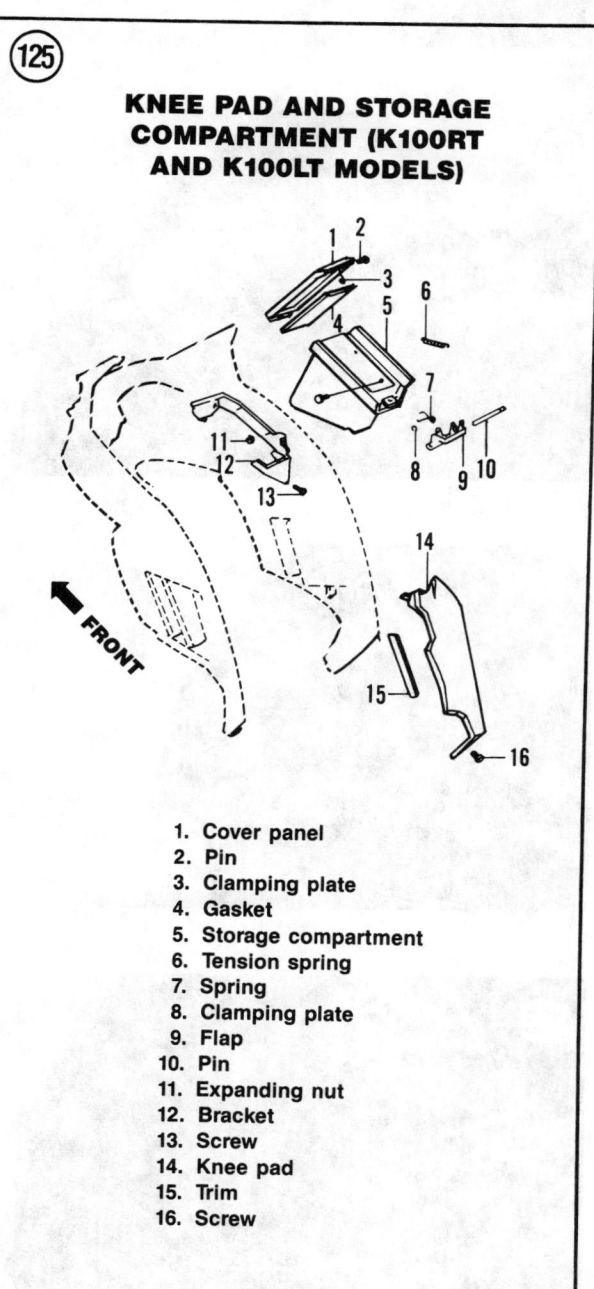

(125)

KNEE PAD AND STORAGE COMPARTMENT (K100RT AND K100LT MODELS)

1. Cover panel
2. Pin
3. Clamping plate
4. Gasket
5. Storage compartment
6. Tension spring
7. Spring
8. Clamping plate
9. Flap
10. Pin
11. Expanding nut
12. Bracket
13. Screw
14. Knee pad
15. Trim
16. Screw

RADIATOR TRIM PANEL
(K100RT AND
K100LT MODELS)

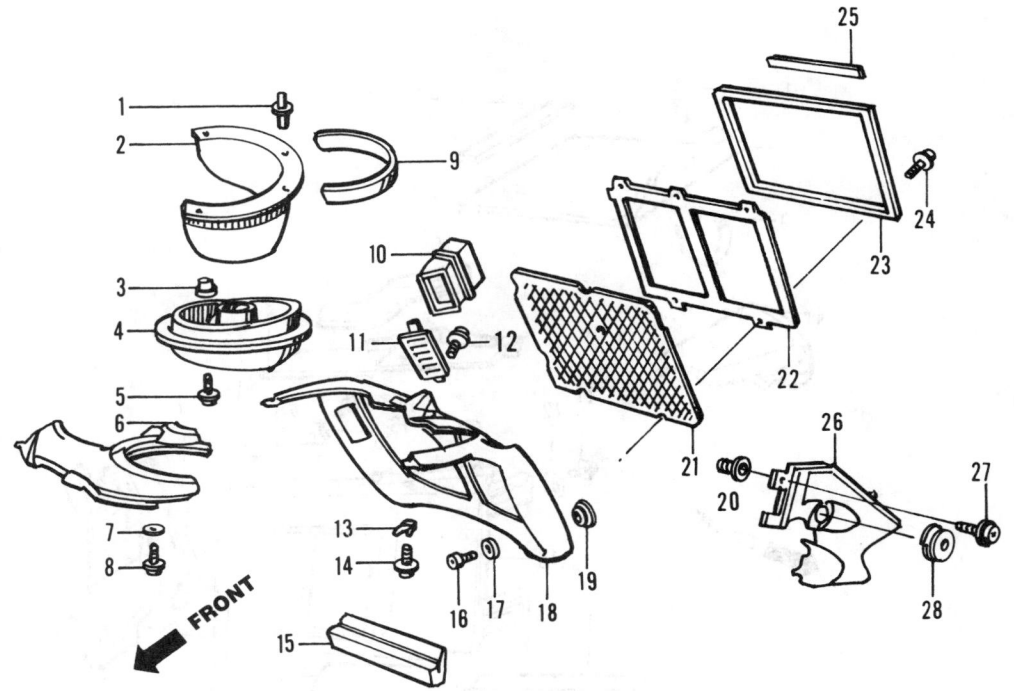

1. Rivet
2. Air inlet
3. Expanding nut
4. Fork tube rubber boot
5. Screw
6. Upper center cover
7. Washer
8. Screw
9. Trim panel
10. Thermovalve housing
11. Mesh screen
12. Bolt
13. Special nut
14. Bolt

15. Gasket
16. Screw
17. Washer
18. Radiator trim panel
19. Nut
20. Expanding nut
21. Grille
22. Frame
23. Gasket
24. Screw
25. Sealing strip
26. Panel cover
27. Screw
28. Rubber grommet

13

**LOWER SIDE PANEL
(K100RT AND
K100LT MODELS)**

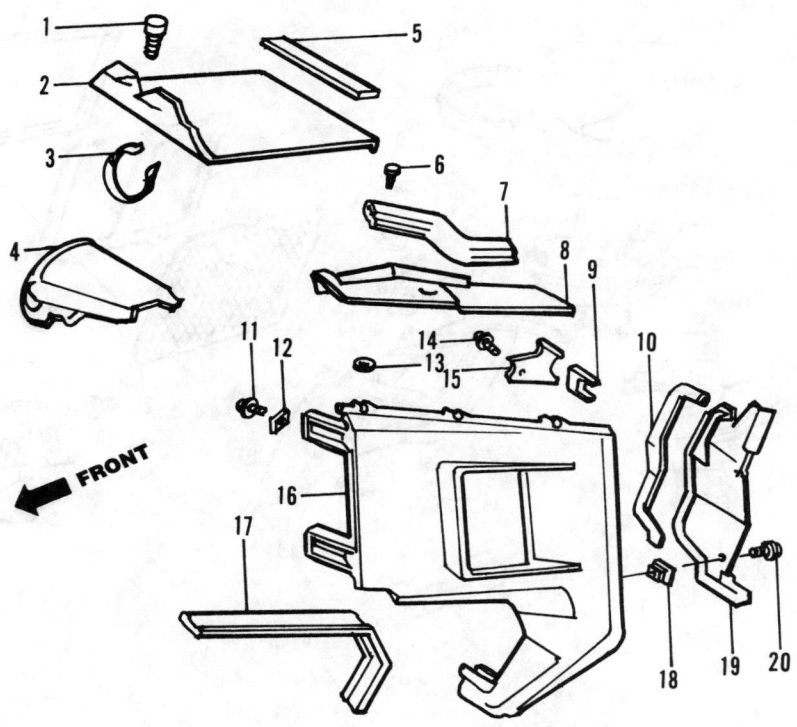

1. Rubber grommet
2. Panel
3. Cable strap
4. Gasket
5. Sealing strip
6. Bolt
7. Gasket
8. Metal inner panel
9. Bracket
10. Trim strip

11. Screw
12. Special nut
13. Special nut
14. Bolt
15. Bracket
16. Lower side panel
17. Gasket
18. Special nut
19. Side panel cover
20. Screw

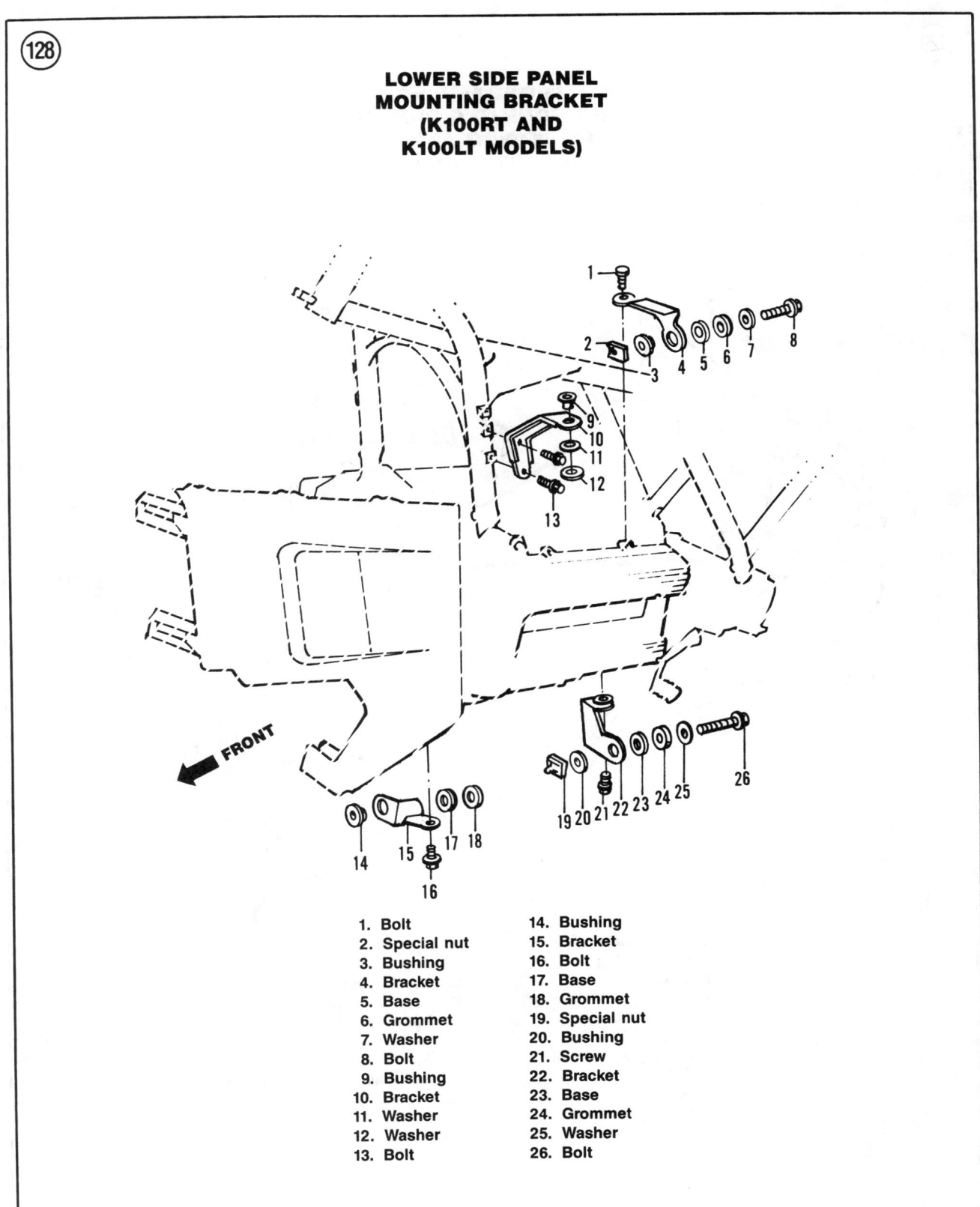

**LOWER SIDE PANEL
MOUNTING BRACKET
(K100RT AND
K100LT MODELS)**

FRONT

1. Bolt
2. Special nut
3. Bushing
4. Bracket
5. Base
6. Grommet
7. Washer
8. Bolt
9. Bushing
10. Bracket
11. Washer
12. Washer
13. Bolt

14. Bushing
15. Bracket
16. Bolt
17. Base
18. Grommet
19. Special nut
20. Bushing
21. Screw
22. Bracket
23. Base
24. Grommet
25. Washer
26. Bolt

13

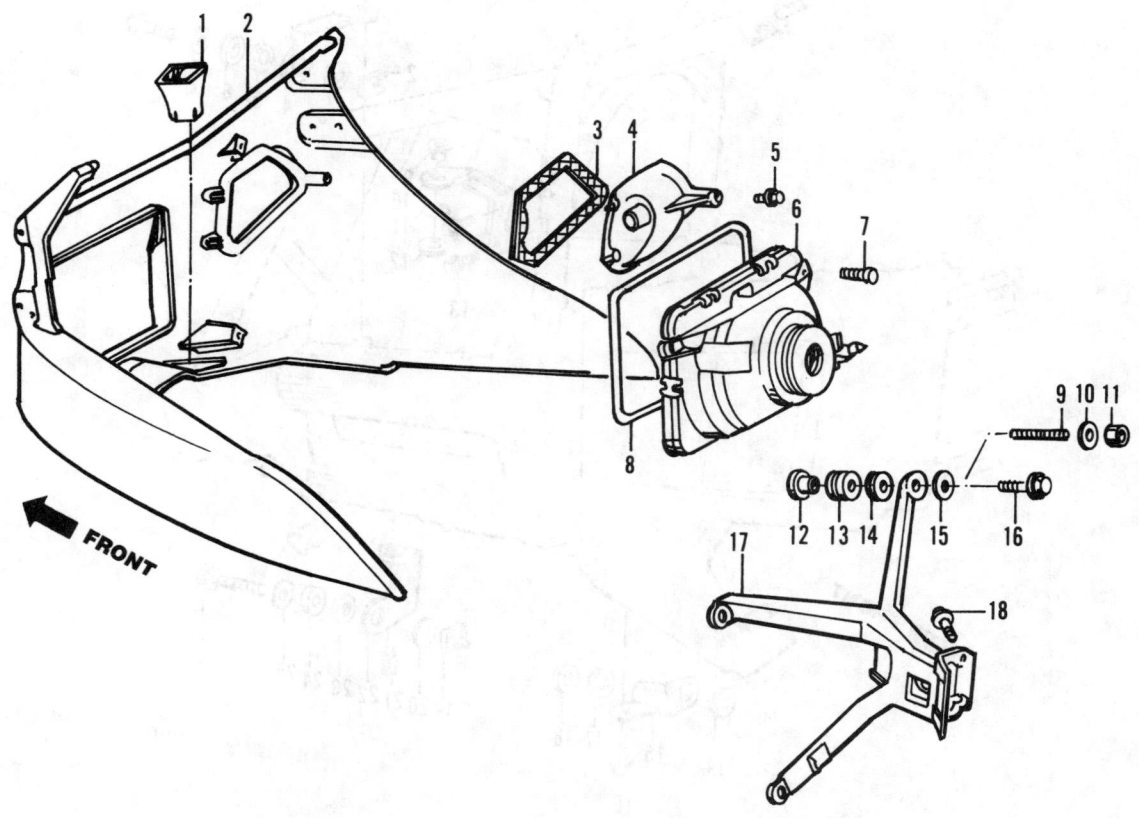

**FRONT FAIRING
AND MOUNTING BRACKET
(K100RT AND
K100LT MODELS)**

FRONT

1. Intermediate piece
2. Front fairing
3. Gasket
4. Turn signal assembly
   right-hand side
5. Screw
6. Headlight assembly
7. Bolt
8. Gasket
9. Spring
10. Washer
11. Nut
12. Metal collar
13. Rubber grommet
14. Base
15. Washer
16. Bolt
17. Front fairing mounting bracket
18. Bolt

The next step requires the aid of an assistant. The fairing is not heavy, but is difficult to hold in place while removing the mounting bolts and nuts.

11. Have an assistant hold onto the front of the front fairing and perform the following:

    a. Remove the bolt on each side securing the front fairing upper portion to the frame.

    b. To protect the finish, place a couple of blankets on the workbench or floor for the front fairing to sit on after removal.

    c. Remove the bolts and washers securing the fairing to the fairing mounting bracket.

    d. Carefully pull the front fairing forward and remove the front fairing from the mounting bracket and set it on the blankets.

12. If necessary, remove the bolts securing the mounting bracket to the frame and remove the mounting bracket.

13. Install by reversing these removal steps, noting the following.

14. Tighten the screws and nuts securely. Don't overtighten the screws or nuts as the plastic mounting bosses may be damaged.

15. Make sure all electrical connectors are free of corrosion and are tight.

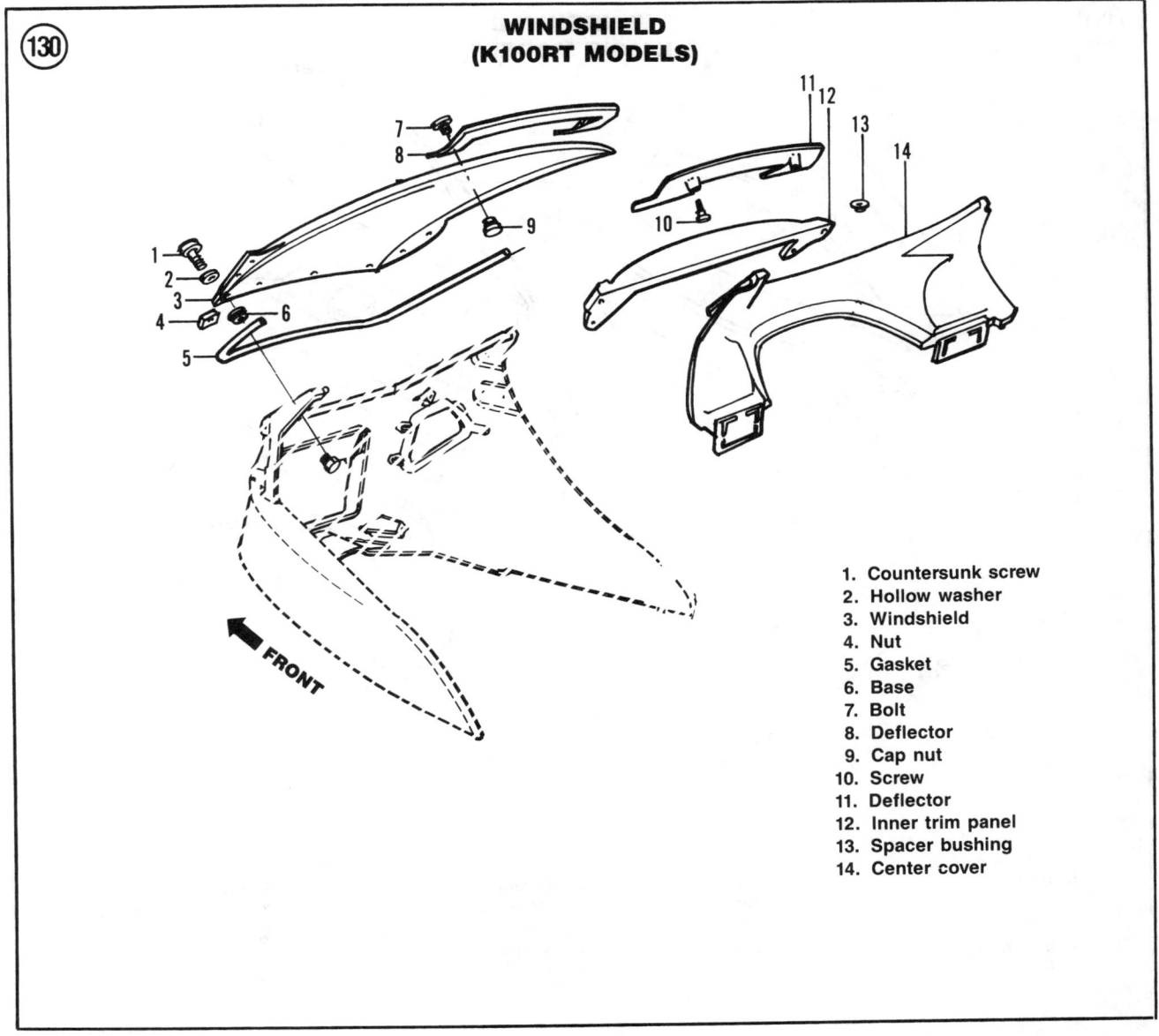

**WINDSHIELD
(K100RT MODELS)**

130

FRONT

1. Countersunk screw
2. Hollow washer
3. Windshield
4. Nut
5. Gasket
6. Base
7. Bolt
8. Deflector
9. Cap nut
10. Screw
11. Deflector
12. Inner trim panel
13. Spacer bushing
14. Center cover

13

Engine Spoiler
Removal/Installation

Refer to **Figure 132** for this procedure.
1. If you are working alone, place wood block(s) (**Figure 133**) or a cardboard box under the spoiler to hold it in place after the mounting bolts are removed.
2. Remove the bolts (**Figure 134**) on each side securing the spoiler.
3. Remove the cardboard box or wood block(s) from under the spoiler and remove the spoiler.
4. If you are working alone, place wood block(s) (**Figure 135**) or a cardboard box under the mounting bracket to hold it in place after the mounting bolts are removed.

5. Remove the bolts (**Figure 136**) on each side securing the mounting bracket.
6. Remove the cardboard box or wood block(s) from under the mounting bracket and remove the mounting bracket.
7. Install by reversing these removal steps, noting the following.
8. Tighten the bolts securely.

LUGGAGE AND RACK

These items are optional and are not installed on all models.

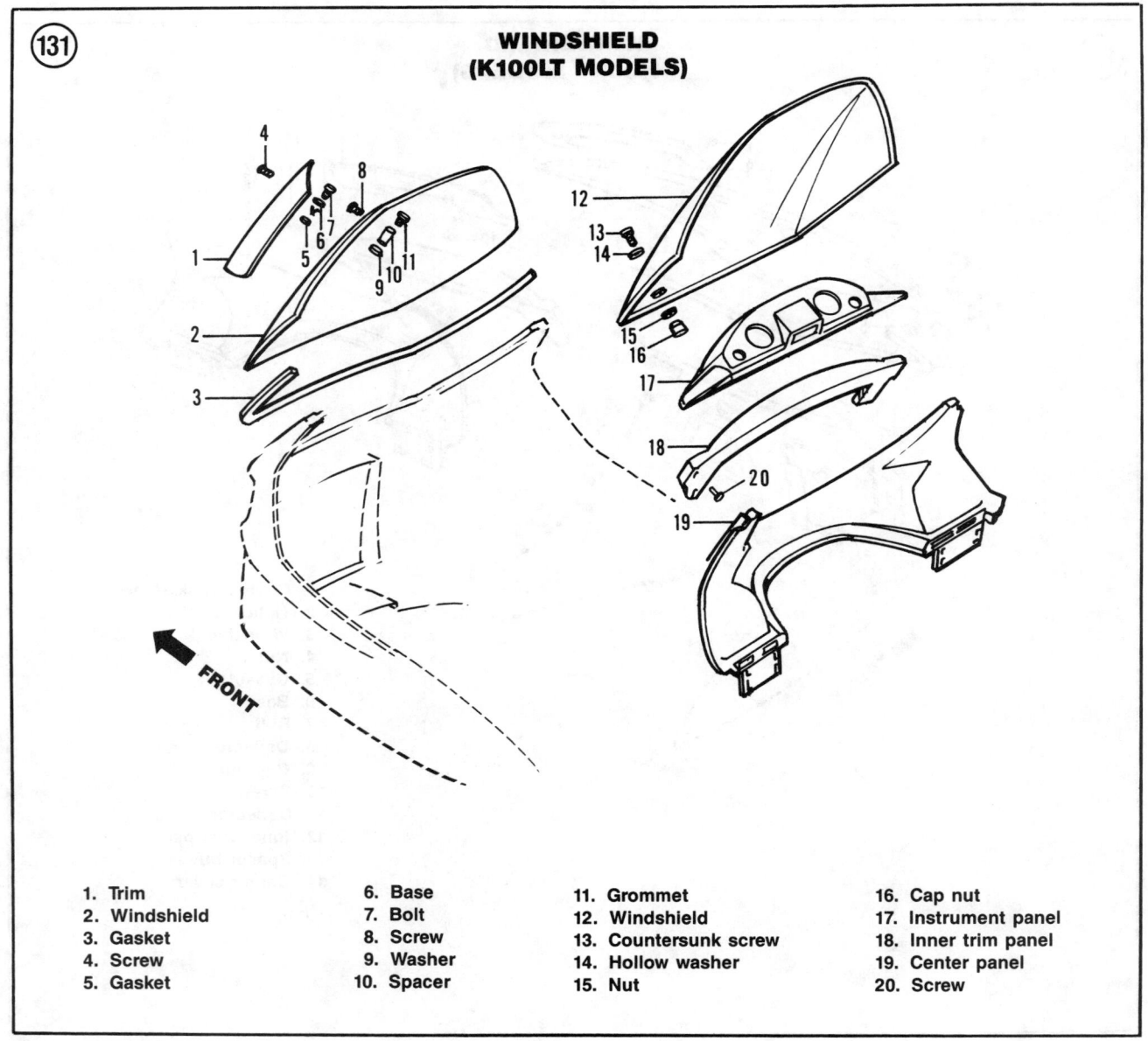

131

WINDSHIELD
(K100LT MODELS)

FRONT

1. Trim	6. Base	11. Grommet	16. Cap nut
2. Windshield	7. Bolt	12. Windshield	17. Instrument panel
3. Gasket	8. Screw	13. Countersunk screw	18. Inner trim panel
4. Screw	9. Washer	14. Hollow washer	19. Center panel
5. Gasket	10. Spacer	15. Nut	20. Screw

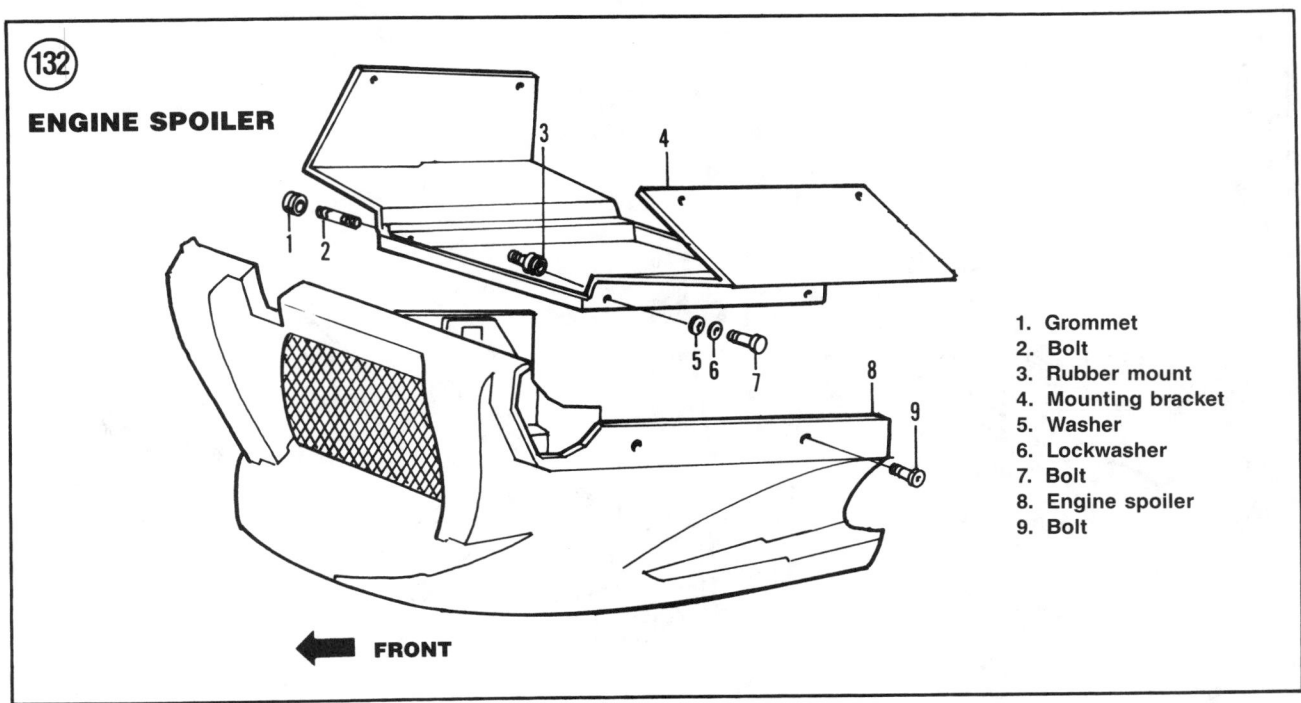

(132)

ENGINE SPOILER

1. Grommet
2. Bolt
3. Rubber mount
4. Mounting bracket
5. Washer
6. Lockwasher
7. Bolt
8. Engine spoiler
9. Bolt

FRONT

(133)

(135)

(134)

(136)

13

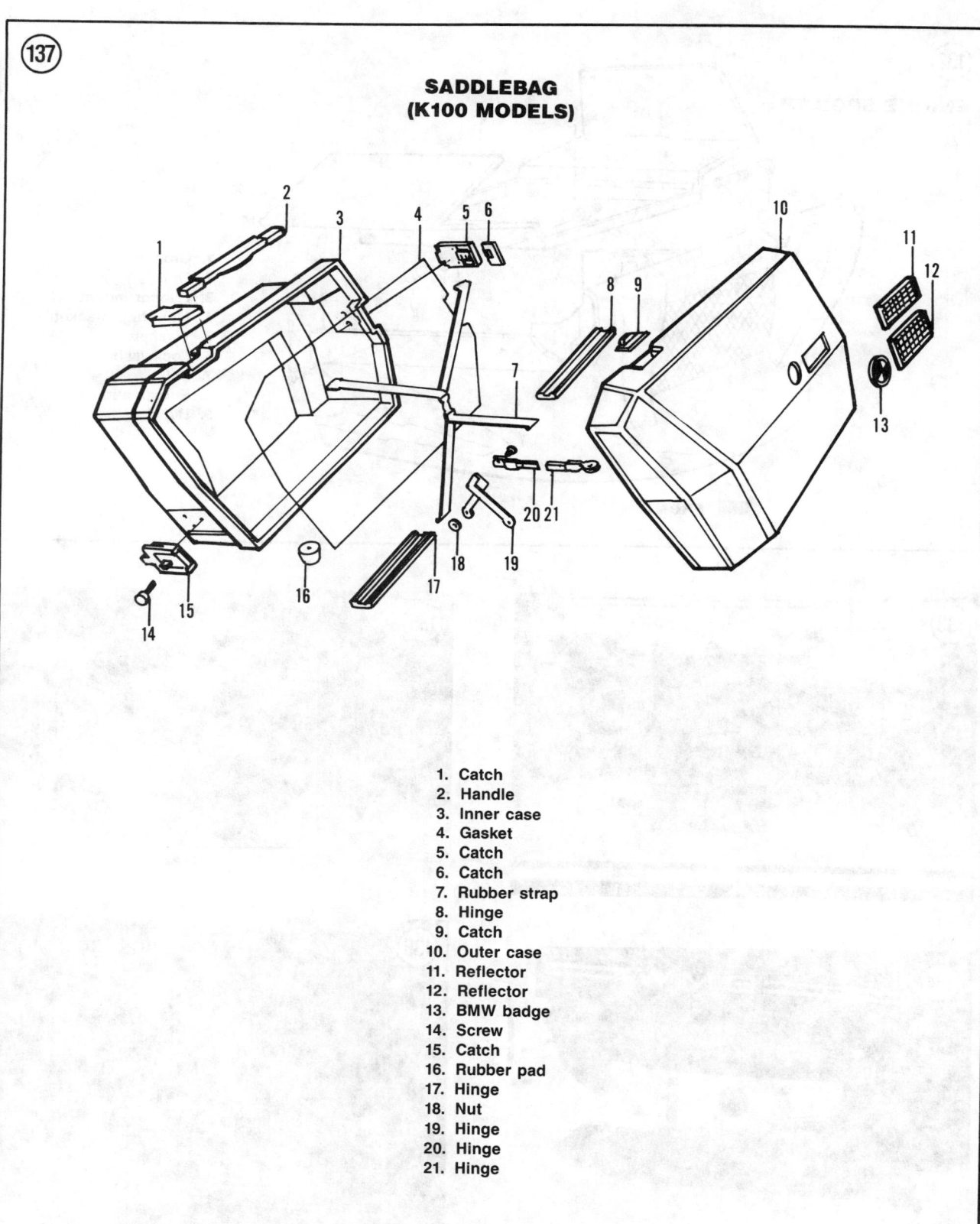

**SADDLEBAG
(K100 MODELS)**

137

1. Catch
2. Handle
3. Inner case
4. Gasket
5. Catch
6. Catch
7. Rubber strap
8. Hinge
9. Catch
10. Outer case
11. Reflector
12. Reflector
13. BMW badge
14. Screw
15. Catch
16. Rubber pad
17. Hinge
18. Nut
19. Hinge
20. Hinge
21. Hinge

(138)   **SADDLEBAG (K75 MODELS)**

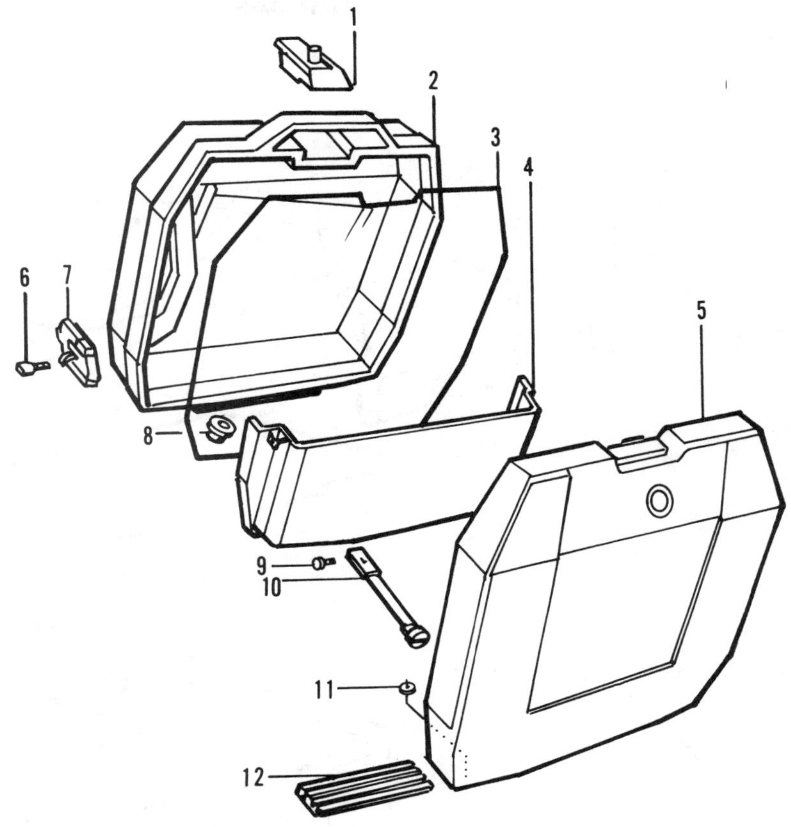

1. Catch
2. Inner case
3. Gasket
4. Divider
5. Outer case
6. Screw
7. Catch
8. Rubber pad
9. Screw
10. Hinge
11. Washer
12. Hinge

(139)

Saddlebag Removal/Installation

Refer to **Figure 137** and **Figure 138** for this procedure.
1. Release the catch (**Figure 139**).
2. Pull out on the bottom of the saddlebag and slide it toward the rear. Unhook and remove the saddlebag from the rack.
3. Install the saddlebag and make sure the catch is securely fastened to the rack.

Top Case Removal/Installation

Refer to **Figure 140** for this procedure.
1. Unlock the catch and open the top cover.
2. Within the lower case, rotate the locking catch and remove the top case from the carrier.
3. Install the top case and make sure the locking catch is securely fastened to the carrier.

13

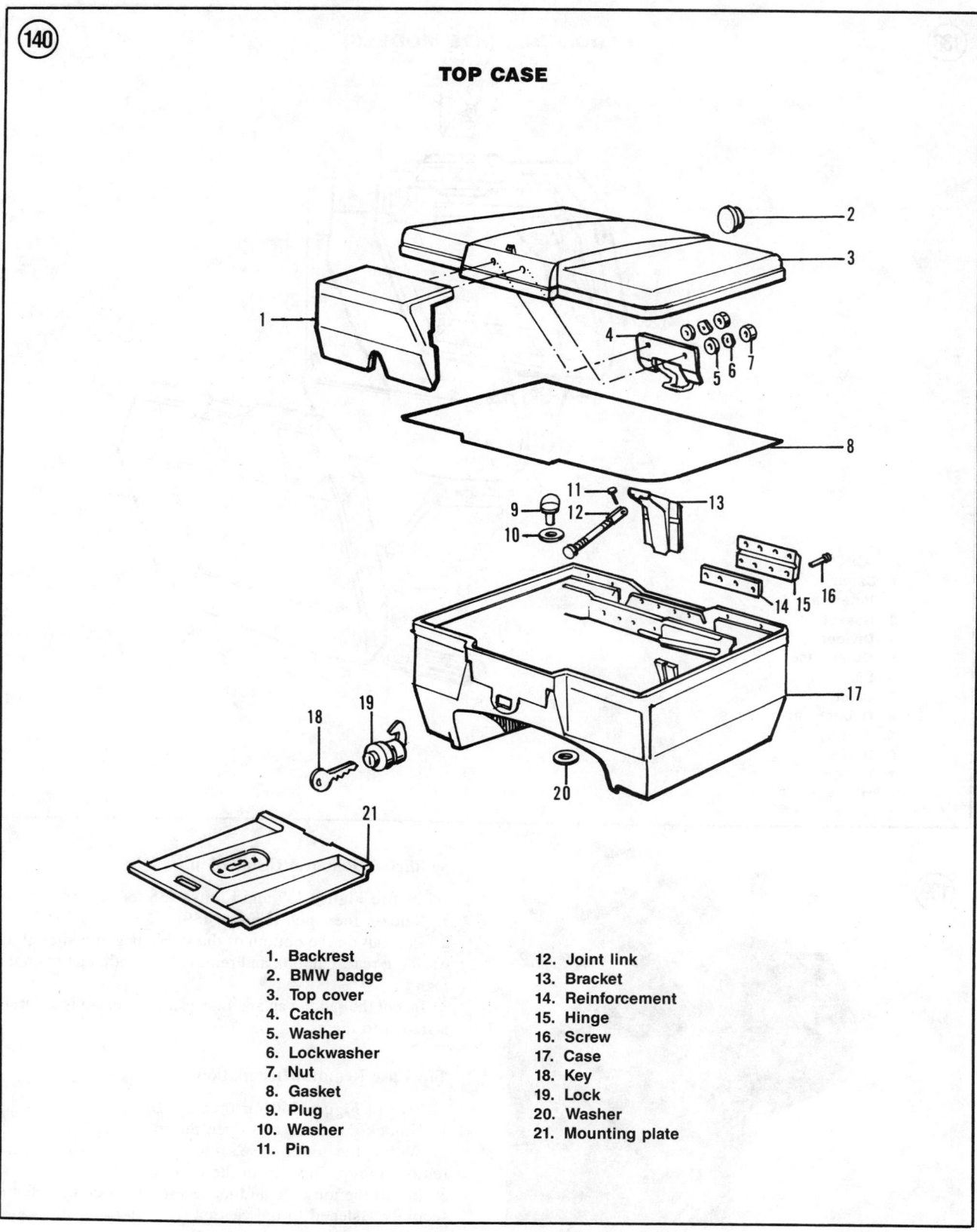

⟨140⟩

TOP CASE

1. Backrest
2. BMW badge
3. Top cover
4. Catch
5. Washer
6. Lockwasher
7. Nut
8. Gasket
9. Plug
10. Washer
11. Pin
12. Joint link
13. Bracket
14. Reinforcement
15. Hinge
16. Screw
17. Case
18. Key
19. Lock
20. Washer
21. Mounting plate

Saddlebag Rack
Removal/Installation

Refer to **Figure 141** for this procedure.
1. Remove the saddlebag as described in this chapter.
2. To remove the right-hand saddlebag rack, perform the following:

   a. Remove the bolts, lockwasher and nuts (A, **Figure 142**) securing the saddlebag rack to the footpeg assembly.
   b. Remove the bolts, washers and nuts (B, **Figure 142**) securing the saddlebag rack to the frame.
   c. Remove the right-hand saddlebag rack.

3. To remove the left-hand saddlebag rack, perform the following:

   a. Remove the bolts, lockwasher and nuts (A, **Figure 143**) securing the saddlebag rack and muffler to the rubber insulator mounted on the footpeg assembly.
   b. Remove the bolts, washers and nuts (B, **Figure 143**) securing the saddlebag rack to the frame.
   c. Remove the saddlebag rack.
   d. If the saddlebag rack is going to be left off for some period of time, reinstall the lower bolts, washers and nuts (B, **Figure 143**) to hold the muffler assembly in place.

4. Install by reversing these removal steps, noting the following.
5. Tighten the bolts and nuts securely.

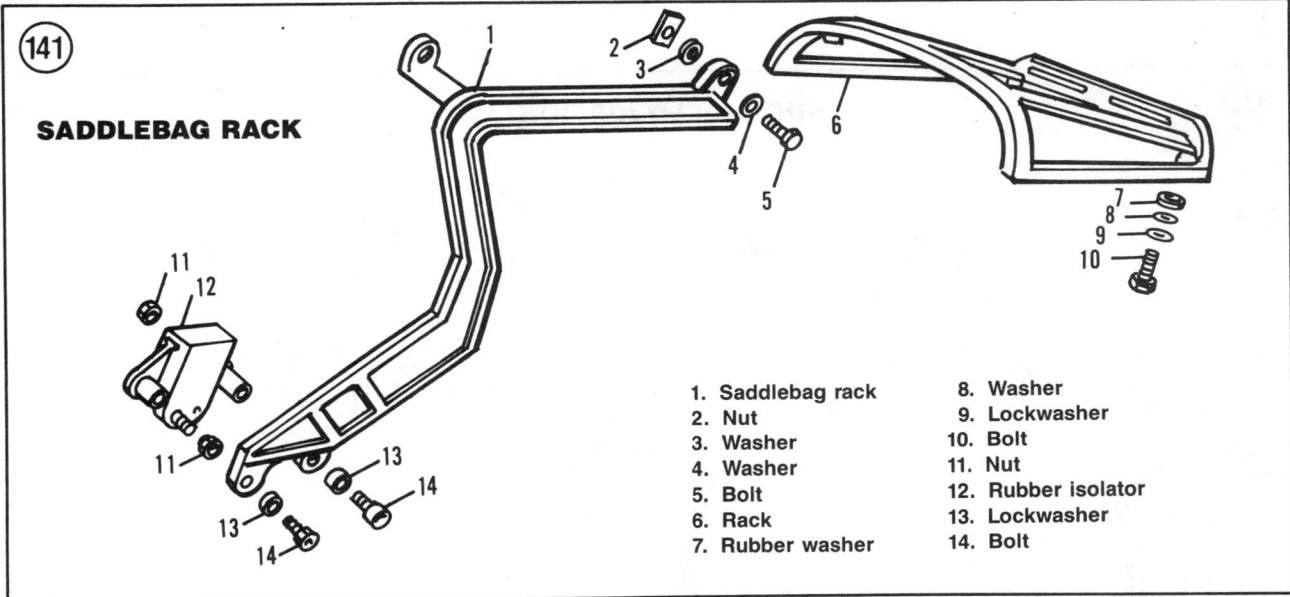

141

SADDLEBAG RACK

1. Saddlebag rack
2. Nut
3. Washer
4. Washer
5. Bolt
6. Rack
7. Rubber washer
8. Washer
9. Lockwasher
10. Bolt
11. Nut
12. Rubber isolator
13. Lockwasher
14. Bolt

142

143

13

OPTIONAL EQUIPMENT

Windshield
Removal/Installation

Refer to **Figure 144** for this procedure.
1. Loosen the cap nuts (**Figure 145**) on each side securing the windshield to the mounting rods and mounting brackets.
2. Remove all cap nuts and washers.
3. Remove the rubber grommet from each of the mounting rods.
4. Leave the upper portion of the windshield held in place on the mounting rods.
5. Remove the bushings and rubber grommet and then remove the bolt and washer from the lower mounting bracket.
6. Carefully pull the windshield off of the upper mounting rod ends and remove the windshield.

7. To remove the mounting bracket, perform the following:
   a. Remove the bolts, washers and nuts (**Figure 146**) securing the mounting bracket to the fork tubes.
   b. Remove the brackets from the fork tubes.
8. Install by reversing these removal steps, noting the following.
9. Be sure to install all rubber grommets and bushings at all attachment points. If the grommets and bushings are not used, the plastic windshield will crack and fracture when the mounting cap nuts are tightened. Do not overtighten the cap nuts.

Optional Instruments and Panel
Removal/Installation

Refer to **Figure 147** and **Figure 148** for this procedure.
1. Remove the frame left-hand side cover.

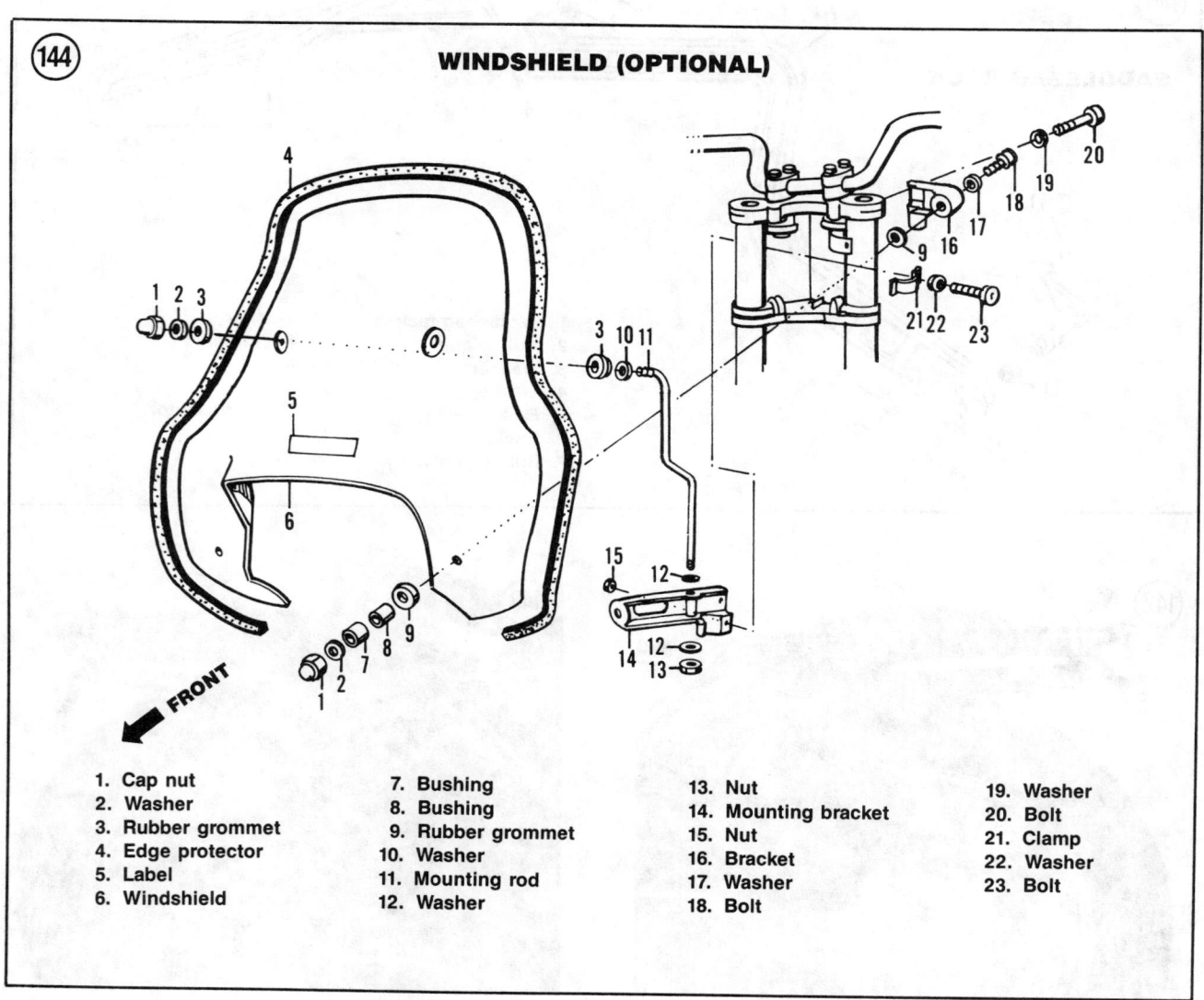

144 WINDSHIELD (OPTIONAL)

1. Cap nut
2. Washer
3. Rubber grommet
4. Edge protector
5. Label
6. Windshield
7. Bushing
8. Bushing
9. Rubber grommet
10. Washer
11. Mounting rod
12. Washer
13. Nut
14. Mounting bracket
15. Nut
16. Bracket
17. Washer
18. Bolt
19. Washer
20. Bolt
21. Clamp
22. Washer
23. Bolt

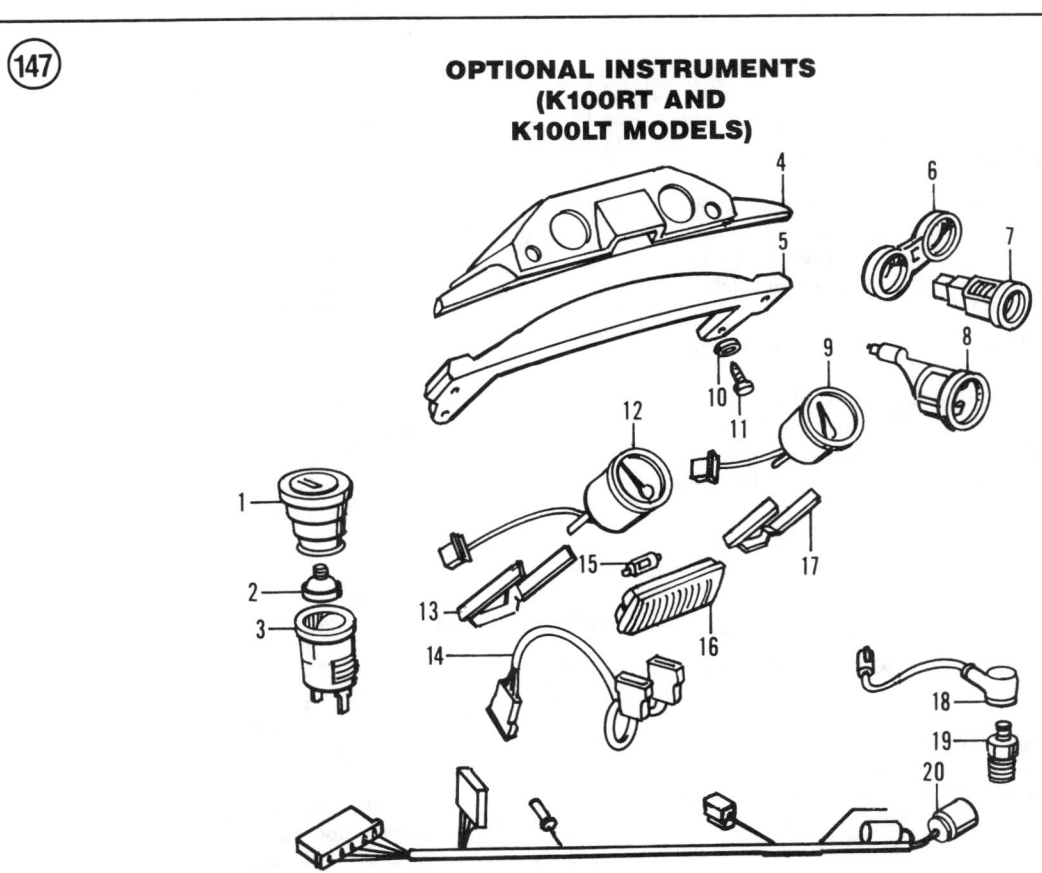

OPTIONAL INSTRUMENTS (K100RT AND K100LT MODELS)

1. Lighter element
2. Filament
3. Lighter socket
4. Instrument panel
5. Panel
6. Cover
7. Plug-in socket
8. Clamping bushing
9. Temperature gauge
10. Hollow washer
11. Bolt
12. Fuel gauge
13. Bracket
14. Wiring harness for instruments
15. Light bulb
16. Interior light
17. Bracket
18. Wiring harness for coolant temperature sensor
19. Coolant temperature sensor
20. Wiring harness

13

2. Disconnect the battery negative lead as described under *Battery* in Chapter Three.
3. Remove the fuel tank as described under *Fuel Tank Removal/Installation* in Chapter Seven.
4. Remove the fasteners securing the instrument panel or center cover.
5. Carefully pull the instrument panel or center cover to locate the electrical wires coming from each attached component.
6. Follow the electrical wire(s) from the component, though the frame and into the area below the fuel tank.
7. Locate the electrical connector(s) and disconnect it from the main wiring harness.
8. Remove any tie wraps securing the electrical wires to the frame members.
9. Install by reversing these removal steps, noting the following.
10. Make sure all electrical connectors are free of corrosion and are tight.

WINDSHIELD CLEANING
(ALL MODELS)

Be careful cleaning the windshield as it can be easily scratched or damaged. Do not use a cleaner with an abrasive or a combination cleaner and wax. Never use gasoline or cleaning solvent. These products will either scratch or totally destroy the surface of the windshield.

For normal cleaning, use a soft cloth or sponge and plenty of water. Dry thoroughly with a soft cloth (like an old plain white T-shirt) or chamois—do not press hard.

To remove oil, grease or road tar use isopropyl alcohol or kerosene. Then wash the windshield with a solution of mild soap and lots of water. Dry thoroughly with a soft cloth or a chamois—do not press hard.

FRAME

The frame does not require routine maintenance. However, it should be inspected immediately after any accident or spill.

Component Removal/Installation

1. Remove both side covers and the seat as described in this chapter.
2. Remove all body components as described in this chapter.
3. Remove the fuel tank as described in Chapter Seven.
4. Remove the battery as described in Chapter Three.
5. Remove the instrument cluster as described in Chapter Eight.
6. Remove the hydraulic brake system flexible hoses as described in Chapter Twelve.
7. Remove the wiring harness from the frame.
8. Remove the front wheel, handlebar, steering head and front forks as described in Chapter Ten.

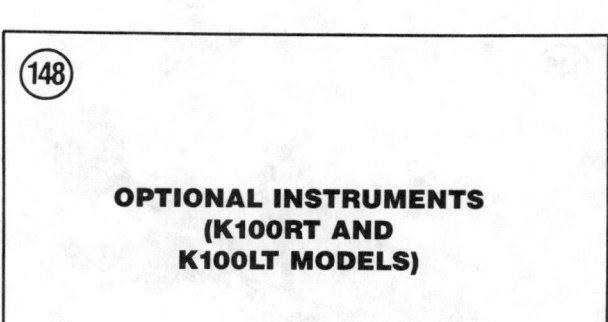

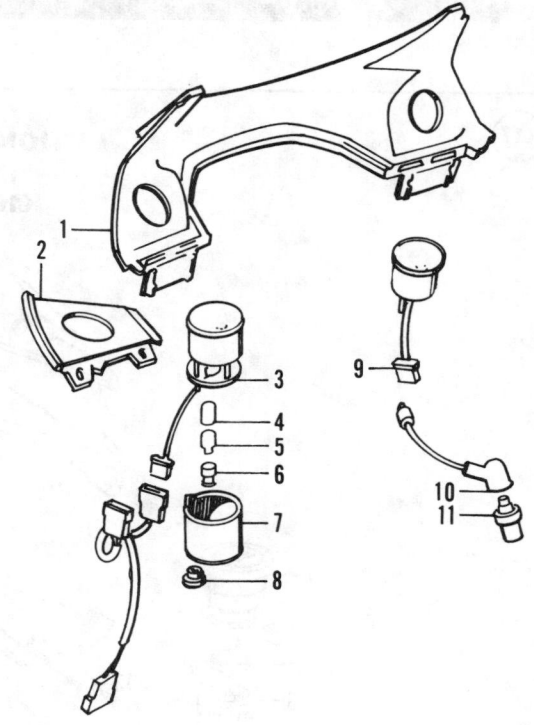

(148)

OPTIONAL INSTRUMENTS (K100RT AND K100LT MODELS)

1. Center cover
2. Side cover
3. Fuel gauge
4. Cap
5. Light bulb
6. Bulb socket
7. Gauge housing
8. Knurled nut
9. Temperature gauge
10. Wiring harness for temperature gauge
11. Coolant temperature sensor

9. Remove the rear wheel, shock absorber and swing arm as described in Chapter Eleven.

10. Remove the engine and transmission housing as described in Chapter Four.

11. Remove the steering head races from the steering head tube as described in Chapter Ten.

12. Inspect the frame for bends, cracks or other damage, especially around welded joints and areas that are rusted.

13. Assemble by reversing these removal steps.

Stripping and Painting

Remove all components from the frame. Thoroughly strip off all old paint. The best way is to have it sandblasted down to bare metal. If this is not possible, you can use a liquid paint remover and steel wool and a fine, hard wire brush.

> *CAUTION*
> *Some of the fenders, side covers, frame covers and air box are molded plastic. If you wish to change the color of these parts, consult an automotive paint supplier for the proper procedure. Do not use any liquid paint remover on these components as it will damage the surface. The color is an integral part of some of these components and cannot be removed.*

When the frame is down to bare metal, have it inspected for hairline and internal cracks. Magnaflux is the most common and complete process.

Make sure that the primer is compatible with the type of paint you are going to use for the finish color. Spray on one or two coats of primer as smoothly as possible. Let it dry thoroughly and use a fine grade of wet sandpaper (400-600 grit) to remove any flaws. Carefully wipe the surface clean and then spray a couple of coats of the final color. Use either lacquer or enamel base paint and follow the manufacturer's instructions.

A shop specializing in painting will probably do the best job. However, you can do a surprisingly good job with a good grade of spray paint. Spend a few extra dollars and get a good grade of paint as it will make a difference in how well it looks and how long it will stand up. It's a good idea to shake the can and make sure the ball inside the can is loose when you purchase the can of paint. Shake the can as long as is stated on the can. Then immerse the can *upright* in a pot or bucket of *warm* water (not hot—not over 120° F).

> *WARNING*
> *Higher temperatures could cause the can to burst. Do **not** place the can in direct contact with any flame or heat source.*

Leave the can in the water for several minutes. When thoroughly warmed, shake the can again and spray the frame. Be sure to get into all the crevices where there may be rust problems. Several light mist coats are better than one heavy coat. Spray painting is best done in temperatures of 70-80° F (21-26° C); any temperature above or below this will give you problems.

After the final coat has dried completely, at least 48 hours, any overspray or orange peel may be removed with a *light* application of Dupont rubbing compound (red color) and finished with Dupont polishing compound (white color). Be careful not to rub too hard or you will go through the finish. Finish off with a couple of coats of good wax before reassembling all the components.

It's a good idea to keep the frame touched up with fresh paint if any minor rust spots, chips or scratches appear.

13

Table 1 FRAME AND BODY TORQUE SPECIFICATIONS

Item	N·m	ft.-lb.
Sidestand pivot bolt	36-46	27-33
Center stand bolt	36-46	27-33
Footpeg assembly mounting bolts	13-17	10-12

CHAPTER FOURTEEN

1990-LATER SUPPLEMENT

This chapter contains all procedures and specifications unique to 1990-1997 K75-K1100 models. If a specific procedure is not included, refer to the procedure for your model in prior chapters. On K1 and K1100 models, refer to K100 procedures in the main body of this book for service information unless otherwise included in this supplement.

The K100RS and the K1 models have a displacement of 1000 cc while the K1100LT and K1100 RSA have a displacement of 1100 cc. The 4-valve cylinder head design is the same on all of these models. The K75 and K100LT models that are covered briefly in this chapter have the 2-valve cylinder head design that is described in Chapter Four in the main body of this book.

The headings in this chapter correspond to those in the other chapter of this book.

CHAPTER TWO

TROUBLESHOOTING

ENGINE STARTING AND ENGINE PERFORMANCE

On all K1, 1991-1992 K100RS and all K1100 models, the ignition control module and fuel injection control module are combined into a single engine management module referred to as the Motronic Control Unit. The Motronic Control Unit is covered in the Chapter Seven and Chapter Eight sections of this supplement.

CHAPTER THREE

LUBRICATION, MAINTENANCE AND TUNE-UP

The service procedures and intervals listed in **Table 1** are recommended by the BMW factory.

ROUTINE MAINTENANCE CHECKS

Coolant Level (K1 Models)

Check the coolant level *when the engine is cold*, since the coolant level in the reserve tank will vary depending on the engine operating temperature.

Always add coolant to the coolant reserve tank as this tank is never pressurized. The remainder of the cooling system is under pressure and the coolant is very hot when the engine has been run.

If the coolant level is very low, it will be necessary to refill the cooling system through the coolant filler cap located under the left-hand side of the fairing inner cover. If this is necessary, refer to *Coolant Change* under *Periodic Maintenance* in this section of the supplement. If the coolant reserve tank requires repeated refilling, inspect the cooling system for the probable cause; correct the problem immediately.

1. Remove the left-hand kneepad as described in the Chapter Thirteen section of this supplement.

2. Remove the left-hand inner fairing panel as described in the Chapter Thirteen section of this supplement.

3. The coolant level should be at the MAX mark on the transparent level check area of the tank.

4. If necessary, remove the reserve tank fill cap and gasket (not the coolant filler cap on the radiator) and add coolant until the level is even with the MAX mark. For the recommended coolant-to-purified water ratio, refer to *Coolant Change* under *Periodic Maintenance* in Chapter Three in the main body of this book.

Tire Pressure

Tire pressure must be checked with the tires cold. Correct tire pressure, listed in **Table 2**, varies with the load you are carrying. Refer to *Tire Pressure* under *Tires and Wheels* in this section of the supplement.

Battery

Remove either side cover and check the battery electrolyte level. The level must be maintained between the MAX and MIN markings (**Figure 1**).

14

SERVICE INTERVALS

The service and intervals shown in **Table 1** are recommended by the BMW factory. Strict adherence to these recommendations will ensure long service from the BMW. If the bike is run in an area of high humidity, the lubrication service must be done more frequently to prevent possible rust damage.

For convenience when maintaining your motorcycle, most of the services shown in this table are described in this section of the supplement or in Chapter Three in the main body of the book. However, some procedures which require more than a minor disassembly or adjustment are covered elsewhere in the appropriate chapter, either in this supplement or in the main body of this book.

TIRES AND WHEELS

Tire pressure should be checked and adjusted to maintain the smoothness of the tire, good traction and handling and to get the maximum life out of the tire. A simple, accurate gauge can be purchased for a few dollars and should be carried in your motorcycle tool kit. The appropriate tire pressures are shown in **Table 2**.

BATTERY

Removal, Electrolyte Level Check and Installation (K100RS, K1, K1100)

The battery is the heart of the electrical system. Check and service the battery at the intervals listed in **Table 1**. Refer to **Figure 2** for this procedure.

1. Remove the seat (A, **Figure 3**) as described under *Seat Removal/Installation* either in the Chapter Thirteen section of this supplement or in the main body of this book.
2. Remove the left-hand side cover.

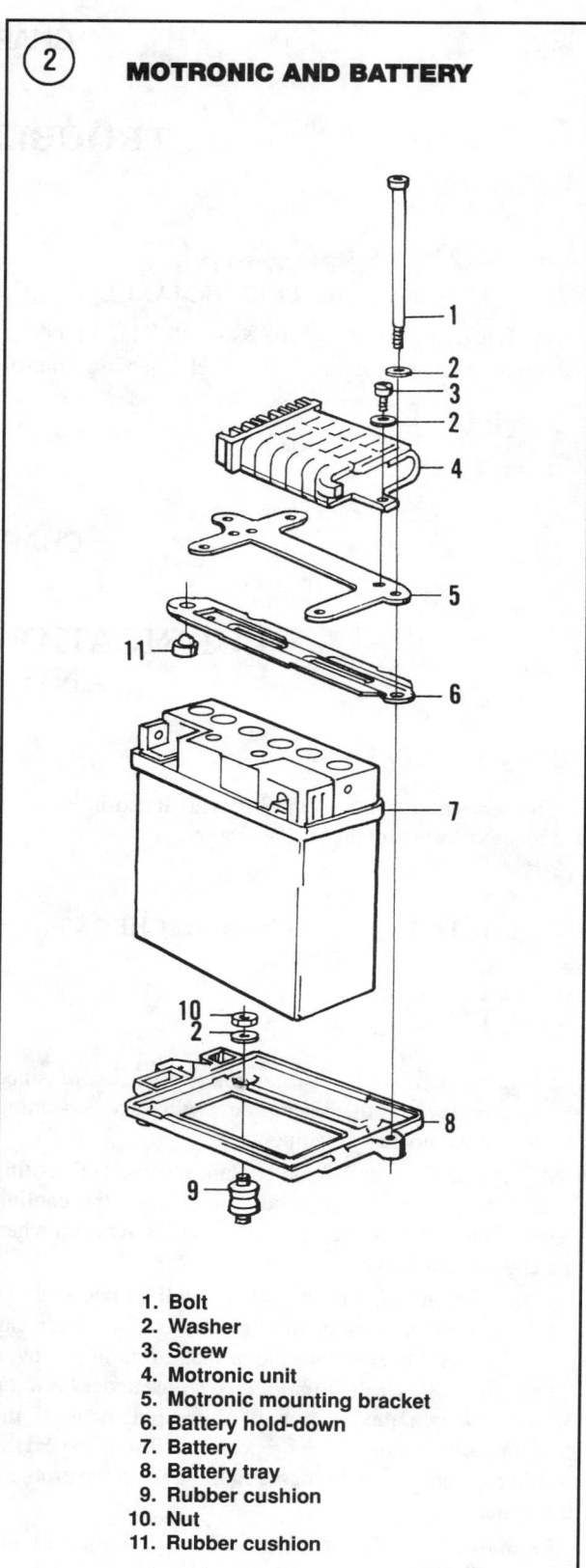

MOTRONIC AND BATTERY

1. Bolt
2. Washer
3. Screw
4. Motronic unit
5. Motronic mounting bracket
6. Battery hold-down
7. Battery
8. Battery tray
9. Rubber cushion
10. Nut
11. Rubber cushion

3. Press the catch (B, **Figure 3**) on the left-hand side of the electrical connector and disconnect the electrical connector (C, **Figure 3**) from the Motronic control unit. Move the connector out of the way.

4. Remove the screws and washers and remove the Motronic control unit (D, **Figure 3**) from the mounting bracket.

5. Remove the long bolts securing the Motronic unit mounting plate and the battery hold-down. Remove the mounting plate and hold down strap from the battery.

6. Press the keeper, pull the electrical connector straight up and disconnect it from the ABS control unit.

7. Remove the screw, washer and nut on each side securing the ABS control unit housing to the battery tray.

8. Carefully pull the ABS control unit and housing straight up and out of the frame.

9. Flip up the protective covers and disconnect the leads. First, disconnect the negative (-) lead then the positive lead (+) from the battery terminals. Move both leads out of the way.

10. Lay several layers of old newspaper on top of your workbench where you intend to place the battery. This will protect the workbench surface if there is electrolyte residue on the sides and/or bottom of the battery.

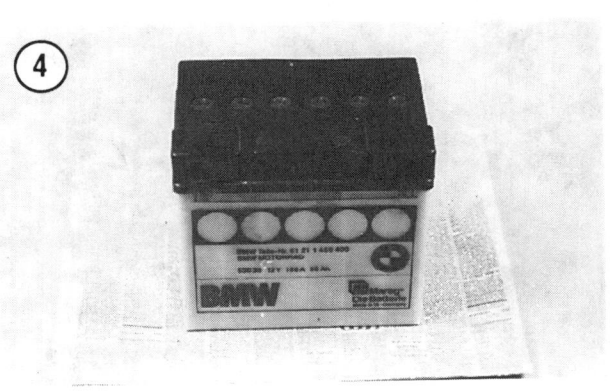

11. Carefully lift the battery straight up and remove it from the frame.

12. Set the battery on the newspapers (**Figure 4**).

13. Perform Steps 15-22 of Removal, Electrolyte Level Check and Installation *in Chapter Three in the main body of this book.*

14. Install the hold-down strap and Motronic mounting bracket on top of the battery case.

15. Install the long bolts--do not overtighten the bolts as the strap may damage the battery case.

16. Install the ABS control unit housing into the frame. Make sure the locating lug on the base of the housing is properly indexed into the receptacle in the battery tray.

17. Install the screw, washer and nut on each side securing the ABS control unit housing to the battery tray. Tighten the screws securely.

18. Connect the electrical connector onto the ABS unit and push it in until it clicks into position. Carefully pull out on the connector to make sure it is properly connected.

19. Position the Motronic control unit with the electrical connector receptacle toward the left-hand side. Install the unit, screws and washers and tighten securely.

20. Connect the electrical connector (C, **Figure 3**) onto the Motronic control unit and push it in until it clicks into position. Carefully pull out on the connector to make sure it is properly connected.

21. Install the left-hand side cover.

22. Install the seat.

PERIODIC LUBRICATION

Refer to **Table 3** for recommended types and quantities of oil for this section.

Final Drive Oil Change (K1, K100RS [1991-1992], K1100LT, K1100RSA)

The oil change service procedure is the same as on previous models with the exception of the oil quantity. Refer to **Table 3** in this section of the supplement.

Front Fork Oil Change

It is a good practice to change the fork oil at the interval listed in **Table 1** or once a year. If it becomes contaminated with dirt or water, change it immediately.

1. Place the bike on the centerstand.

2. On K75 models, remove the plastic trim cap (**Figure 5**) from the top of each fork tube.

3. Place a drain pan under the right-hand and left-hand fork sliders.

14

4. Remove the oil drain plug (**Figure 6**) from each fork slider.

5. Remove the oil filler plug and O-ring from the fork cap bolt.

6. Repeat Step 4 and Step 5 for the other fork leg.

7. Allow the fork oil to drain for 10-15 minutes to ensure that all oil is drained.

8. Sit on the seat and apply the front brake. Lean on the handlebars and compress the front forks several times to expel any additional fork oil. Get off the seat.

9. On models so equipped, remove the engine spoiler as described under *Engine Spoiler Removal/Installation* in the Chapter Thirteen section of this supplement or Chapter Thirteen in the main body of this book.

10. Lean the bike back on the centerstand and place wooden blocks under the oil pan to support the bike with the front wheel off the ground.

11. Inspect the sealing washer on the drain plug, replace if damaged in any way.

12. Install the sealing washer and drain plug in each fork leg and tighten securely.

> *NOTE*
> *On K1 models, it is necessary to use a funnel with a flexible extension tube to gain access to the filler opening in the fork cap bolt beyond the front fairing.*

13. Insert a small funnel into the filler opening in the fork cap bolt.

> *NOTE*
> *Use the recommended weight fork oil or the fork damping will be very stiff.*

> *NOTE*
> *To measure the correct amount of fluid, use a plastic baby bottle. These bottles have measurements in fluid ounces (oz.) and cubic centimeters (cc) on the side.*

14. Fill the fork leg with the correct viscosity and quantity of fork oil. Refer to **Table 3**. Remove the small funnel.

15. Repeat Step 13 and Step 14 for the other fork leg.

16. After the fork oil has been added to both fork legs, remove the wooden blocks from under the oil pan.

17. Sit on the seat and apply the front brake. Lean on the handlebars and compress the front forks several times to expel any trapped air in the fork assemblies and to distribute the fork oil.

18. Inspect the O-ring seal on the oil filler plug, replace if damaged in any way.

19. Install the O-ring seal and oil filler plug in each fork top cap and tighten securely.

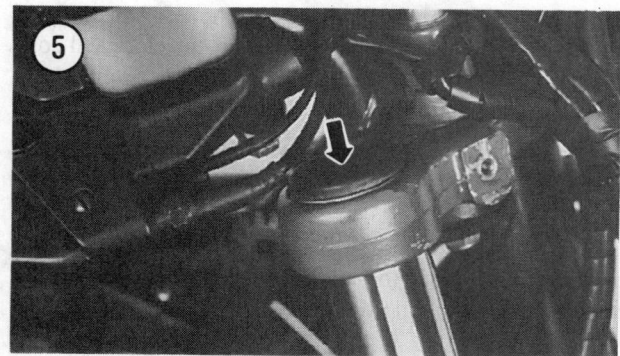

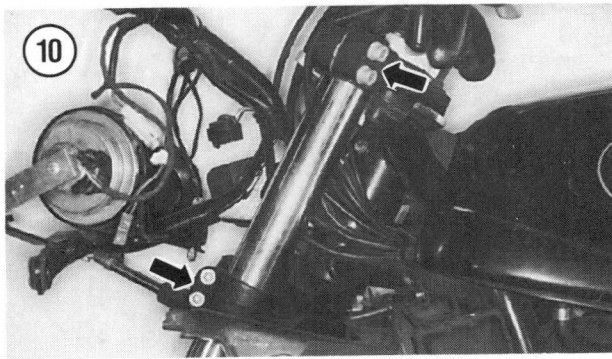

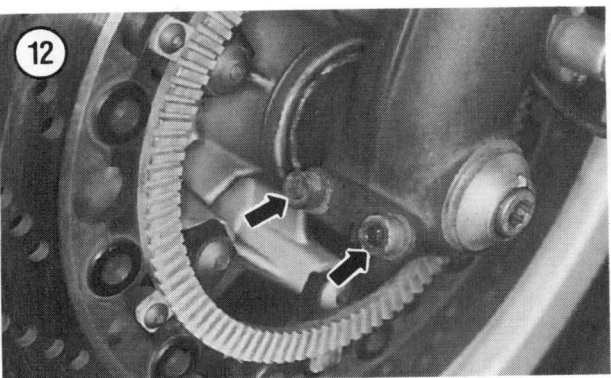

20. On K75 models, install the plastic trim cap on the fork top cap.
21. On models so equipped, install the engine spoiler.
22. Road test the bike and check for leaks.

PERIODIC MAINTENANCE

Disc Brake Pad Wear

Inspect the brake pads for excessive or uneven wear.
1. Look down into the caliper assembly and check the pad thickness.
2. Replace both pads if they are worn to the service limit dimension of 1.5 mm (1/16 in.) as described under *Brake Pad Replacement in* the Chapter Twelve section of this supplement for the front brake (all models except K75) or Chapter Twelve (K75) in the main body of this book for the rear brake.

Exhaust System

Check for leakage at all fittings and mounting fasteners. Refer to **Figure 7**, **Figure 8** and **Figure 9** for K1, K100RS and all K1100 models. If necessary, tighten all bolts and nuts. Replace any gaskets if necessary. Refer to *Exhaust System in* the Chapter Seven section of this supplement.

Front Suspension Check

1. Apply the front brake and pump the forks up and down as vigorously as possible. Check for smooth operation and oil leakage.
2. Make sure the upper and lower (**Figure 10**) fork bridge bolts are tight on each side.
3. On K75 models, remove the plastic trim cap from the top of the fork leg.
4. Make sure the fork cap bolt is tightened securely.
5. To remove the impact pad covering the handlebar upper holder bolts; refer to *Handlebar Removal* as described in the Chapter Ten section of this supplement. Make sure all Allen bolts are tight securing the handlebar upper holders.
6. Make sure the front axle clamp bolts are tight. Refer to **Figure 11** and **Figure 12**.
7. Check the tightness of the front axle bolt (**Figure 13**).
8. Replace the steering head bearings at the interval listed in **Table 1**. The correct service procedure is covered in Chapter Ten in the main body of this book.

CAUTION
If any of the previously mentioned bolts and nuts are loose, refer to the Chapter Ten section

14

of this supplement for correct procedures and torque specifications.

Rear Suspension Check

1. On models so equipped, remove the engine spoiler as described under *Engine Spoiler Removal/Installation* in the Chapter Thirteen section of this supplement or Chapter Thirteen in the main body of this book.

2. Place wooden blocks under each side of the frame to support it securely with the rear wheel off the ground.

3. Push hard on the rear wheel (sideways) to check for side play in the rear swing arm bearings. Remove the wooden block(s).

4. Check the tightness of the shock absorber upper and lower mounting bolt and nut.

5. Make sure the swing arm pivot bolts and locknut are tight as follows:

    a. Refer to the right-hand pivot point, check mounting bolts and lockwashers securing the fixed pivot pin.

    b. Refer to the left-hand pivot point, check the locknut and the adjustable pivot pin for tightness.

6. Remove the cover (**Figure 14**) and make sure the rear wheel bolts are tight (**Figure 15**).

> *CAUTION*
> *If any of the previously mentioned bolts and nuts are loose, refer to Chapter Eleven for correct procedures and torque specifications.*

7. On models so equipped, install the engine spoiler.

TUNE-UP
(K100RS [1991-1992], K1, K1100LT-ABS, K1100RSA)

> *NOTE*
> *All tune-up procedures for the 2-valve cylinder head engines are identical to previous models.*

The only different tune-up procedures required for the 4-valve engine are as follows:

    a. Valve clearance measurement.

    b. Valve clearance adjustment.

To perform a tune-up on your BMW, you need the following tools and equipment:

    a. 5 mm Allen wrench.

    b. BMW spark plug wrench and wheel lug nut wrench (in factory tool kit) or an 18 mm spark plug wrench.

    c. Socket wrench and assorted sockets.

    d. Flat feeler gauge.

    e. Assorted BMW special tools for valve clearance adjustment. These tools are described in the valve clearance adjustment procedure.

Tune up specifications are listed in **Table 4**.

Valve Clearance Measurement

Measure the valve clearance at the interval listed in **Table 1**.

Valve clearance measurement must be performed with the engine cool. The maximum temperature the cylinder

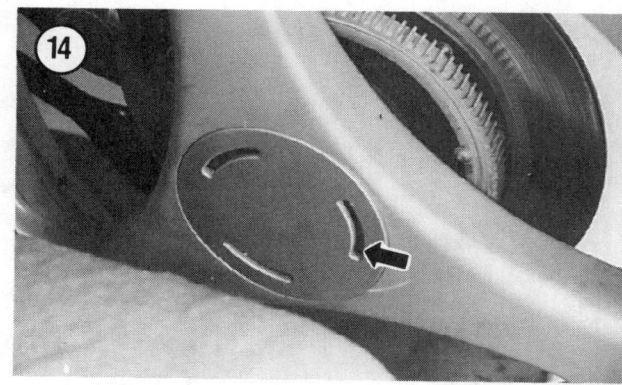

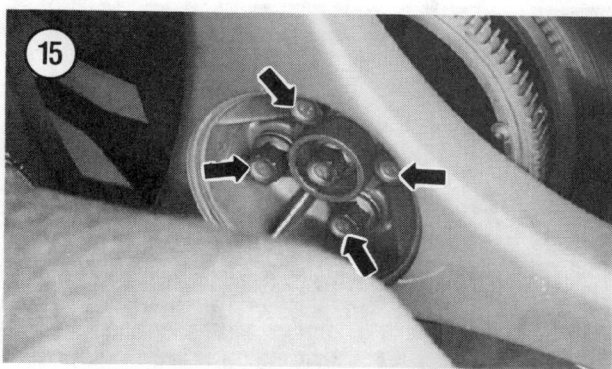

head can be is 35° C (95° F). If the temperature is greater than specified, the clearance measurement will not be correct. The correct valve clearances are listed in **Table 4**. The intake valves are located at the top of the cylinder head and the exhaust valves are located at the bottom.

NOTE
Measure the valve clearance very accurately. This adjustment procedure is quite complicated and you will only want to perform it once. This is not like turning an adjustment screw on a rocker arm adjuster, where you can go back and forth easily until the clearance is correct. If you do not accurately measure the first time, chances are you will have to purchase the valve lifter(s) again and repeat the procedure until the clearance is correct. Once the clearance is correct, it will usually remain correct for many thousands of miles and will probably only have to be checked but not readjusted.

1. Place the bike on the centerstand.
2. Remove any body panels from the left-hand side that may interfere with removal of the cylinder head cover. Refer to Chapter Thirteen in this supplement.
3. Shift the transmission into 5th gear.
4. Remove the screws and lockwashers securing the spark plug cover panel and remove the panel (**Figure 16**).
5. Using a pair of pliers, carefully pull the spark plug cap from each spark plug (**Figure 17**).
6. Using a crisscross pattern, loosen the bolts securing the cylinder head cover (**Figure 18**). Remove the bolts, the cover and the rubber gasket. Don't lose the spring (**Figure 19**) located on one of the camshaft bearing caps.
7. Remove all spark plugs from the cylinder head as described in Chapter Three in the main body of the book. This will make it easier to rotate the engine by hand during this procedure.

NOTE
There is no specific sequence to checking the valve clearance, but to avoid confusion, start at the front of the engine with the No. 1 cylinder and work toward the back checking the remaining 3 cylinders in order.

NOTE
To obtain the correct measurement, the camshaft lobe must be directly opposite the lifter surface.

NOTE
The intake camshaft is located at the upper side of the cylinder head (next to the fuel

14

injectors) and the exhaust camshaft is located at the lower side of the cylinder head (next to the exhaust pipes).

8. Rotate the engine using the rear wheel until the front or No. 1 cylinder is at top dead center (TDC) on its compression stroke. To determine TDC for the No. 1 cylinder, perform the following:

    a. Rotate the rear wheel, in normal forward rotation, until the intake camshaft has completely opened the *intake valves,* and then allowed them to close.

    b. Using a small flashlight, direct the light into the spark plug hole to observe the piston as it moves up in the cylinder.

    c. Continue to rotate the rear wheel until the No. 1 cylinder's piston reaches the top of its stroke. This will be TDC on the compression stroke.

9. With the engine in this position, check the clearance of the No. 1 cylinder's 2 intake and 2 exhaust valves.

NOTE
Measure the valve clearance with a flat metric feeler gauge. If adjustment is necessary, it will be easier to calculate valve lifter spacer selection in the following procedure.

NOTE
Measure the clearance very accurately. The adjustment procedure is quite complicated and you will only want to perform it once. This is not like turning an adjustment screw on a rocker arm adjuster, where you can go back and forth easily until the clearance is correct. If you do not accurately measure the first time, chances are you will have to purchase the valve lifter(s) again and repeat the procedure until the clearance is correct. Once the clearance is correct, it will probably maintain this clearance for many thousands of miles and will probably not have to be readjusted—only remeasured.

10. Check the clearance by inserting a flat *metric f*eeler gauge between the camshaft and the top surface of the valve lifter (**Figure 20**). When the correct feeler gauge is selected, there will be a slight drag on the feeler gauge when it is inserted and withdrawn.

11. Measure the valve clearance for both the 2 intake and 2 exhaust valves on the No. 1 cylinder. Record the clearance for the intake and exhaust valves, noting the cylinder number. The clearance dimensions will be used during the adjustment procedure, if adjustment is necessary.

12. To correct the valve clearance, the valve lifter must be replaced with one having a different top surface thickness. These valve lifters are available from BMW dealers in 0.05

mm increments that range from 2.50 mm to 3.20 mm in thickness. The thickness is marked on the inner surface of the valve lifter body.

13. Repeat Steps 8-11 for the valves in the remaining cylinders. Substitute the No. 1 cylinder designation in these steps for the specific cylinder that you are working on. Record the clearance for both the intake and exhaust valves.

Valve Clearance Adjustment

To adjust the valve clearance on the 4-valve cylinder head, it is necessary to remove both camshafts from the cylinder head to access any valve lifters that must be replaced. Follow the camshaft removal and installation procedure in this section. Do *not* use the procedure described in the Chapter Four section of this supplement since that procedure does not use the special tool used to relieve stress on the camshaft drive chain.

Valve lifter selection

NOTE
The correct valve clearance is 0.15-0.20 mm for the intake valves and 0.25-0.30 mm for the exhaust valves. For the best performance, adjust the valve clearance to the smaller dimension.

There is no specific sequence for adjusting the valve clearance, but to avoid confusion, start at the front of the engine with the No. 1 cylinder and work toward the back. Determine which cylinder(s) require valve clearance adjustment. This procedure takes into account that at least one of the four valves requires adjustment in each cylinder. If all four valves in 1 cylinder are within specification, skip that cylinder and proceed to the next cylinder.

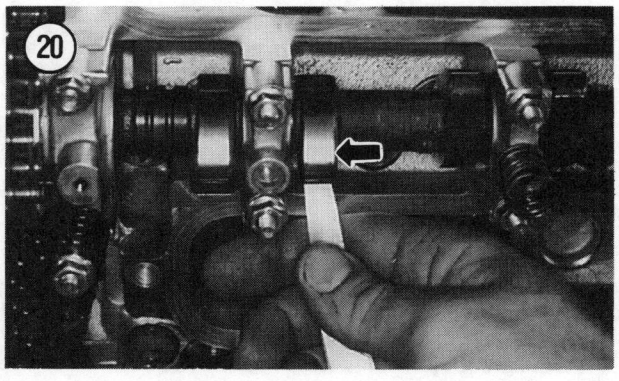

NOTE
If working on a well run-in engine (high mileage), measure the valve lifter head thickness with a micrometer to make sure of the exact thickness of the top surface. If the valve lifter top surface is worn to less than the indicated thickness marked on it, it will throw off calculations when selecting a new valve lifter.

1. For correct valve lifter selection proceed as follows:

NOTE
In the following valve clearance calculations, use the mid-point of the specified clearance. For example, the clearance specification for the intake valve is 0.15-0.20 mm, so use 0.18 mm as the reference value. The clearance specification for the exhaust valves is 0.25-0.30 mm, so use 0.28 mm as the reference value.

NOTE
*The following numbers are for **example only**. Use the numbers written down during the **Valve Clearance Measurement** procedure.*

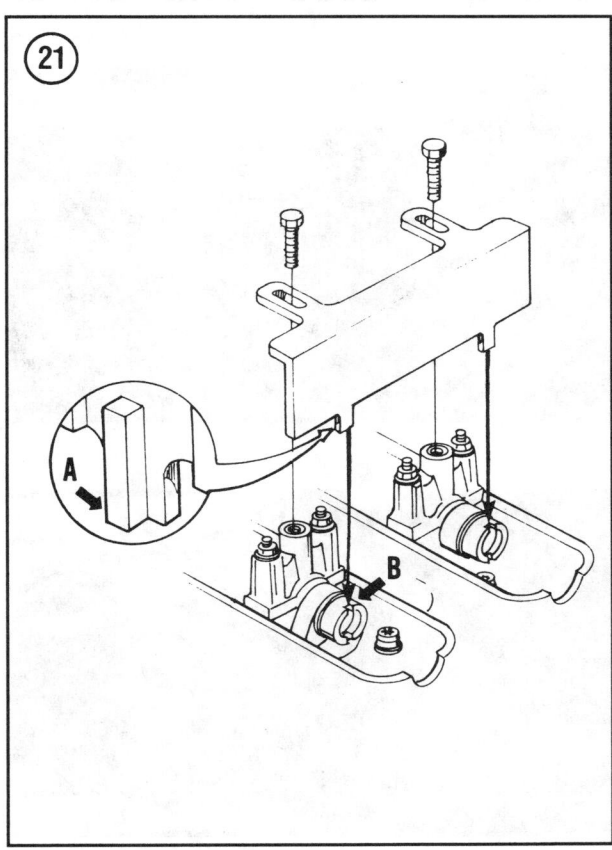

Example:

	Intake	Exhaust
Actual measured clearance	0.50 mm	0.41 mm
Subtract specified clearance	– 0.18 mm	– 0.28 mm
Equals excess clearance	0.32 mm	0.13 mm
Existing valve lifter number	220	245
Add excess clearance	+ 32	+ 13
Equals new valve lifter number	252	258
(round off to the		
nearest spacer number)	250	260

2. Repeat Step 1, for all valve assemblies that are out of specification.

Camshaft removal

NOTE
Remove only the camshaft necessary to replace the valve lifters. Do not remove the intake camshaft, if only the exhaust valve lifters must be replaced.

1. Make sure the No. 1 cylinder is still at TDC on the compression stroke. Refer to Step 8 of *Valve Clearance Measurement* in this section of the supplement.

NOTE
*The following two BMW special tools **are required** to release the tension on the camshaft timing chain. This eliminates the need to remove the timing chain cover and timing chain to remove the camshafts.*

2. Install the BMW setting device (part No. 11 3 700), onto the rear end of the camshafts. Align the raised bosses (A, **Figure 21**) on the special tool with the with the vertical slots on the camshafts (B, **Figure 21**). Secure the special tool to the rear bearing caps with bolts. Tighten the bolts securely.
3. Unscrew the plug (**Figure 22**) in the timing chain cover.
4. Pull back on the pin (A, **Figure 23**) on BMW special tool (part No. 11 2 640) and screw the tool (B, **Figure 23**) into the timing chain cover. Turn it about 3-4 turns.
5. With the tool in this position, push the pin into the timing chain cover behind the timing chain.
6. Slowly turn the pin in a *clockwise* direction to release the tension on the chain tensioner. With the pin in this position, tighten the locknut (C, **Figure 23**) securely.

NOTE
Prior to removing the camshafts, note the identifying grooves on the camshafts. The number of grooves on the intake camshaft

14

(Figure 24) and the exhaust camshaft (Figure 25) varies with years and models. In some cases, the exhaust camshaft may not have any grooves.

7. Remove the nuts (A, **Figure 26**) and the guide rail (B, **Figure 26**) from the front camshaft bearing cap studs.

NOTE
Secure the camshaft with an open-end wrench on the hexagonal area of the camshaft, then loosen the camshaft sprocket bolt(s).

8. Remove the bolt (C, **Figure 26**) and washer (D, **Figure 26**) securing the camshaft sprocket. Disengage the driven sprocket from the timing chain and remove the driven sprocket (E, **Figure 26**).

9. If necessary, repeat Step 8 for the other driven sprocket.

10. Insert the ends of a clean shop cloth into the oil return openings in the cylinder head to prevent small parts from falling into the crankcase.

11. First loosen, then remove the nuts (A, **Figure 27**) and washers (B) securing both front thrust bearing caps (C). Remove these bearing caps and their locating dowels. The front bearing caps take up the thrust movement (end play) of the camshafts and must be removed first.

NOTE
Either camshaft can be removed first. However, remove only the camshaft required for valve lifter replacement.

12. Using a criss-cross pattern, loosen then remove the nuts securing the remaining bearing caps on one of the camshafts and remove the remaining bearing caps (D, **Figure 27**). Mark the location of the bearing caps so they will be reinstalled in the same location (**Figure 28**).

13. Lift up that camshaft and disengage it from the drive chain.

14. If necessary, repeat Step 13 and Step 14 for the other camshaft. After the last camshaft is removed, tie a piece of wire to the timing chain and secure it to the exterior of the engine. This will prevent the timing chain from accidentally slipping into the chain cavity.

15. Use a magnetic tool and remove the valve lifter(s) that requires replacement from the receptacles in the cylinder head. Keep them in the correct order.

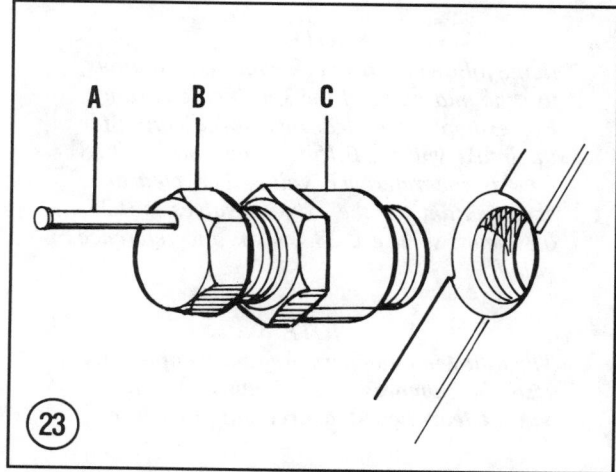

16. Apply clean engine oil to the new valve lifter(s) and install in the cylinder head. Push the valve lifter all the way down until it seats on top of the valve stem. After installation, rotate the valve lifter to make sure it is properly seated in the receptacle in the cylinder head.

Camshaft installation

1. Make sure the No. 1 cylinder is still at top dead center (TDC).

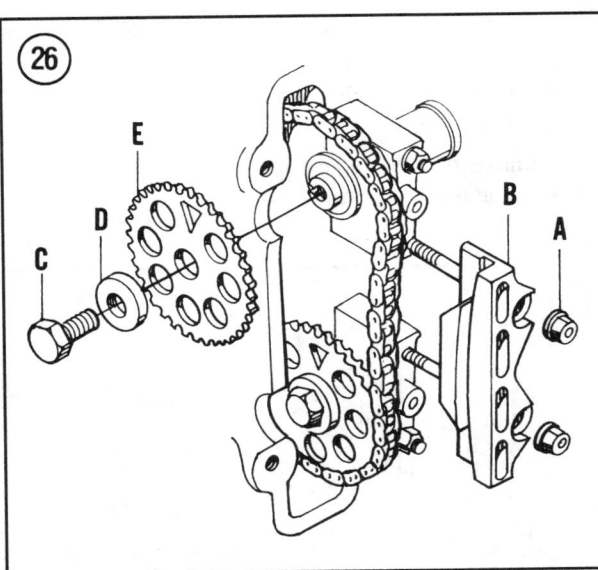

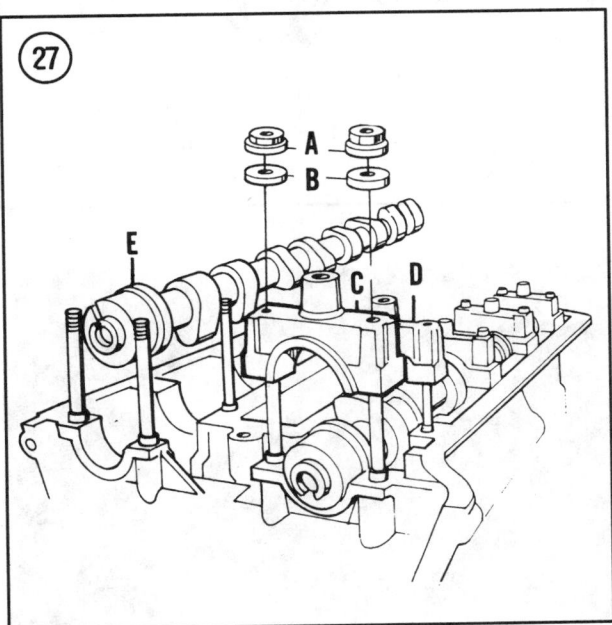

2. Apply clean engine oil to the camshaft bearing journals and lobes. Also apply clean engine oil to the bearing surfaces in the cylinder head and the bearing caps.

3. If used, untie the wire from the timing chain.

NOTE
*Refer to the marks on the camshafts (**Figure 29**) as noted during removal. Be sure to install the camshafts in the correct location in the cylinder head.*

4. Correctly position the camshaft and install the camshaft into the cylinder head. Loop the timing chain over the end of the camshaft.

5. Make sure the locating dowels are in place on the threaded studs for the front thrust bearing caps. These are the only bearing caps equipped with locating dowels.

6. Install the bearing caps in their correct locations in the cylinder head (**Figure 28**). Install the front thrust bearing cap (A, **Figure 30**) *last*. Install the nuts and washers securing the bearing caps and tighten finger-tight.

CAUTION
The camshafts must be correctly positioned within the cylinder head for correct valve timing. If the camshaft is installed incorrectly,

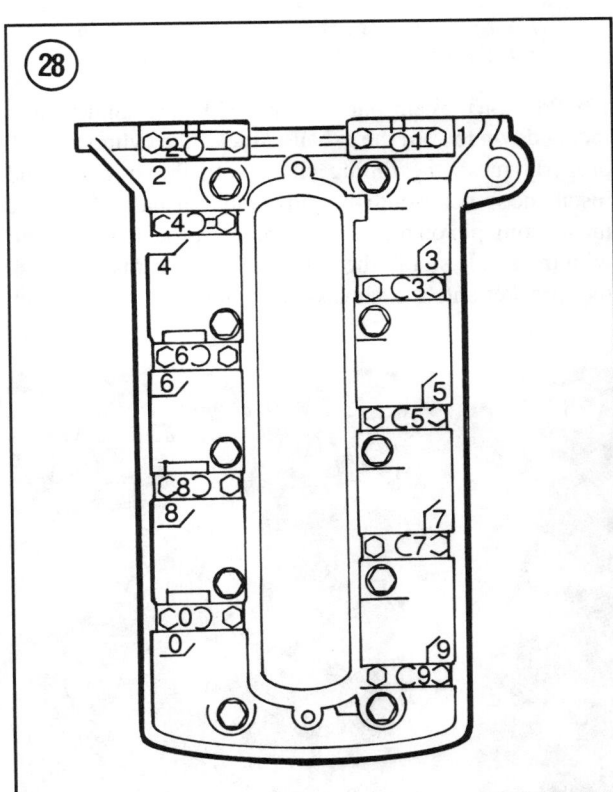

14

there will be severe damage to the valve(s) as well as the piston(s). Be sure to locate the camshaft as described in Step 7.

7. Rotate the camshaft so the single front groove (B, **Figure 30**) points toward the top surface of the cylinder head (C, **Figure 30**), or the crankshaft, and the 2 slots at the rear of the camshaft are facing vertical.

CAUTION
Tighten the bearing caps evenly so the camshafts move down into position evenly, avoiding any undue stress.

8. Tighten the nuts in 2-3 stages in a criss-cross pattern, working from the center of the camshaft out toward each end. Tighten to the torque specification listed in **Table 5**.

9. If necessary, repeat Steps 2-8 for the other camshaft.

10. Remove the shop cloth from the oil return openings in the cylinder head.

11. Install the BMW setting device (part No. 11 3 700), on the rear end of the camshafts. Align the raised bosses (A, **Figure 21**) on the special tool with the with the vertical slots on the camshafts (B, **Figure 21**). Secure the special tool to the rear bearing caps with bolts. Tighten the bolts securely.

NOTE
If both camshafts sprockets are removed, install the exhaust camshaft sprocket first.

12. Position the camshaft sprocket with the triangle cutout facing down toward the exhaust side of the cylinder head, properly mesh the timing chain with the sprocket and install the sprocket onto the end of the camshaft. Make sure the locating pin on the backside of the sprocket is engaged with the single slot in the front end of the camshaft. Push the sprocket onto the camshaft until it bottoms out. Check

to make sure the triangle cutout (**Figure 31**) is facing in the correct direction.

CAUTION
Do not tighten the camshaft sprocket bolt installed in Step 14 while the special tool installed in Step 12 is still in place. If the bolt is tightened with this tool in place, the end of the camshaft will be damaged.

13. Install the washer and bolt and finger-tighten at this time.

14. Repeat Step 12 and Step 13 for the other camshaft sprocket. After installation, make sure both triangle cutouts (**Figure 32**) are facing down toward the exhaust side of the cylinder head.

15. Remove the bolts and the special tool, installed in Step 12, from the rear of the camshafts.

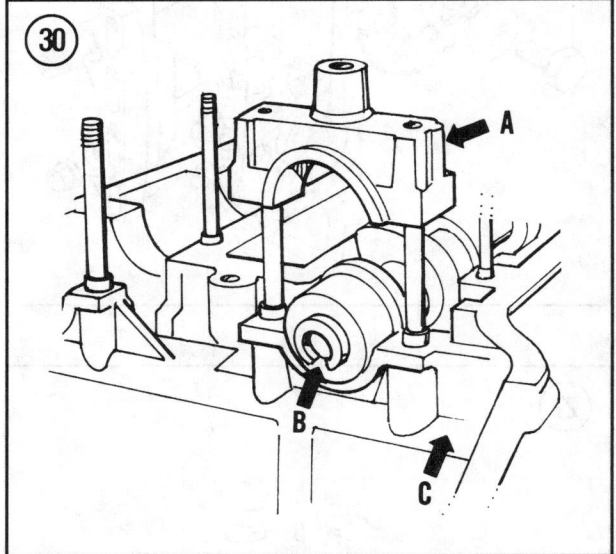

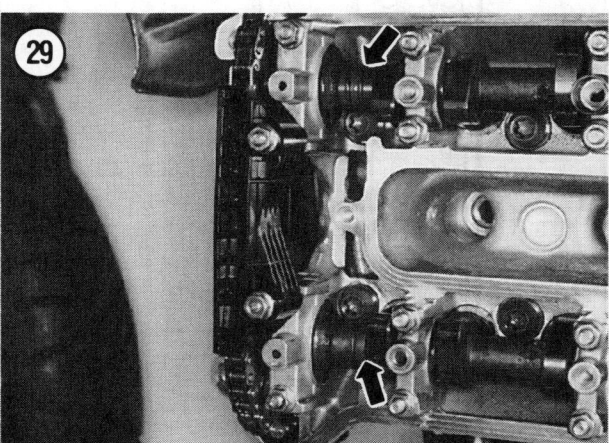

16. Secure the camshaft with an open-end wrench on the hexagon on the camshaft, then tighten the camshaft sprocket bolt to the torque specification listed in **Table 5**.
17. Using the rear wheel, rotate the engine several complete revolutions to seat all new components.
18. Reinspect all valve clearances as described in this chapter. If any of the clearances are still not within specification, repeat this procedure until all clearances are correct.
19. Start the bike and make sure it runs correctly.

Ignition Timing

Check the ignition timing at the interval indicated in **Table 1**.

The ignition procedure is identical to prior models. For 1100cc models, follow the procedures relating to the K100 models.

Fast Idle Adjustment for Cold Starting

On all 4-valve engines, the fuel injection system and the ignition system are controlled by a single engine management computer called the Motronic Control Unit.

The Motronic Control Unit controls all of the fuel injection functions. Any adjustment to any of the components in both systems must be checked by a very expensive piece of BMW test equipment called the Synchrotester (BMW part No. 13 0 800). The service charge for any fuel injection system adjustments by a BMW dealer are minimal compared to the purchase price of this equipment.

Idle Speed Adjustment

Refer to *Fast Idle Adjustment for Cold Starting* in the preceding procedure relating to the Motronic Control Unit.

Table 1 MAINTENANCE SCHEDULE*

Perform these procedures at specific monthly intervals. This is especially true if the bike is not routinely ridden.	
Every 3 months	• Check the battery electrolyte level. Refill if necessary.
Every 3 months or at least every 2,000 miles (1,242 km).	• Change engine oil and filter if the bike is used at temperatures below 0° C (32° F).
Every 6 months or at least every 4,660 miles (7,500 km)	• Change engine oil and filter if the bike is used for short trips only.
	• Lubricate the clutch splines and input shaft splines if bike is used in high humidity areas. Perform this procedure if clutch operation is erratic.
Every 12 months	• Change engine oil and filter.
	• Change transmission oil.
	• Change final drive oil.
	• Change front fork oil.
	• Change brake fluid and bleed the brake system.
	• Lubricate the clutch splines and input shaft splines. Perform this procedure if clutch operation is erratic.
(continued)	

14

Table 1 MAINTENANCE SCHEDULE* (continued)

Every 2 years	• Drain and replace engine coolant.
Before each ride.	• Inspect tire and rim condition. • Check tire inflation pressure. • Check fuel supply. Make sure there is enough fuel for the intended ride. • Check brake operation and for fluid leakage. • Check for fuel leakage. • Check coolant level and for coolant leakage. • Check the oil level in the engine, transmission and final drive unit. • Check for smooth clutch and throttle operation. • Check for smooth gearshift operation. • Check steering for smooth operation with no excessive play or restrictions. • Check headlight, taillight/brake light and turn signal operation. • Check horn operation.
Every 4,660 miles (7,500 km)	• Change engine oil and filter. • Check battery electrolyte level. • Make sure battery cables are clean and properly secured. • Check spark plug condition and gap. Do *not* regap. • Clean or replace air filter element if bike is ridden in dirty or dusty conditions. • Lubricate clutch cable nipples at each end. • Check all fuel line connections for leakage or damage. Tighten hose clamps if necessary. • Check the fuel tank vent and drain lines. • Check brake fluid level in master cylinders. • Check all brake lines and hoses for leakage or damage. • Check brake pads for wear. • Check brake discs for wear or damage. • Lubricate control cables. • Lubricate centerstand and side stand pivot points. • Inspect tire tread depth and inflation pressure. • Check tightness of rear wheel mounting bolts. • Check tightness of muffler heat shield bolts. • Check tightness of sidestand pivot bolt. • Check for smooth clutch and throttle operation. • Check for smooth gearshift operation. • Check steering for smooth operation with no excessive play or restrictions. • Check all running and illumination lights. • Check horn operation.
Every 9,320 miles (15,000 km)	• Replace all spark plugs. • Check valve clearance. • Check ignition timing**. • Have idle speed and CO value checked by a BMW dealer**. • Run a compression test. • Replace air filter element.

(continued)

Table 1 MAINTENANCE SCHEDULE* (continued)

Every 9,320 miles (15,000 km) (continued)	• Replace fuel filter. • Replace transmission oil. • Replace final drive oil. • Replace front fork oil. • Check and adjust throttle free play. • Check and adjust clutch clearance. • Check and adjust brake pedal height. • Check coolant level and antifreeze percentage. • Clean speedometer inductive sensor in final drive unit. • Check ABS sensor clearance. • Check and adjust steering head bearings. • Check and adjust swing arm bearing play. • Check wheel bearings. • Check tightness of front axle bolt and clamping bolts. • Check tightness of side stand and center stand pivot bolts. • Check tightness of shock absorber mounting bolts. • Check tightness of engine mounting bolt and nuts. • Check tightness of exhaust system fasteners.

*This BMW factory maintenance schedule should be considered as a guide to general maintenance and lubrication intervals. Harder than normal use and exposure to mud, water, sand, high humidity, etc. will naturally dictate more frequent attention to most maintenance items.

**Some of the procedures must be performed by a BMW dealer due to the high cost of the test equipment involved and the extensive training required for operation of the equipment.

Table 2 TIRE INFLATION PRESSURE (COLD)*

Model	Rider only		Rider and passenger	
	psi	kPa	psi	kPa
All models				
Front	32	220	36	250
Rear	36	250	42	290

*Tire inflation pressure for factory equipped tires. Aftermarket tires may require different inflation pressure.

14

Table 3 OIL QUANTITY AND RECOMMENDED TYPE

Item	Quantity	Recommended type
Final drive unit oil		Hypoid gear oil GL5
Overhaul	0.25 liter 0.26 qt.)	SAE 90 above 5° C (41° F)
Oil change	0.23 liter (0.24 qt.)	SAE 80 below 5° C (41° F)
		SAE 80W 90 (optional)
	(continued)	

Table 3 OIL QUANTITY AND RECOMMENDED TYPE (continued)

Item	Quantity	Recommended type
Front fork oil		BMW fork oil, ESSO Komfort
K75 models (1992-on)	410 cc (13.8 oz.)	
K100 models	400 cc (13.5 oz.)	
K1	440-450 cc (14.8-15.2 oz.)	
K1100 models		
Left-hand leg	349-351 cc (11.7-11.8 oz.)	
Right-hand leg	399-401 cc (13.4-13.6 oz.)	

Table 4 TUNE UP SPECIFICATIONS

Valve clearance*
  Intake: 0.15-0.20 mm (0.006-0.008 in.)
  Exhaust: 0.25-0.30 mm (0.010-0.012 in.)
Spark plug type
  K75
    Bosch XR5DC or Champion A 85 YC
  K100, K1
    Bosch XR5DC or Beru 12-5DU
  K1100
    Bosch XR5DC or Beru 12 R-5DU
Spark plug gap
  Recommended 0.6-0.7 mm (0.024-0.28 in.)
  Maximum gap limit 0.9 mm (0.036 in.)
Compression pressure
  Good: more than 1000 kPa (145 psi)
  Normal: 850-1000 kPa (123-145 psi)
  Poor: less than 850 kPa (123 psi)
Idle speed 950-1,000 rpm

* Cylinder head maximum temperature: 35° C (95° F).

Table 5 MAINTENANCE AND TUNE UP TORQUE SPECIFICATIONS

Item	N·m	ft.-lb.
Camshaft bearing cap nuts	9	6.6
Camshaft driven sprocket bolt	54	40

CHAPTER FOUR

ENGINES

Refer to **Table 6** for engine specifications that are unique to the 4-valve engines covered in this supplement. Only those specifications listed are unique. If a specification is not listed in **Table 6**, refer to **Table 2** in Chapter Four in the main body of this book.

ENGINE REMOVAL/INSTALLATION (4-VALVE ENGINES)

The engine removal and installation procedure is the same as on previous models with the exception of the front mounting bolts, washers and nuts securing the engine in the frame. On these models, the mounting bolts screw directly into the frames threaded receptacles thus eliminating the nuts. Tighten the bolts to the torque specification listed in **Table 6**.

CRANKSHAFT COVER, CYLINDER HEAD COVER AND TIMING CHAIN COVER

NOTE
The crankshaft cover and the timing chain cover removal and installation procedures are the same as on previous models.

Cylinder Head Cover Removal

NOTE
This procedure is necessary for cylinder head removal.

Refer to **Figure 33** for this procedure.

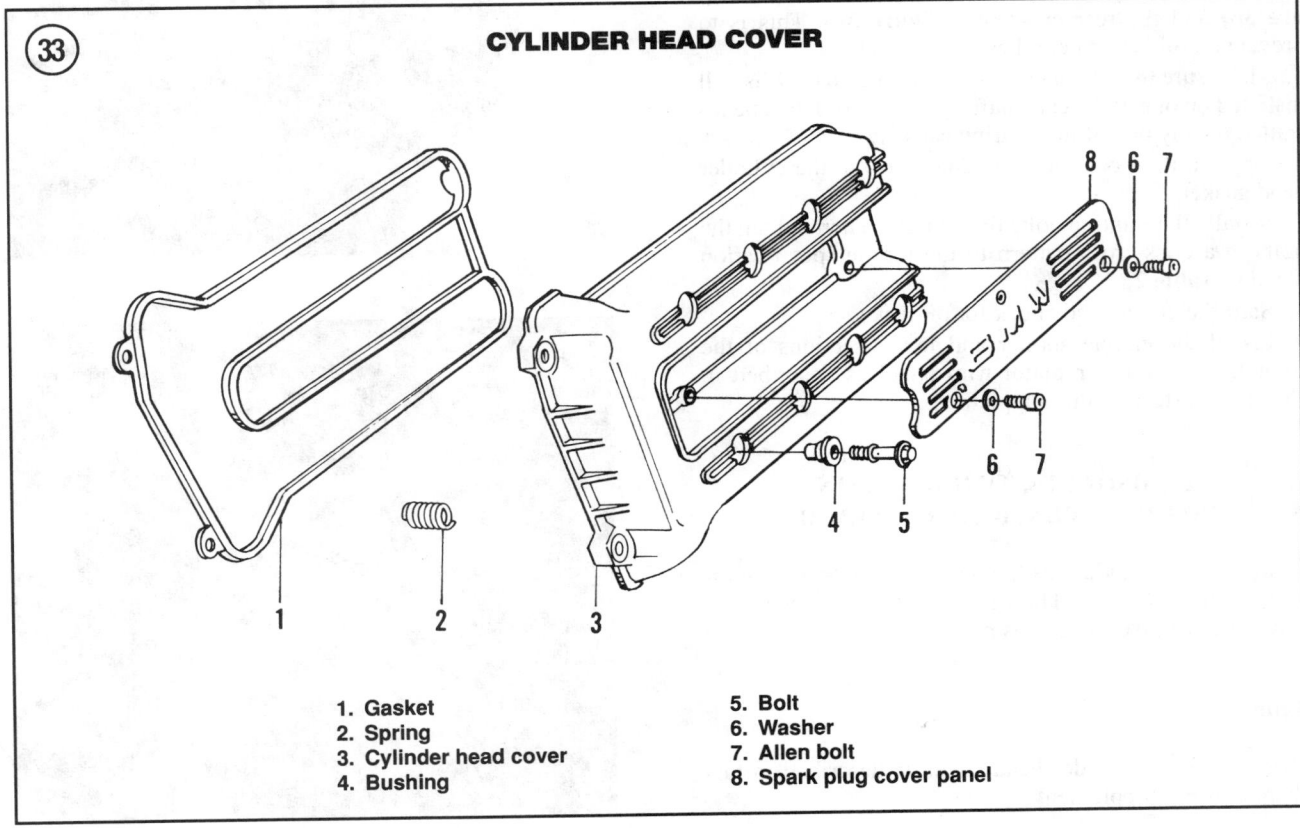

CYLINDER HEAD COVER

1. Gasket
2. Spring
3. Cylinder head cover
4. Bushing
5. Bolt
6. Washer
7. Allen bolt
8. Spark plug cover panel

14

1. Place the bike on the centerstand.

2. Remove the engine spoiler and lower sections of the front fairing and/or radiator trim panel as described in Chapter Thirteen in this supplement.

3. Remove the screws and lockwashers securing the spark plug cover panel and remove the panel (**Figure 16**).

4. Using a pair of pliers, carefully pull the spark plug cap from each spark plug (**Figure 17**).

5. Using a crisscross pattern, loosen the bolts securing the cylinder head cover (**Figure 18**). Remove the bolts, cover and rubber gasket. Don't lose the spring (**Figure 19**) located on one of the camshaft bearing caps.

Cylinder Head Cover Installation

1. Thoroughly clean the mating surfaces of the cylinder head where the cover attaches.

2. Inspect the single rubber gasket around the perimeter of the cylinder head cover. If it is starting to harden or deteriorate it should be replaced.

3. If removed, install the rubber gasket (A, **Figure 34**) into the cylinder head cover starting at the rear and working around to the front. Make sure the crescents at the rear (B, **Figure 34**) are indexed properly into the cover slots.

4. Apply a light coat of ThreeBond No. 1209 gasket sealer to where the timing chain cover mates with the cylinder head (A, **Figure 35**), at the front crescents (B, **Figure 35**) and the rear crescents (**Figure 36**). This is to prevent an oil leak where these parts meet.

5. Make sure the single ground spring (**Figure 19**) is still installed on one of the camshaft bearing caps. It can be installed on any one of the bearing caps.

6. Apply a light coat of clean engine oil to the cylinder head gasket.

7. Install all mounting bolts finger-tight. Then tighten the bolts in a criss-cross pattern to the torque specification listed in **Table 2**.

8. Start the engine and check for oil leaks.

9. Install the engine spoiler and lower sections of the front fairing and/or radiator trim panel as described in Chapter Thirteen in this supplement.

CAMSHAFTS, TIMING CHAIN AND CHAIN PENSIONER ASSEMBLY

On 4-valve cylinder head, refer to *Valve Clearance Adjustment* in the Chapter Three section of this supplement.

Refer to **Figure 37** for this procedure.

Removal

1. Remove the cylinder head cover as described in this chapter of the supplement.

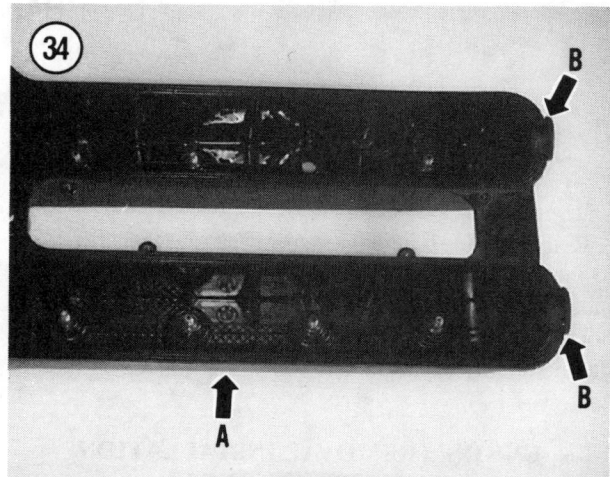

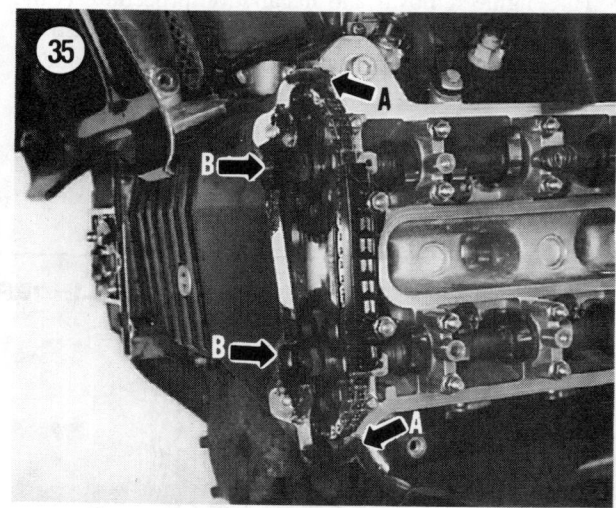

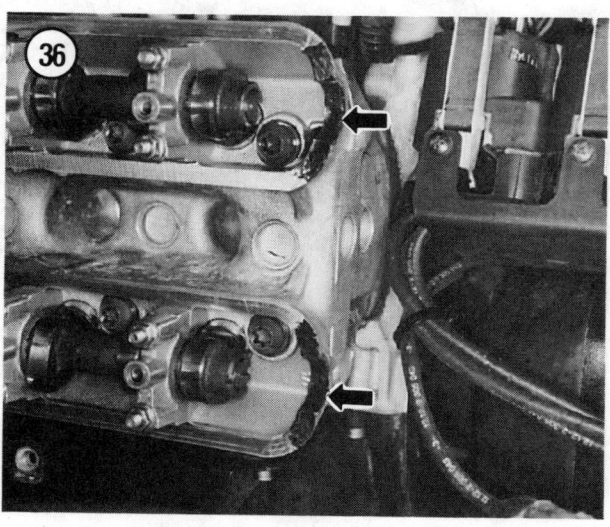

2. Remove the timing chain cover (A, **Figure 38**) and the crankshaft cover as described in Chapter Four in the main body of this book.

3. Remove all spark plugs. This makes it easier to rotate the engine.

NOTE
The following step is not absolutely necessary, but it will even out the stress placed on the camshafts during removal. The engine must also be at this location during camshaft installation.

4. Using an Allen driver on the crankshaft bolt (A, **Figure 39**), rotate the engine in the normal direction of rotation (counterclockwise) until the front or No. 1 cylinder is at top dead center (TDC) on its compression stroke. To determine TDC for the No. 1 cylinder, perform the following:

    a. Rotate the engine in the normal forward rotation, until the intake camshaft (upper camshaft) has completely opened the *intake valves*, then allowed them to close.

    b. Using a small flashlight, direct the light into the spark plug hole to observe the piston as it moves up in the cylinder.

    c. Continue to rotate the engine until the No. 1 cylinder's piston reaches the top of its stroke. This will be TDC on the compression stroke.

    d. At this point, the pin (B, **Figure 39**) on the timing chain drive sprocket will align with the "OT" index mark (C, **Figure 39**) on the cylinder block.

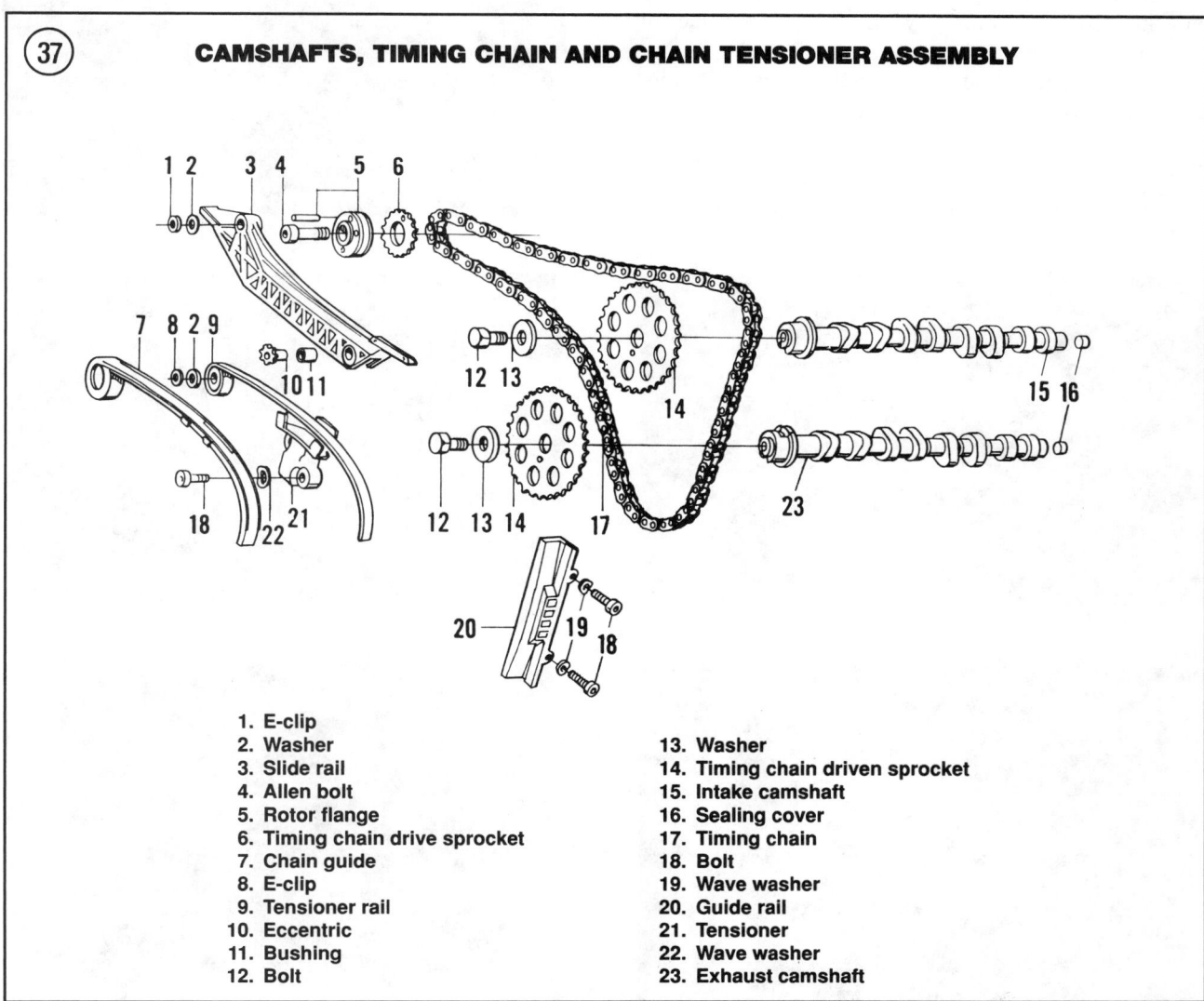

CAMSHAFTS, TIMING CHAIN AND CHAIN TENSIONER ASSEMBLY

1. E-clip
2. Washer
3. Slide rail
4. Allen bolt
5. Rotor flange
6. Timing chain drive sprocket
7. Chain guide
8. E-clip
9. Tensioner rail
10. Eccentric
11. Bushing
12. Bolt
13. Washer
14. Timing chain driven sprocket
15. Intake camshaft
16. Sealing cover
17. Timing chain
18. Bolt
19. Wave washer
20. Guide rail
21. Tensioner
22. Wave washer
23. Exhaust camshaft

14

5. Remove the nuts (B, **Figure 38**) securing the guide rail (C, **Figure 38**) and remove the guide rail.

6. Remove the Allen bolts and washers securing the timing chain tensioner (A, **Figure 40**). Pivot the tensioner counterclockwise and disengage it from the tensioner rail (B, **Figure 40**). Remove the tensioner assembly.

7. Remove the spring clip (**Figure 41**) and the washer (**Figure 42**) securing the timing chain tensioner guide rail and guide to the cylinder block.

8. Remove the timing chain tensioner guide rail and guide (**Figure 43**) from the cylinder block.

9. Remove the upper E-clip and washer (A, **Figure 44**) and the lower E-clip and washer (B, **Figure 44**) securing the timing chain guide rail to the cylinder block.

10. Remove the timing chain guide rail (C, **Figure 44**) from the cylinder block. Don't lose the eccentric (D, **Figure 44**) and the inner eccentric collar from the top mounting boss. The collar may fall out when the guide rail is removed.

11. Remove the nuts and the guide rail (E, **Figure 44**) from the front camshaft bearing cap studs.

NOTE
Prior to removing the camshafts, note the identifying grooves on the camshafts. The

number of grooves on the intake camshaft (**Figure 45**) and the exhaust camshaft (**Figure 46**) varies with years and models. In some cases, the exhaust camshaft may have not have any grooves.

NOTE
Secure the camshaft with an open-end wrench on the hexagonal portion of the camshaft, then loosen the camshaft sprocket bolts.

12. Remove the bolt and washer (F, **Figure 44**) securing each camshaft sprocket. Disengage the driven sprocket from the timing chain and remove the driven sprockets (G, **Figure 44**).

13. Insert the ends of a clean shop cloth into the oil return openings in the cylinder head to prevent small parts from falling into the crankcase.

14. First loosen, then remove the nuts (A, **Figure 47**) and washers (B) securing both front thrust bearing caps (C). Remove these bearing caps and their locating dowels. The front bearing caps take up the thrust movement (end play) of the camshafts and must be removed first.

15. Following a criss-cross pattern, loosen, then remove the nuts securing the remaining bearing caps on one of the camshafts and remove the remaining bearing caps (D, **Figure 47**).

16. Lift up that camshaft and disengage it from the drive chain.

17. Remove the timing chain from the drive sprocket on the end of the crankshaft.

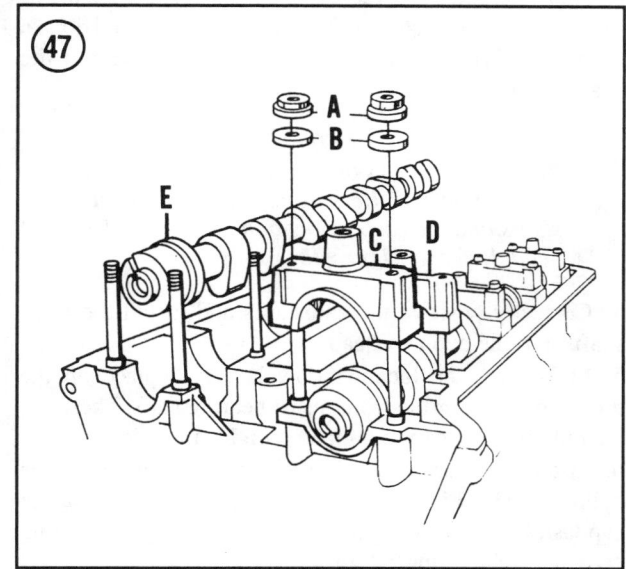

14

Inspection

Inspection of the timing chain and chain tensioner assembly is the same as on previous models. Inspection of the camshafts is the same except there are an additional set of camshaft lobes for each cylinder. On the 4-valve head, each camshaft now has a total of 8 lobes instead of 4 as on previous models. The camshaft inspection procedure also shows the removal and installation of the camshaft driven sprockets and that only relates to the 2-valve cylinder head. On the 4-valve cylinder head, the sprockets are installed after the camshaft have been installed in the cylinder head.

Installation

1. Make sure the No. 1 (front) cylinder is still at top dead center (TDC).

2. To determine if the No. 1 (front) cylinder is at TDC, perform the following:

   a. Using a small flashlight, direct the light into the spark plug hole to observe if the piston is visible in the cylinder.

   b. Using an Allen driver on the crankshaft bolt (A, **Figure 39**), slightly rotate the engine back and forth to make sure the piston is at TDC. If the piston is at TDC, proceed to Step 3. If the No. 1 cylinder is not at TDC, rotate the engine in the normal (counterclockwise) forward rotation until the front or No. 1 cylinder is at top dead center (TDC).

   c. At this point, the pin (B, **Figure 39**) on the timing chain drive sprocket will align with the "OT" index mark (C, **Figure 39**) on the cylinder block. If so, the cylinder is at TDC.

3. Apply a light, but complete, coat of molybdenum disulfide grease to the camshaft bearing journals and lobes. Coat all bearing surfaces in the cylinder head and the bearing caps.

> *NOTE*
> *Refer to the marks on the camshafts as noted during removal. Be sure to install the camshafts into the correct location in the cylinder head. Refer to **Figure 48**.*

4. Correctly position the camshafts and install the camshafts into the cylinder head.

5. Make sure the locating dowels are in place on the threaded studs for the front thrust bearing caps. These are the only bearing caps equipped with locating dowels.

6. Install the bearing caps in their correct locations in the cylinder head (**Figure 49**). Install the front thrust bearing cap last. Install the nuts and washers securing the bearing caps and tighten finger-tight.

> *CAUTION*
> *The camshafts must be correctly positioned within the cylinder head for correct valve timing. If the camshaft is installed incorrectly, there will be severe damage to the valve(s) as well as the piston(s). Be sure to locate the camshaft as described in Step 7.*

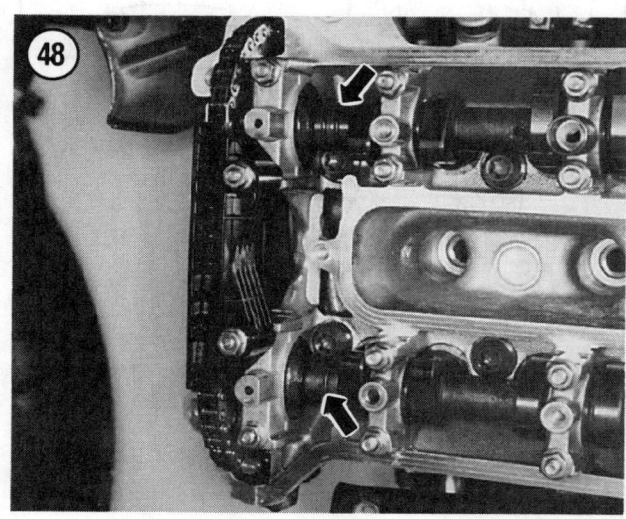

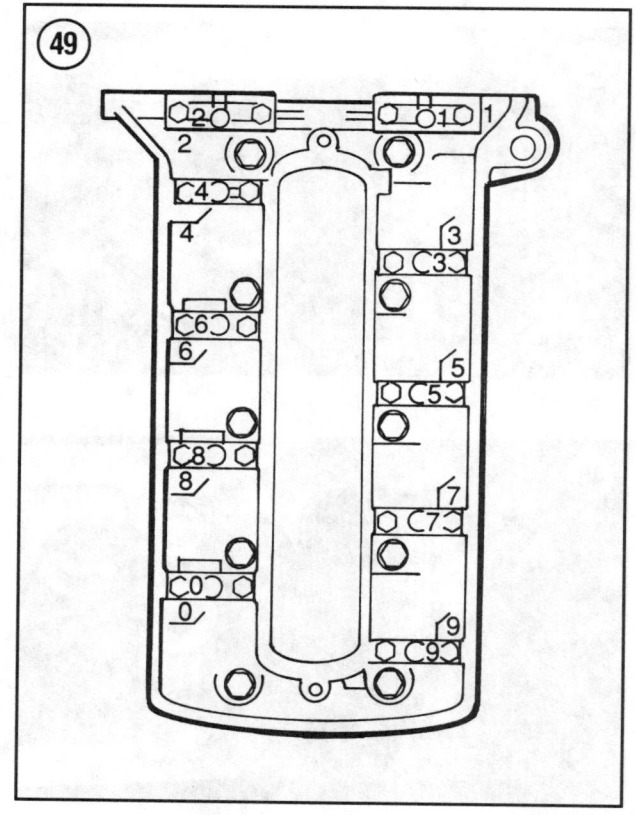

7. Rotate the camshaft so the single front groove points toward the top surface of the cylinder head, or toward the crankshaft and the 2 slots and the rear of the camshaft are vertical.

CAUTION
Tighten the bearing caps evenly so the camshafts move down into position evenly avoiding any undue stress.

8. Tighten the nuts in 2-3 stages in a criss-cross pattern, working from the center of the camshaft out toward each end. Tighten to the torque specification listed in **Table 5**.

9. Repeat Steps 2-8 for the other camshaft.

10. Remove the shop cloth from the oil return openings in the cylinder head.

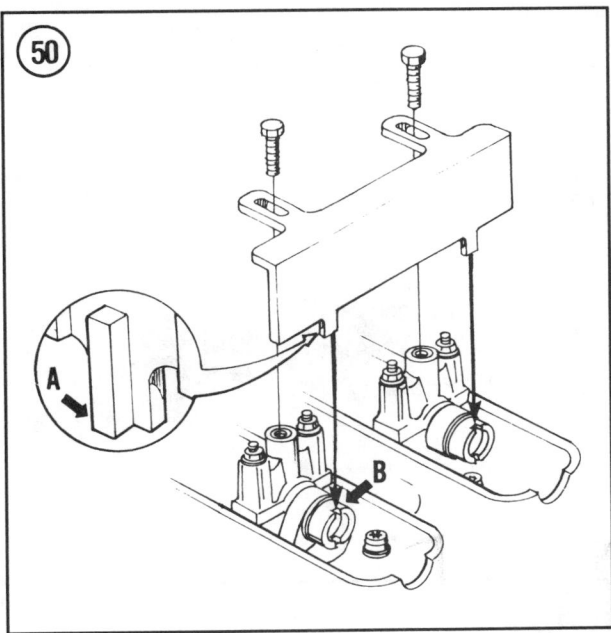

11. Install the BMW setting device (part No. 11 3 700), onto the rear end of the camshafts. Align the raised bosses (A, **Figure 50**) on the special tool with the with the slots on the camshafts (B, **Figure 50**). Secure the special tool to the rear bearing caps with bolts. Tighten the bolts securely.

12. Remove the eccentric (D, **Figure 44**) from the guide rail upper mount.

13. Install the timing chain into the guide rail and install the bushing (H, **Figure 44**) behind the timing chain on the upper mounting hole.

14. Keep the timing chain secure in the guide rail, then install the timing chain onto the drive sprocket (A, **Figure 51**) on the end of the crankshaft.

NOTE
*Make sure the bushing (H, **Figure 44**) is in place in the upper mounting hole when installing the guide rail on the upper post.*

15. Install the guide rail onto the upper and lower mounting posts on the cylinder block. Do not install the upper washer and E-clip at this time.

16. Install the lower washer and E-clip (B, **Figure 44**) securing the guide rail.

17. Position the intake camshaft sprocket with the triangle mark facing down toward the exhaust side of the engine.

18. Make sure the timing chain is still properly meshed with the drive sprocket on the end of the crankshaft, then pull up on the timing chain to remove all slack. The timing chain must be under tension at this time.

19. Properly mesh the timing chain with the intake sprocket and install the sprocket onto the end of the intake camshaft. Make sure the locating pin on the backside of the sprocket is engaged with the single slot in the front end of the camshaft. Push the sprocket onto the intake camshaft until it bottoms out.

20. Install the washer and bolt and finger-tighten at this time.

21. Install the tensioner rail (**Figure 43**) onto the mounting post.

22. Install the large washer (**Figure 42**) and clip (**Figure 41**). Make sure the clip is secured on the groove on the mounting post.

23. Make sure the timing chain is still properly meshed with the drive sprocket on the end of the crankshaft and with the intake camshaft sprocket. Pull on the timing chain to remove all slack in the chain from the intake sprocket. The timing chain must be under tension at this time.

24. Position the exhaust camshaft sprocket with the triangle mark facing down toward the exhaust side of the engine.

25. Properly mesh the timing chain with the exhaust sprocket and install the sprocket onto the end of the exhaust

14

camshaft. Make sure the locating pin on the backside of the sprocket is engaged with the single slot in the front end of the exhaust camshaft. Push the sprocket onto the exhaust camshaft until it bottoms out.

CAUTION
Do not tighten the camshaft sprocket bolt installed in Step 27 while the special tool installed in Step 12 is still in place. If the bolt is tightened with this tool in place, the end of the camshaft will be damaged.

26. Install the washer and bolt and finger-tighten at this time.

27. If the timing chain tensioner was disassembled, reassemble it as follows:
  a. Install the spring into the plunger (**Figure 52**).
  b. Install this assembly into the housing (**Figure 53**).
  c. Push the tensioner foot into the spring (**Figure 54**) and index the pin on the foot with the groove in the plunger. Rotate the foot clockwise while pushing in to compress the spring until the foot bottoms out. Hold the foot in this position.

28. While holding the tensioner foot in place in the housing, install the tensioner assembly onto the cylinder block.

29. Correctly position the tensioner foot onto the tensioner rail and install the mounting bolts and washers. Tighten the bolts to the torque specification listed in **Table 7**.

30. At the guide rails upper mounting post, install the eccentric (A, **Figure 55**) into the bushing (B) that was already installed.

31. Rotate the eccentric in either direction until it pushes the guide rail up against the outer edge of the cylinder head. At this point, push the eccentric (A, **Figure 56**) into the bushing (B, **Figure 56**) and engage the notches with the raised pins (C, **Figure 56**) on the guide rail. Push the eccentric in until it bottoms out.

32. Install the washer (D, **Figure 56**) and E-clip (E, **Figure 56**). Make sure the E-clip is properly seated in the groove in the upper post.

33. Remove the bolts and the special tool, installed in Step 12, from the rear of the camshafts.

34. Secure the camshaft with an open-end wrench on the hexagon on the camshaft, then tighten the camshaft sprocket bolt to the torque specification listed in **Table 5**.

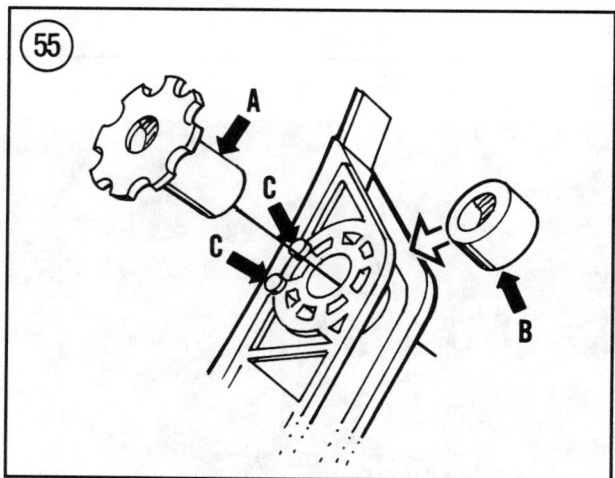

35. Using the rear wheel, rotate the engine several complete revolutions to seat all new components.

36. Inspect all valve clearances as described in the Chapter Three section of this supplement. If any of the clearances are not within specification, perform the adjustment procedure until all clearances are correct.

37. Install all spark plugs.

38. Install the timing chain cover and the crankshaft cover as described in Chapter Four in the main body of this book.

39. Install the cylinder head cover as described in this chapter of the supplement.

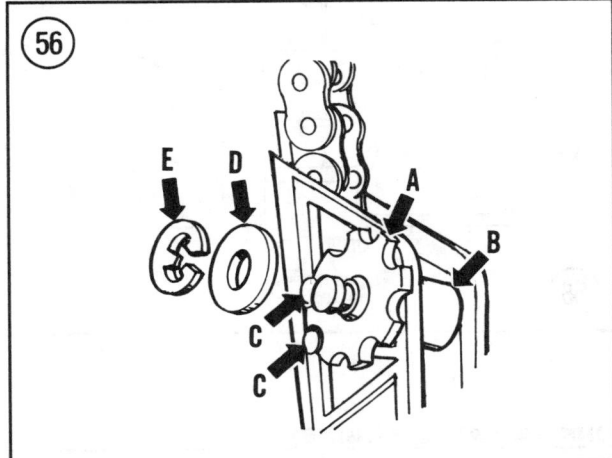

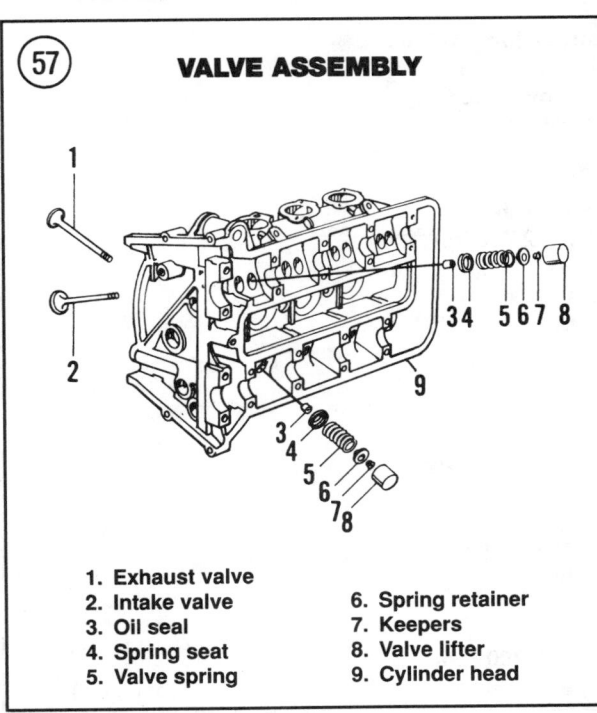

VALVE ASSEMBLY

1. Exhaust valve
2. Intake valve
3. Oil seal
4. Spring seat
5. Valve spring
6. Spring retainer
7. Keepers
8. Valve lifter
9. Cylinder head

40. Start the bike and make sure it runs correctly.

CYLINDER HEAD

Removal and Installation (4-Valve Cylinder Head Engines)

Cylinder head removal and installation on the 4-valve cylinder head is the same as on previous models except there are 4 valves and 4 valve lifters per cylinder instead of 2 valves and 2 valve lifters per cylinder. The other difference is that the spacer previously located on top of the valve lifter has been eliminated on the 4-valve cylinder head. Refer to K100 models for all procedures.

VALVE AND VALVE COMPONENTS (4-VALVE CYLINDER HEAD)

Valve Removal

Refer to **Figure 57** for the components of the 4-valve cylinder head.

Valve and valve component service on the 4-valve cylinder head is the same as on previous models except there are 4 valves per cylinder instead of 2 valves per cylinder.

Inspection

The inspection procedure is the same as on previous models except the specifications are different. Refer to **Table 6** for valve specifications.

Valve Installation

1. Coat the valve stems with molybdenum disulfide grease. To avoid damage to the valve guide, turn the valve (A, **Figure 58**) slowly while inserting it into the cylinder head.

2. Install a new valve seal on each valve guide as follows:
   a. Install BMW assembly sleeve (B, **Figure 58**) (part No. 11 1 960) on the valve stem.
   b. Install the new seal (C, **Figure 58**) onto the valve stem and guide.
   c. Install BMW special tool (part No. 11 1 950) onto the valve stem and seal.
   d. Tap on the special tool with a hammer until the tool bottoms out on the cylinder head.
   e. Remove the special tool and the assembly sleeve from the valve stem.

14

3. Position the spring seat with the flange side facing up and install the spring seat.

4. Install the valve spring. The spring is *not* progressively wound so either end can go on first.

5. Install the valve spring retainer on top of the valve spring.

CAUTION
To avoid loss of spring tension, do not compress the springs any more than necessary to install the keepers.

6. Compress the valve spring with a compressor tool (**Figure 59**) and install the valve keepers. Make sure the keepers fit snugly into the grooves in the valve stem.

7. Remove the valve compressor tool.

8. After the valve has been installed, gently tap the end of the valve stem with a soft aluminum or brass hammer. This will ensure the keepers are properly seated.

9. Repeat for all valve assemblies.

10. Install the cylinder head as described in this section of the supplement and Chapter Four in the main body of this book.

Valve Seat Reconditioning

The reconditioning procedures are the same as on previous models with the exception of specifications. Refer to **Table 6** for valve seat specifications.

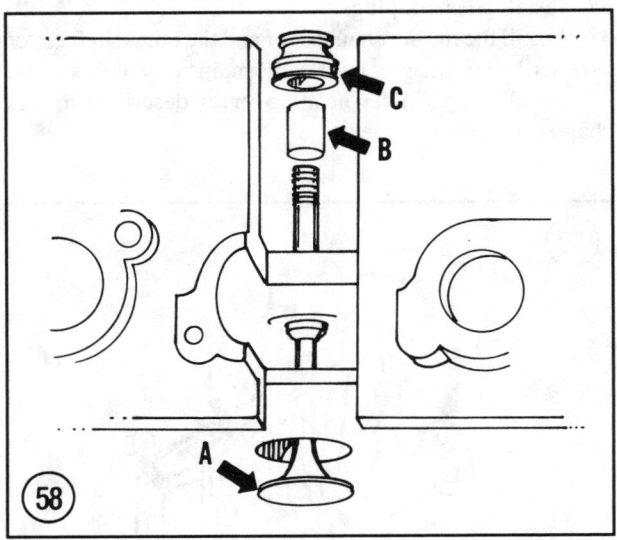

Table 6 ENGINE SPECIFICATIONS (4 VALVE ENGINE)

Item	Specification	Wear limit
General		
Engine type	Water cooled, 4-stroke longitudinal in-line 4 cylinder. Five main bearings with dual overhead camshafts and 4 valves per cylinder	
Bore and stroke		
K1, K100RS	67 × 70 mm (2.638 × 2.756 in.)	
K1100	70.5 × 70 mm (2.775 × 2.756 in.)	
Displacement		
K1, K100RS	980 cc (59.8 cu. in.)	
K1100	1093 cc (66.7 cu. in.)	
Compression ratio	11.0 to 1	
Maximum constant engine speed		
K1, K100RS	8,800 rpm	
K1100	8,500 rpm	
Maximum engine speed		
K1, K100RS	8,900 rpm	
K1100	8,900 rpm	
Engine rotation	Counterclockwise as viewed from front of engine	
Firing order	1-3-4-2	
Maximum engine torque		
K1, K100RS	100 N•m (74 ft.-lb.) at 6,700 rpm	
K1100	107 N•m (79 ft.-lb.) at 5,500 rpm	(continued)

Table 6 ENGINE SPECIFICATIONS (4 VALVE ENGINE) (continued)

Item	Specification	Wear limit
Compression pressure		
Good: more than 1000 kPa (145 psi)		
Normal: 850-1000 kPa (123-145 psi)		
Poor: less than 850 kPa (123 psi)		
Idle speed		
K1, K100RS	950-1,000 rpm	
K1100	900-1,000 rpm	
Engine lubrication		
Output shaft driven oil pump with wet sump		
Full flow oil filter		
Oil bypass valve opens at 150 kPa (22 psi)		
Oil pressure warning light comes on at 20-50 kPa (3-7 psi)		
Oil pressure relief valve opens at 540 kPa (78 psi)		
Maximum oil consumption per 62 miles (100 km): 0.15 liter (0.32 pt.)		
Valves		
Valve clearance (cold)		
Intake	0.15-0.20 mm (0.006-0.008 in.)	
Exhaust	0.25-0.30 mm (0.010-0.012 in.)	
Valve timing		
K1, K100RS		
Intake opens	2° BTDC	
Intake closes	26° BBDC	
Exhaust opens	30° BBDC	
Exhaust closes	2° BTDC	
K1100		
Intake opens	14° ATDC	
Intake closes	18° ABDC	
Exhaust opens	18° BBDC	
Exhaust closes	14° BTDC	
Valve total length		
Intake	115.1 mm (4.531 in.)	
Exhaust	113.7 mm (4.476 in.)	
Head diameter		
Intake	26.45 mm (1.041 in.)	
Exhaust	22.95 mm (1.161 in.)	
Stem diameter		
Intake	5.960-5.975 mm (0.2346-0.2352 in.)	5.950 mm (0.2342 in).
Exhaust	5.945-5.960 mm (0.2340-0.2346 in.)	5.953 mm (0.2343 in.)
Valve head edge thickness		
Intake	1.04 mm (0.041 in.)	—
Exhaust	1.09 mm (0.043 in.)	—
Valve head runout		
Intake and exhaust	—	0.02 mm (0.0008 in.)
Valve seat angle		
Intake and exhaust	44°	—
Valve seat width		
Intake	0.095-1.250 mm (0.0037-0.0492 in.)	2.50 mm (0.098 in.)
Exhaust	1.15-1.45 mm (0.043-0.063 in.)	3.00 mm (0.118 in.)

(continued)

14

Table 6 ENGINE SPECIFICATIONS (4 VALVE ENGINE) (continued)

Item	Specification	Wear limit
Valve guide		
Total length		
Intake	45 mm (1.772 in.)	—
Exhaust	57.5 mm (2.263 in.)	—
Outside diameter	11.533-11.544 mm (0.4540-0.4545 in.)	—
Inside diameter	6.000-6.012 mm (0.2362-0.2367 in.)	6.100 mm (0.2401 in.)
Bore in cylinder head	11.500-11.518 mm (0.4527-0.4534 in.)	—
Repair size	11.700-11.718 mm (0.4606-0.4613 in.)	—
Valve stem clearance		
Intake	0.025-0.052 mm (0.0010-0.0020 in.)	—
Exhaust	0.040-0.067 mm (0.0016-0.0026 in.)	—
Valve springs		
Wire gauge	3.2 mm (0.125 in.)	
Coil winding direction	Clockwise	
Total number of coils	7.8	
Spring free length	41.1 mm (1.618 in.)	39.6 mm (1.559 in.)
Camshaft		
Thrust bearing O.D.	29.970-30.000 mm (1.17991-1.1811 in.)	29.95 mm (1.1791 in.)
All other bearing O.D.	23.970-24.000 mm (0.9437-0.9449 in.)	23.95 mm (0.9429 in.)
Thrust bearing bore in cylinder head I.D.	30.020-30.041 mm (1.1819-1.1827 in.)	—
All other bearing bore in cylinder head I.D.	24.020-24.041 mm (0.9457-0.9465 in.)	—
Oil clearance		
Thrust bearing	0.020-0.071 mm (0.0007-0.0028 in.)	—
All other bearings	0.020-0.071 mm (0.0007-0.0028 in.)	—
Lobe height		
Intake and exhaust	38.824-38.886 mm (1.5285-1.5309 in.)	38.550 mm (1.5177 in.)
Valve lifters		
Outside diameter	26.853-26.840 mm (1.0572-1.0566 in.)	25.970 mm (1.0224 in.)
Receptacle in cylinder head	26.065-26.086 mm (1.0262-1.0270 in.)	26.170 mm (1.0303 in.)
Oil clearance	0.072-0.106 mm (0.0028-0.0042 in.)	0.200 mm (0.0078 in.)
Crankshaft		
Thrust bearing width	23.020-23.053 mm (0.9063-0.9076 in.)	—
Main bearing diameter	45.000-45.076 mm (1.7716-1.7746 in.)	—

(continued)

Table 6 ENGINE SPECIFICATIONS (4 VALVE ENGINE) (continued)

Item	Specification	Wear limit
Connecting rod bearing diameter	38.000-38.076 mm (1.4961-1.4990 in.)	—
Bearing bore diameter in cylinder block	49.000-49.140 mm (1.9291-1.9346 in.)	—
Main bearing journal oil clearance	0.020-0.056 mm (0.008-0.0022 in.)	0.110 mm (0.0043 in.)
Connecting rod journal oil clearance	0.030-0.066 mm (0.0012-0.0026 in.)	130 mm (0.0051 in.)
Crankshaft end float	0.080-0.183 mm (0.0031-0.0072 in.)	0.250 mm (0.0098 in.)
Connecting rods Big end bore I.D.	41.000-41.016 mm (1.6142-1.6148 in.)	—
Big end width	21.973-22.025 mm (0.8651-0.8671 in.)	—
Oil clearance	0.130-0.312 mm (0.0051-0.0123 in.)	0.400 mm (0.0157 in.)
Small end bore I.D.	20.000-20.021 mm (0.7874-0.7882 in.)	—
Maximum weight deviation between rods	± 4 grams	
Cylinder block Bore I.D. (K1, K100RS) Grade A	67.995-67.005 mm (2.6376-2.6380 in.)	67.05 mm (2.6397 in.)
Grade B	67.005-67.015 mm (2.6380-2.6384 in.)	67.06 mm (2.6401 in.)
Bore I.D. (K1100) Grade A	70.495-70.505 mm (2.7754-2.7758 in.)	70.55 mm (2.7775 in.)
Grade B	70.505-70.515 mm (2.7758-2.7762 in.)	70.56 mm (2.7779 in.)
Pistons O.D. (K1, K100RS) KS grade A	66.966-66.980 mm (2.6364-2.6370 in.)	62.92 mm (2.6346 in.)
KS grade B	66.976-66.990 mm (2.6368-2.6374 in.)	62.93 mm (2.6350 in.)
O.D. (K1100) KS grade A	70.466-70.480 mm (2.7742-2.7748 in.)	—
KS grade B	70.476-70.490 mm (2.7746-2.7752 in.)	—
Piston-to-cylinder clearance	0.015-0.039 mm (0.0006-0.0015 in.)	0.130 mm (0.0051 in.)
Piston pin bore I.D.	18.002-18.006 mm (0.7087-0.7089 in.)	—

14

(continued)

Table 6 ENGINE SPECIFICATIONS (4 VALVE ENGINE) (continued)

Item	Specification	Wear limit
Piston pin		
O.D.	17.996-18.000 mm (0.7085-0.7086 in.)	17.96 mm (0.7071 in.)
Pin-to-piston clearance	0.002-0.010 mm (0.00008-0.00039 in.)	—
Pin-to-connecting rod bushing clearance	0.006-0.021 mm (0.00024-0.00083 in.)	0.060 mm (0.0024 in.)
Piston rings		
1st compression ring		
Thickness	1.178-1.190 mm (0.0464-0.0468 in.)	1.10 mm (0.0433 in.)
End clearance (installed)	0.20-0.40 mm (0.008-0.0456 in.)	1.50 mm (0.059 in.)
Side clearance	0.040-0.075 mm (0.0015-0.0029 in.)	0.30 mm (0.012 in.)
2nd compression ring		
Thickness	1.178-1.190 mm (0.0464-0.0468 in.)	1.10 mm (0.0433 in.)
End clearance (installed)	0.10-0.30 mm (0.039-0.0118 in.)	1.50 mm (0.059 in.)
Side clearance	0.030-0.044 mm (0.00118-0.00173 in.)	0.30 mm (0.012 in.)
Oil ring		
Thickness	2.475-2.490 mm (0.0974-0.0980 in.)	—
End clearance (installed)	0.25-0.45 mm (0.098-0.0177 in.)	1.50 mm (0.059 in.)
Side clearance	0.020-0.055 mm (0.0008-0.0022 in.)	0.30 mm (0.012 in.)

Table 7 ENGINE TORQUE SPECIFICATIONS

Item	N•m	ft.-lb.
Engine-to-frame bolts	45	32
Cylinder head cover	8	5.8
Camshaft bearing cap bolts	9	6.6
Timing chain tensioner bolts	9	6.6
Camshaft driven sprocket	54	40

CHAPTER SEVEN

FUEL INJECTION SYSTEM, EMISSION CONTROLS AND EXHAUST SYSTEM (K1, 1991-1992 K100RS AND ALL K1100 MODELS)

On all K1, 1991-1992 K100RS and all K1100 models, the fuel injection control module and the ignition control module are combined into single engine management module referred to as the Motronic Control Unit. The Motronic Control Unit is covered in the Chapter Seven and Chapter Eight sections of this supplement.

THROTTLE HOUSING AND INTAKE MANIFOLD

Removal/Installation

The removal and installation of the throttle housing and intake manifold are identical to previous years. **Figure 60** shows the slight variation of component locations on the throttle housing. The air plenum chamber is now the upper portion of the air filter case and is covered in this section of the supplement.

AIR FLOW METER

The air flow meter is no longer used in the new fuel injection system.

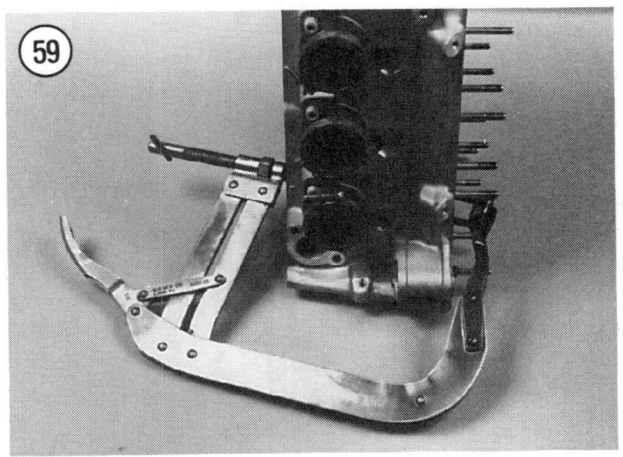

FUEL INJECTION CONTROL UNIT (MOTRONIC)

Removal/Installation

The removal and installation of the Motronic control unit is covered in the Chapter Eight section of this supplement.

FUEL INJECTION SYSTEM ADJUSTMENTS

On all 4-valve engines, the fuel injection system is controlled by a single engine management computer called the Motronic Control Unit.

The Motronic Control Unit controls all the fuel injection functions and any adjustment to any of the components relating to the system must be checked using a very expensive piece of BMW test equipment called the Synchrotester (BMW part No. 13 0 800). The service charge for any fuel injection system adjustments by a BMW dealer is minimal compared to the purchase price of this equipment.

The only adjustment that can still be performed by the home mechanic is the throttle cable adjustment. The throttle cable adjustment procedure is the same as on earlier models covered in Chapter Seven in the main body of this manual.

AIR FILTER CASE

Removal/Installation

14

Refer to **Figure 61** and **Figure 62** for this procedure.
1. Place the bike on the centerstand.
2. Remove the knee pads, storage boxes and front fairing right- and left-hand lower panels as described in the Chapter Thirteen section of this supplement.
3. Remove the fuel tank (A, **Figure 63**).
4. On K1100 models, remove the following:
   a. Disconnect the fuel line (A, **Figure 64**) from the left-hand bulkhead.

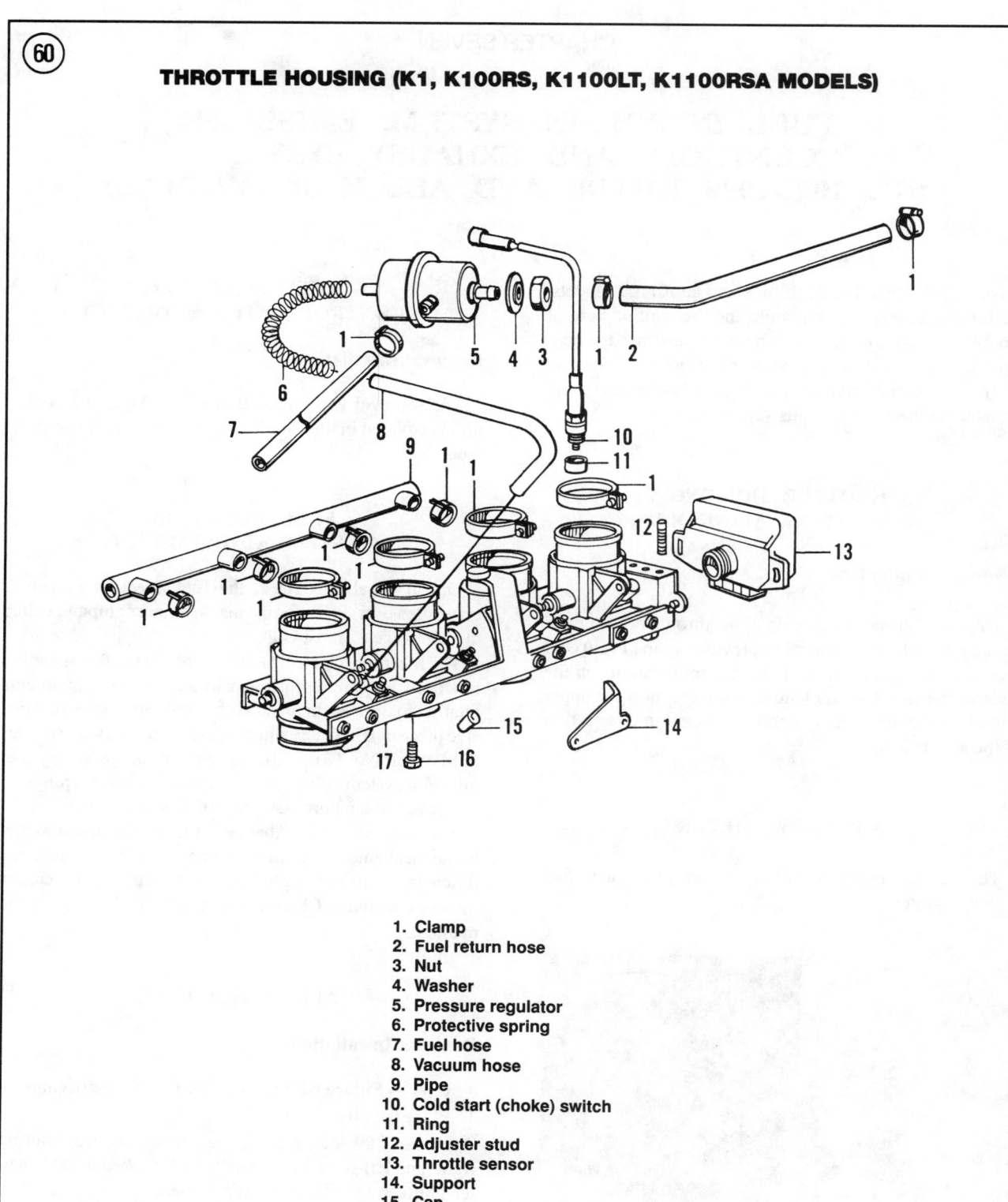

THROTTLE HOUSING (K1, K100RS, K1100LT, K1100RSA MODELS)

1. Clamp
2. Fuel return hose
3. Nut
4. Washer
5. Pressure regulator
6. Protective spring
7. Fuel hose
8. Vacuum hose
9. Pipe
10. Cold start (choke) switch
11. Ring
12. Adjuster stud
13. Throttle sensor
14. Support
15. Cap
16. Adjust screw
17. Throttle housing

AIR FILTER UPPER HOUSING

1. Air temperature sensor
2. Upper case half/air plenum chamber
3. Clamp
4. Rubber intake tube
5. Clamp
6. Cap
7. Bolt
8. Intake manifold
9. O-ring

b. Remove the cable clip (B, **Figure 64**) from the left-hand frame tube.

c. Remove the left-hand bulkhead (C, **Figure 64**).

d. Remove the cable clip (A, **Figure 65**) from the right-hand frame tube.

e. Move the coolant pipe (B, **Figure 65**) from the right-hand bulkhead.

f. Remove the right-hand bulkhead (C, **Figure 65**).

5. On the right-hand side, remove bolts and washers securing the air guide to the radiator and the air filter case. Remove the air guide (B, **Figure 63**).

6. Remove the clamps (A, **Figure 66**) from each rubber intake tube on the cylinder head and discard them. They cannot be reused.

7. Disconnect the intake tubes (B, **Figure 66**) from each rubber intake tube.

8. Unhook the front and rear spring clamps (C, **Figure 63**) securing the upper case to the lower case half.

9. Raise the upper case away from the lower case half and withdraw the air filter element out through the right-hand side.

10. On the right-hand side, remove the wire retainer and disconnect the air temperature sensor electrical connector (D, **Figure 63**) from the upper case half.

11. Loosen the clamp screw and disconnect the crankcase ventilation hose from the engine.

12. Loosen the clamp screws and disconnect the oil delivery hose and the air return hose from the lower case half.

13. Lift up and remove the upper case half (E, **Figure 63**) out through the right-hand side.

14. Remove the screws, O-rings and washers securing the lower case half (F, **Figure 63**) to the engine and remove the lower case half.

15. Install by reversing these removal steps, noting the following.

16. Install the upper case half onto the lower case half and make sure it is seated correctly around the entire perimeter. Secure the upper case half to the lower case half with the spring clamps. Make sure the spring clamps have snapped over-center and are holding tightly.

17. Apply a light coat of rubber lube or Armor All to the to the lower section of the air guide where it fits in the rubber connector on the lower case half. This will make installation easier.

18. Install new clamps on the flexible ducts on each rubber intake tube and crimp securely in place.

19. Install all body panels removed.

14

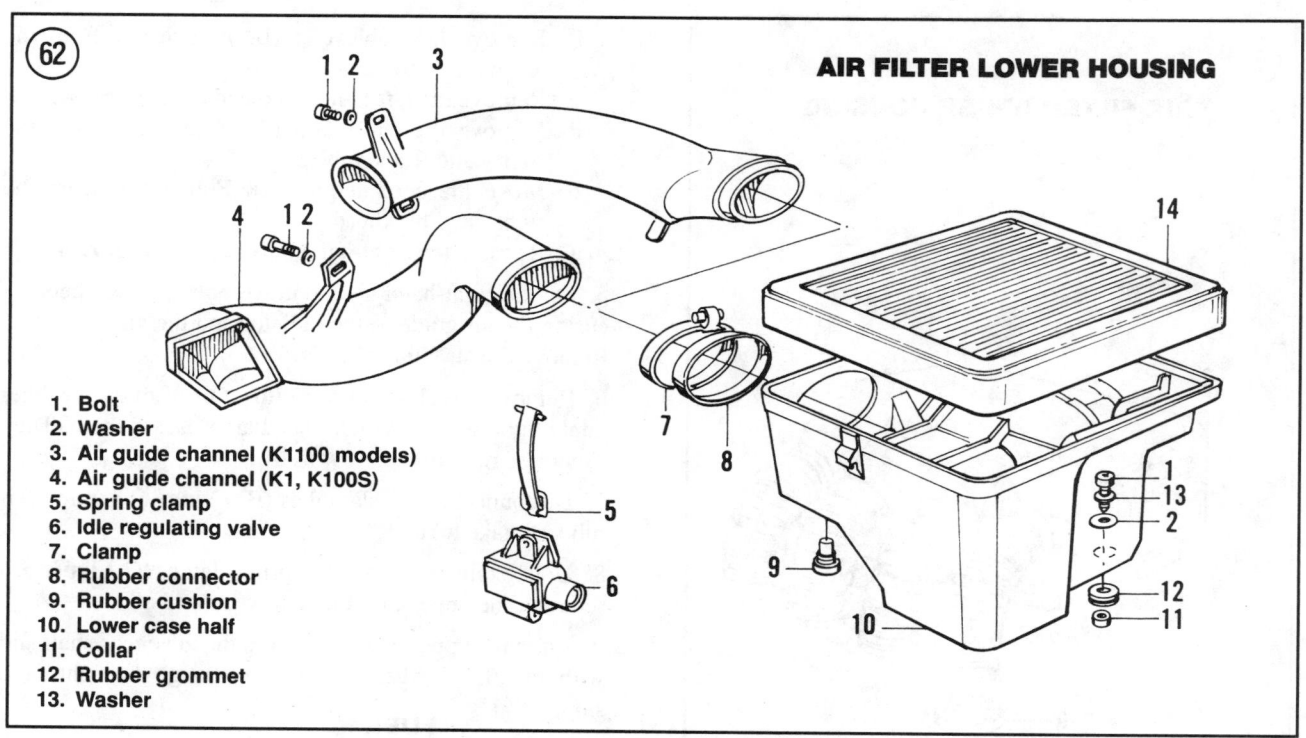

AIR FILTER LOWER HOUSING

1. Bolt
2. Washer
3. Air guide channel (K1100 models)
4. Air guide channel (K1, K100S)
5. Spring clamp
6. Idle regulating valve
7. Clamp
8. Rubber connector
9. Rubber cushion
10. Lower case half
11. Collar
12. Rubber grommet
13. Washer

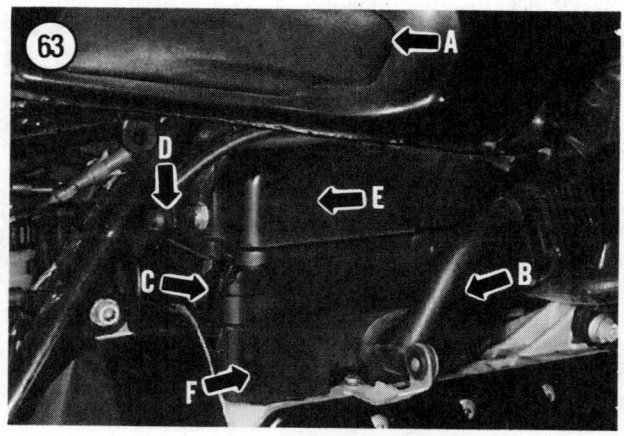

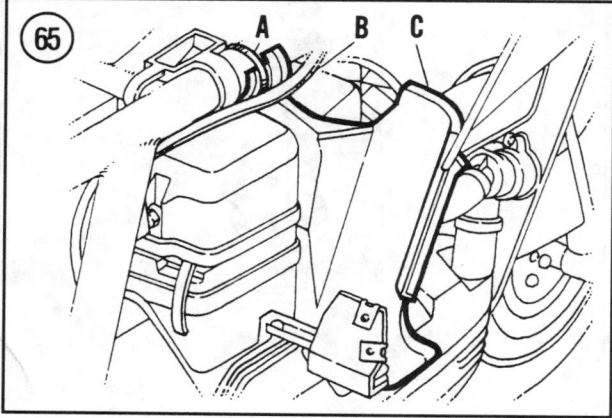

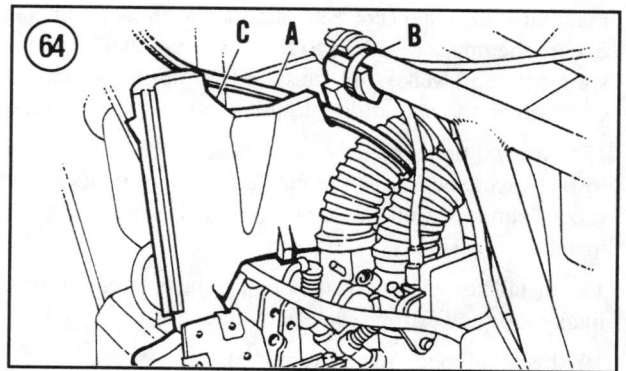

FUEL PUMP

Removal/Installation

The fuel pump and filter are the same as on previous models with the exception of the configuration of the strainer. Refer to **Figure 67**.

EXHAUST SYSTEM

The exhaust system consists of an integrated exhaust pipe and muffler assembly. The entire system is made of stainless steel and should last a long time if well maintained. Protect the finish with a good grade of stainless steel polish and wax.

Refer to **Figure 68** for this procedure.

Removal/installation

1. Place the bike on the centerstand.

2. Remove the engine spoiler as described in the Chapter Thirteen section of this supplement.

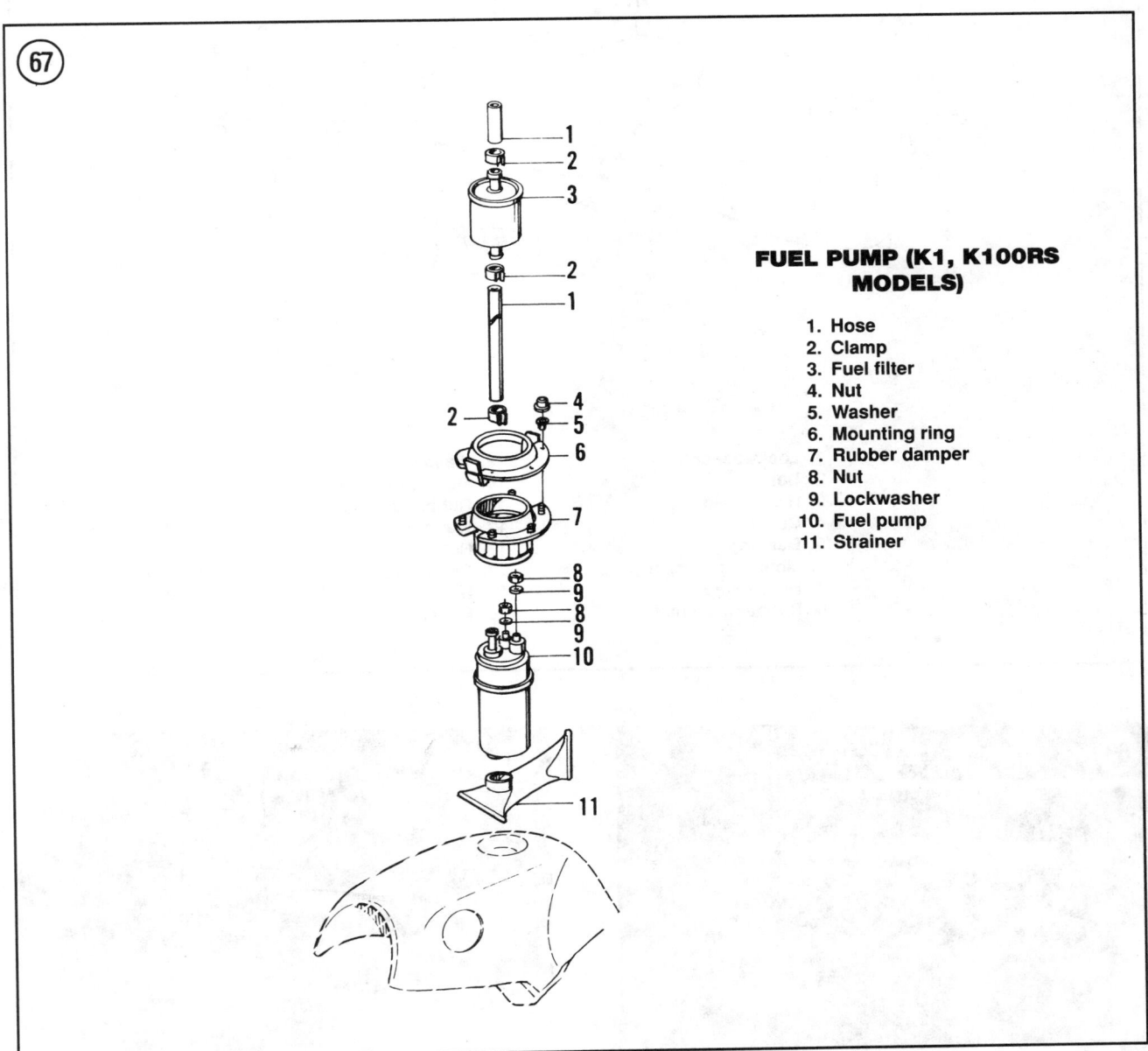

(67)

FUEL PUMP (K1, K100RS MODELS)

1. Hose
2. Clamp
3. Fuel filter
4. Nut
5. Washer
6. Mounting ring
7. Rubber damper
8. Nut
9. Lockwasher
10. Fuel pump
11. Strainer

14

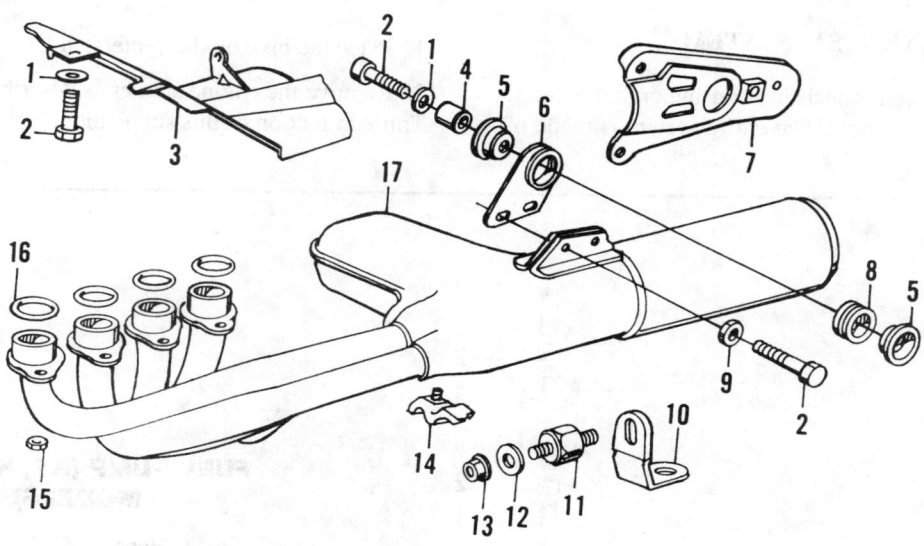

68

EXHAUST SYSTEM

1. Lockwasher
2. Bolt
3. Heat shield
4. Collar
5. Bushing
6. Mounting bracket
7. Heat shield
8. Rubber grommet

9. Washer
10. Mounting bracket
11. Rubber damper
12. Washer
13. Nut
14. Rubber stopper
15. Nut
16. Ring gasket

69

70

3. Loosen the nuts on the mounting flanges (**Figure 69**) securing the exhaust pipes to the cylinder head.

4. Loosen the bolts (**Figure 70**) securing the muffler portion to the footpeg bracket.

5. Loosen the nut (**Figure 71**) securing the muffler portion to the underside of the frame.

6. Remove the nuts from the exhaust pipe mounting flanges.

7. Remove the nut and washer securing the muffler to the under side of the frame.

8. Hold onto the exhaust system and remove the bolts and washers securing the muffler section to the footpeg bracket.

9. Carefully lower the exhaust system, away from the threaded studs on the cylinder head and remove the system from the frame.

10. Remove the ring gasket either from the cylinder head port or from the each exhaust pipe inlet. Discard all ring gaskets--they must be replaced every time the exhaust system is removed to ensure a leak-free seal.

11. Inspect the exhaust system for wear, rust, damage or slight "burn throughs." Replace the exhaust assembly if necessary.

12. Install a new ring gasket in each exhaust port in the cylinder head.

13. Install the exhaust system onto the engine and frame and tighten all bolts and nuts finger-tight at this time.

14. Tighten the bolts and nuts securing the exhaust system to the frame first. Tighten all the fasteners securely.

15. Tighten the exhaust pipe mounting nuts securely.

16. After the exhaust system is completely installed, start the engine and check for exhaust leaks. If any exist, correct the problem immediately.

CHAPTER EIGHT

ELECTRICAL SYSTEM

IGNITION SYSTEM (K100RS [1991-1992], K1 AND ALL K1100 MODELS)

All BMW K-series models are equipped with a solid state transistorized ignition system that uses no breaker points. This system provides longer life for the components and delivers more efficient spark throughout the entire speed range of the engine than breaker point systems.

The ignition system consists of the Motronic Control unit (computer); a trigger assembly or Hall-effect transmitter; 2 individual ignition coils and 4 spark plugs. The Motronic Control Unit also controls the fuel injection system.

There are no test procedures for the Motronic unit that can be performed by the home mechanic. Have the unit tested by a BMW dealer.

IGNITION CONTROL UNIT (MOTRONIC)

Replacement

Refer to **Figure 72** for this procedure.

14

1. Remove the seat (A, **Figure 73**) as described under *Seat Removal/Installation* either in the Chapter Thirteen section of this supplement or in the main body of this book.

2. Remove the left-hand side cover.

3. On K1 and K100RS models, remove the screw and washer securing the dual seat lock mount on each side. Remove the lock mount assembly.

4. Press the catch (B, **Figure 73**) on the left-hand side of the electrical connector and disconnect the electrical connector (C, **Figure 73**) from the Motronic control unit. Move the connector out of the way.

5. Remove the screws and washers and remove the Motronic control unit (D, **Figure 73**) from the mounting bracket.

6. Inspect the exterior of the control unit for damage or deterioration. Make sure the mounting tabs are in good condition.

7. Inspect the contacts on the electrical connector on the control unit for damage or corrosion. Clean the contacts with an aerosol electrical contact cleaner. If damage or corrosion is severe, replace the control unit.

8. Install by reversing these removal steps, noting the following.

9. Make sure the electrical connector is tight and free of corrosion.

IGNITION COILS

Refer to **Figure 74** and **Figure 75** for this procedure.

1. Disconnect the battery negative lead.

2. Remove the left-hand side cover.

3. Remove the screws and lockwashers securing the ignition coil upper cover (A, **Figure 76**). Remove the cover.

4. Remove the screws and lockwashers securing the ignition coil lower cover (B, **Figure 76**). Remove the cover.

5. Disconnect the spark plug secondary leads from the ignition coils.

6. Disconnect the primary electrical connectors from the ignition coils.

7. Remove the bolt and washer securing the starter motor ground lead (C, **Figure 76**).

8. Remove the bolt, lockwasher and nut securing the upper portion of the ignition coils to the mounting boss on the intermediate housing.

9. Remove the bolt, lockwasher and nut securing the lower portion of the ignition coils to the mounting boss on the intermediate housing.

10. Remove the individual ignition coils from the mounting bosses on the engine intermediate housing. Don't lose the rubber grommets or metal collars on the coil mounts

11. Install by reversing these removal steps, noting the following.

12. Make sure the mounting surfaces of each ignition coil and the mounting bosses on the intermediate housing are clean and free of oil. There must be a good metal-to-metal contact at all connection points.

13. Be sure to install the rubber grommets and metal collars along with the mounting bolts. Tighten the bolts and nuts securely.

14. Make sure all electrical connections are tight and free of corrosion.

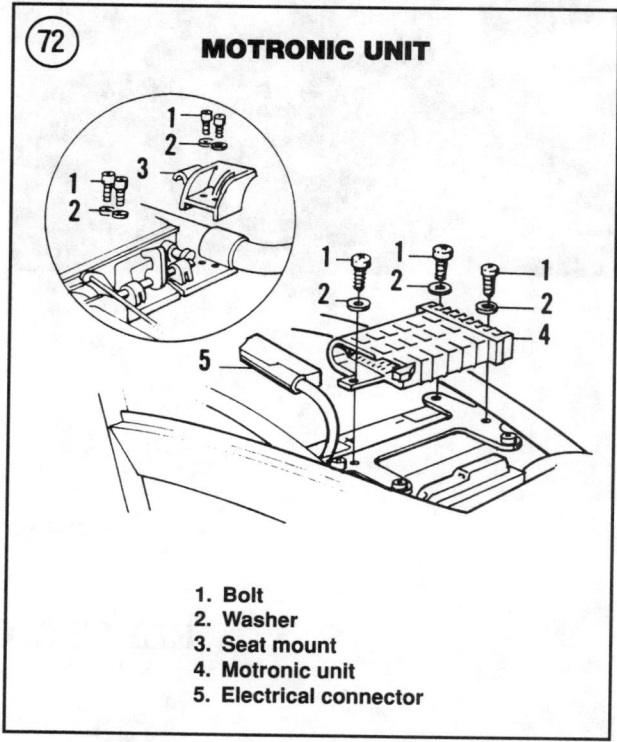

(72) **MOTRONIC UNIT**

1. Bolt
2. Washer
3. Seat mount
4. Motronic unit
5. Electrical connector

15. Route the spark plug wires to the correct cylinder. Each spark plug wire is numbered next to the spark plug rubber boot (**Figure 77**). The cylinders are numbered starting with the No. 1 cylinder at the front of the engine and working toward the back with No. 2, No. 3 and No. 4 cylinders.

IGNITION OUTPUT STAGE

Replacement

Refer to **Figure 78** for this procedure.
1. Disconnect the battery negative lead.
2. Remove the ignition coils as described in this section of the supplement.

3. Remove the nuts securing the ignition output stage to the battery case. Carefully pull the unit away from the battery case.

4. Press on the retaining clip and disconnect the electrical connector from the ignition output stage.

5. Install by reversing these removal steps, noting the following.

6. Make sure the electrical connection is tight and free of corrosion.

7. Coat the backside of the ignition output stage with conducting paste (Curil K2, or equivalent) prior to installation.

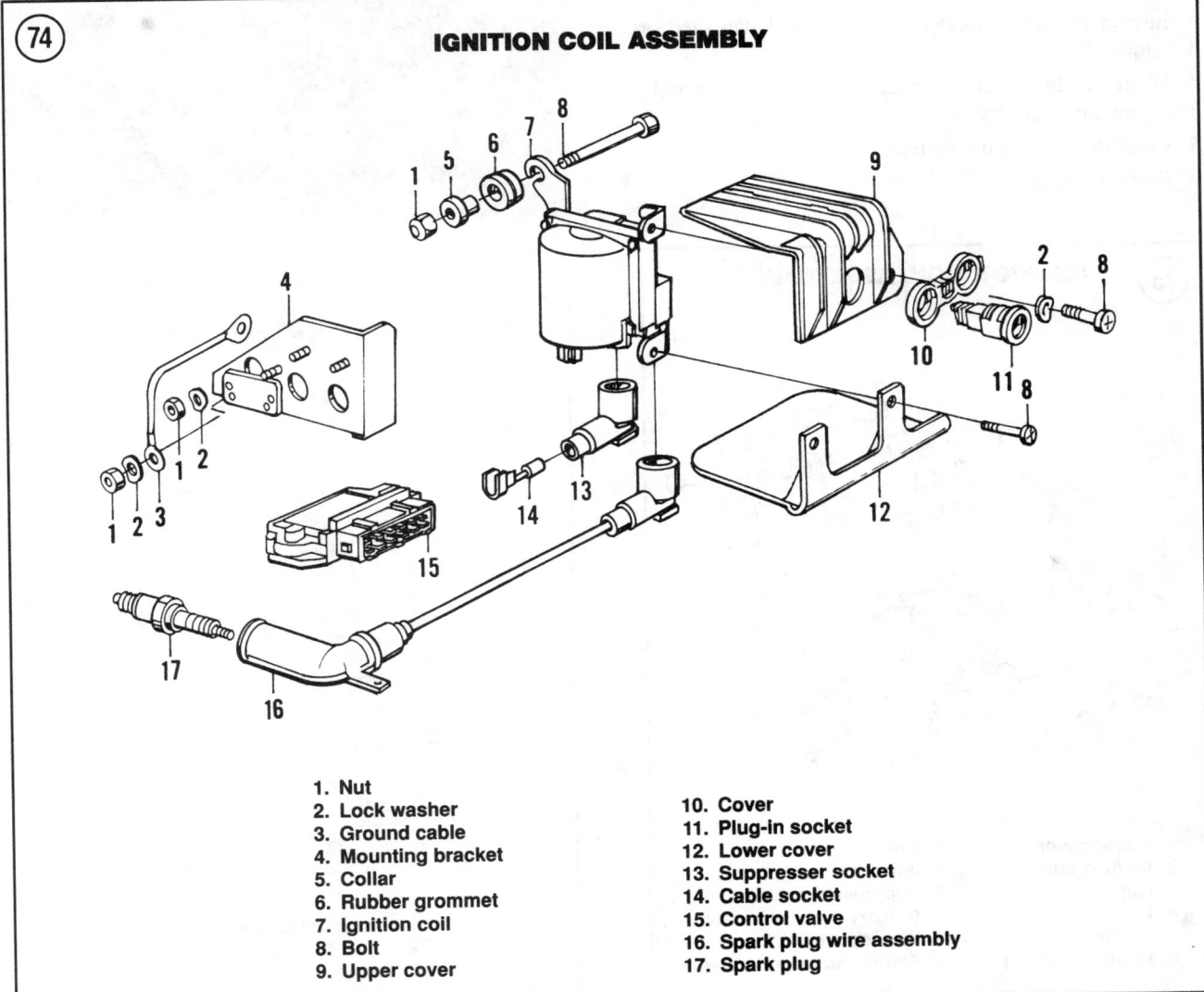

(74) **IGNITION COIL ASSEMBLY**

1. Nut
2. Lock washer
3. Ground cable
4. Mounting bracket
5. Collar
6. Rubber grommet
7. Ignition coil
8. Bolt
9. Upper cover
10. Cover
11. Plug-in socket
12. Lower cover
13. Suppresser socket
14. Cable socket
15. Control valve
16. Spark plug wire assembly
17. Spark plug

14

HEADLIGHT

The headlight assembly used on the K1 and both K1100 models is identical to the assembly used on K100 models. Bulb replacement and headlight assembly replacement procedures are identical to K100 models.

TURN SIGNALS
(K1 MODELS)

Front Turn Signal
Light Assembly

Refer to **Figure 79** for this procedure.

1. Remove the screws securing the lens to the front fairing.

2. Carefully remove the lens and gasket.

3. Inspect the lens gasket and replace it if damaged or deteriorated.

4. Wash the inside and outside of the lens in a mild detergent and wipe dry.

5. Carefully remove the bulb from the socket.

6. Replace the bulb.

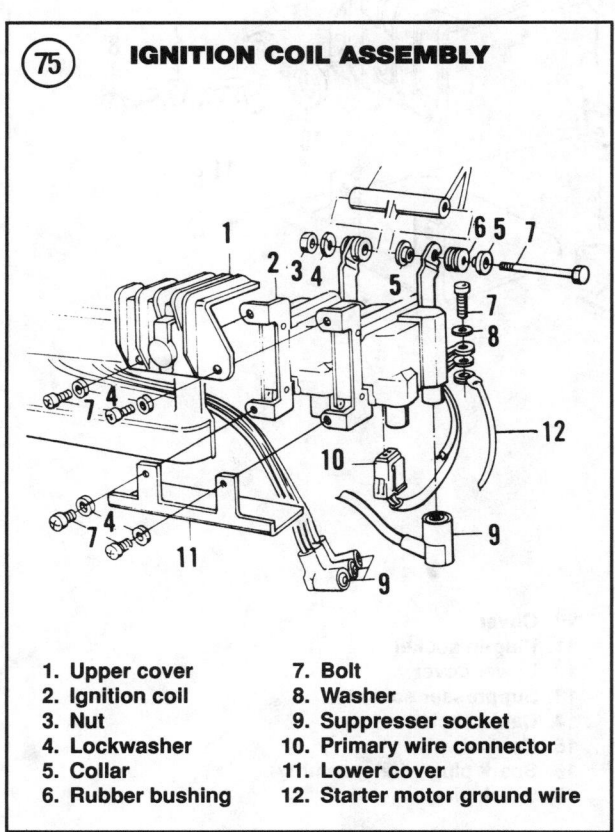

IGNITION COIL ASSEMBLY

1. Upper cover
2. Ignition coil
3. Nut
4. Lockwasher
5. Collar
6. Rubber bushing
7. Bolt
8. Washer
9. Suppresser socket
10. Primary wire connector
11. Lower cover
12. Starter motor ground wire

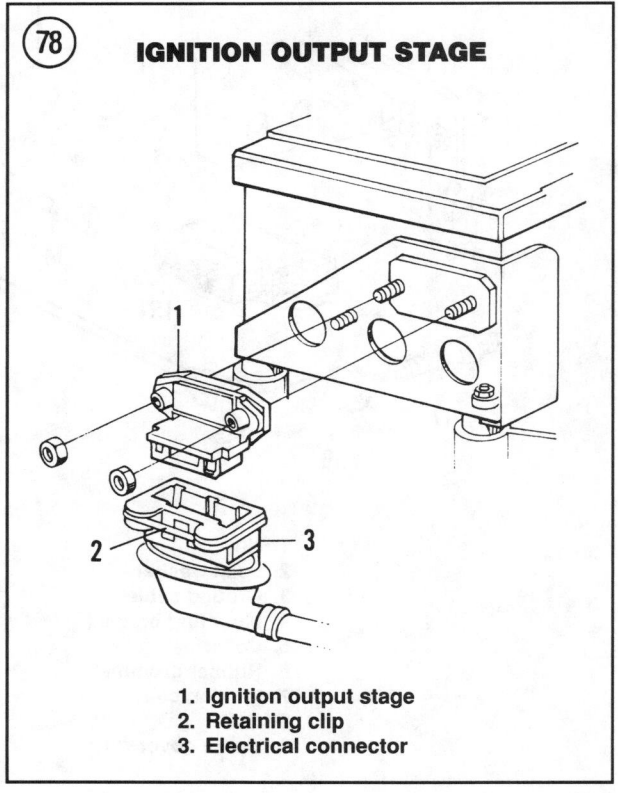

IGNITION OUTPUT STAGE

1. Ignition output stage
2. Retaining clip
3. Electrical connector

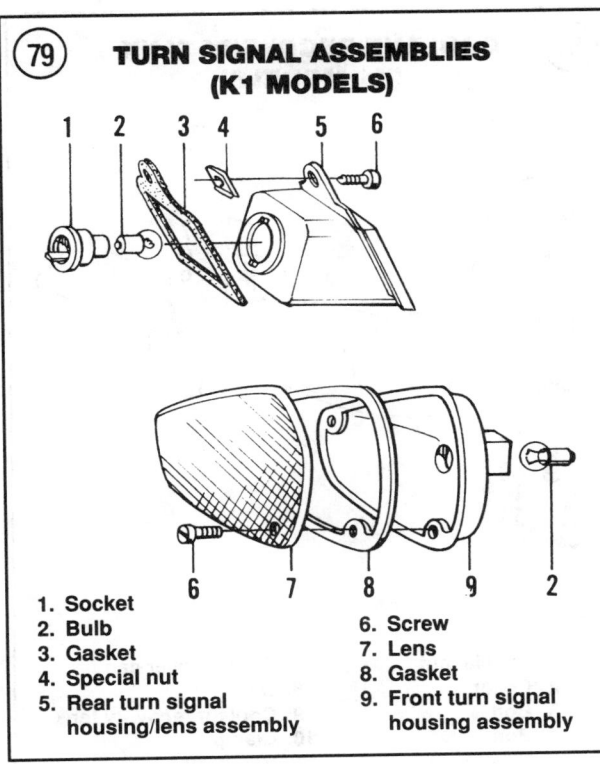

79 **TURN SIGNAL ASSEMBLIES (K1 MODELS)**

1 2 3 4 5 6

6 7 8 9 2

1. Socket
2. Bulb
3. Gasket
4. Special nut
5. Rear turn signal
   housing/lens assembly
6. Screw
7. Lens
8. Gasket
9. Front turn signal
   housing assembly

7. Install the lens and gasket and install the screws. Tighten the screws securely. Don't overtighten the screws as the plastic lens may be damaged.

**Rear Turn Signal
Light Assembly**

Refer to **Figure 79** for this procedure.
1. Remove the screws securing the lens to the rear side panel.

2. Carefully remove the lens and gasket.

3. Inspect the lens gasket and replace it if damaged or deteriorated.

4. Wash the inside and outside of the lens in a mild detergent and wipe dry.

5. Carefully remove the bulb from the socket.

6. Replace the bulb.

7. Install the lens and gasket and install the screws. Tighten the screws securely. Don't overtighten the screws as the plastic lens may be damaged.

CHAPTER NINE

COOLING SYSTEM

RADIATOR

Removal/Installation
(K75RT)

The removal and installation is the same as on previous models except an additional bracket has been added to the rear lower section of the radiator as shown in **Figure 80**. To remove the bracket, remove the screws and remove the bracket from the radiator.

COOLANT RECOVERY TANK

Removal/Installation
(K1 Models)

Refer to **Figure 81** for this procedure.
1. Remove the upper section of the front fairing as described in the Chapter Thirteen section of this supplement.
2. Pull the vent hose free from the cable strap on the front fairing mounting bracket. Keep the vent hose attached to the recovery tank.

14

3. Loosen the screw on the hose clamp on the return hose at the rear of the coolant recovery tank.

4. Remove the special nut and bolt at the front securing the recovery tank to the mounting bracket on the frame.

5. Pull the coolant recovery tank out of the left-hand side of frame.

6. Remove the return hose from the base of the tank. Place your finger over the tank fitting as the coolant within the tank will drain out.

> *NOTE*
> *On some models a dark black residue will come out while draining the coolant. The inside surface of the water pump cover was painted black on some models and this paint has come off, has entered the cooling system and usually settles in the coolant recovery tank. Thoroughly rinse out the inside of the coolant recovery tank to remove this residue prior to installation.*

7. Drain the coolant from the tank.

8. Install by reversing these removal steps, noting the following.

9. Make sure the mounting nut and bolt are secure and that the hose clamp is tight.

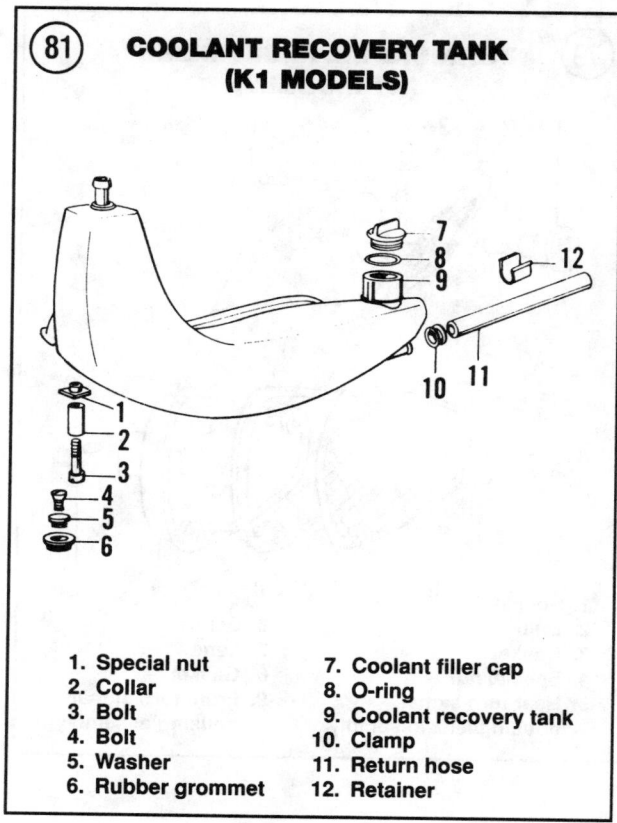

81 COOLANT RECOVERY TANK (K1 MODELS)

1. Special nut
2. Collar
3. Bolt
4. Bolt
5. Washer
6. Rubber grommet
7. Coolant filler cap
8. O-ring
9. Coolant recovery tank
10. Clamp
11. Return hose
12. Retainer

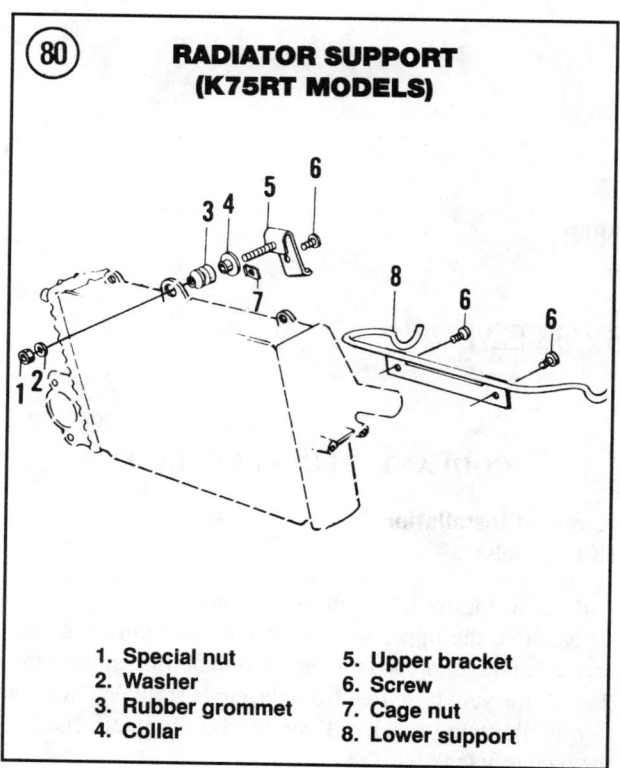

80 RADIATOR SUPPORT (K75RT MODELS)

1. Special nut
2. Washer
3. Rubber grommet
4. Collar
5. Upper bracket
6. Screw
7. Cage nut
8. Lower support

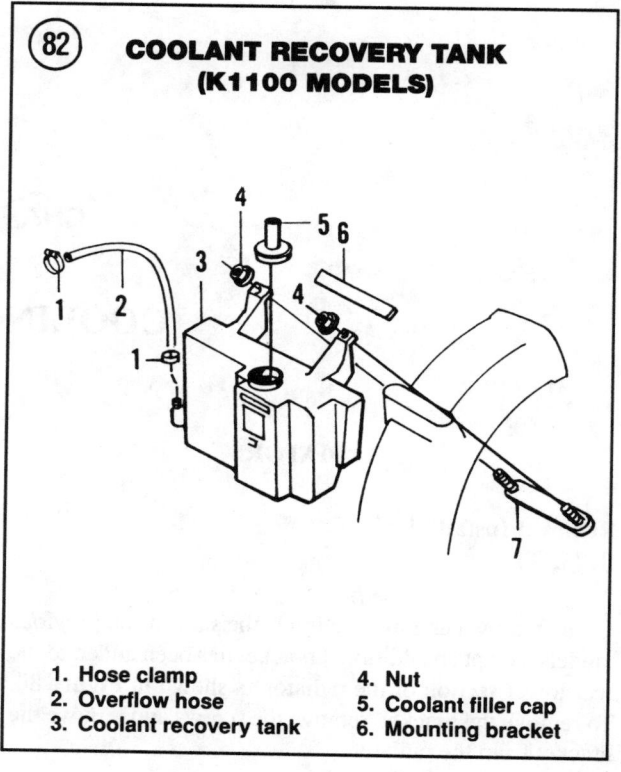

82 COOLANT RECOVERY TANK (K1100 MODELS)

1. Hose clamp
2. Overflow hose
3. Coolant recovery tank
4. Nut
5. Coolant filler cap
6. Mounting bracket

Removal/Installation
(K1100 Models)

Refer to **Figure 82** for this procedure.

1. Remove the frame right-and left-hand side covers.
2. Loosen the screw on the hose clamp on the hose at the base of the coolant recovery tank.
3. Remove the nut on each side securing the recovery tank to the mounting bracket on the rear fender.
4. Pull the coolant recovery tank out of the left-hand side of frame.
5. Remove the hose from the base of the tank. Place your finger over the tank fitting to keep the coolant within the tank from draining out.

NOTE
On some models a dark black residue will come out while draining the coolant. The inside surface of the water pump cover was painted black on some models and this paint

has come off, has entered the cooling system and usually settles in the coolant recovery tank. Thoroughly rinse out the inside of the coolant recovery tank to remove this residue prior to installation.

6. Drain the coolant from the tank.
7. Install by reversing these removal steps, noting the following.
8. Make sure the mounting nuts are secure and that the hose clamp is tight.

HOSES

The service procedure for hoses in Chapter Nine in the main body of this book relates to the K1 except for the location of several of the components and hoses. Refer to **Figure 83** for the K1 models and follow the procedure in Chapter Nine in the main body of this book.

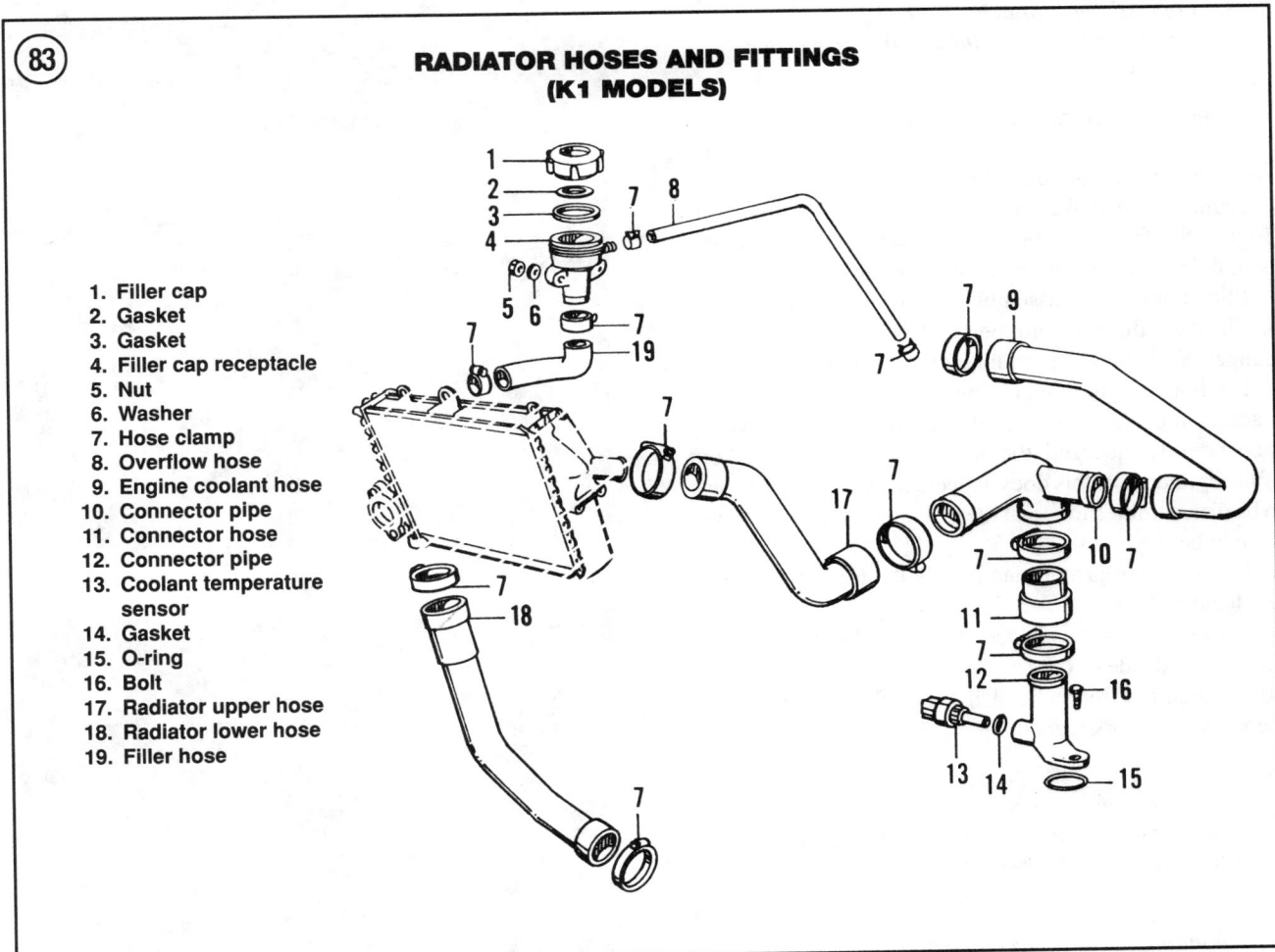

**RADIATOR HOSES AND FITTINGS
(K1 MODELS)**

1. Filler cap
2. Gasket
3. Gasket
4. Filler cap receptacle
5. Nut
6. Washer
7. Hose clamp
8. Overflow hose
9. Engine coolant hose
10. Connector pipe
11. Connector hose
12. Connector pipe
13. Coolant temperature sensor
14. Gasket
15. O-ring
16. Bolt
17. Radiator upper hose
18. Radiator lower hose
19. Filler hose

14

CHAPTER TEN

FRONT SUSPENSION AND STEERING

FRONT WHEEL (3-SPOKE TYPE)

Removal

1. On models so equipped, remove the engine spoiler as described in the Chapter Thirteen section of this supplement.

2. Place the bike on the centerstand or place wooden blocks under the engine oil pan to support it securely with the front wheel off the ground.

NOTE
On ABS equipped models, the ABS electronic trigger sensor is attached to the left-hand fork slider. Do not damage the sensor during caliper removal.

3. Remove the front fender as described under *Front Fender (1-Piece Type) Removal/Installation* in Chapter Thirteen in the main body of this book.

4. Remove the brake caliper assembly mounting bolts (**Figure 84**) from the front fork on each side. Both caliper assemblies must be removed on these models.

5. Slide both caliper assemblies off of the brake discs.

6. Tie the caliper assemblies and brake line up with a Bungee cord to take the strain off the hydraulic brake line.

7. Insert a piece of vinyl tubing or wood in the calipers in place of the brake disc. That way, if the brake lever is inadvertently squeezed, the pistons will not be forced out of the cylinders. If this does happen, the calipers may have to be disassembled to reseat the pistons and the system will have to be bled.

8. Loosen the front axle clamping bolts (**Figure 85**) on the left-hand fork leg.

9. Remove the bolt and special washer (**Figure 86**) from the left-hand side of the front axle.

10. Loosen the front axle clamping bolts (**Figure 87**) on the right-hand fork leg.

NOTE
*Prior to removing the front wheel, note the direction of the tire rotation arrow **Figure 88**. If the tire is not marked, mark a rotation arrow either on the tire or wheel. The wheel must be reinstalled the same way so the arrow will be pointing in the correct direction.*

11. Insert a drift or Allen wrench into the hole (**Figure 89**) in the right-hand side of the front axle.

12. Rotate the axle back and forth and withdraw the front axle from both fork legs.

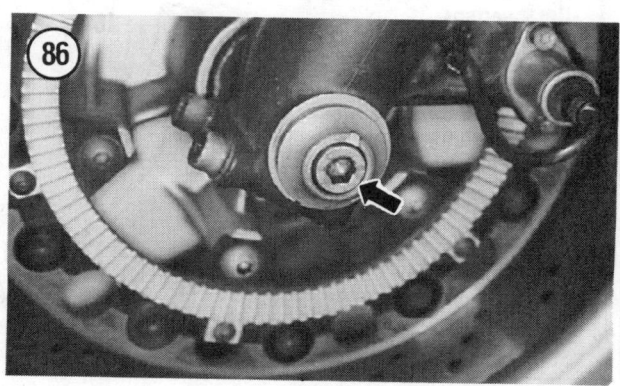

13. Let the wheel come down and forward to remove it. Don't lose the spacer on each side of the front hub. Don't intermix them as they must be reinstalled on the correct side of the wheel during installation.

CAUTION
Do not set the wheel down on the disc surface as it may get scratched or warped. Set the tire sidewalls on 2 wooden blocks.

14. Inspect the front wheel as described in this chapter of the supplement.

Installation

1. Make sure the axle bearing surfaces of both fork sliders and the axle are free from burrs and nicks.
2. Apply a small amount of cold grease to the inner surface of the spacers; this will help hold them in place.
3. Position the spacers onto the correct side of the wheel hub. The narrow spacer goes on the right-hand side.
4. Make sure the front wheel tire rotation arrow (**Figure 88**) is pointing in the correct direction.
5. Apply a light coat of multipurpose grease to the front axle prior to installation.
6. Roll the wheel into position. Lift the wheel up and install the front axle in from the right-hand side (**Figure 89**). Push the axle all the way in until it bottoms out on the left-hand fork leg. Make sure the axle spacers are still in place.
7. Install the special washer and the Allen bolt (**Figure 86**) into the front axle.
8. Install a drift or Allen bolt wrench into the hole in the right-hand end of the front axle. This is to prevent the axle from turning while tightening the Allen bolt on the opposite end.
9. Tighten the Allen bolt to the torque specification listed in **Table 8**.
10. Remove the vinyl tubing or pieces of wood from both brake calipers.

NOTE
On ABS models, the ABS electronic trigger sensor is attached to the left-hand fork slider. Do not damage the sensor during caliper installation.

11. Carefully install the caliper assemblies onto the disc. Be careful not to damage the leading edge of the pads during installation.
12. Install the brake caliper assembly mounting bolts (**Figure 84**).
13. Tighten the caliper mounting bolts to the torque specifications listed in **Table 8**.
14. Install the front fender as described under *Front Fender (1-Piece Type) Removal/Installation* in Chapter Thirteen in the main body of this book.
15. Remove the wooden block(s) from under the engine oil pan and take the bike off the centerstand.
16. Apply the front brakes and pump the front forks up and down several times to seat and center the front axle within the fork tubes.
17. Tighten the front axle clamp bolts on each fork leg to the torque specification listed in **Table 8**. Refer to **Figure 87** and **Figure 85**.

14

18. After the wheel is completely installed, rotate it several times and apply the brakes a couple of times to make sure the wheel rotates freely and that the brake pads are against the discs correctly.

19. On models so equipped, install the engine spoiler.

Inspection

Inspect the front wheel as described in Chapter Ten in the main body of this book.

FRONT HUB

Inspection/Disassembly/Assembly

The inspection, disassembly and assembly of the front hub is the same as on previous models with the exception of the appearance of the wheel and hub center as shown in **Figure 90**. Refer to Chapter Ten in the main body of this book for the inspection, disassembly and assembly of the front hub assembly.

TIRE BALANCING (3-SPOKE TYPE)

The balancing procedure is the same as on prior wheels with the exception of the special tools required to hold the rear wheel in the fixture.

Refer to **Figure 91** for this procedure.

1A. On the front wheel, perform the following:
   a. Install the balance axle through the center of the front hub.
   b. Lightly secure the balance axle with the knurled nut.

1B. On the rear wheel, perform the following:
   a. Install the mounting fixture into the centering collar side of the rear hub and secure it with the wheel mounting bolts.
   b. Install the balance axle through the center of the rear hub.
   c. Lightly secure the balance axle with the knurled nut.

2. Place the wheel on the balancing device as shown in **Figure 92**.

3. Follow the *Wheel Balance* procedure in Chapter Ten in the main body of this book.

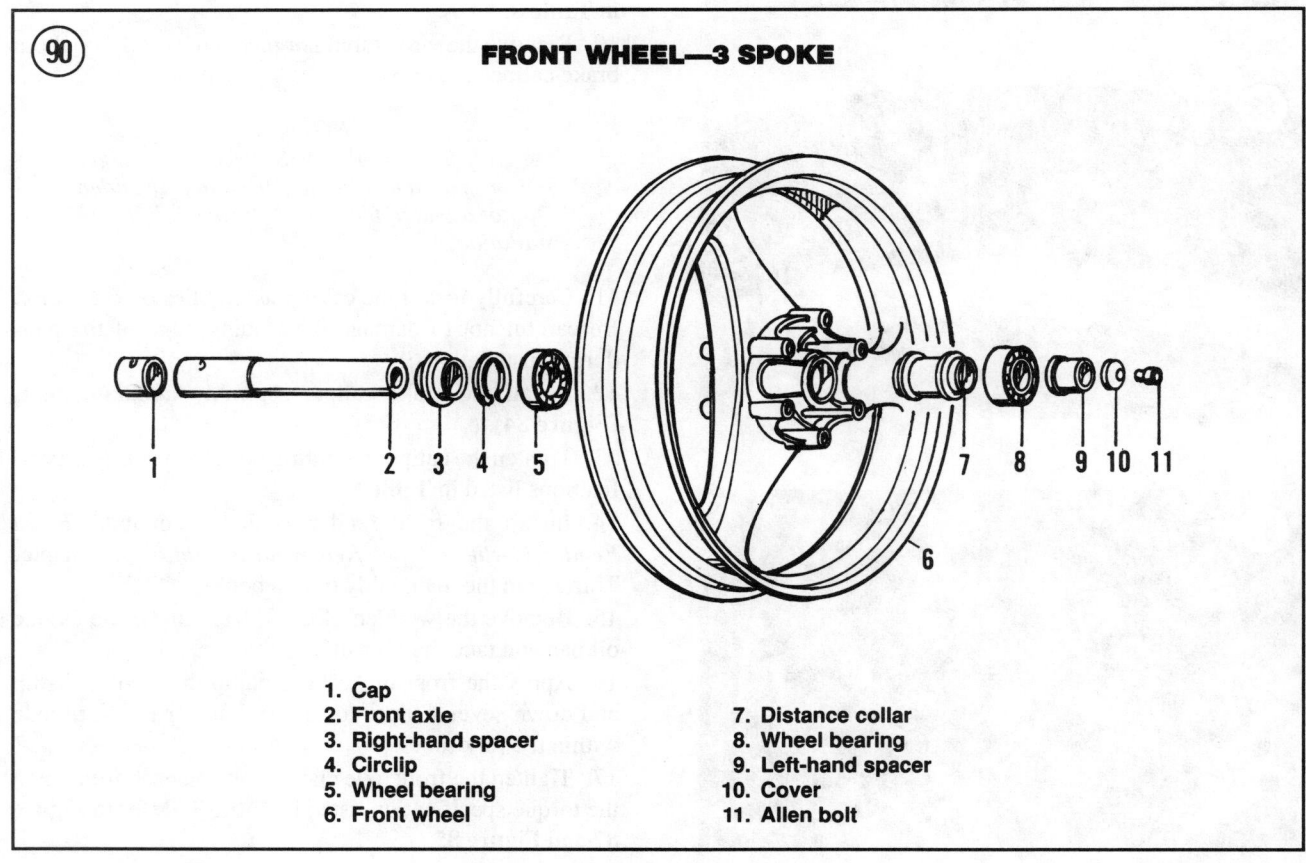

90

FRONT WHEEL—3 SPOKE

1. Cap
2. Front axle
3. Right-hand spacer
4. Circlip
5. Wheel bearing
6. Front wheel
7. Distance collar
8. Wheel bearing
9. Left-hand spacer
10. Cover
11. Allen bolt

HANDLEBAR

Removal/Installation

Refer to the following illustrations for this procedure.
a. K1, K100RS models: **Figure 93**.
b. K1100LT models: **Figure 94**.

NOTE
The handlebar on the K1100RS is the same as on previous models.

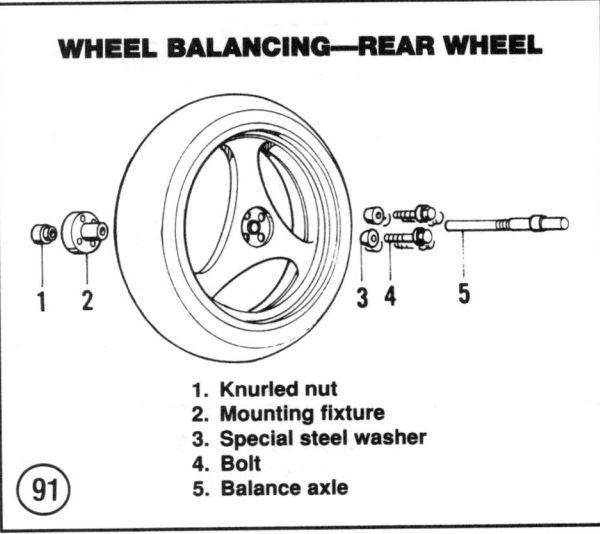

WHEEL BALANCING—REAR WHEEL

1. Knurled nut
2. Mounting fixture
3. Special steel washer
4. Bolt
5. Balance axle

(91)

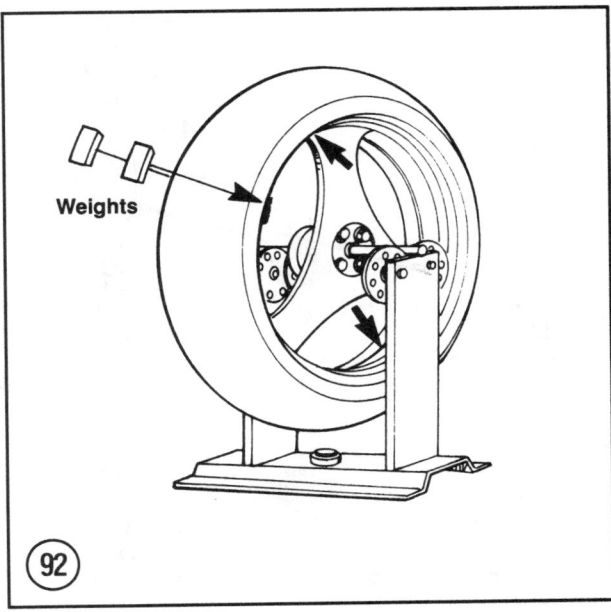

Weights

(92)

The removal and installation procedures are the same as on previous models with the exception of the shape of some of the handlebar components. Refer to the *Handlebar* procedure in Chapter Ten in the main body of this book and the to these illustrations during the removal and installation procedures.

STEERING DAMPER
(K1, K100RS)

Removal/Installation

Refer to the following illustrations for this procedure.
a. K1 models: **Figure 95**.
b. K100RS models: **Figure 96**.
c. K1 models: **Figure 97**.
1. Remove the seat cover and the dual seat as described in the Chapter Thirteen section of this supplement.

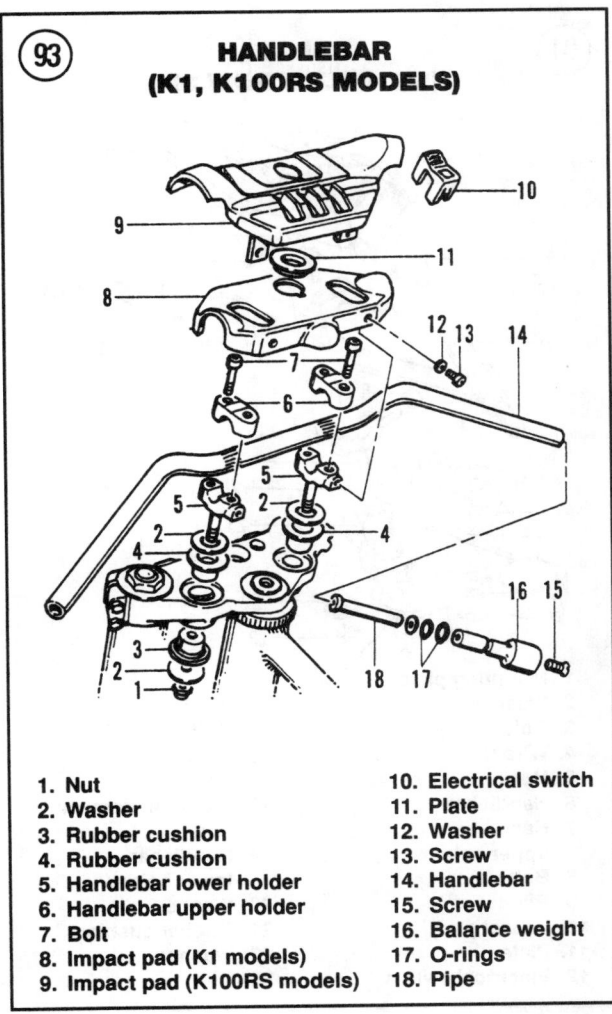

(93)   **HANDLEBAR**
(K1, K100RS MODELS)

1. Nut
2. Washer
3. Rubber cushion
4. Rubber cushion
5. Handlebar lower holder
6. Handlebar upper holder
7. Bolt
8. Impact pad (K1 models)
9. Impact pad (K100RS models)
10. Electrical switch
11. Plate
12. Washer
13. Screw
14. Handlebar
15. Screw
16. Balance weight
17. O-rings
18. Pipe

14

2. Remove the front fairing left-hand knee pad and the left-hand inner cover as described in the Chapter Thirteen section of this supplement.

3. Disconnect the electrical connector from the instrument panel.

4. On K1 models, carefully pry back the plastic cover on the front fairing mounting bracket to expose the mounting bolt.

5. Remove the Allen bolt securing the damper unit (**Figure 98**) to the front fairing mounting bracket.

6A. On K1 models, remove the washer and shim from the front fairing mounting bracket receptacle.

6B. On K100RS models, remove the 2 shims from the front fairing mounting bracket receptacle.

7. Hold onto the damper unit and remove the Allen bolt securing the damper unit to the lower fork bridge (A, **Figure 99**), remove the damper unit (B, **Figure 99**) from the frame.

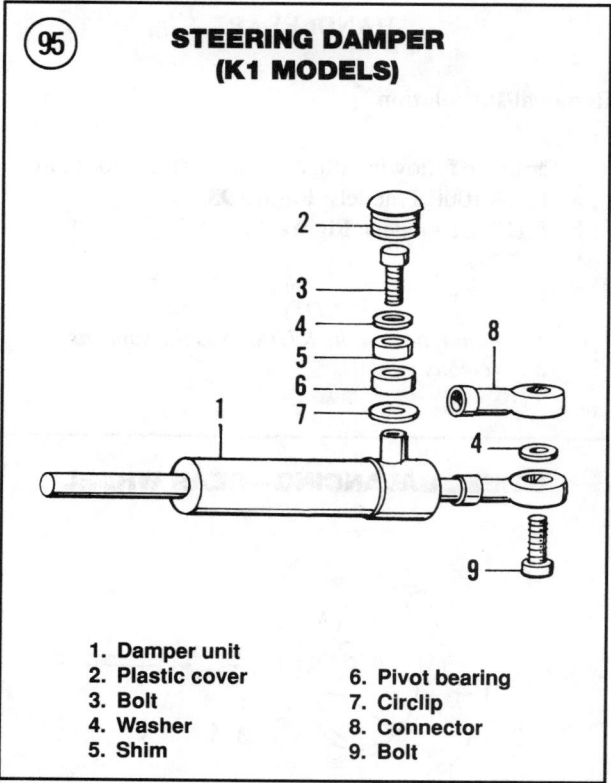

95 STEERING DAMPER (K1 MODELS)

1. Damper unit
2. Plastic cover
3. Bolt
4. Washer
5. Shim
6. Pivot bearing
7. Circlip
8. Connector
9. Bolt

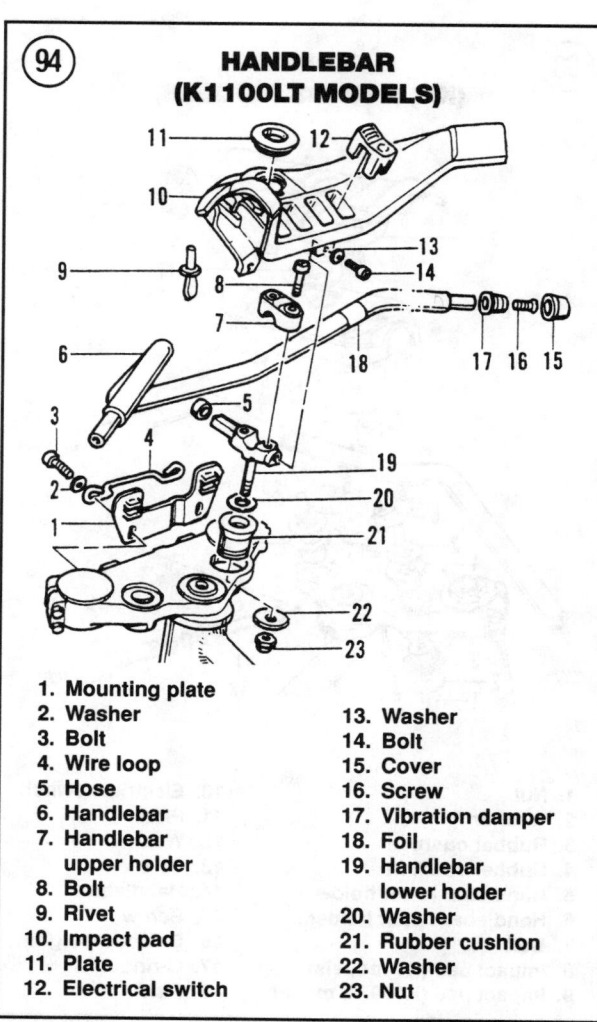

94 HANDLEBAR (K1100LT MODELS)

1. Mounting plate
2. Washer
3. Bolt
4. Wire loop
5. Hose
6. Handlebar
7. Handlebar upper holder
8. Bolt
9. Rivet
10. Impact pad
11. Plate
12. Electrical switch
13. Washer
14. Bolt
15. Cover
16. Screw
17. Vibration damper
18. Foil
19. Handlebar lower holder
20. Washer
21. Rubber cushion
22. Washer
23. Nut

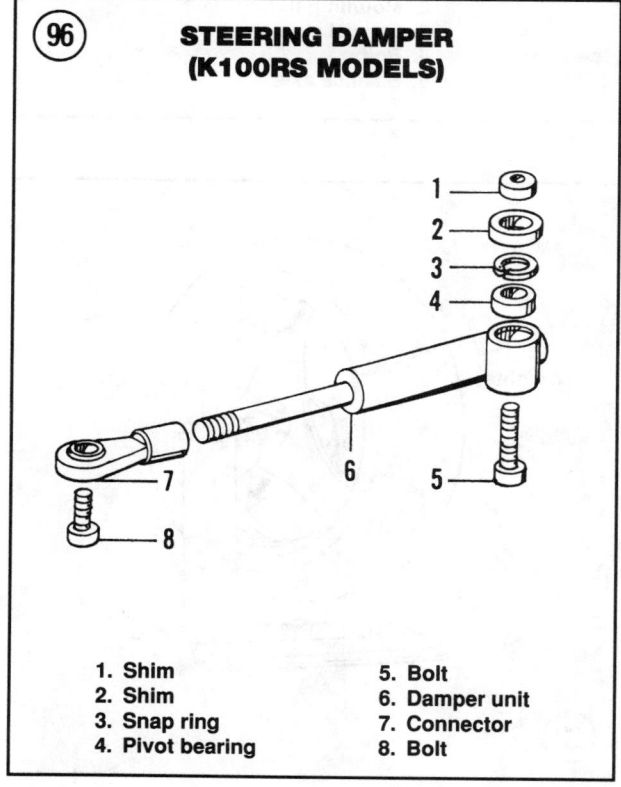

96 STEERING DAMPER (K100RS MODELS)

1. Shim
2. Shim
3. Snap ring
4. Pivot bearing
5. Bolt
6. Damper unit
7. Connector
8. Bolt

8. Remove the felt ring and washer from the lower fork bridge.

CAUTION
Do not remove the pivot bearing for inspection purposes as it will be damaged during the removal process. Remove the pivot bearing only if replacement is necessary.

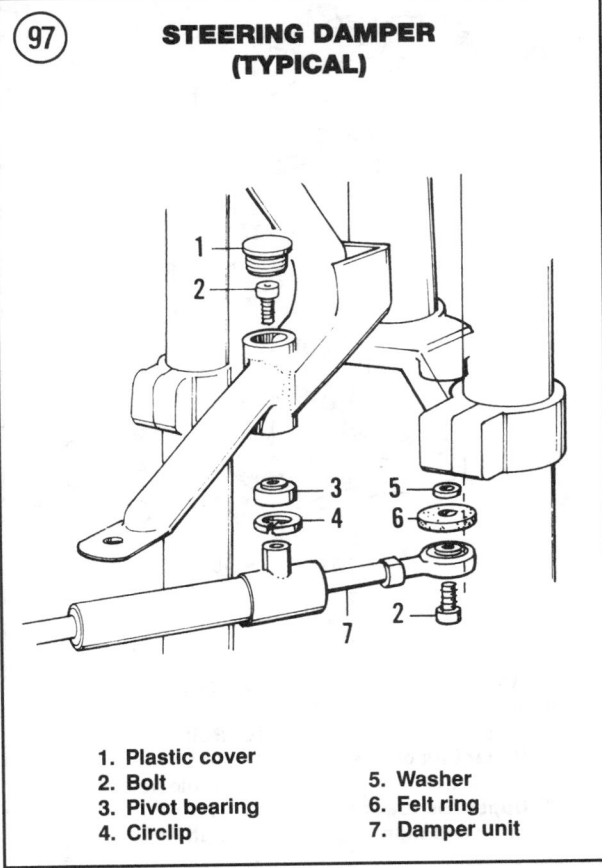

STEERING DAMPER (TYPICAL)

97

1. Plastic cover
2. Bolt
3. Pivot bearing
4. Circlip
5. Washer
6. Felt ring
7. Damper unit

9A. On K1 models, to remove the pivot bearing from the front fairing mounting bracket, perform the following:
  a. Remove the circlip.
  b. Using a suitable size socket, carefully tap the pivot bearing out of the receptacle in the bracket.
9B. On K100RS models, to remove the pivot bearing from the steering damper, perform the following:
  a. Remove the circlip.
  b. Using a suitable size socket, carefully tap the pivot bearing out of the receptacle in the steering damper.
10. Install by reversing these removal steps, noting the following.
11. Install the Allen bolts and tighten to the torque specification listed in **Table 8**.

STEERING HEAD AND STEM (K75, K75RT, K75S)

Disassembly/Assembly

Refer to **Figure 100** for this procedure.
The disassembly and assembly procedures are the same as on previous models with the exception of the number of the clamping bolts and their locations on the lower fork bridge. Refer to the *Steering Head and Stem* procedure in Chapter Ten in the main body of this book and to **Figure 100** during the disassembly and assembly procedures.

FRONT FORK (K75, K75RT, K75S 1992-ON)

Removal/Installation

The removal and installation procedures are the same as on previous models with the exception of the number of the upper and lower fork bridge clamping bolts and their locations (**Figure 101**). Refer to the *Front Forks Removal*

98

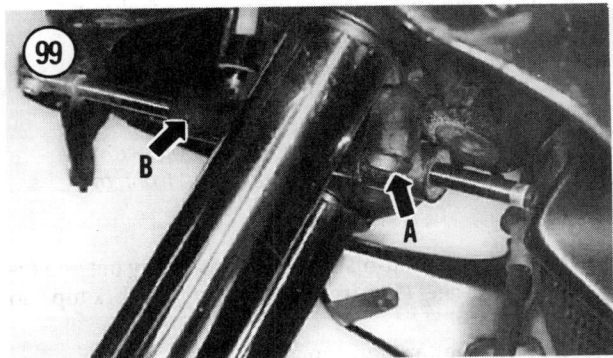

99

14

and Installation procedure in Chapter Ten in the main body of this book.

Disassembly

To simplify fork service and to prevent the mixing of parts, the legs should be disassembled and assembled individually. Some models have different internal components in the right-hand fork assembly than those installed in the left-hand fork assembly.

Refer to **Figure 102** for this procedure.

1. Clamp the slider in a vise with soft jaws.

> *NOTE*
> *This Allen bolt is secured with a locking compound and is often very difficult to remove because the damper rod will turn inside the slider. It sometimes can be removed with an air impact driver. If you are unable to remove it, take the fork tubes to a dealer and have the bolts removed.*

2. Loosen the Allen bolt on the bottom of the slider, then remove the Allen bolt and gasket.
3. Remove the fork slider from the vise.
4. If not already removed, remove the plastic trim cap (**Figure 103**) from the fork tube.
5. Hold the fork top cap with an open end wrench and remove the oil fill plug and O-ring.
6. Pour the fork oil out and discard it. Pump the fork several times by hand to expel most of the remaining oil.
7. Remove the dust seal from the fork slider.
8. Hold the upper fork tube in a vise with soft jaws.
9. Compress the fork top cap with a drift or socket extension.

> *WARNING*
> *Be careful when removing the fork top cap as the spring is under pressure. Protect your eyes accordingly.*

> *NOTE*
> *The spring pressure should push the fork top cap out of the fork slider after the circlip is removed. If it does not come out after the circlip is removed, install a bolt (**Figure 104**) into the oil fill plug threaded hole in the fork top cap. Pull the fork top cap out with a pair of pliers. Unscrew the bolt from the cap.*

10. Using a small flat-bladed screwdriver, pry out and remove the snap ring (**Figure 105**) securing the fork top cap into the slider.
11. Remove the fork top cap and O-ring.

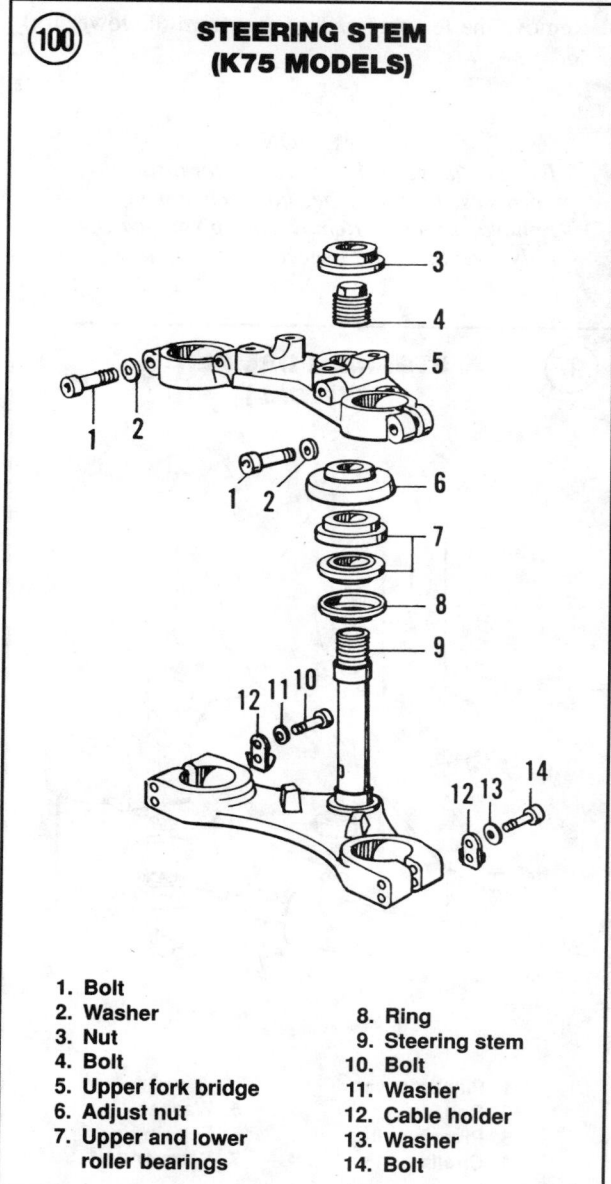

100 STEERING STEM (K75 MODELS)

1. Bolt
2. Washer
3. Nut
4. Bolt
5. Upper fork bridge
6. Adjust nut
7. Upper and lower roller bearings
8. Ring
9. Steering stem
10. Bolt
11. Washer
12. Cable holder
13. Washer
14. Bolt

12. Slide out the distance tube, spring seat and the fork spring from the top of the fork tube.

13. Remove the fork from the vise, pour the fork oil out and discard it. Pump the fork several times by hand to expel most of the remaining oil.

14. Remove the dust seal from the slider.

15. Using circlip pliers, remove the internal circlip from the slider.

16. Install the fork slider in a vise with soft jaws.

NOTE
On this type of fork, force is needed to remove the fork tube from the slider.

17. There is an interference fit between the fork slider guide bushing and the fork tube guide bushing. To remove the fork tube from the slider, pull hard on the fork tube using quick in and out strokes (**Figure 106**). Doing this will withdraw the guide bushing, shim and oil seal from the slider.

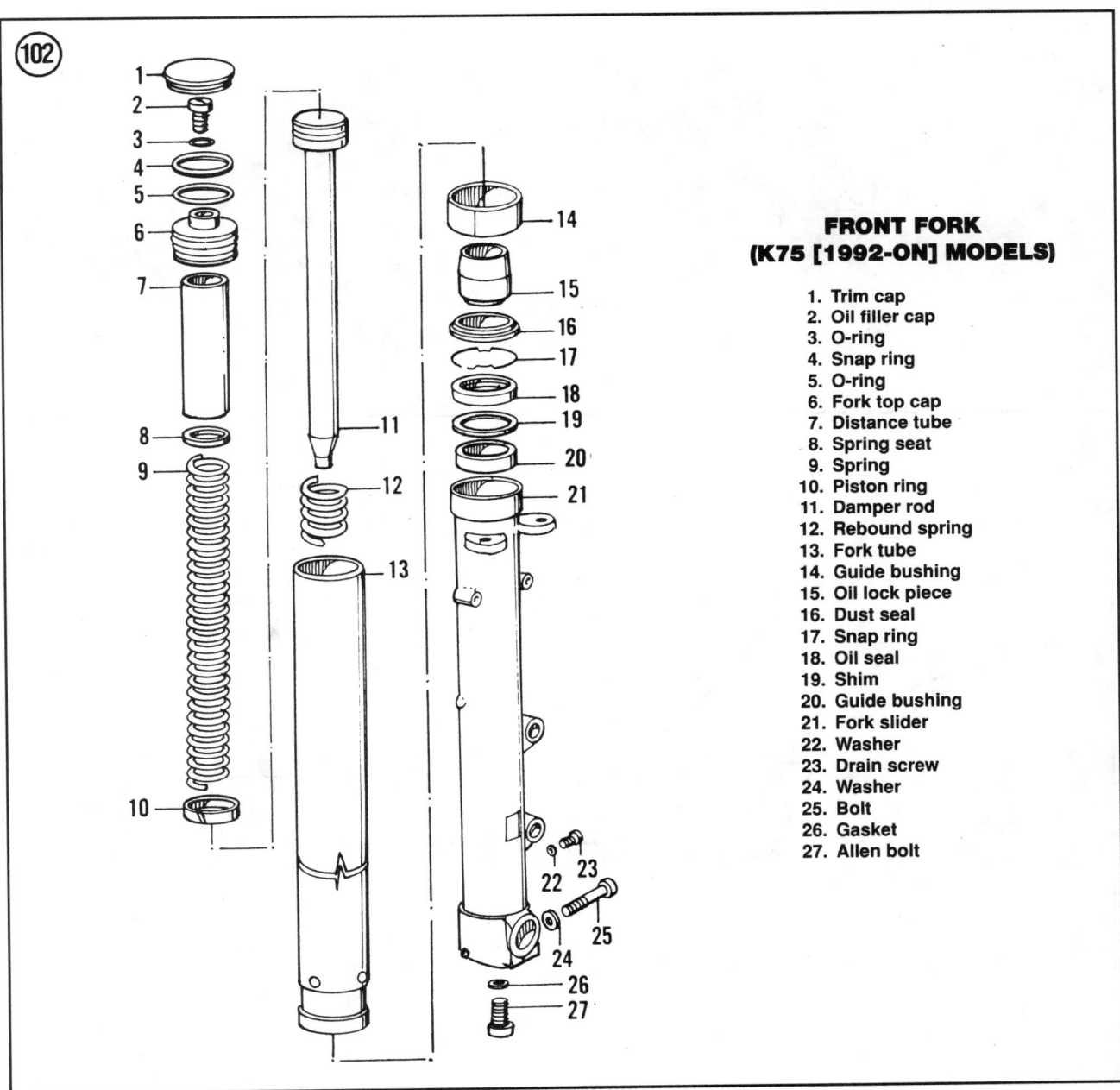

**FRONT FORK
(K75 [1992-ON] MODELS)**

1. Trim cap
2. Oil filler cap
3. O-ring
4. Snap ring
5. O-ring
6. Fork top cap
7. Distance tube
8. Spring seat
9. Spring
10. Piston ring
11. Damper rod
12. Rebound spring
13. Fork tube
14. Guide bushing
15. Oil lock piece
16. Dust seal
17. Snap ring
18. Oil seal
19. Shim
20. Guide bushing
21. Fork slider
22. Washer
23. Drain screw
24. Washer
25. Bolt
26. Gasket
27. Allen bolt

14

18. Withdraw the fork tube from the slider.

NOTE
Do not remove the fork tube guide bushing unless it is going to be replaced. Inspect it as described in this section of the supplement.

19. Turn the fork tube upside down and slide off the oil seal, shim and guide bushing from the fork tube.
20. Remove the oil lock piece, the damper rod and rebound spring from the slider.
21. Inspect all parts as described in this chapter.

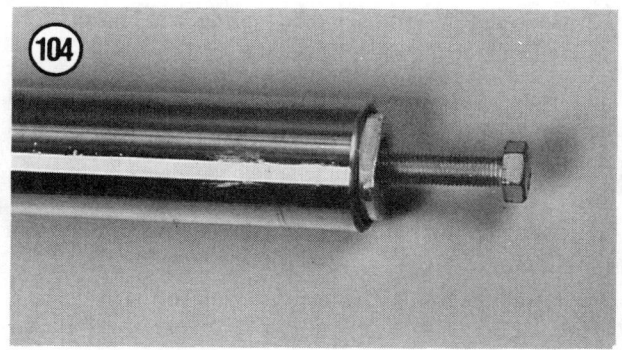

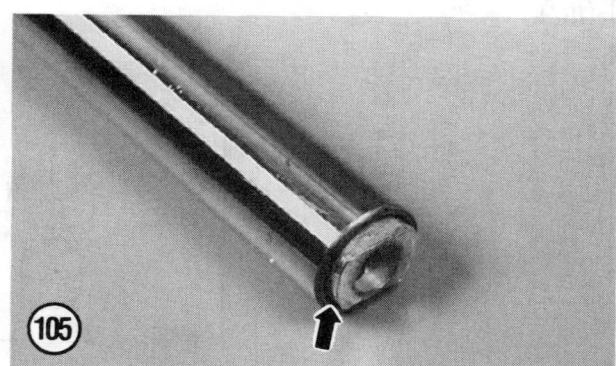

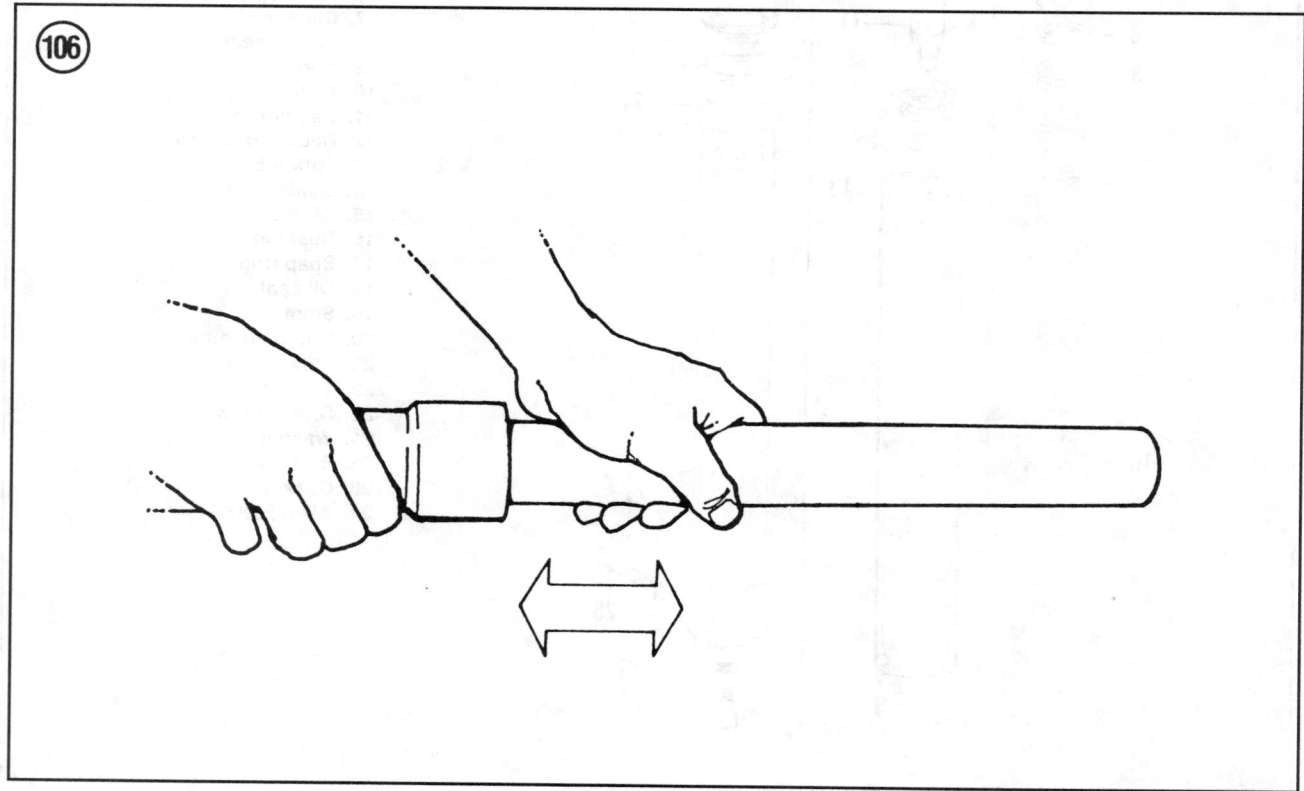

Inspection

1. Thoroughly clean all parts in solvent and dry them. Check the fork tube for wear or scratches.

2. Check the damper rod for straightness (**Figure 107**). BMW does not provide service limit specifications for runout.

3. Carefully check the damper rod and piston ring (**Figure 108**) for wear or damage. Replace if necessary.

4. Inspect the fork oil seal for wear or deterioration. Replace if necessary,

5. Check the fork tube for straightness. If bent or severely scratched, it should be replaced.

6. Check the lower portion of the slider for dents or exterior damage that may cause the fork tube to hang up during riding. Replace if necessary.

7. Check the slider in the area where the fork seal is installed for wear or damage. Replace the slider if necessary.

8. Inspect the snap ring groove (**Figure 109**) in the fork tube for wear, corrosion or damage. Clean out the groove if necessary so that the snap ring can seat correctly during assembly.

9. Check the axle bearing surfaces of the slider (**Figure 110**) for wear or gouges. Clean up the surfaces or replace the slider if necessary.

10. Inspect the axle clamping lugs (**Figure 111**) on the slider for cracks or fractures from over tightening the clamping bolts. If any cracks are found, replace the fork slider.

11. Inspect the fork tube and slider guide bushings (**Figure 112**). If either is scratched or scored, they must be

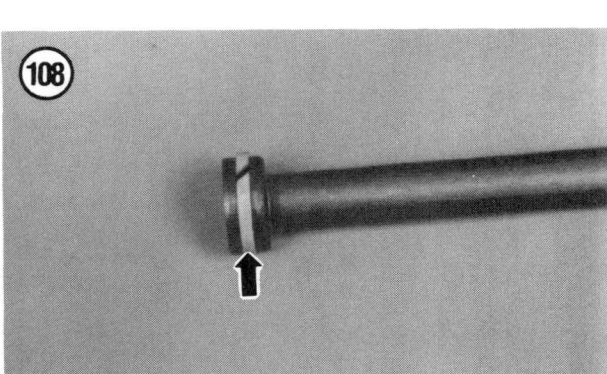

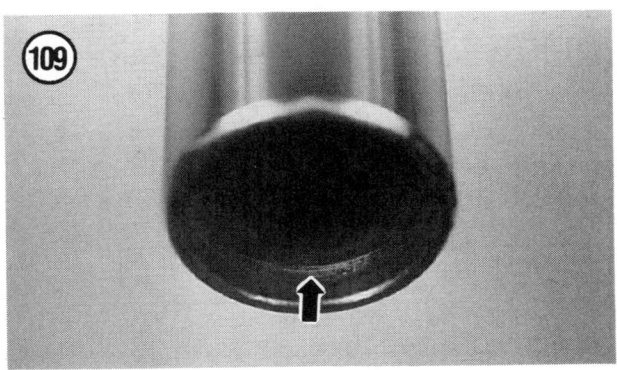

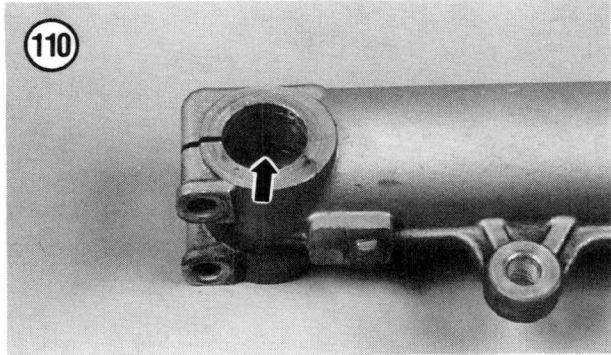

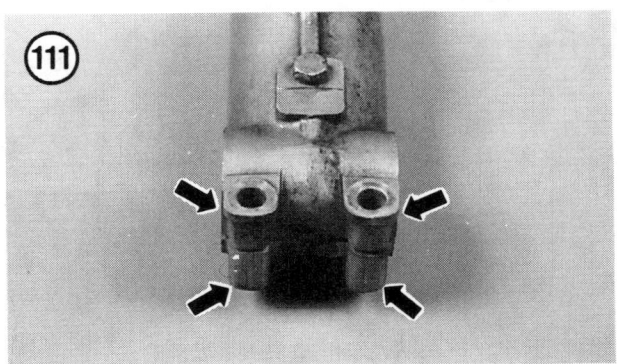

14

replaced. If the Teflon coating is worn off so the copper base material is showing on approximately 3/4 of the total surface, the bushing must be replaced.

12. Inspect the distance tube for wear or damage. Replace if necessary.

13. Any worn or damaged parts should be replaced. Simply cleaning and reinstalling unserviceable components will not improve performance of the front suspension.

Assembly

Refer to **Figure 102** for this procedure.

1. Apply fork oil to all parts prior to installation.

2. If removed, install the new fork tube guide bushing (**Figure 113**).

3. Install the rebound spring onto the damper rod and insert the assembly into the fork tube (**Figure 114**).

4. Install the fork spring (**Figure 115**), spring seat and spacer (**Figure 116**) into the fork tube.

5. Hold the upper fork tube in a vise with soft jaws.

6. Inspect the O-ring seal (**Figure 117**) on the fork top cap; replace if necessary.

7. Install the fork top cap and O-ring (**Figure 118**).

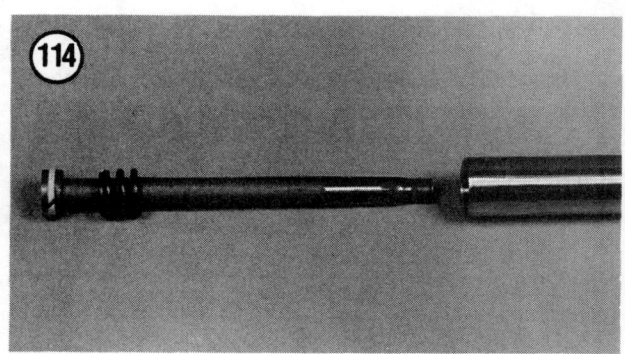

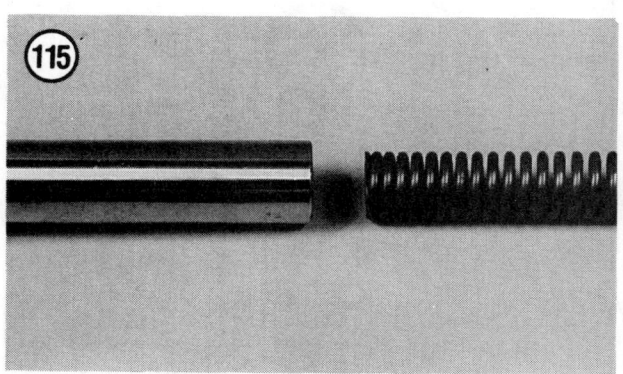

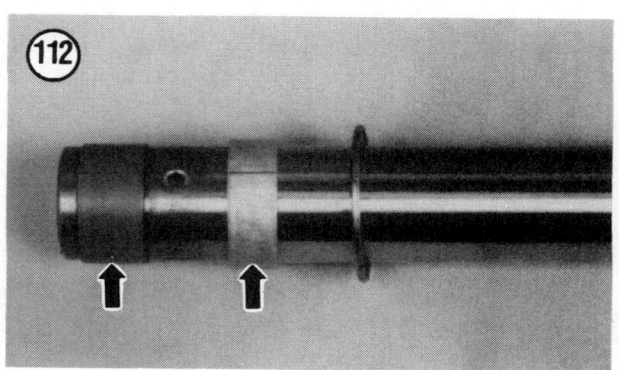

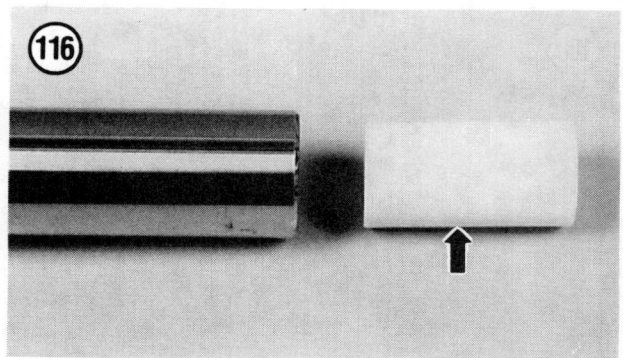

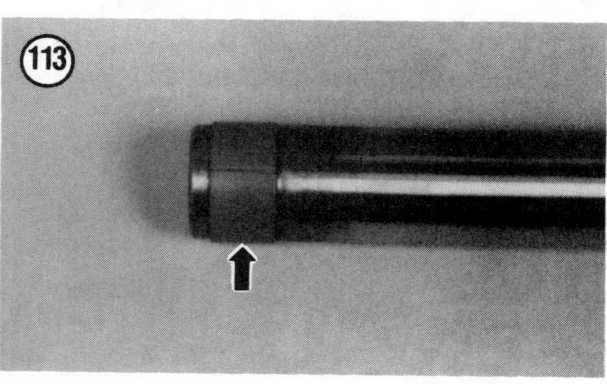

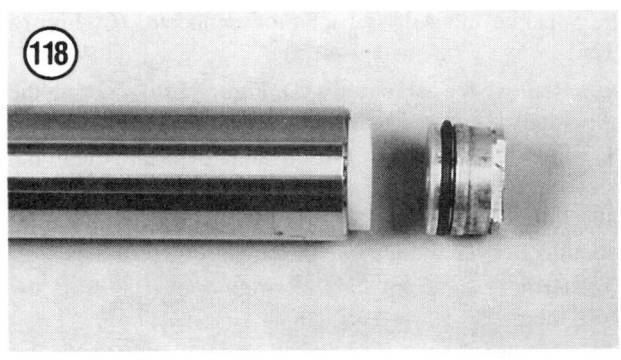

(118)

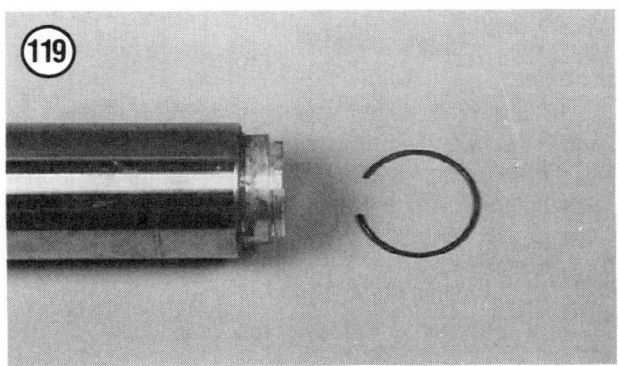

(119)

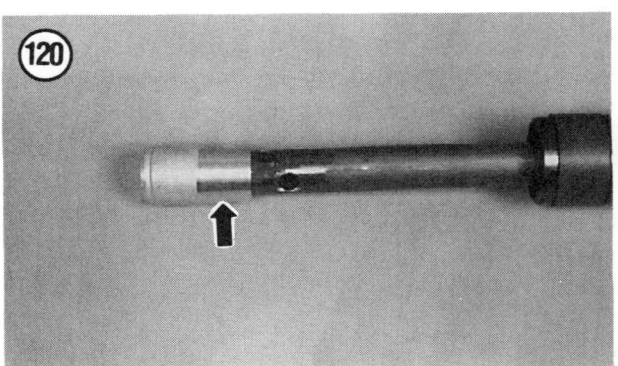

(120)

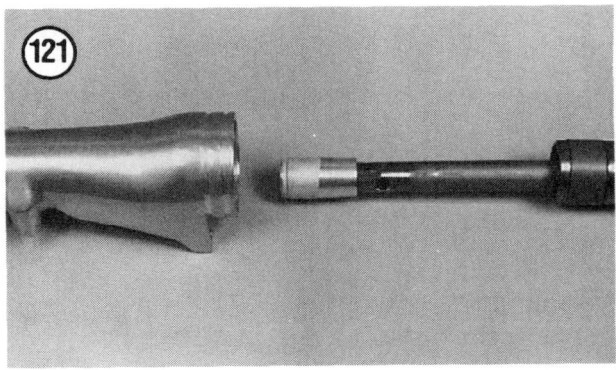

(121)

8. Press down on the fork top cap with a drift or socket extension. While holding the fork top cap down, install the snap ring (**Figure 119**). Make sure the snap ring is correctly seated in the fork tube groove.

9. Install the oil lock piece on the end of the damper rod (**Figure 120**).

10. Install the upper fork assembly into the fork slider (**Figure 121**).

11. Slide the new slider guide bushing down the fork tube and rest it on the slider.

12. Slide the fork slider shim down the fork tube and rest it on top of the guide bushing.

13. Carefully tap the slider guide bushing and shim down into the fork slider.

NOTE
*A piece of pipe can be used as a tool to tap the guide bushing into place. Wrap one end of the pipe with duct tape (**Figure 122**) to prevent the threads from damaging the interior of the slider.*

14. Apply fork oil to the oil seal and slide it down the fork tube (**Figure 123**). Carefully drive the oil seal into the fork slider using the same tool used in Step 13. Drive the oil

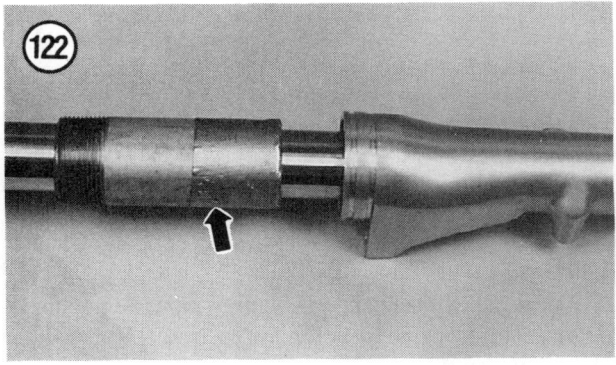

(122)

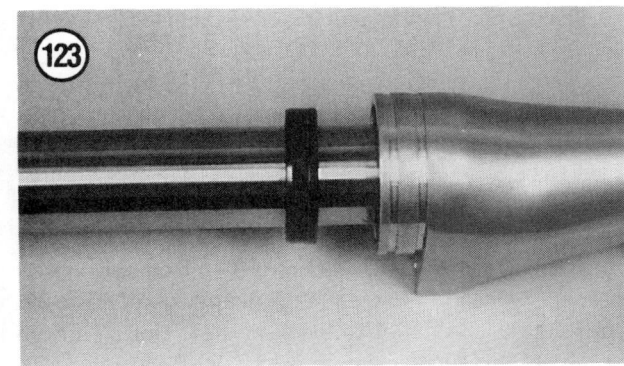

(123)

14

seal in until the groove in the slider can be seen above the top surface of the oil seal.

15. Install the snap ring, making sure it is completely seated in the groove in the fork slider (**Figure 124**).

16. Make sure the gasket is in place on the Allen bolt (**Figure 125**).

17. Install the Allen bolt into the slider and into the damper rod in the fork tube. Tighten the Allen bolt securely.

18. Remove the oil filler plug from the fork top cap.

19. Fill the fork with the correct quantity of fork oil as listed in **Table 9**.

20. Slide the dust seal down the fork tube and into place in the fork slider.

21. Install the fork assemblies as described in this section of the supplement.

FRONT FORK
(K1, K100RS, K100LT)

Removal

1. Remove the engine spoiler as described in the Chapter Thirteen section of this supplement.

2. Place the bike on the centerstand or place wooden blocks under the engine oil pan to support it securely with the front wheel off the ground.

NOTE
The ABS electronic trigger sensor is attached to the left-hand fork slider. Do not damage the sensor during caliper removal.

3. Remove the front fender (A, **Figure 126**) as described in Chapter Thirteen in the main body of this book for K100RS models or for K1 models, refer to the Chapter Thirteen section of this supplement.

4. Remove the brake caliper assembly mounting bolts (B, **Figure 126**) from the front fork on each side. Both caliper assemblies must be removed.

5. Slide both caliper assemblies off of the brake discs.

6. Insert a piece of vinyl tubing or wood in the calipers in place of the brake disc. That way if the brake lever is inadvertently squeezed, the pistons will not be forced out of the cylinders. If this does happen, the calipers may have to be disassembled to reseat the pistons and the system will have to be bled.

7. Remove the front wheel as described in this section of the supplement.

8. Remove the front fairing knee pads and inner covers as described Chapter Thirteen in the main body of this book for K100RS and K100LT models or the Chapter Thirteen section of this supplement for K1 models.

9. Separate the ABS sensor plug connector (C, **Figure 126**).

10. Remove the cable straps (D, **Figure 126**) securing the ABS sensor line and brake line to the left-hand slider.

11. Pull the ABS sensor line out and downward out of the slot in the front fork stabilizer.

12. Remove the bolts and washers securing the front stabilizer cover and remove the cover.

13. Remove the front stabilizer rubber overlay from the fork tubes.

14. Remove the nuts and washers securing the front stabilizer to both fork sliders.

15. Move the front stabilizer and the front brake lines back away from the fork assemblies and secure this assembly to the frame.

16. If the fork assembly is going to be disassembled for service, perform the following:
   a. Loosen the upper fork bridge bolts--do not loosen the lower fork bridge bolts at this time.
   b. Loosen, but do not remove, the fork top cap. It is a lot easier to loosen the fork top cap with the fork tube secure on the lower fork bridge.

17. Loosen the upper and lower fork bridge bolts (**Figure 127**).

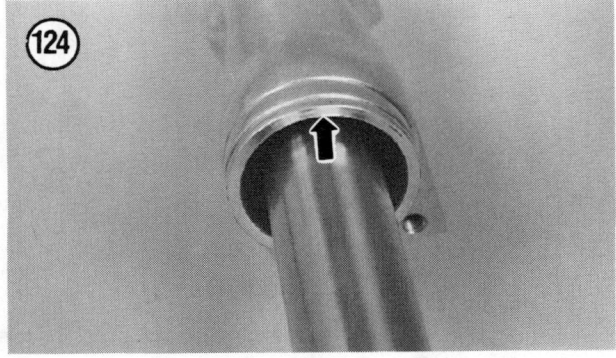

18. Lower the fork assembly down and out of the upper and lower fork bridge. It may be necessary to slightly rotate the fork tube while pulling it out. Remove both fork assemblies.

Installation

1. Clean off any corrosion or dirt on the upper and lower fork bridge fork receptacles.

> *NOTE*
> *The fork assemblies must be reinstalled on the correct side of the bike so the brake calipers, the front fork stabilizer and the front fender can be installed. If the fork assemblies are installed on the wrong side these components cannot be installed onto the fork sliders.*

2. Install the fork assemblies on the correct side. Install the fork tubes up through the lower and upper fork bridges.
3. Push the fork tube up until the top surface is 6 mm (0.24 in.) above the top surface of the upper fork bridge.

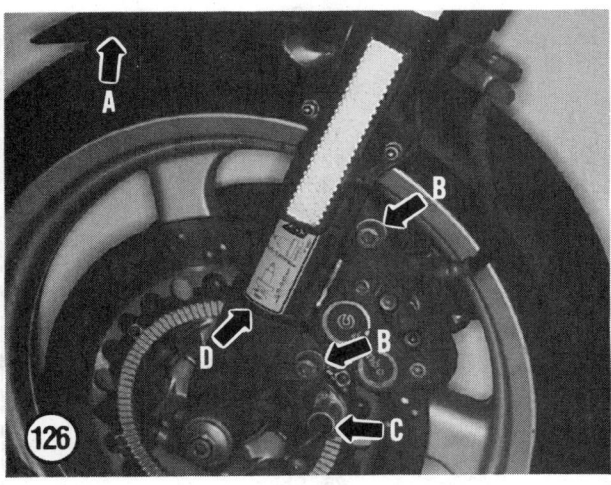

4. Tighten the upper and lower fork bridge clamping bolts to the torque specification listed in **Table 8**.
5. Move the front brake lines and front stabilizer into position on the forks.
6. Install the nuts and washers securing the front stabilizer to both fork sliders. Tighten the nuts to the torque specification listed in **Table 8**.
7. Install the rubber overlay onto the front stabilizer, then install the front stabilizer cover.
8. Install the bolts and washers securing the cover and tighten securely.
9. Move the ABS sensor line back into position in the slot in the front fork stabilizer.
10. Install the cable straps securing the ABS sensor line and brake line to the slider.
11. Connect the ABS sensor connector.
12. Install the front fairing knee pads and inner covers.
13. Remove the pieces of vinyl tubing or wood from the calipers.
14. Install the front wheel as described in this chapter.

> *NOTE*
> *The ABS electronic trigger sensor is attached to the left-hand forks slider. Do not damage the sensor during caliper installation.*

15. Install both brake caliper assemblies and tighten the mounting bolts to the torque specification listed in **Table 8**.
16. Install the front wheel and the front fender.
17. Remove the wooden blocks from under the oil pan.
18. Install the engine spoiler.

Disassembly

To simplify fork service and to prevent the mixing of parts, the legs should be disassembled and assembled individually.

Refer to the following illustrations for this procedure:
   a. **Figure 128**: 1990-1991 models.
   b. **Figure 129**: 1992-1993 models.

1. Drain the fork oil as follows:
   a. Remove the plug and O-ring from the fork top cap.
   b. Position the fork assembly in an upright position and remove the drain screw and washer from the slider.
   c. Allow the fork oil to drain out into the drain pan. Compress the fork assembly by hand several times to expel the residual fork oil. Discard the fork oil properly.
   d. Reinstall the plug and the drain screw and washer to avoid misplacing them.

14

2. Using the front brake caliper mounting bosses, clamp the slider in a vise with soft jaws.

NOTE
The base valve bolt is often very difficult to remove because the damper rod will turn inside the slider. It sometimes can be removed with an air impact driver. If you are unable to remove it, take the fork tubes to a dealer and have the bolts removed.

3. Loosen the base valve bolt on the bottom of the slider.

4. Remove the fork slider from the vise.

5. Install the fork tube in a vise with soft jaws.

WARNING
On 1990-1991 models, be careful when removing the fork top cap as the spring is under pressure. Protect your eyes accordingly.

6. Remove the fork top cap with an open end wrench.

7. Remove the fork tube from the vise.

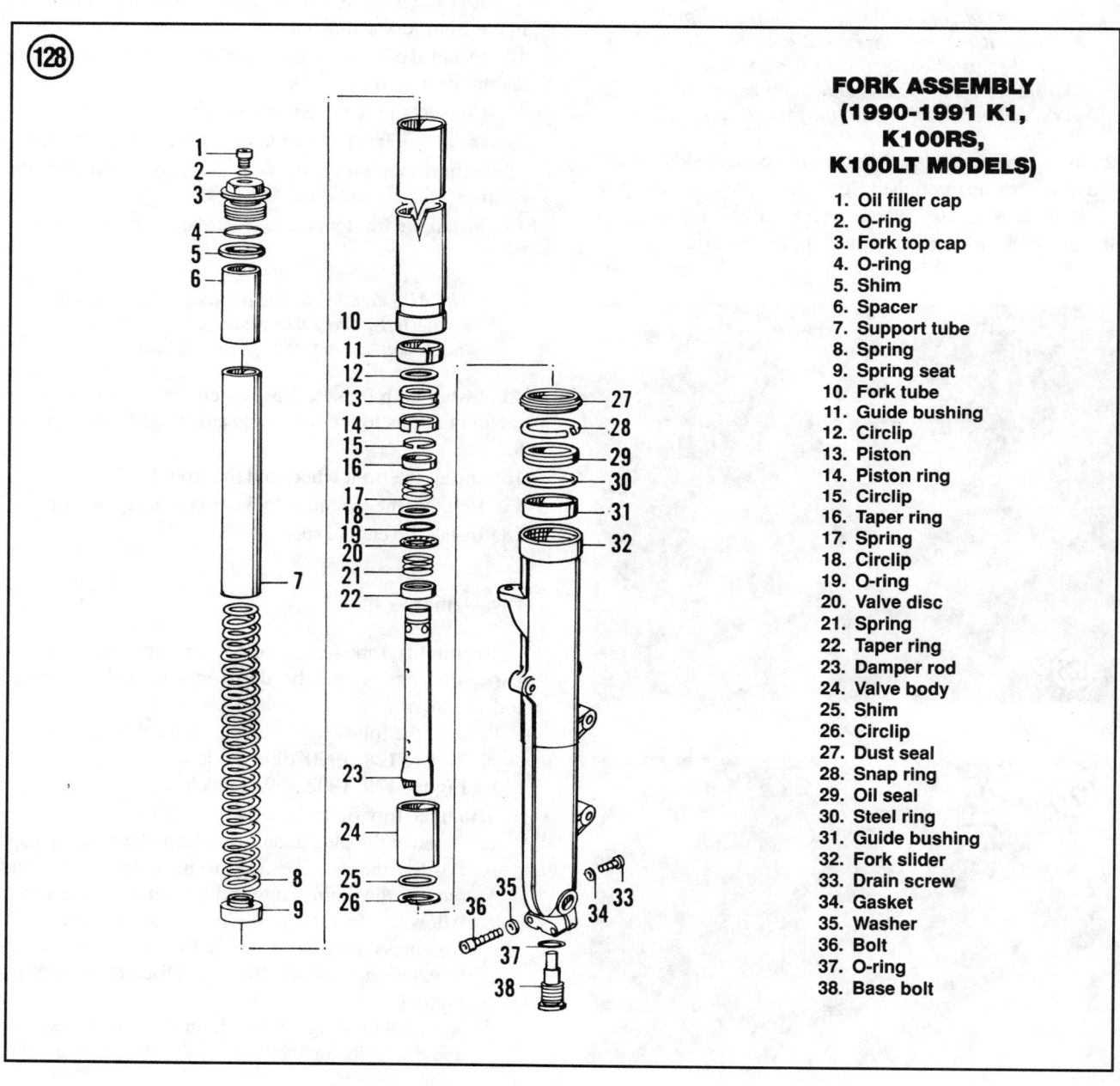

(128)

FORK ASSEMBLY (1990-1991 K1, K100RS, K100LT MODELS)

1. Oil filler cap
2. O-ring
3. Fork top cap
4. O-ring
5. Shim
6. Spacer
7. Support tube
8. Spring
9. Spring seat
10. Fork tube
11. Guide bushing
12. Circlip
13. Piston
14. Piston ring
15. Circlip
16. Taper ring
17. Spring
18. Circlip
19. O-ring
20. Valve disc
21. Spring
22. Taper ring
23. Damper rod
24. Valve body
25. Shim
26. Circlip
27. Dust seal
28. Snap ring
29. Oil seal
30. Steel ring
31. Guide bushing
32. Fork slider
33. Drain screw
34. Gasket
35. Washer
36. Bolt
37. O-ring
38. Base bolt

8. Place your finger over the end of the fork tube, then turn the fork assembly over and pour out any residual fork oil and discard it.

9A. On 1990-1991 models, remove the shim, spacer, support tube spring and spring seat from the fork tube.

9B. On 1992-1993 models, perform the following:

a. Remove the shim.

b. Compress the damper cartridge into the fork tube and remove the clamp ring from the end of the damper cartridge

c. Remove the shim from the top of the fork tube.

d. Remove the snap ring and spacer from the fork tube.

e. Remove the support tube, spring and spring seat from the fork tube.

10. Remove the base valve bolt and O-ring seal from the bottom of the slider.

11. Install the fork slider in a vise with soft jaws.

12. Withdraw the fork tube from the slider.

13A. On 1990-1991 models, perform the following:

a. Remove the circlip, shim and the valve body from the base of the slider.

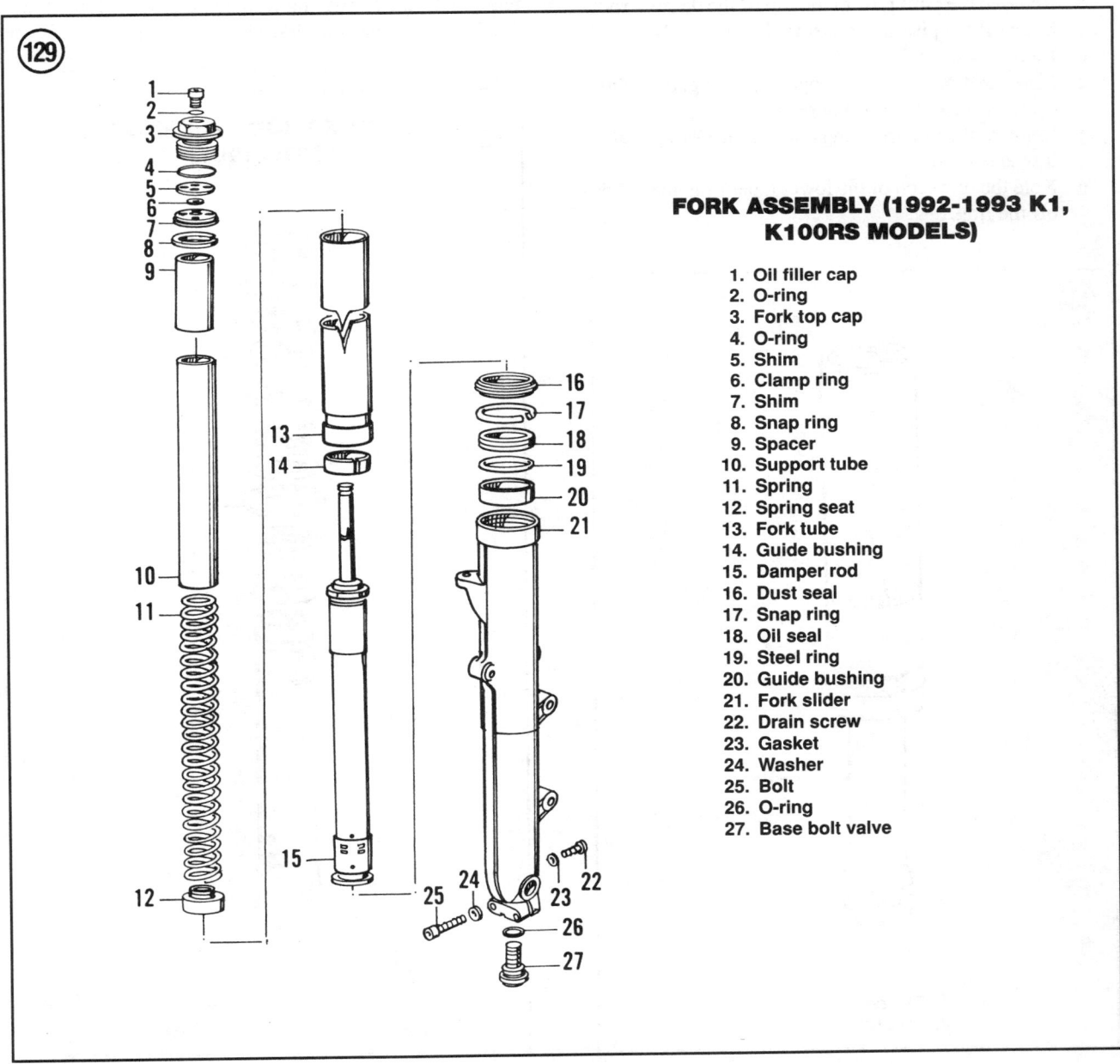

FORK ASSEMBLY (1992-1993 K1, K100RS MODELS)

1. Oil filler cap
2. O-ring
3. Fork top cap
4. O-ring
5. Shim
6. Clamp ring
7. Shim
8. Snap ring
9. Spacer
10. Support tube
11. Spring
12. Spring seat
13. Fork tube
14. Guide bushing
15. Damper rod
16. Dust seal
17. Snap ring
18. Oil seal
19. Steel ring
20. Guide bushing
21. Fork slider
22. Drain screw
23. Gasket
24. Washer
25. Bolt
26. O-ring
27. Base bolt valve

14

b. Withdraw the damper rod assembly from the fork tube (**Figure 130**).

13B. On 1992-1993 models, withdraw the damper cartridge from the fork tube.

14. On 1990-1991 models, examine the damper rod assembly as described in this chapter. Do not disassemble the damper rod assembly for inspection purposes, if one of the components is faulty, refer to **Figure 131** and disassemble as follows:

   a. Thoroughly clean the assembly in solvent and dry with compressed air.
   b. Remove the circlip from the top of the damper rod.
   c. Slide off the piston and piston ring assembly.
   d. Remove the circlip.
   e. Note the direction of the upper taper ring, then slide off the ring and the spring below it.
   f. Remove the circlip, then slide off the O-ring, valve disc and spring.
   g. Note the direction of the lower taper ring, then slide off the ring.

15. Remove the dust seal from the fork slider (**Figure 132**).

16. Carefully remove the snap ring, located above the oil seal, from the top of the fork slider.

17. Protect the edge of the fork slider with a piece of wood or plastic ring (A, **Figure 133**) to keep the screwdriver from making contact with the slider while prying out the oil seal.

18. Using a broad-tipped screwdriver (B, **Figure 133**), carefully pry the oil seal (C, **Figure 133**) out of the fork slider.

19. Remove the steel ring, then using both index fingers, remove the guide bushing from the top of the fork slider.

20. Inspect all parts as described in this chapter.

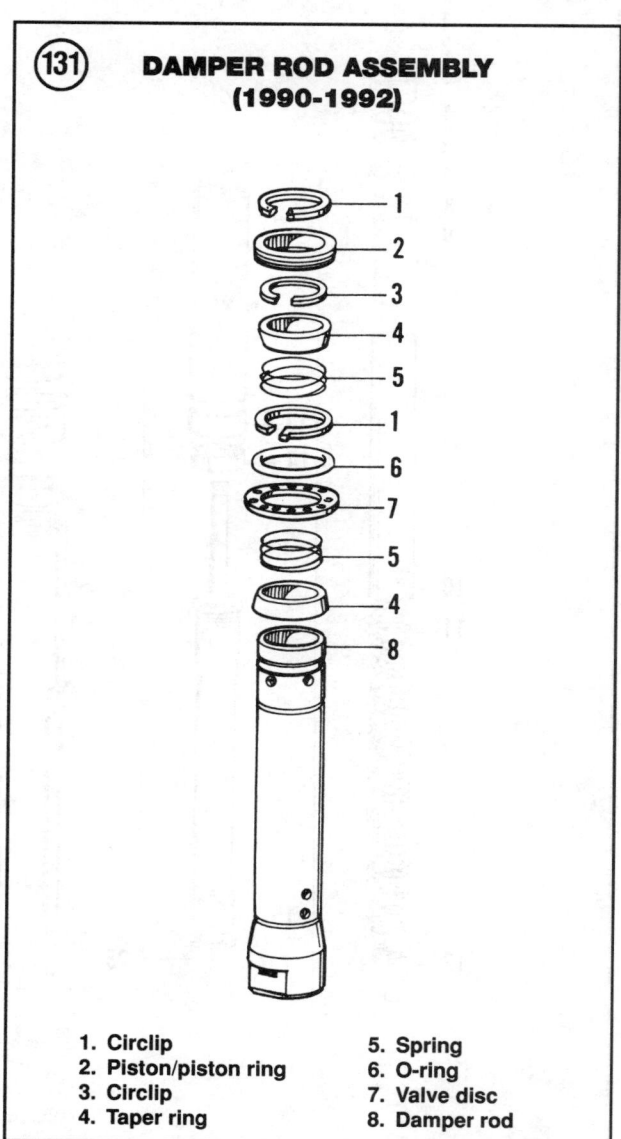

(131) DAMPER ROD ASSEMBLY (1990-1992)

1. Circlip
2. Piston/piston ring
3. Circlip
4. Taper ring
5. Spring
6. O-ring
7. Valve disc
8. Damper rod

(130)

1. Damper assembly
2. Fork tube

Inspection

1. Thoroughly clean all parts in solvent and dry them. Check the fork tube for excessive wear or scratches.

2. Check the damper rod, or damper cartridge, for straightness.

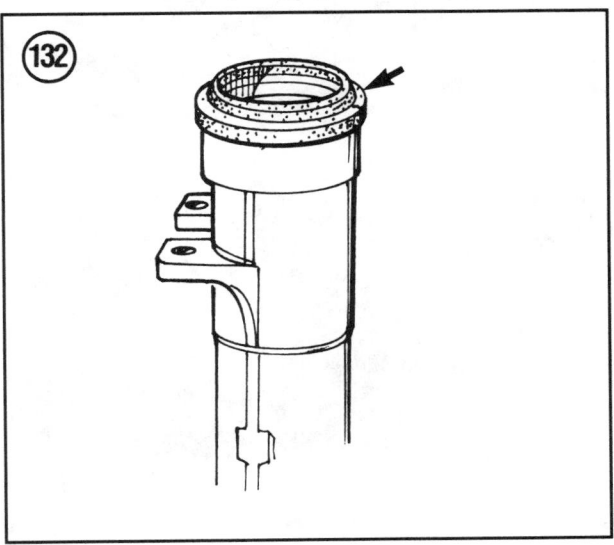

3. On 1990-1991 models, if the damper rod assembly was disassembled, roll it on a piece of plate glass and check for any runout. BMW does not provide service limit specifications for runout.

4. On 1990-1991 models, carefully check the taper rings, the O-ring seal, the valve disc and the piston and piston ring for wear or damage. Replace if necessary.

5. On 1990-1991 models, make sure the oil passage holes in the damper rod are clean. If clogged or congested, clean out with solvent and dry with compressed air.

6. Inspect the fork oil seal for wear or deterioration. Replace if necessary,

7. Check the fork tube for straightness (**Figure 134**). If bent or severely scratched, it should be replaced.

8. Check the slider (**Figure 135**) for dents or exterior damage that may cause the fork tube to hang up during riding. Replace if necessary.

9. Check the slider in the area where the fork seal is installed for wear or damage. Replace if necessary.

10. On 1992-1993 models, inspect the snap ring groove (**Figure 136**) in the fork tube for wear, corrosion or damage. Clean out the groove if necessary so the snap ring can seat correctly during assembly.

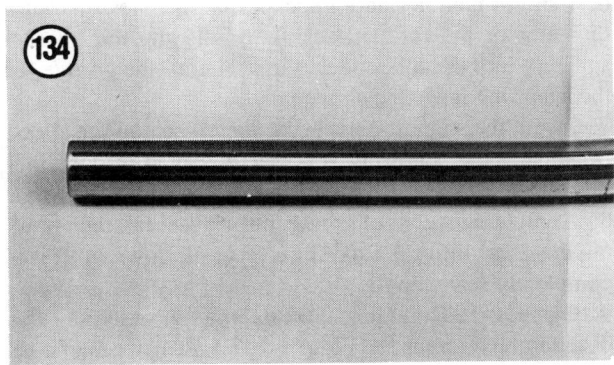

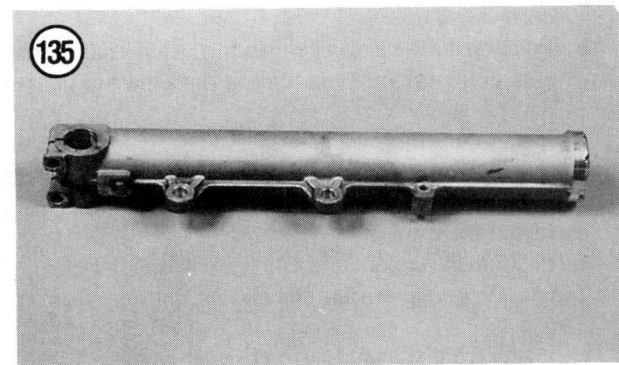

14

11. Check the axle bearing surfaces of the slider (**Figure 137**) for wear or gouges. Clean up the surfaces or replace the slider if necessary.

12. Inspect the axle clamping lugs (**Figure 138**) on the slider for cracks or fractures from over tightening the clamping bolts. If any cracks are found, replace the fork slider.

13. Inspect the spacer (**Figure 139**) for wear or damage. Replace if necessary.

14. Any worn or damaged parts should be replaced. Simply cleaning and reinstalling unserviceable components will not improve performance of the front suspension.

Assembly

Refer to the following illustrations for this procedure:
   a. **Figure 128**: 1990-1991 models.
   b. **Figure 129**: 1992-1993 models.
   c. **Figure 140**: all models.

1. Apply fork oil to all parts prior to installation.

2. Install a new guide bushing into the fork slider. Make sure it is correctly seated in the slider.

3. Install the steel ring on top of the guide bushing.

4. Apply a light coat of grease to the oil seal.

5. Position the new oil seal with the spring on the shaft sealing ring facing up.

6. Using a hammer and a socket that matches the outer diameter of the fork oil seal, carefully tap the oil seal squarely into the fork slider. Tap it in until the groove for the snap ring is visible above it.

7. Install the snap ring to secure the oil seal in the slider. Make sure the snap ring is correctly seated in the slider groove.

8. Apply a light coat of grease to the dust seal, then press the dust seal into the fork slider. Press it down until it is completely seated in the slider.

9. On 1990-1991 models, if the damper rod assembly was disassembled, refer to **Figure 131** and assemble it as follows:
   a. Position the damper rod on the workbench with the correct end up.
   b. Position the lower taper ring with the larger diameter side going on first and slide it onto the top of the damper rod.
   c. Install the spring, valve disc and O-ring.
   d. Install the circlip and make sure it is correctly seated in the groove.
   e. Install the spring.
   f. Position the upper taper ring with the smaller diameter side going on first and slide it onto the damper rod.
   g. Install the piston and piston ring assembly.

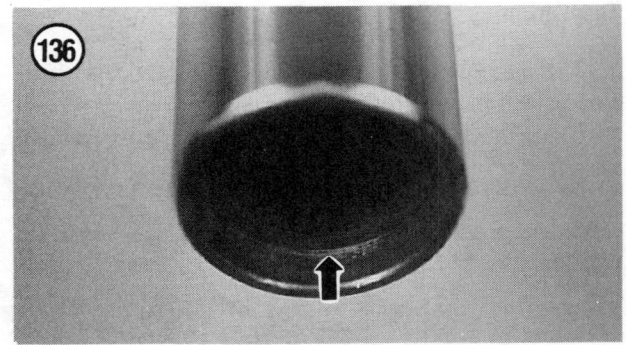

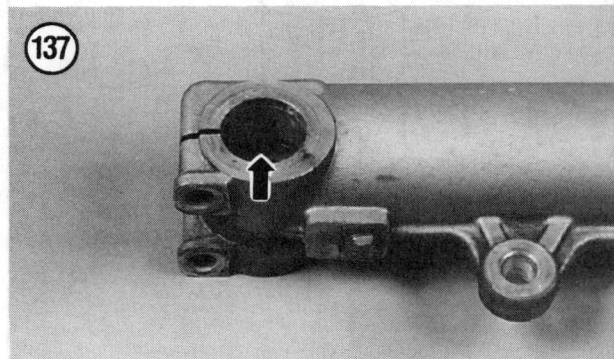

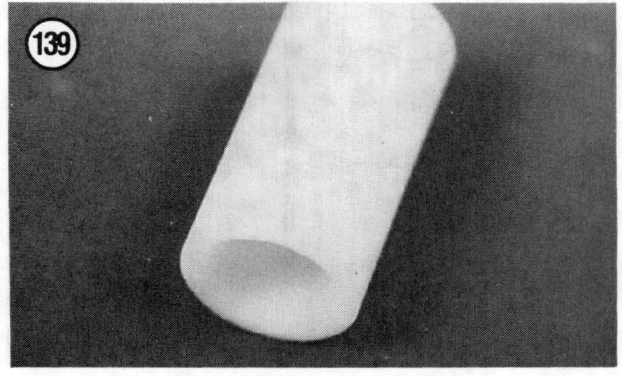

h. Install the circlip and make sure it is correctly seated in the groove.

10A. On 1990-1991 models, refer to **Figure 141** and perform the following:

a. Install the fork tube (A, **Figure 141**) *upside down* in a vise with soft jaws with the lower end (non-threaded end) facing up.

b. Install the BMW Slip Sleeve special tool (part No. 31 4 710) (B, **Figure 141**) into the fork slider.

c. Insert the piston end of the damper rod assembly (C, **Figure 141**) into the slip sleeve. After the piston assembly has passed through the slip sleeve, remove the slip sleeve.

d. Push the damper rod assembly down into the fork tube until it stops.

e. Position the valve body (A, **Figure 142**) with the larger inner diameter end going in first and install it into the fork tube (B, **Figure 142**).

f. Install the shim and circlip (C, **Figure 142**) and make sure the circlip is correctly seated in the fork tube groove.

10B. On 1992-1993 models, install the damper cartridge into the fork tube.

11. Install the fork tube into slider.

12. Using the front brake caliper mounting bosses, install the fork slider in a vise with soft jaws.

13. Make sure the O-ring seal is on the base valve bolt and install the base valve bolt and O-ring seal into the bottom of the slider (**Figure 143**) and into the damper rod or damper cartridge. Tighten the bolt to the torque specification listed in **Table 8**.

14A. On 1990-1991 models, refer to **Figure 144** and perform the following:

a. Install the spring and spring seat assembly, support tube, spacer and shim into the fork tube.

b. Push down on the fork spring and install the fork top cap. Use an open end wrench and tighten to the torque specification listed in **Table 8**.

(140)

1. Snap ring
2. Oil seal
3. Steel ring
4. Guide bushing

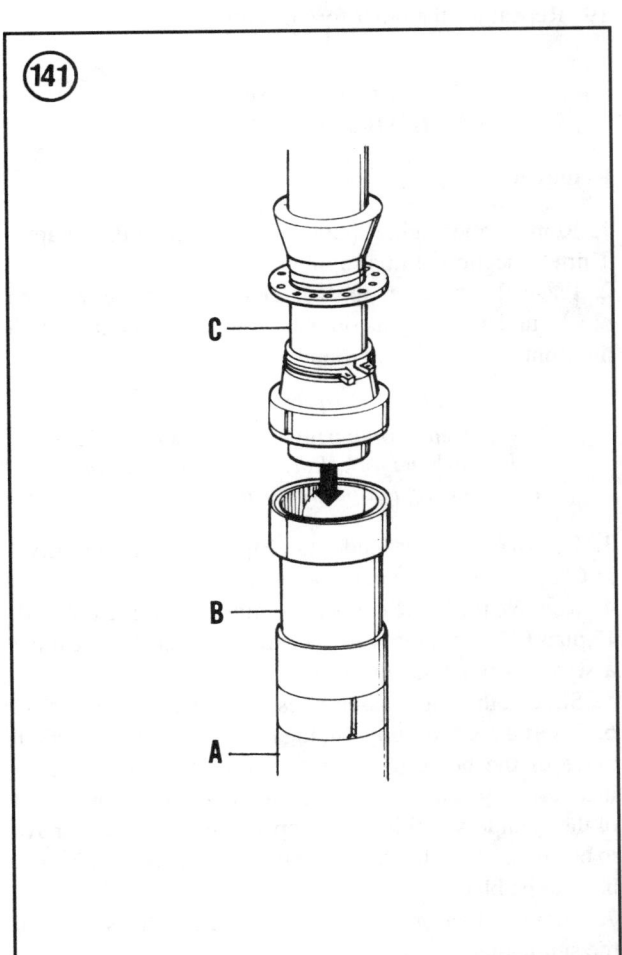

(141)

C

B

A

14

14B. On 1992-1993 models, perform the following:

  a. Install spring and spring seat assembly and the support tube into the fork tube.

  b. Install the spacer and snap ring. Make sure the snap ring is properly seated in the fork tube groove.

  c. Install the shim.

  d. Compress the damper cartridge into the fork tube and install the clamp ring onto the end of the damper cartridge. Make sure it is properly seated.

  e. Install the shim.

  f. Push down on the fork spring and install the fork top cap. Use an open end wrench and tighten to the torque specification listed in **Table 8**.

15. Make sure the washer is in place and securely tighten the drain screw.

16. Add the recommended type and specified amount of fork oil through the small opening in the fork top cap. Refer to **Table 9** for fork oil capacity.

17. Hold onto the fork top cap with an open end wrench and install the oil fill plug. Tighten the plug securely.

18. Install the fork assembly as described in this chapter.

19. Repeat for the other fork assembly.

FRONT FORK
(K1100LT, K1100RS)

Removal

1. Remove the engine spoiler as described in the Chapter Thirteen section of this supplement.

2. Place the bike on the centerstand or place wooden blocks under the engine oil pan to support it securely with the front wheel off the ground.

NOTE
The ABS electronic trigger sensor is attached to the left-hand fork slider. Do not damage the sensor during caliper removal.

3. Remove the front fender (A, **Figure 145**) as described in Chapter Ten in the main body of this book.

4. Remove the brake caliper assembly mounting bolts (B, **Figure 145**) from the front fork on each side. Both caliper assemblies must be removed.

5. Slide both caliper assemblies off of the brake discs.

6. Insert a piece of vinyl tubing or wood in the calipers in place of the brake disc. That way if the brake lever is inadvertently squeezed, the pistons will not be forced out of the cylinders. If this does happen, the calipers may have to be disassembled to reseat the pistons and the system will have to be bled.

7. Remove the front wheel as described in this section of the supplement.

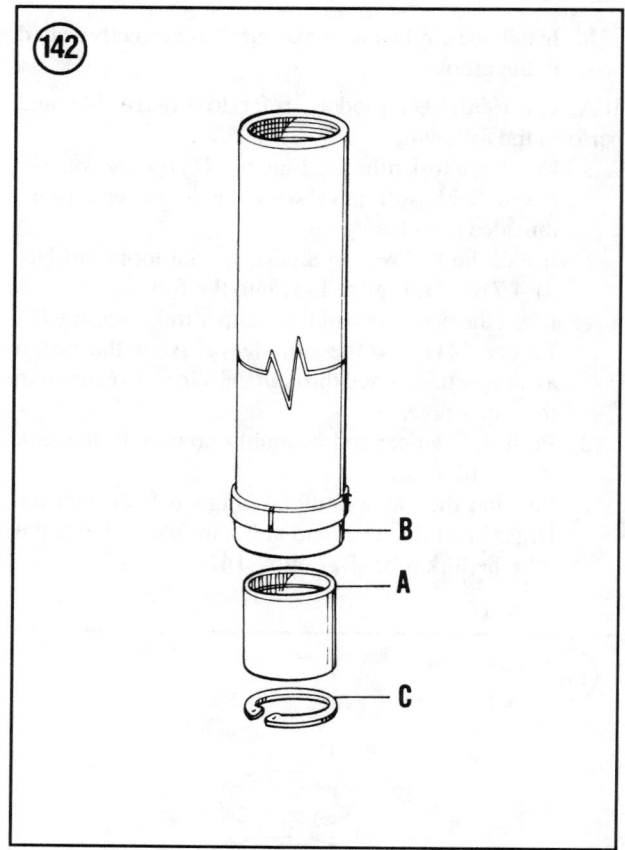

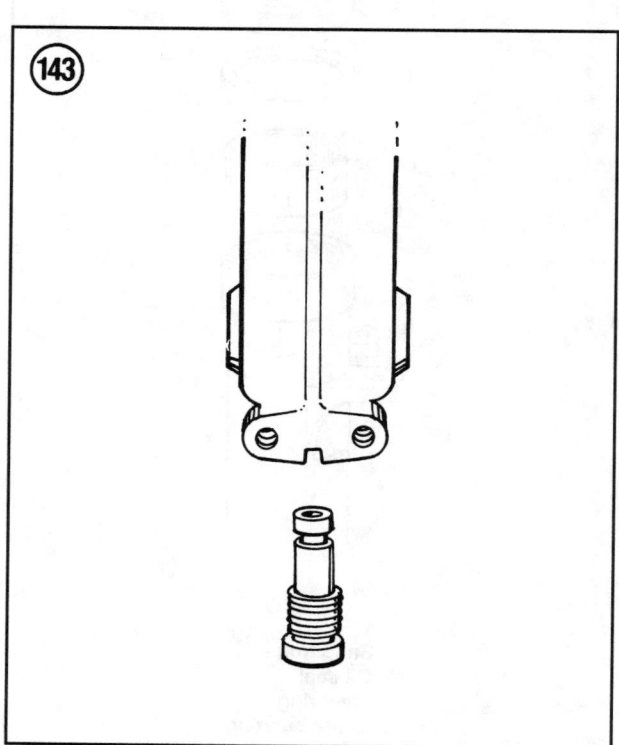

8. Remove the front fairing knee pads and inner covers as described in the Chapter Thirteen section of this supplement.

9. Separate the ABS sensor plug connector (C, **Figure 145**) and remove the sensor from the fork slider.

10. Remove the cable straps (D, **Figure 145**) securing the ABS sensor line and brake line to the left-hand slider.

11. Pull the ABS sensor line out and downward out of the slot in the front fork stabilizer.

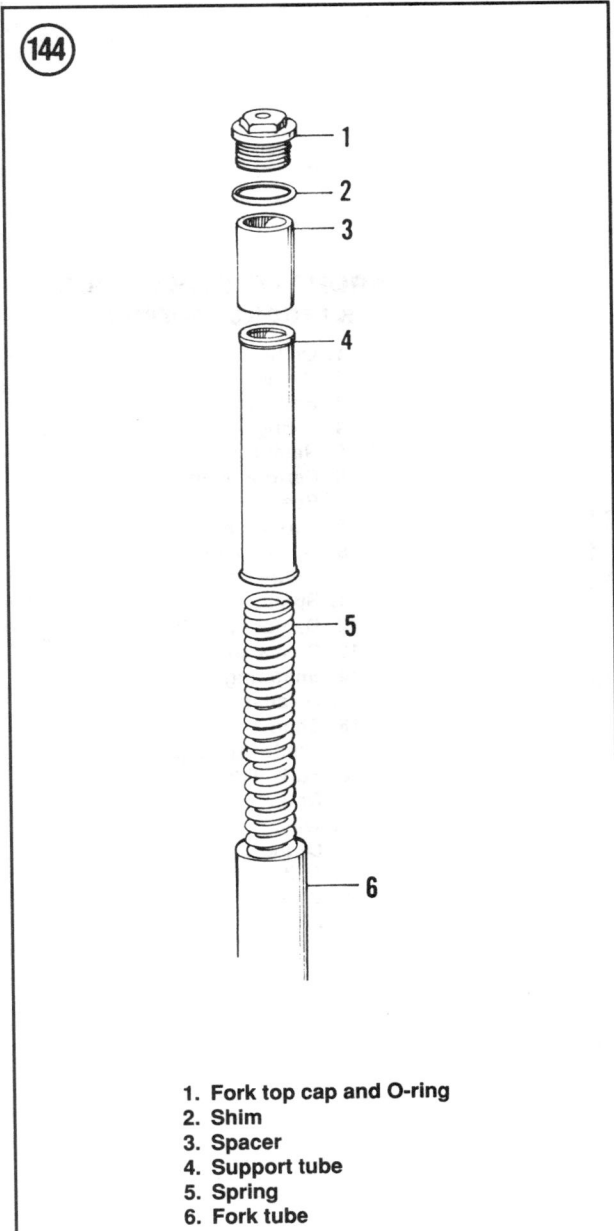

1. Fork top cap and O-ring
2. Shim
3. Spacer
4. Support tube
5. Spring
6. Fork tube

12. Remove the bolt securing the brake joint to the top of the front stabilizer. Move the brake line assembly back and out of the way.

13. Remove the bolts and washers securing the front stabilizer to both fork sliders.

14. Move the front stabilizer and the front brake ABS sensor line back away from the fork assemblies and secure this assembly to the frame.

15. If the fork assembly is going to be disassembled for service, perform the following:
   a. Loosen the upper fork bridge bolts--do not loosen the lower fork bridge bolts at this time.
   b. Loosen, but do not remove, the fork top cap. It is a lot easier to loosen the fork top cap with the fork tube secure on the lower fork bridge.

16. Loosen the upper and lower fork bridge bolts (**Figure 146**).

17. Lower the fork assembly down and out of the upper and lower fork bridge. It may be necessary to slightly rotate the fork tube while pulling it out. Remove both fork assemblies.

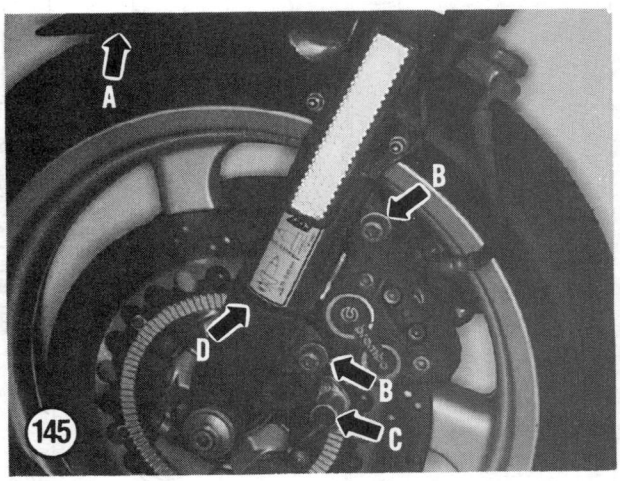

14

Installation

1. Clean off any corrosion or dirt from the upper and lower fork bridge fork receptacles.

NOTE
The fork assemblies must be reinstalled on the correct side of the bike so the brake calipers, the front fork stabilizer and the front fender

can be installed. If the fork assemblies are installed on the wrong side these components cannot be installed onto the fork sliders.

2. Install the fork assemblies on the correct side. Install the fork tubes up through the lower and upper fork bridges.

3. Push the fork tube up until the top surface is 210 mm (8.27 in.) above the top surface of the lower fork bridge.

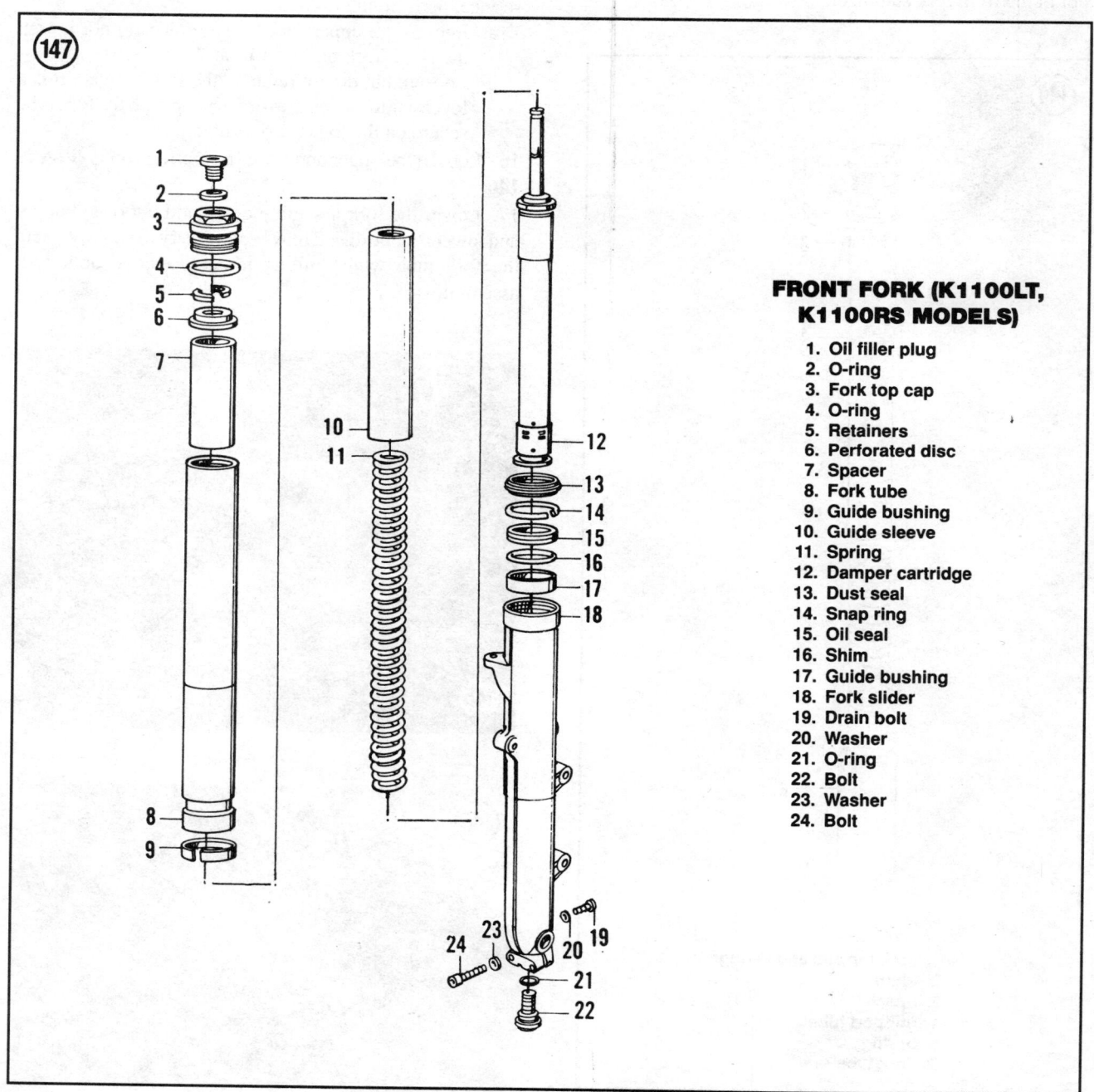

FRONT FORK (K1100LT, K1100RS MODELS)

1. Oil filler plug
2. O-ring
3. Fork top cap
4. O-ring
5. Retainers
6. Perforated disc
7. Spacer
8. Fork tube
9. Guide bushing
10. Guide sleeve
11. Spring
12. Damper cartridge
13. Dust seal
14. Snap ring
15. Oil seal
16. Shim
17. Guide bushing
18. Fork slider
19. Drain bolt
20. Washer
21. O-ring
22. Bolt
23. Washer
24. Bolt

4. Tighten the upper and lower fork bridge clamping bolts to the torque specification listed in **Table 8**.

5. Move the front stabilizer and ABS sensor line back into position on the forks.

6. Install the bolts and washers securing the front stabilizer to both fork sliders.

7. Move the brake line assembly back into position and install the bolt. Tighten the bolt securely.

8. Install the cable straps securing the ABS sensor line and brake line to the slider.

9. Install the ABS sensor and connector the plug connector.

10. Install the front fairing knee pads and inner covers.

11. Remove the pieces of vinyl tubing or wood from the calipers.

12. Install the front wheel as described in this chapter.

NOTE
The ABS electronic trigger sensor is attached to the left-hand fork slider. Do not damage the sensor during caliper installation.

13. Install both brake caliper assemblies and tighten the mounting bolts to the torque specification listed in **Table 8**.

14. Install the front wheel and the front fender.

15. Remove the wood blocks from under the oil pan.

16. Install the engine spoiler.

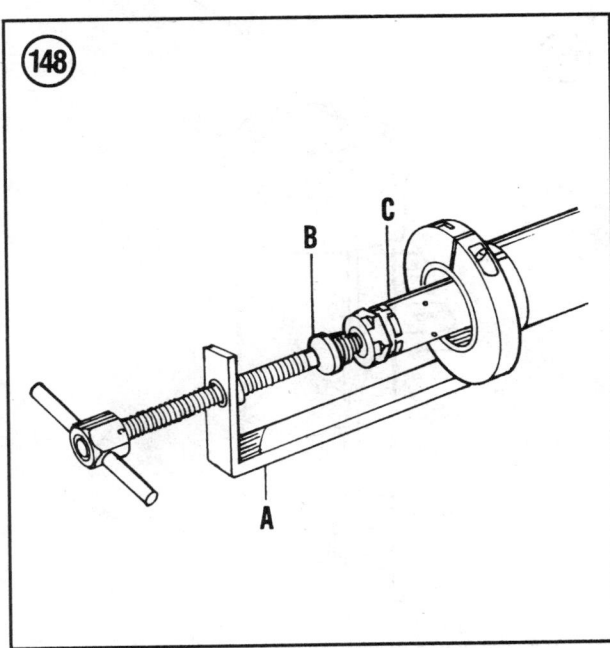

Disassembly

To simplify fork service and to prevent the mixing of parts, the legs should be disassembled and assembled individually.

Refer to **Figure 147** for this procedure.

1. Drain the fork oil as follows:
   a. Remove the plug and O-ring from the fork top cap.
   b. Position the fork assembly in an upright position and remove the drain screw and washer from the slider.
   c. Allow the fork oil to drain out into the drain pan. Compress the fork assembly by hand several times to expel the residual fork oil. Discard the fork oil properly.
   d. Reinstall the plug and the drain screw and washer to avoid misplacing them.

2. Using the front brake caliper mounting bosses, clamp the slider in a vise with soft jaws.

NOTE
The base valve bolt is often very difficult to remove because the damper rod will turn inside the slider. It sometimes can be removed with an air impact driver. If you are unable to remove it, take the fork tubes to a dealer and have the bolts removed.

3. Loosen the base valve bolt on the bottom of the slider.

4. Remove the fork slider from the vise.

5. Install the fork tube in a vise with soft jaws.

6. Remove the fork top cap with an open end wrench.

7. Remove the fork tube from the vise.

8. Turn the fork assembly over and pour out any residual fork oil and discard it.

9. Withdraw the fork tube from the slider.

10. Install the special BMW tools onto the fork tube as follows:
   a. Install the clamping fixture part No. 31 5 550 (A, **Figure 148**) onto the fork tube. Tighten the screw securely.
   b. Install the insert part No. 31 5 553 (B, **Figure 148**) between the clamping fixture and the end of the damper cartridge (C, **Figure 148**).
   c. Tighten the clamping fixture, compressing the spring and press the damper cartridge up into the fork tube. Press the damper cartridge up and out of the spacer until the perforated disc has moved away from the spacer. This is necessary to remove the retainers and the perforated disc in the next step.

11. Use a screwdriver to push the retainers apart, then remove the retainers (A, **Figure 149**) and the perforated disc (B, **Figure 149**) from the top end of the spacer (C, **Figure 149**).

14

12. Remove the spacer from the fork tube.

13. Remove the guide sleeve, spring and damper cartridge from the fork tube.

14. Remove the dust seal from the fork slider (**Figure 150**).

15. Carefully remove the snap ring, located above the oil seal, from the top of the fork slider.

16. Protect the edge of the fork slider with a piece of wood or plastic ring (A, **Figure 151**) to keep the screwdriver from making contact with the slider while prying out the oil seal.

17. Using a broad-tipped screwdriver (B, **Figure 151**), carefully pry the oil seal (C, **Figure 151**) out of the fork slider.

18. Remove the steel ring then, using both index fingers, remove the guide bushing from the top of the fork slider.

19. Inspect all parts as described in this chapter.

Inspection

1. Thoroughly clean all parts in solvent and dry them. Check the fork tube for excessive wear or scratches.

2. Check the damper cartridge for straightness or damage. Replace if necessary.

3. Inspect the fork oil seal for wear or deterioration. Replace if necessary,

4. Check the fork tube for straightness (**Figure 134**). If bent or severely scratched, it should be replaced.

5. Check the slider (**Figure 135**) for dents or exterior damage that may cause the fork tube to hang up during riding. Replace if necessary.

6. Check the slider in the area where the fork seal is installed for wear or damage. Replace if necessary.

7. Check the axle bearing surfaces of the slider (**Figure 137**) for wear or gouges. Clean up the surfaces or replace the slider if necessary.

8. Inspect the axle clamping lugs (**Figure 138**) on the slider for cracks or fractures from over tightening the clamping bolts. If any cracks are found, replace the fork slider.

9. Inspect the spacer (**Figure 139**) for wear or damage. Replace if necessary.

10. Any worn or damaged parts should be replaced. Simply cleaning and reinstalling unserviceable components will not improve performance of the front suspension.

Assembly

Refer to **Figure 147** for this procedure.

1. Apply fork oil to all parts prior to installation.

2. Install a new guide bushing (A, **Figure 152**) into the fork slider. Make sure it is correctly seated in the slider.

3. Position the steel ring as shown in **Figure 153** and install the steel ring (B, **Figure 152**) on top of the guide bushing.

4. Apply a light coat of grease to the oil seal.

5. Position the new oil seal (C, **Figure 152**) with the spring on the shaft sealing ring facing up.

6. Use the BMW special tool (part No. 31 3 620) and a hammer and tap the oil seal into position (**Figure 154**).

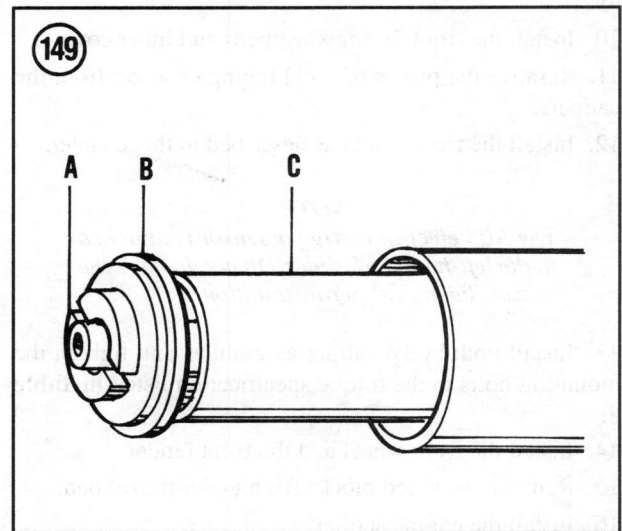

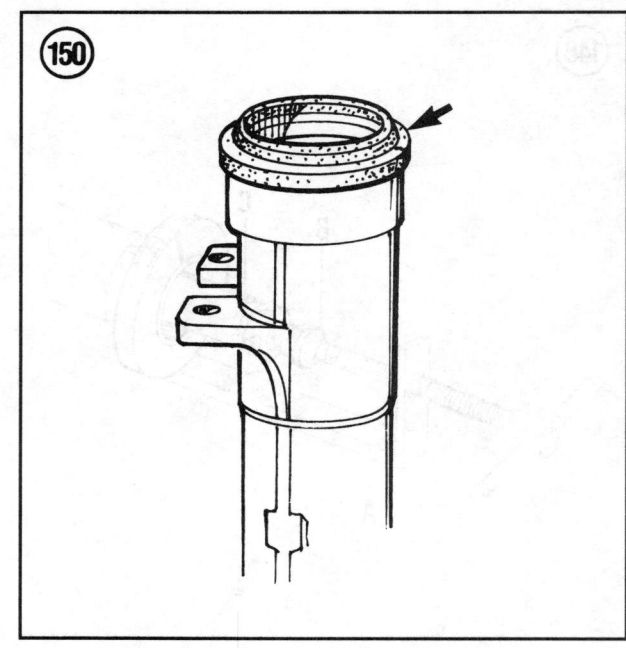

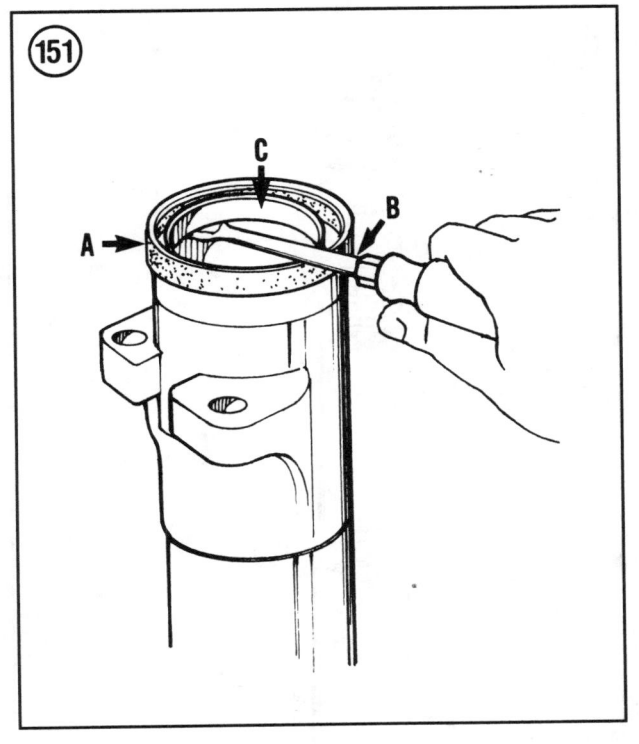

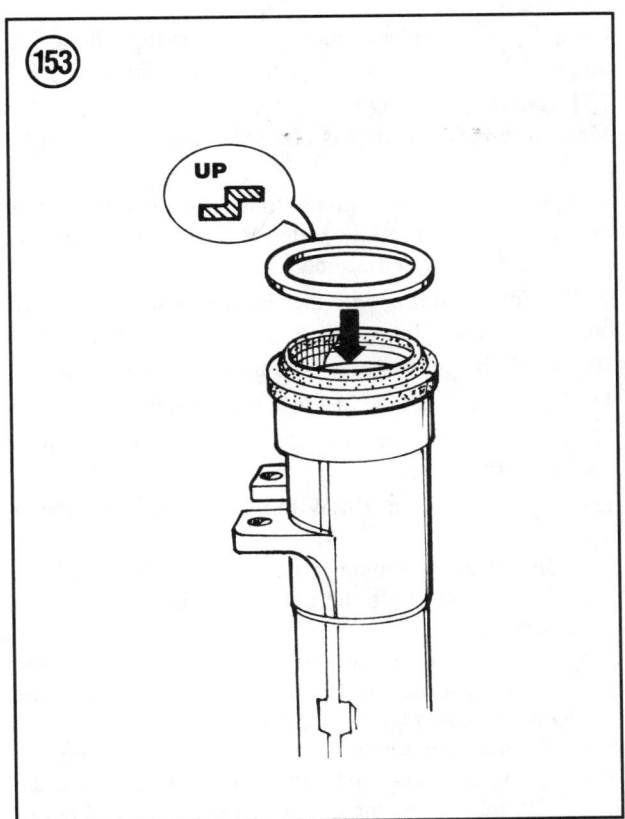

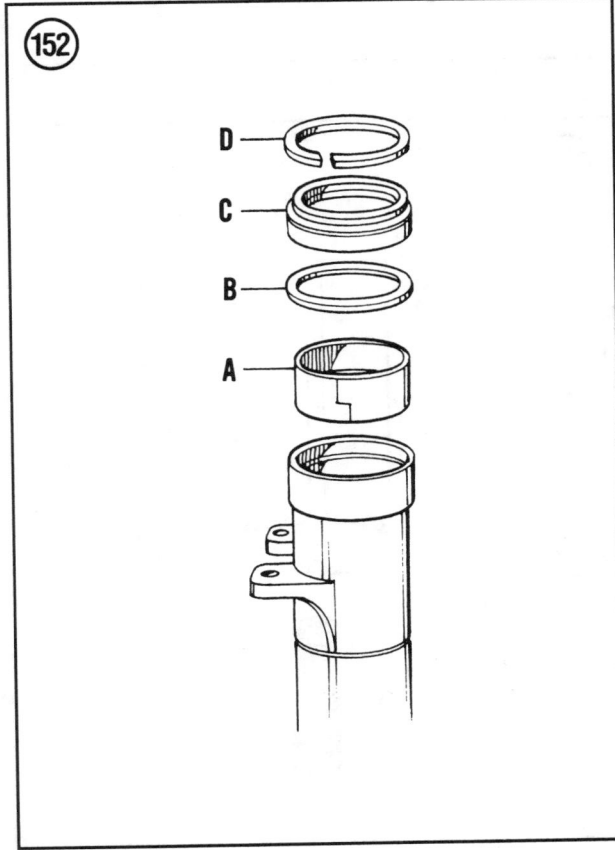

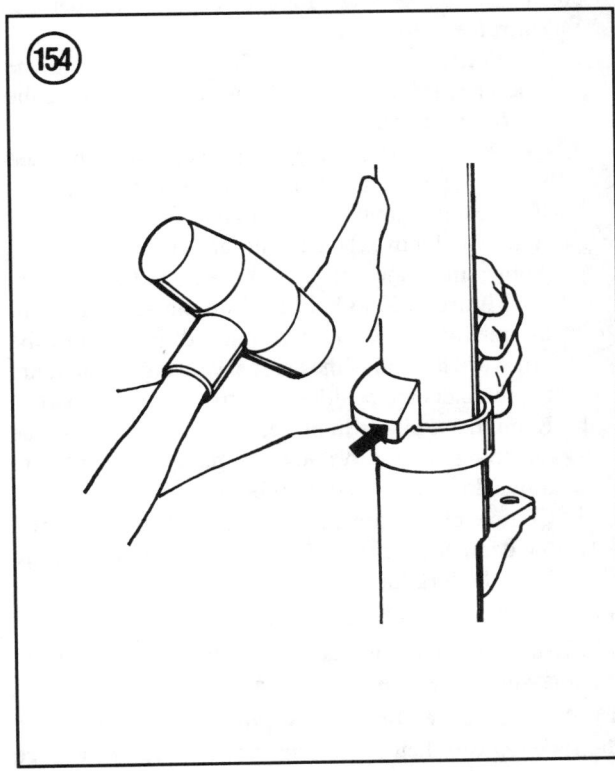

14

Carefully tap the oil seal squarely into the fork slider. Tap it in until the groove for the snap ring is visible above it.

7. Install the snap ring to secure the oil seal in the slider. Make sure the snap ring is correctly seated in the slider groove.

8. Apply a light coat of grease to the dust seal, then press the dust seal into the fork slider. Press it down until it is completely seated in the slider.

9. Position the spring with the closer wound coils toward the top and install the spring onto the damper cartridge.

10. Install the guide sleeve onto the top of the spring.

11. Install the fork tube in a vise with soft jaws.

12. Install the damper cartridge assembly into the lower end of the fork tube.

13. Install the special BMW tools onto the fork tube as follows:

    a. Install the clamping fixture part No. 31 5 550 (A, **Figure 148**) onto the fork tube. Tighten the screw securely.

    b. Install the insert part No. 31 5 553 (B, **Figure 148**) between the clamping fixture and the end of the damper cartridge (C, **Figure 148**).

    c. Tighten the clamping fixture, compressing the spring and press the damper cartridge up into the fork tube. Press the damper cartridge up and out of the top of the fork tube.

    d. Install the spacer (A, **Figure 155**) onto the damper cartridge.

    e. Position the perforated disc (B, **Figure 155**) with the smooth side facing down and install the disc onto the top of the spacer.

    f. Check that the end of the damper cartridge is pressed in far enough to install the retainers into the groove. If necessary, apply more pressure on the clamping fixture and move the end out farther.

    g. Apply small amount of cold grease to the retainers (C, **Figure 155**) to hold them in place, then install the retainers into the perforated disc and into the groove in the end of the damper cartridge. Make sure the retainers are positioned correctly in both parts.

    h. Keep the retainers in place, then slowly release the clamping fixture to allow the damper cartridge to move down into the fork tube.

    i. Completely release the clamping fixture pressure on the damper cartridge. Remove the clamping fixture from the fork tube.

14. Install the fork tube into slider.

15. Using the front brake caliper mounting bosses, install the fork slider in a vise with soft jaws.

16. Make sure the O-ring (D, **Figure 155**) is in place on the fork top cap then install the fork top cap (E, **Figure**

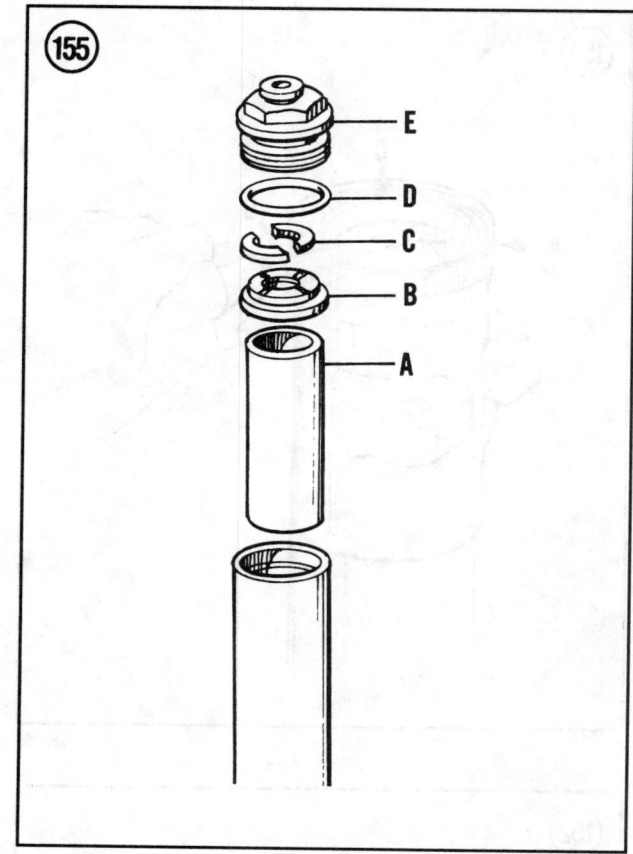

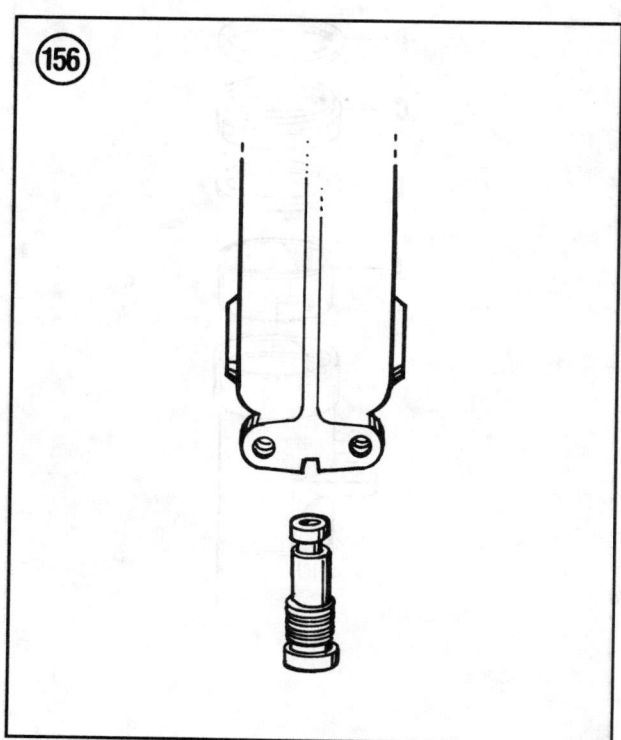

155). Tighten the fork top cap to the torque specification listed in **Table 8**.

17. Make sure the O-ring seal is on the base valve bolt and install the base valve bolt and O-ring seal into the bottom of the slider (**Figure 156**) and into the damper rod or damper cartridge. Tighten the bolt to the torque specification listed in **Table 8**.

18. Make sure the washer is in place and securely tighten the drain screw.

19. Add the recommended type and specified amount of fork oil through the small opening in the fork top cap. Refer to **Table 9** for fork oil capacity.

20. Hold onto the fork top cap with an open end wrench and install the oil fill plug. Tighten the plug securely.

21. Install the fork assembly as described in this chapter.

22. Repeat for the other fork assembly.

Table 8 FRONT SUSPENSION TORQUE SPECIFICATIONS

Item	N·m	ft.-lb.
Front axle		
Allen bolt	33	24
Clamp bolts	14	10
Front caliper mounting bolts	32	25
Steering damper tapered bolts	6.9	5
Fork bridge clamping bolts	14.7-15.5	10.8-11
Front fork brace bolts or nuts	19-23	14-17
Fork slider base valve bolts	43.5-50.5	32-37.2
Fork oil drain bolt	16-24	11.7-17.6
Fork top cap bolt	16-24	11.7-17.6
Fork oil fill plug	12.6-15.4	9.3-11.3

Table 9 FRONT FORK OIL TYPE AND QUANTITY

Model	Quantity	Type
K75 models (1992-on)	410 cc (13.8 oz.)	BMW fork oil, ESSO Komfort
K100 models	400 cc (13.5 oz.)	
K1100 models		
Left-hand leg	349-351 cc (11.7-11.8 oz.)	
Right-hand leg	399-401 cc (13.4-13.6 oz.)	

14

CHAPTER ELEVEN

REAR SUSPENSION AND FINAL DRIVE

REAR WHEEL

Removal/Installation

Refer to **Figure 157** for this procedure.

The removal and installation of the rear wheel is the same as on previous models with the exception of the appearance of the hub cap (**Figure 158**) and the tightening sequence of the 4 wheel bolts and the center bolt. Refer to Chapter Eleven in the main body of this book for the removal and installation of the rear wheel with the following additional steps.

1. Using a crisscross pattern, tighten the four bolts (A, **Figure 159**) to the preload torque specification listed in **Table 1**.
2. Tighten the center bolt (B, **Figure 159**) to the specified torque listed in **Table 1**.
3. Using a crisscross pattern, tighten the four wheel bolts to the *final* torque specification listed in **Table 1**.

CAUTION
Use only bolts with the length code "60" indicated on the top of the bolt head. The use of bolts shorter than specified will result in the loss of the rear wheel.

SWING ARM AND DRIVE SHAFT
(K1, K100RS [1991-1992], K1100LT AND K1100RSA [1993-ON])

Removal/Installation

Refer to **Figure 160** for this procedure.

The removal and installation of the swing arm and drive shaft is the same as on previous models with the exception

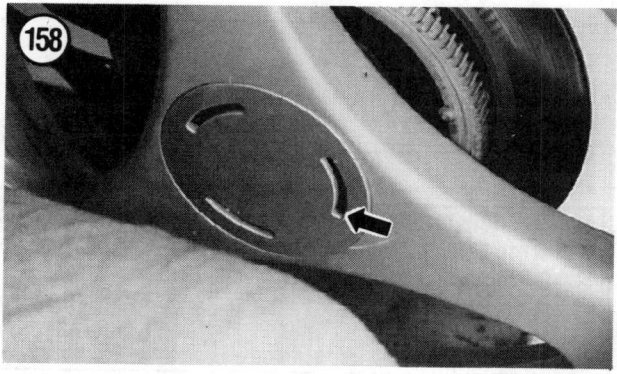

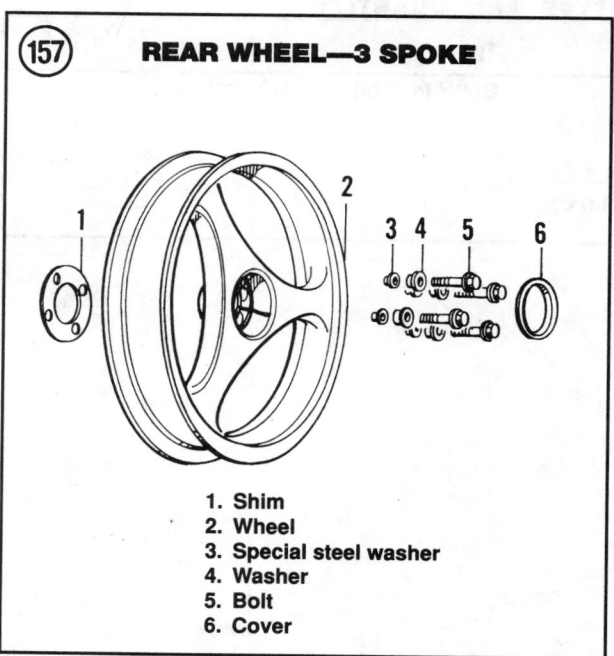

(157) **REAR WHEEL—3 SPOKE**

1. Shim
2. Wheel
3. Special steel washer
4. Washer
5. Bolt
6. Cover

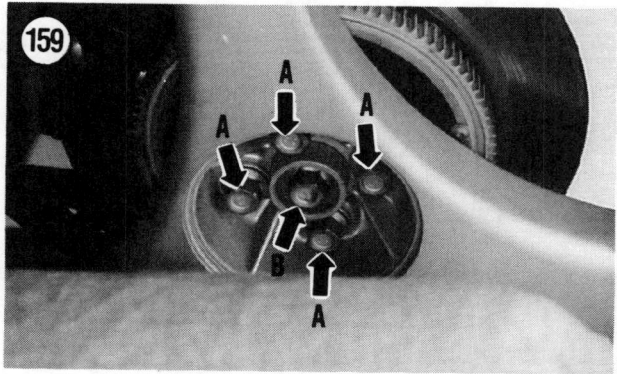

of the design of the rear portion where the final drive unit attaches to the swing arm.

FINAL DRIVE UNIT
(K1, K100RS [1991-1992], K1100LT AND K1100RSA)

Removal

1. Unscrew the clamping screws (A, **Figure 161**) on the rubber boot. Remove both clamps from the rubber boot.

2. Remove the rear wheel (A, **Figure 162**) as described in this chapter.

3. Remove the bolt securing the speedometer sensor. Carefully pry the sensor (B, **Figure 162**) out of the final drive unit.

4. Remove the rear caliper assembly and brake disc (C, **Figure 162**) as described in Chapter Twelve in the main body of this book.

5. Place a wooden block under the swing arm to support it after the shock absorber is removed.

6. Remove the shock absorber (D, **Figure 162**) as described in Chapter Twelve in the main body of this book.

7. Loosen the left-hand pivot pin and the locknut (**Figure 163**) on the right-hand pivot pin.

NOTE
*The left-hand pivot pin had a locking agent applied to the threads during assembly and will be **very difficult** to break loose. Use the correct size and a good quality Allen wrench to avoid rounding off the flats within the pivot pin receptacle for the Allen wrench. It will also be necessary to use a piece of pipe on the end of the Allen wrench to gain enough leverage on the wrench to break the pivot pin loose.*

8. Slide the rubber boot (B, **Figure 161**) off the final drive unit and the swing arm.

9. Remove the bolt, nut and washer (E, **Figure 162**) securing the control rod to the final drive unit. Let the control rod hang down--there is no need to completely remove it.

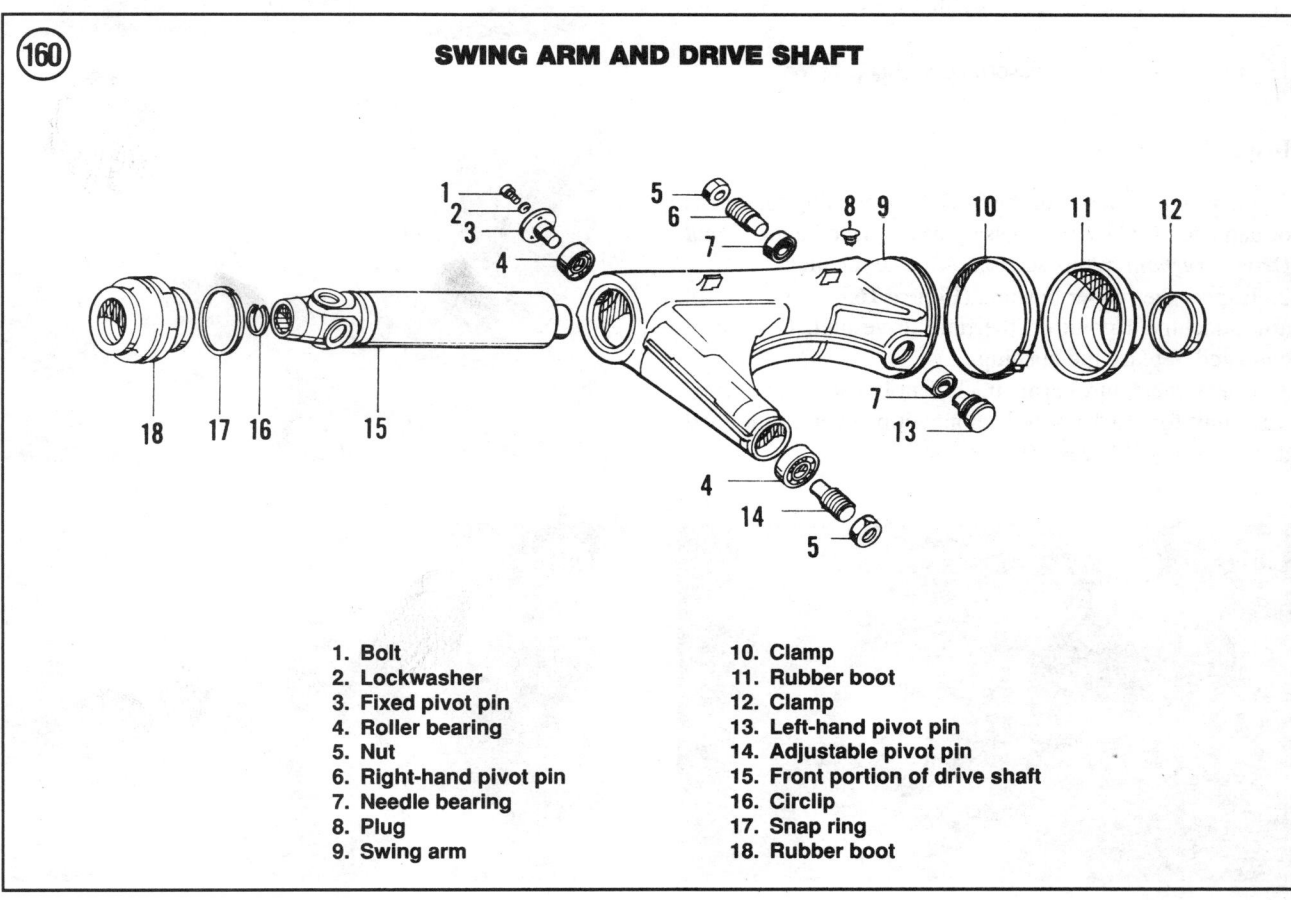

160   **SWING ARM AND DRIVE SHAFT**

1. Bolt
2. Lockwasher
3. Fixed pivot pin
4. Roller bearing
5. Nut
6. Right-hand pivot pin
7. Needle bearing
8. Plug
9. Swing arm
10. Clamp
11. Rubber boot
12. Clamp
13. Left-hand pivot pin
14. Adjustable pivot pin
15. Front portion of drive shaft
16. Circlip
17. Snap ring
18. Rubber boot

14

CAUTION
Place a wooden box under the final drive unit. The final drive unit is heavy and must be supported prior to removing the pivot pins securing it to the rear of the swing arm.

10. Remove the right-hand pivot pin locknut.
11. Completely unscrew both the right-hand (**Figure 164**) and the left-hand pivot pins from the swing arm.

NOTE
The final drive unit is equipped with 2 pivot bearings that have loose inner races. These inner races are held in place with the pivot pins. These races may come out with the pivot pin. When the final drive unit is removed from the swing arm, these inner races may fall out. Be prepared to catch them so they will not fall on the ground and be damaged.

12. Pull back on the final drive unit and separate it, along with the rear portion of the drive shaft, from the front portion of the drive shaft and the swing arm. If necessary, gently tap on the final drive unit with a soft faced mallet or plastic hammer to separate it. Remove the final drive unit and take it to your workbench for inspection or disassembly.
13. Inspect all parts as described in this chapter.

Inspection

1. Inspect the exterior of the final drive housing for cracks or damage. Replace if necessary as described under *Final Drive Overhaul* in this section of the supplement.
2. Inspect the rubber bushing (**Figure 165**) in the control arm attachment point on the final drive unit. If worn or damaged, replace the bushing.
3. Check the control arm attachment bracket on the final drive unit for cracks or hole elongation. Replace the final drive housing if necessary.

4. Check the rear brake caliper mounting tabs on the final drive unit cover for cracks, damage or hole elongation. Replace the cover if necessary.
5. Inspect the exterior of the final drive housing cover for cracks or damage, replace if necessary.
6. Inspect the pinion gear splines. If the splines are worn or damaged, the pinion gear and ring gear assembly must

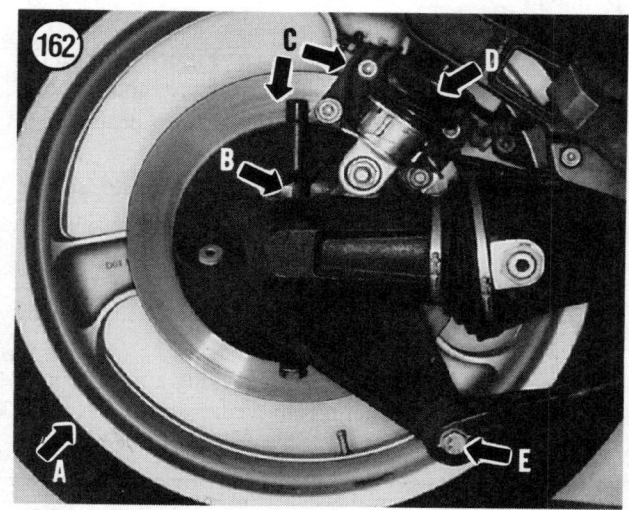

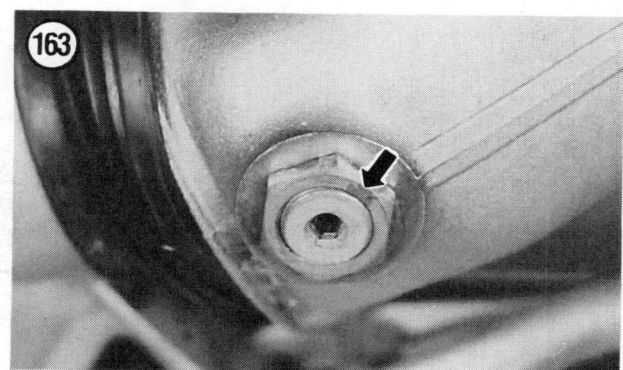

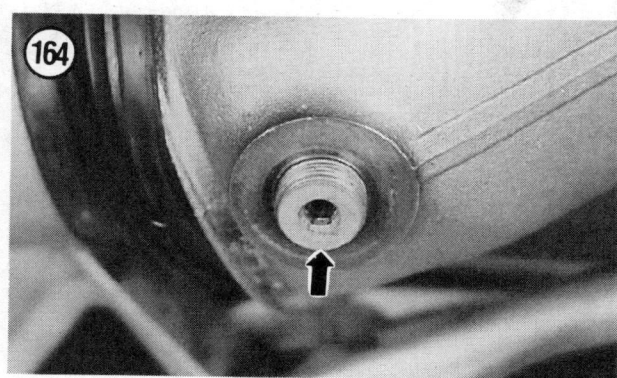

be replaced as described under *Final Drive Overhaul* in this section of the supplement.

NOTE
If the splines are worn or damaged, also inspect the splines on the end of the drive shaft for damage as described in Chapter Eleven in the main body of this book; it may also need to be replaced.

7. Check for oil leakage at the spline portion. If the oil seal has been leaking it must be replaced as described under *Final Drive Overhaul* in this section of the supplement.

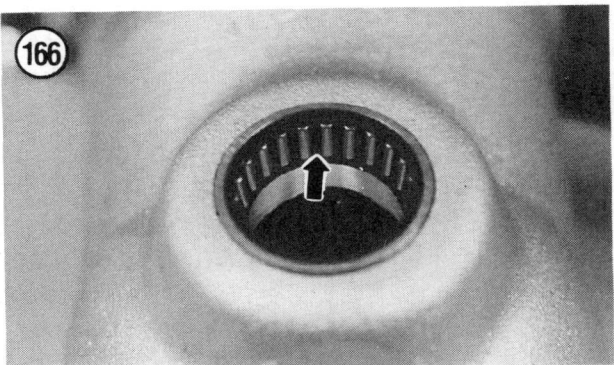

8. Thoroughly clean the pivot pin needle bearings and inner races in solvent and dry with compressed air.

9. Rotate the bearings (**Figure 166**) with your fingers and check for wear. The bearings should rotate freely without binding. Replace the bearing(s) if necessary.

10. Inspect the bearing inner races (**Figure 167**) for wear or damage. If the inner race(s) is worn or damaged, repalce the entire bearing assembly.

11. Make sure the cover mounting bolts (**Figure 168**) are tight. Refer to **Table 1** for torque specifications.

12. Inspect the shock absorber lower mounting stud (**Figure 169**) for wear or damage. If necessary, clean the thread with the correct thread die. Replace the stud if necessary.

13. Thoroughly clean all locking agent residue from the threads on the left-hand pivot pin and frm the pivot pin threads on the swing arm.

14. After the locking compound has been removed, scre the left-hand pivot pin into the threaded hole in the swing arm to make sure the threads are clean and in good condition. Unscrew the pivot pin.

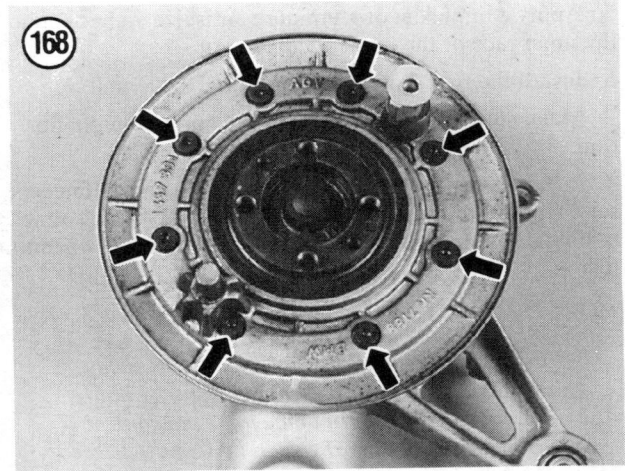

14

15. Inspect the threads of both pivot pins (**Figure 170**) for wear or damage. If necessary, clean the threads with the die. Replace the pivot pin(s) if necessary.

16. Inspect the rubber boot for wear, tears or deterioration. If its condition is in doubt, replace it while the final drive unit is removed.

Installation

1. Shift the transmission into 5th gear. This will prevent the drive shaft from rotating while aligning the final drive splines to the drive shaft splines.

2. Apply a thick coat of Staburags NBU 30PT grease, or an equivalent, to the final drive unit splines and to the splines on both drive shafts.

3. Apply a thick coat of Staburags NBU 30PT grease, or an equivalent, to the pivot needle bearings and to the outer surface of the inner races. Refer to **Figure 171** and **Figure 172**. Avoid getting any grease on the inner race as it will be coated with different material.

4. Install the inner race into the pivot needle bearing in each side of the receptacle in the final drive unit.

5. Apply a light coat of aluminum antiseize compound to the inner race of the pivot needle bearings.

6. Install the rubber boot onto the final drive unit.

7. Make sure the swing arm is in the correct height position.

8. Install the final drive unit onto the swing arm. If necessary, slightly rotate the rear wheel flange until the splines of both drive shafts align. Push the final drive unit on until it stops.

NOTE
In Step 9, do not tighten the pivot pins. They are installed at this time to temporarily hold the final drive unit in place until the control rod and shock absorber can be installed.

9. Hold the final drive unit in this position and install the right-hand and left-hand pivot pins into the swing arm and into the final drive units pivot needle bearing inner races. Slightly move the final drive unit in and out to correctly align the pivot pin needle bearing inner races.

10. Install the shock absorber onto the frame mounting location and onto the stud on the final drive unit. Install the washer and nut on the lower mount and the bolt to the upper mount and tighten the bolt and nut finger-tight at this time.

11. Move the control arm up and into position. Install it onto the mounting receptacle on the final drive unit. Install the bolt, washer and nut finger-tight at this time.

NOTE
In Step 12, do not completely unscrew the left-hand pivot pin as the pivot bearing inner race may come out with it and fall off of the pivot pin. If this happens, you will have to remove the final drive unit and start all over.

12. Hold the final drive unit and partially unscrew the left-hand pivot pin. Apply 2 drops of blue Loctite (No. 242) to the threads and screw the pivot pin back in.

13. Tighten the left-hand pivot pin to 105 N•m (77 ft.-lb.).

14. Using an Allen wrench, hand-tighten the right-hand pivot pin to a "firm hand tightness." This will seat the final drive unit and both pivot needle bearings.

15. Loosen the right-hand pivot pin, then tighten it to 7.3 N•m (65 in.-lb.).

16. Remove the shock absorber lower mounting nut and washer and disconnect the shock absorber from the final drive unit.

17. Move the final drive unit, swing arm and control rod up and down to make sure the entire assembly is moving freely. If everything is okay, proceed to the next step. If not, determine the problem and correct it at this time.

18. Reinstall the shock absorber onto the mounting stud on the final drive unit and install the washer and nut finger-tight.

19. Using an Allen wrench, hold the right-hand pivot pin and tighten the locknut to 105 N•m (77 ft.-lb.). Make sure the pivot pin does not turn while tightening the locknut, as it will apply too much pressure on the pivot needle bearings and cause them to wear prematurely.

20. Tighten the shock absorber upper mounting bolt and nut and the lower nut to the torque specification listed in **Table 1**.

21. Tighten the control rod mounting bolt and nut to the torque specification listed in **Table 1**.

CAUTION
Make sure the rubber boot is installed correctly to prevent moisture and foreign matter from enterint this area.

22. Correctly position the rubber boot onto the swing arm and final drive unit. Make sure it is installed straight with no wrinkles. Install the clamps into position and tighten the screws securely.

23. Remove the wooden block from under the swing arm.

24. Install the rear brake disc and caliper assembly as described in Chapter Twelve in the main body of this book.

25. Install the speedometer sensor into the final drive unit. Install the bolt and tighten securely.

26. Install the rear wheel as described in Chapter Twelve in the main body of this book.

27. Take the bike off the centerstand and depress the rear suspension to make sure all components are working properly.

Overhaul

Overhauling the final drive unit requires many BMW special tools along with a heat gun or hot plate. Before overhauling the final drive unit yourself, compare the price of the expensive BMW special tools versus the cost of having the unit overhauled by a BMW dealer. This unit is

almost "bullet-proof" and rarely requires any type of service. Many units have over 150,000 miles on them without any problems. To maintain the final drive unit in good condition the gear oil should be changed at the recommended intervals listed in Chapter Three.

The following procedure is provided if you choose to perform this procedure yourself.

This procedure is presented as a complete, step-by-step, major overhaul of the final drive unit. However, if you are replacing a part that you know has failed, the disassembly should be carried out only until the failed part is accessible; there is no need to disassemble the final drive unit beyond that point so long as you know the remaining components are in good condition.

Prior to starting this procedure, carefully read the entire procedure. Disassembling the unit is complicated but not nearly as complicated as reassembling it. During assembly there are a lot of tolerances that must be calculated. Also the proper gear backlash between the ring and pinion gear must be achieved in order to have the correct gear tooth contact between the 2 parts. If the gear backlash is incorrect the ring and pinion gears will wear prematurely and will also emit a "howl" while riding.

The following BMW special tools are required for the overhaul procedure:

a. Case holding fixture (part No. 33 1 500).
b. Special socket wrench (part No. 33 1 720).
c. Pin wrench (part No. 33 1 700).
d. Ball bearing puller (part No. 00 7 500).
e. Bearing inner extractor (part No. 00 8 573).
f. Bearing inner extractor support (part No. 00 8 570).
g. Special drift (part No. 33 1 760).
h. Special drift retainer (part No. 00 5 550).
i. Special drift (part No. 36 3 700).
j. Bearing puller and insert (part No.s 33 1 830 and 33 1 307).
k. Internal extractor (part No. 00 8 560).
l. Special drift (part No. 33 1 880).
m. Backlash adjuster (measuring ring) (part No. 33 2 600).
n. Measuring arm (part No. 33 2 604).
o. Depth gauge (part No. 00 2 500).
p. Special drift (part No. 33 1 860).
q. Drift retainer (part No. 00 5 500).

Also needed is a hot plate or a heat gun with a minimum heat capacity of 120° C (248° F).

Disassembly

Refer to **Figure 173** for this procedure.

14

NOTE
*Refer to **Figure 176** for Steps 6-10.*

WARNING
During this procedure many of the components must be heated for removal. Protect your hands when handling hot components. Either wear thick gloves or use heavy household pot holders to hold onto hot parts.

1. Use a screwdriver (A, **Figure 174**) to carefully pry the rear portion of the drive shaft (B, **Figure 174**) from the splines on the pinion gear. Remove the drive shaft.

2. If not already removed, remove the screws securing the rear brake disc. Remove the disc from the final drive unit.

3. If not already drained, remove the drain plug and the filler cap. Drain out all of the gear oil, then reinstall the drain plug and filler cap and tighten both securely.

4. Secure the final drive unit in the BMW retaining fixture, part No. 33 1 500 (A, **Figure 175**), and secure the special tool in a vise. Tighten the mounting bolts to the torque specification listed in **Table 1**.

5. Using a heat gun, heat the pinion gear hex nut to 120° C (248° F).

6. Using BMW special tool (part No. 33 1 720) (B, **Figure 175**), completely unscrew and remove the hex nut from the pinion gear.

7. Remove the thrust ring from the pinion gear shaft.

8. Using a heat gun, heat the final drive unit neck to 120° C (248° F).

9. Using BMW special tool (part No. 33 1 700) (C, **Figure 175**), completely unscrew the threaded ring. Remove the threaded ring and the oil seal.

10. To remove the oil seal from the threaded ring, perform the following:

   a. Using a suitable size socket, press the oil seal out of the threaded ring.

   b. Position in the new oil seal with the lettering facing toward the outside surface of the threaded ring.

   c. Using BMW special tools (part No. 33 1 760 and part No. 00 5 500) drive the new oil seal (A, **Figure 177**) into the threaded ring (B, **Figure 177**).

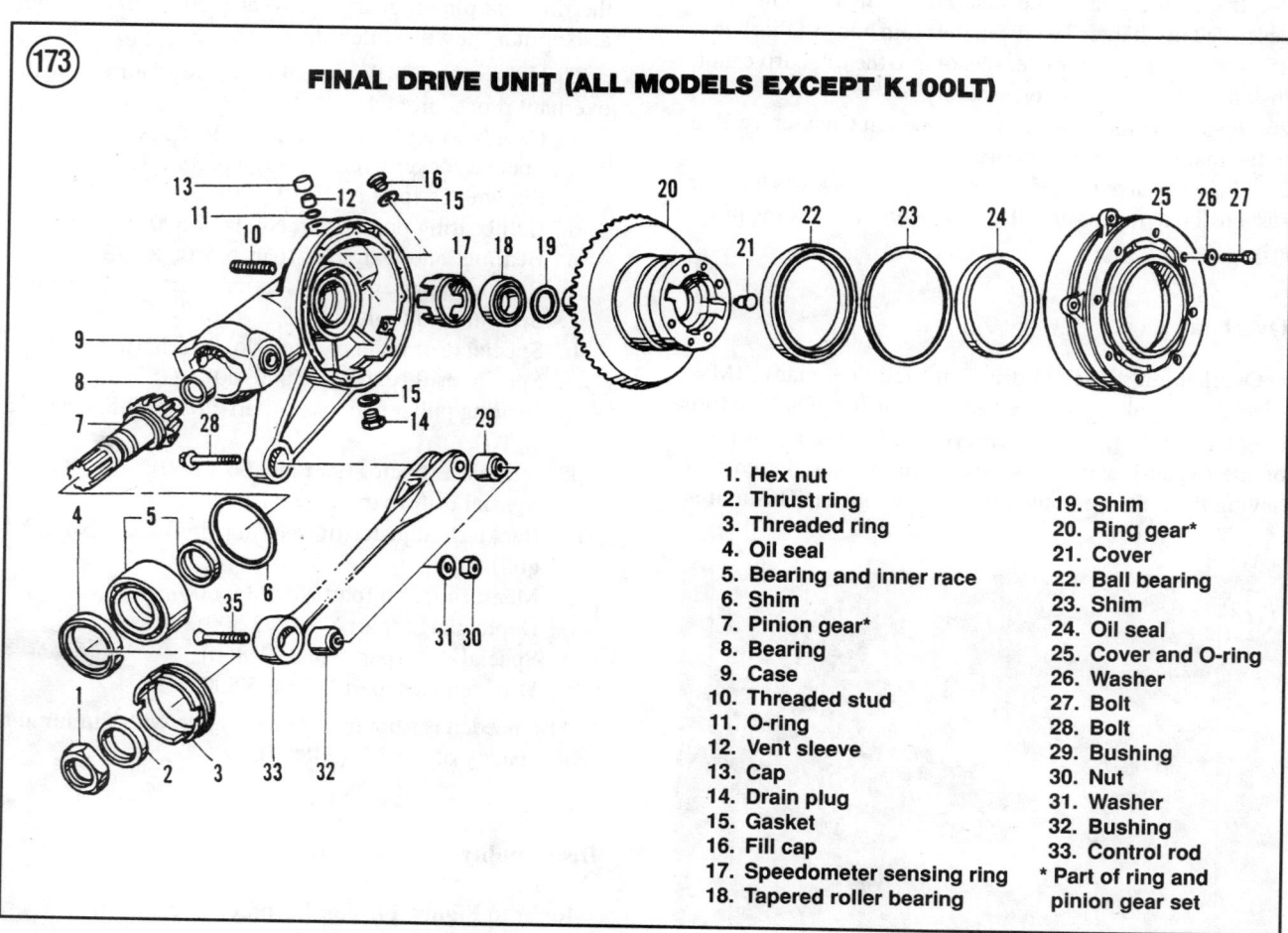

(173) **FINAL DRIVE UNIT (ALL MODELS EXCEPT K100LT)**

1. Hex nut
2. Thrust ring
3. Threaded ring
4. Oil seal
5. Bearing and inner race
6. Shim
7. Pinion gear*
8. Bearing
9. Case
10. Threaded stud
11. O-ring
12. Vent sleeve
13. Cap
14. Drain plug
15. Gasket
16. Fill cap
17. Speedometer sensing ring
18. Tapered roller bearing
19. Shim
20. Ring gear*
21. Cover
22. Ball bearing
23. Shim
24. Oil seal
25. Cover and O-ring
26. Washer
27. Bolt
28. Bolt
29. Bushing
30. Nut
31. Washer
32. Bushing
33. Control rod
* Part of ring and pinion gear set

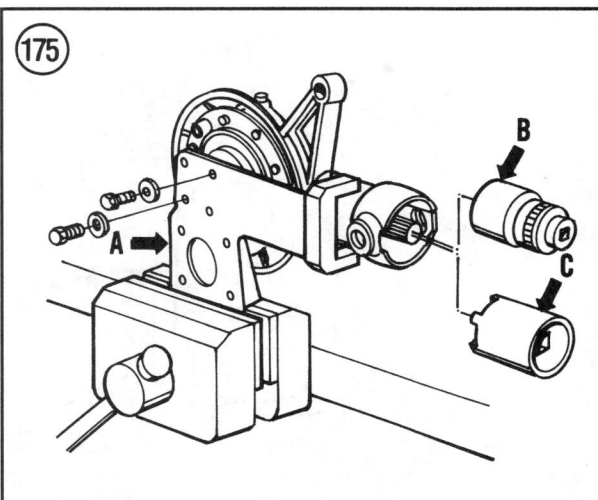

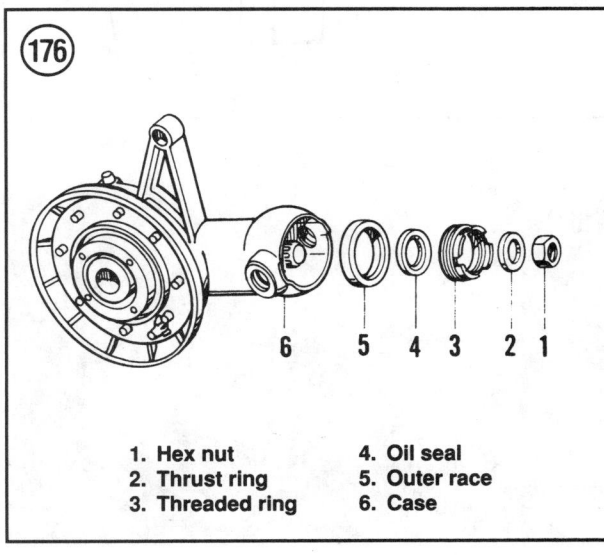

d. Remove the special tools.

11. Using a heat gun, heat the final drive unit neck (surrounding the ball bearing outer race) to 120° C (248° F).

CAUTION
Do not damage the splines on the pinion gear while removing the pinion gear and ball bearing from the final drive unit neck.

12. Use a pair of slip joint pliers or vise-grip pliers and carefully withdraw the pinion gear and the ball bearing from the final drive unit neck. Remove the shim from the pinion gear assembly (**Figure 178**).

13. To remove the bearing assembly from the pinion gear (**Figure 179**), perform the following:

    a. Secure the pinion gear and ball bearing in a vise with soft jaws to protect the gears.

    b. Install BMW special tool (part No. 00 7 500) onto the pinion gear and bearing assembly (A, **Figure 180**).

    c. Hold a pan under the vise as the bearing assembly may separate during removal and the loose bearing balls may fall out.

    d. Tighten the center bolt on the tool (B, **Figure 180**) and withdraw the bearing assembly from the pinion gear.

    e. Disassemble the bearing assembly and place all parts in a box to keep all the small parts together.

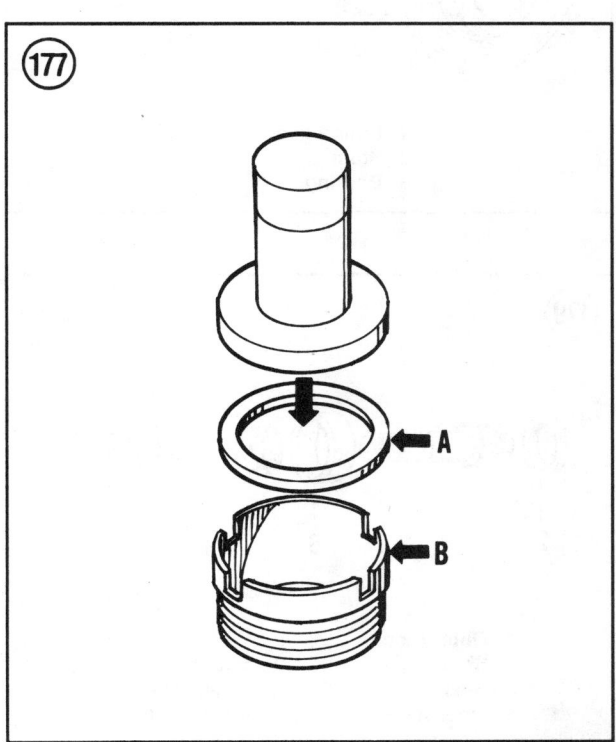

1. Hex nut
2. Thrust ring
3. Threaded ring
4. Oil seal
5. Outer race
6. Case

14

14. Make alignment marks (**Figure 181**) on the case and cover. This will ensure correct alignment of the 2 parts during assembly.

15. Install the final drive unit in the holding fixture and secure it with the left-hand pivot pin (A, **Figure 182**) and tighten with the locknut (B, **Figure 182**).

16. Remove the screws securing the cover to the case.

17. Using a plastic hammer or soft faced mallet, tap around the perimeter of the cover until it is loose.

18. Remove the cover and the ring gear assembly from the case.

19. Using a heat gun, heat the final drive cover to about 80° C (175° F).

20. Use thick gloves or heavy pot holders and separate the ring gear (A, **Figure 183**) from the cover (B, **Figure 183**). Don't lose the shim between the ring gear bearing and the cover. It must be reinstalled.

21. To replace the ring gear oil seal in the cover, perform the following:

   a. Using a hammer and drift, work around the perimeter of the oil seal and carefully tap the seal out of the cover. Discard the oil seal. Be careful not to damage the cover in the area of the oil seal.

   b. Clean out the oil seal area of the cover with solvent and thoroughly dry.

   c. Apply a light coat of oil to the outer surface of the new oil seal (A, **Figure 184**).

   d. Using BMW special tools (part No. 33 1 860 and 00 5 500), carefully tap the new oil seal into the cover

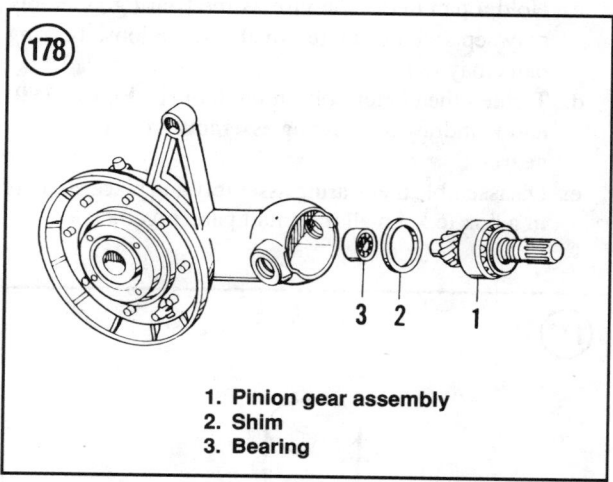

1. Pinion gear assembly
2. Shim
3. Bearing

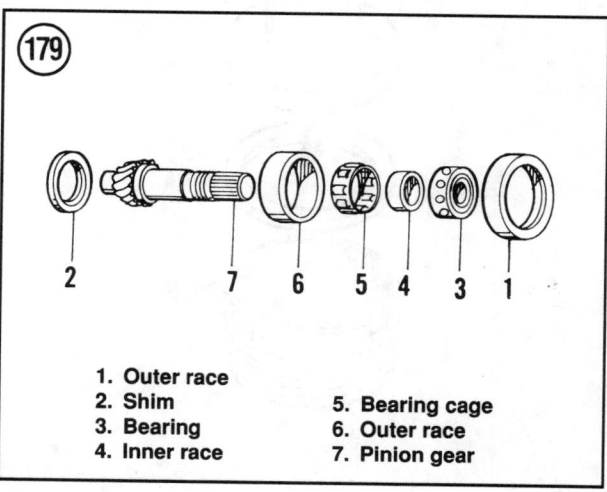

1. Outer race
2. Shim
3. Bearing
4. Inner race
5. Bearing cage
6. Outer race
7. Pinion gear

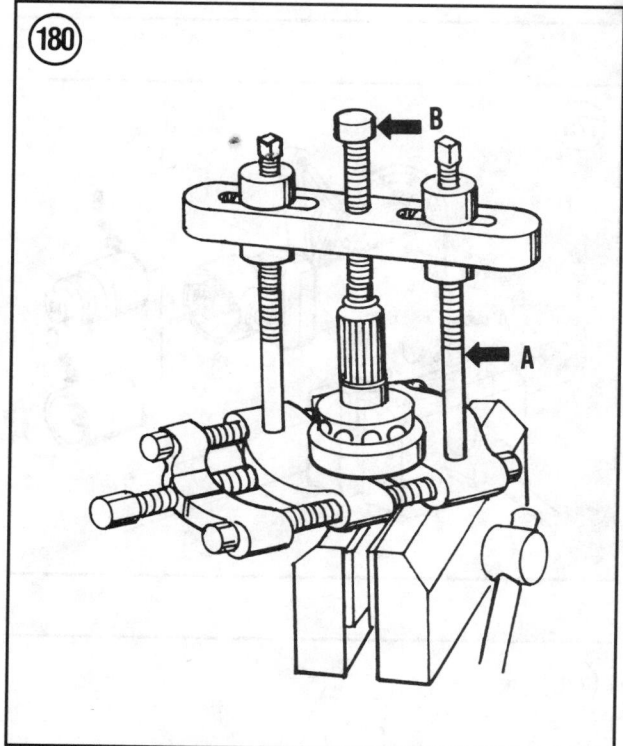

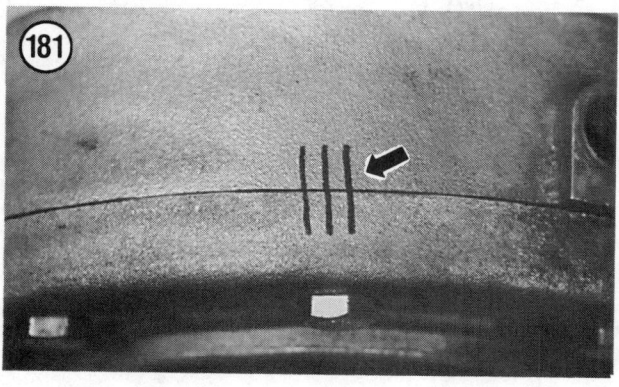

(B, **Figure 184**). Be sure to tap the oil seal in squarely and tap it in until it bottoms out in the cover.

22. To remove the pinion gear needle bearing from the case, perform the following:

    a. Insert BMW special tool (part No. 00 8 573 and 00 8 570) (A, **Figure 185**) into the neck of the case and position it behind the needle bearing (B, **Figure 185**). Turn the special tool end to expand it behind the needle bearing.

    b. Using a heat gun, heat the final drive unit neck (surrounding the needle bearing) to 100° C (212° F).

    c. Carefully and slowly tighten the bearing puller and withdraw the needle bearing from the case.

23. To remove the pivot pin needle bearings from the case, perform the following:

    a. Insert BMW special tool extractor (part No. 00 8 573 and 00 8 570) (A, **Figure 186**) into the neck of the case and position it behind the needle bearing (B, **Figure 186**). Turn the special tool end to expand it behind the needle bearing.

    b. Using a heat gun, heat the final drive unit neck (surrounding the needle bearing) to 120° C (248° F).

    c. Carefully and slowly tighten the bearing puller (A, **Figure 186**) and withdraw the needle bearing from the case.

    d. Repeat for the other bearing if necessary.

24. To remove the ring gear tapered roller bearing outer race (**Figure 187**) from the case, perform the following:

    a. Secure the final drive unit in a vise with soft jaws. Position the open portion of the case facing up to access to the ring gear tapered roller bearing outer race.

    b. Install the internal bearing puller (part No. 00 8 560), onto the outer race (A, **Figure 188**).

    c. Carefully and slowly tighten the bearing puller (B, **Figure 188**) and withdraw the outer race from the case.

    d. Remove the final drive case from the vise.

25. To remove the ball bearing on the ring gear, perform the following:

    a. Secure the ring gear, ball bearing side up, in a vise with soft jaws.

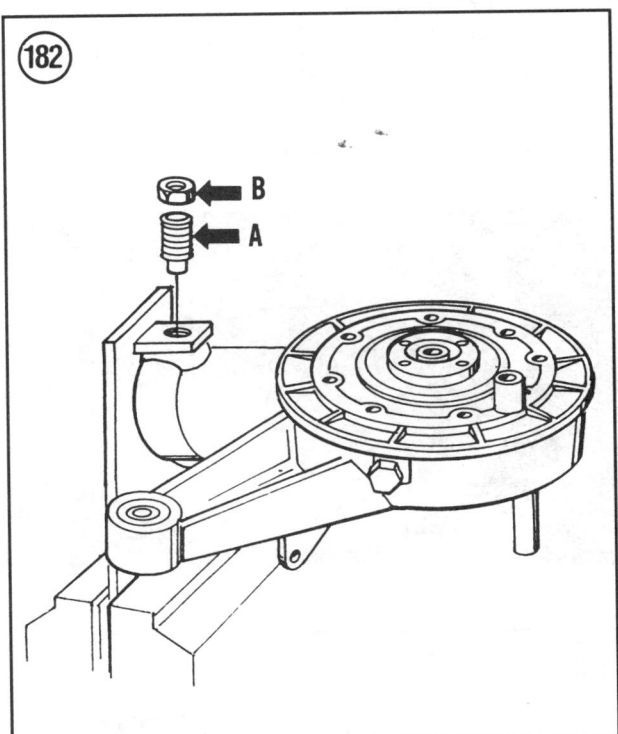

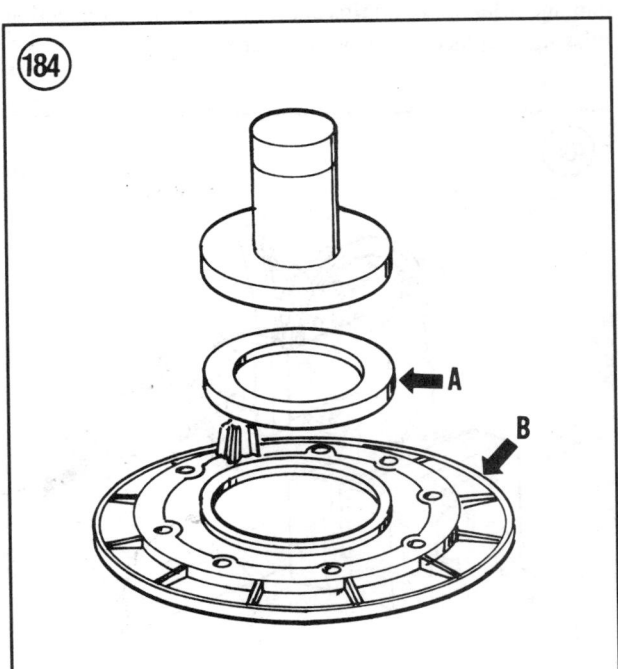

14

b. Insert BMW special tool (part No. 33 1 307) onto the center of the ring gear (A, **Figure 189**).

c. Install the BMW bearing puller (B, **Figure 189**) (part No. 33 1 830), onto the ball bearing.

d. Carefully and slowly tighten the bearing puller and withdraw the ball bearing (C, **Figure 189**) from the ring gear.

e. Remove the special tools from the ring gear.

26. To remove the tapered roller bearing (**Figure 190**), inner race and shim from the ring gear, perform the following:

a. Secure the ring gear, tapered roller bearing side up, in a vise with soft jaws.

b. Install the BMW bearing puller (part No. 00 7 500), onto the tapered roller bearing (A, **Figure 191**).

c. Carefully and slowly tighten (B, **Figure 191**) the bearing puller and withdraw the tapered roller bearing from the ring gear.

d. Remove the tapered roller bearing, inner race and shim from the ring gear.

Inspection

1. Wash all parts in solvent and dry thoroughly with compressed air.

2. Inspect the teeth on the ring gear (**Figure 192**) and the pinion gear set. If the teeth are worn or damaged on either of the gears, both gears must be replaced as a set (the only way they are sold is as a set).

3. Inspect the case and the cover for cracks or other damage. Make sure all ribs and bosses are not damaged or missing. Replace either or both parts.

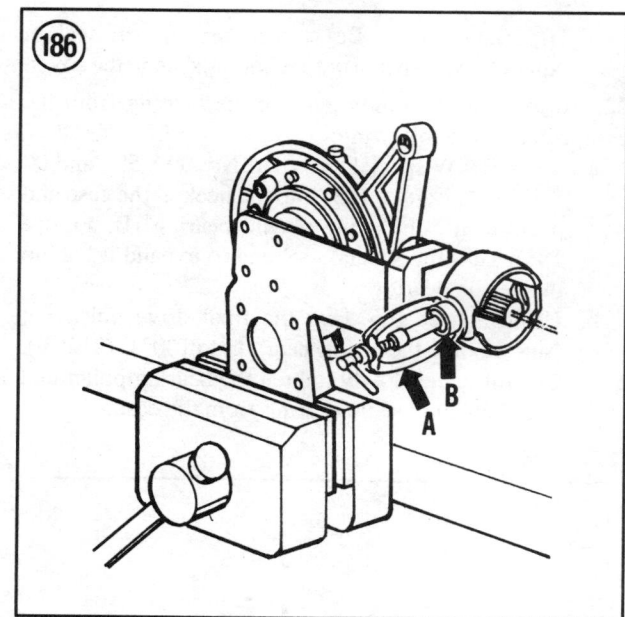

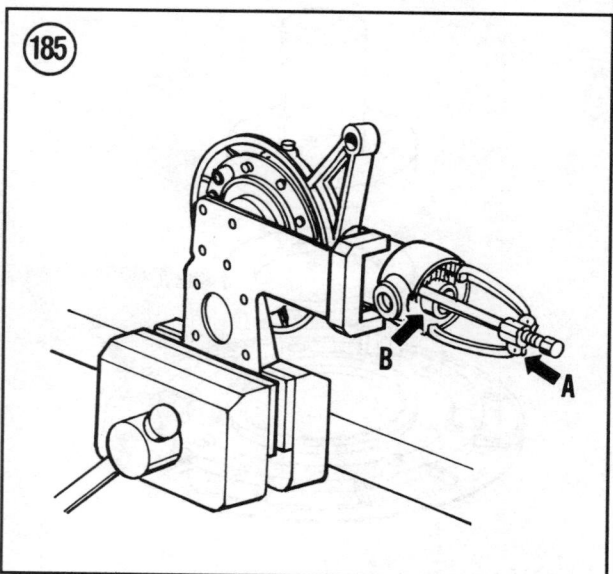
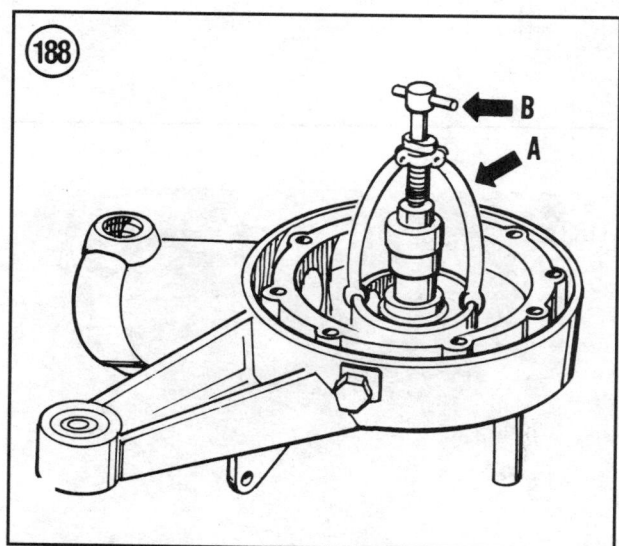

4. Inspect the threads on the threaded ring for wear or damage. Clean the threads with the correct thread tap. Replace if necessary.

5. Inspect the threaded holes (A, **Figure 193**) for the disc mounting screws. Check for wear or damage. If necessary, clean the threads with the correct thread tap. Replace if necessary.

6. On all models, inspect the threaded holes (B, **Figure 193**) for the wheel mounting bolts. Check for wear or

damage. Clean the threads with the correct thread tap. Replace if necessary.

Assembly

Refer to **Figure 173** and **Figure 194** for this procedure.

1. To install the tapered roller bearing, inner race (**Figure 190**) and shim onto the ring gear, perform the following:

    a. Position the ring gear so the portion where the tapered roller bearing is rides facing up.

    b. Secure the ring gear in a vise with soft jaws.

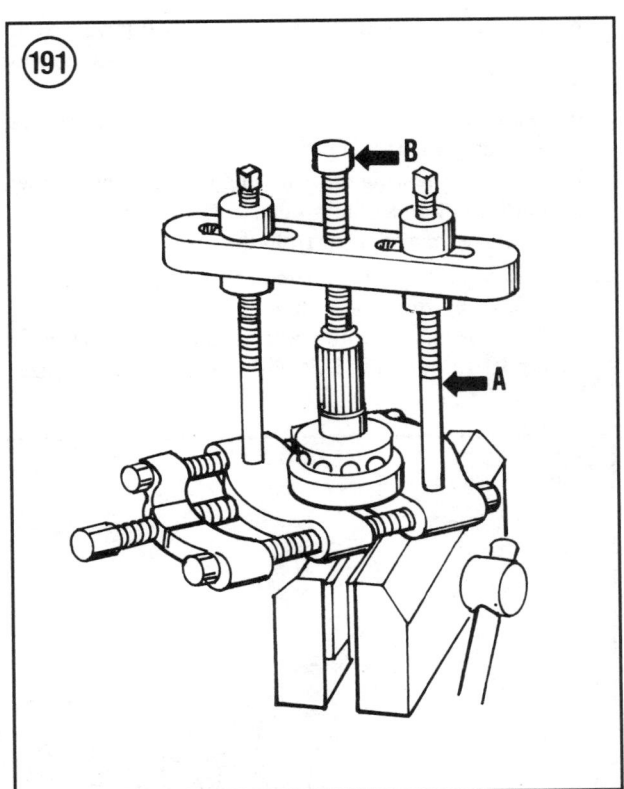

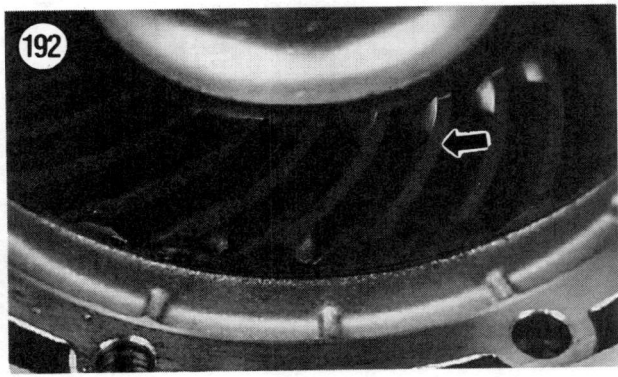

14

c. Position the shim of the correct thickness with the inner diameter chamfer facing down toward the ring gear and install the shim (A, **Figure 195**) onto the ring gear.

d. Using a heat gun or hot plate, heat the bearing and inner race to 80° C (175° F).

e. Install the bearing (B, **Figure 195**) onto the ring gear and tap it down until it bottoms out.

f. Remove the ring gear from the vise.

2. To install the ball bearing on the ring gear, perform the following:

a. Position the ring gear so the portion where the ball bearing is rides facing up.

b. Secure the ring gear in a vise with soft jaws.

c. Install a shim of the correct thickness onto the ring gear.

d. Using a heat gun or hot plate, heat the bearing assembly to 80° C (175° F).

e. Install the bearing onto the ring gear and tap it down until it bottoms out.

f. Remove the ring gear from the vise.

3. To install the ring gear tapered roller bearing outer race into the case, perform the following:

a. Place the tapered roller bearing outer race in a freezer for 10-15 minutes. This will reduce its overall size.

b. Using a heat gun or hot plate, heat the case to 120° C (250° F).

c. Set the case on wooden blocks with the open portion of the case facing up.

d. Install the tapered roller bearing outer race (A, **Figure 196**) into the case.

e. Insert BMW special tools (part No. 33 1 880 and 00 5 500) onto the center of the outer race (B, **Figure 196**) and tap it down in until it bottoms out in the case. Make sure the outer race is installed straight

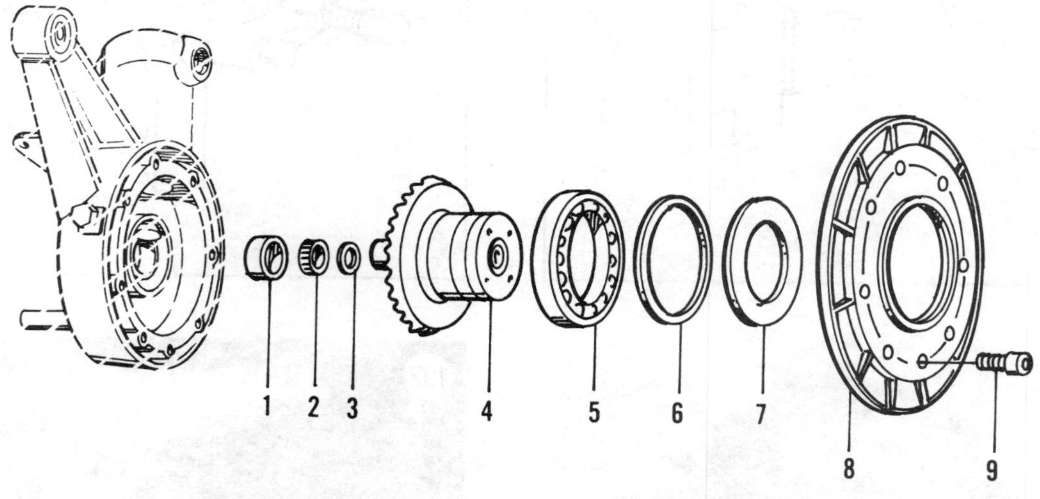

1. Outer race
2. Tapered roller bearing
3. Shim
4. Ring gear
5. Ball bearing
6. Shim
7. Oil seal
8. Cover
9. Bolt

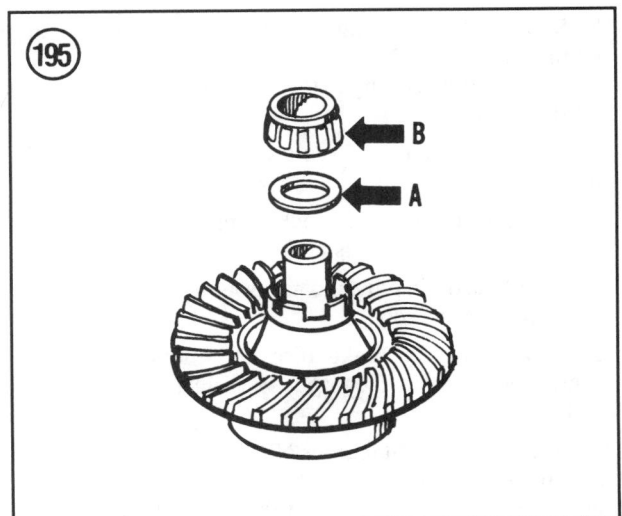

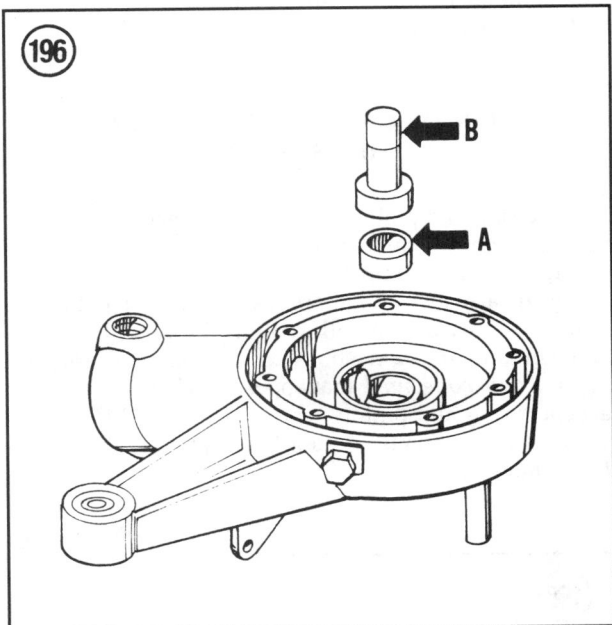

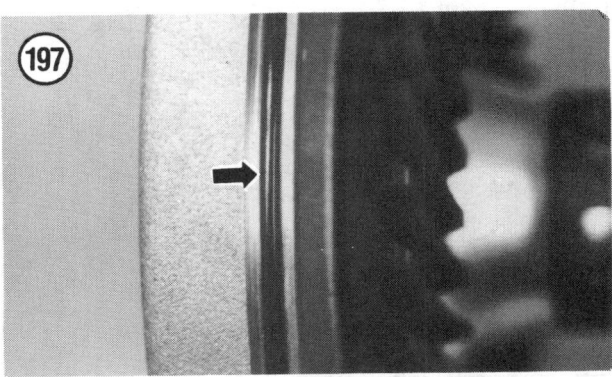

down and that it does not get cocked during installation.

4. To install the pivot pin needle bearings into the case, perform the following:

   a. Clamp the final drive case in the BMW special tool (part No. 33 1 500).

   b. Place the pivot pin needle bearing in a freezer for 10-15 minutes. This will reduce its overall size.

   c. Using a heat gun, heat the case in the area where the needle bearing is to be located. Heat the case to 100° C (212° F).

   d. Position the needle bearing with its identification marks facing out.

   e. Install the needle bearing into the case and tap it in with a suitable size socket or use the pinion gear. Tap it in until it is flush with the outer surface of the case. Make sure the needle bearing is installed straight.

5. To install the pinion gear needle bearing into the case, perform the following:

   a. Clamp the final drive case in the BMW special tool (part No. 33 1 500).

   b. Place the pinion gear needle bearing in a freezer for 10-15 minutes. This will reduce its overall size.

   c. Using a heat gun, heat the case in the area where the needle bearing is to be located. Heat the case to 100° C (212° F).

   d. Position the needle bearing with the identification marks facing out.

   e. Install the needle bearing into the case and tap it in with a suitable size socket or use the pinion gear. Tap it in until it bottoms out in the case. Make sure the needle bearing is installed straight.

6. Place the ring gear assembly in a freezer for about 15-30 minutes. This will reduce its overall size.

7. Install the shim onto the needle bearing in the case.

8. Remove the ring gear assembly from the freezer and install the ring gear onto the case. Using a plastic hammer or soft faced mallet, tap around the perimeter of the ring gear until it bottoms out.

9. If the pinion gear and ring gear were replaced with a new gear set, or if any of the bearings were replaced, perform *Pinion Gear-To-Ring Gear Adjustment* as described in this section of the supplement, prior to installing the cover.

10. Install the shim on the ring gear bearing.

11. Install a new O-ring seal (**Figure 197**) into the groove in the cover.

12. Install the cover onto the case, referring to the alignment marks made in Step 14, under *Disassembly.* in this section. Using a plastic hammer or soft faced mallet, tap around the perimeter of the cover until it bottoms out.

14

13. Install the screws securing the cover to the case. Tighten the screws to the torque specification listed in **Table 1**.

14. To install the bearing assembly on the pinion gear, refer to **Figure 179** and perform the following:

   a. Place the pinion gear in a freezer for about 30 minutes. This will reduce its overall size.

   b. Using a heat gun or hot plate, heat the cylindrical roller bearing inner race to 100° C (212° F) and install the bearing inner race onto the pinion gear shaft.

   c. Carefully tap the cylindrical roller bearing inner race into place until it bottoms out.

   d. Install the cylindrical needle bearing outer race and the cylindrical roller bearing cage into place in the inner race.

   e. Using a heat gun or hot plate, heat the ball bearing assembly to 100° C (212° F) and install the bearing inner race onto the pinion gear shaft.

   f. Carefully tap the ball bearing assembly into place until it bottoms out.

   g. Using a heat gun, heat the final drive unit neck (surrounding the ball bearing outer race) to 120° C (250° F).

   h. Install the pinion gear assembly along with the shim of the correct thickness into the case. Push the assembly in until it bottoms out on the ball bearing in the case (**Figure 178**).

   i. Place the ball bearing outer race in a freezer for about 30 minutes. This will reduce its overall size.

   j. Install the ball bearing outer race into the final drive unit neck and over the ball bearing. Push it in until it seats on the ball bearing.

NOTE
*Refer to **Figure 176** for Steps 15-19.*

15. Thoroughly clean the threaded ring of all oil and/or grease.

16. Secure the final drive unit in the BMW special tool (part No. 33 1 500) and secure the special tool in a vise. Tighten the mounting bolts to the torque specification listed in **Table 1**.

17. Coat the threaded ring with a coat of Hylomar SQ 32 M grease and place it in a freezer for about 15 minutes. This will reduce its overall size.

CAUTION
Do not damage the new oil seal in the threaded ring during installation. After the threaded ring is installed, make sure the oil seal lip is seated correctly around the pinion gear shaft. This is necessary to prevent an oil leak.

18. Start the threaded ring by hand, then using BMW special tool (part No. 33 1 700), screw in the threaded ring. Tighten the threaded ring to the torque specification listed in **Table 1**.

19. Apply Loctite no. 273 to the gear nut and install the nut.

20. Using a suitably sized socket, tighten the gear nut to the torque specification listed in **Table 1**.

21. Install the drain plug and new sealing washer. Tighten the drain plug securely.

22. Install the rear brake disc and mounting screws. Tighten the screws to the torque specification listed in **Table 1**.

23. Apply a coat of Staburags NBU 30 PMT grease, or an equivalent, to the pinion shaft splines and install the rear portion of the drive shaft. Carefully tap the drive shaft onto the splines until it is locked in place.

24. Refill the final drive unit with the recommended type and quantity of oil.

PINION GEAR-TO-RING GEAR ADJUSTMENT

If the ring and pinion gear set is replaced, make sure they are from the same pair that was tested together and "designated as a compatible pair" at the BMW factory. The gears are run on a factory test stand and paired up in sets. This provides smooth running along with the correct amount of backlash. After testing they are then given a *pair code mark* that appears on both gears. Only accept a ring and pinion gear set from a BMW dealer with matching numbers—don't accept a set with 2 different numbers.

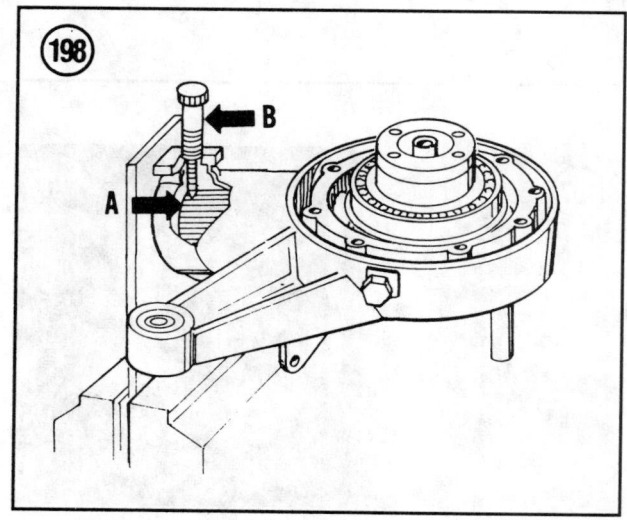

If a *new* ring and pinion gear set is installed into a used case or a *new case* is used with the used ring and pinion set, the tolerance between these parts must be checked. There is a specified distance that provides the correct relation of the ring gear to the pinion gear.

The pinion gear is installed in the case and the ring gear is installed in the cover. When the cover and case are attached to each other the relationship between the ring gear and pinion gear must be correct.

NOTE
If any of the final drive unit bearings are replaced, all of the following procedures must be followed.

The *first section* of the procedure is the adjustment of the ring gear-to-pinion backlash. This adjustment is made to correctly locate the ring gear in relation to the pinion gear. A shim is used to achieve the up and down location of the ring gear in the case.

The *second section* of the procedure is for the pinion gear adjustment. This adjustment is made to correctly locate the pinion gear in relation to the case. A shim is used to achieve the in and out location of the pinion gear in the case and to correctly preload the bearings. This also cor-

rectly aligns the tooth contact pattern or how the pinion gear and ring gear teeth mate to each other. The gear contact must be centered otherwise there will be abnormal stress placed on the gear teeth causing premature wear.

Ring Gear Backlash

To check and adjust gear backlash, several BMW special tools are required. They are as follows:
 a. Holding fixture (part No. 33 1 500).
 b. Measuring ring assembly (part No. 33 2 600).
 c. Measuring arm (part No. 33 2 604).

NOTE
All locking and measuring tools must be tightly secured to the case and gear assembly. If they are loose, they will give a false reading and the measuring procedure results will be incorrect.

1. Mount the gear case in the holding fixture.
2. Lock the pinion gear (A, **Figure 198**) in place with the knurled screw (B, **Figure 198**). The pinion gear must not move during this procedure, otherwise the results will be incorrect.
3. Install the measuring ring assembly (A, **Figure 199**) onto the case and secure with the bolts (B, **Figure 199**).
4. Install the measuring arm (C, **Figure 199**) onto the center of the ring gear and tighten securely.
5. Adjust the measuring ring so the dial gauge is 90° to the rod on the special tool (**Figure 200**).
6. Adjust the dial gauge to zero.

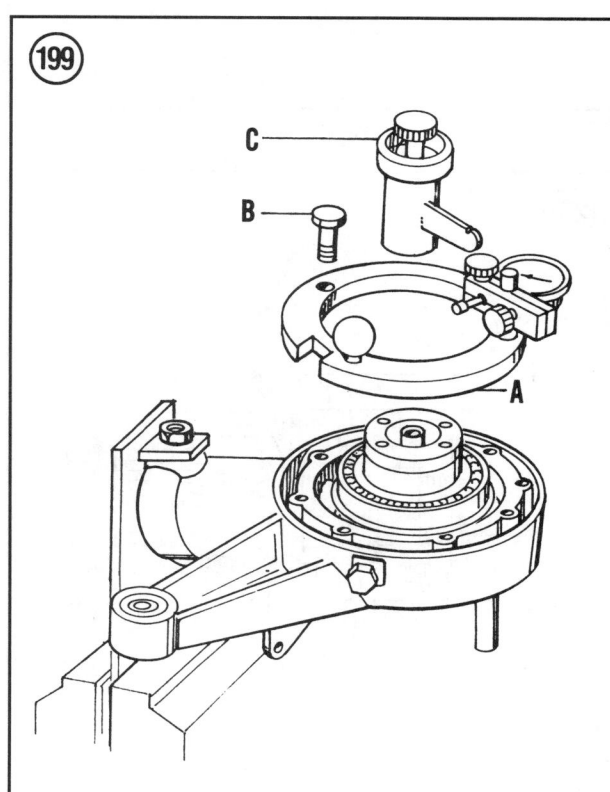

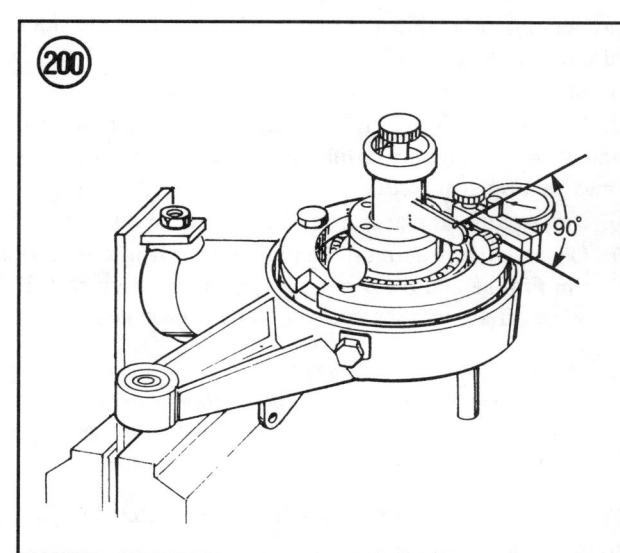

14

7. Using the palm of your hand, press down on the measuring arm and slightly move the ring gear and measuring arm back and forth and note the dial gauge reading.

8. Reposition the measuring ring and check backlash 120° from the point tested in Step 7. Note the reading.

9. Again reposition the measuring ring and check backlash 120° from the point tested in Step 8. Note the reading.

10. The specified backlash is 0.07-0.16 mm (0.003-0.06 in.)

11A. If the backlash is within specification, remove the special tools from the ring gear and gear case.

11B. If the backlash is incorrect, remove the special tool and perform the following:

    a. Remove the ring gear from the final drive unit.

    b. Remove the shim (**Figure 201**) and replace it with a thicker or thinner one.

The shims are available from BMW dealers in thickness from 1.95-2.80 mm in 0.05 increments.

12. Repeat Steps 3-9 until the correct amount of backlash is obtained.

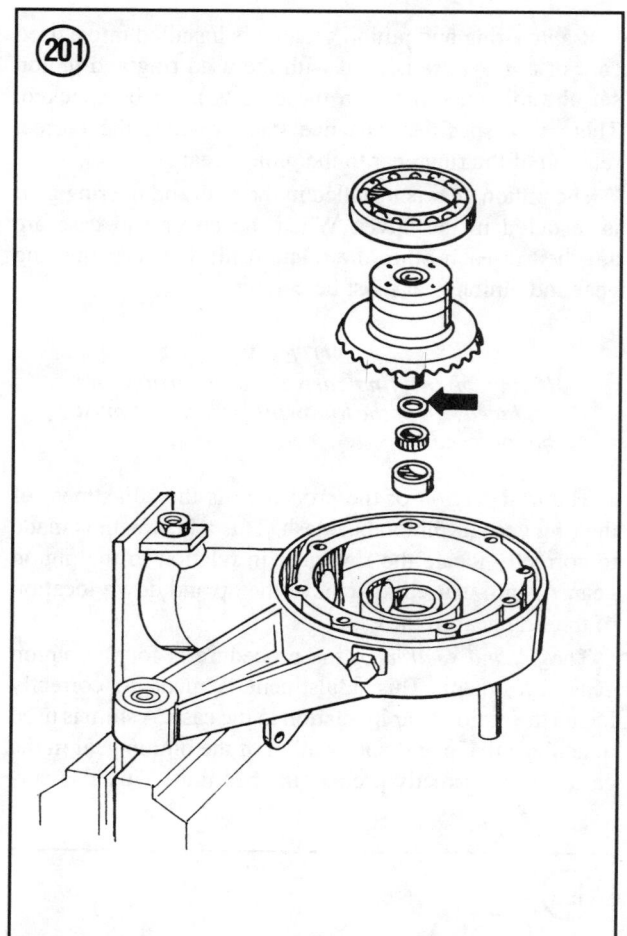

Load Bearing or Tooth Contact Pattern

The load bearing and tooth contact pattern between the ring gear and the pinion gear is controlled by the shim located between the pinion shaft bearing and the gear case surface (**Figure 202**).

1. Remove the ring gear from the final drive case.

2. Thoroughly clean all oil residue from the gear teeth on both the ring and pinion gears. They must be clean so the "paris blue" or gear marking compound applied in the next step can be applied in an even pattern.

3. Apply a light coat of "paris blue," or a light colored printers ink or a white colored artist oil paint to the sides of the teeth on the pinion gear.

4. Install the ring gear into the final drive case.

5. Press down firmly on the ring gear and rotate it back and forth several times so the marking compound transfers onto the ring gear teeth.

6. Remove the ring gear from the final drive case.

7. Observe the pattern on the pinion gear. If it looks like that in **Figure 203** the tooth contact pattern is correct. If so, wipe off all marking compound from each gear.

NOTE
Perform Steps 8-14 only if the tooth contact pattern is not correct and requires shim replacement.

8. If the pattern does not look like **Figure 203**, compare to the following illustrations:

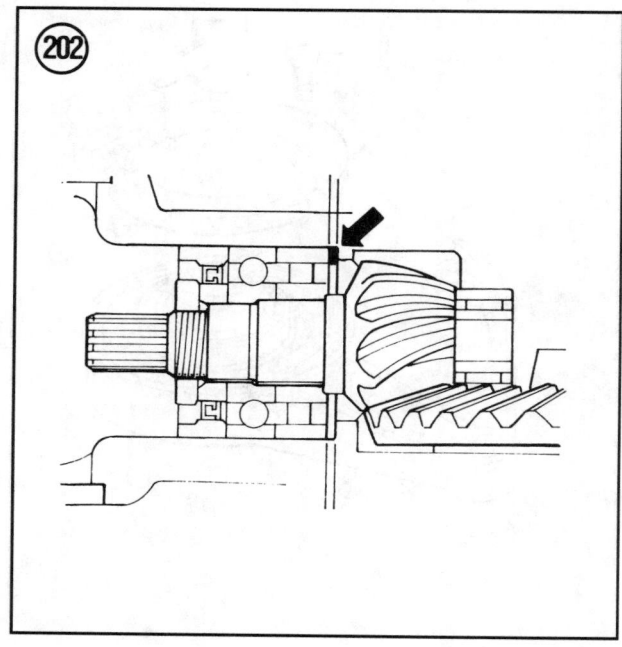

a. **Figure 204**: pinion gear must be moved farther out in the final drive case. Replace the existing shim with a *thicker* shim between the pinion gear and the final drive case.

b. **Figure 205**: pinion gear must be moved farther back into the final drive case. Replace with a existing shim with a *thinner* shim between the pinion gear and the final drive case.

9. Replace the shim (**Figure 202**) between the pinion gear and the final drive case.

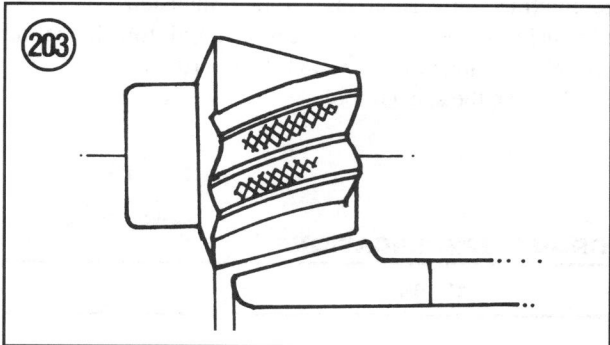

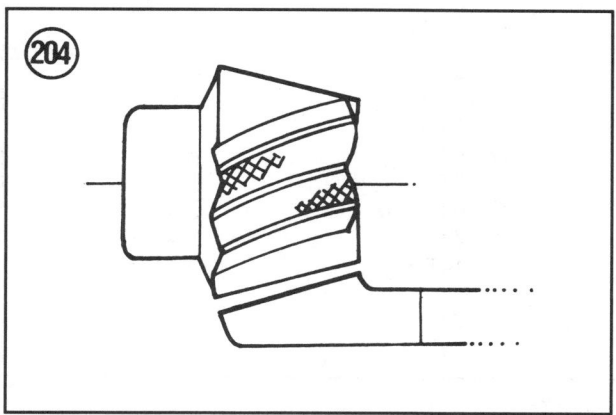

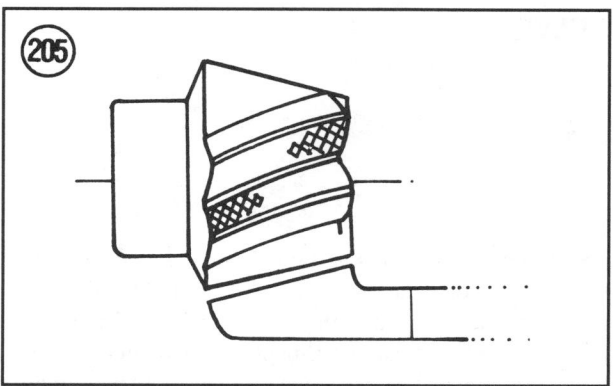

10. Reapply a light coat of "paris blue," marking compound or a light colored printers ink or a white colored artist oil paint to both sides of a couple of teeth on the pinion gear.

11. Install the ring gear into the final drive case and pinion gear.

12. Press down firmly on the ring gear and rotate it back and forth several times so the marking compound transfers onto the ring gear teeth.

13. Remove the ring gear from the final drive case.

14. Observe the pattern on the pinion gear. If it looks like that in **Figure 203** the tooth contact pattern is correct. If not, repeat this procedure until the tooth contact pattern is correct.

15. Remove the ring gear from the final drive case. Wipe off all ink or paint residue from both gears.

TAPERED ROLLER BEARING PRELOAD

The preload on the tapered roller bearing, located on the right-hand side of the ring gear, is controlled by the shim placed between the ball bearing, located on the left-hand side of the ring gear ball bearing and the case cover. The correct spacing of this ball bearing determines the preload on the tapered roller bearing. A specific amount of preload is necessary for the tapered roller bearing to seat correctly and operate properly. The preload dimension is 0.05-0.10 mm. The shims are available from BMW dealers in thickness from 0.1-1.7 mm in 0.1 increments.

1. Place the case cover on the workbench with the inner surface facing up.

2. Place the BMW distance or depth gauge (part No. 00 2 500) on the case-to-cover mating surface of the cover (**Figure 206**).

3. Measure the distance from the mating surface down to the ball bearing seating shoulder of the cover. This is dimension "A."

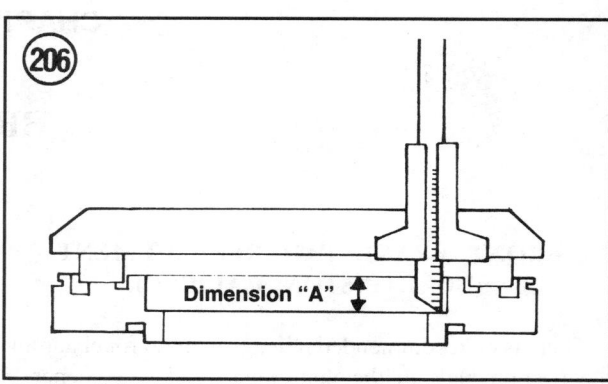

Dimension "A"

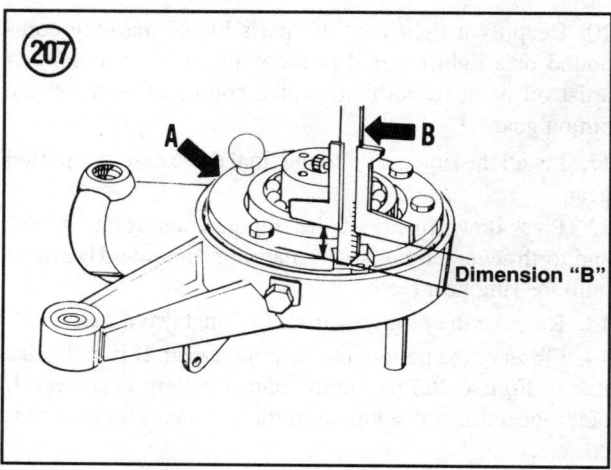

4. Install the ring gear and ball bearing assembly into the final drive case and pinion gear.

5. Place the BMW measuring ring (A, **Figure 207**) (part No. 33 2 601) onto the gear case and secure it with the bolts.

6. Place the depth gauge on the upper surface of the ball bearing on the ring gear. Place the special tool (B, **Figure 207**) in the opening in the gauge ring.

7. Measure the distance from the ball bearing upper surface to the case mating surface of the case. This is dimension "B."

8. Subtract dimension "B" from dimension "A." This dimension is the shim thickness required. to achieve the specified preload dimension of 0.05-0.10 mm.

9. Remove the special tool.

Table 1 REAR SUSPENSION TORQUE SPECIFICATIONS

Item	N•m	ft.-lb.
Rear wheel mounting bolts		
Preload	50	36.8
Final	105	77.4
Rear wheel center bolt	105	77.4
Shock absorber mounting		
bolts and nuts	51	37.6
Final drive unit		
Cover screws	21	15.4
Threaded ring	118	87
Left pivot pin	105	77
Right pivot pin	7.3	64 in.-lb.
Pivot pin locknuts	105	77
Pinion gear hex nut	200	147.4
Final drive unit-to-BMW		
special tool (33-1 500)	105	77.4
Brake disc-to-ring gear bolts	21	15.4

CHAPTER TWELVE

BRAKES

FRONT BRAKE PAD REPLACEMENT (DUAL PISTON CALIPER)

There is no recommended mileage interval for changing the friction pads in the disc brake. Pad wear depends greatly on riding habits and conditions. The pads should be checked for wear every 7,240 km (4,500 miles) and replaced when the lining thickness reaches 1.5 mm (1/16 in.) from the brake pad backing plate. To maintain an even brake pressure on the disc always replace both pads in both calipers at the same time. Always use brake pads from the same manufacturer in both front calipers--never intermix different brands.

CAUTION
Watch the pads more closely when the wear line approaches the disc. On some pads the wear line is very close to the metal backing plate. If pad wear happens to be uneven for some reason, the backing plate may come in contact with the disc and cause damage.

Refer to **Figure 208** for this procedure.

1. To prevent the accidental application of the front brake lever place a spacer between the front brake lever and the hand grip. Hold the spacer in place with a large rubber band, a tie wrap or a piece of tape.

2. Remove the bolts (**Figure 209**) securing the brake caliper to the front fork slider.

3. The pistons must be repositioned within the caliper assembly prior to installing the new *thicker* brake pads. The front master cylinder brake fluid level will rise as the caliper pistons are being repositioned. Perform the following:

a. Clean the top of the front master cylinder of all dirt and foreign matter.

b. Remove the screws securing the top cover and remove the top cover and the diaphragm from the master cylinder.

c. Note the brake fluid level in the reservoir. If it is up to, or close to, the top surface of the reservoir, siphon off some of the fluid at this time.

d. First push the caliper assembly toward the brake disc until it stops. This will reposition the outboard pistons into the caliper cylinder bores.

e. Then pull the caliper assembly toward the brake disc until it stops. This will reposition the inboard pistons into the caliper cylinder bores.

f. Constantly check the reservoir to make sure the brake fluid does not overflow. Remove brake fluid, if necessary, prior to it overflowing.

g. The pistons should move freely during repositioning. If they don't, and there is evidence of them sticking in the cylinders, the caliper should be removed and serviced as described in this section of the supplement.

4. Carefully slide the caliper off the brake disc.

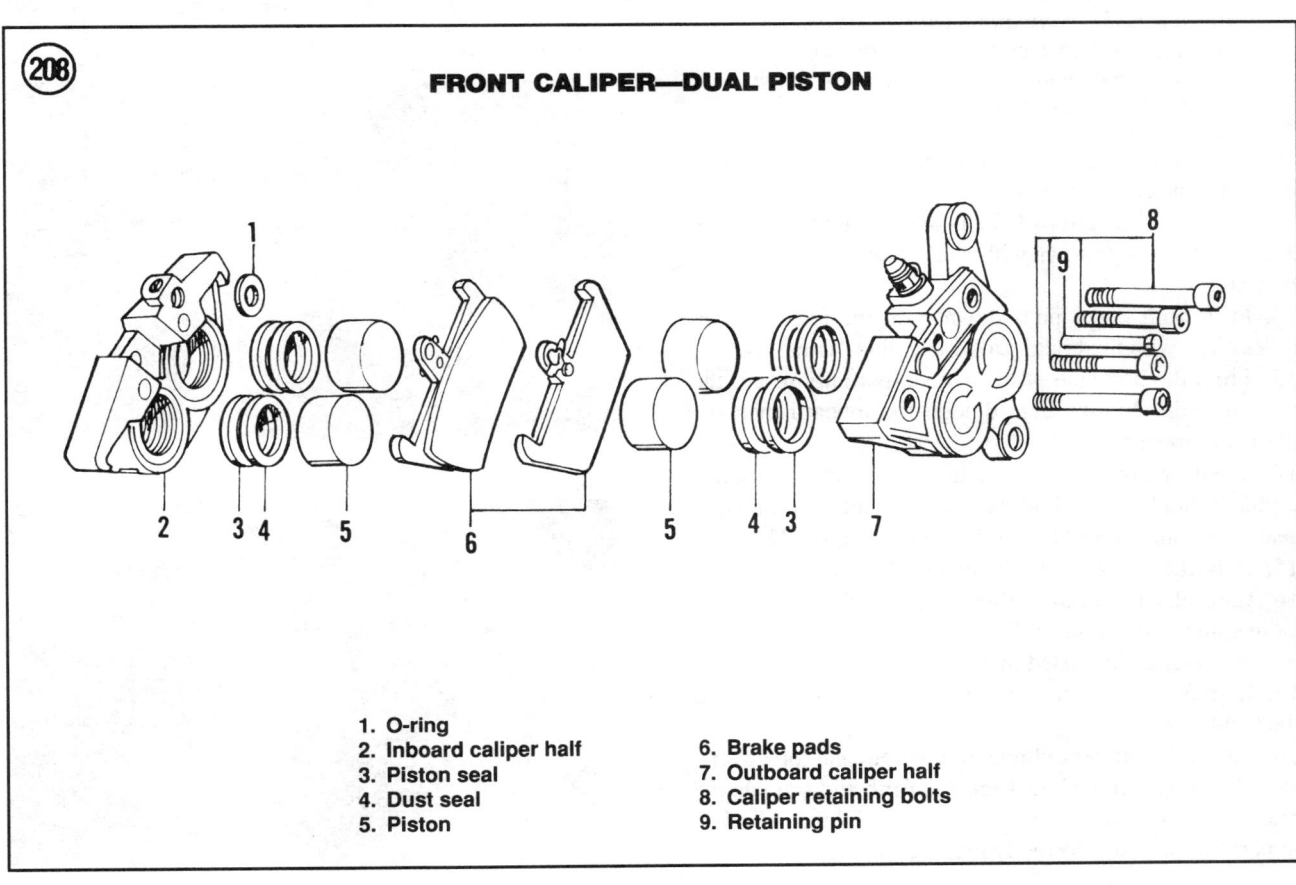

FRONT CALIPER—DUAL PISTON

1. O-ring
2. Inboard caliper half
3. Piston seal
4. Dust seal
5. Piston
6. Brake pads
7. Outboard caliper half
8. Caliper retaining bolts
9. Retaining pin

14

5. Using a drift and small hammer, carefully tap the retaining pin (**Figure 210**) loose, then withdraw the retaining pin (**Figure 211**) from the backside of the caliper.

6. Remove both brake pads (**Figure 212**) from the caliper.

WARNING
When working on the brake system, do not inhale brake dust. It may contain asbestos, which can cause lung injury and cancer. Wear a disposable face mask that meets OSHA requirements for trapping asbestos particles, and wash your hands and forearms thoroughly after completing the work.

7. Clean the pad recess in the caliper and the surfaces of the pistons (**Figure 213**) with a soft brush. Do not use a solvent, wire brush or any hard tool which would damage the pistons.

8. Carefully remove any rust or corrosion from the disc.

9. Lightly coat the end of the pistons and the backs of the new pads (*not the friction material*) with disc brake lubricant.

NOTE
When purchasing new pads, check with your dealer to make sure the friction compound of the new pad is compatible with the disc material. Remove any roughness from the backs of the new pads with a fine-cut file; wipe them clean with a lint-free cloth.

10. Make sure all 4 pistons (**Figure 214**) are still pushed back into the caliper bores.

11. Install the inboard pad, then the outboard pad (**Figure 212**). Push the pads down within the caliper assembly until they stop.

12. Push both brake pads down until the retaining pin holes align with the brake pads and caliper assembly.

13. From the backside of the caliper, partially install the retaining pin (**Figure 211**) though the inboard then the outboard brake pad.

14. Tap the retaining pin in all the way and make sure it is correctly hooked into both brake pads and is completely seated in both sides of the caliper body (**Figure 215**).

15. Repeat Steps 2-14 for the other caliper assembly.

16. Carefully install the caliper onto the disc. Install the caliper mounting bolts (**Figure 209**) and tighten to the torque specification listed in **Table 11**.

17. Remove the spacer between the front brake lever and the hand grip.

18. Install the master cylinder diaphragm and top cover.

19. Carefully roll the bike back and forth and activate the brake lever as many times as it takes to refill the cylinders in both calipers and correctly locate all pads.

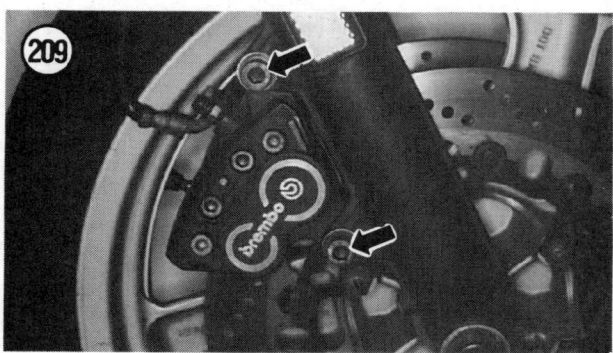

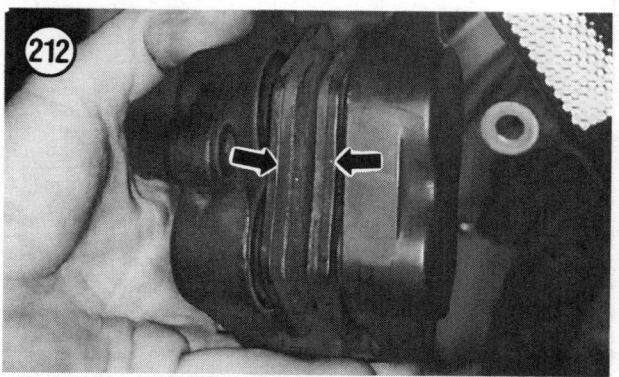

WARNING
Use brake fluid clearly marked DOT 4 from a sealed container. Other types may vaporize and cause brake failure. Always use the same brand name; do not intermix silicone based (DOT 5) brake fluid as it can cause brake component damage leading to brake system failure.

20. Refill the master cylinder reservoir, if necessary, to maintain the correct fluid level.

21. Install the diaphragm and the top cover. Install the screws and tighten securely.

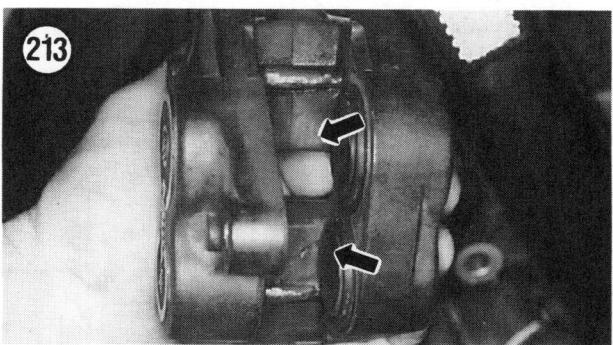

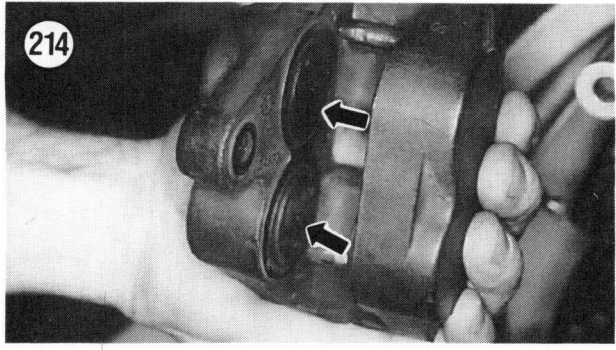

WARNING
Do not ride the motorcycle until you are sure the brakes are operating correctly with full hydraulic advantage. If necessary, bleed the brake as described in this chapter.

22. Bed the pads in gradually for the first 80 km (50 miles) by using only light pressure as much as possible. Immediate hard application will glaze the new friction pads and greatly reduce the effectiveness of the brake.

FRONT MASTER CYLINDER

Removal/Installation

CAUTION
Cover the fuel tank, instrument cluster and front fairing with a heavy cloth or plastic tarp to protect them from accidental brake fluid spills. Wash brake fluid off any painted or plated surfaces immediately, as it will destroy the finish. Use soapy water and rinse completely.

1. Place a couple of shop cloths under the union bolt and remove the union bolt and sealing washers securing the brake hose to the master cylinder. Remove the brake hose. Tie the brake hose up and cover the end with a reclosable plastic bag to prevent the entry of foreign matter.

2. Remove the tie wrap securing the right-hand switch electrical cable to the handlebar.

3. Disconnect the brake light electrical connector from the master cylinder.

4. Remove the screw securing the shut off switch and move the switch out of the way.

5. Remove the screw and cover securing the accelerator cable and disconnect it from the throttle grip.

6. Remove the screw securing the handlebar weight and remove the weight from the end of the handlebar.

7. Loosen the clamping bolt securing the master cylinder to the handlebar, then slide the master cylinder off the end of the handlebar.

8. If necessary, carefully cut through the rubber hand grip and remove the handgrip.

9. Install by reversing these removal steps, noting the following.

10. Make sure the throttle cable is routed properly in the throttle housing and is attached to the throttle wheel receptacle.

11. Install the brake hose onto the master cylinder. Be sure to place a sealing washer on each side of the fitting and install the union bolt. Tighten the union bolt to the torque specifications listed in **Table 11**.

14

12. Bleed the brake as described in Chapter Twelve in the main body of this book.

Disassembly

Refer to **Figure 216** and **Figure 217** for this procedure.
1. Remove the master cylinder as described in this section of the supplement.
2. Remove the screw securing the side cover and remove the side cover.
3. Loosen and remove the brake lever mounting pin.
4. Remove the brake lever from the master cylinder body.
5. Carefully remove the sealing sleeve from the body.

WARNING
The piston is under spring pressure. Be sure to hold onto the piston while unscrewing the stop screw and protect your eyes appropriately.

6. Press in on the piston and remove the stop screw.
7. Remove the piston assembly and spring from the master cylinder body.
8. Remove the screws securing the top cover and remove the top cover and the diaphragm. Pour out the brake fluid and discard it. *Never reuse brake fluid.*

Inspection

BMW does not provide any specifications for wear limits on any of the master cylinder components. Replace any parts that appear to be damaged or worn.
1. Clean all parts in denatured alcohol or fresh brake fluid. Inspect the cylinder bore and piston contact surfaces for signs of wear and damage. If either part is less than perfect, replace it.
2. Check the end of the piston and the sealing sleeve for wear caused by the hand lever. Replace the sealing sleeve and the piston assembly if worn.
3. Replace the piston assembly if the piston cups requires replacement. The cups cannot be replaced separately.
4. Inspect the piston assembly spring for wear or deterioration. Replace if necessary.
5. Make sure the passages on the bottom of the body reservoir are clear. Clean out if necessary.
6. Check the reservoir top cap and diaphragm for damage and deterioration and replace as necessary.
7. Inspect the threads and hole in the bore for the brake hose union bolt. If the threads are slightly damaged, clean them up with a proper size pipe thread tap. If the threads are worn or damaged beyond repair, replace the master cylinder body.

8. Inspect the piston bore in the body for wear, corrosion or damage. Replace the body if necessary.

9. Make sure the fluid passage holes on the union bolt are clear. Clean out if necessary.

Assembly

1. Install the diaphragm and top cover. Install the screws and tighten finger tight at this time as brake fluid must be added after the master cylinder is installed.
2. Soak the new piston assembly in fresh brake fluid for at least 15 minutes to make the cups pliable. Coat the inside of the cylinder bore with fresh brake fluid prior to the assembly of parts.

CAUTION
When installing the piston assembly, do not allow the cups to turn inside out as they will be damaged and allow brake fluid leakage within the cylinder bore.

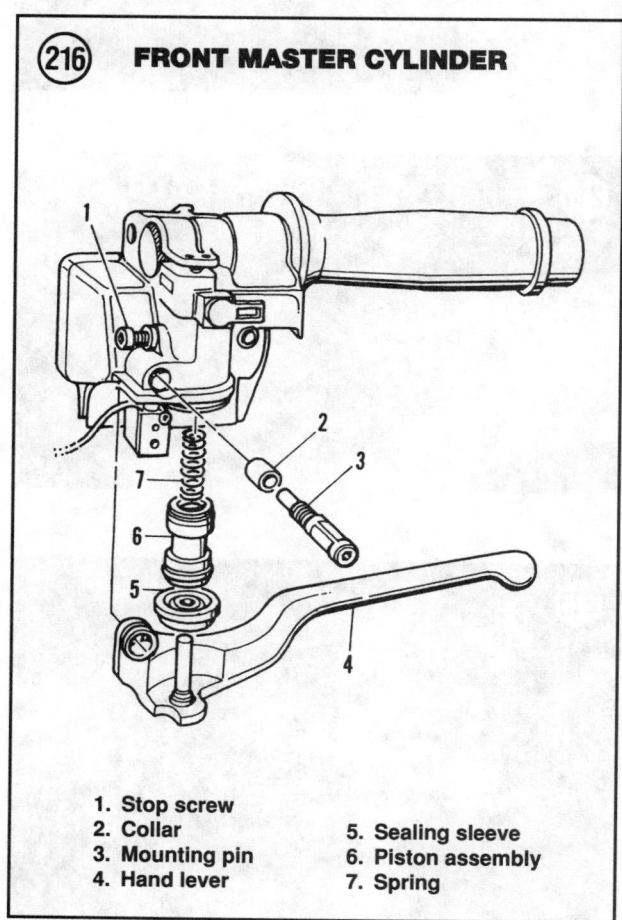

(216) FRONT MASTER CYLINDER

1. Stop screw
2. Collar
3. Mounting pin
4. Hand lever
5. Sealing sleeve
6. Piston assembly
7. Spring

3. Position the piston so the cups' sealing lips face toward the inside. Install the piston assembly and spring into the reservoir cylinder.

4. Apply red Loctite (No. 271) to the threads of the stop screw prior to installation.

5. Push the piston assembly in and make sure it is correctly seated in the cylinder groove. Install the stop screw and tighten finger-tight at this time.

6. Install the sealing sleeve into the body and push it in until it stops.

7. Install the brake lever onto the master cylinder body.

8. Hold the brake lever in place and install the mounting pin. Tighten the pin securely.

9. Turn the stop screw in until the brake lever is free of play, then tighten it an additional one-half turn.

10. Install the side cover and screw and tighten the screw securely.

11. Install the master cylinder as described in this chapter.

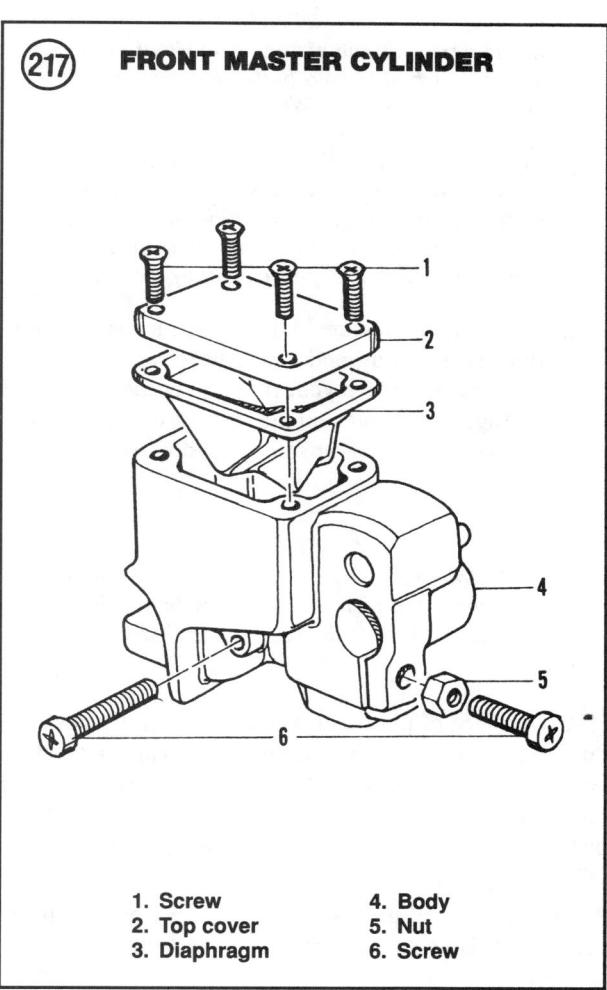

⑵ FRONT MASTER CYLINDER

1. Screw
2. Top cover
3. Diaphragm
4. Body
5. Nut
6. Screw

FRONT CALIPER
(DUAL PISTON CALIPER)

Removal

Refer to **Figure 208** for this procedure.

It is not necessary to remove the front wheel in order to remove either or both caliper assemblies.

> *CAUTION*
> *Do not spill any brake fluid on the painted portion of the front wheel or front fork slider. Wash any spilled brake fluid immediately, as it will destroy the finish. Use soapy water and rinse completely.*

1. Drain the hydraulic brake fluid from the front brake system as follows:
   a. Attach a hose to the bleed valve on the caliper assembly.
   b. Place the loose end of the hose in a container to catch the brake fluid.
   c. Open the bleed valve and continue to apply the front brake lever until the brake fluid is pumped out of the system.
   d. Disconnect the hose and tighten the bleed valve.
   e. Dispose of this brake fluid—*never* reuse brake fluid. Contaminated brake fluid may cause brake failure.

> *NOTE*
> *The ABS electronic trigger sensor is attached to the left-hand fork slider. Do not damage the sensor during caliper removal.*

2. Remove the union bolt and sealing washers (A, **Figure 218**) securing the brake hose to the caliper.

> *NOTE*
> *If the caliper assembly will be disassembled for service, loosen the Allen bolts securing the*

14

caliper assembly halves together. The fork slider makes a good holding fixture.

3. If necessary, loosen the 4 Allen bolts securing the caliper halves together (B, **Figure 218**).

4. Loosen then remove the brake caliper assembly mounting bolts (C, **Figure 218**) from the front fork slider.

5. Carefully slide the caliper assembly off of the brake disc.

6. To prevent the entry of moisture and dirt, cap the end of the brake line.

7. If necessary, repeat Steps 2-6 for the other caliper assembly.

Installation

> *NOTE*
> *The ABS electronic sensor is attached to the left-hand fork slider. Do not damage the sensor during caliper installation.*

1. Carefully install the caliper assembly onto the disc. Be careful not to damage the leading edge of the pads during installation. Do not kink nor damage the brake line assembly.

2. Install the brake caliper assembly mounting bolts (C, **Figure 218**).

3. Tighten the caliper mounting bolts to the torque specifications listed in **Table 11**.

> *NOTE*
> *If the caliper assembly was disassembled for service, securely tighten the Allen bolts securing the caliper assembly halves together. Tighten the caliper retaining bolts to the torque specifications listed in* **Table 11**.

4. Move the brake hose into position on the caliper and install the union bolt and sealing washers (A, **Figure 218**) securing the brake hose to the caliper. Tighten the union bolt to the torque specification listed in **Table 11**.

5. Refill the system and bleed brakes as described in this Chapter Twelve in the main body of this book.

> *WARNING*
> *Do not ride the motorcycle until you are sure that the brakes are operating properly.*

Rebuilding

Refer to **Figure 208** for this procedure.

BMW does not provide any specifications for wear limits on any of the front caliper components. Replace any parts that appear to be damaged or worn.

1. Prior to removing the caliper assembly, loosen the 4 Allen bolts securing the caliper halves together (B, **Figure 218**).

2. Remove the brake pads, then the caliper assembly as described in this section of the supplement.

3. Remove the 2 inner and 2 outer Allen bolts securing the caliper halves together.

4. Separate the caliper halves.

5. Remove the small O-ring seal from the inboard caliper half. Discard the O-ring seal as it must be replaced.

6. To remove the pistons from the caliper halves, perform the following:

    a. Either wrap the caliper half and pistons with a heavy cloth or place a shop cloth or piece of soft wood over the end of the piston.

    b. Perform this step over and close down to a workbench top. Hold the caliper body with the pistons facing away from you.

> *WARNING*
> *In the next step, the pistons may shoot out of the caliper body like a bullet. Keep your fingers out of the way. Wear shop gloves and apply air pressure gradually. Do not use high pressure air or place the air hose nozzle directly against the hydraulic fluid passageway in the caliper body. Hold the air nozzle away from the inlet allowing some of the air to escape during the procedure.*

    c. Apply the air pressure in short spurts to the hydraulic fluid passageway and force the piston out of the caliper body. Place your finger over the other fluid passageways to prevent the air from escaping. Use a service station air hose if you don't have an air compressor.

> *CAUTION*
> *In the following step, do not use a sharp tool to remove the piston seals from the caliper cylinders. Do not damage the cylinder surfaces.*

7. Use a piece of plastic or wood and carefully push the dust seals and piston seals in toward the caliper cylinder and out of their grooves. Repeat for the dust seals and piston seals in the other caliper half. Discard all dust and piston seals, they cannot be reused after removal as they will no longer seal effectively.

8. Inspect the seal grooves in each caliper body half for damage. If damaged or corroded, replace the caliper assembly.

NOTE
The caliper body cannot be replaced separately. If it is damaged in any way the entire caliper assembly must be replaced.

9. Unscrew and remove the bleed screw and cap.

10. Inspect the caliper body halves for damage, replace the caliper body if necessary.

11. Inspect the hydraulic fluid passageway in the base of each cylinder bore. Make sure it is clean and open. Apply compressed air to the opening and make sure it is clear. Clean out if necessary with fresh brake fluid.

12. Inspect the cylinder walls and the pistons for scratches, scoring or other damage.

If either is rusty or corroded, replace the caliper assembly. The pistons cannot be replaced separately.

13. Inspect the caliper mounting bolt holes. If the threads are slightly damaged; clean them up with a proper size metric thread tap. If the threads are worn or damaged beyond repair, replace the caliper assembly.

14. The 2 outer retaining bolts are of the micro-encapsulated type. A self-locking agent was applied to the threads when they were manufactured. Some of this locking agent transfers to threaded holes in the inboard caliper half when the bolts are installed. This locking agent residue must be removed prior to reinstalling the bolts during assembly. Clean out the threads with the proper size metric thread tap and thoroughly clean with solvent and compressed air.

15. Also, thoroughly clean the 2 outer retaining bolt threads with a wire brush and solvent. Remove all locking agent from the threads.

16. Inspect the caliper halves assembly mounting bolt holes. If the threads are slightly damaged; clean them up with a proper size pipe thread tap. If the threads are worn or damaged beyond repair, replace the caliper assembly.

17. Inspect the union bolt hole threads. If the threads are slightly damaged; clean them up with a proper size thread tap. If the threads are worn or damaged beyond repair, replace the caliper assembly.

18. Make sure the hole in the bleed screw is clean and open. Apply compressed air to the opening and make sure it is clear. Clean out if necessary with fresh brake fluid.

19. If serviceable, clean the caliper body halves with rubbing alcohol and rinse with clean brake fluid.

NOTE
Never reuse a dust seal or piston seal that has been removed. Very minor damage or age deterioration can make the seals useless.

20. Coat the new dust seals and piston seals with fresh DOT 4 brake fluid.

21. Carefully install the new piston seals in the groove in each caliper cylinder. Make sure the seals are properly seated in their grooves.

22. Carefully install the new dust seals in the groove in each caliper cylinder. Make sure the seals are properly seated in their grooves.

23. Coat the pistons and the caliper cylinders with fresh DOT 4 brake fluid.

24. Install the piston into each caliper cylinder bore. Push the pistons in until they bottom out.

25. Install the bleed screw and tighten to the torque specification listed in **Table 12**. Install the cap.

26. Install a new O-ring seal into the recess in the inboard caliper half.

27. Lay the inboard caliper half down and install the outboard half on top of it. This is to prevent the small O-ring seal from falling out during assembly. Make sure the O-ring is properly seated between the caliper halves.

28. Hold the caliper halves together and install the 2 inner Allen bolts securing the caliper assembly halves together. Tighten the bolts to the torque specification listed in **Table 12**.

29. Apply red Loctite (No. 271) to the threads of the 2 outer Allen bolts prior to installation. Install the 2 outer Allen bolts and tighten to the torque specification listed in **Table 12**.

30. Install the brake pads, then the caliper assembly as described in this section of the supplement.

REAR MASTER CYLINDER
(K75 [1993-ON], K100 [1990-1992], K1, K1100)

Removal/Installation

Removal and installation of the rear master cylinder is the same as on previous models with the exception of the shape of the master cylinder reservoir and cap. Refer to **Figure 219** and **Figure 220**.

BRAKE HOSE
AND LINE REPLACEMENT
(NON-ABS MODELS)

There is no factory-recommended replacement interval but it is a good idea to replace all flexible brake hoses every four years or if they show signs of cracking or damage.

CAUTION
Cover the fuel tank, front wheel, front fender with a heavy cloth or plastic tarp to protect it from accidental spilling of brake fluid. Wash brake fluid off of any painted or plated surface

14

immediately, as it will destroy the finish. Use soapy water and rinse completely.

Front Hoses and 3-Way Fitting Removal/Installation

Refer to **Figure 221** for this procedure.

1. On models so equipped, remove the front fairing as described under *Front Fairing Removal/Installation* in Chapter Thirteen in the main body of this book or in this supplement.

2. Remove the rear and front portions (A, **Figure 222**) of the front fender as described in Chapter Thirteen in the main body of this book.

> *NOTE*
> *To prevent the entry of moisture and dirt, cap the end of the brake hoses that are not going to be replaced. Place the loose end in a plastic reclosable bag and zip it closed around the hose or line.*

3. Drain the hydraulic brake fluid from the front brake system as follows:

   a. Attach a hose to the bleed valve on each caliper assembly.

   b. Place the loose end of the hose in a container to catch the brake fluid.

   c. Open the bleed valve on each caliper and continue to apply the front brake lever until the brake fluid is pumped out of the front brake system.

   d. Disconnect the hoses and tighten the bleed valves.

   e. Dispose of this brake fluid--*never* reuse brake fluid. Contaminated brake fluid may cause brake failure.

4. Remove the lower union bolt and sealing washer (A, **Figure 223**) securing the lower flexible brake hose to the brake caliper. Drain out any residual brake fluid.

5. Remove the upper union bolt and sealing washer (B, **Figure 222**) securing the lower flexible brake hose to the 3-way fitting on the front fork stabilizer. Remove the lower flexible brake hose.

6. Repeat Step 4 and Step 5 for the other flexible brake hose.

7. To remove the upper brake hose, perform the following:

   a. Remove the union bolt and sealing washer securing the upper flexible brake hose to the front master cylinder.

   b. Remove the union bolt and sealing washer securing the upper flexible brake hose (C, **Figure 222**) to the 3-way fitting on the front fork stabilizer.

   c. Remove the upper flexible brake hose.

8. To remove the 3-way fitting, perform the following:

   a. Remove the upper and lower flexible brake hoses from the 3-way fitting.

   b. Remove the bolt or bolt, nut and washer securing the 3-way fitting to the front fork stabilizer and remove the fitting.

9. Inspect the 3-way fitting as follows:

   a. Check the brake pipe for any cracks or fractures.

   b. Check the condition of the threads at each opening for the union bolts. Clean up with a proper size tap or replace if severely damaged.

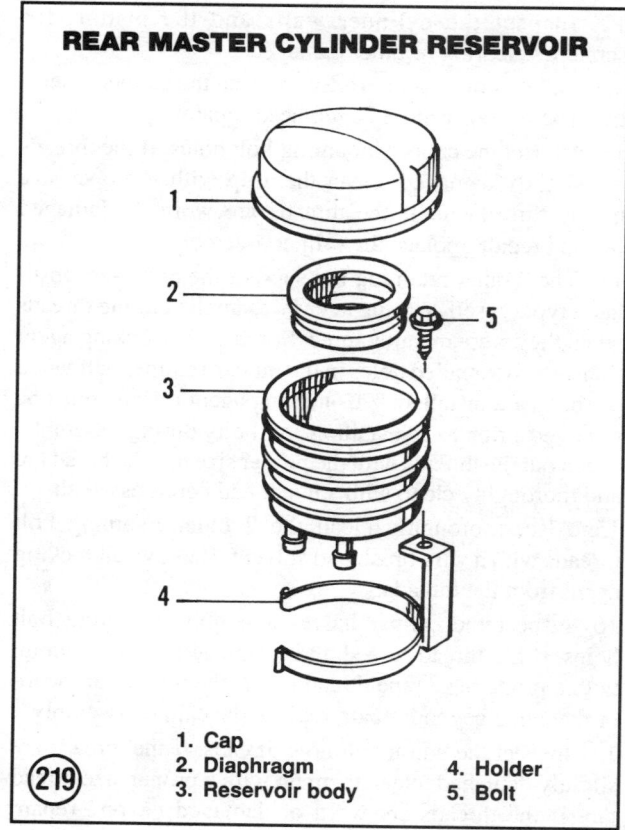

REAR MASTER CYLINDER RESERVOIR

1. Cap	4. Holder
2. Diaphragm	5. Bolt
3. Reservoir body	

(219)

(220)

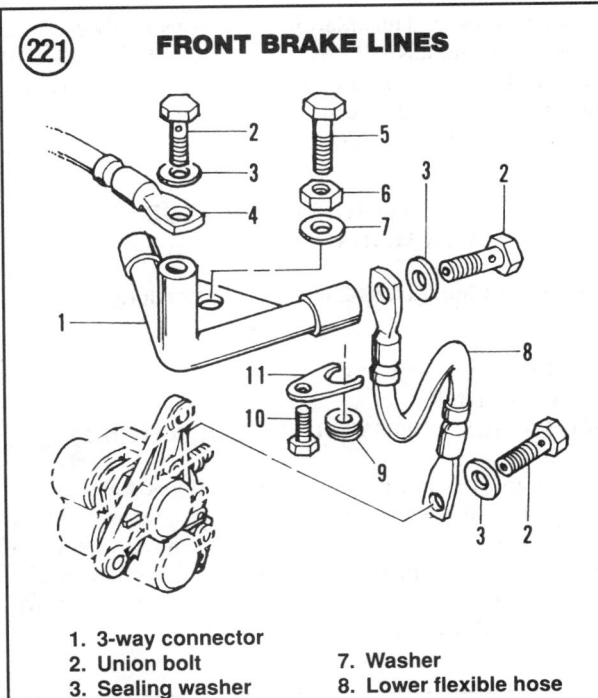

FRONT BRAKE LINES

1. 3-way connector
2. Union bolt
3. Sealing washer
4. Upper flexible hose
5. Mounting bolt
6. Nut
7. Washer
8. Lower flexible hose
9. Rubber grommet
10. Bolt
11. Hose bracket

10. Install new flexible hoses, sealing washers and union bolts in the reverse order of removal. Be sure to install new sealing washers in the correct positions.

11. Tighten all union bolts to torque specifications listed in **Table 11**.

12. Refill the master cylinder with fresh brake fluid clearly marked DOT 4. Bleed the front brake system as described in Chapter Twelve in the main body of this book.

> *WARNING*
> *Do not ride the motorcycle until your are sure that the brakes are operating properly.*

13. On models so equipped, install the front fairing.

BRAKE DISC
(K1, K100RS, K1100LT, K1100RSA)

Front Disc
Removal/Installation

1. Remove the front wheel (A, **Figure 224**) as described in the Chapter Ten section of this supplement.

> *NOTE*
> *Place a piece of wood or vinyl tube in the caliper(s) in place of the disc(s). This way, if the brake lever is inadvertently squeezed, the pistons will not be forced out of the cylinders. If this does happen, the caliper may have to be disassembled to reseat the pistons and the system will have to be bled.*

> *CAUTION*
> *Do not set the wheel down on the disc surface, as it may get scratched or warped. Set the tire sidewall on 2 blocks of wood.*

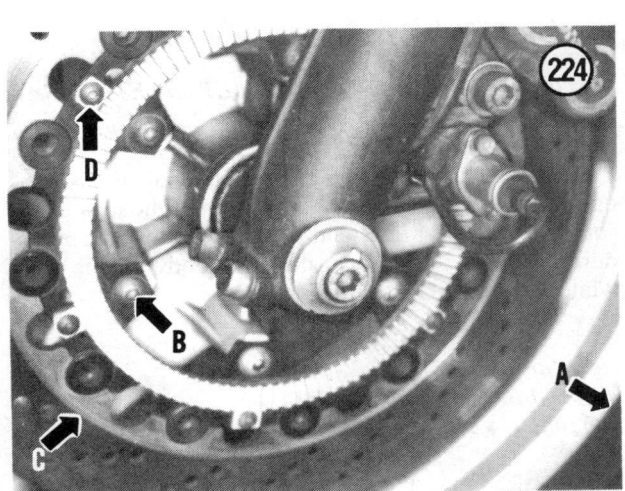

14

NOTE
On the front wheel, if working on a well run-in bike (high mileage), mark the brake disc with a "R" and "L" (on an attached piece of masking tape) so they will be reinstalled on the same side of the wheel from which they were removed. Older parts tend to form a wear pattern and should be reinstalled in the same location. The BMW discs are not marked in regard to right-hand or left-hand side.

2. Remove the Allen bolts and lockwashers (B, **Figure 224**) securing the disc to the front wheel hub. Remove the brake disc (C, **Figure 224**).

3. Inspect the brake discs for wear or damage. Make sure the pulse wheel mounting Allen bolts (D, **Figure 224**) are not damaged and are tight. Tighten if necessary.

4. Install by reversing these removal steps, noting the following.

5. Be sure to place a lock washer under the Allen bolts securing the brake disc. Tighten the bolts to the torque specification listed in **Table 11**.

ABS BRAKE SYSTEM

Brake Hose and
Line Replacement
(ABS Equipped Models)

CAUTION
Due to the sensitivity of the ABS system, brake bleeding should be performed by a BMW dealership. Do not disassemble the ABS system if the bike cannot be safely transported to the dealership.

Front hoses and lines
removal/installation
(K100RS [1993], K1 [1993], K1100LT and K1100RSA)

Refer to **Figure 225** or **Figure 226**.
The removal and installation procedures are the same as on previous models with the exception of the location of some of the hoses, lines and brackets. Follow the procedure in Chapter Twelve in the main body of this book while referring to these illustrations.

Rear hoses and lines
removal/installation
(K1100LT, K1100RSA [1994-on])

Refer to **Figure 227** for this procedure.

The removal and installation procedures are the same as on previous models with the exception of the location of some of the hoses, lines and brackets. Follow the procedure in Chapter Twelve in the main body of this book while referring to this illustration.

PRESSURE MODULATOR AND MOUNTING BRACKET

Refer to **Figures 228-230** for this procedure.

Front Pressure Regulator
Removal/Installation
(K1, K100RS, 1990-1993 K1100RSA, K1100LT)

The removal and installation procedures for the front pressure regulator (**Figure 231**) are the same as on previous models with the exception of the locations of some of the bolts, nuts and brackets. Follow the procedure in Chapter Twelve in the main body of this book while referring to this illustration.

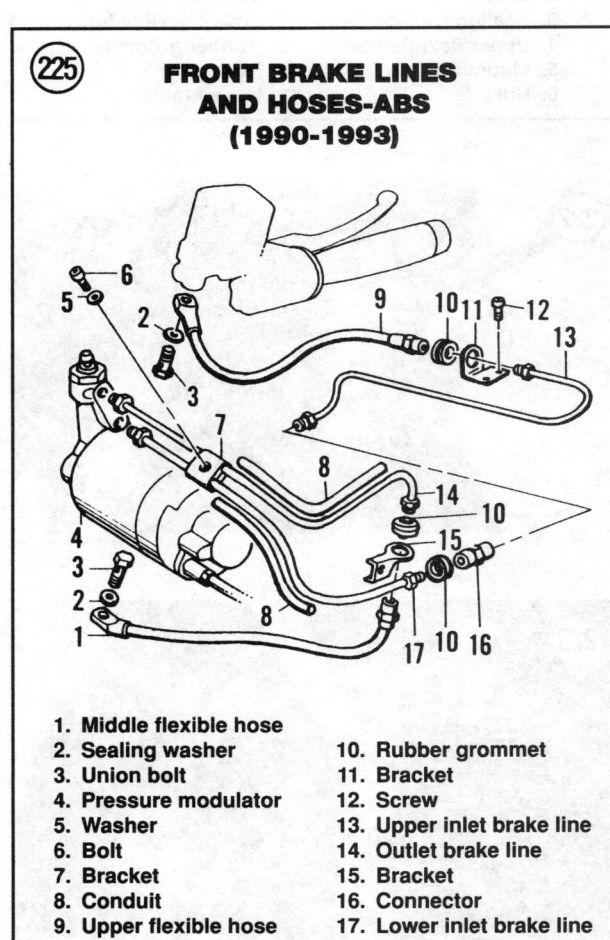

(225) **FRONT BRAKE LINES AND HOSES-ABS (1990-1993)**

1. Middle flexible hose
2. Sealing washer
3. Union bolt
4. Pressure modulator
5. Washer
6. Bolt
7. Bracket
8. Conduit
9. Upper flexible hose
10. Rubber grommet
11. Bracket
12. Screw
13. Upper inlet brake line
14. Outlet brake line
15. Bracket
16. Connector
17. Lower inlet brake line

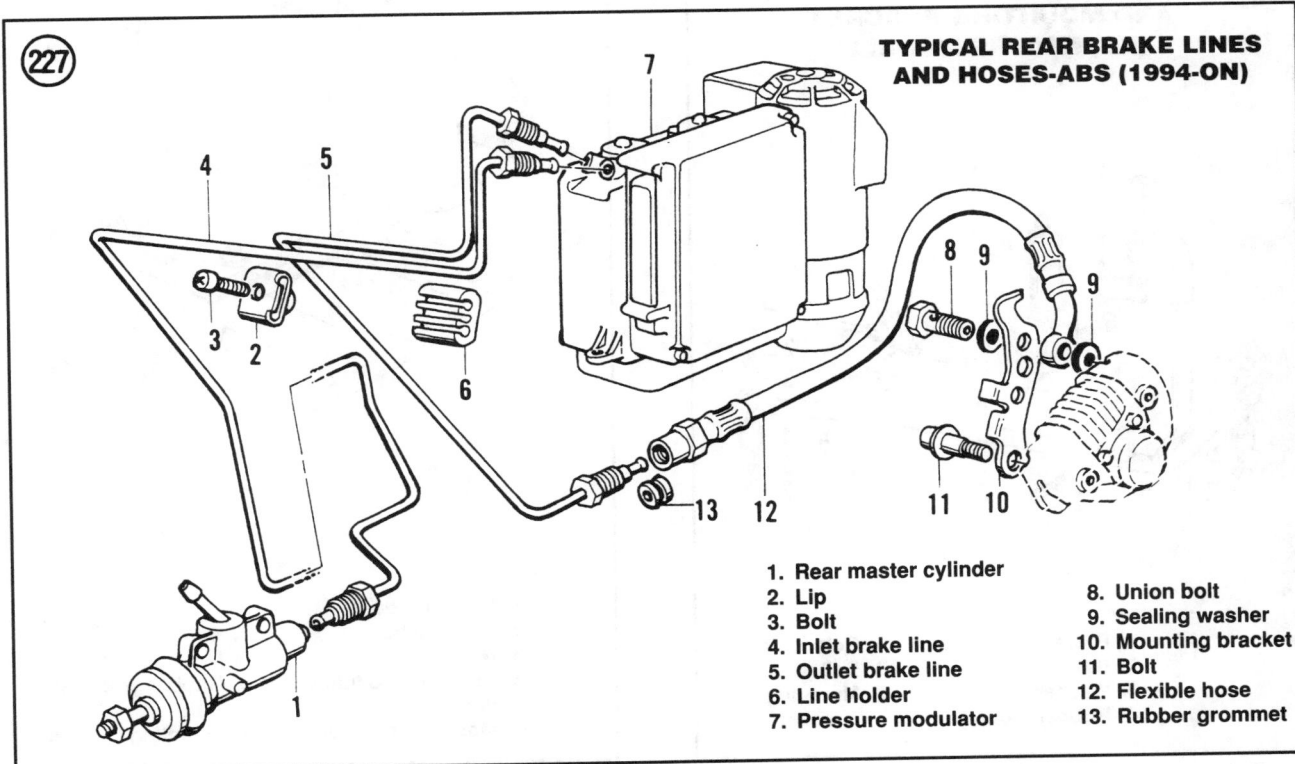

(226)

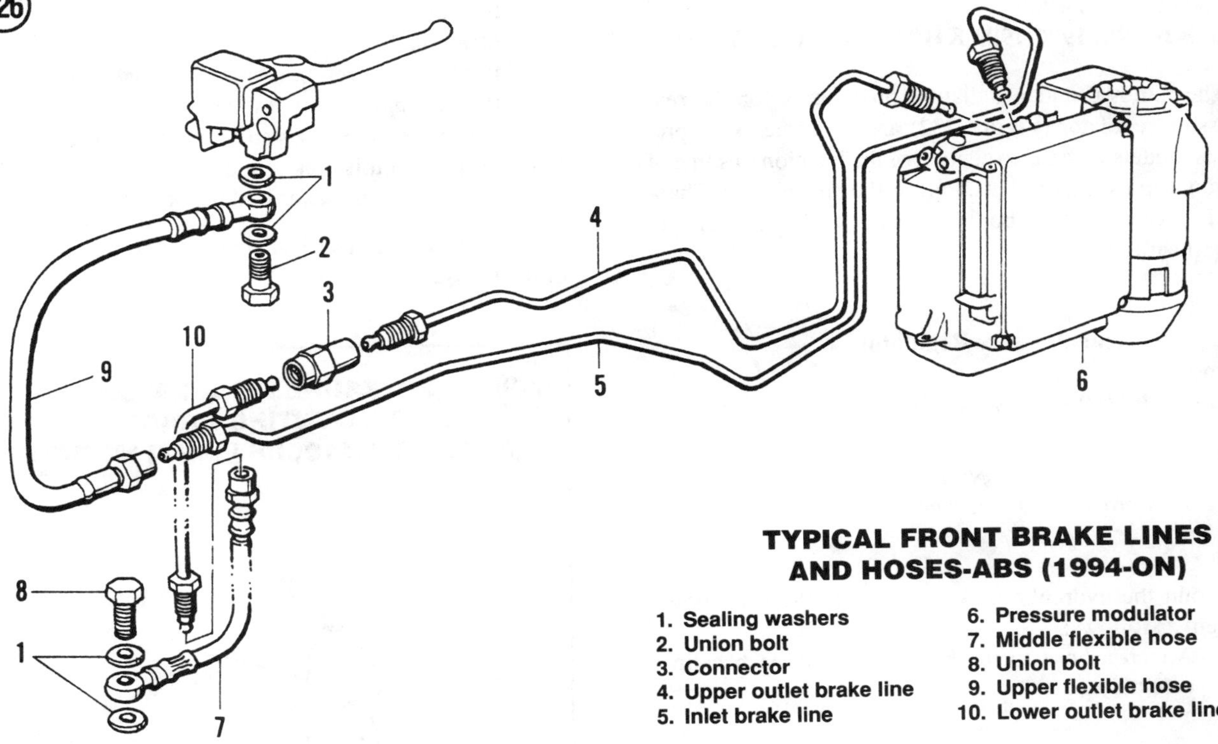

TYPICAL FRONT BRAKE LINES AND HOSES-ABS (1994-ON)

1. Sealing washers
2. Union bolt
3. Connector
4. Upper outlet brake line
5. Inlet brake line
6. Pressure modulator
7. Middle flexible hose
8. Union bolt
9. Upper flexible hose
10. Lower outlet brake line

(227)

TYPICAL REAR BRAKE LINES AND HOSES-ABS (1994-ON)

1. Rear master cylinder
2. Lip
3. Bolt
4. Inlet brake line
5. Outlet brake line
6. Line holder
7. Pressure modulator
8. Union bolt
9. Sealing washer
10. Mounting bracket
11. Bolt
12. Flexible hose
13. Rubber grommet

14

Rear Pressure Regulator
Removal/Installation
(K1, K100RS, 1990-1993 K1100RSA, K1100LT)

The removal and installation procedures for the rear pressure regulator (**Figure 232**) are the same as on previous models with the exception of the location of some of the bolts, nuts and brackets. Follow the procedure in Chapter Twelve in the main body of this book while referring to this illustration.

Front and Rear Pressure Regulator
Removal/Installation
(1994-on K1100RSA, K1100LT)

NOTE
This procedure is the same for both the front and the rear brake system.

1. Drain the hydraulic brake fluid from the front brake system as follows:
   a. Attach a hose to the bleed valve on each caliper assembly.
   b. Place the loose end of the hose in a container to catch the brake fluid.
   c. Open the bleed valve on each caliper and apply the front brake lever, or rear brake pedal until the brake fluid is pumped out of the system.
   d. Disconnect the hoses and tighten the bleed valves.
   e. Dispose of this brake fluid--*never* reuse brake fluid. Contaminated brake fluid may cause brake failure.

2. Disconnect the electrical connector from the backside of the pressure regulator.

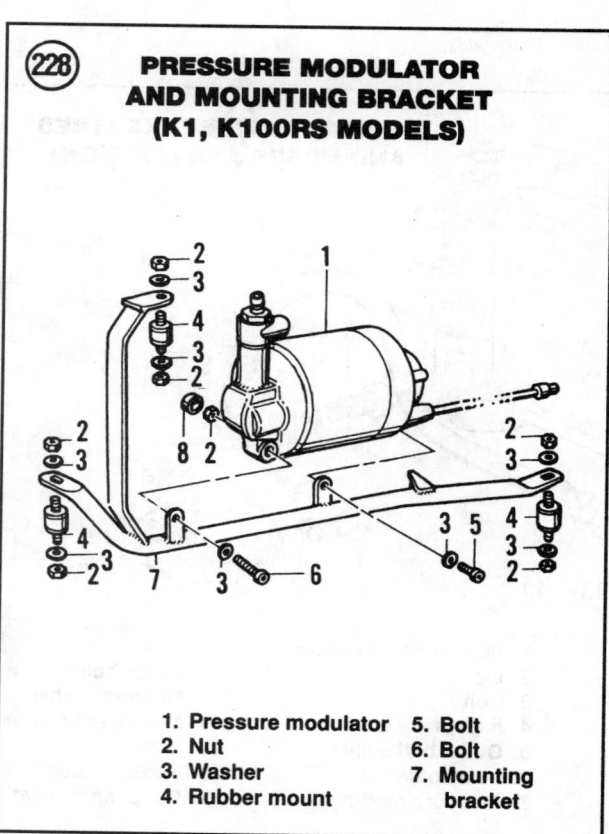

228 **PRESSURE MODULATOR AND MOUNTING BRACKET (K1, K100RS MODELS)**

1. Pressure modulator
2. Nut
3. Washer
4. Rubber mount
5. Bolt
6. Bolt
7. Mounting bracket

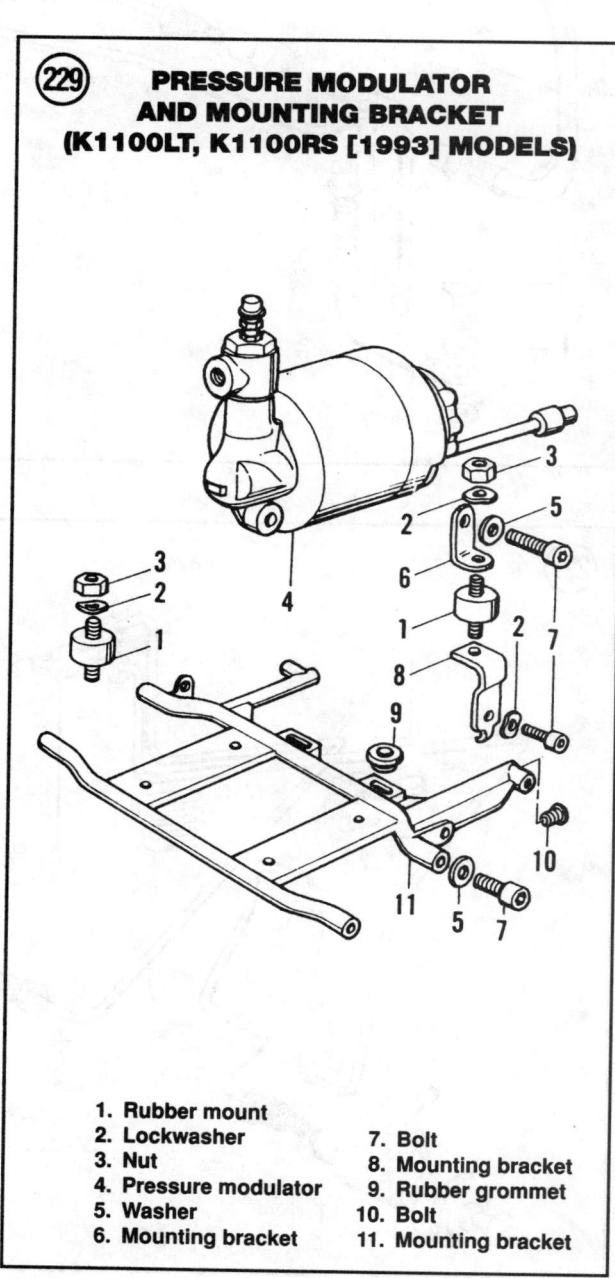

229 **PRESSURE MODULATOR AND MOUNTING BRACKET (K1100LT, K1100RS [1993] MODELS)**

1. Rubber mount
2. Lockwasher
3. Nut
4. Pressure modulator
5. Washer
6. Mounting bracket
7. Bolt
8. Mounting bracket
9. Rubber grommet
10. Bolt
11. Mounting bracket

TYPICAL PRESSURE REGULATOR (K1100LT, K1100RS [1994-ON])

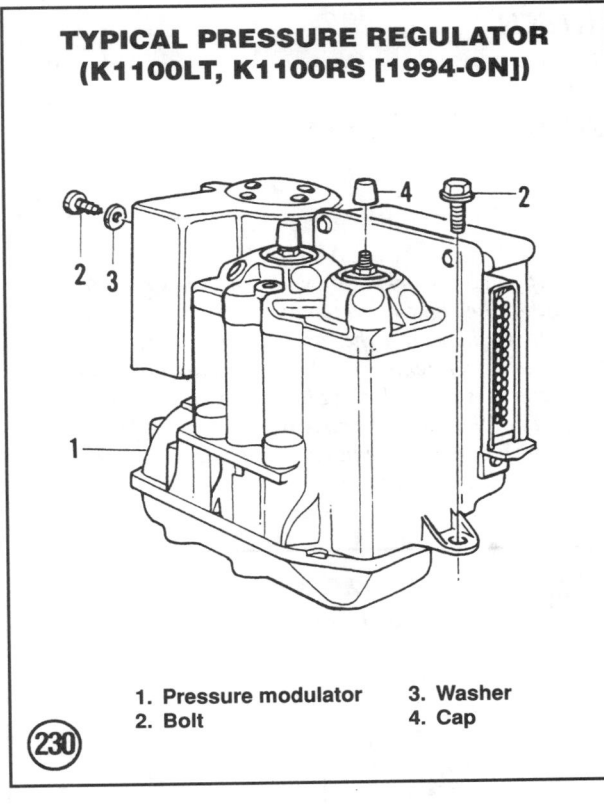

1. Pressure modulator
2. Bolt
3. Washer
4. Cap

(230)

(231)

(232)

3. Using a brake flare nut wrench, loosen and unscrew the flare nuts securing both the inlet and outlet brake lines to the pressure regulator.

4. Remove the bolts (**Figure 230**) securing the pressure regulator to the mounting bracket.

5. Remove the pressure regulator from the frame. Hold the unit in the upright position so the remaining brake fluid will not drain out of the brake line openings in the unit.

6. Install by reversing these removal steps, noting the following.

7. Install the pressure regulator onto the mounting bracket. Tighten the bolts securely.

8. Install the lines and tighten the flare nut fittings securely.

9. Refill the master cylinder(s) with fresh brake fluid clearly marked DOT 4. Have the front and/or rear brake system bled by a BMW dealer.

WARNING
Do not ride the motorcycle until you are sure that the brakes are operating properly.

10. Make sure the electrical connector is free of corrosion and is tight.

14

Table 11 BRAKE SYSTEM TORQUE SPECIFICATIONS

Item	N·m	ft.-lb.
Brake hose union bolts	7	5
Bleed screw	7	5
Front brake caliper mounting bolts		
Outer 2 bolts	5-10	3.6-7.4
Inner 2 bolts	25-35	18.4-25.8
Front brake disc-to-hub bolts	22	16.2

CHAPTER THIRTEEN

FRAME, BODY AND FRAME COMPONENTS

CAUTION
When removing a body component, make sure all of the fasteners have been removed prior to trying to remove the panel from another panel or from a mounting bracket. These body panels are very expensive and some of the mounting tabs are very small and tend to fracture if stressed beyond what they are designed to withstand. If a component will not come off using gentle to medium force—recheck to make sure all fasteners have been removed— you may find a hidden screw.

FOOTPEGS (K1)

Removal/Installation

Refer to **Figure 233** for this procedure. This illustration shows the left-hand footpeg assembly. The right-hand assembly is an exact mirror image and all parts are the identical.

The removal and installation procedures for the footpeg assembly is the same as on previous models with the exception of the location of some of the bolts, nuts and brackets. Follow the procedure in Chapter Thirteen in the main body of this book while referring to this illustration.

FENDERS

Front Fender (K1 Models)
Removal/Installation

NOTE
On this model, the front fender is referred to as a "mudguard." You may have to refer to it this way when ordering parts at a BMW dealer.

Refer to **Figure 234** for this procedure.
1. Place the bike on the centerstand.
2. Remove the bottom screw and washer on each side securing the fender halves to the brackets on the lower mounting bolt of the brake caliper.
3. Remove the 3 top screws and washers securing the right- and left-hand fender halves together.

CAUTION
If you are working by yourself, it is suggested that the right-hand fender half be taped to the fork slider after the top 3 screws and washers have been removed. These parts are not heavy but it is difficult to hold onto both parts after all of the fasteners have been removed. Do not drop either of the parts as the painted surface may be damaged.

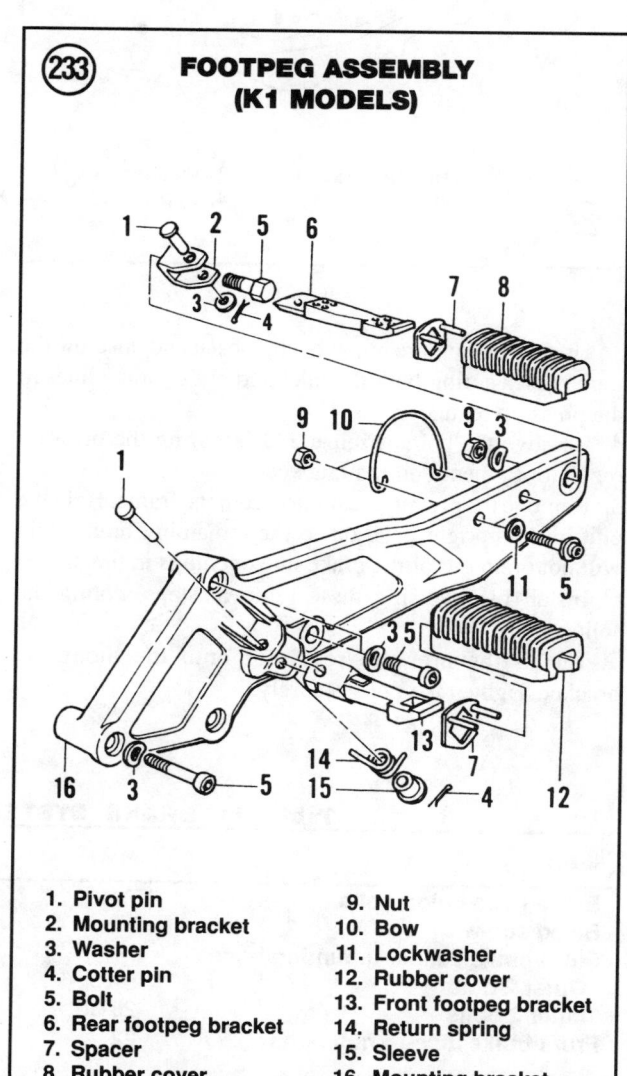

(233) FOOTPEG ASSEMBLY (K1 MODELS)

1. Pivot pin
2. Mounting bracket
3. Washer
4. Cotter pin
5. Bolt
6. Rear footpeg bracket
7. Spacer
8. Rubber cover
9. Nut
10. Bow
11. Lockwasher
12. Rubber cover
13. Front footpeg bracket
14. Return spring
15. Sleeve
16. Mounting bracket

4. Remove the 2 rear screws and washers securing the right- and left-hand fender halves together.

5. Carefully pull the left-hand fender half away from the wheel and out of the rubber sleeve at the fork support plate.

6. Remove the tape from the right-hand fender half.

7. Carefully pull the right-hand fender half away from the wheel and out of the rubber sleeve at the fork support plate.

8. Don't lose the special metal nuts crimped onto the left-hand fender half and on the mounting brackets.

9. Install by reversing these removal steps, noting the following.

10. Be sure to use the special metal nuts are in place on the left-hand fender at the mounting holes on the fender and the mounting brackets.

11. Slowly and in a criss-cross pattern tighten the screws securing the fender. Make sure the fender halves fit together correctly with no gaps or undo stress, then tighten the screws securely. Don't overtighten the bolts as the fender mounting areas may be damaged even with the bushings and special washers in place.

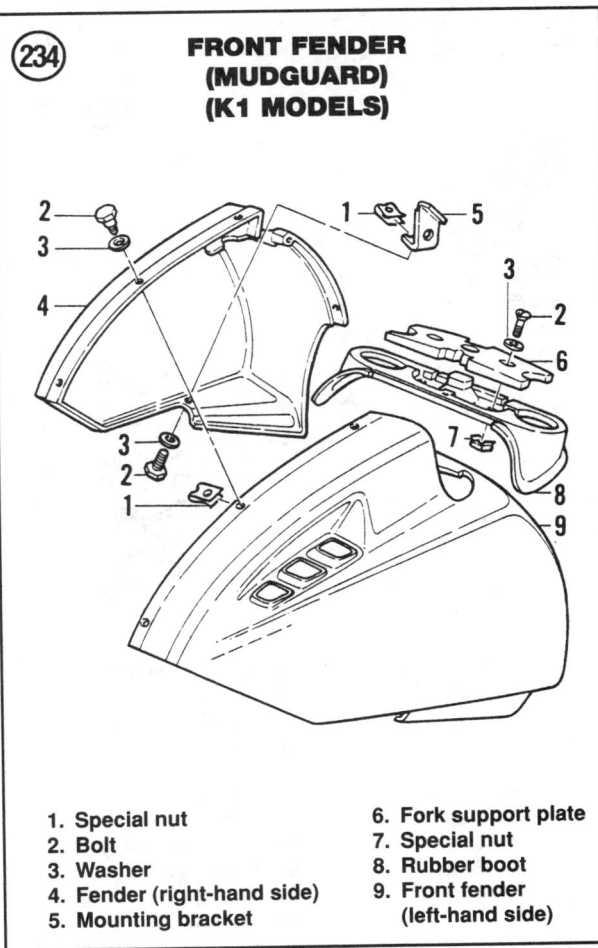

FRONT FENDER (MUDGUARD) (K1 MODELS)

1. Special nut
2. Bolt
3. Washer
4. Fender (right-hand side)
5. Mounting bracket
6. Fork support plate
7. Special nut
8. Rubber boot
9. Front fender (left-hand side)

SEAT

Removal/Installation (K1)

Refer to **Figure 235** for this procedure.

The removal and installation procedures for the seat assembly is the same as on K75C Models. Follow that procedure in Chapter Thirteen in the main body of this book.

Removal/Installation (K1100 LT and K1100RSA)

The removal and installation procedures for the seat assembly is the same as on previous models (all models except K75C) with the exception of the location of some of the bolts, nuts and brackets. Follow the procedure in Chapter Thirteen in the main body of this book.

REAR COWL

The rear cowl on the K1100LT and K1100RS models is the same as the one used on the K75 models except that the storage tray is not used on these models. Refer to Chapter Thirteen in the main body of this book for this procedure. The K1 model is not equipped with this piece of body work since the rear side panels and the seat take the place of this component.

BODY PANELS (K75RT)

The K75RT model is equipped with same body panels at the older model K100RT. Refer to the following illustrations and to the K100RT procedures in Chapter Thirteen in the main body of this book:

    a. *Front Fairing and Mounting Bracket (K100RT and K100LT Models).*

    b. *Knee Pad and Storage Compartment (K100RT and K100LT Models).*

    c. *Radiator Trim Panel (K100RT and K100LT Models).*

    d. *Lower Side Panel (K100RT and K100LT Models).*

    e. *Lower Side Panel Mounting Bracket (K100RT and K100LT Models).*

    f. *Windshield (K100LT Models).*

14

BODY PANELS
(K1 MODELS)

Front Fairing
Removal/Installation

Refer to **Figures 236-241** for this procedure.

The illustrations show mainly the left-hand panels, brackets and the mounting hardware. The right-hand components are an exact mirror image and are attached in the same manner unless otherwise specified.

1. Disconnect the battery negative lead as described under *Battery* in Chapter Three in the main body of this book.

2. Remove the knee pad cover on each side.

3. Remove the single screw at the bottom of the knee pad. Carefully unhook the knee pad from the inner cover above it. Remove both knee pads.

4. On the right-hand side, unlock and remove the tool kit cover.

5. Remove the screws securing the inner cover to the upper portion of the front fairing.

6. Carefully pull the front portion of the inner cover, move it forward to release the retaining hook at the rear. Lift the inner cover up and disconnect the electrical connector(s) from the switch(es). Remove both inner covers.

7. Remove the screws and washers securing the engine spoiler to the front fairing lower side panel on each side. Remove the engine spoiler.

8. Remove the lower side panels as follows:
   a. Remove the rear bolts and washers securing the lower side panel.
   b. Remove the bolts located behind the air duct at the upper rear portion.
   c. Remove the front lower bolt and washer securing the panel to the radiator panel.
   d. Check that all fasteners have been removed, then remove the lower side panel.
   e. Repeat for the lower trim panel on the other side.

9. Remove the radiator trim panel as follows:
   a. Remove the lower screws and washers securing the radiator trim panel to the mounting bracket on each side.
   b. Hold onto the radiator trim panel and remove the screws securing the radiator trim panel to the front fairing upper portion.
   c. Carefully remove the radiator trim panel.

10. Remove the lower side panels as follows:
   a. Remove the rear bolts and washers securing the lower side panel. Don't lose the rubber grommets and metal collar in the mounting hole in the side panel.
   b. Remove the bolts along the upper edge securing the lower side panel to the front fairing upper portion.
   c. Remove the lower side panel and the metal inner panel.
   d. Repeat for the lower trim panel on the other side.

NOTE
The next several steps require the aid of an assistant. The upper portion of the fairing is not heavy but is difficult to hold in place while removing the mounting bolts and nuts.

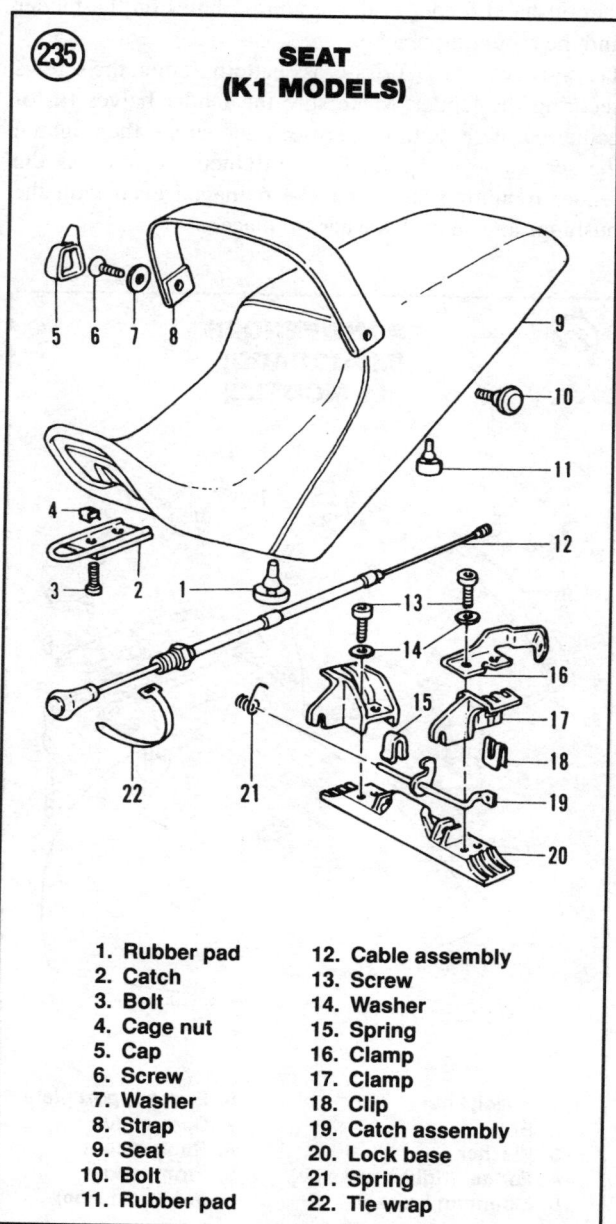

235 **SEAT (K1 MODELS)**

1. Rubber pad
2. Catch
3. Bolt
4. Cage nut
5. Cap
6. Screw
7. Washer
8. Strap
9. Seat
10. Bolt
11. Rubber pad
12. Cable assembly
13. Screw
14. Washer
15. Spring
16. Clamp
17. Clamp
18. Clip
19. Catch assembly
20. Lock base
21. Spring
22. Tie wrap

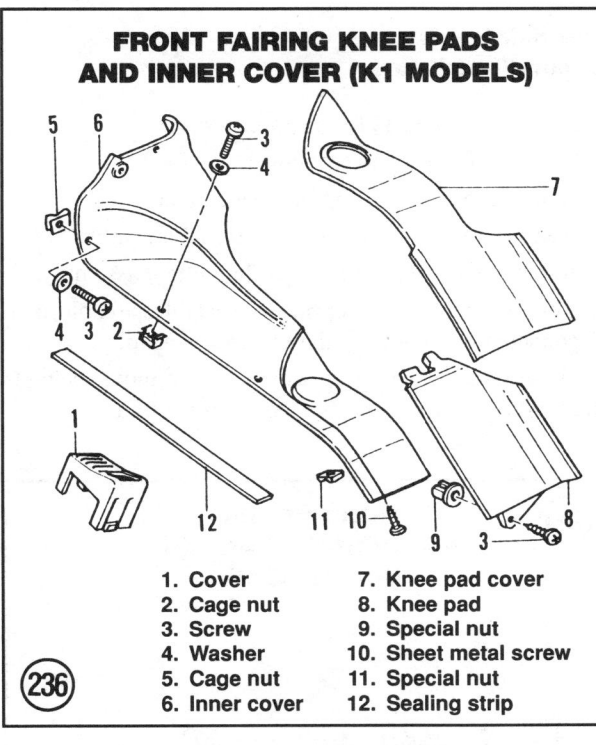

FRONT FAIRING KNEE PADS AND INNER COVER (K1 MODELS)

1. Cover
2. Cage nut
3. Screw
4. Washer
5. Cage nut
6. Inner cover
7. Knee pad cover
8. Knee pad
9. Special nut
10. Sheet metal screw
11. Special nut
12. Sealing strip

(236)

11. Have an assistant hold onto the front of the front fairing and perform the following:

   a. Remove the lower bolt on each side securing the front fairing upper portion to the frame.
   b. Remove the screws and washers securing the front fairing directly under the headlight assembly.
   c. Remove the retaining screw at the holder for the coolant reservoir tank.
   d. Remove the retaining screw at the coolant reservoir tank and disconnect the hoses from the tank.
   e. Disconnect the turn signal electrical connectors from the main wiring harness.
   f. To protect the finish, place a couple of blankets on the workbench or floor for the front fairing to sit on after removal.
   g. Remove the lower bolt and washer and the upper special nuts, lockwasher and washers securing the fairing to the fairing mounting bracket.
   h. Carefully pull the front fairing forward and hold it in the horizontal position.
   i. Have an assistant disconnect the electrical connectors from the headlight and parking lights.
   j. Remove the coolant recovery tank from the fairing.

(237)

FRONT FAIRING LOWER SIDE PANEL AND RADIATOR TRIM PANEL (K1 MODELS)

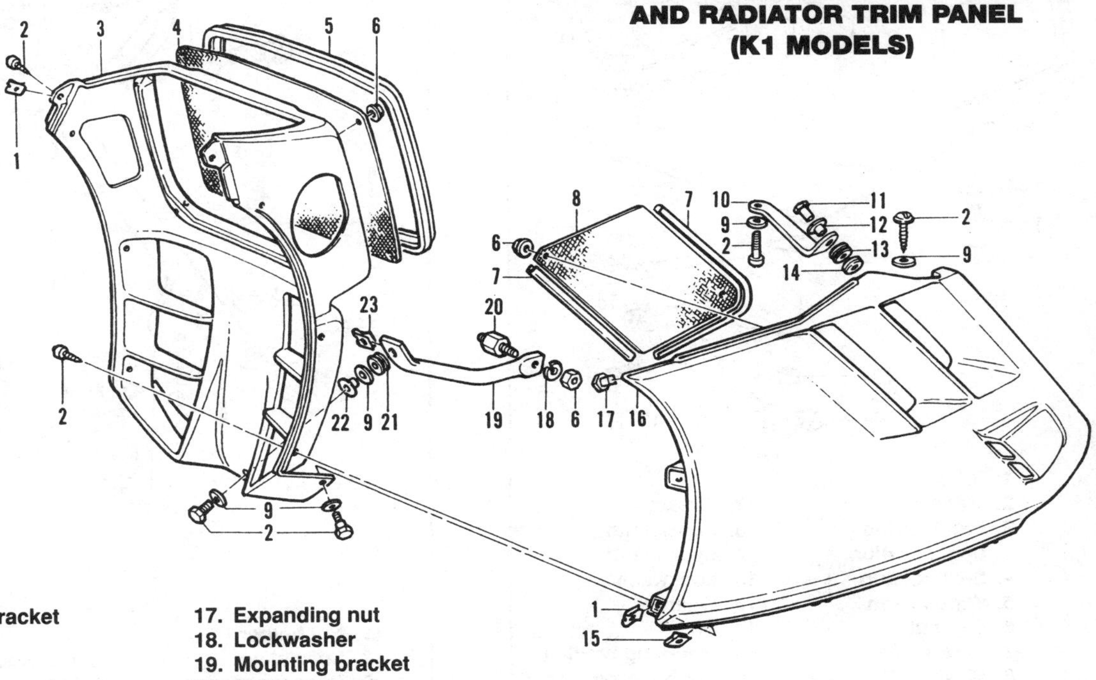

1. Cage nut
2. Sheet metal screw
3. Radiator trim panel
4. Screen
5. Gasket
6. Nut
7. Edge trim
8. Screen
9. Washer
10. Mounting bracket
11. Cap nut
12. Collar
13. Rubber grommet
14. Base fitting
15. Cage nut
16. Lower side panel
17. Expanding nut
18. Lockwasher
19. Mounting bracket
20. Rubber mount
21. Rubber grommet
22. Collar
23. Cage nut

14

k. Remove the front fairing from the mounting bracket and set it on the blankets.

12. If necessary, remove the bolts securing the front fairing mounting bracket and the lower faring mounting bracket to the frame and remove the mounting bracket(s).

13. Install by reversing these removal steps, noting the following.

14. Tighten the screws and nuts securely. Don't overtighten the screws or nuts as the plastic mounting bosses may be damaged.

15. Make sure all electrical connectors are free of corrosion and are tight.

Rear Side Panels
Removal/Installation

Refer to **Figure 242** for this procedure.

1. Remove the seat and seat cover.

2. Remove the storage compartment covers.

3. Remove the holder for the turn signal assembly.

4. Remove the holder for the tail/brakelight assembly.

5. Remove the washer securing the seat release cable, then disconnect the cable from the seat mechanism.

6. Within the storage compartment area, remove the bolts and washers securing the side cover to the frame.

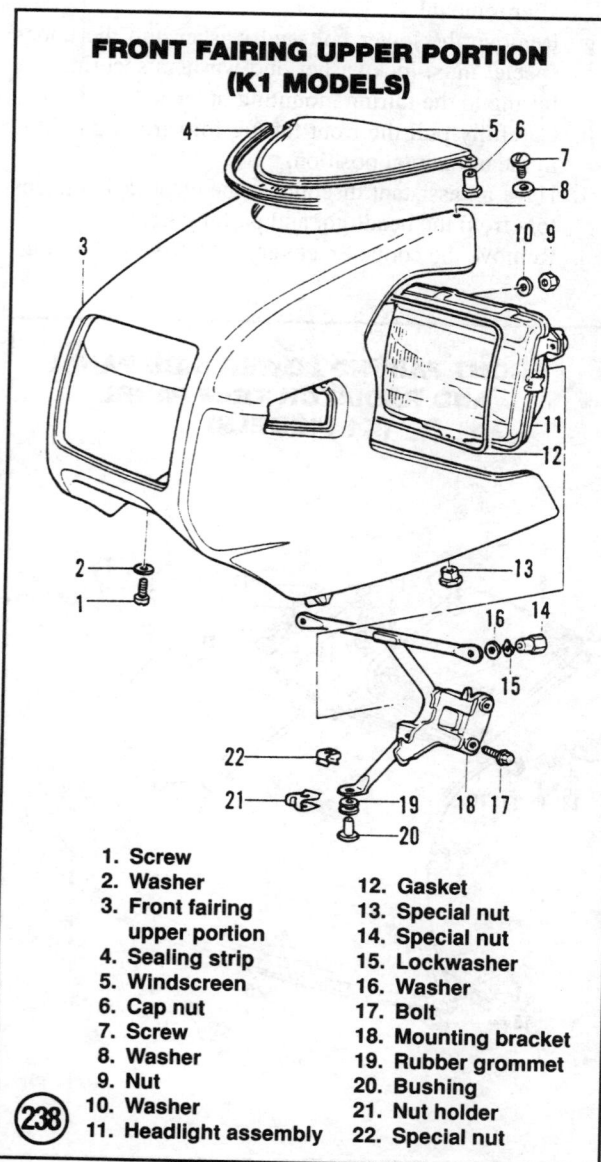

**FRONT FAIRING UPPER PORTION
(K1 MODELS)**

1. Screw
2. Washer
3. Front fairing
   upper portion
4. Sealing strip
5. Windscreen
6. Cap nut
7. Screw
8. Washer
9. Nut
10. Washer
11. Headlight assembly
12. Gasket
13. Special nut
14. Special nut
15. Lockwasher
16. Washer
17. Bolt
18. Mounting bracket
19. Rubber grommet
20. Bushing
21. Nut holder
22. Special nut

(238)

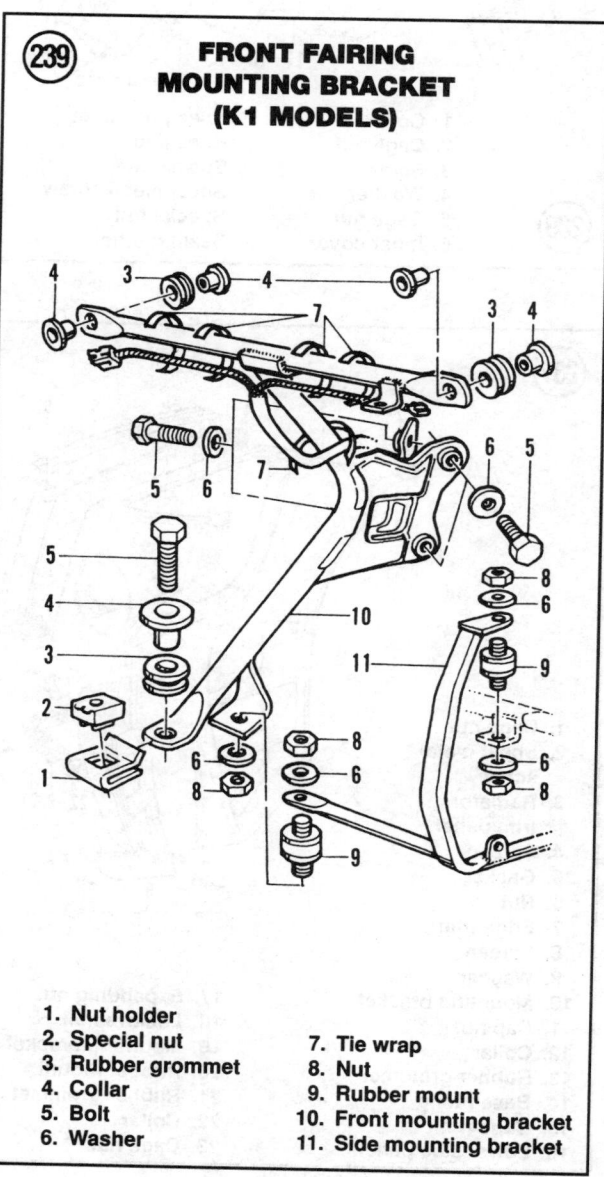

(239) **FRONT FAIRING
MOUNTING BRACKET
(K1 MODELS)**

1. Nut holder
2. Special nut
3. Rubber grommet
4. Collar
5. Bolt
6. Washer
7. Tie wrap
8. Nut
9. Rubber mount
10. Front mounting bracket
11. Side mounting bracket

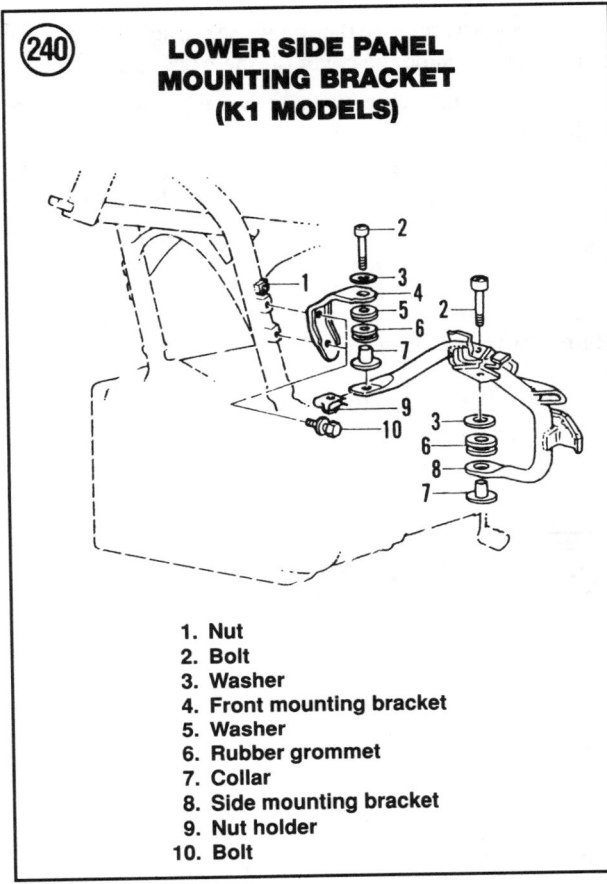

240 **LOWER SIDE PANEL MOUNTING BRACKET (K1 MODELS)**

1. Nut
2. Bolt
3. Washer
4. Front mounting bracket
5. Washer
6. Rubber grommet
7. Collar
8. Side mounting bracket
9. Nut holder
10. Bolt

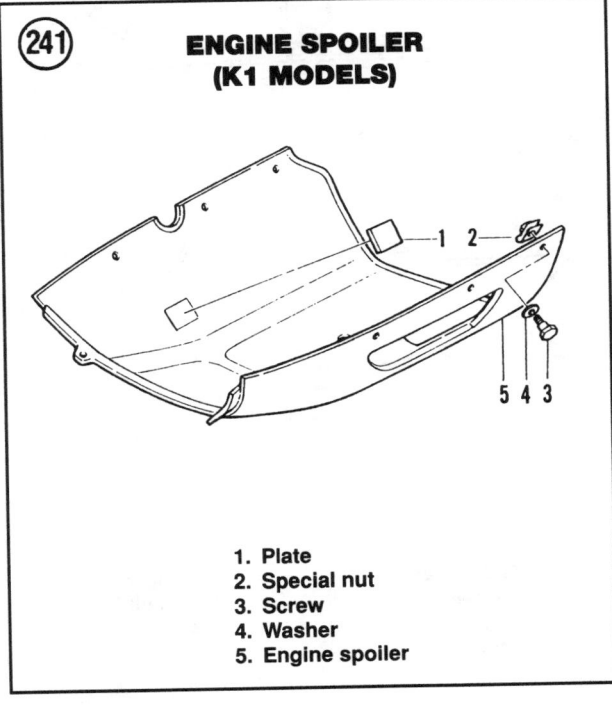

241 **ENGINE SPOILER (K1 MODELS)**

1. Plate
2. Special nut
3. Screw
4. Washer
5. Engine spoiler

7. Remove the bolts securing the rear cover and remove the cover and mount.

8. Remove the bolts and washers securing the top rear portion of the rear side cover to the frame.

9. Remove the bolts and washers securing the rear side cover to the footpeg assembly.

10. Carefully pull the front portion of the rear side cover out of the front retaining clip.

11. Carefully pull the rear side cover up and away from the frame and remove it.

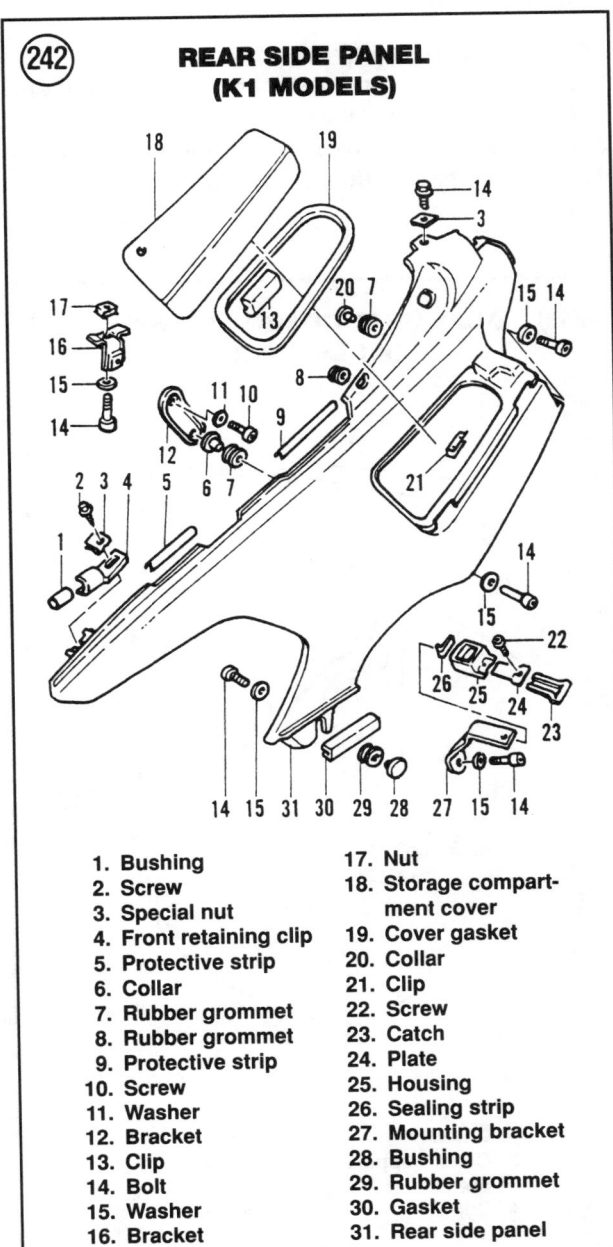

242 **REAR SIDE PANEL (K1 MODELS)**

1. Bushing
2. Screw
3. Special nut
4. Front retaining clip
5. Protective strip
6. Collar
7. Rubber grommet
8. Rubber grommet
9. Protective strip
10. Screw
11. Washer
12. Bracket
13. Clip
14. Bolt
15. Washer
16. Bracket
17. Nut
18. Storage compartment cover
19. Cover gasket
20. Collar
21. Clip
22. Screw
23. Catch
24. Plate
25. Housing
26. Sealing strip
27. Mounting bracket
28. Bushing
29. Rubber grommet
30. Gasket
31. Rear side panel

14

12. If necessary, repeat for the rear side cover on the other side.

13. Install by reversing these removal steps, noting the following.

14. Tighten the screws and nuts securely. Don't overtighten the screws or nuts as the plastic mounting bosses may be damaged.

15. Make sure all electrical connectors are free of corrosion and are tight.

Dual Seat Cover and Pad

Refer to **Figure 243** for this procedure.

1. Remove the screw and washer on each side securing the seat cover to the side of the seat.

2. Carefully pull up on the front of the seat and disengage the holder at the rear from the rear handle. Remove the cover.

3. If necessary, remove the screws securing the pad to the seat cover and slide the cover off the front of the cover.

4. Install by reversing these removal steps, noting the following.

5. Tighten the screws securely. Don't overtighten the screws or nuts as the plastic mounting bosses may be damaged.

Fuel Tank Cover
Removal/Installation

Refer to **Figure 244** for this procedure.

1. Remove the fuel tank as described in Chapter Seven in the main body of this book.

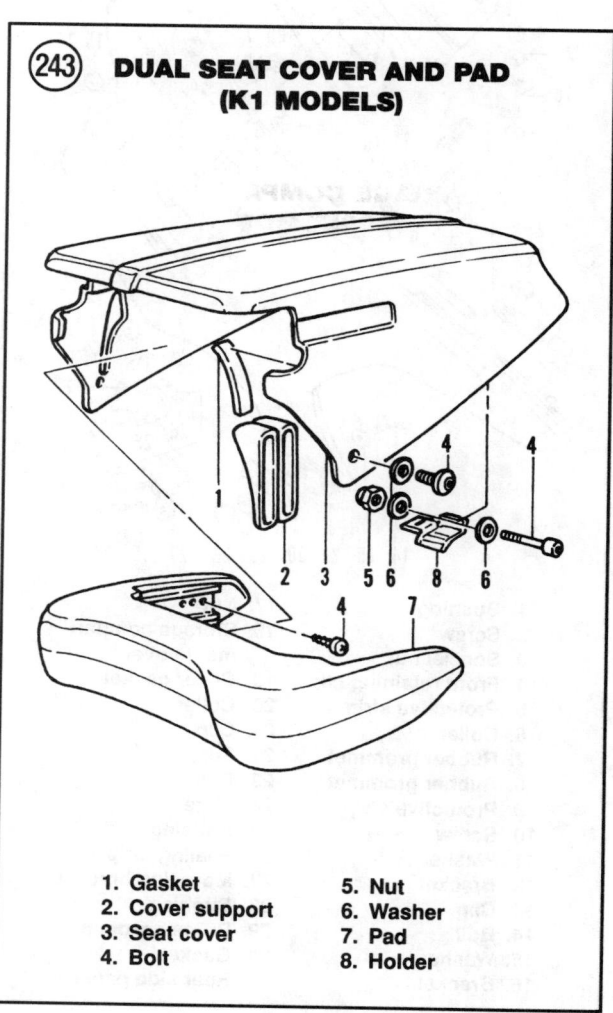

(243) DUAL SEAT COVER AND PAD (K1 MODELS)

1. Gasket
2. Cover support
3. Seat cover
4. Bolt
5. Nut
6. Washer
7. Pad
8. Holder

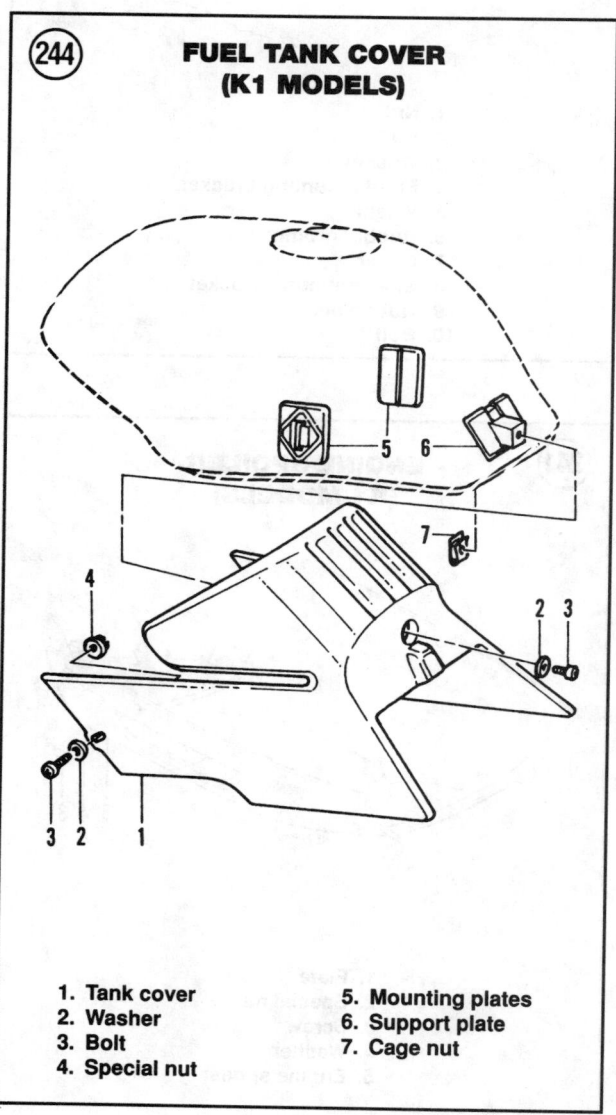

(244) FUEL TANK COVER (K1 MODELS)

1. Tank cover
2. Washer
3. Bolt
4. Special nut
5. Mounting plates
6. Support plate
7. Cage nut

2. Remove the screws and washers on each side and at the rear securing the cover to the mounting plates on the fuel tank. Remove the cover.

3. Install by reversing these removal steps, noting the following.

4. Tighten the screws securely. Don't overtighten the screws as the plastic mounting bosses may be damaged.

Rear Handle
Removal/Installation

Refer to **Figure 245** for this procedure.

1. Remove the seat, seat cover and the rear side panels.

2. Disconnect the electrical connector from the tail-light/brake light assembly.

3. Remove the bolts and washers securing the tail-light/brake light assembly to the carriers and remove the taillight/brake light assembly.

4. Remove the bolts and washers securing the handle to the support brackets and remove the handle.

5. Remove the bolts, washers and cage nuts securing the support bracket to the frame. Remove the bracket from the

frame. Don't lose the bushing located in the lower surface of each rubber bushing at each mounting boss.

6. Discard the cage nuts as new ones must be installed.

7. Repeat for the other support bracket.

8. Install by reversing these removal steps, noting the following.

9. Make sure the rubber grommet and the bushing are installed in each mounting boss.

10. Use new cage nuts as the old ones have lost some of their holding ability.

11. Tighten the bolts securely. Don't overtighten the bolts as the mounting bosses may be damaged.

BODY PANELS
(K1100LT)

Front Fairing
Removal/Installation

Refer to **Figures 246-252** for this procedure.

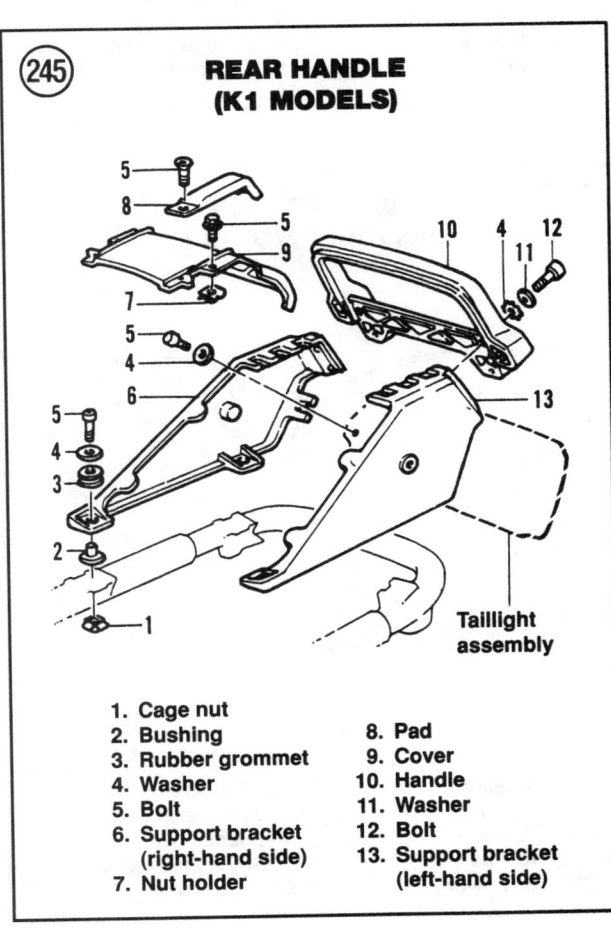

245

REAR HANDLE (K1 MODELS)

Taillight assembly

1. Cage nut
2. Bushing
3. Rubber grommet
4. Washer
5. Bolt
6. Support bracket (right-hand side)
7. Nut holder
8. Pad
9. Cover
10. Handle
11. Washer
12. Bolt
13. Support bracket (left-hand side)

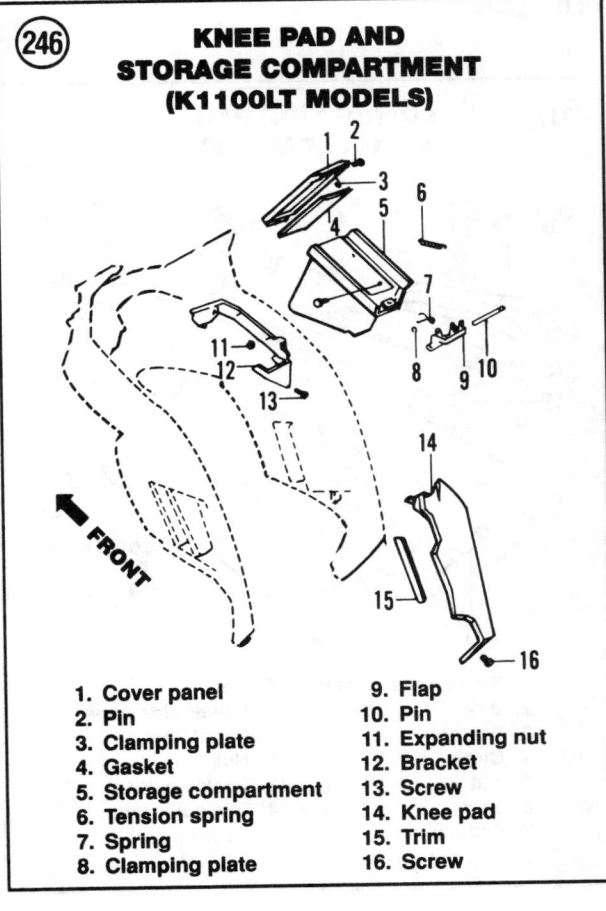

246

KNEE PAD AND STORAGE COMPARTMENT (K1100LT MODELS)

FRONT

1. Cover panel
2. Pin
3. Clamping plate
4. Gasket
5. Storage compartment
6. Tension spring
7. Spring
8. Clamping plate
9. Flap
10. Pin
11. Expanding nut
12. Bracket
13. Screw
14. Knee pad
15. Trim
16. Screw

14

The illustrations show mainly the left-hand panels, brackets and the mounting hardware. The right-hand components are an exact mirror image and are attached in the same manner unless otherwise specified.

1. Remove the frame left-hand side cover.

2. Disconnect the battery negative lead as described under *Battery* in Chapter Three in the main body of this book.

3. Remove the knee pads as follows:
   a. Remove the single screw at the bottom of the knee pad.
   b. Remove the screws at the top of the knee pad.
   c. Carefully remove the knee pad from the front fairing upper portion and lower side panel.
   d. Repeat for the knee pad on the other side.

4. Remove the storage compartment as follows:
   a. Remove the storage compartment cover panel.
   b. Remove the screws securing the storage compartment and remove the storage compartment.
   c. Repeat for the storage compartment on the other side.

5. Remove the fuel tank as described under *Fuel Tank Removal/Installation* in Chapter Seven in the main body of this book.

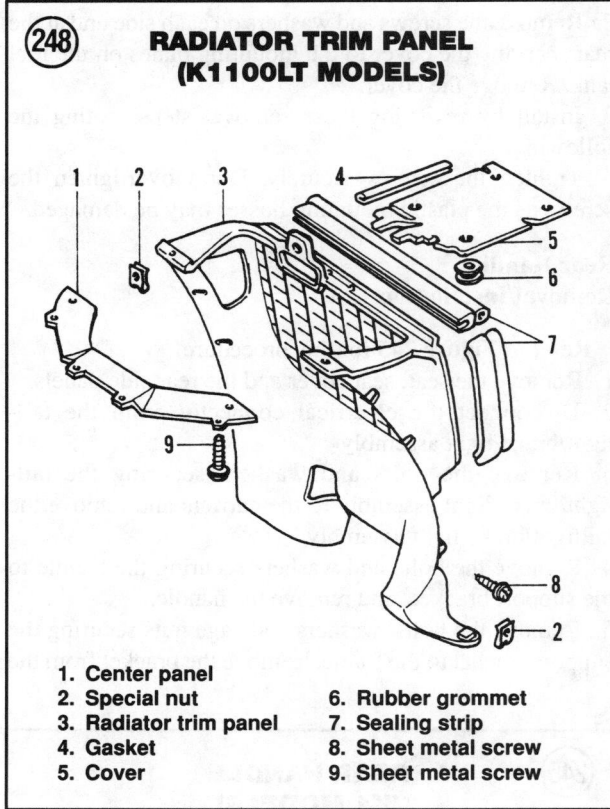

248 RADIATOR TRIM PANEL (K1100LT MODELS)

1. Center panel
2. Special nut
3. Radiator trim panel
4. Gasket
5. Cover
6. Rubber grommet
7. Sealing strip
8. Sheet metal screw
9. Sheet metal screw

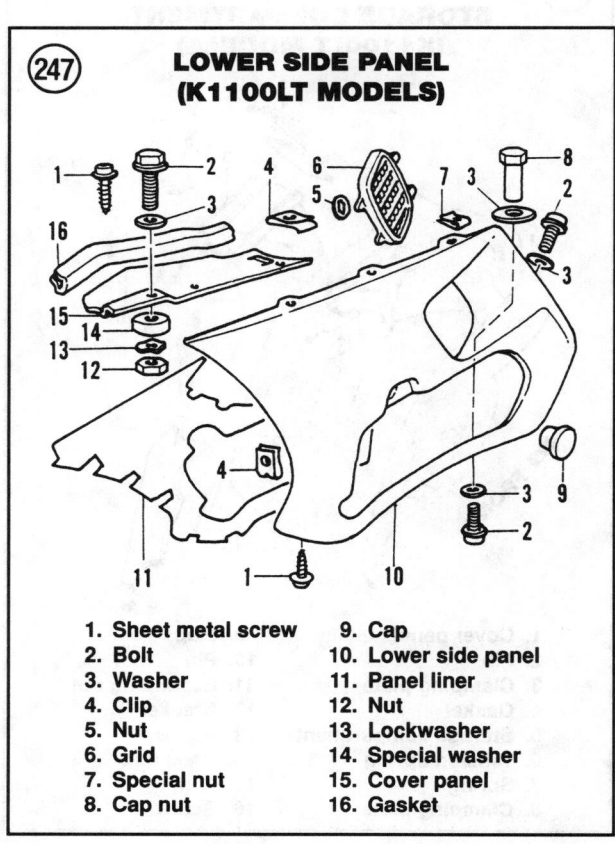

247 LOWER SIDE PANEL (K1100LT MODELS)

1. Sheet metal screw
2. Bolt
3. Washer
4. Clip
5. Nut
6. Grid
7. Special nut
8. Cap nut
9. Cap
10. Lower side panel
11. Panel liner
12. Nut
13. Lockwasher
14. Special washer
15. Cover panel
16. Gasket

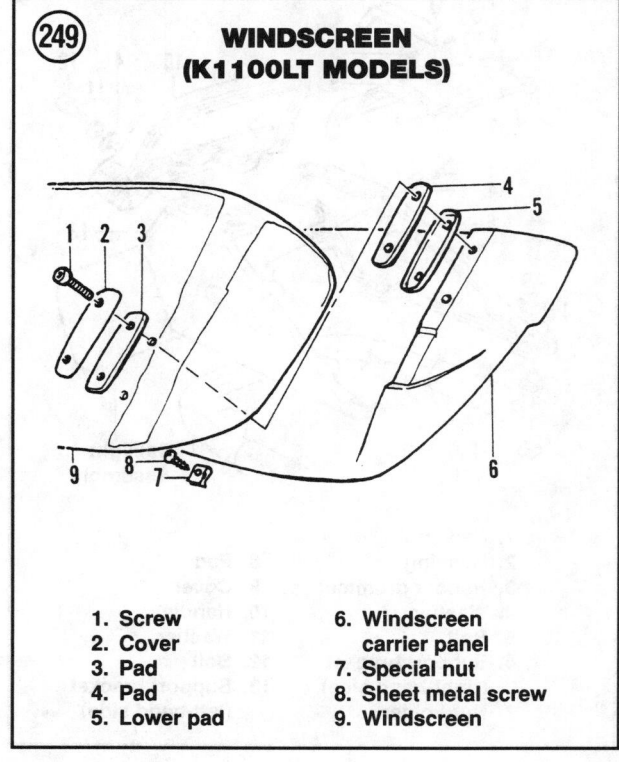

249 WINDSCREEN (K1100LT MODELS)

1. Screw
2. Cover
3. Pad
4. Pad
5. Lower pad
6. Windscreen carrier panel
7. Special nut
8. Sheet metal screw
9. Windscreen

⑳₅₀

**FRONT FAIRING
UPPER SECTION
(K1100LT MODELS)**

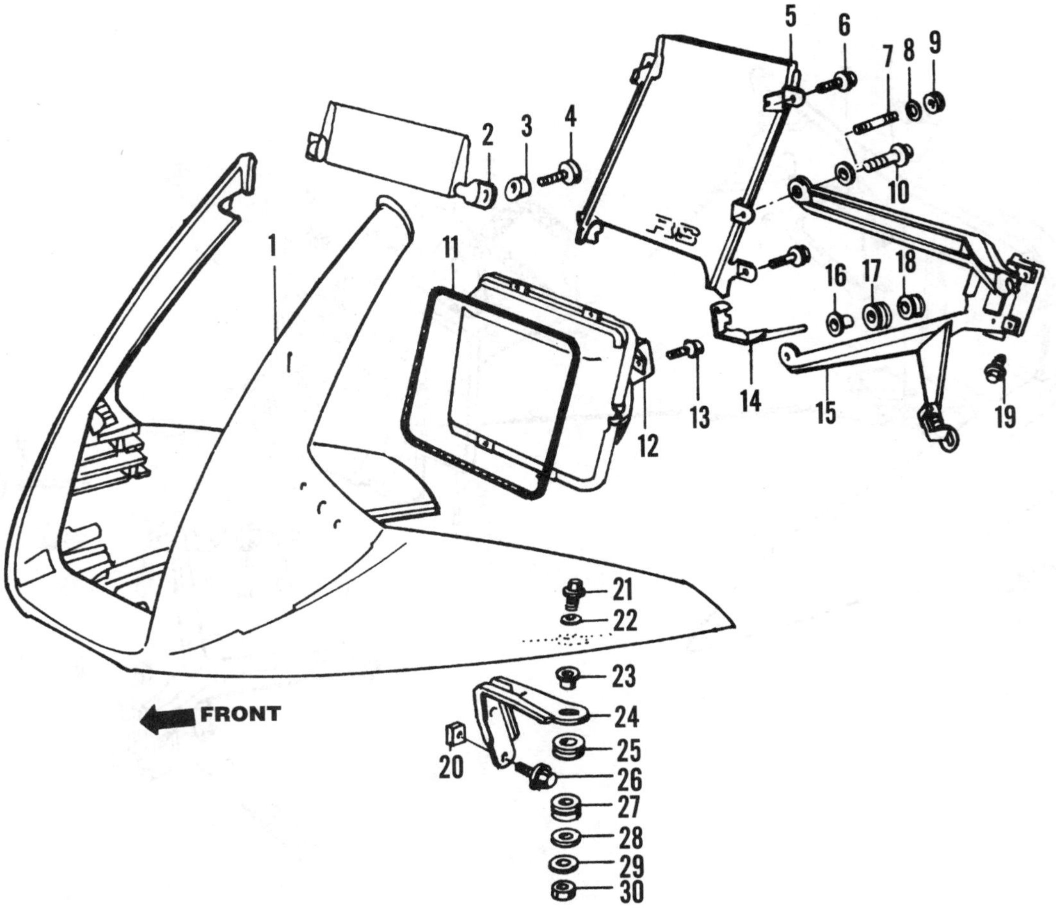

◀ **FRONT**

1. Front fairing upper portion
2. Deflector
3. Clamp
4. Bolt
5. Windscreen
6. Bolt
7. Threaded stud
8. Washer
9. Nut
10. Bolt
11. Gasket
12. Headlight
13. Bolt
14. Bracket
15. Fairing mountng bracket

16. Bushing
17. Rubber grommet
18. Rubber grommet
19. Screw
20. Nut
21. Bolt
22. Washer
23. Bushing
24. Bracket
25. Rubber grommet
26. Bolt
27. Rubber grommet
28. Washer
29. Lockwasher
30. Nut

14

(251)

FRONT FAIRING LOWER SECTION
AND MOUNTING BRACKET
(K1100LT MODELS)

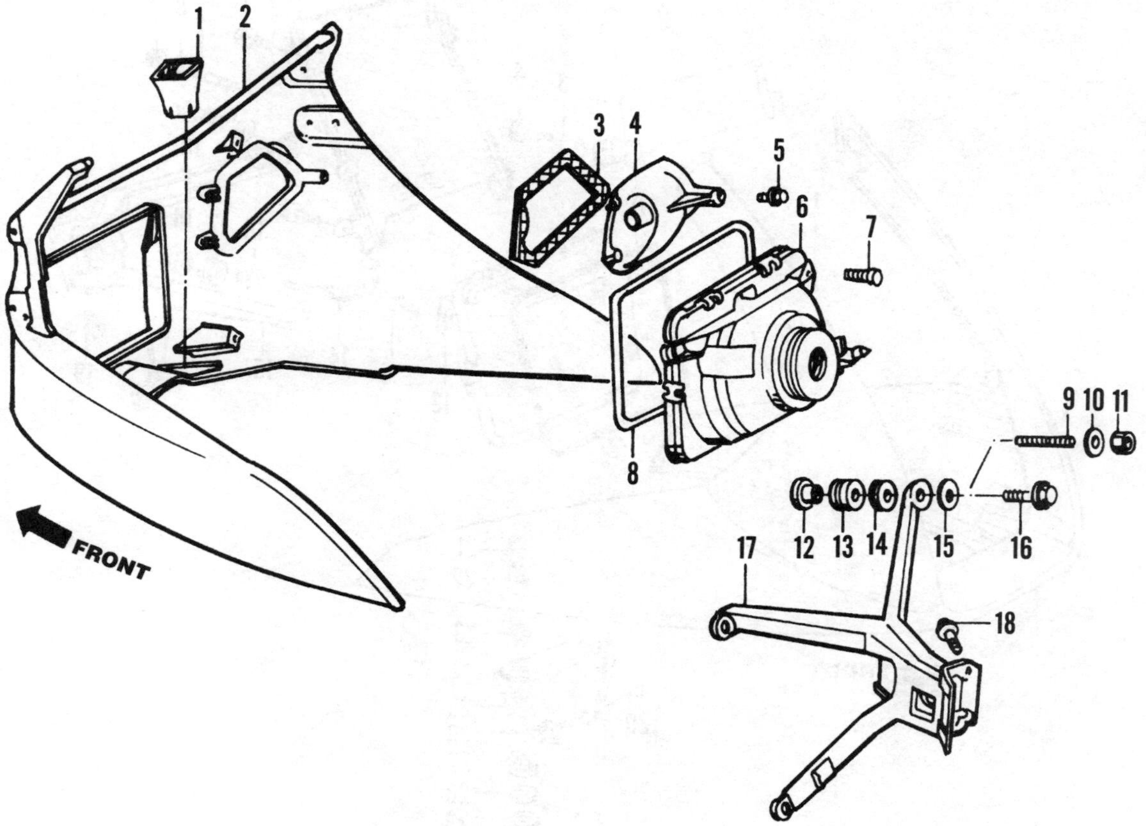

FRONT

1. Intermediate piece
2. Front fairing
3. Gasket
4. Right turn signal assembly
5. Screw
6. Headlight assembly
7. Bolt
8. Gasket
9. Spring
10. Washer
11. Nut
12. Metal collar
13. Rubber grommet
14. Base
15. Washer
16. Bolt
17. Front fairing mounting bracket
18. Bolt

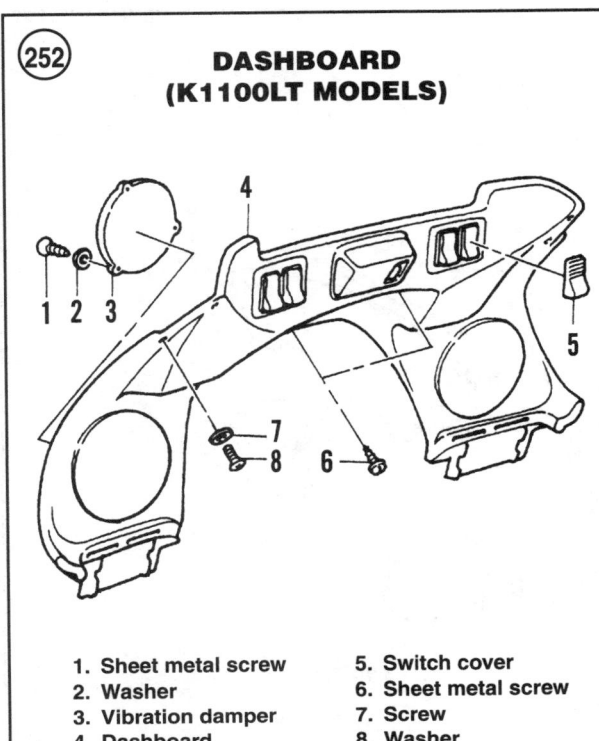

DASHBOARD (K1100LT MODELS)

1. Sheet metal screw
2. Washer
3. Vibration damper
4. Dashboard
5. Switch cover
6. Sheet metal screw
7. Screw
8. Washer

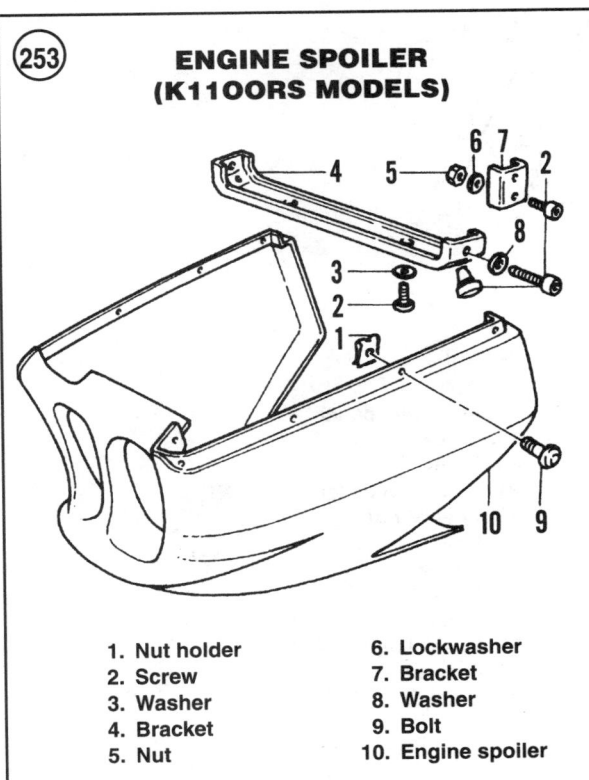

ENGINE SPOILER (K1100RS MODELS)

1. Nut holder
2. Screw
3. Washer
4. Bracket
5. Nut
6. Lockwasher
7. Bracket
8. Washer
9. Bolt
10. Engine spoiler

6. Remove the bolts and washers securing the cover to the top of the lower side panel and remove the cover.
7. Remove the lower side panels as follows:
  a. Remove the rear bolt, washer and nut securing the lower side panel to the small mounting bracket.
  b. Remove the bolts along the front edge securing the lower side panel to the radiator trim panel.
  c. Remove the lower side panel and the inner liner.
  d. Repeat for the lower trim panel on the other side.
8. Remove the instrument panel as follows:
  a. Remove the top bolts and washer securing the instrument panel to the upper section of the front fairing.
  b. Carefully pull the instrument panel out and disconnect the electrical connectors to the instruments.
  c. Remove the instrument panel.
9. Remove the radiator trim panel as follows:
  a. Hold onto the radiator trim panel and remove the screws securing center panel and the radiator trim panel to the bracket.
  b. Carefully remove the radiator trim panel.
10. To remove the windscreen assembly, perform the following:
  a. Remove the screws, covers and pads securing the windscreen to the windscreen panel. After removal, protect the windscreen from scratches and damage.
  b. Remove the screws securing the windscreen panel to the front fairing.
  c. Disconnect the water ducts at the top nipple.
  d. Disconnect the electrical connector from the control motor.
  e. Remove the windscreen assembly from the upper fairing panel.
11. Disconnect the headlight and turn signal electrical connectors from the main wiring harness.

NOTE
The next step requires the aid of an assistant. The fairing is not heavy but is difficult to hold in place while removing the mounting bolts and nuts.

12. Have an assistant hold onto the front of the front fairing and perform the following:
  a. Remove the bolt on each side securing the front fairing upper portion to the frame.
  b. To protect the finish, place a couple of blankets on the workbench or floor for the front fairing to sit on after removal.
  c. Remove the bolts and washers securing the fairing to the fairing mounting bracket.
  d. Carefully pull the front fairing forward and remove the front fairing from the mounting bracket and set in on the blankets.
13. If necessary, remove teh bolts securing the mounting bracket to the frame and remove the mounting bracket.
14. Install by reverseing these removal steps, noting the following.

14

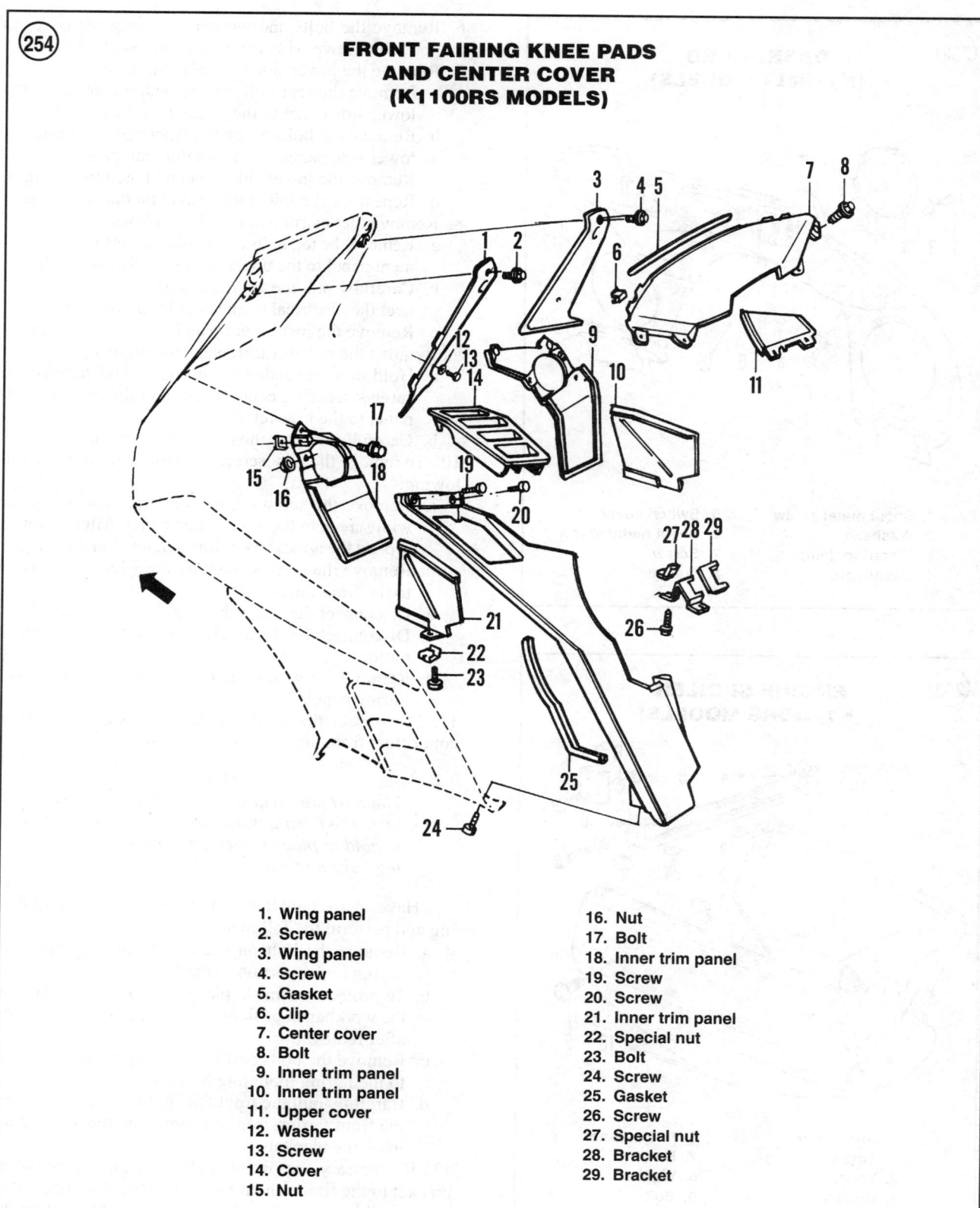

254

FRONT FAIRING KNEE PADS
AND CENTER COVER
(K1100RS MODELS)

1. Wing panel
2. Screw
3. Wing panel
4. Screw
5. Gasket
6. Clip
7. Center cover
8. Bolt
9. Inner trim panel
10. Inner trim panel
11. Upper cover
12. Washer
13. Screw
14. Cover
15. Nut

16. Nut
17. Bolt
18. Inner trim panel
19. Screw
20. Screw
21. Inner trim panel
22. Special nut
23. Bolt
24. Screw
25. Gasket
26. Screw
27. Special nut
28. Bracket
29. Bracket

15. Tighten the screws and nuts securely. Don't overtighten the screws or nuts as the plastic mounting bosses may be damaged.

16. Make sure all electrical connectors are free of corrosion and are tight.

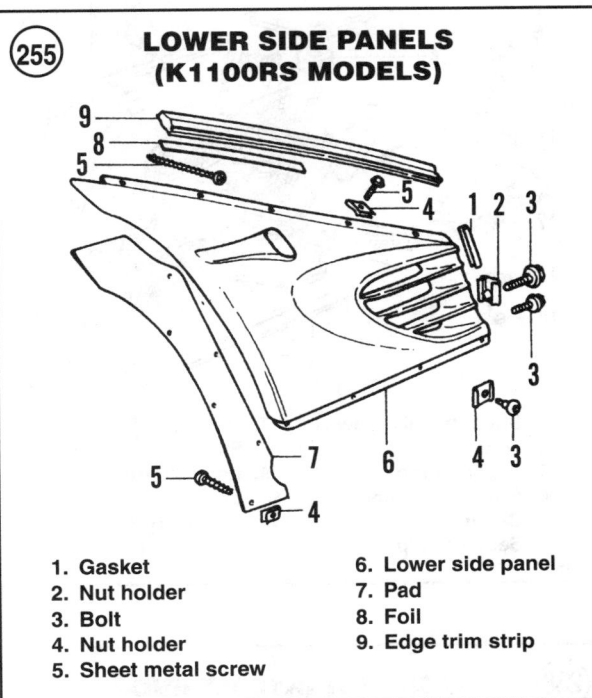

LOWER SIDE PANELS
(K1100RS MODELS)

1. Gasket
2. Nut holder
3. Bolt
4. Nut holder
5. Sheet metal screw
6. Lower side panel
7. Pad
8. Foil
9. Edge trim strip

Engine Spoiler
Removal/Installation

1. If you are working alone, place wood block(s) or a cardboard box under the spoiler to hold it in place after the mounting bolts are removed.

2. Remove the 4 bolts and washers on the bottom surface of the spoiler.

3. Remove the cardboard box or wood block(s) from under the spoiler and remove the spoiler.

4. If you are working alone, place wood block(s) or a cardboard box under the mounting bracket to hold it in place after the mounting bolts are removed.

5. Remove the bolts on each side securing the mounting bracket to the engine.

6. Remove the cardboard box or wood block(s) from under the mounting bracket and remove the mounting bracket.

7. Install by reversing these removal stpes, noting the following.

8. Tighten the bolts securely.

BODY PANELS
(K1100RS)

Front Fairing
Removal/Installation

Refer to **Figures 253-256** for this procedure.

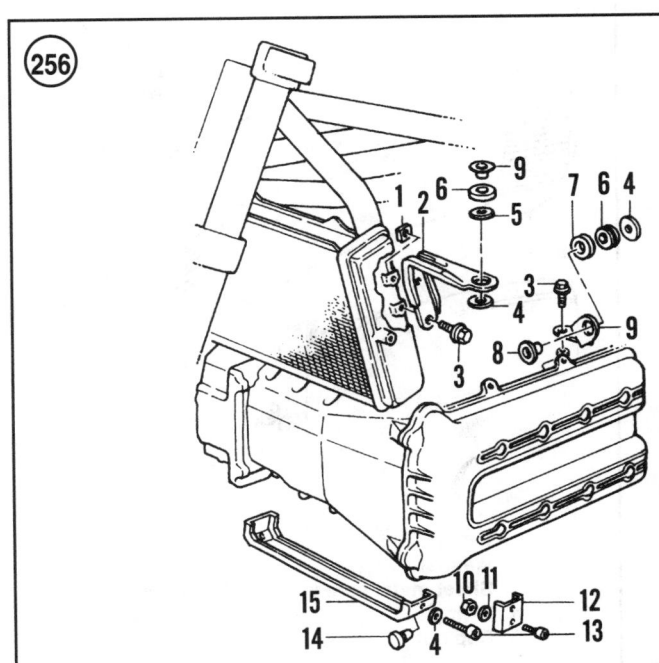

LOWER SIDE PANEL
MOUNTING BRACKETS
(K1100RS MODELS)

1. Nut
2. Upper mounting bracket
3. Bolt
4. Washer
5. Washer
6. Rubbert grommet
7. Base
8. Mounting bracket
9. Collar
10. Nut
11. Lockwasher
12. Bracket
13. Screw
14. Rubber stopper
15. Lower mounting bracket

14

The illustrations show mainly the left-hand panels and brackets. The right-hand components are an exact mirror image and are attached in the same manner unless otherwise specified.

1. Remove the frame left-hand side cover.

2. Disconnect the battery negative lead as described under *Battery* in Chapter Three in the main body of this book.

3. To remove the engine spoiler, perform the following:
   a. If you are working alone, place wood block(s) or a cardboard box under the spoiler in to place after the mounting bolts are removed.
   b. Remove the lower, front and rear bolts on each side securing the spoiler.
   c. Remove the screws securing the upper portion to the lower side panel.
   d. Remove the cardboard box or wood block(s) from under the spoiler and remove the spoiler.

4. Remove the knee pads as follows:
   a. Remove the single screw at the bottom of the knee pad.
   b. Remove the screws at the top of the knee pad.
   c. Unhook the clip at the mid-point of the knee pad, then carefully remove the knee pad from the front fairing upper portion and lower side panel.
   d. Repeat for the knee pad on the other side.
   e. Remove the screws securing the inner trim panel and remove the trim panel from each side.

5. Remove the lower side panel as follows:
   a. Remove the rear lower bolt securing the lower side panel to the mounting bracket on the frame.
   b. Remove the bolts securing the side panel to the radiator trim panel.
   c. Remove the screws along the upper edge securing the lower side panel to the front fairing upper portion.
   d. Remove the lower side panel.
   e. Repeat for the lower trim panel on the other side.

6. Remove the radiator trim panel as follows:
   a. Hold onto the radiator trim panel and remove the screws securing the radiator trim panel to the front fairing upper portion.
   b. Pull out on the lower portion of the radiator trim panel and carefully remove the radiator trim panel.

7. Carefully lift up on the small upper covers and unhook them from the center cover.

8. Remove the bolts securing the wing panel to the side of the windscreen and remove the wing panel. Repeat for the other side.

9. Remove the bolts securing the center cover and remove the center cover.

10. Remove the bolts securing the inner trim panel and remove the trim panel. Repeat for the other side.

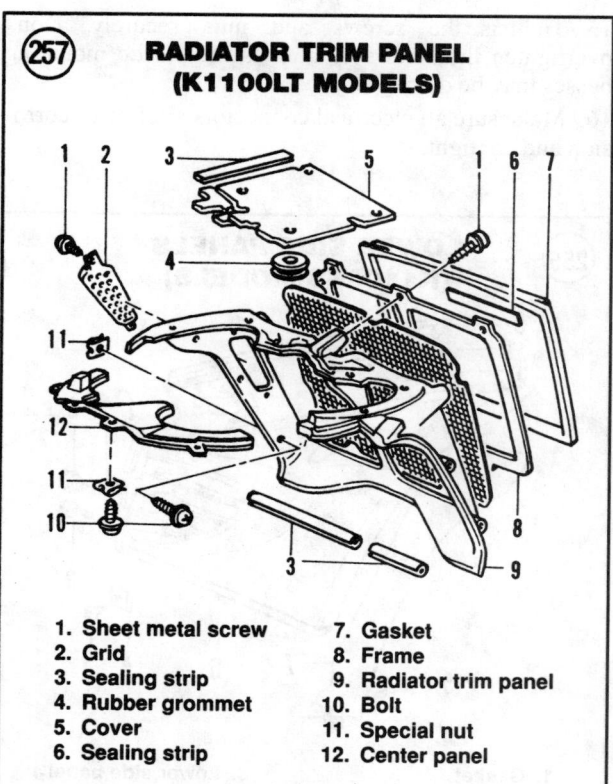

(257) **RADIATOR TRIM PANEL (K1100LT MODELS)**

1. Sheet metal screw	7. Gasket
2. Grid	8. Frame
3. Sealing strip	9. Radiator trim panel
4. Rubber grommet	10. Bolt
5. Cover	11. Special nut
6. Sealing strip	12. Center panel

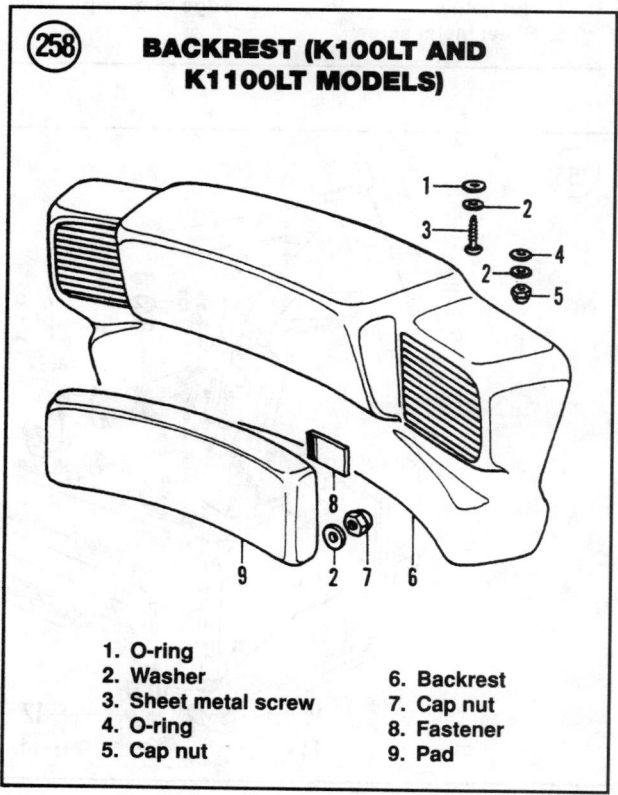

(258) **BACKREST (K100LT AND K1100LT MODELS)**

1. O-ring	
2. Washer	
3. Sheet metal screw	6. Backrest
4. O-ring	7. Cap nut
5. Cap nut	8. Fastener
	9. Pad

11. Loosen the horn mounting nuts and pivot the horns up and out of the way.

12. Remove the screw securing the horn guide channel and remove the guide channel. Repeat for the other side.

13. Disconnect the headlight and turn signal electrical connectors from the main wiring harness.

NOTE
The next step requires the aid of an assistant. The fairing is not heavy but is difficult to hold

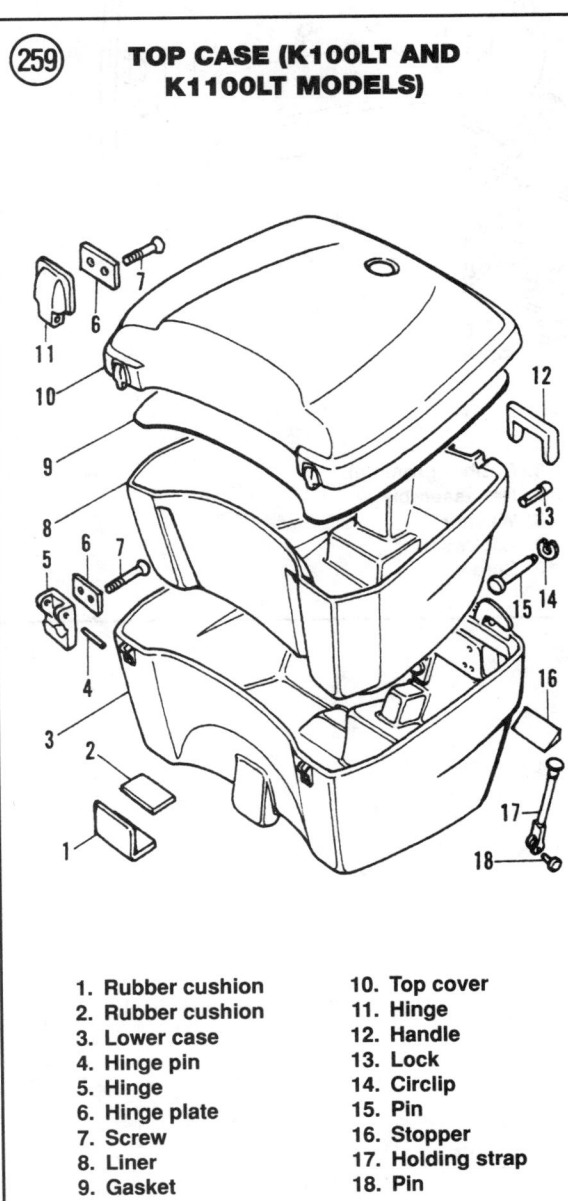

(259) TOP CASE (K100LT AND K1100LT MODELS)

1. Rubber cushion
2. Rubber cushion
3. Lower case
4. Hinge pin
5. Hinge
6. Hinge plate
7. Screw
8. Liner
9. Gasket
10. Top cover
11. Hinge
12. Handle
13. Lock
14. Circlip
15. Pin
16. Stopper
17. Holding strap
18. Pin

in place while removing the mounting bolts and nuts.

14. Have an assistant hold onto the front of the front fairing and perform the following:
   a. Remove the side bolt on each side securing the front fairing upper portion to the side mounting bracket.
   b. Remove the upper bolt on each side securing the front fairing upper portion to the mounting bracket.
   c. Remove the middle bolt on each side securing the front fairing middle portion to the mounting bracket.
   d. To protect the finish, place a couple of blankets on the workbench or floor for the front fairing to sit on after removal.
   e. Carefully pull the front fairing forward and remove the front fairing from the mounting bracket and set in on the blankets.

15. If necessary, remove the bolts securing the mounting bracket to the frame and remove the mounting bracket.

16. Install by reversing these removal steps, noting the following.

17. Tighten the screws and nuts securely. Don't over-tighten the screws or nuts as the plastic mounting bosses may be damaged.

18. Make sure all electrical connectors are free of corrosion and are tight.

LUGGAGE AND RACK

Backrest Removal/Installation (K100LT and K1100LT)

Refer to **Figure 258** for this procedure.
1. Open the top cover of the top case.
2. Remove the cap nuts, washers and O-rings securing the backrest to the top cover and remove the backrest assembly.
3. Install by reversing these removal steps, noting the following.
4. Tighten the cap nuts securely and be sure to install the O-ring seals. The O-rings keep any moisture from entering the top case.

Top Case Removal/Installation (K100LT and K1100LT)

Refer to **Figure 259** and **Figure 260** for this procedure.
1. Unlock the catch and open the top cover.
2. Within the lower case, rotate the locking catch and remove the top case from the carrier.
3. Install the top case and make sure the locking catch is securely fastened to the carrier.

14

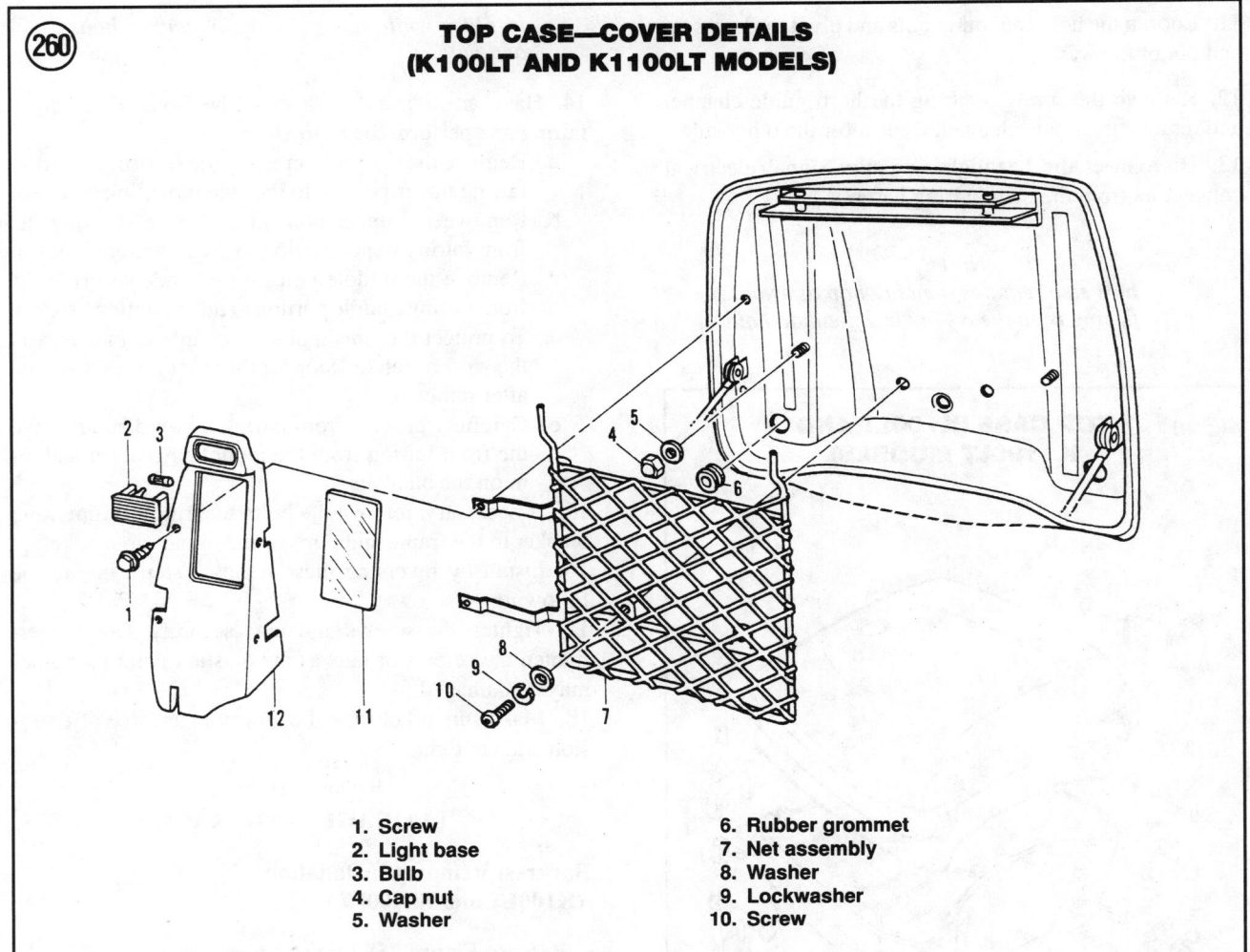

260

TOP CASE—COVER DETAILS
(K100LT AND K1100LT MODELS)

1. Screw
2. Light base
3. Bulb
4. Cap nut
5. Washer

6. Rubber grommet
7. Net assembly
8. Washer
9. Lockwasher
10. Screw

INDEX

A

Air filter case 249-250, 575-578
Air flow meter 240-241, 575
Alternator 275-280

B

Battery 33-37, 546-547
Body panels
 K1 models 650-655
 K100 models 515-534
 K1100LT. 655-660
 K1100RS 660-663
 K75 models 508-514
 K75RT 649
Brake pad replacement
 front 424-427
 rear 441-445
Brake problems 27
Brakes
 ABS 463-464, 644
 bleeding the system 473-476
 caliper, front 432
  dual piston caliper 639-641
 caliper, rear 448-455
 disc
  front and rear 460-463
  K1, K100RS, K1100LT,
   K1100RSA. 643-644
  rear 440
 hose and line replacement
  ABS equipped models 464-468
  non-ABS models . 455-460, 641-643
 master cylinder and
  reservoir, rear 445-448
 master cylinder
  front 427-432, 637-639
  rear, K75 (1993-on), K100
   (1990-1992), K1, K1100 641
 pad replacement
  front 424-427
   dual piston caliper 634-637
  rear 441-445
 pressure modulator and mounting
  bracket 468-471, 644-647
 rear drum, K75C models 477-481

rear pedal 481-483
trigger sensor 471-473
Break-in, engine 162

C

Caliper
 front. 432-440
  dual piston caliper 639-641
 rear 448-455
Camshafts, timing chain and chain
 tensioner assembly . . 92-102, 562-569
Center stand 485-487
Charging system. 274-275
Chassis wiring harness 339
Choke cable replacement 252-253
Clutch 172-183
 cable 187
 release mechanism 183-187
Connector pipe 349-350
Coolant recovery tank. 350-351, 585-587
Cooling system
 check. 344
 connector pipe. 349-350
 fan. 348
 hoses 351-353, 587
 hoses and hose clamps 342-344
 pressure check. 344
 radiator 344-348, 585
 thermostat 348-349
Crankcase breather system, U.S. only 268
Crankshaft. 154-159
 cover, cylinder head cover and
  timing chain cover . 86-92, 561-562
Cylinder block 159-162
Cylinder head 103-108, 569

D

Disc brake, rear. 440

E

Electrical system
 alternator. 275-280
 charging system 274-275
 chassis wiring harness 339

connectors 325
fuses 338-339
hall transmitter unit. 285-286
headlight 301-311, 584
horn 335-338
ignition coils 288-292, 582-583
ignition control unit 287
 Motronic. 581-582
ignition output stage 583
ignition system, K100RS
 (1991-1992), K1 and all
 K1100 models. 581
ignition systems 282-283
 troubleshooting 284-285
ignition output stage 583
instrument cluster 325-334
lighting system 301
relays. 334-335
spark plug secondary wires. . 292-293
starter. 294-300
starter relay 300-301
starting system 294
switches. 314-325
taillight/brake light and
 license plate light 311-312
turn signals 312-314
 K1 models 584-585
voltage rectifier. 280-281
wiring diagrams 339
break-in. 162
camshafts, timing chain and
 chain tensioner
 assembly 92-102, 562-569
crankshaft 154-159
crankshaft cover, cylinder
 head cover and timing
 chain cover 86-92, 561-562
cylinder block 159-162
cylinder head. 103-108, 569
intermediate housing. 122-125
noises. 26-27
oil pan, lower crankcase half
 and output shaft. 130-139
oil/water pump 115-122
performance 25-26
pistons and connecting rods . 140-154
principles. 83

15

removal/installation 83-86
  4-valve engines 561
servicing in frame............. 83
starter clutch and gears..... 125-130
starting 24-25
  and engine performance 545
valves and valve components. 108-115
  4-valve cylinder head 569-570
Evaporative emission control system,
  California models.......... 268-269
Exhaust system..... 269-272, 579-581

F

Fasteners....................... 5-8
Fenders 494-498, 648-649
Final drive unit.............. 405-417
  K1, K100RS (1991-1992),
    K1100LT and K1100RSA . 617-630
Footpegs.................. 487-490
  K1........................ 648
Forks, front
  K1, K100RS, K100LT 600-608
  K1100LT, K1100RS 608-615
  K75, K75RT, K75S 1992-on . 593-600
Frame 542-543
Front forks 375-389
Front suspension and steering 27
Fuel filler cap 258-260
Fuel gauge sensor........... 265-266
Fuel injection control unit 241-242
  Motronic.................... 575
Fuel injection precautions 230
Fuel injection system
  adjustments.......... 243-249, 575
  air flow meter 240-241, 575
  components............... 227-229
  description 225-227
  pressure regulator.......... 239-240
  throttle housing and intake
    manifold 575
Fuel injectors and fuel
  supply pipe 231-235
Fuel level sender, models
  so equipped................. 266
Fuel pump......... 253-258, 579
Fuel system, depressurizing 229-230
Fuel tank.................. 260-265
Fuses.................... 338-339

G

Gasoline/alcohol blend test 266-267
General information
  bike cleaning 30-32
  fasteners 5-8
  information labels.............. 10
  lubricants 8-9
  mechanic's tips 17-18

parts replacement 10
riding safety 18-19
safety first.................... 2
serial numbers................ 10
service hings 2-4
special tips 4-5
supplies, expendable........... 9
test equipment............. 16-17
basic hand 10-16
torque specifications........... 5

H

Hall transmitter unit 285-286
Handle....................... 494
Handlebar 365-370, 591
Headlight............. 301-311, 584
Horn 335-338
Hoses............. 351-353, 587
  and hose clamps 342-344
Hub, front 358-361, 590

I

Ignition coils....... 288-292, 582-583
Ignition control unit 287
  Motronic................. 581-582
Ignition output stage............ 583
Ignition system, K100RS (1991-1992),
  K1 and all K1100 models...... 581
  troubleshooting.......... 284-285
Ignition systems 282-283
Information labels............... 10
Instrument cluster........... 325-334
Intermediate housing 122-125

K

Kickstand (sidestand) 485

L

License plate bracket 498-500
Lighting system 301
Locks.................. 492-494
Lubricants 8-9
Lubrication, periodic ... 37-48, 547-549
Luggage and rack 534-539, 663-664

M

Maintenance checks, routine 545
Maintenance, periodic .. 48-62, 549-550
Master cylinder and
  reservoir, rear 445-448
Master cylinder, front . 427-432, 637-639
Master cylinder, rear, K75 (1993-on),
  K100 (1990-1992), K1, K1100 .. 641
Mechanic's tips.............. 17-18

O

Oil pan, lower crankcase half and output
  shaft.................. 130-139
Oil/water pump 115-122
Operating requirements........... 22
Optional equipment......... 540-542

P

Parts replacement 10
Pinion gear-to-ring
  gear adjustment.... 417-420, 630-633
Pistons and connecting rods ... 140-154
Pressure check............. 344
Pressure regulator 239-240

R

Radiator............... 344-348, 585
Rear cowl 649
  and storage tray........... 503-508
Relays 334-335
Riding safety............... 18-19

S

Safety bars................. 490-492
Safety checks, routine......... 28-30
Seat 500-503, 649
Serial numbers 10
Service
  hints...................... 2-4
  intervals.............. 30, 546
Shock absorber 397-399
Spark plug secondary wires ... 292-293
Starter 294-300
Starter clutch and gears....... 125-130
Starter relay............... 300-301
Starting system 294
Steering damper, K1, K100RS . 591-593
Steering, handlebar 365-370
Steering head and stem 370-374
  K75, K75RT, K75S............. 593
Steering head bearing race ... 374-375
Supplies, expendable............. 9
Suspension and final drive, rear
  pinion gear-to-ring
    gear adjustment......... 417-420
  shock absorber 397-399
  swing arm and drive shaft... 399-405
  taper roller bearing preload.. 420-421
  wheel.............. 392-397, 616
Suspension and steering, front
  forks 375-389
  K1, K100RS, K100LT 600-608
  K1100LT, K1100RS...... 608-615
  K75, K75RT, K75S 1992-on 593-600
  handlebar.................... 591
  hub................. 358-361, 590

steering damper, K1,
    K100RS 591-593
steering head and stem, K75,
    K75RT, K75S 593
tire balancing, 3-spoke type 590
wheel 354-358
    3-spoke type. 588-590
wheel balance 361
Swing arm and drive shaft 399-405
K1, K100RS (1991-1992), K1100LT
    and K1100RSA (1993-on) . 616-617
Switches 314-325

T

Taillight/brake light and license
    plate light 311-312
Taper roller bearing preload 420-421
Tapered roller bearing preload . . 633-634
Test equipment 16-17
Thermostat 348-349
Throttle
    cable replacement. 250-252
    housing and
        intake manifold. 235-239, 575

valve switch 242
Tire
    and wheels 32-33, 546
    balancing, 3-spoke type 590
    changing 361-365
    repairs 365
Tools, basic hand 10-16
Torque specifications 5
Transmission
    and gearshift operation 189-190
    housing 190-197
    shafts. 208-223
        and gearshift mechanism . . . 197-208
Troubleshooting
    brake problems 27
    emergency. 23-24
    engine
        noises 26-27
        performance 25-26
        starting 24-25
        starting and performance 545
    front suspension and steering 27
    fuel injection system. 231
    ignition system 284-285
operating requirements 22

vibration, excessive. 27
Tune-up 62-76
    K100RS (1991-1992), K1,
        K1100LT-ABS,
        K1100RSA 550-557
Turn signals. 312-314
    K1 models. 584-585

V

Valve and valve components. . . 108-115
    4-valve cylinder head 569-570
Vibration, excessive 27
Voltage rectifier. 280-281

W

Wheel
    and tires. 32-33, 546
    balance 361
    front. 354-358
        3-spoke type 588-590
    rear 392-397, 616
Windshield cleaning, all models 542
Wiring diagrams 339

1986-1989 K75C & K75S
ENGINE & FRAME

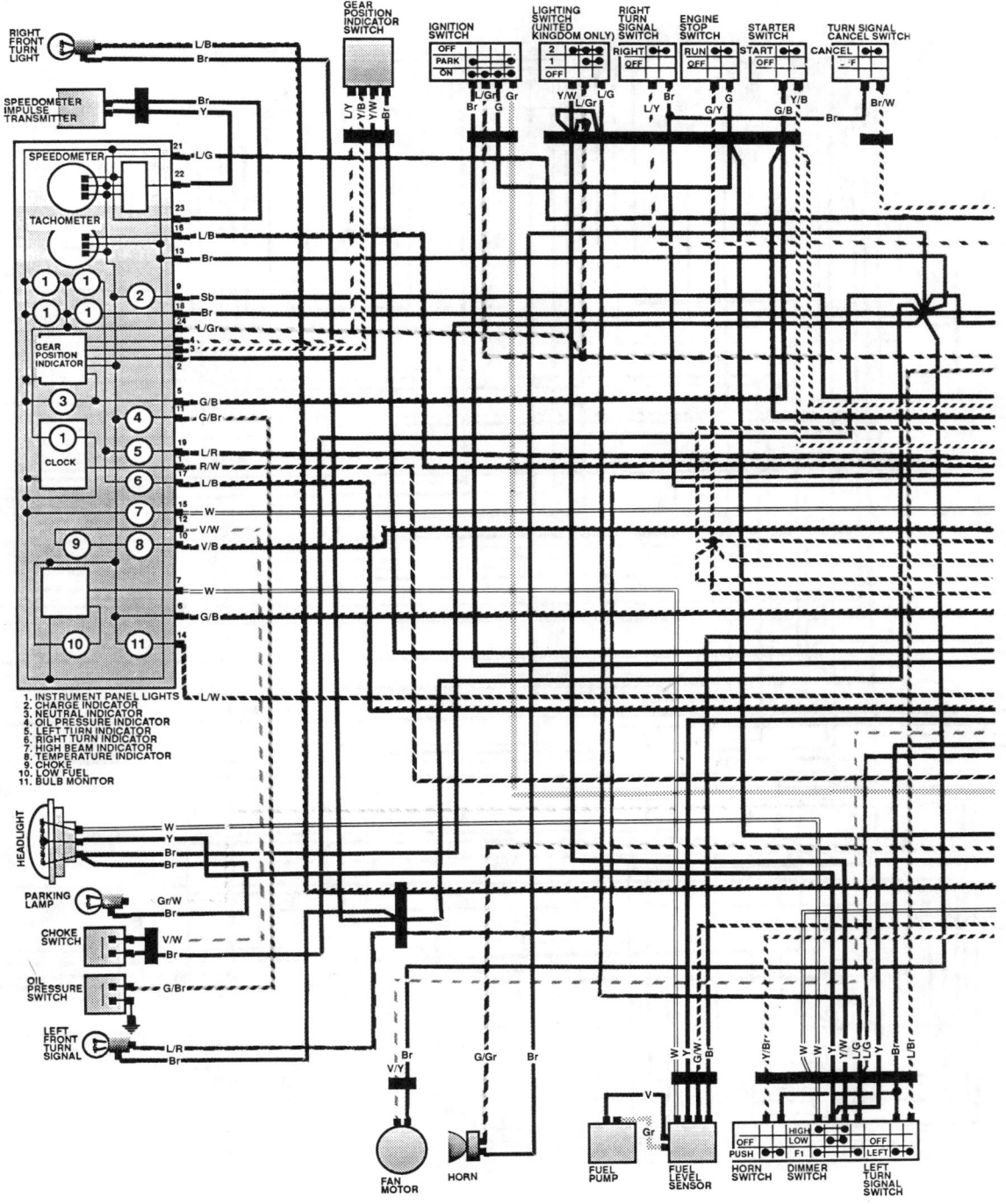

16

PAGE 1 OF 3

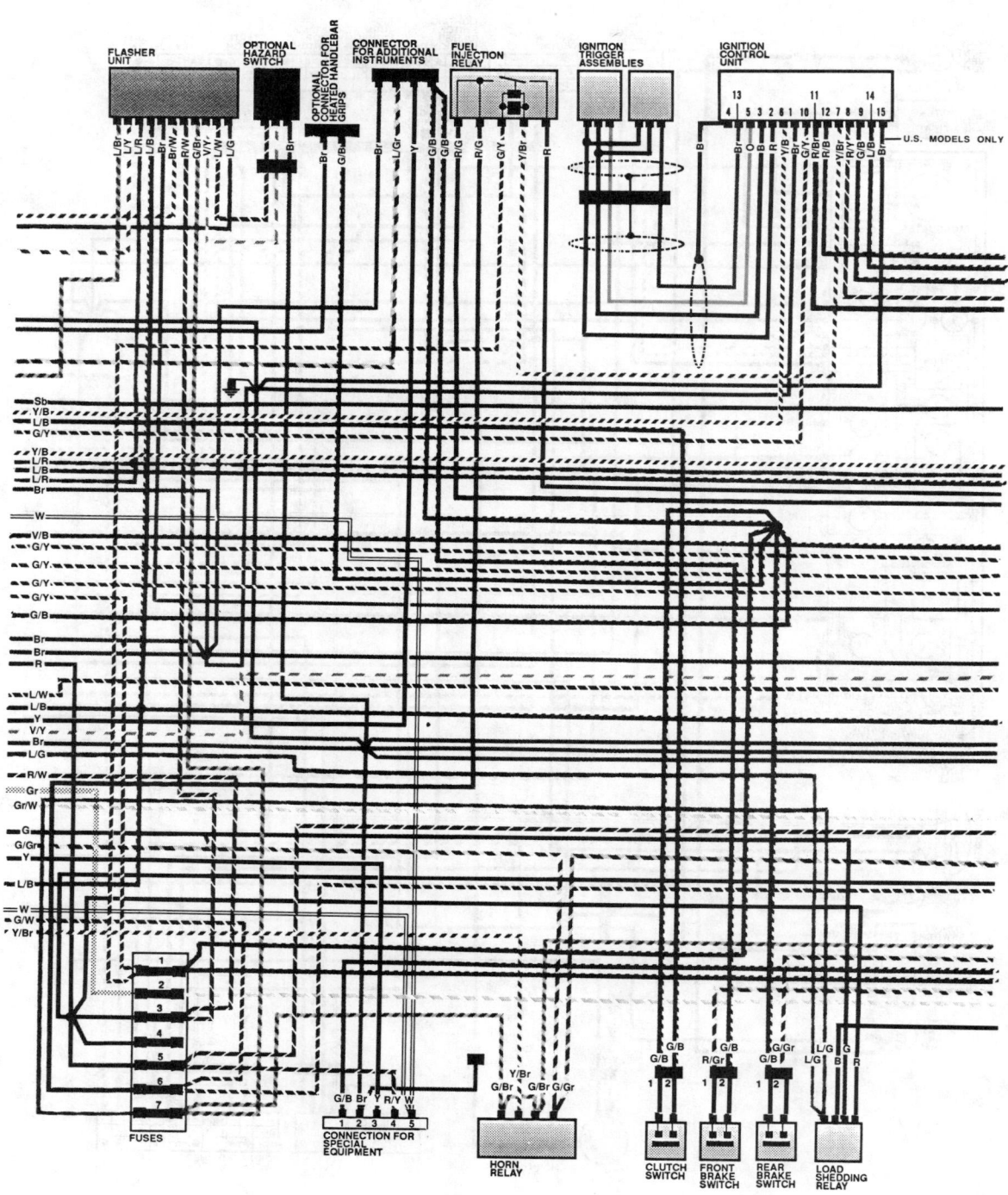

PAGE 2 OF 3

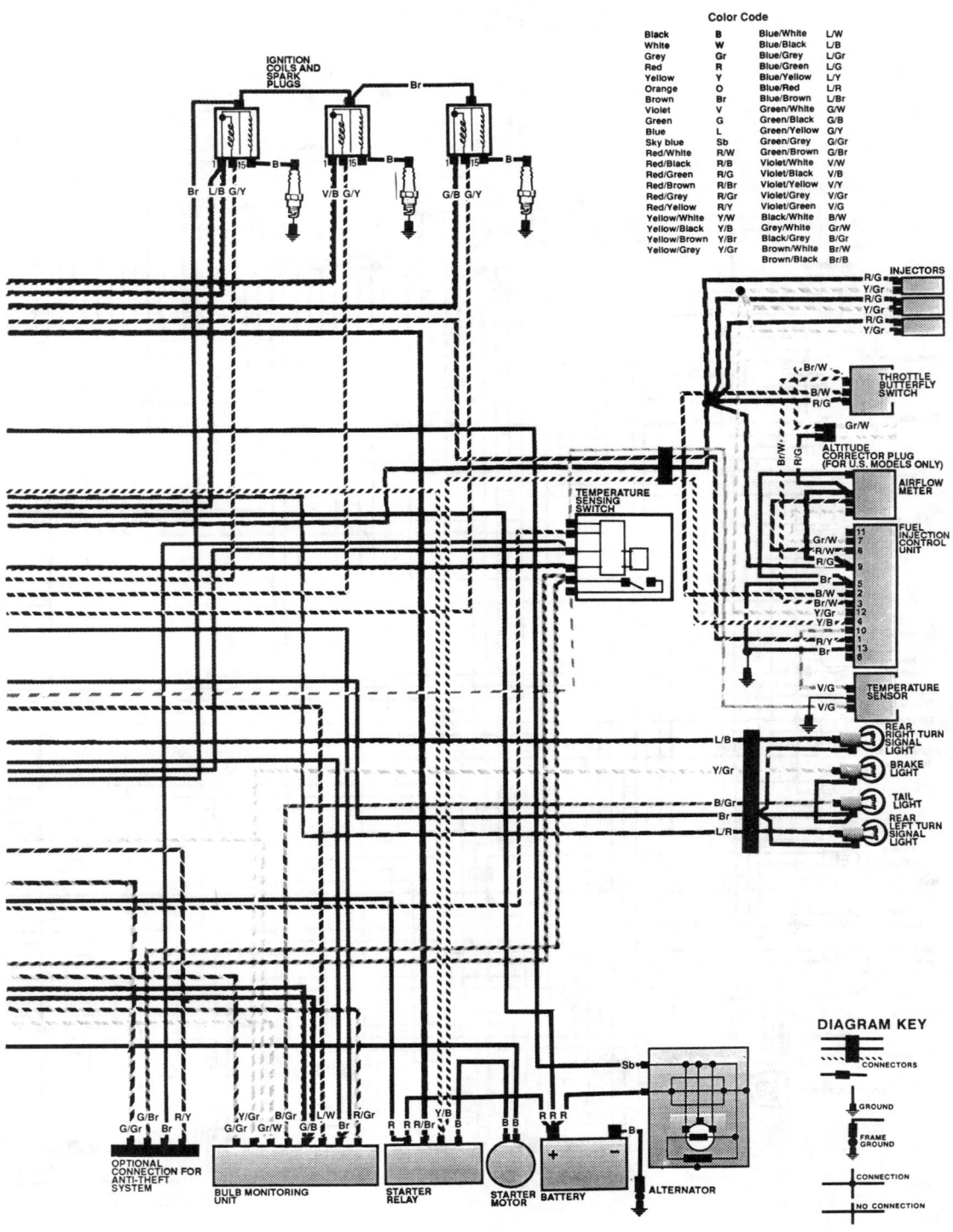

Color Code

Black	B	Blue/White	L/W
White	W	Blue/Black	L/B
Grey	Gr	Blue/Grey	L/Gr
Red	R	Blue/Green	L/G
Yellow	Y	Blue/Yellow	L/Y
Orange	O	Blue/Red	L/R
Brown	Br	Blue/Brown	L/Br
Violet	V	Green/White	G/W
Green	G	Green/Black	G/B
Blue	L	Green/Yellow	G/Y
Sky blue	Sb	Green/Grey	G/Gr
Red/White	R/W	Green/Brown	G/Br
Red/Black	R/B	Violet/White	V/W
Red/Green	R/G	Violet/Black	V/B
Red/Brown	R/Br	Violet/Yellow	V/Y
Red/Grey	R/Gr	Violet/Grey	V/Gr
Red/Yellow	R/Y	Violet/Green	V/G
Yellow/White	Y/W	Black/White	B/W
Yellow/Black	Y/B	Grey/White	Gr/W
Yellow/Brown	Y/Br	Black/Grey	B/Gr
Yellow/Grey	Y/Gr	Brown/White	Br/W
		Brown/Black	Br/B

PAGE 3 OF 3

16

1990-ON K75
ENGINE & FRAME

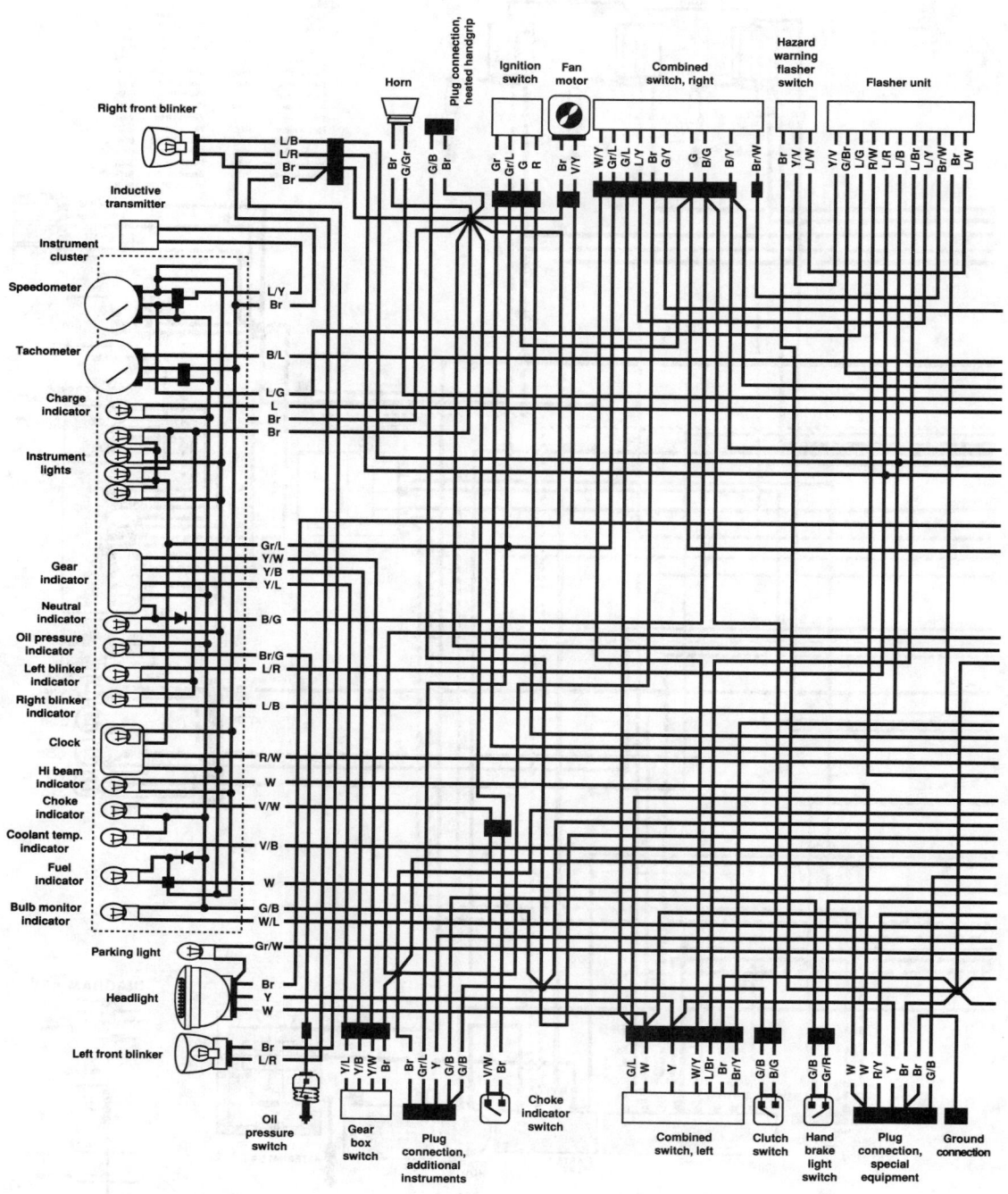

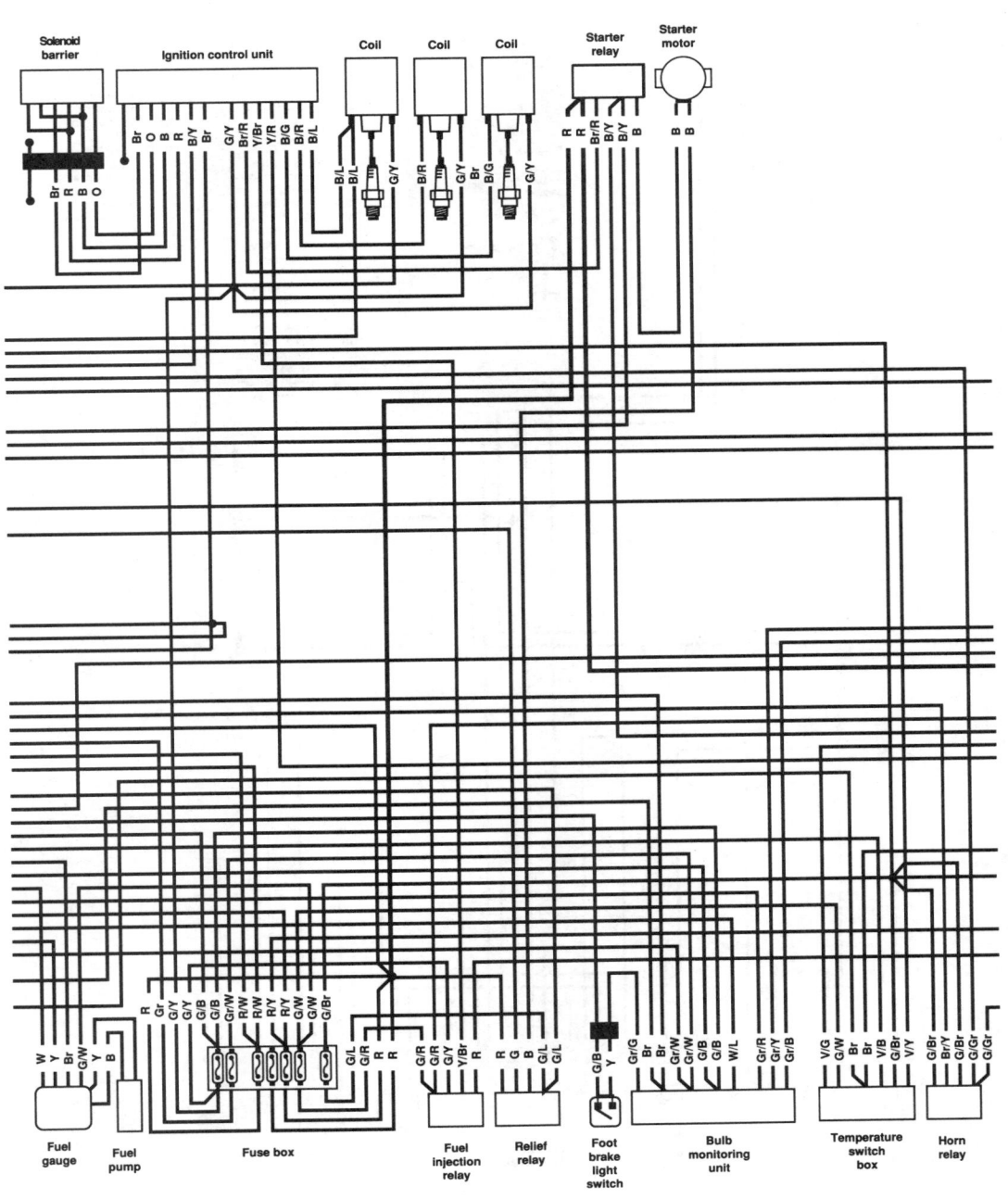

16

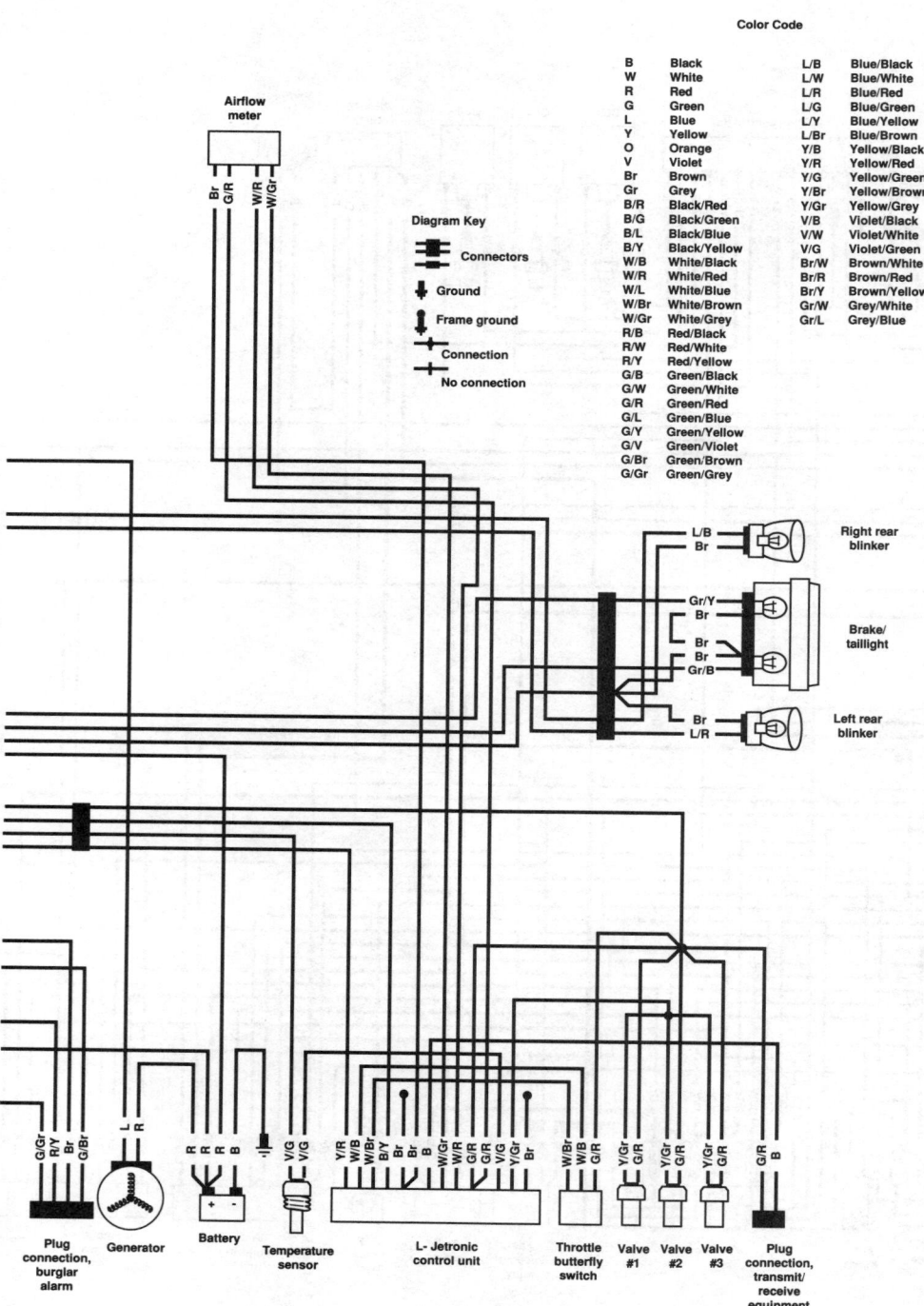

1990-ON K75RT
ENGINE & FRAME

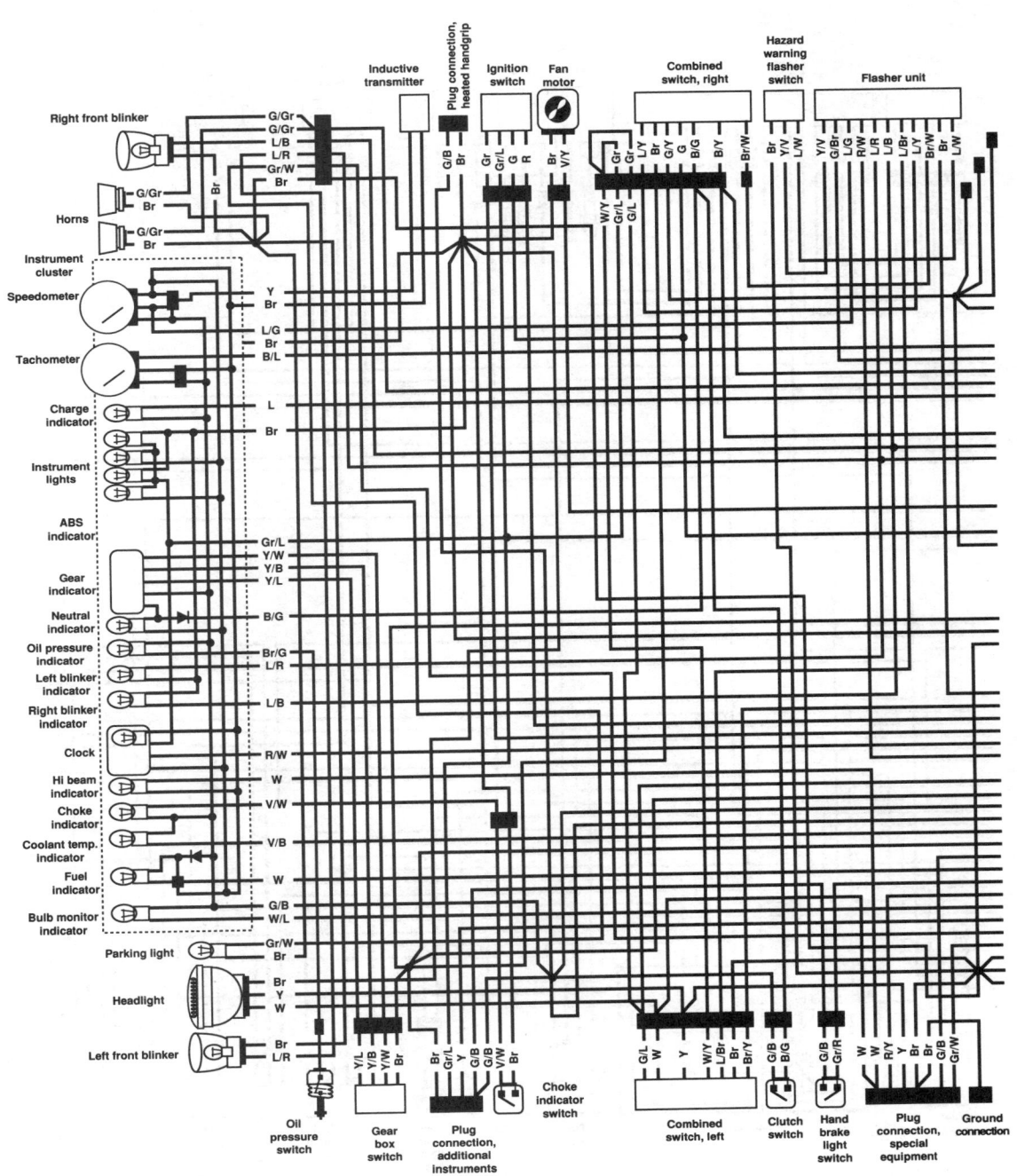

PAGE 1 OF 3

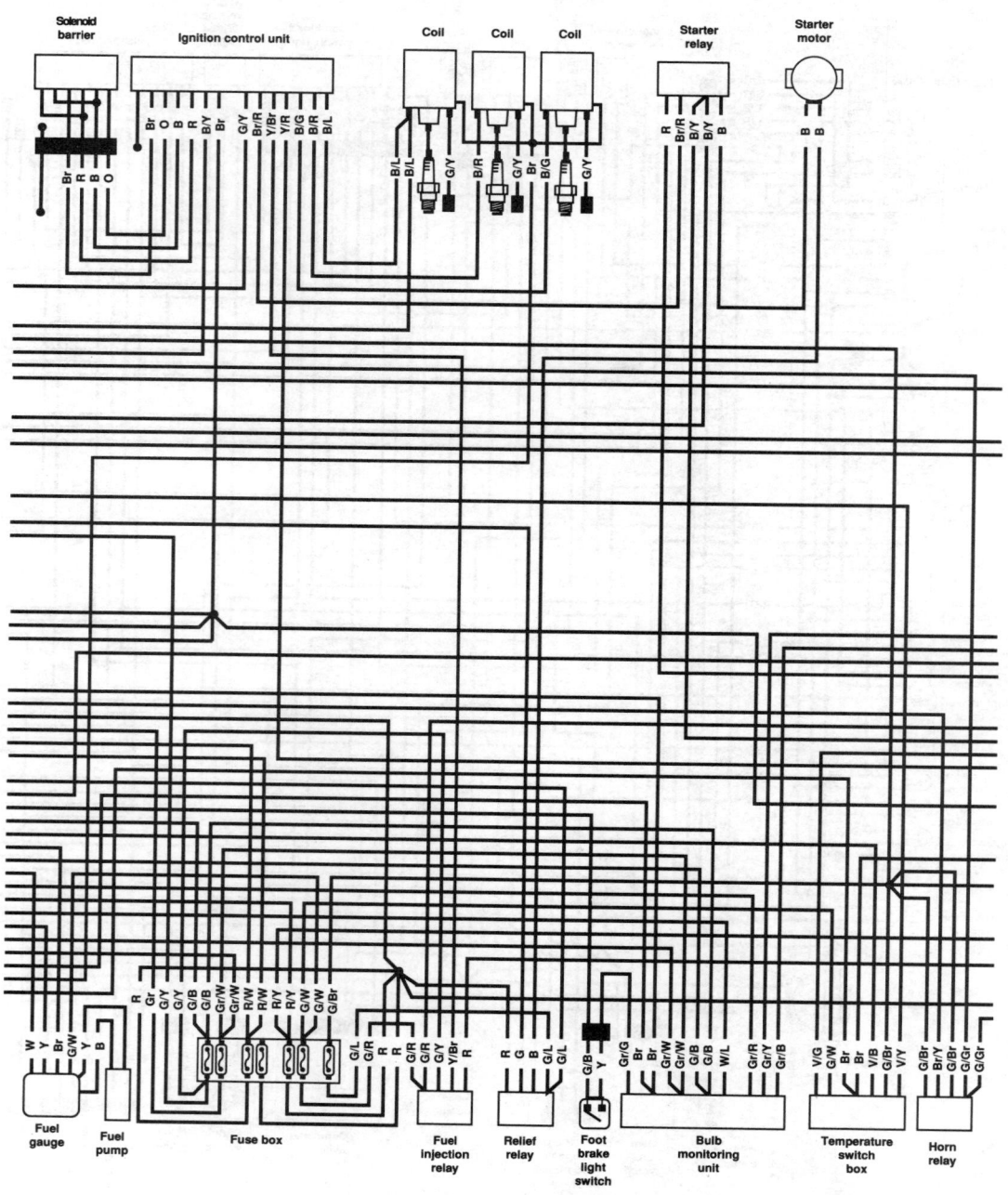

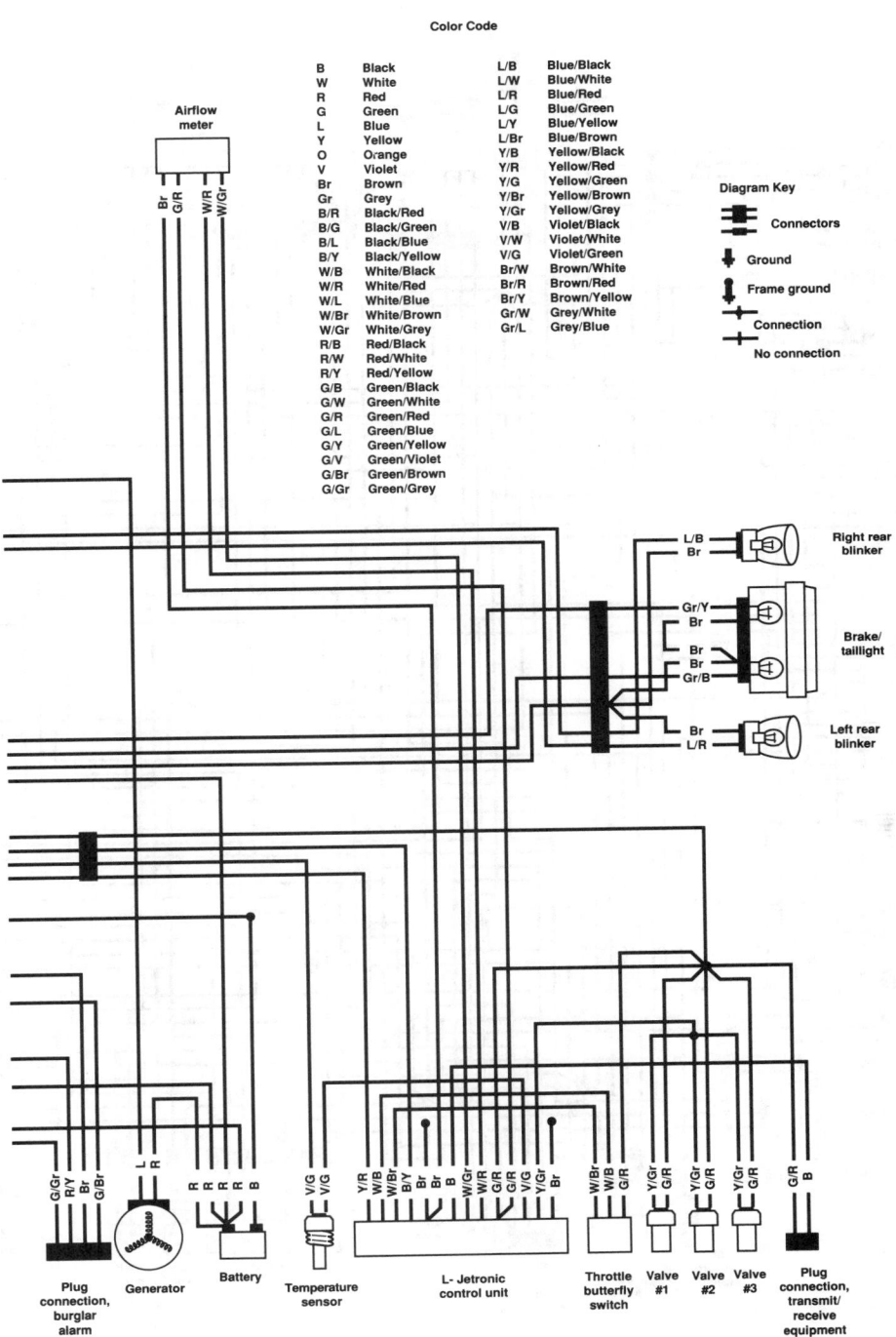

Color Code

B	Black	L/B	Blue/Black
W	White	L/W	Blue/White
R	Red	L/R	Blue/Red
G	Green	L/G	Blue/Green
L	Blue	L/Y	Blue/Yellow
Y	Yellow	L/Br	Blue/Brown
O	Orange	Y/B	Yellow/Black
V	Violet	Y/R	Yellow/Red
Br	Brown	Y/G	Yellow/Green
Gr	Grey	Y/Br	Yellow/Brown
B/R	Black/Red	Y/Gr	Yellow/Grey
B/G	Black/Green	V/B	Violet/Black
B/L	Black/Blue	V/W	Violet/White
B/Y	Black/Yellow	V/G	Violet/Green
W/B	White/Black	Br/W	Brown/White
W/R	White/Red	Br/R	Brown/Red
W/L	White/Blue	Br/Y	Brown/Yellow
W/Br	White/Brown	Gr/W	Grey/White
W/Gr	White/Grey	Gr/L	Grey/Blue
R/B	Red/Black		
R/W	Red/White		
R/Y	Red/Yellow		
G/B	Green/Black		
G/W	Green/White		
G/R	Green/Red		
G/L	Green/Blue		
G/Y	Green/Yellow		
G/V	Green/Violet		
G/Br	Green/Brown		
G/Gr	Green/Grey		

Diagram Key

Connectors

Ground

Frame ground

Connection

No connection

PAGE 3 OF 3

16

1990-ON K75-ABS
ENGINE & FRAME

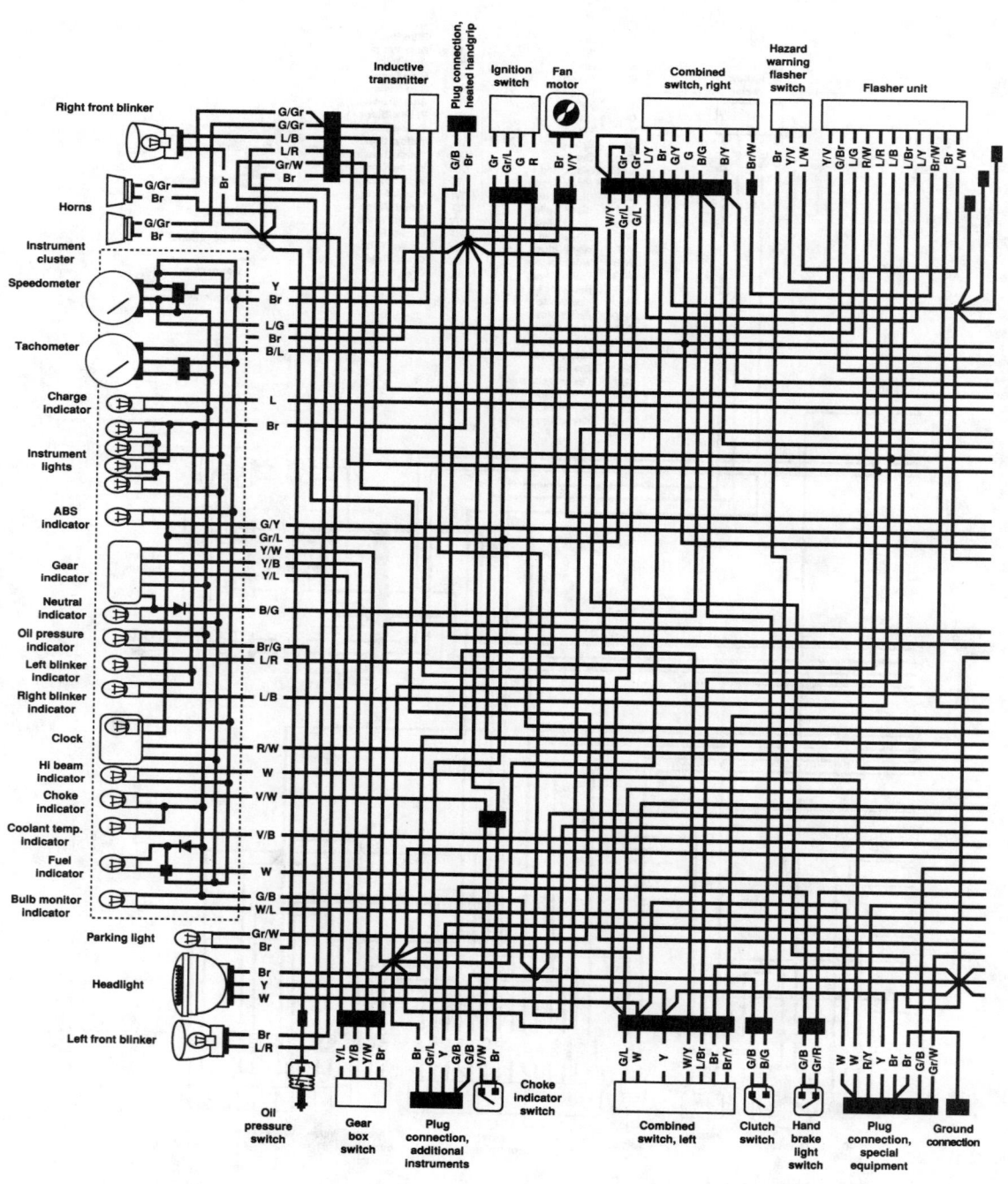

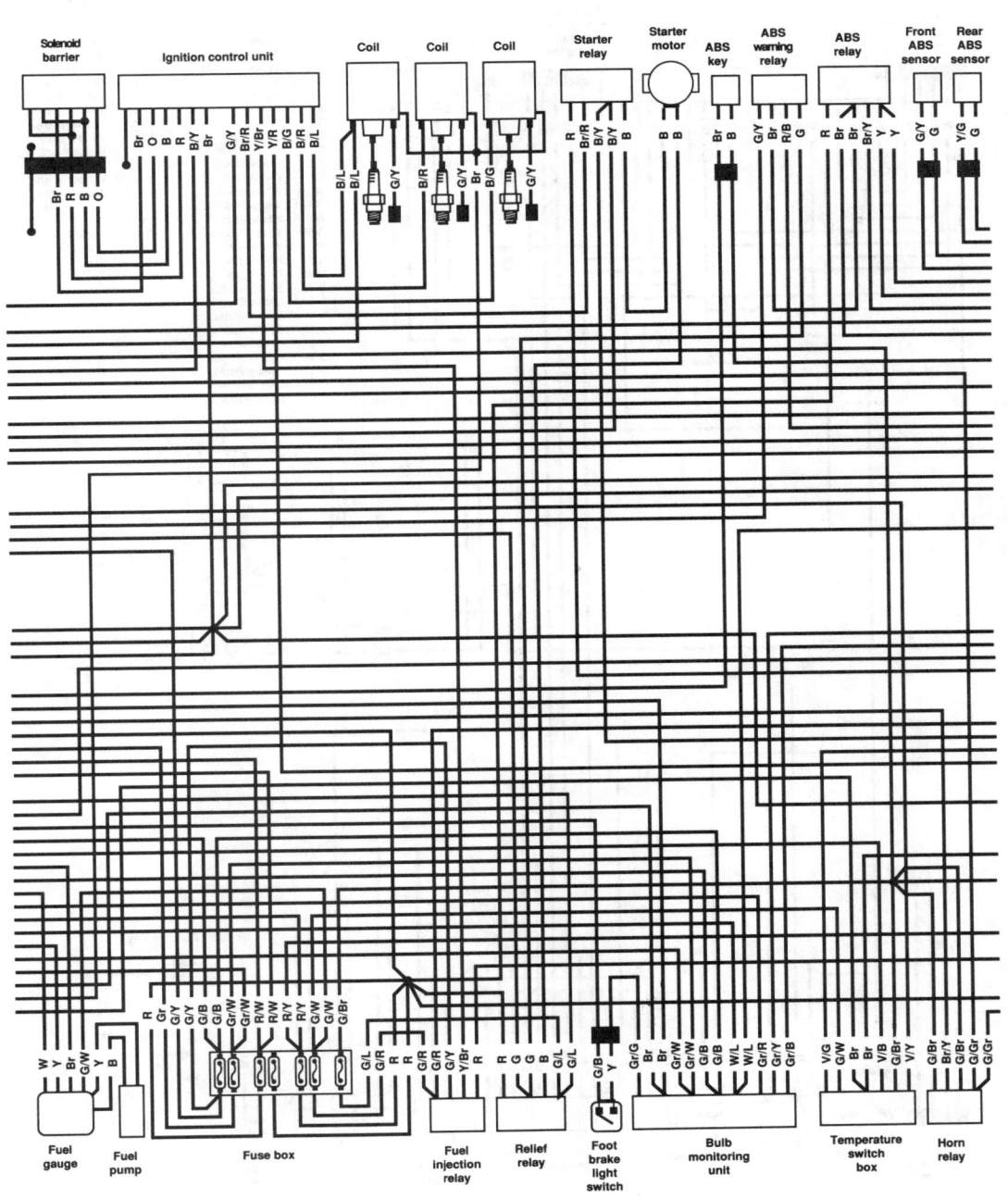

PAGE 2 OF 3

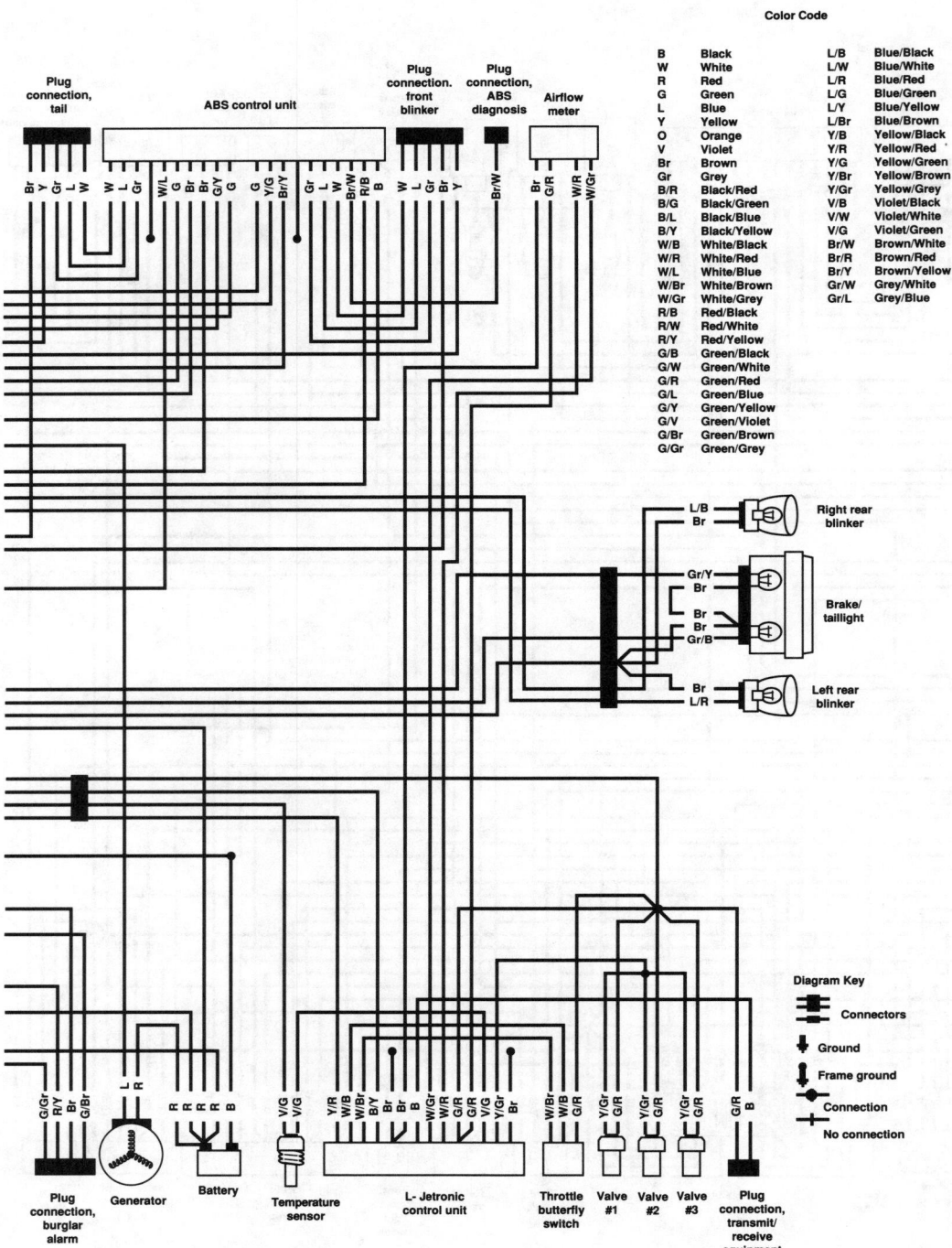

Color Code

B	Black	L/B	Blue/Black
W	White	L/W	Blue/White
R	Red	L/R	Blue/Red
G	Green	L/G	Blue/Green
L	Blue	L/Y	Blue/Yellow
Y	Yellow	L/Br	Blue/Brown
O	Orange	Y/B	Yellow/Black
V	Violet	Y/R	Yellow/Red
Br	Brown	Y/G	Yellow/Green
Gr	Grey	Y/Br	Yellow/Brown
B/R	Black/Red	Y/Gr	Yellow/Grey
B/G	Black/Green	V/B	Violet/Black
B/L	Black/Blue	V/W	Violet/White
B/Y	Black/Yellow	V/G	Violet/Green
W/B	White/Black	Br/W	Brown/White
W/R	White/Red	Br/R	Brown/Red
W/L	White/Blue	Br/Y	Brown/Yellow
W/Br	White/Brown	Gr/W	Grey/White
W/Gr	White/Grey	Gr/L	Grey/Blue
R/B	Red/Black		
R/W	Red/White		
R/Y	Red/Yellow		
G/B	Green/Black		
G/W	Green/White		
G/R	Green/Red		
G/L	Green/Blue		
G/Y	Green/Yellow		
G/V	Green/Violet		
G/Br	Green/Brown		
G/Gr	Green/Grey		

Diagram Key

Connectors
Ground
Frame ground
Connection
No connection

PAGE 3 OF 3

1990-ON K75S-ABS
ENGINE & FRAME

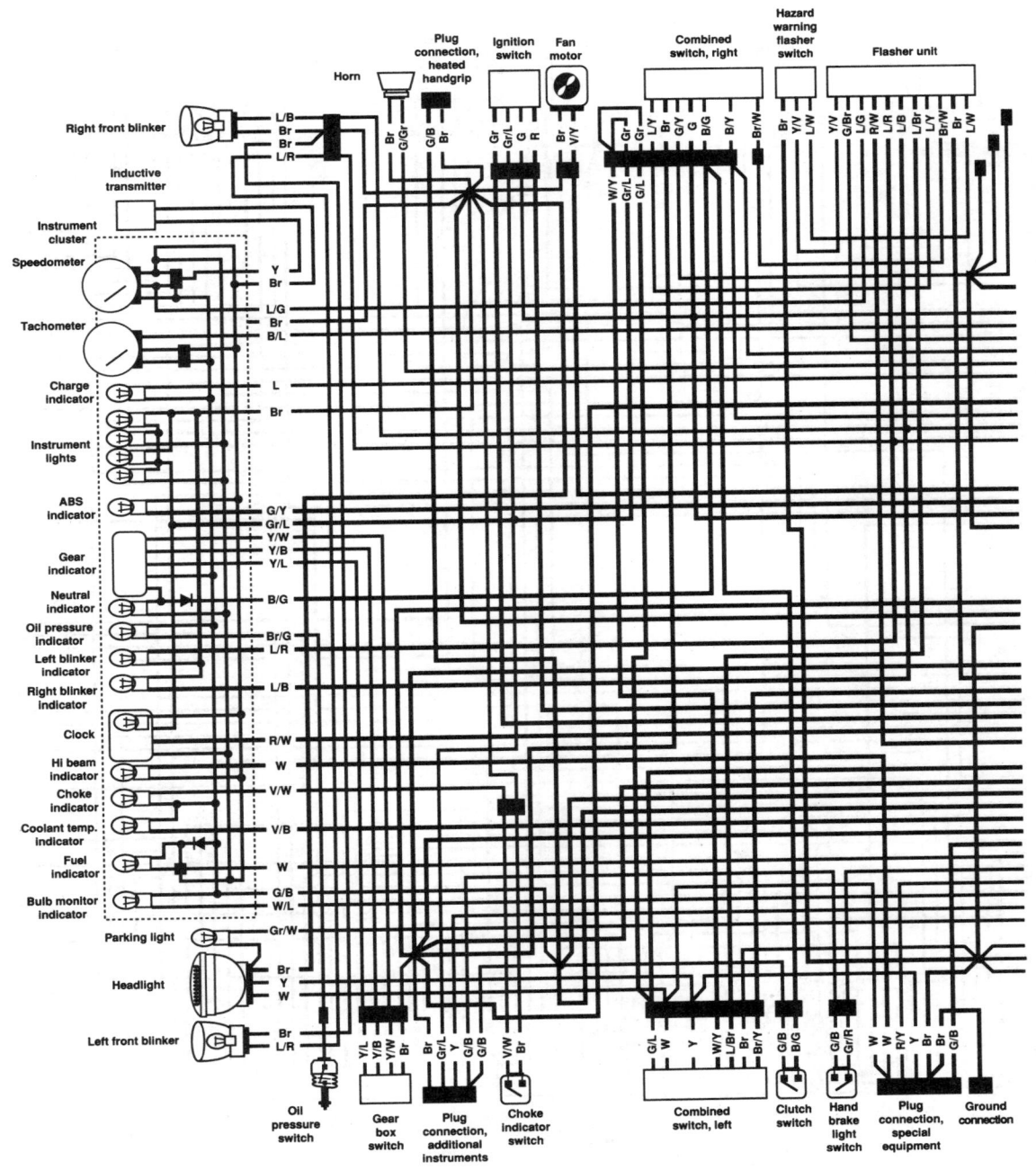

16

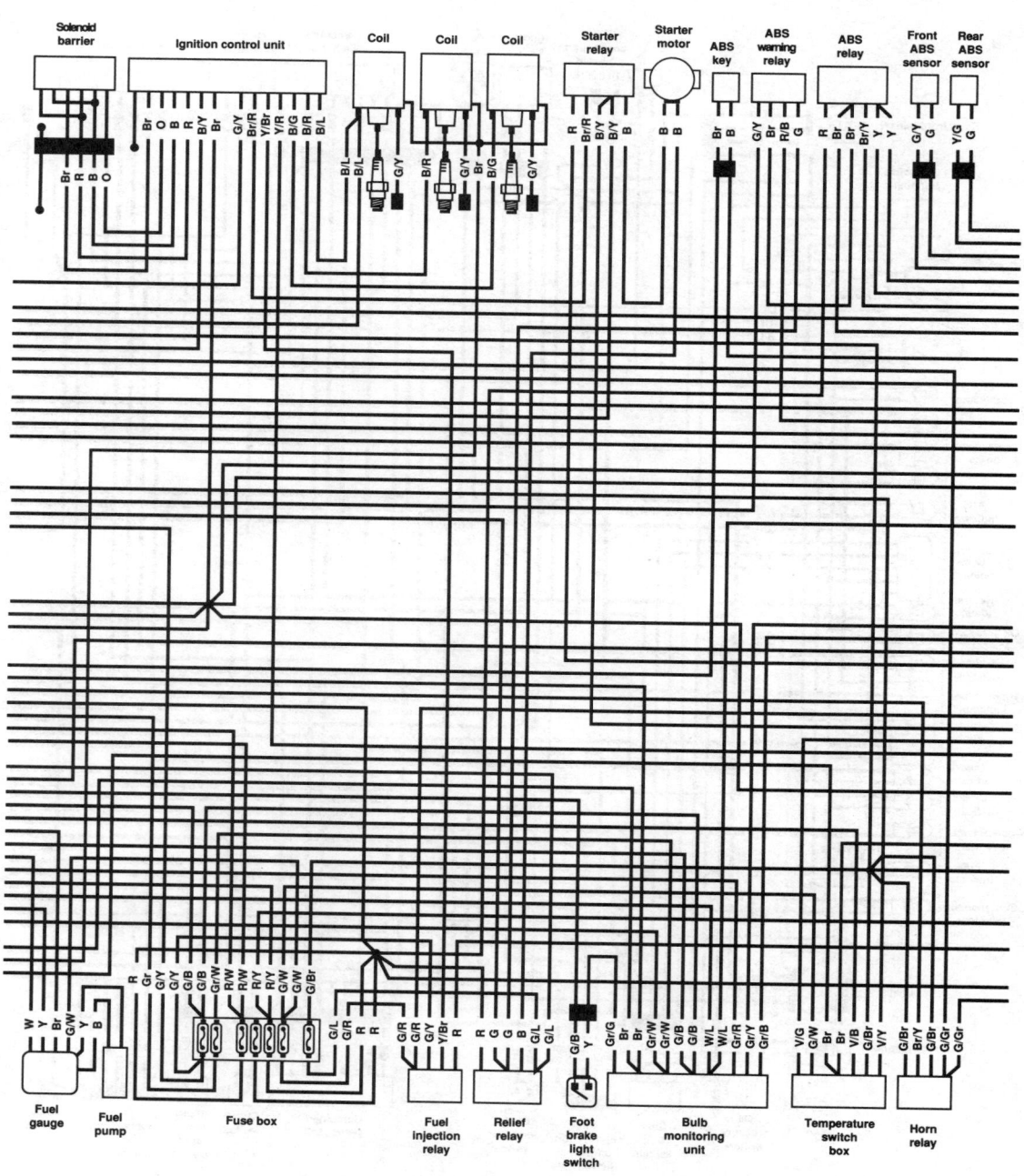

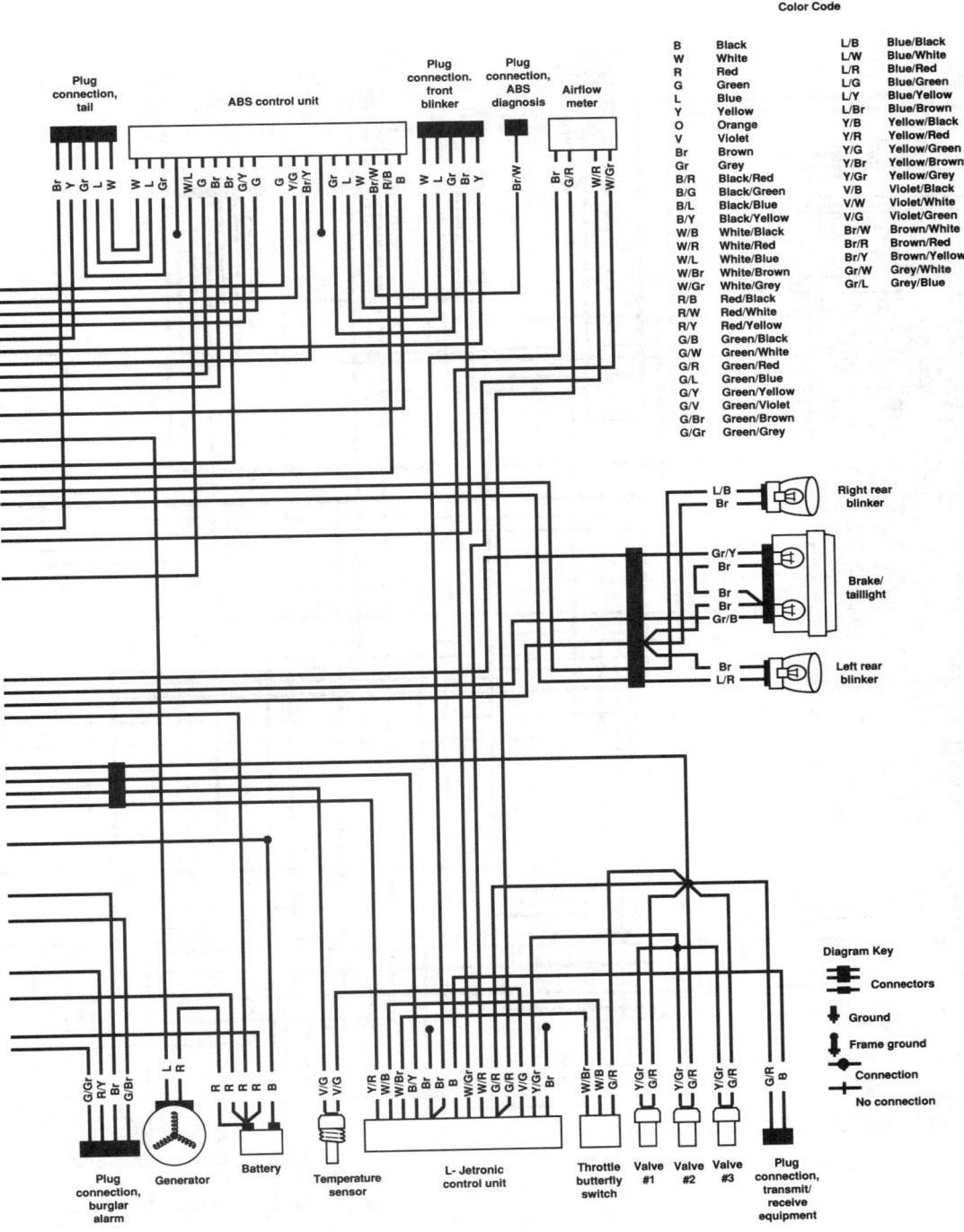

1985-1988 K100
ENGINE & FRAME

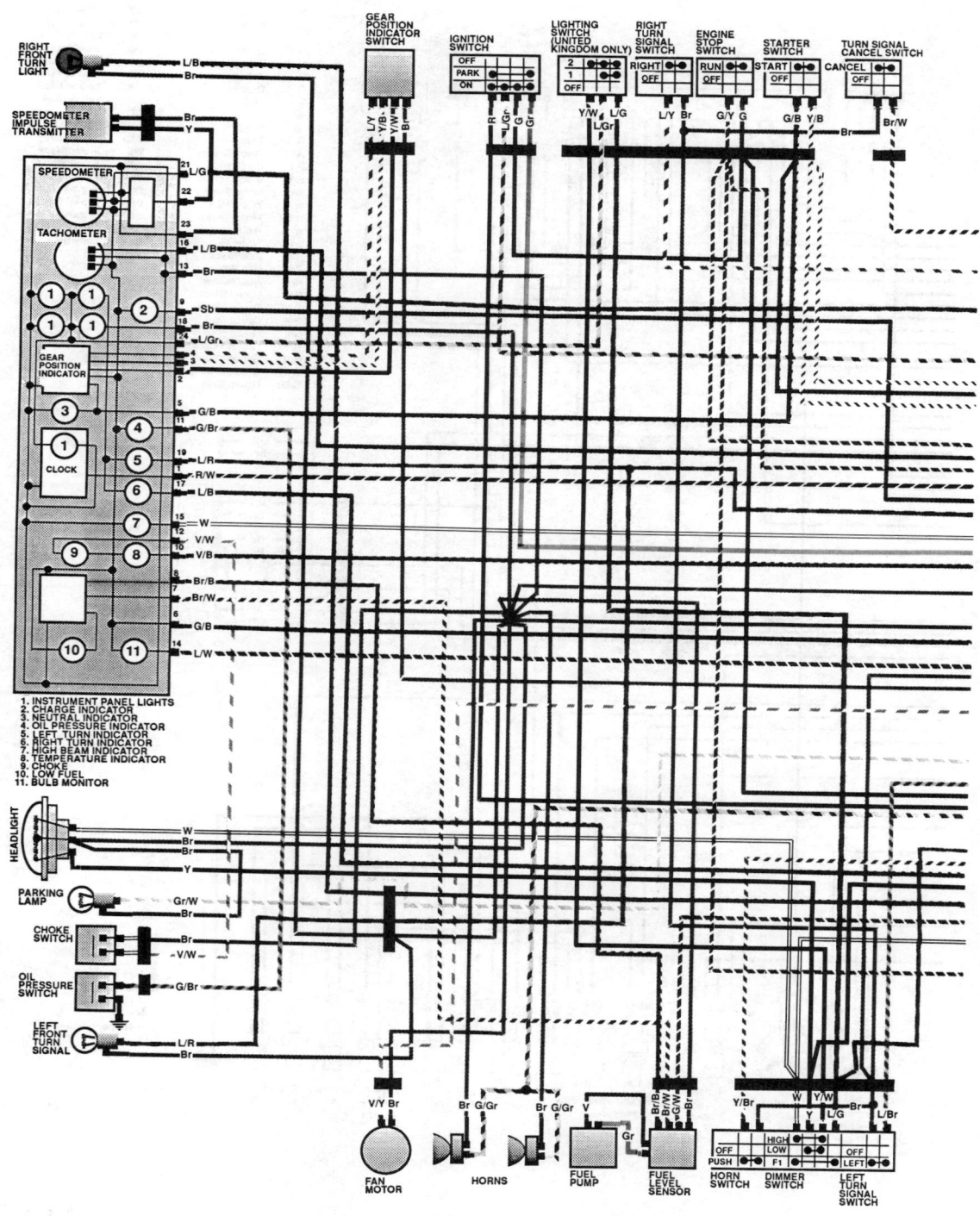

PAGE 1 OF 3

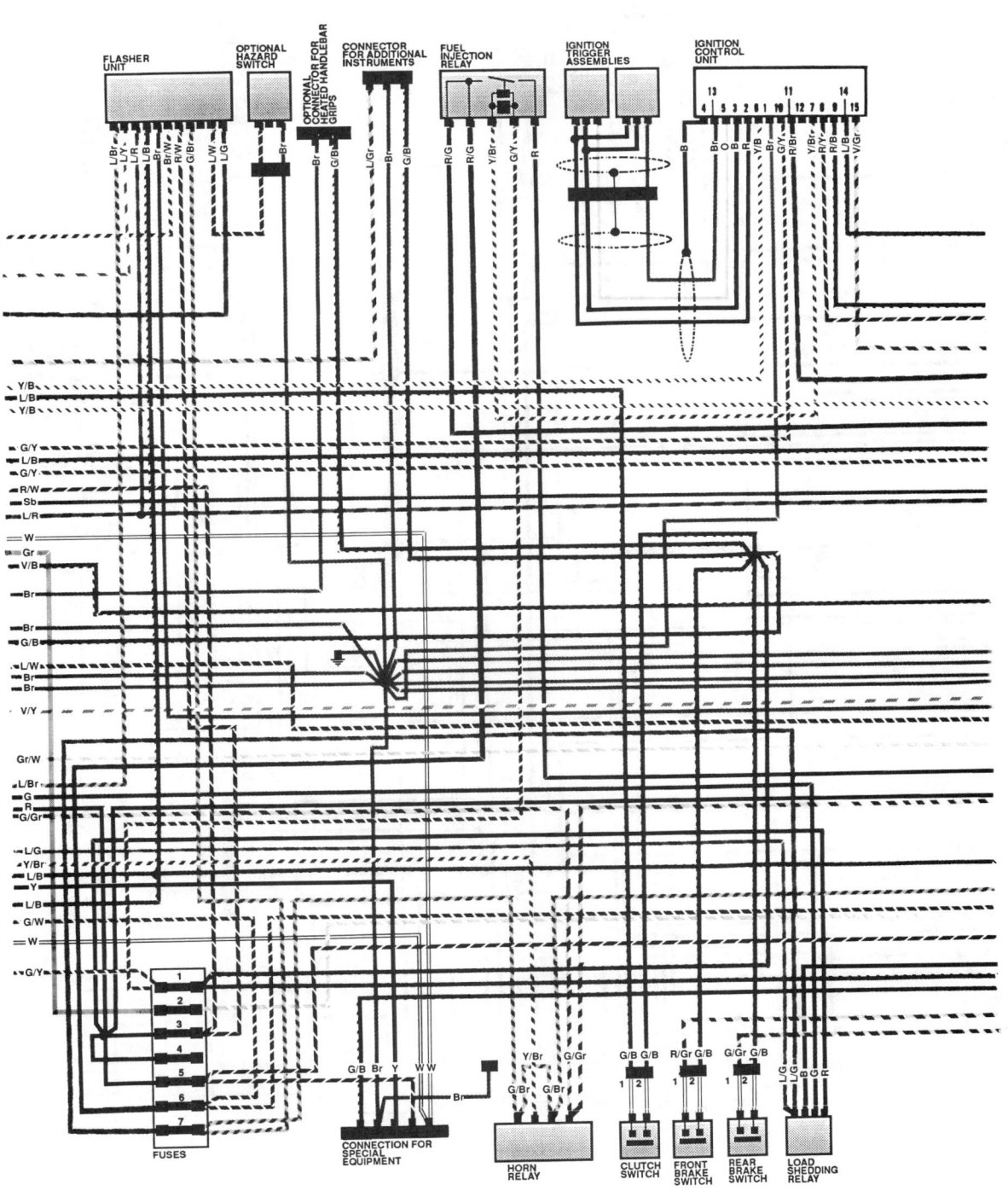

16

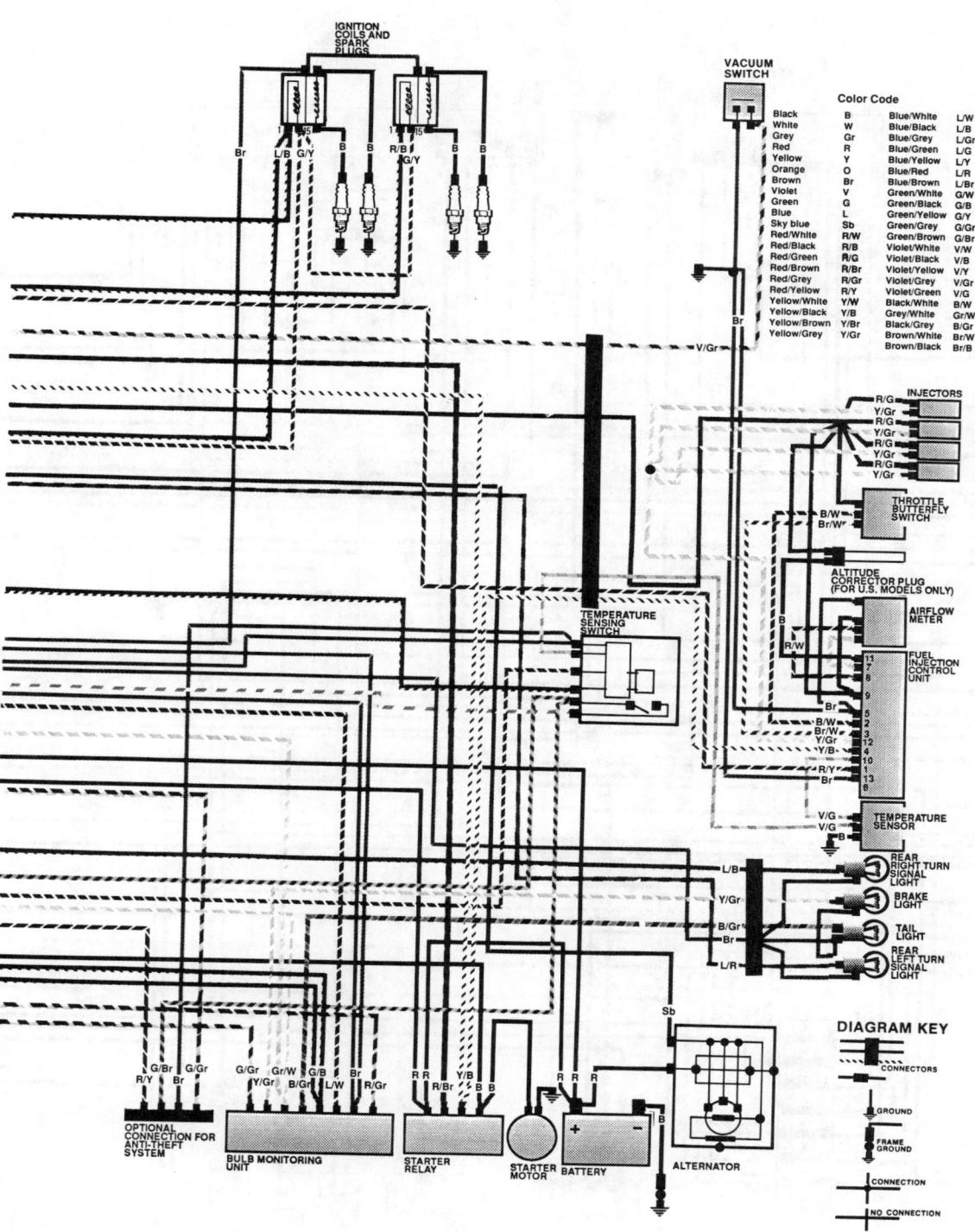

PAGE 3 OF 3

EARLY K100RS & EARLY K100RT
ENGINE & FRAME

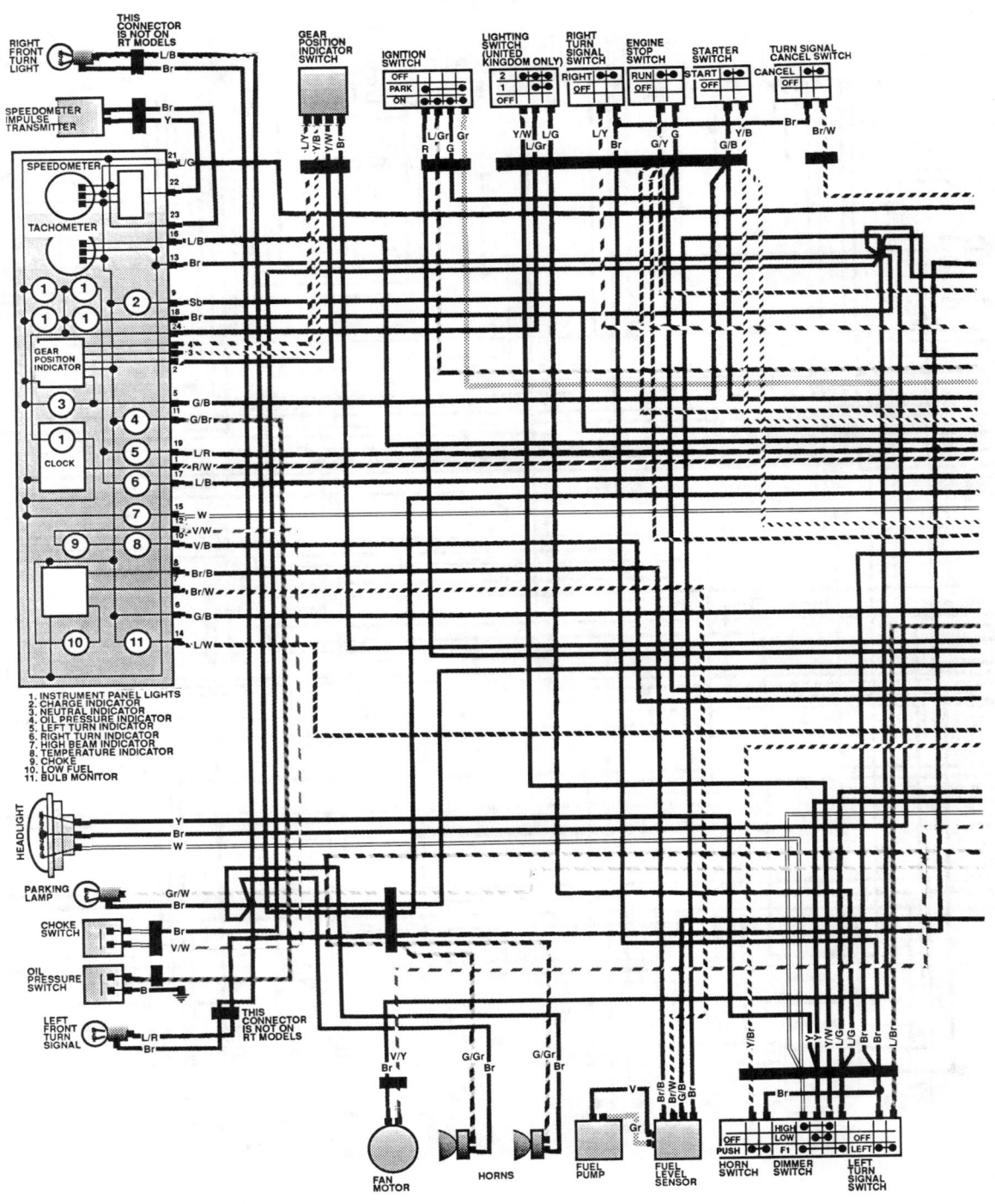

16

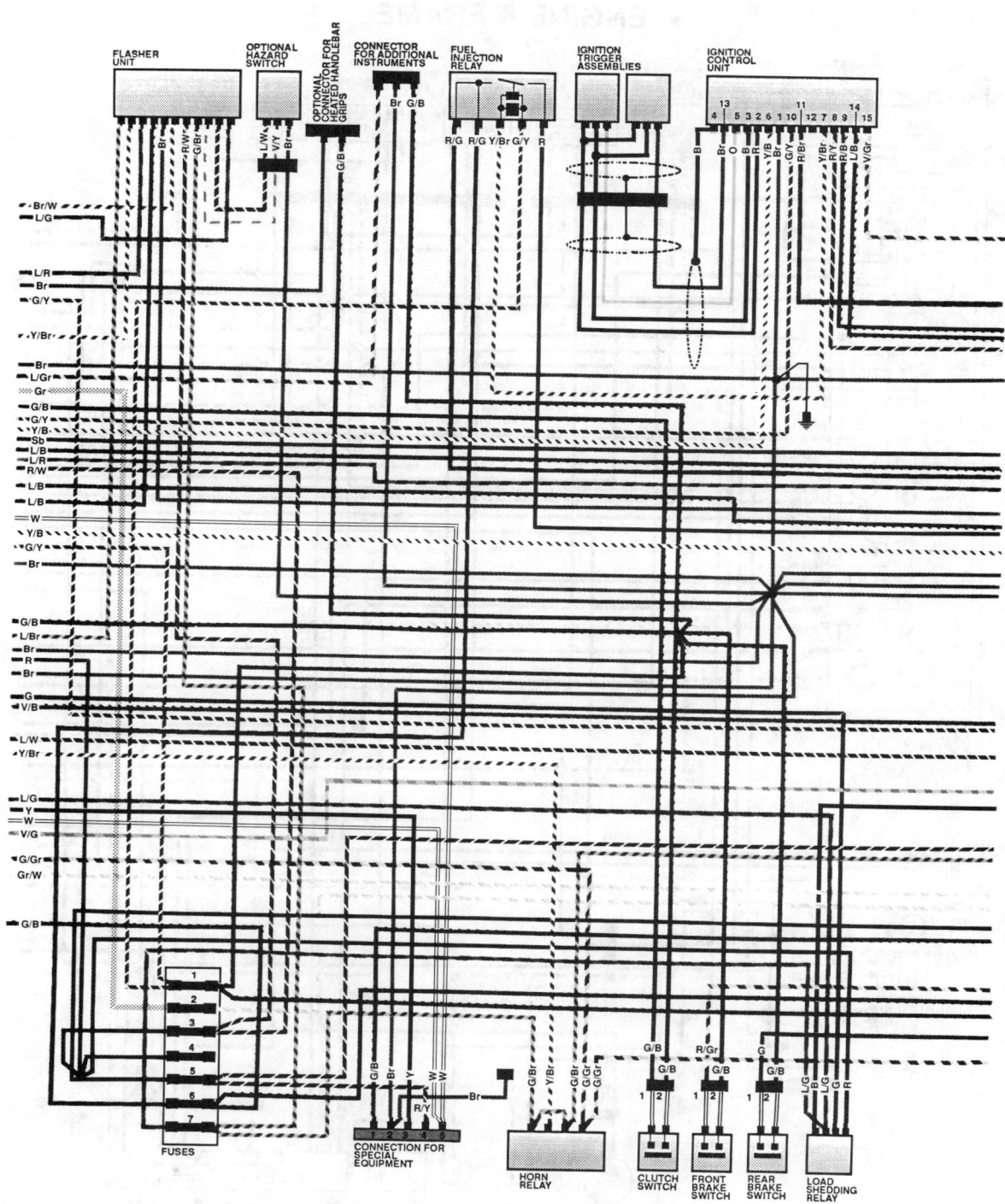

PAGE 2 OF 3

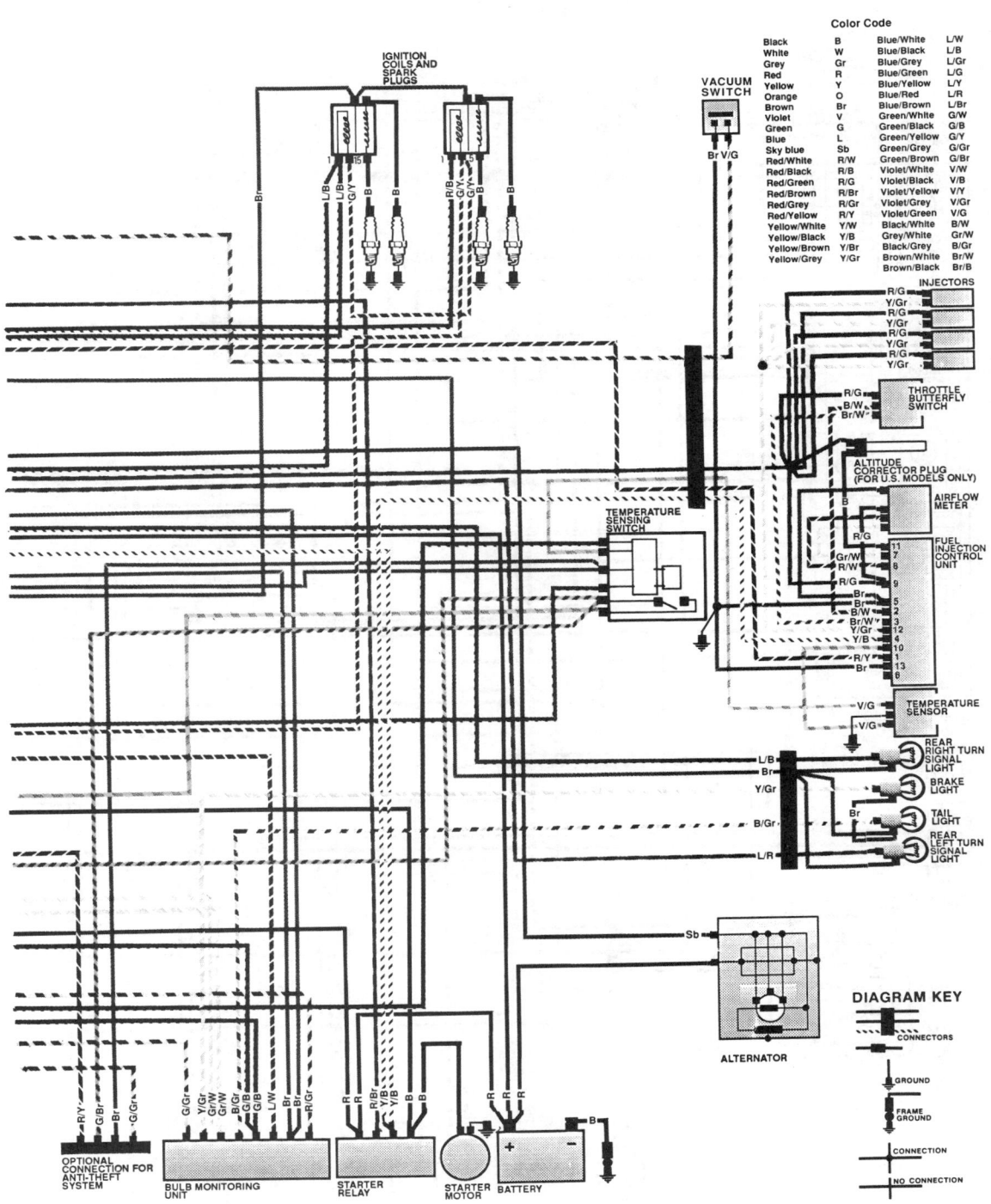

Color Code

Black	B	Blue/White	L/W
White	W	Blue/Black	L/B
Grey	Gr	Blue/Grey	L/Gr
Red	R	Blue/Green	L/G
Yellow	Y	Blue/Yellow	L/Y
Orange	O	Blue/Red	L/R
Brown	Br	Blue/Brown	L/Br
Violet	V	Green/White	G/W
Green	G	Green/Black	G/B
Blue	L	Green/Yellow	G/Y
Sky blue	Sb	Green/Grey	G/Gr
Red/White	R/W	Green/Brown	G/Br
Red/Black	R/B	Violet/White	V/W
Red/Green	R/G	Violet/Black	V/B
Red/Brown	R/Br	Violet/Yellow	V/Y
Red/Grey	R/Gr	Violet/Grey	V/Gr
Red/Yellow	R/Y	Violet/Green	V/G
Yellow/White	Y/W	Black/White	B/W
Yellow/Black	Y/B	Grey/White	Gr/W
Yellow/Brown	Y/Br	Black/Grey	B/Gr
Yellow/Grey	Y/Gr	Brown/White	Br/W
		Brown/Black	Br/B

IGNITION COILS AND SPARK PLUGS

VACUUM SWITCH

INJECTORS

THROTTLE BUTTERFLY SWITCH

ALTITUDE CORRECTOR PLUG (FOR U.S. MODELS ONLY)

AIRFLOW METER

FUEL INJECTION CONTROL UNIT

TEMPERATURE SENSING SWITCH

TEMPERATURE SENSOR

REAR RIGHT TURN SIGNAL LIGHT

BRAKE LIGHT

TAIL LIGHT

REAR LEFT TURN SIGNAL LIGHT

ALTERNATOR

DIAGRAM KEY

CONNECTORS

GROUND

FRAME GROUND

CONNECTION

NO CONNECTION

OPTIONAL CONNECTION FOR ANTI-THEFT SYSTEM

BULB MONITORING UNIT

STARTER RELAY

STARTER MOTOR

BATTERY

16

PAGE 3 OF 3

LATE K100RS & LATE K100RT THROUGH 1989
ENGINE & FRAME

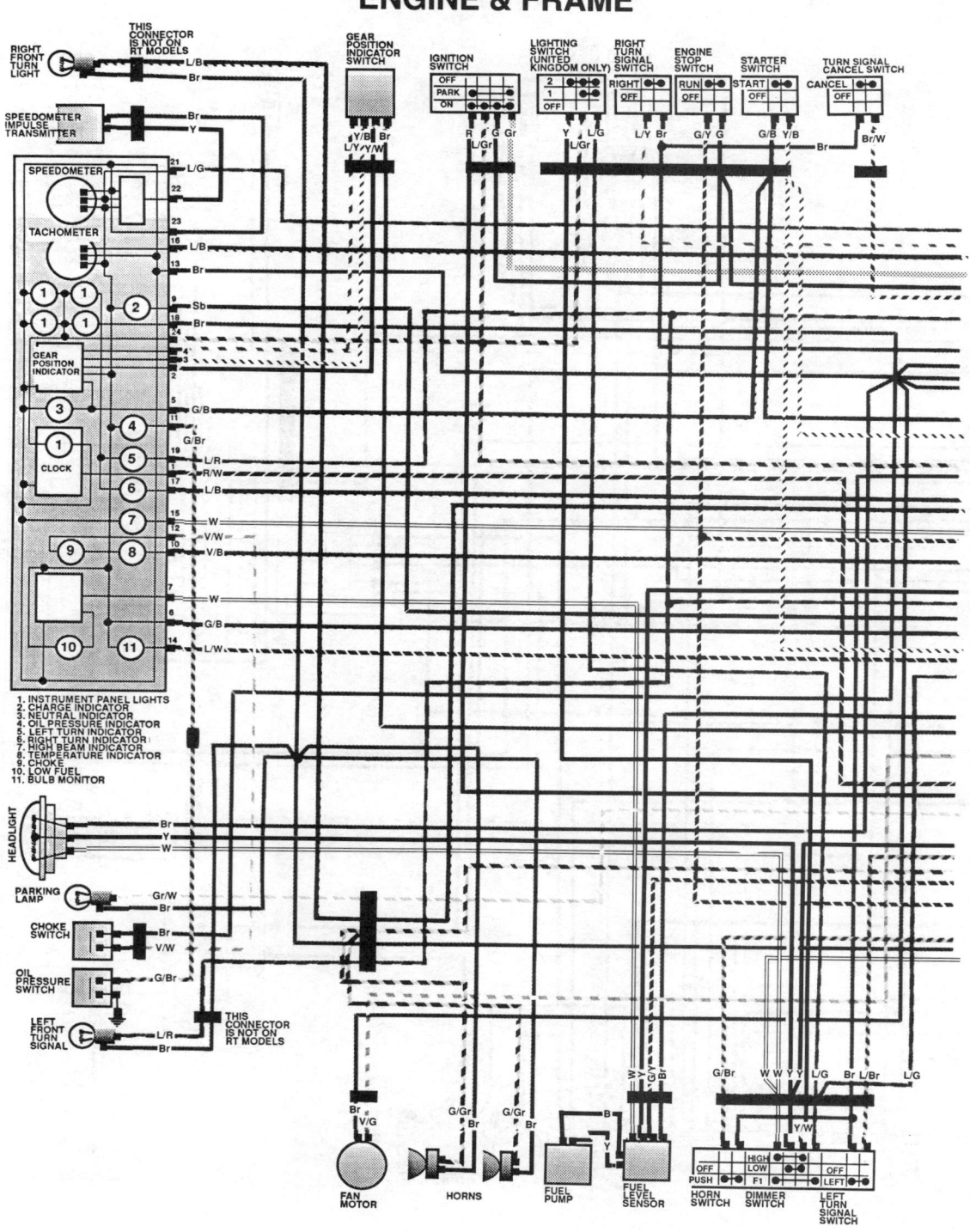

PAGE 1 OF 3

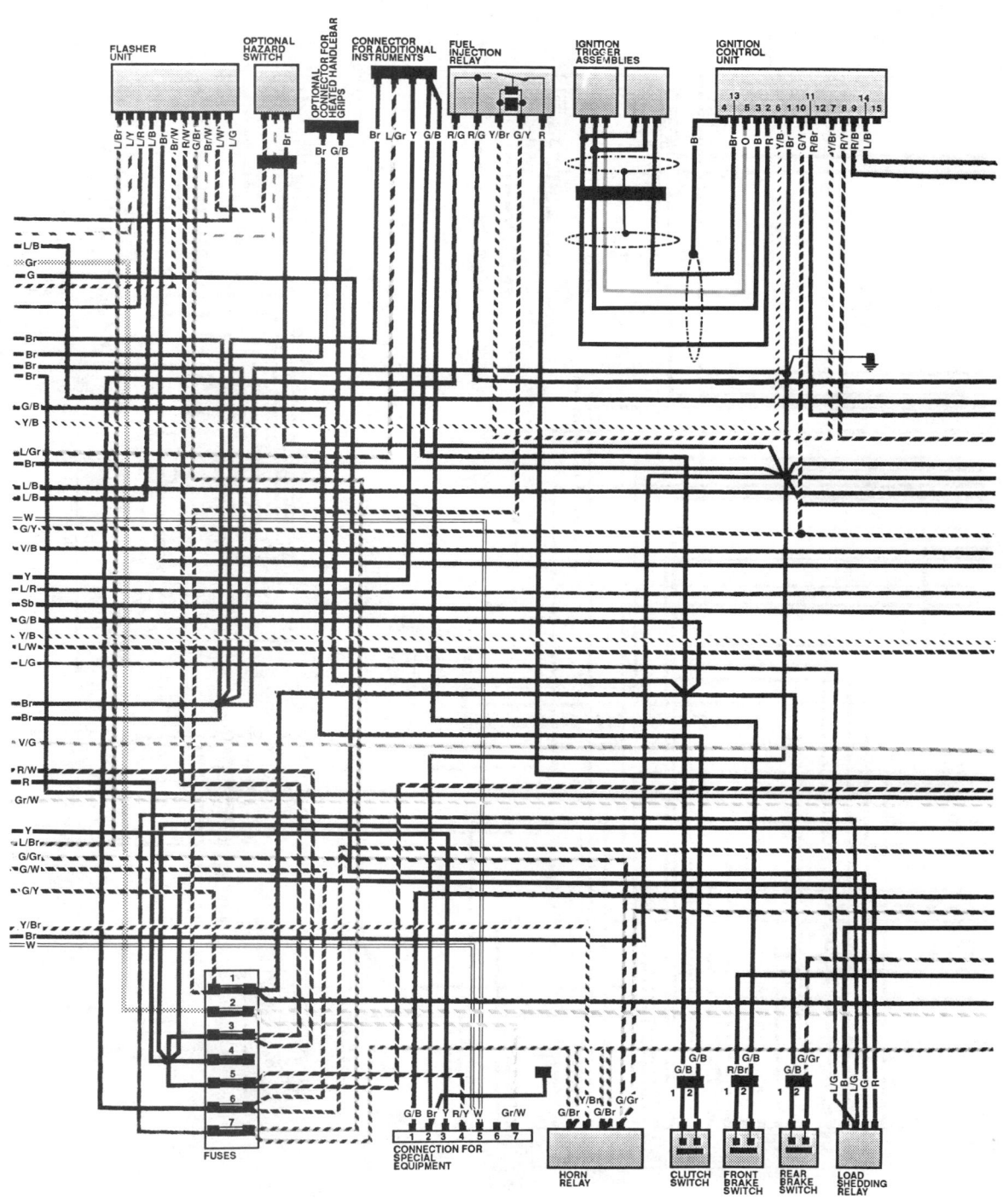

PAGE 2 OF 3

16

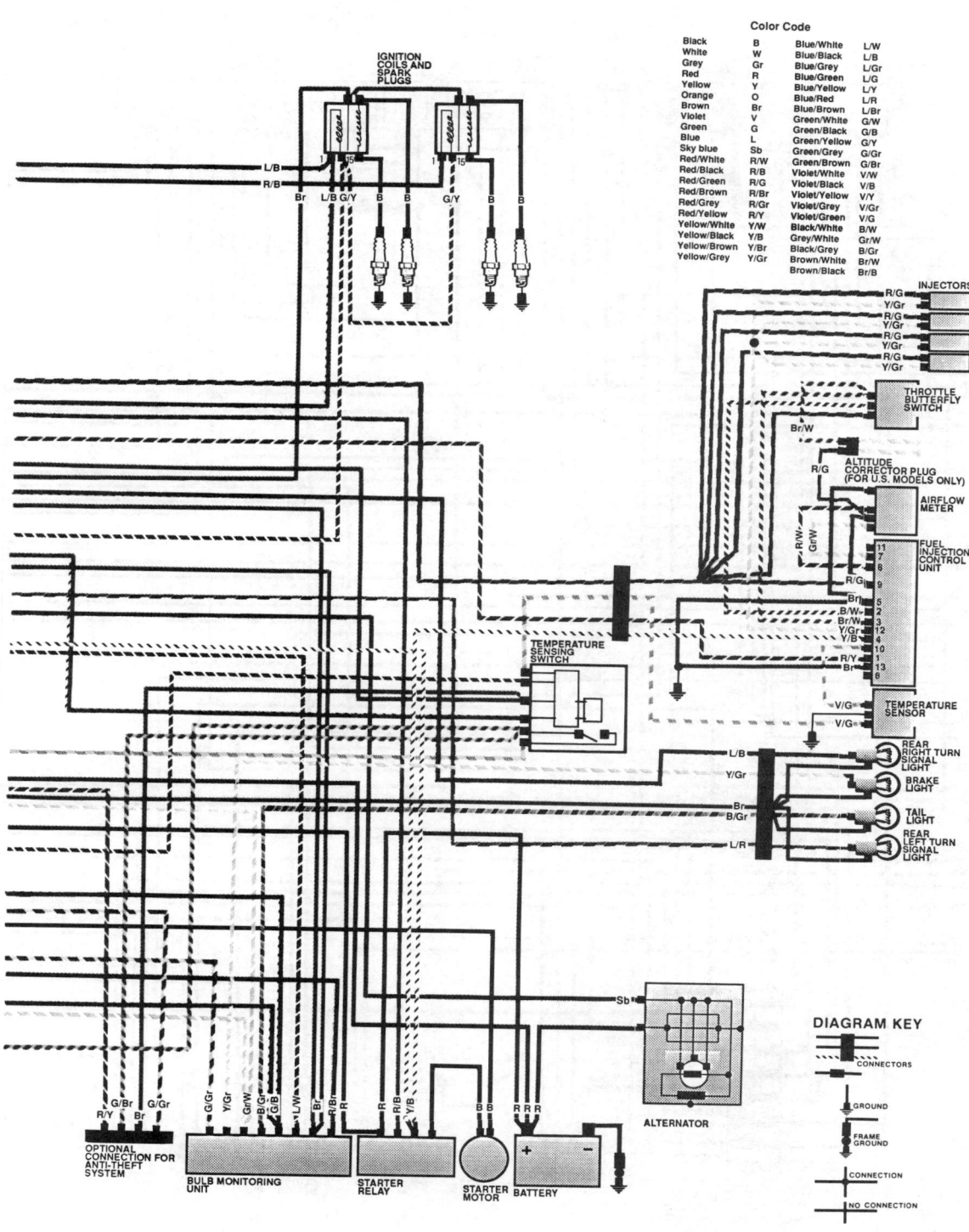

Color Code

Black	B	Blue/White	L/W
White	W	Blue/Black	L/B
Grey	Gr	Blue/Grey	L/Gr
Red	R	Blue/Green	L/G
Yellow	Y	Blue/Yellow	L/Y
Orange	O	Blue/Red	L/R
Brown	Br	Blue/Brown	L/Br
Violet	V	Green/White	G/W
Green	G	Green/Black	G/B
Blue	L	Green/Yellow	G/Y
Sky blue	Sb	Green/Grey	G/Gr
Red/White	R/W	Green/Brown	G/Br
Red/Black	R/B	Violet/White	V/W
Red/Green	R/G	Violet/Black	V/B
Red/Brown	R/Br	Violet/Yellow	V/Y
Red/Grey	R/Gr	Violet/Grey	V/Gr
Red/Yellow	R/Y	Violet/Green	V/G
Yellow/White	Y/W	Black/White	B/W
Yellow/Black	Y/B	Grey/White	Gr/W
Yellow/Brown	Y/Br	Black/Grey	B/Gr
Yellow/Grey	Y/Gr	Brown/White	Br/W
		Brown/Black	Br/B

PAGE 3 OF 3

1987-1989 K100LT
ENGINE & FRAME

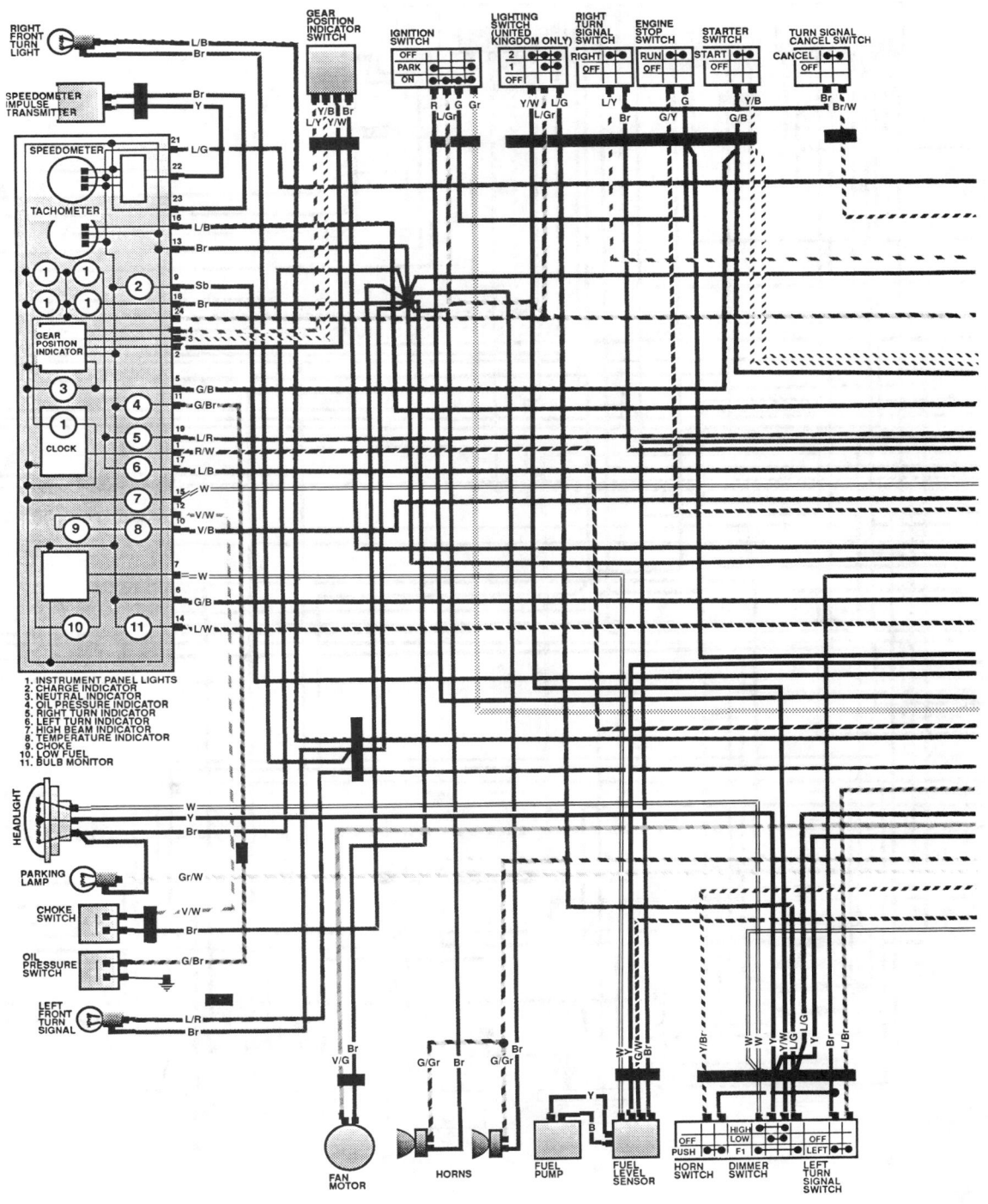

PAGE 1 OF 3

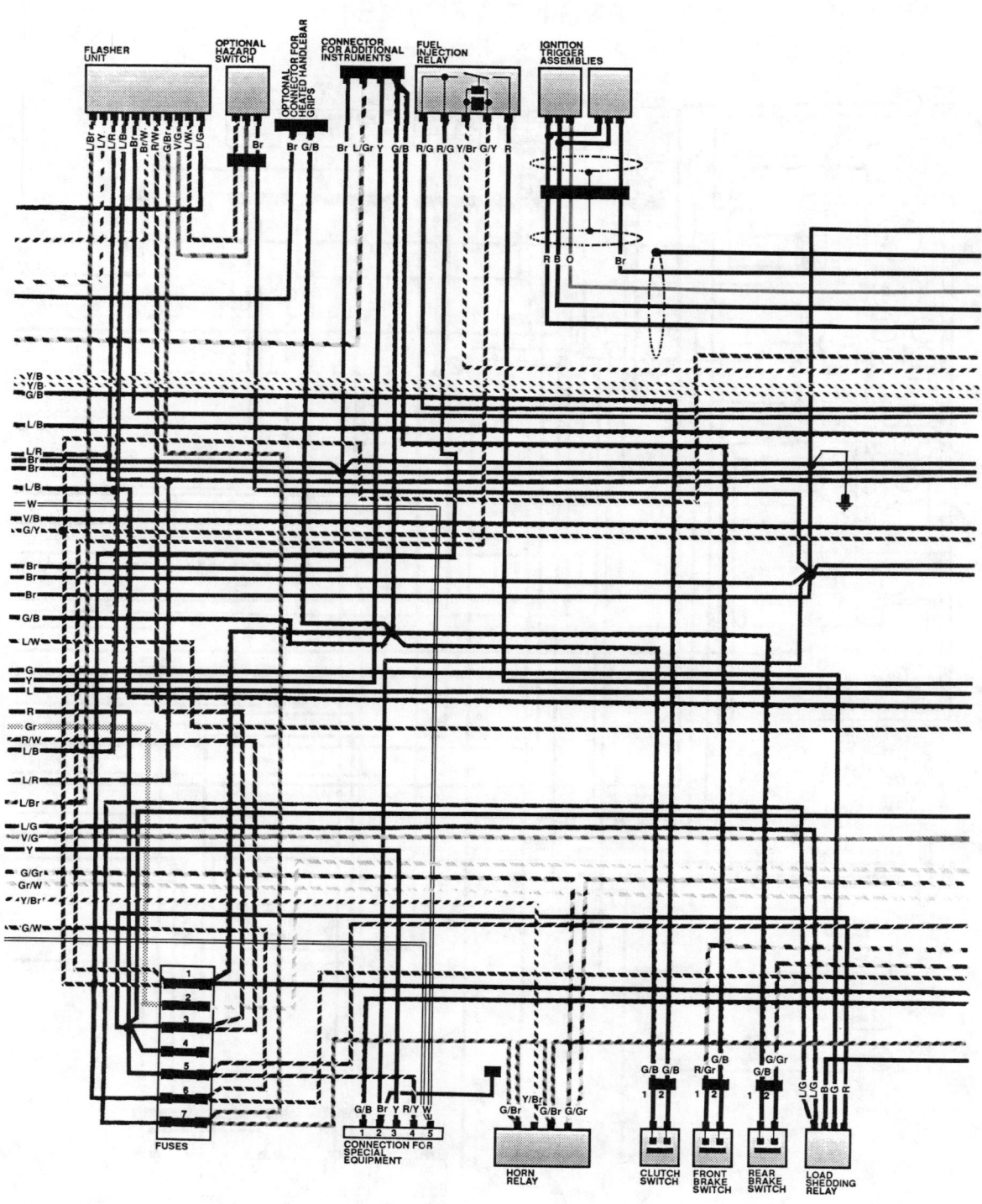

PAGE 2 OF 3

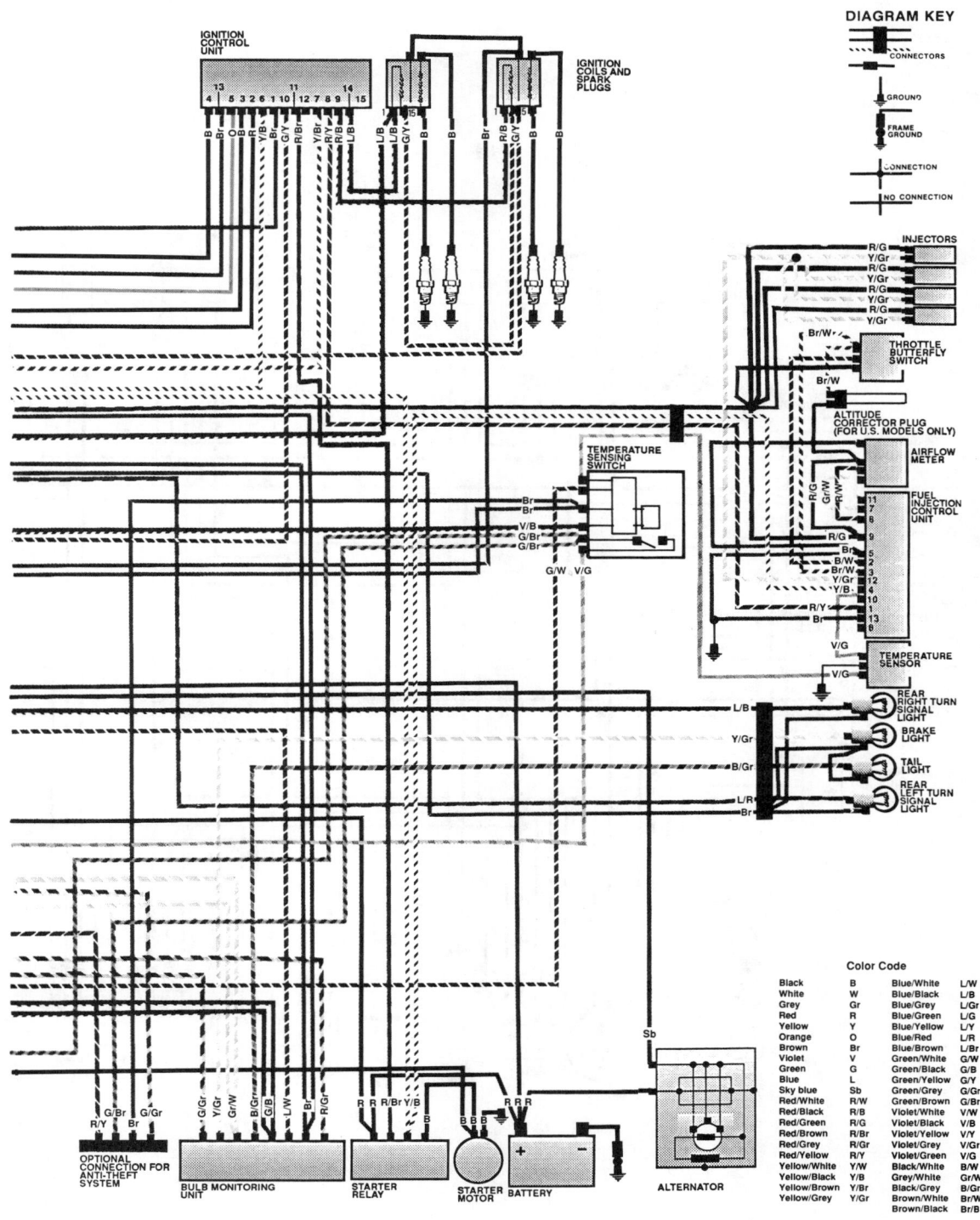

1991-1992 K100RS ENGINE

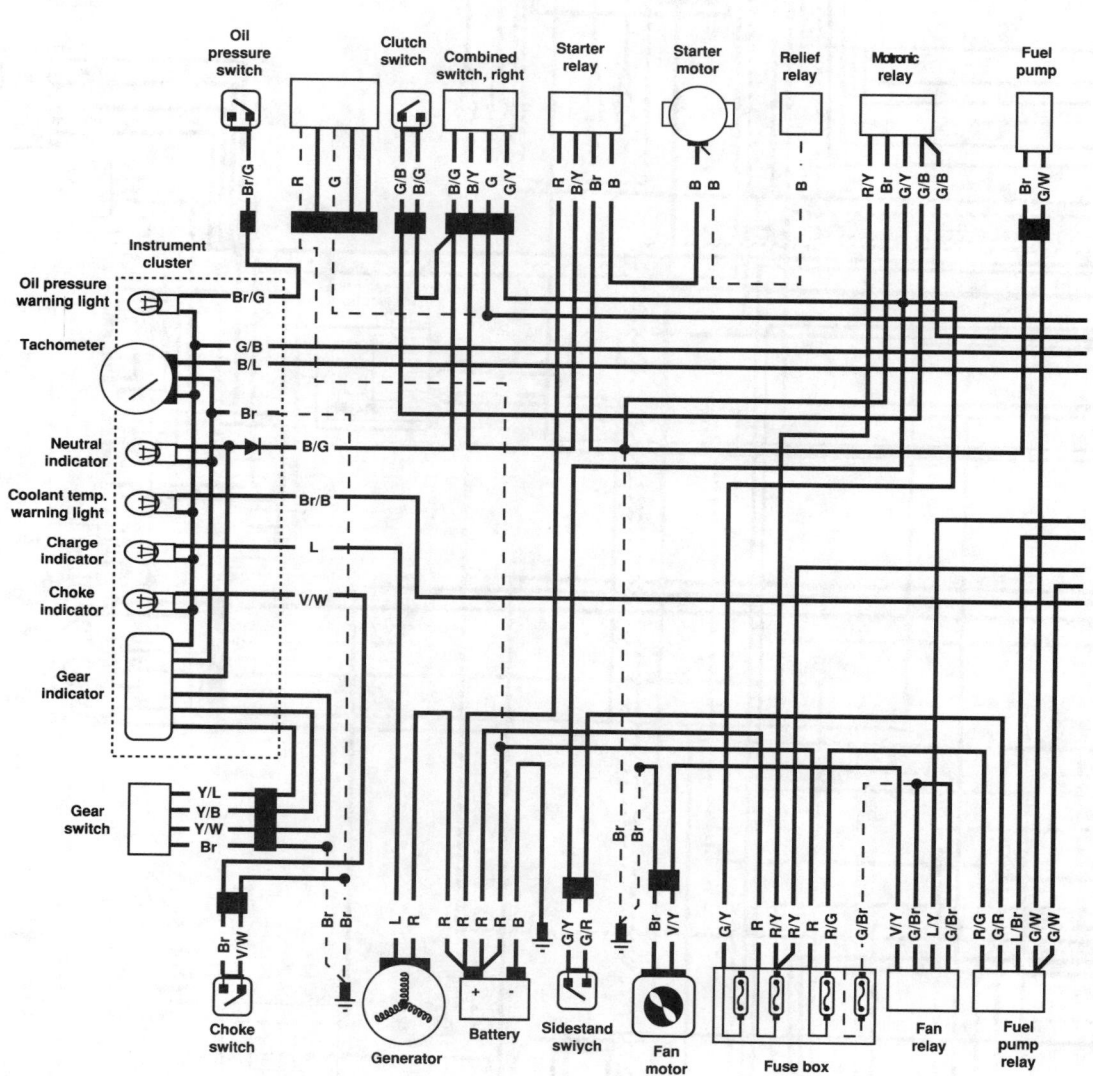

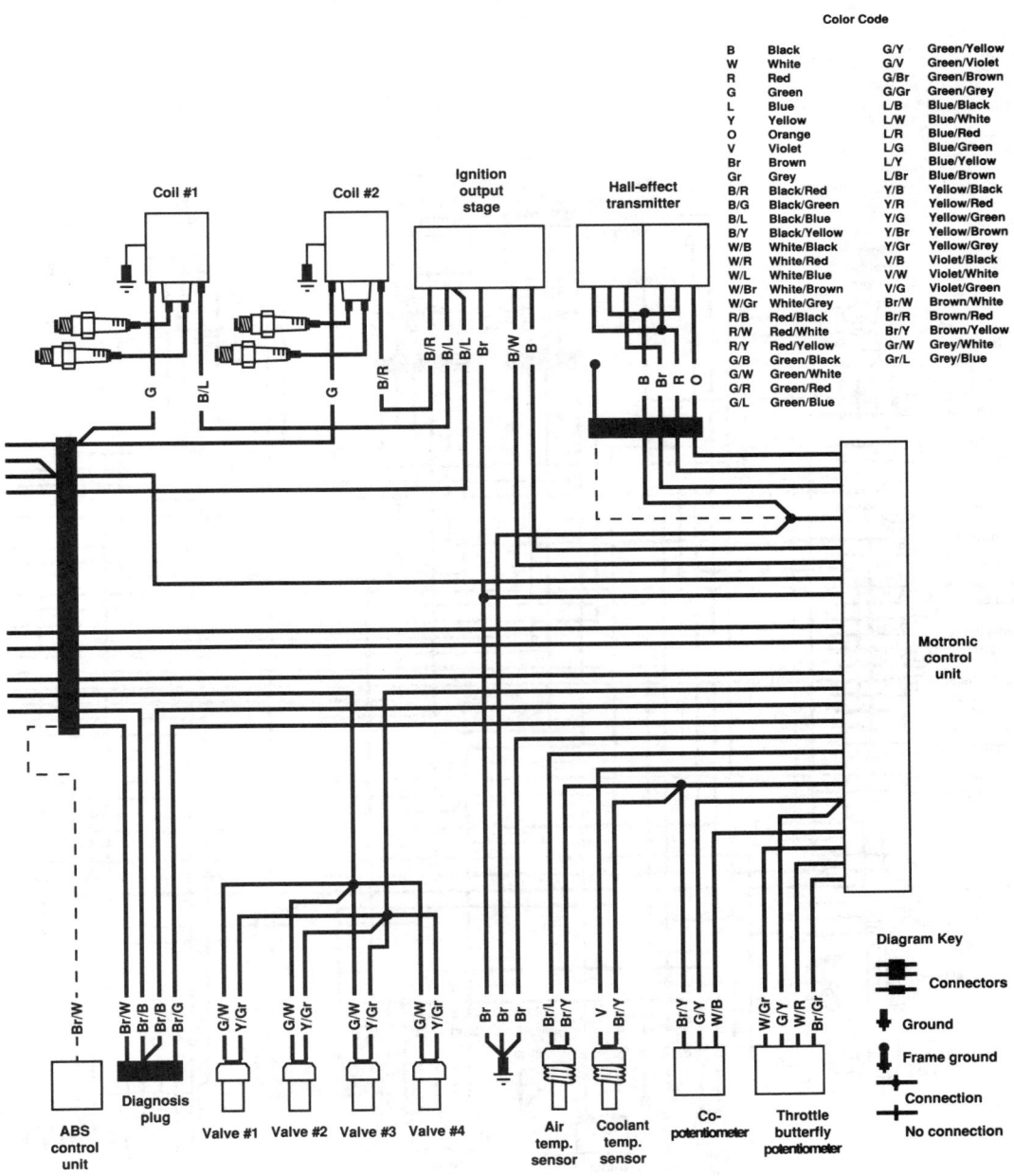

Color Code

B	Black	G/Y	Green/Yellow
W	White	G/V	Green/Violet
R	Red	G/Br	Green/Brown
G	Green	G/Gr	Green/Grey
L	Blue	L/B	Blue/Black
Y	Yellow	L/W	Blue/White
O	Orange	L/R	Blue/Red
V	Violet	L/G	Blue/Green
Br	Brown	L/Y	Blue/Yellow
Gr	Grey	L/Br	Blue/Brown
B/R	Black/Red	Y/B	Yellow/Black
B/G	Black/Green	Y/R	Yellow/Red
B/L	Black/Blue	Y/G	Yellow/Green
B/Y	Black/Yellow	Y/Br	Yellow/Brown
W/B	White/Black	Y/Gr	Yellow/Grey
W/R	White/Red	V/B	Violet/Black
W/L	White/Blue	V/W	Violet/White
W/Br	White/Brown	V/G	Violet/Green
W/Gr	White/Grey	Br/W	Brown/White
R/B	Red/Black	Br/R	Brown/Red
R/W	Red/White	Br/Y	Brown/Yellow
R/Y	Red/Yellow	Gr/W	Grey/White
G/B	Green/Black	Gr/L	Grey/Blue
G/W	Green/White		
G/R	Green/Red		
G/L	Green/Blue		

Coil #1

Coil #2

Ignition output stage

Hall-effect transmitter

Motronic control unit

Diagram Key

Connectors

Ground

Frame ground

Connection

No connection

ABS control unit

Diagnosis plug

Valve #1 Valve #2 Valve #3 Valve #4

Air temp. sensor

Coolant temp. sensor

Co-potentiometer

Throttle butterfly potentiometer

16

1991-1992 K100RS FRAME

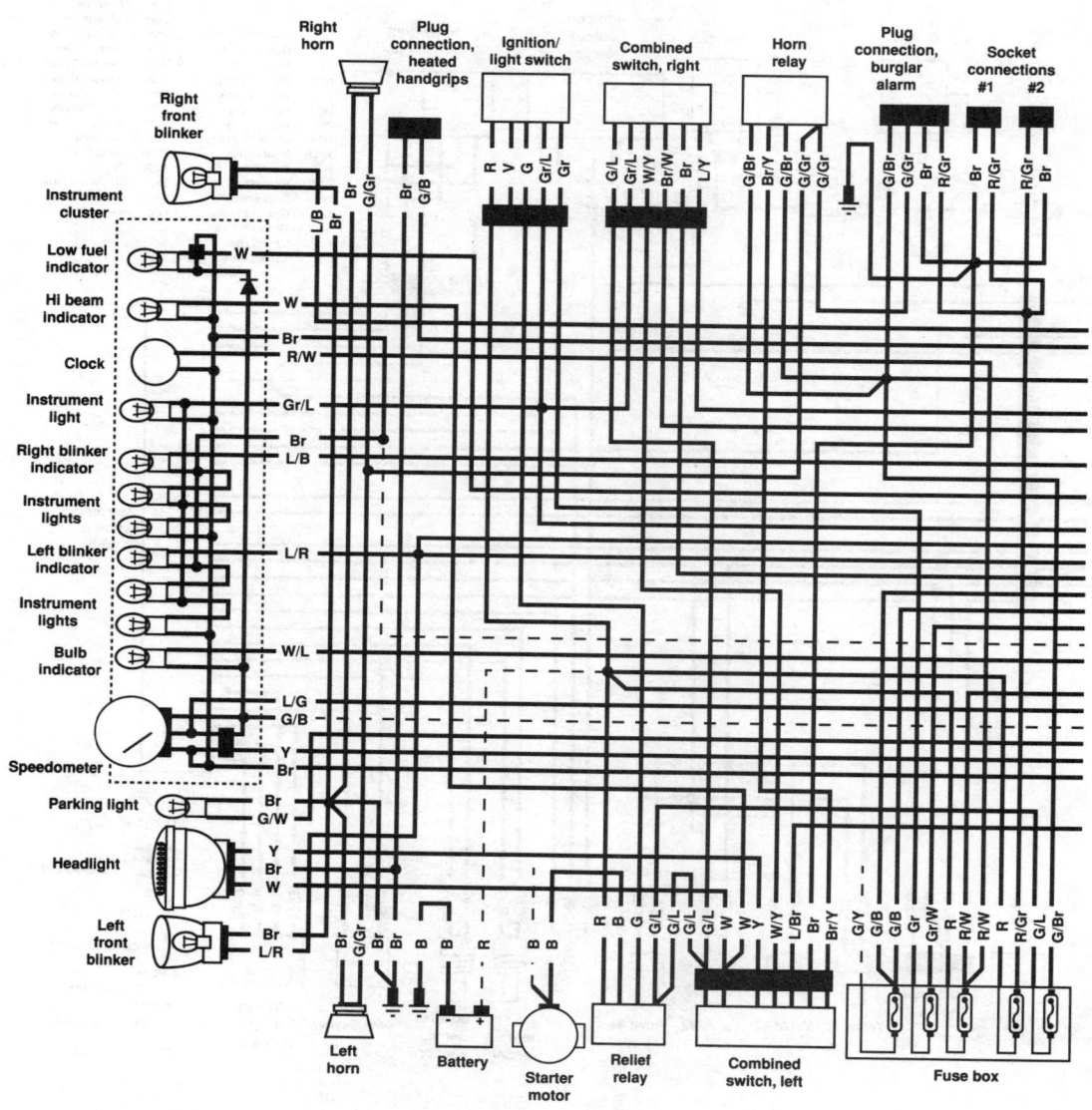

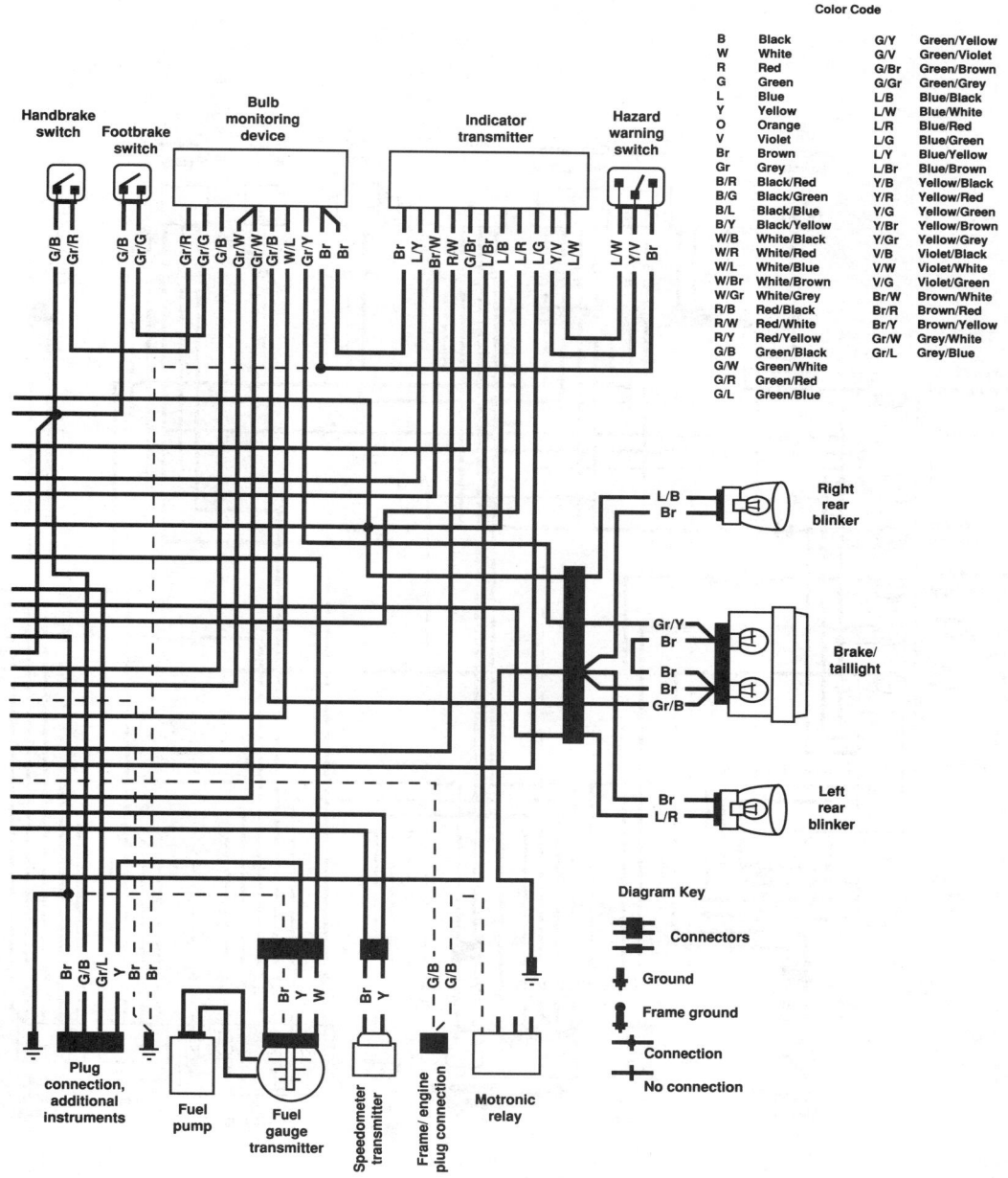

Color Code

B	Black	G/Y	Green/Yellow
W	White	G/V	Green/Violet
R	Red	G/Br	Green/Brown
G	Green	G/Gr	Green/Grey
L	Blue	L/B	Blue/Black
Y	Yellow	L/W	Blue/White
O	Orange	L/R	Blue/Red
V	Violet	L/G	Blue/Green
Br	Brown	L/Y	Blue/Yellow
Gr	Grey	L/Br	Blue/Brown
B/R	Black/Red	Y/B	Yellow/Black
B/G	Black/Green	Y/R	Yellow/Red
B/L	Black/Blue	Y/G	Yellow/Green
B/Y	Black/Yellow	Y/Br	Yellow/Brown
W/B	White/Black	Y/Gr	Yellow/Grey
W/R	White/Red	V/B	Violet/Black
W/L	White/Blue	V/W	Violet/White
W/Br	White/Brown	V/G	Violet/Green
W/Gr	White/Grey	Br/W	Brown/White
R/B	Red/Black	Br/R	Brown/Red
R/W	Red/White	Br/Y	Brown/Yellow
R/Y	Red/Yellow	Gr/W	Grey/White
G/B	Green/Black	Gr/L	Grey/Blue
G/W	Green/White		
G/R	Green/Red		
G/L	Green/Blue		

Handbrake switch
Footbrake switch
Bulb monitoring device
Indicator transmitter
Hazard warning switch

Right rear blinker

Brake/ taillight

Left rear blinker

Diagram Key

Connectors

Ground

Frame ground

Connection

No connection

Plug connection, additional instruments
Fuel pump
Fuel gauge transmitter
Speedometer transmitter
Frame/ engine plug connection
Motronic relay

16

1990-1993 K1 ENGINE

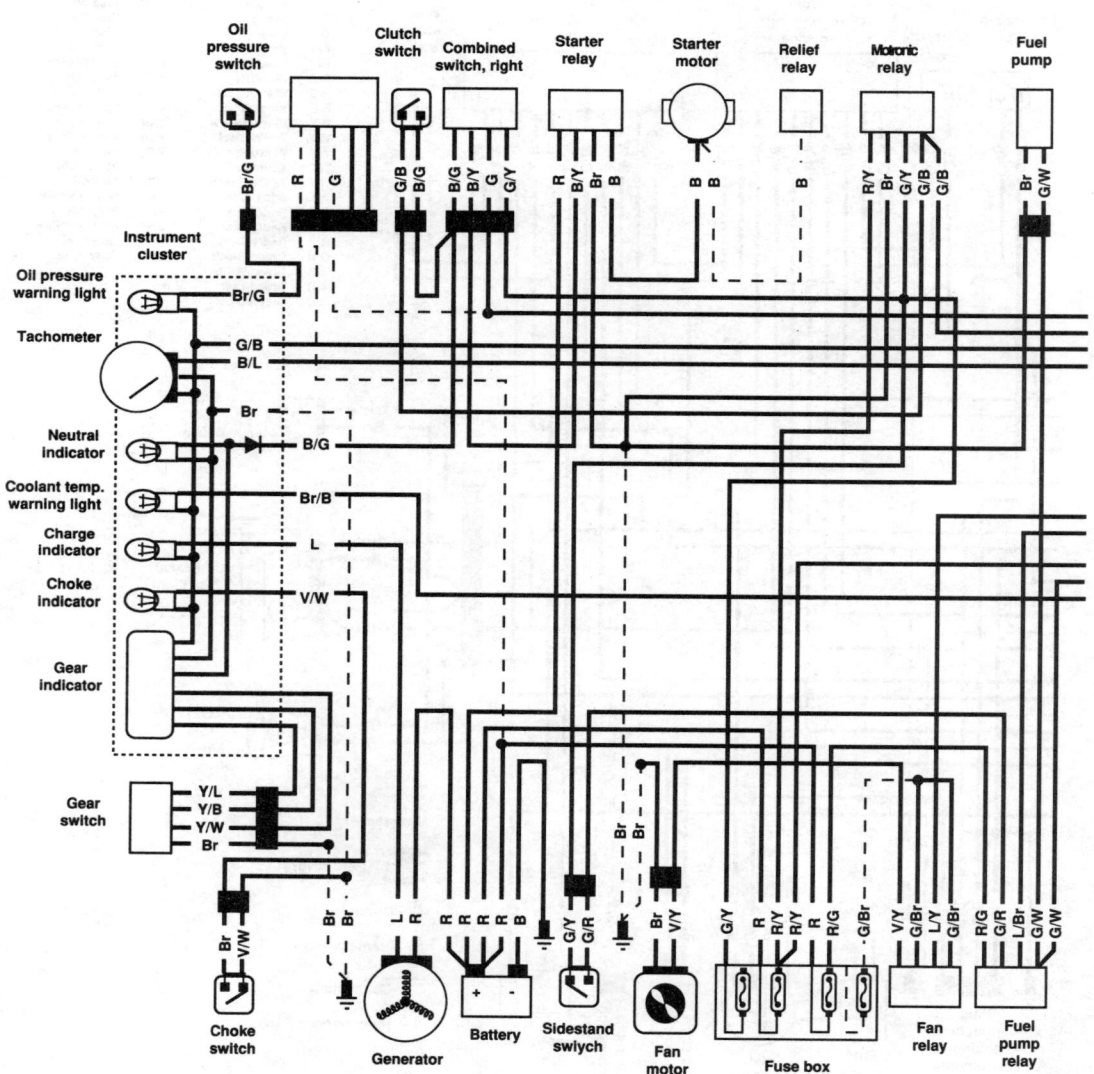

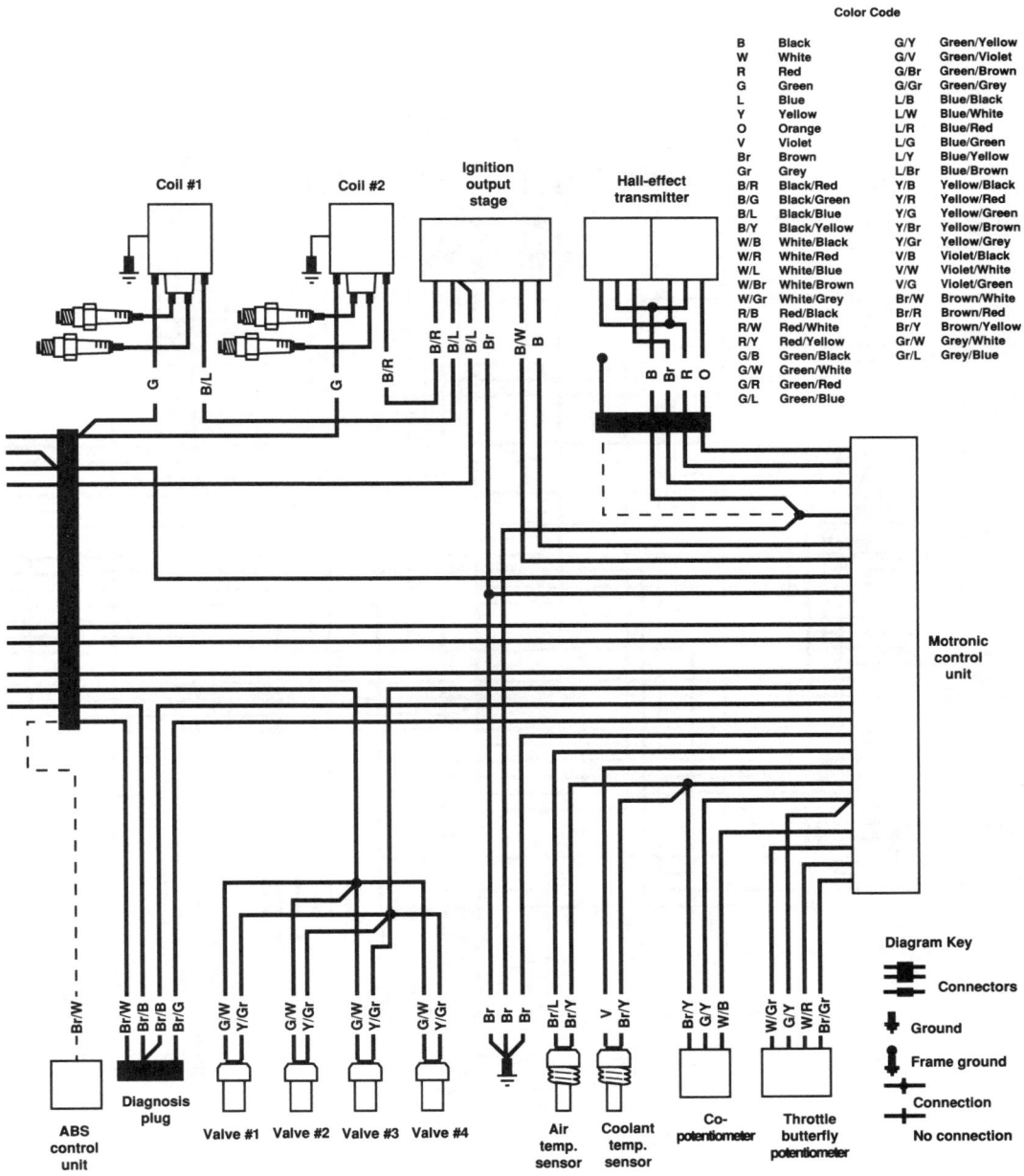

Color Code

B	Black	G/Y	Green/Yellow
W	White	G/V	Green/Violet
R	Red	G/Br	Green/Brown
G	Green	G/Gr	Green/Grey
L	Blue	L/B	Blue/Black
Y	Yellow	L/W	Blue/White
O	Orange	L/R	Blue/Red
V	Violet	L/G	Blue/Green
Br	Brown	L/Y	Blue/Yellow
Gr	Grey	L/Br	Blue/Brown
B/R	Black/Red	Y/B	Yellow/Black
B/G	Black/Green	Y/R	Yellow/Red
B/L	Black/Blue	Y/G	Yellow/Green
B/Y	Black/Yellow	Y/Br	Yellow/Brown
W/B	White/Black	Y/Gr	Yellow/Grey
W/R	White/Red	V/B	Violet/Black
W/L	White/Blue	V/W	Violet/White
W/Br	White/Brown	V/G	Violet/Green
W/Gr	White/Grey	Br/W	Brown/White
R/B	Red/Black	Br/R	Brown/Red
R/W	Red/White	Br/Y	Brown/Yellow
R/Y	Red/Yellow	Gr/W	Grey/White
G/B	Green/Black	Gr/L	Grey/Blue
G/W	Green/White		
G/R	Green/Red		
G/L	Green/Blue		

Coil #1

Coil #2

Ignition output stage

Hall-effect transmitter

Motronic control unit

Diagram Key

Connectors

Ground

Frame ground

Connection

No connection

ABS control unit

Diagnosis plug

Valve #1 Valve #2 Valve #3 Valve #4

Air temp. sensor

Coolant temp. sensor

Co-potentiometer

Throttle butterfly potentiometer

16

1990-1993 K1 FRAME

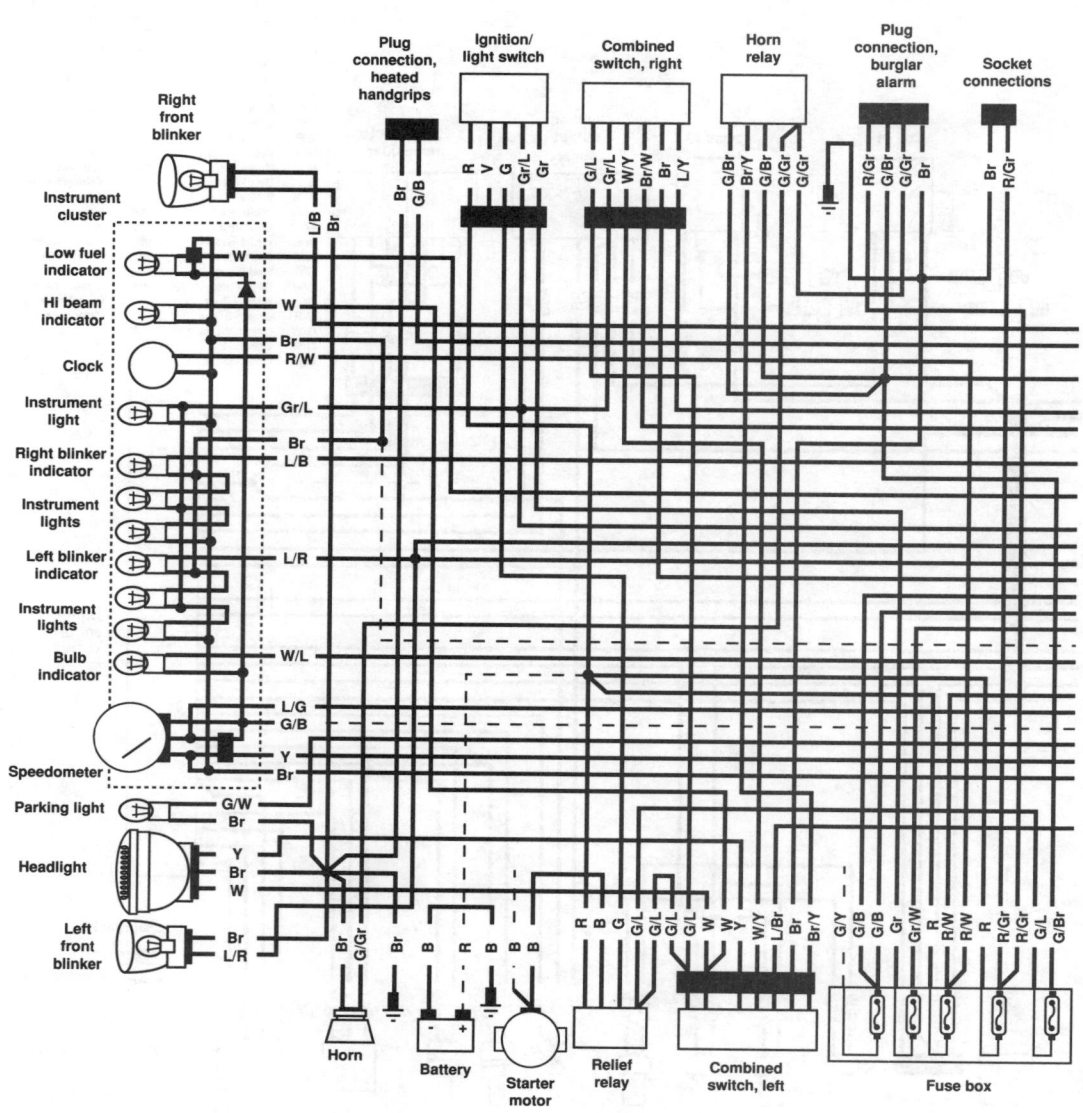

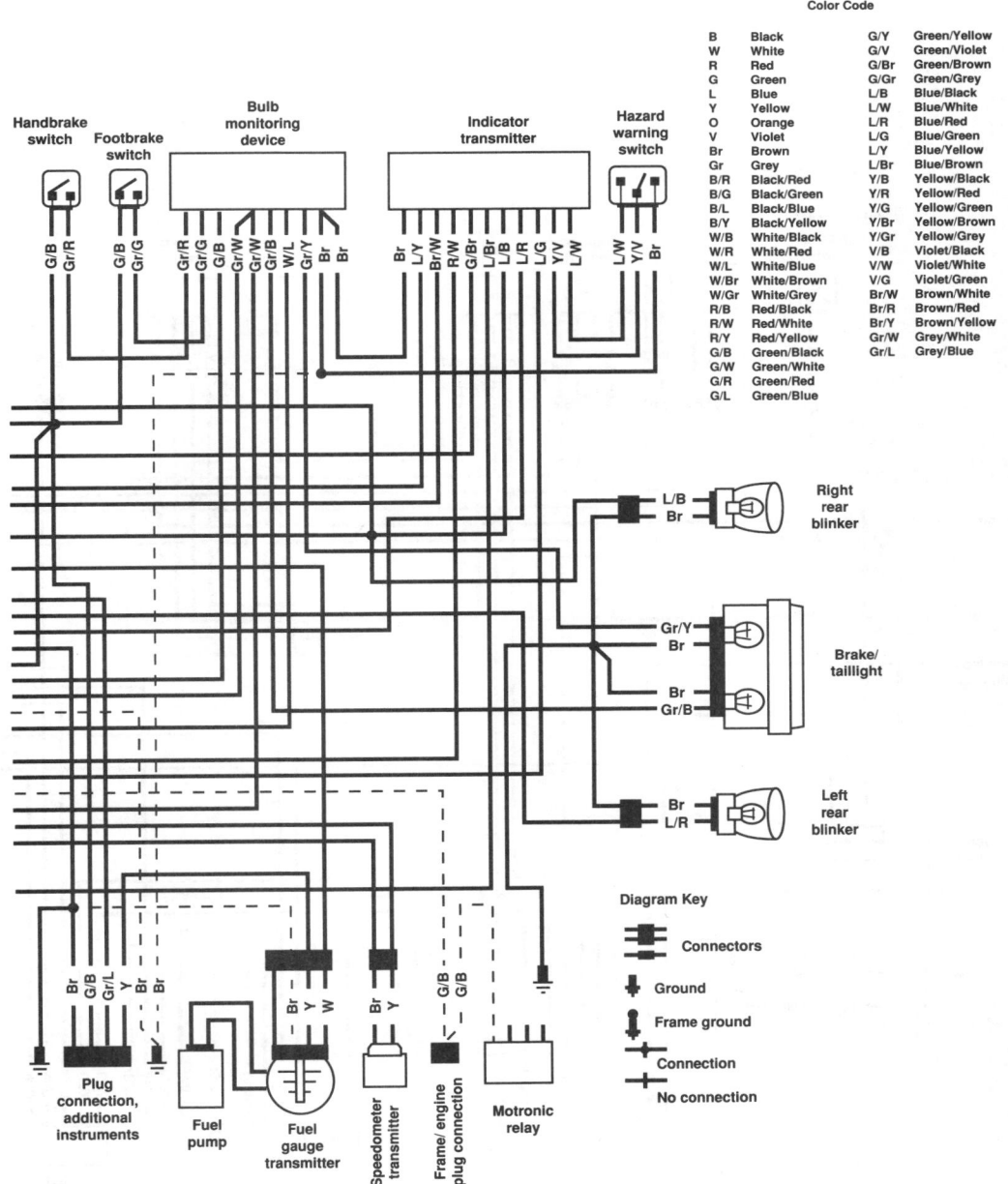

Color Code

B	Black	G/Y	Green/Yellow
W	White	G/V	Green/Violet
R	Red	G/Br	Green/Brown
G	Green	G/Gr	Green/Grey
L	Blue	L/B	Blue/Black
Y	Yellow	L/W	Blue/White
O	Orange	L/R	Blue/Red
V	Violet	L/G	Blue/Green
Br	Brown	L/Y	Blue/Yellow
Gr	Grey	L/Br	Blue/Brown
B/R	Black/Red	Y/B	Yellow/Black
B/G	Black/Green	Y/R	Yellow/Red
B/L	Black/Blue	Y/G	Yellow/Green
B/Y	Black/Yellow	Y/Br	Yellow/Brown
W/B	White/Black	Y/Gr	Yellow/Grey
W/R	White/Red	V/B	Violet/Black
W/L	White/Blue	V/W	Violet/White
W/Br	White/Brown	V/G	Violet/Green
W/Gr	White/Grey	Br/W	Brown/White
R/B	Red/Black	Br/R	Brown/Red
R/W	Red/White	Br/Y	Brown/Yellow
R/Y	Red/Yellow	Gr/W	Grey/White
G/B	Green/Black	Gr/L	Grey/Blue
G/W	Green/White		
G/R	Green/Red		
G/L	Green/Blue		

Handbrake switch

Footbrake switch

Bulb monitoring device

Indicator transmitter

Hazard warning switch

Right rear blinker

Brake/ taillight

Left rear blinker

Diagram Key

Connectors

Ground

Frame ground

Connection

No connection

Plug connection, additional instruments

Fuel pump

Fuel gauge transmitter

Speedometer transmitter

Frame/ engine plug connection

Motronic relay

16

1993 K1100RS & K1100LT ENGINE

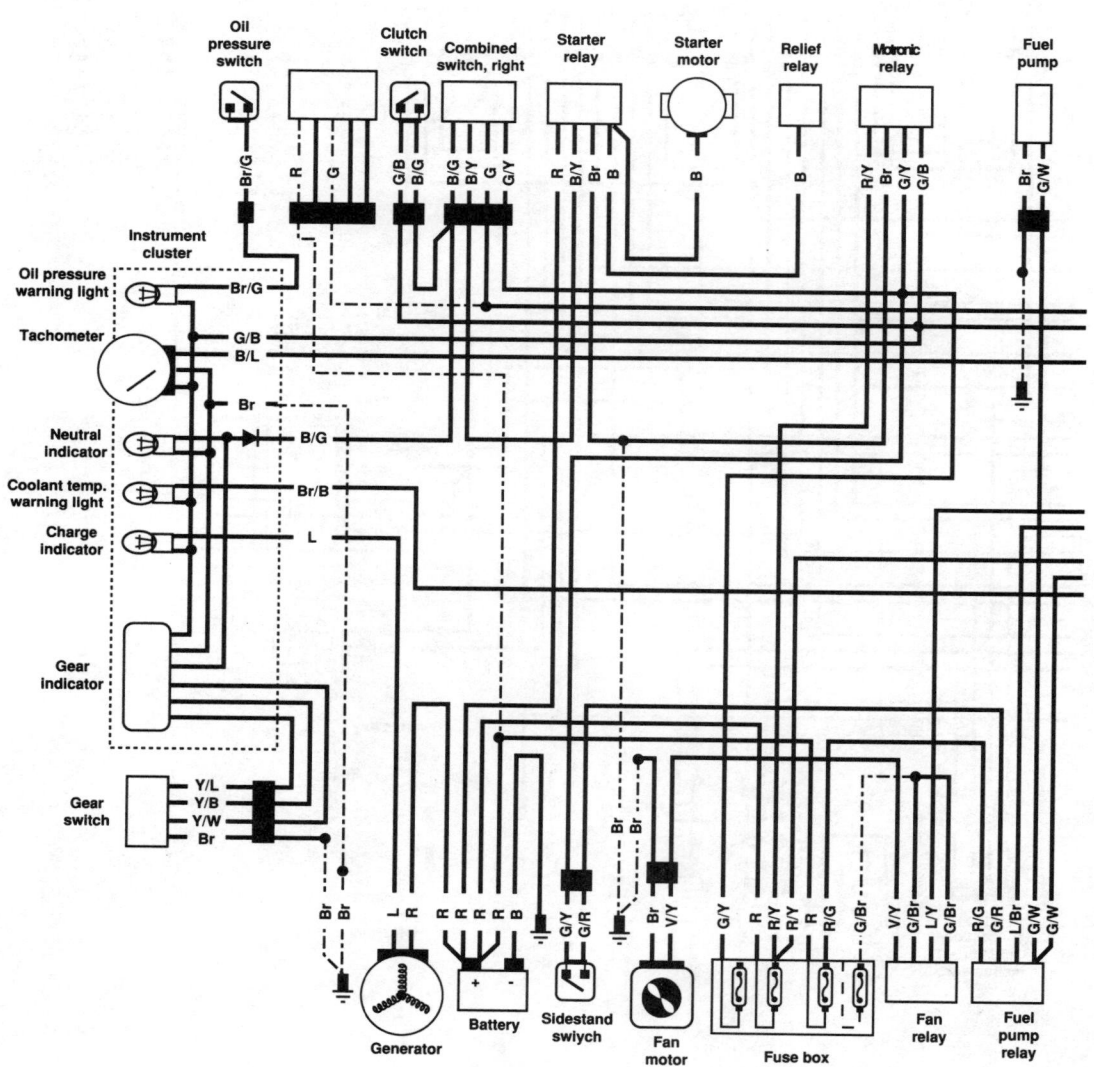

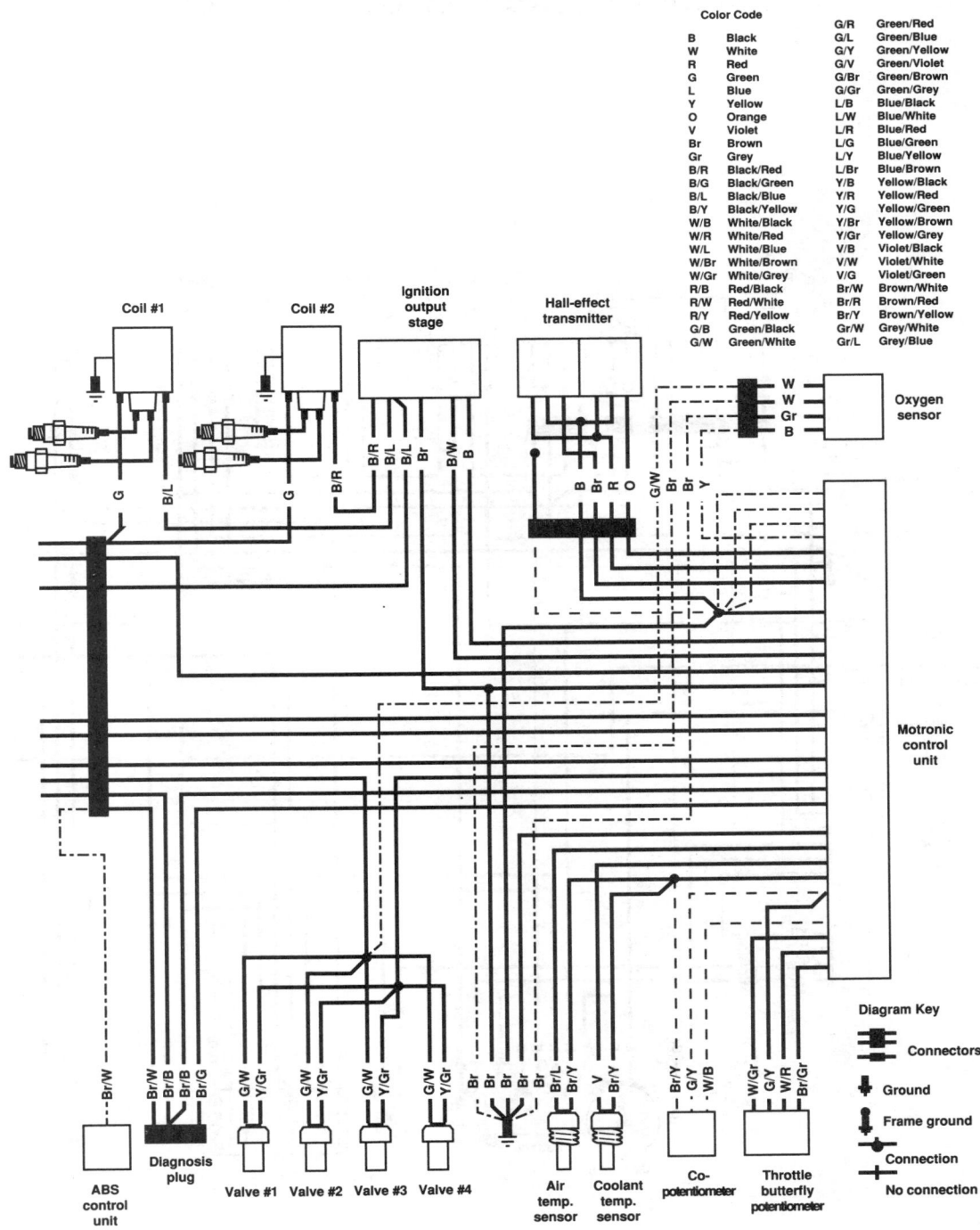

Color Code

B	Black	G/R	Green/Red
W	White	G/L	Green/Blue
R	Red	G/Y	Green/Yellow
G	Green	G/V	Green/Violet
L	Blue	G/Br	Green/Brown
Y	Yellow	G/Gr	Green/Grey
O	Orange	L/B	Blue/Black
V	Violet	L/W	Blue/White
Br	Brown	L/R	Blue/Red
Gr	Grey	L/G	Blue/Green
B/R	Black/Red	L/Y	Blue/Yellow
B/G	Black/Green	L/Br	Blue/Brown
B/L	Black/Blue	Y/B	Yellow/Black
B/Y	Black/Yellow	Y/R	Yellow/Red
W/B	White/Black	Y/G	Yellow/Green
W/R	White/Red	Y/Br	Yellow/Brown
W/L	White/Blue	Y/Gr	Yellow/Grey
W/Br	White/Brown	V/B	Violet/Black
W/Gr	White/Grey	V/W	Violet/White
R/B	Red/Black	V/G	Violet/Green
R/W	Red/White	Br/W	Brown/White
R/Y	Red/Yellow	Br/R	Brown/Red
G/B	Green/Black	Br/Y	Brown/Yellow
G/W	Green/White	Gr/W	Grey/White
		Gr/L	Grey/Blue

Diagram Key

- Connectors
- Ground
- Frame ground
- Connection
- No connection

16

1994-ON K1100RS & K1100LT ENGINE

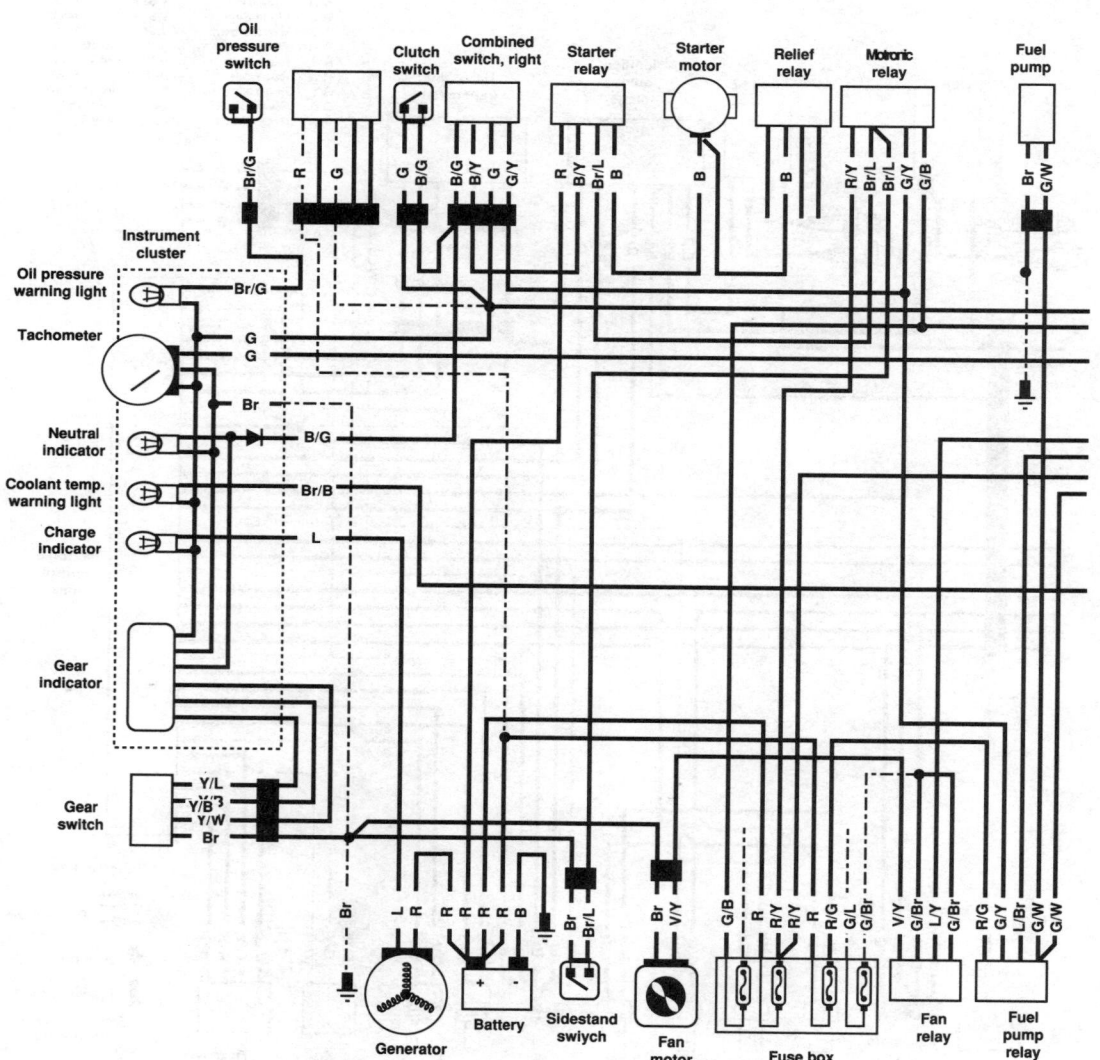

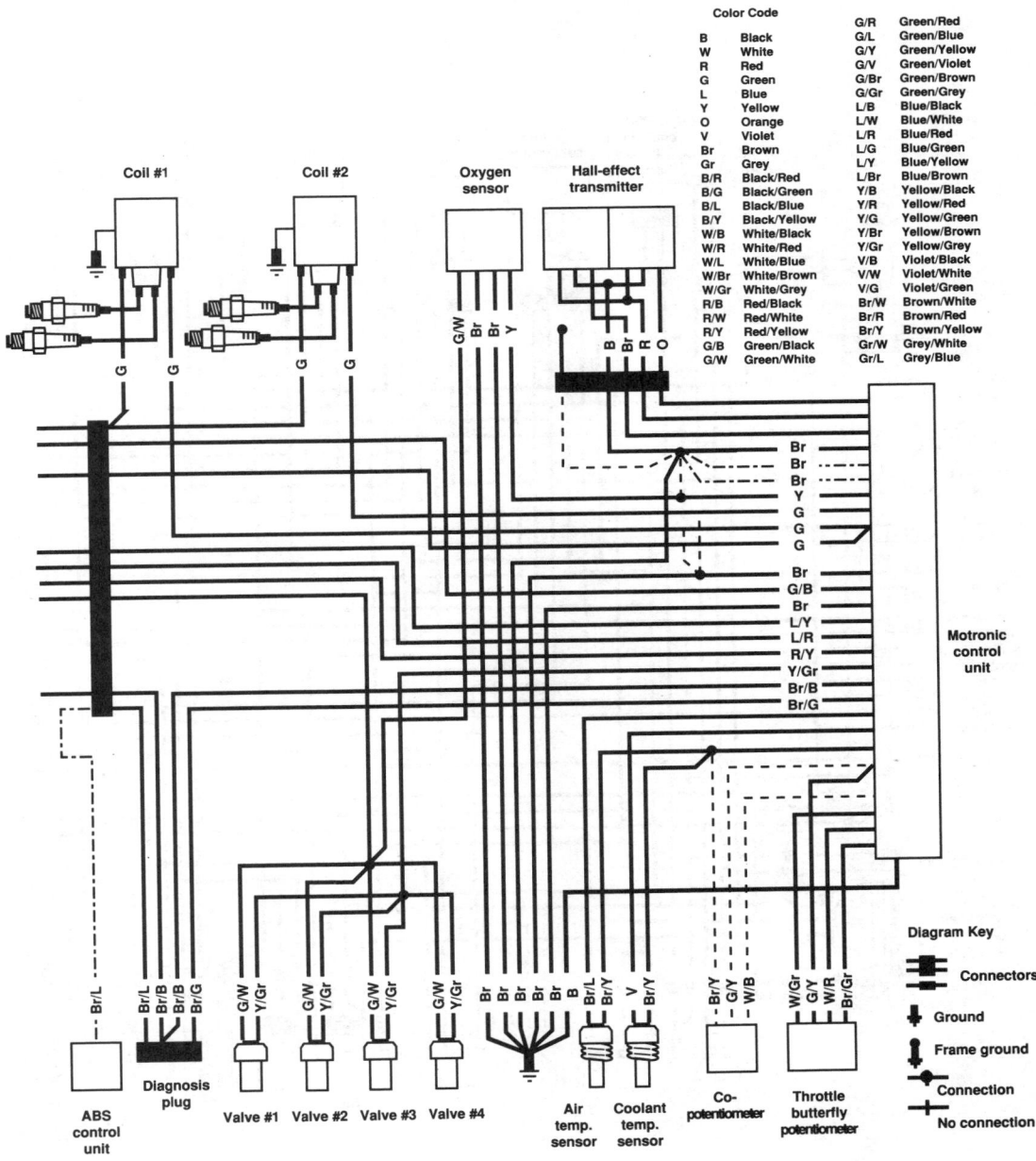

Color Code

B	Black	G/R	Green/Red
W	White	G/L	Green/Blue
R	Red	G/Y	Green/Yellow
G	Green	G/V	Green/Violet
L	Blue	G/Br	Green/Brown
Y	Yellow	G/Gr	Green/Grey
O	Orange	L/B	Blue/Black
V	Violet	L/W	Blue/White
Br	Brown	L/R	Blue/Red
Gr	Grey	L/G	Blue/Green
B/R	Black/Red	L/Y	Blue/Yellow
B/G	Black/Green	L/Br	Blue/Brown
B/L	Black/Blue	Y/B	Yellow/Black
B/Y	Black/Yellow	Y/R	Yellow/Red
W/B	White/Black	Y/G	Yellow/Green
W/R	White/Red	Y/Br	Yellow/Brown
W/L	White/Blue	Y/Gr	Yellow/Grey
W/Br	White/Brown	V/B	Violet/Black
W/Gr	White/Grey	V/W	Violet/White
R/B	Red/Black	V/G	Violet/Green
R/W	Red/White	Br/W	Brown/White
R/Y	Red/Yellow	Br/R	Brown/Red
G/B	Green/Black	Br/Y	Brown/Yellow
G/W	Green/White	Gr/W	Grey/White
		Gr/L	Grey/Blue

Coil #1   Coil #2   Oxygen sensor   Hall-effect transmitter

Motronic control unit

ABS control unit   Diagnosis plug   Valve #1   Valve #2   Valve #3   Valve #4   Air temp. sensor   Coolant temp. sensor   Co-potentiometer   Throttle butterfly potentiometer

Diagram Key

Connectors

Ground

Frame ground

Connection

No connection

16

1993 K1100LT FRAME

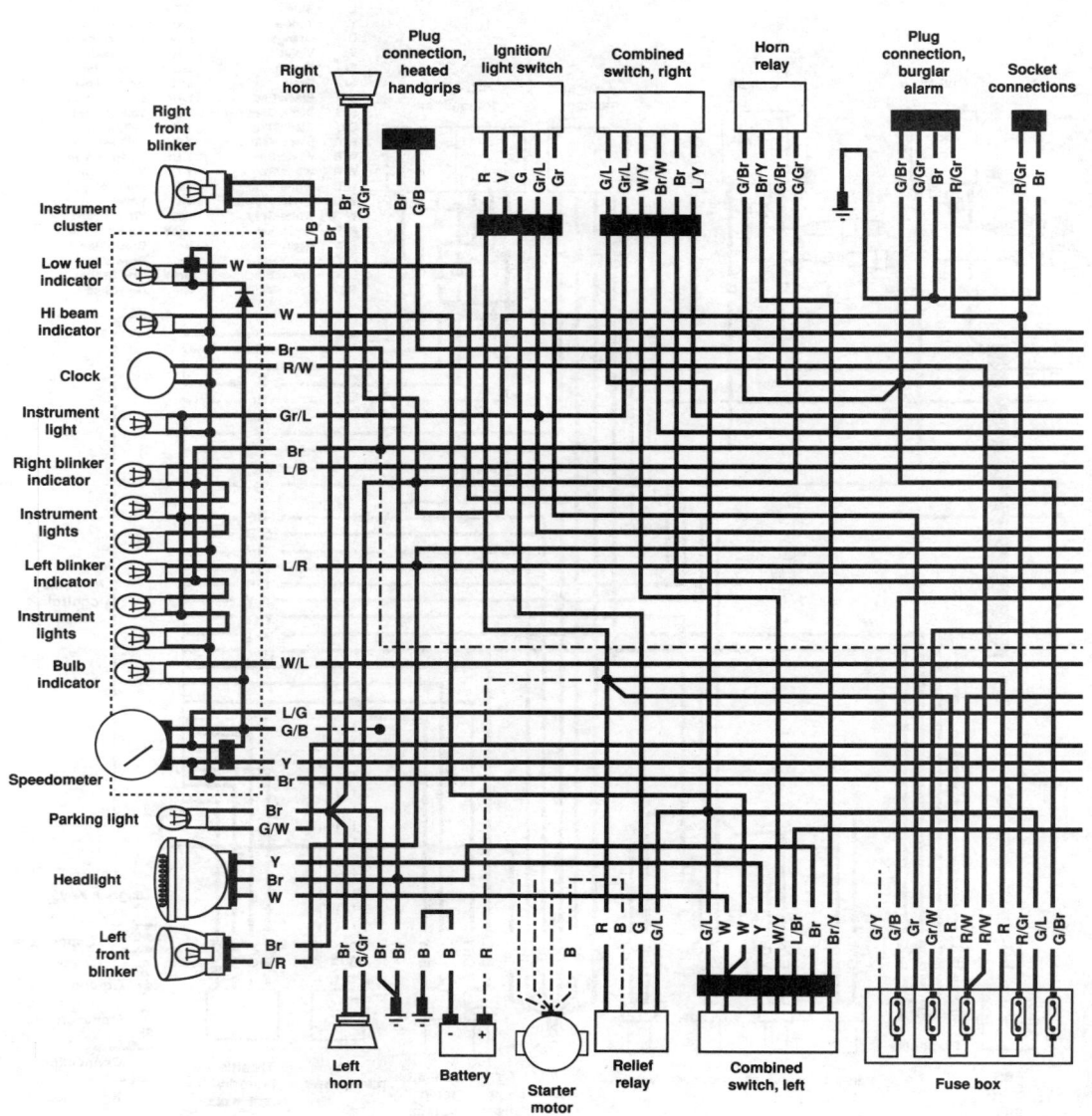

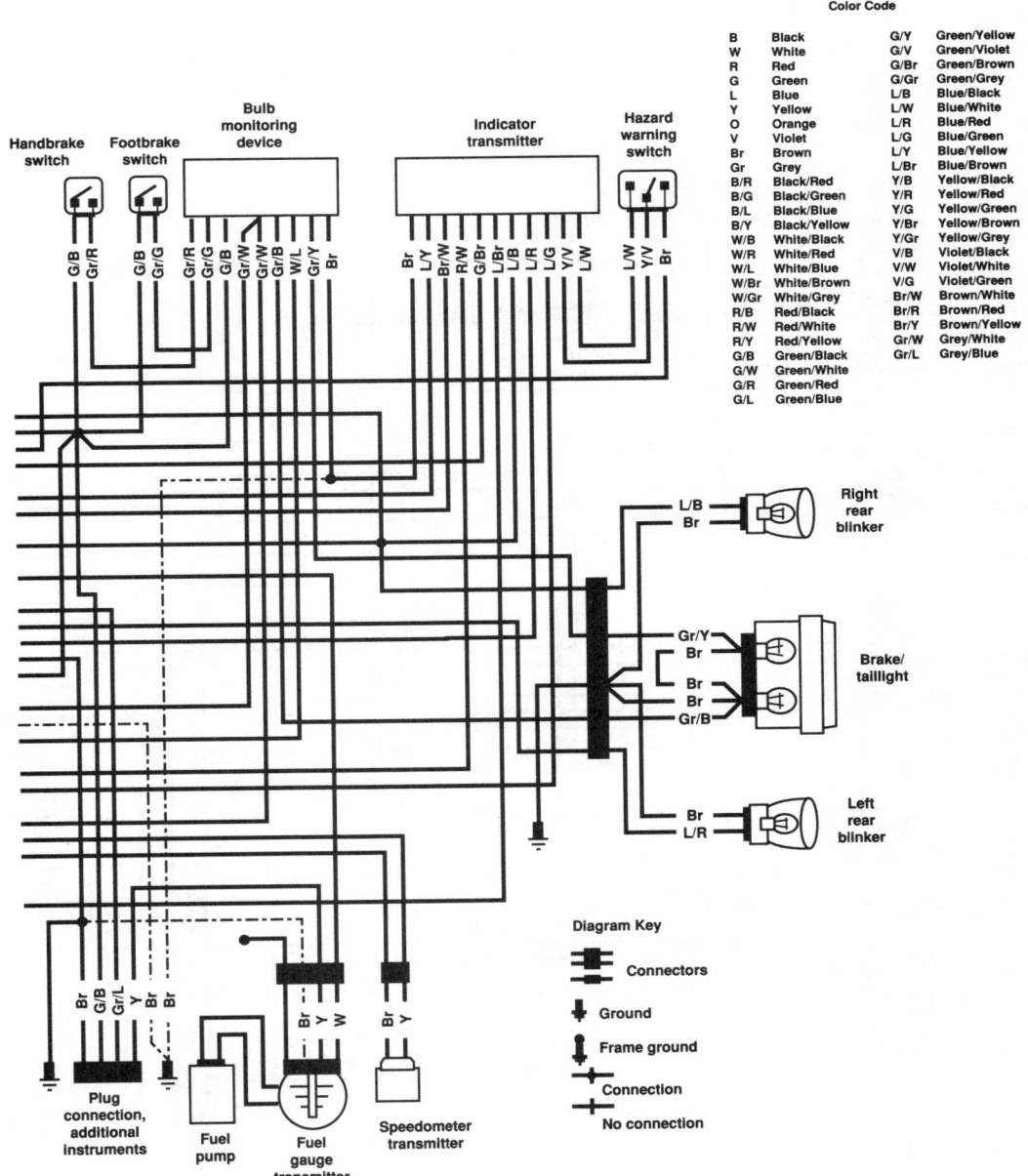

Color Code

B	Black	G/Y	Green/Yellow
W	White	G/V	Green/Violet
R	Red	G/Br	Green/Brown
G	Green	G/Gr	Green/Grey
L	Blue	L/B	Blue/Black
Y	Yellow	L/W	Blue/White
O	Orange	L/R	Blue/Red
V	Violet	L/G	Blue/Green
Br	Brown	L/Y	Blue/Yellow
Gr	Grey	L/Br	Blue/Brown
B/R	Black/Red	Y/B	Yellow/Black
B/G	Black/Green	Y/R	Yellow/Red
B/L	Black/Blue	Y/G	Yellow/Green
B/Y	Black/Yellow	Y/Br	Yellow/Brown
W/B	White/Black	Y/Gr	Yellow/Grey
W/R	White/Red	V/B	Violet/Black
W/L	White/Blue	V/W	Violet/White
W/Br	White/Brown	V/G	Violet/Green
W/Gr	White/Grey	Br/W	Brown/White
R/B	Red/Black	Br/R	Brown/Red
R/W	Red/White	Br/Y	Brown/Yellow
R/Y	Red/Yellow	Gr/W	Grey/White
G/B	Green/Black	Gr/L	Grey/Blue
G/W	Green/White		
G/R	Green/Red		
G/L	Green/Blue		

Handbrake switch

Footbrake switch

Bulb monitoring device

Indicator transmitter

Hazard warning switch

Right rear blinker

L/B
Br

Brake/taillight

Gr/Y
Br
Br
Br
Gr/B

Left rear blinker

Br
L/R

Diagram Key

Connectors

Ground

Frame ground

Connection

No connection

Plug connection, additional instruments

Fuel pump

Fuel gauge transmitter

Speedometer transmitter

16

1994-ON K1100LT FRAME

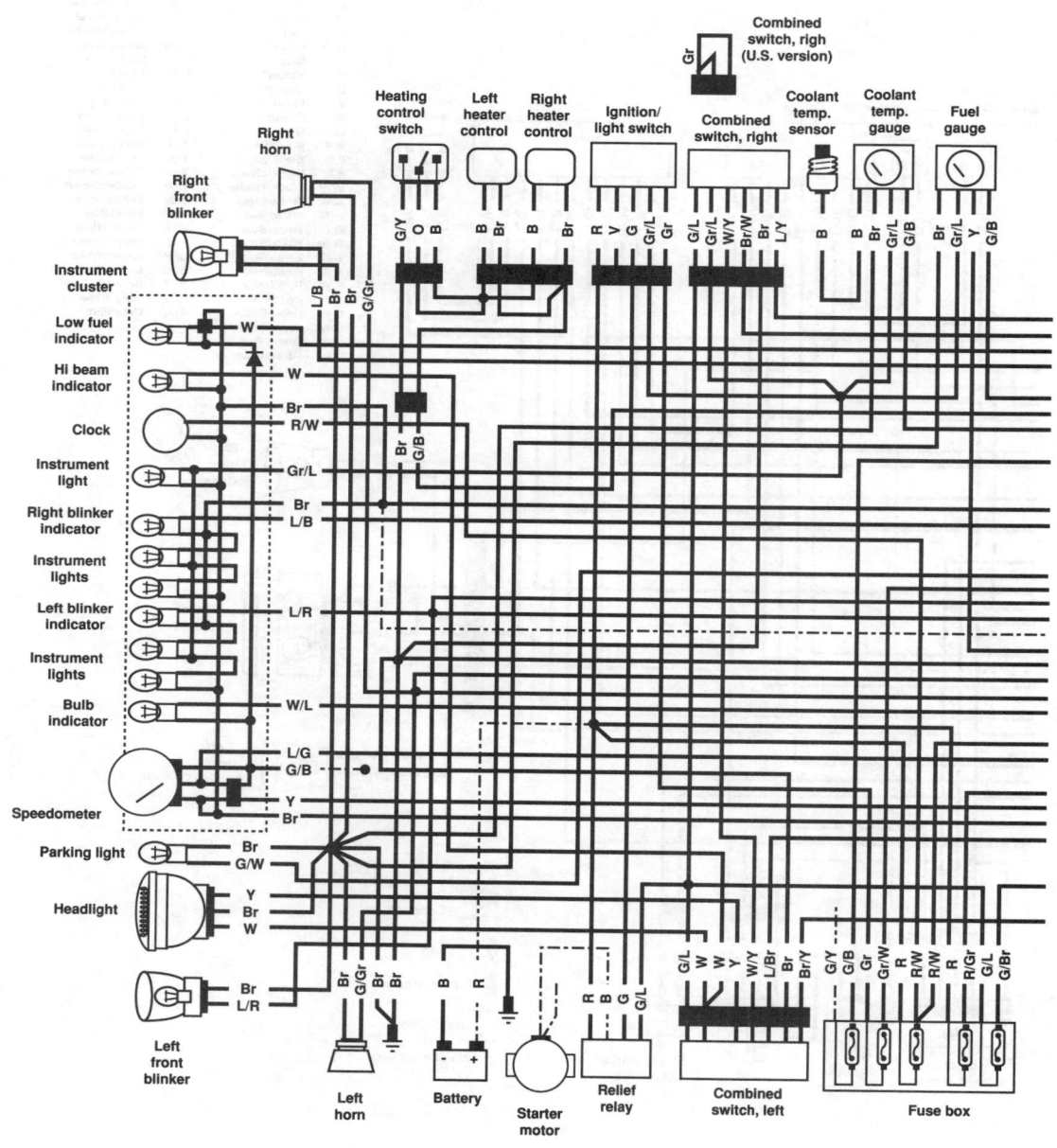

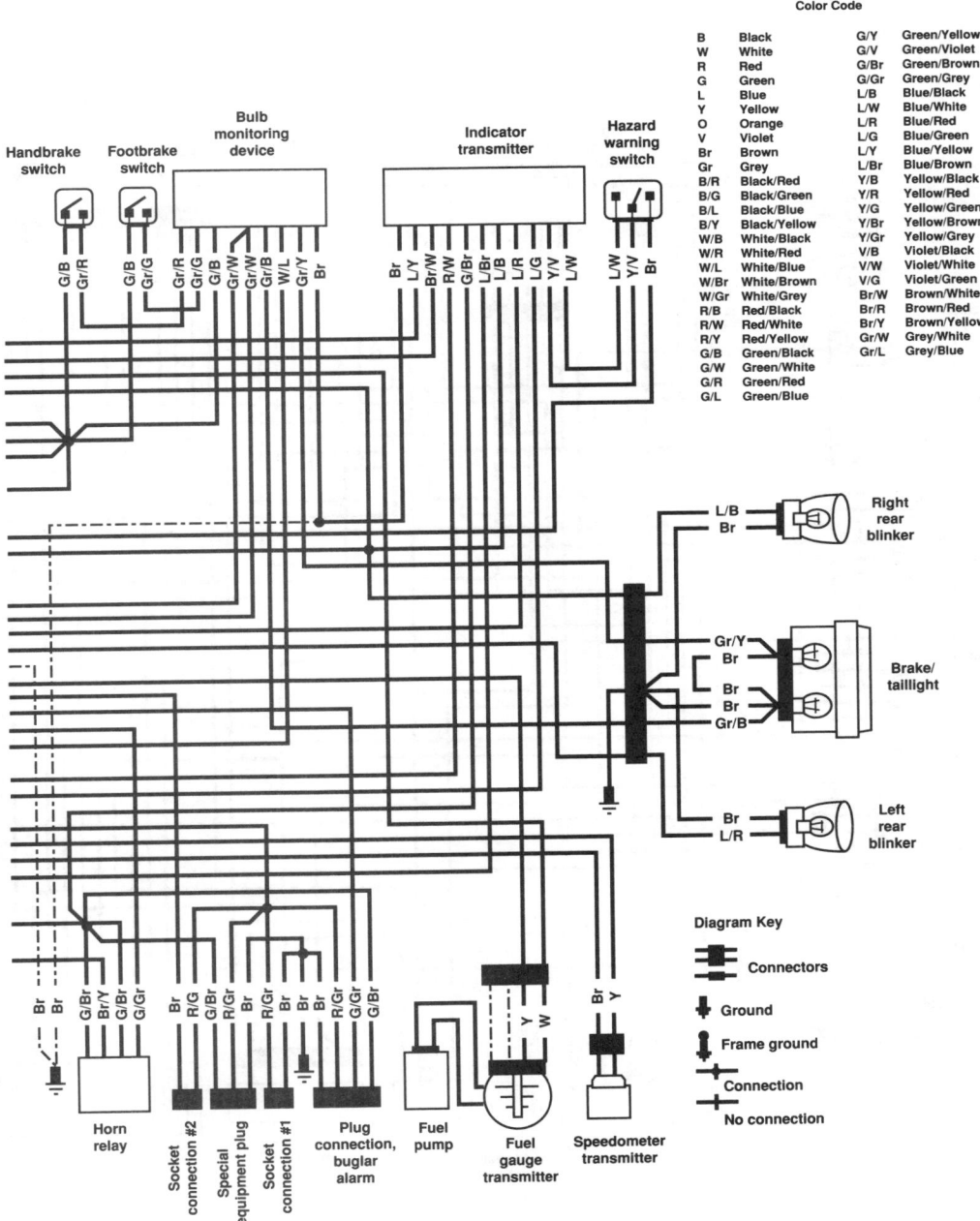

Color Code

B	Black	G/Y	Green/Yellow
W	White	G/V	Green/Violet
R	Red	G/Br	Green/Brown
G	Green	G/Gr	Green/Grey
L	Blue	L/B	Blue/Black
Y	Yellow	L/W	Blue/White
O	Orange	L/R	Blue/Red
V	Violet	L/G	Blue/Green
Br	Brown	L/Y	Blue/Yellow
Gr	Grey	L/Br	Blue/Brown
B/R	Black/Red	Y/B	Yellow/Black
B/G	Black/Green	Y/R	Yellow/Red
B/L	Black/Blue	Y/G	Yellow/Green
B/Y	Black/Yellow	Y/Br	Yellow/Brown
W/B	White/Black	Y/Gr	Yellow/Grey
W/R	White/Red	V/B	Violet/Black
W/L	White/Blue	V/W	Violet/White
W/Br	White/Brown	V/G	Violet/Green
W/Gr	White/Grey	Br/W	Brown/White
R/B	Red/Black	Br/R	Brown/Red
R/W	Red/White	Br/Y	Brown/Yellow
R/Y	Red/Yellow	Gr/W	Grey/White
G/B	Green/Black	Gr/L	Grey/Blue
G/W	Green/White		
G/R	Green/Red		
G/L	Green/Blue		

16

1993 K1100RS FRAME

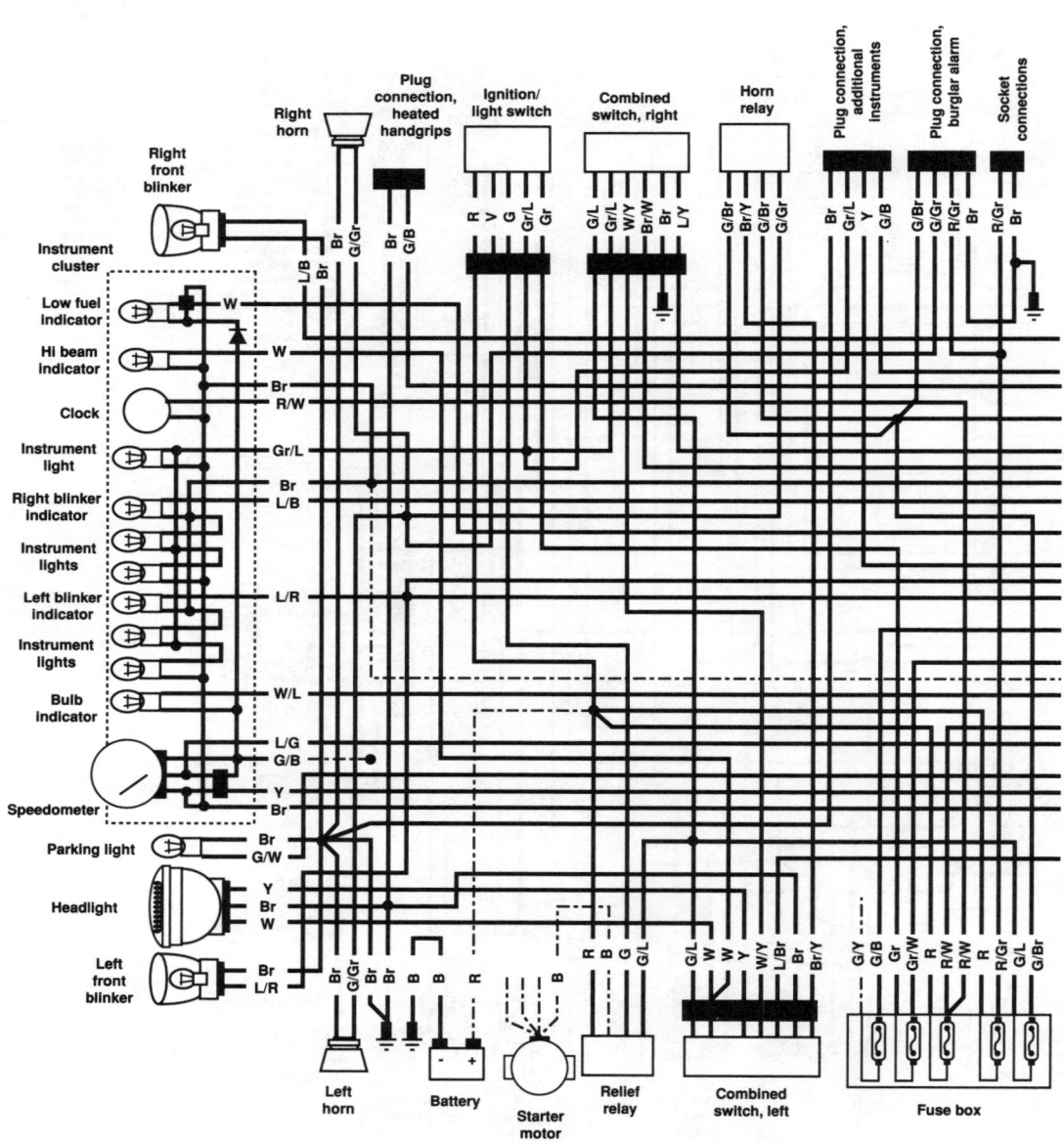

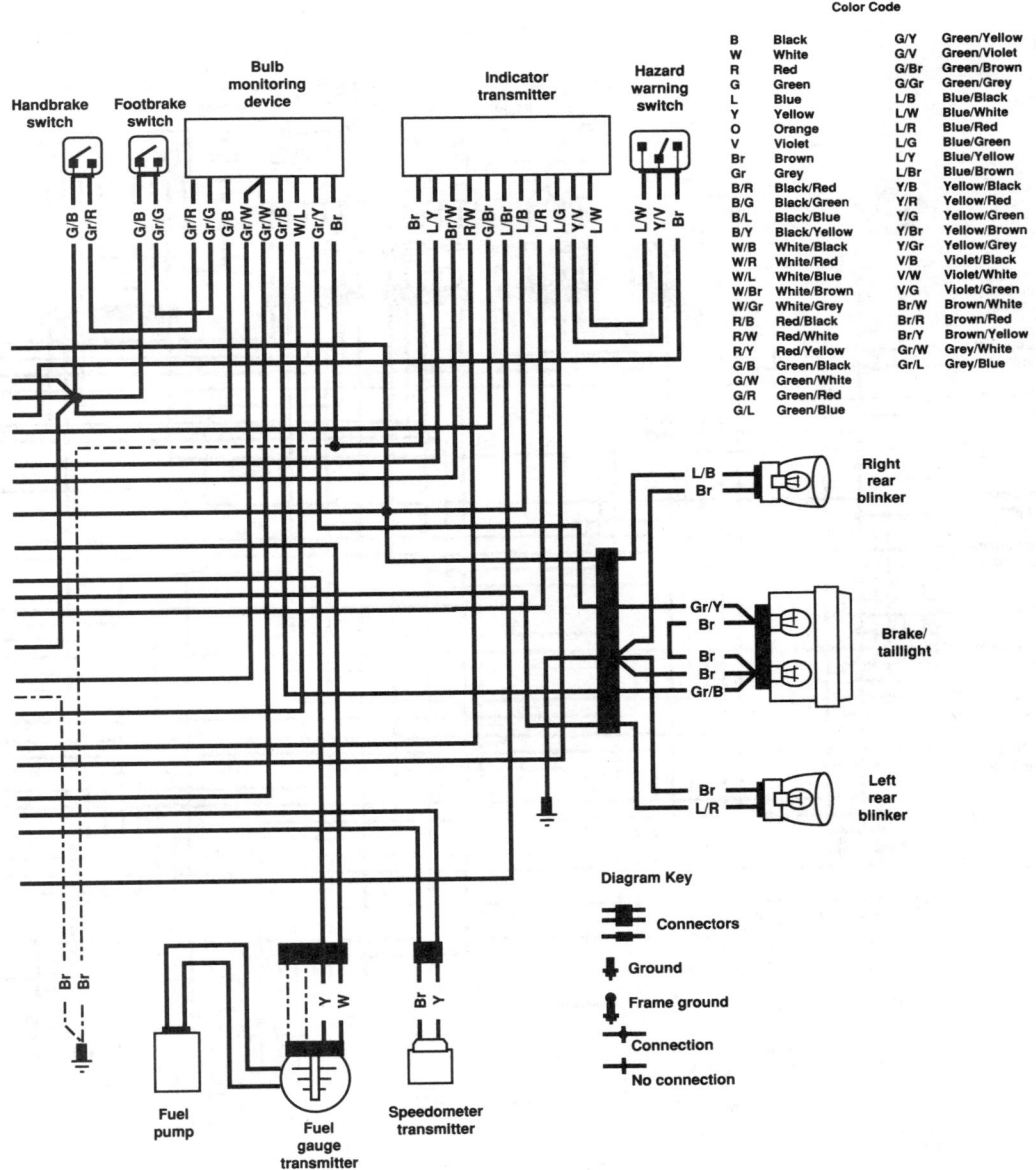

Color Code

B	Black	G/Y	Green/Yellow
W	White	G/V	Green/Violet
R	Red	G/Br	Green/Brown
G	Green	G/Gr	Green/Grey
L	Blue	L/B	Blue/Black
Y	Yellow	L/W	Blue/White
O	Orange	L/R	Blue/Red
V	Violet	L/G	Blue/Green
Br	Brown	L/Y	Blue/Yellow
Gr	Grey	L/Br	Blue/Brown
B/R	Black/Red	Y/B	Yellow/Black
B/G	Black/Green	Y/R	Yellow/Red
B/L	Black/Blue	Y/G	Yellow/Green
B/Y	Black/Yellow	Y/Br	Yellow/Brown
W/B	White/Black	Y/Gr	Yellow/Grey
W/R	White/Red	V/B	Violet/Black
W/L	White/Blue	V/W	Violet/White
W/Br	White/Brown	V/G	Violet/Green
W/Gr	White/Grey	Br/W	Brown/White
R/B	Red/Black	Br/R	Brown/Red
R/W	Red/White	Br/Y	Brown/Yellow
R/Y	Red/Yellow	Gr/W	Grey/White
G/B	Green/Black	Gr/L	Grey/Blue
G/W	Green/White		
G/R	Green/Red		
G/L	Green/Blue		

Diagram Key

Connectors
Ground
Frame ground
Connection
No connection

16

1994-ON K1100RS FRAME

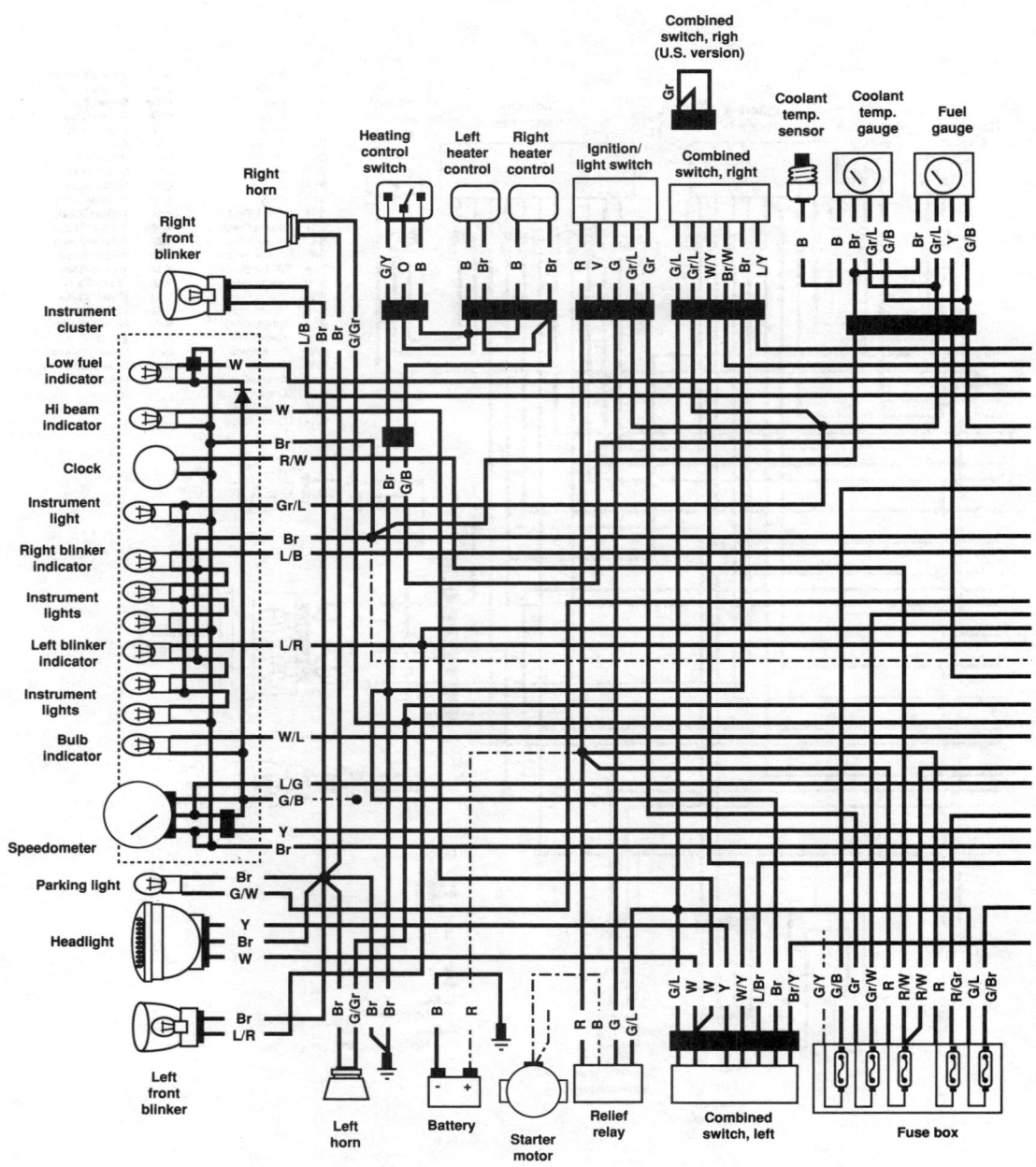

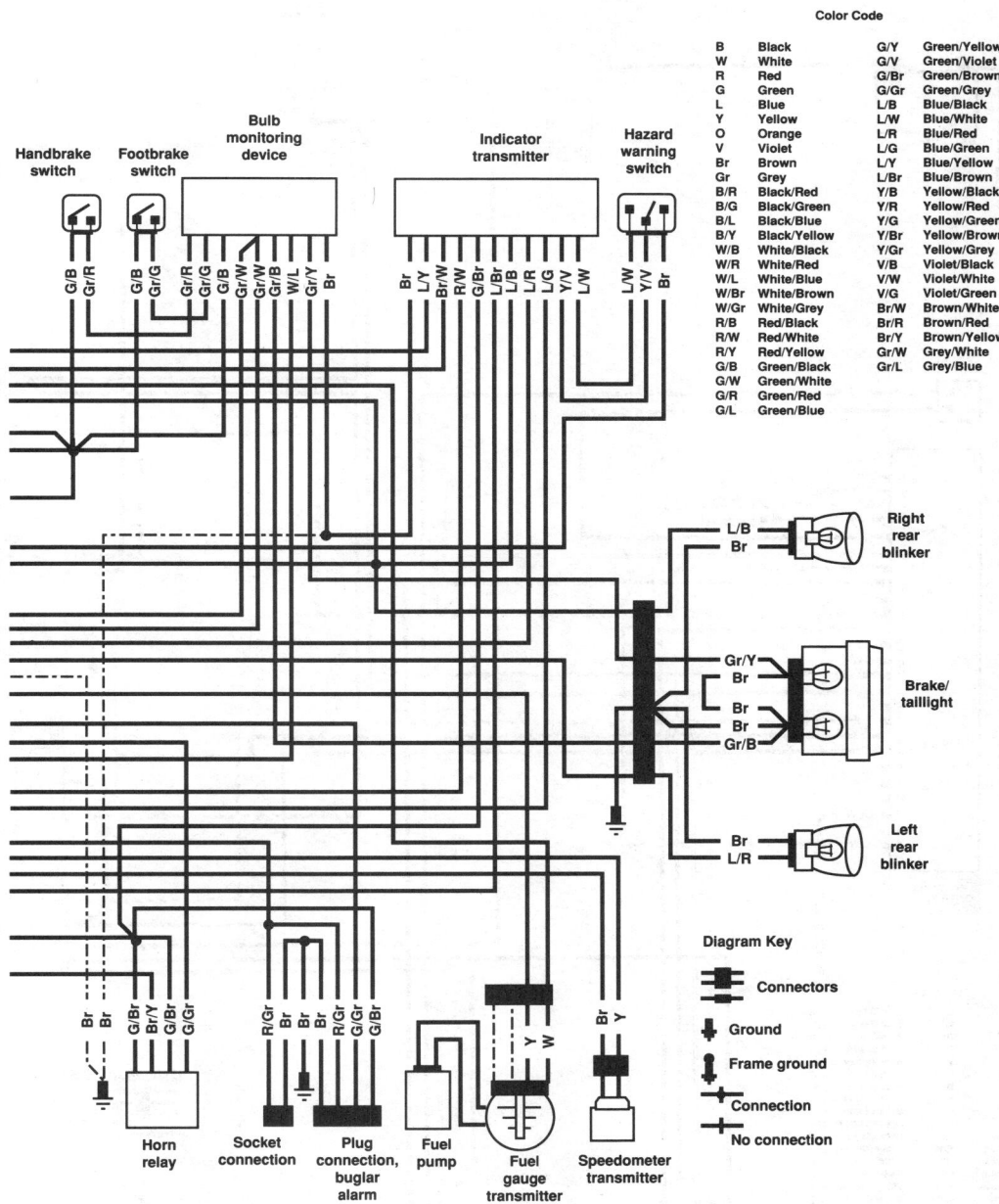

1988-1989 K100RS, K100RT, K100LT
ANTILOCK BRAKE SYSTEM

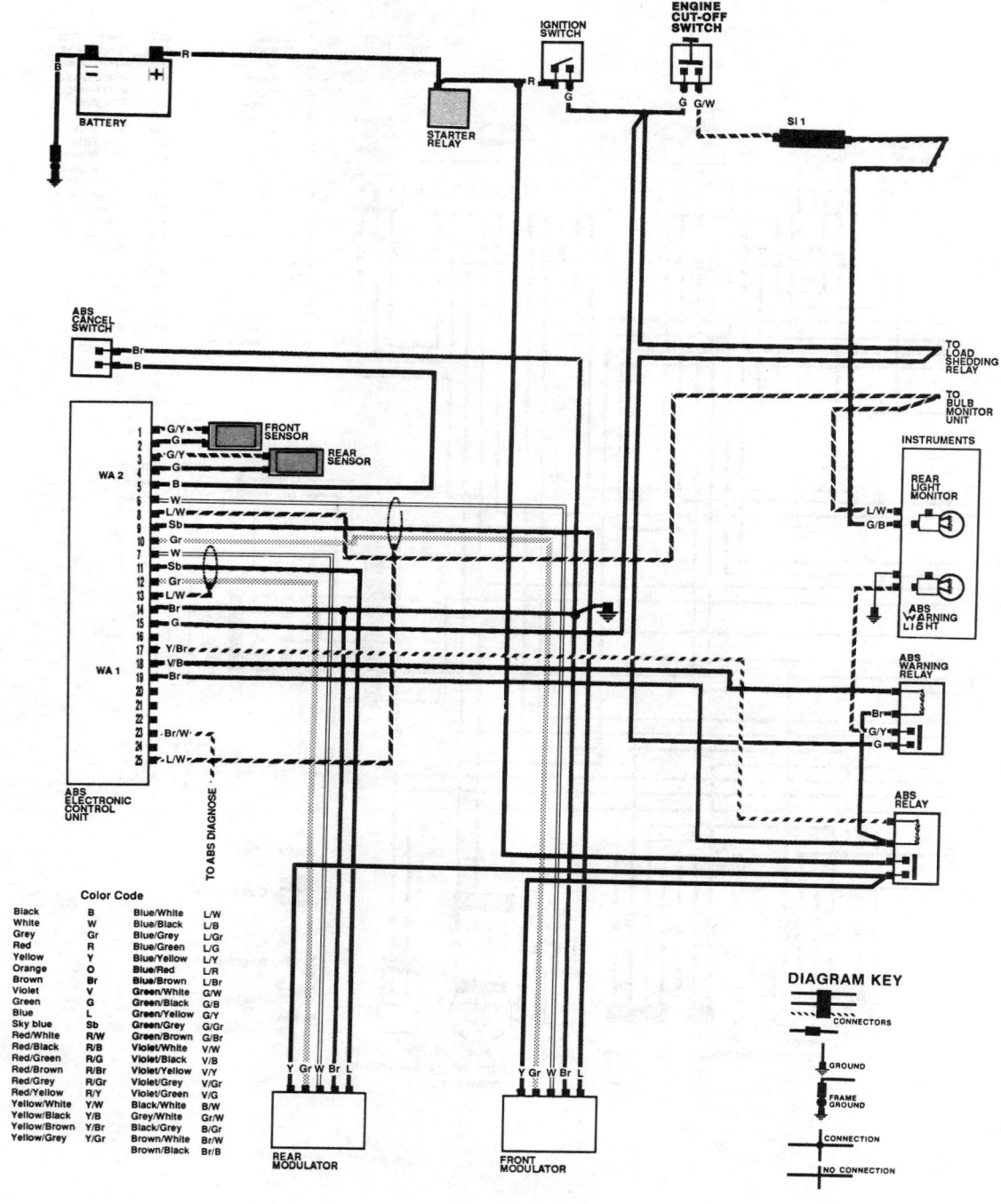

1990-1993 K1, 1991-1992 K100RS, K100LT
ANTILOCK BRAKE SYSTEM

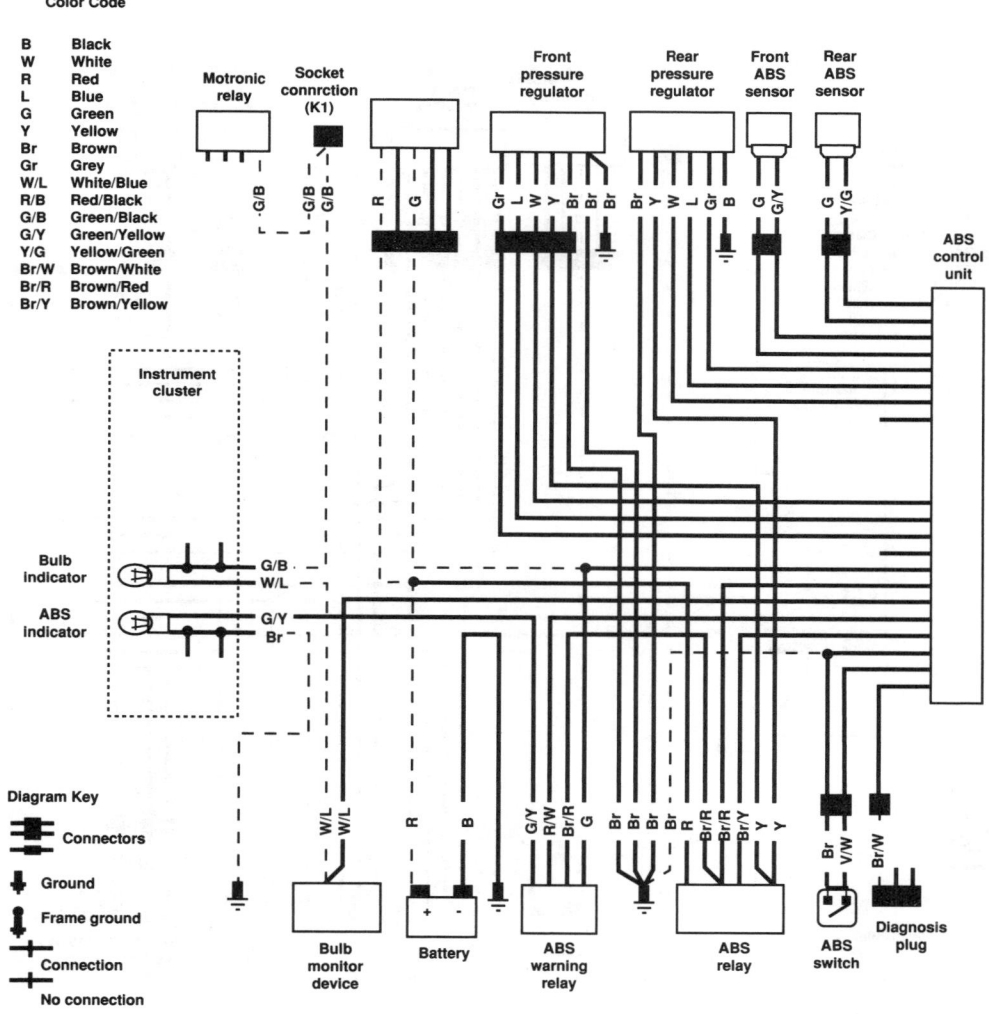

Color Code

B	Black
W	White
R	Red
L	Blue
G	Green
Y	Yellow
Br	Brown
Gr	Grey
W/L	White/Blue
R/B	Red/Black
G/B	Green/Black
G/Y	Green/Yellow
Y/G	Yellow/Green
Br/W	Brown/White
Br/R	Brown/Red
Br/Y	Brown/Yellow

Diagram Key

- Connectors
- Ground
- Frame ground
- Connection
- No connection

1993 K1100RS, K1100LT
ANTILOCK BRAKE SYSTEM

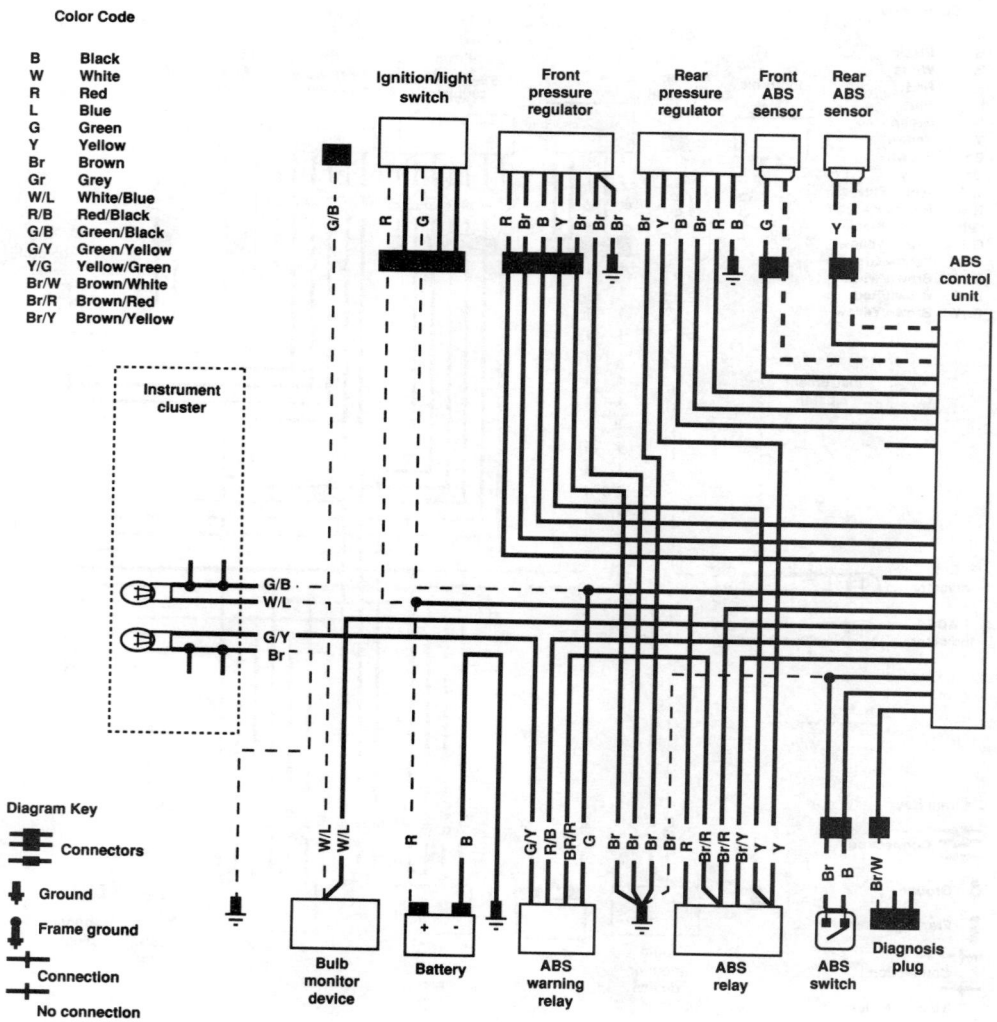

Color Code

B	Black
W	White
R	Red
L	Blue
G	Green
Y	Yellow
Br	Brown
Gr	Grey
W/L	White/Blue
R/B	Red/Black
G/B	Green/Black
G/Y	Green/Yellow
Y/G	Yellow/Green
Br/W	Brown/White
Br/R	Brown/Red
Br/Y	Brown/Yellow

Ignition/light switch

Front pressure regulator

Rear pressure regulator

Front ABS sensor

Rear ABS sensor

ABS control unit

Instrument cluster

G/B
W/L
G/Y
Br

Diagram Key

Connectors

Ground

Frame ground

Connection

No connection

Bulb monitor device

Battery

ABS warning relay

ABS relay

ABS switch

Diagnosis plug

1994-ON K1100RS, K1100LT
ANTILOCK BRAKE SYSTEM

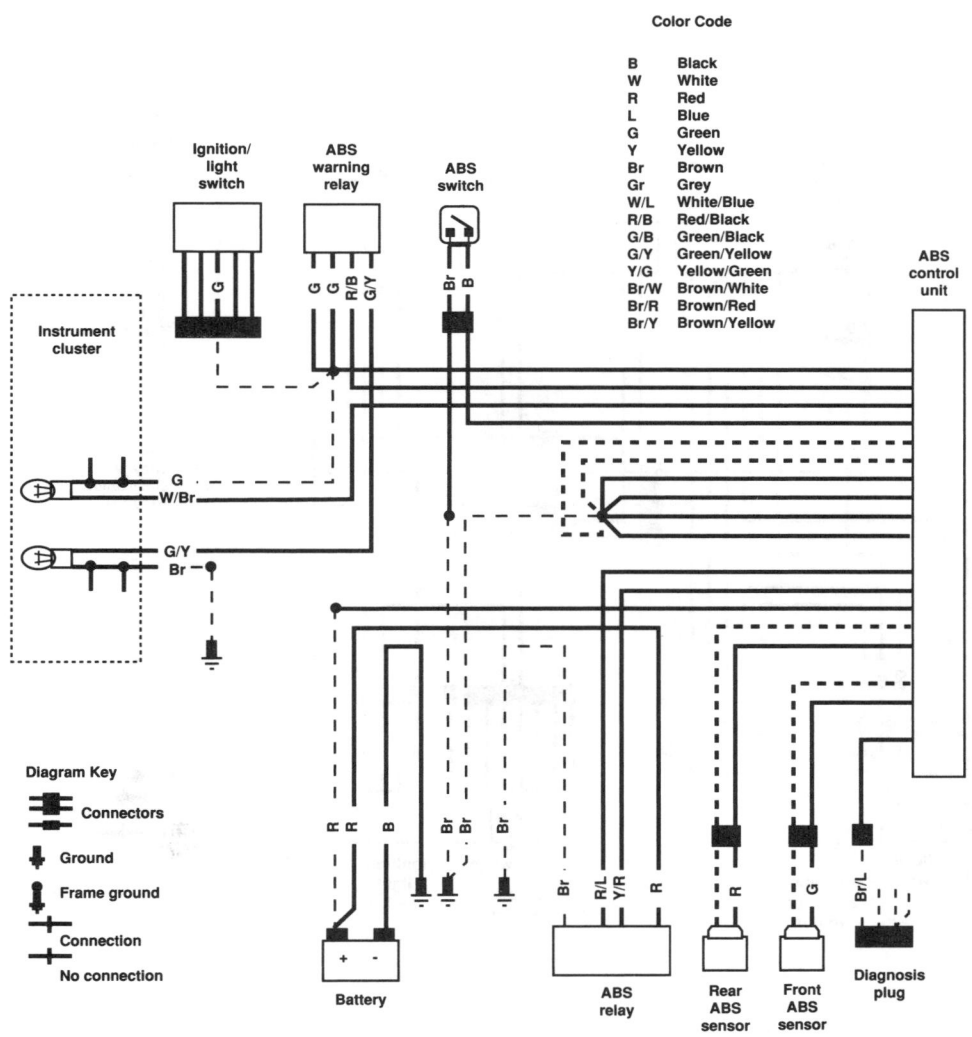

Color Code

B	Black
W	White
R	Red
L	Blue
G	Green
Y	Yellow
Br	Brown
Gr	Grey
W/L	White/Blue
R/B	Red/Black
G/B	Green/Black
G/Y	Green/Yellow
Y/G	Yellow/Green
Br/W	Brown/White
Br/R	Brown/Red
Br/Y	Brown/Yellow

Ignition/ light switch

ABS warning relay

ABS switch

ABS control unit

Instrument cluster

Diagram Key

Connectors

Ground

Frame ground

Connection

No connection

Battery

ABS relay

Rear ABS sensor

Front ABS sensor

Diagnosis plug

16

1993-ON K75RT
WINDSHIELD CIRCUIT

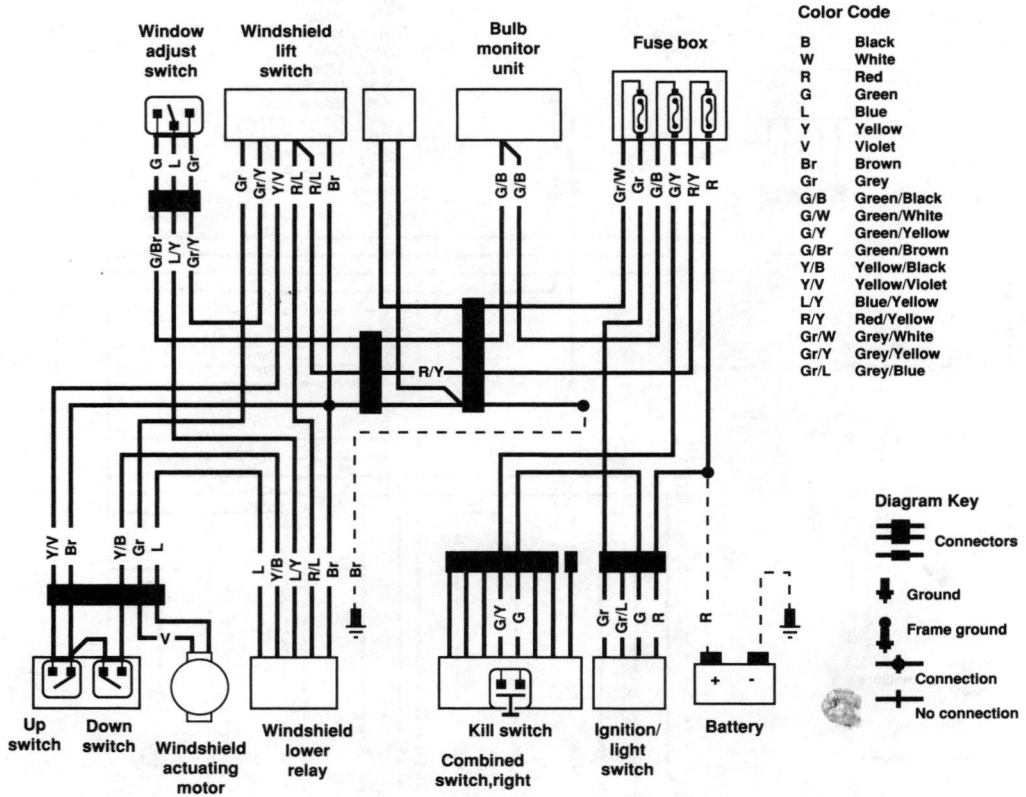

1993 K1100LT
WINDSHIELD CIRCUIT

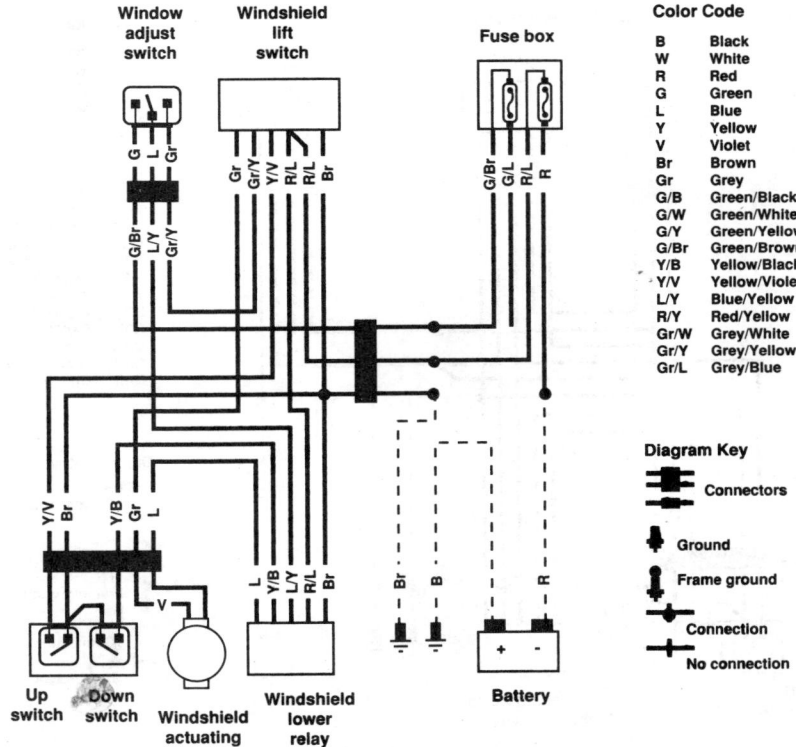

Window adjust switch
Windshield lift switch
Fuse box

Color Code

B	Black
W	White
R	Red
G	Green
L	Blue
Y	Yellow
V	Violet
Br	Brown
Gr	Grey
G/B	Green/Black
G/W	Green/White
G/Y	Green/Yellow
G/Br	Green/Brown
Y/B	Yellow/Black
Y/V	Yellow/Violet
L/Y	Blue/Yellow
R/Y	Red/Yellow
Gr/W	Grey/White
Gr/Y	Grey/Yellow
Gr/L	Grey/Blue

Diagram Key

Connectors

Ground

Frame ground

Connection

No connection

Up switch
Down switch
Windshield actuating motor
Windshield lower relay
Battery

1994-ON K1100LT
WINDSHIELD CIRCUIT

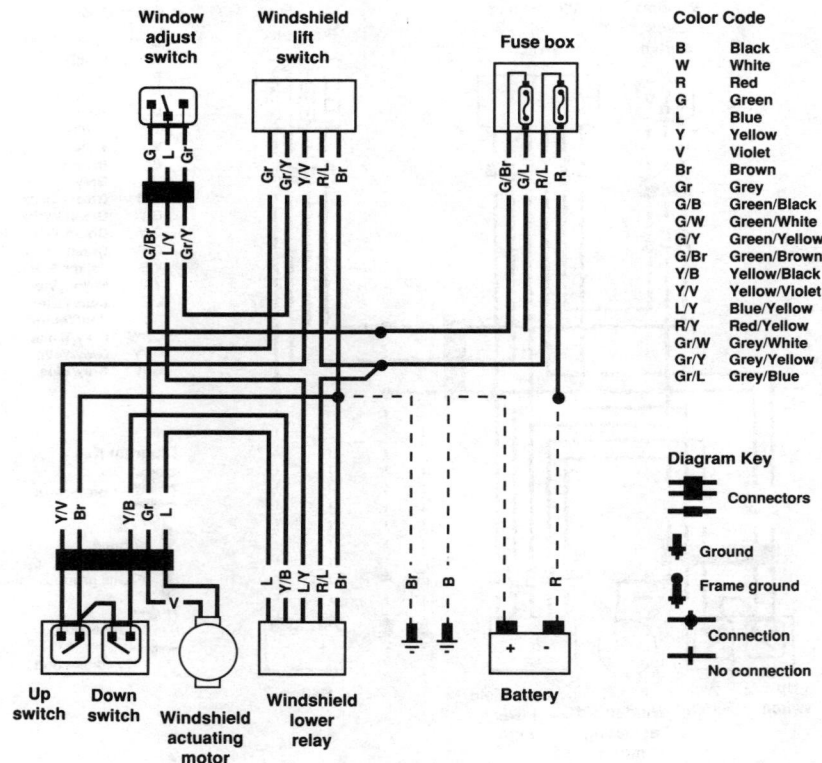

Window adjust switch

Windshield lift switch

Fuse box

Color Code

B	Black
W	White
R	Red
G	Green
L	Blue
Y	Yellow
V	Violet
Br	Brown
Gr	Grey
G/B	Green/Black
G/W	Green/White
G/Y	Green/Yellow
G/Br	Green/Brown
Y/B	Yellow/Black
Y/V	Yellow/Violet
L/Y	Blue/Yellow
R/Y	Red/Yellow
Gr/W	Grey/White
Gr/Y	Grey/Yellow
Gr/L	Grey/Blue

Diagram Key

Connectors

Ground

Frame ground

Connection

No connection

Up switch   **Down switch**   **Windshield actuating motor**   **Windshield lower relay**   **Battery**

1993 K1100LT
RADIO CIRCUIT

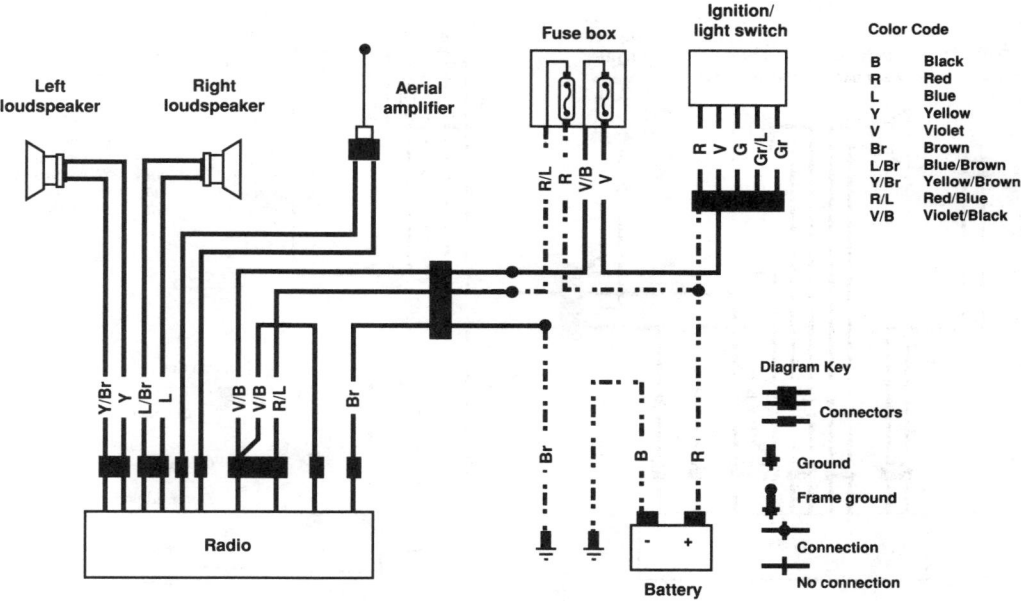

1994-ON K1100LT
RADIO CIRCUIT

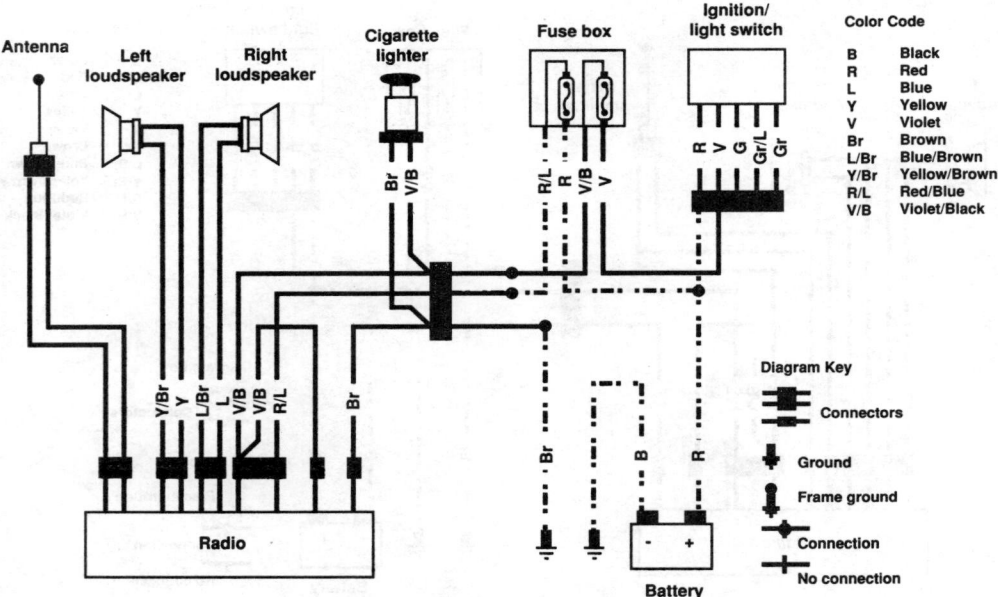

1993-ON K1100RS, K1100LT
HEATED HANDLEBAR GRIP CIRCUIT

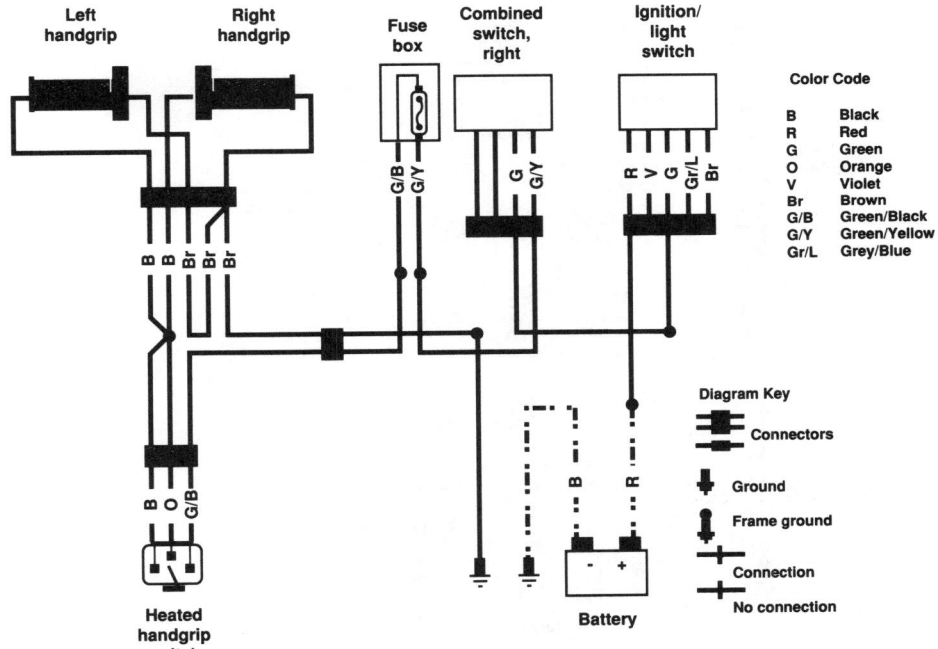

Left
handgrip

Right
handgrip

Fuse
box

Combined
switch,
right

Ignition/
light
switch

Color Code

B   Black
R   Red
G   Green
O   Orange
V   Violet
Br   Brown
G/B Green/Black
G/Y Green/Yellow
Gr/L Grey/Blue

Diagram Key

Connectors

Ground

Frame ground

Connection

No connection

Heated
handgrip
switch

Battery

1993-ON K1100LT
READING LAMP CIRCUIT

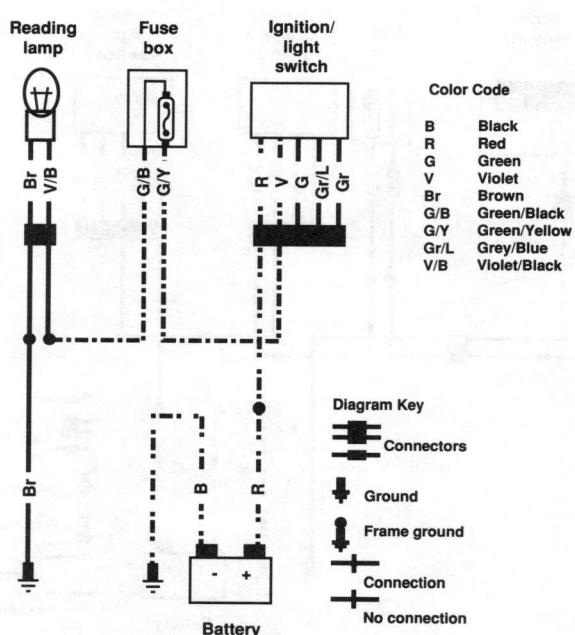

Color Code

B	Black
R	Red
G	Green
V	Violet
Br	Brown
G/B	Green/Black
G/Y	Green/Yellow
Gr/L	Grey/Blue
V/B	Violet/Black

NOTES

NOTES

MAINTENANCE LOG

Date	Miles	Type of Service

BMW

M308	500 & 600 CC Twins, 55-69
M309	F650, 1994-2000
M500-3	BMW K-Series, 85-97
M502-3	BMW R50/5-R100 GSPD, 70-96
M503	R850 & R1100, 93-98

HARLEY-DAVIDSON

M419	Sportsters, 59-85
M428	Sportster Evolution, 86-90
M429-4	Sportster Evolution, 91-03
M418	Panheads, 48-65
M420	Shovelheads, 66-84
M421-3	FLS/FXS Evolution, 84-99
M423	FLS/FXS Twin Cam 88B, 2000-2003
M422	FLH/FLT/FXR Evolution, 84-94
M430-2	FLH/FLT Twin Cam 88, 1999-2003
M424-2	FXD Evolution, 91-98
M425	Dyna Glide Twin Cam, 99-01

HONDA

ATVs

M316	Odyssey FL250, 77-84
M311	ATC, TRX & Fourtrax 70-125, 70-87
M433	Fourtrax 90 ATV, 93-00
M326	ATC185 & 200, 80-86
M347	ATC200X & Fourtrax 200SX, 86-88
M455	ATC250 & Fourtrax 200/ 250, 84-87
M342	ATC250R, 81-84
M348	TRX250R/Fourtrax 250R & ATC250R, 85-89
M456-2	TRX250X 87-92; TRX300EX 93-03
M446	TRX250 Recon 97-02
M346-3	TRX300/Fourtrax 300 & TRX300FW/Fourtrax 4x4, 88-00
M200	TRX350 Rancher, 00-03
M459-2	Fourtrax Foreman 95-01
M454-2	TRX400EX 99-03

Singles

M310-13	50-110cc OHC Singles, 65-99
M319	XR50R-XR70R, 97-03
M315	100-350cc OHC, 69-82
M317	Elsinore, 125-250cc, 73-80
M442	CR60-125R Pro-Link, 81-88
M431-2	CR80R, 89-95, CR125R, 89-91
M435	CR80, 96-02
M457-2	CR125R & CR250R, 92-97
M464	CR125R, 1998-2002
M443	CR250R-500R Pro-Link, 81-87
M432-3	CR250R, 88-91 & CR500R, 88-01
M437	CR250R, 97-01
M312-13	XL/XR75-100, 75-03
M318-4	XL/XR/TLR 125-200, 79-03
M328-4	XL/XR250, 78-00; XL/XR350R 83-85; XR200R, 84-85; XR250L, 91-96
M320	XR400R, 96-00
M339-7	XL/XR 500-650, 79-03

Twins

M321	125-200cc, 65-78
M322	250-350cc, 64-74
M323	250-360cc Twins, 74-77
M324-5	Twinstar, Rebel 250 & Nighthawk 250, 78-03
M334	400-450cc, 78-87
M333	450 & 500cc, 65-76
M335	CX & GL500/650 Twins, 78-83
M344	VT500, 83-88
M313	VT700 & 750, 83-87
M440	Shadow 1100cc, 85-96
M460-2	VT1100C2 A.C.E. Shadow, 95-99

Fours

M332	CB350-550cc, SOHC, 71-78
M345	CB550 & 650, 83-85
M336	CB650, 79-82
M341	CB750 SOHC, 69-78
M337	CB750 DOHC, 79-82
M436	CB750 Nighthawk, 91-93 & 95-99
M325	CB900, 1000 & 1100, 80-83
M439	Hurricane 600, 87-90
M441-2	CBR600, 91-98
M445	CBR600F4, 99-03
M434	CBR900RR Fireblade, 93-98
M329	500cc V-Fours, 84-86
M438	Honda VFR800, 98-00
M349	700-1000 Interceptor, 83-85
M458-2	VFR700F-750F, 86-97
M327	700-1100cc V-Fours, 82-88
M340	GL1000 & 1100, 75-83
M504	GL1200, 84-87
M508	ST1100/PAN European, 90-02

Sixes

M505	GL1500 Gold Wing, 88-92
M506-2	GL1500 Gold Wing, 93-00
M507	GL1800 Gold Wing, 01-04
M462-2	GL1500C Valkyrie, 97-03

KAWASAKI

ATVs

M465-2	KLF220 & KLF250 Bayou, 88-03
M466-2	KLF300 Bayou, 86-98
M467	KLF400 Bayou, 93-99
M470	KEF300 Lakota, 95-99
M385	KSF250 Mojave, 87-00

Singles

M350-9	Rotary Valve 80-350cc, 66-01
M444-2	KX60, 83-02; KX80 83-90
M448	KX80/85/100, 89-03
M351	KDX200, 83-88
M447-2	KX125 & KX250, 82-91 KX500, 83-02
M472-2	KX125, 92-00
M473-2	KX250, 92-00
M474	KLR650, 87-03

Twins

M355	KZ400, KZ/Z440, EN450 & EN500, 74-95
M360-3	EX500, GPZ500S, Ninja R, 87-02
M356-3	700-750 Vulcan, 85-02
M354-2	VN800 Vulcan 95-04
M357-2	VN1500 Vulcan 87-99
M471-2	VN1500 Vulcan Classic, 96-04

Fours

M449	KZ500/550 & ZX550, 79-85
M450	KZ, Z & ZX750, 80-85
M358	KZ650, 77-83
M359-3	900-1000cc Fours, 73-81
M451-3	1000 &1100cc Fours, 81-02
M452-3	ZX500 & 600 Ninja, 85-97
M453-3	Ninja ZX900-1100 84-01
M468	ZX6 Ninja, 90-97
M469	ZX7 Ninja, 91-98
M453-3	900-1100 Ninja, 84-01
M409	Concours, 86-04

POLARIS

ATVs

M496	Polaris ATV, 85-95
M362	Polaris Magnum ATV, 96-98
M363	Scrambler 500, 4X4 97-00
M365-2	Sportsman/Xplorer, 96-03

SUZUKI

ATVs

M381	ALT/LT 125 & 185, 83-87
M475	LT230 & LT250, 85-90
M380	LT250R Quad Racer, 85-88
M343	LTF500F Quadrunner, 98-00
M483-2	Suzuki King Quad/ Quad Runner 250, 87-98

Singles

M371	RM50-400 Twin Shock, 75-81
M369	125-400cc 64-81
M379	RM125-500 Single Shock, 81-88
M476	DR250-350, 90-94
M384-2	LS650 Savage, 86-03
M386	RM80-250, 89-95
M400	RM125, 96-00
M401	RM250, 96-02

Twins

M372	GS400-450 Twins, 77-87
M481-3	VS700-800 Intruder, 85-02
M482-2	VS1400 Intruder, 87-01
M484-3	GS500E Twins, 89-02
M361	SV650, 99-02

Triple

M368	380-750cc, 72-77

Fours

M373	GS550, 77-86
M364	GS650, 81-83
M370	GS750 Fours, 77-82
M376	GS850-1100 Shaft Drive, 79-84
M378	GS1100 Chain Drive, 80-81
M383-3	Katana 600, 88-96 GSX-R750-1100, 86-87
M331	GSX-R600, 97-00
M478-2	GSX-R750, 88-92 GSX750F Katana, 89-96
M485	GSX-R750, 96-99
M338	GSF600 Bandit, 95-00
M353	GSF1200 Bandit, 96-03

YAMAHA

ATVs

M499	YFM80 Badger, 85-01
M394	YTM/YFM200 & 225, 83-86
M488-4	Blaster, 88-02
M489-2	Timberwolf, 89-00
M487-4	Warrior, 87-03
M486-4	Banshee, 87-02
M490-2	YFM350 Moto-4 & Big Bear, 87-98
M493	YFM400FW Kodiak, 93-98
M280	Raptor 660R, 01-03

Singles

M492-2	PW50 & PW80, BW80 Big Wheel 80, 81-02
M410	80-175 Piston Port, 68-76
M415	250-400cc Piston Port, 68-76
M412	DT & MX 100-400, 77-83
M414	IT125-490, 76-86
M393	YZ50-80 Monoshock, 78-90
M413	YZ100-490 Monoshock, 76-84
M390	YZ125-250, 85-87 YZ490, 85-90
M391	YZ125-250, 88-93 WR250Z, 91-93
M497-2	YZ125, 94-01
M498	YZ250, 94-98 and WR250Z, 94-97
M406	YZ250F & WR250F, 01-03
M491	YZ400F, YZ426F & WR400F, 98-00
M417	XT125-250, 80-84
M480-3	XT/TT 350, 85-00
M405	XT500 & TT500, 76-81
M416	XT/TT 600, 83-89

Twins

M403	650cc, 70-82
M395-9	XV535-1100 Virago, 81-99
M495-2	V-Star 650, 98-03
M281	V-Star 1100, 99-04

Triple

M404	XS750 & 850, 77-81

Fours

M387	XJ550, XJ600 & FJ600, 81-92
M494	XJ600 Seca II, 92-98
M388	YX600 Radian & FZ600, 86-90
M396	FZR600, 89-93
M392	FZ700-750 & Fazer, 85-87
M411	XS1100 Fours, 78-81
M397	FJ1100 & 1200, 84-93
M375	V-Max, 85-03
M374	Royal Star, 96-03

VINTAGE MOTORCYCLES

Clymer® Collection Series

M330	Vintage British Street Bikes, BSA, 500-650cc Unit Twins; Norton, 750 & 850cc Commandos; Triumph, 500-750cc Twins
M300	Vintage Dirt Bikes, V. 1 Bultaco, 125-370cc Singles; Montesa, 123-360cc Singles; Ossa, 125-250cc Singles
M301	Vintage Dirt Bikes, V. 2 CZ, 125-400cc Singles; Husqvarna, 125-450cc Singles; Maico, 250-501cc Singles; Hodaka, 90-125cc Singles
M305	Vintage Japanese Street Bikes Honda, 250 & 305cc Twins; Kawasaki, 250-750cc Triples; Kawasaki, 900 & 1000cc Fours